THE LAW SOCIETY'S CONVEYANCING HANDBOOK
10th Edition

THE LAW SOCIETY'S CONVEYANCING HANDBOOK
10th Edition

by

General Editor

Frances Silverman LLM *Solicitor*

Consultant Editors

Annette Goss
Peter Reekie
Michael Taylor
Bernadette Whitters

Editorial Board

Margaret Anstey LLB *Solicitor*
Helen Davies *Solicitor Langsford Davies*
Kenneth Edwards *Solicitor*
Philip Freedman LLB *Solicitor Mishcon de Reya*
Emma Slessenger *Solicitor Dechert*

*nominated by the Law Society's
Conveyancing and Land Law Committee*

The Law Society

The author has asserted the right under the
Copyright, Designs and Patents Act 1988
to be identified as author of this work.

First published January 1992, reprinted June 1992
2nd edition 1993, reprinted April 1993
3rd edition 1994, reprinted February 1995
4th edition 1995
5th edition 1996, reprinted March 1997
6th edition 1997
7th edition 1999, reprinted March 1999 and February 2000
8th edition 2001, reprinted April 2001
9th edition 2002, reprinted October 2002
10th edition 2003

ISBN 1 85328 847 0
ISSN 1350-1852

Published in 2003 by the Law Society
113 Chancery Lane, London WC2A 1PL

Typeset by Columns Design Ltd, Reading
Printed by Biddles Ltd, Guildford and King's Lynn

Contents

C. EXCHANGE

D. TITLE

E. PRE-COMPLETION

F.   COMPLETION

G.   POST-COMPLETION

H.   LENDERS

I.   NEW PROPERTIES

J.   SALES OF PART

K.   LEASEHOLDS

L.   COMMONHOLD

M.   DELAY AND REMEDIES

N.   COSTS

APPENDICES

I.   LAW SOCIETY RULES

II.   LAW SOCIETY CODES

III.   LAW SOCIETY PROTOCOL AND FORMULAE

IV.   LAW SOCIETY WARNING CARDS

VIII. FORMS AND GUIDANCE FROM OTHER ORGANISATIONS

IX. STAMP DUTY

X. INSURANCE

XI. DIRECTORY

XII.   STATUTORY MATERIALS

XIII.   THE LAND REGISTRY

Preface to the 1992 edition

Conveyancing is a much maligned art – an easy option in the eyes of many practitioners. If this is true, why is it that the Legal Practice Directorate and Professional Ethics Department of the Law Society have a constant stream of telephone calls and letters from practitioners anxious to know how to solve conveyancing problems? The idea of this book originated from the Law Society's Land Law and Conveyancing Committee who felt that the time had come to publish a work which attempted to deal with and resolve the many problems encountered on a daily basis by practitioners. The aim of this book, therefore, is to present in readable form a ready reference handbook of the practice of conveyancing. The book does not pretend to be a comprehensive guide to the law – for this the reader is, at various points throughout the text, referred to specialist works dealing with particular areas, but it does seek to deal fully with the practice of conveyancing and to provide guidance on resolving problems which may be encountered by practitioners. The text is, therefore, divided into sections which deal with the conveyancing transaction in chronological sequence. Chapters have been included on matters which, although peripheral to the main issue, nevertheless impinge on it, e.g. advertising, property selling, costs, undertakings and remedies. Although the book does contain some specialist sections, e.g. the purchase of licensed premises, milk quotas in agricultural land, it is intended as a handbook for the general practitioner and does not, therefore, cover in detail specialist areas pertaining to commercial transactions. It does, however, seek to gather together some information which is not found either in other conventional conveyancing texts or in some cases at all, this aspect particularly concentrating on the resolution of practical problems and provision of checklists and guidelines. Precedents are not included within the text since the practitioner has ample scope for finding precedents in many other published works. Some commonly encountered practical areas are no longer dealt with by trainee solicitors during their Finals course, and in such areas, e.g. residential security of tenure, the book aims to provide the solicitor with a brief résumé of the law with reference to a specialist work on the subject should that be required.

It is hoped that this book will form the practitioner's first point of reference and to that end extensive appendices include the text of many of the matters to which a practitioner has cause to refer during the course of each working day, e.g. HM Land Registry Practice Notes, addresses of authorities for the purpose of making searches, stamp duty tables, the Formulae for exchange of contracts.

It is of course vital that any book which purports to be an essential working tool in the hands of a busy practitioner should be up to date with both law and practice. The decision has, therefore, been taken by the Law Society that this book will be completely revised and updated regularly in order to ensure that the practitioner has available to him in one volume the very latest information relating to conveyancing.

No offence is intended to female members of the profession by references in the text to the solicitor as 'he', for which please read 'he or she' as appropriate. To include the words 'he or she' on every occasion where such reference appears would have the effect of extending the text by a considerable amount which in turn would have adverse repercussion on the publication price of the book.

I would like to acknowledge with thanks the permission of HM Land Registry and the Inland Revenue for publication of their various leaflets and guidance notes which appear in the appendices to the book.

I would also like to thank Linklaters and Paines for their help with sections on milk quotas and VAT, Withers for their assistance in preparing the text on agricultural land, Chris Jowett of the Halifax Building Society for his help in relation to mortgages, Martin Wood of HM Land Registry for his assistance with points on registered land, and Tony Donell who read through each section of the manuscript before publication.

I should also record my appreciation to the staff of the Law Society, in particular Joanna Davies-Evitt and Carl Upsall who have been responsible for the co-ordination of the text, preparation of appendices and index and eventual publication of the text itself.

Finally my thanks go to Trevor Aldridge, Margaret Anstey, Murray Ross, Philip Freedman, and Kenneth Edwards who comprised the Editorial Board for this book. They had the unenviable task of sitting through monthly meetings to discuss and correct my indecipherable manuscript. Without their constant help, support and encouragement this book might not have seen the light of day.

The law is stated as at 1 December 1991.

Frances Silverman

Rowfold Grange
West Sussex

1 December 1991

Preface to the 10th edition

It is hard to believe that ten years have gone by since publication of the first edition of this book in 1992. There have been enormous changes in conveyancing law and practice during the intervening years, and this year is no exception.

This edition also marks a change in the way in which the book is presented. Updating a book of this size has become more than a one person job and we have in recent years sought some outside input on specialist areas. This year that outside help has been extended to include three new consultant editors and more specialists to revise specific sections. For my part, I now become the General Editor of this work. We hope this development is an improvement and great care has been taken to ensure that the book retains its unity and reader friendly approach to the subject.

A new section ('AA') has been added to the front of the book which we hope readers will find useful as a quick guide to recent changes in law and practice.

This edition has also been completely revised to take account of the sweeping changes introduced by the Land Registration Act 2002 which comes into force later this year.

The Commonhold and Leasehold Reform Act 2002 has also negotiated its parliamentary hurdles since the last edition was published, but our intention of providing readers with a comprehensive guide to the new law has been thwarted by the fact that the regulations on which the Act depends have not yet been finalised. The commonhold section has been expanded in this edition to explain the principles of the new legislation but sadly the detail will have to wait for the next edition.

My thanks go to the valiant consulting editors who have updated the various sections of the book – Annette Goss, Peter Reekie, Michael Taylor, and Bernadette Whitters; and also to the Editorial Board, Margaret Anstey, Helen Davies, Kenneth Edwards, Philip Freedman and Emma Slessenger for their continuing support and help with this edition.

At the Law Society, my thanks go to Neil Gower, Deborah Manning, Diane Latter and Samantha Barnett (Conveyancing and Land Law Policy), Angela Doran (Professional Ethics), and Steven Durno (Planning and Environmental Policy).

For their help with the updating of this edition, I would also like to thank Nick Lightbody (Environmental Issues), Peter Camp (Financial Services, Mortgage Fraud, Money Laundering), Birketts Solicitors (Agricultural Land and Agricultural Tenancies), Pete Sizer (NLIS), Liz Brady (Pre-Contract Searches and Enquiries), Andrew Boulton (Pre-completion Searches), Dave Jordan (VAT), Reg Nock (Stamp Duty, Land Tax, Stamp Duty and Stamp Duty Savings, Stamping Documents), and Tim Hayden (Licensing).

For their help with permissions and updating this edition, I would like to thank the

following organisations: British Sugar, Council of Mortgage Lenders, Countrywide Legal Indemnities, the Land Registry, Local Government Association, National House Building Council, National Radiological Protection Board, Premier Guarantee, Rural Payments Agency, and Zurich Insurance.

Any errors which remain in the book are my responsibility alone.

Frances Silverman

Rowfold
West Sussex

June 2003

About the Authors

Margaret Anstey is a non-practising solicitor and a member of the Law Society's Conveyancing and Land Law Committee and a member of the editorial board of the Law Society's *Conveyancing Handbook*. She is a former Chairman of the Land Law & Conveyancing Committee and was Chairman of the working parties for the Standard Conditions of Sale, the Standard Commercial Property Conditions and the Law Society's Business Lease. She was one of the original members of the Law Society's TransAction Working Party responsible for the National Conveyancing Protocol and the associated forms and is the present Chairman of that working party.

Andrew Boulton is an associate solicitor at Davies Arnold Cooper where he trained and continued to work since qualifying in 1996. Andrew has experience in all aspects of property work including commercial and residential development, sales and disposals, landlord and tenant (retail, leisure and commercial). He is also author of several articles for the New Law Journal.

Liz Brady is a Property Support Lawyer at Nabarro Nathanson. She has been a practising solicitor for 13 years, 11 in the commercial property department of Nabarro Nathanson. Liz writes Practice Notes, Precedents and Guidance Notes for the Property Department and for clients. She has also written articles for Butterworths' online service.

Peter Camp is a solicitor and is visiting Professor (Chair of Ethics) at The College of Law. He is also Principal of Educational & Professional Services, which provides training and consultancy services to the solicitors' and accountants' professions. Peter is a former member of the Law Society's Financial Services Taskforce. Amongst his numerous publications are: *Solicitors and Financial Services: A Compliance Handbook* (The Law Society, 2002); and *Cordery on Solicitors* (where he contributes sections on Financial Services and Solicitors' Accounts).

Helen Davies is a solicitor and partner at Langsford Davies and Law Society Council Member for Gwent and the South West. Helen specialises in residential and small scale commercial property, business transfers and some agricultural property. She is also President of Cornwall Law Society, Chairman of the LPC Board, Governor of Cornwall College, Chair of County Environmental Trust, and member of the Editorial Board of the Law Society's *Conveyancing Handbook*.

Kenneth Edwards was admitted as a solicitor in 1961 and from 1965 practised at Cardens in Brighton specialising in Building Society law. Kenneth also acted as external Head Office Solicitor to the former Alliance Building Society. He continued in that capacity until the 1980s and played a significant part in the merger with Leicester Building Society. As a member of the Law Society's Conveyancing and Land Law Committee, Kenneth was involved in the bringing together of the Law Society's and National Conditions of Sale and the documentation for the Law Society's TransAction conveyancing protocol (he wrote part of the text for the Buyer's Guide). As member of a joint Law Commission Committee, he authored a paper 'Deposits; no time for a change'. He is a past President of Sussex Law Society.

Philip Freedman is a solicitor and joint managing partner at Mishcon de Reya. He is a member of various committees at the Law Society, including: the Conveyancing and Land

Law Committee, The Standard Conditions of Sale Working Party, The Joint Advisory Committee of the Land Registry and the Law Society, the Local Searches Joint Working Party of the Law Society and the Local Government Association. Philip is also a member of the RICS Working Party on the PACT Scheme and a member of the British Property Federation Working Party on Short Leases. His publications include: *Service Charges: Law and Practice* (Jordans, 2002).

Annette Goss is a solicitor and worked in private practice as a conveyancer and property lawyer before joining the Government Legal Service. She has worked as a Solicitor for the Crown Estate and is currently the Land Registrar at the Land Registry, Nottingham (East) Office. Annette has been involved in designing and developing a professional training course with Michael Taylor on Land Registration Law and Practice for Land Registry staff, and has also prepared and delivered lectures and seminars to Land Registry staff, legal practitioners, academics and other members of the legal profession.

James Harbottle trained with Allen & Overy in the City and qualified into their property department in 1994. He has worked for Burges Salmon from 1996 before joining Birketts in September 2000. His strongest areas of practice are in agricultural, equestrian and commercial property. James is a member of the Agricultural Law Association and a professional member of the CLA.

Tim Hayden is a solicitor-advocate and partner at Clarke Wilmott solicitors. Previously Tim was a prosecutor for HM Inspectorate of Pollution. He has a wide range of prosecution experience relating to waste disposal, contaminated land, air and water pollution and statutory nuisance including noise and odour abatement; and regularly conducts proceedings relating to BSE regulation, county council applications, agricultural accidents and fraudulent subsidy claims. Tim also has an extensive regulatory practice covering licensing (of major retailers, substantial on-licensed premises and night clubs), vehicle licensing disputes and fraud. He has been recognised as an expert in the fields of commercial litigation and environmental law by the Legal Experts directory and for his environmental work by Chambers.

Dave Jordan is an independent VAT specialist with 27 years' experience, including 14 years with HM Customs & Excise. He presents seminars on VAT for Central Law Training, Law South, Croner, and Professional Tax Practice. Dave has also lectured at Bournemouth University on taxation and revenue law. He is author of *Understanding VAT on Property* (Law Society, 2002), co-author of Croner's *A-Z of VAT*, contributor to *CCH UK VAT Planning Guide*, and regularly contributes articles to professional journals.

Nicholas Lightbody is a solicitor and a former partner at both Hobson Audley and Lane & Partners in London. He now undertakes consultancy work and is director of DESKspace Limited (www.deskspace.com). Nick is a member of the Law Society's Planning and Environmental Law Committee and has contributed to the Law Society's *Conveyancing Handbook* and Butterworths' *Encyclopaedia of Forms & Precedents*. He is a past Commodore of the Law Society Yacht Club and still races when he gets the time.

Reg Nock is a barrister with 24 Old Buildings. He is author of *Understanding Stamp Duty on Property* (Law Society, 2003), *Monroe and Nock on The Law of Stamp Duties*, and *Stamp Duties for Property Transactions*. He regularly gives seminars for solicitors on stamp duty.

Peter Reekie was admitted as a solicitor in 1976 and spent some years in private practice dealing with residential and commercial property work. He then moved to The College of Law, where he trained students, wrote for publication and spoke regularly at conferences and seminars. The College has appointed him a Visiting Professor. He was also managing director of Legal Network Television and continues to present programmes for them on property law topics. He is now co-author of www.marplus.co.uk (a property law updating service with John Martin), Property Training Consultant with Penningtons, and a freelance trainer working for law firms and other organisations in the field of property law.

Frances Silverman is a solicitor and formerly a Reader at the College of Law. She has been author of the Law Society's *Conveyancing Handbook* since first publication in 1992. Frances is also author of several other books on conveyancing, sits as as part time Chairman of Employment Tribunal and of the Leashold Valuation Tribunal, and acts as an expert witness.

Emma Slessenger is a solicitor and property support lawyer at Dechert, where she prepares precedents, keeps lawyers up-to-date on developments in property law and practice, edits their property newsletter *Good Title* and organises regular Landlord and Tenant Update seminars. Emma is an editorial board member of the *Conveyancing Handbook* and member of the Law Society's Conveyancing and Land Law Committee. Her publications include the *Landlord and Tenant Factbook* (Sweet & Maxwell) and *Leasehold Liability: the Landlord and Tenant (Covenants) Act 1995* (Jordans). Emma regularly writes articles for the professional press and lectures on landlord and tenant topics for Central Law Training.

Laurence Target is a senior solicitor in the commercial property department at Trowers & Hamlins where he is also a member of the commonhold team. He has made a particular study of successive proposals for Commonhold, as well as of the present legislation and the commercial property and mixed-use opportunities for new commonhold developments. Laurence has delivered seminars and training in relation to commonhold and other areas of practice; as well as having published articles about law in various journals.

Michael Taylor is a solicitor and the senior assistant Land Registrar at the Land Registry, Birkenhead (Rosebrae) Office. Michael spent some years as a conveyancing and property lawyer in private practice before joining the Land Registry. Michael has been involved in designing and developing a professional training course with Annette Goss on Land Registration Law and Practice for Land Registry staff, and has also prepared and delivered lectures and seminars to Land Registry staff, legal practitioners, academics and other members of the legal profession.

Bernadette Whitters is an Associate Professor at the College of Law, currently lecturing Property Law and Conveyancing at the College's Guildford Branch. She qualified as a solicitor in 1980 and from 1980 to 1985 was the Assistant Company Solicitor at the Provident Financial Group, specialising in commercial and residential property matters. In November 1985, Bernadette joined the College of Law as a lecturer specialising in Property Law and Conveyancing. From August 1995 to April 2003 she was responsible for devising, scripting and presenting the residential and commercial property programmes produced by Legal Network Television (LNTV), a wholly owned subsidiary of the College of Law. Bernadette has also devised and presented a number of continuing professional development courses and has written and contributed to a number of College publications as well articles for the New Law Journal and the Homes Overseas magazine.

Richard Williams was admitted as a Solicitor in 1972 and has been in practice as a sole practitioner since 1988. He is currently the Editor of the *Farm Tax Brief* and *Trusts and Estates* newsletters published by Informa Publishing Limited. Richard is also a member of the Law Society's Capital Taxes Sub-Committee.

Table of Cases

Table of Statutes

Table of Statutory Instruments

Table of Checklists

Appendix III, Law Society Protocol and Formulae, contains most of the checklists required by practitioners in the form of:

III.1. National Conveyancing Protocol (4th edition) for domestic freehold and leasehold property
III.2. The Law Society's formulae for exchanging contracts by telephone, fax or telex
III.3. The Law Society's code for completion by post

However, the *Conveyancing Handbook* contains many other checklists in the main text. This table shows:

- paragraph number (bold);
- title of checklist; and
- chapter title (bold)

AAA   Stamp Duty Land Tax

The Finance Bill 2003 makes significant changes to stamp duty with effect from a date to be announced but expected to be 1 December 2003. The two significant sets of changes are that:

- stamp duty in its current form is to be removed from all property other than shares, marketable securities, bearer instruments, dealings in partnership shares and certain transactions involving transfers of land into and out of partnerships by way of capital; and

- stamp duty reserve tax (Finance Act 1986, s.87) continues to apply to the transfer and issue of chargeable securities, broadly, shares and certain loan stocks including certain dealings in bearer securities outside.

A totally new stamp duty land tax is to be imposed upon a wide range of transactions relating to land. It will be much wider and much more rigorously enforced than stamp duty.

Changeover arrangements

'Other property'

For all property, other than land and shares and certain loan stocks, stamp duty ceases to apply to documents executed on or after the implementation date. This will apply where the conveyance is executed pursuant to a contract entered into prior to the implementation date. However, in most situations the contract will be the stampable instrument (Finance Act 1999, Sched.13, para.7) so that parties contemplating arrangements relating to debts, benefits of contract, options and similar arrangements should consider utilising an option being granted before the implementation date for a small premium (*Wimpey* v. *IRC* [1975] 2 All ER 45) to be exercised after implementation date when the contract arising will be free of stamp duty.

Goodwill

Although stamp duty has been abolished upon goodwill one trap remains. Certain types of goodwill can become related to the premises and so are embedded in the value of the land. The price attributable to such goodwill is part of the land price and remains subject to stamp duty and, in time, stamp duty land tax.

Land

For transactions involving land, the transitional position is immensely complicated (Finance Bill 2003, Sched.19). The broad position is:

- contracts entered into on or before Royal Assent (mid-July) which are completed unaltered between the same parties after 1 December will not be subject to stamp duty land tax. It is uncertain whether they also escape stamp duty but this is not intended by the Revenue;

- contracts entered into on or before Royal Assent but varied, assigned or arising from exercise of pre-Royal Assent options after Royal Assent will, if completed after implementation date, be subject to stamp duty land tax;

- for contracts entered into on or before Royal Assent, where there is a subsale after that date and the title is transferred after the implementation date, although a charge to stamp duty land tax will arise in relation to the subsale contract there are to be amendments to the Finance Bill 2003 intended to ensure that the pre-Royal Assent arrangement is not subjected to tax. Details of the charge were not published at the time of writing but it appears that where A contracts to sell land to B prior to Royal Assent, B contracts to sell land to C after Royal Assent and completion from A to C is after implementation date B should not be subject to either tax);

- contracts entered into after Royal Assent if completed after implementation date are subject to stamp duty land tax. This applies even though if the transaction had been completed prior to implementation date no stamp duty would have arisen. Parties should, therefore, give careful thought to completing contracts such as releases of options or modifications of restrictive covenants and certain variations of lease where no stamp duty arises but stamp duty land tax will or the stamp duty regime may produce a lower charge.

Stamp duty land tax

The charge

The tax applies to the 'acquisition' of a 'chargeable interest' in land in the United Kingdom for a chargeable consideration. It applies whether or not the 'acquisition' is by written instrument, statute, order of the Court or operation of law such as constructive trusts (see *Yaxley* v. *Gotts* [1999] 2 WLR 1217). It also applies to foreign mergers involving United Kingdom land but as the reliefs for corporate reconstructions do not contain restrictions upon foreign companies such arrangements may be eligible for relief. The tax does apply to persons not resident in the United Kingdom.

'Acquisition' is extended to include the creation, release, surrender or variation of chargeable interests but not exceptions and reservations, although subsequent dealings in the rights reserved may be taxable.

Chargeable transactions include sales and exchanges of land. Exchanges are treated as two separate transactions each fully taxable. There is a limited exemption for part-exchanges involving new houses where the existing house has a lower value than the new house and the land involved is less than half of a hectare. A similar relief applies to relocation for employees where special relocation companies are involved. Partitions are not treated as exchanges; the land element is ignored and the tax charged only upon any equality adjustment.

Leases

Leases are taxable in respect of any premium and the rent. Rent is defined as including anything that is covered by the definition of 'rent' in the lease such as service charges and VAT if reserved as part of the rent. If not so reserved, service charges are exempt although VAT may be taxable as a premium payable by instalments. No tax is chargeable upon reserve premiums such as inducements to take the lease or a sum paid by the tenant as consideration for the landlord accepting the surrender. Payments by assignors to assignees are to be exempted. Also not chargeable are repairing and insurance covenants or any payments in respect thereof. Payments in respect of dilapidations are exempt but these may be so drafted as to involve a variation of the covenant to repair and run the risk of being taxable as a variation of the lease (see *Banning* v. *Wright* 48 TC 421).

The rent provisions are particularly brutal. There is a formula for 'capitalising' the net present value of the rent which is taxable at one per cent. In practice this means that the new tax upon rents will be four to five times greater than stamp duty in relation to leases for seven years and nine to ten times more expensive in relation to 25 year leases. The Inland Revenue Stamp Taxes Office are to make a facility available online for calculating the rent in accordance with the formula. Assignments of leases are taxable but amendments have been promised so that no tax arises in respect of the covenant to pay the future rent (see *Swayne* v. *IRC* [1900] 1 QB 172).

A variation of a lease involves five areas of potential charge to stamp duty land tax namely:

- the surrender of the existing lease;
- the grant of the new lease;
- any consideration provided by the tenant for the variation of the lease;
- any consideration provided by the landlord for the variation; and
- the new rent.

There is a limited relief for surrenders and regrants which is useless since it applies only where the new lease is for substantially the same term and substantially the same premises and upon the same terms and covenants. It is unlikely that this situation will be frequently encountered in practice. Variations of leases must, in the future, be approached on a cautious basis since alternative methods of avoiding certain of these charges may be available by side-by-side leases or options to renew or partial surrenders. Such arrangements will be taxable but only in respect of a particular transaction entered into not the whole of the land demised and the rent payable.

'Chargeable interests'

These are defined as estates or, interests in or over, or rights in or over, land in the United Kingdom. It applies whether such rights exist at law or in equity. Interests in trusts are within the definition. Special rules are made for foreign trusts so that the interests of beneficiaries are deemed to be interests in United Kingdom land. Variations of trusts and dealings in equitable or deemed equitable interests for consideration will be taxable, as will be an appointment of land to a discretionary beneficiary who provided consideration in order to be included in the class of beneficiaries. Trustee powers appear to be chargeable interests so that exercise of powers of appointment or their variation or release for a consideration may be chargeable. Variations of estates of deceased persons are within the tax but with a limited exemption similar to that available for stamp duty.

Rights in or over land such as mineral rights, easements, restrictive covenants, options and pre-emption rights, rent charges and agreements affecting the value of land such as covenants not to build are chargeable interests. Chargeable interests do not include security interests such as mortgages, although estate rent charges are not specifically dealt with. These it seems are chargeable interests and a transfer in consideration of the grant but not the reservation of an estate rent charge will be a transfer for a periodical payment when there will be tax upon 12 years rent charge. The sale of rent charges or their release or variation will be taxable.

Licenses and tenancies at will are not chargeable interests but entry into possession as a licensee under a contract may operate to trigger tax due in respect of that contract.

Chargeable consideration

There is no charge to stamp duty land tax where there is no chargeable consideration except in relation to acquisitions of land by companies connected with the other party including certain corporate trustees when the market value is subject to stamp duty.

Chargeable consideration is widely defined. It includes any consideration in money or money's worth. It also includes services, beneficial occupation of premises by employees giving rise to taxable benefits in kind and VAT (although where a transaction is completed at a time when no VAT is due the fact that VAT may arise if the option to tax is subsequently exercised is ignored on the initial transaction and the exercise appears not to be a variation of the relationship that requires reporting and payment of additional tax).

The position as regards building works is quite severe. The chargeable consideration includes 'works' which includes not merely construction but also repair, refurbishment and any other works or operations carried out to enhance the value of land. It applies to works carried out on land other than that being acquired. For example, an agreement to grant a lease to a person in consideration of that person constructing a building on the land of the lessor will give rise to stamp duty land tax upon the open market cost of the building. This will include a construction of infrastructure works on adjoining land if part of the consideration and can apply to works constructed by a person upon the land that he has acquired or is about to acquire unless those building works are carried out at his own expense after the acquisition of the land has been 'substantially performed'. Construction works upon the land to be acquired prior to substantial performance of the acquisition agreement will mean that stamp duty land tax is chargeable upon the open market cost of those works even when carried out by the purchaser or tenant in question.

Variable consideration

Where the consideration is payable by instalments the stamp duty land tax is charged upon the full amount without any discount for the deferral. Where the consideration is payable periodically other than rent such as annuities and, possibly, royalties, the tax is charged upon the full amount payable but where the sums are payable for more than 12 years the tax is charged upon the aggregate of the highest 12 years. The poor drafting by putting provisions in the wrong place with wrong terminology leaves open the question of how index-linking of such payments is to operate.

Where there is a contingency arrangement providing for the payment of a fixed sum if certain conditions are satisfied then the parties must pay tax initially on the full amount payable (but with the possibility of payment in respect of the contingent sum by instalments). The tax is refundable if the contingency cannot happen subsequently. Where the consideration is 'uncertain' (i.e. depends upon future factors such as overage payments or turnover rents) the tax is paid initially upon the basis of a reasonable estimate of what the parties think the variable payment will be over time. The question of 'uncertainty' is tested at the effective date which may not be the same as 'completion' in the strict sense. For example, where the consideration is the market value at completion that consideration is *prima facie* 'unascertained' at completion. However, if there is 'substantial performance' creating an effective date earlier than completion it will be 'uncertain' (i.e. linked to value in the future). This matters since different rules may apply to payment and reporting. It is necessary to report and pay any additional tax, or reclaim tax overpaid, every time a payment or adjustment is made or the amount of any instalment becomes settled. This will require multiple reporting in relation to leases, possibly, for example, every time the landlord increases a service charge which is included as part of the rent or where there is a turnover rent. Since the penalties imposed for failure to report or pay on time are of a severe nature this obligation of possibly monthly or quarterly reporting for stamp duty land tax must be noted and observed.

Tax event

A key issue is the 'effective date' which is the date fixing:

- the initial liability to stamp duty land tax;
- the rate;
- the values of relevant property;

- the start of the compliance obligations;
- the nature of the consideration as uncertain or variable;
- the clawback period for certain exemptions; and
- whether a person acquiring land has to pay stamp duty land tax upon building and other works be carries out upon that land.

It is defined basically as 'completion' which is not explained, but will in practice usually be irrelevant since special rules apply where there is a contract which contemplates completion by a written instrument. In such a case the effective date is the earlier of 'completion' or 'substantial performance'. The latter is the key event and is when either the purchaser pays a substantial amount (expected to be 90 per cent) of the consideration or where a purchaser or lessee goes into 'possession' of the land and pays or receives rent. It is unclear whether 'possession' and 'occupation' are to be regarded as the same, but includes entering as a licensee. Where a contract which has been substantially performed is later completed by a written instrument there is a further obligation to report the transaction and pay any additional tax.

Exemptions

The absence of a charge to stamp duty land tax arises for various reasons. Notification depends upon whether the transaction is 'exempt' or there is 'no chargeable consideration'. Other consequences follow for different no charge provisions.

There are exemptions for:

- transactions involving non-residential property in disadvantaged areas. This applies to all transactions. It should be noted that non-residential land includes the acquisition of six or more residential premises in a disadvantaged area. A certificate is required (see Statement of Practice SP1/2003 for guidance on the current relief which is likely to continue into the new tax);

- transactions for no chargeable consideration other than acquisitions by connected companies;

- acquisitions by charities. This is subject to numerous conditions and there is a clawback of the relief for charities if within three years the land ceases to be used for the purposes of the charity;

- land transactions within groups, and in connection with the re-organisation and reconstruction of companies provided the various conditions are satisfied, although it seems that the relief is not to be restricted to United Kingdom companies. This relief is clawed back if the parties cease to be under the same control or within the same group within a period of three years, this is extended if there are arrangements for the parties to cease to be associated or entered into during the three year period;

- certain sale and repurchases and sale and leaseback, by individuals in order to finance the acquisition of property. This is intended to avoid multiple charges upon persons who are restricted in their ability to enter into transactions involving interest;

- land transactions in connection with compulsory purchase and pursuant to planning obligations are exempt;

- incorporation of limited liability partnerships;

- certain acquisitions by registered social landlords providing short-term lets in relation to housing obligations;

- transactions in connection with matrimonial breakdown; and

- certain variations of the estates of deceased persons entered into within two years after the death.

Rates

Rates are expected to be the same as stamp duty, namely:

- consideration not exceeding £60,000 – nil;

- £250,000 – one per cent;

- £500,000 – three per cent; and

- £500,000+ – four per cent.

In the case of rents stamp duty is one per cent of the net present value, a significant increase in duty payable. The rates are modified in certain cases:

- for non-residential property transactions below £150,000 – nil;

- for rent where the net present value does not exceed £60,000 – nil;

- more than £60,000 – one per cent;

- for non-residential or mixed property the nil rate band is increased to £150,000; and

- where there is a lease of land in disadvantaged areas and the lease is granted for a premium and an annual rent exceeding £600 the nil rate band does not apply and the stamp duty is one per cent.

Compliance

Stamp duty land tax is based on self-assessment. Within 30 days after the 'effective date' the taxpayer is required to file a land tax return containing a self-assessment of the tax and pay the tax shown to be due by the return. This will require the taxpayer to carry out valuations determining the open market costs and other matters. Failure to carry out a proper valuation exercise will give rise to penalties for filing a negligent or possibly fraudulent return. The tax is directly enforceable and the Inland Revenue Stamp Taxes Office are given powers to bring court proceedings to collect the tax as a debt.

Although the Inland Revenue Stamp Taxes Office will possibly check the figures, their acceptance of the form and the issue of the certificate is not conclusive that the return is correct. They have power to 'enquire' and assess additional tax in the future.

Notification

The obligation to notify the Revenue applies to:

- grants of leases for a contractual term of seven years or more for a chargeable consideration;

- grants of leases for a contractual term of less than seven years where the stamp duty upon any premium is one per cent or higher or where the consideration includes or consists solely of rent and the tax is chargeable at the rate of one per cent or higher. Such leases must also be notified even if exempt; and

- any other acquisition of major interest in land (i.e. substantial performance of a contract for the freehold or leasehold interest, whether subsisting at law or in equity, unless it is exempt from charge as being for no consideration, in connection with divorce or the variation of the estate of a deceased person or is a lease by a registered social landlord on a short-term basis).

Failure to file a return with the appropriate payment and including the necessary certificate gives rise to penalties which may be tax related if the delay is significant. The Inland Revenue Stamp Taxes Office are given power to demand the production of a return and may issue an assessment of the amount of tax they think is due. The form is to be prescribed by the Inland Revenue Stamp Taxes Office and it will be considerably more complicated than the present PD form and Land Registry TR1.

Certificates

Land transactions may not be registered unless one of two forms of certificate is produced. This is either a certificate from the Inland Revenue Stamp Taxes Office that the return has been delivered and the tax paid or a 'self-certificate' issued by the taxpayer that no return is required in respect of the transaction. Issue of incorrect self-certificates can give rise to tax related penalties.

Continuous reporting

The return or amended return is required on every occasion where the relevant event happens. For example, where there is variable consideration any adjustment in the amount estimated on the return requires the filing of an additional return, possibly including re-claim. Every time rent is varied under a lease, otherwise than pursuant to a rent review to market rent, a return will be required together with payment of additional tax or a reclaim application.

Enquiries

The Inland Revenue Stamp Taxes Office are given wide powers to enquire into land transactions and to challenge returns. Normally this enquiry must be started before the end of nine months after the date on which the return was delivered or amended. However, if the Inland Revenue Stamp Taxes Office subsequently 'discover' that insufficient tax has been paid and this involves fraud or negligence on the part of; the purchaser, a person acting on behalf of the purchaser, or a person who was a partner of the purchaser at the relevant time, the assessment may be made up to 21 years after the effective date.

Record-keeping

Extensive records are required; but the full extent is not made clear by the legislation. For example, when making a self-assessment the parties may be required to carry out a valuation exercise. Unless there is a proper attempt by obtaining suitable professional advice and carrying out other investigations to determine the market value, the Inland Revenue Stamp Taxes Office will regard the return as negligent or possibly fraudulent. In consequence, it is necessary to keep records of all such advice and steps taken to arrive at a reasonable figure. The enquiry can extend to self-certificates so that records are required to justify use of the self-certificate. These records will include the documents themselves or copies of, maps, plans, commercial projections, details of payment receipts and of financial arrangements such as mortgages. Penalties up to £3,000 may be imposed for failure to comply with record-keeping obligations.

Information gathering powers

The Inland Revenue Stamp Taxes Office are given extensive powers to demand copies of documents from the taxpayer, third parties who have documents in their power and, in certain circumstances, from tax accountants. Documents held by legal advisers can be demanded unless protected by a specially defined form of legal privilege. In some cases the approval of a judicial authority is required to the issue of notices requiring production of documents or information.

Appeals

Appeals against liability to tax or matters arising in an enquiry can be made to the General or Special Commissioners. The Regulations are yet to be issued determining jurisdiction in these matters.

Penalties

Penalties are imposed for fraudulently or negligently delivering a land transaction return which is incorrect or for failure to correct a land transaction return subsequently discovered to be incorrect. Penalties may be tax related. A person who assists in or induces the preparation or delivery of any information return or other document that he knows will be used for the purposes of the tax and which he knows to be incorrect is liable to a penalty not exceeding £3,000. This will include professional advisers involved in the preparation of the return or the transaction document. Moreover, a person who is knowingly concerned in the fraudulent evasion of tax by him or any other person, e.g. a client, is liable to a fine and/or imprisonment for a term not exceeding seven years.

AA New Developments in Conveyancing Practice

AA.1. Land Registration Act 2002

Although published prior to the implementation date, this handbook reflects the provisions of both the Land Registration Act 2002 and Land Registration Rules 2003 as at 13 October 2003. The major changes made by the new legislation are summarised in section A22 Land Registration Act 2002. The Appendices include various reference sections, including:

- XII.4.   Land Registration Act (selected Schedules)
- XII.5.   Land Registration Rules 2003 (extracts)
- XII.6.   Land Registration Fees Order 2003
- XIII.1.   Land Registry Forms

The full text of the Act and Rules is available on the Land Registry web site: www.landregistry.gov.uk/legislation/.

AA.2. New Terminology

The Act makes some changes to terminology and the new terminology is adopted in the text. Two terms used in the handbook are of particular relevance:

- The term '*official copy entries of the title*' is used in this handbook to include an official copy of the register and title plan and an official copy of any other document referred to on the register as being filed.

- The Act refers to 'unregistered interests which override' and, for ease of reference, the term '*overriding interests*' is adopted in this handbook.

AA.3. Commonhold and Leasehold Reform

The Commonhold and Leasehold Reform Act 2002 received Royal Assent on 1 May 2002. The commonhold provisions in the first Part of the Act are to be brought into force by Regulations made by the new Department of Constitutional Affairs. It is currently anticipated that commonhold will be introduced in Spring 2004.

A new section L of the Handbook deals with commonhold, but as the regulations have yet to be finalised it is necessarily lacking in detail. The Land Registry has published a report on their Commonhold (Land Registration) Rules consultation, and this is available on their website.

The second Part of the Act containing the provisions on leasehold reform is being implemented by the Office of the Deputy Prime Minister. The Commonhold and Leasehold Reform Act 2002 (Commencement No.1 Savings and Transitional Provisions (England)) Order 2002, brought the right to enfranchisement (RTE) and right to manage (RTM) into force on 26 July 2002.

This edition of the handbook deals with RTM in para. K6.10 and RTE in para K9.3. Readers are advised to monitor the following web sites for further developments:

- www.landregistry.gov.uk/legislation/
- www.housing.odpm.gov.uk/
- www.lcd.gov.uk/

Further information may be obtained from:

Leasehold Reform Team
Office of the Deputy Prime Minister
HPS Division
Zone 2/J6, Eland House
Bressenden Place
London SW1E 5DU
Tel: 020 7944 3462 or 020 7944 3463

Commonhold Team
Department for Constitutional Affairs
Room 3N2
3rd Floor
Southside
105 Victoria Street
London SW1E 6QT
Tel: 020 7210 1227

AA.4. Landlord and Tenant Act 1954 Reform

A draft Regulatory Reform Order entitled The Regulatory Form (Business Tenancies) (England and Wales) Order 2003 has been laid before Parliament, but is being revised following its passage through the House of Lords Select Committee. If successful, the Order will come into force six months after it is made.

The Reform Order proposes changes in the following areas:

- Agreements to exclude security of tenure
- Surrenders
- Termination by tenant
- Notices requiring information
- Landlord's termination notice
- Renewal and termination procedures
- Applications to court by landlord
- Ownership and control of businesses
- Interim rent
- Compensation

The Regulatory Reform Order has yet to be made at the time of going to press with this edition of the handbook. Readers can access all of the background information and the latest news on the progress of the Order on the Cabinet Office's website (www.cabinet-office.gov.uk/regulation/act/proposals.htm).

AA.5. Stamp Duty

The Inland Revenue issued a consultation document 'Modernising Stamp Duty on Land and Buildings' in April 2002. Following the consultation period, provisions outlining a new Stamp Duty Land Tax were included in the Finance Bill 2003 (16 April 2003). In addition to the Finance Bill, regulations are planned to expand the details of the new tax.

The Finance Bill 2003 is published on the HMSO web site. Further explanatory notes are available on the HM Treasury website.

Consultation on the new tax continues throughout the summer of 2003 and any changes that result will be included in the supporting regulations or the next Finance Bill in 2004. The Inland Revenue website includes a document that explains which sections of the Finance Bill are under particular scrutiny.

It is proposed that the Stamp Duty Land Tax will be brought into force on 1 December 2003.

The main provisions of the tax, as provided for in the Finance Bill 2003, are outlined in a new section AAA. Stamp Duty Land Tax. As the final detail of the tax is unknown at the time of going to press, the remainder of the book is up-to-date with the law and practice of Stamp Duty as of 1 June 2003.

Disadvantaged Areas Relief is dealt with in section B10 Pre-contract Searches and Enquiries and section A14 Stamp Duty and Stamp Duty Savings. The Inland Revenue Statement of Practice on Disadvantaged Areas is reproduced in Appendix IX.3.

The Law Society is also organising seminars in conjunction with the Inland Revenue Stamp Taxes Office to explain the implications of the new tax for solicitors. These seminars will be organised by the Law Society's Regional Managers and held throughout England and Wales in the autumn of 2003.

Inland Revenue Stamp Taxes Office Publications

- Stamp Duty – Are you prepared for the changes? (Information Bulletin)
- 'Modernising Stamp Duty: Paper to set out planned consultations during summer 2003'
- Finance Bill 2003 Press Notice (REV55)
- Budget Day 2003 Press Notice (PN08) Inland Revenue Rates and Allowances for 2003–04
- Budget Day 2003 Press Notice (PN05) Modernising the taxation of property.
- Budget Day 2002 Press Notice (REV4 Supplement) Stamp Duty on UK Land and Buildings
- Budget Day 2002 Press Notice (REV4) Stamp Duty on UK Land and Buildings

Inland Revenue Stamp Taxes Office Enquiry Line

The enquiry line (Tel: 0845 603 0135 Mon–Fri 8.30am–5pm) is available to deal with general queries about modernising stamp duty.

AA.6. Money Laundering

HM Treasury is expected to make new Regulations in 2003 (the HM Treasury Public Enquiry line is 020 7270 4558). To date these regulations have not been laid before Parliament. The Treasury has announced that the regulations will come into force 3 months after the laying before Parliament.

When in force the regulations will extend the scope of the present Money Laundering Regulations. The draft regulations suggest that the new scope rule will cover (of particular relevance for property lawyers)

'... the provision of legal services ... which involves participation in a financial or real property transaction (whether by assisting in the planning or execution of transactions or otherwise by acting for, or on behalf of, a client'.

This means that property lawyers will have to comply fully with the regulations including the client verification and record keeping requirements.

In addition, the new scope rule will identify what is meant by 'the regulated sector' within the meaning of the Proceeds of Crime Act 2002. In particular, section 330 of the Act imposes an obligation to report knowledge or suspicion (or reasonable grounds for knowledge or suspicion) of another person's involvement in money laundering where that knowledge or suspicion came to light whilst acting in the 'regulated sector'. Once solicitors recognise that they are acting in the regulated sector (as a result of the new Money Laundering Regulations) systems must be implemented to ensure that all members of staff are made aware of their obligations under the Proceeds of Crime Act.

The Law Society will be updating their guidance once the new Regulations are made. The guidance will be made available on the Law Society's web site when it's published.

AA.7. Planning and Compulsory Purchase

The Government has secured the agreement of the House of Commons to carry the Planning and Compulsory Purchase Bill over into the 2003/4 session. The Bill is now expected to come into force in the summer of 2004. The Government will be introducing new provisions into the Bill so at the time of going to press, the final detail of the legislation is unclear.

However, the key features that are already known include the removal of statutory planning powers from county councils and the introduction of regional spatial strategies to be prepared at the regional level. At the local level, local authorities will have local development frameworks in place of the existing local or unitary plans. Local authorities will be able to introduce local development orders to implement the policies in their local development frameworks. They will also have new powers to decline to determine repeat or similar applications.

Outline planning permission will be replaced by statements of development principles which will not equate to a consent but which will be a material consideration when a developer comes to submit a full application. The period for the implementation of a planning permission will be reduced from the present 5 to 3 years and automatic renewal of a permission will be abolished – the developer would have to submit a fresh application.

Finally the exercise of compulsory purchase powers by local authorities is to be simplified and fairer compensation arrangements will be introduced.

Solicitors can access all the relevant documents on the web site of the Office of the Deputy Prime Minister – www.planning.odpm.gov.uk/consult/greenpap/greenind.htm

AA.8. National Land Information Service

During 2003, there will be changes to take into account the new procedures introduced by the Land Registration Act 2002 and Commonhold and Leasehold Reform Act 2002.

Specifically, NLIS will deliver the following Land Registry products and enhancements during 2003, through its online channels:

- extended hours (Saturday processing);

- retrieval and presentation of a scanned Deed;

- retrieval and presentation of a Land Charges scanned Register;

- submission of Land Charges Search request, including Bankruptcy only, but limited to simple names and limited companies, with PDF result and the result printed and despatched centrally;

- list of documents relating to a Title Number;

- automatic processing of Official Copy requests, with the production of the guaranteed (watermarked) result either in PDF format, or as a centrally printed hard copy;

- Land Registration Act 2002 changes;

- automatic processing of Official Search results with the automatic production of the guaranteed (watermark) result either in PDF format, or as a centrally printed hard copy;

- Commonhold and Leasehold Reform Act 2002 changes.

In the not too distant future, the following items will also be available:

- Vectorised Index Map searching;

- Ability to undertake a property search, using the Unique Property Reference Number (UPRN) from the NLPG.

AA.9. Home Information Packs

'Seller's Packs' first appeared in the Homes Bill on 12 December 2000. That bill failed to complete its passage through Parliament. However, on 31 March 2003 a Draft Housing Bill was published that includes proposals for 'Home Information Packs'.

The draft bill proposes that sellers of residential properties in England and Wales, or their agents, must make a Home Information Pack available before marketing homes for sale, and that they make a copy of the pack available to prospective buyers on request. It is proposed that the pack should include standard documents and information for prospective buyers.

The Government has issued three consultation papers, one of which deals with the contents of the Home Information Packs. The other two papers deal with the draft Housing Bill and the potential impact of the pack in low cost and low demand areas. The consultation papers can be obtained from:

- www.housing.odpm.gov.uk/information/consult/housingbill/
- www.housing.odpm.gov.uk/information/consult/infopack/contents/

The Law Society's responses to the papers can be found on the Law Society's web site (www.lawsociety.org.uk).

AA.10. Land, Valuation and Housing Tribunals

Following publication in 2001 of the Leggatt Review on Tribunals, which recommended reform of the tribunal system as a whole, the Law Commission has been consulting on the reform of land, valuation and housing tribunals. These are the Lands Tribunal, Leasehold Valuation Tribunal, Rent Assessment Committee, Rent Tribunal, Agricultural Land Tribunal, Valuation Tribunal, Commons Commissioners and the new Adjudicator established under the Land Registration Act 2002.

These specialist property tribunals hear hundreds of thousands cases every year including cases about leasehold service charges and the appointment of managers; leasehold enfranchisement; security of tenure and succession in agricultural tenancies; fair rents; restrictive covenants; land compensation and the valuation of property for council tax and rating purposes.

The Law Commission's consultation paper suggests the reform of these tribunals to place them within a more unified structure. It also considers the extent to which there may be overlap between the jurisdictions of these tribunals and the courts. The project aims to meet the need for an expert decision-making forum for property disputes, with a structure that is clear to tribunal users and without unnecessary overlaps between the tribunals and the courts.

Final recommendations for reform will be set out in the Law Commission's report which is published in September 2003. A White Paper setting out further details for the reform of tribunals and the creation of a new Tribunals Service is also anticipated in the Autumn 2003. Further information on the Law Commission project can be obtained on www.lawcom.gov.uk, or by contacting:

The Housing and Administrative Justice Team
The Law Commission
Conquest House
37–38 John Street
Theobalds Road
London WC1N 2BQ
Tel: 020 7453 1228
Email: housingandadmin@lawcommission.gsi.gov.uk

AA.11. Law Society policy and guidance

The current edition of *The Guide to the Professional Conduct of Solicitors* is the 8th edition, published and distributed in 1999.

The current edition of *The Solicitors' Accounts Manual* is the 8th edition published in 2001. The manual includes the Solicitors' Accounts Rules 1998 as updated to 1 September 2001.

The Law Society's web site www.guide-on-line.lawsociety.org.uk includes the full text of the *Guide* and Accounts Rules.

In May 1999, the Regulation Review Working Party was set up by the Law Society Council to start the task of rewriting the rules with a view to simplifying them. The Rules are currently undergoing consultation.

The Law Society's Professional Ethics helpline (Tel: 0870 606 2577) will answer queries relating to professional conduct and the Law Society's Practice Advice line (Tel: 0870 606 2522) will answer queries relating to conveyancing practice.

A selection of the Law Society's client leaflets are reproduced in Appendix VI.

AA.12. The Land Registry

The Land Registration Act 2002 contains provisions that create a framework for the development of electronic conveyancing. A report on the e-conveyancing consultation exercise is available on the e-conveyancing website (www.e-conveyancing.gov.uk).

The Direct Access Service is due to be withdrawn by 13 October 2003, but further changes are planned to Land Registry Direct (www.landregistrydirect. gov.uk). These include the ability for practitioners to create their own official copy entries of the title.

Land Register Online (www.landregisteronline.gov.uk) was launched on 24 March 2003. This service enables members of the public to view registers and title plans via the Internet.

The Land Registry is piloting a new system (EDs) allowing mortgage lenders to discharge their mortgages electronically. If successful, EDs may replace the current ENDs system.

An Action Pack with CD-ROM was distributed in July 2003 to all Land Registry clients and those who registered on the web site (www.landreg.org.uk/legislation/) with all the available forms and explanatory literature from the Land Registry. The Land Registry plan to release a further CD-ROM when more forms and guidance becomes available.

AA.13. Standard Conditions of Sale

This edition of the handbook refers to the third edition of the Standard Conditions of Sale and the first edition of the Standard Commercial Conditions of Sale. Both of which are inconsistent with the Land Registration Act 2002 (i.e. referring to leases of 21 rather than 7 years and to Section 110 of the Land Registration Act 1925).

The Standard Conditions of Sale and the Standard Commercial Conditions of Sale are due to be revised. At the time of going to press a joint working party comprised of representatives from the Law Society and the Solicitors' Law Stationery Society Limited have met to discuss the changes required to bring the Conditions up-to-date. It is hoped that the revised edition of Standard Conditions of Sale will be published in the autumn of 2003, with the revised edition of the Commercial Conditions shortly afterwards.

Further details will be publicised in the Law Society's *Gazette*.

AA.14. Chancel Repair Liability

In 1985 the Law Commission reported that the Chancel Repairs Act 1932 was 'anachronistic and capricious in its modern application' (Law Com No 152, 1985), but since then there has been no move to reform the Act. The liability was a category of overriding interest in the Land Registration Act 1925, s.70(1)(c)) but this has not been replicated in the Land Registration Act 2002. However, the liability has been considered by the High Court, the Court of Appeal, and now the House of Lords.

The High Court held in *Wallbank* v. *Aston Cantlow Parochial Church Council* (2000) *Times*, 30 March that liability to repair the chancel of a church under the Chancel Repairs Act 1932 was not removed by Articles 1, 9, or 14 of the European Convention on Human Rights.

In *Wallbank* v. *Aston Cantlow Parochial Church Council* [2001] EWCA Civ 713 the Court of Appeal overruled the Hight Court decision and found that chancel repair was incompatible with the Human Rights Act 1998. It was held that the Parochial Church Council was a 'public authority' within the meaning of HRA 1998, s.6 and as such it must act within the bounds of the European Convention on Human Rights. In particular, the Court of Appeal decided that chancel repair liability violated Article 1 of the First Protocol (peaceful enjoyment of possessions), and Article 14 (prohibition of discrimination).

However, the House of Lords overturned the Court of Appeal decision on 26 June 2003 in *Aston Cantlow and Wilmcote with Billesley Parochial Church Council* v. *Wallbank and another* [2003] UKHL 37.

It was held that a parochial church council is not a core public authority by virtue of s.6(3)(b) of the Human Rights Act 1998 and there is therefore no relief for lay rectors from chancel repairs under the 1998 Act.

Solicitors are able to conduct a chancel repair search at the Public Records Office according to the procedure in B10. Pre-Contract Searches and Enquiries.

AA.15. The Law Society's Property Section

The Law Society's Property Section is a subscription-based membership group that offers practice-specific advice and guidance to practitioners. The Section works closely with the specialist Committees who advise the Law Society Council and its subsidiary boards on policy in areas of Law.

In response to market research conducted by the Law Society early in 2002, the Property Section was launched with the focus of supporting solicitors when dealing with fundamental changes facing the modern practice.

The Section aims to address the needs and concerns of both residential and commercial property solicitors. Members benefit from a number of resources, including:

- a quarterly magazine 'Property in Practice'
- an email alert service
- an interactive website (yet to be launched at the time of going to press)

For more information about the Section and an application pack, please email to propertysection@lawsociety.org.uk.

AA.15 Licensing Bill

A Bill to reform alcohol and entertainment licensing law in England & Wales was announced in the Queen's Speech on 13 November 2002. The third reading took place in the House of Commons on 16 June 2003 and the Bill returned to the Lords for consideration of Commons amendments. At the time of going to press, the date of Royal Assent and implementation, and the details of transitional provisions are unknown.

The Bill gives responsibility for licensing to District Councils (the Magistrates will hear appeals). The District Councils will have a duty to promote the 'Licensing Objectives':

- Prevention of crime and disorder;
- Public safety;
- Prevention of public nuisance; and
- Protection of children from harm

Properties will require a 'Premises Licence' and need to be supervised by the holder of a 'Personal Licence'. The Premises Licence will be subject to various safety conditions.

Clubs will require a 'Club Premises Certificate' and need to prove to the Council that they are established in good faith for the benefit of club members and have appropriate rules.

'Personal Licences' will be of 10 years duration and renewable. The applicant must hold a licensing qualification from an accredited body.

The Act creates various offences and grants powers to the Magistrates to fine, imprison and close premises down.

AA.17. The Right to Buy Scheme

The Housing Bill, which is also discussed with regard to Home Information Packs in this section, also includes proposed amendments to the Right to Buy Scheme.

In an effort to tackle profiteering, the Bill proposes a number of changes to the scheme. First, the initial qualification period will be increased from two to five years. Thereafter tenants will qualify for the same amount of discount as they do under the current scheme.

Second, the period after sale during which landlords may require owners to repay some or all of their discount on early resale will be extended from three to five years, although there will be a discretion to waive repayment.

Finally, the repayment figure will be altered to reflect a percentage of the resale value of the property rather than the current flat rate basis.

In addition to the changes in the Bill, as from 27 March 2003 the maximum discount available has been lowered to £16,000 in 41 local authority areas in London and the South of England.

AA.18. PACT Scheme

At the time of going to press, a new edition of the guidance notes to the PACT scheme (Professional Arbitration on Court Terms) from the Law Society and the Royal Institute of Chartered Surveyors (RICS) has just been published.

The PACT scheme provides the services of surveyors and solicitors to determine lease renewal disputes as an alternative to litigation. It focuses on unopposed lease renewals under the Landlord and Tenant Act 1954 and offers opportunity for disputes to be resolved without the necessity of going to court.

The scheme provides opportunity for landlords and tenants to have the terms and rent payable under their new lease decided by a surveyor or solicitor acting as either an arbitrator or independent expert. The appointments will be made by RICS or Law Society. The professionals to be appointed are experienced specialists who have been specifically trained under the PACT scheme.

Requests for further information or an application form can be sent to:

- RICS Dispute Resolution Service, Surveyor Court, Westwood Way, Coventry CV4 8JE (Tel: 020 7222 7000); or
- The Arbitration Service, The Law Society, 113 Chancery Lane, London WC2A 1PL (Tel: 020 7242 1222).

A. PRELIMINARY MATTERS

A1. Taking instructions

1.1.　Objectives

1.1.1.　The purpose of taking instructions is to obtain sufficient information from the client to enable the solicitor to conduct the whole transaction: it will be necessary to consult the client further during the course of the transaction, but taking full instructions at an early stage will obviate the need to contact the client frequently to confirm minor details. The need constantly to check minor details with the client is not cost effective nor does it inspire the client with confidence in the solicitor's ability to do the work.

1.1.2.　A further objective is to obtain an overall view of the transaction in order to give the client full and proper advice appropriate to the circumstances: unless full instructions are taken the solicitor is in danger of overlooking matters which are relevant to the transaction, e.g. insuring the property, or the inheritance tax implications of co-ownership.

1.1.3.　*Taxation consequences*

Regard must always be paid to the taxation consequences of the proposed transaction whether or not these are mentioned to the solicitor by the client. Failure to do so may result in an action for breach of contract or negligence by the client against the solicitor.[1]

1. See *Hurlingham Estates Ltd* v. *Wilde, The Times*, 3 January 1997.

1.2.　Where have the instructions come from?

1.2.1.　Instructions to act may be accepted provided there is no breach of Rule 1 Solicitors' Practice Rules 1990 (obtaining instructions). (See below, Appendix I.1.) Thus instructions must be declined *inter alia* in the following circumstances:

(a)　where to act would involve the solicitor in a breach of the law, e.g. a fraudulent conveyance;

(b)　where the solicitor would be involved in a breach of the rules of conduct, e.g. dealing with more than one prospective buyer without disclosing this to all prospective buyers;

(c) where a conflict of interest exists or is likely to exist;

(d) where the solicitor lacks the expertise to carry out the client's instructions competently;

(e) where the solicitor does not have sufficient time to devote to the client's affairs;

(f) where the instructions are tainted by duress or undue influence, e.g. an elderly client is 'persuaded' by her relatives to sell the family home;

(g) where the solicitor, one of his partners, employees or close relatives holds some office or appointment the holding of which might lead the client or the general public to infer that the solicitor had some influence over the outcome of the matter, e.g. a solicitor who is a member of the local planning committee should not accept instructions to act in a planning appeal against the authority of which he is a member;

(h) where another solicitor has already been instructed in the matter and that other solicitor's retainer has not been terminated;

(i) where the client's freedom of choice to instruct the solicitor of his choosing has been impaired in some way, e.g. the client has received a discount from a builder on the condition that a certain solicitor is instructed.

1.2.2.   Subject to the exceptions outlined above the solicitor cannot decline to act on the basis of the colour, race, national or ethnic origins of the client[1] nor on the basis of the client's sex or sexual orientation, marital status[2] or disability.[3]

1.2.3.   Instructions which have been obtained through a referral from an estate agent, mortgage broker or other third party may be accepted provided there is compliance with Rule 3 Solicitors' Practice Rules 1990 (introductions and referrals).[4]

1.2.4.   If instructions are received indirectly through a third party, confirmation of the instructions must be obtained directly from the client in order to clarify the client's exact requirements and to ensure that the instructions are not tainted by duress or undue influence.

1.2.5.   The solicitor should be alert to the possibilities of mortgage fraud and should adhere to the guidelines issued by the Law Society in its leaflet 'Green Card Warning on Property Fraud II' (see Appendix IV.3).

1. Race Relations Act 1976, Law Society's Anti-Discrimination Code and Solicitors' Anti-Discrimination Rule 1995 (Appendix I.3).
2. Sex Discrimination Act 1975 and Law Society's Code.
3. Disability Discrimination Act 1995.
4. See Introductions and referrals, para. A7.

1.3.   Taking instructions in person

1.3.1.   Wherever possible instructions should be obtained from the client in a personal interview. This will enable the solicitor to clarify areas of doubt concerning the transaction, enable the client to ask questions about matters which worry him, and establish a confident working relationship between the solicitor and his client.

1.3.2.   Where the solicitor is instructed by one person to act on behalf of that person and another, e.g. as co-sellers, the non-instructing client's authority to act and consent to the transaction should be confirmed directly with the person concerned.

1.3.3.   If the interviewer is not the person who will conduct the transaction on the client's behalf, the client should be introduced to or at least told the name and status within the firm of the person who will be effecting the client's business and of the person whom he may contact should the need arise and whom the client should contact in the event of a problem or complaint arising about the solicitor's services.[1]

1.3.4.   Under the terms of the Protocol, the solicitor who is acting for the seller is required to obtain his client's answers to the Seller's Property Information Form, to obtain from his client any relevant documents relating to, e.g. guarantees, building regulation consent, etc., and to ask his client to complete the Fixtures Fittings and Contents Form. He must also obtain details of all financial charges over the property (including second and subsequent mortgages, improvement grants and discounts repayable to the local authority), and ascertain the identity of all persons aged over 17 who are resident in the property in order to establish whether or not such persons have an interest in the property.

1. See Rule 15 Solicitors' Practice Rules 1990 (Appendix I.1) and Practice Management Standard F4.

1.4.   Instructions taken by telephone, etc.

1.4.1.   If instructions are received by telephone, e-mail or by any other non-face-to-face method, consideration must be given to the Consumer Protection (Distance Selling) Regulations 2000.[1]

1.4.2.   The Regulations apply where a 'supplier' (the solicitor) is providing services to a 'consumer' (an individual instructing the solicitor on personal business). Corporate clients instructing a solicitor on company business are not consumers within this definition.

1.4.3.   A 'distance contract' is one which is concluded under 'an organised sales or services provision scheme' e.g. in response to an advertisement or where there is no physical communication up to and at the moment when the contract is concluded. Instructions received by letter or e-mail may fall within this definition of a distance contract.

1.4.4.   Contracts relating to financial services are exempted from the regulations but contracts to provide conveyancing services are not currently exempt.

1.4.5.   Where the regulations apply certain information must be supplied to the client in writing.[2] Most of the information required would be contained in a client care letter (e.g. name of solicitor, price, description of service to be provided) but in order to comply with the regulations it is suggested that, in cases where the regulations do or might apply, a clause is included in the client care letter to state that the contract between the solicitor and client will not be concluded until the client signs and returns a copy of the client care letter to the solicitor.

1.4.6. Further, the client care letter must exclude the client's right to cancel the contract once work under it has commenced[3] and should seek the client's agreement to the contract coming into force from the moment the signed client care letter is returned to the solicitor.

1.4.7. It is also essential for the client care letter to obtain the client's agreement to exclude Regulation 19 which provides that if the services provided under the contract are not performed within a maximum of 30 days from the date of the contract, the contract is treated as if it had not been made.

1. S.I. 2000/2334.
2. Regulations 7 and 8.
3. Otherwise a right to cancel and to recover money paid exists under Regulation 10.

1.5.   Identity of the client

1.5.1. A solicitor who purports to act on behalf of a client impliedly warrants to third parties with whom he has dealings (e.g. the other party's solicitor) that he has the client's authority to act. If he does not have the client's authority he may be liable to the third party for breach of warranty of authority.[1] For this reason a solicitor may want to check the identity of a client with whom he is not familiar.

1.5.2. Checking the client's identity may serve as a precaution against mortgage fraud and money laundering and establishes that the client is the person who he says he is, thus ensuring that the solicitor has the client's authority to act in the transaction[2]. The Law Society is due to release guidance on Money Laundering in 2003.

1.5.3.   *Lender's requirements*

When acting for a lender under the terms of the CML Lenders' Handbook,[3] the identity of the client must be verified in accordance with the requirements of paragraph 3.3. of the Handbook.

1. See *Penn* v. *Bristol & West Building Society,* [1997] 3 All ER 470.
2. See Money Laundering, A23; and Mortgage Fraud, A24.
3. See Appendix VIII.3 for Part 1 of the CML Lenders' Handbook.

1.6.   Using checklists

1.6.1. Although checklists cannot be expected to cover every eventuality in every transaction they are useful in standard transactions to ensure that all necessary information is acquired during the course of the interview.

1.6.2. Checklists focus the interviewer's mind on the relevant information, which minimises preparation time and ultimately saves time in the interview itself, but do need to be used sympathetically so that the client does not feel he is being processed in an impersonal way.

1.6.3. Where checklists are used it is helpful to have them printed on a distinct colour of paper so that they are easily located in the file either by the solicitor himself or by another member of his staff who has to work on the file.

1.6.4. A reminder of the matters which will be raised at a first interview with a client is set out in paras. 1.7–1.9 below. Standard checklists for sellers and buyers may be compiled from these guidelines to suit the individual requirements of particular firms.

1.7. Acting for the seller

1.7.1.

Item	Reason for Question	Further Reference
(a) Date instructions taken.	Record keeping.	
(b) Full names, addresses of seller(s) buyer(s) and home and business telephone numbers.	Needed in contract and for contact with client.	
(c) Name and address of person at estate agents.	For contact.	
(d) Find out where title deeds are and obtain client's authority to obtain them if in the hands of a third party.	To deduce title.	Deducing title, D1.
(e) Ask clients for title number (if known).	To obtain official copy entries of the title.	Investigation of title, D2.
(f) Name of other parties' solicitors or representatives.	For contact.	Dealing with non-solicitors, A5.
(g) Do we act for the other party also?	Conflict of interest, breach of Rule 6.	Acting for both parties, A10.
(h) Full address of property to be sold.	Needed in contract.	
(i) Situation of property – position of footpaths/ railways/rivers, etc.	Need for plan or special searches.	Pre-contract searches and enquiries, B10.

Item	Reason for Question	Further Reference
(j) Tenure: freehold/leasehold.	Needed in contract.	
(k) Price.	Needed in contract, stamp duty considerations.	
(l) Has any preliminary deposit been paid? If so, how much? Receipt obtained?	Take account in calculating deposit on exchange.	Preliminary deposits, A12.
(m) Which fixtures are to be removed?	Needed in contract.	Fixtures and fittings, B22.
(n) Which fittings are to remain? Additional price for fittings?	Needed in contract and may affect stamp duty. Need to supply Fixtures, Fittings and Contents Form to client.	Fixtures and fittings, B22.
(o) Anticipated completion date.	To advise client on likely duration of transaction and to assess urgency of matter. To discuss redemption of present mortgage, i.e. interest charges up to end of month.	
(p) Present/proposed use of property.	Planning aspects/ restrictive covenants.	
(q) Does the transaction attract VAT?	May be needed in contract and client may need advice.	VAT, A16.
(r) Who is resident in the property?	Occupiers' rights, overriding interests.	Seller's investigation of title, B3.
(s) Is the transaction dependent on the purchase?	Synchronisation.	Exchange, section C.
(t) Any other terms agreed between the parties?	Needed in contract.	
(u) Any correspondence between the parties?	Existence of a contract, or other terms agreed.	Form of contract, B11.

Item		Reason for Question	Further Reference
(v)	Vacant possession/ details of tenancies.	Needed in contract.	
(w)	Advice as to costs.	Required by Rule 15 (costs information and client care code).[1]	Estimate of costs, A8.
(x)	Interest on deposit.	Deposit interest considerations.	Deposit, B17.
(y)	Do a financial calculation, including costs.	To ensure the client can afford the transaction.	
(z)	Time taken in interview.	Time costing/recording.	
(aa)	Did we act on purchase?	Look at old file prior to interview to gain relevant information.	
(bb)	Are there any outstanding mortgages? How much and to whom?	Calculation of financial statement and will normally need to be redeemed on completion.	
(cc)	Ask for seller's mortgage account number or reference.	Needed in order to obtain deeds from lender and to obtain a preliminary redemption statement.	
(dd)	Advise seller not to cancel mortgage repayments or insurance until completion.	So that redemption figure obtained on completion is not higher than presently anticipated.	
(ee)	How much deposit required?	Advise client on dangers of reduced deposit, use of deposit in related purchase.	Deposit, B17.
(ff)	What is to happen to the proceeds of sale?	Accounting to the client, investment advice.	Financial services, A4. Post-completion, section G.
(gg)	Does the sale attract CGT?	Advise the client.	Capital gains tax, A15.

1. See Appendix II.4.

Item	Reason for Question	Further Reference
(hh) Obtain answers to Seller's Property Information Form and completion of Fixtures, Fittings and Contents Form.	To supply the buyer with this information.	Pre-contract searches and enquiries, B10.
(ii) Discuss advantage of making a local search and enquiries and any other relevant searches.		Pre-contract searches and enquiries, B10.
(jj) Check identity of client.	A precaution against mortgage fraud and money laundering.	Para. A1.4; Money Laundering, A23; Mortgage Fraud, A24.

1.8. Acting for the buyer

1.8.1.

Item	Reason for Question	Further Reference
(a) Date instructions taken.	Record keeping.	
(b) Full names and addresses of seller(s) and buyer(s) and home and business telephone numbers.	Needed in contract and for contact with client.	
(c) Name and address of person at estate agents.	For contact.	
(d) Name of other parties' solicitors or representatives.	For contact.	Dealing with non-solicitors, A5.
(e) Do we act for the other party also?	Conflict of interest, breach of Rule 6.	Acting for both parties, A10.
(f) Full address of property to be bought.	Needed in contract.	
(g) Situation of property – position of footpaths/railways/ rivers, etc.	Need for plan or special searches.	Pre-contract searches and enquiries, B10.

Item	Reason for Question	Further Reference
(h) Tenure: freehold/leasehold.	Needed in contract.	
(i) Price.	Needed in contract, stamp duty considerations.	
(j) Has any preliminary deposit been paid? If so, how much? Receipt obtained?	Take account in calculating deposit on exchange.	Preliminary deposits, A12.
(k) Which fixtures are to be removed?	Needed in contract.	Fixtures and fittings, B22.
(l) Which fittings are to remain? Additional price for fittings? Apportionment of purchase price?	Needed in contract and may affect stamp duty.	Fixtures and fittings, B22.
(m) Anticipated completion date.	To advise client on likely duration of transaction and to assess urgency of matter. Effect of date on first payment under mortgage.	
(n) Present/proposed use of property.	Planning aspects/ restrictive covenants.	
(o) Does the transaction attract VAT?	May be needed in contract and client may need advice.	VAT, A16.
(p) Who is resident in the property?	Occupiers' rights, overriding interests.	Seller's investigation of title, B3.
(q) Is the transaction dependent on the sale of another property?	Synchronisation.	Exchange, section C.
(r) Any other terms agreed between the parties?	Needed in contract.	
(s) Any correspondence between the parties?	Existence of a contract, or other terms agreed.	Form of contract, B11.
(t) Vacant possession/ details of tenancies.	Needed in contract.	

Item	Reason for Question	Further Reference
(u) Advice as to costs.	Required by Rule 15 SPR.	Estimate of costs, A8.
(v) Interest on deposit.	Deposit interest considerations.	Deposit, B17.
(w) Do a financial calculation, including costs.	To ensure the client can afford the transaction.	
(x) Time taken in interview.	Time costing/recording.	
(y) How will the deposit be funded?	Is bridging finance needed? Need to give notice if funds invested? Client's authority if undertaking to be given.	Deposit, B17.
(z) How is the balance of the price to be funded? Has the client obtained a mortgage certificate or offer? Does client have outstanding mortgage on any other property?	Advice on sources of finance and/or tax relief on interest. Lenders may insist that all outstanding mortgages are repaid as a condition of the new loan.	Financial services, A4.
(aa) Survey arrangements.	Advise the client.	Surveys, A13.
(bb) Insurance: Property? Life? Contents? Other? e.g. employee liability.	Advise the client.	Insurance, C3.
(cc) How is property to be held by co-owners?	Advise the client.	Joint purchasers, A9.
(dd) Custody of deeds.	Instructions needed if property not mortgaged.	Post-completion, section G.
(ee) Client's present property?	Need to give notice to determine tenancy? Penalty on mortgage redemption.	
(ff) Check client's identity	A precaution against mortgage fraud and money laundering and required by the Lenders' Handbook.	Para. A1.5; Money Laundering, A23; Mortgage Fraud, A24.

1.9. Instructions in special cases

1.9.1. Additional information will be required where the transaction concerns a newly constructed property, is leasehold, or is a dealing with part only of the seller's property. Further checklists to deal with these situations are contained in sections I (new properties), J (sales of part), and K (leaseholds).

1.9.2. If it appears that the property (or part of it) comprises a flying freehold, the client should be warned of the possible difficulties in obtaining finance for the property as many lenders are reluctant to accept a flying freehold as security for a loan.[1]

1.9.3. If the client is to act as a guarantor to another client's debts (e.g. on a mortgage or as surety to a lender), it may be necessary to consider separate representation for the guarantor in order to avoid any conflict of interests (see A10).

1. See paragraph 5.5 of the Lenders' Handbook (Appendix VIII.3).

1.10. After the interview

1.10.1. Instructions should be confirmed to the client in writing.[1] The letter should include:

    (a) information as to costs;

    (b) information relating to the name and status of the person who will be carrying out the work for the client and, if this person is not a partner, the name of the partner who has overall responsibility for the matter;

    (c) a résumé of the information received and advice given at the interview in order to ensure that no misunderstanding exists between solicitor and client;

    (d) confirmation of any action agreed to be taken by the solicitor;

    (e) a reminder to the client of anything which he promised to do, e.g. obtain service charge receipts;

    (f) details of who the client should contact in the event of a complaint about the solicitor's services;

    (g) a request for a payment on account in relation to disbursements; and

    (h) a copy of the Law Society's client leaflets: 'Your Guide to Buying a Home' and 'The Clients Charter' (where appropriate); or your firms own leaflets.

1.10.2. Provided that the checklist used contains a note of the time expended on the interview, and that a full written record of the interview exists in the form of a follow-up letter to the client, a detailed attendance note may be dispensed with.

1.10.3. If not already done, contact should be established with the representatives of the other parties involved in the transaction, e.g. other solicitor, estate agent, lender. If the identity of the other party's solicitor is not known, his or her status should be checked with the Law Society. If a licensed conveyancer, their status can be checked with the Council for Licensed Conveyancers. This is also a requirement of paragraph 3.2 of the Lenders' Handbook.

1.10.4. For the seller:

   (a) obtain title deeds;

   (b) send for official copy entries of the title (registered land);

   (c) ask estate agent for copy of the particulars;

   (d) requisition local search and enquiries and other searches (if so instructed by the client);

   (e) investigate title before drafting contract;

   (f) prepare abstract or epitome of title (unregistered interest in land);

   (g) make Land Charges Department search against seller;

   (h) check seller's replies to the Seller's Property Information Form.

1.10.5. For the buyer:

   (a) make search applications appropriate to the property and its location (if not to be supplied by seller);

   (b) deal with buyer's mortgage and survey arrangements if required;

   (c) check the identity of the buyer(s);

   (d) check the identity of the seller's representative if not known;

   (e) obtain estate agent's particulars;

   (f) consider draft contract when received from seller.

1. See Practice Management Standard F4, Rule 15 (costs information and client care) *The Guide to the Professional Conduct of Solicitors 1999*, p. 265. In Protocol cases the specimen letters contained in the Protocol documentation may be adapted for use in this situation.

1.11. Lost title deeds

1.11.1. If it appears that the client's title deeds to unregistered land have been lost or destroyed, it may be possible to obtain voluntary registration of the title at the Land Registry.

1.11.2. An application for first registration made by a person who is unable to produce a full, documentary title must be supported by satisfactory evidence of the applicants entitlement to apply, together with, where appropriate, evidence to account for the absence of documentary evidence of title.[1]

1. Land Registration Rules 2003, r.27; and see Land Registry Practice Guide CRPG002.

1.12. Adverse possession

1.12.1. If it appears that the land or any part of it may have been acquired by adverse possession it may be possible to obtain voluntary registration of the title at the Land Registry. Reference should be made to para. A22.8 and the appropriate practice material issued by the Land Registry.

A2. Property selling

See also: Advertising, para. A3
Introductions and referrals, para. A7
Estimate of costs, para. A8
Acting for both parties, para. A10

2.1. General principles

2.1.1. Property selling may be carried out by a solicitor:

- as part of his practice, either through the solicitor's own office or through a separate Solicitors Estate Agency Ltd (SEAL);

- through an individual practice formed for property selling;

- through a joint property selling practice (formed with other firms of solicitors and distinct for all purposes including indemnity rules, accounts rules, practice rules and conflict provisions through a recognised body).

2.1.2. In selling property the solicitor is still acting as a solicitor and therefore remains bound by the Solicitors' Practice Rules 1990, the Solicitors' Accounts Rules 1998, and all other rules, regulations and principles of conduct which affect solicitors in practice.

2.1.3. A solicitor may carry out such valuation as may be necessary to give advice to the client on the price at which the property should be sold, and to prepare the sale particulars. For structural surveys or formal valuations, see Rule 14 SPR 1990 and para. A2.3.4.

2.1.4. The name of a firm of solicitors must comply with Solicitors' Publicity Code 2001, s.1(c) (see Appendix II.3). If incorporated the name will also need to comply with Companies Act 1985 or Limited Liability Partnerships Act 2000.

2.1.5. Property selling may be carried on either as part of the solicitor's business or as a separate business but in the latter case Rule 5 Solicitors' Practice Rules 1990 and the Solicitors' Separate Business Code 1994 must be observed.[1]

2.1.6.   Fees earned by the solicitor through property selling which is carried on through the solicitor's practice or a SEAL must be included in his gross fees return.

2.1.7.   Paragraphs 2.2–2.12 apply where property selling is carried on as part of the solicitor's business.

1. See para. A2.13 and Appendix II.2.

2.2.   Advertising

2.2.1.   Subject to compliance with the Solicitors' Publicity Code 2001, a solicitor may advertise that he undertakes property-selling work and/or may advertise a specific property which he has been instructed to sell.

2.2.2.   An entry or advertisement of a solicitor who undertakes a property-selling service may appear in a directory or 'Yellow Pages' under the heading of 'estate agents' or 'solicitors'.

2.2.3.   Unsolicited visits and telephone calls may be made to a current or former client, another lawyer, an existing or potential professional or business connection, or a commercial organisation or public body. Unsolicited visits and telephone calls to the general public are expressly prohibited by the Solicitors' Publicity Code 2001.

2.2.4.   Solicitors may place 'for sale' boards outside properties which they have been instructed to sell provided that the boards comply with current statutory requirements and with the Publicity Code, s.1(d).

2.3.   Employment and remuneration of unqualified staff

2.3.1.   Unqualified, i.e. non-solicitor, staff may be employed to deal with property selling but they cannot enter into partnership with the solicitor.

2.3.2.   Fee sharing with a genuine employee is permitted by Rule 7 Solicitors' Practice Rules 1990, but this exception to the general prohibition on fee sharing must not be used to disguise a 'partnership' by a solicitor with a non-qualified person.

2.3.3.   An estate agent who is instructed by a solicitor to act as a sub-agent for the sale of a property may be remunerated on the basis of a proportion of the solicitor's professional fee.

2.3.4.   A qualified surveyor employed by the solicitor may carry out surveys on behalf of a client or prospective client provided that the employment of the surveyor falls within Rule 14 Solicitors' Practice Rules 1990 which requires him to be a chartered surveyor or hold another qualification approved by the Council. The solicitor, as the surveyor's employer, would remain liable for breach of duty if the surveyor carried out the survey negligently. The survey work will be covered under the minimum terms and conditions required by the Law Society of qualifying insurers.

2.4. Premises used for property selling

2.4.1. A department or branch office which is used mainly for property selling may be described as an 'estate agency' or 'property centre' or by any other suitable description, provided that the description is not misleading.

2.4.2. Rule 13 Solicitors' Practice Rules 1990 relating to supervision of a solicitor's office applies to premises which are used for property selling. There are special provisions that apply to an office which undertakes only property selling and ancillary services.

2.4.3. A 'property display centre' is a separate office or premises where a solicitor alone or in association with other firms of solicitors, displays or disseminates information relating to the selling of property, but where no other business of a solicitor's firm, particularly negotiating, is conducted. Guidance appears at Principles 26.14 to 26.16 in *The Guide to the Professional Conduct of Solicitors 1999* (8th edition).

2.4.4. The firms operating a joint property display centre may establish a joint service company to carry out the necessary administrative functions concerned with the running of the centre, but the service company cannot carry on any legal practice nor have any dealings with the actual selling of property.

2.4.5. The restrictions on 'flag advertising', which formerly governed the advertising of a joint property display centre, have now disappeared, with the repeal of the Solicitors' Publicity Code 1990. Any stationery used for writing to the property buying and selling public must be the stationery of the individual property selling firm, and not the notepaper of the joint property display centre. However, the centre's name and logo may appear on the notepaper. The words 'regulated by the Law Society' must also appear.

2.5. SEALs

2.5.1. A SEAL is a joint solicitors' property-selling practice. It must be a corporate body recognised under Administration of Justice Act 1985, s.9, by the Law Society (a 'recognised body'). It must be owned by at least four firms of solicitors with no principals in common and none of which has a controlling majority of the shares. It must not itself undertake conveyancing work and must be physically separate from its participating practices.

2.5.2. A SEAL may provide a full range of estate agency services, i.e. act as agent for the seller and provide mortgage services for the buyer.

2.5.3. If the SEAL is acting for the seller on the sale of a property, and

(a) the SEAL is providing mortgage related services to the buyer; or

(b) a participating firm is doing the conveyancing for the buyer;

the buyer and seller must give their written informed consent, and different individuals must deal with the work for seller and buyer.

2.6.   Written agreement as to remuneration

2.6.1.   When accepting instructions to act in the sale of a property, a solicitor must give the client a written statement containing the following information:

(a) the amount of the solicitor's remuneration, or its method of calculation;

(b) the circumstances in which the remuneration becomes payable;

(c) the amount of any disbursements which are to be separately charged, or the basis on which they will be calculated, and the circumstances in which they may be incurred;

(d) whether VAT is payable and whether it is included in the estimate or fixed fee;

(e) whether or not the solicitor is to be a sole agent;

(f) the identity of the property to be sold;

(g) the interest to be sold;

(h) the price to be sought;

(i) an explanation of the phrases 'sole selling rights', 'ready willing and able purchaser' (or similar phrases), if used in the agreement.

2.7.   Amount of remuneration

2.7.1.   The amount of commission charged by the solicitor for selling a property is a matter for agreement between the solicitor and his client.

2.7.2.   Unless the client signs an agreement in relation to charges under Solicitors Act 1974, s.57, the amount of the commission may be subject to the remuneration certificate procedure. The client may in any event be entitled to taxation of the bill by the court.

2.7.3.   A composite fee for both property selling and conveyancing may be quoted or advertised, but must be clearly expressed.

2.8.   Application of Estate Agents Act 1979

2.8.1.   The Estate Agents Act 1979 does not apply to solicitors who are engaged in property selling, but Property Misdescriptions Act 1991 does. This latter Act makes it an offence for a person selling property to attach a misleading description to the property which is being sold. The liability is similar to that incurred under Trades Descriptions Act 1968. The Law Society guidance on property selling (set out in

Appendix V.16) imposes on solicitors similar duties and obligations to those to which estate agents are subject under regulations made under the 1979 Act.

2.9. Insurance

2.9.1. Property-selling activities must be covered by the terms of the solicitors' insurance policy.

2.10. Declining instructions to act

2.10.1. Instructions must be declined where there would be a breach of Rule 1 Solicitors' Practice Rules 1990 (basic principles).

2.10.2. Where the solicitor is asked to sell a property of a type which he is unused to handling he should either decline the instructions or place the property with a sub-agent who is experienced in that type of property.

2.10.3. There may be occasions when a conflict of interest arises between the solicitor and his client when the solicitor is engaged in selling the property as well as undertaking the legal work. As in any situation where a conflict arises or is likely to arise, the solicitor must decline to act or should cease to act further in the transaction. Attention is also drawn to the Law Society's guidance relating to mortgage fraud (see para. A24; Appendix IV.3; and Appendix V.11).

2.11. Introductions and referrals

2.11.1. Provided there is compliance with Rule 3 Solicitors' Practice Rules 1990 (introductions and referrals) and with the Introduction and Referral Code a solicitor may have an arrangement with an estate agent in relation to the sale of property.

2.12. Commissions from third parties

2.12.1. Any commission received by a solicitor as a result of the client having entered into, e.g. an endowment mortgage is subject to Rule 10 Solicitors' Practice Rules 1990 (commissions).

2.13. Property selling as a separate business

2.13.1. Rule 5 Solicitors' Practice Rules 1990 permits a solicitor to control, actively participate in or operate (in each case alone, or by or with others) a separate business, including a property-selling business, provided that there is compliance with the Solicitors' Separate Business Code 1994. The Code contains some principles which are specifically applicable to property selling, which are summarised below.

2.13.2. The property-selling (estate agency) business must be carried out from premises which are physically divided and clearly differentiated from that of any premises of the solicitor in England and Wales. If the estate agency business shares premises or reception staff with any English or Welsh practice of the solicitor, the customers of the estate agency business must be informed both by personal interview or telephone call and by subsequent written confirmation of that interview or telephone call that, as customers of the estate agency business, they do not enjoy the statutory protection afforded to clients of a solicitor.

2.13.3. The name of any practice of the solicitor must have no substantial element in common with the name of the estate agency business and the words 'solicitor', 'attorney' or 'lawyer' must not be used in connection with the solicitor's involvement with the estate agency business.

2.13.4. Paperwork and records relating to customers of the estate agency business must be kept separately from those relating to the solicitor's practice. Money held for the estate agency business and its customers must not be held in the solicitor's client account.

2.13.5. Where the separate business is jointly owned and the solicitor does not do the seller's conveyancing or does the seller's conveyancing under one of the Rule 6 exceptions, the solicitor may carry out conveyancing for the buyer (see Principle 26.17 in the Guide). The buyer and the seller must give their written and informed consent to this arrangement and different individuals must deal with the work on behalf of the seller and the buyer. Alternatively, the solicitor may do conveyancing work for the seller where the separate business has provided mortgage services to the buyer.

2.13.6. All clients who are referred by the solicitor's practice to the estate agency business must be informed of the solicitor's interest in that business and that, as customers of the estate agency business, they do not enjoy the statutory protection afforded to clients of a solicitor. This latter information must be given to the customer at a personal interview or by telephone and subsequently confirmed in writing.

A3. Advertising

See also: Property selling, para. A2
Estimate of costs, para. A8
Solicitors' Publicity Code 2001, Appendix II.3

3.1. Solicitors' Publicity Code 1990

3.1.1. A solicitor may advertise his practice provided that the advertisement complies with Solicitors' Publicity Code 2001. The main points of the Code are summarised below.

3.2. Compliance with the Code and the Consumer Credit Regulations

3.2.1. Advertisements must:

(a) comply with the Publicity Code and the Solicitors' Practice Rules;

(b) not be inaccurate or misleading;

(c) express clearly any publicity as to charges or a basis of charging, making it clear whether disbursements and VAT are included.

3.2.2. The contents of advertisements relating to the provision of credit and related services must comply with Consumer Credit (Quotations) Regulations 1989 (S.I. 1989/1126) which are summarised below. These Regulations apply in circumstances where, e.g. the solicitor is advertising his services and indicates that he can obtain mortgage finance for a client. At the time of publication these regulations are still in force, although the government has recommended their repeal.

3.2.3.   *Summary of the Regulations:*

1. Quotation given to client for 'credit' (including quote about cost of mortgage or life policy) must contain certain information.

2. Regulations apply where request for information is made by client either in person on credit broker's trade premises or by telephone.

3. If exact information not available, an estimate must be given. Estimate should state on what assumptions the estimate is given and give client the right to demand a further quote based on additional information supplied by client.

4. If all information is not contained in the estimate, client must be given notice in writing that this is the case and tell client that a further quote will be given if client so requests, client having supplied such additional facts as are necessary to allow the further quote to be estimated.

5. Information to be supplied (Schedule 1) (NB. Information given under the Regulations must be clear and easily legible):

   (a) APR must be specifically mentioned and given greater prominence than mention of any other charge;

   (b) name and address of person giving quotation;

   (c) statement that security for loan is or may be required;

   (d) where security comprises charge over debtor's home, a statement in the following form: *Your home is at risk if you do not keep up repayments on a mortgage or other loan secured on it*;

   (e) a statement of any contract of insurance required (not buildings or contents insurance) and details of that policy;

   (f) a statement of any requirement to place money on deposit with any person;

   (g) credit broker's fees;

   (h) the amount of credit to be provided;

   (i) nature of any security where security is *not* a charge over the debtor's home;

   (j) frequency and amount of payments;

   (k) other payments or charges;

   (l) total amount payable by debtor; and

   (m) wealth warning in the following form: *Be sure you can afford the repayments before entering into a credit agreement.*

3.3.   Matters prohibited by the Code

3.3.1.   The Publicity Code generally prohibits unsolicited visits or telephone calls to the general public.

3.4.   Application of the Code

3.4.1.   The Code applies to all forms of publicity including stationery, advertisements, brochures, directory entries, media appearances, press releases promoting a practice and direct approaches to potential clients and other persons, and whether conducted in person, in writing or in electronic form.

3.5.   Property selling

3.5.1.   Advertisements placed by the solicitor in relation either to his property-selling services or referring to specific property which the solicitor has been instructed to sell must comply with Solicitors' Publicity Code 2001.

3.5.2.   Unsolicited visits and telephone calls may be made to a current or former client, another lawyer, an existing or potential professional or business connection, or a commercial organisation or public body. Unsolicited visits and telephone calls to the general public are expressly prohibited by the Solicitors' Publicity Code 2001.

3.5.3.   The solicitor would be able to describe himself as a 'solicitor', 'estate agent' or 'solicitor and estate agent' in an advertisement which relates to his property-selling activities, and may be listed under the heading of 'solicitors' or 'estate agents' in a directory.

3.6.   Advertising the solicitor's charges

3.6.1.   References in an advertisement to the solicitor's charges or basis of charging must be clearly expressed.

3.6.2.   Section 1(b) of the Code, which deals with solicitors' charges, states that it must be clear whether disbursements and VAT are included.

3.7.   Advertising placed by third parties

3.7.1.   Where advertisements are placed by third parties which advertise the services of solicitors to whom work may be referred, the solicitor remains responsible for the advertisement. Such advertisements should therefore be checked carefully by the solicitor before publication.

3.8. **Professional stationery**

3.8.1. Requirements for professional stationery are set out in Section 2 of the Publicity Code 2001. From 16 November 2001 all firms are required to put 'regulated by the Law Society' on their letterhead and fax headings.

3.8.2. Stationery should no longer include the words 'regulated by the Law Society in the conduct of investment business' or 'authorised by the Law Society to conduct investment business'.

A4. Financial services

See also: Money Laundering, para. A23
Mortgage Fraud, para. A24

4.1. Activities within Financial Services and Markets Act 2000

4.1.1. The Financial Services and Markets Act 2000 (FSMA) has made major changes to the regulation of the financial services industry. Of necessity, these changes will affect solicitors and since the consequences of providing investment services (referred to in the 2000 Act as 'regulated activities') without authorisation can amount to a criminal offence, solicitors must ensure that any activity caught by the Act is undertaken in an appropriate manner. The Act came into force on 1 December 2001.

The following activities may involve a solicitor in regulated activities:

(a) advising a client about obtaining a mortgage, if this involves a life policy (endowment, unit-linked, ISA) or a pension mortgage;

(b) where a property sale is linked to the sale of a business in the form of a sale of company shares;

(c) where shares in a management company are transferred on completion;

(d) where the sale of a property for a client leads to the client's looking for advice on how to invest the proceeds of sale.

4.1.2. It is a criminal offence to carry on 'regulated activities' as defined in the Financial Services and Markets Act (Regulated Activities) Order 2001, without authorisation. Since 1 December 2001, authorisation must be obtained from the Financial Services Authority. The Law Society has ceased to be a Recognised Professional Body and solicitors can no longer obtain authorisation for the purposes of the Act in this way. However, large numbers of firms of solicitors will fall outside the requirements to be authorised providing they undertake regulated activities strictly in accordance with the statutory exclusions.

4.2. **Regulated activities**

4.2.1. 'Regulated activities' are defined in the Financial Services and Markets Act (Regulated Activities) Order 2001 (RAO).

4.2.2. A regulated activity is potentially undertaken when a solicitor is involved in any one of the activities referred to in articles 5–61 RAO and relating to any one of the specified investments listed in articles 74–89. The most common activities will be advice on the merits of buying or selling a specified investment or arranging on behalf of a client the sale or purchase of a specified investment. Shares, endowment policies, pension policies and ISAs constitute common specified investments.

4.2.3. Advising the client on or arranging the following investments does not constitute a regulated activity:

(a) a normal bank or building society account;

(b) buildings or contents insurance;

(c) a term life insurance policy, e.g. mortgage protection policy.

4.2.4. Generic investment advice is not within the definition of regulated activities in the RAO. Generic advice is advice about general categories of investment, as opposed to specific investments. Recommendations to the client that 'it would be wise to invest capital in equity shares/unit trusts' or 'you should take out a life insurance policy' are both examples of generic advice. A recommendation to the client that he should 'invest £5,000 in x plc unit trusts' or to 'take out a regulated life insurance policy for a 15-year term with y insurance company who do a very good policy' is, however, specific investment advice falling within the definition of a 'regulated activity'.

4.2.5. 'Arranging deals in investments' is a regulated activity within the Act. A solicitor who is involved in arrangements which lead to a client taking out a regulated life insurance policy is potentially carrying on a regulated activity even if he had given no advice about the policy.

4.2.6. Solicitors who arrange deals in investment can avoid the need for authorisation by showing that certain exclusions contained in the RAO apply. The most important are as follows:

(a) Arrangements made with or through an authorised person (i.e. one authorised by the Financial Services Authority under the FSMA) where:

(i) the transaction is entered into on advice given to the client by an authorised person; or

(ii) it is clear in all the circumstances that the client, in his capacity as an investor, is not seeking and has not sought advice from the person as to the merits of the client entering the transaction (or if the client has sought advice the solicitor has declined to give it but has recommended the client to seek advice from an authorised person).

It is important to note, however, that the above exclusion does not apply if the agent receives from any person other than the client any pecuniary reward or advantage, for which he does not account to the client, arising out of his entering into the transaction. The Law Society has taken the view that retaining commission with the informed consent of the client in accordance with Rule 10 Solicitors' Practice Rules 1990 does represent 'accounting to the client' and the benefit of the exception will still apply in these circumstances.

(b) Introductions where a person introduces a client to an authorised or exempt person and the introduction is made with a view to the provision of independent advice.

4.2.7. Solicitors should note that the exclusion arising from the use of an authorised person only applies to arranging; it does not apply to investment advice. Where the activity involves advice or the exclusion for arranging is not available for any reason, an alternative means of avoiding the need for authorisation is to use Part XX FSMA which contains provisions relating to 'exempt regulated activities' carried on by members of a profession which is supervised and regulated by a designated professional body (DPB). The Law Society is a DPB.

4.2.8. Section 327 FSMA provides that the prohibition against carrying on regulated activities contained in the Act does not apply to the carrying on of a regulated activity by a member of a profession if certain conditions apply:

(a) the person must be a member of a profession or controlled or managed by one or more such members;

(b) the person must not receive from anyone other than his client any pecuniary reward or other advantage, for which he does not account to his client, arising out of his carrying on of any of the activities;

(c) the manner of the provision of any service in the course of carrying on the activities must be incidental to the provision by him of professional services;

(d) only regulated activities permitted by the DPB's rules may be carried out.

4.2.9. The Law Society has issued rules (The Solicitors' Financial Services (Scope) Rules 2001), covering the requirements of (d) above. These rules will limit the scope of solicitors benefiting from Part XX. The prohibited activities include:

(a) market making;

(b) buying, selling, subscribing or underwriting as principal where the firm holds itself out as engaging in the business of buying investments with a view to selling them;

(c) acting as a trustee or operator of a regulated CIS;

(d) acting as a stakeholder pension scheme manager;

(e) entering into a regulated mortgage contract as lender or administering a regulated mortgage contract.

4.2.10. There are further restrictions using Part XX where the investment is a packaged product. These are defined as long term insurance contracts (including endowment policies), units or shares in regulated Collective Investment Schemes (e.g. unit trusts or shares in Open Ended Investment Companies) or an investment trust savings scheme, whether or not held within an ISA or PEP or a stakeholder pension scheme. Where such investments are acquired, firms should not use the 'incidental' exception in Part XX but should use an authorised person. Firms may, however, pass on and endorse the advice of an authorised person within Part XX.

4.2.11. The Law Society has also issued the Solicitors' Financial Services (Conduct of Business) Rules 2001, applicable to solicitors seeking exemption under Part XX. These include rules relating to:

Status disclosure. Requiring firms to indicate in writing that they are not authorised by the FSA but are regulated by the Law Society.

Execution of transactions. Requiring firms to carry out transactions as soon as possible.

Records of transactions. Requiring firms to keep records of instructions received and instructions given.

Record of commissions. Requiring firms to keep records of commissions received and records of how such commission has been accounted to clients.

Execution only – packaged products. Requiring firms to give written confirmation of execution only transactions involving packaged products.

4.2.12. There is no provision for the monitoring by the Law Society of firms relying upon Part XX FSMA. However, breach of the rules could amount to (in the case of the Scope rules) a criminal offence and an order by the FSA preventing the firm from carrying on any regulated activities. Breach of the Conduct of Business Rules whilst not amounting to a criminal offence could lead to disciplinary action.

4.3. Trustees and personal representatives

4.3.1. *The solicitor who is a trustee or personal representative*

If a solicitor buys or sells investments for the trust or estate he may be exempted under the RAO, provided he is acting as a principal. Where a solicitor who is a trustee or personal representative advises his fellow trustees or personal representatives or makes arrangements for the acquisition or disposal of investments for his co-trustees or personal representatives or a beneficiary, the RAO provides further exemptions (article 66). These exemptions only apply if the trustee is not remunerated for the arranging or advice in addition to any remuneration received for acting as trustee or personal representative. Article 66 expressly provides that a person is not to be regarded as receiving additional remuneration merely because his remuneration is calculated by reference to time.

Trustees or personal representatives will 'manage' the investments belonging to the trust or estate. The RAO makes it clear, however, that only 'discretionary management' will be caught as a regulated activity. Non-discretionary management will not be a 'regulated activity'. Non-discretionary management will occur when either the firm acts for outside trustees or where a solicitor or employee of the firm is a joint trustee or personal representative with someone from outside the firm. Discretionary management is only likely where a solicitor is a sole trustee or personal representative or where the solicitor is jointly acting as such with someone from within the firm. Article 66 exempts 'discretionary management' where such is undertaken by a person acting as a trustee or personal representative. In addition to the condition relating to 'no additional remuneration' noted above for advising and arranging, solicitors must not hold themselves out as providing a management service if they wish to benefit from this exclusion.

If the article 66 exclusion does not apply, it is open to solicitors who are trustees or personal representatives to show that their activities fall within the general exclusions contained in Part XX FSMA as noted above.

4.3.2. *The solicitor who is acting for trustees or personal representatives*

It should be noted that the exclusion contained in article 66 only applies where a solicitor is a trustee or a personal representative – it does not apply if the solicitor merely acts for trustees or personal representatives. In these circumstances, arrangements can be excluded by using the authorised person exemption noted in para. 4.2.6 above or arrangements and advice may fall within the incidental exclusion contained in Part XX FSMA.

4.4. Mortgages

4.4.1. Arranging mortgage finance for a client or advising about the terms of a mortgage offer is not a regulated activity within the RAO so long as the mortgage does not also involve arranging a life or pension policy (whether endowment, unit-linked or ISA). Where the mortgage is linked to a life or pension policy, arranging the linked investment will be a regulated activity.

4.4.2. Where a client seeks advice about a life policy and the solicitor is not authorised, the solicitor should either seek and pass on the advice of an authorised person or the client should be referred to another adviser who must be an independent financial adviser. Solicitors may not refer clients to tied agents or to providers of financial products. This prohibition is to ensure that the client receives independent and impartial advice. Reference should be made to clauses 4(2) and 4(3) of the Solicitors' Introduction and Referral Code 1990 (see Appendix II.1).

4.4.3. Under article 61(1) RAO, entering into a regulated mortgage contract as lender is a regulated activity. Further, under article 61(2), administering a regulated mortgage contract where the contract was entered into by way of business is also a regulated activity. These provisions were to have been brought into force nine months after N2 (i.e. 1 September 2002). However, the government have announced that in the light of a general review of mortgage regulation, these provisions will not now be implemented until at least 2004.

4.4.4.   A solicitor who is involved in obtaining mortgage finance for a client will be acting as a mortgage broker under Consumer Credit Act 1974. For this activity, the solicitor needs to hold a licence under the 1974 Act. The Law Society holds a group licence from the Director General of Fair Trading which covers all solicitors acting within the ordinary course of practice. Normally, therefore, a solicitor does not need to hold an individual licence.

4.5.   Commissions

4.5.1.   Life assurance companies and the providers of some other types of investment product pay commissions to intermediaries on the sale of their products. A solicitor who introduces a client to an authorised person will usually receive a commission for the introduction.

4.5.2.   Any commission received by the solicitor is subject to Rule 10 Solicitors' Practice Rules 1990 (see Appendix I.1 and para. N1.8). As noted above, a number of the exclusions from the need for authorisation require solicitors to account for any commission. If a solicitor retains commission without the client's consent (even if the commission is not more than the £20 *de minimis* allowed for in Practice Rule 10) these exclusions in the RAO and the Act will not apply. Solicitors risk committing a criminal offence if they undertake regulated activities without being authorised and without the benefit of an appropriate exclusion.

A5. Dealing with non-solicitors

5.1. Licensed conveyancers

5.1.1. Guidance for solicitors dealing with licensed conveyancers is contained in *The Guide to the Professional Conduct of Solicitors 1999*, published by the Law Society, and is summarised below. See further Appendix V.6.

5.1.2. When dealing with a licensed conveyancer who is not known personally to the solicitor, a check on the identity of the conveyancer should be made with the Council for Licensed Conveyancers.[1]

5.1.3. The solicitor should ensure that he deals either directly with the licensed conveyancer or with a person working under the immediate supervision of such a person.

5.1.4. Licensed conveyancers are bound by rules relating to conduct, discipline, insurance and accounts which are similar to those which bind solicitors. It is therefore normally possible to deal with a licensed conveyancer as if the conveyancer was a fellow solicitor subject to the best interests of the solicitor's client.

1. For address see App. XI.5.

5.2. Law Society Formulae and undertakings

5.2.1. The Protocol, the Law Society Formulae for Exchange of Contracts and the Code for Completion by Post (see Appendix III) may be used in dealings with licensed conveyancers. Licensed conveyancers have no equivalent sanction to the court's control over the conduct of solicitors, but the Law Society recommends that they are nevertheless treated by solicitors as being on an equal footing with themselves. It is therefore normally possible to rely on undertakings given by such persons.

5.3.   Employment of licensed conveyancers by solicitors

5.3.1.   A solicitor may employ a licensed conveyancer as a conveyancing clerk or in some other capacity. Work done by the licensed conveyancer must be done as an integral part of the solicitor's practice and is subject to all the practice rules. The licensed conveyancer may be named in the solicitor's publicity (including stationery) provided that his status is made clear. A solicitor may not enter into partnership with a licensed conveyancer nor share his fees with him (except under the exception to Rule 7 Solicitors' Practice Rules 1990 which permits fees to be shared with a genuine employee).

5.3.2.   As with any transaction, the overriding concern is for the best interests of the client. In any situation where there is doubt over the conduct of the matter, guidance should be sought from the Practice Advice Service of the Law Society (see Appendix XI.4 for details).

5.4.   Unqualified conveyancers

5.4.1.   Under Solicitors Act 1974, s.22 (as amended), it is an offence for an unqualified person to draw up or prepare *inter alia* a contract for sale, transfer, conveyance, lease or mortgage relating to land unless that person can prove that the act was not done in expectation of fee, gain or reward.

5.4.2.   'Qualified persons'

The only persons who are 'qualified' under section 22 are solicitors, barristers, notaries public, licensed conveyancers, authorised practitioners, and some public officers. An unqualified person acting in breach of the section commits a criminal offence and his 'client' may be guilty of aiding and abetting the offence.

5.4.3.   A solicitor acting for the other party to the transaction could also be guilty of procuring the commission of an offence by inviting the unqualified person to submit a contract or conveyance.

5.4.4.   Courts and Legal Services Act 1990 contains provisions enabling 'authorised practitioners' (as defined in the Act) to conduct conveyancing services on behalf of their customers. Rules regulating the conduct of authorised practitioners have not yet been made.

5.5.   Dealing with unqualified persons

5.5.1.   The Law Society has published guidance for solicitors who are asked to deal with unqualified conveyancers which are summarised below. See further, Appendix V.7.

5.5.2.   A solicitor should refuse to have any dealings with an unqualified person unless he has clear evidence that no offence under section 22 will be committed.

5.5.3. At the outset of a transaction which apparently involves an unqualified person the solicitor should write to the unqualified person drawing attention to the Law Society's guidelines and asking for satisfactory evidence that no offence will be committed. The solicitor's client should also be informed of the situation.

5.5.4. Drafts of suitable letters are set out in the guidelines.

5.5.5. A letter from a qualified person confirming that he will prepare the relevant documents will be satisfactory evidence that no offence will be committed and the solicitor may proceed with the transaction.

5.5.6. The Protocol can be used with unqualified persons, but no sanctions would lie against them in the event of a breach.

5.5.7. There are provisions in the Land Registration Rules 2003 whereby a conveyancer can satisfy evidential requirements by giving a relevant certificate. The term "conveyancer" includes a solicitor, licenced conveyancer and a fellow of the Institute of Legal Executives.[1]

1. Land Registration Rules 2003, r.217.

5.6. Undertakings

5.6.1. Undertakings should not be accepted from unqualified persons since there is no method of enforcing them. Thus where, e.g. a seller who is represented by an unqualified person has a mortgage subsisting at completion, the buyer's solicitor must require the seller to produce a signed Form DS1 at completion and must not accept an undertaking for its discharge. This may mean that the seller has to obtain bridging finance to repay the loan before completion or that the seller's lender will have to attend at completion. A solicitor who accepts an undertaking from an unqualified person may be in breach of his duty of care to his own client and thus liable to make good to the client any loss sustained as a result of a dishonoured undertaking.

5.7. Completions and agency work

5.7.1. There is no duty on a solicitor to undertake agency work by way of completions by post or to attend to other formalities on behalf of third parties who are not clients and who are represented by an unqualified person. A solicitor who does undertake such work should only do so after having agreed in writing with the unqualified person the precise extent of the solicitor's duties and agreed fee for such services. Where a considerable amount of work is undertaken on behalf of the unqualified person's client there is a danger of the solicitor being in breach of Rule 6 Solicitors' Practice Rules 1990 since he may effectively be acting for both parties in the transaction.

5.8. The contract

5.8.1. It will be necessary for special provisions to be inserted in the draft contract to take account of the fact that the other party is not represented by a qualified person.

Clauses to deal with the following matters should be inserted in the contract:

(a) personal attendance by an unrepresented seller at completion to take up the deeds and purchase price because Law of Property Act 1925, s.69, only applies when a document containing a receipt for the purchase price is handed over by a qualified person or by the seller himself;

(b) payment of the deposit either to an estate agent who is a member of a recognised professional body, or to the buyer's solicitor in the capacity of stakeholder. An alternative to these arrangements would be to insert a condition in the contract providing for the deposit to be placed in a bank or building society deposit account in the joint names of seller and buyer.

5.9. Pre-contract enquiries

5.9.1. The answers to pre-contract enquiries and any other enquiries (including requisitions on title) given by an unrepresented seller should be signed by the seller in person. Although an unqualified person may have the seller's express authority to answer such enquiries on his behalf, an action in misrepresentation (should such become necessary) will more easily be sustained if the answers have been signed by the seller personally.

5.10. Powers of attorney

5.10.1. Any power of attorney which purports to give the unqualified person power to deal with a matter on behalf of his or her 'client' should be carefully checked to ensure its validity and effectiveness for its purported purpose (see para. B23).

5.11. Acting for the lender

5.11.1. A solicitor acting for a lender where the borrower is represented by an unqualified person is under no obligation to undertake work which the buyer's solicitor should normally assume (e.g. drafting the purchase deed) and should not render the unqualified person additional assistance. However, in such a situation the solicitor must bear in mind that the interests of his lender client in obtaining a good title to the property are paramount. The advance cheque should be drawn in favour of a solicitor, licensed conveyancer or person properly authorised to receive the money by the borrower. On redemption of a mortgage similar principles apply.

5.12. **Authorised practitioners**

5.12.1. Authorised practitioners are entitled to carry out conveyancing services on behalf of their clients pursuant to Courts and Legal Services Act 1990 and the regulations made under that Act (none of which have been made as yet). Conveyancing services must be carried out under the supervision of a qualified solicitor. Authorised practitioners are subject to similar rules relating to the handling of clients' money as those which affect solicitors and are also bound to honour undertakings given by them or their staff. They may, therefore, be regarded in the same light as licensed conveyancers.

NB: In cases of doubt or difficulty assistance should be sought from the Practice Advice Service at the Law Society (see Appendix XI.4 for details).

A6. In-house solicitors

6.1. Acting for the lay employer

6.1.1. A solicitor who is employed by a non-solicitor employer must comply with Solicitors' Practice Rules 1990 and all the other rules of professional conduct.

6.1.2. A practising certificate will be needed where the solicitor:

(a) is held out by his employer as practising as a solicitor (e.g. where the solicitor's name and qualifications appear on the employer's notepaper); or

(b) carries out any of the acts which are prohibited to unqualified persons by Solicitors Act 1974 (e.g. drawing a contract for the sale of land for fee or reward); or

(c) administers oaths.

6.1.3. If the employed solicitor uses his employer's notepaper for his professional business, the notepaper must clearly and unambiguously state the status of the solicitor.

6.1.4. Rule 4 Solicitors' Practice Rules 1990 and the Employed Solicitors Code 1990 place restrictions on the type of work which an employed solicitor may undertake. In general he is prohibited from doing work for anyone other than his employer.

6.2. Acting for fellow employees

6.2.1. An employed solicitor may carry out conveyancing on behalf of a fellow employee provided that the work is permitted by his contract of employment and is done free of charge to the fellow employee. The conveyancing must also relate to or arise out of the work of the employee client, i.e. it must be a job-related move. Before accepting the instructions to act the employed solicitor must ensure that the fellow employee does not wish to instruct another solicitor or licensed conveyancer.

6.3. Acting for third parties

6.3.1. If his contract of employment permits him to do so an employed solicitor may undertake work on behalf of private clients in his own time. In this respect he will be treated as a principal in private practice and must comply with the Practice Rules, Accounts Rules and Indemnity Rules. If he practises from home, compliance with Rule 13 Solicitors' Practice Rules will be required and he may need to register his home address with the Law Society as a practising address. Because of the danger of conflict of interests private work must not be undertaken for clients and customers of the employer.

6.3.2. An employed solicitor may act for a joint owner/ buyer and for a lender. A lender may require an indemnity from the employer or insurance cover similar to that provided by Solicitors' Indemnity Rules.

A7. Introductions and referrals

See also: Advertising, para. A3
Financial services, para. A4
Solicitors' Introduction and Referral Code 1990, Appendix II.1.
Solicitors' Publicity Code 2001, Appendix II.3

7.1. Solicitors' Introduction and Referral Code 1990

7.1.1. A solicitor may have an arrangement with a third party for the introduction of clients to the solicitor by the third party, or the referral of clients to the third party by the solicitor. Such arrangements are permitted by Rule 3 Solicitors' Practice Rules 1990 provided that there is no breach of any of the Practice Rules and that there is compliance with the Solicitors' Introduction and Referral Code 1990. The provisions of the Code are summarised below and are set out in full in Appendix II.1.

7.1.2. The Code applies to any arrangement made by a solicitor with, e.g. an estate agent, bank, building society or mortgage broker for the introduction of clients to the solicitor from such third parties or the referral of clients to the third parties by the solicitor but not to introductions and referrals between firms of solicitors. Arrangements are forbidden where the introducer is a builder, developer or seller's estate agent where the conveyancing is to be provided for the buyer, and the buyer's costs are to be paid by the introducer.

7.1.3. Breach of the Code may amount to a breach of Rules 1 (basic principles) and/or 3 (introductions and referrals) Solicitors' Practice Rules 1990 (or breach of one of the other practice rules), and may be conduct unbefitting a solicitor.

7.2. Maintaining the independence of the solicitor

7.2.1. It is of paramount importance that the solicitor should remain independent of any third party to or from whom referrals are made so that the client may be given impartial and objective advice by the solicitor.

7.2.2. To this end, the Code emphasises that Rule 1 Solicitors' Practice Rules 1990 (basic principles) must be complied with at all times.

7.2.3. It should also be noted that Rule 12 Solicitors' Practice Rules 1990 prevents a solicitor from acting as an appointed representative in respect of introductions and referrals made in the field of investment business, other than by having a separate business which is the appointed representative of an independent financial adviser.

7.3. Reliance by the solicitor on limited sources of business

7.3.1. If a solicitor allows himself to become reliant on a limited source or sources of business from introducers there is a danger that the advice given by him to his introduced clients will be influenced by the solicitor's need to maintain his source of business, to the extent that the advice will not be impartial and may not be in the best interests of that particular client.

7.3.2. Solicitors are advised to review their sources of business at regular intervals (see below, para. A7.4) and if it appears that more than 20% of the solicitor's income earned during the period under review has been generated from a single source of introduction, the solicitor should consider whether steps need to be taken to reduce that proportion.

7.3.3. Factors to be taken into account in deciding whether the proportion of business from a single source needs to be reduced include:

    (a) the percentage of income derived from that source;

    (b) the number of clients introduced by that source;

    (c) the nature of the clients and the nature of the work, e.g. where the business is derived from non-commercial sources such as a charity or Law Centre it would not be so important to reduce the volume of work derived from that source as it would be if the large percentage of business was derived from a single commercial client;

    (d) whether the introducer could be affected by the advice given by the solicitor to the client.

7.4. Keeping records

7.4.1. Each firm should keep a record of agreements for the introduction of work and should check at six-monthly intervals:

    (a) that the provisions of the Code have been complied with;

    (b) that referred clients have received impartial advice which has not been tainted by the relationship between the firm and the introducer;

    (c) the amount of income arising from each agreement for the introduction of business.

Records of such reviews must be maintained for inspection by the Law Society and/or the Office for the Supervision of Solicitors.

7.5. Agreements for introductions and referrals to solicitors

7.5.1. When negotiating an agreement for the introduction of business with a potential introducer the solicitor should draw the attention of the potential introducer to the Introduction and Referral Code 1990 and also to the Publicity Code 2001. Arrangements under which the solicitor is to be paid by the introducer to provide conveyancing services for the introducer's customers can only be made with introducers who agree to comply with the Introduction and Referral Code.

7.5.2. Where an introducer wishes to advertise the services of solicitors to whom the introducer will refer work, the introducer should be encouraged to publicise their adherence to the Introduction and Referral Code. A suggested form of wording may be found in the Code. The solicitor remains responsible for any advertisement. Such advertisements should therefore be checked carefully by the solicitor before publication.

7.5.3. Potential introducers should be made aware of the terms on which the solicitor will accept instructions from an introducer and the fees which will be charged to an introduced client.

7.6. Confirming the client's instructions

7.6.1. Any instructions received from or through an introducer must be confirmed directly with the client by sending or giving the client written terms of business.

7.7. Fees and commissions

7.7.1. Although normal hospitality is permitted, a solicitor is forbidden to pay an introducer for his services, whether by commission or otherwise.

7.7.2. Any commission received by the solicitor who has referred a client to a third party is subject to Rule 10 Solicitors' Practice Rules 1990 under which rule the solicitor must account to the client for any commission which exceeds £20 unless the client, having been informed of the amount of the commission in writing, consents to the solicitor keeping the commission.

7.8. Referrals by the solicitor to a third party

7.8.1. A solicitor who recommends a client to a third party must do so in good faith, judging what is in the client's best interests. Any agreement entered into whereby the solicitor recommends clients to a third party must not restrict the solicitor's freedom to recommend clients to other third parties if this would be in the best interests of the client.

7.9.   Agreements to do work for customers of a third party

7.9.1.   A solicitor may enter an arrangement with a third party to provide conveyancing services for customers of the third party under which the solicitor is paid for those services by the introducer.

7.9.2.   The agreement must be in writing and a copy of it must be available for inspection by the Law Society or the Office for the Supervision of Solicitors, together with records of the six-monthly reviews carried out under the Introduction and Referral Code.

7.9.3.   Before making a referral the introducer must give the customer in writing:

    (a) details of the conveyancing service to be provided under the terms of the referral;

    (b) notification of:

        (i) the charge payable by the customer to the introducer for the conveyancing services;

        (ii) the liability for VAT and disbursements and how these are to be discharged; and

        (iii) what charge if any is to be made if the transaction does not proceed to completion or if the solicitor is unable to continue to act;

    (c) notification of the amount the introducer will be paying to the solicitor for the provision of conveyancing services relating to the customer's transaction;

    (d) a statement to the effect that the charge for conveyancing services will not be affected whether or not the customer takes other products or services offered (e.g. a life policy) by the introducer, and that the availability and price of other services will not be affected whether the customer chooses to instruct a solicitor under the referral or decides to instruct another solicitor or conveyancer; and

    (e) a statement to the effect that the advice and service of the solicitor to whom the customer is to be referred will remain independent and subject to the instructions of the customer.

7.9.4.   In publicity material of the introducer which includes reference to any service that may be provided by the solicitor, any reference to the charge for the conveyancing service must be clearly expressed, must not be misleading and must make clear whether disbursements and VAT are included.

7.9.5. The solicitor may be paid by the introducer on a case-by-case basis, or on an hourly, monthly, or other appropriate basis.

7.9.6. Where the solicitor is being paid for his or her services by the introducer rather than by the client there is a danger of conflict of interests arising, and the solicitor must decline to act if such a conflict arises or is likely to arise.

7.9.7. A solicitor is not permitted to enter this type of agreement with a lender, builder, developer or seller or their agent, or with a life office or its tied agent, for the provision of conveyancing services for buyers or borrowers.

7.9.8. The agreement between the introducer and the solicitor must not include any provisions which would:

    (a) compromise, infringe or impair any of the principles set out in Rule 1 Solicitors' Practice Rules (basic principles) or any duties owed by the solicitor to the introducer's customer by virtue of the solicitor/client relationship and/or the requirements of professional conduct; or

    (b) restrict the scope of the duties which the solicitor owes to the customer in relation to the services agreed to be provided by virtue of the professional relationship between the solicitor and client; or

    (c) interfere with or inhibit the solicitor's responsibility for the control of the professional work.

A8. Estimate of costs

See also: Costs, para. N1
Non-contentious costs (available from the Law Society's Practice Advice Service)

8.1. Duty to give estimate

8.1.1. A solicitor should, whenever possible, give a client an estimate of the likely costs of the transaction.[1]

8.1.2. If it is not possible to give an estimate, a general forecast of the approximate costs should be given.

1. See Solicitors' Practice Rule 15 (Appendix I.1), Solicitors' Costs Information and Client Care Code (Appendix II.4).

8.2. Residential conveyancing

8.2.1. In residential conveyancing it is normally possible to give the client an estimate of the costs of the transaction.

8.3. Commercial transactions

8.3.1. A precise estimate of costs may not be possible in the context of commercial transactions; nevertheless the client should still be given a general forecast of likely costs and the method of calculation of those costs at the outset of the transaction, and informed if that figure is likely to vary substantially.

8.4. Bills payable by a third party

8.4.1. Where the client is or will become liable to pay a bill presented by a third party, e.g. to a landlord's solicitor for consent to assignment, the solicitor should obtain an estimate of the third party's bill at the outset of the transaction and should inform the client of the amount of the estimate. If the estimate appears to be an unreasonably high figure, negotiations to attempt to reduce it should be undertaken before a substantial amount of work in the transaction has taken place. Money should be obtained from the client on account of the third party's costs before an undertaking to pay is given.

8.4.2. If the client is entitled to be indemnified by a third party, e.g. by a tenant seeking a licence to assign, an estimate of the costs should be given to the third party's solicitor. Such an estimate should be as firm as possible in the circumstances, but may be qualified by a statement to the effect that the estimate has been given on the basis that the matter proceeds without unforeseen complications.

8.5. Giving an estimate

8.5.1. In order to avoid misunderstandings it is preferable only to give an estimate in writing or, if oral, to confirm the estimate in writing either immediately or, at the latest, when the solicitor is instructed.

8.5.2. In residential conveyancing it is frequently not possible to avoid giving an estimate over the telephone. In such circumstances it should be made clear to the prospective client that the estimate is given on the basis of information supplied by the client and may be subject to variation if unknown factors later emerge which complicate the transaction.

8.5.3. The estimate should be as comprehensive as possible and should be clear as to whether VAT and/or disbursements are included in the given figure.

8.5.4. The client should be warned that if unforeseen complications arise, the estimate may be revised.

8.5.5. Minor expenses, e.g. postage and telephone, which are part of the solicitor's overheads, are to be included in the estimate and must not be added as a disbursement.

8.6. Change in circumstances

8.6.1. If events occur which cause the original estimate to become inaccurate the solicitor must immediately inform the client in writing of the change in circumstances and should revise his estimate accordingly.

8.6.2. Failure to advise the client of a change in the likely level of fees may render the solicitor liable to prosecution for giving misleading information relating to charges under Consumer Protection Act 1987, s.20.

8.7. Quotations for costs

8.7.1. The solicitor should make it clear to the client that an estimate for costs is not a fixed price ('a quotation') for the work unless it is the solicitor's intention to charge a fixed price which will not be altered in any circumstances.

8.7.2. Where a quotation is given the solicitor is not at liberty to charge the client more than the fixed fee even if the transaction turns out to be more difficult or complex than had been anticipated. Petty expenses such as postage and telephone must not be added as disbursements to the fixed fee.

8.7.3. It is recommended that if a fixed fee is quoted the client is informed of that fee in writing and told that the quotation will be valid for a stated period, e.g. three months. If the solicitor has not been instructed by the client within this period he will then be entitled to issue a revised quotation.

8.7.4. Money received for or on account of an agreed fee must not be paid into a client account.[1] It must be paid into an office account.

8.7.5. A quotation for costs which has been accepted by the client may be subject to Solicitors Act 1974, s.57, which provides that it must:

    (a) be in writing;

    (b) embody all the terms of the agreement;

    (c) be signed by the client or his agent;

    (d) be reasonable in amount and in lieu of ordinary profit costs.

8.7.6. Remuneration certificates are not available to a client where a section 57 agreement has been made, but he may seek taxation of the bill in the normal way. The agreement is enforceable by the solicitor under the ordinary principles of contract law.

1. See Rule 19(5) Solicitors' Accounts Rules 1998.

8.8. VAT on solicitors' charges

8.8.1. Where a firm is registered, VAT will be payable by the client on the solicitors' bill and on some of the disbursements paid by the solicitor on the client's behalf.

8.8.2. When giving an estimate or quotation of costs to the client the solicitor should make it clear whether or not that estimate or quotation includes VAT. If no mention of VAT is made the client is entitled to assume that the quoted figure is inclusive of VAT.[1]

8.8.3. Where an individual or firm is registered for VAT, the firm's VAT registration number must appear on the bills issued by the firm or, if a separate tax invoice is issued, on the tax invoice.

8.8.4. Where the client's bill is reduced by the amount of commission which the solicitor has earned, e.g. on an endowment policy taken out by the client, VAT must be charged on the gross amount of the bill. Although the preceding sentence correctly represents the law in this area, in practice VAT is frequently only charged on the net sum.

1. Value Added Tax Act 1994, s.89.

A9. Joint purchasers

9.1. Advising the client

9.1.1. When acting for joint purchasers, it is essential to clarify their intentions as to the method by which they are to hold the property. The solicitor should explain the different methods of co-ownership to the clients in language appropriate to their level of understanding and should advise as to the most suitable type of co-ownership to meet the particular situation. A separate trust deed should be completed to express the clients' wishes. Also a note of the clients' wishes should be made on the file so that appropriate steps may be taken to implement the clients' instructions in the purchase deed.[1]

9.1.2. Instructions should be obtained from both (or all) co-purchasers.[2]

9.1.3. Where the intending co-purchasers are not married to each other it may be necessary to advise each party independently about their rights in the property to be purchased. Solicitors should be alert to the possibility of a conflict of interests arising between the two clients in this situation.[3]

1. See The Purchase Deed, para. E1.
2. See *Penn* v. *Bristol & West Building Society* [1997] 3 All ER 470.
3. See para. A9.8. below.

9.2. Co-ownership or sole ownership?

9.2.1. In the vast majority of cases a husband and wife should be advised to hold a property jointly and this is usually a requirement of any major lending institution. The requirement by lenders for co-ownership by spouses (and co-habitees) is irrespective of the contribution which each party will make to the mortgage repayments.

9.2.2. A non-owning spouse will have rights under Family Law Act 1996 and/or an equitable interest through contribution to the purchase price of the property but neither of these methods of protection of the non-owning spouse's interest is as secure as co-ownership of the legal estate. A contra-indication to co-ownership by a married couple may exist where one or both of the parties is individually wealthy and where consideration must be given to the equalisation of estates for inheritance tax purposes.

9.2.3. Sole legal ownership may be considered prudent if one of the parties is in a 'high-risk' category of unincorporated business where the potential consequences of bankruptcy may need to be considered.

9.2.4. Unmarried purchasers, whether co-habitees, brother and sister or merely friends who are joining together to purchase a property, should normally be advised to hold the property jointly since the existence of an equitable or overriding interest may be costly and difficult to establish in the event of a dispute between the parties. Many lenders will insist that the legal estate is held jointly in these circumstances.

9.2.5. Consideration should always be given to the question of taking out a joint life policy to protect the mortgage over the lives of both spouses/co-habitees even where the property is held in one name alone or where the mortgage repayments are made by one party alone. The joint lives policy will protect the repayments of the mortgage even in the event of death of the non-owning or non-earning spouse/co-habitee.

9.3. The options

9.3.1. In law co-ownership of land can usually only exist through the medium of a trust of land. The legal estate will thus be held by joint tenants on trust for themselves (and possibly other persons) in equity. The legal joint tenancy is not severable and there must be a minimum of two trustees (and maximum of four) in order to deal with the legal estate.

9.3.2. In equity there is a choice between holding as joint tenants or as tenants in common.

9.3.3. The capacity of the buyers, whether as joint tenants or tenants in common, must be expressly stated in the purchase deed itself or in a separate trust deed (in the past, the entry on the certificate only relates to the receipt with no evidence as to the shares held, hence the need for a separate trust deed). The statement in panel 11 of Form TR1 (transfer of whole registered title) contains a declaration of trust to be completed where there is more than one transferee.[1] An express declaration may however be made in the additional provisions panel of the relevant Land Registry form (e.g. panel 12 of TR1).

1. See *Huntingford* v. *Hobbs* [1992] EGCS 38.

9.4. Joint tenants

9.4.1. Where co-owners hold the equitable interest as joint tenants none of the co-owners will be entitled to a distinct or separate proportion of that interest: each one owns all of it. The main distinguishing feature of the joint tenancy is the right of survivorship which leads to the interest accruing to the ultimate sole surviving joint tenant. Because no distinct part of the interest belongs to any individual tenant, no part of it will belong to the estate of a deceased joint tenant and, where the co-owners were married to each other, will not attract inheritance tax. An interest in a joint tenancy cannot be left by will, the deceased's share passing automatically to the surviving joint tenant(s). A beneficial joint tenancy can be severed which has the effect of converting it into a tenancy in common if there were only two joint tenants.

9.5. **Tenants in common**

9.5.1. Where a tenancy in common exists each co-owner holds a quantified proportion of the equitable interest which is capable of being disposed of *inter vivos* or by will or passes on the intestacy of the deceased tenant in common. The proportionate share in the property which belonged to a deceased tenant in common is subject to inheritance tax rules.

9.5.2. Unless the contrary is stated or evidence to the contrary is proved, a court will assume that tenants in common hold the equitable interest in proportion to the parties' original contributions to the property.[1] In order to avoid subsequent disputes and litigation it is desirable that the proportionate shares of each tenant in common are expressly agreed and recorded in a deed of trust (or certified copy transfer) which is signed by the co-owners. In unregistered land an express declaration as to the proportionate shares may be included in the purchase deed. If the parties cannot agree on the amount of their respective shares separate advice for one or all of them is necessary. Unless the proportions in which the equitable interest is held are clearly stated, it may be difficult to determine the ownership of the proceeds of sale when the property is ultimately sold. This will present problems for the solicitor if, e.g. the property is sold and the proceeds are to be divided as a result of a matrimonial breakdown. See the Law Society's guidance on conflicts of interest post Etridge in Appendix V.18.

9.5.3. One drawback to an express statement of the beneficial interest is that it cannot be changed except by deed. If, for example, a deed of trust stated that a husband owned 70% of the equitable interest and his wife 30%, but the wife subsequently paid off the whole mortgage on the house using money which she had inherited on the death of one of her parents, the wife might feel that she had become entitled to a larger proportion of the equitable interest through her contribution to the mortgage but, unless a new deed of trust is drawn up, redefining the proportionate shares of the parties, on sale of the property, the wife would still be entitled only to her original 30%. An alternative solution is that the whole or part of one joint owner's beneficial interest can be transferred to the new owner in writing, signed by the person transferring.[2]

9.5.4. A tenancy in common can be devised by will or will pass on intestacy. Where property is held by this method the parties should be advised as to the desirability of making a will.

9.5.5. Where a tenancy in common is created the deed should make specific provision relating to the appointment of a new trustee in the event of the death of one co-owner. In the absence of such a provision the provisions of Trusts of Land and

Appointment of Trustees Act 1996, s.19 may operate to give beneficiaries who are of full age and competence the right to nominate a new trustee.

1. *Springette* v. *Defoe* [1992] NPC 34; *Savill* v. *Goodall* [1992] NPC 153.
2. Law of Property Act 1925, s.53.

9.6.   Suitability of each method

9.6.1.   *Joint tenancy*

The automatic right of survivorship makes this method of co-ownership both suitable and attractive to prospective co-owners who are married to each other. Exceptionally, a joint tenancy may be unsuited to a married couple where one or both of the buyers is individually wealthy and where equalisation of estates for inheritance tax purposes is a consideration. Survivorship rights may well not be intended by co-owners who are not married to each other, and would not normally be considered suitable when dealing with property held in a business partnership.

9.6.2.   *Tenancy in common*

Prospective co-owners who are not married to each other will usually be advised to hold by this method. This is also the most appropriate method by which partnership property can be dealt with. Consideration should be given to this method where the contributions made by each of the co-owners to the purchase price are in unequal proportions and where the parties are married to each other but one (or both) of them has offspring from a previous relationship who might reasonably expect to inherit on the death of their natural parent.

9.7.   Gifts

9.7.1.   Where the purchase price of the property is supplied by one party alone, but the property is purchased in the joint names of the person who paid the purchase price and another, equity generally deems the property to be held on a resulting trust on behalf of the buyer, unless there is an indication to the contrary (such as an express declaration of trust in the transfer), or the circumstances are within the limited cases where a presumption of advancement applies.[1]

1. See Appendix V.8., Gifts of Property Guidelines.

9.8.   Co-habitees

9.8.1.   Co-habitees may need to be advised independently about their respective rights in the property to be purchased. Solicitors should be alert to the possibility of a conflict of interests arising in this situation.

9.8.2.   It is advisable for co-habitees who are to be co-owners to enter a separate deed of trust (separate from but to be kept with the title deeds) which sets out their respective interests in the property. The rights and obligations conferred by this document can only be altered by the execution of a further deed of trust but this disadvantage is outweighed by the advantage of having certainty as to the parties' rights and interests.

9.8.3.   If the property is to be purchased in the sole name of one co-habitee, the other should be advised (where appropriate) to protect his or her interest by lodging an application for registration of an appropriate restriction at the Land Registry.[1]

1. Land Registration Rules 2003, r.92.

A10. Acting for both parties

See also: Mortgages: acting for lender and borrower, para. A11
Contract races, para. B2
Appendix V.13, V.14, V.15

10.1. Conflict of interests

10.1.1. As a general principle of professional conduct a solicitor or firm of solicitors should not accept instructions to act for two or more clients in the same transaction where there is a conflict or a significant risk of a conflict between the interests of those clients.[1]

10.1.2. Neither should a solicitor or his firm continue to act for two or more clients if a conflict of interests arises between those clients.[2]

1. See *The Guide to the Professional Conduct of Solicitors 1999,* Principle 15.01.
2. See *The Guide to the Professional Conduct of Solicitors 1999,* Principle 15.03.

10.2. Rule 6 Solicitors' Practice Rules 1990

10.2.1. Subject to certain exceptions, acting for both parties in a conveyancing transaction at arm's length is generally prohibited by Rule 6 Solicitors' Practice Rules 1990.[1] The rule should be considered carefully before a decision is taken to act for more than one party.

10.2.2. In most circumstances, therefore, a solicitor who is asked to act for both parties to a transaction will decline to act for both either because of the potential conflict of interest between the parties or because of the application of Rule 6 Solicitors' Practice Rules 1990.

10.2.3. Provided there is no conflict of interest the same solicitor may act for both seller and buyer where the transaction is not at arm's length (e.g. a transaction between parties who are related by blood, adoption or marriage).

1. See Appendix I.1.

10.3.   **Exceptions to Rule 6**

10.3.1.   A solicitor must not act for seller and buyer:

  (a) without the written consent of both parties;

  (b) if a conflict of interest exists or arises; or

  (c) if the seller is selling or leasing as a builder or developer.

If a builder or developer acquires a property in part exchange, and sells it on without development, he or she is not selling as a builder or developer.

10.3.2.   Subject to para. A10.3.1. above, a solicitor may act for both seller and buyer, but only if:

  (a) both parties are established clients (the test here is an objective one, i.e. whether a reasonable solicitor would regard the person as an established client. A person who is related by blood, adoption or marriage to an established client counts as an established client. A seller or buyer who instructs the solicitor for the first time is not an established client. A person who is selling or buying jointly with an established client counts as an established client); *or*

  (b) the consideration is £10,000 or less and the transaction is not the grant of a lease (the value of any property taken in part exchange must be taken into account in calculating the £10,000); *or*

  (c) there is no other qualified conveyancer in the area whom either the seller or the buyer could reasonably be expected to consult; *or*

  (d) seller and buyer are represented by two separate offices in different localities and

   (i) different solicitors who normally work at each office, conduct or supervise the transaction for seller and buyer; and

   (ii) no office of the practice (or an associated practice) referred either client to the office conducting his or her transaction; *or*

  (e) the only way in which the solicitor is acting for the buyer is in providing mortgage related services; *or*

  (f) the only way in which the solicitor is acting for the seller is in providing property selling services through a SEAL.

10.3.3.   When a solicitor's practice (including a SEAL) acts in the property selling for the seller and acts for the buyer, the following additional conditions must be met:

  (a) different persons must conduct the work for the seller and the work for the buyer; and if the person conducting the work needs supervision, they must be supervised by different solicitors; *and*

  (b) the solicitor must inform the seller in writing, before accepting instructions to deal with the property selling, of any services which might be offered to a buyer, whether through the same practice or any practice associated with it; *and*

(c) the solicitor must explain to the buyer, before the buyer gives consent to the arrangement:

(i) the implications of a conflict of interest arising; *and*

(ii) the solicitor's financial interest in the sale going through; *and*

(iii) if the solicitor proposes to provide mortgage related services to the buyer through a SEAL which is also acting for the seller, that the solicitor cannot advise the buyer on the merits of the purchase.

10.4. Mortgages

10.4.1. *Standard mortgages*

A mortgage is a standard mortgage where:

(i) it is provided in the normal course of the lender's activities;

(ii) a significant part of the lender's activities consists of lending; and

(iii) the mortgage is on standard terms.

A solicitor, or solicitors practising in associated practices, must not act for both lender and borrower on the grant of a mortgage of land if a conflict of interest exists or arises or if, in the case of a standard mortgage of property to be used as the borrower's private residence only, the lender's mortgage instructions extend beyond the limitations contained in paragraphs (3)(c) and (3)(e) of Rule 6 or do not permit the use of the certificate of title required by paragraph (3)(d) of Rule 6.[1] In the case of standard mortgages of other premises the solicitor must not act where the lender's instructions extend beyond paragraphs (3)(c) and (3)(e). A solicitor who proposes to act for both lender and borrower on the grant of a standard mortgage must first inform the lender in writing of the circumstances if the solicitor or a member of his immediate family is a borrower or if the solicitor proposes to act for seller buyer and lender in the same transaction. The limitations contained in paragraphs (3)(c) and (3)(e) are set out in Appendix I.1.

1. Rule 6(3)(c) applies to both commercial and residential properties, but it is only in the case of residential properties that the approved Certificate of Title must be used. (See the Certificate of Title, Appendix VII.2.)

10.4.2. *Individual mortgage*

An individual mortgage is any mortgage other than a standard mortgage (see para. 10.4.1 above). A solicitor, or solicitors practising in associated practices, must not act for both lender and borrower unless the transaction is not at arm's length and no conflict of interest exists or arises on the grant of an individual mortgage.

10.4.3. *Acting for seller, buyer and lender*

A solicitor, or solicitors practising in associated practices, must not act for seller, buyer and lender in the same transaction unless no conflict of interest exists or arises, and, in the case of a standard mortgage, the solicitor has given written notification of the circumstance to the lender.

10.5. **Contract races**

10.5.1. If the transaction involves a contract race the same firm may not act for two or more prospective buyers, nor may the firm act for both seller and one of the prospective buyers.[1]

1. Rule 6A Solicitors' Practice Rules 1990 (Appendix I.1).

10.6. **Merger of firms**

10.6.1. As a result of a merger or amalgamation a firm may find that it is acting for both seller and buyer in the same transaction. Unless the circumstances of the transaction fall within one of the exceptions to Rule 6 above the firm should cease to act for one or both of the parties from the date of the merger. It is, however, recognised that to cease to act for one client during the course of the transaction might cause hardship and inconvenience to both clients and provided that there is compliance with the guidelines set out below the firm may continue to act for both clients in order to finalise the transaction.

10.6.2. *Guidelines*

The individual solicitors within the merged firm who are representing the respective parties should, in relation to this particular transaction, regard themselves as belonging to separate firms and should not communicate with each other (except formally about the outcome of the transaction) until the transaction has been concluded. *The Guide to the Professional Conduct of Solicitors 1999* contains guidelines relating to this matter in Principle 15.03 and Annex 15A.

10.6.3. New instructions received for clients of the merged firm will be subject to the provisions of Rule 6 above.

10.7. **Solicitor who moves to another firm**

10.7.1. *Client's pending business is taken over by the new firm*

In these circumstances the solicitor may find that his new firm is already acting for the other party to the transaction and a situation analogous to that which occurs on a merger of firms pertains. The guidelines set out above should be followed.

10.7.2. On moving to the new firm the solicitor finds he is now acting for the buyer in a transaction where he had previously been acting for the seller in the same transaction (or vice versa): although in this situation there is no question of the same solicitor or same firm acting for both parties the solicitor, while working for his previous firm, will have acquired information which is confidential to his (now) former client and which may affect or prejudice the way in which he handles the transaction for the client of the new firm. In order to preserve his duty of confidentiality to his former client the solicitor should not act for the client of the new firm in this transaction, but there is no objection to the matter being handled by another fee-earner in the solicitor's new firm.

10.8. Property selling

10.8.1. As part of the solicitor's business

See para. A10.3.3 above.

10.8.2. As a separate business

Where the solicitor conducts property selling through a separate jointly owned business and the solicitor does not do the seller's conveyancing or does the seller's conveyancing under one of the Rule 6 exceptions, he may do the buyer's conveyancing. Alternatively the solicitor may do a seller's conveyancing where the estate agency business provides mortgage services to the buyer. The buyer and the seller must give their written informed consent and different individuals must deal with the work for seller and buyer.[1]

1. See Property selling, para. A2.

10.9. Joint borrowers

10.9.1. Where joint borrowers are obtaining a mortgage for the purchase of property, there is no objection to the same solicitor advising both of them, provided that their interests coincide. Where, however, one party is acting as surety for the other's debts, e.g. a wife who is guaranteeing her husband's mortgage of the matrimonial home to secure the husband's business debts, the parties' interests will almost certainly be in conflict with each other (see Appendix V.18 Undue influence – solicitors duties post Etridge). In these circumstances, separate and independent advice must be given to each party. It may be possible for the same solicitor to advise both clients in these circumstances, but each client should be seen separately and the advice given to each party must be consistent with that party's interests.[1] When instructions are being carried out under the terms of the Lenders' Handbook, paragraph 8 of the Handbook will normally prohibit the same solicitor from advising any borrower who does not benefit personally from the loan or any guarantor or any non-owning occupier. Such persons must have independent advice (also see para. A10.4).

1. See *Barclays Bank* v. *O'Brien* [1993] 4 All ER 417; *Midland Bank plc* v. *Serter* [1994] EGCS 45; *Clark Boyce* v. *Mouat* [1993] 3 WLR 1021, PC; *Banco-Exterior Internacional* v. *Mann* [1995] 1 All ER 936 (CA). Also see *Bank Melli Iran* v. *Samadi Rad* [1995] 2 FLR 367, where the court said that a wife who had been advised separately by a different solicitor in the firm which was also advising her husband had not received 'independent' advice.

A11. Mortgages: acting for lender and borrower

See also: Acting for both parties, para. A10
Lenders, section H
Costs, para. N1
CML Lender's Handbook, Appendix VIII.3

11.1.   General principles

11.1.1.   The buyer's lender will frequently instruct the buyer's solicitor also to act for him in connection with the grant of the mortgage. The same situation commonly occurs in relation to the discharge of an existing mortgage when acting for a seller client.

11.1.2.   As soon as the solicitor accepts instructions to act for the lender he is acting for both parties in one transaction (i.e. for both lender and borrower) and owes a duty to both clients.[1] Their respective interests are not necessarily identical and need to be separately considered.

11.1.3.   Subject to para. A10.4 above, acting for both parties is permissible provided that no conflict of interest arises between the two clients.

11.1.4.   The lender's instructions to act and (in the case of a purchase) terms of offer must be carefully scrutinised to ensure that there is no conflict or potential conflict between the interests of the lender and the buyer/seller.

11.1.5.   In many cases the lender's instructions will require the solicitor to observe the terms of the Lenders' Handbook (which is certified for compliance with Rule 6).

11.1.6.   A solicitor may not act for a lender where the terms of the lender's instructions exceed the limitations imposed by Rule 6 Solicitors' Practice Rules 1990 (as amended).

1. *Mortgage Express* v. *Bowerman & Partners* [1995] 2 All ER 769 (CA).

11.2. Conflict of interests

11.2.1. If a conflict should occur the solicitor must decline to act (or to continue to act) for both parties unless he can, with the consent of one party, continue to act for the other.

11.3. Examples of conflict

11.3.1. Conflict may arise if, for example:

(a) the terms of the mortgage offer are inequitable;

(b) instructions reveal that the buyer would be in breach of one of the terms of the offer;

(c) the buyer/seller is unable to comply with the lender's terms;

(d) the buyer is offering inadequate security.

11.3.2. A conflict will also arise if the buyer's solicitor becomes aware that the buyer is misrepresenting the purchase price to the lender, e.g. where the buyer and seller have agreed that the actual purchase price of the property will be lower than that shown in the contract and purchase deed, or where the buyer receives an inducement such as a free holiday to persuade him to buy the property. Solicitors have a duty of confidentiality to their clients, but this does not affect their duty to act in the best interests of each client. Subject to the instructions received from the particular lender concerned, any information regarding variations to the purchase price should be forwarded to the lender with the consent of the buyer. If the buyer will not consent to the information being disclosed to the lender the solicitor must cease to act for the lender and must consider carefully whether he is able to continue to act for the buyer. Any attempt to defraud the lender may lead to criminal prosecutions of both the buyer and the buyer's solicitor. The solicitor would also be guilty of unprofessional conduct. If a solicitor is aware that his client is attempting to perpetrate fraud in any form he should immediately cease to act for that client. Attention is drawn to the Law Society's Property Fraud Warning Card II (Appendix IV.3) and the Law Society's guidance on mortgage fraud – variation in purchase price (Appendix V.11).

11.4. Confidentiality

11.4.1. If a conflict does arise between the borrower and his lender where the same solicitor is acting for both parties it should be borne in mind that all information received by the solicitor from his client is confidential and cannot be disclosed to the lender without the client's consent. Knowledge acquired in the course of acting for the client is not imputed to the lender.[1] Where, for example, the solicitor is told by his borrower client that the client intends to breach the terms of the mortgage offer by letting the premises to a tenant, the solicitor, when informing the lender that he can no longer act for him, must tell the lender that the reason for the termination of the retainer is because a conflict of interests has arisen, but is not at liberty to disclose the nature of the conflict without the borrower client's consent.

1. *Halifax Mortgage Services Ltd.* v. *Stepsky, The Times,* 27 June 1995.

11.5. Individual mortgages

11.5.1. The solicitor must not act for both lender and borrower in an individual mortgage at arm's length.

11.5.2. An individual mortgage is defined by Rule 6(3) Solicitors' Practice Rules 1990 as 'any mortgage other than a standard mortgage'. A standard mortgage is one on standard terms provided in the normal course of the lender's activities.

11.5.3. Subject to the general principles of conflict of interests it would be possible to act in an individual mortgage which is not at arm's length (e.g. a loan between father and son), but it is advisable to ensure that the borrower receives independent advice about the terms of the loan.

11.6. Lender's costs

11.6.1. See Costs, N1.

11.7. Sureties

11.7.1. Where the lender requires a surety to enter into the transaction, the surety should be advised to take independent advice before signing the security document. This is of particular importance where the intended surety is the wife of the borrower since the courts take the view that a security should not be enforced against a married woman unless the lender can show that he has taken reasonable steps to show that she understood the transaction.[1] Under the terms of the Lenders' Handbook (paragraph 8) a solicitor cannot act for both the borrower and a surety without the lender's consent and the surety must have independent advice.

11.7.2. If the proceeds of a life policy fall into the deceased's estate (e.g. because the policy was not formally assigned to the lender) the surety has no claim against the deceased's estate.

1. See *Barclays Bank plc* v. *O'Brien* [1993] 3 WLR 786, HL; *C.I.B.C. Mortgages* v. *Pitt* [1993] 3 WLR 802, HL; guidance in Appendix V.18.

11.8. Mortgage fraud

11.8.1. Mortgage fraud can occur in either a residential or commercial transaction and can assume many different guises. Solicitors must be alert to the possibility of fraud and should be careful not to participate, even unknowingly, in a transaction where such a fraud is being perpetrated.[1]

1. See Mortgage Fraud, para. A24 and Appendix IV.3).

11.9. Ownership of documents and confidentiality

11.9.1. The following guidance relates to the position where the same firm of solicitors acted for the buyer/borrower and for the lender on a contemporaneous purchase and mortgage and the lender asks to see documents on the 'conveyancing file'.

11.9.2. Where all the documentation is kept on one file, the solicitor will have to sort through the file to determine ownership of the various papers. Annex 12A of *The Guide to the Professional Conduct of Solicitors 1999* contains guidance on the legal subject of ownership of documents on a solicitor's file.

11.9.3. The documents which the lender will be entitled to see fall into two categories. The first category is documents prepared or received by the solicitor on behalf of the lender. The second category is documents prepared or received by the solicitor on behalf of the borrower which, it is considered, the lender is nonetheless entitled to see. The rationale is that these documents relate to that part of the solicitor's work where the lender and borrower can be said to have a common interest, i.e. the deduction of title, the acquisition of a good title to the property and ancillary legal issues, such as the use of the property. Examples of the most common items in these two categories are set out below.

11.9.4. Documents held by the solicitor on behalf of the lender are:

(a) the lender's instructions to the solicitor;

(b) copy mortgage deed;

(c) copy report on title;

(d) any correspondence between the solicitor and the lender or between the solicitor and a third party written or received on the lender's behalf.

11.9.5. Documents held by the solicitor on behalf of the borrower are:

(a) contract for sale;

(b) property information form/enquiries before contract;

(c) abstract or epitome of title/official copy entries of the title;

(d) requisitions on title;

(e) draft purchase deed;

(f) draft licence to assign (where appropriate);

(g) Land Registry application forms.

11.10. **The CML Lenders' Handbook for England and Wales**[1]

11.10.1. *Introduction*

The Lenders' Handbook forms the contract between the solicitor (or licensed conveyancer) and lender where the solicitor (or licensed conveyancer) is representing a lender who has agreed to be a party to the Lenders' Handbook. A number of major lenders have agreed to be parties to the Lenders' Handbook and other mortgage lenders may instruct solicitors to act on the terms of the Lenders' Handbook. The instructions apply whether or not the solicitor is acting for both borrower and lender or for the lender only.

11.10.2. Modifications of the instructions specific to the transaction in hand will be notified to the solicitor in the lender's written instructions to the solicitor and/or in Part 2 of the Lenders' Handbook.

11.10.3. It is the solicitor's responsibility to ensure that the property has a good and marketable title which can safely be accepted by the lender as security and that the property is validly charged to the lender to secure the advance made to the borrower.

11.10.4. Communications between the solicitor and the lender must be in writing (or confirmed in writing) and must quote the mortgage account or roll number, the borrower's name and initials, the address of the property and the solicitor's reference.

11.10.5. Documents contained in the 'joint file' (as defined in the Lenders' Handbook) must be retained by the solicitor for at least six years from the date of the mortgage. The borrower is not permitted to have documents from the file without the lender's consent. Equally, the lender is not permitted to have documents from the file without the borrower's consent. Each would be entitled to certified copies, but the lender only to those documents relevant to its retainer because of the right of the borrower to confidentiality (see para. A11.9.4 and A11.9.5).

11.10.6. The solicitor must use the lender's standard documentation the wording of which must not be varied without the lender's consent.

---

1. Some lenders started to use the Lenders' Handbook before 1 October 1999, on which date the amended Rule 6(3) affecting mortgage instructions applies. See Appendix VIII.3 for Part 1 of the CML Lenders' Handbook and Appendix V.13, V.14, V.15 for further guidance on Rule 6(3).

A12. Preliminary deposits

12.1. **General law**
12.2. **Payment to estate agents**

12.3. **New properties**
12.4. **Action by solicitor**

See also: Deposit, para. B17

12.1. General law

12.1.1. There is no requirement in law for either party to pay a preliminary deposit since neither party is committed to the sale and purchase until contracts have been exchanged.

12.2. Payment to estate agents

12.2.1. An estate agent will sometimes ask a prospective buyer to pay a preliminary deposit as an indication of the buyer's good intentions to proceed with negotiations. The buyer should be advised to resist pressure from the agent to make such a payment since no advantage to the buyer derives from it.

12.2.2. If a preliminary deposit is to be paid the buyer should ensure that the agent has the seller's authority to take the deposit. Without such authority the buyer has no recourse against the seller if the agent misappropriates the money.[1]

12.2.3. A signed receipt must be obtained in respect of any preliminary deposit which is paid, a copy of which should be placed on the solicitor's file for reference. The terms of the receipt should be scrutinised before signature to ensure that the deposit will be refundable if the transaction does not proceed.

12.2.4. Any preliminary deposit paid is normally fully refundable to the buyer if the transaction does not proceed.

12.2.5. Preliminary deposits are usually paid to the estate agent who will hold the money in the capacity of agent for the seller. Interest on a preliminary deposit which exceeds £500 may be payable under Estate Agents Act 1979.

12.2.6. Where a preliminary deposit is taken by a solicitor who is acting as an estate agent, consideration should be given to holding that deposit in the capacity of agent for the buyer in accordance with the Solicitors' Property Group Code of Practice.[2]

1. See *Sorrell v. Finch* [1977] AC 728.
2. See www.solicitorspropertygroup.co.uk

12.3.   New properties

12.3.1.   A seller who is a builder or developer will invariably require a prospective buyer to pay a preliminary deposit. In this situation the payment of the deposit may operate as an option to purchase a numbered plot at a stated price, the seller promising that he will not sell that plot elsewhere nor raise the price provided that contracts are exchanged within a stated period. Here the buyer may have little choice but to pay the deposit, but a receipt should always be obtained and a copy of it placed on the buyer's solicitor's file for reference. The terms of the receipt should be scrutinised to ascertain whether the deposit is refundable to the buyer if he later changes his mind and withdraws from the transaction. Since this type of preliminary deposit often buys an option on a numbered plot it is not unusual to find that the deposit is not returnable to the buyer in any circumstances, although it will be credited as part of the purchase price if the matter proceeds.

12.4.   Action by solicitor

12.4.1.   The solicitor should always enquire whether a preliminary deposit has been paid, and if so how much and to whom. A copy of the receipt should be obtained and a note of the amount of the deposit made on the file so that this may be taken into account when calculating the balance of deposit needed on exchange.

12.4.2.   The solicitor should also enquire whether the prospective buyer has signed any authority or other documents held by the estate agent which may be relevant to the contract.

A13. Surveys

See also: Environmental issues, para. B25
Other causes of action, para. M6

13.1. When should a survey be commissioned?

13.1.1. Ideally the buyer should always have a survey carried out before exchange of contracts, but many buyers, particularly first-time buyers for whom the expense of a survey is a major consideration, do not commission an independent survey, preferring to rely instead on the valuation undertaken by their lender. Most lenders disclose their written valuation reports to their customers.

13.1.2. In the case of commercial premises a buyer will have much more detailed concerns relating to the structure, use, and floor loading capabilities of the property. Compliance with statutory requirements must also be checked. The comments contained in the following paragraphs do not reflect the detail required in a commercial transaction.

13.2. Reasons for a survey

13.2.1. The *caveat emptor* rule places on the buyer the onus of discovering any physical faults in the property agreed to be sold. For this reason alone, a survey is always advisable in order to discover physical defects which are not readily apparent on inspection of the property by the lay client, except perhaps where a property in the course of construction is being purchased with the benefit of structural defects insurance.

13.2.2. In addition to the above the surveyor's report should:

(a) confirm whether or not the value of the property equates with the price agreed to be paid for it;

(b) point out any major structural defects which exist;

(c) give the buyer early warning of potential structural problems or major repair work which will be required in the foreseeable future so that these may be taken into account in deciding whether the buyer is able and/or prepared to undertake the responsibility for such future expenditure;

(d) bring to the attention of the buyer's solicitor the existence of factors which may be indicative of third party rights or overriding interests over the property and which need to be the subject of further enquiries by the solicitor;

(e) point out minor matters which may need remedial work in the near future;

(f) confirm whether or not the boundaries on the ground correspond with those shown in the title deeds.

13.3. Advice to the client

13.3.1. If the client has not already instructed a surveyor, the reasons for having a survey done should be explained to the client and a note made on the file that the client was so advised and of the client's decision following the receipt of the advice. The advice given should include information relating to the different types of survey available and their relative cost.

13.3.2. The client should be advised to commission a survey as soon as a firm offer has been accepted by the seller. The results of the survey must be obtained before exchange of contracts since once exchange has taken place the client will no longer have the right to withdraw from the transaction on the grounds of a physical defect in the property. The results of the survey may reveal matters which will require further investigation by the buyer's solicitor, or even give grounds for the negotiation of a reduction in the purchase price, both of which must, where appropriate, be conducted before a binding contract is entered into.

13.3.3. Although there is no reported decision on the point, it is possible that a court might hold that a solicitor who had not advised a client to have a survey done was in breach of his duty of care towards his client or in breach of Supply of Goods and Services Act 1982, s.13 which implies an obligation to perform a contract for services with reasonable skill and care.

13.3.4. If the solicitor does go through the surveyor's report prepared for the client, he is expected to exercise his own judgment and expertise in relation to the interpretation of the report and should emphasise to the client the limitations on the advice which can be given by the solicitor about the report (i.e. that he is looking at the report as a lawyer and not as a surveyor).

13.4. Types of survey

13.4.1. In broad terms the client has three options open to him:

(a) to rely on the valuation made by his lender;

(b) to commission a 'Home Buyer's Valuation and Survey Report';

(c) to instruct an independent surveyor to do a full structural survey.

13.4.2. *Valuation*

This will be undertaken by the buyer's lender in order to establish whether the property being purchased will be adequate security for the amount of the loan. The buyer pays the cost of this valuation and is usually permitted to see the valuer's report, but the report will not necessarily reveal sufficient information about the state of the property to allow the buyer to make a reasoned judgment as to whether or not to proceed with his purchase. Where the amount required by the buyer on mortgage represents a high percentage of the purchase price of the property, the interests of the buyer and his lender in the valuation broadly coincide, in that if the value of the property does not provide adequate security for the loan, then neither does it represent a wise investment for the client. In these circumstances therefore it may be considered that a lender's valuation report alone will provide sufficient protection of the client's interests. A valuation alone may also be considered adequate in circumstances where the client is purchasing a property in the course of construction which is to be covered by a structural defects insurance scheme.

13.4.3. *Home Buyer's Valuation and Survey Report*

This option represents a compromise between the mortgage valuation and the full survey and is thus an attractive option for a client who, for reasons of expense or otherwise, is reluctant to commission a full survey. In many cases the buyer's lender will agree (for an additional fee) to instruct the lender's valuer to undertake the survey concurrently with the mortgage valuation with consequent savings in time and expense for the client. This type of survey may provide adequate information for the client who is purchasing an ordinary suburban property built within the last 100 years, but the client should not be misled into thinking that the survey result is an absolute guarantee of the state and condition of the property. Although of much more value to the client than a mere valuation, this type of survey is still relatively superficial in scope.

13.4.4. *Full survey*

The potential expense of a full survey deters many clients from choosing this option. The client might be reminded that £500 abortive expense on a survey is preferable to discovering that £30,000 worth of structural repairs needs to be done to the property he has just purchased without the benefit of a survey. This option is undoubtedly the most expensive of the three on offer, the exact expense and value to the client depending on what the surveyor has been instructed to investigate. A full survey will only reveal the true state and condition of the entire property if the surveyor is correctly instructed to investigate all aspects of the property.

13.4.5. *Guidelines*

The need for a full structural survey may be indicated by the presence of one or more of the following factors:

(a) the property is of a high value;

(b) the amount of the buyer's intended mortgage represents a low proportion of the purchase price, e.g. less than 70%;

(c) the property is more than 100 years old;

(d) the buyer intends to alter or extend the property after completion;

(e) the property is not of conventional brick and mortar construction;

(f) the proximity of the property to features which may cause subsidence or other structural problems, e.g. mines, filled-in gravel pits, rivers, vibration damage from aircraft or railways;

(g) the property is not detached.

13.4.6. Surveys in special cases

A surveyor, even when instructed to carry out a full structural survey, will not normally investigate drainage or electrical systems. A property which does not have the benefit of mains drainage will require a separate drainage survey from an expert in that field, since the cost of repair or replacement of a private drainage system can be prohibitive. Liability for escaping effluent can also involve civil and criminal penalties. If the electric wiring system in the property has not been inspected during the past five years a report on the adequacy and safety of the electrical installations may also be desirable. Where environmental issues are relevant, e.g. on purchases of development land a separate environmental survey may also be desirable to ensure that the land does not harbour any hazardous substances which may incur liability on the landowner under Environmental Protection Act 1990 or Environment Act 1995. The local authority for the area can supply information relating to the presence of radon in the area. The National Radiological Protection Board publishes definitive maps, provides information on radon, and offers a written report on the radon potential for a property (see B25.9).

13.4.7. Flats and other attached properties

Where the property to be purchased is a flat or is a property which is structurally attached to neighbouring property, a full survey is desirable. The structural soundness of the property being bought is in these circumstances dependent on the soundness of the neighbouring property also, and the surveyor must therefore be instructed to inspect the adjoining property (if possible) as well as the property actually being purchased.

13.4.8. Water supply pipes

The owner or occupier of land may be responsible for the maintenance of a water supply pipe which crosses privately owned land before joining the publicly maintained mains supply pipe. A full structural survey may not deal with the water supply system (particularly where the pipes supplying the property being surveyed pass through or under adjoining property). The client may be advised to obtain a separate survey of the water supply pipes from his water supply company. A fee may be payable for this service.

13.5. Surveyor's liability

13.5.1.   The surveyor owes a duty of care to his client to carry out his survey with reason-able skill and care. This common law duty is reinforced by Supply of Goods and Services Act 1982, s.13 which implies into a contract for services a term that the work will be carried out with reasonable skill and care.

13.5.2.   Where a client suffers loss as a result of a negligent survey an action can be sustained against his surveyor, subject to the validity of any exemption clause which may have formed part of the surveyor's terms of work. The normal rules relating to remoteness of damage apply; thus the client will not sustain a successful action unless the area of the client's complaint lies within the scope of what the surveyor was instructed to do, and hence the importance of giving full and explicit instructions when the survey is commissioned.

13.5.3.   An exclusion clause which seeks to limit or to exclude the surveyor's liability in contract or tort will be subject to the reasonableness test in Unfair Contract Terms Act 1977, s.11. Where a lay client has suffered loss the burden of showing that the clause satisfies the reasonableness test will be a difficult one for the surveyor to discharge,[1] but the clause may give some protection where the client who commissioned the survey was experienced in the property field.[2]

13.5.4.   Where the client suffers loss after having relied on a lender's valuer's report an action in tort may lie against the surveyor. No action in contract can be sustained because, the survey having been commissioned by the lender, there is no contrac-tual relationship between the buyer and the surveyor. The success of such an action may again depend on the validity of any exclusion clause contained in the valua-tion; however, it was held by the House of Lords in *Smith* v. *Eric S. Bush* (a firm); *Harris* v. *Wyre Forest District Council*[3] that a valuer instructed by a lender to carry out a mortgage valuation of a modest house, in the knowledge that the buyer would rely on the valuation without obtaining an independent survey, owed a duty of care to the buyer to exercise reasonable care and skill in carrying out the valuation. Similarly in *Beresforde* v. *Chesterfield Borough Council*,[4] where the lender presented the valuer's report to the buyer on its own headed notepaper, the Court of Appeal allowed the buyer to proceed with a claim based on loss arising out of an allegedly negligent valuation directly against the lender. However, the court's decision in this case was interlocutory and as no trial took place it cannot be assumed that a lender will always be liable in such circumstances. The decisions in these cases may assist lay purchasers of ordinary modestly priced houses or small businesses,[5] but may not assist in other circumstances where it would be reasonable to assume that the buyer would commission his own independent survey.

13.5.5.   A complaint about a negligent valuation/survey made in-house by a lender may be investigated by the Building Society's Ombudsman provided the complainant is an existing borrower from that Society.[6]

13.6. Lenders' Handbook[7]

13.6.1 Paragraph 4 of the Lenders' Handbook requires the solicitor to check that certain assumptions made by the valuer in his report are correct.

13.6.2. The solicitor is recommended by the Lenders' Handbook to advise the buyer client that the valuation may contain omissions or inaccurate information.

1. See *Yianni* v. *Edwin Evans & Sons* [1982] 1 QB 438.
2. See *Stevenson* v. *Nationwide Building Society* (1984) 272 EG 663.
3. [1990] 1 AC 831, HL.
4. [1989] 39 EG 176.
5. See *Qureshi* v. *Liassides* (unreported 22 April 1994). See commentary in *Estates Gazette*, 11 November 1994, p.123.
6. *Halifax Building Society* v. *Edell* [1992] Ch 436.
7. Part 1 of the CML Lender's Handbook is reproduced as Appendix VIII.3.

A14. Stamp duty and stamp duty savings

See also: Stamp Duty, para. AA4
VAT, para. A16
Sub-sales, para. B14
Title, section D
Post-completion, section G
Stamping documents, para. G2
Leaseholds, section K

14.1. Introduction

The Finance Bill 2003 makes provision for a new Stamp Duty Land Tax, which is planned for implementation on 1 December 2003. However, the detail of the new tax is unknown at the time of going to press so this book is up-to-date with stamp duty as at 1 June 2003. An outine of the new tax and related provisions in the Finance Bill is given in section AAA. Stamp Duty Land Tax and Disadvantaged Areas relief is explained in para. A14.2.4, section B10 and in the Inland Revenue Statement of Practice at Appendix IX.3.

14.1.1. Statutory framework

An estimate of the stamp duty to be incurred will need to be included in the costs estimate given to the buyer or lessee. Although there is no general statutory obligation to pay stamp duty (*Marx* v. *Estates and General* [1975] 3 All ER 1064), non-payment gives rise to penalties and interest under Stamp Act 1891 and Finance Act 1999 and difficulties in establishing title or enforcing security or producing evidence in litigation (Stamp Act 1891, ss.14 and 17). Evasion of stamp duty will expose the client and his solicitor to prosecution. A solicitor who is aware of an intention to defraud the Inland Revenue in this way, or who assists his client to do so, may also be subject to disciplinary proceedings. Duty is payable on the instrument within 30 days after execution.

14.1.2. Type of stamps

Stamps which have to be impressed upon the face of the document are of two kinds:

- stamps indicating that stamp duty has been paid whether *ad valorem* or the fixed duty of £5;

- stamps indicating that certain compliance procedures have been satisfied such as adjudication indicating that the correct duty has been paid, denoting stamps and the produced stamp.

Failure to obtain these stamps usually means that the document is not a duly stamped instrument of title, even where the duty is only £5 or nil because of an exemption.

14.1.3. Avoidance schemes

It has recently been stated that arrangements intended to mitigate duty are not particularly vulnerable to attack under the decision in *Furniss* v. *Dawson* [1984] AC 474 (see also *Westmoreland* v. *MacNiven* [2001] STC 237).

There is an increasing body of anti-avoidance legislation which must be understood by conveyancers if they are to satisfy their statutory obligations to prepare documents and forms correctly and to protect the interests of their clients by investigating title and carrying out due diligence upon transactions. For conveyancers the key areas of anti-avoidance for land transactions are:

- transfers in contemplation of a sale (FA 1965, s.90);

- transfers and leases of land to connected companies (FA 2000, ss.119 to 121);

- transfers and leases of land in exchanges (FA 1994, s.241; FA 2000, s.118);

- transfers of property subject to mortgages or in satisfaction of debt (Stamp Act 1891, s.57; Statement of Practice SP6/90);

- transfers of leases of reversionary interests subject to an agreement for lease for a term exceeding 35 years (FA 1984, s.111);

- surrenders of leases by operation of law (FA 2000, s.128);

- contracts in the chain of title where at some stage the consideration has exceeded or will or may exceed £10 million which contracts have to be stamped after 90 days (FA 2002, s.115; Sched. 36);

- clawback of exemptions and reliefs upon transfers or leases of land between associated companies when the parties cease to be associated within two years (3 years under the Finance Bill 2003, cl.127) after the transfer or lease is executed (FA 2002, ss.111 and 113; Scheds. 34 and 35).

14.2. Purchase of freehold property for value

14.2.1. Contracts for the sale of freehold land

Contracts for the sale of land are not subject to stamp duty except where:

- they are for the sale of the equitable interest (FA 1999, Sched. 23 para. 7);

- they are for a consideration exceeding £10 million and there is no stamped transfer after 90 days (FA 2002, s.115); or

- they are so drafted that they are in law 'conveyances' (*Peter Bone Ltd* v. *IRC* [1995] STC 921).

Notices exercising options to purchase land may be dutiable under these provisions.

14.2.2. Transfers

Transfers of freehold property at a consideration of £500,000 or less will require a certificate of value (as outlined below). In the absence of a certificate of value stamp duty will be payable at the rate of 4%. Transfers of land for a consideration or deemed consideration of more than £500,000 are subject to duty at 4%.

Where the consideration or deemed consideration for the transfer is £60,000 or less and the transaction does not form part of a larger transaction or series of transactions, no duty is payable provided an appropriate certificate of value is included in the document.

Where the consideration or deemed consideration for the transfer exceeds £60,000 but does not exceed £250,000 and the transaction does not form part of a larger transaction or series of transactions, duty is payable at the rate of 1% provided an appropriate certificate of value is included in the document.

Where the consideration for the transfer exceeds £250,000 but does not exceed £500,000 and the transaction does not form part of a larger transaction or series of transactions, duty is payable at the rate of 3% provided an appropriate certificate of value is included in the document.

14.2.3. Form of certificate of value

'It is certified that the transaction effected does not form part of a larger transaction or of a series of transactions in respect of which the amount or value or the aggregate amount or value of the consideration exceeds [£60,000: (£250,000) (£500,000)]'.

Misuse of a certificate of value can be fraud on the Revenue and/or professional misconduct.[1] A larger transaction or series of transactions require a contractual linkage; so purely commercial linkage (i.e. one contract would not be signed without the other) does not prevent the inclusion of a certificate of value where the contracts are not legally interdependent. However, provisions requiring simultaneous completions, where a party can refuse to complete without completion of the other contract, would constitute contractual linkage.

All of the consideration must be included except that which is attributable to intellectual property other than knowhow and goodwill other than goodwill embedded in the land and goods which includes equipment attached to the land which has not become a fixture (*Stamp Tax Bulletin*, August 2001).

The wording of the certificate of value does not permit the contract for the purchase of a single piece of land to be sub-divided into separate small transfers with the intention of bringing the value of each small unit under the stamp duty threshold, so avoiding the payment of duty on the whole unit.

14.2.4. *Enterprise land and 'disadvantaged areas'*

Disadvantaged Areas Relief is provided for by the Finance Act 2001, s.92 and Schedule 30. It has been given temporary approval by the European Commission until 31 December 2006. From 10 April 2003 no stamp duty is payable on:

- purchases or leases of non-residential property in a designated disadvantaged areas

- residential purchases in designated disadvantaged areas where the purchase price does not exceed £150,000; and

- the grant of leases where the average rent does not exceed £15,000 pa and/or where any premium does not exceed £150,000.

Designated Areas are contained in The Stamp Duty (Disadvantaged Areas) Regulations 2001 (SI. 2001/3747), but see para. B10.5.10 for an explanation of how to search and the problems surrounding the list of wards.

Residential, non-residential, and mixed use are defined in The Stamp Duty (Disadvantaged Areas) (Application of Exemptions) Regulations 2003 (S.I. 2003/1056), and the Stamp Taxes Office interpretation given in Inland Revenue Statement of Practice SPI/2003 Stamp Duty: Disadvantaged Area Relief (see Appendix IX.3).

14.3. **VAT**

14.3.1. Where the consideration for the property attracts VAT, stamp duty is payable on the whole of the consideration including the VAT element of the price.

14.3.2. Stamp duty itself does not attract a charge to VAT.

14.3.3. Where an election to waive the VAT exemption has already been exercised at the time of the transaction, stamp duty is chargeable on the purchase price, premium or rent including VAT. Where, however, the election has not at that time been exercised, VAT at the current rate is to be included in the calculation of the stamp duty in respect of any payments to which such an election could apply.[1]

---

1. See Inland Revenue Practice Statement 11/91, and VAT, para. A16.

14.4.   Assignment of an existing lease

14.4.1. *Contracts*

A contract for the sale of the legal title to a lease is not dutiable unless it includes tenant's fixtures, i.e. those items attached to the land which are fixtures that the tenant is entitled to sever and remove during or at the end of the tenancy (FA 1999, Schedule 13 paragraph 7).

14.4.2. *Transfer*

The transfer (assignment) of an existing lease attracts stamp duty at the same rate as that applicable to freehold property, calculated on the consideration for the assignment and ignoring the rest payable under the lease.

14.5.   Grant of lease

14.5.1. *Agreements for lease*

Where an agreement for lease is entered into, or where a notice is given exercising an option to call for or to renew a lease, it is stampable as if it were a lease. Duty need not be paid immediately since sub-sections 240(2) and (3) of the Finance Act 1994 will apply to prevent interest or penalties being due if the agreement for lease is presented for stamping at the same time as the lease. If both the lease and the agreement for lease are submitted 30 days or more after the execution of the lease, penalties will be applied to both documents. A problem will arise where there is an agreement for lease and, for whatever reason, the lease is not subsequently executed. In these circumstances, the agreement for lease will need to be presented for stamping if it is to be enforced. If, as is likely, presentation occurs more than 30 days after execution section 240 will not apply so interest and penalties will be payable. It must be noted that in dealings in interests reversionary upon agreements for lease for a term exceeding 35 years (which can include leases which have been granted but not registered (see Land Registration Act 2002, s.4)) the deed creating the reversionary interest must bear a stamp denoting that the agreement for lease has been duly stamped.

14.5.2. *Assessment of stamp duty on grant of a lease*

Stamp duty on the grant of a lease is assessed by reference to the premium paid for the grant and the average or market rent and the length of the term. Where the premium or rent is 'unascertainable' on stamp duty principles, in whole or in part, the stamp duty is charged upon the market premium or market rent (FA 1994, s.242). Where a lease is granted to a connected company it is stamped upon the market value not necessarily the contractual consideration (FA 2000, s.121). Where VAT is chargeable, or may become chargeable should the option to tax be exercised, this is included in the stamp duty computation. Current stamp duty tables should be consulted to inform the client of the amount of duty which will be incurred on completion. The lease itself bears full duty but with a deduction for the stamp duty paid upon the agreement for lease. A counterpart lease bears fixed duty of £5.[1]

14.5.3. *Presenting a lease for stamping*

When a lease is presented for stamping, it must either contain a certificate to the effect that there was no prior agreement for lease or be denoted with the duty paid (if any) on the agreement to which the lease gives effect (see para.A14.5.1). The form of certificate suggested by the Stamp Office is as follows:

'We certify that there is no agreement for lease to which this lease gives effect.'

The certificate should be included in the lease itself (and not presented as a separate document) and signed by the parties who have executed the instrument. A counterpart lease does not require a certificate.

1. Leasehold stamp duties are discussed further in section K.

14.6. **Variation of leases**

14.6.1. *Rent reviews*

No stamp duty is payable upon an instrument or memorandum endorsed upon a lease recording the effect of a rent review carried out in accordance with the provisions of the lease. An instrument increasing the rent otherwise than pursuant to a review is dutiable as if it were a lease for the amount of the increase in the rent.

14.6.2. *Other variations*

Other variations in a lease do not attract stamp duty unless these amount to a surrender and regrant (*Friends Provident* v. *British Rail* [1996] 1 All ER 336) such as enlarging the term or extending the demised premises. A surrender and regrant involves duty upon:

- the surrender in respect of any payment by the landlord and the value if any of the new lease (FA 2000, s.128;)

- the rent payable under the new lease;

- any actual premium provided by the tenant such as a payment to extend the term;

- any hidden premium represented by the value of the lease surrender (FA 1994, s.241) unless the new lease relates to the same land as the old lease (FA 2000, s.128(3); Stamp Act 1891, s.77).

Parties should look to less expensive alternatives such as options to renew or to break or a parallel lease of the additional land or a reversionary lease (subject to Law of Property Act 1925, s.149).

14.7. **Transactions at an undervalue**

Unless a transfer made for a consideration which is below market value is specifically exempt from stamp duty (e.g. under a statutory provision such as Church Building Act 1882) or falls within Stamp Duty (Exempt Instruments) Regulations 1987[1] stamp duty will be payable on the transfer, the amount to be assessed on adjudication of the transfer after completion. The duty is generally charged upon the actual consideration rather than the market value; but there are an increasing number of situations where the stamp duty rules provide for duty upon some amount other than the actual consideration.

1. S.I. 1987/516. See below, para. 14.9.3 and Appendix XII.2.

14.8. **Chattels**

Stamp duty is not payable on the value of chattels which are not included in the land transfer. For this reason it is permissible to apportion the value of the land from the value of included chattels, e.g. carpets and curtains, paying stamp duty only on the value of the land.

14.8.1. *Apportionment of purchase price*

Where chattels, including chattels attached to the land[1], are included in the sale and the seller has not apportioned the purchase price to reflect the value of the chattels, the buyer may wish to amend the draft contract to make such an apportionment and thus reduce his liability to stamp duty. Such an apportionment is of most value to the buyer where the purchase price of the property (including chattels) is marginally above the stamp duty threshold including the £10 million threshold for stamp duty upon uncompleted land contracts[2] and the effect of the apportionment is to reduce the price of the land[3] to bring it below the stamp duty limit. The buyer must seek the seller's permission to make an apportionment of the price. Provided the apportionment is a true reflection of the value of the chattels the seller has no reason to object to it since he will, on completion, still be receiving the full amount of the agreed price of the property, unless there are tax implications for him as mentioned below.

14.8.2. *Valuation of chattels*

The apportionment of the value of chattels must be a realistic estimate of their actual worth. Any purported over-valuation of the chattels will be a fraud on the Inland Revenue which may give rise to the sanctions mentioned above. Additionally, the effect of an over-valuation may be to render the contract illegal (and thus unenforceable) on the grounds of public policy.

Where fixtures, fittings and stock in trade are included in a commercial sale, a professional valuation of their worth should be obtained. Although it will, in most cases, be possible to determine the value of fixtures and fittings at the outset of the transaction, stock in trade may have to be purchased at a price to be agreed pursuant to a valuation made on the day of completion, since the amount of stock held by a trading business will fluctuate from day to day.

14.8.3. *Other tax liabilities*

In some cases the apportionment of the price of chattels may lead to other tax liabilities on the seller (*Re Hollebone* [1959] 2 All ER 152) or affect the purchaser's own tax liability in due course.

Even where the sale of the land is exempt from VAT, the sale of chattels may attract VAT.[4]

Where the contract is for the sale of the assets of a business, some of those assets may attract stamp duty while others will be exempt. Stamps Form 22[5] showing the apportionment of the price between the various assets should be completed and submitted to the Stamp Office.

1. *Stamp Taxes Bulletin*, August 2001.
2. FA 2002, s.115.
3. *Saunders* v. *Edwards* [1987] 2 All ER 651.
4. See para. B14.3.
5. Form 22 is reproduced in Appendix IX.2.

14.9.   **Exemptions and reliefs**

14.9.1. Ad valorem *duties*

Certain conveyances on sale and leases are exempt from stamp duty. These reliefs are subject to numerous conditions being satisfied and usually must be adjudicated. The major reliefs for land are:

- sales and leases to charities[1] and similar bodies including registered social landlords;[2]
- transfers and leases within a group,[3] but this is now subject to a three year clawback;[4]
- certain land transfers to connected companies;[5]
- transfers (but not leases) in connection with company reconstructions,[6] but certain of these are now subject to a two year clawback;[7]
- relief for disadvantaged land is expected in mid 2003;
- subsale relief;[8]
- transfers of mortgages.[9]

14.9.2. *Fixed duty*

Many instruments are subject to the fixed duty of £5 and some of those also require adjudication to be duly stamped.

14.9.3. *Stamp Duty (Exempt Instruments) Regulations 1987*

Where the document falls within one of the categories listed in Stamp Duty (Exempt Instruments) Regulations 1987 (see Appendix XII.2) and contains an appropriate certificate, no duty is payable and adjudication is not required.[10]

The most commonly encountered documents which will fall within these Regulations are:

- conveyance or transfer to a beneficiary named in the will (or his nominee);
- appointment of a new trustee;
- conveyance or transfer to a beneficiary (or his nominee) under the intestacy rules;
- variations of estates of deceased persons within two years after death;
- transfers in connection with divorce settlements;
- a voluntary disposition *inter vivos* for no consideration in money or money's worth except where the gift is subject to a mortgage (but see Statement of Practice SP6/90) or is to a connected company.[11]

The exemption conferred by the above Regulations applies provided that the document contains a certificate which specifies the category of exemption within the Regulations which is relied on.

14.9.4. *Form of certificate*

'It is certified that this instrument falls within category [X] in the Schedule to Stamp Duty (Exempt Instruments) Regulations 1987.'

The certificate which is contained in the purchase deed must be signed by the buyer. The document does not need to be sent to the Stamp Office nor for adjudication.

14.9.5. *Exempt bodies*

The transfer of land by certain bodies (e.g. the Church Commissioners in respect of a sale of church property) is exempt from stamp duty under various statutory provisions. Where the seller is a government department or public authority the buyer's solicitor should check his client's liability to stamp duty on the transaction and inform his client accordingly.

1. FA 1982, s.129.
2. FA 2000, s.130.
3. FA1930, s.42; FA 1995 s.151.
4. FA 2002, s.111 and Schedule 34.
5. FA 2000, s.120.
6. FA 1986, ss.75 and 76; FA 2002, s.112.
7. FA 2002, s.113.
8. Stamp Act 1891, s.58(4) and (5); but also see FA 2002, s.115 and Schedule 36.
9. FA 1999, Schedule 13 para.25
10.S.I. 1987/516.
11.FA 2002, ss.119 and 120.

14.10. Exchanges and part exchanges

14.10.1. Exchange of equal consideration

An exchange of freehold land for other freehold land attracts stamp duty at *ad valorem* rates. Subject to the drafting of the document duty is charged on each transfer and the reduction in duty pursuant to FA 2000, s.118 may not be available unless properly drafted. The duty in each case is calculated by reference to the 'consideration' (i.e. the value) given for the transfer: where the consideration consists of property, its open market value will be taken.[1]

For example, if one house worth £100,000 is exchanged for another house worth £100,000, duty of £1,000 (1% of £100,000) is charged on each transfer. The £250,000 threshold is applied separately to each side of the exchange. Also, if there is a straightforward exchange of one house worth £50,000 for another worth £50,000, both transfers are within the £60,000 threshold and so no duty would be payable on either.

14.10.2. Exchanges of unequal consideration

Where the market values of the two properties being exchanged are not equal, a payment of money (or some other consideration) may often be given with the lower value property, so as to equalise the bargain. The treatment of such cases for stamp duty purposes will depend on the facts and the effect of the relevant documents.

For example, where one house worth £100,000 is exchanged for another worth £80,000 plus £20,000 money, the conveyance for the transfer of the £100,000 house will normally say that the consideration for the transfer consists of the £80,000 house and the £20,000 money; and the conveyance will be stamped accordingly with duty on £100,000.

On the conveyance of the £80,000 house, the Stamp Office charges duty by reference to the consideration expressed in the conveyance:

(a) where the conveyance provides that the consideration for the transfer of the cheaper property is the appropriate proportion of the value of the more expensive property, stamp duty is applied accordingly. Thus if the conveyance provides that the consideration for the £80,000 house is the appropriate proportion of the £100,000 house, the amount charged to duty on the transfer of the £80,000 house is limited to £80,000;

(b) more commonly the conveyance may say simply that the consideration for the transfer of the £80,000 house consists of the £100,000 house. In these circumstances, the Stamp Office will charge duty by reference to the value of the £100,000 house.

14.10.3. *Equality money*

In many cases, the wording of the transfer of the cheaper property may not fully reflect the consideration expressed in the initial contract or agreement. Where it is clear from the contract that the intention of the parties to the transaction is that the cheaper property should be transferred for the more expensive property less the equality money, the Stamp Office will limit the charge to duty accordingly.

For example, if the initial contract provided for an £80,000 house to be exchanged for a £100,000 house, and for £20,000 to be paid as equality money, the amount charged to duty on the transfer of the £80,000 property would be limited to £80,000.

The result in an individual case will depend on the facts of the case and the relevant documents. The Stamp Office will need to see the relevant contract with the transfer which is to be stamped.

Where there is a multiple exchange of properties, an apportionment on similar lines may be made to determine how much of the consideration is attributable to each of the transfers. For example, two or more properties may be exchanged for one larger property, with or without a payment of equality money. Here again, the precise result will depend on the facts of each case.

14.10.4. *Application of lower band thresholds*

Sales of property (other than shares) for a price not exceeding the £60,000 threshold are exempted from duty, provided that a 'certificate of value' is given stating that the transfer is not part of a larger transaction, or a series of transactions, for a total consideration of more than £60,000. The threshold is applied separately to each side of an exchange of properties. Similar principles apply to the £250,000 band threshold.

14.10.5. *Sales*

In many cases, transactions which in the past have been structured and documented as exchanges could equally well be carried out as sales for a price which may be partly satisfied in kind.

For example, when a builder offers a property for sale, he may receive the price from the buyer in the form either of money, or partly of money and partly of the buyer's old house. Such a transaction can be carried out and documented (commencing with the initial contract) as a single sale by using wording such as the transfer is in consideration of a specified cash sum to be satisfied by the transfer of the other property and the payment of cash equally (*Tax Bulletin*, August 1995).

Stamp duty is charged on the consideration for the sale. So if, for example, the buyer is buying a new house for £100,000, and pays for it with £30,000 in cash plus his old house worth £70,000, duty of £1000 (1% of £100,000) would be charged on the transfer of the £100,000 house. The house which the builder accepts as part payment for the sale is regarded as a separate sale for stamp duty purposes but the amount of stamp duty is reduced by reference to the stamp duty paid upon the other land.[2] It would be charged only to the fixed duty.

14.10.6. *Further reference*

In cases of doubt about how a particular document of the types mentioned above would be treated by the Stamp Office for stamp duty purposes, The Technical Section, The Stamp Office, Ridgeworth House, Liverpool Gardens, Worthing BN11 1XP, will be willing to help but will refuse to give a binding clearance.

1. FA 1994, s.241.
2. FA 2000, s.118.

14.11. Non-merger of freehold and leasehold interests

Where the transaction comprises the purchase of an unmerged freehold and lease-hold interest, and two purchase deeds are executed to transfer the respective estates in the land, the parties are entitled to decide which deed is the 'principal' instrument and that document will bear *ad valorem* stamp duty at the rates applicable to freehold land. A denoting stamp should be affixed to the other deed. This problem does not arise if a single transfer document is used, which is only suitable when both interests are either registered or registrable.

14.12. Sale and leaseback

A sale and leaseback transaction is treated by the Inland Revenue as two separate transactions. The sale will attract *ad valorem* duty at the normal rates applicable to a transfer of freehold land, and the lease will bear the appropriate lease duty. However, the possible application of the land exchange rules[1] must be investigated if there is any possibility that the price paid or the rent reserved might be below the open market value or rent.

1. FA 1994, s.241.

14.13. Associated companies

Some transfers of land between associated companies are eligible for relief from *ad valorem* stamp duty under the provisions of Finance Act 1930, s.42, as amended. This exception also applies to the grant of a lease, and to an agreement for a lease.

14.14. Sub-sales

Provided that the transfer is made directly between the seller and the sub-purchaser, the two transactions are regarded as one, thus incurring only one amount of stamp duty which will be borne by the sub-purchaser. If two purchase deeds are executed, one from the seller to the buyer and a second from the buyer to the sub-purchaser, two transactions will have taken place and stamp duty will be payable by both the buyer and the sub-purchaser on their respective purchase deeds.

Where there is a previously uncompleted contract in the chain of the title for the sale of United Kingdom land for a consideration in excess of £10 million this is dutiable (FA 2002, s.115). Subsequent contractual purchasers liable to stamp duty upon their contract will be entitled to a credit for the stamp duty paid upon earlier contracts, or part thereof, where they purchase part of the land. A similar credit is available against the stamp duty upon the transfer of the legal title. Where the stamp duty upon the transfer is less than the stamp duty paid upon the prior contracts, the transfer may not be dutiable and the excess stamp duty paid upon the contracts is refundable. Solicitors must take appropriate steps to ensure that the necessary information is made available to ensure their client's credit or refund.

Where there is a restriction on sub-sales in the contract it may be possible for the buyer to assign the benefit of his contract with the seller to the third party and then to complete the purchase as nominee for the third party. The contract to assign the benefit of the contract is subject to stamp duty and payment of this duty franks the subsequent assignment of the contract. The duty is charged upon the consideration paid for the assignment; no duty is chargeable upon the outstanding purchase price (*Swayne* v. *IRC* [1899] 1 QB 335). If the property is transferred directly to the assignee this transfer is dutiable upon the original contract price. If the property is transferred to the assignor, i.e. the original purchaser, it will be dutiable upon the contract price and it may be possible to persuade the Inland Revenue Stamp Taxes Office that the subsequent transfer from the assignor to the assignee is dutiable only at £5 as a transfer from nominee to beneficial owner. However, this will require that duty has been paid in respect of the assignment and for the assignee to have provided the completion money used by the assignor and it is by no means certain that the Revenue will accept the analysis particularly where the assignment has attracted one of the lower rates of stamp duty. Usually assignments are less stamp duty efficient than sub-sale.

14.15. New properties

The Inland Revenue have issued a statement relating to stamp duty on new properties and building plots the text of which is set out in Appendix IX.1.

14.16. Transfers subject to a debt

Where property is transferred subject to a debt (e.g. subject to an existing mortgage), the stamp duty on the debt element of the transaction is payable if the buyer expressly or impliedly undertakes an obligation to discharge the debt. If, however, the buyer passively accepts the property which is subject to the charge and is indemnified by the transferor, no duty is payable.[1]

A transfer of mortgaged property between spouses may (in the absence of evidence to the contrary) be regarded as imposing on the transferee an implied obligation to discharge the outstanding mortgage, in which case the assumption of the debt will (together with any cash payment) constitute the consideration for stamp duty purposes and the transaction is treated as a sale on which duty is payable and not as a gift. By concession where there is a transfer of a part interest in the property an equivalent proportion of the mortgage is dutiable.

For example: A gifts a half share in land to B. There is a mortgage of £100,000. As the consideration is treated as being £50,000 a certificate of value for nil stamp duty can be included.

A transfer of the matrimonial home between spouses which arises out of a divorce or separation arrangement between them is usually treated by the Inland Revenue as being a transaction on which no duty is payable.[2]

Where the sale is of a council house with outstanding discount duty, is not payable on the amount of the discount.

1. Stamp Act 1891, s.57.
2. See Inland Revenue Statement of Practice 6/90.

14.17. **Property which is sold for unascertained price**

Where property is sold for a price which cannot be ascertained or where a lease is granted at a premium which cannot be ascertained at the date of grant, stamp duty will be payable on the market value of the land interest transferred or lease granted immediately before the stampable document is executed. Where a lease is granted at an unascertainable rent, lease rental duty will be calculated by reference to the market rent at the time when the lease was executed.[1]

1. See *LM Tenancies 1 plc* v. *Inland Revenue Commissioners* [1998] NPC 13.

14.18. **Documents executed outside the UK**

An instrument relating to property other than land within the UK but which is executed outside the UK does not attract stamp duty until the document is brought back to the UK when duty must be paid within 30 days and penalties run from the expiry of the 30 days.[1] Interest runs from 30 days after execution. Where UK land is involved in the transaction both penalties and interest run from 30 days after execution and not from the later 30 days after bringing the document into the UK.[2] There is generally no longer any stamp duty benefit in executing land documentation abroad, especially where it will have to be produced for registration. A document executed outside the UK which relates solely to a transaction involving only property outside the UK does not attract stamp duty,[3] but a document relating to foreign property which is executed within the UK or relates to something done in the UK bears duty at the normal rate applicable to that type of document.

1. Stamp Act 1891, s.15B. See also para. 14.19 below.
2. FA 2002, s.114.
3. But see *Maples (Paris) Ltd* v. *IRC* (1908) AC 22.

14.19. Interest and penalties

As from 1 October 1999, all instruments executed on or after this date have been subject to new provisions with regard to late stamping of documents.[1]

Interest will be payable on the stamping of an instrument if it is not paid or deposited within 30 days after the day of execution.[2] Interest is payable at a rate which is varied from time to time[3] and is calculated on the amount of the unpaid duty for the period from the end of the 30-day period until the date of payment. Interest will still be payable even if the instrument is executed and held outside of the UK.

A penalty will be also payable if an instrument is presented late for stamping.[4] This will be 30 days from the date of execution, or if the document was executed outside the UK and does not relate to a transaction involving land in the UK, 30 days after the day the instrument was first received in the UK. If the instrument is presented within a year after the due date for stamping the penalty for late stamping will be a maximum of an amount equivalent to the amount of duty due or £300, whichever is less. For documents stamped more than one year late the penalty will be the minimum of £300 or an amount equivalent to the duty due, whichever is greater.

1. See Inland Revenue leaflet SO10, *Stamp duty interest and penalties.*
2. Stamp Duty Act 1891, s.15A as inserted by Finance Act 1999, s.109(1).
3. The Stamp Office Customer Newsletter; *New interest and penalty arrangements*, September 1999.
4. Stamp Duty Act 1891, s.15B as inserted by Finance Act 1999, s.109(1).

A15. Capital gains tax

15.1. Liability to CGT

15.1.1. A liability to CGT may arise on the disposal of an interest in land. A seller's solicitor should be aware of the possibility of potential liability and advise his client accordingly. Similarly, a buyer who is purchasing property other than for use as his principal private dwelling should be made aware of potential tax liability which may be incurred in his subsequent disposal of the property.

15.1.2. The definition of 'chargeable assets' within Taxation of Chargeable Gains Tax Act 1992 includes an interest in the proceeds of sale of land held by co-owners. Thus a disposition by a beneficial joint owner of his equitable interest in land could give rise to a charge to CGT.[1]

15.1.3. Some transactions which are incidental to the sale of land also give rise to a charge to CGT, e.g. where a separate payment is made for the release or modification of an easement or covenant.

15.1.4. For the purposes of the Act, a sale and leaseback transaction is technically treated as two separate disposals, but in practice the Inland Revenue may regard them as one, namely the part disposal of land by the seller of the freehold.

15.1.5. Subject to certain reliefs, gifts fall within the meaning of 'disposal'.

1. *Kidson* v. *Macdonald* [1974] Ch 339.

15.2. The principal private dwelling house exemption

15.2.1. The disposal of an individual's principal private dwelling house including garden or grounds is exempt from CGT. Up to 0.5 hectare (including the site of the house) is within the exemption.[1]

15.2.2. To qualify for the exemption the seller must have lived in the dwelling house as his only or main residence throughout his period of ownership. A degree of permanence and expectation of continuity is required for the exemption to be claimable. A short period of residence (e.g. of a few months) may not qualify for relief.[2]

15.2.3. Certain periods of absence are disregarded when deciding the question of residence:[3]

    (a) the last 36 months of ownership;

    (b) by extra-statutory concession, the first 12 months of ownership (in order to facilitate the sale of another property). If there are good reasons for this period exceeding one year, which are outside the individual's control, it will be extended up to a maximum of two years;

    (c) any period(s) not exceeding three years in total throughout the period of ownership. Absence within this exception may be for any reason, e.g. an extended holiday and can be made up of several separate periods of absence provided that the total under this exception does not exceed three years;

    (d) any period(s) during which the individual was working outside the UK. This exception applies to employees only, not to self-employed persons;

    (e) any period(s) not exceeding four years in total during which the individual was prevented from living in his dwelling house because he was required by his conditions of employment to live elsewhere. This exception would be applicable, e.g. to a headmaster who was required to live in accommodation provided by the school, or to an employee who was temporarily seconded to a branch office beyond commuting distance from his home.

15.2.4. The periods of absence outlined above are cumulative, and if exceeded a proportion of the exemption relative to the length of the absence in proportion to the length of ownership of the property will be lost and the non-exempt part chargeable to CGT.

15.2.5. Where a dwelling house has grounds of more than 0.5 hectare, the excess is prima facie taxable, but the Inland Revenue has a discretion to allow land in excess of 0.5 hectare to be included within the principal private dwelling house exemption if the extra land can be shown to be necessary for the reasonable enjoyment of the house.

15.2.6. The sale of land alone, where the ownership of the house is retained, enjoys the benefit of the exemption so long as the land sold does not exceed 0.5 hectare. It should be noted that if the house is sold and land retained, a subsequent sale of the land will usually attract CGT.

15.2.7. *Duality of user*

Where part of a principal private dwelling house is used for business purposes, e.g. a doctor who has a consulting room in his home, a proportion of the exemption may be lost, relative to the area of the 'business premises' in relation to the total area of the dwelling house. If, however, a 'duality of user' can be shown, the full exemption may be available. Thus a person who works from home, but who does not have a separate room for his business from which the other members of the family are prohibited from entering, may still take full advantage of the principal private dwelling house exemption.

15.2.8. Only one exemption is available to married couples. Where a married couple own more than one house an election must be made as to which property is to take the benefit of the exemption. An election in respect of one property is not irrevocable and can be switched, e.g. if it appears that one property is increasing in value at a faster rate than the other.

15.2.9. The principal private dwelling house exemption is available where the disposal is made by trustees provided that the person in occupation of the property was a person who was entitled to be in occupation under the terms of the settlement, e.g. a tenant for life.[4]

15.2.10. Tenants in common may be liable for CGT on their respective shares in the equitable interest in the property.

15.2.11. An individual who buys his dwelling house in the name of a company will not be able to claim the principal private dwelling house exemption.

1. Taxation of Chargeable Gains Act 1992, s.222.
2. *Goodwin* v. *Curtis, The Times,* 14 August 1996.
3. Taxation of Chargeable Gains Act 1992, s.223.
4. Taxation of Chargeable Gains Act 1992, s.28(1) and (2).

15.3. Chargeable gains

15.3.1. Any gain is chargeable at the highest rate at which the individual pays income tax, subject to the availability of proper relief. Corporations pay CGT at the corporation tax rate applicable to them, subject to roll-over relief. Separate taxation is applied to married couples; each spouse therefore has his or her own annual allowance for CGT purposes.

15.3.2. *Guidelines*

When taking instructions from an individual in relation to the sale of a dwelling house, the answers to the following four questions will indicate to the solicitor whether there is likely to be a CGT liability on the property. If the client's answers to all the questions set out below match the suggested answers, there is unlikely to be a CGT liability arising out of the transaction. If any of the client's answers differ from those suggested, further enquiries should be raised with the client.

1. Question: Did you move into the house immediately after you bought it?
   Answer: Yes.

2. Question: Have you lived anywhere else since moving into this house?
   Answer: No.

3. Question: Does the house and the garden cover more than 0.5 hectare?
   Answer: No.

(The answer to this question may already be apparent from the estate agent's particulars of the property.)

4. Question: Do you own another house?
   Answer: No.

15.4. **Business premises**

15.4.1. Subject to certain reliefs, business premises are subject to CGT. The matter should be referred to the client's accountant for him to check the correct apportionment of the purchase price as between the property and any goodwill paid for the business.

15.5. **Charities**

15.5.1. Generally charities are exempt from CGT.

15.6. **Time of disposal**

15.6.1. The time of disposal of the property affects the year of assessment for the calculation of gains and losses for CGT purposes. A disposal of an interest in land is made at the time of the contract and not at the later time of completion.[1] However, no charge to tax arises unless the contract is completed, since until completion there will have been no disposal within the tax. Where a contract is conditional, the disposal is made at the time when the contract becomes unconditional, or in the case of an option, when it is exercised.[2] See the Taxation of Chargeable Gains Act 1992, s.144 for more about options and in particular the treatment of a payment for the grant of an option.

1. Taxation of Chargeable Gains Act 1992, s.28(1).
2. Taxation of Chargeable Gains Act 1992, s.28(2).

A16. Value added tax

See also: VAT on solicitors' charges, A8.8

Stamp duty and stamp duty savings, para. A14

VAT, para. A14.3

Agricultural land, para. B8

Taxation consequences, para. B8.5

Completion statement, para B8.14.4

VAT, para B20.12

VAT, para N1.3.

16.1. VAT on property transactions

16.1.1. *The charge to tax*

VAT at standard rate has been chargeable on certain commercial property transactions since 1 April 1989. Non-compliance with the legislation (where relevant) will involve the client in heavy penalties and interest payments, as well as unforeseen VAT liability. It is therefore essential that the relevance of VAT to a transaction is considered at an early stage and the client advised accordingly.

16.1.2. Generally VAT will not be chargeable on transactions involving residential property but may be relevant to both freehold and leasehold commercial property and to land. This chapter does not deal with problems associated with the self-supply of services.

16.2. Residential property

16.2.1. The sale of an existing building (i.e. not new) which is a dwelling or is used for a qualifying residential purpose or qualifying charitable purpose is generally exempt from VAT.

16.2.2. 'Qualifying residential purposes' include premises which are used as a hospice; accommodation for the armed forces; a children's home; a care home; and the accommodation element of a residential school, a monastery or nunnery and any other residential premises which is the sole or main residence of at least 90% of its residents. Specifically excluded from this category are hospitals, prisons and hotels or similar accommodation. 'Qualifying Charitable Purposes' include use as a village hall or similar or use by a charity otherwise than in the course or furtherance of a business.

16.2.3. Supply of construction work

The construction or development of new dwellings, qualifying residential or qualifying charitable property is zero-rated. A garage built at the same time as the dwelling for use with it will usually also benefit from zero-rating. Services supplied to a registered housing association for the conversion of a non-residential building are also zero-rated. Work of converting a non-residential property into residential property and of converting, for example, a house into flats, and renovation of a dwelling which has been empty for three years or more, is chargeable at the 5% rate.

16.2.4. Time share, holiday, and other accommodation with restrictions on its use does not fall within the zero-rated category.

16.2.5. A residential developer, building new houses and flats for sale, will be able to recover his input tax (e.g. on agents, solicitors, architects and other professional fees) since the sale of a major interest in his property to a private buyer will be zero-rated. The buyer pays no VAT on his purchase. The same position applies to sales of substantially reconstructed listed buildings and the first sale of buildings converted into residential from non-residential property. It should be noted that certain purchases, including white goods, fitted furniture except in kitchens, and carpets are specifically blocked for input tax recovery purposes.

16.2.6. Subsequent sales by private individuals will be exempt from VAT.

16.2.7. Owners of residential accommodation who did not construct the building in question, and who subsequently sell the building in the course of a business, will be making an exempt supply with no right to opt to tax.

16.2.8. Change of use

If the use of a building designed as a dwelling is subsequently changed to a non-residential use, this has no immediate VAT consequences. If, however, the use of a building intended for a qualifying residential purpose as defined above (i.e. a communal residential building) or qualifying charitable (non-business) use is changed to a non-residential or non-charitable use within 10 years of its construction, a charge to VAT at the standard rate arises in order to claw back the charge which would have arisen if there had not initially been a qualifying residential or charitable use. The value of the charge to VAT is dependent on how many years the building has been used for qualifying purposes.

16.3. Mixed developments

16.3.1. Where only part of a building qualifies for zero-rating, e.g. a shop with a residential flat above, the non-zero-rated element of the building (in the example given, the shop) will either be exempt or standard rated. The proceeds received from the development must be apportioned between the two differently rated parts of the building on a fair and equitable basis. It is unclear how the apportionment of common areas of the building, e.g. foundations and roof, is to be made. As a precaution the client should be advised to seek clearance from HM Customs and Excise before development is commenced.

16.4. Land

16.4.1. The sale of a freehold interest in land (without buildings or civil engineering works on it), grant of a lease, or of a licence is generally exempt from VAT, subject to the right in most cases (except outright sales of freeholds in new buildings or civil engineering works under three years old which are standard rated in any case) to exercise the option to tax. The grant of certain short term rights over land, such as car parking, mooring of boats, storage of aircraft, sporting rights over land, or the right to fell and remove standing timber and certain other freehold supplies listed in Item 1, Group 1, Schedule 9 VATA 1994 attract VAT at the standard rate.

16.5. Commercial property

16.5.1. The freehold sale of a new building (within 3 years of the date of completion)[1] is standard rated. Other dealings with commercial property are exempt subject to the option to waive that exemption (commonly known as the option to tax). If the option to tax has been exercised and notified to Customs within 30 days the standard rate will apply, or if the property is a new freehold to which the compulsory standard rate charge applies on a mandatory basis. The sale of a let property by a VAT-registered seller to a VAT-registered buyer who elects to waive the VAT exemption for the property and notifies it to Customs prior to the tax point for the transaction, may be treated as the sale of a business as a going concern so that VAT will not be chargeable. Clearance for transfer of a going concern transaction is not generally provided by Customs and Excise for straightforward transactions and reference should be made to HM Customs and Excise Notice 700/9. It is advisable to ensure the buyer provides evidence of having opted to tax by the relevant date.

1. See para. A16.6.

16.6. Freehold sales of new commercial buildings

16.6.1. Every freehold sale of a new commercial property (including civil engineering works) before it is completed and within the first three years after its completion attracts VAT at standard rate.

16.6.2. 'Completion' of the building is either the date of the architect's certificate of practical completion or the date when the building was first fully occupied, whichever first occurs.

16.6.3. The buyer of such a building must therefore raise additional enquiries of the seller to ascertain whether the transaction (and any subsequent disposal of the building by the buyer) will attract VAT and the parties must agree on the contractual provisions which are to be inserted relating to the payment of VAT.

16.6.4. *Guidelines*

(a) Matters to be considered on taking instructions:

    (i) will the sale be a standard rated supply so that VAT will be chargeable?

    (ii) if not, what evidence (if any) is needed to satisfy HM Customs and Excise that the sale will be an exempt or zero-rated supply or a transfer of a going concern?

(b) Additional enquiries:

[If the contract requires the buyer to pay VAT he will want to be certain that VAT is chargeable and will also wish to have evidence to establish whether or not there is a mandatory charge to VAT on a subsequent sale. If the contract does not require the buyer to pay VAT he may be inclined not to raise the issue with the seller, but he should still ensure that the supply is in fact an exempt supply and that he has sufficient evidence to establish that a future sale by him will be exempt.]

    (i) why does the seller consider that the sale is a standard-rated supply?

    (ii) please provide a copy of the architect's certificate of practical completion;

    (iii) when was the building first fully occupied?

    (iv) what evidence is available to verify the date when the building was first fully occupied?

    (v) please confirm that if VAT is paid on completion the seller will at that time deliver a VAT invoice to the buyer;

    (vi) has the seller previously elected to waive his exemption from VAT or does he intend to do so before completion?

    (vii) if the answer to question (vi) is 'yes', please confirm that the exercise of the option to tax has been or will be notified to Customs within 30 days of its being made. The buyer's solicitor should request a copy of the option to tax document (if any) and of the letter of notification to ascertain the extent of the land to which the option will apply and to check that it is valid. It should also be noted that it is Customs' policy to acknowledge receipt of an option to tax and this can therefore be acceptable evidence.

[Note that if the seller agrees not to charge VAT, the contract should either specify that the price stated is inclusive of any VAT or should expressly provide that the seller has not elected to waive the VAT exemption in respect of the property and agrees not to do so.]

(c) The deposit:

If the seller's solicitor receives the deposit in the capacity of 'agent for the seller', a VAT tax point arises on exchange of contracts in relation to the amount of the deposit. If the deposit is held as 'stakeholder' the tax point for both the deposit and the balance of the purchase price will not arise until completion. This can be particularly important when dealing with the transfer of a going concern rules – see A16.15.

16.6.5. A special condition on the printed version of the Standard Conditions of Sale Form provides that the sale is exclusive of VAT.[1]

1. See Appendix VII.13.

16.7. Commercial leases

16.7.1. Commercial leases are normally treated as giving rise to exempt supplies by the landlord to the tenant, and no VAT will be payable on the premium or rent unless the landlord has exercised his option to waive the VAT exemption in respect of the building on or before completion or before rent is paid (or invoiced if earlier). If the landlord exercises that option, he must account to HM Customs and Excise for VAT on the rent from all tenants of the building whether or not he obtains that VAT from the tenant. The landlord will normally want the tenant to pay the VAT, but whether the tenant will be liable to do so depends upon the date and wording of the lease. If the landlord makes the election after the grant of the lease, he can compel the tenant to pay VAT in addition to the rent unless there is anything in the lease to the contrary (and for this purpose a contrary provision must expressly refer to VAT; a general reference to the tenant not being liable to pay for tax on rent will not preclude the landlord from holding the tenant liable to pay the VAT).[1] Conversely, where a lease is granted after the landlord has elected to waive the VAT exemption for the building, the rent specified in the lease will be inclusive of VAT unless the lease states otherwise.[2] If the landlord exercises his option to tax during the term of a lease which expressly exonerates the tenant from paying VAT, or exercises his option and then grants a lease which is silent as to VAT, the landlord will have to account to HM Customs and Excise for VAT as if the rent payable by the tenant was inclusive of VAT, i.e. seven forty-sevenths of the rent will be regarded as VAT.

16.7.2. Any lease which might be subject to VAT should contain a covenant by the tenant to pay to the landlord any VAT chargeable on the rent or on any payment made under the lease in addition to the rent. The clause should also provide that in any situation where the tenant is required by the lease to reimburse the landlord for expenditure incurred by the landlord, e.g. for insurance premiums or service charge, the tenant should also reimburse any VAT paid by the landlord in respect of those payments unless VAT on those payments is recoverable by the landlord. Generally the service charge follows the rent, i.e. if the rent is standard rated, so is the service charge.

16.7.3. Where in a lease a landlord has covenanted not to elect for VAT during the currency of the lease, that covenant, being personal in nature, may not be binding on a subsequent purchaser of the reversion unless a direct covenant has been entered into by that purchaser. It is therefore safer for the tenant to negotiate a lease which includes a covenant given by the landlord that he will undertake to obtain a non-opting covenant from any buyer.

16.7.4. Exempt tenants

If the tenant of a lease makes exempt supplies he will be seriously disadvantaged by having to pay VAT on his rent (since he will not be able to recover some or all of that VAT). An exempt tenant in a market dominated by taxable tenants should consider taking a valuer's advice about the consequences of the VAT implications in his lease.

16.7.5. Guidelines

(a) Options checklist for landlords:

Consider:

(i)   how much irrecoverable VAT has/does the landlord incur?

(ii) the VAT status of tenants/potential tenants/purchasers;

(iii) the short- and long-term consequences of exercising an option which is only revocable in limited circumstances (generally after 20 years);

(iv) the consequences of agreeing a premium rent with an exempt tenant;

(v)   the costs of any additional administration which would be incurred in collecting VAT and issuing VAT invoices;

(b) Reminders for tenants:

(i)   check whether or not VAT is included in the rent;

(ii) remember that if the lease is silent section 89 could apply;

(iii) if the tenant makes taxable supplies only, the main adverse consequence of paying VAT on his rent may be a cash flow disadvantage, set against which there may also be cash benefits for the tenant, e.g. the recovery of VAT on his service charge payments;

(iv) if the tenant makes exempt or mainly exempt supplies he may be seriously disadvantaged by having to pay VAT on his rent since he will not be able to recover some or all of that VAT.

16.7.6. Purchases subject to leases

The leases to which the property is subject should be checked to discover whether the buyer will be able to charge VAT should he wish to exercise his option to tax. The following matters should also be considered:

(a) does the lease expressly provide that VAT is payable in addition to rent and other payments made or consideration given by the tenant or if not will section 89 apply?

(b) will the landlord be able to recover from the tenant VAT on supplies received from a third party? or

(c) is the landlord under an obligation to attempt to recover VAT from HM Customs and Excise before he can look to the tenant for indemnity?

(d) are all other sums referred to in the lease expressed to include any VAT which will be chargeable?

(e) are the rent review provisions adequate if the landlord decides to elect to tax?

1. Value Added Tax Act 1994, s.89.
2. Value Added Tax Act 1994, s.10.

16.8. The option to tax

16.8.1. Where a dealing with a commercial building or land is exempt from VAT the seller or landlord normally has the right to elect to waive the VAT exemption for the building, with a result that VAT will be chargeable both on the rents received from lettings and on the proceeds of any sale.[1]

16.8.2. The option to tax relates to the landlord's interest in an entire building. Thus an election made by a landlord who owns a whole office block affects all his tenants. Buildings consisting of a number of units under one roof or which are linked by covered walkways or internal access are treated as one building as are complexes consisting of a number of units grouped around or fully enclosed concourse. If a tenant wishes to sub-let premises the VAT treatment does not depend upon the landlord's election to waive exemption. The tenant must himself elect to waive exemption if he wishes to charge VAT to the sub-tenant and retain the right to recover input tax charged to him by the landlord.

16.8.3. An option cannot be exercised retrospectively. When ownership of the building changes hands, the new owner can make his own election to tax. A transfer by one company to a subsidiary or holding company will be a change of ownership giving rise to a fresh election to tax so long as the transferee company is not in the same VAT group as the transferor. Normally such a transfer would have to be at the market price, that price being subject to VAT, so that the VAT on the purchase would be irrecoverable by the transferee if it did not itself make the election unless the transferee was occupying the building for the purposes of its taxable business.

16.8.4. A common problem encountered is where the owner of the property has charged VAT on rent but there is no formal option to tax in place. Where the option to tax was exercised prior to 1 March 1995 and the total rental income was under £20,000 pa, then there was no requirement to notify the election to Customs. In cases where the election took place subsequent to that date, Customs will generally accept that the election was exercised but there was a failure to notify it, and a belated notification will usually be accepted. Alternatively it could be argued that as no notification was made, the election is invalid and the supply should be exempt from VAT.

16.8.5. Written notice of an election must be given to the Commissioners not later than 30 days from the date of the election. This can be done by a letter to the local VAT office or on Form VAT1614 (available from the HM Customs and Excise website – see Appendix XI.6). The letter must include a clear description of the property involved including the building name and postcode. Plans or maps should be supplied if these are necessary to identify the land and buildings. The letter should be signed by an appropriately authorised person, for example, a director, a partner (or trustee), an authorised administrator or by a sole proprietor.[2] In cases where any other person notifies the election, it must be accompanied by a letter of authority.

16.8.6. An election which is under three months or over 20 years old can be revoked upon application to HM Customs and Excise and obtaining their agreement in writing. If the election is under three months old, no output VAT must have arisen, no input VAT must have been reclaimed and no 'transfer of a going concern' treatment applied to the land in question.

16.8.7. A buyer who has had to pay VAT on his purchase may wish to charge VAT on a letting or a subsequent disposition of the property by him in order to recover the VAT which he incurred on his purchase. VAT incurred before the date of election is irrecoverable (except with the consent of HM Customs and Excise) unless no exempt supplies have been made in the meantime; thus the buyer's election to tax must normally be made before completion, particularly where the building is bought subject to existing tenancies.[3] Similar considerations apply to developers who have incurred substantial input tax as a result of construction work on the building.

16.8.8. Exempt or partially exempt tenants, e.g. those whose business is in the financial sector, banks, building societies, etc., will be reluctant to pay VAT on their rent because they cannot usually recover the tax in full.

16.8.9. Persons who wish to make an election may need to seek permission from Customs *before* they elect when the land or buildings concerned have *already* been the subject of an exempt supply by them, usually an exempt letting. If Customs are satisfied that there would be a 'fair and reasonable' attribution of input tax between the exempt supplies already made and the taxable supplies to be made following the election, the person will be authorised to waive exemption on the land or buildings from a current date. Alternatively, prior consent is not needed provided the conditions for automatic consent published by HM Customs and Excise are met. Under the capital goods scheme, recovery of some of the VAT incurred on the land or buildings may then follow by means of annual adjustments and, usually, a 10-year period beginning with the time the VAT was incurred. No input tax incurred before 1 August 1989 can be recovered by election under any circumstances.

16.8.10. Statutory block to the option to tax

The Finance Act 1997 changed the option to tax regime to counter tax avoidance in this area (e.g. lease and leaseback between associated traders) but it can catch 'innocent' transactions. The provisions are complex the following is only a summary. If it appears that a transaction may be caught by the provisions reference to the detail of the legislation is essential and specialist advice may be necessary. The disapplication of the option to tax could have serious effects on the viability of a development as it may result in the recovery of input tax incurred on the project being forfeited.

16.8.11. Paragraph 2(3AA) and 3A of Schedule 10 VATA 1994 were inserted by the Finance Act 1997 and apply to supplies made on or after 19 March 1997.[4] Paragraph 2(3AA) provides that where an option to tax has been made a supply will not be treated as a taxable supply in situations where:

    (a) the grant giving rise to the supply was made by a person ('the grantor') who was a developer of the land; and

    (b) at the time of the grant, it was the intention or expectation of either:

        (i) the grantor; or

        (ii) a person responsible for financing the grantor's development of the land for exempt use,

    that the land would become exempt land.

16.8.12. A grant of land made by any person in relation to any land is a grant made by a developer if

    (a) the land or building or part of a building on that land is an asset which can be treated as a capital item in respect of which the input tax incurred is subject to adjustment under the capital goods scheme;[5]

    (b) that person or the person financing the development, intended or expected either of them or a person connected with either of them occupying it for ineligible purposes, that the land would be occupied for ineligible purposes during the capital goods scheme adjustment period applicable to it.

16.8.13. A person does not occupy for eligible purposes unless he is a taxable person. A taxable person must also occupy the land for the purpose of making supplies which are in the course or furtherance of his business and the supplies are taxable supplies (whether zero, lower or standard rated) such that any input tax of his which was wholly attributable to those supplies would be input tax for which he would be entitled to a credit. Customs' rule of thumb is that at least 80% of the person's supplies must be taxable.

16.8.14. Occupation of land by a body to which section 33 applies (local authorities and various other statutory bodies) is occupation of the land for eligible purposes to the extent that the body occupies the land other than for the purposes of a business. Occupation of land by a Government department (within the meaning of VATA 1994, s.41) is also occupation of the land for eligible purposes.

16.8.15. 'Funding the development of the property' includes all the following:

    (a) directly or indirectly providing funds for meeting the whole or any part of the cost of the grantor's development of the land or building;

(b) directly or indirectly procuring the provision of such funds by another;

(c) directly or indirectly providing funds for discharging, in whole or in part, any liability that has been or may be incurred by any person for or in connection with the raising of funds to meet the cost of the grantor's development of the land or building;

(d) directly or indirectly procuring that any such liability is or will be discharged, in whole or in part, by another.[6]

16.8.16. References to the provision of funds for a purpose referred to in paragraph 3A(4) include:

(a) the making of a loan of funds that are or are to be used for that purpose;

(b) the provision of any guarantee or other security in relation to such a loan;

(c) the provision of any of the consideration for the issue of any shares or other securities issued wholly or partly for raising those funds; or

(d) any other transfer of assets or value as a consequence of which any of those funds are made available for that purpose.[7]

16.8.17. *Transitional provisions*

The rules above apply to supplies made on or after 19 March 1997 unless the supply arises from a 'relevant pre-commencement grant'.

A 'relevant pre-commencement grant' is a grant which was either made before 26 November 1996; or made after 26 November 1996 but before 30 November 1999 in pursuance of an agreement in writing entered into before 26 November 1996 on terms fixed in that agreement.[8]

16.8.18. *Capital goods scheme*

The following types of land are covered by the capital goods scheme:

(a) land or a building or part of a building where the value of the interest supplied to the owner, by a taxable supply is £250,000 or more (excluding any part of that value consisting of rent);

(b) a building or part of a building where the owner's interest in, right over or licence to occupy it is treated as self-supplied to him. The value of the supply must be £250,000 or more;

(c) a building where the aggregate value of the land on which the building is constructed and the goods and services in connection with the construction supplied to the owner by way of taxable (standard rated) supply is £250,000 or more;

(d) a building which the owner alters, or an extension or an annex which he constructs, where additional floor area is 10% or more of the original floor area before the work was carried out. The value of all taxable (standard rated) supplies of goods and services, made or to be made to the owner on or after 3 July 1997 for, or in connection with, the alteration, etc., must be £250,000 or more;

(e) a refurbishment of property costing more than £250,000 where the goods or services involved are supplied to the landlord on or after 3 July 1997. Refurbishment includes fitting out but is otherwise undefined. This gives rise to a practical difficulty in distinguishing between refurbishment and repair.

16.8.19. Where a buyer inherits the balance of the seller's capital goods scheme adjustment period, as is the case where a building is acquired under the transfer of a going concern rules, the method of scheme adjustments for that balance of the adjustment period must be agreed in advance with HM Customs and Excise. Enquiries should therefore be raised with the seller as to whether there is an existing capital goods scheme adjustment period. If so, the seller must be asked to supply details of the cost of the property, of the VAT initially recovered by the seller, any subsequent adjustments to that recovery and the timing of the intervals in the adjustment period.

1. See para. A16.5.1.
2. See Business Brief 17/99, dated 5 August 1999.
3. But, see the decision in *Higher Education Statistics Agency Limited* v. *Customs and Excise Commissioners* [2000] STC 332 where it was held that the relevant date when an election had to be made by is the date of payment of the deposit. In the case of HESA the election to tax was made after the deposit was paid at auction but prior to completion. HESA were found liable to pay VAT on the purchase price.
4. See para. A16.8.16.
5. See para. A16.8.18.
6. VATA 1994, Sched. 10, para. 3A(4).
7. VATA 1994, Sched. 10, para. 3A(5).
8. See s.37(5) Finance Act 1997).

16.9. Surrenders

16.9.1. Surrenders in the course of a business are exempt from VAT. They may be taxable if the tenant has exercised his option to tax in respect of his leasehold interest.[1]

16.9.2. If the tenant has exercised his option to tax in respect of his leasehold interest, and if the landlord is paying the tenant for the surrender, the tenant is making a supply of an interest in the land. Where the consideration for the surrender is other than in money VAT is payable on the value of the interest surrendered. Thus if the landlord in return for the surrender grants a long lease to the tenant, VAT is payable on the value of the surrendered lease, but a precise value may be difficult to assess. If a proposal involves a surrender by operation of law, liability to VAT should be agreed in writing before the surrender is made.

16.9.3. Variations to a lease will be treated as being part of the supply of the lease. Variations will therefore be exempt unless the landlord has opted to tax, in which case the lease and the variations will be subject to VAT at the standard rate. A variation of a lease is regarded as the surrender of the lease and the grant of another in its place. HM Customs and Excise have published the following revised Statement of Practice[2] which will apply in circumstances where a deemed surrender and re-grant occur by operation of law:

'(A)　Where there is no monetary consideration passing from lessor to lessee as a result of or in connection with the variation, then Customs Policy is that there is no surrender of the old lease for non-monetary consideration when:

(i)　the new lease is for the same building (or the same part of the building) but the new lease is for an extended term; or

(ii)　the new lease is for a larger part of the same building than the old lease but the term is for the same or an extended term; or

(iii)　the new lease is for the same land and for an extended term.

However, (i)–(iii) above do not embrace 'new for old' ground leases or building leases, i.e. leases granted on condition that the lessee will undertake development. Very often, the negotiations between the parties will result in agreement for demolition of an old building and the construction of a new one, or partial demolition and reconstruction or enlargement. In the case of these ground/building leases and in any other cases not covered above, Customs would expect to find that the terms of the new lease will be more favourable to the lessee as a result of the surrender of the old lease. They would be likely to rule that the old lease was being surrendered in consideration of the grant of the new on favourable terms and that the surrender supply by the lessee should be valued at its open market value. Where there is doubt, the position should be discussed with Customs.

(B)　Where the surrender and re-grant involves ground leases or building leases, i.e. leases granted on condition that the lessee will undertake development, very often the negotiations between the parties will result in demolition of an old building and the construction of a new one, or partial demolition and reconstruction or enlargement. Customs may find that the terms of the new lease will be more favourable to both the lessee and the lessor but do not consider this in itself indicates that the old lease was surrendered in consideration of the grant of the new one. However, if the lessee receives a direct benefit in return for undertaking the construction works (e.g. a rent-free period, or reduced rent for a period) Customs are likely to see a consideration passing from the lessee to the lessor in return for the benefit. In cases where there is doubt you should agree the position with Customs.

(C)　Where monetary consideration passes from lessor to lessee, Customs would normally regard the monetary consideration as the sole consideration for the surrender.

Where monetary consideration passes to the lessor from the lessee Customs would normally see this as consideration for the grant of the new lease which would be exempt subject to the lessor's election to waive exemption (option to tax). However, the circumstances may indicate that the payment is consideration for the lessor's supply of the acceptance of the surrender of an onerous lease from the lessee (sometimes known as a reverse surrender). From 1 March 1995, we say these payments are for an exempt supply, with the option to tax. When the payment received by the lessor is seen as consideration for the grant of a new lease, there would be no surrender by the lessee.'

1. *Lubbock Fine & Co.* v. *Commissioners of Customs and Excise* (Case C-63/92) [1994] STC 101.
2. *Gazette* 1 May 1991, p. 16.

16.10. Charities

16.10.1. The sale of a major interest in a building which is constructed or converted from non-residential use for use for a 'relevant charitable purpose' is zero-rated. Where the charity is using the premises for the purpose of a business carried on by it (e.g. a shop run by the charity where goods are sold to the public or a school where fees are charged for attendance), the rules for commercial property apply as this is not a use for a relevant charitable purpose.

16.11. Conversions

16.11.1. The cost of reconstruction, alteration or enlargement of an existing building generally attracts VAT at the standard rate. However, the sale by a developer of a major interest in a building which has been converted to a dwelling or for residential use from a non-residential building is zero rated. A 'major' interest is a freehold sale or the grant of a lease for over 21 years. However, there are problems in applying the zero rate where the non-residential premises contained residential accommodation prior to the conversion, such as in the case of a public house. In such cases the zero rate only applies to the extent that an additional dwelling is formed not containing any part of the pre-existing residential accommodation.

16.11.2. The reduced rate of VAT (5%) is chargeable on works for the conversion of a property into a different number of dwellings; conversions of dwellings into residential communal homes; and the renovation of dwellings that have been empty for at least three years with effect from 11 May 2001. This will cover the qualifying conversion/renovation services, and building materials supplied with those services. In addition, from 1 August 2001 the sale of the freehold, or the premium or first payment of rent on a lease in excess of 21 years, in a renovated dwelling which has been empty for 10 years or more prior to the sale is zero rated.

16.12. Listed buildings

16.12.1. Alterations to listed and other protected buildings (scheduled monuments) which required and have received listed building consent are zero rated, whereas repairs and maintenance to such buildings is standard rated. The grant of a major interest in a substantially reconstructed protected building is zero rated. If a building is simply in a conservation area it does not qualify for the zero rating.

16.13. Agricultural land[1]

16.13.1. The option to tax applies to agricultural land in a broadly similar way to other kinds of land. Marshland and moorland which is used for grants of sporting rights comes within the definition of agricultural land in this context. Agricultural dwelling houses are exempt and no option to tax can be exercised in respect of them, but an apportionment of their value will have to be made where they are part of a sale of agricultural land.

1. See Agricultural land, para. B8.

16.14. **Sporting rights**

16.14.1. Where sporting rights are sold as part of the sale of freehold land, the whole supply is treated as exempt subject to the option to tax, unless the value of the sporting rights is more than 10% of the total value in which case an attribution must be made and standard rate VAT accounted for on the sporting rights. In the case of supplies of sporting rights where the freehold of the land over which they are to be exercised is not sold to the same person, VAT at standard rate applies.

16.15. **Property sold as a going concern**

16.15.1. Where property is sold as a going concern, the transaction will only be exempt from VAT if the buyer satisfies all the criteria for relief. If he does not do so, the seller will be liable for VAT.

16.15.2. To qualify for relief the buyer must carry on the business previously conducted by the seller. The relief may therefore be lost if the buyer contracts a sub-sale or re-sells the property within a short period.

16.16. **Summary checklist of application of VAT to property transactions**

Type of dealing	Rate of tax
A. Freehold sales	
Buildings designed as dwellings built or converted and sold by developer.	Zero.[1]
Communal residential buildings sold by developer.	Zero.[1]
Non-business charitable buildings sold by developer.	Zero.[1]
Domestic and other non-commercial buildings sold by others.	Exempt.
New commercial buildings.	Standard.[2]
Other commercial buildings.	Exempt subject to option.
B. Leases[3]	
New buildings or converted from non-residential buildings where dwellings, communal residential buildings or non-business charitable buildings if for more than 21 years where built by and granted by developer.	Zero on premium or first payment of rent.[1]

Type of dealing	Rate of tax
B. Leases[3]	
Similar to above but lease for 21 years or less	Exempt.
Domestic and non-commercial buildings granted by others.	Exempt.
New commercial buildings.	Exempt subject to option.
Other commercial buildings.	Exempt subject to option.
Assignments.	Exempt subject to option.
Surrenders.	Exempt subject to option.
Reverse surrenders	Exempt subject to option.
C. Listed buildings	
Approved alterations to dwellings, communal residential and non-business charitable buildings.	Zero.
Other work on similar buildings.	Standard.
Freehold sales by developer of substantially reconstructed similar buildings.	Zero.[1]
Leases for more than 21 years from developer of substantially reconstructed similar buildings.	Zero on premium or first payment of rent.[1]
Any works to commercial listed buildings.	Standard.
Sales and leases of substantially reconstructed commercial listed buildings.	Exempt subject to option.

Type of dealing	Rate of tax

D. Building land

Sales and leases.	Exempt subject to option.[4]

E. Refurbished buildings

Sales and leases of residential buildings.	Exempt subject to option.[5]
Sales and leases of non-residential buildings	Exempt subject to option.

F. Conversions

Freehold sale by developer of conversion from non-residential building into dwelling or communal residential building.	Zero.[1]
As above but grant of lease for over 21 years.	Zero on premium or first rent.[1]
Construction services supplied to registered housing association on conversion of non-residential building into a dwelling or communal residential building.	Zero.
Conversion of a property into a number of dwellings or of a dwelling into residential communal homes.	5%

G. Building services

Construction of new buildings designed as dwellings (including sub-contractors' services).	Zero.
Construction of communal residential and non-business charitable buildings provided an appropriate certificate is obtained from the customer, and the customer is the person using the building for qualifying purposes.	Zero.
Construction of new commercial buildings.	Standard.

Type of dealing	Rate of tax
G. Building services	
Repairs and alterations.	Standard.
Demolition.	Standard.
Professional services.	Standard.
Renovations of dwellings which have been empty for at least three years.	5%
H. Civil engineering work	
New work.	Standard.
Repairs, maintenance and alteration of existing buildings.	Standard.
I. Options	
Option to undertake a transaction which itself is chargeable to VAT.	Standard on option fee.

1. Zero on first grant, subsequent supplies exempt.
2. All freehold sales are taxable at standard rate while building remains 'new'.
3. In relation to leases, 'grant' includes assignment.
4. Except for sales to housing associations where a certificate for residential development is supplied or sales to DIY housebuilders, where the option to tax is not available.
5. Unless the property has been empty for 10 or more years when freehold sale, or lease over 21 years is zero rated.

A17. Tax relief on mortgages

17.1. Introduction	**17.3. Companies**
17.2. Business premises	

17.1. Introduction

17.1.1. Tax relief on the interest element of mortgage repayments relating to the purchase of an individual's private dwelling house ceased to be available as from 6 April 2000.

17.2. Business premises

17.2.1. Where a loan is taken out in respect of the purchase or improvement of business premises interest on that loan may qualify as an allowable expense of the business for tax purposes and thus some element of tax relief will be obtained against an individual's income tax liability or a company's corporation tax liability.

17.3. Companies

17.3.1. A company which takes out a loan for the purchase or improvement of business premises may obtain corporation tax relief on the interest element of the loan provided it is an allowable business expense.

A18. Transfers on breakdown of marriage

See also: Stamp duty and stamp duty savings, para. A14
Capital gains tax, para. A15
Tax relief on mortgages, para. A17
Pre-contract searches and enquiries, para. B10

18.1. Introduction

18.1.1. Special considerations apply to the transfer of property between husband and wife on the breakdown of a marriage. This chapter does not deal with giving advice on the terms of the settlement between husband and wife, only on its implementation (see the guidance on Undue Influence in Appendix V.18).

18.1.2. *Conflict of interests*

Even in cases where the settlement is amicable and is not made pursuant to a court order in matrimonial proceedings, the parties must be independently advised because of the inevitable risk of conflict of interests which arises in this situation.

18.2. Acting for the transferor

18.2.1. *Mortgages*

The solicitor acting for the transferor should ascertain the extent of existing mortgages over the property to be transferred. It must be decided whether the property is to be transferred free of the mortgage to the other spouse, and if so, whether the transferring spouse will redeem the mortgage or will continue to make repayments. If the property is to be transferred free of the mortgage, steps must be taken to discharge those charges before completion of the transfer. This may involve advising the transferor about refinancing and taking a new loan secured over another property in order to discharge his indebtedness over the property to be transferred. The lender's consent to the transfer will be required if either the mortgage deed requires it or if the borrower-spouse is to be released from his or her covenant under the mortgage. The borrower's continuing liability under the mortgage may affect his or her ability to obtain another loan on a different property. Arrangements must be made for the continuation of payments under the mortgage. Any life policy taken out in connection with an existing mortgage should be checked to ascertain the name(s) of the person(s) insured under the policy. If the property is to be transferred free of the mortgage to which the policy related, a re-assignment of the policy should be effected on discharge of the mortgage. If the benefit of the policy is to be transferred, the consent of the lender should be obtained and the insurance company notified of the change. The transfer of the benefit of the policy may attract CGT liability.[1]

18.2.2. Outstanding discount on purchased local authority housing

A disposal of property which had been bought from a local authority under the provisions of Housing Act 1985, Pt. V made in pursuance of an order under Matrimonial Causes Act 1973, s.24 does not trigger the repayment of discount provisions under the Housing Act 1985.[2] Thus no discount is repayable where the property is transferred under a court order for the transfer or a property adjustment order made under section 24. Where the court order is for the sale of the property under Matrimonial Causes Act 1973, s.24A a proportion of the discount may be repayable if the property is sold within three years after its purchase from the local authority.

1. See para. A15.
2. Housing Act 1985, s.160(1)(c).

18.3. Acting for the transferee

18.3.1. The transferee's solicitor should undertake the normal pre-contract searches and enquiries to ensure that no adverse entries exist which might adversely affect the property or its value[1].

18.3.2. Any charge which had been registered to protect the spouse's rights of occupation under Family Law Act 1996 ceases to be effective on issue of a divorce decree absolute.

18.3.3. In appropriate cases advice should be given in relation to raising finance to purchase the share in the property to be transferred.

18.3.4. If the property is to be transferred subject to an existing mortgage, the lender's consent to the transfer must be obtained if the borrower is to be released from the covenant and/or if the mortgage so requires and arrangements made for the continuance of payments under the mortgage. If the benefit of a life policy is to be transferred, the lender's consent may be necessary and notice of the transfer must be given to the insurance company after completion.

18.3.5. Where the transferred property is mortgaged, consideration should be given to the protection of the mortgage by either an endowment policy or a mortgage protection policy. A lender may also insist that a policy to insure against the transferor's subsequent insolvency is acquired.

18.3.6. Transfers made in connection with divorce settlements do not attract stamp duty on the purchase deed provided that the requirements of the Finance Act 1985, s.83 and the Stamp Duty (Exempt Instruments) Regulations 1987 are met.[2]

18.3.7. A transfer of land between spouses for which 'value' is not given, that is, full consideration or something like it, in some form may be set aside by the court, under Insolvency Act 1986, ss.339–342 at the request of the trustee in bankruptcy if the transferring spouse becomes bankrupt within five years of the transfer. The solvency of the transferring spouse at the time of the transfer may be a material factor in the decision whether the transfer can or should be set aside, so the transferee spouse may want to get a declaration of solvency from the transferor at the time when the transfer is made. The transferee might also want to consider the possibility of insuring against the risk of the transferor's becoming bankrupt within five years. Should the transferee want to mortgage or sell the property within five years, this should not cause difficulties because of the amendments made to the 1986 Act by Insolvency (No.2) Act 1994 – see para. D2.10.6.

1. See para. B10.
2. See Appendix XII.2.

18.4.   Public funding

18.4.1. The cost of conveyancing work necessary to give effect to the terms of a court order will usually be covered by the client's public funding certificate. This applies equally to consent orders and the work which is undertaken to implement such orders.[1]

1. See *S.* v. *S.* (Legal Aid Taxation) [1991] Fam. Law 271; *Copeland* v. *Houlton* [1955] 3 All ER 178.

18.5.   Lenders' Handbook

18.5.1. The provisions of paragraph 16.3 of the Lenders' Handbook must be observed in appropriate cases.[1]

1. See Appendix VIII.3.

A19. The National Conveyancing Protocol ('TransAction 2001')

See also: Law Society Protocol and Formulae, Appendix III
Standard Conditions of Sale, Appendix VII.13

19.1. Aim of the Protocol

19.1.1. The Protocol for domestic conveyancing was first introduced in March 1990 in an attempt to standardise and streamline the procedures involved in domestic transactions. The revised edition, updating the third edition of 1994, came into force in May 2001.

19.2. Domestic transactions

19.2.1. Solicitors are recommended to use the Protocol in domestic transactions and should agree with the other party's solicitor at the outset of each transaction whether or not the Protocol will be used in that transaction.

19.2.2. *Developers*

Not all of the Protocol procedures will be appropriate for use when a developer is selling individual houses on an estate but, as far as possible, developers who have chosen to use the Protocol should adhere to the Protocol procedures, having notified the buyer's solicitors of any changes which have been made.

19.2.3. *Local authority transactions*

The Law Society's Local Government Group recommends that a local authority which is selling property should consider whether or not the transaction is one where it is appropriate to use the Protocol in whole or in part. In cases where the authority dispenses with a formal contract of sale use of the Protocol may not be appropriate.

19.3.   Departure from the Protocol

19.3.1.   If the Protocol is not being used in a residential transaction, or is to be substantially varied, the solicitor who intends to depart from the Protocol must inform the solicitor acting for the other party of this fact at the earliest opportunity. For the avoidance of doubt, variations to the Protocol should be recorded in writing between the parties. A departure from the Protocol when it has been agreed that it should be used in the transaction, or a failure to notify the other party of a departure from the Protocol, may be professional misconduct.

19.4.   Standard Conditions of Sale

19.4.1.   The Standard Conditions of Sale will be used to form the basis of the contract of sale in transactions which are regulated by the Protocol. The drafting of the Standard Conditions reflects the requirements of the Protocol, and thus an amendment to the Standard Conditions may itself be a departure from the Protocol which will need to be notified to the other party.

19.5.   Disclosure of related transactions

19.5.1.   When a solicitor is instructed to buy or sell a residential property on behalf of his client he will explain the use of the Protocol to the client and will discuss with him the advantages and disadvantages of disclosing information to the other party about the progress of any related sale or purchase transaction. Disclosure of such information may be helpful to the other party but might not be helpful to the solicitor's own client if, e.g. the client was experiencing difficulties in selling his own property. Disclosure of information about related transactions can only be made with the client's consent, and the client's refusal to give such consent is not deemed to be a departure from the Protocol.

19.6.   Non-solicitors

19.6.1.   *Licensed conveyancers*

Where it is in the interests of a client that the Protocol procedures are followed, a licensed conveyancer acting for the other party should be invited to adopt them. Licensed conveyancers are to be regarded in the same light as solicitors; it is therefore possible to rely on a licensed conveyancer's agreement to use the Protocol in a transaction.

19.6.2.   *Unqualified persons*

There is no reason why an unqualified person should not agree to comply with the Protocol procedures and use the related standard forms in the course of a transaction but no sanction would lie against such a person who departed from the Protocol. Not all of the standard forms are available to unqualified persons.

Since undertakings cannot be accepted from unqualified persons it follows that an exchange of contracts using the Law Society formulae and completion using the Code for Completion by Post (both required under the Protocol) cannot be used when dealing with an unqualified person.[1]

1. See Dealing with non-solicitors, para. A5.

19.7. Text of the Protocol

19.7.1. The full text of the Protocol is set out in Appendix IV, and the procedures referred to in the Protocol are dealt with in context in other sections of this book.

19.8. Use of forms

19.8.1. Where the Protocol is used the Standard Conditions of Sale should be used to form the basis of the agreement between the parties. While the Standard Agreement for Sale (front and back pages of the printed form) may be reproduced on a solicitor's word processor, the text of the Conditions themselves, for copyright reasons, may not.[1]

19.8.2. Pre-contract enquiries under the Protocol are conducted using the Seller's Property Information Form, which may be reproduced on a solicitor's word processor as may the Fixtures, Fittings and Contents Form and the Completion Information and Requisitions on Title Form.

19.8.3. Any form which is reproduced under the general licence outlined above, which applies to solicitors only, must be presented in a format as close as possible to the original form with no textual alterations and must state in a prominent position 'This form is part of the Law Society's TransAction Scheme'. The forms may not be photocopied except for the purpose of taking a file copy.

1. See para. A21.

A20. Interest on clients' money

20.1. Solicitors' Accounts Rules 1998

20.1.1. A solicitor who holds money on behalf of a client may be required to pay the client interest or a sum in lieu of interest on the money he is holding. The circumstances when the client is entitled to interest and the amount of that interest are governed by Solicitors' Accounts Rules 1998 a summary of which is set out below. The text of Part C of the Rules appears in Appendix I.2.

20.1.2. The Rules can be varied by agreement in writing between the solicitor and his client, but contracting out is never appropriate if it is against the client's interests.[1]

20.1.3. If a solicitor pays a lender's cheque into his client account in anticipation of completing the mortgage and completion is postponed, he may be liable to pay interest at the mortgage rate if the money is not returned to the lender within the time stipulated in the lender's instructions.

1. See Rule 27 SAR 1998.

20.2. Deposits in conveyancing transactions

20.2.1. The Rules apply to all money held by a solicitor on behalf of a client, including a deposit held by a solicitor whether as agent for the seller or as stakeholder.

20.2.2. Where the Rules apply, interest must be paid to the client irrespective of whether the money was held in a deposit or current account.

20.3. Stakeholder deposits

20.3.1. A deposit which is held in the capacity of stakeholder does not belong to either client until completion, but an entitlement to interest on that deposit arises under Rule 26 Solicitors' Accounts Rules 1998.

20.3.2. In the absence of express agreement to the contrary the interest will follow the stake.

20.3.3. Standard Condition 2.2.3 provides for the seller to receive the interest earned on a stakeholder deposit, provided the contract is completed but not if it is rescinded.[1]

1. See Appendix VII.13.

20.4. Designated accounts

20.4.1. Where client money is held in a separate designated client account, the solicitor must account to the client for the interest actually earned on that account. A separate designated client account is a deposit or share account for money relating to a single client.

20.5. General client account

20.5.1. If the money is held in a general client account the duty to pay interest depends on the amount of money held and the period for which it is held, but there is no requirement to pay interest if the amount calculated is £20 or less.

20.5.2. *Table of minimum balances*

No interest need be paid if the money held does not exceed the amounts set out in the table below for times not exceeding the periods shown.

Time in weeks	Amount
8	£1,000
4	£2,000
2	£10,000
1	£20,000

20.6. Sums exceeding £20,000

20.6.1. If a sum exceeding £20,000 is held for one week or less, a solicitor is not required to pay interest unless it is fair and reasonable to do so in all the circumstances. Although this part of the rule allows some discretion to be exercised by the solicitor in deciding whether or not to pay interest, such discretion should be exercised in the client's favour. Thus, if a sum of £1,000,000 were held on behalf of a client for two days, the considerable amount of interest which would accrue during that short time should be paid to the client.

20.7. Intermittent amounts

20.7.1. There will be occasions when the solicitor either holds money intermittently for the client, or when the amount being held varies from time to time. In these circumstances the solicitor must account to the client for interest where it would be fair and reasonable to do so, having regard to the amounts of money held and to the length of time for which it is held. The discretion permitted by this rule should be exercised in favour of the client.

20.8. Rate of interest

20.8.1. The rate of interest (for money not held in a separate designated client account or held on a general client account) is the same rate as would have been payable if the money had been kept in a separate designated client account. Where money is held in a separate designated client account (which should be a deposit account with a major clearing bank or a deposit or share account with a building society) the amount of interest payable is the sum actually earned on that money while on deposit. However, for money held in a general client account, Rule 25(2) Solicitors' Accounts Rules 1998 requires payment (if higher) of the rate of interest payable on money placed on deposit on similar terms by a member of the business community.

20.8.2. Interest on a contractual deposit held under the terms of the Standard Conditions of Sale is governed by Standard Condition 1.1.1.(a).[1] The difference between a fair sum in lieu of interest and any higher rate payable in respect of a much larger general account may be retained by the solicitor.

1. See Appendix VII.13.

20.9. Trustees

20.9.1. The Rules apply to money held by a solicitor which belongs to a trust (not being a controlled trust) of which the solicitor is a trustee, where the solicitor is acting for the trust. If interest arises under a controlled trust, all of the interest must be paid to the beneficiaries.[2]

2. See Rule 15, note (vi)

20.10. Client's right to certificate

20.10.1. A client who feels that he ought to have been paid interest on money held on his behalf by his solicitor may apply to the Law Society for a certificate as to whether or not interest ought to have been paid and, if so, the amount of that interest.

20.11. Tax on interest

20.11.1. In some circumstances deduction of tax at source may be applicable to interest which is paid on clients' money. The Law Society guidance on this matter is set out in full in Appendix V.17.

A21. Reproduction of standard forms

21.1. Standard Conditions of Sale and Standard Commercial Property Conditions

21.1.1. Solicitors may reproduce on their own word processors the agreement for sale which incorporates the Standard Conditions of Sale or Standard Commercial Property Conditions by reference but are not permitted to reproduce (whether on a word processor or by other means of reproduction) the text of the General Conditions of Sale without express permission from the copyright holder. Copyright is jointly held by the Law Society and the Solicitors' Law Stationery Society (OYEZ). Enquiries relating to copyright should, in the first instance, be addressed to Law Society Publishing (for address see Appendix XI.4). The Conditions are reproduced in Appendix VII.12 and VII.13.

21.2. Protocol forms

21.2.1. It is in the interests of both the solicitor and his client that uniformity of presentation should be maintained where forms form part of the TransAction scheme.

21.2.2. The forms are Law Society copyright but may be reproduced by a solicitor on a word processor in a version which resembles the printed form as closely as possible. No additions, deletions, adaptations or alterations of the text of the printed version must be made. Additionally each word-processed copy must bear in a prominent position the following phrase 'This form is part of the Law Society's TransAction Scheme' in order to indicate to a person who reads the form that the document is a genuine reproduction of a Protocol form.

21.3. Enquiries of Local Authority Forms

21.3.1. A general licence has been granted to solicitors to reproduce CON 29 Part I Standard Enquiries of Local Authority 2002 and CON 29 Part II Optional Enquiries of Local Authority 2002 on word processors provided that the quality of the form produced is of a standard acceptable to local authorities.

21.3.2. As a general guideline, reproduction on paper which weighs no less than 80gsm, at a resolution of no less than 300 dpi, in 12 point Roman typeface should satisfy these requirements. The local authority has the right to reject a form which does not meet an acceptable standard of reproduction.

21.3.3. The forms may be reproduced on separate sheets of A4 paper. Permission has been granted for practitioners to reproduce and submit to the local authority only the front page of the printed CON 29 Parts I and II. The local authority may insist that the format of the printed form is followed as closely as is possible and in particular that the boxes which appear on the front page of the printed form are reproduced in the word-processed version.

21.4.   Land Registry forms

21.4.1. Land Registry forms may be downloaded from the Land Registry website *www.landreg.gov.uk* and may be freely reproduced. They may also be obtained from the Stationary Office or through a law stationer.

21.4.2. All Land Registry forms are Crown copyright and all rights are reserved. The forms may not be sold to a third party in hard copy or machine readable format.

21.4.3. Schedule 1 forms may be reproduced in accordance with rules 210 and 211 of the Land Registration Rules 2003 and must be printed on durable A4 size paper.

21.4.4. Documents for which no form is prescribed must be in such form as the registrar may direct or allow.[1]

21.4.5. Any queries about adaptation or licensing should be referred to the Forms Unit, Land Registry, 32 Lincoln's Inn Fields, London, WC2A 3PH. Telephone no. 0207 917 8888. Any queries regarding copyright may be emailed to *copyright@landreg.gov.uk*.

21.4.6. Detailed guidance on reproduction of Land Registry forms can be found in Land Registry Practice Guide 46 Land Registry Forms (March 2003).

1. Land Registration Rules 2003, r.212.

A22. Land Registration Act 2002

See also: Investigation of Title, para. D2
Registration of Title, para. G3
Rectification and Indemnity, para. M7
Land Registration Act 2003 (selected schedules), Appendix XII.4
Land Registration Rules 2003 (selected schedules), Appendix XII.5

22.1. Introduction

22.1.1. The Land Registration Act 2002 (the Act) and Land Registration Rules 2003 (the Rules) came into force on 13 October 2003. The legislation is designed to improve and modernise land registration law and thus bring added certainty, simplicity and economy to the system of registered land. The Act contains the major principles of law and the supporting details are contained in the Rules. The major changes made by the new legislation are summarised in this section.

22.1.2. The fundamental objective underpinning the legislation is set out in paragraph 1.5 of Law Commission Report 'Land Registration for the Twenty-First Century' No 271:

'... the register should be a complete and accurate reflection of the state of the title of the land at any given time, so that it is possible to investigate title to land on line, with the absolute minimum of additional enquiries and inspections'.

22.1.3. One of the main aims of the new Land Registration Act and Rules is to extend registration of land to achieve complete registration of the whole of England and Wales over a relatively short period of time. The register will also be made more comprehensive. However, certain interests will continue to affect a title even though not contained in the register of the title.[1] The legislation also provides a framework for the development and regulation of a system of electronic conveyancing.

22.1.4. Schedule 1 of the Land Registration Rules 2003 contains the prescribed forms. Where a form is prescribed its use is compulsory.[2] These forms are greater in number than those prescribed by the Land Registration Rules (as amended) 1925 although many follow the earlier format. Schedule 9 to the Land Registration Rules 2003 sets out the compulsory forms of execution of scheduled forms.[3]

1. See paragraph 22.5 as to overriding interests.
2. Land Registration Rules 2003, r.206(1).
3. Land Registration Rules 2003, r.206(3).

22.2. First registration

22.2.1. Compulsory registration

The events which trigger first registration remain largely the same as under the previous legislation. However, such events are extended to include leases granted for more than seven years and leases assigned where they have over seven years left to run.[1] The reduction in the length of leases and assignments subject to compulsory registration is an important change in the law. Most commercial leases will now become compulsorily registrable on grant or assignment.

22.2.2. A reversionary lease of any term granted to take effect more than three months after the date of grant is now subject to compulsory registration.[2] The existence of such a lease may be difficult to discover in the absence of registration as the tenant may not be in occupation.

22.2.3. The Act contains provisions enabling the Lord Chancellor, by order, to add to the events that will trigger compulsory first registration.[3]

22.2.4. Voluntary registration

Discontinuous leases of any length may be voluntarily registered.[4] Such leases are sometimes used in timeshare arrangements. A discontinuous lease is only compulsorily registrable if the periods in possession when added together total more than 7 years.

22.2.5. Both profits à prendre in gross (for example fishing and sporting rights) and franchises (for example, a right granted by the Crown to hold a market) may now be voluntarily registered with their own titles.[5] Such rights often have considerable economic value.

1. Land Registration Act 2002, s.4(1).
2. Land Registration Act 2002, s.4(1)(d).
3. Land Registration Act 2002, s.5.
4. Land Registration Act 2002, s.3(4).
5. Land Registration Act 2002, s.3(1).

22.3. Dispositions of registered land

22.3.1. Powers of disposition

A registered proprietor is to be taken to have power to make any disposition permitted by the general law unless there is any contrary entry in the register such as a restriction limiting this power.[1] Disponees are entitled to assume that there are no limitations on an owner's powers unless this is reflected by an entry in the register. The purpose of these provisions is to prevent the title of a disponee being questioned, but does not affect the lawfulness of a disposition.[2] For example, if trustees were to sell land in breach of trust, in the absence of a restriction on the register, the transfer could not be impeached but the trustees would be liable for the breach.

22.3.2. Registrable dispositions

The Act details those dispositions which must be completed by registration.[3] Failure to complete a disposition by registration prevents it from operating at law. The dispositions that must be registered include the following:

(a) a transfer;

(b) the grant of a legal charge;

(c) a lease for a term of more than 7 years;

(d) a reversionary lease of any length which takes effect more than 3 months from the date of the grant;

(e) a discontinuous lease of any length;

(f) a rentcharge;

(g) the express grant or reservation of easements and profits à prendre over or out of registered land.

22.3.3. Effect of dispositions on priority

The general principle of priority under the Act is that the priority of any interest in registered land is determined by the date of its creation.[4] However, where a disposition is made for valuable consideration,[5] completion of the disposition by registration has the effect of giving priority to that disposition order any interest affecting the estate immediately before the disposition whose priority is not protected at the time of registration.[6] Priority is protected if the interest is:

(a) a registered charge;

(b) the subject of a notice in the register;

(c) an overriding interest falling within Schedule 3 of the Land Registration Act 2002;

(d) an interest that appears from the register to be excepted from the effect of registration (for example where title is other than absolute); and

(e) in the case of a disposition of a leasehold estate, the burden of an interest that is incident to the estate (for example, covenants in the lease).[7]

22.3.4. *Relative priority of registered charges*

Registered charges are to be taken to rank as between themselves in the order shown on the register.[8] Any alteration of this priority should be entered on the register.[9] Registration of charges and the priority of further advances are dealt with in more detail in para. H3.

1. Land Registration Act 2002, ss.23 and 26(1) and (2). However, charges of registered land can no longer be made by demise or sub-demise.
2. Land Registration Act 2002, s.26(3).
3. Land Registration Act 2002, s.27.
4. Land Registration Act 2002, s.28.
5. 'Valuable consideration' does not include marriage consideration or a nominal consideration in money: see Land Registration Act, s.132(1).
6. Land Registration Act 2002, s.29(1).
7. Land Registration Act 2002, s.29(2).
8. Land Registration Act 2002, s.48.
9. Land Registration Rules, 2003 r.102.

22.4. **Investigation of title to registered land**

22.4.1. The provisions of Land Registration Act 1925, s.110 are not replicated in the new legislation. The Land Registration Act 2002 provides that rules may be made about the obligations of a seller to prove or perfect his title under a contract for the transfer or other disposition for valuable consideration of registered land.[1] No rules have been made however and the seller and buyer are free to make their own bargain as to the evidence of title to be deduced.

22.4.2. The current position of the register can be ascertained by obtaining official copy entries of the title. The term official copy entries of the title is used in this handbook to include an official copy of the register and title plan and an official copy of any other document referred to on the register as being filed.

22.4.3. Investigation of title to registered land is dealt with in more detail in paragraph D2.3. Official searches are covered in paragraph E2.

22.4.4. The Act makes no provision for land and charge certificates and none will be issued on or after 13 October 2003.

22.4.5. A title information document will be issued by the Land Registry where an application leads to a change of ownership. The title information document does not constitute a guarantee of title nor is it admissible in evidence. It does not need to be lodged on the registration of any dealing with the land.

1. Land Registration Act 2002, Sched.10, para.2.

22.5. Overriding interests

22.5.1. Introduction

The Act refers to unregistered interests which override and, for ease of reference, the term overriding interests will be adopted in this handbook. These interests will bind a proprietor of registered land although they are not entered on the register of the title.[1] The legislation redefines such interests and they are reduced in scope. The Act lists separately those interests that override first registration and those that override registered dispositions.[2]

22.5.2. Duty of disclosure

A person applying for either first registration or registration of a registrable disposition must provide the registrar with information as to certain overriding interests which affect the estate.[3] This information will enable the interests to be noted on the register thereby losing their overriding status. This disclosure obligation relates only to interests within the actual knowledge of the applicant; and does not extend to, for example:

(a) an interest arising under a trust;

(b) a lease for a term of three years or less which is not required to be registered; and

(c) a local land charge.

(d) a public right; and

(e) on first registration, an interest that is apparent from the deeds and documents of title accompanying the application.

Where an overriding interest is disclosed the registrar may enter notice of it in the register.

22.5.3. The overriding interests most frequently met in practice are:

(a) short leases;

(b) interests of persons in actual occupation;

(c) easements and profits à prendre; and

(d) adverse possession rights.

22.5.4. Short leases

Leases that are not capable of registration are overriding interests. Thus most leases for a term of seven years or less will be overriding interests. Under the transitional provisions, a lease granted for a term of 21 years or less which prior to 13 October 2003 was an overriding interest will continue to be an overriding interest.[4]

22.5.5. Interests of persons in actual occupation

These interests have a narrower definition than in the Land Registration Act 1925. The major changes are as summarised below:

(a) The protection is for persons in actual possession of the land. There is no protection for the rights of persons who are are only in receipt of rents and profits. Such persons, however, have limited protection in the case of registered land under the transitional provisions.[5]

(b) Where a person occupies only part of the land, the interest is protected only as to that part.[6]

(c) In the case of dispositions of registered land only, the following interests of persons in occupation are not overriding:

    (i) an interest of a person of whom inquiry was made before the disposition and who failed to disclose the interest when he could reasonably have been expected to do so; and

    (ii) an interest which would not have been obvious on a reasonably careful inspection of the land at the time of disposition and of which the person to whom the disposition is made did not have actual knowledge at that time.

Neither of these exceptions apply on first registration.

22.5.6. *Easements and profits à prendre*

On first registration, a legal easement or profit à prendre is an overriding interest. An equitable easement is not protected.[7]

22.5.7. On registrable dispositions, a legal easement or profit à prendre will only override a registered disposition if:

    (a) it is within the actual knowledge of the person to whom the disposition was made; and

    (b) it is obvious on a reasonable inspection of the land; or

    (c) it has been exercised within the year before the disposition; or

    (d) registered under the Commons Registration Act 1965.[8]

22.5.8. The effect of the above provisions is that no easement or profit expressly granted or reserved out of registered land after the commencement of the Land Registration Act 2002 can be an overriding interest.

22.5.9. Under the transitional provisions, any easement or profit existing as an overriding interest on 13 October 2003 will continue to be overriding.

In addition, for three years from 13 October 2003, any legal easement or profit will be an overriding interest.[9] In practice, this provision protects easements and profits arising by implication or prescription during the three-year period. Expressly granted easements and profits are equitable unless and until they are registered.

22.5.10. *Adverse possession*

For three years, a right acquired under Limitation Act 1980 or Land Registration Act 1925 before the Land Registration Act 2002 came into force will be an overriding interest. From 13 October 2006 such a right can only be protected if the squatter is in actual occupation. A person who has acquired a title by receipt of rent or who has acquired a title but ceased to occupy the land will need to apply for registration.

22.5.11. Certain miscellaneous interests will lose their overriding status after 10 years (13 October 2013) and will need to be protected before then by notice in the case of registered land or by a caution against first registration in the case of unregistered land.[10] There is no Land Registry fee for entering such protection.

1. Land Registration Act 2002, s.11(4)(b) and s.29(2)(a)(ii).
2. Land Registration Act 2002, Scheds.1 and 3.
3. Land Registration Act 2002, s.71 and Land Registration Rules 2003, r.28 and r.57.
4. Land Registration Act 2002, Sched.12, para.12.
5. Land Registration Act 2002, Sched.12, para.8.
6. This reverses the Court of Appeal decision in *Ferrishurst Ltd* v. *Wallcite Ltd* [1999] Ch. 355
7. Land Registration Act 2002, Sched.1, para.3.
8. Land Registration Act 2002, Sched.3, para.3.
9. Land Registration Act 2002, Sched.12, paras. 9 and 10.
10. Land Registration Act 2002, s.117.

22.6. Protection of third party interests

22.6.1. Introduction

Cautions against dealings and inhibitions were abolished with prospective effect from 13 October 2003. Thereafter, third party interests in registered land may only be protected by the entry of either a notice or a restriction. However, transitional provisions protect existing cautions against dealings which will continue to be dealt with under provisions of the 1925 Act.[1] Existing inhibitions are treated as restrictions.

22.6.2. Notices

A notice is used to protect interests that will not be overreached on a disposition (for example, restrictive covenants and equitable easements) and will therefore continue to affect the land. Certain interests are excluded from protection by way of notice.[2] The main excluded interests are:

(a) an interest under a trust of land;

(b) a lease for a term of three years or less which is not required to be registered; and

(c) a restrictive covenant between lessor and lessee so far as it relates to the property leased.

Where an interest protected by a notice is valid then the notice will protect the priority of that interest.[3] A notice may be either an agreed notice or a unilateral notice.

22.6.3. Agreed notices

The proprietor's consent is normally required for an application for an agreed notice. An agreed notice may also be used without the proprietor's consent if the registrar is satisfied as to the validity of the claim.[4] In practice, this might be the case where there is, for example, an application relating to a document signed by the registered proprietor, such as a contract for sale.

22.6.4. There are some special cases (for example, a matrimonial home rights notice, or an inheritance tax notice) which can be protected only by agreed notice.[5]

22.6.5. *Unilateral notices*

A unilateral notice is entered without the consent of the registered proprietor. A unilateral notice must indicate that it is such a notice and identify who is the beneficiary of the notice. Where the registrar enters a unilateral notice in the register notice of the entry will be given to the registered proprietor who may at any time apply for its cancellation.[6] This is similar to the 'warning off' of a caution against dealings under the 1925 Act. Unlike, a caution, notice will not be served on the beneficiary of the notice on registration of a disposition. The notice remains on the register until such time as it is withdrawn or cancelled.

22.6.6. *Restrictions*

Where a restriction is entered on the register, a disposition cannot be registered otherwise than in accordance with the terms of the restriction.[7] A restriction may be used, for example:

   (a) to require that the proceeds of sale of land held on a trust of land are paid to at least two trustees or a trust corporation thus overreaching the beneficial interests under the trust; or

   (b) to ensure that any required consents to a disposition are obtained.

A restriction, however, cannot be entered for the purpose of protecting the priority of an interest which could be protected by notice.[8]

22.6.7. An application for entry of a restriction may be made by the registered proprietor or with his consent. A third party who can show a sufficient interest can also make an application. The Rules list persons who are to be regarded as having a sufficient interest for this purpose.[9] These include a person with a beneficial interest under a trust of land, a person who has applied for a freezing order and a person with the benefit of a charging order over a beneficial interest under a trust of land. The corresponding standard forms of restriction are set out in Schedule 4 of the Rules.

22.6.8. The registrar has power to enter restrictions without application in certain cases and to disapply or modify a restriction.[10]

22.6.9. *Cautions against first registration*

Although cautions against dealings with registered land have been abolished, cautions against first registration of unregistered land remain, although there are certain changes. Owners of a registrable estate can no longer register cautions against first registration to protect their own interest against third parties.[11] The most appropriate course is for such an owner to apply for the first registration of his interest. Transitional provisions allow cautions against first registration to be lodged by landowners during a two year transitional period. Any such cautions lodged during that period will cease to have effect after 13 October 2005.[12]

22.6.10. The transmission of the cautioner's interest can now be recorded on the register and it is now possible for an application to be made for the cancellation of a caution against first registration.

22.6.11. A caution against first registration merely entitles the cautioner to be notified of an application for first registration. It does not confer any validity or priority on the interest claimed. Where necessary, such interest should be protected by registration at the Land Charges Department.

22.6.12. *Duty to act reasonably*

It is important to note that a person must not lodge a caution against first registration or apply for entry of a notice or restriction without reasonable cause.[13] A duty of care is owed to any person who suffers damage in consequence of its breach.[14]

1. Land Registration Act 2002, Sched.12, paras. 1 and 2(3) and (4).
2. Land Registration Act 2002, s.33.
3. Land Registration Act 2002, s.32.
4. Land Registration Act 2002, s.34(3)(c).
5. Land Registration Rules 2003, r.80.
6. Land Registration Act 2002, s.36.
7. Land Registration Act 2002, s.41(1).
8. Land Registration Act 2002, s.42(2).
9. Land Registration Rules 2003, r. 93.
10. Land Registration Act 2002, s.41(2).
11. Land Registration Act 2002, s.15.
12. Land Registration Act 2002, Sched.12, para.14.
13. Land Registration Act 2002, s.77(1).
14. Land Registration Act 2002, s.77(2).

22.7.   **Access to information**

22.7.1. The general principle is that any person can inspect and make copies of:

  (a) the register of title;

  (b) any document kept by the registrar which is referred to in the register of title;

  (c) any other document kept by the registrar which relates to an application that has been made to him; or

  (d) the register of cautions against first registration.[1]

22.7.2. There are exceptions to this general right to inspect. An exemption may be claimed for prejudicial commercial or personal information contained in such documents. Any person may apply to the registrar for a document to be designated as an exempt information document if he claims that the document contains prejudicial information. Any such application must be made in Form EX1 and EX1A.[2] During the transitional period to 13 October 2005 leases, charges and other documents which did not fall within the previous open register provisions can only be inspected at the discretion of the registrar.[3]

22.7.3. The Act contains provisions whereby the registrar may, on application, provide information about the history of a registered title. Historical editions of the register will be available where the register is held in electronic form.[4]

1. Land Registration Act 2002, s.66.
2. Land Registration Rules 2003, rr.131 and 136.
3. Land Registration Rules 2003, r.139.
4. Land Registration Act 2002, s.69.

22.8. Adverse possession

22.8.1. Unregistered land

The Limitation Act 1980 continues to apply unamended to adverse possession of unregistered land. A person claiming to be in adverse possession of unregistered land may make an application to the Land Registry for first registration on the basis that, under the provisions of section 15 of the Limitation Act 1980, the documentary title owner is barred from obtaining possession of the land. The application must be accompanied by a statutory declaration providing evidence of the adverse occupation for a minimum of twelve years. There is no change to the way in which the Land Registry deals with claims to adverse possession of unregistered land.

22.8.2. Registered land

The provisions of the Limitation Act 1980 are disapplied in relation to registered land.[1] The relevant provisions relating to the registration of an adverse possessor of registered land are contained in Schedule 6 of the Land Registration Act 2002.[2] A squatter on registered land will be able to apply for registration if adverse possession has been enjoyed for at least 10 years. The substantive law regarding what constitutes adverse possession has not been changed, for example, as to the requirements of factual possession and the intention to possess.

22.8.3. If, on an application for registration, there appears to be sufficient evidence of adverse possession for at least 10 years' notice will be served on the owner, chargee and other interested parties.[3] A person in receipt of a notice has the following options:

(a) He can take no action. If no response is received to the notices, the applicant will be registered as the owner of the registered title.

(b) He may object to the application on the basis that the applicant has not been in adverse possession for 10 years.[4] In the absence of agreement the dispute will need to be resolved judicially.[5]

(c) He may serve a counter notice on the registrar requiring that the matter be dealt with under Sched.6, para.5 of the Act.[6]

22.8.4. Where a counter notice has been served, the applicant can only be registered if he meets one of three conditions. Summarised, these are that:

(i) an equity by estoppel has arisen by reason of which the applicant should be registered as proprietor;

(ii) the applicant is for some other reason entitled to be registered as proprietor; or

(iii) the squatter is the owner of adjacent land and has been in adverse possession of the land in the application under the reasonable but mistaken belief that the land belonged to him. (This condition will be brought into force on 13 October 2004.)

22.8.5. Where an application is rejected, then, if still in adverse possession, the squatter may re-apply in two years time.[7] If the owner has not either evicted the squatter or agreed terms within that period then on re-application the squatter will be registered in place of the owner.[8]

1. Land Registration Act 2002, s.96.
2. Land Registration Act 2002, s.97.
3. Land Registration Act 2002, Sched.6, para.2.
4. Land Registration Act 2002, s.73.
5. Land Registration Act 2002, s.73 (7).
6. Land Registration Act 2002, Sched.6, para.3.
7. Land Registration Act 2002, Sched.6, para.6.
8. Land Registration Act 2002, Sched.6, para.7.

22.9. Miscellaneous matters

22.9.1. Objections

Any person may object to an application to the registrar.[1] The objection must be in writing, signed by the objector or his conveyancer, state the ground for the objection, give the full name of the objector and the address to which communications may be sent and be delivered to the appropriate office.[2]

22.9.2. A person objecting to an application must not do so without reasonable cause; and owes a duty to any person who suffers damage in consequence of its breach.[3]

22.9.3. If the objection is not groundless and cannot be disposed of by agreement it must be referred to the Adjudicator.[4]

22.9.4. The Adjudicator

The Act creates the office of the Adjudicator to the Land Registry.[5] The Adjudicator is independent of the Land Registry. His role is to determine references made to him by the registrar where there is a dispute between a person who has made an application to the registrar and some other person. He will also hear certain appeals in relation to network access agreements when electronic conveyancing is in place.[6] The decision of the adjudicator is enforceable as an order of the Court.

22.9.5. *Alteration of the register*

The court and the registrar are both given powers under the Act to alter the register in order to correct a mistake, to bring the register up to date or to give effect to any estate right or interest excepted from the effect of registration. The registrar may also alter the register for the purpose of removing a superfluous entry.[7]

22.9.6. Rectification may be defined as a particular type of alteration which involves the correction of a mistake and which prejudicially affects the title of a registered proprietor.[8] A right to indemnity will flow from rectification. Rectification and indemnity is dealt with in more detail in para. M7.

22.9.7. *The Crown*

The Act enables the Crown to register its demesne land. Demesne land is where the Crown is the direct owner of the land and does not hold an estate. Provision is also made to ensure that where land escheats to the Crown it remains on the register.[9]

1. Land Registration Act 2002, s.73(1).
2. Land Registration Rules 2003, r.19.
3. Land Registration Act 2002, s.77.
4. Land Registration Act 2002, s.73(6) and (7).
5. Land Registration Act 2002, s.107.
6. Land Registration Act 2002, s.108.
7. Land Registration Act 2002, Sched.4, paras.2 and 5.
8. Land Registration Act 2002, Sched.4, para.1.
9. Land Registration Act 2002, ss. 80, 81 and 82.

22.10. **Electronic conveyancing**

22.10.1. The legislation aims to create the necessary legal framework to allow registered land conveyancing to be conducted electronically. Electronic conveyancing is to be developed in stages over the next 3–7 years and will be the subject of further consultation and parliamentary scrutiny. The Act provides for:

    (a) the formal requirements for electronic dispositions;[1]

    (b) the creation of a secure electronic Land Registry network;[2] and

    (c) the power to require the use of electronic conveyancing.[3]

1. Land Registration Act 2002, s.91.
2. Land Registration Act 2002, s.92.
3. Land Registration Act 2002, s.93.

A23. Money laundering

See also: Financial services, para. A4

Mortgage fraud, para. A24

Property Fraud Warning Card II ('Green Card'), Appendix IV.3.

Money Laundering Warning Card ('Blue Card'), Appendix IV.2.

23.1. What is money laundering?

Money laundering is the process through which criminals attempt to conceal the true origin or ownership of the proceeds of their criminal activities so as to retain control over them and ultimately make it appear as though the proceeds come from a legitimate source. Solicitors should be alert to the possibility of their clients using them to launder money, which may expose the solicitors themselves to criminal offences. Failure to report a client where there is a suspicion that a money laundering offence may be, or has been, committed can result in the solicitor being prosecuted, as can assisting a money launderer.

Solicitors are advised to study the following documents from the Law Society:

- *Money Laundering Legislation: Guidance for Solicitors* (1999)

- *Money Laundering Warning Card ('Blue Card')*

- *Money Laundering Legislation: Guidance for Solicitors Update February 2002*

- *Money Laundering Legislation: Guidance for Solicitors Update September 2002*

- *Consultation – minimising the risk of money laundering – proposed amendments to the accounts rules* (*March 2003*)

New comprehensive guidance will be issued once all of the regulatory and legislative changes are complete.

23.2. The offences

The current offences relating to money laundering are contained in the Proceeds of Crime Act 2002. Many offences carry a penalty of between five and 14 years' imprisonment. The offences divide into three categories:

23.2.1. *Offences where the firm is involved in a client matter or transaction*

It is an offence:

  (a) to acquire, use or possess the proceeds of criminal conduct;

  (b) to conceal, disguise, convert, transfer or remove from the UK the proceeds of criminal conduct;

  (c) to be involved in an arrangement which facilitates the acquisition, retention, use or control of another person's proceeds of criminal conduct, where there is knowledge or suspicion that this is the case.

Criminal conduct for these purposes means any conduct which constitutes a crime in the UK or if undertaken abroad, would have constituted a crime if committed in the UK.

A defence is available where disclosure of knowledge or suspicion is made to an appropriate person (i.e. a firm's Money Laundering Reporting Officer (MLRO)).

23.2.2. *Offences following a disclosure report made to the firm's Money Laundering Reporting Officer (MLRO)*

It is an offence to disclose to any person (including your client) that a report has been made to the firm's MLRO in circumstances where this is likely to prejudice an investigation (tipping off).

Further, once a report has been made to the MLRO it may be an offence to continue to act for the client without the consent of the MLRO. The MLRO can only give consent if he has disclosed details to the National Criminal Intelligence Service (NCIS) and NCIS have, in turn, given consent for the firm to continue to act.

23.2.3. *Offences involving a failure to disclose knowledge or suspicion of money laundering*

It is an offence for a person who knows or suspects or who has reasonable grounds for knowing or suspecting that another is engaged in money laundering not to disclose that information where the information came to him in the course of business in the regulated sector. (After the implementation of the amended money laundering regulations (expected on or after 15 September 2003) most conveyancing transactions will be within the 'regulated sector' for these purposes.)

23.3. **The conduct issues**

Money Laundering Legislation: Guidance for Solicitors, Update February 2002 (Law Society) warns solicitors that they should not use their client account without being instructed in relation to an underlying transaction as this might lead to a suspicion of dishonesty on the part of the solicitor.

23.3.1. Disclosure and legal professional privilege

Legal professional privilege may prevent the solicitor reporting their suspicions in some circumstances. However, privilege does not extend to information communicated in order to further a criminal purpose. Disclosure in accordance with the relevant statutory provision does not amount to a breach of duty of confidentiality. By Principle 16.06 of *The Guide to Professional Conduct of Solicitors 1999*, published by the Law Society, a solicitor usually has the duty to pass on to the client all the information which is material to the client's business, regardless of the source of that information. The 'tipping-off' provisions create an exception to this principle (see above).

23.3.2. The Money Laundering Warning Card

The best approach for solicitors is to exercise extreme vigilance before accepting instructions. The Law Society has issued a 'Blue Card' warning, which contains suspect factors, which should alert solicitors to the possibility of money laundering, e.g. clients who use large amounts of cash. The 'Blue Card' is reproduced here in Appendix IV.2. and copies are available from Professional Ethics (tel. 0870 606 2577) or online at *www.guide.lawsociety.org.uk* (at Annex 16D).

23.4. Money laundering regulations

23.4.1. Amendments to the Money Laundering Regulations 1993

The Regulations were passed as a result of EC Council Directive 91/308/EEC of 10 June 1991, and were recently amended to adopt the new language of the Financial Services and Markets Act 2000 (S.I. 2001 No. 3641).

It is anticipated that the UK implementation of the Second European Money Laundering Directive (Council Directive 2001/97/EC of 4 December 2001) will mean that in the future the Regulations will apply to more areas of solicitors' practice, including all property transactions. Therefore the Law Society recommends that solicitors begin to adapt to the requirements of the Regulations now.

23.4.2. Scope of the 1993 Regulations

The Regulations came into force on 1 April 1994. They only apply if a person is carrying on 'relevant financial business' which includes regulated activities within the meaning of Financial Services and Markets Act 2000.

23.4.3. Money Laundering Regulations 2003

The draft Money Laundering Regulations 2003 (expected to be brought into force on or after 15 September 2003) extends the regulations to include:

(a) regulated activities within the meaning of the Financial Services and Markets Act 2000 but only if undertaken by an authorised person with permission under the 2000 Act to carry on that activity;

(b) any of the following activities when carried on by way of business:

    (i) operating a bureau de change;

    (ii) transmitting money (or any representation of monetary value) by any means; or

    (iii) cashing cheques which are made payable to customers;

(c) estate agency work;

(d) any activity of the following persons acting in the course of their profession:

    (i) a person who acts as an insolvency practitioner; or

    (ii) a person appointed to give advice about the tax affairs of another person;

(e) the provision of legal services by a body corporate or unincorporate or, in the case of a sole practitioner, by an individual and which involves participation in a financial or real property transaction (whether by assisting in the planning or execution of transactions or otherwise by acting for, or on behalf of, a client);

(f) the provision by way of business of services in relation to the formation of a company or the formation, operation or management of a trust.

23.4.4 *Systems and training to prevent money laundering (Regulation 5)*

When conducting relevant financial business, no business relationship is to be formed or one-off transaction carried out unless the solicitor maintains:

    (i) identification procedures;

    (ii) record-keeping procedures;

    (iii) if the solicitor is an employer or in partnership, internal reporting procedures; and

    (iv) such other procedures of internal control and communication as may be appropriate for the purposes of forestalling and preventing money laundering.

The solicitor must also ensure that employees who handle relevant financial business are aware of the procedures and of the law and provide employees with training in the recognition and handling of suspect transactions. The maximum penalty for failing to comply with these provisions is two years in prison.

A business relationship exists where at least one person involved is acting in the course of a business and where:

(i) the purpose of the arrangement is to facilitate the carrying out of transactions between the persons concerned on a frequent, habitual or regular basis; and

(ii) the total amount of any payment to be made is not known or capable of being ascertained at the time the arrangement is made.

Once satisfactory evidence is obtained of the client's identity, the relationship becomes an *established business relationship*. Any transaction which is not carried out in the course of an established business relationship is regarded as a 'one-off transaction'.

23.4.5. *Identifying the client (Regulations 7–11)*

These regulations apply in all cases where the solicitor is forming a business relationship with his client. They also apply to one-off transactions where the value of the transaction is 15,000 Euros or more, or where the solicitor knows or suspects the client is either himself engaged in money laundering or is acting for someone who is engaged in money laundering.

The solicitor must, as soon as is reasonably practicable after first contact, ask the client for production of satisfactory evidence of identity or take steps which will result in evidence being produced. The evidence must be reasonably capable of establishing that the client is who he says he is and the person obtaining evidence must be satisfied that it does that, e.g. current document bearing a photograph, a passport or an identity card. The client's address should also be checked. If satisfactory evidence of identity is not produced, the transaction must not proceed any further (regulation 7(1)).

23.4.6. *Keeping records (Regulations 12 and 13)*

Records must be kept for five years after completion of the transaction of the evidence obtained of identity and of all transactions carried out by the client.

23.4.7. *Internal reporting (Regulation 14)*

Internal reporting procedures are necessary where persons are employed who are handling relevant financial business or where the solicitor practices in partnership. In such cases, there must be a person within the firm to whom all information about known or suspected money launderers is to be given – 'the appropriate person' – or another designated person who has the task of deciding whether the information does amount to knowledge or suspicion and, if it is decided that it does, of reporting the matter to 'a constable'. The appropriate person or designated person will probably be a partner.

23.4.8. *Reporting to a constable*

All reports are dealt with nationally by the National Criminal Intelligence Service (NCIS). It is recommended that reports are made on the standard form which can be found at www.ncis.gov.uk.[1]

1. See Appendix XI.5 for address.

A24. Mortgage fraud

See also: Financial services, para. A4
Money laundering, para. A23
Mortgage offers, para. B19
Mortgages: acting for lender and borrower, para. A11
Property Fraud Warning Card II ('Green Card'), Appendix IV.3
Mortgage Fraud – variation in purchase price, Appendix V.11

24.1. Guidance from the Law Society

24.1.1. Solicitors need to be alert to the possibility of a mortgage fraud. The Law Society has issued the following guidance to solicitors:

- Property Fraud Warning Card II ('Green Card') – Appendix IV.3

- Mortgage Fraud – variation in purchase price, Appendix V.11

The following paragraphs outline the most common types of fraud and the solicitor's duty in relation to a suspected fraud.

24.2. Solicitor's duty

24.2.1. The Law Society's guidance on mortgage fraud states that if a solicitor is aware that his or her client is attempting to perpetrate fraud in any form, he or she must immediately cease acting for that client.

24.2.2. Principle 12.02 of *The Guide to the Professional Conduct of Solicitors 1999* states that:

'A solicitor must not act, or where relevant, must stop acting, where the instructions would involve the solicitor in a breach of the law or a breach of the principles of professional conduct, unless the client is prepared to change his or her instructions.'

24.2.3. Failure to comply with the above principle carries with it the risk of criminal prosecution (for having aided and abetted a fraud) and/or civil action (breach of contract or negligence by, e.g. a lender who suffers loss) and of being disciplined for breach of the principles of professional conduct.

24.2.4. A solicitor may be guilty of conspiracy to defraud by undertaking the conveyancing work for a client who is himself engaged in a fraudulent transaction. The solicitor's active knowledge of or participation in the fraud is not necessary; if the work involved in the conveyancing falls below the standard expected of a normal solicitor, this may indicate that the solicitor had no genuine belief in the transaction in which he was acting and imply that the solicitor was involved in the conspiracy. A solicitor who is found guilty of fraud is likely to be struck off the Roll.

24.3. Types of fraud

24.3.1. *Status*

24.3.1.1. Income

The borrower overstates his income in the mortgage application, usually with the sole aim of securing a higher mortgage. A solicitor who knows that his client is unemployed or that there are substantial arrears owing on the client's current mortgage should be alert to the possibility of mortgage fraud but is not under a duty to inform the lender of this fact unless the lender's instructions expressly require him to do so.[1]

24.3.1.2. Identity

The borrower conceals his true identity, perhaps to disguise the fact that he has another subsisting mortgage. Fraud can also occur where a husband forges his wife's signature (or vice versa). An indication of this type of fraud is where the solicitor is asked to contact the husband at his business address rather than his home address. Another example in this category is the sale at an inflated price to an individual by a company controlled by him. This device is used to raise additional finance for the company. This type of fraud is sometimes carried out on a large scale and often involves other fraud, e.g. tax, improvement grants. Instructions to purchase or transfer the property into the name of nominees may indicate a fraud of this type. In all cases where the client is not personally known to the solicitor, it may be prudent to check the identity of the client. Where there are co-buyers (e.g. husband and wife), instructions must be confirmed from both of them.[1]

24.3.2. *Property*

24.3.2.1. Price reduction

The price to be shown in the purchase deed is less than that agreed to be paid by the buyer, or situations where the client instructs that a reduced price has been agreed to take account of an allowance for 'repairs to the property'. In some cases, the amounts shown in the contract and purchase deed will be identical but fraud occurs because the full amount of the purchase price is never in fact paid, e.g. the buyer says he has paid money directly to the seller, or that part of the price has been set off by the buyer against money owed to him by the seller.

24.3.2.2. Fraudulent valuations

Where it appears that the valuation of the property is higher than might be expected for a property of that type or is considerably higher than the figure in a recent (say within the last 12 months) disposal of the property. A solicitor is not an expert in valuations and cannot be expected to advise on the accuracy of a valuation obtained by the client; nevertheless, a valuation which is patently out of line with the apparent value of the property may give rise to suspicion.

24.3.2.3. Roll-over fraud

This occurs where the borrower sells a property to an associate at an inflated price. As a result, the associate is able to obtain a higher mortgage. No repayments are made under the mortgage. Before the lender is able to repossess the property, it is sold to another associate for a higher figure, and so on.

24.3.2.4. Use of sub-sales

A client instructs a solicitor in the purchase of a property for, say, £100,000. The solicitor is told that the property is to be bought in the name of B who is selling to C at a price of £160,000. B and C are either the same person (using assumed identities) or associated persons. A may also be a party to the fraud, although in some cases he may be an innocent seller. C obtains a mortgage of £150,000 based on the higher value and secures an immediate profit of £50,000. The balance between the original sale price and the higher sub-sale price is never paid, or is said to be paid direct by B to C, or is allegedly set off by B against money owed to him by C. A simultaneous exchange of contracts followed by a quick completion is often a feature of these transactions. The lender is then left with a property worth only £100,000 as security for the loan.[2] A variation on this theme is where A grants a lease to B at a ground rent; B then assigns the lease to C at a premium. The purpose of this type of transaction is to give C a legal interest on which he can then obtain a mortgage.

24.3.2.5. Money paid direct

A deposit or balance of the purchase price which is paid (or said to be paid) direct to the seller from the buyer may indicate a mortgage fraud.

1. *Penn* v. *Bristol & West Building Society* [1997] 3 All ER 470.
2. *Bristol & West Building Society* v. *Kramer, The Independent,* 26 January 1995

24.4.   The conduct issues

24.4.1.   A solicitor must act in the best interests of the client. Where he is acting for both the buyer and his lender, he owes a duty to both. There is a duty to report to the lender any alteration in the purchase price and any other information specifically identified in the lender's instructions.[1]

24.4.2. The solicitor's duty of confidentiality means that the buyer/borrower must consent to disclosure being made to the lender. This situation may give rise to a conflict of interests between the lender client and the buyer client. The solicitor cannot then continue to act for both clients and cannot continue to act for one client without the consent of the other. The safest course of action to adopt is to cease to act for both clients in these circumstances. Where the solicitor is obliged to cease to act for the lender, he should return the papers to the lender, stating that they are returned on the grounds of conflict of interests.

1. *Alliance & Leicester Building Society* v. *Edgestop Ltd* [1994] 2 EGLR 229; *Bristol & West Building Society* v. *May, Merriman* [1997] 3 All ER 206.

B. PRE-EXCHANGE

B1. Pre-contract negotiations

See also: Form of contract, para. B11

Conditional contracts, para. B13

1.1. Effect of 'subject to contract'

1.1.1. The phrase 'subject to contract' may no longer be of great importance in view of the fact that Law of Property (Miscellaneous Provisions) Act 1989, s.2, requires the contract for the sale of land to be in writing and signed by both parties. It is unlikely that a contract would inadvertently be entered into by correspondence between the parties.[1]

1.1.2. The inclusion of the phrase 'subject to contract' will normally act as a suspensory condition which will prevent the formation of a binding contract until such time as the effect of the condition is removed, e.g. on exchange.

1.1.3. Once introduced, the phrase will continue to govern subsequent correspondence until its effect is expressly or impliedly removed. It is thus not essential that every item of pre-contract correspondence carries the suspensory condition.

1. See para. B1.6.3.

1.2. A contract already exists

1.2.1. The phrase 'subject to contract' can only give protection to the parties where no contract exists. If a contract has already come into existence the phrase cannot invalidate or eradicate that contract.

1.3. Removal of suspensory condition

1.3.1. The condition will normally remain in effect until removed with the consent of both parties on exchange. It cannot be removed unilaterally.[1]

1.3.2. However, care should be taken to ensure that the wording of correspondence or telephone conversations does not imply the current existence of a contract which will negate the effect of the 'subject to contract' formula.[2]

1.3.3. The phrase should thus be used with care and not regarded as a magic formula which will protect the parties in all circumstances.

1. *Sherbrooke* v. *Dipple* (1980) 255 EG 1203.
2. See *Griffiths* v. *Young* [1970] Ch 675; *Michael Richards Properties Ltd* v. *Corporation of Wardens of St. Saviour's Parish Southwark* [1975] 3 All ER 416.

1.4. Protracted negotiations

1.4.1. In *Cohen* v. *Nessdale*,[1] it was held that the phrase 'subject to contract' continued to govern negotiations despite an interval of some eight months; however, it is unwise to rely on this decision as the continued protection of the phrase cannot be guaranteed in all circumstances.

1.4.2. Where negotiations for the property have become interrupted or protracted a solicitor should not rely on the continued effect of the phrase 'subject to contract'. When negotiations recommence after an interval the 'subject to contract' formula should be repeated in all subsequent correspondence to ensure its continued protection pending the resolution of the negotiations.

1. [1982] 2 All ER 97.

1.5. Contract denied

1.5.1. Difficulties have in the past arisen over the use of the phrase 'subject to contract'[1] and some solicitors prefer to use the words 'contract denied' in preference to 'subject to contract'. However, there is no reported decision on the effect of the phrase 'contract denied' and the phrase should therefore, for safety's sake, be regarded as being similar in operation and effect to the words 'subject to contract'.

1. See *Law* v. *Jones* [1974] Ch 112; *cf. Tiverton Estates* v. *Wearwell Ltd* [1975] 1 Ch 146.

1.6. Need for written contract

1.6.1. In most cases the requirement for a written contract for the sale of land will be satisfied by the formal exchange of contracts by the parties, following negotiations conducted by their respective solicitors.

1.6.2. To ensure that no contract inadvertently comes into existence before the parties are ready to exchange it is customary to qualify all pre-contract correspondence with the words 'subject to contract' or 'contract denied'.

1.6.3. In exceptional cases an exchange of correspondence may satisfy the requirements of section 2 Law of Property (Miscellaneous Provisions) Act 1989, but only where:

(a) the letters set out or incorporate all the terms of the agreement; and

(b) there is an intention that the exchange of letters will result in a binding contract.[1]

Correspondence which is headed 'subject to contract' cannot fulfil the above conditions.[2]

1. *Commission for New Towns* v. *Cooper* [1995] 26 EG 129 (CA).
2. *Commission for New Towns* v. *Cooper* [1995] 26 EG 129 (CA).

1.7. Collateral contracts

1.7.1. Section 2 of the Law of Property (Miscellaneous Provisions) Act 1989 requires that all agreed terms be incorporated into the written contract. As a result, a contract will be invalid if it omits any of the terms agreed between the parties.

1.7.2. One way around this rule was for the party attempting to enforce the contract to argue that the omitted terms form a collateral contract, and do not have to be included in the main contract. The courts are increasingly reluctant to accept such argument so care should be taken to include all the terms in the main contract.[1]

1.7.3. It may be possible to avoid this problem by including a clause in the property contract to the effect that all matters agreed in correspondence between the parties' solicitors should be deemed to be included in that contract.[2]

1. *Grossman* v. *Hooper* [2001] 2 EGLR 82.
2. *Jones* v. *Forest Fencing* [2001] PLSCS 249.

1.8. Lock-out agreements

1.8.1. A lock-out agreement where the seller agrees not to negotiate with any third party for a specified period of time is capable of being a valid collateral contract and does not need to satisfy the requirements of Law of Property (Miscellaneous Provisions) Act 1989, s.2.[1] A lock-in agreement, i.e. to negotiate with these parties only, is never valid.[2]

1.8.2. Breach of a lock-out agreement does not give rise to a claim for substantial damages nor for long-term injunctive relief.[3]

1. *Pitt* v. *PHH Asset Management Ltd* [1993] EGCS 127; *Walford* v. *Miles* [1992] 2 AC 128, HL.
2. *Courtney & Fairburn Ltd* v. *Tolaini Bros Ltd* [1975] 1 WLR 297.
3. *Moroney* v. *Isofam Investments* [1997] EGCS 178; *Tye* v. *House* [1997] 41 EG 160, CA.

B2. Contract races

See also: Solicitors' Practice Rules, Appendix I.1.
        Guidance on Rule 6, Appendix V.13, V.14, V.15

2.1. Solicitors' Practice Rules 1990

2.1.1. Where a seller's solicitor is asked by his client to deal simultaneously with more than one prospective buyer he is required to comply with Rule 6A Solicitors' Practice Rules 1990, the text of which is summarised below. The full text of the Rule is reproduced in Appendix I.1.

2.1.2. Compliance with the Rule is mandatory and breach thereof can lead to disciplinary action being taken against the solicitor.

2.1.3. The Rule applies irrespective of whether the prospective buyers are supplied with their contracts simultaneously or whether contracts are issued to different prospective buyers one after the other. The supply of documentation such as a plan of the land or Land Registry title number in order to facilitate the transfer of the premises to a buyer is covered by the Rule. It is not necessary for each prospective buyer to be supplied with a 'contract', nor need each contract be in identical terms. The Rule applies to both domestic and commercial transactions. The Rule also applies where the seller's solicitor knows that the second (and subsequent) buyer(s) are being dealt with directly by the seller without the solicitor's involvement.

2.1.4. Where, having supplied a prospective buyer with a draft contract or other documentation, the seller later receives a further offer for the property which later offer he would prefer to accept, the seller may accept the second offer but his solicitor should give notice of withdrawal to the first prospective buyer's solicitor prior to dealing with the second prospective buyer and submitting draft papers to him. If notice of withdrawal is given, Rule 6A does not apply. Similarly, if the first prospective buyer's solicitor returns the papers to the seller's solicitor before papers are submitted to the second prospective buyer, only one buyer would be in possession of draft papers at any given time, thus a contract race does not exist and Rule 6A does not apply. The Rule does not apply to the distribution of auction papers to potential bidders or their solicitors, but does apply where a prospective buyer by private treaty is part of a draft contract and the seller then decides to put the property into auction.

B

2.2. Solicitor acting for seller

2.2.1. Where a solicitor is acting for the seller he must explain to his client that the solicitor is required to comply with the Practice Rule referred to above, and if the seller refuses to allow the solicitor to notify all the prospective buyers of the contract race the solicitor must decline to act. The duty to notify the buyers only arises if a contract race situation exists.

2.2.2. Since buyers are themselves wary of entering into contract races, the seller should also be warned of the danger of losing the prospective buyers altogether if a race is commenced. It is normally preferable to avoid a contract race if at all possible.

2.3. Disclosure of race to buyers

2.3.1. Having obtained his client's authority, the solicitor must at once disclose the seller's decision to conduct a contract race direct to the solicitor acting for each prospective buyer or (where no solicitor is acting) to the prospective buyer(s) in person. Such disclosure, if made face to face, or by telephone, must at once be confirmed in a letter, or by fax.

2.3.2. When the seller's solicitor informs the prospective buyers of the race, he must make it clear to each of them the precise terms of the race, i.e. what has to be done by a buyer in order to secure the property. Commonly the terms of the race are that the first buyer who presents a signed contract and deposit cheque at the seller's solicitor's office will secure the property.

2.4. Acting for seller and buyer

2.4.1. Even where a solicitor would normally be entitled to act for both the seller and buyer, e.g. because the situation falls within one of the exceptions to Rule 6(2) Solicitors' Practice Rules 1990, the contract race gives rise to a significant risk of conflict of interests between the two clients and the solicitor must not continue to act for both.

2.5. Acting for more than one buyer

2.5.1. Where forms of contract are submitted to more than one prospective buyer, a solicitor must not accept instructions to act for more than one such buyer.

2.6. Licensed conveyancers

2.6.1. Licensed conveyancers may be regarded in the same light as solicitors; thus, for the purpose of the Rule, disclosure of a contract race to a licensed conveyancer can be treated as disclosure of the race to the client of the conveyancer. Disclosure of the existence of the race must, however, be made directly to the buyer if that buyer is represented by an unqualified person. Authorised practitioners may be regarded in the same light as licensed conveyancers.

B3. Seller's investigation of title

3.1. Seller's investigation of title

3.1.1. Having obtained official copy entries of the title (registered land) or the seller's title deeds or a copy of them (unregistered land), the seller's solicitor should investigate title before drafting the contract for sale. The manner and method of such investigation is dealt with in para. D2.

3.2. Reasons for investigation

3.2.1. The investigation of the title by the seller's solicitor at this stage of the transaction is a precautionary measure to ensure that:

(a) the seller is the owner of or is otherwise entitled to sell the whole of the estate in accordance with the instructions given to his solicitor;

(b) any incumbrances on the title can be revealed in the draft contract in order to satisfy the seller's duty of disclosure;

(c) any defects in the title may be spotted and appropriate steps taken to rectify them before exchange of contracts;

(d) any consents which may be necessary from third parties may be obtained;

(e) any requisitions on title by the buyer can be anticipated, and if necessary an appropriate special condition may be included with the draft contract.

3.3.   **Registered land**

3.3.1.   Obtain up-to-date official copy entries of the title and check to ensure that no entries have been made which will affect the seller's right to sell the property as instructed, e.g. there may be a restriction or a caution against dealings on the register. (Although cautions against dealings have been abolished with prospective effect by the Land Registration Act 2002, existing cautions will be unaffected.)

3.3.2.   On first registration of the title positive covenants may have been omitted from the register; in such a case the seller will need to take an indemnity covenant from the buyer and provide the buyer with a copy of the transfer which imposed the covenants in order to prove the need for indemnity. This latter will involve the inspection of pre-registration title deeds.

3.4.   **Unregistered titles**

3.4.1.   Check when the compulsory registration order came into force in the area and that no dealings which would have induced registration have occurred since that date.

3.4.2.   In most cases the land will require registration after completion of this transaction. Although this will primarily be the responsibility of the buyer, this factor should be borne in mind by the seller's solicitor in his pre-contract investigation of title so that any areas of difficulty which might be the subject of a requisition by the Land Registry may be clarified.

3.4.3.   If it transpires that the land should have been registered on a previous disposition, an immediate application for late registration must be made by the seller's solicitor, a full disclosure of the situation being made to both the seller and the buyer's solicitor. Title will then need to be dealt with as if the seller's title was awaiting registration at the Land Registry (see para. B4).

3.4.4.   An index map search should be made to ensure that no part of the land has already been registered without the owner's knowledge and that no caution against first registration affects the land (see para. B10).

3.4.5.   A Land Charges Department search should be made against the name of the seller to ensure that no incumbrances exist other than those revealed by the title deeds (see para. B10).

3.4.6.   *Freeholds*

    (a) Decide which document is to be used as the root of title, and check the validity of the chain of title forwards from that time.

    (b) Does the root document refer to any earlier documents which the buyer may be entitled to call for?

    (c) Are there any pre-root covenants which need to be disclosed to the buyer?

(d) Are all documents within the chain correctly stamped and executed?

(e) Watch for change of names, e.g. on marriage or change of a company name. Obtain evidence of the changes if necessary.

(f) If in doubt as to the effectiveness of restrictive covenants, options or third party rights revealed by the title a Land Charges Department search should be made to clarify the position.

(g) Obtain copies of any necessary death certificates or grants of representation.

3.4.7. Existing leaseholds

The Law of Property Act 1925, s.44 limits the right of an intended lessee or assignee of an existing lease to require production of the reversionary title or titles. This limitation, however, does not apply to:

(a) registered land or a term of years to be derived out of registered land; or

(b) a contract for the grant of a lease to which the compulsory registration provisions apply.[1]

Where the lease falls outside the compulsory registration provisions and there is little or no premium payable for its assignment the buyer may be content not to insist on deduction of the reversionary title.

3.4.8.   Problems may, however, arise if the title to the freehold was not called for on the original grant of the lease. The following points should be checked:

(a) Is a marked copy of the freehold title available or can it be obtained? If not, check that the contract excludes the buyer's right to deduction of the freehold.

(b) Check the chain of title from the lease (or sub-lease) including evidence of surrenders and copies of any necessary consents, e.g. to assignments or alterations.

(c) Is consent to this assignment required? If so, obtain the names of referees from the buyer's solicitor and forward them to the landlord's solicitor. Obtain a firm estimate from the landlord's solicitor before giving an undertaking for costs.

(d) Is the freehold or superior leasehold title registered? Whether or not this is so can be ascertained by making an index map search. Where the freehold or superior title is registered official copy entries of the title can be obtained by the buyer. This may overcome the limitation posed by the seller being unable to deliver the freehold or superior leasehold title.

1. Law of Property Act 1925, s.44; as amended by Land Registration Act 2002, Sched.11, para.2.

3.5. Title in name of sole owner

3.5.1. Instructions will have revealed whether anyone other than the seller is living at the property. If there is, consideration should be given to the question of whether the occupants have any rights in the property which may impede the seller's intention of selling with vacant possession.

3.5.2. Is the seller married?

The seller's spouse may have statutory rights of occupation under the Family Law Act 1996 and/or an equitable interest in the property through a contribution to the purchase price. Enquiries should also be made to ascertain whether the non-owning spouse has the benefit of an occupation order under Family Law Act 1996.

3.5.3. Matrimonial homes rights

Current registration of such rights can be verified by inspecting official copy entries of the title (registered land) or by making a Land Charges Department search against the seller (unregistered land). Even if such rights are not presently protected by registration the spouse may still effect a registration at any time until actual completion.

3.5.4. Rights are already registered

It will be a condition of the contract that such registration is removed before completion.[1] Negotiations must be entered into with the spouse's solicitors for the removal of the charge and a satisfactory solution obtained before exchange of contracts.

3.5.5. Rights in existence but not registered

It is unsafe to assume that the spouse will not exercise the right to register a charge under Family Law Act 1996 and instructions should be obtained directly from the spouse (through a separate solicitor if there is any possibility of conflict of interests) to confirm the spouse's acquiescence in the proposed sale. A formal release of rights and agreement not to enforce any such rights against the seller should be prepared for signature before exchange by the non-owning spouse.

3.5.6. A registration under Family Law Act 1996 can be removed on production of:

(a) an application made by the person with the benefit of the rights;

(b) a divorce decree absolute;

(c) a court order to that effect;

(d) the death certificate of the spouse.

3.5.7. *Equitable interests*

If it is thought that the spouse may also be entitled to an equitable interest in the property it should be assumed that the property is held by the seller on constructive trust for himself and his spouse. The spouse's independent confirmation of agreement to the sale must be obtained and the spouse joined as a party to the contract. A solicitor would be well advised to explain to the spouse that his/her written consent to the sale is required, that giving such consent may affect his/her legal rights and that the spouse should obtain independent advice before signing the release. The dangers of negligence and undue influence should also be noted where the owning spouse 'persuades' the non-owning spouse to consent to the transaction (see Appendix V.18).

3.5.8. Suggested form of wording for release of rights:

(a) 'In consideration of the buyer entering this agreement I (*name of spouse*) agree:

   (i) to the sale of the property on the terms of this agreement; and

   (ii) that I will not register rights in relation to the property, whether under Family Law Act 1996 or otherwise, and that I will procure before completion the removal of any registration made by me; and

   (iii) that I will vacate the property by the completion date.'[2]

or

(b) 'In consideration of your today entering into a contract with (*name of owning spouse*) for the purchase of the property known as (*insert address of property to be sold*), I agree:

   (i) to release any equitable interest which I may have in the property (such interest, if any, being transferred to the proceeds of sale of the property), such release to be effective from the date of completion of the sale of this property;

   (ii) to procure the cancellation of any registration which may have been effected by me or on my behalf on or before completion, including any registration in respect of rights of occupation which I may have under Family Law Act 1996; and

   (iii) to vacate the property by the completion date.'[3]

3.5.9. *Sharers and co-habitees*

Sharers and co-habitees may be able to establish an equitable interest in the property through contribution to the purchase price. Investigation must be made of the exact status of each occupier. If necessary a release of rights should be obtained, or they may be joined as parties to the contract. The solicitor should advise the sharer/co-habitee in similar terms to those suggested in para. B3.5.7. Enquiries should also be made to ascertain whether the non-owning occupier has the benefit of an occupation order under Family Law Act 1996, s.33.

3.5.10. *Overriding interests*

Persons in actual occupation of registered land may have overriding interests.[4] A formal release of such rights should be obtained. The occupiers may also be joined as contracting parties.

3.5.11. *Tenants*

If vacant possession is to be given of the property on completion effective steps must be taken to terminate the tenancies.

If vacant possession is not to be given on completion full details of the tenancies must be obtained since disclosure of the tenancies must be made in the draft contract. Accurate information will be required by the buyer in relation to the amount of rent payable by the tenants, the dates of rent reviews, and the effect of any security of tenure legislation on the tenancies.

1. Family Law Act 1996, Sched.4, para. 3(1).
2. This clause should be included in the contract of sale.
3. This clause may either be incorporated in the contract or drawn up as a separate document and attached to the contract. In either case the clause should be signed by the non-owning spouse.
4. Land Registration Act 2002, Sched.1, para. 2, Sched.3, para. 2 and Sched.12, para. 8.

3.6. **Death of a joint proprietor**

3.6.1. *Registered land*

3.6.1.1. Registration of restriction

A restriction in either Form 62 or Form A registered in the proprietorship register indicates that the equitable interest was held on a tenancy in common and two trustees will be needed to transfer the legal estate. A buyer will normally insist that the seller obtains the appointment of a new trustee or the removal of the restriction before taking a transfer from him. If he does not do this then, on lodging his application for registration of the transfer, the buyer would need to produce to the Land Registry such evidence as will satisfy the Registrar that the registered estate is no longer subject to a trust of land.[1] Such evidence might comprise a statutory declaration by the sole survivor that in stated circumstances the declarant has become entitled legally and beneficially to the registered land, that he has not encumbered his undivided share, and that he has not received notice of any incumbrance upon the undivided share of the deceased proprietor. A certificate by the seller's conveyancer will be accepted in place of a declaration if the conveyancer is able to speak from his knowledge of all the relevant facts.

3.6.1.2. Appointment of second trustee

The seller's solicitor may be appointed as the new trustee provided that there is no conflict of interest between the instructing client and the other person(s) now entitled to the remainder of the property. The appointment of the second trustee should be dealt with as a matter of urgency so that there are two trustees named in the contract. If there is difficulty over the appointment of a second trustee the contract may include a clause providing that a second trustee will be appointed prior to execution of the purchase deed, the existing trustee contracting alone at this stage of the transaction. This latter situation should be avoided if possible because it is less satisfactory to the buyer who in contracting with one trustee alone has no guarantee that the matter will proceed smoothly to completion.

3.6.1.3. No restriction registered

Where no restriction is registered the equitable interest may be presumed to have been held under a joint tenancy and the sole surviving joint tenant may sell on production of the death certificate of the deceased.[2]

3.6.2. Unregistered land

Check the document under which the joint owners acquired the property to ascertain whether it was held on a joint tenancy or tenancy in common.

3.6.2.1. Tenancy in common

The existence of two trustees of the legal estate gives the buyer the assurance that any subsisting beneficial interests will be overreached on completion, thus removing any doubt which may exist as to whether the deceased had disposed of his interest in the property during his lifetime (see above).

3.6.2.2. Joint tenancy

Check the deed by which the joint tenants bought the property to ensure that no memorandum of severance is endorsed on it and make a bankruptcy search in the Land Charges Department to establish that no bankruptcy proceedings were or are pending against either joint tenant (see para. B10). Provided that these conditions are satisfied, the sole survivor may sell with a certificate that he is a sole beneficial owner on production of the death certificate of the deceased joint tenant. Again, provided that these conditions are satisfied, the personal representatives of a last surviving joint tenant can convey the land on production of the grant so long as the conveyance contains a statement that the survivor was solely and beneficially entitled to the property. If the joint tenancy has been severed or if bankruptcy proceedings are pending the tenancy must be treated as a tenancy in common and dealt with by the appointment of a second trustee (see above).

1. Land Registration Rules 2003, r.99.
2. Land Registration Rules 2003, r.164.

3.7. Breach of restrictive covenant/other defect in title

3.7.1. Restrictive covenants

If the breach cannot be remedied, e.g. by obtaining belated consent of the person entitled to the benefit of the covenant, consider obtaining restrictive covenant indemnity insurance in an appropriate sum.

3.7.2. Other defects in title

Defects which can be remedied, e.g. the appointment of a new trustee or missing stamp duties should be rectified as soon as possible and in any event before exchange of contracts. Defects which are irremediable will have to be revealed in the draft contract and insurance cover obtained as appropriate (see para. B6 and Appendix X.1).

3.8. Planning

3.8.1.
Although not strictly a matter of title, the seller's solicitor should check at this stage that any necessary planning or building regulation consents have been obtained and complied with. If not with the deeds copies of such consents should be requisitioned from the local authority for the buyer's use.

3.9. Donatio mortis causa

3.9.1.
It is possible, although extremely rare, for the seller to have acquired the land through a *donatio mortis causa*.[1] In such a case there will be no documentary evidence of the devolution of title from the deceased to the present seller. Proof of the validity of the seller's title will have to be shown to the buyer; it may be possible to do this by means of a statutory declaration made by the seller.

1. See *Sen* v. *Headley* [1991] 2 All ER 636.

3.10. Action after investigation of title

3.10.1. Registered land

Official copy entries of the title and any other supporting documentation, e.g. evidence of tenancies or overriding interests should be prepared for delivery to the buyer with the draft contract.

3.10.2. Unregistered land

An epitome of title should be prepared for delivery to the buyer with the draft contract.

B4. Seller's title awaiting registration

See also: Land Registration Act 2002, para. A22.
Registration of title, para. G3
Land Registration Rules 2003 (selected schedules), Appendix XII.5
Land Registration Act 2002 (selected schedules), Appendix XII.4

4.1. The nature of the problem

4.1.1. A seller, after completion of a recent purchase of registered land, may seek to sell the land to a third party before registration of his own transfer has been completed at the Land Registry. As such, he will not at that stage be the registered proprietor of the land.

4.1.2. A similar problem exists where, having bought unregistered land which is subject to compulsory registration, the seller wishes to sell that land before his application for first registration has been completed. In this latter situation he should not sell on his unregistered title to the buyer, leaving the buyer to apply for registration on completion of his purchase, since the seller's title will become void if no application for registration is made by the seller within two months of the completion of his own purchase.[1] A safer course of action is for the seller to submit his application to the registrar for first registration and then to sell on with registration of title pending.

1. Land Registration Act 2002, s.7; and see *Pinekerry* v. *Needs (Contractors)* (1992) 64 P & CR 245.

4.2. Seller's right to deal with land

4.2.1. The seller is entitled to exercise owner's powers in relation to a registered estate if he is the registered proprietor or entitled to be registered as the proprietor.[1]

1. Land Registration Act 2002, s.24.

4.3. Delay

4.3.1. In practice, if the buyer was to insist that completion of his purchase be delayed until the seller became the registered proprietor of the land through completion of the pending application for registration, the transaction might be delayed by several months which would result in adverse practical and financial consequences for both parties. The buyer will normally agree to complete provided that the seller's own title to the land is registered at some time before the buyer's application for registration is completed.

4.3.2. The buyer's lender must be informed of the position and his requirements observed.

4.4. Contractual condition for deduction of title

4.4.1. The seller must prove to the buyer's satisfaction that the seller is a person who is entitled to be registered as proprietor of the land concerned. This is normally achieved by producing to the buyer official copy entries of the title (which will show the seller's predecessor as registered proprietor), together with a copy of the stamped transfer from the registered proprietor to the seller, appropriate evidence as to those matters upon which the register is not conclusive, a clear Land Registry search against the title, and evidence that the seller lodged a correct application for registration preferably within the priority period afforded by his own search.

4.4.2. Where the land is presently unregistered, the buyer will insist on deduction of the unregistered title together with evidence that the seller has lodged a properly completed application form for first registration of the title. Deduction of title by this method requires the insertion of a special condition to this effect in the contract.

4.4.3. The contract should require the seller to expedite the application and assist the buyer in answering any requisitions which might be raised by the Land Registry in relation to the pending registration.

4.4.4. If the contract requires the buyer to purchase the seller's existing equitable interest in the property (the seller does not have the legal estate until registration is complete), the seller must be required to give an undertaking to transfer the legal estate to the buyer on completion of the seller's registration of title.

4.4.5. Any clause in the contract which relates to obligations that remain in existence after completion will not merge on completion under Standard Condition 7.4.

4.5. Provision for payment of interest by buyer

4.5.1. In order to discourage the buyer from delaying completion by insisting on the seller actually becoming registered as proprietor it is not uncommon to find a contractual provision to the effect that if the buyer does insist on the seller completing his own registration before completion of the sale to the buyer, the buyer will pay interest on the balance of the purchase price at the contract rate for the period between the agreed contractual completion date and actual completion. The Court of Appeal upheld such a provision.[1]

1. *P & O Overseas Holdings Ltd* v. *Rhys Braintree Ltd* [2002] EWCA Civ 296.

4.6. Protection of the buyer

4.6.1. The buyer may insist that the seller includes a provision in the contract whereby he agrees to expedite his application for registration by paying any appropriate expedition fee, and that he will assist the buyer by answering any requisitions relating to the pending application which are raised by the Land Registry. Such a condition should be expressed so that it remains extant after completion of the buyer's contract and does not merge with the transfer on completion. Some risks are inherent in this situation and the buyer should protect his contract by registration.

4.7. Protection of the lender

4.7.1. The mortgage, until registration, takes effect only as a charge on the equitable interest and will not comply with the provisions of Building Societies Act 1986. The borrower would, however, be estopped from denying the validity of the charge.[1]

1. *First National Bank plc* v. *Thompson* [1995] NPC 130.

B5. Seller's duty of disclosure

5.1. Reasons for disclosure

5.1.1. It is an implied term of a contract for the sale of land that the seller is selling free from incumbrances. If this is not to be so the seller must reveal the incumbrances to which the property is subject. Failure to disclose incumbrances may give the buyer the right to rescind the contract and to claim damages.

5.2. What must the seller disclose?

5.2.1. As an exception to the *caveat emptor* principle the seller is under a duty to disclose to the buyer latent incumbrances and defects in his title. This duty exists irrespective of whether the buyer raises enquiries about such matters.

5.2.2. Meaning of latent

Legally a defect is latent if it is not apparent, but the distinction between latent and patent defects is, in practice, unclear: see, e.g. *Yandle & Sons* v. *Sutton*[1] where a right of way which was apparent on inspection of the property was nevertheless held to be a latent defect. A seller should err on the side of caution and make a full disclosure of defects and incumbrances.

5.2.3. Law of Property Act 1969, s.24

Although a defect is not latent if the buyer has constructive notice of it under Law of Property Act 1925, s.198, the effect of Law of Property Act 1969, s.24 is to place a duty on the seller to reveal matters which are registered at the Land Charges Department. A buyer who enters into a contract knowing of an irremovable incumbrance impliedly agrees to take subject to that incumbrance (i.e. cannot rescind because of it), but the effect of section 24 is that mere registration under Land Charges Act 1972 is not knowledge for this purpose.

5.2.4. Occupiers

A buyer of an unregistered title who inspects the property will be deemed to have notice of the rights of occupiers.[2] Where the title is registered, the rights of occupiers may be overriding interests. It is uncertain whether the rights of occupiers fall within the duty of disclosure. Following *Williams & Glyn's Bank Ltd* v. *Boland*[3] the accepted view is that a full disclosure of occupiers' rights should be made.

5.2.5. Local land charges

Unless the contract provides to the contrary, the duty of disclosure includes matters which would be revealed by a local land charges search. Where the contract does not contain an effective clause excluding such matters from the duty of disclosure the seller should make a local land charges search before drafting the contract.[4]

5.2.6. Matters outside the seller's knowledge

It was held in *Re Brewer & Hankin's Contract*[5] that the seller's duty of disclosure may extend even to matters of which he was unaware. However, standard contractual conditions will normally exclude the seller's liability for non-disclosure in these circumstances (see Standard Condition 3, Appendix VII.13). Knowledge acquired by the seller's solicitor in the course of acting for his client is imputed to the seller.[6]

5.2.7. Overriding interests[7]

The seller is under a duty to disclose latent overriding interests. In practice a disclosure of all overriding interests known to the seller should be made.

1. [1922] 2 Ch 199.
2. *Hunt* v. *Luck* [1902] 1 Ch 428.
3. [1981] AC 487.
4. *Rignall Developments Ltd* v. *Halil* [1988] Ch 190.
5. (1889) 80 LT 127.
6. *Strover* v. *Harrington* [1988] Ch 390.
7. See para. A22.5.

5.3. Matters falling outside the duty of disclosure

5.3.1. Matters known to the buyer

There is no duty to disclose matters which are already known to the buyer, but the seller must ensure that the buyer has actual knowledge of such matters and cannot assume that a matter is within the buyer's knowledge. Even where an incumbrance is contained within one of the title deeds (or appears on the register in registered land) supplied to the buyer with the draft contract, the buyer's knowledge of the incumbrance cannot be assumed and the seller should take steps, whether by inclusion of a contractual condition or otherwise, specifically to draw the defect to the buyer's attention.

5.3.2. Matters apparent on inspection

Matters which can readily be discovered on an inspection of the property do not fall within the duty of disclosure.[1]

5.3.3. *Physical defects*

Physical defects, whether latent or patent, do not generally fall within the duty of disclosure, but the buyer may seek a remedy in misdescription if the contractual description of the land is rendered inaccurate through this omission.[2] Rescission may also be available to a buyer who, through the non-disclosure of a physical defect, is unable to use the land for the specific purpose for which it was sold.[3] The deliberate concealment of a known physical defect may give rise to an action in the tort of deceit.[4]

5.3.4. *Planning matters*

Planning matters are not matters of 'title' and are therefore not strictly within the duty of disclosure. It is, however, considered good practice to make disclosure of such matters.

1. But see *Yandle & Sons* v. *Sutton* [1922] 2 Ch 199.
2. *Re Puckett & Smith's Contract* [1902] 2 Ch 258.
3. *Re Puckett & Smith's Contract* [1902] 2 Ch 258.
4. *Gordon* v. *Selico Co. Ltd* (1986) 278 EG 53.

5.4. Non-disclosure by buyer

5.4.1.
As a general rule a prospective buyer who is not already in a fiduciary relationship with his seller owes no duty of disclosure to his seller. Exceptionally such a duty may exist, e.g. *English* v. *Dedham Vale Properties*,[1] where the buyer was held liable to account to the seller for profit ultimately received from an undisclosed planning application made by the buyer.

1. [1978] 1 WLR 93.

5.5. Consequences of non-disclosure

5.5.1.
The buyer's remedies for non-disclosure will be rescission of the contract if the non-disclosure is judged to be substantial. If the non-disclosure is not substantial the buyer can be forced to complete and will obtain his remedy through an abatement in the purchase price. A substantial non-disclosure is one where its effect is substantially to deprive the buyer of his bargain. A remedy may also lie in misrepresentation since non-disclosure effectively amounts to a misrepresentation by silence.[1]

1. *Pankhavia and anon* v. *Hackney London Borough Council and anon* [2002] All ER (D) 22.

5.6. Contractual exclusion clauses

5.6.1.
Clauses which purport to exclude liability for non-disclosure and misrepresentation are common, e.g. Standard Condition 7.1 (Appendix VII.13), and as far as

the latter is concerned are subject to the reasonableness test in Unfair Contract Terms Act 1977.[1] Their effectiveness in protecting the seller cannot therefore be guaranteed. Some restriction of the seller's duty of disclosure may be felt desirable but a total exclusion of liability would probably not be upheld by the courts save in exceptional circumstances.

1. *Pankhavia and anon* v. *Hackney London Borough Council and anon* [2002] All ER (D) 22.

5.7. Conclusion

5.7.1. Despite the various recognised exceptions to the duty of disclosure outlined above, a prudent seller will make a full disclosure of all defects and incumbrances to the buyer, protecting himself where necessary by the inclusion of appropriate contractual clauses to prevent the buyer from exercising a right to rescind in respect of the disclosed matters. Some restriction of the seller's duty of disclosure may be incorporated by way of an exclusion clause in the contract, but care must be exercised to ensure that the clause is reasonable in the light of the circumstances of the particular transaction.

B6. Defective title and restrictive covenant insurance

See also: Seller's investigation of title, para. B3
Seller's duty of disclosure, para. B5
Covenants for title, para. M9.
CML Lenders' Handbook Part 1, Appendix VIII.3.
Countrywide Legal Indemnities, Appendix X.1.

6.1. Discovery of defects

6.1.1. The seller's solicitor should make a full investigation of the seller's title prior to drafting the contract for sale. Any potential defects in that title must be disclosed to the buyer in the contract and accepted by him, otherwise the seller may be called upon to remove the incumbrance.

6.1.2. Where it appears that a defect in title exists which is not remediable, the seller's solicitor may consider obtaining defective title insurance to cover liability arising out of the defect. Many, but not all, defects can be insured against in this way.

6.1.3. Before obtaining the policy the seller's instructions should be obtained, authorising the solicitor to proceed with this course of action. The seller should be fully advised of the problem and of the likely cost of a policy.

6.1.4. Some lenders insist on the borrower obtaining an indemnity policy against the seller's insolvency, for example where it is apparent that a voluntary transaction has been effected within the past five years. A typical policy will cost a minimum of £175.

6.2. Obtaining a policy

6.2.1. Countrywide Legal Indemnities offers a policy which has been negotiated by the Law Society (Appendix X.1). Some other major insurance companies will issue policies to cover defects in title. To ensure that a proper premium, commensurate with the risk involved, is paid, quotations should be obtained from more than one company.

6.2.2. The defect in title is the seller's responsibility because he will be contractually bound to prove a good title to his buyer. The seller should therefore normally expect to meet the costs of obtaining the policy. If the policy is obtained at the request of the buyer it may be possible to negotiate to share the expense with him. In any event the contract should deal with the liability for the expense of obtaining such a policy.

6.2.3. The policy will be a single premium policy the benefit of which will attach to the land. The policy should be mentioned in the contract (if the policy is available at that time) and handed over to the buyer on completion to be kept in a safe place with the documents of title.

6.3. Information needed by insurance company

6.3.1. Before issue of the policy the insurance company will need to assess the risk involved. As a general rule, defects which have occurred in the recent past, e.g. during the last 15 years will be more expensive and difficult to insure against than those which occurred many years ago. The seller's solicitor should be prepared to provide the insurance company with the following information or documents:

(a) the precise nature of the defect;

(b) where relevant, a copy of the document in which the defect appears;

(c) the date when the defect arose, or date when the problem giving rise to the defect occurred;

(d) what steps (if any) have been taken to remedy the defect;

(e) whether any third party has taken steps to assert rights against the land because of the defect;

(f) an approximate estimate of the amount of cover needed.

6.4. Restrictive covenants

6.4.1. The breach of a restrictive covenant affecting the title is a common reason for needing defective title insurance. In some cases the need for the policy will arise, not because a covenant has been broken, but because some contemplated action with or on the land will cause a breach. For example, it is common to find a restrictive covenant which prevents use of the property except as a single private dwelling house and the client wishes now to convert the property into flats, which action would cause a breach of covenant. In such a case it may be possible to obtain an insurance policy which will cover liability for the future breach of covenant. Where the seller is contracting to sell with planning permission for development, he should obtain and bear the cost of the policy; in other cases this matter will be the buyer's responsibility.

6.4.2. Apart from the matters listed above in para. B6.3, the insurance company will also need the following information or documents:

(a) a copy of the document imposing the covenant or, if this is not available, a copy of the exact wording of the covenant;

(b) the exact nature of the breach which has occurred or details of the action which is contemplated which will cause the breach;

(c) the date when the covenant was imposed;

(d) whether or not the covenant is registered on the charges register of the title (or as a Class D(ii) charge in unregistered land where the covenant was imposed after 1925);

(e) the nature of other properties in the immediate neighbourhood. This is to enable the insurance company to assess the risk of enforcement of the covenant more precisely. Taking the example given above of a potential breach being caused by a conversion of a dwelling into flats, if many of the neighbouring properties have already been converted into flats, the likelihood of this particular covenant being enforced if breached is more remote than if the surrounding properties remain in single ownership. A plan which shows the property in the context of the surrounding locality is often useful;

(f) a copy of any planning permission which permits the development to be undertaken by the client and copies of any objections which were lodged in respect of the application;

(g) what steps have been taken (if any) to trace the person(s) with the benefit of the covenant and the results of those enquiries. The identity of the person who has the benefit of the covenant should be revealed if known, but steps should not be taken to approach that person without the prior consent of the insurance company since such an approach may have an adverse effect on the outcome of the situation and the consequent insurance risk;

(h) details of any complaints which have been received from persons with the benefit of the covenants.

6.5. Accepting the policy when acting for the buyer

6.5.1. Where a buyer is asked to accept a policy taken out by the seller or his predecessor which purports to cover liability for a defect or breach consideration should be given to the following matters:

(a) check that full disclosure of all relevant facts was made to the insurer prior to the issue of the policy;

(b) ensure that the policy enures to the benefit of successors and is not restricted to a named person;

(c) check that the policy covers the defect or breach in question;

(d) check that the amount of cover offered by the policy appears to be adequate;

(e) if the policy is already in existence enquire whether any claims have been made under the policy and the result of those claims;

(f) ensure that the original policy will be handed over on completion. Where the policy has been taken out by a developer to cover the building of several properties, an examined or certified copy of the policy should be handed over on completion;

(g) where a policy already exists, consideration should be given to taking an express assignment of the benefit of the policy from the seller and, after completion, giving notice of the assignment to the insurance company;

(h) obtaining any proposed lender's approval to the policy terms and amount of cover.

6.6. Positive covenants

6.6.1. Similar considerations apply where indemnity has been given in relation to a positive covenant.

6.7. Lenders' Handbook

6.7.1. The Lenders' Handbook outlines a number of situations in which indemnity insurance will be required by the lender. The terms on which the lender will accept a policy are contained in paragraph 9 of the Handbook.

B7. Capacity

See also: Powers of attorney, para. B23
The purchase deed, para. E1
Death and insolvency, para. E6
Covenants for title, para. M9
Gifts of property guidelines, Appendix V.8.

7.1. Introduction

7.1.1. In general a seller cannot convey a legal estate unless that estate is vested in him, although in very limited cases he may, under a power, convey a legal estate vested in some other person, e.g. a lender exercising a power of sale.

7.1.2. Although the nature of the seller's capacity no longer affects the extent of the covenants which are implied in the buyer's favour in the purchase deed, certain points relating to the seller's capacity to deal with the interest in land which he is purporting to dispose of still need to be addressed. These points are outlined in the paragraphs below. Implied covenants are discussed in para. M9.[1]

7.1.3. A registered proprietor has unfettered powers of disposition.[2] A buyer of registered land is concerned only to ensure that any restrictions on the register are complied with. The statutory provisions have effect only for the purpose of preventing the title of a buyer being questioned (and do not affect the lawfulness of a disposition).[3] The seller will in any event be bound to comply with any fiduciary duties he has, but a buyer is not concerned with them unless they are reflected in a restriction on the register. Where the title to the property is registered with title absolute, and there is no restriction placed on the proprietorship register, the seller is deemed to have the capacity to transfer the land (subject to the provisions relating to alteration of the register) and further enquiry into the seller's capacity is in such cases unnecessary.

1. See Law of Property (Miscellaneous Provisions) Act 1994 and para. M9.
2. Land Registration Act 2002, s.26(1).
3. Land Registration Act 2002, s.26(2).

7.2. Provision for capacity in the contract

7.2.1.   For contracts entered into on or after 1 July 1995, it is no longer necessary to state the seller's capacity in the contract.[1]

1. See Law of Property (Miscellaneous Provisions) Act 1994 and para. M9.

7.3. Beneficial owner

7.3.1.   A beneficial owner is a single estate owner who owns the whole of the legal and equitable interest in the property for his own benefit. Either an individual or a corporation may satisfy this requirement. No other person must have any beneficial interest in the interest in land if the capacity of beneficial owner is to apply. Co-owners cannot satisfy this requirement since they hold the property on a trust of land.[1]

7.3.2.   If it appears that someone other than the seller named in the contract is in occupation of the property, the buyer must make full enquiries about the status of such occupier in order to establish what interest he has in the property and to establish whether or not the seller is in fact a beneficial owner.

7.3.3.   An occupier may claim a beneficial interest in the property through, e.g. contributing to the purchase price. In such a case, it will be necessary for a second trustee to be appointed to act with the seller in order to overreach the beneficial interest of the occupier.[2] Alternatively (or additionally) it may be thought desirable for the occupier to sign a release of his or her rights. Such a release may be included as a contractual term, in which case the occupier will need to sign the contract before exchange. The validity of such disclaimers seems to have met with the court's approval.[3]

7.3.4.   In registered land the rights of persons in actual occupation may be overriding interests.[4] If so, a buyer will take subject to these rights (including those which are capable of registration but which are not in fact registered). However, where the sale is by trustees, the rights arising under the trust will be overreached provided the capital money arising is paid to at least two trustees or a trust corporation.

7.3.5.   In unregistered land a buyer is deemed to buy with notice of occupiers' rights, other than those capable of registration but which are not registered as land charges;[5] thus the buyer needs to inspect the property and to make full enquiries about the rights of any occupiers.

7.3.6.   A surviving co-owner may be a beneficial owner.[6]

1. See *Re Robertson's Application* [1969] 1 All ER 257.
2. See *City of London Building Society* v. *Flegg* [1988] AC 54; *Lloyds Bank* v. *Rossett* [1991] 1 AC 107.

3. *Appleton* v. *Aspin* [1988] 1 WLR 410.
4. Land Registration Act 2002, Sched.1, para.2 and Sched.3, para.2.
5. *Hunt* v. *Luck* [1902] 1 Ch 428.
6. See para. B7.4.

7.4. Trustees of land

7.4.1. Where land is held on a trust of land any conveyance or transfer of the land must be made by the trustees, being at least two individuals or a trust corporation, in order to overreach the equitable interests of the beneficiaries.

7.4.2. Co-owners hold land on a trust of land.[1]

7.4.3. Where a trust of land exists, whether expressly created or arising under statute (e.g. on intestacy), the trustees are under a duty to consult with, and, so far as is consistent with the general interests of the trust, give effect to the wishes of the adult competent beneficiaries who are entitled to a beneficial interest in possession of the land, when exercising their powers under the trust (e.g. to sell the land).[2] A trust which is created by an *inter vivos* disposition (but not by will) can expressly exclude the duty to consult.[3] A buyer is not concerned to check compliance with the obligation to consult.[4] In registered land the buyer is only concerned to see that the terms of any restriction on the register are complied with.

7.4.4. Where the trust was expressly created, a power to postpone the sale is implied and cannot be excluded by contrary provision in the trust instrument.[5]

7.4.5. Where the trust arises under statute (e.g. on intestacy), the trustees have a power (but not a duty) to sell the land.[6]

7.4.6. Difficulties may arise if there are only two acting trustees who disagree over the decision to sell, since one trustee alone cannot transfer the legal estate. It may therefore be necessary in these circumstances to apply to the court under Trusts of Land and Appointment of Trustees Act 1996, s.14 to resolve the dispute. On an application under this section the court may make any order it thinks fit (including an order for sale), and thus may, but is not obliged to, order the sale of the property.

7.4.7. In making such an order the court must have regard to the factors listed in section 15 of Trusts of Land and Appointment of Trustees Act 1996 including the purpose of the trust and the interests of any secured creditor or beneficiary.

7.4.8. If a disposition creating a trust of land requires the trustees to obtain the consents of a person or persons before exercising their power of sale, the buyer is only concerned to see that a maximum of two consents have been obtained (even if the trust deed requires a greater number) and is never concerned with the consents of persons suffering mental incapacity. Where a person whose consent is required is not of full age, the buyer is not concerned to see that such consent has been obtained, but the trustees must obtain the consent of a parent or guardian of the under age beneficiary.[7] In registered land the buyer is only concerned to see that the terms of any restriction on the register are complied with.

7.4.9.   Trustees' powers to sell, mortgage, and grant leases are the same as those of an absolute owner but they must exercise those powers having regard to the rights of the beneficiaries.[8]

7.4.10.   Trusts of Land and Appointment of Trustees Act 1996 has converted existing trusts for sale into 'trusts of land'. From 1 January 1997, co-owners will hold land on a trust of land (formerly trust for sale).

7.4.11.   Where the purpose of the trust is to sell the land it is still possible to create an express. The requirement for the trustees to sell must however be expressly stated since it is no longer implied under the general law.

1. Law of Property Act 1925, ss.34 and 36.
2. Trusts of Land and Appointment of Trustees Act 1996, s.11.
3. *Ibid.* s.11(2).
4. *Ibid.* s.16(1).
5. *Ibid.* s.4(1).
6. *Ibid.* Sched 2.
7. *Ibid.* s.10.
8. *Ibid.* s.6.

7.5.   Personal representatives

7.5.1.   Personal representatives have all the powers of trustees of land but are only entitled to exercise those powers during the administration.[1] They are not, however, subject to ss.10, 11 and 14 of Trusts of Land and Appointment of Trustees Act 1996 (duties to obtain consents, consultation with beneficiaries and the court's power of sale).[2]

7.5.2.   Their powers are joint as to land, whether freehold or leasehold; therefore all proving personal representatives must be made parties to the contract and purchase deed (conveyance, lease, etc.).[3] A single proving personal representative may, however, act on his own.

7.5.3.   The buyer should always see a copy of the grant to ascertain the names of all of the proving personal representatives.

7.5.4.   In registered land a buyer is only concerned to see that the terms of any restriction on the register are complied with.

1. Administration of Estates Act 1925, s.39.
2. Trusts of Land and Appointment of Trustees Act 1996, s.18.
3. Law of Property (Miscellaneous Provisions) Act 1994, s.16.

7.6.   Settled land

7.6.1.   The following sub-paragraphs should be read in the light of Trusts of Land and Appointment of Trustees Act 1996 which abolishes the creation of new strict settlements (with very limited exceptions) on or after 1 January 1997. The Act is not retrospective in effect and existing strict settlements are unaffected by the legislation. Land which is held under Universities and Colleges Estates Act 1925 will continue to be settled land and is unaffected by the 1996 Act.

7.6.2. The tenant for life is the person in whom the legal estate in settled land is vested via the vesting instrument. Where there is no tenant for life, or he is a minor, the legal estate is vested in statutory owners who are usually the trustees of the settlement. The tenant for life (or, if none, the statutory owners) will therefore be the seller of settled land, but the trustees of the settlement must be joined as parties to the purchase deed in order to give a valid receipt for capital moneys arising and thus to overreach the interests of the beneficiaries.

7.6.3. The trust deed itself is generally 'behind the curtain' and thus of no concern to a buyer. The buyer is bound and entitled to assume that the person in whom the legal estate is vested by the vesting instrument is the person rightfully entitled to the legal estate and that the persons named as trustees are the properly constituted Settled Land Act trustees.

7.6.4. A sale or other disposition of settled land can only be made for the purposes of the settlement and must be made for the best consideration in money reasonably obtainable.[1] Unless expressly extended by the terms of the settlement certain restrictions on dispositions are imposed by Settled Land Act 1925. The main restrictions relate to mortgages and leases, e.g. the Act permits leases for building or forestry to be granted for a term not exceeding 999 years, for mining, not exceeding 100 years, and for agricultural or occupational purposes, not exceeding 50 years. Powers to grant options to purchase or to take a lease and to grant easements are limited by Settled Land Act 1925, s.51. A disposition which is not authorised either by the Act or by the terms of the settlement is void, even if the buyer was unaware of the settlement.[2]

7.6.5. Where settled land is registered, the tenant for life (or statutory owners) will be registered as proprietor and appropriate restrictions are entered on the proprietorship register. A buyer is only concerned to see that the terms of the restrictions are complied with.

1. Settled Land Act 1925, s.39(1).
2. *Weston* v. *Henshaw* [1950] Ch 510; *cf. Re Morgan's Lease; Jones* v. *Norsesowicz* [1972] Ch 1.

7.7. Mortgagees

7.7.1. In order to sell the property the lender must have an express or implied power of sale and that power must have arisen and become exercisable. A power of sale is implied in every mortgage made by deed unless expressly excluded.[1] A legal mortgage must be made by deed.[2] It therefore follows that a lender who has taken a legal mortgage will always have a power of sale unless (exceptionally) that power has been expressly excluded. An equitable mortgage need not be made by deed;[3] it will therefore be necessary to check carefully the existence of the lender's power to sell. In some cases an equitable mortgage may give the lender an irrevocable power of attorney which would give the lender power to convey the legal estate vested in the borrower in exercise of the power of sale.

7.7.2. Under Land Registration Act 2002, s.52, subject to any entry in the register to the contrary, the proprietor of a registered charge is to be taken to have the powers of disposition conferred by law on the owner of a legal mortgage. Conversely, the owner of a charge which is not substantively registered has no power of sale.

7.7.3. As far as a buyer is concerned, he need only check the existence of the power of sale and that it has arisen. The power of sale arises on the legal date for redemption of the mortgage which is usually specified to be a date early on in the mortgage term (e.g. one month after creation of the mortgage).

7.7.4. A lender who is exercising his power of sale must ensure that:

(a) his power of sale exists;

(b) the power has arisen; and

(c) the power has become exercisable.

7.7.5. The lender's power becomes exercisable if one of the three following conditions is met:[4]

(a) notice requiring payment of the principal money has been served on the borrower and default has been made in payment of the principal money for three months; or

(b) some interest under the mortgage is in arrears and unpaid for two months after becoming due; or

(c) there has been breach of some other provision contained in the mortgage deed or Law of Property Act 1925.

7.7.6. A lender who sells in a situation where his power has arisen but not become exercisable will nonetheless pass good title to the buyer but may be liable in damages to the borrower.

7.7.7. *Borrowers*

Subject to any contractual restriction in the mortgage (e.g. restricting further the limited statutory power to grant leases of the property) which may be reflected by a restriction on the register of the title, a borrower may be treated as a beneficial owner.

1. Law of Property Act 1925, s.101.
2. Law of Property Act 1925, s.85.
3. But must be in writing and signed by both parties to satisfy Law of Property (Miscellaneous Provisions) Act 1989, s.2.
4. Law of Property Act 1925, s.103.

7.8. **Charities**

7.8.1. If there is no restriction on the proprietorship register, a buyer may safely deal with the charity as if it were an absolute owner. If there is a restriction on the register, the following subparagraphs should be considered. Reference should also be made to the Land Registry's Practice Guide 14 Charities (March 2003).

7.8.2. Unless a charity is an exempt charity, no disposition (the term disposition applies to the transfer or conveyance of land and not to the contract for sale)[1] can be made by the charity without an order of the court or Charity Commissioners unless all the following conditions are satisfied:[2]

   (a) the trustees must obtain a written report about the proposed disposition from a qualified surveyor (FRICS, ARICS, SVA or ASVA);

   (b) the property is advertised for the period and in the manner advised by the surveyor;

   (c) the trustees decide that in the light of the surveyor's report they are satisfied that the terms of the disposition are the best that can be obtained;

   (d) prescribed words are inserted in both the contract and purchase deed.

7.8.3. The prescribed words must be in one of the following forms:

   (a) the land transferred (or as the case may be) is held by [(proprietors) in trust for] (charity), an exempt charity; or

   (b) the land transferred (or as the case may be) is held by [(proprietors) in trust for] (charity), a non-exempt charity, but this transfer (or as the case may be) is one falling within paragraph ((a) or (b) or (c)) of section 36(9) of the Charities Act 1993; or

   (c) the land transferred (or as the case may be) is held by [(proprietors) in trust for] (charity), a non-exempt charity, and this transfer (or as the case may be) is not one falling within paragraphs (a) (b) or (c) of section 36 of the Charities Act 1993, so the restrictions on disposition imposed by section 36 of that Act apply to the land.[3]

Note that when there is no trust (i.e. the land is the corporate property of the registered proprietor charity) the words 'XXXX in trust for' are omitted.

7.8.4. Where the prescribed words are included in the disposition, the buyer and persons who subsequently acquire the property for money or money's worth are entitled to rely on the conclusiveness of the facts stated and rely on a certificate in the purchase deed that the trustees have power under the trusts of the charity to effect the disposition and that they have complied with the provisions of Charities Act 1993, s.36 so far as applicable to it. The buyer may also rely on such a certificate where the land is registered with a restriction in Form 12 or Form E.[4]

7.8.5. *Dealing with land owned by a charity*

When dealing with land owned by a charity the following points should be checked:

   (a) Is the transaction authorised by the statute or deed which governs the charity?

(b) Is the charity exempt? If so, the transaction can proceed without delay; if not an exempt charity:

(c) Can the trustees give the certificate referred to in para. 7.8.4 above?

(d) If not, has an order of the court or the Charity Commissioners been obtained?

7.8.6. Where an order is needed it must either be obtained before exchange of contracts or the contract must be made conditional on the order being obtained.[5]

7.8.7. The purchase deed containing the certificate must be signed by the charity trustees, or by two or more of them acting under an authority given by the trustees.[6] In the case of a corporate charity this usually means the directors. It is not sufficient for the deed to be sealed by the company in the presence of a director and the secretary.

7.8.8. Land held on charitable, ecclesiastical and public trusts ceased to be settled land and became subject to a 'trust of land' on 1 January 1997 (with the exception of land to which the Universities and College Estates Act 1925 applies).[7]

1. *Osborn and Co Ltd* v. *Dior; Marito Holdings SA* v. *Borhane* CA [2003] All ER (D) 185 (Jan).
2. Charities Act 1993, ss.37–40.
3. Land Registration Rules 2003, r.180.
4. Land Registration Rules 2003, Sched.4.
5. See Conditional contracts, para. B13.
6. See Charities Act 1993, s.82.
7. Trusts of Land and Appointment of Trustees Act 1996.

7.9. Companies

7.9.1. A company which is regulated by the Companies Acts may deal with land so long as the transaction is within the scope of the objects clause of its memorandum of association. In favour of a person dealing with a company the validity of an act done by a company shall not be called into question on the ground of lack of capacity by reason of anything in the company's memorandum. The good faith of the buyer is irrelevant and it is no longer necessary to make a company search to ensure that the power to conduct the transaction exists.[1] A company may hold property jointly with another company or individual.[2] Where a company applies to become the proprietor of registered land, details of the company's powers must be supplied to the registrar[3] and, if those powers are limited, an appropriate restriction will be entered on the register. A buyer is only concerned to see that the terms of any restriction are complied with.

7.9.2. The powers of a company incorporated by Royal Charter are not restricted by the terms of its Charter; it may therefore be regarded as having the same powers as an individual.

7.9.3. The powers of a company which is incorporated by some other statute are governed by the enabling statute which should in each case be checked and the requisite procedures followed. A transaction outside the terms of the statute will be void.

7.9.4. The powers of a foreign company should be expressly checked and the requisite procedures followed. Checks may include confirmation from a lawyer entitled to practise in the jurisdiction in which the foreign company was incorporated that the company exists in law and has power to buy, sell and hold land, etc.[4]

7.9.5. *Transactions between a company and one of its directors*

Companies Act 1985, s.320, applies to arrangements under which a director acquires an asset from the company. The word 'arrangement' covers freehold and leasehold transactions and options made between the director and the company. Transactions under which the company purchases assets from one of its directors are also covered by section 320(1)(*b*). Under these provisions, a transaction to which the section applies must be sanctioned by the company in general meeting. The company's approval should be obtained before exchange of contracts, but a retrospective approval, obtained before completion, will validate the transaction. The resolution should identify the property, the buyer and the price and may approve the transaction on such other terms as the board of directors may agree. A private company may pass a written resolution (without holding a formal meeting) provided that the vote is unanimous. Where a formal meeting is held, a bare majority will suffice to pass the resolution. Minor transactions, defined as those which are below £2,000 in value or those with a value of between £2,000 and £100,000 where the value represents less than 10% of the company's assets, do not need approval. The term 'director' includes persons connected with the director so that a transfer by a company to a director's wife or to another company with which the director is associated will invoke the provisions of the section. The consequences of failure to comply with section 320 are contained in section 322: broadly, the transaction is voidable at the instance of the company. The company is entitled to be compensated for any loss it has suffered as a result of the unapproved transaction and to account for any gain.

7.9.6. *Transactions before company formed*

A person who purports to act on behalf of a company or as agent for it at a time when the company has not been formed will be personally liable on the contract, Companies Act 1985, s.36C(1). This provision can result in the solicitor acting on a sale or purchase for a company in the process of incorporation becoming personally liable for the contract and being entitled to enforce the contract.[5]

1. Companies Act 1989, s.108.
2. Bodies Corporate (Joint Tenancy) Act 1899, s.1.
3. See Land Registration Rules 2003, rr.181 and 183.
4. See para. E.7 as to execution by foreign companies.
5. *Brayhurst Limited* v. *Wise Finance Co. Ltd* [2002] EWCA Civ 127, [2002] 2 All ER 333 CA.

7.10. **Minors**

7.10.1. A person aged under 18 years cannot hold a legal estate in land but may hold an equitable interest. If, however, there is no restriction on the register of the title, the buyer is entitled to assume that the seller has full capacity. A conveyance to a minor alone takes effect as an agreement to create a trust of land and in the meantime to hold the land on trust for him. A contract for sale to a minor is binding on him unless repudiated by him during minority or within a reasonable time after attaining majority.[1]

1. See Minors' Contracts Act 1987.

7.11. Persons suffering from mental disability

7.11.1. A contract for the sale or purchase of land, entered into by a person who is suffering from mental incapacity sufficient to deprive him of understanding of the nature of the transaction, is voidable at the option of the incapacitated party, provided he can prove that at the time of the transaction the other contracting party was aware of the disability.[1]

7.11.2. Once a receiver is appointed under Mental Health Act 1983, s.99, the patient loses all contractual capacity and any purported *inter vivos* disposition by him is void. The receiver has power, subject to the court's approval, to deal with the patient's property.[2]

7.11.3. On the appointment of a receiver a restriction is not normally entered on registered land unless the receiver or other authorised person requests its entry and, on a dealing with registered land, the registrar will require a copy of the order which provides the receiver's authority to act. Where the receiver is registered as proprietor a restriction is automatically entered.[3]

7.11.4. See also para. D2.8.6.

1. *Broughton* v. *Snook* [1938] Ch 505.
2. See Mental Health Act 1983, ss.95 and 96.
3. Land Registration Act 2002, s.42(1)(a).

7.12. Universities and colleges

7.12.1. Universities and Colleges Estates Act 1925 confers powers to sell and exchange land and to purchase land as an investment on the universities of Oxford, Cambridge and Durham (and their respective colleges) and on Winchester and Eton Colleges and restrictions are entered in registered land reflecting the limitations on their powers under the statutes governing them. Other universities and colleges may be educational charities and are subject to the rules on charities outlined above.

7.13. Local authorities

7.13.1. A local authority may acquire land, inside or outside its own area, for the purpose of any of its functions under any Public General Act or for the benefit, improvement or development of its area. Power to acquire land for the provision of accommodation is given by Housing Act 1985, s.17. Powers of compulsory purchase of land are conferred by many statutes.[1]

7.13.2. Ministerial consent is required for certain disposals of land by a local authority. In such a case, consent must be obtained before contracts are exchanged, or alternately the contract made conditional on such consent being forthcoming. A conveyance made without the requisite consent may be void. In certain cases a buyer is entitled to assume that the transaction is within the powers of the local authority and does not have to investigate whether or not ministerial approval has been given. Under Housing Act 1988, s.44 (which does not apply to right to buy sales and leases), any disposal of residential property by a local authority for which the consent of the Secretary of State for the Environment is required is void if made without consent unless:

(a) the disposal is in favour of an individual or two or more individuals; and

(b) the disposal comprises only a single house or flat.

7.13.3. The protection afforded by Local Government Act 1972, s.128 does not apply in respect of residential premises unless both these conditions are satisfied. Where the land is registered, a buyer is only concerned to see that the terms of any restriction are complied with.

1. Compulsory purchase is outside the scope of this book.

7.14. Parish and community councils

7.14.1. Land may be acquired by such a council (whether inside or outside its own area) for the purposes of any of its functions under Local Government Act 1972 or any other Public General Act.

7.14.2. Ministerial consent is required for disposals of land, but buyers from parish and community councils are protected against breach of the consent provisions.[1]

1. Local Government Act 1972, s.128.

7.15. Building societies, friendly societies, trade unions

7.15.1. A building society may acquire and hold land for the purpose of its business or for commercial purposes under Building Societies Act 1986, ss.16 and 17. It will also have power to sell land as a lender where it has lent money on mortgage and the lender's power of sale has become exercisable.[1]

7.15.2. Registered friendly societies and industrial and provident societies have power to buy, sell and hold land, subject to the rules of each individual society.

7.15.3. Property belonging to a trade union is usually vested in trustees on trust for the union. Powers of acquisition and disposition are subject to the rules of the union, the general law relating to trustees, and some special provisions contained in Trade Union and Labour Relations Act 1974, s.2.

1. See para. B7.7.

7.16. Fiduciary relationships

7.16.1. Where a fiduciary relationship exists between the parties to the transaction, there is a presumption of constructive fraud which is rebuttable on proof (by the dominant party to the relationship) that the transaction was at a fair price (an independent valuation is highly desirable), that all the circumstances of the transaction were known to the subordinate party, and that each party received, or was given a proper opportunity to take, independent legal advice. The transaction is prima facie voidable at the instance of the subordinate party.

7.16.2. A fiduciary relationship is deemed to exist in dealings between the following persons:

(a) solicitor and client;

(b) trustee and beneficiary;

(c) parent and child (where the influence of the parent over the child may be held to have endured beyond the child's majority);

(d) doctor and patient;

(e) religious advisor and disciple;

(f) teacher and pupil;

(g) fiancés (but not between husband and wife).

7.16.3. A fiduciary relationship may exist in circumstances other than those listed above, but is not presumed to exist, and the dominance of one party over the other would have to be proved before the court would apply the doctrine of constructive fraud.[1]

7.16.4. If a solicitor is asked to act in dealings between any of the parties listed above, in para. B7.16.2, or in any other situation where he feels that the relationship between the contracting parties may be classed as fiduciary, he should ensure that:

(a) an independent valuation of the property is obtained;

(b) all the facts pertaining to the transaction are known by and understood by both parties;

(c) the parties are separately represented.[2]

1. See, e.g. *Lloyds Bank* v. *Bundy* [1975] QB 326 (fiduciary relationship proved to have existed between bank manager and customer).
2. See Acting for both parties, para. A10.

7.17. Death and insolvency[1]

7.17.1. The death of one of the contracting parties between contract and completion does not affect the validity of the contract. The party's personal representatives step into the shoes of the deceased and are obliged to continue with the transaction.

7.17.2. Where one of the contracting parties has a bankruptcy order made against him between contract and completion, his capacity to contract is transferred to his trustee in bankruptcy who, subject to his power to disclaim the contract, will take over the rights and obligations of the bankrupt under the contract. Where the seller is bankrupt a disclaimer of the contract by the trustee can only be made if the trustee also disclaims the property.

1. See Death and insolvency, para. E6.

7.18. One-man companies

7.18.1. It is permitted for a company to have only one shareholder. That shareholder may also be a director of the company. If he is the only director a second person must be appointed to act as company secretary.

7.19. Administrative receiver

7.19.1. An administrative receiver must be a qualified insolvency practitioner and must accept his appointment to act by the business day following the receipt by him of his appointment.

7.19.2. When buying a property from an administrative receiver the validity of the receiver's appointment should be checked, including:

    (a) the validity of the floating charge under which the appointment was made;

    (b) that the charge covered the whole or substantially the whole of the company's property;

    (c) that the charge is not likely to be invalidated, e.g. for want of registration, or fraudulent preference;

    (d) that the receiver's appointment does not exceed any powers in the charge;

    (e) that the receiver has power to conduct the transaction in question;

    (f) in a case where two receivers have been appointed, whether they are able to act jointly and severally or jointly only.

7.19.3. A certified copy of the receiver's appointment should be obtained by the buyer since this document will have to be produced to the Land Registry on registration of the transfer.

7.19.4. As a matter of practice the receiver may decline to give any warranties or covenants and may seek to exclude his personal liability. A buyer may, where appropriate, prefer to take a transfer from the lender in exercise of his power of sale where the buyer will benefit from the limited covenants given by lenders and will also have the guarantee of overreaching subsequent incumbrances.

7.20. **Attorneys**

7.20.1. A power of attorney can be general (giving the attorney power to do anything that the donor can lawfully do) or specific (giving the attorney power to sell a specific property).

7.20.2. Where the seller is a beneficial owner he can delegate his power to sell land to an attorney by using a general power of attorney.[1]

7.20.3. Where the land is held by co-owners the land is held on a trust of land. A trustee with a beneficial interest in the land can appoint an attorney using a general power and can appoint his sole co-trustee to be his attorney. The attorney must make a statement that the donor is beneficially entitled either at the time of the disposition or within three months following the disposition.[2]

7.20.4. A trustee who is not beneficially entitled under the trust should use a general trustee power. He can appoint his sole co-trustee to be his attorney, however, the power will be limited to a maximum period of 12 months.[3]

7.20.5. If a sole co-trustee has been appointed to be an attorney using a general power or a general trustee power of attorney, he cannot give a good receipt for the purchase price, overreaching will not operate. In such a case the donor should appoint a third party to act as attorney.

7.20.6. The buyer must insist on seeing a certified copy of the power of attorney and he must carry out a bankruptcy search against the donor. Provided that the buyer is not aware of any event that would revoke the power, the buyer will get a good title.

7.20.7. When the person who bought from the attorney comes to sell the property, his buyer will want to ensure that the power had not been revoked prior to the sale by the attorney. He can conclusively presume that it was not revoked if the sale by the attorney took place within 12 months of the power being granted. If the sale took place more than 12 months after the date of the power then the current buyer must obtain a statutory declaration from his seller stating that the seller was not aware of any revocation of the power at the time of his purchase. This statutory declaration must be produced either before the sale to the buyer or within three months of that sale having taken place.

1. Powers of Attorney Act 1971, s.10.
2. Trustee Delegation Act 1999, s.1.
3. Trustee Delegation Act 1999, s.5.

B8. Agricultural land

See also: Capital gains tax, para. A15
VAT, para. A16
Milk quotas, para. B9
Pre-contract searches and enquiries, para. B10
Plans, para. B21
Planning, para. B24
Pre-completion searches, para. E2
Long-term residential tenancies, para. K6
Agricultural tenancies, para. K8

8.1. Introduction

8.1.1. The procedure when buying agricultural land will be similar to that employed when buying any piece of freehold or leasehold land (as appropriate). The following paragraphs merely draw attention to some matters to which particular attention needs to be paid because of the nature of agricultural land. For more detailed information reference should be made to a specialist text on the subject.

8.2. Plans

8.2.1. The boundaries of agricultural land need to be checked carefully so that both parties understand clearly and precisely the extent of the land to be sold or let. The seller and buyer and/or their respective surveyors should inspect the land and agree the boundaries which should be marked on a plan to be attached to the contract and, in due course, the form of lease or transfer. The plan should be of sufficiently large scale, e.g. 1:2500, and dimensions to clearly identify the land and its salient features. A large scale Ordnance Survey map may be used for this purpose. The route of any services and other easements which cross the land should be identified.

8.2.2. Where possible 'T' marks should be marked on the plan to indicate the future responsibility for maintenance of boundaries with specific reference in the wording of the lease or transfer to those responsibilities. Where no definite indications as to boundaries exist, reference may be made to the common law presumptions, e.g. where there is a hedge and ditch boundary, the boundary lies on the far side of the ditch from the hedge. At common law the *ad medium filum* rule applies to roads and rivers.

8.2.3. Rights of way and access to the property should be checked.

8.3. Pre-contract searches

8.3.1. The situation of the land may indicate that some of the less usual pre-contract searches should be undertaken, e.g. rivers, railways.[1] A commons registration search should always be undertaken. It will also be necessary for the buyer's solicitor to require the local authority to answer some of the questions on Part II of Enquiries of Local Authority Search Form. Particular attention should be paid to questions relating to public rights of way.

8.3.2. If only part of land which enjoys rights of common is being sold, an apportionment of those rights between the two parcels of land may be considered.

8.3.3. Specific enquiries should be raised with the seller about sites of special scientific interest or other environmental designations where the local search replies indicate that such a site is included in the land to be bought.

8.3.4. A search may be made with the owning authority where it is necessary to establish the routes of pipelines and cables passing under, through or over the property.

8.3.5. A corn rent and corn annuity search may be necessary where the land is in the vicinity of an ancient parish church.

8.3.6. Geological workings may necessitate searches, e.g. for coal, oil, sand and gravel.

8.3.7. *Enquiries of the seller*

In addition to the normal pre-contract enquiries, a form of agricultural tenancy enquiries may be required where the land to be bought includes tenanted property and some of the following additional enquiries may be relevant to the purchase:

    (a) planning enquiries concerning agricultural buildings and whether or not they fall within Agricultural General Development Order;

    (b) enquiries concerning listed buildings and scheduling under Ancient Monuments and Archaeological Areas Act 1979;

    (c) information should be sought on all grant or subsidy schemes relating to the property ascertaining whether the conditions applicable to them have been properly observed and ensuring no money will become repayable;

(d) enquiries concerning crop and other quotas which may benefit the property and whether they are transferable to the buyer;

(e) enquiries concerning boundaries and their maintenance;

(f) enquiries relating to services benefiting the property (especially water supplies);

(g) enquiries relating to sites of special scientific interest or other environmental designations whether or not these come to light in answer to a local search;

(h) enquiries relating to abstraction and discharge licences granted by the Environment Agency under Water Resources Act 1991, Environmental Protection Act 1990 or Environment Act 1995;

(i) enquiries as to the history of the occurrence of notifiable diseases on the property;

(j) specific enquiries relating to sporting rights;

(k) enquiries relating to the existence of standing timber felling licences and grant conditions.

Particular attention should be paid to matters arising in (c) and (d) above in view of imminent proposals by the European Commission to reform the subsidy payment system under the mid-term review.

1. See Pre-contract searches and enquiries, para. B10.

8.4. Planning

8.4.1. The authorised use of the land under the Town and Country Planning Act 1990 should be ascertained. This information may be revealed in answer to enquiries of the local authority where planning permissions have been granted or a certificate confirming lawful use has been obtained from the planning authorities. In the absence of these the seller should be asked to disclose detailed information on the use of the property. Any restrictions on the use of the property should be discussed by the buyer's solicitor with his client to ensure that they do not conflict with the client's requirements. The seller should only give a warranty in the contract relating to the authorised use of the property if he is sure that the information which he is warranting is correct.

8.4.2. In most cases a change of use to agricultural use needs no consent. In some cases the erection of agricultural buildings does not require consent.

8.5. Taxation consequences

8.5.1. If the transaction involves the sale of a business as a going concern, value added tax should not be paid where both the seller and the buyer are registered for VAT. The VAT rules for a going concern transaction are more rigorous where land is included. If the buyer is not registered but the seller is, the seller must charge VAT on the assets which are subject to VAT at the standard rate. This may include the agricultural land if the option to tax has effect in relation to it.[1] In other cases value added tax may be payable on the transaction, in which case an appropriate clause to this effect needs to be included in the contract.

1. Value Added Tax Act 1994, s.40 and VAT (Special Provisions) Order 1995 (S.I. 1995/1268).

8.5.2. This type of transaction will often raise taxation issues in relation to capital gains tax and/or corporation tax as well as inheritance tax. Both the seller and the buyer should ensure they take appropriate advice before the structure of the transaction is finalised.

8.6. Grants and subsidies

8.6.1. The buyer should enquire of the seller whether any grants or subsidies have been received or are payable in respect of the land. If any part of these grants or subsidies is repayable on sale of the land, the seller should be required to fulfil this obligation before completion.

8.7. Growing crops, livestock, machinery

8.7.1. The seller must agree with the buyer which items of livestock and/or plant and machinery are to be included in the sale. A valuation of these items is often required and the contract should contain an appropriate clause to cover the valuation issues. A schedule of items to be included in the sale should be annexed to the contract.

8.7.2. Similarly agreement must be reached between the parties relating to growing crops, i.e. whether the seller is to be entitled to return to the property after completion in order to harvest his crops, or whether the benefit of the growing crops will pass to the buyer. Where the buyer is to take over responsibility for livestock and/or growing crops he may require the seller to give a warranty in the contract that the seller will use his best (or reasonable) endeavours to maintain standards of good husbandry over the land until completion. The buyer may consider it prudent to employ a veterinary surgeon to inspect livestock and to certify their state of health. The seller may be required to produce current vaccination certificates for livestock (where appropriate) and livestock passports. It should be noted that a contract to fell and remove standing timber is a contract for the sale of an interest in land which is, by Law of Property (Miscellaneous Provisions) Act 1989, s.2, required to be in writing.

8.8. Water

8.8.1. If the land currently has a water abstraction licence under Water Resources Act 1991, enquiries should be raised to confirm that the benefit of the licence is assignable; a condition providing for the licence to be assigned to the buyer must then be included in the contract. The buyer must then notify the water authority of the change of ownership of the licence within 15 months of completion. Failure to do so results in the licence becoming void and there is no guarantee that a new licence would be granted. Forms supplied by the Environment Agency (in duplicate and accompanied by a plan of the land) may be used to notify the authority of the assignment. Assignment of a licence is only possible where the buyer takes over the whole of the land to which the licence applies. If the licence relates to only part of the land sold, no assignment is possible and the buyer will need to apply for apportionment of the existing licence with the seller's cooperation. The contract should contain an appropriate clause to deal with any proposed apportionment.

8.8.2. Where the water supply to the property is metered, the water authority must, in addition to being notified of the change of ownership, be asked to read the meter on the day of completion, in order that apportioned accounts can be sent to seller and buyer.

8.8.3. Some or all of the following enquiries may need to be raised in connection with the water supply to the property:

(a) does the property have a mains water supply?

(b) if there is a mains water supply, does the mains pipe (which is maintained by the water company) run through the property or immediately adjacent to the property in a public highway?

(c) if there is no direct access to the mains water pipe, how is the property connected to the mains, who owns and is liable for the private spur, and does the property have the benefit of private easements for the continued use of the pipe, its maintenance repair and replacement and the taking of water through it?

(d) where is the mains water meter?

(e) if the property has a private water supply its source should be identified and enquiries raised as to whether the source supplies this property exclusively;

(f) are special water uses required, e.g. for spray irrigation?

(g) if the property is supplied by a private water source from an adjoining property enquiries should be raised to ascertain the contractual rights and obligations of the parties.

8.9. Tenancies

8.9.1. In order to fulfil his duty of disclosure the seller must give the buyer full details of any tenancies or licences which affect the property. Such details having been supplied, the buyer is, by Standard Condition 3.2.2(a) and Standard Commercial Property Condition 3.3.2, deemed to enter the contract knowing and accepting the tenancy terms. By Standard Condition 3.2.2(e), it is the buyer's responsibility to check the effects of any security of tenure legislation affecting such tenancies. Some tenant farmers may have significant protection under Agricultural Holdings Act 1986 or some protection under Agricultural Tenancies Act 1995,[1] and farm workers living in tied accommodation may be protected by Rent (Agriculture) Act 1976 or Housing Act 1988.[2]

8.9.2. If the property is sold subject to existing tenancies the buyer should covenant with the seller to observe and perform those conditions which remain to be observed and performed by the landlord and to indemnify the seller against them.

1. See Agricultural tenancies, para. K8.
2. See Long-term residential tenancies, para. K6.

8.10. Wayleave agreements

8.10.1. Any wayleave agreements which affect the property (e.g. for pylons, pipelines, etc.) should be expressly assigned to the buyer with the consent of the appropriate authority. Wayleave payments need only be apportioned if they are of substance. Generally a plan of the property sold is sent to the utility board after completion and they will apportion the wayleave and issue refunds and demands as appropriate.

8.10.2. The utility companies generally offer a pre-contract search where the seller wishes to establish exactly what wayleaves exist over the property.

8.11. Quotas

8.11.1. Milk quota must be expressly transferred to the buyer. This topic is further considered in para. B9. The sale of milk quotas is a standard-rated supply of services for VAT purposes if it is done in the course of a business and the seller is VAT registered. If the quota is sold together with the land, Customs have indicated that they will treat it as a simple supply of the land.

8.11.2. Sugar beet contracts with British Sugar plc are not quotas[1]. They are standard form contracts agreed through the NFU under the industry's Inter Professional Agreement (IPA). They are personal to the grower and except in limited circumstances provided in the IPA or where special dispensation has been given by British Sugar plc, they cannot be assigned (in whole or in part) or charged or dealt with in any way. All changes are subject to the agreement of British Sugar without which the contract may be terminated. All queries or proposed changes should be referred to British Sugar plc, Oundle Road, Peterborough, PE2 9QU.

1. For address see App. XI.5.

8.12. Agricultural credits search

8.12.1. A fixed or floating charge made by a farmer in favour of a bank over agricultural stock or assets is void against anyone other than the farmer himself unless the charge is registered with the Land Registry within seven days of its execution.[1]

8.12.2. A person who is buying farming stock or assets or a mortgagee who is lending money on the security of such items should make an agricultural credits search at the Land Registry in order to check the existence and validity of subsisting charges. The search should be made by the buyer before contracts are exchanged in order to find out whether any charges affect the property; in such a case the seller must be required to provide evidence of their discharge at completion. A further search is advised, to be made just before completion, to ensure that no further charges have been registered since the date of the earlier search.

8.12.3. The search is made by submitting Form AC6 in duplicate to The Superintendent, Agricultural Credits Department, Plumer House, Tailyour Road, Crownhill, Plymouth PL6 5HY. No personal or telephone search facilities currently exist. Current search fees are listed in Appendix XII.1.

8.12.4. A certificate of search is conclusive but affords no priority period in favour of the searcher. Copies of the register entries can be obtained on application on Form AC5.

8.12.5. An agricultural credits search can only be made against a private individual. Where the seller is a company, the buyer should make a search at Companies House to establish whether any floating charges exist over the company's farming stock or assets.

1. Agricultural Credits Act 1928, s.9.

8.13. Company search

If buying or leasing land from a limited company or granting a mortgage to a limited company, a company search will normally be desirable. This search should be made before exchange of contracts and updated before completion, particularly where farming stock or assets form part of the sale (see para. E2.10).

8.14. Post-exchange matters

8.14.1. *Mortgages*

Appropriate releases should be obtained from the seller or the relevant chargee in relation to any mortgages which affect the property being sold.

8.14.2. Where a floating charge is discovered against a company seller, a certificate of non-crystallisation should be obtained from the lender.

8.14.3. Duplicate purchase deed

When a part only of agricultural land is sold or where the buyer is giving indemnities to the seller, it is advisable to have the purchase deed drawn up in duplicate, the duplicate being kept by the seller as evidence of, e.g. restrictive covenants imposed on the buyer. The duplicates will need to be submitted together for stamping after completion and the contract should make provision for this.

8.14.4. Completion statement

In addition to the normal requirements for a completion statement (see Preparing for completion, para. E4) the following may need to be considered on a dealing with agricultural land:

(a) VAT on vatable supplies, e.g. farming stock and assets, sporting or fishing rights and quota;

(b) apportionment of agricultural rents, cottage rents, wayleave payments, sporting or fishing rents;

(c) payment for fittings being purchased;

(d) payment for any seeds, cultivations or labour at valuation (plus VAT if applicable);

(e) allowance for any agreed retentions for holdover;

(f) where VAT is payable, a separate VAT invoice should be supplied with the completion statement on receipt of the VAT from the buyer.

8.15. Post-completion matters

8.15.1. On the sale of the whole or part of a freehold which is subject to an agricultural tenancy, written notice of the change of ownership should be served on the tenant including details of the rent apportionment.

8.15.2. Transfer forms for the transfer of milk quota must be registered with the Rural Payments Agency by 1 March where land is transferred by lease and 31 March where the land is transferred by other means.[1]

8.15.3. If the benefit of a grant is taken over with the granting authority's consent, registration of the new owner must be made in accordance with the granting authority's requirements.

8.15.4. Notice of transfer of a water abstraction licence must be given to the Environmental Agency within 15 months of the transfer.

1. See para. B9.

8.16. **Environmental aspects**

8.16.1. Any discharge which may pollute controlled waters will require a licence/consent from the Environment Agency under Water Resources Act 1991. Discharge from slurry tanks or yard washing may be sufficiently contaminated to require such a consent.[1]

8.16.2. Enquiries should be made as to whether the agricultural processes carried out on the property fall within the scope of the regulations made under Environmental Protection Act 1990 as amended or other statutes governing the environment.

8.16.3. Enquiries should be raised as to whether the property has been the subject of a past land use which has left residual contamination likely to interfere with the buyer's proposed use of the property or which may cause pollution.

1. See Control of Pollution (Silage, Slurry and Agricultural Fuel Oil) Regulations (S.I. 1991/324).

8.17. **Sporting and other rights**

8.17.1. Occasionally sporting rights are reserved by the seller. These may include game under Ground Game Acts, deer (not included in Ground Game Acts) and fishing rights for the seller and his licensees. The rights will include rights of access both to exercise the sporting rights and to retrieve fallen game, any damage caused being made good by the seller. The terms of the contract should be checked to see which, if any, of such rights are being reserved by the seller.

8.17.2. If it is likely that minerals are contained under the land being sold, consideration should be given to their reservation to the seller, including, where appropriate, rights to work and take away the minerals. A bare reservation of minerals does not allow either seller or buyer to work them. Alternatively, a restrictive covenant may be imposed on the buyer preventing him from working any minerals in the land. If this is done a buyer who wished in the future to work the minerals would have to seek a release of the covenant from the seller (or his successor in title), but no further transfer of the mineral rights would be needed.

8.17.3. Unless there is a specific reservation in the purchase deed, most incorporeal hereditaments (including a lordship of the manor) will pass with the land. Lordships and manorial rights are frequently reserved to the seller when land is sold since they are saleable commodities in themselves.

8.17.4. The reservation of sporting rights, minerals and incorporeal hereditaments all impact on the value of the interest being transferred or leased. The buyer should ensure that appropriate valuation advice is taken where the seller requires reservations of this kind.

B9. Milk quotas

See also: Agricultural land, para. B8
Agricultural tenancies, para. K8

9.1.   General principles

9.1.1.   Milk quotas were introduced in the UK on 2 April 1984 to regulate the quantity of milk and milk products being produced in the EU. Farms producing milk and other milk products were given an allocation (a quota) the amount of which was normally based on their production levels in 1983. A levy may be payable if a producer exceeds his quota. Quota attaches to the land and will thus pass to a buyer or tenant of the land.

9.2.   Buying land with quota attached

9.2.1.   *Pre-contract enquiries*

Additional pre-contract enquiries will be necessary to establish:

(a) the exact amount of quota attaching to the land;

(b) the composition of the quota (i.e. does it include direct sales, or SLOM quota);

(c) that the seller is the freehold owner of the whole holding to which the quota attaches;

(d) that the quota does not attach to any land outside the land agreed to be sold;

(e) that if the seller is not the freehold owner of the entire holding, all other persons with an interest in the holding, such as landlords or lenders, who will be affected by the disposal of the quota have signified their agreement to the disposal on Form MQ/1; or

(f) if an apportionment of the quota has been made within the previous six months and notified to the Rural Payments Agency by means of Form MQ/8.

9.2.2. If a third party, other than persons referred to in (e) above, has an interest in the land (e.g. lender or trustee) that person's consent to the transfer of the quota should be required on Form MQ/1.

9.2.3. The seller should be required to supply the buyer with his most recent computer print-out from the Rural Payments Agency (see Appendix XI.5)[1] which will show the allocation of quota and the registration of the quota in the seller's name. The seller will also need to produce his latest statement from his purchaser(s) of milk, showing deliveries to date, to assess the used/unused element of the quota to be sold.

9.2.4. To assist the buyer in dealing with future transfers of quota or claims for compensation from tenants the seller's records relating to livestock cropping in 1983 and details of the use of the land and buildings, tenant's improvements and rent paid in 1983 should be produced to the buyer and handed over to him on completion.

9.2.5. A seller who sells milk direct to the public must have a licence, a copy of which should be supplied to the buyer and arrangements made for the transfer of the licence to the buyer on completion. Farmhouse cheesemakers are classified as direct sellers if they use their own milk for cheese production within a single business entity. If a farmhouse cheesemaker buys milk directly from a producer or processes his own milk in a separate business entity, the cheesemaker must be approved by the Rural Payments Agency to act as a purchaser. The producer will need to ensure that the quota is registered with the farmhouse cheesemaker to cover deliveries.

9.2.6. *The contract*

The contract must contain a clause dealing with the transfer of the quota to the buyer (see paras. B1 and B11). Wording similar to that set out below will be appropriate for this purpose:

> 'The seller is the proprietor of wholesale/direct sales quota for … litres of milk per annum. On completion the seller shall hand over to the buyer an application form for the transfer of the said quota duly signed and completed so far as the seller is able together with a signed statement as required by the Rural Payments Agency and thereafter shall use his best endeavours to obtain the transfer of the said quota to the buyer by providing any further evidence as the Agency shall require.'

9.2.7. *The purchase deed*

The purchase deed must contain a clause assigning the benefit and burden of the specified amount of quota to the buyer.

9.2.8. *Completion*

On completion (in addition to normal completion requirements) the buyer must ensure that such of the following documents as are relevant to the transaction are handed over:

(a) completed Form MQ/1 (consent to transfer of quota);

(b) any documentation relevant to an apportionment of quota;

(c) the quota notification from the Rural Payments Agency;

(d) the seller's records for 1983;

(e) a direct seller's licence.

9.2.9. *Post-completion*

The buyer must give notice of change of occupation to the Rural Payments Agency on a quota transfer form (Form MQ/1).

If the change happens at the end of the quota year MQ/1 forms must be submitted by:

- 1 March if the transfer is a lease of land

- 31 March if the quota is by inheritance, gift or sale

- 31 March if the quota is being transferred back to a landlord or on to a new tenant on termination of a tenancy.

The buyer should also be advised to keep accurate records of his milk production, use of land, tenant's improvements, etc., for use in future transfers or disputes relating to a tenant's right to compensation.

9.3.   Sales of part of land

9.3.1.   Where a buyer buys part of the seller's land he will become entitled to a proportionate amount of the quota attaching to the holding. If the parties (including interested parties) cannot agree on the apportionment of the quota taking account of areas used for milk production within 28 days then the matter must be referred to arbitration.

9.3.2.   (a) Where apportionment is to be carried out by arbitration the transferor and transferee may, by arrangement and within 28 days of completion, appoint an arbitrator, and the transferee must give notice of such appointment to the Rural Payments Agency within 14 days of the appointment; or

(b) the transferor or transferee may, within 28 days of completion, make application to the President of the Royal Institution of Chartered Surveyors (RICS) for the appointment of an arbitrator. The party which makes the application must, within 14 days of making the application, notify the Rural Payments Agency of the application. The arbitrator will base his award on the areas used milk production during the last 5 year period in which production took place. A fee will be charged by the RICS; or

(c) where neither of the above have taken place during the 28 days of completion, the Rural Payments Agency may make application to the President of RICS for the appointment of an arbitrator.

9.3.3. The provisions in para. B9.2 will also be relevant to a sale of part of a holding. In particular the contract must contain a clause to deal with the transfer of the quota. Provisions similar to those set out below will be appropriate:

'(a) in addition to the property the seller shall transfer on completion … litres of wholesale/direct sales quota;

(b) on completion the seller shall hand over to the buyer's solicitors an application form for the transfer of the said quota duly signed and completed (so far as the seller is able) together with a signed statement the contents of which are in accordance with the provisions of the relevant regulations.[1] The documentation shall be submitted to the Rural Payments Agency forthwith;

(c) if the seller fails to hand over the requisite forms the buyer may rescind the contract and the seller shall repay the deposit money to the buyer;

(d) the seller shall supply the buyer and the Rural Payments Agency (or as appropriate) with all necessary evidence required to substantiate the amount of quota transferred with the property and shall use the seller's best endeavours to obtain a transfer of that share of the quota.'

1. The Dairy Produce Quotas (General Provisions) Regulations 2002 (S.I. 2002/458); The Dairy Produce Quotas Regulations 2002 (S.I. 2002/457); The Dairy Produce Quotas (Wales) Regulations 2002 (S.I. 2002/897).

9.4. Selling land with the benefit of quota

9.4.1. The seller should be prepared to supply the buyer with the information specified in para. A9.2.1 and, on completion, such of the documents listed in para. A9.2.8 as are relevant. The contract and purchase deed must contain a clause dealing with the transfer of the quota (see para. A9.2.6).

9.5. Tenancies[1]

9.5.1. Clauses to deal with the following matters should be considered for inclusion in any tenancy agreement which relates to land which has the benefit of quota:

(a) prohibition of alienation of the quota by the tenant;

(b) maintenance of milk production on the land to prevent loss of quota;

(c) the benefit of the quota on termination of the tenancy;

(d) tenant's rights to compensation for loss of quota at the end of the tenancy.

9.5.2. The quota will revert to the landlord on termination of the tenancy but the tenant may be entitled to compensation for the loss of the quota. Where the quota reverts to the landlord Form MQ/1 needs to be completed and sent to the Rural Payments Agency.

1. See para. K8.

9.6. Compensation payable to tenants for loss of quota

9.6.1. Agriculture Act 1986 provides for payment by the landlord to certain agricultural tenants on termination of a tenancy which is subject to the provisions of Agricultural Holdings Act 1986. Agricultural Tenancies Act 1995 applies to farm business tenancies entered into on or after 1 September 1995. The 1995 Act entitles a tenant to compensation at the end of a tenancy for physical improvements made to a holding and for intangible advantages which increase the value of the holding, provided they are left behind by a departing tenant and the landlord's written consent to the improvements has been obtained. Intangible advantages include milk quota obtained during the course of a tenancy. For tenancies covered by the 1995 Act the milk quota provisions in section 13 and Schedule 1 Agriculture Act 1986 do not apply.

9.6.2. *Eligible tenants*

To be eligible for compensation under Agriculture Act 1986 a tenant must:

(a) have the quota registered in his own name (not in the name of a company or partnership through which the tenant carries on business); and

(b) have been in occupation of the land as tenant on 2 April 1984; or

(c) have succeeded to a tenancy since 2 April 1984 under the succession provisions of Agricultural Holdings Act 1986, so long as the party from whom the tenant succeeded was himself in possession on 2 April 1984.

9.6.3. Assignors of tenancies assigned after 2 April 1984 are not eligible, but the assignee is, subject to satisfying the qualifications outlined above.

9.6.4. The statutory entitlement to compensation relates to only one transfer of occupation. There is no entitlement on subsequent transfers. It is therefore open to a landlord to determine the terms under which new tenants can enjoy the quota attached to the holding, i.e. whether they will be charged for quota at the beginning of the tenancy and whether or not they will be entitled to any payment at the end of the tenancy. If the land being vacated comprises only part of the tenant's holding there is an apportionment of the quota for compensation purposes.

9.6.5. *Calculation of payment*

Payment is calculated by taking:

(a) the value of the allocated quota in excess of the standard quota for the land (or if allocated quota is less than the standard quota a proportionate reduction is made); and

(b) the value of the tenant's fraction of the standard quota; and

(c) the value of the transferred quota (this will be the entire value where the tenant has borne the whole cost of the transfer and proportionately where the tenant has only borne part of the cost).

9.6.6. *Valuation of quota*

Value = value at the termination of the tenancy taking into account available evidence of the value of the quota including the value of the land with and without quota.

9.6.7. Standard quota is calculated by multiplying the relevant number of hectares by the prescribed quota per hectare.

9.6.8. Prescribed quota is defined by Milk Quota (Calculation of Standard Quota) (Amendment) Order 1992 (S.I. 1992/1225) as 7,140 litres per hectare. There is a lower figure for land in less favoured areas (areas eligible for hill livestock compensatory allowance) and different figures apply for different breeds.

9.6.9. The relevant number of hectares is the average number of hectares used during the relevant period (the period to which allocated quota was determined, normally 1983) for feeding of dairy cows kept on the land.

9.6.10. *Method of assessing quantum*

The quantum of compensation (called the 'tenant's fraction') is ascertained by comparing the annual rental value of the tenant's dairy improvements and fixed equipment with the rent paid for the land during the relevant period.

9.6.11. The formula used is $\dfrac{r}{r+R}$

where r = the annual rental value at the end of the relevant period of the tenant's dairy improvement and fixed equipment and R = the rent of the land.

9.6.12. Liability for compensation does not arise until the termination of the tenancy but either landlord or tenant may at any time prior to termination seek determination of the standard quota or the tenant's fraction by agreement or arbitration.

9.6.13. The procedure for claiming compensation is similar to that for claiming tenant right under Agricultural Holdings Act 1986.

9.7 Quota transfers without land

9.7.1. An application may be made to the Rural Payments Agency to transfer quota without land 'to improve the structure of milk production at the level of the holding'.[1] The transferor and transferee must explain on the application form MQ/2 (Application for approval to transfer quota without land) how the transfer is necessary to improve the structure of their businesses.

9.7.2. WARNING: Transferor and transferee must comply with the following restrictions, on transferring *any* quota to or from their holding after they have been involved in a transfer without land:

9.7.3. The seller

Sellers or 'transferors' must get permission from everyone with a legitimate interest in their holding before they apply to transfer quota without land. (A holding is all the land and production units operated by a quota holder.)

9.7.4   They must also declare that they have not:

(a) bought or leased in quota under the 'transfer without land' provisions during the quota year in which the application was made;

(b) bought or leased in quota under the 'transfer without land' provisions during the previous quota year.

9.7.5. The buyer

The buyer or 'transferors' must declare on the form MQ/2 that they are in milk production or intend to commence milk production on their holding within six months of the intended date of transfer. They must undertake to remain in milk production, or have commenced and remain in milk production, at the end of that six-month period. If the transferee is not in milk production at the end of the six-month period the quota may be confiscated.

9.7.6. Applying for approval

An application for approval is made:

(a) using form MQ/2 (*Application for approval to transfer quota without land*);

(b) at least 10 working days before the intended date of transfer.

9.7.7. Used and unused quota

The transferor and transferee must agree how much quota is used or unused. When calculating how much of the original wholesale quota is used it is necessary to take into account deliveries which have already been made with the butterfat adjustment, and without the butterfat adjustment. The higher figure must be used.

9.7.8.   If used quota is transferred with unused quota, the Rural Payments Agency will:

(a) permanently transfer the unused quota to the new owner (the transferee);

(b) recalculate their ongoing and permanent butterfat bases to take account of the newly-acquired unused quota for the current quota year;

(c) leave the used quota with the transferor for the remainder of the quota year in question. The used quota will be moved to the transferor as unused quota following the end of the quota year.

9.7.9.   The producer taking over the used quota cannot produce against it until the beginning of the next quota year. The quota will remain registered with the original purchaser or producer group until the end of the current quota year.

9.7.10. *Geographical restrictions on transfers*

Quota cannot be transferred to or from any of these groups of Scottish islands:

(a) the Orkneys;

(b) the Kintyre Peninsula south of Tarbert and the islands of Jura, Gigha, Arran, Bute, Great Cumbrae, Little Cumbrae.

9.7.11. These groups of islands form separate units of production and are known as 'ring-fenced areas'. A temporary transfer of quota is permitted where it increases quantities available to dairy enterprises within the ringfenced areas. Quota is freely transferable within each ringfenced area as long as the normal transfer requirements are met. Quota may be transferred to any other producer in the UK, provided that the general transfer requirements are met.

9.7.12. *Changes in butterfat base after a permanent transfer*

9.7.12.1. 'Permanent' butterfat base is the figure attached to permanent quota, after being adjusted for transfers, permanent conversions and special allocations. If the butterfat base of any wholesale quota transferred in is higher or lower than the transferor's ongoing or permanent butterfat base, the new ongoing or permanent butterfat base will be recalculated as the weighted average of the butterfat base of the quota transferred in and the transferee's existing quota and butterfat base. A quota holder who has leased in quota and then leases/permanently transfers quota out, will have their ongoing butterfat base reweighted after each quota movement.

9.7.13. *Confirmation of transfer*

The Rural Payments Agency will write to the transferor to confirm:

(a) that the transfer has been entered on the quota register;

(b) the changes to the transferor's quota and permanent and ongoing butterfat bases (where applicable);

(c) the details of the producers and purchaser(s) involved.

They will also notify the purchaser of the change in the amount of quota registered with them and the changes to the producer's permanent and ongoing butterfat bases. The Rural Payments Agency will also write to the transferee (and transferee's purchaser, where appropriate) to confirm the results of the transfer in.

9.7.14. *Temporary reallocation of quota*

Farmers affected by herd movement restrictions can apply for a temporary re-allocation of quota using Form MQ/16. For details see Form MQ/16A Explanatory Notes.

---

1. See Council Regulation (EEC) 3950/92, Art. 8, as amended, and Dairy Produce Quotas Regulations 1997, reg. 13(1) (S.I. 1997/73).

B10. Pre-contract searches and enquiries

See also: Seller's duty of disclosure, para. B5; Pre-completion searches, para. E2

10.1. Reason for making searches

10.1.1. Subject to the seller's duty of disclosure,[1] it is up to the buyer to make sure of his bargain. Thus the buyer needs to find out as much about the property as possible before he commits himself to a binding contract to purchase the property. At common law the seller is generally under no obligation to disclose physical defects in the property to the buyer; therefore if the seller does not reveal information about the physical aspects of the property the buyer must obtain such information from other sources, much of which can be obtained through making proper pre-contract searches and enquiries.[2] Failure to make these searches may give rise to liability in negligence to the buyer if as a result the buyer suffers loss.[3] However, the seller must not fraudulently conceal know defects or reply dishonestly to questions on pre-contract enquiries or information forms.

1. Discussed in para. B5. The common law duty of disclosure is often modified by contractual condition, e.g. Standard Condition 3.
2. See Standard Commercial Property Conditions of Sale (First Edition) 3.1.2 (d) on 'searches and enquiries which a prudent buyer would have made before entering into the contract'. Reproduced in Appendix VII.12.
3. *Cooper* v. *Stephenson* (1852) Cox M & H 627.

10.2. Who should make the searches and enquiries?

10.2.1. The onus of making searches rests with the buyer, but in some cases the seller may make all appropriate pre-contract searches and pass the results of these searches to the buyer as part of the pre-contract package. It will frequently assist the progress of the transaction if the seller chooses to instigate pre-contract searches on behalf of the buyer and thus gives the buyer a complete package of documentation at an early stage in the transaction, but he is not obliged to do so. The liability provisions on Form CON 29 (see Appendix VII.4) acknowledge a duty of care in negligence by the council to a buyer who relies on replies obtained from another party.

10.2.2. In any case where the seller does not make all the appropriate pre-contract searches, the buyer should do so. Since the risk of buying the property subject to undiscovered defects broadly rests with the buyer, it is up to the buyer to ensure that all necessary pre-contract searches have been made, whether by the buyer himself, or by the seller on the buyer's behalf.

10.3. When should searches be made?

10.3.1. Where the searches are being undertaken by the seller's solicitor, they should be put in hand in sufficient time to ensure that their results will be available to send to the buyer with the draft contract. Where it is anticipated that delay in receiving the search result will be experienced this may mean that it is necessary to submit a search application as soon as instructions for the sale of the property are received notwithstanding that a buyer has not at that time been found for the property. In other cases the search application need not be submitted until a buyer for the property has been found since, the more recent the date of the search result, the more benefit it will be to the buyer. If the buyer's solicitor is to make searches, he should put his searches in hand as soon as firm instructions to proceed are received from his client. In Protocol cases, the buyer's solicitor, on receipt of the pre-contract package from the seller's solicitor, should check which searches (if any) have been made by the seller, and immediately submit additional search forms if he considers that any additional searches need to be made to meet the requirements of the particular transaction. Search applications should always be submitted without delay since some authorities take a long time to reply to them. It is unwise for a buyer to exchange contracts before having analysed the results of his pre-contract searches; thus delay in submitting search applications may result in delay to the transaction itself.

10.4. Which searches should be made?

10.4.1. Details of the searches listed below are contained in para. B10.5.

10.4.2. *All transactions*

The following searches are regarded as 'usual' and should be undertaken in every transaction:

- search of the local land charges register;
- enquiries of the local authority and, if appropriate, additional enquiries;
- standard drainage and water enquiries of the water service company;
- pre-contract enquiries of the seller.

10.4.3. Registered land

Depending on the circumstances of the transaction the following searches may need to be undertaken in addition to obtaining official copy entries of the title:

- commons registration search;
- mining search;
- index map search if dealing with an unregistered interest in registered land;
- any of the less usual searches which may be applicable in the circumstances (see para. B10.6).

10.4.4. Unregistered land

In addition to the searches listed in the preceding two paragraphs, a Land Charges Department search against the name of the seller and prior estate owner whose names appear on the abstract or epitome of title should be undertaken.

10.4.5 Contaminated Land

The Law Society's Contaminated Land Warning Card (reproduced in Appendix IV.1) explains that 'solicitors should be aware that environmental liabilities may arise and consider what further enquiries and specialist assistance the client should be advised to obtain'. The Warning Card does not impose a professional requirement on solicitors to conduct searches, but advises them to 'exercise their professional judgement to determine the applicability of this advice to each matter in which they are involved'.

10.5. **Summary of usual searches**

10.5.1. Local land charges search

- **When to make:** in every transaction.
- **Form:** LLC1 in duplicate (LLC1 is a prescribed form provided for by Local Land Charges Rules 1977, Schedule 1, form C).
- **Search methods:**
  - National Land Information Service Channel (NLIS, see para. B10.17);
  - post/DX to local authority (see Appendix XI.2 for addresses);
  - personal search.
- **Plan:** needed if land cannot be clearly identified from postal address.
- **Fee:** yes. Contact the relevant local authority. Also available through your NLIS channel – VAT is payable on a personal search but not on one made by post.
- **Summary of information to be obtained from search:** the most impor-

tant are: some planning decisions, compulsory purchase orders, financial charges affecting the property, tree preservation orders.

- **Protection given by search:** none: search result only shows state of register at time when search is made but warning of impending land charges can sometimes be obtained by making an Enquiries of Local Authority search on Form CON 29 (see para. B10.5.2). A third party can take benefit of search made by someone else (e.g. a seller can make a search to pass the result to buyer or his lender). The Local Land Charges Act 1975, s.10 provides compensation in limited circumstances where there is an error on the search certificate, or where a matter is binding on the land but is not revealed by the search, because it was not registered at the time of the search. An entry is binding on the land whether or not it is revealed by the search.

- **Personal search facility:** there is a statutory right to make a personal search, but local authorities do not guarantee the accuracy of the result. It should only be undertaken where time does not permit an official search to be made.

- **Special points:** can be made personally or by agent, but the result is not guaranteed. Insurance may be available if exchange has to take place before result of search received.

10.5.2. *Standard and optional enquiries of local authority*

- **When to make:** standard enquiries in every transaction, optional enquiries where appropriate.

- **Form:** The enquiry form CON 29 is split into two forms and both should be submitted in duplicate:
  - CON 29 Part I Standard Enquiries of Local Authority (2002 edition).
  - CON 29 Part II Optional Enquiries of Local Authority (2002 edition).

- **Search methods:**
  - National Land Information Service Channel (NLIS, see para. B10.17);
  - post/DX to local authority (see Appendix XI.2 for addresses);
  - personal search.

  In view of local government boundary changes, care should be exercised to ensure that the search forms are sent to the correct local authority.

- **Plan:** always include a plan with search requests. Some local authorities have specific requirements in relation to the submission of forms and plans (e.g. Cornwall County and District Councils). Non-compliance with these procedures may result in delay in receiving the answers to enquiries.

- **Fee:** yes. Contact the relevant authority for details. Fees will differ between authorities and between standard and optional enquiries. VAT is payable on a personal search but not on one made by post.

- **Summary of information to be obtained:** relates only to the property being searched against. Matters which affect neighbouring properties are not disclosed in the search replies.

  – *from standard enquiries:* planning and building regulations; roads; land for public purposes; land for road works; drainage agreements and consents; road schemes; railway schemes; traffic schemes; outstanding notices; infringements of building regulations; notices, orders, directions and proceedings under planning acts; conservation areas; compulsory purchase; contaminated land; radon gas. See Appendix VII.4 for the full enquiries and Appendix V.2 for the guidance notes.

  – *from optional enquiries:* road proposals by private bodies; public paths and byways; advertisements; completion notices; parks and countryside; pipelines; houses in multiple occupation; noise abatement; urban development areas; enterprise zones; inner urban improvement areas; simplified planning zones; land maintenance notices; mineral consultation areas; hazardous substance consents; environmental and pollution notices; food safety notices; hedgerow notices.

- **Protection given by search:** the buyer is bound by matters even if not discovered by search. The authorities 'do not accept legal responsibility for an incorrect reply, except for negligence. Any liability for negligence will extend to the person who raised the enquiries and the person on whose behalf they were raised. It will also extend to any other person who has knowledge (personally or through an agent) of the replies before the time when he purchases, takes a tenancy of, or lends money on the security of the property or (if earlier) the time when he becomes contractually bound to do so' (extract from the notes to Form CON 29, see Appendix VII.4).

- **Personal search facility:** some authorities permit personal searches, but do not guarantee the accuracy of the result; it should only be undertaken where time does not permit an official search to be made. Even where facilities are granted for personal searches, these may not cover all the matters normally covered by Form CON 29 and may not be acceptable to the buyer's lender.

  There are limitations on personal searches and some lenders will not accept them. The accuracy of a personal search depends on the ability and diligence of the searcher. It is not guaranteed by the local authority. If a personal search is undertaken, clients should be told of this and advised of the limitations on personal searches and their possible implications.

- **Special points:** can be made personally or by agent, but the result is not guaranteed. Insurance is available if exchange has to take place before result of search received, but check lender's requirements. Where a local authority refuses to answer a question relating to whether or not a property abuts a public highway consideration should be given to undertaking a commons registration search (see para. B10.5.6) and to making an inspection of the property. See the full guidance notes reproduced at Appendix V.2.

- **Notes:** both the local search and enquiries of the local authority contain questions relating to planning matters. In most cases the local authority to whom the search application is submitted will also be the planning authority for the area who will therefore answer the planning enquiries on the standard forms. In a few cases, e.g. new town development corporations, the planning authority is separate from the local authority and planning enquiries have to be separately addressed to the planning authority. If in doubt, telephone the local authority prior to submitting the search application in order to check the position.

10.5.3. Standard drainage and water enquiries

- **When to make:** standard enquiries in every transaction, optional enquiries where appropriate.

- **Form:** CON 29DW (2002) Standard Drainage and Water Enquiries.

- **Search methods:**

  - National Land Information Service Channel (NLIS, see para. B10.17);

  - post/DX to relevant company(ies) (see Appendix XI.5 for addresses);

  - fax – 24 hour expedited search is available from all companies.

  Care should be exercised to ensure that the search forms are sent to the correct company. In some cases enquiries will need to be made of more than one company. The website www.drainageandwater.co.uk has a post-code search facility that will return the correct company for a property.

- **Plan:** insisted on by some water service companies, always needed if land cannot be clearly identified from postal address.

- **Fee:** yes, contact the appropriate regional water service company for details or visit www.drainageandwater.co.uk. All regional water service companies answer standard drainage and water enquiries (and for a higher fee, answer an expedited standard search made by fax). Also, at the time of going to press, both Severn Trent and Thames Water offer a 'commercial search' at a higher fee. Solicitors should be aware that the Law Society has only been involved in approving the form and content of the standard drainage and water search. Some areas, such as those served by Dee Valley Plc water supply, may be subject to further administrative charges – always check with the appropriate water service company before sending fees.

- **Summary of information to be obtained from search:** location of public sewers within boundaries of the property or its vicinity; whether foul water and surface drainage from property drain to a public sewer; whether any sewers or proposed sewers are adopted; location of public water mains and whether the property is connected; the basis of charging for sewerage and water supply to the property (see Appendix VII.5 for full enquiries and Appendix V.3 for the full guidance notes).

- **Protection given by search:** The standard drainage and water enquiries were aimed primarily at residential property but were not intended to exclude commercial properties, however when first launched the liability was limited to £5,000. Following representations from the profession and discussion between the Law Society and the regional water service companies, an interim measure was agreed in September 2002 – an increase in professional indemnity cover maintained by each water company to £2 million for commercial property transactions. However, at the time of going to press the level of cover provided by Southern Water, United Water, Wessex Water and Welsh Water remains limited to £5,000. Standard searches made with the other companies (Anglian, Northumbrian, Severn, South West, Thames and Yorkshire) on commercial land/property using form CON 29 DW Standard Drainage and Water Enquiries will benefit from the increased professional indemnity cover of £2 million. Practitioners should enquire as to the extent of professional indemnity cover for the 'commercial search' offered by Severn Trent and Thames Water before making one of these searches. This information is correct at the time of going to press, practitioners are advised to check the level of liability cover with individual water service companies before making a search.

- **Personal search facility:** none.

- **Special points:** protection extends to the person, company or body who is the recipient of the report with an actual or potential interest in the property. The property may be located where two different water companies separately provide water and sewerage services. Check carefully for this before submitting the search form to avoid unnecessary delays.

10.5.4   *Pre-contract enquiries of seller*

- **When to make:** in every transaction.

- **Form:**

  - Seller's Property Information Form (3rd edition) (SPIF) for domestic freehold properties and leasehold properties;

  - Seller's Leasehold Information Form (2nd edition) (SLIF) for domestic leasehold properties;

  - Commercial Property Standard Enquiries (CPSE) (available from the Practical Law Company's website, www.practicallaw.com; also see Appendix VIII.5 for further information);

  - Other forms from legal stationers are also available.

  In domestic leasehold cases, both the SPIF and the SLIF must be submitted; the information on these two forms does not overlap and answers to both sets of enquiries will be needed by the buyer.

- **Search methods:** send to seller's solicitor.

- **Plan:** no.

- **Fee:** no.

- **Summary of information to be obtained from:**

  - *Seller's Property Information Form:* ownership of boundaries; disputes about the property; occupiers' interests; planning requirements; guarantees affecting the property; approximate completion date; fixtures and fittings; details of notices received by the seller which affect the property.

  - *Seller's Leasehold Information Form:* management company information; landlord's details; maintenance charges; notices; consents; complaints; building insurance; decoration; alterations; occupation; enfranchisement; fire certificates; differences to letting arrangements of other units in the building; problems with maintenance charges; whether the property is part of a conversion; planning permission or established use certificates.

  - *Commercial Property Standard Enquiries (general – for all transactions):* boundaries and extent; party walls; rights benefiting the property; adverse rights affecting the property; title policies; access to neighbouring land; access to and from the property; physical condition; contents; utilities and services; fire certificates and means of escape; planning and building regulations; statutory agreements and infrastructure; statutory and other requirements; environmental; occupiers and employees; insurance; rates and other outgoings; capital allowances; value added tax; transfer of a business as a going concern; other VAT treatment; standard-rated supplies; exempt supplies; zero-rated supplies; transactions outside the scope of VAT; notices; disputes.

- **Protection given by search:** none. Seller may be liable in misrepresentation for inaccurate replies.

- **Personal search facility:** none.

- **Special points:** Solicitors are required to check Part 2 of the Solicitors Property Information Form and the Solicitors Leasehold Information Form. Enquiries additional to those on the prescribed forms should only be raised where relevant and necessary to the particular transaction. Do not raise additional enquiries about matters that can be resolved by a survey or personal inspection of the property. Seller's replies should be factual and accurate and not based on statements of opinion. The seller's solicitor must take his client's instructions before answering the enquiries.

  Seller may supply replies as part of pre-contract package, in which case it is unnecessary for buyer to send form to seller. In other cases buyer should send forms to seller as soon as possible at the start of the transaction, and seller should reply as quickly as possible.

  In commercial property cases where CPSEs are used it is standard practice for the solicitor to submit the request form to the seller's solicitors (usually via email) while the CPSEs referred to in the request are available to all parties on the Practical Law Company's website (www.practicallaw.com). The CPSEs are due to be updated in Autumn 2003.

10.5.5. *Official copy entries of the title*

- **When to make:** in every registered land transaction.
- **Form:**
  - OC1 Application for Official Copies of Register/Title Plan and/or certificate in Form C1.
  - OC2 Application for Official Copies of Documents Only.
- **Search methods:**
  - National Land Information Service Channel (NLIS, see para. B10.17);
  - Land Registry Direct (www.landregistrydirect.gov.uk);
  - post/DX to the Land Registry (see Appendix XI.1 for addresses);
  - telephone – application can be made by a credit account holder between 8.30am–6.30pm Monday to Friday and 8.30am–1.00pm Saturdays and on the national number 0845 308 4545 or 0845 307 4535 for the telephone centre for Wales (specialising in Welsh place names and offering a Welsh speaking service). This number deals with all telephone applications irrespective of where the land is situated.
- **Plan:** no.
- **Fee:** yes, see the Land Registration Fee Order 2003 (see Appendix XII.6).
- **Summary of information to be obtained from search:** up-to-date copy of entries affecting seller's title.
- **Protection given by search:** none.
- **Personal search facility:** none.
- **Special points:** application usually made by seller who supplies results to buyer.

10.5.6. *Commons registration search*

- **When to make:** in any case where the property to be purchased abuts a village green or common land, where property is to be built on previously undeveloped land, where a verge strip, not owned by the property, separates the property from the public highway.
- **Form:** CR1 in duplicate.
- **Search methods:**
  - National Land Information Service Channel (NLIS, see para. B10.17);
  - post/DX/fax to local authority (see Appendix XI.2 for addresses).
- **Plan:** a large-scale plan needed.

- **Fee:** £6

- **Summary of information to be obtained from search:** whether any land is registered under Commons Registration Act 1965.

- **Protection given by search:** none.

- **Personal search facility:** none.

- **Special points:** where land has been registered under the 1965 Act it is difficult to remove that land from the register and not possible to obtain planning permission for development over the land. Third parties may have rights over the land which is registered, e.g. rights to graze cattle. Registers relating to land in East Sussex were destroyed by fire in 1994. Reconstituted registers have been validated under Commons Registration (East Sussex) Act 1994.

10.5.7. Coal mining search

- **When to make:** in any case where the property is situated in an 'Affected Area' in which coal mining takes place or has done so in the past. To determine whether a coal mining search is required, conveyancers should consult *Coal Mining Searches: Directory and Guidance*, 5th edition (Law Society Publishing, 2003). Conveyancers may also check online using a post code search service operated freely by the Coal Authority at www.coalminingreports.co.uk.

- **Form:** CON 29M (2003) Coal Mining Search.

- **Search methods:**

  - National Land Information Service Channel (NLIS, see para. B10.17);

  - the Coal Authority's Mining Report Online Service (www. coalminingreports.co.uk);

  - fax – expedited 48 hour service;

  - post/DX to the Coal Authority (see Appendix XI.5 for address).

- **Plan:** yes.

- **Fee:** subject to change and different for the Residential Property Search and the Non-Residential or Development Site Search. Current fees information is available from the Coal Authority by telephone, 0845 762 6848 and at www.coalminingreports.co.uk, or from your NLIS channel.

- **Summary of information to be obtained from search:** whether the property is in an area where coal mining has or is likely to take place; the existence of underground coal workings and mine entries which may cause problems with subsidence; whether compensation for subsidence has been paid in the past or repairs carried out or any claim is current.

- **Protection given by search:** Any liability of the Coal Authority for negligence in giving mining reports shall be for the benefit of not only enquirers but also a person (being a purchaser for the purpose of s.10(3) of the Local Land Charges Act 1975) who or whose agent had knowledge before the relevant time (as defined in that section) of the contents of the mining report. Such extension of liability to another (who did not purchase the mining report from the Authority) is limited to a purchaser, lessee or mortgagee of the property and not others (e.g. other recipients of reports on title, etc.). Full Terms and Conditions and guidance on liability can be found in *Coal Mining Searches: Directory and Guidance* and on the Coal Authority's website (www.coalminingreports.co.uk).

- **Personal search facility:** none.

- **Special points:** disused mines exist in many areas where coal mining has not been carried on within living memory. The dangers of subsidence exist in any area where mining has at some time taken place. Provisions for compensation for subsidence are complex: in some cases, once a sum has been paid in compensation, no further claim can be sustained despite further subsidence damage to the land.

10.5.8. *Land Charges Department search*

- **When to make:** in all cases when dealing with unregistered land. Strictly not relevant to land registered with an absolute title but sensible for seller's solicitor to make search against his own client's name to ensure no bankruptcy proceedings pending.

- **Form:**
  - Form K15 Application for an Official Search: not applicable to registered land.
  - Form K16 Application for an Official Search (bankruptcy only).

- **Search methods:**
  - National Land Information Service Channel (NLIS, see para. B10.17);
  - Land Registry Direct (www.landregistrydirect.gov.uk);
  - post/DX to Land Charges Department, Plymouth (see Appendix XI.5 for address);
  - personal search at Plymouth address only (see Appendix XI.5 for address).

- **Plan:** none.

- **Fee:** £1 per name for written applications, £2 per name for telephone, fax and computer searches.

- **Summary of information to be obtained from search:** this is the quickest method of checking that no bankruptcy proceedings are registered against a client (although it must be borne in mind that bankruptcy entries are normally cancelled automatically after five years). In addition, in unregistered land, information relating to incumbrances over the land, e.g. post-1925 restrictive covenants, second and subsequent mortgages, estate contracts, and matrimonial home rights.

- **Protection given by search:** full search: 15 working days from date of official search certificate provided completion takes place within this period. Where an entry is revealed which appears to be irrelevant to the transaction in hand, the seller's solicitor may be asked to certify that the entry does not apply to the transaction (by endorsing the search certificate to this effect). Such endorsement does not alter the legal significance of the search result, but an unqualified endorsement by the seller's solicitor would commit him to personal liability if loss were subsequently suffered by the buyer resulting from that particular entry.

- **Personal search facility:** at Land Charges Department, Plymouth only, but no protection given by personal search.

- **Special points:** the effect of Law of Property Act 1969, s.24 (by displacing the 'registration is notice' rule contained in Law of Property Act 1925, s.198) is to place the burden of disclosure of incumbrances on the seller and thus renders this search strictly unnecessary at the pre-contract stage of the transaction. Since the search needs to be made against all estate owners of the land whose names are revealed in the evidence of title, it is only possible for a buyer to make proper searches if title is deduced to him before exchange. These points notwithstanding it is advisable for the buyer to make a search at least against the seller's name at this stage in order to ensure that no bankruptcy or other financial charges are pending against the seller and that no Class F charge protecting the seller's spouse's matrimonial home rights have been registered at that time. Additionally, if the documentation supplied by the seller reveals the existence of restrictive covenants which if valid would impede the buyer's proposed use of the land, a check may be made against the name of the person on whom the burden of the covenants was imposed to check whether the covenants were registered as Class D(ii) land charges (if not the covenants are not enforceable against a subsequent purchaser if entered into after 1925). To take advantage of the protection period afforded by the search it will usually need to be repeated shortly before completion. In registered land, bankruptcy entries or a notice protecting a spouse's matrimonial home rights will be entered on the register and so revealed by official copy entries of the title so long as those copies are up to date.

10.5.9. *Index map search*

- **When to make:** in all cases when buying an interest in unregistered land. It is also useful when buying an area of land comprised in more than one registered title.

- **Form:** SIM Application for an Official Search of the Index Map.

- **Search methods:**

  - National Land Information Service Channel (NLIS, see para. B10.17);

  - Land Registry Direct (www.landregistrydirect.gov.uk);

–   post/DX/fax/telephone to the Land Registry (see Appendix XI.2 for addresses).

● **Plan:** a large-scale plan needed.

● **Fee:** See the Land Registration Fee Order 2003 (see Appendix XII.6).

● **Summary of information to be obtained from search:** whether the land is already registered or is subject to a pending application or caution against first registration or existence of a registered rentcharge.

● **Protection given by search:** none, although if search result is inaccurate, a right to indemnity may arise (see para. M7).

● **Personal search facility:** not available.

● **Special points:** if it is discovered that the land is already registered or that a compulsory registration order came into force before the date of the most recent conveyance on sale on the title the seller must be asked to rectify the situation before this transaction proceeds.

10.5.10. *Disadvantaged Areas Search (Relief from Stamp Duty)*

● **When to make:** When acting for the buyer or seller, a search should be made to determine whether a property is located within a designated disadvantaged area. This will be necessary in every:

–   purchase or lease of non-residential property

–   purchase of residential property where the purchase price does not exceed £150,000

–   lease of residential property with an average rent of £15,000 pa.

From 10 April 2003, the disadvantaged areas relief was extended so that no stamp duty is payable on:

–   purchases or leases of *non-residential* property in a designated disadvantaged area;

–   *residential* purchases in designated disadvantaged areas where the purchase price does not exceed £150,000; and

–   *the grant of leases* where the average rent does not exceed £15,000 pa and/or where any premium does not exceed £150,000.

The Inland Revenue Statement of Practice SP 01/03, which is reproduced in Appendix IX.3, defines residential, commercial, and mixed-use property. In mixed use property (part residential and part non-residential) the value has be apportioned and the £150,000 limit applied to the residential part.

The scope of the exemption is such that it applies to property which on 7 May 1998 was situated in specified qualifying wards included in the current indices of deprivation for England and Wales (which are the Indices of Deprivation 2000).

The exemption will apply to a property falling outside a qualifying ward if on 27 November 2001 it had the same postcode as land which on the 7 May 1998 was within a qualifying ward.

Where a property is partly inside a qualifying ward, the purchase price must be apportioned and the part outside will be subject to stamp duty.

This complicated definition can give rise to a number of problems, not least that searches currently available too establish whether property falls within a qualifying ward for the purposes of disadvantaged areas stamp duty exemption are not always conclusive.

- **Form:** not applicable
- **Search method for properties with a postcode:**
  - Check the postcode lies in a disadvantaged area by using the postcode search on the Inland Revenue's web site (www.inlandrevenue.gov.uk/so/pcode_search.htm)
  - Check which ward the property was located in on 7 May 1998 by visiting www.neighbourhood.statistics.gov.uk and searching against the property's postcode
  - Check the ward is listed on the Inland Revenue's web site (www. inlandrevenue.gov.uk/so/disadvantaged.htm).

If the results of these three checks are positive, then the property is exempt.

If the postcode search is positive but the ward search shows part or all of the property is outside the relevant ward, the property will still be exempt if the property on 27 November 2001 has the same postcode as land which on 7 May 1998 fell within a qualifying ward.

Warning: The Inland Revenue postcode search is not up-to-date, and is therefore inconclusive. If the postcode search shows that the property is outside a designated area or no postcode is found it may be prudent to follow the steps for properties without postcodes below.

- **Search method for properties without a postcode**
  - Check with the local authority to find out which ward the property was located in on 7 May 1998 (see Appendix XI.2 for contact details). Maps showing wards as at 1998 can be viewed as pdf files on www.neighbourhood.statistics.gov.uk.
  - Check whether the ward is listed on the Inland Revenue website (www.inlandrevenue.gov.uk/so/disadvantaged.htm).
  - Obtain a copy of the 7 May 1998 boundary ward map from the Ordnance Survey Boundaries Service (Tel. 023 8030 5092) and check that the property is within the boundaries shown. The Neighbourhood Statistics website also holds pdf files of the 1998 ward boundary maps.

If the results of these checks above show the property within the ward, it is exempt. Any part outside the ward is subject to stamp duty.

- **Alternative search method**

  The procedures to ascertain whether a property qualifies for the relief can be time-consuming and not always conclusive. An alternative may be to submit a good plan of the property together with the relevant transaction document to the appropriate Stamp Office and seek its written advice. However, you are only able to obtain a binding opinion of the stamp duty due on the document if you send the actual signed document and inform the Inland Revenue of everything they need to know about the transaction (Stamp Act 1891, s.12). If the advice of the Inland Revenue is sought when the document is unsigned or in draft form, the Inland Revenue will assist you but any opinion they give will be an informal opinion and will not bind them to assess the document in the same way when it has been signed/completed. Telephone enquiries made on the Stamp Taxes Helpline on 0845 603 0135 may also be of general assistance.

- **Plan:** a copy of the 7 May 1998 ward map clearly showing the property within a ward boundary.

- **Fee:** none.

- **Summary of information to be obtained from search:** an indication of whether the property falls within one of the designated areas that qualify for relief.

- **Protection give by search:** none.

- **Personal search facility:** not applicable. Queries may be directed to the Stamp Taxes Helpline on tel. 0845 603 0135.

- **Special points:** a contract providing for the transfer of six or more properties is classed as commercial (see Inland Revenue SP 01/03 at Appendix IX.3). Schedule 30 to Finance Act 2001, together with the Regulations, determines how property situated partly within and partly outside a designated disadvantaged area is to be treated for the purposes of the relief (queries may be referred to Inland Revenue Stamp Taxes Office). The extended relief (lifting of the upper limit from £150,000 on commercial and mixed use properties) applies to documents executed on or after 10 April 2003, irrespective of whether the contract was entered into before or after that date. There is no scope to reclaim stamp duty already paid in respect of transfers executed on or before 9 April 2003. The European Commission granted approval for the Disadvantaged Areas Relief on 21 January 2003, its approval is limited in time until 31 December 2006.

- **Notes:** For further information, see:

  - the Inland Revenue Customer Newsletter: Disadvantaged Areas Stamp Duty Exemption (December 2001);

  - the Inland Revenue Statement of Practice SP01/03 on Disadvantaged Area Relief (reproduced in Appendix IX.3);

  - the Stamp Duty (Disadvantaged Areas) Regulations 2001 (S.I. 2001/3474);

- **Summary Checklist (from IR Customer Newsletter):** All instruments in respect of which relief is claimed must be formally adjudicated. To prevent delay in processing claims it will greatly assist if all the following information is supplied at the time the instrument is presented for stamping:

  - The document contains a certificate confirming it is within the provisions of Section 92 Finance Act 2001.

  - The full postcode for the property being transferred is supplied.

  - The relevant PD form is enclosed, if appropriate.

  - A full photocopy of the transfer document is provided.

  - A copy of the contract or sale agreement is provided

  - The document contains a £250,000 certificate of value.

  - If the document is a lease, a payment in respect of the rent element is enclosed.

Appropriate evidence to support the application for exemption should be submitted with the application, e.g. a copy of the ward map with the location of the property clearly marked.

10.6. Less usual searches

10.6.1. The buyer's solicitor must in all cases be alert to the need to make additional searches since his client will normally be bound by any matters which those searches would have revealed if made. If a less usual search is not made, in circumstances where it would have been relevant, and as a result of this omission the client suffers loss, the buyer's solicitor will be liable in negligence[1]. In some cases the seller's solicitor may make the appropriate searches and supply the results to the buyer's solicitor, but it remains the buyer's solicitor's duty to ensure that all the correct searches have been undertaken and that their results are satisfactory. A summary of some of the less usual pre-contract searches appears below.

10.6.2. *Underground railways*

- **When to make:** land adjoins railway, railway passes through land, property built close to underground railway network.

- **Form:** letter.

- **Search methods:**

  - National Land Information Service Channel (NLIS, see para. B10.17);

  - post to appropriate underground authority (see Appendix XI.5 for addresses).

- **Plan:** yes.

- **Fee:** yes.

- **Summary of information to be obtained from search:** ownership of track, routes of underground tunnels.

- **Protection given by search:** none.

- **Personal search facility:** not available.

- **Special points:** although a search may be requested electronically through an NLIS channel the response will arrive by post/DX.

10.6.3. Overground railways

There is no statutory basis for response to property enquiries by the railway industry in Great Britain. The main infrastructure controller is Network Rail (formerly Railtrack plc) and a variety of train operators use the track, occupy stations and other railway land. None of these bodies has a system to respond to search letters. Enquiries may be made of Network Rail requesting information as to any existing rights or obligations regarding boundaries or access, on rights of reverter or pre-emption to Network Rail. However, Network Rail may not respond to such enquiries. This search is only required for land bordering a railway or land with a railway through or under it, whether used or disused. Enquiry 3.5 'Nearby Railway Schemes', on Form CON 29 (Part 1) Standard Enquiries of Local Authority 2002, will give details of railways within 200m of the proposed property.

10.6.4. Waterways

- **When to make:** where a river, stream or canal passes through or adjoins the property.

- **Form:** letter.

- **Search methods:**

  - National Land Information Service Channel (NLIS, see para. B10.17);

  - for rivers, streams or brooks post to the Environment Agency (see Appendix XI.5 for address);

  - for canals post to the British Waterways Board (see Appendix XI.5 for address).

- **Plan:** yes.

- **Fee:** yes.

- **Summary of information to be obtained from searches:** ownership of river banks and canals; liability for repairs of and maintenance of river banks and canals; fishing rights; licences to abstract water; drainage rights; liability for flooding from rivers; rights of way affecting towpaths along sides of canals.

- **Protection given by searches:** none.

- **Personal search facility:** none.

- **Special points:** The local authority may be responsible for smaller waterways within its own area. Although a search may be requested electronically through an NLIS channel, the response will arrive by post/DX.

10.6.5. *Tin mining*

- **When to make:** mainly applicable to land to be purchased in West Devon or Cornwall.
- **Form:** letter.
- **Search methods:**
  - National Land Information Service Channel (NLIS, see para. B10.17);
  - post to Cornwall Consultants (see Appendix XI.5 for address).
- **Plan:** yes.
- **Fee:** yes.
- **Summary of information to be obtained from search:** presence of disused underground workings which could cause subsidence damage.
- **Protection given by search:** none.
- **Personal search facility:** not available.
- **Special points:** although a search may be requested through an NLIS channel, the response will arrive by post/DX.

10.6.6. *Clay mining*

- **When to make:** mainly applicable to land to be purchased in Dorset, West Devon or Cornwall.
- **Form:** letter.
- **Search methods:**
  - National Land Information Service Channel (NLIS, see para. B10.17);
  - post to Kaolin and Ball Clay Association (see Appendix XI.5 for address).
- **Plan:** yes.
- **Fee:** yes.
- **Summary of information to be obtained from search:** presence of workings which could cause subsidence damage.
- **Protection given by search:** none.
- **Personal search facility:** not available.
- **Special points:** although a search may be requested through an NLIS channel, the response will arrive by post/DX.

10.6.7. *Brine*

- **When to make:** land to be purchased in Cheshire or Greater Manchester, Droitwich (Hereford & Worcester).

- **Form:** letter.

- **Search methods:**
    - National Land Information Service Channel (NLIS, see para. B10.17);
    - post to Cheshire Brine Subsidence Compensation Board (see Appendix XI.5 for address).

- **Plan:** yes.

- **Fee:** yes.

- **Summary of information to be obtained from search:** presence of disused brine extraction workings which could cause subsidence damage; an indication of whether there have been any claims for damage made by the owner or a previous owner against the Brine Board for past or suspected past damage; whether the Board has made a 'once-and-for-all' payment commuting the property from any further claim for compensation: such a commutation will usually result in the value of the property being reduced and making it difficult to mortgage. If the search result reveals that a claim for compensation has been lodged but not yet adjudicated the buyer must after completion give notice of the change of ownership to the Board.

- **Protection given by search:** none.

- **Personal search facility:** not available.

- **Special points:** although a search may be requested through an NLIS channel, the response will arrive by post/DX.

10.6.8. *Limestone*

- **When to make:** land to be purchased in Dudley, Sandwell, Walsall or Wolverhampton.

- **Form:** letter.

- **Search methods:**
    - National Land Information Service Channel (NLIS, see para. B10.17);
    - post to local, district or metropolitan council (see Appendix XI.2 for addresses).

- **Plan:** yes.

- **Fee:** yes.

- **Summary of information to be obtained from search:** presence of disused underground workings which could cause subsidence damage.

- **Protection given by search:** none.

- **Personal search facility:** not available.

- **Special points:** although a search may be requested through an NLIS channel, the response will arrive by post/DX.

10.6.9. Rent registers

- **When to make:** land to be purchased is subject to a Rent Act 1977 tenancy.

- **Form:** CON 29E Request for a search of the register kept pursuant to section 79 of the Rent Act 1977 (in duplicate).

- **Search methods:** post to the relevant Rent Assessment Panel (see Appendix XI.5).

- **Plan:** no.

- **Fee:** £1.

- **Summary of information to be obtained from search:** the form of enquiry is as follows: 'Are there any, and if so what, subsisting entries in the Register in respect of the above property or any part of it kept pursuant to Section 79 of the Rent Act 1977, as amended by Paragraph 43 of Schedule 25 to the Housing Act 1980'.

- **Protection given by search:** the replies are furnished in the belief that they are correct but on the distinct understanding that neither the President nor any member of his staff is legally responsible therefore, except in negligence.

- **Personal search facility:** not available.

- **Special points:** if a rent is registered, it is an offence for the landlord to charge more than the registered rent for the property. Rent charged in excess of the registered amount is recoverable by the tenant. Registration of a revised rent can normally only be made after two years have elapsed since the last registration. There are now five Rent Assessment Panels covering England, and one covering Wales. For details of their coverage, visit the web site of the Residential Property Tribunal Service (www.rpts.gov.uk). Form CON 29E was agreed between the Law Society of England and Wales and the Department of the Environment, it has not been updated since 1996.

10.6.10. Chancel repairs

- **When to make:** chancel repair liability can only affect land within a Church of England parish which has a vicar (not a rector) and has a church dating from the medieval period or earlier.

- **Form:** personal search.

- **Search methods:**
  - National Land Information Service Channel (NLIS, see para. B10.17);
  - visiting the Public Records Office, Kew (see Appendix XI.5 for address and telephone number).

- **Plan:** yes.

- **Fee:** no.

- **Summary of information to be obtained from search:** potential liability to contribute to cost of repairs to chancel of a church.

- **Protection given by search:** none.

- **Personal search facility:** available Monday to Saturday.

- **Special points:** it is not easy to define with certainty those properties which are affected by liability since the records held at the Public Records Office are incomplete. If it appears that liability may exist, a buyer should consider taking out insurance to cover this liability. A Court of Appeal decision from 2001 that chancel repair liability was unenforceable under the Human Rights Act 1998 was overturned by the House of Lords on 26 June 2003 in *Aston Cantlow and Wilmcote with Billesley Parochial Church Council v. Wallbank and another* [2003] UKHL 37. The High Court, Court of Appeal, and House of Lords decision in this case are covered in more detail at section AA. New Developments in Conveyancing Practice.

10.6.11. *Environmental Data Search*

- **When to make:** there is no professional obligation to undertake an environmental data search in the course of property transactions. Solicitors must, however, consider whether contamination is an issue in every transaction and advise clients of the potential liabilities associated with environmental issues, without overstating them. In all commercial transactions, and in residential cases where contamination is considered a potential issue, solicitors should consider making specific pre-contract enquiries of the seller, and other enquiries of statutory and regulatory bodies and if there is a possibility that the site is contaminated, or the buyer or lender requests one, an environmental data search should be made, see section B25 Environmental Issues and the *Environmental Law Handbook, 5th edition* (Law Society, 2002).

- **Form:** there is no standard form.

- **Search methods:**

  - National Land Information Service (NLIS, see para. B10.17)

  - Online with search providers: Ground Sure Ltd, Landmark Information Group Ltd, Sitescope (see Appendix XI.6)

  - Post to search providers (see Appendix XI.7)

  - Fax to search providers (see Appendix XI.7)

- **Plan:** it is essential to confirm the location of the land by reference to a plan (paper or online) or by National Grid reference.

- **Fee:** From £25–£200 (differs for residential or commercial).

- **Summary of information to be obtained from search:** (depending on provider) all information held by regulatory bodies, a detailed land use survey highlighting current and historic uses, floodplain data, risk assessment.

- **Protection given by search:** none.

- **Personal search facility:** none.

- **Special points:** the purpose of this search is to establish that there is no cause for concern regarding environmental issues or, if there is a concern, to inform further enquiries and advice to the client. For further guidance see section B25 Environmental Issues, the Law Society's Contaminated Land Warning Card at Appendix IV.1 and the *Environmental Law Handbook* (Law Society, 2002).

1. See *G. & K. Ladenbau (UK) Ltd* v. *Crawley & De Reya* [1978] 1 All ER 682.

10.7.   **Results of searches**

10.7.1.   On receiving the results of searches the buyer's solicitor must check the answers given to ensure that the information supplied complies with his client's instructions. Any reply which is unclear must be pursued with the appropriate authority (or seller in the case of pre-contract enquiries) until a satisfactory explanation is received. Failure to pursue an unsatisfactory reply which results in loss being suffered by the client may result in the buyer's solicitor being liable to his own client in negligence.[1] Any reply which is for any reason not satisfactory must be referred to the client for further instructions. Contracts should not be exchanged until satisfactory results of all searches have been received. A summary of the information received from the searches should be communicated to the buyer by his solicitor.

1. *Computastaff Ltd* v. *Ingledew Brown Bennison Garrett & Co.* (1983) 133 NLJ 598.

10.7.2.   When reporting back to the client it is essential that the client is made aware of the type of issues that cannot be identified from the local search and enquiries.

10.8.   **Checklist**

10.8.1.   *Making searches*

(a) Decide which searches need to be made and which method is most appropriate.

(b) Is a plan required, is it accurate, and is it on a sufficiently large scale to clearly identify the property and the surrounding area?

(c) What questions (in addition to those on the printed form) need to be asked?

(d) Correct application form and fee?

(e) Correct address for submission of the search?

(f) Diarise the file and chase up delayed responses.

10.8.2. Search replies

(a) Analyse the answer to each question – does it accord with what you would expect to find and with what the client wants?

  – If it does: place a tick in the margin against that question.

  – If it does not: place a cross in the margin by the question, pursue the question with the relevant authority until a satisfactory reply is received, then replace the cross with a tick, take the client's further instructions if the ultimate reply is not satisfactory.

(b) Where an answer contains information which should be communicated to the client or on which the client's further instructions are needed, place a 'C' in the margin beside that question and contact the client.

(c) Do not exchange contracts until all search replies have been received and all answers are marked with a tick.

10.9. Liability on searches

10.9.1. Local land charges

Where a person suffers loss as a result of an error in an official certificate of search, compensation may be payable under Local Land Charges Act 1975, s.10.

10.9.2. Pre-contract enquiries of the seller

An incorrect reply to pre-contract enquiries may lead to liability in misrepresentation. A reply expressed in terms such as 'the seller is not aware (etc.)' may import a warranty that the seller has made reasonable enquiries relating to the matter in question.[1] Any exclusion clause purporting to avoid or minimise liability for misrepresentation will be subject to the reasonableness test in Unfair Contract Terms Act 1977, s.11 and cannot therefore be guaranteed to afford protection to the seller.[2] Even a carefully worded reply to an enquiry, insisting upon caveat emptor, may not excuse the seller from a misrepresentation.[3] Where the erroneous reply stems from the seller's solicitor's negligence he will be liable to his own client,[4] he may also owe a duty of care to the buyer under *Hedley Byrne* v. *Heller* principles.[5] Knowledge acquired by the solicitor while acting on his client's behalf is imputed to the client (regardless of whether the client had actual knowledge of the matter in question); thus a seller may be liable in misrepresentation to the buyer for a statement made by his solicitor without his knowledge. In such a case indemnity against the seller's liability could be sought from the seller's solicitors.[6] Where the answers to the enquiries are to be completed by the seller personally (and not by his solicitor), e.g. the SPIF in Protocol cases, the seller's solicitor should advise his client to complete the form with care, since an inaccurate or misleading reply could lead to liability in misrepresentation[7]. The seller should also be advised of the need to notify the buyer if circumstances change, thus rendering inaccurate the original reply given to a question on the search form.

1. *William Sindall* v. *Cambridgeshire County Council* [1996] 3 All ER 932.
2. See Standard Condition 7.1. Some forms of pre-contract enquiries also contain an exclusion clause. See also *Walker* v. *Boyle* [1982] 1 All ER 634.
3. *Morris* v. *Jones* [2002] EWCA Civ 1790.
4. *Cemp Properties* v. *Dentsply* [1989] 35 EG 99.
5. *Hedley Byrne & Co. Ltd* v. *Heller and Partners Ltd* [1964] AC 465 and *Wilson* v. *Bloomfield* (1979) 123 SJ 860.
6. See *Strover* v. *Harrington* [1988] Ch 390.
7. See *McMeekin* v. *Long* (Portsmouth County Court, October 2002). Mr. Justice Astill ruled that the Longs should have answered yes to a question on SPIF asking whether there were any neighbourhood disputes.

10.10. Relying on searches made by a third party

10.10.1. In relation to enquiries of local authorities on Form CON 29 and those other enquiries whose terms and conditions include similar provisions as to liabilities, the results of searches are not personal to the searcher; thus their benefit may be transferred to a third party. Where the seller makes pre-contract searches and passes their results to the buyer, the buyer and his lender may in such cases take the benefit of the results. The buyer must check that the seller has undertaken all the searches and enquiries which the buyer deems necessary for the transaction in hand and, if not, he must effect the additional searches himself. If the buyer is not satisfied with the results of the searches made by the seller because, e.g. he considers that they are out of date, or that insufficient questions have been raised, he should repeat the search himself.

There are limitations on personal searches and some lenders will not accept them. The accuracy of a personal search depends on the ability and diligence of the searcher. It is not guaranteed by the local authority. If a personal search is undertaken, clients should be told of this and advised of the limitations on personal searches and their possible implications.

10.11. Inspection of the property

10.11.1. Inspection of the property should be undertaken by the client in all cases. There is no obligation on the solicitor, either in law or conduct, to carry out an inspection in every transaction, but he should do so if his client so requests or if matters reported by the client's inspection give rise to suspicion on the part of the buyer's solicitor. The client should be advised to look for (and to report their existence to his solicitor) any of the following matters:

(a) a discrepancy or uncertainty over the identity or boundaries of the property;

(b) evidence of easements which adversely affect the property;

(c) the existence and status of non-owning occupiers;

(d) discrepancy between the fixtures and fittings which the client understood to belong to the property and those actually existing.

10.11.2. It is useful for the client to take a plan of the property with him in order to check its accuracy. An appointment to inspect should be arranged with the seller. The client's surveyor may be able to obtain the necessary information whilst carrying out a survey, but must be instructed to do so.

10.11.3. A solicitor who carries out an inspection on behalf of his client may be liable in negligence if he fails to discover a matter which he ought reasonably to have discovered,[1] for example, the existence of a right of way crossing the property, but the solicitor should stress to the client that the inspection has been carried out by the solicitor in his role as solicitor, and that he does not profess to have the same knowledge about, for example, structural defects in the property as possessed by a surveyor.

1. *Barclay-White* v. *Guillame & Sons* [1996] EGCS 123.

10.12. Tithes

10.12.1. Tithes were abolished in 1936. The 60-year annuities which replaced them were themselves extinguished by Finance Act 1977. There is therefore no need to consider any search for tithes.

10.13. Company search

10.13.1. Where either the seller or buyer is a corporate body a company search prior to exchange should be undertaken in order to check that the company actually does exist. Company searches are discussed under Pre-completion searches, para. E2.

10.14. Assignment of guarantees

10.14.1. Where the answers to pre-contract enquiries reveal that the property has the benefit of a structural defects policy (for example, NHBC, Zurich, Premier Guarantee) or other guarantee (such as, for woodworm or damp treatment) the benefit of which will pass to the buyer on completion, consideration should be given to whether a formal assignment of the benefit of the policy or guarantee will be needed.

10.15. Properties without mains drainage

10.15.1. Some rural properties may not have the benefit of mains drainage. The client's surveyor should be asked to ascertain the type of drainage provided at the property and if necessary a drainage survey may need to be undertaken to ensure that the system is functional and adequate to meet the needs of the property and its occupants. In some cases it will be necessary to obtain the consent of the Environment Agency for the operation of the drainage system (because the system may discharge effluent into the land or into an adjacent watercourse). The seller should be asked to supply a copy of any such consents in his possession. It may be necessary to transfer such consents to the buyer on completion.

10.15.2. *Cesspools*

A cesspool is a covered watertight tank used for receiving and storing sewage. It has no outlet but must be regularly emptied either by the local authority or by a private contractor. The tank must be, and remain, impervious to the ingress of groundwater or surface water and to leakage. No consent from the Environment Agency is required for a cesspool.

10.15.3. *Septic tanks*

A septic tank is a sewage system (usually consisting of two or three chambers) in which the sewage is retained for sufficient time to allow it to partially break down (anaerobic decomposition) before the contents are discharged. Discharge may be by soakage into the ground. The effluent cannot be discharged into a watercourse without further treatment. Environment Agency consent may be required for discharge into the ground.

10.15.4. *Package sewage treatment plants*

Package sewage treatment plants are similar to septic tanks but treat the sewage to a higher standard than the former before discharging the effluent. Environment Agency consent is required for the discharge.

10.15.5. *Environmental Agency consent*

Under Water Resources Act 1991, Environmental Agency consent is required for any discharge of sewage effluent into a watercourse, lake or pond, and may also be required for any discharge into or onto land. Separate consent is required under Land Drainage Act 1991 if the discharge is made into a main river. An administration charge is made by the Environmental Agency for an application for consent together with an annual fee to cover monitoring and other costs.

10.16. **Lenders' Handbook**

10.16.1. When acting under the terms of the Lenders' Handbook paragraph 5.2 gives details of the pre-contract searches which must be made (see paragraph 5.2.4 for specific details on mining searches). Note that except where the search result carries a priority period the search must not be more than six months old at the date of completion. The lenders' specific requirements should also be checked since some lenders will not accept personal searches or search insurance.

10.17. **National Land Information Service (NLIS)**

10.17.1. *Introduction*

The National Land Information Service (NLIS) is a joint initiative between central and local government. It brings together and delivers land and property related information held by many different organisations.

NLIS delivers integrated land and property information search facilities that support the conveyancing process and assists the conveyancing process through faster and more accurate property identification available through the National Land and Property Gazetteer (NLPG).

Conveyancing searches are requested and delivered, where possible, electronically. Solicitors and licensed conveyancers can retrieve land and property information from the Land Registry and conduct local authority searches, as well as searching for other information – such as coal mining activity, utility services, environmental or geological data – relating to the property.

10.17.2. Benefits

NLIS aims to provide faster turnaround times for searches. It is a flexible and transparent service, with improved access to information.

10.17.3. Concept and features

NLIS provides nationwide access to information gathered and maintained at a local level, by the people who are well placed to maintain the quality of the information.

It also provides a means of using electronic and automated systems to directly benefit the public.

10.17.4. Issues

NLIS seeks to obtain a price for the search results it provides which is no higher than that being offered by individual data providers for their own 'over-the-counter' service.

Security and integrity of data are paramount to NLIS. It is essential for the organisation to understand security threats and where they come from. The NLIS hub and channels have specifically addressed privacy, authentication, non-repudiation and data integrity.

Since much of the data is held by local and central government, the connections from the hub to data providers and to channels are also extremely secure. Best practice, Internet security technologies (including encryption) and e-commerce techniques are used to secure connections, and provide maximum confidence in the services.

10.17.5 How the process works

The NLIS hub acts as the gateway to the information held by NLIS data providers such as local authorities, the Land Registry and the Coal Authority. It also provides workflow management, which tracks all requests for information from the channels and responses from data providers. The hub provides 'service level monitoring', as well as billing and payment mechanisms for both channels and data providers.

There are three channels licensed by government to provide NLIS services to solicitors and licensed conveyancers:

- NLIS Searchflow (www.searchflow.co.uk);

- TM Property Service (www.tmproperty.co.uk); and

- TransAction Online (www.transaction-online.co.uk).

These channels act as e-retailers, interacting directly with practitioners via the Internet.

10.17.6. *The search request process*

The solicitor submits a search request via a secure Internet connection to a channel, which in turn, passes it to the hub. The hub interrogates each of the appropriate data providers concurrently, and reports back to the channel, which formats and presents the consolidated search results for delivery to the practitioner. The whole process is streamlined, and in some cases only takes a matter of hours to complete.

An important additional benefit is the simplified charging, billing and payment arrangements that NLIS makes possible, where the practitioner makes only a single payment to a channel for these services, and can even be billed monthly.

10.17.7. *Information*

Further information may be found on the websites of the National Land Information Service (www.nlis.org.uk) and the National Land and Property Gazetteer (www.nlpg.org.uk). Contact details for the channels can be found in Appendix XI.5 and XI.6.

B11. Form of contract

See also: Pre-contract negotiations, para. B1

Capacity, para. B7.

The contract, para. B9.2.6

Standard Conditions of Sale and Standard Commercial Property Conditions of Sale, para. B12

Plans, para. B21

Powers of Attorney, para. B23

11.1. Statutory provisions

11.1.1. Law of Property (Miscellaneous Provisions) Act 1989 repealed Law of Property Act 1925, s.40. The 1989 Act requires all contracts for the sale or other disposition of land or an interest in land to be made in writing and signed by the parties. The writing must incorporate all the terms which have been expressly agreed by the parties and the document must then be signed by or on behalf of all the parties. Where contracts are to be exchanged each part of the contract must contain all the agreed terms and be signed by the appropriate party. It is possible for the signed document to refer to another document which itself contains the agreed terms. If the document does not contain all the agreed terms an order for rectification may be sought.[1]

11.1.2. The requirement for a written contract does not apply to contracts:

(a) to grant a lease for a term not exceeding three years taking effect in possession without a fine;

(b) made at public auction.

11.1.3. *Joining two documents together to satisfy the section*

Where the signed document does not itself contain all the agreed terms it is possible to join two (or more) documents together in order to constitute a complete contract and thus satisfy the statutory requirements. Little case law yet exists under the 1989 Act, but the rules which applied to the joining of documents under Law of Property Act 1925, s.40 (predecessor to section 2) will not necessarily be applied to actions brought under the new section.[2] It is possible, e.g. to draft a contract which incorporates the Standard Conditions of Sale or Standard Commercial Property Conditions[3] by reference without setting out the full text of those conditions. In such a case the Standard Conditions or Standard Commercial Conditions (as appropriate) will be deemed to be incorporated as part of the contract although contained in a different document from that which was signed by the parties. Since the court's interpretation of this aspect of section 2 is as yet unknown, it is not possible to speculate in what circumstances the court will allow documents to be joined together to form a contract. It should be borne in mind that failure to satisfy the requirements of section 2 results in there being no contract at all between the parties, and the court has no equitable jurisdiction to allow the enforcement of a contract which does not meet the statutory requirements.[4] Care should therefore be taken to ensure that the contract does satisfy section 2 and to this end it is recommended that the full text of the general conditions of sale which are being used (e.g. the Standard Conditions of Sale) is set out in the contract itself.[5]

1. *Wright* v. *Robert Leonard Developments Ltd* [1994] EGCS 69.
2. See *Firstpost Homes Ltd* v. *Johnson* [1995] 1 WLR 1567.
3. See Appendices VII.12 and VII.13.
4. See however *Pagemanor* v. *Ryan* [1998] NPC 37 where a buyer under contract which did not fulfil s.2 obtained an alternative remedy in quasi-contract.
5. See *B. Ltd* v. *T. Ltd* [1991] NPC 47 where it was held that incorporation of the National Conditions of Sale by reference did satisfy s.2 of the Act. See also *Commission for New Towns* v. *Cooper, The Independent*, 15 March 1995 (CA) where it was held that an exchange of letters did not satisfy s.2.

11.2. Satisfying the statutory requirements

11.2.1. The statutory requirements are normally satisfied by the preparation by the seller's solicitor of a formal contract. The contract is usually prepared in two identical parts based on the Standard Conditions of Sale or Standard Commercial Property Conditions as amended to fit the particular circumstances of the transaction. A summary of both sets of Standard Conditions is contained in para. B12. The contract comes into being when exchange of contracts takes place. For signature and exchange of contracts see section C.

11.2.2. *Collateral contracts*

To be enforceable, options, equitable mortgages[1] and side letters issued in connection with sale of land transactions also need to satisfy the requirements of section 2. This will mean that these documents need to be in writing and signed by both parties. An agreement not to negotiate with any other buyer (a 'lock-out' agreement) can be enforceable as a separate collateral contract provided good consideration is given. This type of agreement does not fall within the scope of section 2.[2] A 'lock-in' agreement (i.e. to negotiate with these buyers only) is not an enforceable contract.[3] Also see paras. B1.7 and B1.8.

11.2.3. *Variation of contract*

A variation of a contract to which section 2 applies must itself comply with the section.[4]

1. *United Bank of Kuwait* v. *Sahib* [1996] NPC 12.
2. *Pitt* v. *PHH Asset Management Ltd* [1993] EGCS 127.
3. *Courtney & Fairburn* v. *Tolaini Bros.* [1975] 1 WLR 297.
4. *McCausland* v. *Duncan Lawrie* [1996] NPC 94. An exception to this is a variation of the payments to be made under a mortgage which are not required to satisfy the section: *Target Holdings* v. *Priestly* [1999] *Gazette*, 6 May.

11.3.   Contents of the contract

11.3.1. In addition to the formal parts, i.e. date, parties, signature, the contract comprises two main elements:

> (a) the particulars, which describe the physical extent of the property to be sold and its tenure; and
>
> (b) the conditions which set out the terms on which the seller is prepared to sell the property.

11.4.   The particulars

11.4.1. These must contain a clear description of the physical extent of the property to be sold and whether the estate to be sold is freehold or leasehold. The title number of a parcel of registered land is its sole distinguishing feature and thus must be referred to in the particulars. The class of title under which the land is registered (e.g. absolute) must also be included in order to give the buyer an accurate description of the estate which is being sold. Where the boundaries are well defined and the property has a regular postal address, the postal address may suffice to describe the land itself. In other cases a more detailed description may be necessary, referring where appropriate to the measurements of the property and/or a plan (see para. B21). Any inaccuracy in the particulars may give rise to an action in misdescription or misrepresentation (see Delay and remedies, section M).

11.5.   Conditions of sale

11.5.1.   *Open contract rules*

Where a contract makes no reference to a particular matter the contract is said to be 'open' on this point and is thus governed by the open contract rules which are laid down either by common law or by statute. Some of the open contract rules are satisfactory in operation, e.g. the rules for deduction of title on the sale of unregistered freeholds, and are invariably used without alteration. Others, e.g. the time for completion, which under the open contract rules is set at 'a reasonable time after the contract', are less satisfactory and are frequently altered by special condition in the contract itself. The Standard Conditions of Sale normally vary the open contract rules, but may themselves require amendment to suit the particular circumstances of the transaction.

11.5.2. Assuming that the Standard Conditions of Sale have been used to form the basis of the contract, special conditions will still be needed to deal with any variations which are required, and any features peculiar to the particular transaction. Even in the most straightforward transaction special conditions will invariably be required to deal with the matters listed below.

11.5.3. Checklist of usual special conditions

Condition to deal with	Reason for inclusion	Standard Condition	Further reference
Title	Buyer is entitled to know what title is being offered.	4.2	Section D
Deposit	No provision at common law, variation of general conditions may be required.	2.2	B17
Interest on deposit	Interest is payable under Solicitors' Accounts Rules.	2.2.3	A20
Completion date	Open contract rule and general conditions not satisfactory.	6.1	
Title guarantee	Defines scope of implied covenants for title.	4.5.2	M9
Incumbrances	Seller's duty of disclosure.	3	B5
Fixtures and fittings	To create an obligation and to avoid disputes between the parties.	9	B22
Vacant possession	Implied by common law unless stated to the contrary. Normally included for certainty and must deal with requirement for completion to take place at the property if so required.		B3

11.6. Full/Limited Title Guarantee

11.6.1. On the seller can sell with either full or limited title guarantee irrespective of the capacity in which he could have sold the property under the pre 1 July 1995 law (Law of Property (Miscellaneous Provisions) Act 1994). The guarantees apply to the sale of both freehold and leasehold property and on the grant of a lease. They can also be used on the transfer of personal property including intellectual property and rights in shares. The extent of the warranties given under the full and limited title guarantees is discussed under Title Guarantees at paragraph M9.[1]

11.6.2. The front of the Standard Contract form the seller should specify whether he sells with full or limited title guarantee. Should the seller fail to specify the nature of the title guarantee, Standard Condition 4.5.2, and Standard Commercial Property Condition 4.5.2, provides that the seller will sell with full title guarantee.

11.6.3. The warranties given under the full and limited guarantees can be amended in the agreement. If the seller is concerned about incumbrances he should disclose them in the contract and ensure that the buyer agrees to take the property subject to them. See also Standard Condition 4.5.3. Under s.6 of the 1994 Act (as amended by the Land Registration Act 2002) the sale of a registered title will also be subject to any matters entered on the register of title at the time of the disposition. As a result any such matters will not be covered by the title guarantee.

11.6.4. If the seller is a beneficial owner he will usually provide full title guarantee. If the seller is a trustee, personal representative or mortgagee, he will usually provide a limited title guarantee.

11.6.5. Where the disposition is of an interest the title to which is registered the seller will not be liable under any of the covenants for title for anything which at the time of the disposition was entered in the register in relation to that interest.[2]

1. Land Registry Rules 2003, rr. 67 to 69, incorporate the provisions as to implied covenants into registered conveyancing.
2. Law of Property (Miscellaneous Provisions) Act 1994, s.6 as inserted by Land Registration Act 2002, Sched. 11, para. 31.

11.7. Drafting the contract

11.7.1. Although drafting the contract is the prerogative of the seller, the relative bargaining strength of the parties rarely permits the seller to draft a contract which is entirely to his own satisfaction. Contract drafting is therefore an exercise in the art of compromise. The seller must seek to preserve his own interests without misleading the buyer, but will frequently have to include or concede some terms which favour the buyer in order to achieve a prompt conclusion to the transaction. A solicitor, whether acting for seller or buyer, who obstinately insists on the total protection of his own client's interests in the contract terms will at best prolong the transaction unnecessarily or at worst find that negotiations break down entirely and in neither case can he be said to be providing a proper service to his client. Where the Protocol is used amendments of the standard terms should be kept to a minimum.

11.8. Style of drafting

11.8.1. The contract must clearly state what the seller is offering to sell and on what terms including price. Use of anachronistic language should be avoided but clarity must not be sacrificed for brevity. Conditions should only be included where they are relevant and necessary and not through force of habit. Bearing in mind that it is the solicitor's duty to draft a contract which will avoid disputes or litigation between the parties, it becomes a matter of judgment as to the extent of the inclusion of clauses which cater for unforeseen eventualities.

11.8.2. *Guidelines*

    (a) Does the contract describe clearly what is to be sold?

    (b) Is a plan necessary?

    (c) Does the contract accord with the client's instructions as to the conditions on which the property is to be sold?

    (d) Are the conditions concise and unambiguous?

11.9. Looking at the contract from the buyer's point of view

11.9.1. No two draftsmen will ever produce identically worded contracts for the sale of the same property. Drafting is a personal skill and the draftsman's choice of words must be respected by the buyer's solicitor. Amendments should not be made to suit the individual whim of the buyer's solicitor but should be confined to those which are necessary and relevant to the particular transaction. The primary questions in looking at the contract from the buyer's point of view are:

    (a) does the clause accord with the client's instructions? and

    (b) does the clause do what it is intended to do?

11.9.2. If the answers to these questions are in the affirmative – leave the wording alone. If not, alter the clause until it does meet the above criteria.

11.9.3. Amendments should be clearly inserted on both copies of the draft contract in a distinctive colour.

11.10. National Conditions of Sale

11.10.1. Prior to the introduction of the Standard Conditions of Sale in 1990 there were two standard forms of contract in common use in England and Wales: The Law Society's Conditions of Sale (1984 revision) and the National Conditions of Sale (20th edition). The Standard Conditions of Sale (first edition) represented a merger of these two popular forms and the current (third edition) of the Standard

Conditions describes itself in a sub-title as 'National Conditions of Sale 23rd edition, Law Society's Conditions of Sale 1995'. The National Conditions are therefore no longer published as an independent set of conditions and many former Nationals users have adopted the Standard Conditions as the basis of contracts drafted by their firms, but a few firms continue to base their contracts on the 20th edition of the National Conditions.

11.10.2. In view of the number of changes in both law and practice which have occurred since the last independent revision of the National Conditions in 1981 or the Law Society Conditions in 1984, it is considered unwise to base a contract on either of these conditions which, as time goes by, become increasingly out of date.

11.11. Unfair Terms in Consumer Contracts Regulations 1994

11.11.1. Unfair Terms in Consumer Contracts Regulations 1994[1] affect all contracts (oral or written) made between a seller or supplier and a consumer (this latter expression applies to individuals only). Unlike Unfair Contract Terms Act 1977, the new regulations probably apply to land contracts, including mortgages and tenancy agreements. Agreements for financial services made between an individual and his broker are also potentially within the Regulations. The EU Directive from which the English Regulations derive may have intended land contracts to be included within its scope and some national versions of the Regulations do apply to land (e.g. France), but the English Regulations use the expression 'goods' (although land is not specifically excluded in the list of exclusions from the Regulations). There is therefore some doubt as to the application of the Regulations to contracts affecting land, but the Department of Trade and Industry has issued a statement which indicates that, in their view, the Regulations do apply to land contracts.

The English Regulations could be amended in future to clarify the position, or could be challenged by application to the European Court of Justice on the basis that the English Regulations do not correctly implement the EU Directive. Practitioners should therefore be aware of the Regulations and of their possible effects on land transactions.

11.11.2. Situations in which the Regulations apply

The Regulations do not apply to a contract for sale made between two private individuals but catch contracts made between a corporate or business seller and a private individual. Thus contracts for new houses or plots on a building estate where the seller is a developer and the buyer a private individual are potentially affected since in these circumstances the contract is usually in standard form and there is little or no freedom for the buyer to negotiate terms. Similarly mortgages, where the lender is in business and the borrower is not, are caught, as also are sales by mortgagees.

Tenancy agreements and contracts for financial services are potentially within the scope of the Regulations.

11.11.3. *Effect of the Regulations*

If a term is held to be unfair, that term is to be treated as void, but the rest of the contract remains binding on the parties, so long as it is capable of continuing without the offending term.

A term will be regarded as unfair if, contrary to the requirement of good faith, it causes a significant imbalance in the parties' rights and obligations arising under the contract to the detriment of the consumer. Various factors, similar to those contained in Unfair Contract Terms Act 1977, are contained in the Regulations to act as guidelines as to whether 'good faith' exists, e.g. the strength of the bargaining position of the parties, the circumstances surrounding the contract, and whether the consumer has received any special inducement, such as a discount, to agree to the term.

The burden of proof will lie on the consumer to show that a term included in the contract which was not individually negotiated between the parties is unfair.

The Regulations also require all contracts to be drafted in plain intelligible language.

See also para. A21 for information on the reproduction of the contract.

1. S.I. 1994/3159.

B12. Standard Conditions of Sale and Standard Commercial Property Conditions

See also: The National Conveyancing Protocol ('TransAction'), para. A19

Form of contract, para. B11

12.1. Standard Conditions of Sale

12.1.1. Most contracts for the sale of residential property will be made either on the Standard Conditions of Sale Form or by reference to the Standard Conditions.[1]

12.1.2. The text of the Standard Conditions of Sale (3rd edition) with accompanying notes for guidance is set out in Appendix VII.13. Individual conditions are referred to in context in the text of this book.

12.1.3. The Standard Conditions of Sale (3rd edition) and the Standard Commercial Property Conditions are both being revised in 2003. See section AA. New Developments in Conveyancing Practice for details.

1. The Standard Conditions of Sale (first edition) came into force on 21 March 1990 and replaced the Law Society Conditions of Sale (1984 revision) and the National Conditions of Sale (20th edition). The third edition came into force on 1 July 1995.

12.2. Standard Commercial Property Conditions

12.2.1. The Standard Commercial Property Conditions (first edition) are based on the Standard Conditions of Sale (third edition) but apply to commercial transactions. They came into effect in May 1999 and the full text of the conditions is set out in Appendix VII.12. Many of the conditions in the Standard Commercial Property Conditions are identical both in wording and numbering to their Standard Conditions counterparts, but there are some notable exceptions. Sub-sales are prohibited by Standard Commercial Property Condition 1.5. Risk in freehold property passes to the buyer on exchange of contracts under Standard Commercial Property Condition 5.1 and the method of calculating compensation for late completion under Standard Commercial Property Condition 7.3 is not based on the concept of relative fault.

12.3.   Incorporating Standard Conditions of Sale

12.3.1.   To satisfy Law of Property (Miscellaneous Provisions) Act 1989, s.2 a contract for the sale or other disposition of land must be in writing, incorporating all the terms which have been agreed between the parties. These terms will normally include the Standard Conditions of Sale or the Standard Commercial Property Conditions. Where a solicitor prepares a contract on a word processor or by other duplicated means incorporation of either set of the Standard Conditions by reference may satisfy the requirements of section 2 (but see para. B11.1.3). Failure to satisfy section 2 means that no contract exists between the parties.[1]

1. See *B. Ltd* v. *T. Ltd* [1991] NPC 47.

12.4.   Using Standard Conditions of Sale

12.4.1.   Not all of the Standard Conditions will be appropriate for use in every transaction. Solicitors should, in every transaction, give careful thought to the application of the conditions and expressly amend those which are inappropriate to the particular circumstances of the current transaction. As in all cases, amendments should be restricted to those which are essential to meet the circumstances of an individual case.

12.5.   Protocol[1]

12.5.1.   The Standard Conditions of Sale (third edition) are one of the standard documents forming part of the Protocol. The proposed use by the seller's solicitor of a different form of conditions would be a departure from the Protocol which would need to be disclosed to the buyer's solicitor at the commencement of the transaction. The drafting of the Standard Conditions mirrors the requirements of the Protocol; thus an amendment to the Standard Conditions may itself be a departure from the Protocol requiring notification to the other party. Since the aim of the Protocol is to simplify and speed up the conveyancing process it is recommended that in transactions where the Protocol is being used, solicitors alter the Standard Conditions as little as possible, subject to their paramount duty of acting in the best interests of their client.

1. See para. A19.

B13. Conditional contracts

See also: Pre-contract negotiations, para. B1

Capacity, para. B7

Form of contract, para. B11

13.1. When are conditional contracts appropriate?

13.1.1. Conditional contracts carry with them some risks and uncertainties which make them inappropriate for everyday use, but they may be considered for use in the following circumstances:

(a) where the buyer has not had the opportunity before exchange of contracts to make searches and enquiries or to conduct a survey or where his mortgage arrangements have not been finalised;

(b) where the contract is dependent on planning permission being obtained for the property;

(c) where the sale requires the consent of the Charity Commissioners under Charities Act 1993 (see para. B7.8);

(d) where the sale is dependent on permission being obtained from a third party, e.g. ministerial consent, landlord's consent;

(e) where the parties wish to be bound to a contract but there is some other unresolved matter which prevents commitment to an unconditional contract for the time being, e.g. the seller has to get in part of the legal estate.

13.2. Desirability of conditional contracts

13.2.1. Conditional contracts are generally not desirable since they leave an element of doubt as to the very existence and validity of the contractual obligations between the parties. Most of the situations in which conditional contracts are proposed for use benefit the buyer more than the seller (e.g. 'subject to planning permission'), and the seller should resist the suggestion of entering a conditional contract if at all possible. A conditional contract may, however, be inevitable where the seller needs the consent of the Charity Commissioners to the sale under Charities Act 1993 since an unconditional contract which is entered into without such consent is not lawful.

13.2.2. Conditional contracts should never be used where one or both of the parties has an unconditional sale or purchase contract which is dependent on the conditional contract. In this situation, if the conditional contract were to be rescinded for non-fulfilment of the condition, this would give rise to great difficulties in the fulfilment of the linked unconditional contract and may result in a breach of that contract.

13.2.3. Before agreeing to enter a conditional contract the seller should consider whether there are any viable alternative solutions. Where it has been suggested that the sale is 'subject to planning permission', it may be preferable to delay exchange until the results of the planning application have been received by the buyer, rather than enter into a hastily drafted conditional contract. An alternative solution may be to grant the buyer for a nominal consideration an option to purchase the property to be exercised within a stated period.

13.3. Conditions precedent and subsequent

13.3.1. Conditions precedent

A condition precedent has the effect of suspending the operation of the contract until the terms of the condition have been met. If the condition has not been fulfilled by the appropriate time-limit, the party with the benefit of the condition may withdraw and the contractual obligations of the parties never come into existence.

13.3.2. Conditions subsequent

Where the contract is subject to a condition subsequent, the contractual obligations of the parties arise on the creation of the contract and continue to exist until terminated by the party with the benefit of the condition on its non-fulfilment.

13.3.3. If the wording of the condition reads 'subject to x', this indicates a condition precedent.

13.3.4. If the wording of the condition reads 'until x', this indicates a condition subsequent.

13.4. Requirements for a valid conditional contract

13.4.1. Certainty

The terms of the condition must be clear and certain. In *Lee Parker* v. *Izzett* (*No. 2*),[1] an agreement to sell a freehold house 'subject to the buyer obtaining a satisfactory mortgage' was held to be void because the word 'satisfactory' was too nebulous and there was thus no certainty regarding the circumstances in which the buyer would validly be able to withdraw from the contract. It should be noted, however, that not all 'subject to mortgage' clauses will suffer the same fate. A similarly worded clause in *Janmohamed* v. *Hassam*[2] was held to be valid.

13.4.2. *Time for performance*

It was held in *Aberfoyle Plantations Ltd* v. *Cheng*[3] that the time for performance of the condition is of the essence and cannot be extended either by agreement between the parties or by the court. The same case also laid down the rules relating to the time for performance of the condition which are summarised as follows:

(a) where the contract contains a completion date, the condition must be fulfilled by that date, irrespective of whether time was of the essence of the contractual completion date;

(b) if a time is stated for the fulfilment of the condition, that time-limit must be complied with or the contract will fail;

(c) if no time-limit is specified the condition must be fulfilled within a reasonable time. This provision is patently unsatisfactory since it leaves room for argument about what is a reasonable time.

1. [1972] 2 All ER 800.
2. (1976) 241 EG 609.
3. [1960] AC 115.

13.5. Withdrawal from the contract

13.5.1. Only the party with the benefit of the condition may withdraw from the contract, and only for reasons connected with the condition. No other reason will justify withdrawal, although there is no obligation on the resiling party to prove that he is being reasonable in exercising his rights to withdraw. It is a question of construction of the condition itself as to whether a party may withdraw before performance of the condition.[1]

1. *Tesco Stores Ltd* v. *William Gibson & Co. Ltd* (1970) 214 EG 835.

13.6. Waiver of the condition

13.6.1. Where the condition benefits one party only, it may be waived unilaterally. In other cases the waiver amounts to a variation of the contract and requires the consent of both parties. If to remove the condition takes away the whole purpose of the contract, the whole contract will fail for uncertainty.

13.7. Drafting

13.7.1. The drafting of a condition requires extreme care to ensure that the requirements outlined in para. B13.4 have been satisfied. No such provision is included in the

Standard Conditions of Sale although a contract to assign a lease may be conditional on the landlord's consent being obtained under Standard Condition 8.3.

13.7.2. Guidelines

(a) Consider the precise event(s) on which the contract is to be made conditional.

(b) By what time must the condition be fulfilled? (Bear in mind that the specified time-limit cannot be extended.)

(c) Consider the precise terms on which the party with the benefit of the condition may rescind.

(d) Ensure that there are no loopholes which would enable one party to escape from the contract other than for the non-fulfilment of the event(s) contemplated in (a) above.

(e) Use an established precedent, tailoring it to fit your exact requirements.

(f) Take your time: a condition which is hastily drafted may contain unforeseen errors.

(g) Having drafted your 'perfect' condition, leave it on the desk overnight and review the wording objectively in the cold light of day. Does the condition achieve its objectives? Is it clear and certain? Do any unforeseen or unwanted consequences flow from the wording?

13.7.3. Precise terms for rescission

13.7.3.1. 'Subject to searches'

(a) Which searches?

(b) Which adverse entries will give rise to the right to rescind?

(c) By when must the search result(s) be received?

(d) Can buyer rescind if he changes his mind and never makes search applications?

13.7.3.2. 'Subject to mortgage'

(a) Specify name of lender(s) to whom application made.

(b) Specify amount of required advance.

(c) Specify acceptable interest rates.

(d) Should the buyer be entitled to rescind if the mortgage offer is subject to conditions or a retention – what conditions attached to the offer would be acceptable/unacceptable?

(e) Time-limit by which application must be determined?

(f) Can buyer rescind if he changes his mind and never puts in an application for a mortgage?

13.7.3.3. 'Subject to survey'

    (a) Named surveyor?

    (b) What type of survey?

    (c) Which defects revealed by survey report will entitle buyer to withdraw?

    (d) Should a financial limit be placed on the entitlement to rescind? e.g. buyer can rescind if survey reveals defects which exceed £x in total – if so who assesses the value?

    (e) Time-limit for obtaining result of survey.

    (f) Can buyer rescind if he changes his mind and never instructs the surveyor?

13.7.3.4. 'Subject to planning permission'

    (a) Form of application to be agreed between the parties.

    (b) What conditions attached to the consent would entitle the buyer to rescind?

    (c) Can buyer rescind if he changes his mind and never puts in a planning application?

    (d) Time-limit for result of application.

    (e) Which party is to make the application and pay the fee?

    (f) The non-applying party should agree in writing not to oppose the application and to support it.

    (g) Is the application to be for outline or detailed permission?

    (h) Which party is to pay the architect's and other professional fees in connection with the application?

B14. Sub-sales

See also: Stamp Duty and Stamp Duty Savings, para. A14
Capital Gains Tax, para. A15
Value Added Tax, para. A16

14.1. Definitions

14.1.1. In this section of the text only, the following expressions have the meanings set out below:

   (a) 'the buyer' means the person who has contracted to buy land and who is selling the land under a sub-sale contract before completion of his own purchase;

   (b) 'the seller' means the person from whom the buyer (as defined above) is purchasing the land and in whom the legal title to the property will be vested pending completion;

   (c) 'the third party' means the person who is buying the land from the buyer (as defined above) under the sub-sale contract.

14.2. Buyer's position pending completion

14.2.1. A buyer who has exchanged contracts for the purchase of property is the owner of the beneficial interest in the land, but does not obtain the legal estate until registration of the transfer to him (or completion in the case of unregistered land). However, in the case of registered land the buyer is nevertheless empowered to deal with the land as if he was registered as proprietor.

14.3. Contractual restriction on sub-sales

14.3.1. Where a buyer intends to sell the property to a third party by way of sub-sale he must ensure that his existing contract to purchase the land contains no restriction which would prevent the sub-sale. The Standard Conditions of Sale do not restrict sub-sales of freehold land nor assignments of existing leases, but Condition 8.2.5

prevents a sub-sale where the contract is for the grant of a new lease. A seller should resist a buyer's request to remove Condition 8.2.5 from the contract, because its presence ensures that the seller will take the benefit of the covenants given by the first tenant. Covenants given by an original tenant endure throughout the term of the lease notwithstanding its assignment to an assignee. The Standard Commercial Property Conditions do restrict sub-sales (Condition 1.5).

14.3.2. If a restriction against sub-sales is included in the buyer's contract, he will be able to contract to resell the land to a third party, but will have to complete this second transaction separately and subsequent to his own purchase.

14.3.3. Provided there is no such restriction, the buyer may enter a contract for sale with a third party, prior to completion of his own purchase. In such a case, the buyer may, if he wishes, draft the transfer document to reflect the sub-sale (i.e. the seller transfers direct to the sub-purchaser with the original buyer joining in as a party to transfer his beneficial interest in the estate being transferred). Provided the buyer's transfer is technically correct, the seller cannot refuse to sign even if he had previously been unaware of the sub-sale.

14.3.4. Where there is a restriction on sub-sales in the contract it may be possible for the buyer to assign the benefit of his contract with the seller to the third party and then to complete the purchase as nominee for the third party. The subsequent transfer of the property from the buyer (as nominee) to the third party will not attract *ad valorem* stamp duty.

14.4. Special conditions in the sub-sale contract

14.4.1. Special conditions may need to be inserted in the sub-sale contract to deal with the following matters:

(a) **The contract**

When drafting the sub-sale contract, care must be taken to take account of any relevant provisions in the principal contract, e.g. as to length of a notice to complete; the buyer needs to be in a position to give the third party a notice to complete expiring not later than the date of expiry of any notice to complete which the buyer receives from the seller.

(b) **Title**

The third party should be required by contractual condition to accept the buyer's entitlement to be registered by the production of official copy entries of the seller's registered title, and the contract between seller and buyer. In unregistered land the buyer, having investigated title with his own seller, can usually satisfy Law of Property Act 1925, s.44 by supplying a good root of title and subsequent documentation, but will need to produce his own purchase contract to the third party as evidence that he can compel the seller to convey the legal estate.

(c) **The purchase deed**

The purchase deed will usually consist of a transfer or conveyance from the seller direct to the third party. The buyer will need to be made a party to the document in order to transfer his equitable interest in the property to the third party.

(d) **Apportionment of the price**

Where the amount payable by the third party exceeds the consideration due from the buyer to the seller, the purchase deed will need to contain an apportionment of the price as between buyer and seller, with a receipt for their respective portions being given by each.

14.5. Completion

14.5.1. Depending on the arrangements which have been made between the parties, special provisions may need to be considered in relation to actual completion of the transaction, e.g.

(a) where completion is to take place;

(b) transmission of the money;

(c) custody of deeds;

(d) undertakings for the discharge of the seller's mortgage(s) over the property.

14.6. Stamp duty

14.6.1. Provided that the transfer or conveyance is made directly between the seller and the third party, the two transactions are regarded as one, thus incurring only one amount of stamp duty which will be borne by the third party. If two purchase deeds are executed, one from the seller to the buyer and a second from the buyer to the third party, two transactions will have taken place and stamp duty will be payable by both the buyer and the third party on their respective purchase deeds. Where there is a previously uncompleted contract in the chain of the title for the sale of United Kingdom land for a consideration in excess of £10 million this is dutiable (Finance Act 2002, s.115). Subsequent contractual purchasers liable to stamp duty upon their contract will be entitled to a credit for the stamp duty paid upon earlier contracts, or part thereof where they purchase part of the land. A similar credit is available against the stamp duty upon the transfer of the legal title. Where the stamp duty upon the transfer is less than the stamp duty paid upon the prior contracts the transfer may not be dutiable and the excess stamp duty paid upon the contracts is refundable. Solicitors must take appropriate steps to ensure that the necessary information is made available to ensure their client's credit or refund. Where there is a restriction on sub-sales in the contract it may be possible for the buyer to assign the benefit of his contract with the seller to the third party and then to complete the purchase as nominee for the third party. The contract to assign the benefit of the contract is subject to stamp duty and payment of this duty franks the subsequent assignment pursuant thereto. The duty is charged upon the consideration paid for the assignment; no duty is chargeable upon the outstanding purchase price (*Swayne* v. *IRC* [1899] 1 QB 335). If the property is transferred directly to the assignee this is dutiable upon the contract price. If the property is transferred to the assignor i.e. the original purchaser it will be dutiable upon the contract price and it may be possible to persuade the Inland Revenue Stamp Taxes Office that the subsequent transfer from the assignor to the assignee is dutiable only £5 as a transfer from nominee to beneficial owner but this will require that duty has been paid in respect of the assignment and it is by no means certain that the Revenue will accept the analysis particularly where the assignment has attracted one of the lower rates of stamp duty. Usually assignments are less stamp duty efficient than sub-sale.

14.7. Registration of third party

14.7.1. Whether the transaction proceeds by way of a direct transfer from the seller to the third party or by two separate purchase deeds, the third party will still be able to effect registration of his own title at the Land Registry without needing to insist that the buyer obtains a registered title in his own name first. Where two purchase deeds have been executed, the third party will need to produce the transfer or conveyance from the seller to the buyer to the Registry as proof of the devolution of title.[1]

1. See Seller's title awaiting registration, para. B4.

14.8. Protection of sub-sale contract

14.8.1. The third party is in a more vulnerable position than a normal buyer since completion of his contract is dependent on the buyer's completion of his own contract with the seller. It may therefore be advisable for the third party to protect his contract by registration. Registration of a contract for sale as a class C(iv) land charge can only be effected against the owner for the time being of an unregistered legal estate, i.e. the seller.[1] When the title is registered protection is by the entry of notice in the register of the title.

1. See Protection of the contract, para. C5.3.

14.9. Notice to complete

14.9.1. The buyer cannot serve a notice to complete on the third party unless and until he has completed his own contract with the seller. Until this happens the buyer is not 'ready able and willing' to complete within the terms of Standard Condition 6.8.2[1] or Standard Commercial Property Condition 6.8.1. This problem can be overcome by the insertion of a special condition in the contract which allows the buyer to serve a notice notwithstanding that he has not yet completed his own contract. Once a notice to complete is served, time will be of the essence of the contract; the buyer should therefore not serve such a notice unless he is confident that he can complete his own purchase (from the seller) within the time-limit which he has imposed on the third party.

1. See generally *Cole* v. *Rose* [1978] 3 All ER 1121.

14.10. Capital gains tax[1]

14.10.1. Where a capital gains tax liability is incurred by either the seller or buyer as a result of the sale(s) the Inland Revenue treats a sub-sale transaction as being two separate sales (even if completed by one deed), the sale from seller to buyer being regarded as having taken place before the transaction between the buyer and the third party.

1. See Capital Gains Tax, para. A15.

14.11. VAT

14.11.1. The VAT implications of a sub-sale will also need to be considered and provision made in the contract for the responsibility for payment of VAT where applicable.[1]

1. See VAT, para. A16.

B15. Supply of evidence of title before exchange

15.1. Supply of evidence of title before exchange	**15.2. Registered land** **15.3. Unregistered land**

See also: Seller's investigation of title, para. B3
Deducing title, para. D1

15.1. Supply of evidence of title before exchange

15.1.1. Having investigated title prior to drafting the contract it will be possible in most cases for the seller to supply the buyer with evidence of title concurrently with the draft contract. Where the Protocol is being used, the seller is obliged to supply his evidence of title to the buyer at this stage of the transaction (Protocol, para. 4.4, see Appendix III.1).

15.1.2. The supply of such evidence of title before exchange is recommended as it will enable the buyer to obtain a comprehensive view of the property which he is buying and will obviate delays after exchange since problems which arise on the title will be brought to light and dealt with at an early stage in the transaction.

15.1.3. Where this is done, it is common for the seller to include a contractual condition which precludes the buyer's right to raise requisitions on the evidence of title. Such a condition does not bind the buyer's lender. Such a condition will exclude the normal contractual condition allowing requisitions to be raised within a certain time after exchange of contracts (see Standard Condition 4.1.1 and Standard Commercial Property Condition 4.1.1). Where such a condition is included in the contract the buyer must obtain satisfactory answers to his queries on the evidence of title before exchange of contracts. He will not be able to rescind the contract after exchange if he discovers a defect arising out of the evidence of title which was supplied to him prior to exchange. The buyer should ensure that any condition excluding his right to raise requisitions should be limited to requisitions upon the evidence of title actually supplied by the seller prior to exchange of contracts. It should not prohibit requisitions being raised on undisclosed matters which are only revealed by pre-completion searches at the Land Registry or the Land Charges Department.

15.2. Registered land

15.2.1. Up-to-date official copy entries of the title together with supporting documents, e.g. evidence of overriding interests, tenancies, title plan, etc., should be supplied by the seller at his own expense. The copies supplied to the buyer must be *original* official copies. Photocopies of official copies do not satisfy this requirement.

15.3. Unregistered land

15.3.1. An epitome of title together with clear photocopies of the documents referred to in it should be supplied to the buyer.

B16. Undertakings for bridging finance

See also: Accepting undertakings on completion following *Patel* v. *Daybells*, Appendix V.1.
Undertakings Warning Card, Appendix IV.4.
Agreed form of wording with banks for undertaking for bridging finance, Appendix VII.1

16.1. General points on undertakings

16.1.1. An undertaking is a promise by a solicitor (or a member of the solicitor's staff) to do, or to refrain from doing, something. The promise is enforceable against the solicitor personally, even where the promise was given by a member of staff and not by the solicitor himself. An undertaking given in the firm's name binds all the partners. Undertakings are binding because they are given and no other considerations impinge on their enforceability; thus the normal period of limitation of actions imposed by the Limitation Acts does not apply and an undertaking may be enforced against the giver irrespective of the fact that the normal limitation period has expired.[1]

16.1.2. Failure to honour an undertaking is professional misconduct.[2]

16.1.3. Because of the personal liability which attaches to undertakings it is important that both the giver and recipient of the promise understand precisely what the terms of the promise are. To avoid any misunderstanding it is recommended that undertakings are always given in writing. Any ambiguity in the terms of the promise is construed against the giver of the undertaking. The guidelines contained in the Law Society's Undertakings Warning Card should be observed (see Appendix IV.4).

16.1.4. An undertaking is enforceable because it has been given and thus needs no consideration for its validity, although in practice consideration will often be present.

16.1.5. A promise to give an undertaking is enforceable as an undertaking.

16.1.6. A solicitor is responsible for honouring any undertaking given by his staff. In order to ensure that no undertaking is given which is outside the control of the solicitor to perform it is recommended that undertakings should only be given by partners in the firm, or by other staff with the prior consent of a partner.

16.1.7. Where an undertaking is given by a member of staff without having obtained or exceeding the requisite authority from a partner, the firm will still be bound to honour that undertaking unless the recipient was aware of the lack of authority on the part of the giver.

16.1.8. Any exclusion of the personal liability of the giver of the undertaking must be clear and explicit. Such undertakings should be regarded with great caution since the primary value of the undertaking, i.e. its enforceability may have been seriously eroded by the exclusion clause. A solicitor may give an undertaking on behalf of a client provided that the wording of the undertaking makes it clear that the primary responsibility for performance of the promise lies with the client and not with the solicitor.

16.1.9. The solicitor must ensure that whatever is promised by the undertaking is capable of performance and is totally within his own control to perform. An undertaking will be enforceable even if the circumstances which prevailed at the time when the undertaking was given subsequently change. Any change in circumstances which potentially affects the fulfilment of an undertaking must be notified to the recipient and, if necessary, the terms renegotiated to ensure that whatever promise has been given is capable of performance.[3]

16.1.10. An undertaking to do something which is not within the direct control of the giver should, if it is appropriate to give such an undertaking at all, only be given in qualified form, e.g. an undertaking to procure the client's signature to a document is not totally within the solicitor's own control since he cannot force the client to sign; thus the undertaking should be worded on the basis that the solicitor will use his best (or reasonable) endeavours to procure the required signature.

16.1.11. Undertakings given by licensed conveyancers or authorised practitioners are enforceable as if they were given by solicitors.

16.1.12. Undertakings given by unqualified persons who are not acting through a solicitor's practice are only enforceable under the ordinary law of contract and should never be accepted.

16.1.13. *Guidelines*

(a) Obtain the client's irrevocable written authority before giving an undertaking.

(b) Ensure the wording of the undertaking is clear, unambiguous, and totally capable of performance.

(c) Only give written undertakings, signed or authorised by a partner.

(d) Mark the client's file conspicuously to ensure that the undertaking is not overlooked.

(e) When the undertaking has been fulfilled obtain a written release from the recipient.

1. *Bray* v. *Stuart West & Co.* [1989] EGCS 60.
2. *The Guide to the Professional Conduct of Solicitors 1999*, Principle 18.02.
3. *Udall* v. *Capri Lighting Ltd* [1997] 3. All ER 262.

16.2. Bridging finance for the deposit

16.2.1. Where bridging finance is being extended for the deposit on the client's purchase the bank or other lender will normally require the solicitor to give an undertaking to repay the loan, usually out of the proceeds of sale of the client's existing property.

16.2.2. Such an undertaking should only be given where:

    (a) the solicitor is sure that sufficient funds will be available on completion to repay the loan with interest;

    (b) the solicitor knows the client well enough to feel confident of making a binding commitment on that client's behalf;

    (c) the client has given his irrevocable authority for the undertaking to be given. If in doubt, obtain the authority in writing.

16.3. When should the undertaking be given?

16.3.1. Until contracts have been exchanged on the client's related sale transaction there is no guarantee that any funds will be available to repay the loan. Ideally, therefore, such an undertaking should not be given until contracts have been exchanged on the sale. In practice it may be necessary to give the undertaking shortly before exchange in order to ensure the availability of funds for a simultaneous exchange on both sale and purchase contracts. The undertaking should not be given until negotiations for the sale contract are close to the point of exchange, with no outstanding unresolved problems.

16.4. Terms of the undertaking

16.4.1. The Law Society has agreed a form of wording for use by solicitors when giving undertakings to banks for bridging finance. The full form of this undertaking is set out in Appendix VII.1.

16.4.2. Even where an undertaking is presented to the solicitor in the standard form or a familiar and frequently used form of wording, the entire wording should be read carefully in the light of the particular transaction to ensure that the wording is appropriate for those circumstances. If the wording is not wholly appropriate to the circumstances in hand, the undertaking should be amended to reflect the particular requirements of the transaction.

16.4.3. Confine the terms of the undertaking to repayment:

    (a) of a stated figure, plus interest on that sum if so instructed;

    (b) from a defined source, e.g. the proceeds of sale of a named property;

(c) of the net proceeds of sale, having defined what is understood by the word 'net', i.e. after deduction of specified loans, estate agents' commission, solicitor's fees, disbursements on the sale and purchase, and any other known and defined liabilities which will reduce the amount available to repay the loan;

(d) when the proceeds of sale are actually received by the solicitor. This protects the solicitor against having to honour the undertaking in circumstances where the sale of the property is completed but for some reason the funds are never received by him, e.g. the client intercepts the money and absconds with it.

16.5. Change of circumstances

16.5.1. If, having given an undertaking, the circumstances of the client's sale and purchase transactions change, e.g. the consideration for the sale is reduced to take account of a structural defect, the terms of the undertaking must be considered carefully to ensure that they are still capable of performance. The recipient of the undertaking must be informed of the changed circumstances irrespective of whether they affect the obligations covered by the undertaking. Where the undertaking has become impossible of performance because of the changed circumstances the solicitor must renegotiate the undertaking to obtain either a release of his obligations or a form of wording which is capable of performance in the light of the current situation.

16.6. Checklist

16.6.1. (a) Do I know the client well enough to feel confident about giving the undertaking?

(b) Have I got the client's irrevocable written authority to give the undertaking?

(c) Has the client disclosed all subsisting mortgages and liabilities which will or might affect the amount of money which will be available to discharge the loan?

(d) Is there sufficient equity to repay the loan with interest?

(e) Are the terms of the undertaking totally acceptable?

(f) Are negotiations for the client's sale sufficiently firm and advanced to make it safe to give the undertaking?

(g) Has the undertaking been authorised by a partner?

(h) Has the cover of the client's sale file been clearly marked to show that an undertaking has been given, to whom, and for what amount?

16.7. **Loan guarantees**

16.7.1. A solicitor who gives an undertaking which is effectively a guarantee of a loan being taken out by the client will be bound by that undertaking even if it is not given 'in the normal course of practice'. Such an undertaking may, however, be outside the scope of the solicitors' indemnity insurance.

B17. Deposit

B

See also: Dealing with non-solicitors, para. A5
Preliminary deposits, para. A12
Interest on clients' money, para. A20
Form of contract, para. B11
Standard Conditions of Sale and Standard Commercial Property Conditions of Sale, para. B12
Undertakings for bridging finance, para. B16

17.1. Is a deposit necessary?

17.1.1. In law a deposit is unnecessary and neither common law nor statute provides for such to be payable. The payment of a deposit is a purely customary arrangement which is expressly incorporated into the contract for the benefit of the seller.

17.1.2. *Purpose of deposit*

The payment of a deposit acts as part payment of the purchase price, demonstrates the buyer's good intentions of completing the contract, and gives the seller leverage to ensure the fulfilment of the contract since he is usually able to forfeit the deposit if the buyer defaults, thereby recouping part or all of the loss occasioned by the buyer's default.

17.2. How much deposit?

17.2.1. No deposit at all is payable unless the contract expressly makes provision for one.

17.2.2. A deposit of 10% of the purchase price has until recently been standard practice and is the figure provided by the Standard Conditions of Sale and the Standard Commercial Property Conditions unless specifically amended.

17.2.3. In recent years deposits of less than 10% have become more widespread in residential transactions due in part to the increase in 95% or 100% mortgage offers to buyers, and to the fact that high property prices, with consequently high deposits, place an unfair financial burden on the buyer whilst over-compensating a seller who forfeits that deposit on the buyer's default.

17.2.4. It is clearly to the seller's advantage to demand a 10% deposit; if, however, he is asked by the buyer to accept a reduced amount the following factors should be considered:

    (a) the risk of the sale going off, with the consequent need to forfeit the deposit to compensate for loss;

    (b) the buyer's mortgage arrangements – are they firm and settled? Is the offer of advance for the whole of the purchase price (taking into account the amount of the reduced deposit)?

    (c) the likely amount of loss which the seller would suffer if the buyer were to default, e.g. cost of bridging finance or interest needed to complete a related purchase, length of time and costs of resale of the property.

17.2.5. The seller's solicitor must explain the consequences of taking a reduced deposit to his client and obtain his client's express authority before agreeing the reduction with the buyer's solicitor or representative. *Morris* v. *Duke Cohan*[1] suggests that it may be professional negligence for a solicitor to accept a reduced deposit without the client's express authority.

17.2.6. If a reduced deposit is taken on exchange, the contract should provide for the balance of the 10% to become immediately payable on service of a notice to complete.[2]

17.2.7. Only in exceptional circumstances should the transaction proceed without any deposit being taken. Examples might include family transactions or sales to sitting tenants.

17.2.8. Deposits in excess of 10% are very rare, and cannot be justified in normal circumstances. The risk is that a defaulting buyer may be able to obtain repayment of the whole of an excessive deposit (not just the amount in excess of 10%).[3]

17.2.9. The amount of the deposit actually payable on exchange will take into account any preliminary deposit already paid, but, unless the contract provides otherwise, is calculated exclusive of the value of chattels which are to be paid for in addition to the purchase price of the land.

1. (1975) 119 SJ 826.
2. See Standard Condition 6.8.4.
3. See *Dojap Investments Ltd* v. *Workers Trust and Merchant Bank Ltd* [1993] AC 573 where the forfeiture of a 24% deposit was held to be a penalty.

17.3. How is the deposit to be funded?

17.3.1. The answer to this question should be obtained when initial instructions are taken from the client. It is safest to assume at this stage that the seller will require a full 10% deposit, and if the buyer wishes to pay a reduced deposit the matter will have to be raised during negotiations with the seller's solicitor.

17.3.2. From an investment account

(a) How much notice does the buyer need to give to withdraw his funds without losing a significant amount of interest?

(b) Ensure sufficient money is transferred to a short-term investment account in time for it to be immediately available on exchange.

17.3.3. Bridging finance

Bridging finance from a bank or other lender will often be needed in a situation where the purchase is dependent on a related sale:

(a) It should be apparent at an early stage in the transaction that bridging finance will be required and arrangements should be made as soon as possible so that the money is immediately available when required on exchange.

(b) An undertaking to repay the bridging loan out of the proceeds of sale of the client's existing property will often be required from the solicitor. Should an undertaking be given and, if so, are its terms acceptable?

(c) Has the client been properly advised about the costs and risks of bridging finance, e.g. high interest rate payable over an uncertain period if the sale goes off, arrangement fees?

(d) Tax relief on the amount of the bridging finance is available where the loan is taken on a separate loan account, but not where the loan is taken by way of overdraft on a current account. If the client has a high cash flow passing through his current account it may be more cost effective to forgo the tax relief and take advantage of the lower interest rates payable on the current account.

17.3.4. Deposit guarantee

Check buyer's eligibility – the conditions of the scheme may provide, e.g. that the scheme is not available for first-time buyers, or that the deposit must not exceed either 10% of the purchase price or £15,000, or that the completion date in the contract must not be more than six weeks from the date of exchange.

17.3.5. The seller's agreement to use of the scheme must be obtained as soon as possible and arrangements put in hand to obtain the guarantee so that it is available to be handed to the seller on exchange of contracts.

17.3.6. Before agreeing to accept deposit by way of guarantee the seller should consider:

    (a) the fact that he may not be able to use the deposit towards the deposit on his own purchase (depending on the scheme used) although this factor will be of no consequence if a deposit guarantee is to be used in that transaction also;

    (b) the consequences (including costs and delay) of attempting to enforce payment through the scheme if the reasons for the buyer's ultimate default are either disputed or not covered by the scheme.

17.3.7. Lenders' deposit-free schemes

The terms of these schemes vary from lender to lender. The terms of the particular scheme should be considered carefully by both parties before a decision to use them is taken. In particular the seller should have regard to the possible consequences (including costs and delay) if the reasons for the buyer's ultimate default are either disputed or not covered by the scheme.

17.4. Clearing funds

17.4.1. The seller will normally require the deposit to be paid either by solicitor's cheque or banker's draft.[1] The buyer's solicitor must therefore ensure that he receives the amount of the deposit from his own client in sufficient time to allow the client's cheque to be cleared through the solicitor's clients' account before drawing the cheque in favour of the seller for the deposit.

17.4.2. Under Standard Commercial Property Condition 2.2.2 the deposit is payable by direct credit only. The Conditions require that the direct credit arrive not later than the date of the contract in cleared funds at the bank nominated by the seller's solicitors (see SCPC 1.1.1(e), 2.2.1 and 2.2.2). This may be impossible to fulfil if exchange takes place in the late afternoon. Agreeing between solicitors to send the money the next working day may avoid the buyer's solicitor being in breach of the undertaking implied in Formula B but will not operate to amend the contract because of Law of Property (Miscellaneous Provisions) Act 1989 s.2 – so (a) his client will technically be in breach of contract and (b) is the seller entitled to the overnight interest which his solicitor has forgone?

1. See Standard Condition 2.2.1, Appendix VII.13.

17.5. Capacity in which deposit is held

17.5.1. The deposit is held in one of the three capacities listed below:

    (a) agent for the seller;

    (b) agent for the buyer;

    (c) stakeholder.

17.5.2. In the absence of contrary agreement solicitors and estate agents hold in the capacity of agent for the seller, but an auctioneer holds as stakeholder.[1] This general rule may be varied by express contractual condition.

17.5.3. The capacity of agent for the buyer is rarely used since in most situations the seller will be reluctant to agree to the deposit being held in this way. It may, however, be necessary to use this capacity where the seller is represented by an unqualified person.

17.5.4. If the deposit is held as agent for the seller, the agent may hand the money over to the seller before completion. In this situation the seller can use the money towards the deposit on his own purchase, but where this occurs the buyer may have difficulty in recovering the money if the seller defaults on completion. The buyer should be advised of the risks involved in agreeing to the deposit being held in the capacity of agent.

17.5.5. A stakeholder is the principal for both parties and where this capacity is used the money can be handed to either party without the consent of the other provided the stakeholder is confident that circumstances exist which justify his decision to make payment.

17.5.6. Most deposits are paid to the seller's solicitor in the capacity either of agent for the seller or stakeholder.

17.5.7. The Standard Conditions of Sale (Condition 2.2.1) and Standard Commercial Property Conditions (Condition 2.2.2) generally provide for the deposit to be held as stakeholder and this is the capacity recommended by the Law Society.[2] The capacity of agent for the seller will, however, apply if the seller is to use all or part of the deposit towards the deposit on his related residential transaction in England and Wales (Standard Condition of Sale 2.2.2), and may be necessary in some circumstances where an exchange under the Law Society's Formula C is contemplated, see para. B17.9.7.

17.5.8. Where the seller is represented by an unqualified person the buyer's solicitor should ensure that he or a reputable estate agent holds the deposit (in either case in the capacity of stakeholder) or that it is placed in a deposit account in a bank or building society in the joint names of seller and buyer.

17.5.9. *Fiduciary vendors*

Where the sellers are selling as trustees the money arising from the sale will be trust money and should never be outside the control of the trustees.[3] This requirement will be satisfied if the deposit is paid to some person in the capacity of agent for the seller.

17.5.10. Where the deposit or any part of it is proposed to be held as agents of the seller, it is recommended that the buyer client should be advised of the risks involved in agreeing to this.

1. *Edgell* v. *Day* (1865) LR 1 CP 80; *Ryan* v. *Pilkington* [1959] 1 All ER 689.
2. [1975] *Gazette*, 184.
3. [1957] *Gazette*, 327.

17.6. Solicitor holding the deposit

17.6.1. The money is client money and must be placed in a client account in accordance with Solicitors' Accounts Rules 1998.[1]

1. See Solicitors' Accounts Rules 1998 (Appendix I.2).

17.7. Interest on the deposit

17.7.1. Whether the money is held in the capacity of agent for the seller or stakeholder interest may be payable under Solicitors' Accounts Rules 1998.[1]

17.7.2. Where the money is held as stakeholder interest is payable on the stake money under the provisions of Solicitors' Accounts Rules 1998. It is up to the parties to decide which of them should be entitled to the interest on the stake money and an appropriate clause must be included in the contract to deal with the payment of interest in these circumstances. The Law Society's recommended form of wording for such a clause is as follows: 'The stakeholder shall pay to the seller/buyer a sum equal to the interest the deposit would have earned if placed on deposit (less costs of acting as stakeholder).'

17.7.3. Standard Condition 2.2.3 provides that where the deposit, or part of it, is held in the capacity of stakeholder, interest on the deposit will be payable to the seller on completion. If the buyer negotiates an agreement that he is to be credited with interest on the deposit, a special condition must be inserted in the contract to that effect. Standard Commercial Property Condition 2.2.2 contains provisions similar to Standard Condition 2.2.3.

1. See Solicitors' Accounts Rules 1998 (Appendix I.2).

17.8. Deposits paid to estate agents

17.8.1. At common law an estate agent holds the deposit as agent for the seller, but this capacity may be changed to stakeholder by express contractual provision.

17.8.2. In whichever capacity the deposit is held the risk of its loss through the default of the agent generally falls on the buyer.[1]

17.8.3. This risk has been minimised by Estate Agents Act 1979, s.16 which requires agents to carry insurance to cover clients' money. 'Clients' money' is defined by section 12 of the 1979 Act to include any contract or pre-contract deposit.

17.8.4. The money must be placed in a clients' account (*ibid.* s.14), and is held on trust by the agent for the person who is or who will become entitled to the money. Since the money is trust money it will not vest in a trustee in bankruptcy should the agent be made bankrupt.[2]

17.8.5. An estate agent who holds in the capacity of agent for the seller is under a duty to account to the client for interest on any deposit exceeding £500.[3] It is not clear whether an estate agent who holds in the capacity of stakeholder is subject to the provisions relating to the payment of interest.

1. *Sorrell* v. *Finch* [1977] AC 728.
2. Estate Agents Act 1979, s.13(1).
3. Estate Agents (Accounts) Regulations 1981 (S.I. 1981/1520), reg.7.

17.9. Contractual terms relating to the deposit

17.9.1. Standard contractual conditions will normally provide for the seller's solicitor to hold a 10% deposit as stakeholder, the deposit to be paid by banker's draft or solicitor's cheque (see Standard Condition 2.2.1) or by direct credit (Standard Commercial Property Condition 2.2.2).

17.9.2. The standard clauses represent the safest method both of payment and of holding the deposit. Variations of these provisions by express contractual term is possible but should only be done where the substituted term is necessary to meet the circumstances of the individual transaction and sufficiently safeguards the interests of both parties.

17.9.3. Variation of the standard provisions may be required where the seller is represented by an unqualified person, or where a less than 10% deposit is being taken. In the latter case provision should be included in the contract for the balance of the 10% to become immediately payable in the event of a notice to complete being served so that the seller is able to forfeit the full 10% sum should it become necessary to do so. (See Standard Condition 6.8.4 and Standard Commercial Property Condition 6.8.4.)

17.9.4. Any preliminary deposit which was paid to an estate agent before exchange should be handed over to the solicitor who is holding the deposit once exchange has taken place. If this does not occur the seller will technically be in breach of contract because the contract requires the solicitor to hold 'the deposit', and this may in turn cause problems for a buyer who seeks the recovery of his deposit on the seller's default. In practice estate agents are reluctant to part with the preliminary deposit, seeking to retain it in part payment of their commission. The solicitor who is to hold the deposit should check the terms on which any preliminary deposit is held by the estate agent to ascertain if it can be taken into account in the completion statement.

17.9.5. *Checklist for contract terms*

(a) How much deposit is required in total?

    (b) Has a preliminary deposit been paid – if so, how much and to whom?

    (c) Who is to hold the deposit and in which capacity?

    (d) Method of payment?

    (e) If in cash, provide for payment by banker's draft or equivalent.

    (f) If less than 10%, provide for balance to be immediately payable on service of a completion notice.

17.9.6. The Protocol and the Standard Conditions of Sale recognise the existing practice in many areas for the deposit received on the sale of the property to be used to pay the deposit on the purchase of another property.

17.9.7. The presence of Standard Condition 2.2.3 may mean that a special condition will be necessary if the Law Society's Formula C is used on exchange of contracts and the person at the end of the chain will not agree to the deposit being held as stakeholder. In this event, it would be necessary for all parties in the chain to be notified and a special condition would be required only in the last contract in the chain. It is suggested that this should be:

> 'The deposit shall be paid to the seller's solicitor as agent for the seller and Standard Condition 2.2.3 is varied accordingly.'

17.10. Methods of payment of deposit

17.10.1. The seller may insist on the payment of the deposit in cash unless he has agreed to accept some other method of payment.[1] Standard Condition 2.2.1 requires payment to be made by banker's draft or solicitor's cheque only, except where the contract is made at auction. Standard Commercial Property Condition 2.2.2 requires payment only by direct credit except at sales by auction where other methods of payment are acceptable.

17.10.2. If a cheque taken in payment of the deposit bounces, this constitutes a fundamental breach of contract which gives the seller the option either of keeping the contract alive for the benefit of both parties, or of treating the contract as discharged by the breach, and in either event of suing for damages.[2] A separate cause of action arises out of the cheque itself. The contract should be drafted to indicate precisely what the rights of the parties are in the event of the dishonour of the deposit cheque.

17.10.3. The option of treating the contract as discharged is of little consolation to a seller who, on the strength of his sale contract, has exchanged contracts for the purchase of another property. Provision should therefore be made in the contract to ensure that the deposit is only payable by a method which will be honoured on presentation, e.g. banker's draft or solicitor's clients' account cheque.

1. *Johnston* v. *Boyes* (1898) 14 TLR 475.
2. *Millichamp* v. *Jones* [1983] 1 All ER 267, and see Standard Condition 2.2.4.

17.11. Using the deposit to fund another transaction

17.11.1. A seller who is a builder or developer, or one who is involved in the purchase of another property, may wish to use part or all of the deposit received from his sale before completion of that transaction takes place.

17.11.2. The deposit may only be used by the seller in this way if it is held in the capacity of agent for the seller.

17.11.3. Although totally satisfactory for the seller, this situation is less than satisfactory for the buyer who may find that he has difficulty in recovering his money if the sale is not completed through the default of the seller or if the seller goes bankrupt or absconds with the money. The buyer should be advised of these risks.

17.11.4. Before agreeing to allow the seller to have use of the deposit pending completion the buyer should try to ensure that the contract contains some protection for him against the seller's default. In an exceptional case it would be possible for the buyer to secure the deposit by taking an equitable charge over the seller's existing and new properties. Such a charge would need to be protected by registration of a notice (registered land) or Class C(iii) land charge (unregistered land) to bind a purchaser and could only be enforced by a court order for the sale of the property.

17.11.5. Standard Condition 2.2.2 allows the seller to use all or part of the deposit to fund his own deposit on a related residential transaction in England and Wales but for no other purpose. No equivalent provision is contained in the Standard Commercial Property Conditions.

17.12. Buyer's lien

17.12.1. From the moment when he pays the deposit to the seller in the capacity of agent (but not stakeholder) the buyer has a lien over the property for the amount of the deposit. The lien is only enforceable by a court order for sale of the property and must be protected by a notice (registered land) or Class C(iii) land charge (unregistered land) in order to bind a purchaser. If the buyer is in occupation his lien may be an overriding interest in registered land under Land Registration Act 2002.[1]

17.12.2. If the buyer defaults on completion he has no right to the return of his deposit. This is subject to the court's discretion to order the return of a deposit under Law of Property Act 1925, s.49(2).

17.12.3. If the contract is terminated for any other reason the buyer has a lien which may be enforced either by the buyer himself or by a person claiming under him.[2]

17.12.4. When the reason for non-completion of the sale is a defect in the seller's title the lien extends to the deposit, interest, and the costs of investigating title, and where the sale is by auction under the direction of the court, costs incurred by the buyer in connection with the auction are also included.[3]

17.12.5. A buyer who pays a deposit to a stakeholder is not entitled to recover through his lien the costs of an unsuccessful action for specific performance brought against him by the seller.[4]

1. Sched. 1, para. 2 and Sched. 3, para. 2.
2. *Levy* v. *Stogdon* [1898] 1 Ch 478.
3. *Holliwell* v. *Seacombe* [1906] 1 Ch 426.
4. *Combe* v. *Lord Swaythling* [1947] Ch 625.

17.13. Deposits paid direct to the seller

17.13.1. A buyer's solicitor should be wary of a situation in which the buyer has apparently paid a deposit directly to the seller. This may indicate the existence of a mortgage fraud.[1]

17.13.2. The Protocol envisages the deposit being passed by the buyer's solicitor to the seller's solicitor. Solicitors are reminded of the Law Society's guidance on mortgage fraud. In many cases of such fraud, the deposit is allegedly paid direct between the parties.

17.13.3. A solicitor should not confirm to another solicitor that deposit payments have been made or received unless the moneys have been paid into that solicitor's client account or that solicitor has actual evidence that the payment has been made or received by a third party.

17.13.4. Solicitors are reminded of Principle 16.01 of the Guide to the Professional Conduct of Solicitors (General duty of confidentiality). Any solicitor with a query about a suspected mortgage fraud should contact the Law Society Practice Advice Service on 0870 606 2522.

1. See Mortgage Fraud, para. A24; Property Fraud Warning Card, Appendix IV.3; Mortgage Fraud – variation in purchase price, Appendix V.11.

B18. Liquor licensing and food safety

See also: Pre-contract Searches and enquiries, para B10
Local Authorities of England and Wales, Appendix XI.2

18.1. Pre-contract enquiries

18.1.1. Additional enquiries of the seller should be made in relation to the following matters:

(a) to require copies of all current licences, certificates and permits applicable to the premises;

(b) to ascertain whether notice has been received by the seller of any application to revoke any licence or certificate;

(c) to ascertain whether the seller has received notice of any application for a restriction order or notice of the imposition of a closure order;

(d) to find out whether any alterations have been made to the premises under s.20 of the Licensing Act 1964;

(e) to require copies of all correspondence relevant to the licence between the licensee and the court, police, fire and local authorities since the date of the last renewal;

(f) to confirm that the seller is not aware of any current investigations or proceedings which would place any of the licences, certificates or permits at risk;

(g) to supply copies of any undertakings or assurances given by the licensees on the last grant, renewal or transfer of the licence;

(h) to provide details of any special orders of exemption granted to the licensees or copies of any applications pending.

18.2. Checking the current licences

18.2.1. The licences supplied by the seller should be checked to see:

(a) that they are valid and subsisting;

(b) what (if anything) they cover in addition to a justices' licence, e.g. a certificate under s.68 of the Licensing Act 1964, a special hours certificate (s.77) or public entertainment licence;

(c) what restrictions the licences or certificates impose on the use of the premises. Restrictive conditions will frequently be found on the liquor licence itself, on the special hours certificate and on children's certificates;

(d) care should be taken to check the public entertainment licence thoroughly. Such licences are normally accompanied by extensive schedules of conditions. Note also that any failure to renew the public entertainment licence will terminate the special hours certificate.

18.3. The premises

18.3.1. The premises themselves should be inspected to ensure that they accord with any plan deposited with the licensing justices which defines the licensed area.

18.3.2. Particular care should be taken on inspection to see whether any unauthorised alterations have taken place. Apart from issues over planning consent or building regulations, unauthorised alterations can result in a licence being forfeited or a direction being made that the premises shall be restored to their original condition. Since alterations cannot be approved retrospectively, the only way for the seller to obtain authorisation for alterations is to apply to the licensing justices for a new licence which incorporates them.

18.3.3. The client's intentions in relation to future development of the premises should be noted and their feasibility considered in view of any restrictions imposed by the current licences and certificates. Bear in mind that the licensing committee are likely to require the client to give undertakings or assurances in the same terms as any currently required of existing licensees.

18.3.4. If there are tenants occupying the premises then normal enquiries should be made as to the extent of their security of tenure.

18.4. Transfer of licence

18.4.1. Except where the transfer can be synchronised with the completion of the purchase, arrangements must be made to authorise sales between completion and the date of transfer.

18.4.2. The licence cannot be transferred unless the transfer is approved by the justices who meet by way of a licensing committee at approximately monthly intervals. In the interim either a protection order or an interim authority should be obtained in order to authorise sales of intoxicating liquor until the transfer takes place.

18.4.3. A protection order protects the holder from prosecution for the offence of selling liquor without being the holder of a licence. It is obtained by application to the magistrates' court and seven days notice to the court and to the police is required. Often these applications are taken on a particular day of the week and so enquiries should be made of the magistrates' court. The magistrates will need to be satisfied that the applicant is a fit and proper person.

18.4.4. Alternatively, application may be made for an interim authority. If this route is taken then a deemed grant will be made for a period of 14 days beginning with the date on which the application is submitted. Such authority will cease if the police (who must be given the appropriate notice) serve notice of objection. Within the 14 day period the court will normally list the application and then deal with it in the same way as they would for a protection order.

18.4.5. The date of the next licensing session should be obtained from the clerk to the licensing justices. A protection order ceases to have effect at the second transfer sessions after its grant. In the case of an interim authority the actual grant is limited to a period of 28 days. This means that where a protection order has been obtained the notice of application for the transfer of the licence should be served in time to be heard by the date of the second sessions after its grant. Where an interim authority has been obtained an application for transfer should be submitted within the 28-day period. The authority will remain in force until that application for transfer is heard.

18.4.6. If either a protection order or an interim authority cannot be obtained before contracts are exchanged then the contract will need to be made conditional on such an order being made and should contain a clause stating that the seller will consent to the buyer's application for a protection order/interim authority and to the subsequent transfer of the licence. It should be noted that the grant of either a protection order or an interim authority does not guarantee that the subsequent transfer of the licence will be granted.

18.4.7. Informal enquiries should be made of the clerk to the local licensing justices to obtain a copy of their procedural guidelines. At the same time enquiries should be made of the clerk as to the commencement of permitted hours in the relevant licensing division. Many areas have now approved a 10 a.m. commencement for the sale of intoxicating liquor.

18.4.8. Although there is no legal reason why a corporation cannot hold a licence, the invariable practice is for a corporation to nominate individuals to hold the licence on its behalf. The number of licensees required will normally depend on the nature of the premises, but checks should be made with the clerk to the licensing committee as to policy in a particular area. Some committees prefer one licensee but many others require more in order to extend the amount of time during which a licensee will be upon the premises.

18.4.9. In order to determine whether an applicant (whether for an interim authority/ protection order or transfer) is fit and proper, the court or committee will consider their previous experience. Increasingly it is becoming an entry point for new licensees that they should hold the National Licensee's Certificate or an accreditation of an equivalent standard.

18.5. The buyer

18.5.1. The buyer should be fully advised about the extent of the licence which he is proposing to take over, the items which are permitted by it (and by any other certificates or permits), the restrictions on hours and the date on which licences are next to be renewed.

18.5.2. The buyer's solicitor should check that his client is eligible to take a transfer of the licence and that no order has been made under the Licensing Act 1964, s.100 disqualifying him from holding a licence. In view of the requirements of fitness, the buyer's solicitor should also ascertain whether his client has any previous convictions.

18.5.3. Enquiries should be made as to whether the licensing justices have made any regulation under Licensing Act 1964 s.8(4) determining the time which must elapse between the grant of the transfer and any further applications for the same licence to be transferred.

18.6. Food Safety

18.6.1. The Food Premises (Registration) Regulations 1991 (as amended), made under the Food Safety Act 1990, make it an offence to carry on a food business from premises that are not registered. Food business is defined as any business in the course of which commercial operations with respect to food or food sources are carried out.

18.6.2. Application for registration must be made on a prescribed form to the appropriate local authority at least 28 days before the commencement of the business.

18.6.3. There is no fee for registration, and no requirement for renewal of registration once registered, but any changes in the information supplied must be notified to the registering authority.

18.6.4. Registration is required for:

(a) premises where a food business is carried on for five or more days (whether or not consecutive) in any five consecutive week period;

(b) premises where two or more food businesses are carried on by the same or by different people/organisations for five or more days (whether consecutive or not) within any five consecutive week period.

Where the premises are used by more than one person, it is the aggregate of use by all of them which counts towards the five-day period.

18.6.5. A large building containing smaller permanent premises where several different food businesses are carried on (e.g. the food court of an airport terminal) will not need to be registered, but each of the smaller individual food businesses must be registered. Where all of the smaller premises are used by the same food business, only one registration is required.

18.6.6. In markets where vehicles, moveable stalls and barrows (not provided by or used by the market controller) are used, the individual stalls etc. will have to be registered and, in most cases, registration will also be required for the market itself.

18.6.7. In markets where moveable stalls, barrows etc. are provided by the market controller for the use of others, individual registration of the stalls etc. is not required, but the market itself must be registered.

18.6.8. Vehicles used for food businesses, such as ice cream vans or mobile food stalls, are exempt from registration unless used within a market (as explained above). However, the premises where the vehicles are stored must be registered.

18.6.9. Staff canteens, directors' dining rooms and their kitchens attract registration under the regulations.

18.6.10. Exemptions from registration:

(a) slaughterhouses;

(b) poultry meat slaughterhouses and cutting premises;

(c) meat export cutting premises, cold stores and transhipment centres;

(d) meat product plants approved for export to another country in the EU;

(e) dairies or dairy farms;

(f) milk distribution centres;

(g) places where game is killed for sport, e.g. grouse moors;

(h) places where fish is taken for food, but not processed, e.g. river banks;

(i) places where crops are harvested, cleaned, stored and/or packed, except where the crops are wrapped in the way in which they will be sold to the consumer;

(j) places where honey is harvested;

(k) egg production or packing premises;

(l) livestock farms and markets and shellfish harvesting areas;

(m) places where no food is kept, such as kitchens used only for washing up;

(n) private cars, aircraft, and ships, except where the latter are permanently moored or used for pleasure excursions in inland or coastal waters.

(o) tents, marquees, awnings and similar structures (not including stalls);

(p) places supplying food or drink in the course of religious ceremonies;

(q) premises where the only food sold is through vending machines;

(r) places where the supply of biscuits, cakes, drinks is ancillary to the main business which is not the sale of food (e.g. hairdressers);

(s) places run and used by voluntary/charitable organisations where no food (except, tea, coffee, sugar, biscuits etc.) is stored (e.g. some village and church halls);

    (t) some domestic premises where food is prepared for another food business;

    (u) houses where bed and breakfast accommodation is provided in not more than three bedrooms.

18.6.11. The Local Authority is required to keep a register containing the name and address of each registered food premise and the type of business operated there. This is open to inspection by the public and copies can also be requested, although the local authority may charge a fee for the latter.

18.6.12. The Local Authority is also required to maintain a Supplementary Record which contains the other details supplied by food business on the registration forms. This is confidential and therefore not open to the public, but is open to inspection by the police and authorised officers. The proprietor of a food business should be allowed access to any information supplied on the registration form relating to their business.

18.6.13. Clients may be advised to obtain Code of Practice 11 published by HMSO (ISBN: 0-11-321478-2) which deals with the application and enforcement of these regulations.

B19. Mortgage offers

See also: Financial services, para. A4
Acting for both parties, para. A10
Mortgages: acting for lender and borrower, para. A11
Mortgage Fraud, para. A24

19.1. Acceptance of offer

19.1.1. Where the client is purchasing a property with the aid of mortgage finance, the solicitor must ensure that the client has received and (where necessary) accepted a satisfactory offer of a mortgage before advising the client to exchange contracts. Advice given to the client about the terms of a mortgage offer may be a regulated activity within the terms of Financial Services and Markets Act 2000.[1]

1. See Financial services, para. A4.

19.2. Conditions attached to offer

19.2.1. Before acceptance of the offer or committing his client to the purchase, the solicitor should ensure that the client understands the conditions attached to the mortgage offer and the terms of the mortgage and will be able to comply with them. Conditions may be general, e.g. a condition that the property must not be let without the lender's consent, or special, having application to this offer only, e.g. a condition that the buyer obtains an endowment policy as security for the mortgage. The mortgage offer, if formally accepted, may constitute a contract between the buyer and his lender, and the lender may not be able to withdraw his offer once accepted. The solicitor should check the offer to see whether this is the case and whether or not the lender requires a formal acceptance of the offer.

19.2.2. If the conditions attached to the mortgage offer are not wholly acceptable to the client, e.g. the offer requires the client to take out a new endowment policy when the client would be better advised to extend and re-assign an existing policy, an attempt should be made to renegotiate the terms with the lender. Such a term may be invalid under Part IV Courts and Legal Services Act 1990. In extreme cases an alternative source of finance may need to be investigated.

19.2.3. In this situation, where the buyer's solicitor has also been instructed to act for the lender, a conflict exists between the interests of the buyer client and the lender client. Unless such conflict can be resolved to the satisfaction of both clients, the solicitor cannot continue to act for either, unless with the consent of one client he is permitted to continue to act for the other. The solicitor's duty of confidentiality towards his client may prevent him from continuing to act for either client in this situation.

19.2.4. If it comes to the notice of the solicitor that the client will be in breach of the terms of the mortgage offer, e.g. where the purchase price for the property has been misrepresented to the lender, the lender must be informed of the problem.[1] The duty to inform the lender exists throughout the transaction, not just at the time when the offer is being considered. Failure to inform the lender of circumstances in which it appears that the buyer client is attempting to perpetrate a fraud on the lender may lead to the criminal prosecution of the solicitor and to disciplinary proceedings being taken against him. This gives rise to a conflict of interests between the buyer client and the lender client since the lender may, in the light of the information received, choose to adjust the terms of the mortgage offer to the detriment of the buyer client. Attention is drawn to the Law Society's guidelines on mortgage fraud which are reproduced in Appendix V.11 and Law Society's Property Fraud Warning Card in Appendix IV.3.

1. See also Mortgages: acting for lender and borrower, para. A11.

19.3. Duty of confidentiality

19.3.1. In any of the above circumstances where a conflict of interests exists between the buyer client and the lender client the solicitor, acting in his capacity of adviser to the buyer, may only disclose the nature of the conflict to the lender with the consent of the buyer client. Disclosure of information without the buyer client's consent will be a breach of the solicitor's duty of confidentiality (see also para. A24 Mortgage Fraud).

19.4. Consumer Credit Act 1974

19.4.1. Consumer Credit Act 1974, s.58 may be applicable if the mortgage is:

  (a) for a sum less than £15,000; and

  (b) to be granted to an individual or partnership by a non-exempt lender; and

  (c) is not a loan for the *purchase* of land.

19.4.2. Consumer Credit Act 1974 does not generally apply to loans exceeding £15,000 and, by regulations made under the Act,[1] loans granted by most major banks, building societies and insurance companies are exempted from the provisions of the Act.

19.4.3. The requirements of section 58 will thus not normally be relevant in circumstances where the buyer client is purchasing land with the assistance of a first mortgage from an institutional lender. Where, however, the client already owns the land in question and is refinancing or taking out a second or subsequent mortgage the provisions of section 58 should be borne in mind, particularly where the solicitor is acting also for the lender.

19.4.4. Section 58 provides that the borrower must be given a 'cooling-off' period (normally of 14 days) after the mortgage documentation has been sent to him by the lender. The purpose of this period is to allow the borrower to reflect on and to take independent advice on the terms of the loan without being subjected to pressure from the lender or anyone acting on behalf of the lender. During the 'cooling off' period neither the lender nor anyone acting on his behalf (which includes the solicitor acting for the lender) may make contact with the borrower, whether by letter, telephone or any other means of communication. During this time the solicitor may speak or write to his borrower client if the client approaches him, but client contact should not be initiated by the solicitor whilst the consideration period is running. Failure to comply with this provision will render the mortgage unenforceable except with leave of the court, which will not automatically be granted. Thus a solicitor who is acting for a lender in circumstances where section 58 applies must establish precisely when the consideration period begins to run and must not prejudice the enforceability of the loan by voluntarily contacting his client during this period.

1. Consumer Credit (Exempt Agreements) Order 1989 (S.I. 1989/869).

19.5. Discharge of existing mortgage

19.5.1. It is usually a term of a mortgage offer for a first mortgage over property that any existing mortgage which the client has should be discharged on or before completion of the new loan. The solicitor must ensure the buyer client is aware of and can comply with this condition.[1]

19.5.2. Some lenders charge interest on an existing loan until the end of the calendar month notwithstanding that the mortgage is repaid earlier. Since this extra amount of interest can add up to a considerable sum, the solicitor should enquire of the lender whether such interest will be charged on the discharge of the existing mortgage and advise his client accordingly.

1. See para 5.8 of the CML Lenders' Handbook (see Appendix VIII.3).

B20. Auctions

See also: Conditional contracts, para. B13

20.1. Acting for the seller

20.1.1. Where property is to be sold by auction the contract generally consists of particulars, describing the land to be sold, conditions stating the terms of the sale, and a memorandum of the sale which will be signed by or on behalf of the buyer at the auction itself.

20.1.2. The special conditions of the contract are normally prepared by the seller's solicitor in conjunction with the auctioneer who will prepare the particulars of sale. The contract will frequently incorporate the Standard Conditions of Sale although many auctioneers have their own general conditions of sale and some have adopted the Common Auction Conditions (promoted by RICS).

20.2. Preparing the contract

20.2.1. In addition to the usual contractual clauses particular attention should be paid to the matters listed below. Most of these matters are normally dealt with either in the auctioneers' general conditions or by the Standard Conditions of Sale and by the Standard Commercial Property Conditions but it is advisable to check their relevance to the particular property concerned and to ensure that any necessary amendments or additions to the Standard Conditions are included in the special conditions of the contract. Some, but not all, of the matters listed below are included in Standard Condition 2.3 and in Standard Commercial Property Condition 2.3.

(a) Reserve price

By Sale of Land by Auction Act 1867, s.5 the contract must state whether or not the property is subject to a reserve price. Unless a reserve is placed on the property the auctioneer will be bound to sell to the highest bidder.

(b) Right to bid

Where the property is subject to a reserve price the seller may, under Sale of Land by Auction Act 1867, reserve the right to bid at the auction. This right when reserved by special condition in the contract may be exercised by the seller or his agent.

(c) The auctioneer's control over the bidding

In order to avoid uncertainty the contract should make it clear whether the auctioneer has the right to refuse a bid; or to fix the amount of bids; and should contain provisions whereby the auctioneer may settle any dispute which arises over the bidding.

(d) Payment of deposit

The contract should provide for the amount of the deposit to be paid, the time when it is to be paid, and the methods of payment which are acceptable. It is usual at an auction to provide for a full 10% deposit to be paid. At common law the deposit must be tendered in cash.[1] Standard Condition 2.2.1 and Standard Commercial Property Condition 2.2 provide for a 10% deposit to be payable but does not limit the methods of payment (e.g. to solicitor's cheque); therefore unless this condition is amended the seller would have to accept payment by the buyer's own cheque with the attendant risks of that cheque not being honoured on presentation.

(e) Seller's right to withdraw from auction

In the absence of a special condition it is uncertain whether the seller is entitled to withdraw the property from auction once bidding has commenced unless the sale is subject to a reserve price.

(f) Retraction of bids by buyer

It is common to include a condition precluding the retraction of a bid once made. Such a condition is probably unenforceable at common law under the general principles of offer and acceptance. A bid made at auction is an offer, and the offeror (buyer) is free to withdraw his offer at any time until acceptance by the auctioneer. Acceptance takes place with the fall of the hammer. It should be noted that auction contracts are excluded from the provisions of Law of Property (Miscellaneous Provisions) Act 1989, s.2 (requiring a contract for the sale of land to be in writing); an auction contract will therefore be binding and enforceable even if oral and no memorandum is signed.

(g) Division of property into lots

If required, an express right to divide the property into separate lots should be included in the contract.

(h) Buyer's right to rescind

Where the buyer has not been given the opportunity to make searches or to inspect copies of searches made by the seller prior to the auction, it may be felt appropriate to include a provision which allows the buyer to rescind within a certain time if the results of his searches are not satisfactory. The inclusion of such a condition will introduce an element of uncertainty into the contract, which is not primarily in the interests of the seller. Any such condition must be carefully drafted to ensure that it will not render the contract void for uncertainty and will not allow the buyer to escape from the contract except in precisely worded given circumstances.

(i) Tenancies

The seller's duty of disclosure requires that accurate details of all tenancies to which the property is subject must be revealed in the contract.

(j) Inspection of title deeds and searches

It is common to include a clause in the auction particulars which entitles any prospective buyer to inspect the title deeds and any searches which have been made by the seller. The clause should provide for a time and place for the inspection.

1. *Johnston* v. *Boyes* (1898) 14 TLR 475.

20.3. Other preparatory steps by the seller

20.3.1. In addition to the preparation of the contract the seller's solicitor should, before the auction, undertake the following preparatory steps.

20.3.2. *Searches*

A buyer will frequently not have sufficient time before the auction in which to make the usual searches and enquiries. In order to avoid having to include a clause in the contract entitling the buyer to rescind if the results of searches are not satisfactory, it is preferable for the seller to undertake such searches himself and to make them available for inspection by prospective buyers both before the auction and at the sale itself. A local authority search and enquiries may be requisitioned by the seller's solicitor, as well as any other searches which are relevant to the particular transaction. The seller's solicitor should also prepare and make available answers to standard enquiries before contract.

20.3.3. *Title*

As with the preparation of any draft contract, the seller's solicitor should investigate his client's title prior to drafting the contract so that any imperfections may either be disclosed in the contract or put right before the auction takes place. Particular care is needed to ensure that full details of any existing tenancies are obtained.

20.3.4. *Inspection of deeds*

It is helpful to the buyer if the seller can allow a prospective buyer an opportunity to inspect the title deeds and search results at the seller's solicitors' office or other named place at a convenient time prior to the auction. The deeds and search results should also be available for inspection at the auction itself.

20.4. Attending the auction

20.4.1. The seller's solicitor should attend the auction in order to make the title deeds and search results available for inspection to prospective buyers and to answer any queries which may arise.

20.5. Memorandum of sale

20.5.1. The memorandum of sale is usually annexed to the printed auction particulars and conditions. It is common to include a condition that the buyer will sign the memorandum immediately after the sale. The auctioneer has implied authority to sign on behalf of both seller and buyer. An auctioneer's clerk has no such implied authority but may be expressly authorised to sign for one or both of the parties. As far as the buyer is concerned, the auctioneer's authority is limited to 'the time of the sale' which expression has no legal definition but must be taken to mean either at the sale itself or within a short time afterwards. In *Chaney* v. *Maclow*[1] the auctioneer's signature, effected at the auctioneer's own offices some two hours after the sale, was held to bind the buyer; *cf. Bell* v. *Balls*[2] where a signature made one week after the sale was not effective to bind the buyer. If the buyer refuses to sign and the auctioneer will not sign as the buyer's agent the seller cannot force the buyer to sign, because an oral agreement to put a contract into writing and to sign it cannot be enforced by specific performance, but it seems that damages may be recovered for breach of such a condition.[3] It should be noted that auction contracts are excluded from the provisions of Law of Property (Miscellaneous Provisions) Act 1989, s.2 (requiring a contract for the sale of land to be in writing); an auction contract will therefore be binding and enforceable even if oral and no memorandum is signed.

1. [1929] 1 Ch 461.
2. [1897] 1 Ch 663.
3. See *Wood* v. *Midgely* (1854) 5 De M & G 41.

20.6. Acting for the buyer

20.6.1. *Searches*

The buyer will frequently not be aware of the auction and/or instruct his solicitor in sufficient time to permit the usual searches and enquiries to be undertaken. If there is time, then searches should be made in the usual way. If not, the buyer's solicitor should at least attempt to make a local authority search and enquiries either in person or through an agent unless up-to-date search results are available for inspection from the seller's solicitor or the auctioneer.

20.7. Survey

20.7.1. Where time permits the buyer should be advised to have the property surveyed prior to the auction.

20.8. Contract and title

20.8.1. A copy of the auction particulars, containing the contract terms, should be obtained and scrutinised prior to the auction. Where searches have not been made by the buyer it should be ascertained whether the contract contains a provision allowing the buyer to rescind if the results of searches undertaken after the auction are adverse. If no such provision is included, the buyer should be advised of the consequences of entering a contract without having made searches and enquiries.

20.8.2. The seller's solicitor will often allow the buyer the opportunity to inspect the title deeds (and sometimes also searches which he has undertaken) before the auction. The buyer's solicitor should inspect the deeds and make such further enquiries as are relevant to the property at the earliest possible opportunity. The buyer may take the benefit of searches requisitioned by the seller, but reliance on such searches is inadvisable if the search results are more than two months old. If inspection of the deeds is not possible prior to the auction the buyer's solicitor should attend the auction and make such inspection before the bidding commences.

20.8.3. The terms of an auction contract are often less favourable to the buyer than would be the case in a sale by private treaty. Auction contract terms are generally non-negotiable as far as the buyer is concerned and therefore the terms of the contract need to be carefully scrutinised before the auction and the buyer advised about the consequences of any adverse terms. Occasionally, the special conditions of the contract will be altered by an oral statement made at the time of the auction itself and the buyer should be advised to listen carefully and note the effect of any such amendments. Examples of terms which might be onerous to the buyer include the following:

(a) terms precluding the buyer's right to raise enquiries or requisitions after the auction;

(b) restrictions on sub-sales by the buyer;

(c) obligations on the buyer to pay the arrears of rent or service charge on a leasehold property;

(d) terms requiring the buyer to reimburse the seller for search fees and/or the cost of supplying an engrossment of the transfer deed;

(e) on the sale of a freehold reversion of a block of flats, terms excluding any warranty by the seller that the provisions of Landlord and Tenant Act 1987 have been complied with. This statute is discussed in para. K9.

20.8.4. Any information supplied by the seller to the potential buyers prior to the auction must be accurate. Despite the terms of the contract, inaccuracies in any documents provided by the seller may lead to an action in misrepresentation.[1]

1. *Pankhavia and anon* v. *Hackney London Council and anon* [2002] All ER (D) 22.

20.9. Finance

20.9.1. The buyer should be warned of the possibility of abortive expenditure if his bid is not successful. As the contract to purchase will come into existence at the time of the auction itself it is essential that the buyer's financial arrangements have been finalised prior to the auction. Arrangements must be made for the deposit to be available at the auction, in cash (banker's draft) if this is required by the auction particulars.

20.10. Insurance

20.10.1. The buyer should also make arrangements for the property to be placed on insurance cover from the moment of the fall of the auctioneer's hammer since, depending on the terms of the contract, risk in the property may pass to him at this time.

20.11. Rights of first refusal

20.11.1. If the property to be sold at auction is affected by Landlord and Tenant Act 1987 which gives the tenants of some leasehold flats the right to purchase the landlord's reversionary interest (see para. K9) the landlord must comply with section 5B Landlord and Tenant Act 1987 (as amended by Housing Act 1996). This section requires the landlord to serve notice on at least 90% of the qualifying tenants between four and six months before the auction. Failure to comply with the Act is a criminal offence.

20.12. VAT

20.12.1. The auctioneer usually holds deposits for the seller as agent. This means that when the hammer goes down, a tax point is created for the transaction. Therefore, if the property is subject to the election to waive exemption, and it is intended to make the purchase under the TOGC rules (so that no VAT is payable) the purchaser must exercise their election to waive exemption and notify it to Customs & Excise prior to the day of auction, otherwise TOGC procedures cannot be invoked. If the purchase does not take place, the purchaser can then revoke the election to waive exemption (see Value Added Tax, para. A16).

B21. Plans

See also: Form of contract, para. B11
Land Registration Rules 2003 (selected Schedules), Appendix XII.5.

21.1. When is a plan necessary?

21.1.1. Before drafting the contract the seller's solicitor should consider whether it is necessary to identify or describe the property by reference to a plan. On receipt of the draft contract from the seller's solicitor, the buyer's solicitor should also consider whether a plan is required. The buyer is entitled to demand a plan on the purchase deed (at the seller's expense) only if the description of the property through the contract and evidence of title is inadequate without one; therefore this matter must be addressed at the pre-contract stage. In other circumstances the buyer might be able to insist on the inclusion of a plan provided that he offered to prepare and pay for it. The buyer's solicitor may need a plan of the property in order to make pre-contract searches and enquiries.[1]

21.1.2. A plan must be used on a sale of part of land (which includes the grant of leases of flats) and may be desirable in other cases, e.g. where the boundaries of the property are not self-evident, but should not be used indiscriminately[2]. The sale of the whole of a registered title can usually be described adequately by reference to its title number and, where applicable, its postal address.

21.1.3. Land Registration Rules 2003, r.213, provides that a document lodged at the Land Registry dealing with part of the land in a registered title must have attached to it a plan identifying clearly the land dealt with. However, if the land dealt with is identified clearly on the title plan it may instead be described by reference to that title plan. On building estates, the seller should normally submit his estate layout plan to the Land Registry for approval before the sale of the individual plots is commenced. Any changes in the approved estate layout plan should be notified by the seller to the Land Registry.

21.1.4. Whatever type of plan is used it must be of sufficient size and scale to enable the boundaries and other features of the property to be readily identified.[3] A plan on a scale of 1:1250 will suffice for most cases, but a larger scale will usually be required for sales of flats or the division of buildings into separate units.

21.1.5. Boundaries shown on the majority of plans prepared by the Land Registry are general boundaries only and do not therefore show the exact line of the boundaries.[4] The registered proprietor may apply to the Land Registry for the exact line of the boundary, or any part of the boundary, to be determined.[5] The procedure for fixing boundaries under the Land Registration Rules 1925 was rarely used in practice.

21.1.6. A plan will be required where the sale is by reference to a fence line or where the boundaries of the property are otherwise unclear. In such a case the parties should be asked to agree the boundaries (if necessary by a site inspection and with the co-operation of the owner of neighbouring property) and the fence line or boundary should be staked out on the site.

1. See Pre-contract searches and enquiries, para. B10.
2. See *Land Registry Practice Guide 40 Land Registry Plans*.
3. See *Scarfe v. Adams* [1981] 1 All ER 843.
4. Land Registration Act 2002, s.60.
5. Land Registration Rules 2003, r.118.

21.2. Preparing the plan

21.2.1. Plans used in deeds may emanate from a variety of sources. Generally, any plan that has been professionally prepared and is drawn accurately to a scale referred to in para. B21.2.3 should be satisfactory for use in a deed. Hand drawn sketches should not be used.

21.2.2. There are some occasions where a professionally drawn plan may be unsuitable, e.g. if it was drawn for an architectural or engineering purpose (large scale) or it was drawn for a location plan or road map (small scale). The most commonly acceptable base plans for use in any deed lodged for registration are copies of Ordnance Survey maps (see para. B21.2.5) or copy estate layout plans (see para. B21.1.3).

21.2.3. Where a plan is required for any new deed or for any application lodged at the Land Registry it should be prepared having regard to the following guidelines:

- it should be drawn true to scale and show its orientation (e.g. north point);

- the preferred scales are 1/1250–1/500 for urban and semi-urban properties and 1/2500 for rural properties (farms, etc.);

- metric scales must be used – scales using imperial measurements, e.g. 16 feet to 1 inch, are not permitted;

- it should not be marked or referred to as being for identification only;

- statements of disclaimer intended to comply with the Property Misdescriptions Act 1991 are not acceptable for registration purposes where the plan is, or is about to be, part of a conveyancing deed. They are also inappropriate to any preliminary services applications;

- it must show sufficient detail to enable the position and precise extent of the property to be related to the Ordnance Survey map, e.g. roads and road junctions and other landmarks;

- the property which is the subject of the transaction must be clearly identified, e.g. edged, coloured or hatched;

- multiple parcels of a property, e.g. house, parking space, dustbin space etc. must be separately identified by suitable plan markings;

- different floor levels must be identified both on the plan and in the parcels of the deed;

- intricate boundaries may require a larger scale or inset plan;

- where it is necessary for any measurement to be shown, e.g. the boundary needs to be described to the nearest centimetre, metric units must be used;

- undefined boundaries, i.e. no physical feature, should be drawn accurately, and where necessary, located by reference to metric measurements on the plan;

- where measurements are considered necessary then the dimensions shown on the plan should correspond, so far as is possible, to the scaled measurements;

- the plan should show buildings in their correct position on their plots together with access drives and pathways which form plot boundaries.

Note: The Land Registry does not consider it necessary to specify in any deed or on any plan the area of the property described.

21.2.4. Where it is clear that the plan contained in any deed is a reduced copy of a layout plan drawn to a recognised scale, e.g. 1/500, the reduced plan is acceptable provided:

- the original scale has been deleted;

- the plan has been endorsed with a suitable form of words to indicate that it is a reduced copy;

- the actual scale has been calculated and shown on the face of the plan in place of the original scale.

In all cases the reduced plan must be clear and unambiguous so that relevant details can be identified.

Where the plan attached to the copy transfer or lease is a reduced copy of the plan to the original transfer, it is acceptable provided:

- the original scale has been deleted;

- it has been endorsed with a statement to the effect that it is a reduced copy of the plan to the original deed;

- the actual scale of the copy plan, where known, is stated.

21.2.5. Current Ordnance Survey mapping is only available from authorised Ordnance Survey Superplan Agents. (For details of Agents, contact Ordnance Survey, see Appendix XI.5 for address.)

21.2.6. The Land Registry is not authorised to supply Ordnance Survey maps.

21.2.7. Where the value or complexity of the transaction justifies the expense, an architect or surveyor may be instructed to prepare a plan. The client's authority should be obtained prior to incurring such expenditure.

21.2.8. If there is any doubt as to the size or extent of the property an inspection should be carried out and measurements taken.

21.2.9. Guidance on the preparation of plans can be found in the appropriate practice material issued by the Land Registry.

21.3. Showing features on the plan

21.3.1. The plan must be clearly drawn so that it is capable of being read in isolation from the accompanying contract or purchase deed. The wording of the contract or purchase deed will, however, need to make reference to the plan and its various features and this point should be borne in mind when the plan is drawn, e.g. a right of way may be more easily described in words in the contract if its beginning and end points are marked 'A' and 'B' on the plan in addition to the demarcation of the route.

21.3.2. *Points to note*

(a) Markings should be clear and precise.

(b) Land to be sold should be outlined or coloured in red.

(c) Retained land (if any) should be outlined or coloured in blue.

(d) Other land referred to should be coloured or hatched in distinct colours other than red or blue. If possible it is best to avoid the use of green on a plan where red has already been used since the most common form of colour blindness relates to the inability to distinguish between these two colours. Reference should also be made to the appropriate practice material issued by the Land Registry in relation to the Registry's preferred practice for colouring plans.

(e) The ownership of boundaries should be indicated by 'T' marks with the 'T' on the side of the boundary line within the land which bears responsibility for the maintenance of the boundary. In the absence of a specific request the Land Registry will only show 'T' marks on the title plan if referred to in a covenant or other provision in the transfer.

(f) Rights of way and routes of services should be tinted or marked with broken or dotted lines of a distinct colour, with each end of the route being additionally identified with separate capital letters.

(g) Where the plan is to scale the scale should be shown.

(h) If the plan is not to scale, metric measurements should be shown along each boundary. An imperial measurement can be used in addition to the metric measurement provided that the metric measurement is placed first and the imperial measurement is in characters no larger than the metric figure.

(i) A compass point indicating the direction of North should be shown.

(j) A key should be included to explain the meaning of the various colours and lines used on the plan.

21.4.   Referring to the contract plan

21.4.1. The contract (and subsequent purchase deed) may refer to the plan as being 'for identification purposes only', or will describe the land as being 'more particularly delineated on the plan'. These two phrases are mutually exclusive and a combination of the two serves no useful purpose.[1]

21.4.2.   'Identification purposes only'

Where there is a discrepancy between the land shown on the plan and the contract description and the plan has been described as being for identification purposes only, the verbal description of the land will normally prevail over the plan. The court may, however, refer to such a plan to define the boundaries of the property where the verbal description is unclear.[2] Plans described as 'for identification purposes only' are not satisfactory for land registration purposes.

21.4.3.   'More particularly delineated'

In the event of a discrepancy between the verbal description of the land and the plan, the plan will prevail over the words where the phrase 'more particularly delineated' has been used. This phrase should not be used unless the plan is to scale.

21.4.4. A plan which is included in the purchase deed but which is not referred to by use of one of the above phrases may be looked at in order to identify the land only if the description of the property as afforded by the purchase deed and other available evidence (e.g. title deeds) is unclear.[3]

1. *Neilson* v. *Poole* (1969) 20 P & CR 909.
2. See *Wiggington & Milner Ltd* v. *Winster Engineering Ltd* [1978] 3 All ER 436.
3. *Leachman* v. *L. & K. Richardson Ltd* [1969] 3 All ER 20.

B22. Fixtures and fittings

See also: Form of contract, para. B11

22.1. Distinction between fixtures and fittings

22.1.1. *Fixtures*

Fixtures are generally items which are attached to and form part of the land and which will therefore be included as part of the property on sale of the land unless the seller expressly reserves the right to remove them.

22.1.2. *Fittings*

Fittings or chattels do not form part of the land and so are not included as part of the property on sale of the land unless the seller expressly agrees to leave them behind.

22.1.3. *Practical distinction*

The legal distinction between fixtures and fittings as outlined in the above sub-paragraphs is quite clear. The practical distinction between the two categories is sometimes less obvious. Movable objects which are not attached to the land, e.g. carpets, curtains and free-standing furniture clearly fall within the definition of fittings, but items which are attached to the land such as gas boilers and satellite dishes are not always classified as fixtures. Case law in this area is unclear and there have been reported cases where items such as greenhouses, garden ornaments, plumbed-in kitchen appliances and even freezers have been held to be fixtures, and other cases where the same items have been held to be fittings.[1]

1. See *TSB Bank* v. *Botham* [1996] EGCS 149, and *Elitestone* v. *Morris* [1997] 2 All ER 513.

22.2. Need for certainty in contract

22.2.1. In view of the uncertainty of the status of some items in law it is essential that in appropriate circumstances the contract deals expressly with:

(a) fixtures which the seller intends to remove on or before completion (including, where appropriate, the tenant's right to remove tenant's trade fixtures);

(b) compensation for the buyer if the seller causes damage in the course of the removal of fixtures;

(c) fittings which are to remain at the property;

(d) any additional price which the buyer is to pay for the fittings;

(e) the apportionment of the purchase price to exclude from the total the price paid for the fittings;

(f) deferment of passing of title to fittings until completion because in the absence of such a condition Sale of Goods Act 1979, s.18 will provide that title to the fittings passes to the buyer on exchange;

(g) a warranty that fittings are free of incumbrances (e.g. subsisting hire-purchase agreements). Although Sale of Goods Act 1979, s.12 will imply such a warranty its express inclusion in the contract prevents the matter from being overlooked by the seller (see Standard Condition 9).

22.2.2. Disputes over the unexpected removal of fixtures and fittings are common and frequently cost more to resolve than the value of the disputed items. The buyer may require the seller to supply written confirmation that fixtures and fittings which were seen by the buyer on inspection of the property will not be removed from the property and are included in the sale, or in appropriate cases the contract may contain a warranty given by the seller that he has not removed any fixtures from the property since a stated date.

22.2.3. The estate agent's particulars should be scrutinised to see which items are listed as being included or excluded from the sale, and checked with the client to ensure their accuracy.

22.2.4. When taking instructions it will be necessary to ascertain from the client which items are to be removed, which items he expects to remain at the property, and whether any price in addition to the price of the land is required for the fittings.

22.3. Apportionment of purchase price

22.3.1. No stamp duty on chattels

The sale of chattels, including chattels which although attached to the land have not become fixtures, does not attract *ad valorem* stamp duty unless included in the conveyance. The value of chattels which have been included in the purchase price of the land may therefore be subtracted from the total purchase price and ignored in deciding whether a certificate of value for below £500,000 can be inserted in the transfer, thereby effecting a reduction in the value of the land and a possible consequent reduction in the rates and or amount of *ad valorem* stamp duty payable by the buyer.

22.3.2. This apportionment of the purchase price between the land and the chattels is of most value to the buyer when the value of the land and chattels together is marginally above the current stamp duty threshold.

22.3.3. *Consequences of over-valuation*

Only the true value of the chattels may be deducted from the purchase price for this purpose. Any over-valuation of the price of the chattels is a fraud on the Inland Revenue which may render both the solicitor and his client liable to criminal sanctions. Such conduct would also be conduct unbefitting the solicitor which could result in disciplinary proceedings being brought against him. A further consequence of the over-valuation is that the contract for the sale of the land would be unenforceable by court action since it could be construed by the courts as being a contract to defraud the Inland Revenue, such contracts being unenforceable on the grounds of public policy.[1]

22.3.4. If the draft contract does not make provision for the apportionment of the purchase price in a situation where such apportionment would be appropriate, the buyer should, as a matter of courtesy, seek the seller's consent before making the necessary adjustment to the contract.

1. See *Saunders* v. *Edwards* [1987] 2 All ER 651.

22.4. **Protocol**

22.4.1. Paragraph 2.9 of the Protocol requires the seller's solicitor to obtain information relating to fixtures and fittings from the seller, using the standard Fixtures, Fittings and Contents Form. The completed form should then be sent to the buyer's solicitors with the draft contract (Protocol, para. 4.4). See Appendix III.1. for the full text of the Protocol.

22.5. **Guidelines**

22.5.1. In order to avoid future disputes between the parties the solicitor is advised to check with the client which items are included/excluded from the sale and whether any additional price is payable for the included items. Items which would normally be considered to be fixtures (e.g. fitted wardrobes) should not be charged for in addition to the contract price nor removed from the property unless there is an express reservation of the right to do so in the contract. Items which are normally removable as fittings, e.g. carpets will not be included in the contract unless the parties agree to their inclusion, possibly at a price additional to the sum payable for the land. Where there are items which may be regarded either as fixtures or fittings depending on the circumstances, e.g. a greenhouse, the solicitor will need to make further enquiries of his client and should consider express mention of these items in the contract for the avoidance of doubt. In residential transactions use of the Fixtures, Fittings and Contents Form is strongly recommended. This form, the contents of which will be agreed by the parties, will be annexed to and form part of the contract.

22.6. Passing of title to chattels

22.6.1.   Under Standard Condition 9 both the risk and title in chattels does not pass to the buyer until completion.

22.6.2.   Under Standard Commercial Property Condition 9 title in chattels remains with the seller until completion but risk passes on exchange. It may be difficult for a buyer to obtain insurance over chattels which he does not own.

B23. Powers of attorney

See also: Capacity, para. B7
Title, section D
Completion, section F

23.1. When is a power needed?

23.1.1. The solicitor should consider the preparation of a power of attorney for his client if the client:

(a) is elderly and/or physically infirm; or

(b) is likely to be unavailable at the time when it will be necessary to obtain his signature to documents.

23.2. What type of power?

23.2.1. *General power under Powers of Attorney Act 1971*

This type of power will give the attorney authority to deal with all of the donor's assets including the sale or purchase of property.

23.2.2. *Special power under Powers of Attorney Act 1971*

A special power will give the attorney authority to deal only with the matters specified in the power and thus may be limited to, e.g. the sale of a named property. Except where it is intended to allow the attorney to assume complete control of the donor's affairs this type of power would be more appropriate than a general power in the context of the sale or purchase of land.

23.2.3. *Enduring power under Enduring Powers of Attorney Act 1985*

This type of power must be executed in the form prescribed by the Regulations made under the 1985 Act[1] and is not revoked on the subsequent mental incapacity of the donor. It cannot be used by a trustee to confer power on his sole co-trustee where, e.g. property is jointly owned by husband and wife and one party wishes to appoint the other as his or her attorney during a period of absence abroad. See the Trustee Delegation Act 1999.

23.2.4. Security powers

A security power under Powers of Attorney Act 1971, s.4 may be taken by a lender who has taken an equitable mortgage in order to give him a power to sell the property if the borrower defaults on the mortgage. This type of power is irrevocable and may be incorporated in the mortgage document or given by separate deed.

23.2.5. Trusts and Powers of Attorney

23.2.5.1. Prior to 1 March 2000, if a trustee (including a co-owner) wished to appoint an attorney to act in connection with a sale or purchase of a property, he could not use a general power of attorney. The donor had to use a specific power of attorney under Trustee Act 1925 s.25. This was limited in duration to 12 months. In addition the power could not be used by a trustee to delegate to his sole co-trustee, in such a case he would have to use an enduring power of attorney under the Enduring Powers of Attorney Act 1985.

23.2.5.2. From 1 March 2000 a trustee who is beneficially entitled under the trust (e.g. a co-owner) can now use a general power (s.1 of the Act). He can also appoint his sole co-trustee to be his attorney. If the trustee is not beneficially entitled under the trust, s.5 of the Act states that he can use a general power but that it must be limited to a period of 12 months. The trustee can appoint his sole co-trustee to be his attorney. In either case, if the sole co-trustee has been appointed, such an attorney cannot give a valid receipt for capital money and overreaching will not operate. In such a case a third party should be appointed to act as attorney. An enduring power of attorney can no longer be used by a trustee to appoint a sole co-trustee to act as attorney.

1. See Enduring Powers of Attorney (Prescribed Forms) Regulations 1990 (S.I. 1990/1376). A power which is executed under a prescribed form which is not current at the time of execution is probably not valid and a new power using the form prescribed by the current regulations must be executed. Acts done by the attorney under an invalid power can be ratified by execution of a deed of ratification by the donor, provided the donor is still mentally capable.

23.3. Who should be the attorney?

23.3.1. The client should be advised of the consequences of giving a power of attorney, i.e. that the attorney will (depending on the terms of the power) have a wide authority and discretion to deal with the client's affairs. Only a person whom the client trusts absolutely should be considered for appointment as attorney. The solicitor may be appointed as attorney provided that no conflict of interests exists between himself and his client(s). The solicitor should advise the client of his charges in relation to so acting. The limitations on the appointment of an attorney in the case of trust property have been noted above.

23.4. When should the appointment be made?

23.4.1. The power of attorney should be drawn up and executed as soon as the decision to appoint an attorney has been made. This is necessary because it is courteous to inform the other party to the transaction at the earliest opportunity that the documents will be signed under a power of attorney.

23.5. The client who already has a power

23.5.1. Where a client comes to the solicitor with an existing power of attorney, the solicitor should examine the power to ascertain its type and validity for the transaction proposed.

23.6. Informing the other party of the appointment

23.6.1. It is courteous to inform the other party to the transaction at the earliest opportunity that the documents will be signed under a power of attorney. A copy of the power should be supplied to the other party as soon as possible so that its validity and suitability for the transaction in progress may be confirmed.

23.6.2. Except in the case of a security power or an enduring power which has been registered with the Court of Protection, if the power will be more than 12 months old at the date when it is purportedly exercised, the person who buys from the attorney will need to make a statutory declaration immediately after completion stating that he believed the power to be valid and had no knowledge of its revocation at the time of its exercise.[1]

1. See Powers of Attorney Act 1971, s.5.

B24. Planning

See also: Planning and compulsory puchase, para. AA6.
Conditional contracts, para. B13
Environmental issues, para. B25

24.1. Relevance of planning to the transaction

24.1.1. Heavy penalties may ensue from breach of planning legislation; it is therefore important to check at the start of a transaction that any necessary planning requirements have been or will be complied with. It may also be necessary to check whether any restrictive covenants on the property conflict with the present structure(s) and/or use, and if so whether consent to the buildings and/or their current use/or a release or indemnity insurance has been obtained.

24.1.2. The development of land will normally require the grant of planning permission. Development is defined by Town and Country Planning Act 1990 (as amended) as 'the carrying out of building, engineering, mining or other operations in, on, over or under land, or the making of any material change in the use of any buildings or other land'. This definition encompasses the erection of new buildings, the demolition of and alterations and additions to existing buildings, fish farming and in certain circumstances changing the use of a building.

24.1.3. A house which has been in multiple occupation will need planning permission for use as a single dwelling unless it has been occupied by not more than 6 residents living together as a single household (including a household where care is provided for residents). See Class C3 of the T&CP (Use Classes) Order 1987.

24.2. Acting for the seller

24.2.1. Although planning matters do not necessarily fall within the seller's duty of disclosure, the buyer's solicitor will raise various enquiries about planning matters and will be reluctant to proceed with the transaction unless he can be reassured that the buildings and use of the property satisfy current planning regulations. In Protocol cases, a number of matters pertaining to planning will be revealed by the seller on the Seller's Property Information Form which is supplied to the buyer. The following matters should therefore be checked either from the documents in the solicitor's possession, from information obtained from the client, or from the local planning authority (usually the district council):

(a) the date when the property was first built;

(b) whether any additions, alterations or extensions have been made to the property or within its grounds since the property was first built and, if so, the date of each addition, etc.;

(c) if the property has been built or any alteration to it has been made within the past four years, either that planning consent was obtained (either expressly or by virtue of General Permitted Development Order) or was not required. Any conditions attached to the planning consent should, if possible, be checked to ensure that they have been complied with. Proceedings to enforce planning restrictions in respect of development which consists of 'building works' must normally be taken within four years of the breach;

(d) if the property is leasehold, in addition to (c) above, whether any additions, alterations, etc., have been made since the date of the grant of the lease and, if so, whether any restriction on development contained in the lease has been complied with;

(e) what the property is used for, whether any material change of use to the property has occurred during the past 10 years and, if so, whether the appropriate consent has been obtained. There is a 10-year time-limit on the enforcement of breach of planning control through change of use. If no enforcement proceedings are taken within the 10-year period the previously unlawful use becomes an authorised use. The change of use from one use class to another requires consent, as does the change from use as a single dwelling house to use of the premises for multiple occupation or sub-division into separate units;

(f) where alterations or additions to the property have been made within the past 12 months, whether building regulation consent has been obtained and complied with (see para. B24.6);

(g) whether the property is a listed building or in a conservation area. Special provisions apply to such buildings and areas and the restrictions on development are more stringent than those applied in other cases. Where a building is listed, separate listed building consent may be required.

24.2.2. Any irregularity in the planning situation should ideally be corrected by the seller before contracts are exchanged. Realistically this may not always be possible and the seller may have to reveal the irregularity to the buyer who, depending on the nature of the problem, may be prepared to proceed with the transaction subject to a reduction in the price or an indemnity against liability given by the seller in the contract.

24.2.3. Paragraph 2.4 of the Protocol requires the seller's solicitor to obtain copies of all relevant planning decisions and to submit these to the buyer's solicitor as part of the pre-contract documentation (see Appendix III.1 for the full text of the Protocol).

24.3. Acting for the buyer

24.3.1. The matters itemised in para. B24.2.1 should be raised as pre-contract enquiries with the seller. Any irregularity revealed by the seller's answers should either be corrected at the seller's expense or, depending on the nature of the breach, an indemnity taken from the seller in the contract. Liability for breach of planning legislation enures with the land; thus any breach which exists on completion will become the responsibility of the buyer.

24.3.2. Instructions should be taken from the buyer in relation to the following matters:

(a) Does the buyer's intended use of the property correspond with its present authorised use? If not, will planning permission be required for the buyer's intended use and is it realistic to expect that consent from the local planning authority would be forthcoming?

(b) Is it apparent on inspection of the property that new buildings or alterations have been made within the last four years? If so, check with the seller whether planning consent for the new buildings was needed/obtained/ complied with.

(c) Does the buyer intend to alter the property in any way after completion? If so, will the proposed alterations require planning consent or consent from the person with the benefit of an existing restrictive covenant against development and is it realistic to expect that such consent(s) will be forthcoming?

24.3.3. The answers to the local search and enquiries should be checked carefully to ensure that no breach of planning law is revealed in those answers. Any matters of doubt should be clarified with the local authority and the seller before the matter proceeds to exchange of contracts.

24.3.4. Where the client's instructions reveal that his proposals for the property will require planning permission to be obtained it should first be ascertained whether or not the client would wish to proceed with his purchase in the event of an application for permission being refused by the local authority. If the client would not wish to pursue his purchase in such circumstances, he should be advised either to delay exchange until planning permission for his proposed development is obtained, or to ask the seller to make the contract conditional on obtaining such consent.[1] Even where the client is prepared to take the risk of planning permission ultimately being refused, he should be advised about the procedure for making such application (including the costs) and the consequences of developing the land without permission. The register of planning applications maintained by the local authority under Town and Country Planning Act 1990 may be inspected to obtain an insight into the authority's policy for the area, and thus the likelihood of obtaining permission for the proposed development. Generally an authority will not permit development which conflicts with its local plan for the area, e.g. industrial development would not be permitted in an area designated for residential use or vice versa.

24.3.5. Even where the client's proposals will not require planning permission, consideration should still be given to the necessity for building regulation consent (for building works of any description) and compliance with or insurance against any restrictive covenants on the property which would prevent the client's intended development.

1. See Conditional contracts, para. B13.

24.4. Matters which do not require specific planning permission

24.4.1. Certain matters which would otherwise fall within the definition of development (and thus require planning permission) are specifically excluded from that definition by the Act itself or by General Permitted Development Order. A summary of the main cases where permission is not required either by the statute or by regulation is listed below. In any case of doubt, the Act and the various regulations made under it should be checked, and/or advice sought from the planning department of the local authority:

(a) maintenance works to buildings, e.g. painting the exterior;

(b) internal works which do not materially affect the appearance of the exterior, e.g. sub-dividing a room by the erection of a non-load-bearing partition wall;

(c) the use of buildings or land within the curtilage of a dwelling house for any purpose incidental to the use of the dwelling house, e.g. using an existing outhouse as a playroom. The 'curtilage' of a dwelling house is the land immediately surrounding the house and except where the grounds are large will normally encompass the whole of the garden area;

(d) change of use within the same use class as specified by Town and Country Planning (Use Classes) Order 1987, e.g. changing from use as a newsagent's shop to an ironmonger's shop. Changing a single dwelling house into two or more units is a material change of use which requires planning permission, as is a change from one use class to another, e.g. changing from use as a shop to use as an office;

(e) development which falls within Town and Country Planning (General Permitted Development) Order 1995, e.g. erection of fences (subject to a height restriction), some demolition works, development within the curtilage of a dwelling house. This latter provision will permit the building of a small extension to an existing dwelling house without the need for express planning permission but is subject to strict conditions on the extent and siting of the extension; once the size limit for extensions under General Permitted Development Order has been used, all further extensions to the house require express permission. The conditions attached to General Permitted Development Order must be strictly observed, and if they cannot be complied with express permission for the development is needed. The local authority has power to restrict General Permitted Development Order in whole or in part in relation to its area. Before the client proceeds to effect works which ostensibly fall within the Order it should be confirmed that the relevant part of the Order is in force in the area concerned.

24.4.2. Enquiries of the local authority, which will be undertaken in every transaction, contain several questions relating to planning matters. The answers to these questions should be analysed carefully by the buyer's solicitor.

24.4.3. Special rules apply to listed buildings and the provisions outlined above may not apply.

24.5. Planning rules which apply in special cases

24.5.1. If the land is covered by a Special Development Order, or is within an enterprise zone or a simplified planning zone, special rules apply which alter the general law.

24.5.2. In some cases the rules relating to the need for planning permission are relaxed within these special zones, in others parts of General Permitted Development Order may be restricted. The replies to enquiries of the local authority will reveal whether or not the property is affected by any of these special zonings. If so, the provisions of the relevant Order should be checked before advice is given to the client on the need for planning permission.

24.6 Building regulations

24.6.1. Building Regulations compliance is necessary whenever building works are to be undertaken. The need for this is separate from planning consent and is required even where the development falls within the General Permitted Development Order and does not require express planning permission.

24.6.2. The regulations cover various aspects of the structure including its structural stability, fire resistance and means of escape, weather resistance, sound resistance, ventilation, drainage, heating and the conservation of fuel and power, stairways, ramps and guards and facilities for disabled people and the safety of glazing.

24.6.3. Since 1 April 2002 the regulations have applied to the installation of replacement windows and doors. All replacement windows, roof lights, and glazed doors will have to be covered by either a certificate issued by the Local Authority Building Control or by FENSA. The Glass and Glazing Federation has established a self-assessment scheme, FENSA, and FENSA members must carry out the work to the appropriate standard and can then issue a certificate with the local authority within 10 days of the work being completed. These provisions apply to contracts entered into on or after 1 April 2002. The provisions will apply to orders placed before 1 April 2002 if the work was not completed before 1 July 2002. The solicitor needs to check that the appropriate consents are available (appropriate questions are included in the third edition of the seller's property information form).

24.6.4. Certain buildings do not need Building Regulation consent, for example, certain detached buildings not used for sleeping and some extensions, provided they are under certain size restrictions. In addition the construction of a greenhouse, porch, conservatory (with transparent or translucent roof), covered yard or car port are exempt from Building Regulation control where the floor area of the addition does not exceed 30 square metres. The installation of heat producing appliances when carried out by an approved installer does not require consent.

24.6.5. A person who intends to undertake building works must make an application for consent before starting work. There are two forms of application, the Full Plans Application and the Building Notice method. For a Full Plans application detailed plans are required and full details of the construction must be submitted. The Building Notice differs from the Full Plans Application in that all that is necessary is the completion and submission of a simple form describing the proposed work. With the Building Notice application the Building Control Surveyor will inspect the work on site and will expect any problems to be rectified immediately.

24.6.6. A key element of building control is the inspections conducted by the Building Control Officer. Statutory inspections have to be carried out at specified stages in the construction and the Building Control Officer may also inspect at other stages in the construction.

24.6.7. The Local Authority issues a Certificate of Compliance when the building work is finished and the final inspection has taken place. This confirms that the work is in accordance with the regulations. In some cases an independent building inspector will carry out the inspections and issue the Certificate of Compliance to the local authority. It is essential that a copy of this certificate is provided to the buyer on the sale of the property.

24.6.8. Proceedings for breach of Building Regulations must generally be taken within 12 months of the infringement. However in some circumstances the local authority may be able to enforce the regulations outside the 12-month time limit.[1] A buyer should therefore seek confirmation of compliance with the regulations in respect of works completed since the property was built and if this is not available the buyer should consider insurance against the risk of enforcement.[2] The buyer could ask the seller to obtain a Regularisation Certificate from the Building Control Department at the Local Authority. The Building Control Officer will inspect the property and provide a list of work required to bring the building up to the correct standard. Depending upon the level of work required the buyer might choose to ask the seller to carry out the work prior to completion, negotiate a reduction in the purchase price to cover the cost of carrying out the work after completion or withdraw from the transaction. The buyer's lender may also need to be informed.

1. Building Act 1984, s.36(1) and Public Health Act 1936, s.65.
2. See Building Act 1984, s.36(6) and *Cottingham v Atley Bower and Jones* [2000] PNLR 557.

24.7. Environmental issues[1]

24.7.1. Where a planning application is made for 'environmentally sensitive development' as defined in Town and Country Planning (Assessment of Environmental Effects) Regulations 1988 (S.I. 1988/1199) the local planning authority may require the applicant to submit an environmental statement with his application. Some local authorities ask for an environmental assessment to be submitted in connection with all applications for major development irrespective of the above Regulations.

1. See Environmental Issues, para. B25.

B25. Environmental issues

25.1. **Introduction**
25.2. **Advising buyers and lenders**
25.3. **Pre-contract enquiries**
25.4. **Insurance**
25.5. **Contravention**

25.6. **Contaminated water**
25.7. **Statutory nuisance**
25.8. **Contaminated land**
25.9. **Radon**
25.10. **Flooding**

See also: Pre-contract searches and enquiries, para. B10

25.1 Introduction

25.1.1 The responsibility for polluting substances in or on land rests on the owner or occupier of the land for the time being under Environmental Protection Act 1990 (EPA 1990) and Environment Act 1995 (EA 1995). Civil liability may also exist in tort.[1] Statutory guidance attributes liability to various classes of potentially liable persons, failing which it attributes liability to the owner or occupier of the land subject to a 'hardship' test intended to protect the domestic owner. This minimal protection should not be relied upon.

25.1.2. EA 1995 inserts detailed provisions regarding liability for contaminated land into EPA 1990. These provisions have been implemented by extensive statutory guidance which came into force on 1 April 2000 in England and 1 July 2001 in Wales.[2]

The Law Society's 'Contaminated Land Warning Card' was issued in June 2001 (reproduced in Appendix IV.1). The key provision of the Card is that 'In every transaction you must consider whether contamination is an issue'. The steps that should be taken in purchases, mortgages and leases are given below:

1. Advise the client of potential liabilities associated with contaminated land (generally clients should be advised of the possibility and consequences of acquiring interests in contaminated land and the steps thaty can be taken to assess the risks).

2. Make specific enquiries of the seller.

In all commercial cases, and if contamination is considered likely to be a risk in residential cases, e.g. redevelopment of brown field land:

3. Make enquiries of statutory and regulatory bodies.

4. Undertake independent site history investigation, e.g. obtaining site report from a commercial company.

In commercial cases, if there is a likelihood that the site is contaminated:

THE LAW SOCIETY'S CONVEYANCING HANDBOOK 10TH EDITION   293

5. Advise independent full site investigation.

6. Consider use of contractual protections and the use of exclusion tests.

This may involve specific disclosure of known defects, possibly coupled with price reduction, requirements on seller to remedy before completion, and in complex cases the use of warranties and indemnities.

If there are unresolved problems, consider:

7. Advising withdrawal, and noting advice;

8. Advising insurance (increasingly obtainable for costs of remediation of undetected contamination and any shortfall in value because of undisclosed problems).

25.1.3. A lender who has taken possession of land (but not a receiver) is liable as an owner or occupier under these provisions, which enable the relevant authority to require polluted land to be cleaned up.

25.1.4. The cost of compliance with the Act is potentially a major liability in connection with land and potentially polluted land may be difficult to sell or to mortgage. A perception of pollution, even if incorrect, may lead to similar difficulties.

25.1.5. When buying property, whether residential or commercial, remember that many newer developments are on land previously used for a potentially contaminative use such as: petrol station, sewage farm, light industrial, brickworks, railway sidings, town gas works and landfill.

25.1.6. Although it is not possible to be certain of contamination of a site, or non-contamination, without a fairly expensive investigation including soil or ground water analysis, it is possible to be reasonably certain of the likelihood of contamination occurring based on the historic use of the site. Alternatively, one may be reasonably confident that there is no particular cause for concern if no sign of historic activity exists in any records or on the property itself. Certain past uses have been shown to consistently result in contamination with certain substances. Whether possible contamination of a site poses a significant risk to the potential buyer will also depend on the geological structure of the ground, the height and flow of groundwater, whether the site is over an aquifer which is abstracted for drinking purposes or other sensitive types of consumption and what is the current and proposed new use of the site by the buyer. Sites can be contaminated by the leaching of contaminants from neighbouring land. Some substances will leach in groundwater from a considerable distance. Methane will migrate up to 400 metres or more from its source in an old landfill, through strata above the water-table. In addition to landfills, many old industrial sites are 'methanogeric' producing methane from gradual degradation of soils contaminated by oils.

25.1.7. Inspection of old plans and maps forming part of the title deeds and pre-registration deeds can prove invaluable in identifying earlier contaminative uses. There are presently several organisations (see para. B25.1.8) selling site-specific environmental data in England and Wales. A search from one of these will identify whether there may, or may not, be cause for concern based on past use. It is more difficult, and expensive, to accurately assess the risk where there is possible cause for concern.

25.1.8. To obtain information about past historic land use of both the property and surrounding land the following options are presently available:

(a) consider the title deeds, including pre-registration deeds, going back to a green field site, if possible;

(b) search Ordnance Survey Maps (back to about 1840) and old trade directories for details of previous occupiers and obvious features or activities;

(c) make personal enquiries of local authority and Environment Agency personnel who may know the site's history: make use of the Access to Environmental Information Regulations 1992 (S.I. 1992/3240) where information exists but is not shown on public register;

(d) employ an environmental auditor to undertake a 'desk-top' study or Phase 1 audit which will comprise the three preceding areas of enquiry with others that the consultant may be able to access (typical cost £750–£1500);

(e) purchase an environmental data search through an NLIS channel (see para. B10) or direct from one of the commercial suppliers: GroundSure Ltd, Landmark Information Group Ltd, and Sitescope (see Appendix XI.5 for addresses).

25.1.9. *Questions to ask of search providers*

- Do their products include Environment Agency flood plain data?

  Note: Unless you want to obtain this from another source.

- What are the names of the products that they produce for residential purchase/mortgage purposes and for commercial property, and what are the differences between them?

- What is the delivery time and price for each such product?

  Note: The delivery time can range from 10 minutes (via the Internet) to several days, and the price from £25 to several hundred pounds.

- Does each product include a conclusion/certificate stating whether further investigation would be prudent or confirm that there is no cause for concern and that, in consequence, the search is 'clear' from a contaminated land and/or flooding perspective?

  Note: Given the length of such reports, something authoritative and brief that avoids having to review the whole report before advising the client is useful.

- Are further services available to assist should further investigation be prudent?

- What insurance cover does the provider have for each such product and, if they provide a conclusion, what cover supports the conclusion?

Note: Expect an answer giving a maximum value for each claim and the total value of their coverage.

- Do they sell environmental risk insurance? Are you required to buy a search in order to obtain the insurance? Does the policy include coverage for those potential risks identified by the search, if any? At what cost, for what term and under what policy wording?

- On what basis are the various data sets on which each product is based updated?

Note: This may vary but you would expect the provider to be able to give a detailed response.

25.1.10. Each of the above search services will provide the data which they think most suitable for a potential purchaser's needs and will include maps. If in any doubt, you may need to seek further advice on the significance of the search report that you have obtained from an environmental auditor, an appropriately qualified specialist surveyor, or a similarly qualified person.

25.1.11. Search providers will sell their products direct, through an NLIS channel, or through their respective network of resellers.

25.1.12. Under EA 1995, the Environment Agency has responsibility for the enforcement of environmental matters under both EPA 1990 and EA 1995 other than air pollution functions exercised by local authorities.

1. See *Scott-Whitehead v. National Coal Board* (1987) 53 P & CR 263; *cf. Cambridge Water Co.* v. *Eastern Counties Leather plc* [1994] 1 All ER 53, HL.
2. See Contaminated Land (England) Regulations 2000 (S.I. 2000/227); Contaminated Land (Wales) Regulations 2001 (S.I. 2197/W.157); and DETR Guidance on Contaminated Land, April 2000. These regulations are retrospective.

25.2. Advising buyers and lenders

25.2.1. Prospective buyers who are contemplating buying or leasing development land or land which is to be used for an industrial use where chemicals are involved may consider taking certain precautions before completing the transaction. They may consider having an environmental audit undertaken, setting up, maintaining and regularly reviewing a policy for the control of pollution on the land and taking out an insurance policy to cover liability against contamination of the land, if such a policy is available (an environmental impairment liability policy). As protection against future liability it may be prudent to have a Phase 2 audit carried out, including soil and ground water tests, to establish existing contamination as a 'bench mark' against claims of future liability.

25.2.2. Paragraph 5.2 of the CML Handbook provides that lenders will inform solicitors whether or not they require an environmental audit to be carried out. Where the lender does not want to see such a report the solicitor need not carry one out unless of course the buyer client requests one. Nevertheless the solicitor must report any adverse information discovered on any search actually carried out, for example on the local authority search. See Appendix VIII.3 for Part 1 of the CML Lenders' Handbook.

25.2.3. A full environmental investigation is also necessary in support of any planning application where the local authority believes that the land may be contaminated. If the result of the investigation is unsatisfactory in the local authority's view, they may require remediation of the land at the applicant's expense as a condition of the planning consent.

25.2.4. Prospective buyers of land which is being acquired for development and their lenders may consider making full enquiries relating to neighbouring land as well as the land which they are buying. Contaminating chemicals and gases, especially methane and radon, may migrate or leach from neighbouring land and contaminate the land being purchased.

25.2.5. The contract to purchase the land might contain warranties from the seller relating to the absence of actions or events which may otherwise have contaminated the land during the period of the seller's ownership. The seller should not give such warranties unless he is fully aware of the commercial risks involved. They should in any event be limited to the period of the seller's use of the land.

25.2.6. Lenders and landlords may consider taking covenants from their borrowers/ tenants to cover some or all of the following matters:

(a) not to bring hazardous material on to the property

(b) to comply with environmental law

(c) to remedy any breach of environmental law, with power reserved for the lender/landlord to remedy the breach himself and recoup the resulting cost from the borrower/tenant;

(d) to notify the lender/landlord of any circumstances which could give rise to liability for environmental damage;

(e) to provide periodical environmental investigations and audits (in each case specifying the detail required to be covered by the investigation or audit);

(f) reservation of the right for the lender/landlord to enter to inspect the property.

25.2.7. A Phase 1 environmental audit consists of documentary evidence only; a physical investigation, or Phase 2 audit, may include geotechnical and chemical data obtained from samples of soil, water or building materials.

25.3. Pre-contract enquiries

25.3.1. The 'Contaminated Land Warning Card' specifies that in purchases, mortgages and leases solicitors should make specific enquiries of the seller (see para. B10). It may be difficult to ascertain likely previous use, especially if time is short. Thus, in the absence of information showing no cause for concern a range of questions covering areas of possible concern should be asked.

25.3.2. Pre-contract enquiries should be raised with the seller/borrower in relation to some or all of the following matters as may appear relevant in the circumstances, unless it is clear that the property cannot previously have been used for industrial or waste disposal purposes:

(a) whether to the seller's knowledge there is now or has been carried out at the property a process controlled under EPA 1990;

(b) whether to the seller's knowledge there is now or has been kept or deposited at the property any substance controlled under EPA 1990;

(c) whether there is or ever has been on the property the disposal, storage, deposit, treatment, recycling or transportation of controlled waste as defined by EPA 1990, s.75;

(d) permission for the buyer or his authorised agent to take samples of air, water and soil from the property;

(e) whether there are any old storage tanks on, or under, the site;

(f) whether the seller or its predecessor has had any environmental audit or investigation into the site, if so please provide a copy;

(g) whether the seller has any reason to believe, or does believe, that the site is contaminated with any noxious, toxic or dangerous substances or has been used for any activity which may have caused such contamination.

For a comprehensive set of environmental definitions and enquiries see forms 35 and 36 in the Encyclopaedia of Forms and Precedents v.38(1) 2000 and reissue published by Butterworths.

25.3.3. Control of Pollution (Silage, Slurry and Agricultural Fuel Oil) Regulations 1991 (S.I. 1999/324) will also be of concern when acting in a manner where any of these items are to be used or stored on land. Escape of these substances will be an offence under the Regulations.

25.3.4. Environmental Protection (Prescribed Processes and Substances) Regulations 1991 (S.I. 1991/1472, amended by S.I. 1992/614) gives details of the business activities for which a licence is required under Integrated Pollution Control regime (IPC). Enquiries should be raised with a seller as to whether such a licence is required and/or has been detained.

25.4. Insurance

25.4.1. Insurance policies are available to provide to purchasers and/or lenders where contamination of land presents a potential problem. Such policies may set rigorous requirements before the risk is accepted. Possible coverage can be arranged from the following companies (see Appendix XI.5 for details):

- Certa: Bespoke Environmental Liability Insurance
- Countrywide Legal Indemnities
- Pollution Liability through AIG Europe (UK) Ltd

- Suppliers of environmental data searches (e.g. GroundSure Ltd, Landmark Information Group Ltd, Sitescope).

25.4.2. Established insurance products providing coverage for new build residential property may include an environmental element in the risks covered. Purchasers of new build should enquire of the developer what guarantee will be provided in this respect.

25.5. Contravention

25.5.1. The Environment Agency has the task of enforcing the rules made by the Secretary of State for the Environment relating to the regulation system under EPA 1990. The Agency works through regional offices. Some enforcement procedures are carried out by the local authority for the area. The local authority retains responsibility for Air Pollution Control. Contravention of environmental law will generally result in committing an offence leaving the committer open to a criminal charge. Some penalties can be heavy. Some company directors have been imprisoned for repeated flagrant breaches of environmental law.

25.5.2. Certain specified industrial processes must be licensed under the Integrated Pollution Control Regime (IPC) before they can be carried out. The Environment Agency maintains the registers of information relating to applications for authorisations under EPA 1990 and EA 1995. These registers are open to public inspection.

25.5.3. Activities which fall into the following general categories should be checked to ensure that any necessary licence has been obtained and its terms have been complied with. The Agency has power to enforce the terms of a licence and to prosecute the breach:

    (a) production of fuel and power

    (b) metal production

    (c) mineral industries

    (d) chemical industries

    (e) waste disposal and recycling.

25.6. Contaminated water

25.6.1. The Environment Agency has power under the Water Resources Act 1991, s.161 to clean up polluted water and to recover the expenses reasonably incurred from the party who caused or knowingly permitted the pollution to occur. The meaning of 'caused or knowingly permitted' is well established and includes those who fail to take reasonable precautions against the occurrence of a contaminating event; those who fail to take reasonable steps which would have alerted them to the need to take reasonable precautions and those who deliberately fail to find out about their possible liabilities.

25.6.2. Most instances of contaminated land involve contaminated controlled water – ground and surface water. Whether or not contamination of a site is likely to cause the owner problems is closely linked to whether or not groundwater used for drinking and other purposes is affected.

25.6.3. The Groundwater Regulations 1998 (S.I. 1998/2746) control standards for clean up of ground water. However, these standards may not be uniformly applied by the Environment Agency.

25.7. Statutory nuisance

25.7.1. Under EPA 1990, ss. 79–82, statutory nuisances include the following:

(a) any premises in such a state as to be prejudicial to health or a nuisance;

(b) emission of smoke, fumes or gases which are prejudicial to health or a nuisance;

(c) dust, steam or other effluvia arising on trade or industrial premises which are prejudicial to health or a nuisance;

(d) any accumulation or deposit which is prejudicial to health or a nuisance;

(e) noise emitted from premises so as to be prejudicial to health or a nuisance.

25.7.2. Local authorities have a duty to inspect their areas to detect statutory nuisances and to take steps to investigate complaints made by individuals.

25.7.3. Where an authority is satisfied that a statutory nuisance exists or is likely to occur or recur it is under a duty to serve an abatement notice on the person responsible for the nuisance or, if that person cannot be found, on the owner or occupier of the premises. Non-compliance with an abatement notice is a criminal offence penalised by a maximum fine of £20,000 and/or an injunction.

25.8. Contaminated land

25.8.1. The requirement to maintain registers relating to matters arising in respect of contaminated land is contained in EA 1995, s.57 which inserts sections 78A–78YC into EPA 1990. EPA 1990, s.78R requires every enforcing authority to maintain a register containing prescribed particulars of, or relating to, inter alia:

(a) remediation notices;

(b) remediation statements or declarations;

(c) designation of special sites;

(d) termination of designation as a special site;

(e) notification of claimed remediation;

(f) convictions for offences for failure to comply with a remediation notice.

25.9. Radon

25.9.1. Radon is a naturally occurring radioactive gas which is present in the ground and is found at low levels in all buildings. High levels, which can increase the life-time risk of lung cancer, occur in some dwellings. The recommended limit for radon in UK homes is called the Action Level. A Radon Affected Area is declared when the estimated percentage of dwellings at or above the Action Level is 1% or more.

25.9.2. The majority of dwellings requiring remedial measures are concentrated in the Radon Affected Areas. The answer to question 3.13 of Form CON 29 (Part 1) Standard Enquiries of Local Authority will reveal whether a property is in a Radon Affected Area.[1] If this is the case, the seller should be asked for the results of any radon measurements made in the property. Additionally, NRPB offers an information service to provide information on the radon potential of a dwelling. Alternatively the data are published in two reports:

  (a) *NRPB-W26 Radon Atlas of England and Wales*, ISBN 0–85951–497–8 (available from NRPB Information Services or as a downloadable PDF at www.nrpb.org).

  (b) *NRPB-R308 Radon in Dwellings in Northern Ireland: Atlas and 1999 Review* (available direct from the Environment and Heritage Service, Calvert House, Belfast, BT1 1FY).

25.9.3. In Affected Areas the National Radiological Protection Board (NRPB) recommends that dwellings are measured and that two detectors are used in separate rooms over a three-month period to average out the short-term variations. An estimate of the annual average radon concentration for the whole dwelling is calculated from the two results and compared to the Action Level. Shorter measurement-periods, such as a fortnight or less, increases the uncertainty of the estimate of the annual average but the estimate may be low enough to be reasonably certain that the true annual average is below the Action Level. However, this is not always the case and further measurements may be needed. Measurements are available from NRPB and other validated laboratories. The current NRPB charge for two detectors (inclusive of analysis, postage and VAT) is £36.19.

25.9.4. The result of the survey is confidential and NRPB will advise the householder and/or whoever commissioned the test of the result and, if necessary, what steps can be taken to reduce the radon level. NRPB will not reveal the survey result or the fact a survey has been undertaken to a potential buyer or his solicitor. The seller's solicitor should be asked for a copy of the survey result. In cases where no result is available, a retention (often referred to as a radon bond) can be negotiated between the buyer and seller to cover the cost of radon reduction works (typical costs are in the region of £500–£1,000) if indicated by a validated measurement. The bond's life must be realistic, allowing for example, six months from completion of the house sale to initial radon test result. If the result is at or above the Action Level, another nine months should be allowed for completion of reduction works and a further three month test.

25.9.5. Special requirements under the Building Regulations are also in force for new homes in some parts of the country. See *BR 211 Radon: Guidance on Protective Measures for New Dwellings 1999 edition.* ISBN 1–86081–328–3, available from CRC Ltd, 151 Rosebery Avenue, London EC1R 4GB. Also see *BR 413 Radon: Guidance on Protective Measures for New Dwellings in Northern Ireland.* ISBN 1–86081–469–7. Both of these titles can be ordered online at *www.brebookshop.com.*

25.9.6. A free information pack on radon is available from NRPB. Private householders can also obtain background information by leaving their name, address and post-code on the 24-hour radon freephone 0800 614529. For contact details see Appendix XI.5 and their web site at *www.nrpb.org.*

1. NRPB Response Statement R3/02, 9 September 2002 – see www.nrpb.org.

25.10. Flooding

25.10.1. The Environment Agency (see Appendix X1.5 and X1.6 for details) has been given responsibility for warning the public about the risk of flooding. They have floodplain maps that can be accessed on their web site and, along with water companies, hold data on historic occurrences of flooding. Environmental search reports from the organisations mentioned in para. B25.1.8 will generally indicate whether a property is located within a flood plain but may not cover the existence of flood defences, which may have relevance to insurance. Practitioners are recommended to ensure that they consider this issue in relation to any transaction.

25.10.2. The Environment Agency definition of a floodplain is as follows:

'All land adjacent to a watercourse over which water flows in the time of flood, or would flow but for the presence of flood defences where they exist. The limits of flood-plain are defined by the peak water level of an appropriate return period event on the watercourse or at the coast. On rivers, this will normally be the greater of the 1 in 100 year return period or the highest known water level. In the coastal areas the 1 in 200 year flood or the highest known flood will be used, whichever is the greater. In both instances where a flood defence exists which protects to a greater standard than those defined, then the floodplain is the area defended to the design water level.'

B26. Easements and boundaries

26.1. Checking boundaries
26.2. Evidence of boundaries
26.3. Party walls
26.4. Access to neighbouring land

26.5. Hedgerows
26.6. Vehicular access over common land

See also: New properties, para. I1
Sales of part, para. J1

26.1. Checking boundaries

26.1.1. The burden of discovering the identity and ownership of boundaries usually lies with the buyer since Condition 4.3.1 Standard Conditions of Sale and Standard Commercial Property Condition 4.3.1 will (unless excluded from the contract) relieve the seller of the obligation to define precisely their route or to prove title to their ownership.

26.1.2. The buyer's solicitor should therefore check the boundaries as shown on the title deeds, accompanying plans, and (where supplied) the estate agent's particulars. Where from investigation of the above documents the boundaries are unclear or a discrepancy exists, further enquiries should be undertaken to clarify the position.

26.1.3. The client should be asked to check the boundaries by a site inspection or the client's surveyor should specifically be asked to undertake this task in the course of his own inspection of the property. The solicitor is not generally under an obligation to inspect the property but may need to do so where a discrepancy or query over the boundaries exists which is not resolved by inspection of the deeds and plans or by other enquiries made by the solicitor. An inspection may be required in the case of the purchase of a newly constructed property to ensure that the site plans accord with the property as it stands on the ground. Where the solicitor does accept the obligation of inspecting the property he will be liable in negligence if he does not carry out that duty with proper care.[1]

26.1.4. The following enquiries and investigations may also assist to determine the extent and ownership of boundaries:

(a) specific pre-contract enquiries of the seller;

(b) application of the common law presumptions (see para. B26.2.2);

(c) a site inspection of the property;

(d) an inspection of pre-root or pre-registration title deeds (if available);

(e) an Index Map search at the Land Registry (see para. B10 Pre-contract searches and enquiries);

(f) inspection of Ordnance Survey Maps.

26.1.5. The Lenders' Handbook, para. 6.2 requires the solicitor to ensure that the boundaries of the property are clearly defined by reference to a suitable plan or description (see Appendix VIII.3).

1. See *Barclay-White* v. *Guillame & Sons* [1996] EGCS 123.

26.2. Evidence of boundaries

26.2.1. Registered land

Provided that provisions relating to the ownership of boundaries were clearly set out in the documentation accompanying the application for registration, these will be recorded on the register of the title. The extent of the boundaries shown on the title plan will usually not show the exact position since boundaries shown on plans drawn by the Land Registry are general boundaries only unless shown on the register as determined.[1]

26.2.2. Common law rebuttable presumptions as to boundaries

The *ad medium filum* rule

A person who owns land abutting on a private or public highway is presumed to own the soil or sub-soil respectively of the highway up to the middle line. The surface of a public highway is vested in the highway authority. Registered titles do not show ownership of the sub-soil to the centre of an adopted road even where expressly included in the transfer.

The hedge and ditch rule

Where two properties are separated by a hedge and a man-made ditch, the boundary line is presumed to lie on the far side of the ditch from the hedge.[2]

Foreshore

In the absence of contrary evidence, the boundary of land adjoining the sea lies at the top of the foreshore. The foreshore is that part of the shore lying between the ordinary high and low water marks. Land below the medium line of the foreshore belongs to the Crown.

Non-tidal rivers and streams

The *ad medium filum* rule applies so that the owners of properties on either bank of the stream or river own the bed up to the middle of the stream or river. The owner of the river is also presumed to own the right to fish in the river but this presumption may be rebutted and it is common to find that fishing rights have been separately sold to third parties.

Tidal rivers and sea inlets

The bed and foreshore of a tidal river is prima facie vested in the Crown subject to the public's rights of navigation and fishing. The Crown's rights extend to that point in the river where the tide ebbs and flows, beyond which point the *ad medium filum* rule applies.

Trees

A tree belongs to the owner on whose land it was planted even if its trunk, roots or branches extend on to a neighbouring property. Where it cannot be established who planted the tree (e.g. because the trunk straddles the boundary of the land) ownership may be inferred from the circumstances. Regular maintenance (e.g. lopping or topping) by one person may be indicative of ownership by that person.

26.2.3 *Accretion and diluvion*

Where land is bounded by water the land owner's boundary extends to that land as added to by accretion or lost by diluvion (erosion). This doctrine applies only where the changes in the boundary are gradual and imperceptible in the ordinary course of nature. It does not apply where a substantial and recognisable change in the boundary has suddenly taken place.[3] The doctrine applies to registered land unless an agreement as to its operation has been noted in the register.[4]

26.2.4. *Ordnance survey maps*

It is the practice of ordnance survey maps to show the centre line of boundary features as the boundary. These maps may therefore give a general indication of the placing of a boundary subject to tolerances of scale but will not show the precise delineation of the boundary.

1. Land Registration Act 2002, s.60.
2. See *Alan Wibberley Building Ltd* v. *Insley* [1999] *The Times*, 30 April.
3. *Southern Centre for Theosophy Inc.* v. *State of South Australia* [1982] 1 All E.R. 283.
4. Land Registration Act 2002, s.61.

26.3. **Party walls**

26.3.1. *Party Wall Act 1996*

Party Wall Act 1996 in substance re-enacts London Building Acts (Amendment) Act 1939 which previously only applied to London. The 1996 Act applies its provisions throughout England and Wales.

26.3.2. New party structures

Section 1 requires a building owner to give at least one month's notice if he wishes to build a party structure where none exists. If the adjoining owner consents within 14 days, the wall is to be built half on the land of each owner or in such position as they agree. The expense of building is agreed between them or in an appropriate proportion considering the use and the cost of labour and materials. If consent is not forthcoming, the building owner may only build on his land. He may, subject to certain conditions, place footings below the land of the adjoining owner. He must compensate the adjoining owner and any occupier for any damage caused. Any dispute which arises is to be determined in accordance with the dispute resolution procedure in section 10.

26.3.3. Existing party structures

Section 2 gives a building owner wide powers to deal with party structures. Rebuilding may be to a height of not less than two metres where the wall is not used by the adjoining owner. A building owner may not cause unnecessary inconvenience and must compensate the adjoining owner and occupier for any loss or damage caused. If he opens any part of the adjoining land or building, he must maintain hoarding or shoring for its security. He must usually make good all damage caused to adjoining premises, internal furnishings and decorations, and may be required to pay expenses in lieu. He must also pay a fair allowance for disturbance and inconvenience.

26.3.4. Procedure

Section 3 requires a building owner to serve the adjoining owner with a party structure notice stating the building owner's name and address, details of the proposed work and the date on which it is to start at least two months before any proposed work is to start. Section 20 defines 'owner' to include anyone with a tenancy for more than a year and any purchaser under an agreement for purchase or lease. The notice ceases to have effect if work is not started within 12 months and if it does not proceed with due diligence. If an adjoining owner does not consent to the notice within 14 days, a dispute arises and section 10 applies. An adjoining owner may serve a counter notice within one month requiring the owner to build chimney breasts, recesses or other such works. The works must be specified and plans, sections and particulars must accompany the counter notice. The counter notice may require the existing height of the wall to be maintained if a building owner proposes to reduce it to not less than two metres. A building owner must comply with a counter notice unless this would injure him, cause unnecessary inconvenience or delay. If he does not consent to the counter notice within 14 days, section 10 applies. The procedure differs where a building owner wants to construct special foundations. If the adjoining owner does not consent, they may not be put in.

26.3.5. Dispute resolution procedure

Where a dispute arises, it is to be settled by surveyors (section 10). Both parties must agree on the appointment of a surveyor or appoint their own surveyor and the two surveyors must select a third surveyor. Either of the other two may then call on him to settle the matter. All appointments must be in writing and cannot be rescinded. Provision is made to deal with the situation where a surveyor dies, becomes incapable of acting, or refuses or neglects to act effectively. An award cannot authorise interference with an easement of light or rights in the party wall but may deal with the right, time and manner of carrying out work and any other matter arising from the dispute. The surveyor's award is conclusive, subject to the right of either party to appeal to the county court within 14 days of the date of the award. The court may rescind or modify the award.

26.3.6. Payment for the work

The building owner generally pays for all work. Where work is due to lack of repair, required by the adjoining owner or the latter makes use of the work, he must pay or contribute to the cost of the work. The building owner must serve him with an account within two months of completion. If the adjoining owner objects within one month, the matter is to be settled under section 10. Security for costs may be required before any work starts.

26.3.7. Miscellaneous

A building owner who proposes to excavate and construct a building or structure within three to six metres of any building or structure of the adjoining owner may, and must if required by the adjoining owner, strengthen or safeguard at his own expense the foundations of the adjoining owner if certain conditions are met. Finally, the Act gives rights to enter and remain on land for carrying out works and an occupier who refuses to permit this may be guilty of an offence.

26.4. Access to neighbouring land

26.4.1. Access to Neighbouring Land Act 1992 allows the court to grant the applicant a temporary right of access to another person's land for the purpose of carrying out basic preservation work, i.e. work necessary to protect, repair or maintain (but not to improve) the applicant's property. The fact that the repairs would be substantially more expensive to carry out without access to the neighbour's land is not itself a ground for making the order. For an order to be made, the proposed works must be either impossible or substantially more difficult to carry out without an access order. The applicant need not be the owner of the land in question.

26.4.2. The county court must refuse an access order where it is satisfied that the respondent or any other person would suffer interference with or disturbance of his use or enjoyment of the land to such a degree that it would be unreasonable to make the order.

26.4.3. An order, if made, will be binding on successors in title of the respondent, provided it is registered. Although the applicant need not own the land, if he does the Act does not seem to provide for the benefit of the order to enure for the benefit of successors in title to the applicant's land. Where the land is unregistered an application under the Act is registrable as a pending action, an order as a writ and order. Where the land is registered, an application under the Act can be protected by either an agreed or unilateral notice. An order under the Act can only be protected by an agreed notice (Land Registration Rules 2003, r.80).

26.4.4. The Act contains provisions for compensation for loss of privacy, inconvenience, pecuniary loss, damage or injury. Except where the dominant land concerned is residential payment of a fee for the access may be ordered by the court.

26.4.5. Pre-completion searches at the Land Registry (or the Land Charges Department in the case of unregistered land) will identify cases where access orders have been registered under the Act.

26.4.6. It is not possible to contract out of the provisions of the Act.

26.5. Hedgerows

26.5.1. The Hedgerow Regulations 1997[1] reg. 3 prevents or inhibits the removal of hedgerows growing in or adjacent to common land, a nature reserve, a SSSI, or land used for agriculture, forestry, or the keeping of horses, ponies or donkeys. Optional enquiry 21 on Form CON 29 (Part II) asks: if there are entries in the record under reg. 10, how can they be obtained, and where can the record be inspected.

26.5.2. The Regulations apply where a hedgerow has a continuous length of at least 20 m. (or if less than 20 m. must meet by intersection or junction another hedgerow). They do not apply to hedgerows within or marking the boundary of a domestic curtilage.

26.5.3. The local planning authority has power to prevent the removal of an 'important hedgerow' which is defined by reg. 4 as one which has existed for 30 years or more and which satisfies at least one of the criteria set out in Part II of Schedule 1 to the Regulations. These criteria relate to archaeological/historical matters and to wildlife/landscape considerations.

26.5.4. An owner (which includes a tenant) who wishes to remove a hedgerow which is covered by the Regulations must serve a 'hedgerow removal notice' on the local planning authority. The form of notice is specified in Schedule 4 and must include a plan. The local planning authority may then either serve a notice saying that the hedgerow can be removed or serve a 'hedgerow retention notice'. If no notice has been served at the expiry of 42 days, the hedgerow can be removed.

26.5.5. Exceptions, where hedgerow removal is permitted, include:

(a) making a new access to replace an existing access;

(b) making a temporary access in an emergency;

(c) national defence;

(d) development for which planning permission has been granted;

(e) flood defence or land drainage;

(f) work preventing plant or tree pests;

(g) felling, etc., to prevent obstruction with electric lines;

(h) proper management.

26.5.6. An appeal against a retention notice lies to the Secretary of State for Environment within 28 days. It is an offence to remove a hedgerow without the necessary permission.

26.5.7. As an alternative to prosecution the local planning authority can serve a notice requiring a new hedge to be planted. The local planning authority can apply for an injunction in the county or high court to restrain an actual or apprehended offence.

1. S.I. 1997/1160.

26.6. Vehicular access over common land

26.6.1 It is not possible, under ordinary rules of property law, to acquire by prescription a right of way for vehicles over common land to a property, even if it would be otherwise land-locked. However, the Countryside and Rights of Way Act 2000 s.68 provides for the grant of easements for vehicular access over common land.

26.6.2 The regulations under s.68 allow a property owner with at least 20 years use of a privately owned access way over common land or a village green to claim a statutory easement.

26.6.3 The property owner will have to pay compensation to the owners of the common land or village green. The level of compensation is determined by fixed criteria and will depend upon the current open market value of the property benefiting from the easement at the time the easement is being claimed and the age of the property.

26.6.4 Properties in existence before 1905 wil pay 0.25% of their current market value. Those in existence by 1930 will pay 0.50% of their current market value and newer properties will pay 2% of their current market value.

C. EXCHANGE

C1. Preparing to exchange

1.1.	**Introduction**	1.3. **Reporting to the buyer**
1.2.	**Checklist**	

See also: Surveys, para. A13
Pre-contract searches and enquiries, para. B10
Undertakings for bridging finance, para. B16
Deposit, para. B17
Mortgage offers, para. B19
Fixtures and fittings, para. B22
Signature of contract, para. C2
Insurance, para. C3
Law Society Protocol and Formulae, Appendix III
Report on Proposed Purchase (domestic), Appendix VII.10
CLLS Certificate of Title and Short Report on Title, Appendix VIII.2.

1.1. Introduction

1.1.1. On exchange a binding contract will come into existence, after which time neither party will normally be able to withdraw from the contract without incurring liability for breach. It is therefore essential to check that all outstanding queries have been resolved and that both parties' financial arrangements are in order before the client is advised to commit himself to the contract.

1.2. Checklist

1.2.1. Although the checklist below largely reflects matters which are of concern to a buyer, many of the items will also be of concern to a seller. The seller should pay particular attention to those items marked with an asterisk.

1.2.2. *Searches*

    (a) Have all necessary searches and enquiries been made?

    (b) Have all the replies to searches and enquiries been received?

    (c) Have all search and enquiry replies been checked carefully to ensure that the replies to individual questions are satisfactory and accord with the client's instructions?

    (d) Has Part 2 of the Sellers' Property Information Form or Part 2 of the Sellers' Leasehold Information Form been checked by the solicitor?

    * (e) Have all outstanding queries been resolved satisfactorily?

1.2.3. *Survey*

(a) Has a survey of the property been undertaken?

(b) Is the result of that survey satisfactory?

1.2.4. *Mortgage arrangements*

(a) Has a satisfactory mortgage offer been made and (where necessary) accepted by the client?

(b) Are arrangements in hand to comply with any conditions attached to the advance, e.g. in relation to an endowment policy?

(c) Taking into account the deposit, the mortgage advance (less any retention) and the costs of the transaction (including stamp duty and Land Registry fees), has the client sufficient funds to proceed with the purchase?

* (d) Are arrangements in hand to discharge the seller's existing mortgage(s)?

* (e) If the transaction is a sale of part, has the seller's lender (if any) agreed to release the property to be sold from the mortgage?

1.2.5. *Deposit*

* (a) How much (if any) preliminary deposit has been paid?

* (b) How much money is needed to fund the deposit required on exchange?

(c) Has a suitable undertaking been given in relation to bridging finance?

* (d) To whom is the deposit to be paid?

NB: where Formula C is to be used for exchange, the deposit may have to be paid to someone other than the immediate seller.

(e) Have the deposit funds been obtained from the client and cleared through clients' account?

NB: Contractual conditions (e.g. Standard Condition 2.2) normally require that payment is to be made only by banker's draft or solicitor's cheque or by direct credit (Standard Commercial Property Condition 2.2).

1.2.6. *The contract*

* (a) Have all outstanding queries been satisfactorily resolved?

* (b) Have all agreed amendments been incorporated clearly in both parts of the contract?

* (c) Has the approved draft been returned to the seller?

* (d) Is a clean top copy of the contract available for signature by the client?

* (e) Have the terms of the contract been explained to the client?

* (f) Has the list of fixtures and fittings been agreed between the parties?

1.2.7. *Insurance*

    (a) Have steps been taken to insure the property?

    * (b) If the buyer is to rely on the seller's insurance policy, has the buyer's interest been noted on that policy?

    (c) Have steps been taken to obtain any life policy required under the terms of the buyer's mortgage offer?

1.2.8. *Completion date*

    *   Has a completion date been agreed?

1.2.9. *Method of exchange*

    *   Which method of exchange is most suitable to be used in this transaction?

1.2.10. *Synchronisation*

    *   Where the client requires a simultaneous exchange on both sale and purchase contracts, ensure that both transactions are ready to proceed and that all related transactions in the chain are also ready.

1.2.11. *Signature of contract*

    *   Has the client signed the contract?

1.2.12. *Occupiers*

    *   Has the concurrence of all non-owning occupiers been obtained?

1.3.   **Reporting to the buyer**

1.3.1.   When the buyer's solicitor has completed his investigations into the property (including having finalised any amendments to the draft documentation) he should prepare and send or give to his client a report on the proposed purchase which should explain to the client (in language appropriate to the client's level of understanding) the nature of the solicitor's investigations into the property and its legal title, the results of these investigations, and a summary of conclusions or advice to the client.

1.3.2.   An example of such a report is set out in Appendix VII.10. The precise content of the report will vary from transaction to transaction and in the case of commercial property a more detailed report may be desirable. A report on leasehold property should explain the terms of the lease to the client (see Acting for the tenant, para. K3). Also see Appendix VIII.2 CLLS Certificate of Title and Short Report on Title.

C2. Signature of contract

2.1. Requirement for signature

2.1.1. Both parties must sign the contract (or each must sign one of two identical copies) in order to satisfy Law of Property (Miscellaneous Provisions) Act 1989, s.2. Such signature need not be witnessed.

2.2. Signature by the client

2.2.1. Ideally the client should be asked to sign the contract in the presence of his solicitor, the solicitor first having ensured that the client understands and acquiesces in the terms of the contract.

2.2.2. In cases where it is not practicable for the client to sign in the solicitor's presence, the contract may be sent to the client for signature with an accompanying letter which clearly explains where and how the client is required to sign the document. If not already done, the letter should explain the terms of the contract in language appropriate to the client's level of understanding, and also request a cheque for the deposit indicating by which date the solicitor needs to be in receipt of cleared funds. The client should be asked to return the signed contract to the solicitor as soon as possible. (There is an example Report on proposed purchase at Appendix VII.10.)

2.3. Signature by solicitor on behalf of client

2.3.1. A solicitor needs his client's express authority to sign the contract on behalf of the client.[1]

2.3.2. Unless the solicitor holds a valid power of attorney, it is recommended that such an authority be obtained from the client in writing, the client previously having been informed of the legal consequences of giving such authority (i.e. signature implies authority to proceed to exchange, and exchange creates a binding contract). Failure to obtain authority may render the solicitor liable in damages for breach of warranty of authority.[2]

1. *Suleman* v. *Shahsavari* [1989] 2 All ER 460.
2. *Suleman* v. *Shahsavari* [1989] 2 All ER 460.

2.4. Special cases

2.4.1. Co-owners

One co-owner may sign the contract on behalf of all the co-owners, but the solicitor should ensure that all co-owners have voluntarily given their consent to the transaction and have authorised the signature of the contract.

2.4.2. Trustees

One trustee alone may sign the contract for sale on behalf of his co-trustees. The solicitor should ensure that all co-trustees have voluntarily given their consent to the transaction and have authorised the signature of the contract.

2.4.3. Partners

Provided that the transaction has been authorised by the partnership, one partner may be given authority to sign the contract on behalf of the partners.

2.4.4. Companies

Provided that the transaction has been authorised by the company, an officer of the company (usually a director or the secretary) may be authorised to sign on behalf of the company.

2.4.5. Attorneys

A person who holds a valid power of attorney on behalf of another may sign the contract on behalf of the donor of the power. The attorney may sign either in his own name or that of the donor. The solicitor acting for the other party should be notified that the contract will be signed by an attorney and a properly certified copy of the power supplied to him so that he may satisfy himself as to the validity of the power and that it contains proper authority for the conduct of the particular transaction (see para. B7.20 and para. B.23).

2.4.6. Personal representatives

All proving personal representatives must be parties to the contract and purchase deed.[1]

2.4.7. Occupiers

A non-owning occupier may be joined as a party to the contract in order to give a release of his or her purported interest in the property. Where this occurs the non-owning occupier must sign the contract.[2]

1. Law of Property (Miscellaneous Provisions) Act 1994, s.16.
2. See para. B3.5.8 for an appropriate form of wording to release rights.

C3. Insurance

See also: Financial services, para. A4
After exchange, para. C5
Insurance, Appendix X

3.1. Risk in the property

3.1.1. At common law and unless the contract provides otherwise, the risk in the property passes to the buyer from the moment of exchange; the buyer thus bears the risk of loss or damage, except where it can be shown that the loss or damage is attributable to the seller's lack of proper care.[1] The buyer should therefore normally insure the property from exchange of contracts onwards. A solicitor who fails to advise his client of the consequences of failure to insure, or who fails to carry out his client's instructions to insure the property, will be liable in negligence if the client suffers loss as a result of the lack of insurance.

3.1.2. Since it is impossible to predict at which precise moment exchange will occur, it is essential that the buyer's insurance arrangements have been made in advance of actual exchange so that the policy will be effective immediately upon exchange.

1. *Clarke* v. *Ramuz* [1891] 2 QB 456; *Phillips* v. *Lamdin* [1949] 2 KB 33.

3.2. Insuring the property

3.2.1. Where the buyer's solicitor has in force a block policy which covers all properties currently being handled by the firm, the property should be noted on the policy in accordance with the firm's standard procedures and, at the latest, by the morning of the day on which it is anticipated that exchange will occur.

3.2.2. If the buyer is financing his purchase with the assistance of a building society mortgage, the lender will normally attend to the insurance arrangements on being requested to do so by the buyer's solicitor. The building society's standing instructions to solicitors should be checked to ensure that:

(a) the amount of cover will be adequate;

(b) the property will be put on cover from the time of exchange;

(c) the lender's insurance requirements do not conflict with the terms of the contract or of any lease to which the property is subject.

3.2.3. If neither of the preceding subparagraphs apply the buyer must obtain a policy which will cover the property from exchange.

3.3. The terms of the policy

3.3.1. The terms of the policy should be checked to ensure that:

(a) the amount of cover is adequate;

(b) the sum insured is index linked;

(c) the risks insured against are adequate, e.g. is flood damage covered where the property is situated in a low-lying area?

(d) particular features of the property have been disclosed to the insurance company and are adequately insured, e.g. thatched roofs, garden walls, interior decorative plasterwork;

(e) where the property consists of a flat within a larger building, or is otherwise attached to adjoining property, the insurance cover extends to damage to neighbouring property where practicable.

3.3.2. The client should be alerted to possible exclusions under the policy. In particular damage caused by terrorist activity may not be covered; in a leasehold context damage caused to the property by, e.g. a terrorist bomb would not be an insured risk; nevertheless the tenant or prospective tenant would remain liable under the terms of the lease, including the covenant to pay rent. Similarly, some policies will not cover damage to empty properties (or to blocks of flats where a resident is claiming social security benefits).

3.4. Property at seller's risk

3.4.1. In some cases, and commonly with property which is in the course of construction, the contract will provide that the property is to remain at the seller's risk until completion. Standard Condition 5.1 also provides for the seller to bear the risk in the property until completion and permits rescission if the property is substantially damaged between exchange and completion. Except in certain cases applicable to the sale of leaseholds, the seller is not obliged by the condition to maintain his own insurance policy after exchange. Where the risk in the property remains with the seller the buyer need not take out his own policy until completion but should ensure, before exchange, that:

(a) the seller will maintain his policy until completion and the terms of that policy provide sufficient protection for the buyer;

(b) the buyer receives written confirmation that his interest has been noted on the seller's policy;

(c) the contract contains a provision requiring the seller to transfer the property in substantially the same physical condition as it was in at the time of exchange, failing which the buyer is entitled to rescind the contract (Standard Condition 5.1 contains this type of provision). This type of clause is not necessary where the property is in the course of construction because the contract for such a property will normally contain provisions requiring the seller to complete the building in accordance with specifications, failing which the buyer is under no obligation to complete.

3.4.2. Where the property is in the course of construction and the risk is to remain with the seller until completion, the buyer should clarify with the seller whether the word 'completion' is intended to refer only to completion of the building works, or whether it is intended that the seller will retain the risk in the property until actual completion of the transaction.

3.5. Standard contractual conditions

3.5.1. Standard Condition 5.1 permits the seller to cancel his insurance policy (except in certain cases related to the sale of an existing lease), thus implicitly obliging the buyer to insure. This condition also excludes Law of Property Act 1925, s.47 which would otherwise give the buyer the right, in certain circumstances, to claim off the seller's policy in the event of damage to the property. However, Standard Condition 5.1 also requires the seller to transfer the property in the same physical condition as it was in at the date of the contract, failing which a right to rescind exists.

3.5.2. Standard Commercial Property Condition 5.1 passes risk to the buyer on exchange and provides that the seller is under no obligation to the buyer to insure the property. Condition 8.1.3 applies to leasehold property and in this context may require the seller to maintain his policy if so required by the lease.

3.6. Maintenance of seller's policy

3.6.1. Except where the seller is obliged by a condition of his mortgage or lease to maintain his policy, the seller could, with little risk, cancel his insurance policy on exchange of contracts, but in practice he would be ill advised to do so, e.g. in case the buyer failed to complete.

3.6.2. In practice the seller will not usually cancel his policy until after completion; thus for the period between exchange and completion there will often be two policies in force (one having been taken out by the buyer on exchange), both covering the same property against the same risks.

3.6.3. Should the property be damaged or destroyed during the period when the two policies subsist difficulty may sometimes be experienced in obtaining payment from the insurer, since each insurer may maintain that the responsibility for payment lies with the other. This difficulty may be resolved by including a special condition in the contract which requires the buyer to complete, subject to an abatement in the purchase price, leaving the seller to resolve the dispute with his own insurers. For a suitable form of wording see the Law Society Conditions of Sale (1984 revision), Condition 11(1). Standard Commercial Property Condition 5.1.1(b) contains an abatement clause similar to Law Society Condition 11(1).

3.7. Damage to the property

3.7.1. Under the common law the buyer will have to bear the cost of any damage caused to the property after exchange unless one of the provisions outlined below can be utilised. Additionally, the buyer's solicitor may be liable to his client in negligence.

3.7.2. Law of Property Act 1925, s.47 provides that a buyer may claim his loss from the policy maintained by the seller provided that:

(a) the contract does not exclude the operation of the section;

(b) the buyer pays a proportionate part of the insurance premium; and

(c) the insurance company consents to noting the buyer's interest in the policy.

3.7.3. The contract will normally exclude the operation of section 47, rendering the section ineffective so far as the buyer is concerned. (See Standard Condition 5.1 and Standard Commercial Property Condition 5.1.4.)

3.7.4. Fires Prevention (Metropolis) Act 1774, s.83 allows a person interested in or entitled to a property to require an insurance company to apply the proceeds of the policy towards the reinstatement of the property in the event of its damage by fire. Despite its title, the operation of the Act is not confined to London, but there is no direct authority for the proposition that a buyer under a contract for sale is a 'person interested' under the section.[1]

1. *Rayner* v. *Preston* (1881) 18 Ch 1 suggests *obiter* that a buyer can claim under the Act.

3.8. Other types of insurance

3.8.1. In appropriate cases the buyer should be advised to take out insurance to cover other risks, e.g. house contents, as well as life insurance in accordance with the terms of the mortgage offer.

3.8.2. Steps should be taken before or immediately after exchange to put such policies on foot although they will not normally need to be effective until completion. Advice given by the solicitor to his client about the terms of a life insurance policy will be subject to the provisions of Financial Services and Markets Act 2000.[1]

The seller should be advised not to cancel his house contents or other policies (including life policies linked to his mortgage) until completion.

1. See para. A4.

C4. Exchange of contracts

4.1. The practice of exchange	**4.5.** Standard Conditions of Sale and Standard Commercial Property Conditions
4.2. Authority to exchange	
4.3. Methods of exchange	
4.4. The Protocol	

See also: Acting for both parties, para. A10
Undertakings for bridging finance, para. B16
Preparing to exchange, para. C1

4.1. The practice of exchange

4.1.1. The physical exchange of contracts between the parties is not a legal requirement for a contract for the sale of land but where a contract is drawn up by solicitors acting for the parties it is usual for the contract to be prepared in two identical parts, one being signed by the seller, the other by the buyer. When the two parts are physically exchanged, so that the buyer receives the part of the contract signed by the seller and vice versa, a binding contract comes into existence. The actual time when the contract comes into being depends on the method which has been employed to effect the exchange.[1]

4.1.2. The practice of exchange was given legal recognition in *Eccles* v. *Bryant and Pollock*[2] where Lord Greene in his judgment stated in relation to the then existing law under Law of Property Act 1925, s.40[3] that the three essential ingredients of a contract for the sale of land were:

(a) compliance with the requirements of Law of Property Act 1925, s.40;[4]

(b) certainty in respect of the existence of the contract; and

(c) certainty in respect of the terms of the contract.

4.1.3. All three of the above requirements are satisfied by the practice of exchange of contracts, because where a contract is to come into existence through exchange both parties have the assurance of knowing that no contract exists until that time, i.e. either party is free to change his mind and withdraw from the negotiations until exchange. In the same way, once exchange has taken place, there is certainty for both parties as to the existence of an enforceable contract, and also certainty over the terms which have been agreed since each party retains a copy of the contract signed by the other in identical form to the one which he himself signed. Where contracts are to be exchanged both parts of the contract must be identical. This includes the filling in of the date of the contract and the date of completion. If this requirement is not met no contract will come into existence whether or not the exchange takes place.[5]

4.1.4. Since exchange is not a legal necessity there is no reason why the contract should not be embodied in a single document which is signed by both parties. In such a case the contract becomes binding and enforceable as soon as the second signature has been put on the document.[6] This situation will not frequently occur and in any event the same solicitor is usually forbidden from acting for both parties by Rule 6 Solicitors' Practice Rules 1990 (as amended).

4.1.5. An exchange of faxes is not an exchange of contracts to satisfy section 2 Law of Property (Miscellaneous Provisions) Act 1989.[7] In *Commission for the New Towns* v. *Cooper (Great Britain) Ltd*[8] an exchange of letters was held not to satisfy section 2.

1. See para. C4.3.
2. [1948] Ch 93.
3. [1948] Ch 93 at 99.
4. Now replaced by Law of Property (Miscellaneous Provisions) Act 1989, s.2.
5. *Harrison* v. *Battye* [1975] 1 WLR 58.
6. *Smith* v. *Mansi* [1963] 1 WLR 26.
7. *Milton Keynes Development Corporation* v. *Cooper (Great Britain) Ltd* [1993] EGCS 142.
8. [1995] 2 All ER 929 (CA).

4.2. Authority to exchange

4.2.1. A solicitor who exchanges contracts without his client's express or implied authority to do so will be liable to the client in negligence. In *Eccles* v. *Bryant and Pollock*[1] Lord Greene said that where a contract was to come into existence using the standard form of contract (now the Standard Conditions of Sale or Standard Commercial Property Conditions), it was implicit that the contract would come into existence on exchange, and that the client therefore impliedly authorised his solicitor to effect an exchange. In *Domb* v. *Isoz*[2] it was held that, once the solicitor has his client's authority to exchange, he has the authority to effect the exchange by whichever method the solicitor thinks most appropriate to the situation.

4.2.2. Although *Eccles* v. *Bryant and Pollock*[3] suggests that a solicitor's authority to exchange may be implied, it is better practice to obtain express authority from the client at the time of signature of the contract. Where an exchange of contracts by telephone is contemplated, it is suggested that, for the avoidance of doubt, express authority to use this method should be obtained. Where Formula C is to be used, it is a requirement of that Formula that express authority be obtained, preferably in writing. The Formula contains a suggested form of wording to meet this situation.[4]

1. [1948] Ch 93.
2. [1980] Ch 548.
3. [1948] Ch 93.
4. Formula C is set out in full with notes for guidance in App. III.2.

4.3.   Methods of exchange

4.3.1.   Whichever method is chosen the exchange is usually initiated by the buyer indicating to the seller that he is now ready to commit himself to a binding contract. Once contracts have been exchanged neither party will be able to withdraw from the contract; it is therefore essential that the parties' solicitors have checked that all necessary arrangements are in order before proceeding to exchange. Also, where the purchase of one property is dependent on the sale of another the solicitor must ensure that the exchange of contracts on both properties is synchronised to avoid leaving his client either owning two houses or being homeless. Failure to synchronise the exchange where the client has instructed that his sale and purchase transactions are interdependent is professional negligence.

4.3.2.   *Telephone*

Exchange by telephone is now the most common method of effecting an exchange of contracts. Legal recognition of the practice was given by the Court of Appeal in *Domb* v. *Isoz*.[1] With the exception of personal exchange this method represents the quickest way of securing an exchange of contracts and is thus particularly useful in a chain of transactions. The method is not, however, risk free. Where exchange is effected by telephone, the contract between the parties becomes effective as soon as the parties' solicitors agree in the course of a telephone conversation that exchange has taken place. The telephone conversation is usually followed by a physical exchange of documents through the post in the normal way, but the existence of the contract is not dependent on this physical exchange; the contract already exists by virtue of the telephone conversation. If one party were subsequently to change his mind about the contract there is ample scope with this method for disputing the contents of the telephone conversation and thus the existence of the contract itself. To avoid the uncertainties arising out of this method of exchange the parties' solicitors must agree prior to exchange that the telephonic exchange will be governed by one of the Law Society's Formulae which were drawn up by the Law Society in response to the decision in *Domb* v. *Isoz*. The text of these Formulae appears in Appendix III.2. An accurate attendance note recording the telephone conversation must also be made as soon as practicable.

4.3.3.   *Using the Formulae*

(a) The text of the Formulae with their accompanying guidance notes is set out in Appendix III.2 and III.3.

(b) Whichever Formula is used, the client's express authority to exchange must be obtained before the procedure to exchange is commenced.

(c) If any variation to a Formula is to be made, such variation must be expressly agreed and noted in writing by all the solicitors involved before exchange takes place. Any agreement relating to the payment of a less than 10% deposit should be finalised at the preliminary enquiries stage of the transaction and not left until exchange is imminent. Any agreed variation to the Formula which has been made orally must be confirmed in correspondence between the solicitors.

(d) Subject to (c) above, the conditions attached to the Formula being used must be strictly adhered to. In particular, where an undertaking is given to remit a deposit cheque and/or contract to the solicitor acting for the other party, such undertaking must be complied with on the day on which exchange takes place or, if compliance on the same day is not practicable, e.g. because exchange takes place after normal working hours, at the earliest opportunity on the next working day.

(e) To ensure compliance with the conditions attaching to the Formulae it is recommended that only qualified staff be authorised to effect an exchange by telephone.

(f) The Formulae may be used where the other party to the transaction is represented by a licensed conveyancer. The Formulae must never be used where the other party is represented by an unqualified person whose undertaking is not enforceable in the same way as those given by solicitors and licensed conveyancers.

(g) Extreme care needs to be exercised when using Formula C (for use in chain transactions) where, in certain circumstances, a solicitor is required to give an undertaking, the performance of which is outside his direct control, e.g. solicitor A undertakes to solicitor B that solicitor C will send the deposit cheque to solicitor B. The Standard Conditions of Sale only permit a deposit to be used for an exchange of contracts along the chain if that contract contains similar provisions as to the deposit. This almost inevitably means that the second contract must also be made by reference to the Standard Conditions.

(h) Under Formula C the ultimate recipient of the deposit must hold as stakeholder. No other capacity is permitted.

(i) An attendance note recording full details of the exchange by telephone must be made immediately exchange has taken place.

(j) A solicitor's failure to honour an undertaking given in relation to use of one of the Formulae (e.g. failure to send the deposit cheque on the same day as exchange takes place) is professional misconduct but probably does not affect the validity of an otherwise valid contract.[2]

(k) Fax can be used to activate the Formulae.

4.3.4. *Personal exchange*

By this method the solicitors for the parties meet, usually at the seller's solicitor's office, and the two contracts are physically exchanged. A contract exists from the moment of exchange. Although this type of exchange represents the safest and most instantaneous method of exchange it is frequently not possible to use personal exchange because the physical distance between the offices of the respective solicitors make it impractical to do so. Personal exchange is little used today, but it should be considered for use when the parties' solicitors are located in sufficient geographical proximity to make personal exchange feasible. A personal exchange has the benefit not only of being instantaneous, and thus leaving no uncertainty over the timing of the creation of the contract, but also of enabling both parties to see the other party's part of the contract before exchange actually takes place, so that both may be reassured that the parts of the contract are identical in form and have been properly signed.

4.3.5.   Postal exchange

Where exchange is to take place by post the buyer's solicitor will send his client's signed contract and the deposit cheque to the seller's solicitor who on receipt of these documents will post his client's signed contract back to the buyer (see Appendix III.3 for the Law Society's Code for Completion by Post). Generally a contract does not come into being until the buyer has *received* the seller's contract. Exchange of contracts by post forms an exception to this rule and the contract is made when the seller *posts* his part of the contract to the buyer.[3] Posting the contract means that the seller must actually place the letter in the letter box. Handing the letter to a third party with instructions that it should be posted is not sufficient.[4] The postal rules of acceptance may be displaced by contrary intention in the contract itself.[5] It follows from the above that a contract will be formed even if the seller's part of the contract is lost in the post and is thus never received by the buyer. Using the post as a method of exchange is reasonably satisfactory when dealing with a single sale or purchase which is not dependent on another related transaction, but even in this simple scenario some dangers exist. There will inevitably be a delay between the buyer sending his contract to the seller and the seller posting his part back, during which time the buyer is uncertain of whether he has secured the contract. There is also no guarantee that the seller will complete the exchange by posting his part of the contract back to the buyer. Until he actually does so he is free to change his mind and withdraw from the transaction. Although these dangers are minimal where a single sale or purchase is being undertaken, the risks assume a much greater importance where a chain of transactions is involved; thus, the use of postal exchange is not to be advocated in linked transactions.

4.3.6.   Document exchanges

A document exchange would be used to effect an exchange of contracts in a similar way to the normal postal service and is subject to the same risks as are outlined in the preceding subparagraph. The court has approved the use of document exchanges for the service and delivery of documents in non-contentious matters in *John Wilmot Homes* v. *Reed*.[6] The rules on postal acceptance do not apply to document exchanges and unless the contract contains a contrary provision the contract will come into existence when the seller's part of the contract is received by the buyer.[7] Where the Standard Conditions of Sale in each case are used, Condition 2 provides that the contract is made when the last copy of the contract is deposited at the document exchange. Standard Commercial Property Condition 2 provides to identical effect. If the Standard Conditions of Sale or Standard Commercial Property Conditions do not form the basis of the contract, the contract probably comes into existence when the last part of the contract is placed in the solicitor's box at the document exchange. There is no decided case on the making of a contract for the sale of land where a document exchange has been used to effect an exchange, and the proposition outlined above would be subject to the rules of the particular document exchange which was being used.

4.3.7. Telex

The use of telex as a method of exchanging contracts has largely been superseded by telephone and more recently by fax. In operation the use of telex for exchange is very similar to the telephone and the Law Society's Formulae have equal application to this situation.[8] It is suggested that the contract comes into existence when the seller's telex message activating the Law Society's Formulae is received on the buyer's telex terminal.[9] The advantage of telex over the telephone is that the actual message transmitted between the parties' solicitors is reduced into writing, thus eliminating any possibility that one party might later deny the existence of the contract. A physical exchange of contracts should follow the telex messages but is not essential since the contract will already be in existence. It should be noted, however, that if the physical exchange is not made, and one party subsequently refuses to complete, without the documentary evidence supplied by the contract itself, the party seeking to enforce the contract will have difficulty in demonstrating that the requirements of Law of Property (Miscellaneous Provisions) Act 1989, s.2 have been satisfied.

4.3.8. Fax

Exchange of contracts by using facsimile transmission is similar in operation to telex but is probably to be preferred to telex in that with facsimile transmission a copy of the contract signed by the buyer is transmitted to the seller's terminal and may thus be verified by him before he transmits his copy of the contract in return. A physical exchange of documents must follow the faxed messages; if this were never to happen a party seeking enforcement of the contract would have difficulty in demonstrating that the requirements of Law of Property (Miscellaneous Provisions) Act 1989, s.2 have been satisfied.[10] The main use of fax is to transmit the messages which activate the Law Society's Formulae. In this context fax is merely a substitute for using the telephone. Standard Condition 1.3.3 and Standard Commercial Property Condition 1.3.3 do not permit fax to be used as a valid method of service of a document where delivery of the original document is essential (as it is with the contract), thus effectively ruling out an *exchange* by this method, although there is no objection to the parties using fax in order to activate the Law Society's Formulae.[11]

1. [1980] Ch 548.
2. See *Khan* v. *Hamilton* [1989] EGCS 128.
3. Despite doubts expressed about these rules in *Eccles* v. *Bryant and Pollock* (above), it is generally accepted that the postal rules as established in *Adams* v. *Lindsell* (1818) 1 B & Ald 681 do apply.
4. *Re London and Northern Bank, ex p. Jones* [1900] Ch. 220.
5. *Holwell Securities* v. *Hughes* [1974] 1 All ER 161.
6. (1985) 51 P & CR 90.
7. See Standard Conditions 1 and 2 and Standard Commercial Property Conditions 1 and 2.
8. See para. C4.3.2.
9. *Entores Ltd* v. *Miles Far East Corporation* [1955] 2 QB 327.
10. *Milton Keynes Development Corporation* v. *Cooper (Great Britain) Ltd* [1993] EGCS 142. An exchange of faxes was held not to be an exchange of contracts.
11. See *Hastie & Jenkerson* v. *McMahon* [1991] 1 All ER 255 where the court, in a contentious case, approved fax as a valid method of service of a document but said that, to be valid as a method of service, the onus was on the sender of the document to prove that the document, in complete and legible form, had arrived at the recipient's terminal.

4.4. The Protocol

4.4.1. Paragraph 8 of the Protocol (see Appendix III.1 for the full text of the Protocol) provides as follows:

> 'On exchange the buyer's solicitor shall send or deliver to the seller's solicitor:
>
> 8.1 The signed contract with all names, dates and financial information completed.
>
> 8.2 The deposit provided in the manner prescribed in the contract. Under the Law Society's Formula C the deposit may have to be sent to another solicitor nominated by the seller's solicitor.
>
> 8.3 If contracts are exchanged by telephone, the procedures laid down by the Law Society's Formulae A, B or C must be used and both solicitors must ensure (unless otherwise agreed) that the undertakings to send documents and pay the deposit on that day are strictly observed.
>
> 8.4 The seller's solicitor shall, once the buyer's signed contract and deposit are held unconditionally, having ensured that details of each contract are fully completed and identical, send the seller's signed contract on the day of exchange to the buyer's solicitor in compliance with the undertaking given on exchange.
>
> 8.5 Notify the client that contracts have been exchanged.
>
> 8.6 Notify the seller's estate agent or property seller of exchange of contracts and the completion date.'

4.5. Standard Conditions of Sale and Standard Commercial Property Conditions

4.5.1. Condition 2.1 of both sets of conditions governs the making of the contract and allows contracts to be exchanged by document exchange, by post, or by telephone using the Law Society's Formulae (see Appendices VII.12 and VII.13).

C5. After exchange

See also: Insurance, para. C3

5.1.   The effects of exchange

5.1.1.   A binding contract exists from which normally neither party may withdraw without incurring liability for breach.

5.1.2.   The beneficial ownership in the property passes to the buyer who becomes entitled to any increase in value of the property, but also bears the risk of any loss or damage; hence the need to ensure that insurance of the property is effective from the moment of exchange.[1] Standard Condition 5.1 states that the risk in the property is to remain with the seller until completion. However, Standard Commercial Property Condition 5.1 passes risk to the buyer on exchange of contracts.

5.1.3.   The seller retains the legal title to the property until completion, but holds the beneficial interest on behalf of the buyer. During this period the seller is entitled to remain in possession of the property and to the rents and profits (unless otherwise agreed). He must also discharge the outgoings, e.g. water rates until completion. He owes a duty of care to the buyer and will be liable to the buyer in damages if loss is caused to the property through neglect or wanton destruction.[2] This duty continues so long as the seller is entitled to possession of the property and does not terminate because the seller vacates the property before completion.[3]

5.1.4.   From the moment that a binding contract exists between the parties two equitable liens arise, enforceable only through a court order for sale of the property. The seller's lien on the buyer's equitable interest is for the balance of the purchase price and if this is not paid in full on completion the lien attaches to the legal estate in the hands of the buyer. The buyer's lien is on the seller's legal estate for any deposit paid to the seller in the capacity of agent (but not as stakeholder), and in the case of unregistered land would not bind another buyer from the seller unless registered as a Class C(iii) land charge under Land Charges Act 1972. In the case of registered land the lien could be protected by the registration of a notice, although this might not be necessary if the buyer was already in occupation of the property as the lien may then constitute an overriding interest within Land Registration Act 2002.[4] Protection of the lien by registration is not normally considered to be necessary, but should be undertaken immediately if problems arise between the parties in the period between contract and completion.

1. In *National Carriers Ltd* v. *Panalpina (Northern) Ltd* [1981] AC 675 it was held that the doctrine of frustration can, in exceptional cases, apply to leases. Thus if a leasehold property were to be totally destroyed between exchange and completion, it is arguable that the buyer could not be forced to complete. The same case contains dicta to the effect that the doctrine may also be applicable to freehold land, but to date there has been no decided case where the doctrine has been held to apply, and it is therefore unsafe to assume that the buyer will be discharged from his obligations following total destruction of the property.
2. *Clarke* v. *Ramuz* [1891] 2 QB 456; *Phillips* v. *Lamdin* [1949] 2 KB 33.
3. *Lucie-Smith* v. *Gorman* [1981] CLY 2866.
4. Land Registration Act 2002, Sched. 1, para. 2 and Sched. 3, para 2, and see also *London & Cheshire Insurance Co. Ltd* v. *Laplagrene Property Co. Ltd* [1971] Ch 499.

5.2. After exchange

5.2.1. *The seller*

(a) Inform the client and estate agent that exchange has taken place and enter completion date in diary or file prompt system.

(b) Where, immediately after exchange, the seller is in possession of both copies of the contract, the seller's solicitor should check that both parts of the contract have been dated and bear the agreed completion date. The copy of the contract signed by the seller should immediately be sent to the buyer's solicitor to fulfil any undertaking given in the course of an exchange by telephone.

(c) Any deposit received must immediately be paid into an interest-bearing clients' deposit account.

(d) If any preliminary deposit has been held by an estate agent, the agent should be asked to remit such sum to the seller's solicitor who is normally required under the contract to hold 'the deposit', i.e. the whole of the amount specified in the contract as the contractual deposit (see Standard Condition 2.2 and Standard Commercial Property Condition 2.2). The agent may be reluctant to part with the money, preferring to hold it on account for any commission due to him.

(e) If not already done, the seller should deduce title to the buyer.

5.2.2. *The buyer*

(a) Inform the client and his lender that exchange has taken place and enter completion date in diary or file prompt system.

(b) Where exchange has taken place by telephone, immediately send to the seller (or as directed by him) the signed contract and deposit cheque in accordance with the undertaking given, having first checked that the contract is dated and bears the agreed completion date.

(c) Where appropriate, protect the contract by registration (see para. C5.3).

5.3.   Protection of the contract

5.3.1.   Registered land

The contract constitutes an interest which, in order to be binding on future buyers of an interest in the land, needs to be protected by entry of a notice on the register of the title. The contract, once protected on the register, will bind all future buyers of interests in the land, but would not take priority over another buyer who had made an official search before registration of the contract and who lodged his own application for registration within the priority period afforded by his search. Where a buyer is in possession the contract could constitute an overriding interest.[1] In this case protection of the contract by registration may not be necessary.

1. Land Registration Act 2002, Sched. 1, para. 2 and Sched. 3. para. 2.

5.3.2.   Unregistered land

The contract is an estate contract within the Class C(iv) category of land charge and will be void against a buyer of the legal estate for money or money's worth if not registered. Registration must be made against the name of the legal estate owner for the time being.[1] Care needs to be exercised when effecting the registration of sub-contracts, where the buyer under the sub-contract needs to register his C(iv) against the current owner of the legal estate who will not be his immediate seller. For example:

A contracts to sell to B.
Before completion of this contract B contracts to sell to C.
If C seeks to protect his estate contract, he must register a Class C(iv) land charge against A who will be the owner of the legal estate until completion of the contract between himself and B.

5.3.3.   Options to purchase and rights of pre-emption also require registration within this category.

5.3.4.   Registration of the contract

Since the contract is capable of registration, a solicitor who fails to register, thereby causing loss to his client, may be liable in negligence to the client. However, since completion of most contracts occurs within a very short period following exchange, in practice registration of the contract is uncommon. Consideration should always be given to the question of whether or not a particular contract requires protection by registration and the contract should always be registered if any of the circumstances listed in para. C5.3.5 apply.

5.3.5.   Guidelines

Registration of the contract is desirable in any of the situations listed below. The following is not an exhaustive list of all the circumstances in which registration is desirable. If the solicitor is in any doubt, he should err on the side of caution and register the contract in order to protect his client's interests:

(a) there is to be a long interval (e.g. more than two months) between contract and completion;

(b) there is reason to doubt the seller's good faith;

(c) a dispute arises between the seller and buyer;

(d) the seller delays completion beyond the contractual date;

(e) the purchase price is to be paid by instalments, the conveyance or transfer to be executed after payment of the final instalment;

(f) the transaction is a sub-sale.

1. *Barrett* v. *Hilton Developments Ltd* [1975] Ch 237.

D. TITLE
D1. Deducing title

See also: Seller's investigation of title, para. B3
Defective title and restrictive covenant insurance, para. B6
Acting on grant of lease, para. K1
Assignment of leases, para. K11

1.1. Time for deduction of title

1.1.1. Historically the seller deduced title after exchange of contracts but this practice had serious disadvantages because the buyer was committed to a contract without knowing the state of the seller's title. This could cause problems, particularly if the transaction was one of a chain.

1.1.2. Only in exceptional cases should deduction of title be delayed until after contracts have been exchanged.

1.1.3. Where the Protocol is used, by para. 4.4, the seller is required to send evidence of his title to the buyer with the draft contract and other pre-contract documentation.

1.1.4. Standard Condition 4.1.1 and Standard Commercial Property Condition 4.1.1 which both require evidence of title to be supplied 'immediately after making the contract', reflect the traditional practice of supplying the evidence of title after exchange of contracts. Despite these conditions, in most cases deduction of title will in practice take place before exchange of contracts.

1.2. Seller's obligation

1.2.1. The seller's obligation in relation to the deduction of his title is to supply sufficient documentary evidence to the buyer to prove that the seller is either the outright owner of the land he has contracted to sell or, if not, that he is in a position to compel someone else to transfer the land to the buyer or is a lender whose power of sale has arisen and become exercisable, thus entitling him to sell the land. It is not enough to show that the seller is able to ask a third party to transfer the land to the buyer; the seller must be able to force or oblige the third party to execute the purchase deed, e.g. where the land is held in the name of a company, the seller would need to own a controlling shareholding in that company in order to be able to compel the company to convey to the buyer.[1]

1. See *Re Bryant and Barningham's Contract* (1890) 44 Ch 218; *cf. Elliott* v. *Pierson* [1948] Ch 452.

1.3. Method of deduction in registered land

1.3.1. Land Registration Act 1925, s.110 contained detailed provisions as to the documents that a seller was required to supply to the buyer. These provisions have not been carried forward into the Land Registration Act 2002. The Act does provide that rules may be made about the obligations of a seller to prove or perfect his title under a contract for the transfer or other disposition for valuable consideration of registered land.[1] No rules have been made, however, and the seller and buyer are free to make their own bargain as to the evidence of title to be deduced.

1.3.2. The Protocol, Standard Condition 4.2.1 and Standard Commercial Property Condition 4.2.1 all require the seller at his own expense to supply official copy entries of the title to the buyer. Official copy entries of the title should always be supplied since they usually show the up-to-date position of the register. The official copy entries of the title supplied to the buyer must be originals (not photocopies) and of recent date. Later, when making a search at the Land Registry, the buyer will need to search from the date of such an official copy (or the date of an access by remote terminal).[2]

1. Land Registration Act 2002, Sched. 10, para. 2.
2. Land Registration Rules 2003, r.129.

1.4. Method of deduction in unregistered land

1.4.1. The seller will prove his ownership of unregistered land by supplying the buyer with an abstract or epitome of the documents comprising the title. In some cases the evidence supplied will be made up of a combination of these two styles of presentation.

1.4.2. An abstract of title is in essence a summary of all the documents comprised in the title. The preparation of an abstract in traditional form is a skilled and time-consuming task which has largely been superseded by the practice of supplying an epitome of the title supported by photocopies of all the documents referred to.

1.4.3. An epitome of title is a schedule of the documents comprising the title. The documents should be numbered and listed in chronological order, starting with the earliest in time. Each document should be identified as to its date, type (e.g. conveyance, assent, etc.), the names of the parties to it, whether a copy of the document is supplied with the epitome, and whether or not the original of the document will be handed to the buyer on completion. Photocopies of the documents which accompany the epitome must be of good quality, marked to show the document's corresponding number on the list shown by the epitome, and any plans included in the documents must be coloured or marked so that they are identical to the original document from which the copy has been made. Before the epitome and copy documents are sent to the buyer the seller's solicitor should check that all the copies are legible and bear the appropriate markings as outlined in the preceding sentence, and that all pages are complete and assembled in the correct sequence. The paper on which the epitome is supplied must be sufficiently permanent and durable to last in a clearly legible state throughout the likely period of its need as evidence of the title. An epitome which is supplied by means of a faxed copy may not at present satisfy these requirements unless the originals of all the documents referred to are to be handed over on completion. Thus if a seller delivers the epitome by fax, in a situation where all of the original documents will not be handed over on completion, he should deliver a further copy of the abstract to the buyer, by post or document exchange, such further copy being produced on non-glossy A4 size durable paper.

1.4.4. Documents to be included in the epitome

1.4.4.1. Root of title

The epitome must commence with a good root of title, as specified by a special condition in the contract. A good root of title is a document which, at the date of the contract:

(a) is at least 15 years old;[1]

(b) deals with or shows the ownership of the whole legal and equitable interest contracted to be sold;

(c) contains an adequate description of the property; and

(d) contains nothing to cast any doubt on the title.

1.4.4.2. A conveyance on sale or legal mortgage which satisfies the above requirements is generally acknowledged to be the most acceptable root of title because it effectively offers a double guarantee on the title. The buyer in the present transaction will be investigating the seller's title for a minimum period of 15 years; the buyer under the root conveyance would similarly have investigated title over a period of at least 15 years when he bought the property. Thus the present buyer is provided with the certainty of the soundness of the title over a period of at least 30 years. If there is no conveyance on sale on the title which satisfies the requirements of a good root, a legal mortgage provides an acceptable alternative. Since a lender will not lend money on the security of a property without investigating the title, a legal mortgage used as a root document provides a similar double guarantee of the title to that afforded by a conveyance on sale. In the absence of both a conveyance on sale and a legal mortgage, title may be commenced with either a voluntary conveyance or an assent dated after 1925.[2] Since both of these documents effect gifts of the land, no investigation of prior title would have taken place at the time when they were executed, and they do not therefore provide the double check on the title which is given by the conveyance on sale or the legal mortgage and for this reason are less satisfactory to a buyer when offered as roots of title. They should therefore only be offered as roots of title (and accepted as such by the buyer) where, after investigation of all the title documents available to the seller, no better root can be found. The nature of the root document will be specified by special condition in the contract, and if the buyer does not consider the root being offered to be adequate he must raise this problem with the seller before contracts are exchanged; once contracts have been exchanged, it is too late to vary the terms of the contract. If, however, it transpired that the seller was ultimately unable to prove his title to the property, the buyer could withdraw from the contract.

1.4.4.3. Less than statutory minimum title is offered

Only in very rare cases will it be found that the seller cannot provide the buyer with a root of title which satisfies the statutory minimum period of 15 years prescribed by Law of Property Act 1925, s.44 (as amended). A buyer who is offered a short title should not accept the situation until he has received a satisfactory explanation for the reasons for the short root from the seller and should be advised that, in accepting less than his statutory entitlement under Law of Property Act 1925, he is also assuming the risk of being bound by incumbrances on the title which he has had no opportunity of discovering or investigating. The risk of being bound by undiscovered incumbrances stretches backwards in time, not just to the statutory 15-year period, but to the date of the first document on the title (however old) which would satisfy the requirements for a good root. A short root should not be accepted by the buyer without a full investigation of the circumstances, the concurrence of his lender, and investigation of the possibility of obtaining defective title insurance, preferably at the seller's expense. The acceptance by the buyer of a short root of title may also affect his ability to obtain registration with an absolute title at the Land Registry.

1.4.4.4. Documents to be included in the abstract or epitome

From the root of title, all dealings with the legal and equitable interests in the land down to and including the interests of the present seller must be shown, thus constituting an unbroken chain of ownership stretching from the seller named in the root document to the present day. This includes the following:

(a) evidence of devolutions on death (death certificates, grants of representation, assents);

(b) change of name of an estate owner, e.g. marriage certificate, deed poll or statutory declaration;

(c) discharge of legal mortgages;

(d) documents prior to the root which contain details of restrictive covenants which affect the property;

(e) memoranda endorsed on documents of title, e.g. recording a sale of part, assent to a beneficiary, or severance of a beneficial joint tenancy;

(f) powers of attorney under which a document within the title has been executed.

1.4.4.5. Documents which need not be included in the abstract or epitome

Certain documents need not be included in the abstract or epitome, although in some cases their inclusion will be helpful to the buyer and may forestall queries on the title raised by the buyer. They include:

(a) documents of record and Land Charges Department search certificates (but it is good practice to include these so that the buyer can see which searches have been correctly made in the past, in which case he need not repeat the search during his own investigation of the title). It is recommended that documents of record should always be abstracted so that the buyer receives a complete picture of the title and one on which he can act immediately. Failure to supply such documents may lead to delay while, e.g. the buyer obtains a document which was not supplied by the seller;

(b) documents relating to equitable interests which will be overreached on completion of the current transaction (the buyer may discover these charges when he makes his pre-completion searches and if he has already been supplied with information about them he will not need to raise last-minute queries with the seller or to delay completion while he investigates them; therefore as a matter of good practice some notice of their existence should be given to the buyer);

(c) leases which have expired by effluxion of time (but if the tenant is still in possession of the property, possibly with the benefit of security of tenure, evidence of the terms on which the tenant enjoys the property should be supplied). Although leases which have been surrendered should be abstracted, together with evidence of the surrender, it is common practice not to provide evidence of leases which no longer affect the title;

(d) documents which pre-date the root of title except where a document within the title refers to the earlier document[3] (note that where a document within the title has been executed under a power of attorney, the power must be abstracted whatever its date);

(e) documents relating to discharged equitable interests in the land, e.g. receipted equitable mortgages.

1.4.4.6. Standard Condition 4.2.3 and Standard Commercial Property Condition 4.2.3 require the seller to produce to the buyer (at the seller's expense) the original of every relevant document, or an abstract, epitome or copy with an original marking by a solicitor of examination either against the original or against an examined abstract or an examined copy.

1.4.4.7. If the title documents produced by the seller do not adequately show the physical extent of the property or its title, the seller may have to supplement the evidence of title with a statutory declaration. By Standard Condition 4.3 and Standard Commercial Property Condition 4.3 the seller is relieved of the obligation to define precisely the boundaries of the property, or to show the ownership of fences, hedges, ditches or walls, or to identify separately parts of the property with different titles, further than he is able to from information in his possession, but the buyer may, if reasonable, call for a statutory declaration as to the facts of these matters. If the land cannot be properly identified or described from its description in the title deeds and contract, the buyer is entitled to call for a plan, to be prepared at the seller's expense. In other cases if the buyer insists on describing the property by means of a plan, he must bear the cost of preparation of the plan himself.

1.4.4.8. Documents which will not be handed over on completion

The epitome must specify which documents will be handed to the buyer on completion and which will be retained by the seller. The buyer is entitled on completion to take the originals or marked abstracts or marked copies of all the documents within the title except those which relate to an interest in the land which is retained by the seller, e.g. on a sale of part the seller will retain the title deeds in order to be able to prove his ownership of the land retained by him. Similarly, a general power of attorney will be retained because the donee of the power needs to keep the original document in order to deal with other property owned by the donor, and personal representatives will retain their original grant in order to administer the remainder of the deceased's estate.

1. Law of Property Act 1925, s.44, as amended by Law of Property Act 1969.
2. Before 1926 there was no requirement for an assent to be in writing, and an oral assent alone would not have been capable of satisfying the definition of a good root of title.
3. Law of Property Act 1925, s.45.

1.5.   Sub-sales

1.5.1.   The Law of Property Act 1925, s.44 does not appear to apply to a contract for a sub-sale. The buyer of unregistered land will require his immediate seller to deduce title to him as if this section did apply to the transaction, otherwise the buyer will not be sure of purchasing a good title, but the seller, until he completes his own purchase, may not be in a position to deduce such a title to the buyer. In any event the requirements for the deduction of title in these circumstances must be specifically dealt with by a special condition in the contract since there are no common law rules applicable to this situation.[1]

1.5.2.   Where the land is registered the requirements for deduction of title must again be dealt with by a special condition in the contract.

1. See also paras. B4 and B14 and see *Urban Manor* v. *Sadiq* [1997] NPC 24, CA.

1.6.   Leaseholds

1.6.1.   Deduction of title to leaseholds is discussed in section K.

D2. Investigation of title

See also: Mortgages: acting for lender and borrower, para. A11

Seller's investigation of title, para. B3

Defective title and restrictive covenant insurance, para. B6

Requisitions on title, para. D3

Pre-completion searches, para. E2

Lenders, section H

2.1. Purpose of investigation

2.1.1. The seller having supplied the buyer with evidence of his title, the buyer's task is to investigate that evidence to ensure that the seller is able to transfer that which he has contracted to sell and that there are no defects in that title which would adversely affect the interests of the buyer or his lender.

2.1.2. Any matters which are unclear or unsatisfactory on the face of the documentary evidence supplied by the seller may be raised as queries (requisitions) with the seller within the time-limits specified in the contract for raising requisitions.[1]

2.1.3. Investigation will be carried out by the solicitor on behalf of his buyer and/or lender client. Where the same solicitor is acting for both the buyer and his lender in a simultaneous transaction investigation is carried out only once, bearing in mind the particular requirements of each client.[2]

2.1.4. If ultimately the seller cannot show a good title, the buyer is entitled to withdraw from the contract. Prima facie the seller's inability to show title is a breach of contract entitling the buyer to a remedy in damages, but in practice the buyer's right to damages may, in certain circumstances, be curtailed or precluded by express provision in the contract.[3]

1. See Requisitions on title, para. D3.
2. See Mortgages: acting for lender and borrower, para. A11; The buyer's mortgage, para. E3; Lenders, section H.
3. See Requisitions on title, para. D3; Delay and remedies, section M.

2.2. Time for investigation

2.2.1. Conventionally investigation of title follows deduction of title as a procedure which is undertaken after exchange of contracts and is subject to time-limits imposed by the contract.[1]

2.2.2. In practice the seller will usually supply his evidence of title at the draft contract stage of the transaction (and in Protocol cases must do so) and may, by inclusion of a contractual provision to such effect, prevent the buyer from raising his requisitions after exchange, thus compelling the buyer to carry out his investigation at that stage of the transaction.

1. See Standard Condition 4.1 (Appendix VII.13) and Standard Commercial Property Condition 4.1 (Appendix VII.12).

2.3. Registered land

2.3.1. Investigation of title comprises:

(a) an examination of the official copy entries of the title supplied by the seller (including a copy of the lease where the title is leasehold and documents which are referred to on the register and evidence relating to matters as to which the register is not conclusive);[1]

(b) checking for evidence of overriding interests as these are not entered on the register but are binding on the buyer irrespective of notice; and

(c) pre-completion searches.[2]

2.3.2. Particular points which may arise out of the examination of the official copy entries of the title are dealt with below and in paras. D2.6 *et seq.*

2.3.3. The existence of most overriding interests can be discovered through:

(a) pre-contract enquiries of the seller under which the seller will normally be asked to reveal details of adverse interests and occupiers' rights. A seller who did not disclose such matters might be liable to the buyer for non-disclosure;[3]

(b) a local land charges search (local land charges not protected on the register are overriding interests);

(c) inspection of the property before exchange which may reveal, e.g. occupiers, easements, or adverse possession. The buyer may also be advised to re-inspect immediately prior to completion.

2.3.4. The examination of official copy entries of the title in registered land is a relatively quick and simple process. So long as a note is made of any matters on which requisitions need to be raised the method of investigation to be employed with a registered title is a matter to be decided by the solicitor concerned.

2.3.5. *Official copy entries of the title*

The following points should be checked:

(a) on the property register:

    (i)   the description of the land accords with the contract description;

    (ii) the title number corresponds with that given on the contract;

    (iii) the estate – is it freehold or leasehold?

    (iv) easements enjoyed by the property (if they are entered on the register);[4]

    (v) has any land been removed from the title? If so, does this affect the land being purchased?

(b) on the proprietorship register:

    (i)   is the class of title correct?

    (ii) is the seller the registered proprietor? If not, who has the ability to transfer the land?

    (iii) the existence and effect of any other entries (restrictions, or pre-Land Registration Act 2002 cautions or inhibitions);

(c) on the charges register:

    (i)   are there any incumbrances or other entries?

    (ii) how do these affect the buyer?

    (iii) which of them will be removed or discharged on completion and how will their removal be effected?

(d) on the title plan:

    (i)   is the land being bought included within the title?

    (ii) check any colourings/hatchings which may indicate rights of way, the extent of covenants or land which has been removed from the title;

(e) the date of issue of the official copy entries of the title.

2.3.6. *Adverse entries in the proprietorship register*

The most commonly found entry on the proprietorship register will be a restriction which regulates the circumstances in which a disposition of a registered estate may be the subject of an entry in the register.[5] The wording of the restriction will indicate what procedure must be followed in order to conduct a valid disposition of the land. The buyer must therefore either follow that procedure (e.g. payment of money to two trustees in the case of land held on a trust of land) or require the seller to procure the removal of the restriction from the register on or before completion. In some cases a pre-Land Registration Act 2002 inhibition will be found on the proprietorship register (usually in connection with the bankruptcy of the proprietor) which will prevent any disposition of the land until it is removed. Similarly, a caution may have been entered on the register before the implementation of the Land Registration Act 2002. In the absence of a withdrawal no dealing with the land could be registered until the cautioner has been given the opportunity by the Chief Land Registrar to show cause why the dealing to the buyer should not proceed.

1. See Standard Condition 4.2.1 (Appendix VII.13) and Standard Commercial Property Condition 4.2.1 (Appendix VII.12).
2. See Pre-completion searches, para. E2.
3. See Seller's duty of disclosure, para. B5.
4. See also Access to neighbouring land, para. B26.4.
5. Land Registration Act 2002, s.40(1).

2.4.   Unregistered land

2.4.1.   Investigation of title comprises:

(a) an examination of the documents supplied in the abstract or epitome to check that:

    (i) the root document is as provided for by the contract or, if none is specified, complies with Law of Property Act 1925, s.44.[1] The root document will usually have been specified by special condition of the contract. Once contracts have been exchanged it is too late to object to the date or nature of the deed being offered as a root of title. If the wrong document has been supplied, the buyer is entitled to insist on the correct document being supplied in its place. Both parties may agree to substitute a different document as the root of title;

    (ii) there is an unbroken chain of ownership beginning with the seller in the root document and ending with the present seller;

    (iii) there are no defects in the title which will adversely affect the buyer's title or the interests of his mortgagee;

(b) verification, i.e. inspection of the original deeds;[2]

(c) checking for evidence of occupiers (this is normally done by inspection of the property);

(d) pre-completion searches.[3]

1. See Deducing title, para. D1.
2. See para. D2.13.
3. See Pre-completion searches, para. E2.

2.5.   Method of investigation (unregistered land)

2.5.1.   Examination of an unregistered title can be a complex and time-consuming business. It is essential that each of the documents within the abstract or epitome is carefully scrutinised to ensure that it is in order and a note made of any irregularities which need to be clarified by way of requisitions with the seller.[1]

2.5.2. To ensure that nothing is overlooked on investigation it is recommended that the solicitor adopts and follows a systematic and thorough method of investigation of an unregistered title and allows himself sufficient time in which to carry out this procedure at an unhurried pace. Except in the simplest cases, written notes of the title should be made while carrying out the investigation so that these notes can be used as the basis for framing requisitions and, if needed, will be available for reference at a later stage of the transaction.

2.5.3. *Method*

(a) Check each document chronologically starting with the root.

(b) Is the root as provided for in the contract?[2]

(c) Is there an unbroken chain of title from the root to the present day?

Then, in each document within the abstract or epitome, check the following points, making written notes of any matter which needs to be clarified or rechecked:

(d) Date

A deed is not invalid because it is not dated or is wrongly dated, but the date of the document will:

(i)   establish whether a root document is a good root;[3]

(ii)   affect the amount of stamp duty payable;

(iii) affect its vulnerability under the Insolvency Act 1986 in the case of a voluntary disposition;

(iv) assist in making a reasoned judgment on an apparent defect in title, e.g. a technical defect in a document which is over 15 years old may be less detrimental to the title than one contained in a more recent document.

(e) Stamp duties

Ad valorem duties and particulars delivered stamp. The amount of duty will depend on the nature of the document, the value of the consideration and the date of the document. The seller must be required to rectify any irregularities of this nature. If no certificate of value is included in the document, stamp duty at full rate should have been paid on the conveyance. In the event of doubt the party should insist that the earlier document is adjudicated and any additional duty, penalties and interest paid.

(f) Parties

For example, are the seller's names as shown on the previous document?

(g) Description of the property

Does it accord with what the buyer is purchasing?

(h) Acknowledgments for production of earlier deeds?

(i) Execution

Have all formalities been observed?

(j) Powers of attorney

Is the disposition by the attorney valid and are subsequent buyers protected?

(k) Endorsements on deeds

Are those that are necessary present, and are there any adverse memoranda?

(l) Incumbrances

What are they? Are they as expected? Is there a chain of indemnity covenants where required?

(m) Easements and rights

Are these as expected? Do they follow down the chain? Have any been added or taken away?[4]

(n) Receipt clause

This is evidence (although not necessarily conclusive evidence) that the seller's lien for the unpaid purchase price has been extinguished.[5]

(o) Searches supplied with the abstract

Have searches against all previous estate owners been abstracted or are there gaps? Are the names and periods searched against correct? Did completion take place within the priority period?

(p) Compulsory registration

Check:

(i) that there has been no conveyance on sale since the area became one of compulsory registration. The date of the compulsory registration order can be checked from the appropriate practice material issued by the Land Registry;

(ii) that there has been no dealing of any kind since 1 April 1998.

If necessary the seller should be required to register before completion.

1. Particular points which may arise out of the examination of the abstract or epitome are dealt with in paras. D2.6 *et seq.*
2. See para. D2.4.1.
3. See para. D2.4.1.
4. See also Access to neighbouring land, para. B26.4.
5. See *London & Cheshire Insurance Co. Ltd* v. *Laplagrene Property Co. Ltd* [1971] Ch 499.

2.6.   Root of title

2.6.1. Documents which are capable of being used as a good root of title are listed in para. D1.4.4.1.

2.6.2. The document which is to constitute the root will be specified by a special condition in the contract and once contracts have been exchanged cannot be changed except with the consent of both parties (and, where relevant, the buyer's lender).

2.6.3. Generally the buyer cannot require evidence of title prior to the root except:[1]

(a) he is always entitled to a copy of a power of attorney under which any abstracted document is executed;

(b) where an abstracted document refers to an earlier document, he may call for that earlier document, e.g. where an abstracted document refers to restrictive covenants imposed by a pre-root conveyance, the document imposing the covenants may be called for;

(c) where an abstracted document describes the property by reference to a plan which is attached to or referred to in an earlier document, that earlier document may be called for so that the plan may be examined;

(d) any document creating any limitation or trust by reference to which any part of the property is disposed of by an abstracted document may be called for even if dated pre-root.

1. Law of Property Act 1925, s.45.

2.7.   Conveyance by trustees to themselves

2.7.1. If on the title there is a conveyance by trustees or personal representatives to one of themselves, enquiry must be made into the circumstances of the transaction since, on the face of it, such a conveyance is in breach of trust and is voidable by the beneficiaries without enquiry as to fairness.

2.7.2. Such a transaction can be justified if one of the following situations exists:

(a) there is proof of a pre-existing contract to purchase, an option or right of pre-emption in favour of the trustee or personal representative;

(b) the personal representative was a beneficiary under the will or intestacy of the seller;

(c) the consent of all the beneficiaries being legally competent was obtained to the transaction;

(d) the conveyance was made under an order of the court;

(e) the transaction was sanctioned by the trust instrument.

2.8.   Particular capacities

2.8.1.   Trustees of land

2.8.1.1. Registered land

In registered land, a Form A restriction may be entered on the proprietorship register indicating what must be done to overreach the beneficial interests. A further restriction may also be entered reflecting any other limitations on the trustees' powers to dispose of the land. Provided the terms of any restriction are complied with the buyer will get good title. Where trustees hold the land on trust for themselves as joint tenants in equity, no restriction is placed on the register and the buyer may safely deal with the survivor on proof of death of the other trustee.

2.8.1.2. Unregistered land

(a) Such trustees have a wide power of sale,[1] and if consents are required to a sale a buyer is not concerned to see that the consents of more than two persons are obtained and is never concerned with the consents of persons under disability (i.e. minors, persons under mental incapacity).

(b) A buyer paying his money to the trustees, being at least two individuals or a trust corporation, will take the land free from the equitable interests of the beneficiaries, but not otherwise.[2] Thus a conveyance on the title by a sole individual trustee will require investigation.

2.8.2.   Personal representatives

2.8.2.1. Registered land

On production of the grant, personal representatives may become registered as proprietors of the land, in which case, provided the buyer deals with the registered proprietors and complies with any restriction on the register, he will get good title. Personal representatives would not normally register themselves as proprietors unless they intended to hold on to the land without disposing of it for some period of time, e.g. during the minority of a beneficiary. In other cases the personal representatives will produce their grant of representation to the buyer as proof of their authority to deal with the land. Provided the buyer takes a transfer from all the proving personal representatives and submits an office copy or certified copy of the grant with his application for registration, he will obtain a good title.[3] A transfer or assent made by personal representatives must be in the form prescribed.[4]

2.8.2.2. Unregistered land

(a) Personal representatives have the wide powers of trustees of land. If there is only one proving personal representative he has all the powers of two or more personal representatives and consequently (unlike a sole individual trustee) can convey the land on his own and give a valid receipt for the proceeds of sale. If, however, the grant is made to two or more personal representatives, they must all join in the assent or conveyance, but a sole proving personal representative of an absolute owner is entitled to act on his own. A buyer must therefore call for the grant to see who have been appointed as personal representatives, and must insist that all the personal representatives named in the grant join in the assent or conveyance, or call for evidence of the death of any personal representative who will not be a party to the purchase deed.

(b) An assent made by personal representatives must be in writing in order to pass the legal estate in the land to the beneficiary. The beneficiary who is to take the land must be named in the document, which must be signed by the personal representatives. If the document contains covenants given by the beneficiary (e.g. indemnity in respect of existing restrictive covenants) it must be by deed. Even where the beneficiary is also the sole personal representative (as may be the case where a widow is her deceased husband's sole personal representative and sole beneficiary) a written assent is required.[5]

(c) The effect of Administration of Estates Act 1925, s.36 is that an assent in favour of a beneficiary may be defeated by a later sale of the land by the personal representatives in favour of a buyer who takes from them a written statement that they have made no previous assent or conveyance of the land. However, this will not be the case if either there was an endorsement of a previous assent on the grant or there had been a previous sale by the assentee. It follows that a conveyance on sale by personal representatives should contain a section 36(6) statement and that an assentee (and a buyer) should require an endorsement on the grant. This may be done at the cost of the estate. Where the transaction induces first registration (as it almost always will) an endorsement on the grant is not required.

(d) A disposition by personal representatives should contain an acknowledgment of the right to production of their grant of representation as this is a document of title the inspection of which may be required by subsequent buyers of the land. The grant should be inspected to check for endorsements which have been made on it.

(e) An assent or conveyance by personal representatives of a legal estate is sufficient evidence in favour of a buyer that the person in whose favour it is made is the person entitled to have the legal estate conveyed to him, unless there is a memorandum of a previous assent or conveyance on the grant. This in effect means that a buyer from an assentee of land, having checked the grant and found no adverse endorsements, does not have to look at the deceased's will to check that the assentee was rightly entitled to the land, but this provision will not protect the buyer if it is apparent from some other source (e.g. the assent itself) that it was made in favour of the wrong person.[6]

(f) On a sale by the personal representatives of the survivor of beneficial joint tenants, a statement should be included in the conveyance to the effect that the survivor was solely and beneficially entitled so that the buyer has the protection of Law of Property (Joint Tenants) Act 1964. If such personal representatives did not sell the land but made an assent in favour of a beneficiary, the assent should properly include the above statement in order to protect a buyer from the assentee. If the statement was missing from the assent, consideration should be given to joining the personal representatives of the survivor into the conveyance by the assentee in order to give the statement.

(g) If a sole or sole surviving trustee of a trust of land dies in a case where a buyer cannot rely on the 1964 Act (because the survivor was not solely and beneficially entitled), his personal representatives can exercise all the powers of that trustee. If a sole personal representative is appointed in such a situation, he can act on his own in dealing with the deceased's private property (including land), but he must act jointly with another trustee in making a disposition of the trust property under which capital money arises.

2.8.3. Co-owners

2.8.3.1. Co-owners hold land on a trust of land and the remarks relating to trustees in para. D2.8.1 apply.

2.8.3.2. Registered land

If the co-owners are tenants in common in equity, there will generally be a restriction on the proprietorship register to the effect that no disposition by a sole proprietor of the registered estate (except a trust corporation) under which capital money arises is to be registered unless authorised by an order of the court. In the event of the death of one or more of the co-owners, so that at the time of sale there is only one surviving trustee, a second trustee must be appointed to join with the survivor in the transfer. Alternatively, the buyer can deal with the survivor alone provided that the restriction is removed from the register, or the survivor provides the buyer with documentary evidence which will enable the restriction to be removed on the buyer's application for registration. Such proof might consist of a statutory declaration by the survivor that in stated circumstances the declarant had become entitled legally and beneficially to the registered estate and that he has not encumbered or dealt with his own share nor has he received notice of any incumbrance on or dealing with the deceased's share. A certificate by the seller's conveyancer will be accepted in place of a declaration if the conveyancer is able to speak from his knowledge of all the relevant facts. In practice, it is better either for the seller to procure the removal of the restriction or to appoint a second trustee to act with the seller.

2.8.3.3. If the co-owners are joint tenants in equity, no restriction is placed on the register and a buyer may deal with the survivor of them on proof of the death of the deceased co-owner.

2.8.3.4. Unregistered land

(a) Inspection of the conveyance under which the co-owners bought the land will reveal whether they held as joint tenants or tenants in common in equity.

(b) The sole survivor of tenants in common does not automatically become entitled to the whole equitable estate in the land since a tenancy in common is capable of passing by will or on intestacy. The trust therefore still subsists and a buyer from the survivor should insist on taking a conveyance only from two trustees in order to overreach any beneficial interests which may subsist under the trust. Alternatively, if the survivor has become solely and beneficially entitled to the whole legal and equitable interest in the land, he may convey alone on proof to the buyer of this fact. Such proof would consist of the death certificate of the deceased, a certified or office copy of the grant of representation and an assent made in favour of the survivor.

(c) The survivor of beneficial joint tenants becomes entitled to the whole legal and equitable interest in the land but a buyer from him will only accept a conveyance from the survivor alone if he can be satisfied that he will gain the protection of Law of Property (Joint Tenants) Act 1964. This Act (which is retrospective in operation to 1925) allows the buyer to assume that no severance of the joint tenancy (turning it into a tenancy in common) had occurred before the death of the deceased joint tenant. To gain the protection of the Act the following three conditions must all be satisfied:

    (i)   there must be no memorandum of severance endorsed on the conveyance under which the joint tenants bought the property;

    (ii) there must be no bankruptcy proceedings registered against the names of either of the joint tenants;

    (iii) the conveyance by the survivor must contain a recital stating that the survivor is solely and beneficially entitled to the land.

If any of the above conditions is not met, the survivor must be treated as a surviving tenant in common and the procedure in para. (b) above followed.

2.8.4. *Settled land*

2.8.4.1. Section 2 of Trusts of Land and Appointment of Trustees Act 1996 prohibits the creation of new strict settlements (except in limited circumstances). The following sub-paragraphs will generally be relevant only to settlements which were in existence on 1 January 1997.

2.8.4.2. Registered land

The tenant for life (or, if none, the statutory owners) will be registered as proprietor of the land and an appropriate restriction entered on the register. This will usually require capital money arising on a disposition to be paid to the trustees of the settlement. Provided the buyer complies with the terms of the restriction he will take a good title.

2.8.4.3. Unregistered land

    (a) Where land is settled land within Settled Land Act 1925, the legal estate in the land will be vested in the tenant for life under the Act by a vesting instrument, which will be a vesting deed in the case of an *inter vivos* settlement and may be a vesting assent by the personal representatives of the deceased where the settlement arises under a will. In exceptional cases, e.g. where the person who would otherwise be tenant for life is a minor, the legal estate will be vested in the trustees of the settlement as statutory owners. Both the tenant for life and the statutory owners have a wide power of sale under the Act (which can be extended by the terms of the settlement itself) but it is provided by Settled Land Act 1925, s.18 that where the land is the subject of a vesting instrument and the trustees of the settlement have not been discharged, any disposition which is not authorised by the Act or by the settlement is void. Further, where capital money arises on a disposition of the land, the disposition is of no effect for the purposes of the Act unless the money is paid to the trustees of the settlement, being at least two individuals or a trust corporation.

(b) A vesting instrument under Settled Land Act 1925 must describe the land, name the person in whose favour it is vested and name the trustees of the settlement for the purposes of the Act. Except in exceptional circumstances, a buyer is bound and entitled to rely on these statements and cannot call for the trust instrument.

2.8.5.   Lenders

2.8.5.1. A power to sell the legal estate vested in the borrower, subject to prior incumbrances but discharged from subsequent ones, is given by Law of Property Act 1925, s.101 to every lender whose mortgage is made by deed. Thus unless expressly excluded the power is available to a lender who has taken a legal mortgage and to one whose equitable mortgage is made by deed. In order actually to convey the legal estate of the borrower to the buyer an equitable lender whose mortgage is not made by deed must adopt some conveyancing device such as an irrevocable power of attorney granted by way of security in his favour by the borrower. An equitable lender whose mortgage is made by deed can apply to the court under Law of Property Act 1925, s.90 for an order for sale and an order appointing a person to convey the land.

2.8.5.2 In relation to registered land, the proprietor of a registered charge is taken to have the powers of disposition conferred by law on the owner of a legal mortgage in the absence of any entry in the register to the contrary.[7] The owner of a charge which is not substantively registered has no statutory power of sale.

2.8.5.3. The power of sale arises when the mortgage money becomes due under the mortgage, i.e. on the legal date for redemption which is usually set at an early date in the mortgage term. The power only becomes exercisable by the lender when one of the events specified in Law of Property Act 1925, s.103 has occurred.[8] A buyer from the lender must check (by looking at the mortgage deed) that the power of sale has arisen, but is not concerned to enquire whether the power has become exercisable.

2.8.5.4. The sale must be genuine; a sale to the lender's nominee or to a company controlled by him will not be treated as a valid exercise of the power of sale.

2.8.6. *Attorneys*

2.8.6.1. The buyer is entitled to a copy of any power of attorney which affects the title (even if in unregistered land the power is dated earlier than the root of title). The buyer must check that the power authorises the transaction and that it has not been revoked before the transaction in question.[9]

2.8.6.2. Where the seller is a sole legal owner he can delegate his power to sell using a general power under Powers of Attorney Act 1971, s.10. A certified copy of the power should be handed over on completion.

2.8.6.3. Where co-owners are concerned the requirements vary according to the date of the transaction.

(a) Before 1 March 2000 a co-owner who wanted to appoint an attorney to act for him on the sale had to use a specific power of attorney under Trustee Act 1925, s.25. This power was only effective for a period of 12 months. Under a Trustee Act power a co-owner or trustee could not appoint his sole co-trustee to be his attorney. If a co-owner or trustee wished to appoint his sole co-trustee an enduring power of attorney under the Enduring Power of Attorney Act 1985 should have been used.

(b) On or after 1 March 2000 a co-owner can use a general power of attorney and can appoint his sole co-trustee to be his attorney (Trustee Delegation Act 1999, s.1).

(c) Under the Trustee Delegation Act 1999, trustees who are not beneficially entitled to the land may use a general trustee power (Trustee Delegation Act 1999, s.5). However, the general trustee power is only effective for a period of 12 months. The trustee can appoint his sole co-trustee to be his attorney under the general trustee power.

(d) Whether a general power or general trustee power is used, if a sole co-trustee has been appointed to act as attorney he cannot give a valid receipt for capital money. Overreaching cannot operate in these circumstances. The donor of the power should therefore appoint a third party to act as attorney. From 1 March 2000, enduring powers of attorney cannot be used to appoint a sole co-trustee to be an attorney.

2.8.6.4. Registered land

(a) If any document executed by an attorney is delivered to the Law Registry there must be produced to the registrar either the instrument creating the power of attorney or a sufficient copy of the power or a certificate by a solicitor in Form 1.[9]

(b) If the transaction between the attorney and the buyer is not made within 12 months of the date on which the power came into operation the registrar may require evidence to satisfy him that the power has not been revoked. This may consist of or include a statutory declaration by the buyer or a certificate given by the buyer's solicitor in Form 2.[10]

2.8.6.5. Unregistered land

(a) *Security powers under Powers of Attorney Act 1971, s.4*

A buyer from an attorney holding such a power will take good title provided that he had no actual knowledge that the power had been revoked with the attorney's consent.

(b) *Other non-enduring powers*

A person who buys directly from the attorney will take good title under Powers of Attorney Act 1971, s.5(2) provided he buys in good faith without knowledge of the revocation of the power. The power is revoked automatically if the doner dies, becomes bankrupt or becomes incapable of managing his own affairs. Thus the buyer cannot take good title if he is aware of the death, bankruptcy or incapacity of the donor. A subsequent purchaser gains the protection of Powers of Attorney Act 1971, s.5(4) if either:

(i) the dealing between the attorney and his immediate purchaser took place within 12 months of the grant of the power; or

(ii) the person who buys directly from the attorney makes a statutory declaration within three months of completion of his transaction to the effect that he had no knowledge of the revocation of the power.

Where a person buys directly from an attorney more than 12 months after the date of the grant of the power, the buyer's solicitor should require his client immediately on completion of the transaction to make the requisite statutory declaration, since this document will be required as evidence of non-revocation on a subsequent disposition of the property. If not made immediately, and the buyer client dies before making the declaration, there will be a defect in title, since the subsequent buyer will not be able to take the protection of Powers of Attorney Act 1971, s.5(4).

(c) *Enduring powers*

Until the incapacity of the donor the power takes effect as an ordinary power and the Act contains provisions to protect buyers which are similar to those outlined above. On the incapacity of the donor the attorney's authority to act becomes limited to such acts as are necessary for the protection of the donor and his estate until such time as the power is registered with the Court of Protection. Once registered, the power is incapable of revocation and the attorney's full authority to act is restored. Where a person is buying from an attorney who holds an enduring power he should conduct a search at the Court of Protection to ensure that no application for registration of the power is pending. If the power has already been registered, the attorney should produce the registration certificate to the buyer. An office copy of the power can be produced as evidence both of the contents of the power and of its registration.

(d) Powers granted before 1 October 1971
Such powers are governed by Law of Property Act 1925, ss.126–128 and
not by Powers of Attorney Act 1971.

1. Trusts of Land and Appointment of Trustees Act 1996, s.6.
2. Law of Property Act 1925, ss.2 and 27.
3. Land Registration Rules 2003, r.162.
4. Land Registration Rules 2003, r.58.
5. *Re Kings Will Trusts* [1964] Ch 542.
6. Administration of Estates Act 1925, s.36.
7. Land Registration Act 2002, s.52.
8. See para. B7.7.4.
9. Land Registration Rules 2003, r.61 and Sched. 3
10. Land Registration Rules 2003, r.62 and Sched. 3.

2.9. Discharged mortgages

2.9.1. Registered land

A mortgage over registered land which has been discharged will be deleted from
the charges register of the title and is thus of no further concern to the buyer. As
far as the seller's existing mortgage is concerned the buyer should raise a requisition requiring this to be removed on or before completion.

2.9.2. Unregistered land

(a) Discharged legal mortgages should be abstracted by the seller and checked
by the buyer's solicitor to ensure that the discharge was validly effected.
Discharged equitable mortgages will not normally be abstracted and once
discharged no longer affect the title.

(b) Where a sale has been effected by a lender in exercise of his power of sale,
the mortgage deed will not bear a receipt.

(c) Building society mortgages
Provided that the receipt (usually endorsed on the mortgage deed) is in the
form of wording prescribed by Building Societies Act 1986, and is signed
by a person authorised by the particular society, the receipt may be treated
as an effective discharge of the mortgage without further enquiry being
made.

(d) Other mortgages
By Law of Property Act 1925, s.115 a receipt endorsed on the mortgage
deed (even if the receipt is not executed as a deed) operates to discharge
the mortgage provided it is signed by the lender and names the person
making repayment. However, where the money appears to have been paid
by a person not entitled to the immediate equity of redemption, the receipt
will usually operate as a transfer by deed of the mortgage. Thus if the
person making repayment is not the borrower named in the mortgage or a
personal representative or trustee acting on his behalf, the receipt should

make it expressly clear that the receipt is to operate as such and is not intended to be a transfer of the mortgage to the person making payment. If the borrower makes repayment of the mortgage debt, but the receipt is dated later than the date of the conveyance by the borrower to a buyer of the land charged, at the date of the receipt the borrower will not be the person immediately entitled to the equity of redemption under the mortgage, because the mortgage had not been discharged at the date of completion of the sale of the land; thus the buyer will technically have bought the land subject to this incumbrance. In these circumstances the receipt operates to transfer the mortgage to the borrower (and not as a receipt) and it is, in theory, undischarged. In reality, any rights which the borrower has under the mortgage are unlikely to be enforced since he may be estopped from setting up the mortgage against the buyer. The borrower's position is at best that of a puisne mortgagee, since the title deeds will have passed to the buyer on completion of the sale, and unless registered as a Class C(i) or C(iii) land charge would be unenforceable against a subsequent buyer of the land for valuable consideration.[1] A buyer should therefore check the mortgage receipt to see who made repayment and also check that the receipt is dated no later than the date of the next transaction in the chain. If the mortgage receipt appears inadvertently to have transferred the mortgage and not discharged it a requisition should be raised to ensure that the seller or his lender is in possession of the title deeds (so that no mortgage supported by deposit of deeds can have come into existence as a result of the transfer) and the buyer should make a Land Charges Department search against the name of the person who bought from the borrower to ensure that no land charge has been registered against his name. Provided that the present seller or his lender has the deeds and the result of the land charges search reveals no adverse entries the defect can be ignored.

1. See *Cumberland Court (Brighton) Ltd* v. *Taylor* [1964] Ch 29.

2.10.   Transactions at an undervalue

2.10.1.   Dispositions which are made by way of gift or at an undervalue (whether *inter vivos* or by assent) are not generally acceptable as roots of title in unregistered land because no investigation of title would have been made by the donee at the time of the transaction. They do not therefore provide the double check on title which is afforded by an arm's length conveyance.

2.10.2.   Where a prospective buyer or mortgagee of land, whether registered or not, has notice that the land has been the subject of an undervalue transaction, it may be necessary to consider whether the courts' powers to set aside, under Insolvency Act 1986, s.238 or s.339, apply. An undervalue transaction may be the result of a gift, a partial gift (made for a consideration but a substantially below market value one), financial arrangements following a marriage breakdown, or a deed of variation in relation to an inheritance. If sections 238 or 339 do apply, it will then be necessary to see whether the protection provided by Insolvency (No.2) Act

1994 operates. The courts' sections 238 and 339 powers are exercisable for periods of two or five years, respectively, from the date of the transaction (depending on whether the transferor was a company or an individual), but the 1994 Act's provisions protect a person acquiring in good faith and for value during those periods – see para. D2.10.6.

2.10.3. *Dispositions by companies*

If a company has made a disposition at an undervalue within the last two years, the transaction can be set aside if the transaction was with a person connected with the company, or if the present buyer knows that the company was insolvent at the time of the transaction or knows that the company would have become insolvent as a result of that transaction at an undervalue.

In any dealing where a company has made a transaction at an undervalue more than two years ago, a company search must be carried out to whether the company went into liquidation or administration within two years of the voluntary disposition.

The term 'connected person' includes a director (Insolvency Act 1986, s.249).

2.10.4. *Dispositions by individuals*

If an individual becomes bankrupt after having made a disposition at an undervalue, the transaction can be set aside if the transaction was made within the last two years. If the transaction was made within the last five years it can be set aside if the present buyer knows that the donor was insolvent at the time of the transaction or knows that he would have become insolvent as a result of the transaction. It can also be set aside if the transaction at an undervalue was made within the last five years and it was made to an 'associate' of the donor. The word associate is widely defined in the Insolvency Act 1986, s.435 to include the donor's spouse, ex-spouse, partner, partner's relatives, employers and employees. Buyers must carry a Land Charges Department search against the donor in a transaction at undervalue to find out if they have become insolvent within five years.

2.10.5. *Protection of the buyer*

2.10.5.1. The courts can set aside transactions at an undervalue against subsequent owners of the property if the insolvency occurred within the two or five year periods. Insolvency Act 1986, ss 241(2) and s.342(3), provide protection for subsequent buyers. For dispositions made on or before 26 July 1994, the transaction cannot be set aside where:

(a) the purchaser was not a party to the transaction at an undervalue;

(b) acted in good faith;

(c) provided value for the purchase (i.e. the open market price) and was without knowledge that the transaction was an undervalue.

2.10.5.2. Where the transaction at an undervalue was made after 26 July 1994, it cannot be set aside where the buyer bought in good faith and for value. Insolvency (No.2) Act 1994 amended s.241(2) and s.342(3) to the effect that the clawback will be limited to cases where either:

(a) the purchaser is an associate of the donor or donee to the transaction at an undervalue; or

(b) the buyer has notice that the transaction was at an undervalue and that the donor has become insolvent or was about to become insolvent.

If one of these two exceptions applies the buyer is presumed not to have bought in good faith. Provided the buyer does the appropriate searches and has no knowledge of any insolvency and provided he is not an associate (he will be protected from the clawback provisions).

2.10.6. Notice

Insolvency (No.2) Act 1994 was passed to deal with difficulties caused by those provisions of Insolvency Act 1986 which apply to undervalue transactions. Various questions had arisen about its effect since it came into force in July 1994. As a result, the Law Society obtained the opinion of leading counsel, Gabriel Moss Q.C., on certain points. Appendix V.10. sets out his views.

2.10.7. Registered land

On first registration the registrar must enter a notice in the register of the burden of any interest which appears from his examination of the title to affect the registered estate.[1] Land Registry practice is at present to enter a note, on first registration, that the land may be affected by sections 238 or 339, either where the transfer to the applicant appears to be an undervalue transaction; or where an undervalue transaction appears in the title deduced, unless it is shown that the two or five-year period (company or individual transferor) had expired by the time the transaction took place, or that the applicant is protected by the 1994 Act.

2.10.8 Also consider the issues raised in the Law Society guidance on gifts of property reproduced in Appendix V.8.

1. Land Registration Rules 2003, r.35.

2.11. Effect of failure to register land charges (unregistered land)

2.11.1. Charges of Classes C(i), C(ii), C(iii) and F are void against a purchaser of any interest in the land for valuable consideration (including marriage).

2.11.2. Charges of Classes C(iv) and D are void only against a purchaser of a legal estate for money or money's worth.

2.12. Checking stamp duties

2.12.1. *Registered land*

Once the buyer has become registered as proprietor, the transfer and/or pre-registration deeds, in general, no longer concern a subsequent buyer and in any event are not generally available to be checked. However, the Land Registry is bound to investigate the stamping of documents prior to registering any change of title and parties submitting a transfer or application for registration may find that they have to adjudicate the documents supporting their application for registration and to pay any duty, penalties and interest assessed. Additionally, the adequacy of the stamp upon any documentation may become relevant if any party subsequently challenges the registration such as where it is a forgery or made in breach of trust or is set aside on insolvency. The party seeking to preserve the registration may have to rely upon such documents in the litigation and ensure that they are properly stamped. The registration may not protect against the inadequacy of the stamping.

2.12.2. *Unregistered land*

(a) Unstamped or incorrectly stamped documents or documents not bearing adjudication or denoting stamps where these are required by the legislation are not good roots of title, nor good links in the chain. They cannot be produced in evidence in civil proceedings and will not be accepted by the Chief Land Registrar on an application to register the title.

(b) A buyer is entitled to insist that all documents within the title are properly stamped at the expense of the seller. If, therefore, on examination of the title stamping defects are found, the buyer or mortgagee should raise a requisition requiring the seller to remedy the deficiency at his own expense.[1]

(c) Stamp duty may be *ad valorem* or fixed duty, the rates of which vary from time to time. Each document in the title should be checked against a table of stamp duties to ensure that it bears the correct duty in relation to the nature of the instrument, its date, and the amount of its consideration. The presence of a certificate of value in a document may have the effect of reducing the liability to duty or of exempting it from duty altogether. Where VAT has been paid on the consideration, stamp duty is payable on the VAT element of the price.

(d) In addition to stamp duty, conveyances on sale (including registered land transfers) and leases granted for a term of seven years or more and assignments of such leases must be produced to the Inland Revenue under Finance Act 1931. On production a Produced Stamp (Particulars Delivered Stamp) is affixed to the document. The consequences of failure to produce a document are the same as for lack of stamp duty and the seller must be required to rectify any deficiency at his own expense.

1. Stamp Act 1891, s.117.

2.13. Verification of title

2.13.1. Verification of title consists of checking the evidence of title supplied by the seller against the original deeds.

2.13.2. In registered land the true state of the register can be confirmed by the buyer when making his pre-completion search at the Land Registry.

2.13.3. In unregistered land, the abstract or epitome should be checked against the seller's original deeds. The buyer's time-limit for making this inspection expires with his time-limit for raising requisitions. Verification should therefore be carried out as part of the investigation of title procedure. In most cases, where the title is not complex, and the photocopy documents supplied by the seller are of good quality, the buyer's solicitor postpones his verification until actual completion. If, however, he then finds an error on the title it will be too late to query the error since his time-limit for raising requisitions will have expired. If there is any doubt over the validity of the title, or it is of a complex nature, verification should be carried out at the proper time. Unless the contract provides to the contrary the costs of verification are borne by the buyer. Standard Condition 4.2.3 and Standard Commercial Property Condition 4.2.3 require the seller to produce to the buyer (without cost to the buyer) the original of every document within the title or, if the original is not available, an abstract, epitome or copy with an original marking by a solicitor of examination either against the original or against an examined abstract or an examined copy.

2.14. Acting for the lender

2.14.1. The solicitor will be instructed to ensure that the property has a good and marketable title free from unspecified defects.

2.14.2. The lender may not be prepared to accept as security any property which is registered with a title other than absolute or any property which is a flying freehold.

2.14.3. Where the solicitor has been instructed under the terms of the Lenders' Handbook the provisions of the Handbook must be observed. See in particular paragraph 5.4 relating to a good and marketable title.

2.14.4. Under the Lenders' Handbook specific conditions are applicable to good leasehold titles (paragraph 5.4.2) and to flying freeholds (paragraph 5.5). See Appendix VIII.3 for the full text of Part 1 of the Lenders' Handbook.

D3. Requisitions on title

See also: Investigation of title, para. D2
Delay and remedies, section M

3.1. Purpose of requisitions

3.1.1. The purpose of requisitions on title is to require the seller's solicitor to clarify and if necessary to rectify matters on the title supplied which the buyer's solicitor finds unsatisfactory. In practice they are commonly used also to resolve administrative queries relating to the arrangements for completion.

3.2. Time for raising requisitions

3.2.1. By Standard Condition 4.1.1 and Standard Commercial Property Condition 4.1.1 written requisitions on the title supplied must be raised within six working days after either the date of the contract or the day of delivery of the seller's evidence of title, whichever is the later. The buyer will lose his right to raise requisitions if he does not do so within the time-limits prescribed by this condition. If the evidence of title is incomplete and this fact is pointed out to the seller within the above period, under Standard Condition 4.1.1 and Standard Commercial Property Condition 4.1.1, the buyer's solicitor has six working days from the supply of additional evidence to raise requisitions on that additional evidence. By Standard Condition 4.1.4 and Standard Commercial Property Condition 4.1.4 , this time-limit may be adjusted *pro rata* to fit a completion date which is less than 15 working days from the date of the contract.

3.3. Standard form requisitions

3.3.1. A standard form of requisitions (the Completion Information and Requisitions on Title Form) is published by the Law Society for use in Protocol transactions. Most law stationers produce a standard form of requisitions on title which includes many commonly asked questions, e.g. confirmation that the seller's mortgage on the property will be discharged on or before completion. The seller's solicitor should be asked to confirm that the answers given to enquiries before contract or information volunteered on the Seller's Property Information Form remain correct. Additionally the printed questions frequently deal with the administrative arrangements for completion itself, e.g. method of payment of money. Queries which are specific to the title under consideration may be added to the end of the standard form or typed on a separate sheet. The buyer's solicitor should send two copies of the form to the seller's solicitor who will return one copy with his answers appended, keeping the other copy on his own file for reference. Standard Condition 4.1.1 and Standard Commercial Property Condition 4.1.1 require the seller's solicitor to reply to requisitions within four working days after receiving them from the buyer's solicitor.

3.4. Further queries

3.4.1. On receipt of replies from the seller's solicitor, the buyer's solicitor should ensure that the answers given to his queries are satisfactory both in relation to the title and to the client's interests. Any replies which are unsatisfactory should be taken up with the seller's solicitor and further written queries raised until the matter is resolved.

3.4.2. Standard Condition 4.1.1 and Standard Commercial Property Condition 4.1.1 govern the time-limits for raising observations on the seller's replies to requisitions.

3.4.3. In some cases the replies given to requisitions may be construed as undertakings, e.g. to discharge the seller's outstanding mortgage on the property. Where such an undertaking is given the seller's solicitor should ensure that he has only committed himself to do what is within his power to do; an undertaking to discharge the seller's mortgage(s) on the property or one which is simply worded 'confirmed' or 'noted' will be interpreted as meaning that *all* subsisting charges will be removed. The seller's solicitor should therefore ensure that he is fully aware of the details of all such charges before committing himself to such an undertaking. Alternatively, the seller's solicitor or licensed conveyancer may prefer to undertake to discharge certain named charges only.

3.4.4. From the buyer's point of view, the buyer's solicitor should ensure that he asks the seller's solicitor to supply a list of all outstanding charges and obtains a specific undertaking in relation to each of them. He should only accept an undertaking from a solicitor or licensed conveyancer, such undertaking being in the form approved by the Law Society, failing which the buyer's solicitor should raise a requisition requiring the mortgages actually to be discharged on or before completion.

3.5. Restrictions on subject matter of requisitions

3.5.1. The buyer's solicitor is only entitled to raise requisitions on the title which he has, by contractual condition, agreed to accept. Except where Law of Property Act 1925, s.45 applies, he cannot in the case of unregistered land require production of documents prior to the root of title.[1] The buyer's right to raise requisitions may be curtailed or excluded by a condition in the contract.[2] Such a restriction only takes effect on exchange of contracts and does not preclude the buyer from raising queries in relation to that particular matter before contracts are exchanged. If the seller wishes to curtail or exclude the buyer's right to raise requisitions he must make a full disclosure of all defects in his title. In strict theory, the seller is only obliged to answer requisitions which relate to title, and not those which relate to, e.g. the form of the purchase deed. In practice the distinction between true requisitions on title and those relating to other matters is largely ignored and the seller's solicitor will answer all reasonable queries raised by the buyer's solicitor. Contractual conditions may also require the buyer in certain circumstances to waive a defect in title. At common law the buyer is deemed to accept the seller's title (and thus loses his right to raise requisitions or further requisitions) when he delivers a draft purchase deed to the seller. In practice the draft purchase deed is usually submitted to the seller simultaneously with requisitions and the buyer's right to raise requisitions will be expressly preserved by a contractual condition, e.g. Standard Condition 4.5.1.

1. See para. D2.6.
2. Special Condition 2 of the Standard Conditions of Sale Form excludes requisitions in relation to the matters defined in the contract as 'incumbrances'. The same limitation applies under Standard Commercial Property Condition 2 (see Appendix VII.12 and VII.13).

3.6. Vendor and purchaser summons

3.6.1. If the seller's solicitor refuses to answer a proper requisition, the buyer can compel an answer by means of the vendor and purchaser summons procedure under Law of Property Act 1925, s.49 which provides a summary method of resolving disputes between the parties. This procedure is intended to be used to resolve an impasse between the parties where agreement cannot be reached over a specific point in relation to the title and not as a general sounding-board to test the validity of the whole title or of the contract.

3.7. Seller's right to rescind

3.7.1. Neither the Standard Conditions of Sale (3rd edition) nor the Standard Commercial Property Conditions contain clauses entitling the seller to rescind the contract where the buyer raises a requisition with which the seller is unable or unwilling to comply. However, if the seller had not answered a requisition by contractual completion date it might be possible for the buyer to serve a notice to complete under Standard Condition 6.8.2(a) or Standard Commercial Property Condition 6.8.1.

E. PRE-COMPLETION

E1. The purchase deed

See also: Plans, para. B21

1.1. Who prepares the deed?

1.1.1. It is normally the buyer's duty to prepare the purchase deed, although the seller may, by Law of Property Act 1925, s.48(1), reserve the right by contractual condition to prepare the deed himself. This right is usually only used in estate conveyancing where the seller commonly supplies an engrossment of the purchase deed in standard form, a draft of the deed having been annexed to the contract. If the seller charges a fee for the engrossment, such fee must be reasonable and is deemed to include VAT unless stated otherwise.

1.2. Time for preparation of deed

1.2.1. Conventionally the purchase deed is prepared after completion of the buyer's investigation of title, but in practice the deed is usually prepared shortly after exchange of contracts and submitted to the seller for his approval with the buyer's requisitions on title. At common law the buyer is deemed to have accepted the seller's title when he submits the purchase deed for approval, and thus the submission of the purchase deed simultaneously with requisitions would preclude the buyer's right to raise requisitions on the seller's title. This problem is surmounted by Standard Condition 4.5.1 and Standard Commercial Property Condition 4.5.1 which both preserve the buyer's right to raise requisitions in such circumstances. By Standard Condition 4.1.2 and Standard Commercial Property Condition 4.1.2, the buyer is required to submit the draft purchase deed to the seller at least 12 working days before the contractual completion date. Under para. 9.1 of the Protocol the buyer's solicitor is required to submit the draft purchase deed simultaneously with his requisitions on title as soon as possible after exchange of contracts and in any case within the time-limits specified in the contract.

1.3. Form of the deed

1.3.1. The purchase deed must be a deed in order to transfer the legal estate in the land to the buyer.[1]

1.3.2. The purchase deed puts into effect the terms of the contract and so must reflect its terms.

1.3.3. Where the property being transferred is registered land the form of the purchase deed is prescribed by rules made under Land Registration Act 2002 and, subject to permitted variations, the prescribed form of wording and layout must be used. Almost all of the standard Land Registry forms are reproduced by law stationers, and these may be used as the basis of the purchase deed.

1.3.4. Most of the forms (such as TR1 and TR2) can also be reproduced electronically by using commercial forms packages or, with the approval of the Forms Unit at Land Registry headquarters, using the firm's own software. The District Land Registry for Wales will accept a document which is prepared in Welsh and do not require a translation to be supplied (see Reproduction of standard forms, para. A21).

1.3.5. No prescribed form of wording exists for a conveyance of unregistered land. The buyer is thus free to choose his own form of wording subject to the seller's approval and provided that it accurately reflects the terms of the contract. Instead of using a traditional conveyance the buyer may prepare his purchase deed as a Land Registry transfer.

1. Law of Property Act 1925, s.52.

1.4. Drafting the deed

1.4.1. When drafting the purchase deed the buyer's solicitor needs to have access to:

(a) the contract – because the purchase deed must reflect the terms of the contract;

(b) the official copy entries of the title/title deeds – because the contract may refer to matters on the title which need to be repeated or reflected in the purchase deed;

(c) except in straightforward cases, a precedent on which to base the deed under preparation.

1.4.2. *Using a precedent*

Except in the simplest cases it is advisable to refer to a precedent if only to focus the mind on the types of clause which will be required in the draft deed. Use the precedent as a guide and not as a model to be followed slavishly. Consider whether a clause is really necessary before copying it from a precedent and check that the law has not altered since the precedent was published.

1.5. Seller's approval of draft deed

1.5.1. When the draft has been prepared two copies should be submitted to the seller's solicitor for his approval. A further copy of the draft should be retained by the buyer's solicitor so that amendments can be agreed over the telephone if required. By Standard Condition 4.1.2 and Standard Commercial Property Condition 4.1.2 one of the copies submitted to the seller's solicitor can be of engrossment quality enabling the seller to use this as a top copy for signature in cases where no amendments are needed and where the buyer does not need to sign the deed.

1.5.2. On receipt of the draft, the seller's solicitor should check it carefully to ensure that the document accurately reflects the terms of the contract. Amendments should be confined to those which are necessary for the fulfilment of the document's legal purpose, bearing in mind that the choice of style and wording is the buyer's prerogative. Minor amendments may be agreed with the buyer's solicitor by telephone in order to save time. More substantial amendments should be clearly marked in a distinct colour on both copies of the draft, one copy being returned to the buyer's solicitor for his consideration, the other being retained in the seller's solicitor's file for reference. By Standard Condition 4.1.2 the seller's solicitor is to approve or return the revised draft document within four working days after delivery of the draft transfer by the buyer's solicitor.

1.6. Engrossment

1.6.1. When amendments (if any) to the draft deed have been finalised, the buyer's solicitor should prepare an engrossment of the deed on good quality paper. A deed which is to be submitted to the Land Registry should be engrossed on durable A4 size paper.[1]

1.6.2. The engrossment must be checked carefully (if necessary by comparing the draft document with the engrossment) to ensure the accuracy of the typing and that all agreed amendments have been incorporated. A copy of the engrossment should be kept on the buyer's solicitor's file for reference.

1.6.3. The completed engrossment should then be sent to the seller's solicitor for execution by his client. Where the buyer is required to execute the deed it is common practice for the buyer to execute the deed prior to delivery of the deed in escrow to the seller for his signature. The condition attached to the escrow should be defined. By Standard Condition 4.1.2 and Standard Commercial Property Condition 4.1.2 the buyer must deliver the engrossment of the purchase deed to the seller at least five working days before completion.

1. Land Registration Rules 2003, r.210.

1.7. Execution

1.7.1. To be valid in law a deed must be clear on the face of it that it is a deed, signed by the necessary parties in the presence of a witness, and delivered.[1] Use of a seal is no longer required either by individuals or bodies corporate. A company seal may, however, still be used and is a valid method of execution of a document.

1.7.2. Where land is registered, the form of transfer and certain other deeds affecting the land must follow the prescribed form.[2] The forms of words of execution are also prescribed.[3] Reference should also be made to the appropriate practice material issued by the Land Registry.

1.7.3. Signature by the seller is always required in order to transfer the legal estate.[4]

1.7.4. The buyer is required to execute the deed if it contains a covenant or declaration on his behalf. Thus execution by the buyer will be needed where the document contains an indemnity covenant in respect of existing restrictive covenants or a declaration by the buyers relating to the trusts on which they hold the property.

1.7.5. Where other parties are joined in the deed, e.g. to release the property from a mortgage or to give a valid receipt for money paid under the deed, they should also sign the document.

1.7.6. Signature by an individual must be made by him in person, preferably in ink.

1.7.7. Where an individual is incapable of signing the document himself, e.g. as a result of illness or disability, another person may execute it on his behalf. If necessary the document should be read over to the individual, or its contents clearly explained to him, before signature. Two witnesses are required to the signature.[5]

1.7.8. Any responsible person may be a witness to the signature of an individual. There is no legal restriction on one party to a document being a witness to the other party's signature nor on one spouse being a witness to the signature of the other spouse, but an independent witness is preferable since if the validity of the document was ever challenged in court, the independent witness would provide a stronger testimony. The witness should sign his name, and add underneath the signature his address and occupation. If the name of the witness is not clear from the signature it is sensible to ask the witness also to write his full name in block capitals after his signature. Two witnesses are required whenever the document is signed by one person on another's behalf.

1.7.9. Where an individual is capable of signing the document but cannot read it, e.g. because he is blind or the document is in a foreign language, he should familiarise himself with its contents. It is preferable that a solicitor witnesses the signature to confirm that the correct procedure was followed.

1.7.10. A solicitor should always be satisfied before submitting a document for signature that the client understands the nature and contents of the document. Where the solicitor invites his client to sign the purchase deed in the solicitor's presence the deed can be explained to the client before signature, and actually signed in the presence of the solicitor who can then act as a witness to the signature. If this is not possible, the purchase deed may be sent to the client for signature and return. The letter which accompanies the purchase deed should:

(a) explain the purpose and contents of the document;

(b) contain clear instructions relating to the execution of the deed;

(c) specify a date by which the signed document must be returned to the solicitor;

(d) request that the client leaves the document undated.

1.7.11. *Attorneys*

A person who holds a power of attorney on behalf of another may execute a deed on that person's behalf. The attorney may sign either in his own name or in that of the person on behalf of whom he is acting, e.g. 'X by his attorney Y' or 'Y as attorney on behalf of X'.

1.7.12. *Companies*

A company will normally execute a deed by using its common seal which is impressed on the document in the presence of a director of the company and its secretary (who for this purpose must be two separate individuals) or two directors who will then sign the document to witness the execution by the company. Alternatively, the document may simply be signed by a director and the secretary or by two directors on behalf of the company. Use of a common seal is no longer compulsory but the document must make it clear on the face of it that it is a deed.[6]

If either of these methods is used, due execution by the company may be presumed under Companies Act 1985, s.36A(6) and a buyer need not investigate whether the manner of execution is authorised by the company's articles. In some cases a company's articles may permit execution of a document by a method different to those outlined above, e.g. signature by an authorised person acting alone. In such a case the procedure prescribed by the articles should be followed and a copy of the signatory's authorisation attached to the deed to prove the validity of its execution. The requirements for execution of documents by companies incorporated outside the UK are dealt with in para. E7.

1.7.13. *Other bodies*

The requirements for execution of deeds by other bodies, e.g. corporations sole (e.g. a bishop), district councils, government departments or statutory undertakings, will vary depending on the body concerned. The precise procedure for execution should be checked well in advance of execution. The document should then be executed in accordance with the prescribed method, and a copy of the authority of the signatory to sign attached to the deed to prove the validity of its execution. The relaxation on the use of corporate seals which was granted to registered companies by Companies Act 1989 does not extend to these bodies.

1.7.14. *Patients*

Following Court of Protection Rules 1994, deeds affecting sale and purchase transactions are no longer required to be sealed by the Court of Protection.

1.7.15. In addition to signature a deed must be delivered. A deed takes effect on its delivery. When the buyer delivers the engrossment to the seller for execution by him, he does not normally intend the deed to become effective at that time. It is therefore common practice for the buyer to deliver the deed to the seller in escrow, i.e. conditionally, so that the operation of the deed is postponed until completion. In the case of a company, delivery is presumed at the date of execution unless the contrary is proved.[7]

1. Law of Property (Miscellaneous Provisions) Act 1989, s.1.
2. Land Registration Rules 2003, r.206(1) and Sched. 1.
3. Land Registration Rules 2003, r.206(3) and Sched. 9.
4. Law of Property Act 1925, s.52.
5. Law of Property (Miscellaneous Provisions) Act 1989, s.1.
6. Companies Act 1989, s.130.
7. Companies Act 1985, s.36A(5).

1.8.   Plans

1.8.1. If the contract provides for the use of a plan the purchase deed will also refer to the plan. In other cases the buyer is not entitled to demand that a plan is used with the purchase deed unless the description of the property as afforded by the contract and title deeds is inadequate without one. If the buyer wishes to use a plan in circumstances where he is not entitled to demand one, he may do so with the seller's consent but will have to bear the cost of its preparation.

1.8.2. Where the sale is of the whole of the seller's property use of a plan is not normally considered necessary, and unless very clearly drawn may confuse rather than clarify the deed as well as adding unnecessary expense.

1.8.3. On a sale of part (including flats and office suites) a plan is highly desirable and where the land is registered generally must be used.[1]

1.8.4. The plan(s) to be used with the purchase deed should be checked for accuracy, including all necessary colourings and markings, and firmly bound into the engrossment of the deed which should in its wording refer to the use of the plan(s). Measurements must be expressed in metric values.

1.8.5. In registered land cases the transferor must sign the plan. In unregistered land signature of the plan is not compulsory but is highly desirable. Such signatures need not be witnessed. Where a company seals the purchase deed, it should also seal the plan.

1.8.6. The preparation and use of plans is further discussed in para. B21.

1. Land Registration Rules 2003, r.213.

1.9. **Parties**

1.9.1. Anyone whose concurrence is necessary in order to transfer the legal estate or who is to give a valid receipt for capital money arising out of the transaction must be joined as a party to the deed.

1.9.2. The seller and buyer will usually be the only parties to the deed, but in view of the principle outlined in para. E1.9.1 it may be necessary to join, e.g. the trustees of a Settled Land Act settlement or a non-owning occupier.

1.9.3. Where the seller is bankrupt, his trustee in bankruptcy will transfer the property and the seller is not a party to the deed.

1.9.4. If the seller is a company which is in liquidation or under receivership, the company itself transfers the property with the receiver or liquidator joining in the deed to give a receipt for the purchase price. In such a case the liquidator actually executes the deed. Exceptionally, if an order has been made by the court under Companies Act 1989 vesting the legal estate of the company's property in the liquidator, the liquidator will be the seller and the company will not be a party to the deed.

1.9.5. In a sub-sale transaction, the seller transfers the property directly to the sub-purchaser, but the original buyer will join in the document to give implied covenants and, where appropriate, to give a receipt for all or part of the purchase price.

1.9.6. On a sale of part of registered land which is subject to a mortgage, the lender will not be a party to the purchase deed since he will release the part sold from his charge by using Form DS3. In the same situation in unregistered land the lender may join in the conveyance in order to release the part sold from the mortgage and, where appropriate, to give a receipt for such part of the purchase price as is paid to him. Alternatively, a lender in the case of unregistered land may give a separate deed of release to the buyer. The seller must ascertain from his lender which of these methods of release the lender wishes to employ and inform the buyer accordingly so that the buyer can, if necessary, include appropriate clauses relating to the lender in the draft purchase deed.

1.9.7. On a sale by a mortgagee in possession the mortgagee will be the seller and the owner will not enter into the deed.

1.10. **Transfer of whole**

1.10.1. A transfer of whole must be in Form TR1 (or, in the case of a transfer under power of sale, TR2).[1] The following paragraphs relate to a transfer to give effect to one sale.

1.10.2. The title number and short description of the property, i.e. its postal address, may be taken from the official copy entries of the title supplied by the seller.

1.10.3. The date of the document is inserted on actual completion.

1.10.4. The amount of consideration must be stated[2] in both words and figures in the consideration panel. The receipt in the consideration panel renders any other form of receipt for the purchase price unnecessary and acts as a sufficient discharge to the buyer.[3] The presence of this receipt also gives the buyer authority to pay the purchase price to the seller's solicitor.[4] The receipt is also evidence, but not necessarily conclusive evidence, that the seller's lien over the property for the unpaid purchase price has been extinguished. The purchase price in the transfer should exclude the amount of any consideration attributable to chattels for which a separate receipt should be prepared.[5]

1.10.5. The seller's name should be inserted as it appears on the proprietorship register of the title. If the seller is not the current registered proprietor, the seller's name should be inserted as it appears in, for example, his transfer.

1.10.6. There is provision on the form for the seller's title guarantee, which will imply covenants for title under Law of Property (Miscellaneous Provisions) Act 1994.[6] Any modification of the covenants must be set out expressly on the face of the transfer and must refer to the section of the 1994 Act which is being modified or excluded.

1.10.7. The buyer's full name and address should be inserted. The buyer's address or addresses for service given in the Transfer Form or AP1 (Application to change the register) will be placed on the proprietorship register on registration of the buyer's interest and is the address which will be used by the Chief Land Registrar should it become necessary for him to contact the registered proprietor of the land, e.g. to serve notices on him.[7] The address given should therefore be one at which it is certain that the buyer can be contacted. In the case of residential property where the buyer will be moving into the property on completion, the address should therefore be the address of the property being purchased and not the address at which the buyer is currently living.

1.10.8. Where the sale is subject to existing covenants the contract will usually provide for the purchase deed to include an indemnity covenant to be given by the buyer.[8] An indemnity covenant will be required in respect of positive covenants and restrictive covenants which are not limited to seisin.[9] Where such a covenant is necessary it should be added expressly to the transfer form, there being no such covenant included on the printed forms. A covenant which gives indemnity only is enforceable in breach by an action for damages. One which is 'to observe perform and indemnify' is enforceable by injunction and damages and thus provides fuller protection for the seller. Standard Condition 4.5.3 provides for the full form of covenant to be given. Where there are joint purchasers, the covenant should be given by both or all of them.

1.10.9. Joint purchasers should indicate in the transfer the capacity in which they will hold the equitable interest in the property, i.e. as joint tenants or tenants in common. On registration of the buyers as proprietors a restriction in Form A will automatically be entered on the register, if required. Instructions as to the method in which the beneficial ownership is to be held should have been taken by the buyer's solicitor at an early stage in the transaction, and those instructions will now be effected in the transfer. Where the buyers have decided to hold as tenants in common, instructions should also have been obtained in relation to the proportionate shares which each co-owner will hold in the equitable interest. In the absence of evidence to the contrary it will be assumed by the court that they hold the equity in proportion to their original contributions to the property.[10] In order to avoid costly and time-consuming litigation at a later date, it is recommended that full details of the beneficial interests of the co-owners are recorded in writing at the time of their purchase. There is provision in the form of transfer to record the respective beneficial interests. Alternatively, a short deed of trust may be drawn up to give effect to the buyers' wishes, in which case it should be referred to in the transfer and kept safely for future reference.

1.10.10. Where the consideration for the transaction is below the current threshold for payment of stamp duty a certificate of value should be included in the transfer.[11]

1.10.11. The transfer should provide for execution by all parties in the presence of a witness. The form of attestation is prescribed by Schedule 9 to the Land Registration Rules 2003 and will vary dependent on the identity of the signatory.[12] Reference should be made to the appropriate practice material issued by the Land Registry which sets out the Land Registry's requirements in relation to the execution of deeds.

1.10.12. Additional provisions may be required in the deed in accordance with special conditions of the contract. There is a panel on the new Land Registry forms for these.

1. Land Registration Rules 2003, r.58.
2. Stamp Act 1891, s.5.
3. Law of Property Act 1925, s.67.
4. Law of Property Act 1925, s.69.
5. The amount of the consideration affects the amount of stamp duty payable on the document and, since chattels are not subject to stamp duty, any sum payable for them does not need to be included in the purchase deed. Where VAT is payable the amount of the consideration stated should include the VAT element of the price.
6. See below, Delay and remedies, section M.
7. Land Registration Rules 2003, r.198.
8. See Standard Condition 4.5.3 and Standard Commercial Property Condition 4.5.2.
9. See *Rhone* v. *Stephens, The Times,* 18 March 1994, HL; *Austerberry* v. *Oldham Corporation* (1885) 29 ChD 750.
10. *Springette* v. *Defoe* (1993) 65 P & CR 1 (CA).
11. See Stamping documents, para. G2.
12. Land Registration Rules 2003, r. 206(3) and Sched.9.

1.11. Transfer of part

1.11.1. A transfer of part of a registered title must be in Form TP1 (or in the case of a transfer of part under power of sale, TP2).[1] All of the matters referred to in para. E1.10 will be relevant to a sale of part but the following will also be required either in addition to or in substitution for the above.

1.11.2. At this stage the sale is made by reference to the seller's existing title number. A new title number for the part being sold will be allocated by the Land Registry on registration of the transaction.

1.11.3. A clear description of the land being sold must be included with reference to the plan annexed to the transfer. When necessary, the land retained by the seller should also be expressly defined and identified on the plan. When the postal address of the property is not yet known, the property may be described by the plot number on the seller's approved estate layout plan. However, it will not then be possible to give the property as the buyer's address for service. In this case a care of address may be inserted in the transfer. If the postal address is available when application is made for registration of transfer, it may be inserted in the application Form AP1.

1.11.4. Where the contract made provision for the grant of easements to the buyer or reservations in favour of the seller, these easements must be expressly inserted into the transfer.

1.11.5. The contract will usually provide for the exclusion of rights of light and air from the transfer. This contractual provision (see Condition 3.4.2 in both sets of conditions reproduced in Appendix VII.12 and VII.13) must be implemented by a declaration to this effect in the transfer.

1.11.6. New restrictive covenants are frequently imposed in a contract for the sale of part of land; these too must be expressly set out in the transfer. Except where the land forms part of a building scheme, to be enforceable against subsequent owners of the land sold, the covenants must be taken for the benefit of land retained by the seller and the burden annexed to the land sold. Express words to give effect to these principles are advisable.

1.11.7. The new forms provide sub-headings within the additional provisions panel under which full details of the rights granted and received, restrictive covenants, and other matters may be inserted. These sub-headings may be added to, amended, repositioned, or omitted as desired.

1. Land Registration Rules 2003, r.58.

1.12. Conveyance

1.12.1. A conveyance of unregistered land fulfils the same purpose as a Land Registry transfer and contains similar information but is presented in a different manner and consequently looks, on its face, entirely different from a registered land transfer. Each conveyance of unregistered land has slightly different requirements and thus each has to be individually drafted to fit the situation in hand. Although not all of the clauses which are mentioned below will be relevant to every transaction, where they are required they will normally be inserted in the deed in the order in which they are given in the following paragraphs. It is not obligatory to insert the clauses in this particular order but by convention they do so appear and it is of assistance to another solicitor who looks at the document at a later date to be able to locate a particular clause quickly because it has been placed in the recognised order. If desired, a registered land transfer may be used instead of a conveyance.

1.12.2.   The conveyance will start with the words 'This conveyance' followed by the date (which is inserted on actual completion) and the full names and addresses of all the parties to the deed.

1.12.3.   *Recitals*

Recitals are not included in Land Registry forms nor by draftsmen who favour a modern approach to drafting. If a traditional approach to drafting is taken, recitals may be used in the conveyance. These do not form an operative part of the body of the deed but are more in the nature of a preamble, the function of which is to introduce the nature of and to set the scene for the deed which follows, e.g. by explaining the recent history of the title. Although recitals do not form an operative part of the deed, where they are included they must still be drafted with care and accuracy since a party is estopped from later denying the accuracy of a statement of fact made in a recital. Recitals of fact which are contained in a deed which is 20 years old are by Law of Property Act 1925, s.45(6) deemed to be correct. Where there is an ambiguity in an operative part of the deed, recitals may be looked at and used to clarify that ambiguity.[1] Where personal representatives are required to give a statement under Administration of Estates Act 1925, s.36(6) that they have not made any previous assent or conveyance, such statement is usually dealt with by way of recital. Similarly a statement that the survivor of joint tenants is solely and beneficially entitled to the property (required under Law of Property (Joint Tenants) Act 1964) is commonly dealt with in this way.

1.12.4.   A consideration and receipt clause will be included. See para. E1.10.4.

1.12.5.   The operative word ('convey(s)') is followed by a statement of title guarantee which imports covenants for title.[2]

1.12.6.   The parcels clause must clearly and adequately describe the land being sold. An adaptation of the description of the land in the particulars of the contract may be used for this purpose. Where the sale is of part of the seller's land, reference must generally be made to the land which is retained by the seller, such land being identified on the plan annexed to the deed.

1.12.7.   Express reference should be made to benefits previously enjoyed by the land which are to pass to the buyer.

1.12.8.   Clauses should be included to deal with exceptions, i.e. those matters which are excluded from the land and which do not therefore pass to the buyer, and to reservations, i.e. those matters which (usually on a sale of part) are being regranted by the buyer for the benefit of the seller. If reservations are to be reserved, a clause in the contract will have specified which rights were to be reserved to the seller in the purchase deed and those clauses are now activated by inclusion in the purchase deed itself.

1.12.9.   Easements which are to be expressly granted to the buyer (usually only on a sale of part) will have been set out in the contract and are now included in the purchase deed to give effect to them.

1.12.10. The habendum ('to hold') is followed by express references to the estate conveyed (fee simple) and existing incumbrances, e.g. existing restrictive covenants subject to which the property is sold.

1.12.11. Declarations may be inserted, e.g. on a sale of part to negate the implied grant rules especially in respect of rights of light and air following a contractual provision to this effect.[3] Declarations may also be used to define the ownership of party walls.

1.12.12. Where the property is bought by co-owners a statement of their capacity must be included, i.e. as joint tenants or tenants in common. Where the co-owners are tenants in common the division of the beneficial interest between them may be specified either in the purchase deed or by separate deed of trust.[4] It is no longer necessary to include a clause to extend the powers of the trustees to make them co-extensive with those of an absolute owner because these powers are implied by Trusts of Land and Appointment of Trustees Act 1996, s.6.

1.12.13. On a sale of part, new restrictive covenants may be imposed and these should be inserted following the contractual provision to this effect. See para. E1.11.

1.12.14. Where existing positive covenants or restrictive covenants which are not limited to ownership will continue to bind the land after completion of the sale to the buyer an indemnity covenant will be required in fulfilment of the contractual obligation to that effect.[5]

1.12.15. If any of the documents of title which the seller has are not to be handed over to the buyer on completion, e.g. a grant of probate or all the title deeds on a sale of part, an acknowledgment for their production and undertaking for safe custody should be included in the document. By Law of Property Act 1925, s.64 the acknowledgment gives a right to production of the named document(s) at the cost of the person requiring production. Production may be required, e.g. to satisfy requisition raised by a sub-purchaser. The undertaking gives a right of damages (but no other remedy) if the named document(s) is lost or destroyed otherwise than by fire or inevitable accident. These rights are reiterated by Standard Condition 4.5.5. All sellers will give an acknowledgment for production (where relevant), but only a beneficial owner gives the undertaking for safe custody. Such an undertaking is not appropriate in a situation where the seller is not the true owner of the deeds. If the title deeds which are being retained are not in the seller's possession at the time of completion, e.g. on a sale of part, they may be in the hands of his lender; the seller may be asked to give a covenant that he will give an undertaking for safe custody as and when the title deeds come into his possession.

1.12.16. In appropriate circumstances a certificate of value should be included in the document (see para. E1.10.10).

1.12.17. The document concludes with schedules (if any), e.g. of covenants, etc., testimonium (in witness) and attestation clauses. The attestation clause should contain the words 'signed as a deed' to comply with Law of Property (Miscellaneous Provisions) Act 1989, s.1.

1. The converse situation is not true. An ambiguous recital cannot be clarified by a statement in the operative part of the deed.
2. See Delay and remedies, section M.
3. See para. E1.11.5.
4. See para. E1.10.10.
5. See Standard Condition 4.5.4, in both sets of Conditions reproduced in Appendix VII.12 and VII.13, and see para. E1.10.9.

1.13. Assent

1.13.1. Where personal representatives transfer land to a beneficiary they will use an assent. If they sell land to a third party the purchase deed will be a transfer or conveyance depending whether or not the land is registered.

1.13.2. One exception to the rule that a legal estate can only be conveyed by a deed is an assent by personal representatives which must be in writing but need not be by deed unless it contains a covenant by the assentee, e.g. for indemnity in respect of restrictive covenants.

1.13.3. An assent of registered land must be in a transfer in Form AS1 or AS3 as prescribed by r.58 of the Land Registration Rules 2003. An assent of unregistered land is not subject to any restraints on its form or contents except that it must be in writing and must name the person(s) in whose favour it is given.

1.13.4. On a sale or assent by personal representatives all proving personal representatives must be parties to the document.

1.13.5. In unregistered land the assent may contain recitals, and will otherwise be similar to an unregistered conveyance. Since the land will be subject to first registration of title following the assent, it may be more convenient to use Form AS1 or AS3 in preference to an unregistered form of assent. A memorandum of the assent should be noted on the grant after completion, although this is not strictly necessary where the land is to be registered on completion of the assent.

1.14. Assignment

1.14.1. An assignment of an existing registered lease is the transfer of a registered estate and the purchase deed will be a Land Registry transfer form. The form is the same as for the transfer of a freehold. An assignment of an unregistered lease is similar in form to a conveyance of unregistered land, subject to some modifications.

1.14.2. Frequently the contract contains provision modifying the effect of the implied covenants for title in leasehold cases (e.g. Standard Condition 3.3.2) and the purchase deed will contain a provision giving effect to this contractual term. In a transfer, this will appear in the title guarantee panel.

1.14.3. An express indemnity covenant will be inserted if required by the contract (if any) (see Standard Condition 4.5.4). No indemnity covenant is implied by statute in new leases (granted after 1 January 1996).[1] In leases granted before this date an indemnity covenant is implied except where in unregistered land value is not given by the assignee for the transaction.

1.14.4. In addition, an unregistered assignment may contain recitals relating to the recent history of the lease, the agreement to sell and, where appropriate, the fact that the landlord has consented to the assignment. The estate transferred will be the unexpired residue of the term, subject to the terms and conditions of the lease itself. The benefit of options should be expressly assigned to ensure that their benefit is transferred to the buyer.

1. Landlord and Tenant (Covenants) Act 1995, s.14.

1.15. Sellers' cashback schemes

1.15.1. These schemes appear to be operated by brokers who, in conjunction with a small number of lenders, participate in enabling a seller to offer an incentive to a buyer. In essence the seller and lender state that, e.g. the property is to be sold for £40,000 but that on completion the seller agrees to pay £5,000 to the buyer. Traditionally the contract discloses the arrangement, but the price inserted in the contract will be the higher figure, e.g. £40,000 rather than £35,000, which is the net price the seller receives from the buyer.

1.15.2. In these schemes the lender is normally aware of the circumstances, and so the schemes do not, in fact, involve a fraud on the lender in the usual sense. Solicitors (whether acting for sellers or buyers) should always check that the lender is aware of the proposed cashback.

1.15.3. As the transfer is a matter of public record, it is a solicitor's duty not to be a party to any mis-statement of the sale price. Inserting the higher price would be a mis-statement. If solicitors are instructed in relation to such schemes, they should make it clear from the outset that the figure they will insert in the transfer will be the net figure, and should decline to act if the client instructs otherwise.

1.15.4. These schemes should be distinguished from cases where the lender gives an incentive 'cashback' to borrowers, as such cashbacks do not affect the price paid to the seller.

E2. Pre-completion searches

2.1. Who makes the searches?
2.2. Reason for making searches
2.3. When to make searches
2.4. Which searches to make
2.5. Land Registry search
2.6. Land Charges Department search
2.7. Acting for the lender
2.8. Bankruptcy search
2.9 Probate and administration
2.10 Company search
2.11 Enduring powers of attorney
2.12 Local land charges search and enquiries
2.13 Other searches
2.14 Results of searches

See also: Pre-contract searches and enquiries, para. B10

2.1. Who makes the searches?

2.1.1. In accordance with the *caveat emptor* principle it is up to the buyer to make sure of his bargain. Therefore it is the buyer's solicitor's responsibility to ensure that such pre-completion searches as are relevant to the transaction are carried out and that the results of those searches are satisfactory to his client.

2.1.2. Where the buyer is purchasing with the assistance of a mortgage, his lender also has an interest in the soundness of the title to the property and some or all of the pre-completion searches may be carried out by the lender's solicitor acting at this stage on behalf of both the lender and the buyer.

2.2. Reason for making searches

2.2.1. The principal reason for making pre-completion searches is for the buyer's solicitor to confirm that information obtained about the property prior to exchange remains correct. In some situations searches additional to those which were made before exchange of contracts will also be undertaken at this stage either to verify information received after exchange or where the circumstances were such that the buyer did not have sufficient time to make the relevant search before contracts were exchanged.

2.3. When to make searches

2.3.1. The searches must be done in sufficient time to ensure that the results are received by the buyer's solicitor in time for completion to take place on the contractual completion date.

2.3.2. Pre-completion searches should generally be made about seven days before the contractual completion date but may be left until closer to the completion date if,

THE LAW SOCIETY'S CONVEYANCING HANDBOOK 10TH EDITION 377

e.g. a telephone, computer or fax search is to be made. Searches will need to be done earlier than seven days before completion if some delay in the receipt of replies, e.g. through industrial action, is anticipated.

2.3.3.   The principal searches which are made at this stage of the transaction (the Land Registry and/or Land Charges Department searches) generally confer protection on the searcher against later entries (i.e. they give a priority period); thus a balance has to be drawn between making the search at the latest moment before completion in order to gain the benefit of a long priority period after completion, and the risk, if a search is submitted at the last moment, of completion being delayed (and compensation payable by the buyer for the delay) because the search result has not been received by the date of completion.

2.4.   Which searches to make

2.4.1.   The following searches should be made:

     (a) for registered land, search against title number at the Land Registry (see para. E2.5);

     (b) for unregistered land, including an unregistered reversion to a lease, search at Land Charges Department against names of estate owners of the land (see para. E2.6);

     (c) if acting for a lender, a bankruptcy search against the name of the borrower (see para. E2.8);

     (d) such other of the searches listed in paras. E2.9–E2.13 as are applicable to the transaction.

2.5.   Land Registry search

2.5.1.   Introduction

When acquiring an interest in a registered estate in land, a pre-completion search should be made at the appropriate Land Registry Office. Guidance on making these searches can be found in the appropriate practice material issued by the Land Registry. A fee of £4 per title is payable (£2 if made by Land Registry Direct or NLIS).[1] Fees can be paid by cheque (if the application is lodged by post, DX or in person) or credit account, provided that the applicant's solicitor's key number is quoted in the application.

2.5.2.   Official search of the register with priority

An application for an official search with priority can only be made by a 'purchaser'. This term is defined in the Rules as a person who for valuable consideration has entered into or intends to enter into a registrable disposition of a registered estate or registered charge.[2]

2.5.3.   *Application by post or DX: Search of Whole*

Where the interest being purchased, leased or mortgaged concerns the whole of a registered title, the search application should be made on Form OS1. The application will give details of the title number of the property to be searched, a brief description of its situation, i.e. postal address, county and district, and the names of the registered proprietors. The applicant's name must also be given together with his reason for making the search, i.e. he intends to purchase/lease/take a charge on the land. Where a solicitor is acting both for a buyer and his lender the search application should be completed in the name of the lender client. If this is done the buyer may take the benefit and protection of the search and a separate search in the buyer's name is unnecessary.

2.5.4.   The form requests the registrar to provide information on any adverse entries made in the register or daylist[3] since a specified date. This 'search from' date can be either:

   (a) the date shown as the 'subsisting entries' date on an official copy of the register; or

   (b) the date shown as the 'subsisting entries' date when register entries were accessed by remote terminal.[4]

2.5.5.   The search result contains the applicant's name but where, for example, the clients are both the chargor and chargee and the applicant is the chargee, the chargor's name will not be shown. Further, the result does not contain the address of the property, but it does include an applicant's reference of not more than 25 characters (including spaces). It is therefore suggested that the applicant's reference stated on OS1 should include sufficient detail (e.g. applicant's or chargor's name and the address of the property or solicitor's file number) to ensure that the incoming search can be returned to its proper file without delay.

2.5.6.   *Application by post or DX: Search of Part*

Where the interest being acquired comprises only part of a registered title, the search application is made on Form OS2 and must identify the part of the land against which the search is to be made either by the submission of a clearly marked plan of the land with sufficient detail to identify the land in relation to features shown on the Ordnance Survey plan, or by its plot number where the Land Registry has already approved an estate layout plan. Where the application is made in Form OS2 and an accompanying plan is required, the plan must be delivered in duplicate. It is advisable that the same plan is used for the contract, search application and purchase deed. Care should be taken not to search against more land than is included in the contract as the priority conferred by the search may delay transactions in relation to the additional land. In other respects the application is similar to that made on Form OS1.

2.5.7.   *Application by fax*

This facility is available at all Land Registry offices but only to credit account holders. No additional fee is charged for this service. Applications may be faxed to the specified fax number at the proper office at any time on a working day except:

(a) where the previous day was not a working day, applications cannot be made before 8.00 a.m.; and

(b) where the following day is not a working day, applications cannot be made after 4.00 p.m.

The search must be a search of whole of a title or of a pending first registration on Form OS1, or a search of part of a title on Form OS2 provided that the search is in respect of a plot number of an approved estate plan or the land to be searched is clearly depicted on an A4 size plan that is drawn to a stated scale of not less than 1/1250; a north point must be included and sufficient detail to identify the land in relation to features shown on the Ordnance Survey plan. Applications must be completed in black ink or black type and, where the facility is available, sent in fine mode. The result of the search cannot be sent by fax but is posted to the applicant in the normal way.

2.5.8. *Application by telephone*

An application can be made (through the Telephone Service Centre) by an applicant who is or who acts for an intending buyer (including lessee and chargee) and must be for a search of the whole title. The telephone call, using the special number allocated for this service, will only be accepted between 8.30 a.m. and 6.30 p.m. (Monday to Friday) excluding Christmas Day, Good Friday or a statutory bank holiday and 8.30 a.m. and 1.00 p.m. on Saturday. The application can only be made by a credit account holder. (Official copy entries can also be obtained by this procedure.) On telephoning the registry the following information must be supplied in the order given below:

(a) the applicant's key number;

(b) name and address of firm holding the account;

(c) if different from (b) above, the name and address to which the result of search is to be sent;

(d) title number of the land;

(e) the name of the registered proprietor (or applicant for first registration);

(f) (if requested) the county and district or London borough in which the land is situated;

(g) where the land is already registered, the date from which the search is to be made;[5]

(h) the applicant's reference (maximum 25 characters);

(i) whether the search is intended to protect a purchase lease or charge;

(j) the name of the applicant on whose behalf the search is being made;

(k) the name and telephone number of the person making the search telephone call or the person to be contacted if there is an enquiry.

A paper result of the search is normally dispatched to the applicant's solicitor on the same or following working day. The priority period commences from the time the application is entered on the day list, usually at the time of the telephone call. If the search is 'clear' (if there are no relevant adverse entries in the register or pending applications), a guaranteed result will be given over the telephone. Several search applications may be made during the course of one telephone call including searches of the Land Charges Registers. Informal disclosure of entries revealed by the search can be made over the telephone if so requested by the applicant. Such information is not, however, guaranteed by the Registry. Further, a result of a search of the Land Charge Registers (including a result that reveals no entries) given over the telephone is never guaranteed.

2.5.9. *Application by personal attendance*

A buyer or a person acting for a buyer may apply orally for an official search with priority of the whole of the land in a registered title. Application may only be made by the applicant attending a Customer Information Centre at a Land Registry office. Such applications may be made between 8.30 a.m. and 6.00 p.m. Mondays to Fridays (other than public holidays).

2.5.10. *Application by Land Registry Direct*

An application can be made through Land Registry Direct by an applicant who is or who acts for an intending buyer (including lessee and chargee) and must be a search of the whole title or of a pending first registration of land in England and Wales. A fee of £2 is charged for this service. The application will only be accepted between 7.00 a.m. and 10.00 p.m. Monday to Friday and 7.00 a.m. and 5.00 p.m. on Saturdays (excluding public holidays). The application can only be made by a credit account holder who is already connected to Land Registry Direct. (Official copy entries of the title can also be obtained by this procedure.) When making the application the information set out in para. E2.5.8 above must be supplied. Full directions on the use of the service are provided to users on installation.

2.5.11. *Application via the National Land Information Service*

An applicant can apply via NLIS for any type of search, subject to the usual requirements. An applicant must also provide similar information to that required for an application made by Land Registry Direct (see para. B10.17).

2.5.12. *Sub-sales*

(a) *Of whole of a registered title or pending first registration title* — Where A has contracted to sell to B, and before B completes his purchase he contracts to resell to C, the sub-purchaser (C) will need to make a search against the title quoting A's name as proprietor since at the time of C's application B will not be the registered proprietor of the land.

(b) *Sub-sales of part of a registered title or pending first registration title* — Where A, has contracted to sell part of his estate to B, and before B completes his purchase he contracts to resell that estate or part of it to C, the sub-purchaser (C) will, to reserve priority, need to made a search. The title to be searched will depend upon whether the application to register B's interest is pending in the Land Registry or not. If the application to register B's interest is pending in the Land Registry, the search should be made against the title number allocated to B's application quoting B as the proprietor. If the application has not been lodged, the search sould be made against A's title quoting A as the proprietor.

2.5.13. Official search with priority where application for first registration pending

Where an applicant has applied for first registration of his title and has contracted to sell, lease or charge the land to a third party before completion of the first registration, the third party can make a search as if the land were already registered. A search against the whole of the land in a pending application may be made by post, DX or NLIS on Form OS1 or by using the other methods of searching against the whole of a registered title explained above. A search of part can only be made by post DX on Form OS2. The purpose of the search, in relation to a pending first registration, is to ascertain whether any adverse entry has been made in the daylist (i.e. list of applications received by the Land Registry) since the date of the pending first registration application. The date of the pending first registration application does not have to be specified by the searcher. The effect of the result of search will be to give the searcher priority against any other intervening application if he lodges his own application before the expiry of the priority period.

2.5.14. Result of official search

On completion of the application for the official search with priority, a result of search is issued giving the result of the search as at the date and time that the application was entered on the daylist. The information to be included in the result of an official search is specified in Schedule 6 of the Land Registration Rules 2003.

2.5.15. Priority period

Currently an official certificate of search issued by the Land Registry following an application for an official search with priority gives a priority period to the searcher of 30 business days.[6] A buyer will also take advantage of this protection where a search was made on his behalf in the name of his lender. The searcher will take priority over any entry made during the priority period provided that completion takes place and a correct application for registration of the transaction is received by the appropriate Land Registry office within the priority period given by the search.

2.5.16. The date of expiry of the priority period is shown on the search certificate and should be marked on the outside of the client's file and entered in the solicitor's diary or file prompt system to ensure that it is not overlooked.

2.5.17. The priority period given by an official search cannot be extended. If completion is delayed and cannot take place within the priority period given by the search, a new search application will have to be made. The new search certificate will give another priority period but does not extend the original priority period from the first search. This means that if a third party has made a search or lodged an application in the intervening period, the third party's interest may have priority.

2.5.18. *Withdrawal of official search*

A person who has made an application for an official search with priority of a registered title or in relation to a pending first registration application, may withdraw that official search by application to the registrar.[7] Such an application cannot be made if an application for an entry in the register in respect of the purchase made pursuant to that official search has been made and completed.

2.5.19. *Official search of the register without priority*

The searches with priority are only available for use by a 'purchaser': see para. E2.5.2. In other situations or where a priority search is not required an application for a search of the register may be made in the following ways:

(a) by post or DX – on Form OS3 for searches of whole or part;

(b) by fax – on Form OS3 for searches of whole or part; and

(c) by telephone – for searches of whole of a registered title.

2.5.20. A search without priority can be used in the following circumstances, e.g.:

(a) when acting for a buyer of an equitable interest in the land;

(b) a lender who is selling under a power of sale should make a search to discover subsequent incumbrances (if any).

2.5.21. *Mortgagee's search for matrimonial homes rights*

This search is of limited application and may only be used by the proprietor of a charge of registered land which consists of or includes a dwelling house. The search is available to any chargees regardless of whether or not the charge is registered. The purpose of the search is for the chargee of a dwelling house to ascertain whether any entry has been made on the register to protect a non-owning spouse's matrimonial homes rights under Family Law Act 1996. A chargee is required to serve notice on such a person before taking action to enforce his security. The search is made in Form MH3.

2.5.22. *Outline applications*

An outline application can be used to reserve a period similar to a short period of priority for certain interests that cannot be protected by an official search such as a charging order. The interest claimed must be in existence at the time that the application is made.[8] An outline application can only be made by telephone, personal attendance or electronic means.[9]

1. For address see App. XI.1.
2. Land Registration Rules 2003, r. 131.
3. The daylist is a record of all pending applications and unexpired priority searches kept by the registrar under Land Registration Rules 2003, r. 12.
4. Land Registration Rules 2003, r. 131.
5. Land Registration Rules 2003, r. 131.
6. Land Registration Rules 2003, r. 131.
7. Land Registration Rules 2003, r.150.
8. Land Registration Rules 2003, r.54(2)(b).
9. Land Registration Rules 2003, r.54(3).

2.6. Land Charges Department search

2.6.1. Unregistered land

This search is only of relevance to unregistered land.

2.6.2. Applications

The search is made by submitting Form K15 to the Land Charges Department at Plymouth with the appropriate fee.[1] Fees can be paid by credit account provided the applicant's solicitor's key number is stated on the application form. An official certificate of result of search confers a priority period of 15 working days on the applicant.[2] The search application can be made by post, or by telephone, telex or fax by a credit account holder. Applications can also be made through the Land Registry's direct access service, Land Registry Direct or NLIS. A personal search of the register can be made but it confers no protection or priority period on the applicant.

2.6.3. Name based system

The register comprises a list of the names of estate owners of land, with details of charges registered against those names. The search is therefore made not against the land itself but against the names of the estate owners. In the case of unregistered land it is necessary for the search to be made against the names of all the estate owners whose names appear on the abstract or epitome of title supplied by the seller, including those who are merely referred to in the bodies of deeds (as opposed to being parties to the deeds themselves) or in schedules attached to deeds which form part of the title. There is no need to repeat searches where a proper search certificate made against previous estate owners has been supplied with the abstract of title.

2.6.4. Variation in names

The register is maintained on a computer which will only search against the exact version of the name as shown on the application form. It is therefore important to check that the name inserted on the application form is identical to that shown on the title deeds and that if any variations of that name appear in the deeds, e.g. if Frederick Brown is variously referred to as 'Frederick Brown', 'Frederick Browne' and 'Fred Brown', all the given variations of the name are separately entered on the search form and a separate fee paid in respect of each. Guidance on filling in the application form together with a list of accepted abbreviations and variations which the computer will search against is given in Land Charges Department Practice Leaflet No. 2.

2.6.5. *Periods of ownership*

It is only possible for an effective entry to be made against a name in relation to that person's (or company's) period of estate ownership of the land in question. Except as below it is therefore only necessary to search against a name for the period during which the estate owner owned the land. For the purposes of the search form, periods of ownership must be stated in whole years and can be ascertained by looking at the abstract or epitome of title supplied by the seller. If the estate owner's period of ownership is not known, as will be the case when searching against the name of the person who was the seller in the document forming the root of title, the search is in practice made from 1926 (the year when the register was opened). Where there is a voluntary disposition on the title which is, at the date of the contract, less than five years old, it is necessary to search against the donor's name for a period up to and including the fifth year after the date of the voluntary disposition to ensure that no bankruptcy of the donor occurred during this period. The bankruptcy of the donor during this period could lead to the disposition being set aside by the trustee in bankruptcy. Since it is possible to register a land charge against a deceased estate owner after his death, it is necessary to extend the period of search against the deceased to cover the period between his death and the current date.

2.6.6. *Description of the land*

Unless a description of the land is inserted on the search application form, the computer will produce entries relating to every person of the given name in the whole of the county or counties specified. In order to avoid having to read through and then reject multiple search entries revealed by the certificate of search, a brief description of the land which is sufficient to clearly identify it should be included on the application form. Although the intention of describing the land is to curtail the number of irrelevant entries produced by the computer, care should be taken in supplying the description, since an inaccurate description of the land may result in a relevant entry not being revealed by the search. Particular care is needed when the abstract shows that the land was formerly part of a larger piece of land, e.g. is one plot on a building estate, since the land may previously have been known by a different description to its current postal address. If the search is limited to the present postal address, entries registered against its former description will not be revealed by the search. In such a case both the present address and former description of the land should be entered on the search application form. Similarly, there is a possibility that the land was previously situated in a different administrative county to that in which it is now situate. For the reasons given above, both the present and former county must be included in the description of the land given on the search application form. In some cases the postal address of the property differs from its actual address, e.g. the village of Rogate is in the administrative county of West Sussex, but its postal address is Hampshire. In such cases the search must be made against the actual address of the property and not its postal address.

2.6.7. Pre-root estate owners

The buyer is not concerned to search against estate owners who held the land prior to the seller in the root of title supplied to him except in so far as the names of such persons have been revealed to him in documents supplied by the seller.

2.6.8. Conclusiveness of the search

An official certificate of search is conclusive in favour of the searcher provided that the search has been correctly made, i.e. it extends over the whole period of the title supplied by the seller and has been made against the correct names of the estate owners for this period, against the correct county or former county, and for the correct periods of ownership of each estate owner. In order to ensure that the buyer gains the protection afforded by the search, and the accompanying priority period, it is vital to check that the search application form is accurately completed.

2.6.9. Priority period

An official certificate of search issued by the Land Charges Department gives a priority period of 15 working days from the date of the certificate: in that time the searcher will take free of any entries made on the register between the date of the search and the date of completion (except pursuant to a priority notice) provided that completion takes place during the priority period given by the search. The date of expiry of the priority period is shown on the search certificate and should be marked on the outside of the client's file and entered in the solicitor's diary or file prompt system to ensure that it is not overlooked.

2.6.10. The priority period given by land charge searches cannot be extended. If completion is delayed and cannot take place within the priority period given by the search, a new search application will have to be made. The new search certificate will give another priority period but does not extend the original priority period from the first search. This means that if a third party has made a search in the intervening period, the third party may have priority.

2.6.11. Previous search certificates

Where the seller provides previous search certificates as part of the evidence of title, it is not necessary to repeat a search against a former estate owner provided that the search certificate supplied by the seller reveals no adverse entries and was made:

    (a) against the correct name of the estate owner as shown in the deeds;

    (b) for the correct period of ownership as shown in the title deeds; and

    (c) against the correct description of the property as shown in the deeds,

and the next disposition in the chain of title took place within the priority period afforded by the search certificate. If any of the conditions outlined above cannot be met, a further search against the previous estate owner must be made.

2.6.12. *Sub-sales*

Where A has contracted to sell to B, and before B completes his purchase he contracts to sub-sell to C, the sub-purchaser (C) will need to make a search against A's title since at the time of C's search application B will not be the estate owner of the land. B's name should be included on the search (although B will not be an estate owner in the land within the terms of Land Charges Act 1972) because the search may reveal bankruptcy entries against him. If, however, B does become an estate owner before completing the second sale to C, B's name must also be searched against.

1. For fee see App. XII.1 and for address see App. XI.5.
2. See para. E2.14.

2.7 **Acting for the lender**

2.7.1. The lender is, like the buyer, concerned to ensure that the property being purchased has a good and marketable title.

2.7.2. Where the same solicitor is acting both for the buyer and his lender, pre-completion searches in The Land Charges Department are normally carried out once on behalf of both clients each of whom is able to claim the protection (if any) afforded by the search certificate.

2.7.3. Where a Land Registry search is being made the buyer is able to take the protection of the search if it is made in the name of the lender but not vice versa. It is therefore important in this situation to remember to complete the search application form in the name of the lender client. If the application form is completed in the name of the buyer client a second search must be made on behalf of the lender. The Lenders' Handbook requires the search to be made in the name of the lender.

2.7.4. If the buyer and his lender are separately represented, subject to para. E2.7.3, the lender will frequently accept the results of searches made by the buyer's solicitor, but in some cases may insist on carrying out the pre-completion searches himself. The lender's requirements in relation to this matter should be ascertained in good time to avoid the duplication of work and expense involved in making two separate sets of searches.

2.7.5. No lender will lend money to a buyer who is bankrupt. The lender will therefore always insist that his solicitor obtains a clear result of a bankruptcy search against the buyer (see para. E2.8) before releasing the advance.

2.7.6. Some lenders may also insist that a search is made against the buyer's name in the Register of Voluntary Arrangements.

2.7.7. Where instructions are being carried out under the terms of the Lenders' Handbook paragraph 5.12 requires that the solicitor must certify that entries revealed by a Land Charges Department search certificate do not apply to the borrower client. If they do, the solicitor must report this to the lender.

2.8. Bankruptcy search

2.8.1. Irrespective of whether the transaction relates to registered or unregistered land, a lender will require a clear bankruptcy search against the name of the buyer and also against any guarantor of the buyer for the purposes of the mortgage before releasing the advance.

2.8.2. Unless a full search of the register has been made on Form K15 (see para. E2.6) the lender's solicitor should submit Form K16 to the Land Charges Department, completed with the full and correct names of the borrower(s) and guarantor(s) (if applicable).[1]

2.8.3. A search certificate will be returned by the Department.

2.8.4. In the event of there being an adverse entry revealed by the search, the solicitor should seek to establish without delay whether or not his client is the person to whom the search entry relates. For this purpose he can obtain an office copy entry, and enquiries of the Official Receiver's office may assist in this investigation. The lender must be informed immediately if the search entry does relate to the borrower client (or guarantor). If there is any doubt about whether the entry does relate to the borrower or guarantor, the lender's instructions should be obtained. The solicitor should only certify the search entry as not relating to the borrower or guarantor if he is absolutely certain that this is the case. A certification is tantamount to a warranty given by the solicitor. The client's self-certification of the entry may not satisfy a lender client.

2.8.5. Where a mortgage is being taken out independently from the purchase of unregistered land the lender's solicitor should make a full search on Form K15 (see para. E2.6) against the names of the borrowers and any guarantor(s) to ensure that there are no bankruptcy entries or priority notices registered against them. A bankruptcy only search will not reveal priority notices or deeds of arrangement under Insolvency Act 1986. In respect of the latter a search should be made at the Register of Voluntary Arrangements. This register is maintained by the Insolvency Practitioners Control Unit and a search can be undertaken, without fee, by letter or by telephone.[2]

1. For fee see App. XII.1 and for address see App. XI.5.
2. For address see App. XI.5.

2.9. Probate and administration

2.9.1. Where a grant of representation is relevant to the title and it appears from replies given to requisitions on title that the seller cannot produce the original or a marked copy of the grant on completion, the buyer should consider making a pre-completion search at the Principal Probate Registry to ensure that the grant has not been revoked or, in the case of a limited grant, that it has not expired. Alternatively, where the grant forms a link in the chain of title to unregistered land, the buyer's solicitor may ask the seller's solicitor to produce written evidence (i.e. a clear probate search) on or before completion that the grant was valid at the time of the purported disposition. Where the grant was issued by a District Registry there may be some delay before it is noted at the Principal Registry. Therefore a clear search result may not be conclusive. There is a case for saying that the search should be made in all cases where a grant forms a link in the title but in practice this is not the case.

2.9.2. The protection given to a buyer by Administration of Estates Act 1925, s.27(2) that the payment of money to a personal representative in good faith acts as a good discharge to the payer only operates where the grant is valid and had not been revoked at the time of payment. A probate search confers no priority period on the searcher and if where the buyer is buying directly from personal representatives there is doubt as to the validity of a grant, the buyer may consider whether he should require the seller to insist on the registration of the personal representatives as proprietors at the Land Registry before completion takes place.

2.9.3. The search may be made in person by searching the year book for the year of the issue of the grant. If the grant has been revoked, a note of this fact will be recorded next to the entry recording the issue of the grant.

2.9.4. Alternatively an application may be made by letter for a postal search enclosing the appropriate fee.[1] The application should specify the full names of the deceased, the date of death, and the last known address of the deceased.

1. For fee see App. XII.1 and for address see App. XI.5.

2.10. Company search

2.10.1. The effect of Land Registration Act 2002 is that a buyer is not bound by a charge created by a company unless that charge is registered at the Land Registry, or otherwise protected on the register. However, it is suggested that a company search should still be made even in the case of registered land. The company search might reveal, e.g. impending insolvency or that the company had been struck off the register and therefore no longer exists in law.

2.10.2. When buying unregistered land from a company, a company search ought to be undertaken in order to ensure that there are no adverse entries which would affect the buyer. Adverse entries would include, e.g. fixed or floating charges, or the appointment of a receiver or liquidator.

2.10.3. No official search procedure exists for making a company search which must be made either in person or through an agent by attendance at the Companies Registration office or on-line (www.direct.companies-house.gov.uk).[1]

2.10.4. The search is made by requisitioning the company's filed documents. For documents filed prior to 31 December 2002, these are available on microfiche but after that date copies must be obtained on-line or by applying for hard copies (available by post or fax). The information obtained from the search is thus dependent on both the extent of the instructions given to the searcher and his diligence in carrying out those instructions. The search will only reveal matters registered against companies which are registered in England and Wales (not foreign companies). Equivalent facilities are available in Scotland for Scottish companies. Since company charges need only be registered within 21 days of creation, and are valid in the intervening period, a company search may not reveal a very recently created charge.[2]

2.10.5. Where the search is carried out through an agent, care must be taken to instruct the agent fully as to the information which it is desired to obtain from the search.

1. For fee see App. XII.1 and for address see App. XI.5.
2. See *Burston Finance* v. *Speirway* [1974] 3 All ER 735.

2.11. Enduring powers of attorney

2.11.1. Where the purchase deed is to be executed by a person who is acting under the authority of an enduring power of attorney a search should be made at the Court of Protection on Form EP4[1] to check whether or not registration of the power has been effected or is pending. The search fee is currently £20.

2.11.2. If no registration has been made or is pending the transaction may proceed to completion.

2.11.3. If the power has been registered the attorney may deal with the land and thus, provided the donor is still alive, completion may proceed, since the power is no longer capable of revocation without notification to the Court of Protection.

2.11.4. While registration is pending the transaction may only proceed if it is within one of the limited categories permitted by Enduring Powers of Attorney Act 1985.

1. For further details see the Court of Protection (Enduring Powers of Attorney) (Amendment) Rules 2002, S.I. 2002/832 and for address see App. XI.5.

2.12. Local land charges search and enquiries

2.12.1. These searches are invariably made before exchange of contracts and are discussed at para. B10. Although the local land charges search only shows the state of the register at the time of issue of the search certificate and neither search confers a priority period on the buyer, a repeat of these searches before completion is not normally considered to be necessary provided that completion takes place within a short time after receipt of the search results or (in the case of the local land charges search) adequate insurance has been taken out. Delay in receipt of the replies to these searches also frequently makes it impracticable for them to be repeated at this stage of the transaction.

2.12.2. These searches should, however, be repeated prior to completion if:

    (a) there is to be a period of two months or more between exchange of contracts and completion and the search has not been covered by insurance or replaced by insurance;

    (b) information received by the buyer's solicitor suggests that a further search may be advisable in order to guard against a recently entered adverse entry on the register;

    (c) the contract was conditional on the satisfactory results of later searches;

    (d) required under paragraph 5.2 of the Lenders' Handbook.

2.12.3. In the absence of a special condition in the contract the discovery of a late entry on such a search is not a matter of title and will not thus entitle the buyer either to raise requisitions about the entry or to refuse to complete. Where there is to be a long gap between exchange of contracts and the contractual completion date, the buyer should try to negotiate a special condition enabling him to raise requisitions prior to completion in respect of any local land charges or adverse schemes and proposals revealed by a local search and enquiries made prior to completion and not revealed by the searches and enquiries made before exchange. Such a condition may be resisted by the seller.

2.13. Other searches

2.13.1. The buyer's solicitor should check to ensure that all other searches which are relevant to the circumstances of the transaction have been carried out and that their results are satisfactory. A checklist of the most common pre-contract searches appears at para. B10. These searches should normally have been carried out before exchange of contracts but may be required at this stage of the transaction if either there was insufficient time to make them before exchange or since that time additional information has come to light which indicates that a particular search may be relevant. Inspection of the property is dealt with in para. E4. It should be noted that paragraph 5.2 of the Lenders' Handbook requires searches which have no priority period attaching to them to be not more than six months old at the date of completion.

2.14. Results of searches

2.14.1. The results of searches must be received by the date when completion is due to take place. Completion cannot proceed until these results have been received and are considered to be satisfactory to the interests of the client.

2.14.2. In the majority of cases the results of searches will either show no subsisting entries or will merely confirm information already known, e.g. an entry on the register protecting the contract between the buyer and the seller or, in the case of unregistered land, the registration of existing restrictive covenants. In such circumstances no further action on the search results is required from the buyer's solicitor.

2.14.3. If an unexpected entry (other than a Class D(ii) protecting restrictive covenants, which cannot generally be removed) is revealed by the search result, the buyer's solicitor should:

(a) find out exactly what the entry relates to;

(b) if the entry appears adversely to affect the property, contact the seller's solicitor as soon as possible to seek his confirmation that the entry will be removed on or before completion;

(c) in the case of a Land Charges Department search, apply for an office copy of the entry using Form K19.[1] The office copy consists of a copy of the application form which was submitted when the charge was registered and will reveal the name and address of the person with the benefit of the charge who may have to be contacted to seek his consent to its removal;

(d) keep the client, his lender and, subject to the duty of confidentiality, other solicitors involved in the chain of transactions informed of the situation since negotiations for the removal of the charge may cause a delay in completion.

2.14.4. An application form for the removal of an entry from the register in either registered or unregistered land will generally only be accepted by the Chief Land Registrar if it is signed by the person with the benefit of the charge or a person acting on his behalf. An application form signed by the seller's solicitors or an undertaking given by them on completion to secure the removal of the entry may not therefore suffice unless the seller is the person with the benefit of the entry.[2] In the case of registered land, the cancellation of a registered charge is normally made on Form DS1 or by ENDs. Withdrawals of cautions and restrictions are effected on Forms WCT and RX4 respectively. The application for cancellation of a unilateral notice must be made in Form UN4. An application for the cancellation of a notice (other than a unilateral notice or a matrimonial home rights notice) must be in Form CN1. As to bankruptcy entries, evidence needs to be lodged that the bankruptcy no longer affects the property.

2.14.5. Charges which are registered at the Land Charges Department can only be entered against the name of an estate owner in relation to the period during which he was the owner of the land in question. Thus an entry which was made before or after this time cannot prejudice the buyer. The computerised system which is used to process these searches will sometimes throw up entries which are clearly irrelevant to the transaction in hand, particularly where the name searched against is a very common one, e.g. John Smith. Having checked that the entry is irrelevant , it may either be disregarded or the seller's solicitor may at completion be asked to certify the entry as being inapplicable to the transaction. Certification by a solicitor is tantamount to a warranty, the consideration for it being completion of the transaction.

2.14.6. The court has a discretion to remove entries which are redundant but which cannot be removed from the register because the person with their benefit will not consent to their removal or cannot be contacted.

2.14.7. Entries protecting a spouse's matrimonial homes rights under Family Law Act 1996 can be removed on production of the death certificate of the spouse or a decree absolute or by an order of the court. In the absence of these items, the charge can only be removed with the consent of the spouse who has the benefit of the charge.

2.14.8. An official certificate of search issued by the Land Registry is not conclusive in favour of the searcher who will thus take his interest in the land subject to whatever entries are on the register irrespective of whether or not they were revealed by the search certificate.[3] However, where a person suffers loss as a result of a mistake in an official search he will be able to claim compensation under Land Registration Act 2002, Schedule 8, para.1.

2.14.9. An official certificate of search issued by the Land Charges Department is conclusive in favour of the searcher who will thus take his interest in the land free of any entries which are on the register but which were not revealed by the search certificate. Where a person suffers loss as a result of an error in an official certificate of search he may be able to claim compensation from the Chief Land Registrar, but there is no statutory right to compensation in these circumstances. No liability will attach to the solicitor who made the search provided that a correctly submitted official search was made.[4]

1. For fee see App. XII.1 and for address see App. XI.5.
2. See *Holmes* v. *Kennard & Son* (1985) 49 P & CR 202.
3. *Parkash* v. *Irani Finance Ltd* [1970] Ch 101.
4. Land Charges Act 1972, s.12.

E3. The buyer's mortgage

See also: Mortgages: acting for lender and borrower, para. A11
Investigation of title, para. D2
Pre-completion searches, para. E2
Post-completion, section G
Lenders, section H
Costs, para. N1

3.1. Instructions from lender

3.1.1. Instructions from the lender to act will usually be received at the same time as an offer of mortgage is made to the buyer, i.e. shortly before exchange of contracts. Since each lender's requirements will differ slightly from another, the precise instructions of the lender for whom the solicitor is acting in the present transaction must be noted and strictly observed. The instructions should comply with Practice Rule 6(3) of the Solicitors' Practice Rules 1990 (see Appendix I.1). Any queries which arise in relation to those instructions, whether at the outset of the transaction or during its course, must be immediately clarified with the lender. Where the solicitor is acting also for the buyer, the problems of conflict of interests and confidentiality must be borne in mind. Where the same solicitor is acting for both borrower and lender he owes a duty to both clients.[1] These issues are further discussed in para. A11. Many lenders require their solicitors to obtain evidence of the client's identity (e.g. a passport) and to keep a copy of the evidence of identity on file.[2]

3.1.2. Where a mortgage is being taken from an institutional lender over residential property it is likely that the solicitor will be instructed to follow the Lenders' Handbook (see Appendix VIII.3). The solicitor must check which specific variations to the Handbook are required by the lender to suit both the lender's own requirements and the transaction in hand.

1. See *Mortgage Express* v. *Bowerman & Partners* (1994) 34 EG 116; and *Bristol & West Building Society* v. *May, May and Merriman* [1997] 3 All ER 206.
2. See paragraph 3.3 of the CML Lenders' Handbook reproduced in Appendix VIII.3.

3.2. Investigation of title

3.2.1. When instructed to act both for the buyer and his lender, investigation of title on behalf of both clients will be carried out simultaneously, but the particular requirements (if any) of the lender must be considered when carrying out this procedure. Any queries which arise during the course of the investigation should immediately be clarified with the mortgagee client since if they are deferred until a later stage in the transaction some delay in completion may result.

3.2.2. When acting only for the lender, the lender's solicitor should request the buyer's solicitor to send him copies of the following documents as soon as the buyer's solicitor has completed his own investigation of title:

    (a) all pre-contract searches and enquiries with their results;

    (b) the contract;

    (c) evidence of title;

    (d) requisitions on title with their answers;

    (e) the draft and subsequently the approved purchase deed;

    (f) at a later stage, all pre-completion searches with their results;

    (g) any other documents which are relevant to the acquisition of a good title by the lender or which are specifically required by the lender's instructions.

3.2.3. On receipt of these documents from the buyer's solicitor, the lender's solicitor should conduct his own investigation of the title in accordance with instructions received from his client. Any queries on the title should be raised with the buyer's solicitor who will in turn seek an answer from the seller's solicitor. Investigation must be carried out as quickly as possible so that no delay in completion occurs.

3.3. Report on title

3.3.1. Investigation of title having been completed, the solicitor will be required to make a report on title to his lender client certifying that he has carried out a full investigation in accordance with the lender's instructions and that the title to the property is good and marketable. In residential transactions the report on title will be in the form of the certificate set out in Rule 6 of the Solicitors' Practice Rules 1990 (see Appendix VII.2); in other transactions the CLLS Certificate and Short Form Report on Title may be used (see Appendix VIII.2). At the stage when the Report on Title or Certificate is submitted to the lender, there should be no remaining queries on the title, any such queries having been clarified during the course of investigation of title. Notification of queries at this late stage may well result in completion being delayed pending their resolution. If a plan has been supplied by the lender for verification this must be carefully checked before certification. The solicitor may also be asked to advise whether a further inspection of the property by the lender's surveyor before completion will be required. This is usually only required in connection with property which is in the course of construction.

3.3.2. If the enquiries before contract indicate that works have been carried out to the property, paragraph 5.3 of the CML Lenders' Handbook makes it clear that the solicitor must ensure that all the necessary consents are available (i.e. both planning and building regulations consents) and there should be no evidence of any breach of any condition attached to any consent. This should be done before exchange of contracts. Solicitors will rarely be in a position to give an unqualified assurance that all the conditions attached to a planning consent have been complied with.

3.3.3. Local land charge searches on Form LLC1 will reveal if there are any planning charges and proceedings for building regulation breaches. The reply to question 1 of CON 29 Part I Standard Enquiries of Local Authority (2002 edition) should reveal if proceedings have been authorised for any infringement of building regulations. Enquiries of the seller's solicitors, or the borrower himself if he is in occupation, should reveal whether any notices have been received from the local authority complaining of building regulation or planning breaches.

3.3.4. Any certificate relating to planning matters by the borrower's solicitor should be limited to matters revealed by the usual local searches and by their enquiries of the seller/borrower. It is suggested that reporting solicitors should decline to certify that they are not aware of any matters which would give rise to a breach of planning conditions or building regulation control. Such a statement might lead a lender to assume that the solicitor has undertaken more extensive enquiries than a solicitor would reasonably be expected to make.

3.3.5. A reporting solicitor can properly go no further than confirm to the lender that searches and enquiries do not reveal evidence of any breach. This should be done before exchange of contracts.

3.3.6. Part 1 of the CML Lenders Handbook states at 5.2.5:

'You must advise us of any contaminated land entries revealed in the local authority search. Check part 2 to see if we want to receive environmental or contaminated land reports (as opposed to contaminated land entries revealed in the local authority search). If we do not, you do not need to make these enquiries on our behalf'.

Individual lender's requirements are set out in Part 2 of the CML Lenders Handbook, which can be viewed online at www.cml.org.uk. Also see para. B10.6.11, section B25 Environmental Issues, and Appendix IV.1 of this Handbook for solicitors' duties to the buyer.

3.3.7. A solicitor is liable for a report on title signed by his employee. (*Nationwide Building Society* v. *Lewis* [1997] 3 All ER 498.)

3.4. Searches before completion

3.4.1. Searches before completion are an integral part of the investigation of title procedure and should be strictly carried out before a report on title or certificate is submitted to the lender. If time does not permit this, the report on title or certificate should be qualified by a statement saying that the report is given subject to the results of such searches being satisfactory. The searches which need to be undertaken are identical to those which are conducted on behalf of a buyer, subject to the following modifications, and when the same solicitor is acting both for the buyer and his lender will be carried out once on behalf of both clients. Where two separate solicitors are acting for the buyer and his lender, the lender's solicitor should indicate to the buyer's solicitor whether he will accept the results of pre-completion searches made by the buyer, or whether he wishes to conduct his own searches. Where the title being purchased is registered, the buyer may take the benefit and protection of a search made in the name of the lender; thus only one search application is necessary.[1] The converse is not true, so that if the search application is made in the name of the buyer, a second application must be submitted in the name of the lender. Whether or not the land is registered, the lender will invariably instruct his solicitor to make a Land Charges Department search for bankruptcy against the name of the borrower(s) and to obtain a clear result to that search before releasing the mortgage funds into the buyer's hands. Where the borrower is a company a company search should be made against the borrower both as a safeguard against liquidation, receivership or administration and also for potential incumbrances, e.g. debentures which charge after-acquired property.

3.4.2.   All searches, both pre-contract and pre-completion must be no older than six months at completion, the CML Lenders' Handbook, para. 5.2.3.

1. Land Registration Rules 2003, r.151.

3.5.   Life policies

3.5.1.   The lender's instructions in relation to any life policy which is to protect or act as collateral security to the mortgage must be carried out before completion (see Mortgages and life policies Appendix V.12). In a case where a solicitor is acting both for the buyer and his lender, in his capacity as buyer's solicitor and irrespective of whether the lender requires an endowment policy to be on foot by actual completion, or whether his instructions permit the policy to be obtained within a certain period after completion has taken place, the solicitor owes a duty to the buyer to ensure that the policy is on foot at the date of actual completion,[1] failing which the solicitor might be liable to the buyer or his personal representatives in negligence for any resulting loss, e.g. if the buyer died after completion so that the mortgage had to be repaid before the policy became effective. It is also usual in the case of a new policy to check that the first premium has been paid and that it states that the age of the insured is admitted. If age is not admitted and the age of the policy holder turns out to be wrong, this could have the effect either of invalidating the policy or of reducing the proceeds which are payable under the policy.

3.5.2.   Some lenders require a formal assignment to them of the benefit of the policy, in which case such assignment must be prepared (usually on a standard form supplied by the lender) and executed by the borrower. The assignment should be kept with the title deeds to the mortgaged property and after completion sent to the lender for safe custody or otherwise in accordance with the lender's instructions. The deed of assignment is not submitted to the Land Registry when an application for registration of title is made. Where the lender does not require a formal mortgage or deposit of the policy, the proceeds of the policy will fall into the deceased's estate on his death, and may not therefore be available to pay off the mortgage debt. This problem is particularly relevant where one of two unmarried co-owners dies, and the policy taken out by the deceased will fall into his estate and not into the hands of the surviving co-owner. The consequences of non-assignment or non-deposit of the policy should be explained to the policy holder and to potential beneficiaries under the policy at the time when the policy is taken out.

3.5.3.   To preserve the priority of the lender's claim to the benefit of the policy moneys, notice of the assignment of the benefit of the policy should, after completion, be given to the insurance company in accordance with Policies of Assurance Act 1867. If the lender does not supply a standard form on which to make this notification, a letter may be sent to the insurance company informing them of the assignment, the name of the assignee (the lender), and the details of the policy which has been assigned. Two copies of this letter or standard form notice should be sent to the insurance company, requesting them to sign one copy in acknowledgement of its receipt and to return it to the solicitor. The receipted copy must then be placed with the title deeds of the property for safe custody.

3.5.4.   The lender may require that an endowment policy is put on risk on or before completion of the mortgage.

1. But see *Lynne* v. *Gordon Doctors & Walton* (1991) 135 SJ (LB) 29.

3.6.   The mortgage deed

3.6.1.   Where the mortgage is granted by an institutional lender, e.g. a bank or building society, drafts and engrossment copies of the lender's standard form of mortgage will be supplied to the solicitor for completion and execution by the borrower. In other cases the lender's instructions (if any) as to the form and contents of the mortgage must be followed and his approval obtained to the draft deed before engrossment. A legal mortgage must be made by deed to comply with Law of Property Act 1925, s.87. In registered land cases, the mortgage deed must identify the registered land which is to be charged, i.e. by its title number or by reference to a suitable plan. A legal charge of a registered estate may be made in Form CH1.[1]

3.6.2.   The mortgage deed will be prepared simultaneously with the purchase deed and will be executed by the borrower prior to completion. The borrower is required to execute the deed in the presence of a witness, but in the case of a legal mortgage the lender does not usually sign the deed. If the mortgage is equitable it will generally be a contract for a disposition of an interest in land within Law of Property (Miscellaneous Provisions) Act 1989, s.2 which is required to be in writing and signed by both contracting parties.

3.6.3.   The contents and effect of the mortgage deed must be explained to the borrower before signature to ensure that, e.g. the borrower understands that the lender will be entitled to sell the property if the borrower defaults in his repayments. Any prohibitions contained in the mortgage, e.g. as to letting the property or particular conditions attached to it, must also be explained to the borrower and where the charge is an all-moneys charge the effect of this type of charge should be explained to the client.

3.6.4. The solicitor acting for the lender should take reasonable steps to check that the security effected over the property will be valid and enforceable. Problems can arise where, e.g. a 'friend' of one of the co-borrowers ostensibly pretending to be the co-borrower's wife signs the mortgage deed in the wife's place thus vitiating the security. It would appear that a solicitor does not generally have a duty to ensure that the mortgage deed is validly executed by the named borrower(s) but he should be alert to the issues involved and should do what he can to ensure proper execution by the correct persons. Execution by the borrower(s) in the solicitor's presence is a sensible precaution to take, although even this will not guard against forgery where the identity of the borrowers is not known personally to the solicitor.[2] The Lenders' Handbook does not specifically require the mortgage deed to be executed in the presence of the solicitor but it does require normally the solicitor to check the identity of signatories to documents and to ensure that the lender is supplied with a fully enforceable first charge by way of legal mortgage over the secured property. The Lenders' Handbook also recommends that the mortgage should be signed in the presence of a solicitor.

3.6.5. The lender's instructions will frequently also require the solicitor to discuss repayment of the mortgage with the borrower and may require the solicitor to obtain a signed banker's standing order for repayments from the borrower.

1. Land Registration Rules 2003, r.103.
2. See Mortgage Fraud, para. A24; Property Fraud Warning Card II, Appendix IV.3, and Mortgage Fraud – variation in purchase price, Appendix V.11.

3.7. Mortgage funds

3.7.1. The effect of any retentions from the mortgage advance must be explained to the buyer in advance of completion and, if necessary, the buyer should be advised to seek estimates for any works which are to be effected on the property.

3.7.2. The lender will not release the mortgage advance to the solicitor until he is satisfied that all conditions attached to the advance have been complied with and he has been requested to release the funds by the solicitor acting for him. Such request is commonly made on the Report on Title Form or Certificate of title, or on a separate form supplied by the lender (see Appendices VIII.2 and VII.2). The solicitor should ensure that he is in receipt of cleared funds (in order to avoid any breach of Solicitors' Accounts Rules) by the morning of the day of actual completion. The mortgage advance is clients' money and must be placed in a clients' account. If completion does not take place on the anticipated date, the amount of the mortgage advance must be returned to the lender or dealt with in accordance with his instructions, and a further cheque requested for the re-arranged completion date. If the solicitor pays the advance cheque into his clients' account and completion is delayed the solicitor may be liable to pay interest on the amount of the advance if the cheque is not returned to the lender within the time specified in the lender's instructions. The mortgage advance is held by the solicitor (pending completion) on trust for the lender. If the solicitor deals with the funds during this time, except in accordance with the lender's instructions, a breach of trust will occur.[1]

3.7.3. Any conditions relating to the discharge of the borrower's existing mortgage(s) over the same or another specified property identified by the lender must be complied with before the mortgage advance is released for his use.

3.7.4. If it is not possible to synchronise a sale and purchase transaction or in any other situation where it becomes apparent that the mortgage funds will not be available in time to complete the purchase, the buyer must be advised of the consequences of a delayed completion and of any decision to use bridging finance in order to complete the purchase on the due date.

3.7.5. Where different solicitors are acting for the buyer and his lender, it will be necessary for the two solicitors to liaise in order to ensure that the mortgage funds reach the seller's solicitor's bank account in time for completion.

1. *Target Holdings* v. *Redferns (a firm)* [1995] NPC 136 (HL) and see *Bristol & West Building Society* v. *May, May and Merrimans* [1997] 3 All ER 206.

3.8. Duty to lender

3.8.1. Solicitors who do not apply the advance in the manner required by their instructions or who release it before the lender's title is complete may be liable to repay the advance. Until the mortgage is completed, the solicitor may hold the advance on the borrower's client account but it must be clearly identifiable as coming from the lender and will be returned to the lender on demand.

3.8.2. Where the lender instructs that separate advice must be given to joint borrowers, the joint borrowers must be seen separately.

3.8.3. Where the solicitor signs a certificate saying that he has independently advised the borrowers,[1] the lender is not under a duty to enquire as to the nature of the advice given.[2]

1. In *Bank Melli Iran* v. *Samadi Rad* [1995] 2 FLR 367 the court suggested that advice given by a separate solicitor in the same firm was not considered to be 'independent'.
2. *Bank of Baroda* v. *Rayorel* [1995] NPC 6, and see Acting for both parties, para. A10.

3.9. Completion of the mortgage

3.9.1. Since it is not possible for the buyer to mortgage a property which he does not own, it follows that formal completion of the mortgage cannot take place until after completion of the purchase, irrespective of the fact that the mortgage funds will have been released to the use of the borrower on completion of the earlier purchase. As soon as completion of the purchase of the property has taken place, the mortgage deed can be completed by insertion of the date of completion and any other formalities which have to be entered in it, e.g. date of first repayment. The lender client may require to be informed that completion has taken place. If there is any doubt over whether vacant possession will be given the client should be advised to inspect the property immediately prior to completion.

3.9.2. Following completion of the mortgage, the lender's charge must be protected by registration on the charges register of the title. The solicitor acting for the lender should take possession of all the necessary documents on completion and should effect the registration on behalf of his client. Where separate solicitors are acting for the buyer and the lender, it is usual for the lender's solicitor to require the buyer's solicitor to hand over on completion completed and signed Land Registry application forms and PD forms as appropriate.

3.9.3. Charges created by companies must, in addition to any registration at the Land Registry, be registered at the Companies Registry within 21 days of their creation in accordance with Companies Act requirements. The practice now is to file a memorandum of the charge with the appropriate form at Companies House. Additionally evidence must be lodged at the Land Registry that the charge has been registered at Companies House.[1]

1. See Post-completion, section G.

3.10. Custody of deeds

3.10.1. On completion of the post-completion formalities, any relevant documents, e.g. life policy and assignments and notices relating to it, should be sent to the lender for safe custody. The documents to be sent should be listed in triplicate, one copy of the list being retained on the solicitor's file, the remaining two being sent to the lender with the deeds with a request that one copy of the list is signed by the lender and returned to the solicitor as an acknowledgement of their receipt. The deeds should be despatched by a method which ensures their safe arrival at their destination, e.g. registered post, document exchange or insured post. If there is to be any delay in the despatch of the deeds, e.g. because of delays in registration at the Land Registry, the lender should be informed of the delay, the reason for it and its likely duration.

3.11. Costs

3.11.1. The lender's costs in relation to the grant of the mortgage are primarily the lender's responsibility since he is the client who has instructed the solicitor, but the lender commonly seeks indemnity for those costs from the buyer who should be informed of this fact and their likely amount at the outset of the transaction. In other cases the amount to be charged must be agreed between the solicitor and his lender client (see Costs, para. N1).

E4. Preparing for completion

See also: Undertakings for bridging finance, para. B16
The purchase deed, para. E1
Pre-completion searches, para. E2
The buyer's mortgage, para. E3
The buyer in occupation, para. E5
Completion, section F
Acting on grant of lease, para. K1
Delay and remedies, section M
Costs, para. N1

4.1. Introduction

4.1.1. In order to ensure that completion proceeds smoothly, both parties need to under-take a number of preparatory steps. Most of these steps have been examined in depth in other areas of this book. The following paragraphs therefore concentrate on summarising the matters to be dealt with at this stage of the transaction by way of checklists with some additional commentary.

4.2. Seller's checklist

4.2.1. (a) Ensure purchase deed has been approved and requisitions answered.

(b) Receive engrossed purchase deed from buyer – has buyer executed the deed (where appropriate) and plan (if used), or has an acceptable under-taking been given that he will execute after completion?

(c) Get seller to execute purchase deed and return it to solicitor in time for completion.

(d) Obtain redemption figure(s) for seller's mortgage(s) and check that they are correct and ensure that the seller's solicitor is aware of *all* the mort-gages which need to be redeemed.

(e) Obtain last receipts, etc., where apportionments are to be made on completion.

(f) Prepare completion statement (where necessary) and send two copies to buyer in good time before completion.

(g) Remind client to organise final readings of meters at the property.

(h) Prepare forms for discharge of land charges where necessary (unregistered land).

(i) Approve any memorandum which the buyer has requested be placed on retained title deeds or grant of representation (unregistered land).

(j) Prepare any undertaking which needs to be given on completion (e.g. for discharge of seller's mortgage if also acting for the lender).

(k) Contact lender to confirm final arrangements for discharge of seller's mortgage, method of payment, etc.

(l) Prepare authority addressed to tenants relating to payment of future rent (tenanted property).

(m) Check through file to ensure all outstanding queries have been dealt with.

(n) Prepare list of matters to be dealt with on actual completion.

(o) Locate deeds and documents which will need to be inspected/handed over on completion and prepare certified copies for the buyer of those documents which are to be retained by the seller.

(p) Prepare two copies of schedule of deeds to be handed to buyer on completion.

(q) Prepare inventory of chattels and receipt for money payable for them.

(r) Check arrangements for vacant possession and handing over keys.

(s) Receive instructions from buyer's solicitor to act as his agent on completion and clarify instructions with him if necessary.

(t) Make final arrangements with buyer's solicitor for time and place of completion.

(u) Ensure estate agents are aware of completion arrangements.

(v) Prepare bill for submission to client.

4.3.   Buyer's checklist

4.3.1.   (a) Ensure purchase deed has been approved and requisitions satisfactorily answered.

(b) Engross purchase and mortgage deeds.

(c) Get buyer to execute mortgage deed, purchase deed and plan (if necessary) and return it to solicitor.

(d) Send (executed) purchase deed to seller's solicitor for his client's execution in time for completion. The submission of the deed should be in escrow subject to the express condition that the buyer may withdraw if the seller fails to complete.[1]

(e) Make pre-completion searches and ensure their results are satisfactory.

(f) Make report on title to lender and request advance cheque in time for completion.

(g) Receive completion statement (where necessary) and copies of last receipts in support of apportionments and check it is correct.

(h) Remind client of arrangements for completion.

(i) Prepare forms for discharge of land charges where necessary (unregistered land).

(j) Obtain seller's approval of the wording of any memorandum which the buyer has requested be placed on retained title deeds or grant of representation (unregistered land).

(k) Prepare and agree the form of wording of any undertaking which needs to be given or received on completion.

(l) Contact lender to confirm final arrangements for completion.

(m) Ensure that any life policy required by the lender is on foot and check with client that any other insurances required for the property (e.g. house contents insurance) have been taken out. Prepare and engross assignments of other insurance policies to the buyer (e.g. for damp treatment) if appropriate.

(n) Check through file to ensure all outstanding queries have been dealt with.

(o) Prepare statement of account and bill for client and submit together with a copy of the completion statement, requesting balance due from client be paid in sufficient time for the funds to be cleared before completion.

(p) Receive advance cheque from lender, pay into clients' account and clear funds before completion.

(q) Receive balance of funds from client and clear through clients' account before completion.

(r) Arrange for final inspection of property if necessary.

(s) Prepare list of matters to be dealt with on actual completion.

(t) Check arrangements for vacant possession and handing over keys.

(u) Instruct seller's solicitor to act as agent on completion if completion not to be by personal attendance.

(v) Make final arrangements with seller's solicitor for time and place of completion.

(w) Ensure estate agents are aware of completion arrangements.

(x) Make arrangements for transmission of completion money to seller's solicitor (or as he has directed).

1. Under Companies Act 1985, s.36A execution by a company is deemed to be delivery of the deed: this re-emphasises the need for execution subject to an express condition in such cases.

4.4. Apportionments

4.4.1. Where completion does not take place on a date when outgoings on the property fall due, outgoings which attach to the land may be apportioned between the parties on completion, the calculations of the apportioned sums being shown on the completion statement.

4.4.2. Uniform business rate and water rates can be apportioned but it is normally considered better practice to inform the relevant authority after completion of the change of ownership and request them to send apportioned accounts to seller and buyer.

4.4.3. Where applicable rent and service charge payments may have to be apportioned. These matters are further dealt with in paras. K1 and K5.

4.4.4. Standard Condition 6.3 deals with apportionments and allows a provisional apportionment to be made where exact figures are not available at completion (e.g. in respect of service charges).

4.4.5. The seller must be asked to produce the last demands or receipts for all sums which are to be apportioned so that the calculations of the amounts due or to be allowed on completion may be made. Copies of these receipts should be sent to the buyer with the completion statement to enable him to check the accuracy of the calculation.

4.5. Completion statement

4.5.1. A completion statement, to be prepared by the seller's solicitor, showing the amount of money required to complete the transaction and how that figure is calculated, will be requested by the buyer when he submits his requisitions on title.

4.5.2. It is only necessary to provide the buyer with a completion statement where the sum due on completion includes apportionments or other sums in excess of the balance of the purchase price.[1]

4.5.3. If not sent to the buyer with the answers to his requisitions on title, the completion statement should be supplied in good time before completion to enable the buyer to check its accuracy and to make arrangements for the amount due to be available.

4.5.4. The statement should show clearly the total amount due on completion, and how that total sum is made up. Depending on the circumstances it may be necessary to take account of some or all of the following items:

    (a) the purchase price, giving credit for any deposit paid;

    (b) apportionments of outgoings;

(c) money payable for chattels;

(d) compensation if completion is delayed;

(e) a licence fee if the buyer has been in occupation of the property.

4.5.5. Two copies of the completion statement should be sent to the buyer together with copies of any receipts or demands on which apportioned figures have been based.

1. *Carne* v. *Debono* [1988] 3 All ER 485; *Hanson* v. *SWEB* [2001] EWCA Civ 1377.

4.6. Statement to client

4.6.1. The buyer's solicitor should prepare and submit to his client a financial statement which shows clearly the total sum which is due from him on completion and how that sum is calculated.

4.6.2. In addition to the matters dealt with on the completion statement, the financial statement should also take account of such of the following matters as are relevant to the transaction:

(a) the mortgage advance and any costs and/or retentions made in respect of it;

(b) disbursements, e.g. stamp duty, Land Registry fees, fees payable for registration of notices or search fees;

(c) the solicitor's costs.

4.6.3. The financial statement, accompanied by a copy of the completion statement and the solicitor's properly drawn bill, should be sent to the client in sufficient time before completion to allow the client to forward the required balance of funds to the solicitor in time for those funds to be cleared by completion.

4.7. Money – the buyer

4.7.1. On being informed of the amount required to complete, the buyer's solicitor should check the figures for accuracy, verifying any apportionments made against the copy receipts or demands supplied by the seller. Any discrepancies must be clarified as a matter of urgency.

4.7.2. The solicitor should then make a final calculation of the sums due on completion, preparing his financial statement and bill for submission to the client.

4.7.3. If at this stage it appears that there is any shortfall in funds the client must immediately be informed and steps taken to remedy the shortfall. If bridging finance or a further loan are necessary in order to complete the transaction arrangements must be made to effect such arrangements without delay. An undertaking given by the solicitor to repay bridging finance must only be given where the promise given by the solicitor is wholly capable of performance by him.[1]

4.7.4. The mortgage advance requested by the solicitor from the lender should be received in sufficient time to permit the funds to be cleared through clients' account before completion.

4.7.5. The client must be asked to put the solicitor in funds for the balance of the completion money (over and above the mortgage advance) in sufficient time to permit the funds to be cleared through clients' account before completion. On receipt of the funds from the client, the cheque should be credited to a ledger account in the name of that client.

4.7.6. On the day of completion arrangements must be made to remit the amount due to the seller's solicitor in accordance with his instructions.

1. See Undertakings for bridging finance, para. B16.

4.8. Completion checklist

4.8.1. When preparing for completion the buyer's solicitor should make a checklist of the matters which need to be dealt with on actual completion to ensure that nothing is overlooked. Where the transaction is complex, the list should be submitted to the seller's solicitor for his agreement as to its contents. Where the buyer instructs a person to act as his agent on completion he should, when instructing the agent, send him a copy of the checklist so that the agent is fully informed as to the matters which need to be dealt with.

4.8.2. Some or all of the items in the following checklist will need to be attended to on actual completion.

4.8.3. The list should contain an itemised list of the documents which need to be inspected/marked/handed over/received at completion.

    (a) Documents to be available at completion

        (i)   contract;

        (ii) evidence of title;

        (iii) copy purchase deed;

        (iv) answers to requisitions;

        (v) completion statement.

    (b) Documents to be inspected by buyer

        (i)   title deeds where in unregistered land these are not to be handed over on completion (e.g. on a sale of part);

        (ii) general or enduring power of attorney;

        (iii) grant of administration;

        (iv) receipts/demands for apportionments if not previously supplied.

(c) Documents, etc., to be handed to buyer on completion

    (i)   title deeds;

    (ii)   original lease;

    (iii)   executed purchase deed;

    (iv)   schedule of deeds;

    (v)   Form DS1/discharged mortgage or undertaking in respect of discharge of mortgage(s);

    (vi)   receipt for money paid for chattels;

    (vii)   authority addressed to tenants relating to payment of future rent and original tenancy agreements/leases (tenanted property);

    (viii)   keys of the property (if these are not available the seller's solicitor should be asked to telephone the key holder to request the release of the keys);

    (ix)   certified copy of any memorandum endorsed on retained deeds;

    (x)   landlord's licence.

(d) Documents, etc., to be handed to seller on completion

    (i)   banker's draft for amount due on completion;

    (ii)   executed duplicate purchase deed/counterpart lease/licence (where appropriate);

    (iii)   receipted schedule of deeds received from seller;

    (iv)   release of deposit if held by third party in capacity of stakeholder.

(e) Endorsements on documents if required by buyer

    (i)   endorsement of assent or conveyance on grant of representation (unregistered land);

    (ii)   endorsement of sale on most recently dated retained document of title (sale of part of unregistered land);

    (iii)   mark up abstract or epitome as compared against the original deeds (unregistered land in respect of any document the original of which is not handed over on completion).

E5. The buyer in occupation

See also: Licence or tenancy, para. K12
Delay and remedies, section M

5.1. Introduction

5.1.1. In many cases the seller will be in actual occupation of the property until completion and thus the question of the buyer taking possession before completion does not arise. The seller is entitled to retain possession until completion unless otherwise agreed.

5.1.2. The buyer's request to enter and occupy the premises before completion should be regarded with some caution by the seller since once the buyer takes up occupation he may lose his incentive to complete on the contractual completion date and, if ultimately he does not complete the transaction at all, it may be difficult to evict the buyer from the property. Where the seller has a subsisting mortgage on the property, his lender's consent should be obtained before the buyer is allowed into occupation.

5.1.3. It is essential that the nature of the buyer's occupation is a licence and not a tenancy in order to avoid the possibility of the buyer claiming security of tenure against the seller.[1] Even where a licence is granted a court order will always be necessary to remove a residential occupier who does not voluntarily vacate the property,[2] and may be necessary in non-residential cases where the tenant will not peaceably surrender his occupation.

1. See Licence or tenancy, para. K12. An outline of the major statutes affecting security of tenure is given in section K.
2. Protection from Eviction Act 1977, s.2.

5.2. Conditions to be imposed on buyer

5.2.1. Where it is agreed to allow the buyer into possession the seller may consider imposing some restrictions or conditions of occupation on the buyer. If the contract does not make provision for occupation by the buyer (e.g. Standard Condition 5.2), the terms of the occupation should be agreed in writing and signed by both parties prior to the commencement of the buyer's occupation.

5.2.2.   Some or all of the following conditions may be considered:

    (a) the occupation shall be a licence and not a tenancy;[1]

    (b) payment of a further instalment of the purchase price as a precondition of occupation;

    (c) payment of a licence fee during occupation (frequently this is calculated by reference to the rate at which compensation for late completion is payable under the general conditions of the contract);

    (d) the licence should be non-assignable;

    (e) restrictions on who may occupy the property;

    (f) restrictions on the use of the property during the buyer's occupation (including an obligation to comply with the terms of the lease in the case of leasehold property);

    (g) payment by the buyer of all outgoings on the property;

    (h) the buyer to be responsible for insuring the property and/or paying the insurance premium;

    (i) the buyer to be responsible for repairs and maintenance;

    (j) prohibition on alterations and improvements;

    (k) provisions for termination of the licence by either party;

    (l) entitlement to the income of the property (if any).

5.2.3.   Some but not all of the above conditions are provided by Standard Condition 5.2 which restricts the occupation of the property to the buyer and his household.

5.2.4.   Alternatively, the seller may consider granting the buyer a licence for access only, e.g. for measuring up for alterations, such licence to be restricted to access at specified times and for a specific purpose.

---

1. But see Licence or tenancy, para. K12. Where the terms of the original contract do not provide for the buyer's occupation, care must be exercised in drawing up the terms of the licence agreement. Such an agreement does not fall within Law of Property (Miscellaneous Provisions) Act 1989, s.2 but for certainty should be in writing and signed by both parties.

5.3.   Delay

5.3.1.   Where there is a delay in completion and the seller sues for specific performance, the court usually gives the buyer the option either of paying the balance of the purchase price with interest into court or of giving up possession.[1] This provision is, however, thought not to apply where the buyer takes possession under a provision to that effect contained in the contract to purchase the property, e.g. Standard Condition 5.2.[2]

5.3.2.   The seller has an equitable lien over the property which endures until the purchase price is paid in full.[3]

1. This order is known as a 'Greenwood and Turner' order after the case of that name: *Greenwood* v. *Turner* [1891] 2 Ch 144.
2. *Attfield* v. *D.J. Plant Hire and General Contractors Ltd* [1987] Ch 141.
3. See Delay and remedies, section M.

5.4. Common law provisions

5.4.1. The seller's position as quasi-trustee of the property on behalf of the buyer, from which stems the seller's duty to take care of the property pending completion, is not affected by the buyer's occupation. Therefore the seller should expressly pass this duty of care (and to do repairs) on to the buyer as part of the licence to occupy.

5.4.2. The buyer becomes entitled to receive the income of the property and is responsible for outgoings.

5.4.3. Unless the contract provides to the contrary, the buyer, by taking possession, will be deemed to have accepted the seller's title and thus loses his right to object to any defects of which he knew at that time.[1] Standard Condition 5.2.7 and Standard Commercial Property Condition 5.2.5 reverse this common law rule by providing that the buyer's right to raise requisitions is unaffected by his occupation of the property.

1. See After exchange, para. C5.

5.5. The buyer

5.5.1. Since the terms of the occupation agreement will normally be construed as a licence and not a tenancy the buyer's position as occupier is somewhat tenuous and he will face certain eviction if he does not ultimately complete the purchase. The buyer should therefore be advised not to spend money on altering or improving the property until completion has taken place. The terms of the occupation agreement will often prohibit the buyer from altering or improving the property pending completion.

5.5.2. If delay in completion is anticipated, the buyer may seek to protect his contract by applying for registration of a notice (a Class C(iv) estate contract in unregistered land) although this may strictly be unnecessary in registered land cases since by being in occupation the buyer may be able to establish an overriding interest under Land Registration Act 2002.[1]

5.5.3. The terms of the occupation agreement should be fully explained to the buyer. In particular his attention should be drawn to the financial provisions since the buyer is often required to pay a further instalment of the purchase price together with a daily licence fee as one of the terms of his occupation. Where the purchase is being financed by a mortgage, the lender's consent to the terms of the occupation agreement should be obtained.

1. Land Registration Act 2002, Sched. 1, para. 2 and Sched. 3, para. 2.

5.6.   Sitting tenants

5.6.1.   Where the property is being sold to a sitting tenant there is ample justification for accepting a less than 10% deposit on exchange of contracts, or even for dispensing with the deposit altogether.[1]

5.6.2.   Although the tenant will already be familiar with the physical condition and structure of the property, he should still consider the merits of a survey of the property. In cases where the landlord is responsible for repairs, the tenant will on completion become responsible for the maintenance and upkeep of the property and will thus need to be aware of any major structural defects in it which might affect his decision to proceed with the purchase or his ability to resell the property at a later date. Even in cases where the tenant is currently responsible for repairs he may still consider it wise to have a survey of the property made.

5.6.3.   Even where the tenant is not raising a mortgage to finance his purchase, full deduction of title by the landlord should be required to ensure that the tenant will become registered with an absolute freehold title and thus able to resell the property should he wish to do so. If the title to the tenant's lease is already registered, an application for merger of the freehold and leasehold titles may be made after completion. If the tenant's leasehold interest in the property is subject to a mortgage which is not discharged on completion of the purchase of the reversion, the freehold and leasehold titles cannot be merged.[2]

5.6.4.   The landlord should include a contractual provision to the effect that the tenant will remain liable on the tenant's covenants contained in the lease until actual completion. Without such a clause it could be argued that the lease under which the tenant currently holds the property comes to an end on the contractual completion date irrespective of whether actual completion occurs then or later. This would mean that the landlord would be unable to enforce covenants or to recover any rent from the tenant during the period between the contractual completion date and actual completion. Alternatively a contractual condition may be inserted to the effect that the sale of the property is subject to the terms of the lease, the lease merging with the freehold on completion. The landlord should consider the effect of the contract for sale on his insurance policy covering the property.

5.6.5.   Standard Condition 5.2 and Standard Commercial Property Condition 5.2 (occupation by buyer) do not apply to a sale to a sitting tenant.

1. See Deposit, para. B17. Standard Condition 2.2.1 and Standard Commercial Property Condition 2.2.1 provide for payment of a 10% deposit.
2. See Registration of title, para. G3.

E6. Death and insolvency

See also: Delay and remedies, section M

6.1. Death of a contracting party

6.1.1. The death of one of the contracting parties between contract and completion does not affect the validity of the contract; the benefit and burden of the contract passes to the deceased's personal representatives who are bound to complete.

6.2. Death of sole seller

6.2.1. The seller's personal representatives are bound to complete the contract, but cannot actually do so until issue of the grant of representation. Executors derive their authority from the will, administrators from the grant, but in either case the grant is necessary in order to make title to the buyer. Even in the case of executors, it is unsafe for a person dealing with them to rely on evidence of their appointment other than by production of the grant.

6.2.2. If completion does not take place on the contractual completion date, a breach of contract will occur (irrespective of whether time was of the essence of the completion date) and remedies, e.g. compensation or damages, will be available to the innocent party.[1]

6.2.3. A delay in obtaining the grant of representation will have adverse consequences for a buyer who is involved in a chain of transactions since he may be forced to complete his sale, but unable to complete his purchase simultaneously because of the death of the seller and delay in the issue of the grant of representation. Loss suffered by the buyer, e.g. the cost of temporary accommodation may be claimable as a head of damage against the seller's personal representatives.

6.2.4. If time was not originally of the essence of the completion date, it can be made so by service of a notice to complete. Such a notice can be served on the executor(s) named in the seller's will (if any) and a separate copy of the notice served on the Public Trustee.

6.2.5. The practical answer to the problem of the seller's death is for the seller's solicitor immediately to inform the solicitors for the other party (or parties in a chain of transactions) and (with the authority of those concerned) to apply for an expedited grant of probate or letters of administration. Obviously the closer the death to the date of completion, the more acute the problem, but even in a chain transaction the parties may agree in the circumstances to postpone completion until a grant is obtained if assured that this can be done with expedition. In any circumstances where delay in completion is likely, consideration should be given to the protection of the contract by registration by the buyer's solicitor of a notice (registered land) or a Class C(iv) land charge (unregistered land).

6.2.6. Although generally probate cannot issue within seven days of death (administration within 14 days), there is an exception in case of emergency with leave of two registrars. It is considered that leave would normally be granted in this situation where there is a possibility of damages being awarded against the estate and the Probate Registry will assist with quick responses and advice in such a situation.

6.2.7. A possible solution to the problems caused by the death of the seller before completion is for the executors named in the will to negotiate to allow the buyer into possession pending formal completion. On taking possession the buyer would normally be required to pay a licence fee under the terms of the contract[2] which could be offset against the compensation payable by the personal representatives for late completion.

1. See Delay and remedies, section M.
2. Standard Condition 5.2 and Standard Commercial Property Condition 5.2. See The buyer in occupation, para. E5.

6.3. Death of co-owner

6.3.1. Property owned by beneficial co-owners is held on trust and all the trustees must join in any conveyance of the legal estate.[1] The death of one trustee between contract and completion does not, however, affect the validity of the contract.

6.3.2. Where following the death there still remain at least two trustees of the legal estate, the transaction can proceed to completion without delay. It will be necessary to produce the death certificate of the deceased in order to provide the buyer with evidence of the death. The purchase deed will need to be redrawn to reflect the change of parties to the transaction.

6.3.3. Frequently the legal estate is held by only two trustees (e.g. husband and wife) and the death of one of them will leave only one trustee of the legal estate which will prima facie be insufficient to satisfy Law of Property Act 1925, s.27. If the trustees held the property as joint tenants in equity, the surviving joint tenant will become entitled to the deceased's equitable interest through the law of survivorship (*jus accrescendi*) and can deal with the property as a beneficial owner provided that there is no restriction on the proprietorship register of a registered title or, in unregistered land, that the requirements of Law of Property (Joint Tenants) Act 1964 are satisfied.

6.3.4. *Surviving beneficial joint tenant*

Where the sole surviving joint tenant is to transfer registered land the buyer should:

(a) check that no restriction is entered on the proprietorship register of the title;

(b) redraft the transfer to reflect the change of parties and capacity of the seller;

(c) require the seller to provide evidence of the death,[2] for example, an official copy of the death certificate of the deceased co-owner.

6.3.5. Where the land is unregistered the buyer should:

(a) check the conveyance under which the co-owners *bought* the property to ensure that no memorandum of severance of the joint tenancy has been endorsed on it;

(b) redraft the purchase deed to reflect the change in parties. The conveyance should recite the death and state that the sole seller has become solely and beneficially entitled to the property;

(c) make a Land Charges Department search against the names of both the deceased and the survivor to ensure that no bankruptcy proceedings have been registered against either name.

6.3.6. Steps (a) and (c) immediately above would be done as a matter of course during the normal investigation of title procedure and thus do not put the buyer to extra inconvenience or expense.[3]

6.3.7. If these conditions are not satisfied, another trustee should be appointed to act with the survivor. Where the survivor has become solely and beneficially entitled to the property, delay in completion should be minimal, but normal remedies for delay would in any event be available.[4]

6.3.8. *Surviving beneficial tenant in common*

In all circumstances another trustee should be appointed to act with the surviving tenant in common. This appointment can be effected either by separate deed of appointment or by including the appointment in the purchase deed. In either case the purchase deed will have to be redrafted to reflect the change in parties. The seller's solicitor may act as the second trustee provided that there is no potential conflict of interests between the survivor and other beneficiaries (if any). Alternatively, the other beneficiary (or one of them, being of full age and competence) may be appointed as second trustee of the legal estate.[5] If a dispute arises between the trustees in relation to the sale, delay may occur. The contract is, however, binding and such delay will incur liability to the buyer[6] and the refusal of the new trustee to, e.g. sign the purchase deed will not frustrate the transaction

since the buyer could seek specific performance of the contract or serve a notice
to complete.

6.3.9. Settled land

On the death of a sole tenant for life under Settled Land Act 1925 the position
depends on whether the land remains settled land after the death. If it does, the
trustees of the settlement are entitled to a grant of probate or administration
limited to the settled land, and they will be the persons with capacity to make good
title. If, however, the settlement ends on the death, the former settled land is
included in the grant made to the deceased's ordinary personal representatives
who will perform the contract.

1. Law of Property Act 1925, s.27.
2. Land Registration Rules 2003, r.164.
3. See Investigation of title, para. D2.
4. See Delay and remedies, section M.
5. See Trusts of Land and Appointment of Trustees Act 1996, s.19 in relation to the appointment of new trustees.
6. See Delay and remedies, section M.

6.4. Death of sole buyer

6.4.1. The personal representatives step into the shoes of the deceased and will be bound
to complete the contract. Even in the most straightforward case some delay in
completion may be experienced because the purchase deed will have to be redrafted to reflect the change in parties and the personal representatives cannot
complete until they obtain the grant of representation. Where the purchase was
due to be financed by a mortgage, the death of the borrower (the buyer) will
usually mean that the offer of mortgage is revoked and the personal representatives may therefore find themselves with insufficient funds to complete unless an
alternative source of finance can be found. Where the deceased buyer intended to
purchase the house for his own sole occupation the personal representatives may
feel that since the purpose of the transaction has been defeated they no longer
wish to proceed with the transaction. Unless they can negotiate a written release
with the seller they will, however, be bound to complete (and may then attempt
to resell the property) or face an action in damages from the seller.

6.5. Death of joint buyer

6.5.1. The survivor remains bound by the contract and can be forced to complete. The
joint buyers obtained an equitable interest in the property on exchange of
contracts and it is possible that the deceased's share in the property may on his
death have passed to a third party (not to the co-purchaser) under his will or intestacy. In order to avoid delay while this matter is resolved it may be advisable to
transfer the property into the names of two trustees on completion. In any event
the purchase deed will have to be redrafted to reflect the change in parties.
Finance may have to be rearranged and a new mortgage deed prepared. Some
delay seems to be inevitable and the seller will have a claim against the buyer for
loss caused by the delay.[1] In cases where the surviving buyer (being solely

entitled to the benefit of the contract) decides that he/she no longer wishes to proceed with the purchase, an attempt may be made to negotiate a written release with the seller, but he is under no obligation to accede to this request. Failing a negotiated release the buyer will have to proceed with the purchase and then attempt to resell the property.

1. See Delay and remedies, section M.

6.6. Service of notices on deceased estate owner

6.6.1. If the person serving the notice is at the time of service unaware of the death, service on the deceased at his last known address is valid.

6.6.2. If at the time of service the person serving the notice was aware of the death, notice should be served on the deceased and his personal representatives at the deceased's last known address and a copy of the notice served on the Public Trustee.[1]

1. Law of Property (Miscellaneous Provisions) Act 1994, ss.10–14.

6.7. Bankruptcy of seller

6.7.1. A buyer will usually only be affected by the bankruptcy of the seller if there is a bankruptcy entry shown on the result of his official search or on official copy entries of the title. Such entry may reveal either the presentation of the petition and/or the making of a bankruptcy order.

6.7.2. On the bankruptcy of an individual who is the sole proprietor of the land, the legal estate in the property owned by him passes to his trustee in bankruptcy and the buyer must from that time deal only with the trustee and not the seller. The trustee may be forced to complete the sale by an action for specific performance, subject to his right to disclaim under section 315 of Insolvency Act 1986. Under that section the trustee may, by the giving of a prescribed notice, disclaim any onerous property, which is defined as 'any unprofitable contract, and any other property comprised in the bankrupt's estate which is unsaleable or not readily saleable or is such that it may give rise to a liability to pay money or perform any other onerous act'. 'Onerous' does not in this context extend to disclaiming the contract simply because the trustee can realise more money by entering into some other contract. The trustee might in an appropriate case take the view that the contract constituted a transaction at an undervalue or a preference, in which event he might refuse to complete the transaction on this ground. Assuming the matter proceeds to completion, the purchase deed will have to be redrafted to show the trustee as the seller and the bankrupt will not be a party to the deed.

6.7.3. Between the making of a bankruptcy order and the time at which the bankrupt's estate vests in a trustee, the Official Receiver is the receiver and manager of the bankrupt's estate, but under section 287 of Insolvency Act 1986 his powers in this period are very limited and it is doubtful whether in most cases he would be entitled to complete the transaction. The Official Receiver has, under section 293 of Insolvency Act 1986, 12 weeks following the bankruptcy order in which to decide whether to convene a meeting of creditors to appoint a trustee. If the Official Receiver decides not to summon such a meeting then he must give notice of his decision to the court and to every creditor of the bankrupt known to him or identified in the bankrupt's statement of affairs and as from the giving to the court of such notice the Official Receiver becomes the trustee of the bankrupt's estate (section 293(3)).

6.7.4. If a creditors' meeting is held then a trustee may be appointed at such a meeting. Trust property, which includes property held by co-owners, does not vest in a bankrupt's trustee.

6.7.5. The making of a bankruptcy order effects a severance of a joint tenancy. The bankrupt's beneficial interest in the property will vest in the trustee in bankruptcy. Consequently on the bankruptcy of one co-owner the legal estate is unaffected and completion may proceed, the bankrupt and the co-owner being entitled to convey the legal estate. If the bankrupt will not co-operate it is open to his or her co-trustee to replace the bankrupt on the grounds of the bankruptcy under the provisions of Trustee Act 1925. A buyer should attempt to get the trustee in bankruptcy to join in the purchase deed to give his consent to the sale of the beneficial interest and preferably to give a receipt for the part of the purchase money attributable to the beneficial interest, but cannot insist on this happening, nor can the trustee insist on joining in the deed.

6.8. Bankruptcy of buyer

6.8.1. The benefit of the contract passes to the buyer's trustee in bankruptcy who may complete the transaction subject to his right to disclaim onerous contracts. Where the transaction was to be financed by a mortgage the buyer's mortgage offer will have been revoked by the bankruptcy, and there will obviously be no other available funds to complete the purchase. The trustee is in this situation more likely to disclaim, although he would in so doing forfeit the deposit already paid and be subject to an action brought by the seller against the bankrupt's estate to recover loss suffered. Some delay is inevitable pending the appointment of the trustee and while waiting for his decision whether or not to disclaim. Where one of two or more co-purchasers goes bankrupt, the bankrupt's equitable interest will pass to his trustee.

6.8.2. The remaining buyer(s) may have difficulty in completing on the contractual completion date, or at all, since a joint mortgage offer may have been vitiated by the co-purchaser's bankruptcy. If the non-bankrupt buyer can refinance his purchase he may complete the purchase on his own (he is contractually bound to do so) but would hold the bankrupt's equitable interest in the property on trust for the trustee who might at a later stage wish to sell the property in order to realise this asset for the benefit of the bankrupt's creditors.

6.8.3.   A seller who wished to force completion on a buyer's trustee in bankruptcy must give written notice to the trustee requiring him within a period of 28 days (or such longer period specified by the court) in which to perform or disclaim the contract and the property. If the trustee does not disclaim within this period the right to disclaim is lost. The seller may at all times pursue the remedies open to a seller where a buyer defaults, including bringing an action for specific performance.

6.8.4.   If the seller completes the transaction with the buyer between the presentation of a petition but before the bankruptcy order is made, but having effected a priority search on which no bankruptcy entry appears, the trustee cannot reclaim the purchase price from the seller: this is probably the case even if he is able to prove that after the making of the priority search the seller became aware of the presentation of a bankruptcy petition.

6.9.   Appointment of liquidator

6.9.1.   Every disposition of a company's property after presentation of a winding-up petition to the court is void if a winding-up order is subsequently made unless sanctioned by the court. Accordingly where a petition for the compulsory winding-up of a company is presented the buyer must insist on obtaining the sanction of the court to the completion of the transaction or he must await the result of the petition. In the case of a voluntary liquidation the directors' powers cease on the appointment of a liquidator whether the liquidation is a members' voluntary liquidation or a creditors' voluntary liquidation. A liquidator can complete a sale on behalf of the company and can bring proceedings to force a buyer to complete a transaction. In the case of a compulsory winding up the liquidator will require the sanction of the court to bring proceedings, but in the case of a voluntary winding up no such sanction is required. When a seller company goes into liquidation the liquidator will normally complete the transaction. The company will normally remain as 'seller' and the liquidator will attest the deed on the company's behalf. The liquidator will only become the 'seller' in the purchase deed if an order vesting the legal estate in him has been made by the court, which happens only very rarely. The formalities of a liquidator's appointment are dealt with by Insolvency Rules 4.100–4.105 and a buyer from a liquidator should ensure that those formalities have been complied with.

6.9.2.   Where a liquidator is appointed to a company which is buying land, the liquidator has the power to complete or to disclaim an onerous contract in which latter case the position is the same as already discussed under para. E6.7.1 in the case of an individual buyer becoming insolvent. Non-availability of funds may present practical problems in proceeding to completion. Where the buyer company is in liquidation and does not complete the seller may exercise his contractual rights, including the ability to forfeit any deposit, and in the converse situation the buyer has the right to recover his deposit from any stakeholder. If the matter does not proceed to completion then any damages will be a proveable debt in the liquidation.

6.10. Appointment of administrative receiver

6.10.1. The appointment of an administrative receiver does not affect the validity of the transaction. The powers of the receiver will be those contained in the instrument under which he was appointed and in addition he will have the powers conferred upon him by Schedule 1 Insolvency Act 1986. Most of the powers of the directors will be suspended by virtue of the appointment of the administrative receiver. The appointment of a receiver has the effect of crystallising floating charges created by the company and a buyer from a company in receivership will have to take steps to obtain the release of the property from the now fixed charge. The receiver may join in the purchase deed on sale to give a receipt for the purchase price and will execute the purchase deed on behalf of the company. The company normally remains the 'seller' under the contract or purchase deed since if the receiver enters the transaction in his own name he will assume personal liability for it. For this reason, any contract entered into by the receiver in the name of the company will normally contain a clause excluding the receiver's personal liability and excluding the effect of any implied covenants for title from the purchase deed. Where the company is buying land, the receiver will execute the purchase deed on behalf of the company, but in this situation the financing of the purchase may have to be re-arranged and this may result in some delay. A certified copy of the document appointing the receiver should be handed over on completion.

6.11. Signature of documents

6.11.1. *Trustee in bankruptcy*

A trustee in bankruptcy should sign a contract using the following wording: 'trustee in bankruptcy of XY a bankrupt [without personal liability]'.

6.11.2. The attestation clause of the purchase deed can be expressed in the following way: 'signed as a deed by CD in the presence of .... (trustee of the estate of XY, a bankrupt)'.

6.11.3. Many insolvency practitioners seek to limit their liability by adding the words 'without personal liability' to the attestation clause. It is understood that these words imply that the trustee can still be sued *qua* trustee, but that liability in him in his personal capacity is excluded. These words do not preclude negligence liability for which most insolvency practitioners will carry indemnity insurance.

6.11.4. *Supervisor of voluntary arrangement*

The company, individual or mortgagee will execute the document in the normal way unless the scheme is such that the land has been vested in the supervisor or trustee. If this occurs the supervisor must transfer and execute as a trustee.

6.11.5. A contract signed or transfer executed by a supervisor may use the following wording: 'Supervisor of XY acting in the voluntary arrangement of XY [without personal liability]'.

6.11.6. The words 'without personal liability' have the same effect as is noted in para. E6.11.3.

6.11.7. *Law of Property Act receiver*

A Law of Property Act receiver can sign a contract or execute a transfer provided that the appointing lender delegates this power. The authority from the lender should be in writing but under section 1 of Law of Property (Miscellaneous Provisions) Act 1989 does not need to be under seal. A receiver signs a contract as agent for the borrower. It is normal practice in these circumstances for the appointing lender to sign the contract and execute the transfer using his power of sale. The capacity in which the lender sells will affect the nature of the implied covenants for title given to the buyer in the purchase deed.

6.11.8. *Debenture holder*

A debenture holder can sign in the name of the company provided that he holds a valid power of attorney from the company.

6.11.9. *Administrative receiver*

In the absence of any provision to the contrary, Insolvency Act 1986, s.42 and Sched. 1 gives power to an administrative receiver to execute deeds and other documents in the name of and on behalf of the company using the company's seal.

6.11.10. *Company in administration*

A deed should be executed using the common seal of the company in the presence of the administrator.

6.11.11. *Administrative receiver of company in liquidation*

The following form of wording is accepted by the Land Registry:

Signed as a deed by [*the company*] (in liquidation) by its administrative receiver *AB* appointed under a [*debenture*] dated [*date*] in favour of [*the debenture holder*] in the presence of:

[*the company*] by its receiver *AB*

Signature of witness . . . .

Name (in BLOCK CAPITALS) . . . .

Address . . . .

. . . .

6.11.12. The receiver should provide evidence of his appointment and acceptance of office.

6.11.13. *Execution on behalf of insolvent company*

(a) Execution by receiver (whether or not the company is in liquidation)

The following form of execution is acceptable to the Land Registry:

Signed as a deed by [*the company*] by
its administrative receiver
AB appointed under a [*debenture*] dated
[*date*] in favour of [*the debenture holder*]
in the presence of:

[*the company*]
by its receiver *AB*

Signature of witness ....

Name (in BLOCK CAPITALS) ....

Address ....

....

(b) Execution by administrative receiver (whether or not the company is in liquidation)

As for receiver (para. E6.11.11) omitting reference to the liquidation where appropriate.

(c) Execution by administrator

Using the common seal of the company in the presence of the administrator:

Common seal of company

The common seal of *(name of company)*
in administration was affixed in the
presence of:

....
Administrator

(d) Execution by liquidator

Using the common seal of the company in the presence of the liquidator:

Common seal of company

The common seal of *(name of company)*
(in liquidation) was affixed in the
presence of *(name of liquidator)*:

....
Liquidator

6.11.14. *Transfer by Law of Property Act receiver*

The powers of administrative receivers do not extend to receivers appointed under section 101(1)(iii) of Law Property Act 1925. Therefore, even if sales are arranged by receivers appointed under Law of Property Act 1925, it is better practice to arrange for the appointing lender to sign the contract once his power of sale has arisen and thereafter for the lender to execute the conveyance or to transfer as lender.

6.11.15. Although the case of *Windsor Refrigeration Co. Ltd* v. *Branch Nominees Ltd*[1] states that if a receiver uses a power of attorney to sell under a contractually extended power, his appointment should be by deed rather than under hand, conventionally administrative receivers are appointed under hand and the appointment is regarded as merely identifying the receiver upon whom the debenture confers the power of attorney.

6.11.16. In *Phoenix Properties Ltd* v. *Wimpole Street Nominees Ltd*[2] one of the questions addressed by the court was whether a receiver appointed by a debenture holder *in writing* and not under seal had the power to bind a borrower to a conveyance of the legal estate in the property charged by the debenture. It was held that, since the irrevocable appointment of the receiver as attorney for the company was contained in a debenture executed as a deed by the company itself, the common law rule requiring that a receiver should be appointed under seal was satisfied. In other words, provided that the company has executed the debenture under seal, the receiver can then validly be appointed by the debenture holder in writing alone.

6.11.17. If a receiver sells with a power of attorney in place of a lender, he will not be able to sell the property free of incumbrances and a deed of release will also need to be executed by the lender and any other charge holders. In this instance, care should be taken to ensure the deed of release is executed by the lender after the execution of the transfer, as otherwise there is a risk that the receiver has no power to sell the property due to the determination of his power of sale and power of attorney under the debenture. However, if the lender sells as outlined above, the property will automatically be sold free of the mortgage and will remove subsequent charges from the title.

6.11.18. *Transfer by debenture holder*

A debenture holder can sign in the name of the company provided he holds a valid power of attorney from the company. The attestation clause should read as follows:

Signed as a deed by *(name of company)* acting by *(name of attorney)* duly appointed to execute as an officer of *(name of Bank)* pursuant to clause [of a debenture dated] in the presence of:	Sign here the name of the company and your own name with details of the resolution appointing you *(Example: John Smith Limited by its attorney Jane Brown duly appointed officer of* [ ] Bank by a resolution of [ ] Bank plc dated [ ]

6.11.19. *Signature of contracts*

Due to the doubt cast by Lord Reading in the case of *Brandt (H.O.) & Co.* v. *Morris (H.N.) & Co.*[3] the better view is that agreements should be signed by including the extra words 'without personal liability' in order to ensure that a signatory signs as agent and not principal. The following is a suggested example of how agreements should be signed:

'Signed as agent for ABC LIMITED without personal liability	Signature of supervisor/ administrator/ administrative receiver/ liquidator/trustee'

6.11.20. After winding up, or after the presentation of a winding-up petition, a better wording may be:

'Signed in the name of ABC LIMITED by its [administrator/ administrative receiver] JOHN SMITH ESQ. Without personal liability'	Signature: ABC LIMITED [in liquidation]

1. [1961] Ch 88.
2. [1989] Ch 737.
3. [1917] 2 KB 784.

E7. Foreign companies

7.1.	What is the status of the foreign company?	7.3.	Execution of documents
7.2.	What are the powers of the company?	7.4.	Disposals by foreign companies

7.1. What is the status of the foreign company?

7.1.1. If it is recognised as a corporation under its foreign law it will be treated as such by English law.

7.1.2. If the status of the company is not clear from its documents, further evidence of status will be needed before an application for registration of title can be made. This will consist either of an unequivocal certificate by the company's solicitors that it is a corporation validly incorporated under the law of its country of origin or a letter from a lawyer practising in the foreign country confirming that the applicant is a corporation under that law. Confirmation should also be obtained of the corporation's power to enter the particular transaction and of the authenticity of a named person or persons to sign the contract/purchase deed on the corporation's behalf.

7.1.3. The information in para. E7.1.2 does not apply to companies incorporated in Scotland. Companies registered in the Channel Isles or Isle of Man, however, are foreign companies.

7.1.4. Solicitors acting for the foreign company should ensure that any local consent needed for the transaction is obtained. The documents relating to the transaction should also make it clear which jurisdiction is applicable to the transaction.

7.1.5. If the original documents are not in English or Welsh a certified translation should be supplied with an application to register at the Land Registry.

7.2. What are the powers of the company?

7.2.1. This question is not usually relevant in the case of companies incorporated in the European Union nor where there is evidence that the law of the country of origin contains provisions equivalent to the powers conferred by the Companies Acts on trading companies. In other cases any limitation on the power of the company will be reflected on the register of title by an appropriate restriction. The constitution of the company will be perused to see what its powers are and, if not clear, evidence of the powers will be requested.

7.3. Execution of documents

7.3.1. The Foreign Companies (Execution of Documents) Regulations 1994 (S.I. 1994/950) have the effect of making Companies Act 1985, s.36(A) (as amended) apply to foreign companies. Section 36(A) abolished the requirement for a company to execute a deed by using its company seal. Prior to 1994 this section was until then of little use to foreign companies, which in many cases did not have company seals of the type used in England and Wales. Although the intention of the Rules is to allow foreign companies to execute deeds by the same method as applies to English companies, thus dispensing with the need for proof of due execution under the jurisdiction of incorporation, the Rules actually deem a deed to be correctly executed by a foreign company if the execution complies with the rules of execution under the jurisdiction of the company's incorporation. It may still therefore be necessary to provide proof that the execution of the document complies with foreign law. Schedule 9 of the Land Registration Rules 2003 contains a form of execution to deal with execution by foreign companies without using a common seal. The prescribed form of execution in Form E is as follows:

Signed as a deed on behalf of *(name of company)* a company incorporated in (territory), by *(full name(s) of person(s) signing),* being [a] person[s] who, in accordance with the laws of that territory, [is] [are] acting under the authority of the company.	Signature Authorised signatory (*or* signatories)

In the case of an overseas company having a common seal, the form of execution appropriate to a company registered under the Companies Acts may be used, with such adaptations as may be necessary, in place of execution by a person or persons acting under the authority of the company. See also the appropriate practice material issued by the Land Registry.

7.4. Disposals by foreign companies

7.4.1. When a foreign company is disposing of property which it owns the following question is relevant: does the company have power to make the disposition? This will only be of concern where a restriction is already on the register. Provided the terms of the restriction can be complied with the transaction can proceed.

F. COMPLETION

F1. Date and time of completion

1.1. **Date**	1.2. **Time**

See also: Delayed completion, para. M1

1.1. Date

1.1.1. The date of completion will be agreed between the solicitors for the parties (after consultation with their respective clients) shortly before exchange of contracts.

1.1.2. Where the buyer's purchase is dependent on his sale of another property the completion dates in both contracts must be synchronised. It follows that the completion dates in all transactions in a chain of transactions must also be synchronised if the chain is not to break.

1.1.3. In residential transactions a completion date 28 days or less from the date of exchange is common. Sufficient time must be allowed between exchange and completion for the respective solicitors to undertake the pre-completion steps in the transaction. If it is anticipated that the clients will wish to complete very quickly after exchange, arrangements can usually be made for some of the pre-completion steps in the transaction to be effected before exchange, e.g. preparation of the purchase deed.

1.1.4. In the absence of express agreement Standard Condition 6.1.1 provides that completion shall take place on the 20th working day after exchange. Standard Commercial Property Condition 6.1.1 contains identical wording.

1.1.5. Under Standard Condition 6.1.1 and Standard Commercial Property Condition 6.1.1 time is not of the essence of the completion date (unless a notice to complete has been served); thus although a delay in completion beyond the date fixed in the contract would give rise to an action in damages at the instigation of the innocent party and would activate the compensation provisions of Standard Condition 7.3 and Standard Commercial Property Condition 7.3, the delay would not of itself entitle the innocent party to withdraw from the contract at that stage.[1] In the absence of this provision time would be of the essence of the completion date (thus enabling the innocent party to withdraw from the contract if delay occurs) where the common law so provides, e.g. in the case of the sale of a business as a going concern. Since delay in completion can occur for reasons beyond the control of the contracting parties, e.g. postal delays, it is not generally a good idea to make time of the essence of the completion date. If exceptionally it is desired to make time of the essence, this may be done by inserting an express provision to this effect in the contract, e.g. by adding the words 'as to which time shall be of the essence' alongside the insertion of the contractual completion date.

1. See Delayed completion, para. M1.

1.2. Time

1.2.1.   Where a buyer's purchase is dependent on the receipt of money from a related sale, the solicitor must ensure that arrangements are made to complete the sale before the purchase to allow funds received from the sale to be utilised in the purchase.

1.2.2.   Where the transaction is part of a chain such arrangements may be complex. Most contracts do not require completion to take place by a certain time, but merely provide that, where the completion money arrives at the nominated bank after a specified time (e.g. 2 p.m.), it is deemed to have arrived on the next working day for certain purposes (e.g. so as to entitle the seller to interest). Special conditions may however require completion to take place at a specified time. In practice, particularly if the chain is long, funds will be transferred from the first (time) buyer as early as 9 a.m. and the funds will travel by a series of inter-bank tele-graphic transfers until the deadline of 2 p.m. or even later. Security is maintained in two ways. First each solicitor will not transmit purchase funds until after the sale proceeds reach his bank. Second, the keys to the property being sold will not be released to the buyer or his agent until the seller's solicitor has received the purchase funds.

1.2.3.   Even where a seller has no related purchase, he should ensure that the com-pletion time agreed allows sufficient time for the proceeds of sale to be banked on the day of completion. If the money is not banked or remitted to the mortgagee until the following working day the seller will suffer loss of interest on his money. To this end a completion time later than 2 p.m. is inadvisable.

1.2.4.   Provided each set of funds reaches its destination before bank closing on the day of completion, the strict timetable of 2 p.m. is unlikely to be enforced. Nevertheless, Standard Condition 6.1.2 and Standard Commercial Property Condition 6.1.2 provide that if completion does not take place by 2 p.m. on the day of completion, interest for late completion becomes payable. It is therefore important for the solicitor to ensure that there is as little delay as possible between receipt of the sale proceeds and release of the purchase money so that his client does not become liable to pay compensation at the contractual interest rate for the delay which he cannot, in turn, recover from his buyer. Standard Condition 6.1.2 does not apply where the sale is with vacant possession and the seller has not vacated the property by 2 p.m. on the date of actual completion.

F2. Place of completion

2.1. Place of completion

2.1.1. By Standard Condition 6.2 completion is to take place in England and Wales, either at the seller's solicitor's office or at some other place which the seller reasonably specifies. Standard Commercial Property Condition 6.2 contains an identical provision.

2.1.2. These conditions mirror the convention that the money goes to the deeds.

2.1.3. Where the seller has an undischarged mortgage over the property and the seller's solicitor is not also acting for the lender, completion may be required to take place at the offices of the seller's lender's solicitors.

2.1.4. Where there is a complex chain of transactions it may sometimes be convenient for some or all of the solicitors for the parties involved in the chain to meet at a mutually convenient location in order to complete several of the transactions in the chain within a very short interval.

2.1.5. Under Standard Condition 6.2 and Standard Commercial Property Condition 6.2 the choice of venue for completion is given to the seller. If completion is not to take place at the seller's solicitor's office he should give the buyer's solicitor sufficient notice of the chosen venue to allow the buyer's solicitor to make his arrangements for attendance at completion and/or transmission of funds. If possible, the buyer's solicitor should be informed of the venue for completion in the answers given to his requisitions on title.

2.1.6. Although traditionally the buyer's solicitor attends the seller's solicitor's office in person to effect completion, it is more common today (especially in residential transactions) for completion to be effected by using the Law Society's Code for Completion by Post[1] with the transmission of funds being made directly to the seller's solicitor's bank account. In such cases the actual place of completion is of little significance to the transaction so long as both parties' solicitors are able to contact each other by telephone, fax or email to confirm the transmission and receipt of funds on the day of completion itself.

2.1.7. If the sale is with vacant possession and the buyer is in doubt whether or not the seller will comply with this condition (e.g. because of the presence of tenants or other non-owning occupiers in the property) he may consider the benefits of insisting on completion taking place at the property itself following an inspection of the property. The buyer may also wish to complete at the property if he, for other reasons, needs to inspect the property or its contents before completion, e.g.

to check an inventory of stock or fittings. In such cases the buyer should have included a special condition in the contract stating that completion shall take place at the property, or, if this was not possible, make his request to the seller's solicitor in adequate time before completion to permit the necessary arrangements to be made. Unless such a term is included as a contractual condition, the seller is under no obligation to accede to the buyer's request since the choice of location for completion is, by Standard Condition 6.2 and Standard Commercial Property Condition 6.2, given to the seller.

1. The text of the Code is set out in full in Appendix III.3.

F3. The money

See also: Financial services, para. A4
Preparing for completion, para. E4
Completion, para. F4

3.1. Method of payment

3.1.1. Standard Condition 6.7 provides that the buyer is to pay the money due on completion in one or more of the following ways:

(a) legal tender;

(b) a banker's draft drawn by and on a clearing bank (defined as meaning a bank which is a member of CHAPS Ltd, see Appendix VIII.1);

(c) a direct credit to a bank account nominated by the seller's solicitor;

(d) an unconditional release of a deposit held by a stakeholder.

3.1.2. Under Standard Commercial Property Condition 6.7 money is to be paid by direct credit and payment by any other method requires an express amendment to Condition 6.7.

3.1.3. In the absence of agreement to the contrary, the seller's solicitor is entitled to refuse payment tendered by any method other than those mentioned in the contract. A special condition in the contract is required if payment is to be made in foreign currency or out of the jurisdiction.

3.1.4. Notes and gold coins are legal tender up to any amount,[1] but other coins are subject to the limits imposed in Coinage Act 1971, s.2. Currently these limits restrict payment by cupro-nickel or silver coins with a value exceeding 10p (including £1 coins) to a maximum face value of £10. Payment by cupro-nickel or silver coins with a face value not exceeding 10p are limited to a maximum of £5, and bronze coins to a maximum of £0.20.

3.1.5. Provided the parties agree, payment of money on completion may be made by a solicitor's clients' account cheque or building society cheque, but in practice payment by such methods is uncommon since there is the danger that the cheque could in theory be stopped. A 'stop' on a building society cheque would in practice be very rare and is generally confined to cases of theft, forgery, or fraud.

1. Currency and Bank Notes Act 1954, s.1.

3.2. Banker's draft

3.2.1. Where completion is to take place in person payment by banker's draft is the most common method of payment.

3.2.2. The buyer's solicitor may have the draft drawn in favour of the seller's solicitor (or as he has directed) or may prefer to have the draft drawn to show the buyer's solicitor as payee. In the latter case, the draft will be endorsed in favour of the seller's solicitor at actual completion, but can easily be paid back into the buyer's solicitor's clients' account should completion for some reason not take place on the due date. The draft should not be marked 'account payee only' or 'not negotiable' since the seller's solicitor may wish to endorse the draft to a third party, e.g. to use towards payment in another transaction.

3.2.3. A banker's draft can be regarded as being analogous to cash. It is therefore sensible to take precautions against forgery and theft of a draft. For this reason it may be considered to be unwise to send a banker's draft through the post and, where completion is to take place through the post or through the attendance of an agent, some other method of transmission of funds should be used.

3.3. Telegraphic transfer of funds

3.3.1. Frequently completion will take place using the Law Society's Code for Completion by Post (see Appendix III.3). In such a case the parties will normally agree to transfer the amount of money needed to complete the transaction through the telegraphic transfer (or similar) system. Payment under a contract governed by the Standard Commercial Property Conditions must be by way of direct credit (unless the contract has been amended to provide otherwise).

3.3.2. The seller's solicitor should inform the buyer's solicitor of the amount needed to complete the transaction and of the details of the account to which the funds are to be remitted. This information is normally given in response to the buyer's requisitions on title.

3.3.3. The buyer's solicitor should instruct his bank to remit funds from the buyer's solicitor's clients' account to the account nominated by the seller's solicitor. Instructions to the bank must be given sufficiently early on the day of completion to ensure that the funds arrive at their destination before the time-limit for receipt of funds, as specified in the contract, expires. Some delay in the transmission of funds may be experienced where the funds are to be transmitted from one bank to another as opposed to transfers between different branches of the same bank.

3.3.4. The seller's bank should be asked to telephone the seller's solicitor to inform him of the receipt of the funds immediately they arrive. Completion may proceed as soon as the seller's solicitor is satisfied as to the arrival of the funds in his clients' account, and it is courteous for him to confirm the safe arrival of the funds to the buyer's solicitor.

3.4. Cleared funds

3.4.1. In order to avoid breach of Rule 22 Solicitors' Accounts Rules 1998, payment of completion money should only be made from cleared funds in client account. This means that the buyer's solicitor must ensure that he is put in funds by his client in sufficient time for those funds to clear through client account before it becomes necessary to draw against them.

3.5. Time for payment

3.5.1. Standard Condition 6.1.2 and Standard Commercial Property Condition 6.1.2 encourage the payment of money on the day of completion by 2 p.m. in default of which payment is treated (for compensation purposes only) as having been received on the next following working day which may result in the buyer becoming liable to pay compensation for late completion under Condition 7.3 of both sets of conditions. Standard Condition 6.1.2 does not apply where the sale is with vacant possession and the seller has not vacated the property by 2 p.m. on the date of actual completion.

3.5.2. Where the transaction forms part of a chain of transactions it may be necessary to insert a time-limit for the payment of completion money imposing a contractual obligation to complete by this specified time (see para. F1.2.2.). If this is not done, there is a danger that the seller will not receive the funds from his sale in sufficient time to allow him to meet the time-limit in his related purchase transaction.

3.6. Chain transactions

3.6.1. As noted in para. F3.5.2, it will frequently be necessary to insert a special condition relating to the time of completion in order to allow sufficient time for funds to be received by the seller's solicitor and then utilised to complete a purchase transaction later on the same day.

3.6.2. Where it is known that the transaction forms part of a chain arrangements may be made by the solicitors involved for the funds to be sent directly to their ultimate destination. Thus if A is selling to B and buying from C, he may need to use part of the proceeds of sale (to be paid by B) towards payment for his purchase from C. In this case A's solicitor may ask B's solicitor to send a specified part of the sale money direct to C's solicitor, the remainder being sent to A's solicitor in the normal way. C's solicitor must be asked to telephone A's solicitor when he receives the funds from B's solicitor so that the transaction between A and B can be completed. C's solicitor will also be asked to undertake to hold the funds received from B's solicitor to A's order until completion of the transaction between A and C is ready to proceed. Such an arrangement can help to avoid delays in the transmission of funds, since fewer telegraphic transfers are required (particularly in a long chain), and thus it ultimately helps to ensure that all transactions within the chain are completed within their relevant time-limits. The solicitors involved must nevertheless be careful to obtain the written authority of the parties since the protection given by Law of Property Act 1925, s.63, only applies where the money is paid to the seller's solicitor. It is a breach of trust for the buyer's solicitor to part with the money without having the title deeds in his possession or without knowing that the seller's solicitor is holding the deeds to the buyer's solicitor's order.

3.7. Discharge of seller's mortgage

3.7.1. The seller's existing mortgage over the property being sold will frequently be discharged immediately after completion of the sale using part of the proceeds of sale to make payment to the lender.

3.7.2. The seller's solicitor may choose to ask the buyer to draw separate banker's drafts for completion, one in favour of the lender for the amount needed to discharge the mortgage and the other, for the balance of the money due, in the seller's solicitor's favour.

3.7.3. Alternatively, where payment is to be made by telegraphic transfer, the seller's solicitor may request that a direct transfer is made to the separately represented mortgagee's solicitor, and a second transfer, for the balance of funds due, to the seller's solicitor. The method for achieving this is broadly similar to the method described in para. F3.6.2.

3.8. Undertakings to remit funds

3.8.1. In some circumstances the seller's solicitor may be prepared to complete the transaction against the buyer's solicitor's undertaking to remit funds within a specified time, the actual transfer of the money occurring after completion has taken place. The seller's solicitor should only do this if he has his client's authority to do so, and the client understands the consequences of completing against an undertaking. In such circumstances the seller should consider protecting his lien against the property for the unpaid purchase price by the registration of a notice against the title. It should, however, be noted that Standard Condition 6.5.1 and Standard Commercial Property Condition 6.5.1 have the effect of removing the seller's lien over documents of title. He may, however, have an equitable lien over the property for money not paid. If the land is unregistered a priority notice should be lodged before completion.

3.8.2. Such an undertaking given by the buyer's solicitor is binding on him and should therefore not be given unless the buyer's solicitor is absolutely certain that he will be put in funds in sufficient time to comply with his promise to the seller's solicitor.

3.8.3. If completion does take place on the strength of the buyer's solicitor's undertaking, the seller is bound to complete and may not retain possession of the title deeds and other documents even if the money does not arrive when promised. The common law lien which the seller may exercise over documents of title until he receives payment in full would be overridden by the seller's solicitor's acceptance of an enforceable undertaking from the buyer's solicitor. Standard Condition 6.5.1 and Standard Commercial Property Condition 6.5.1 remove the seller's lien over documents of title.

3.9. Release of deposit

3.9.1. A deposit which is held in the capacity of agent for the seller belongs to the seller and does not need to be released on completion.

3.9.2. Where a deposit is held by some person in the capacity of stakeholder, the buyer's solicitor should on completion provide the seller's solicitor with a written release addressed to the stakeholder, authorising payment of the deposit to the seller or as he directs. Where the deposit is being held by the seller's solicitor as stakeholder, a written release is often neither asked for nor provided, the release being given orally once completion has taken place. If the deposit is being held by a third party, e.g. an estate agent in the capacity of stakeholder, a written release will be required. In the absence of a written release the stakeholder, on being satisfied that the conditions under which he holds the money have been fulfilled, may pay the stake money to the party whom he considers entitled to receive it, subject to his becoming liable to account to the other party if he makes the wrong judgment in relation to the handing over of the money.[1]

1. *Hastingwood Property Ltd* v. *Saunders Bearman Anselm* [1991] Ch 114.

3.10. Retentions from the purchase price

3.10.1. Where it has been agreed that a retention should be deducted from the purchase price on completion, e.g. to cover the cost of outstanding works to be done by the seller, the agreement should be expressly clear as to whether interest is payable on the retained sum and to whom, and whether the buyer is to withhold the sum on completion or, e.g. to pay the full purchase price to the seller's solicitor with the amount of the agreed retention being held by the seller's solicitor in a deposit account opened in the joint names of the seller and buyer until the matter is resolved. It is also desirable to agree that if the obligation secured by the retention money has not been performed by a particular date, the retention money would be remitted back to the buyer to deal with the matter instead, and if it costs more than the retention money to do so, the buyer can claim the deficit from the seller.

3.11. Money laundering[1]

3.11.1. Where a transaction is being funded by the client in cash, or via a third party (other than a recognised lender) or from a foreign bank, the solicitor should be alert to the possibilities of money laundering and should take appropriate steps to check the identity of the client and the source of the funds.

1. See Money laundering, para. A23; Mortgage fraud, para. A24; Money Laundering Warning Card, Appendix IV.2.; Property Fraud Warning Card II, Appendix IV.3.

F4. Completion

See also: Preparing for completion, para. E4
Date and time of completion, para. F1
Place of completion, para. F2
The money, para. F3
After completion, para. G1
Delayed completion, para. M1
Code for Completion by Post, Appendix III.3

4.1. Introduction

4.1.1. The date and time of actual completion will be specified in the contract but may be varied by subsequent agreement between the parties. Similarly the place and method of completion will previously have been agreed by the parties.

4.1.2. Completion may take place by personal attendance by the buyer's solicitor or his agent or through the post using the Law Society's Code for Completion by Post (see Appendix III.3).

4.2. Completion by personal attendance

4.2.1. Personal attendance by the buyer's solicitor on the seller's solicitor or seller's lender's solicitor is the traditional method by which completion takes place but is not commonly used in uncomplicated transactions where, particularly in residential conveyancing, it is now more common for completion to take place through the post.

4.2.2. If the transaction is complex or of a high value, consideration should be given to the benefits of completing the matter in person since, when this method is employed, the buyer's solicitor is able physically to inspect all the relevant documents prior to handing over the purchase price; he takes possession of those documents immediately completion has taken place instead of having to rely on the seller's solicitor's undertaking to forward the documents to him, and there is therefore absolute certainty that all the documents are in order and that completion has taken place at a specific time. Against these benefits may be set the time and expense involved in the buyer's solicitor having to travel to the seller's solicitor's office in order to attend personally at completion.

4.2.3. A few days before the date arranged for completion the buyer's solicitor should telephone the seller's solicitor to arrange a mutually convenient appointment for completion.

4.2.4. On the morning of completion a banker's draft for the amount required to complete the transaction should be drawn by the buyer's solicitor and kept in a safe place until it is needed.[1]

4.2.5. The representative from the buyer's solicitors who is to attend completion should take with him to the seller's solicitor's office the following items:

(a) the contract (queries which arise may sometimes be resolved by checking the terms of the contract);

(b) evidence of title (in order to verify the title);

(c) a copy of the approved draft purchase deed and of any other documents which are to be executed by the seller and handed over on completion (in case there is any query over the engrossments);

(d) answers to requisitions on title (some queries which arise, e.g. over who has the keys may be resolved by the answers previously given to requisitions);

(e) the completion checklist and completion statement;[2]

(f) banker's draft;

(g) any documents which are required to be handed over to the seller's solicitor on completion, e.g. release of deposit.

4.2.6. Verifying title

The buyer's time-limit for verifying title, i.e. comparing the original deeds against the evidence of title supplied by the seller, expires with the time-limit for raising requisitions.[3] Strictly therefore the buyer has no right to verify at this stage. In practice verification is not normally carried out at the requisitions on title stage of the transaction unless the transaction is complicated and the buyer's solicitor will check the evidence of title against the original deeds at completion itself. It should, however, be remembered that since the time-limit for verification has now expired, the buyer will have no right to query any defect which he discovers on verification, nor to refuse to complete because of a defect discovered at this stage. In the case of registered land verification is unnecessary since official copy entries of the title will show the true up-to-date position of the register. On a sale by a lender under his power of sale, it is not necessary to obtain discharges relating to subsequent mortgages which will be overreached on the completion of the sale by the selling lender.

4.2.7. When the buyer's solicitor is satisfied as to the title, he should ask the seller's solicitor to hand over the documents necessary to complete the transaction. These documents including the title deeds (in unregistered land) will have been previously agreed in a list drawn up between the parties and itemised on the completion checklist. Except where these documents have recently been checked by verification, the buyer's solicitor should check each document to ensure it is as he expects to find it, and tick each off on his list as he receives it. The purchase deed will be among the documents to be received by the buyer's solicitor and should be dated at completion after being checked by the buyer's solicitor to ensure it has been validly executed and has not been altered since the buyer last saw the document. The seller's solicitor will have prepared a schedule of deeds in duplicate, one copy of which will be handed to the buyer's solicitor to keep; the other should be signed by the buyer's solicitor when he is satisfied that he has received all the documents listed on it, and returned to the seller's solicitor as evidence for his file of the handing over of the deeds.

4.2.8. Depending on the circumstances it may be necessary for the buyer's solicitor to inspect receipts for, e.g. last payment of outgoings where such items have been apportioned on the completion statement. Copies of these receipts should have been supplied to the buyer's solicitor with the completion statement in order to allow him to check the amount of the apportionments. By Standard Condition 6.6 and Standard Commercial Property Condition 6.6 the buyer is required to assume that whoever gave any receipt for the payment of rent, rentcharge or a service charge which the seller produces was the person or agent of the person then entitled to that rent or service charge. In the absence of this condition from the contract Law of Property Act 1925, s.45(2) requires the buyer to make the same assumptions in respect of rent and rentcharges.

4.2.9. Where the sale includes fittings or chattels, a separate receipt for the money paid for those items should be signed by the seller's solicitor and handed to the buyer's solicitor. A copy of the receipt should be retained by the seller's solicitor. The receipt clause in the purchase deed only operates as a receipt for the money paid for the land; therefore a separate receipt for the money paid for chattels is necessary.

4.2.10. *Discharge of seller's mortgage*

Arrangements for the discharge of the seller's mortgage(s) over the property will have been agreed between the parties at the requisitions on title stage of the transaction. Where the mortgage is a first mortgage of the property in favour of a building society lender, the parties will frequently have agreed to permit the seller to discharge his mortgage after completion takes place by using part of the proceeds of sale to make payment to the lender. In such a case it will have been agreed that the seller's lender's solicitor should hand to the buyer's solicitor on completion an undertaking in the form of wording recommended by the Law Society to discharge the mortgage (para. F4.2.11.) and to forward the receipted deed or Form DS1 to the buyer's solicitor as soon as this is received from the lender. Alternatively the mortgage may be discharged by using the Land Registry END system.[4] An undertaking to discharge the seller's mortgage should only be accepted from a solicitor or licensed conveyancer because of the difficulties of enforcement of undertakings against unqualified persons.[5] The undertaking should also be in the form of wording approved by the Law Society. The current guidance from the Law Society is that it will not normally be advisable to accept an undertaking if the mortgagee is not a member of the

CML, and/or where the amount required to redeem the mortgage exceeds the maximum level of solicitors indemnity insurance (£1 million per claim). In such a case an undertaking should not be accepted and it may be necessary for completion to take place at the lender's solicitors' offices (not the seller's solicitors' offices) or for the lender's solicitor to attend personally at completion in order to discharge the mortgage. If the amount of the mortgage exceeds £1 million consider asking for a warranty from the seller's solicitor that his insurance cover does exceed the amount required to redeem the mortgage. See the Law Society's guidance at Appendix V.1.

4.2.11. The buyer's solicitor must ensure that any undertaking given mentions every subsisting mortgage on the title. The form of wording recommended by the Law Society for undertakings to discharge building society mortgages is as follows:

> 'In consideration of you today completing the purchase of [*insert description of property*] we hereby undertake to pay over to [*insert name of lender*] the money required to discharge the mortgage/legal charge dated [*insert date of charge*] and to forward the receipted mortgage or Form DS1 to you as soon as it is received by us from [*insert name of lender*].'

4.2.12. When the buyer's solicitor is satisfied as to the documents received from the seller's solicitor and the documents which he has inspected, he should hand to the seller's solicitor any documents which the seller's solicitor requires in accordance with the list agreed prior to completion, e.g. release of deposit, and a banker's draft for the amount specified on the completion statement or otherwise notified to the buyer's solicitor by the seller's solicitor.

4.2.13. Where the banker's draft has been made out in the name of the buyer's solicitor it will have to be endorsed over to the seller's solicitor or as he directs. An endorsement may be general or special. To effect a general endorsement the buyer's solicitor simply signs the reverse of the draft using the payee's name as shown on the front of the draft. To effect a special endorsement the buyer's solicitor writes on the reverse of the draft 'pay to the order of [*name of seller's solicitor or as he directs*]' and then signs the endorsement. In either case the buyer's solicitor must ensure that his signature is in an identical form of wording to that used on the front of the draft where the payee is named. In default of this the endorsement may not be accepted by the bank when the draft is presented for payment.

4.2.14. Release of deposit

An unconditional written release of deposit should be supplied in any situation where the deposit under the contract has been held in the capacity of stakeholder. In practice, where the deposit has been held by the seller's solicitor in that capacity, an oral release will suffice. A written release is only therefore necessary where the deposit has been held by a third party, e.g. an estate agent as stakeholder.

4.2.15. Endorsement of memoranda

Where in unregistered land a document affecting the title is not to be handed over on completion, the buyer may want the seller to endorse a memorandum of the transaction on the deed(s) retained by the seller. The endorsement of such a memorandum protects the buyer against a subsequent mistaken or fraudulent re-conveyance of the same property. This is most likely to be needed on the sale of part of unregistered land where the buyer is entitled to insist on the endorsement of the memorandum on the most recent in date of the seller's retained title deeds under Law of Property Act 1925, s.200 (where the seller enters into new restrictive covenants), or where the purchase is from personal representatives of a deceased seller where Administration of Estates Act 1925, s.36(4) gives the buyer the right to insist on the endorsement of a memorandum on the grant of representation. The form of wording to be used for the endorsement should be drafted by the buyer's solicitor and agreed with the seller's solicitor at the requisitions on title stage of the transaction. A copy of the endorsement should be given to the buyer's solicitor for retention by him as evidence that this has been done. In registered conveyancing this procedure is not necessary since once the buyer is registered as proprietor of the land, previous documents relating to the title become irrelevant.

4.2.16. If in unregistered land the seller is entering into new restrictive covenants he should either retain a copy of the conveyance which imposes those covenants or a copy of the covenants themselves. The covenants will be contained in the purchase deed which will be handed to the buyer on completion and unless a copy is retained by the seller, he will have no documentary evidence of the covenants to produce to a buyer on a subsequent sale of the retained land. An alternative is for the conveyance or transfer to be prepared and executed in duplicate, the seller's solicitor retaining the duplicate on completion (or the buyer's solicitor having it denoted for stamp duty when he stamps the original part, and then sending the duplicate to the seller's solicitor).

4.2.17. In some cases the buyer will only be entitled to have copies of documents relating to the seller's title and not the originals. Chiefly this will occur on a sale of part of unregistered land where the seller is entitled to retain the title deeds which relate to the land retained by him. Other examples would include purchases from personal representatives where they are entitled to retain the original grant and purchases from attorneys who hold a general or enduring power. Where a power is a special power, relating only to the sale of this property, the buyer is entitled to the original power. In any case where an original document relevant to the title is not being handed over, the buyer's solicitor should call for the original document and examine his copy against the original. The copy should then be marked to show that it has been examined against the original and is a true copy of the original document. On a sale of part of unregistered land all the documents contained in the abstract or epitome of title will have to be so marked and each examined document should bear the wording 'examined against the original at the offices of [*insert name of seller's solicitors or as appropriate*] signed [*by buyer's solicitor's representative either in his own name or in the name of the firm*] and dated [*insert date of examination*]'. Where a certified copy of a document will be required by the Land Registry the certification should be carried out by a conveyancer for such other person as the registrar may permit) by writing on the document clearly and in a conspicuous position the words 'I certify this to be a true copy of the [*insert type of document*] dated [*insert date of document being* *certified]* signed *[signature of conveyancer]* and dated *[insert date of certification]'*. The name and address of the signatory should also be endorsed.[6] This will assist in the event of the certification later having to be checked in a subsequent transaction. It should be noted that under Powers of Attorney Act 1971, s.3(1)(*b*)(ii), a copy of a power of attorney must be certified on every page.

1. See The money, para. F3.
2. See Preparing for completion, para. E4.
3. Under Standard Condition 4.1.1 and Standard Commercial Property Condition 4.1.1 the buyer must raise his requisitions within six working days after the date of the contract or delivery of evidence of title by the seller, whichever is later. In practice, where title is deduced before exchange of contracts, the right to raise requisitions on certain matters after exchange may be precluded by special condition.
4. See para. G1.10.
5. See *Patel* v. *Daybells* [2001] EWCA Civ 1229 where the Court of Appeal expressed the view that the acceptance of a solicitor's undertaking for Form DS1 could in exceptional circumstances be negligent. Possible examples of exceptional circumstances are for example where the lender was not a member of the Council of Mortgage Lenders or where the amount to be redeemed exceeded the minimum level for solicitors' indemnity insurance. Also see Accepting undertakings on completion following *Patel* v. *Daybells*, Appendix V.1.
6. Land Registration Rules 2003, r.217(1).

4.3. Completion through the post

4.3.1. In many cases, particularly with simple residential transactions, the buyer's solicitor will not wish to attend completion personally. In such a case arrangements may be made with the seller's solicitor to complete the transaction through the post.

4.3.2. Arrangements to complete through the post should be made at the latest at the requisitions on title stage of the transaction, although it is courteous for the buyer's solicitor to ask the seller's solicitor whether this method of completion will be convenient at an earlier stage so that the seller can if necessary obtain the consent of his lender's solicitor to this procedure.

4.3.3. The Law Society's Code for Completion by Post should be used.[1] The buyer's solicitor should agree any variations to the Code in writing with the seller's solicitor well before completion is due to take place. He should also send written instructions to the seller's solicitor specifying precisely what the buyer's solicitor requires the seller's solicitor to do on the buyer's solicitor's behalf at completion and agreeing a time on the day of completion itself when completion will take place.

4.3.4. The seller's solicitor will effectively act as the buyer's solicitor's agent for the purpose of carrying out the completion procedure. The instructions given by the buyer's solicitor should therefore encompass such of the matters detailed in para. F4.2 as the buyer's solicitor would have carried out had he attended personally at completion. If the seller's solicitor perceives any difficulty or ambiguity in the instructions received from the buyer's solicitor, he must resolve that query or ambiguity before completion is due to take place.

4.3.5. The buyer's solicitor must either send the banker's draft to the seller's solicitor to arrive in time for completion and to be held by the seller's solicitor to the buyer's solicitor's order until completion takes place, or, more commonly, remit the necessary funds by telegraphic transfer to the seller's solicitor's nominated bank account to arrive there in time for completion to take place at the agreed time.

4.3.6. On being satisfied as to the proper payment of the completion money, either by draft or telegraphic transfer, the seller's solicitor must carry out the buyer's instructions and effect completion on his behalf. He should then immediately telephone (or fax) the buyer's solicitor to inform him that completion has taken place and post to the buyer's solicitor, by first class post or document exchange, the documents which the buyer is entitled to receive on completion. Where documents are required to be marked, certified or endorsed, the seller's solicitor will carry out these operations on behalf of the absent buyer's solicitor.

4.3.7. Under the Law Society's Code, the seller's solicitor is not entitled to make a charge to the buyer's solicitor for acting as his agent in carrying out completion.

1. The text of the Code is set out in App. III.3.

4.4. Using an agent

4.4.1. If the buyer's solicitor is unable to attend personally at completion, but does not wish to complete through the post, he may appoint another solicitor to act as his agent, the agent attending completion in person and carrying out the same procedures that the buyer's solicitor would have done had he been present.

4.4.2. The agent will generally be a solicitor who practises within the vicinity of the office where completion is due to take place and should be given instructions to act in good time before actual completion day.

4.4.3. The instructions given to the agent should be full and explicit so that the agent is in no doubt as to what he is required to do. Copies of all the documents which the buyer's solicitor would normally take to completion with him should be supplied with the instructions and the agent should be put in funds either by banker's draft or telegraphic transfer so that he has cleared funds in his own clients' account against which to draw the draft for the completion money.

4.4.4. The agent is entitled to charge a reasonable sum for carrying out his duties as agent. The fee should be agreed in advance between the agent and the buyer's solicitor to avoid any later dispute. The buyer's solicitor is then bound to pay the agent's fee after completion irrespective of whether he has received reimbursement from his own client. It should be made clear to the client at the outset of the transaction that if the employment of an agent is required in order to attend completion, the agent's fee will be added as a disbursement on the client's bill.[1]

4.4.5. The agent should attend completion in person and carry out the buyer's solicitor's instructions. As soon after completion as possible he should telephone (telex or fax or email) the buyer's solicitor to confirm that completion has taken place and should send the documents which he has received at completion to the buyer's solicitor by first class post or document exchange.

1. See Estimate for costs, para. A8.

4.5. Synchronisation

4.5.1. Where the client is to complete a sale and purchase of property on the same day, it is essential that the sale actually takes place before the purchase so that the proceeds of sale can be utilised in the later purchase transaction. Sufficient time should be allowed between the times of completion of sale and purchase to permit the funds received from the sale transaction to be transmitted to and received by the seller's solicitor in the purchase transaction within the time-limits specified in the purchase contract.

4.6. Deemed late completion

4.6.1. By Standard Conditions 6.1.2 and 6.1.3, where the sale is with vacant possession and the money due on completion is not paid by 2 p.m. on the day of actual completion (or such other time as may have been agreed by the parties), for compensation purposes completion is deemed to have taken place on the next following working day unless the seller had not vacated the property by 2 p.m. (or other agreed time). The Standard Commercial Property Conditions contain a similar provision. The buyer's solicitor must therefore instruct his bank to remit the completion money in sufficient time to ensure its arrival at its destination bank within the time-limit specified in the contract. In default the buyer may find himself liable to pay compensation to the seller under Standard Condition 7.3 or Standard Commercial Property Condition 7.3.[1]

1. Compensation is discussed in para. M1.4.

4.7. Lender's requirements

4.7.1. The buyer's solicitor will often also be acting as solicitor for the buyer's lender. In such a case the buyer's solicitor should check the lender's requirements for completion when he is preparing his checklist and making arrangements for completion. In most cases the lender's requirements will be identical to the buyer's solicitor's own requirements, but a check on the lender's instructions should always be made to ensure that nothing is overlooked.

4.8.   Problems with vacant possession

4.8.1.   If the buyer's solicitor suspects that there may be practical problems in obtaining vacant possession, he should deal with this matter at an early stage in the transaction. Taking a written release of rights from an occupier and/or joining the occupier as a party to the contract will in most cases resolve the problem, but a signed release is of little comfort if on the day of completion the occupier refuses to vacate the property. If it is suspected that this might happen, the buyer's solicitor may take the precaution of inserting a contractual condition specifying that completion shall take place at the premises themselves so that an inspection of the property can be carried out immediately before completion takes place. Such a condition would have to be inserted into the contract before exchange and it is too late to try and impose such a term just before completion. Standard Condition 6.2 and Standard Commercial Property Condition 6.2 give the seller the right to decide where completion will take place.

4.8.2.   In the absence of a term allowing completion to take place on the premises themselves, the buyer's solicitor may, in appropriate cases, either inspect the property himself on the day of completion, or ask the client or the client's surveyor to do so and then to telephone the buyer's solicitor to confirm that the premises are vacant before completion proceeds. An inspection will also be necessary if the lender's instructions require the solicitor acting for the lender to ensure that vacant possession is obtained. Such an instruction places a heavy responsibility on the lender's solicitor who should seek to delete this term from his instructions.

4.9.   Effect of completion

4.9.1.   In unregistered land, title in the property passes to the buyer on completion.

4.9.2.   In registered land, the legal title does not pass until the buyer has become registered as proprietor of the land.

4.9.3.   On completion the contract merges with the purchase deed in so far as the contract and purchase deed cover the same ground; thus after completion it is not possible to bring an action which arises out of one of the terms of the contract unless that provision has been expressly left extant by a term of the contract itself. For this reason it is common for the contract to contain a non-merger clause. Standard Condition 7.4 and Standard Commercial Property Condition 7.4 say that the provisions within the contract do not merge on completion in so far as there is outstanding liability under these provisions.

4.9.4.   In the absence of a non-merger provision an action on the contract may not be possible after completion has taken place, but an action in tort or for misrepresentation would still be available since neither of these actions is based on the contract.

4.9.5. The principal remedy available to the buyer after completion is an action on the title guarantee or covenants for title, which is further discussed in para. M9.

1. Land Registration Act 2002, s.27(1).

G. POST-COMPLETION

G1. After completion

See also: Undertakings for bridging finance, para. B16
Stamping documents, para. G2
Registration of title, para. G3

1.1. Seller's checklist

1.1.1. Where appropriate to the transaction the following steps should be taken by the seller's solicitor as soon as possible after completion has taken place:

(a) Where completion has taken place by post, telephone the buyer's solicitor to inform him that completion has taken place.

(b) Telephone the estate agent to inform him of completion and to direct him to release the keys to the buyer.

(c) Inform client that completion has taken place.

(d) Where completion has taken place by post, send purchase deed, title deeds and other relevant documents to buyer's solicitor by first class post or document exchange.

(e) If part of the proceeds of sale are to be used towards the purchase of another property on the same day, make arrangements for the transmission of these funds in accordance with instructions received.

(f) Deal with the discharge of the seller's existing mortgage(s) by sending a clients' account cheque for the amount required (as per redemption statement previously obtained) to the lender together with the engrossment of the Form DS1 (or deed of release relating to unregistered land) requesting him to discharge the mortgage and to forward the receipted Form DS1 to you as quickly as possible.[1] If the mortgage is over unregistered land, the lender will, instead of using a Form DS1, complete the receipt clause on the reverse of the mortgage deed and forward the receipted deed to the seller's solicitor. If in unregistered land the lender is not a building society, the lender should be requested to date the receipt with the date of completion in order to avoid the risk of a transfer of the mortgage under Law of Property Act 1925, s.115. Where necessary, the reassignment of collateral security, e.g. a life policy, should also be dealt with, and a lender who has insured the property will also need to be told to cancel the property insurance cover.

(g) If instructed to do so, pay the estate agent's commission and obtain a receipt for the payment.

(h) Account to the seller's bank for the proceeds of sale in accordance with any undertaking given to them.

(i) Account to the client for the balance of the proceeds of sale in accordance with his instructions.

(j) If not already done, draft and remit bill of costs to the client.

(k) Where money is being held by the solicitor on account of costs, it may be transferred to office account provided that the client has expressly or impliedly agreed to this being done.

(l) If the land is to remain unregistered after completion of this transaction make application for registration of land charges at the Land Charges Department.[2]

(m) On receipt of the completed Form DS1 or receipted mortgage from the lender, check the form or receipt to ensure it is correct, then send it to the buyer's solicitor and ask to be discharged from the undertaking given on completion.

(n) Remind the client of the need to notify the local and water authorities of the change of ownership of the property.

(o) Remind the client to cancel insurance cover over the property (and associated insurances if relevant).

(p) Advise the client about the payment of capital gains tax on assessment.

(q) Deal with the custody of deeds in accordance with the client's instructions. Most, if not all, original deeds will have passed to the buyer's solicitor on actual completion, but the seller will have retained custody of such deeds on a sale of part, or may have, e.g. an original grant of representation or power of attorney.

(r) Check through the file to ensure that all outstanding matters have been dealt with before sending the file for storage.

1. Alternatively the mortgage may be discharged using the END system.
2. See section G3 as to the events giving rise to compulsory first registration.

1.2. Buyer's checklist

1.2.1. Where appropriate to the transaction the following steps should be taken by the buyer's solicitor as soon as possible after completion has taken place:

(a) Inform client and his lender that completion has taken place.

(b) Complete the mortgage deed by insertion of the date and any other information which still has to be completed, e.g. date when first repayment is due.

(c) Complete file copies of the mortgage, purchase deed and other relevant documents.

(d) Attend to payment of stamp duty on purchase deed and other appropriate documents.

(e) Submit purchase deed for production to the Inland Revenue (PD stamp).

(f) Register any charge created by a company at Companies House within 21 days of its creation in accordance with Companies Act requirements. This time-limit is absolute and cannot be extended without an order of the court. Failure to register within the time-limit may prejudice the lender's security and will be an act of negligence on the part of the defaulting solicitor.

(g) Account to the buyer's bank for any bridging finance in accordance with any undertaking given to them and ask to be released from that undertaking.

(h) If not already done, draft and remit bill of costs to the client.

(i) Where money is being held by the solicitor on account of costs, it may be transferred to office account provided that the client has expressly or impliedly agreed to this being done.

(j) If the seller's land is to remain unregistered after completion of this transaction make application for registration of land charges at the Land Charges Department within the period given by the previously lodged priority notice, e.g. new restrictive covenants by the seller on a sale of part.

(k) On receipt of the completed Form DS1 or receipted mortgage from the seller's lender's solicitor, check the form or receipt to ensure it is correct, acknowledge its receipt and release the sender from the undertaking given on completion. Alternatively, discharge the mortgage using the END system.

(l) Make copies of all documents which are to be sent to the Land Registry to ensure that file copies exist in case requisitions are raised by the Registry or the documents are lost or damaged before registration is complete.

(m) Make copies of any documents where a request is to be made to the registrar for the original to be returned.[1]

(n) Certify copy documents which are to be sent to the Land Registry.[2]

(o) Make application for registration of title within the relevant priority period (land already registered) or within two months of completion (application for first registration).

(p) Make diary or file prompt entry recording the approximate date when the title information document may be expected to be received from the Land Registry and send a reminder if the document is not received by that time.

(q) Send notice of assignment of a life policy to the insurance company and place their acknowledgement of receipt with the title deeds.

(r) Give notice to the landlord's solicitors of an assignment, mortgage, etc., in accordance with a requirement to that effect in the lease or in the mortgagee's instructions and place their acknowledgement of receipt with the title deeds.

(s) Notify tenants of the change of ownership of the property.

(t) Make application for the discharge of any entry which was lodged to protect the contract.[3]

(u) On receipt of the title information document from the Land Registry, check its contents carefully and ask the Registry to correct any errors which have been made.

(v) Deal with the custody of deeds in accordance with the client's instructions.

(w) Check through the file to ensure that all outstanding matters have been dealt with before sending the file for storage.

NB: Where a separate solicitor has been instructed to act for the buyer's lender, the lender's solicitor will normally have taken custody of the purchase deed and other title deeds on completion and he will assume responsibility for the stamping and registration of the documents in place of the buyer's solicitor.

1. See section G3.
2. See para. F4.2.17.
3. In registered land this will be combined with any application for registration.

1.3. Undertakings

1.3.1. Failure to honour an undertaking is professional misconduct. Any undertaking given must therefore be honoured and the obligations promised must be fulfilled without delay.

1.3.2. A solicitor who has performed his undertaking should formally ask the recipient to release the giver from his undertaking so that the giver has written evidence of the fulfilment of the undertaking. The recipient may either acknowledge the giver's release by letter, or return the original undertaking to the giver, and in either case the evidence of release is to be kept on the giver's file.

1.4. Stamping documents[1]

1.4.1. Documents should be submitted for stamping as soon as possible after completion has taken place to ensure that they will be returned to the buyer's solicitor in sufficient time for an application for registration of title to be made within the appropriate time-limits and to avoid the accrual of interest charges that arise where the duty is not paid or deposited within the 30 days after execution of the instrument.

1.4.2. It is not possible to delay the initial application for registration until the documents have been correctly stamped because in doing so the client might lose the protection of the priority period afforded to him by his pre-completion search. However, the Land Registry's rejection policy is to reject leases and transfers which are unstamped, if it is clear that they should have been stamped. The Land Registry will accept applications in respect of documents which have been sent for adjudication provided a copy of the unstamped document accompanies the application. The Land Registry will also accept applications where the deed requires *ad valorem* duty but has not yet been stamped, provided that at least 20 days have passed since completion, a copy of the dated deed is supplied and it is clear that the original deed is missing as it has not yet been returned by the Stamp Office. Where it is anticipated that there is likely to be a significant delay in stamping the documentation because, for example, valuations are involved or there are technical issues to be debated with the Inland Revenue Stamp Taxes Office, in addition to depositing the duty to avoid interest costs which run during an adjudication the parties should consider completing by means of a declaration of trust and submitting this for stamping as the principal instrument. The legal title can then be transferred upon payment of the fixed duty of £5 as a conveyance not on sale permitting prompt registration of title. Occasionally the Land Registry and the Inland Revenue Stamp Taxes Office will agree to a provisional stamping of the instrument to permit registration upon payment of an agreed amount of stamp duty and a solicitor's undertaking to pursue the adjudication expeditiously and to pay any additional duty and interest eventually assessed. However, this practice is unpublished and not always applied in practice.

G

1.4.3. Where a transfer on sale has to be produced to the Inland Revenue under Finance Act 1931, and is certified as not exceeding the current stamp duty thresholds, the completed Form L(A)451 (PD) may be sent to the Land Registry with the application for registration of title and the Registry will then stamp the form with the Agency's 'received' stamp before forwarding the Form L(A)451 to the Inland Revenue. This procedure circumvents any delay which might otherwise be experienced in separate submission of the document for stamping prior to registration. New leases must be presented to the Stamp Office even if no duty is payable.

1.4.4. Depending on the nature of his instructions and report on title, a lender's solicitor may be under a duty to stamp documents and register at the Land Registry even if the buyer has not put him in funds to do so.

1. See Stamping documents, para. G2.

1.5. **Registration of title**

1.5.1. It is essential that the relevant time-limits for submission of an application for registration of the client's title are complied with. Failure to make an application for first registration within two months of completion results in the transfer of the legal estate becoming void.[1] Failure to make an application for a registration of a dealing within the priority period of 30 business days given by a pre-completion Land Registry search may have the consequence of the client's interest losing priority to another application.[2] In either case, if the client suffered loss as a result of the late application, the solicitor would be liable in negligence.

1.5.2. Delays caused by late return of the documents from the Inland Revenue following an application for stamping or registration at the Companies Registry can be avoided if the procedure outlined in para. G1.4.2 is followed.

1.5.3. The Land Registry will accept an application without a mortgage discharge provided the application contains an explanation for the delay in providing the discharge and confirmation that it will be provided. The Land Registry will allow 20 business days for the discharge to be produced. Before the end of that period an extension can be applied for. The application must state the reason for the delay and give an explanation of the steps taken to obtain the discharge.[3]

1.5.4. Registration of title is further dealt with in para. G3.

1. Land Registration Act 2002, s.7.
2. See Land Registration Rules 2003, r.131 for the definition of 'priority period'.
3. Land Registration Rules 2003, r.16.

1.6. Registration of company charges

1.6.1. Legal charges created by a company are registrable at the Land Registry (or the Land Charges Department in the case of a charge over unregistered land which is not supported by a deposit of title deeds) and, as a separate obligation in relation to any charge on land, at the Companies Registry under Companies Act requirements. Failure to register the charge under the Companies Act 1985 within the 21 days following its creation renders the charge void against a liquidator or another creditor of the company. This time-limit can only be extended by an order of the court which is not automatically granted. Fixed equitable charges and floating charges must also be noted on the register if they are to affect registered land.

1.7. Notices of assignment

1.7.1. Where following completion notice has to be given to a landlord of an assignment or mortgage, or notice given to an insurance company of the assignment of a life insurance policy, such notice should be given in duplicate. The recipient of the notice should be requested to sign one copy of the notice in acknowledgement of its receipt, and to return the receipted copy to the sender. The receipted copy will then be kept with the title deeds as evidence of compliance with this requirement.

1.7.2. In the case of the assignment of a life policy, the notice of assignment should be given as soon as possible after completion, since the giving of the notice establishes the priority of charges and is required to be given by Policies of Assurance Act 1867.

1.7.3.   Where notice is being given under the terms of a lease, it should be delivered within the time-limits specified in the lease together with the appropriate fee.

1.8.   Certifying documents

1.8.1.   Where a certified copy of a document will be required by the Land Registry the certification should be carried out by a conveyancer (or such other person as the registrar may permit) by writing on the copy clearly and in a conspicuous position the words 'I certify this to be a true copy of the [*insert type of document*] dated [*insert date of document being certified*] signed [*signature of conveyancer*] and dated [*insert date of certification*]'. The name and address of the signatory should also be endorsed.[1] This will assist in the event of the certification later having to be checked in a subsequent transaction. It should be noted that under Powers of Attorney Act 1971, s.3(1)(b)(ii), a copy of a power of attorney must be certified on every page.

1. See Land Registration Rules 2003, r.217(1) and para. F4.2.17.

1.9.   Custody of deeds

1.9.1.   Instructions relating to custody will have been obtained from the client at an earlier stage in the transaction.

1.9.2.   In many cases the client's lender will require custody of the deeds after completion or, if this is not the case, the client may have been advised to deposit the deeds with his bank or in the solicitor's strongroom.

1.9.3.   Where the original deeds are not to be sent to the client himself, it is courteous to photocopy (the principal title deeds) and send these copies to the client who will thus have immediate access to the relevant information in the case of, e.g. a dispute over a right of way or restrictive covenant.

1.9.4.   Before deeds are sent to a mortgagee (or other third party) for custody, they should be checked for accuracy and a schedule of deeds drawn up in duplicate. The recipient should be asked to acknowledge the receipt of the deeds by signing and returning one copy of the schedule. This signed acknowledgement will then be placed on the buyer's solicitor's file as evidence that the deeds have been sent to the recipient.

1.9.5.   Deeds should normally be sent by recorded delivery, insured post or document exchange to ensure their safe arrival at their destination.

1.9.6.   If deeds are to remain in the solicitor's own strongroom, a schedule of the deeds should be drawn up in duplicate, one copy being placed with the deeds, the other remaining in the solicitor's file. In no circumstances should original deeds be left in the solicitor's file when the file is sent for storage. If deeds are kept in the solicitor's strongroom, the solicitor owes a duty of care to his client and, if the deeds are lost, the solicitor may not charge the client with the cost of replacement.

1.10. Electronic Notification of Discharge (END)[1]

1.10.1. An END is an electronic message sent from an authorised lender to the Land Registry via a computer link using the information supplied on Form END1. This method of discharge is an alternative to Form DS1 in registered land transactions. Like the paper form of discharge, an END does not cause the charge to be cancelled, it must be combined with a formal application to the Land Registry using Form AP1 or DS2, to discharge the charge.

Form END1 is completed by the borrower's solicitor and sent to the lender as a request for an END to be transmitted to the Land Registry. Lenders will tell you if they belong to the scheme in the redemption statement or when the deeds packet is issued.

1.10.2. The borrower's solicitors send Form END1 to the lender when they remit the amount required to redeem the mortgage. The lender will then transmit an END to the Land Registry. An authorised lender will normally use the END system in all cases where the whole of the land in a title is discharged from a charge in place of Form DS1.

1.10.3. The lender will send the borrower's solicitors confirmation of receipt of Form END1 or the receipted form.

1. See the appropriate practice material issued by the Land Registry.

G2. Stamping documents

See also: Stamp duty, para. AA4
Stamp duty and stamp duty savings, para. A14
After completion, para. G1
Registration of title, para. G3
Stamp duty, Appendix IX.

2.1. Introduction

This section contains only a summary of the information given in para. A14, where the rates of duty on the various instruments are also set out.

2.1.1. Payment of stamp duty

Stamp duty must be paid on certain documents within 30 days of execution or, if a document is delivered subject to conditions, within 30 days of the date when the conditions are fulfilled.

The stamp duty cheque should be made payable to 'Inland Revenue – Stamp Duties' and should include the firm's reference number where such a number has been allocated.

2.1.2. Stamp duty definitions

Although the tax is imposed only on documents and not transactions, it must not be overlooked that the stamp duty definitions of what are dutiable documents are much wider than for conveyancing purposes. Thus certain powers of attorney, declarations of trust, receipts and memoranda have been held to be 'conveyances' which also include the grant of options and annuities, and written notices exercising options to renew leases and certain buildings agreements are 'agreements for lease' liable to stamp duty.

2.1.3. Responsibility for bearing stamp duty

Apart from the liability imposed on purchasers in relation to contracts for sale (but not conveyances) and special rules for bearer instruments there is no general legislation which sets out who is responsible for bearing the stamp duty. The convention is that it is the transferee or lessee who pays the duty but persons who are not parties to an instrument may have to stamp it where it forms part of their chain of title.

2.1.4. Late stamping of documents

A document can be stamped outside the 30-day period mentioned in para. G2.1.1 but that delay in stamping involves problems. Primarily late stamping and payment is available only on payment of a penalty and interest.[1]

If the duty is not paid or deposited with the Revenue within 30 days after execution of the instrument then interest runs on the duty or the amount not deposited from the end of the 30 days until payment.

2.1.5. Effect of unstamped documents

Unstamped or insufficiently stamped documents are not admissible in evidence and it is now the duty of the advocate and the judge to take the point (Stamp Act 1891, s.14(4)). This applies even where the litigant relying upon the document is not a party to it such as a lender seeking to enforce his security. This can provide an expensive surprise and failure to take stamp objections to the other side's documents is a breach of duty to the client.

Consequently, the Land Registry and Companies Registry will not accept unstamped or incorrectly stamped documents for registration and they may insist that the instrument is presented to the Inland Revenue Stamp Taxes Office and adjudicated (Stamp Act 1891, s.17). Duty must therefore normally be paid before an application for registration of title is submitted.

Unstamped or incorrectly stamped documents cannot be used in evidence in civil proceedings. Such a document is not therefore a good root or link in the chain of title to land and since certain documents other than Land Registry transfers, including certain contracts for sale, may be subject to stamp duty these can affect the title to registered and unregistered land.

2.1.6. Avoidance by inserting false information

An agreement to avoid the payment of the correct duty by inserting false information in a document may be a fraud on the Inland Revenue which could result in the transaction being declared void as being illegal on the grounds of public policy. This liability extends to the parties' professional advisers involved in the preparation of the documentation.[2]

2.1.7. Advising the client

The buyer's potential liability to pay stamp duty on the transaction must be discussed with him when instructions are taken. Third parties such as lenders or purchasers of reversions upon leases must be advised if there are unstamped or insufficiently stamped documents in the chain of title or security since they may have to pay the duty, interest and penalty in order to protect or register their title or enforce their security. In such cases agreements to indemnify the third party against the stamp duty liability are void.

1. See Stamp Office Leaflet SO10.
2. See *Saunders* v. *Edwards* [1987] 2 All ER 651.

2.2. Particular instruments

2.2.1. *Conveyance or transfer on sale*

An instrument which in stamp duty terms is a 'conveyance on sale' is dutiable at the rate of 4% of the consideration where the consideration or deemed consideration exceeds £500,000.

No duty is payable where the consideration is £60,000 or less provided an appropriate certificate of value is included in the document (see para. A14.2.3).

Where the consideration for the transfer exceeds £60,000 but does not exceed £250,000 and the transaction does not form part of a larger transaction or series of transactions, duty is payable at the rate of 1% provided an appropriate certificate of value is included in the document.

Where the consideration for the transfer exceeds £250,000 but does not exceed £500,000 and the transaction does not form part of a larger transaction or series of transactions, duty is payable at the rate of 3% provided an appropriate certificate of value is included in the document.

The Finance Acts 2000 and 2001 make provision for the total exemption from stamp duty for conveyances and leases of land in certain designated areas (see para. A14.2.4).

Increasingly stamp duty is chargeable by reference to value and in several cases the actual consideration is ignored with duty being charged upon the market value. These include:

- land exchanges and conveyances for an unascertainable consideration (FA 1994, ss.241 and 242);

- transfers of land to connected companies (FA 2000, ss.119 and 120); and

- transfers in contemplation of a sale (FA 1965, s.90).

2.2.2. *Voluntary conveyance or transfer*

In general no duty is payable upon a transfer for no consideration provided the document bears an appropriate certificate under Stamp Duty (Exempt Instruments) Regulations 1987 (see Appendix XII.2). However, *ad valorem* duty is payable where:

- the transfer is land in the United Kingdom to a connected company which is deemed to be a sale at market value (FA 2000, s.119 – a 'connected company' is widely defined and subject to limited exceptions includes corporate trustees and certain nominees);

- the transfer is in contemplation of a sale (FA 1965, s.90, and see Inland Revenue Stamp Taxes Office Customers Newsletter, July 2002);

- the transfer is subject to a mortgage unless the transferor agrees to indemnify the transferee (Stamp Act 1891, s.57, and see Inland Revenue Stamp Taxes Office Statement of Practice SP6/90).

2.2.3. Assent under hand

No duty is payable.

2.2.4. Assent under seal

No duty is payable provided the document bears an appropriate certificate under Stamp Duty (Exempt Instruments) Regulations 1987.

2.2.5. Mortgages and vacating receipts

No duty is payable upon dealings in mortgages unless they are marketable securities.

2.2.6. Powers of attorney

In general no duty is payable, but a power of attorney given to a purchaser can be dutiable as an equitable assignment on sale (see para. B23).

2.2.7. Leases

Duty is assessed upon the premium paid or the deemed premium for the grant by reference to sale duty and in relation to the average rent by reference to the length of the term. An agreement for lease is liable to the same duty as if it were the actual lease but this duty is deducted from the duty payable on the lease. Under the terms of Finance Act 1994, s.240 all leases must either contain a statement that there is no agreement for lease to which the lease gives effect or they must be denoted to show that the proper stamp duty has been paid on the relevant agreement.

2.2.8. Assignments of existing leases

These are treated as conveyances and bear the same duty as a conveyance.

2.2.9. Duplicate and counterpart leases

Fixed duty of £5 is payable even where the lease itself is not stamped.

2.2.10. *Agreements to surrender leases*

An agreement to surrender a lease may be liable to stamp duty as if it were a conveyance or transfer of the interests surrendered (FA 1994, s.243). Notification to the Land Registry of the surrender of lease by operation of law is stampable as a conveyance (FA 2000, s.128).

2.2.11. *Declaration of trust*

Fixed duty of £5 is payable. Certain declarations of trust are liable to *ad valorem* duty as a conveyance or transfer on sale.

2.2.12. *Transfer in consideration of a debt*

Where a conveyance or transfer is made so that the transferee takes over liability for a debt without there being any other money consideration for the transfer, e.g. a transfer of property subject to a mortgage, the Inland Revenue may treat the transfer as a sale of property and *ad valorem* duty will be payable on the amount of the debt.

2.3. **VAT**

2.3.1. *Where consideration attracts VAT*

Where the consideration paid for an interest in land includes VAT, the tax is treated as part of the value of the land and attracts stamp duty. This may influence whether the contract is dutiable because the consideration including VAT exceeds £10 million. Duty is therefore payable on the whole of the consideration including the VAT element of the price.

2.3.2. *VAT on stamp duty*

Stamp duty itself does not attract a charge to VAT.

2.3.3. *Transfer of a going concern*

The obligations of the parties in relation to completing PD forms and producing undertakings to the Inland Revenue Stamp Taxes Office where the transaction involves a possible transfer of a going concern are contained in an Inland Revenue Stamp Taxes Office Customer Newsletter (reproduced in the Law Society's *Gazette*, 16 September 1998). This Newsletter was later amended in the Law Society's *Gazette*, 15 January 1999:

'If the document allows for VAT to be charged later on, for instance, if Customs & Excise refuse clearance, then we will stamp the document on the initial consideration stated and ask you to confirm that:

- the transaction is believed to involve the transfer of a going concern and consequently no VAT has been added to the consideration stated in the document;

- you have advised your client that they are obliged to tell the Stamp Office if that position changes, in line with their obligations under s.5 of the Stamp Act 1891; and

- that the client undertakes to arrange for the document to be returned to the Stamp Office and to pay the extra duty due if VAT does become payable.

A written undertaking from the client to that effect should be enclosed with your letter.

2.4. Particulars delivered stamp

2.4.1. *When to produce instruments*

Under Finance Act 1931 certain instruments are required to be produced to the Inland Revenue within 30 days of their execution. Failure to comply with this requirement where applicable results in the same penalties and consequences as for lack of stamp duty.

These provisions apply to a conveyance (or transfer) on sale of freeholds, leases which are granted for a term exceeding seven years and agreements to lease and to assignments of such leases. The obligations are satisfied if the agreement for lease is not presented at once but subsequently with the lease when granted.

2.4.2. *Form LA451 (PD)*

To comply with Finance Act 1931, the relevant document must be produced to the Inland Revenue with a completed Form LA451 (PD) which must contain all information relevant to the stamping of the instrument such as, undertakings to pay VAT if the transaction is not a transfer of a going concern, overage or earnout arrangements and lease premiums payable to persons other than the landlord.

Failure to include such information is a breach of s.5 of the Stamp Act 1891 and may be regarded as fraud. The Inland Revenue will stamp the document (a Particulars Delivered or 'PD' stamp) to show that this requirement has been complied with. A plan showing the land should be submitted with the Form LA451 if the postal description of the land is not adequate to identify it clearly.

2.4.3. *Registration without stamp duty*

Where the transfer on sale being produced does not require stamp duty and registration of title is required, the document, with its completed Form LA451, may be sent direct to the Land Registry as part of an application for registration of the title and the Land Registry will deal with the production of the document as agents for the Inland Revenue. Separate submission of the document to the Inland

Revenue is in such cases unnecessary. Leases which need to be produced must be sent to the Inland Revenue irrespective of whether stamp duty is also payable (see para. G1.4.3).

2.5.   Denoting stamps

Certain documents are not properly stamped unless they have a special stamp indicating that the proper duty has been paid on some other instrument. This denoting stamp is required in addition to any stamps impressed to show that the particular instrument is itself fully stamped. The circumstances where denoting stamps are required include:

- duplicates and counterparts;

- conveyances where the contract for sale is dutiable;

- leases where there is a dutiable agreement for lease;

- bearer instruments; and

- transfers and leases which are reversionary on an agreement for lease for a term exceeding 35 years.

2.6.   Adjudication

The presence of stamp duty on a document is not conclusive proof that the correct duty has been paid. If conclusive proof of payment of the correct duty is needed, the document must be submitted for adjudication by the Inland Revenue. An adjudication stamp placed on the document will then be conclusive as to the payment of duty. Persons who are doubtful as to the stamp upon a document of title, such as a lender, should insist that it be adjudicated since indemnities in this context are void (Stamp Act 1891, s.117).

2.7.   Payment of duty

2.7.1.   *Payment by the client*

The client should be asked to pay his solicitor the amount necessary to cover the stamp duty before completion, so that the solicitor has funds available to make this payment on behalf of the client immediately following completion. Where the solicitor is acting also for the buyer's lender, the documents must be stamped within the relevant period, regardless of whether the buyer client has paid his solicitor the amount required to discharge the stamp duty. Failure to do so would put the solicitor into breach of his duty to the lender.

2.7.2.   Time-limits for payment post completion

It is important that payment of stamp duty is made as soon as possible following completion, not only in order to comply with the 30-day period for payment of duty, after the expiration of which interest runs (Stamp Act 1891, s.15A), but also so that the stamped documents may be submitted to the Land Registry for registration within the relevant time-limits applicable. Where the application is for registration of a dealing (i.e. the land is already registered), the application for registration must be received by the Land Registry within 30 business days of the date of the official certificate of search issued prior to completion.[1] If stamping is not carried out with reasonable expedition, it is likely that this latter time-limit will not be complied with (see para. G3 for consequences of a late application for registration).

2.7.3.   Administration

Documents to be stamped may either be taken to an Inland Revenue Stamping Office or, if this is not convenient, delivered by post to the Inland Revenue (see Appendix XI.5 for addresses). A cheque for the correct amount of duty must accompany the documents. The cheque should be made payable to 'Inland Revenue – Stamp Duties' and bear the solicitor's registered number where such a number has been allocated.

2.7.4.   Where duty is unknown

If the amount of duty payable is not known by the solicitor presenting the document, he may ask the Inland Revenue to assess the duty, 'mark' the document accordingly and return it to the solicitor who will then resubmit the document for stamping with a cheque for the assessed duty. The instrument may have to be adjudicated where the stamp duty is charged upon the value of property. This course of action will inevitably delay the date when the document can be submitted to the Land Registry during which time interest will be running unless it has been paid on account. This re-emphasises the necessity to deal with the stamping of documents at the earliest possible opportunity.

1. See Land Registration Rules 2003, r.131 for the definition of the 'priority period' conferred by an official search.

G3. Registration of title

See also: Land Registration Act 2002, para. A22
Rectification and Indemnity, para. M7
Land Registration Act 2002 (selected Schedules), Appendix XII.4.
Land Registration Act 2003 (selected Schedules), Appendix XII.5.

3.1. Introduction

Registration of title is governed by the Land Registration Act 2002 (the Act) and Land Registration Rules 2003 (the Rules), which came into force on 13 October 2003. Registration guarantees the title to registered land. Thus, a person who suffers loss as a result of a mistake in the register is entitled to be indemnified for that loss.[1]

1. See para. M7.

3.2. Compulsory registration

3.2.1. Extension of compulsory registration

The extension of compulsory registration to the whole of England and Wales became effective on 1 December 1990 under Registration of Title Order 1989.[1]

3.2.2. When title must be registered

Registration is compulsory on specified types of transfers, leases and mortgages of a qualifying estate, which is defined as either a legal freehold estate or a legal lease with more than seven years to run. They are:[2]

(a) a transfer:

    (i) for valuable[3] or other consideration, by way of gift or in pursuance of a court order; or

    (ii) by means of an assent;

(b) the grant of a legal lease:

(i) for a term of more than seven years; and

(ii) for valuable or other consideration, by way of gift or in pursuance of a court order;

(c) the grant of a legal lease to take effect in possession more than three months after it is granted;

(d) the creation of a first legal mortgage where the mortgage is protected by the deposit of documents.

3.2.3. Certain disposals under the Housing Act 1985

The following disposals under the Housing Act 1985 also trigger compulsory registration:

(a) the transfer or grant of a legal lease of an unregistered estate where Housing Act 1985, s.171A applies (a disposal by a landlord which leads to a person no longer being a secure tenant); or

(b) the grant of a 'right to buy' lease under the Housing Act 1985, Part 5.

3.2.4. Transfers not subject to compulsory registration

The compulsory registration provisions do not apply to:

(a) a transfer by operation of law (for example, the vesting of land in personal representatives);[4]

(b) an assignment of a mortgage term; or

(c) a surrender of a lease where the term is to merge into the reversion.[5]

3.2.5. Duty to apply for registration

Where registration is compulsory, the transferee, lessee or mortgagor is under a duty to apply for first registration.[6] In the case of a mortgage, the mortgagee may make an application in the name of the mortgagor whether or not the mortgagor consents.[7] The application for first registration must be made within two months. This period may be extended by the registrar if he is satisfied that there is a good reason for doing so.[8]

3.2.6. Effect of failure to register

Where an application is not lodged within the registration period the transfer, lease or mortgage is void as regards the legal estate.[9] In the case of a transfer, the legal estate reverts to the transferor. A lease or mortgage takes effect as a contract made for valuable consideration to grant the lease or mortgage concerned.[10] Although the registration period can be extended, a client is at risk of being registered subject to interests which would not have otherwise bound the land.

3.2.7. *Liability for making good void transfers, etc.*

If the transaction has to be repeated because of a failure to register, the transferee, lessee or mortgagor:

(a) is liable to the other party for the costs involved; and

(b) must indemnify the other party for any other liability reasonably incurred due to the failure to register.[11]

1. S.I. 1989/1347.
2. Land Registration Act 2002, s.4(1).
3. If the estate transferred or leased has a negative value it is to be regarded as transferred or leased for valuable or other consideration. Valuable consideration does not include marriage consideration or a nominal consideration in money. See Land Registration Act 2002, ss.4(6) and 132(1).
4. Land Registration Act 2002, s.4(3).
5. Land Registration Act 2002, s.4(4).
6. Land Registration Act 2002, s.6(1)–(3).
7. Land Registration Rules 2003, r.21.
8. Land Registration Act 2002, ss.6(4) and (5).
9. Land Registration Act 2002, s.7(1).
10. Land Registration Act 2002, s.7(2).
11. Land Registration Act 2002, s.8.

3.3.   **Voluntary registration**

3.3.1.   *When title may be registered*

Under Land Registration Act 2002, s.3, the following legal estates and interests may be registered under their own title numbers:

(a) a freehold estate;

(b) a lease for a term of which more than seven years are unexpired;[1]

(c) a lease for a discontinuous term whatever its length;

(d) a franchise;

(e) a profit à prendre in gross

3.3.2.   *Reasons for voluntary registration*

The benefits of the registered system of conveyancing, such as, simplified methods of deduction of title, are such that a client should be encouraged to make an application for voluntary registration in appropriate circumstances. This might be particularly appropriate where, for example, an unregistered title is complex or has minor defects in it, since on first registration the registrar has a discretion to 'cure' such defects.[2]

1. Where a reversionary lease is to take effect in possession on, or within one month of, the end of the lease in possession, the terms may be treated as one continuous term. If this exceeds seven years, the lease can be registered: see Land Registration Act 2002, s.3(7).
2. Land Registration Act 2002, ss.9(3) and 10(4).

3.4.   Applications for first registration

3.4.1.   The application for first registration must be made to the proper land registry office. See para. G3.10 as to the proper office for the receipt of applications and other general matters relating to applications to the Land Registry.

3.4.2.   The application must be made in Form FR1.[1] It must be accompanied by:[2]

(a) sufficient details, by plan or otherwise, so that the land can be identified clearly on the Ordnance Survey Map;[3]

(b) where the land is leasehold, the lease, if in the control of the applicant, and a certified copy;

(c) all deeds and documents relating to the title in the control of the applicant;

(d) a list in duplicate in Form DL of all the documents delivered.

3.4.3.   The registrar needs to investigate title on an application for first registration in order to decide which class of title can be allocated to the title. He therefore needs to have access to all the documents which form the evidence of title to the land. The documents should be individually listed and numbered in chronological sequence in the Form DL. They should include:

(a) all the documents which formed the evidence of title supplied by the seller's solicitor;

(b) all the buyer's pre-contract searches and enquiries with their replies (including any variations or further information contained in relevant correspondence);

(c) the contract;

(d) requisitions on title with their replies;

(e) all pre-completion search certificates;

(f) the purchase deed;

(g) the seller's mortgage, duly receipted;

(h) the buyer's mortgage;

(i) where the transaction is leasehold, the original lease and a certified copy;

(j) PD form, where no stamp duty is payable.

3.4.4.   There is a case for retaining copies of all documents which are to be submitted to the registry on the applicant's solicitor's file pending completion of the registration. The registrar may need to raise requisitions on an application (particularly for first registration) and it assists in the speedy reply to those requisitions if the solicitor has retained copies of the documents which may contain information relevant to the query raised by the registry. Delay may also be experienced with the application for first registration. A further reason for retaining copies of the documents is so that any queries which arise in relation to the land pending completion of the registration for example, over boundaries or the exercise of a right of way, can be resolved from the copies in the solicitor's possession.

. Land Registration Rules 2003, r.23.
. Land Registration Rules 2003, r.24(1).
. On an application to register a rentcharge, franchise or profit à prendre in gross, the land to be identified is the land affected: see Land Registration Rules 2003, r.24(2).

3.5. Classes of title

3.5.1.
On first registration the registrar will decide which class of title should be granted to the estate which is being registered. The class of title granted is shown in the proprietorship register of the title.[1]

3.5.2. Absolute title

The vast majority of titles are registered with absolute title. An absolute title may be approved if the registrar is of the opinion that title to the estate is such that a willing buyer could properly be advised by a competent professional adviser to accept.[2] The registrar may disregard a defect in the title if he is of the opinion that the defect will not cause the holding under the title to be disturbed.[3] Where the title is leasehold, absolute title is granted where the registrar also approves the lessor's title to grant the lease.[4]

3.5.3. Qualified title

A person may be registered with qualified title if the registrar is of the opinion that title has been established only for a limited period or subject to certain reservations which cannot be disregarded.[5] A qualified title is very rare in practice. It might be approved where, for example, the title submitted for first registration showed that a transaction within the title had been carried out in breach of trust. In this situation the proprietor would take his interest in the land subject to the interests (if any) of the beneficiaries under the trust. Qualified title can be given to either a freehold or a leasehold estate in the land.

3.5.4. Possessory title

Possessory title may be granted where the registrar considers that the applicant is in possession of the land, or in receipt of rents and profits, and there is no other class of title with which he may be registered.[6] In practice, a possessory title will be granted where the applicant's title is based on adverse possession or where title cannot be proved satisfactorily because the title deeds have been lost or destroyed. Possessory title can be given to either a freehold or leasehold estate in the land.

3.5.5. Good leasehold title

Registration with good leasehold title will be granted where the registrar is satisfied only as to the title to the leasehold estate.[7] Such a title will therefore generally only result where the title to the freehold reversion is unregistered and where the applicant for registration of the leasehold interest does not submit evidence of title to the freehold reversion when making his application. A good leasehold title is regarded by some mortgagees as being unsatisfactory, and for this reason is sometimes difficult to sell or mortgage.[8]

1. Land Registration Rules 2003, r.8(1).
2. Land Registration Act 2002, ss.9(2) and 10(2)(a).
3. Land Registration Act 2002, ss.9(3) and 10(4).
4. Land Registration Act 2002, s.10(2)(b).
5. Land Registration Act 2002, ss.9(4) and 10(5).
6. Land Registration Act 2002, ss.9(5) and 10(6).
7. Land Registration Act 2002, s.10(3).
8. The problems of a good leasehold title are discussed in para. K1. See also Standard Condition 8.2.4 and Standard Commercial Property Condition 8.2.4 which require a seller on the grant of a new lease for over 21 years to deduce to a buyer such evidence of title as will enable the buyer to obtain registration of his title with an absolute title.

3.6. Effect of first registration

3.6.1. Freehold estates

On first registration with absolute title, the legal estate is vested in the proprietor together with all interests subsisting for the benefit of the estate, such as appurtenant easements.[1] The registered estate is subject only to the following interests affecting the estate at the time of registration:[2]

    (a) interests which are entered in the register;[3]

    (b) overriding interests falling within Land Registration Act 2002, Sched.1;[4] and

    (c) interests acquired under the Limitation Act 1980 of which the proprietor has notice.[5]

3.6.2. Where the proprietor is a trustee, the estate is vested in him subject to the rights of the beneficiaries under the trust of which he has notice.[6]

3.6.3. Registration with qualified title has the same effect as registration with absolute title except that it does not affect the enforcement of any estate, right or interest appearing from the register to be excepted from the effect of registration.[7]

3.6.4. Registration with possessory title has the same effect as registration with absolute title, except that it does not affect the enforcement of any estate, right or interest, adverse to, or in derogation of, the title subsisting at the time of registration.[8]

3.6.5. Leasehold estates

In general terms the registration of a proprietor with absolute, qualified or possessory title to a leasehold estate has the same effect as registration with the corresponding freehold estate. The significant difference is that a leaseholder is also subject to implied and express covenants, obligations and liabilities incident to the leasehold estate. The proprietor, therefore, takes subject to interests such as restrictive covenants contained in the lease.[9]

3.6.6. Registration with good leasehold title has the same effect as registration with absolute leasehold title except that it does not affect the enforcement of any estate, right or interest affecting, or in derogation of, the title of the lessor to grant the lease.[10]

1. Land Registration Act 2002, s.11(3).
2. Land Registration Act 2002, s.11(4).
3. The only interests entered on first registration will be charges, notices and restrictions.
4. As to overriding interests, see para. A22.5.
5. During a three year transitional period, a right acquired under the Limitation Act 1980 before the coming into force of the Act will be an overriding interest: see Land Registration Act 2002, s.11(4)(b) and (c) and Sched.12, para.7.
6. Land Registration Act 2002, s.11(5).
7. Land Registration Act 2002, s.11(6).
8. Land Registration Act 2002, s.11(7).
9. Land Registration Act 2002, s.12.
10. Land Registration Act 2002, s.12(6).

3.7. Upgrading title

3.7.1. The registrar has power to upgrade a title in the following circumstances:[1]

(a) from possessory or qualified freehold title to absolute freehold title if he is satisfied as to the title to the freehold estate;

(b) from good leasehold title to absolute leasehold title if he is satisfied as to the superior title;

(c) from possessory or qualified leasehold title:

    (i) to good leasehold title, if he is satisfied as to the title to the leasehold estate; and

    (ii) to absolute leasehold title if he is satisfied both as to the title to the leasehold estate and as to the superior title;

(d) from possessory freehold title to absolute freehold title or from possessory freehold title to good leasehold title if the title has been registered for at least 12 years and he is satisfied that the proprietor is in possession[2] of the land.

3.7.2. The registrar cannot exercise his power to upgrade a title if there is any outstanding adverse claim under any estate, right or interest whose enforceability is preserved by the existing class of title.[3] Any adverse claim must be resolved before the title can be upgraded.

3.7.3. An application to upgrade a title must be made in Form UT1.[4]

1. Land Registration Act 2002, s.62(1)–(5).
2. See Land Registration Act 2002, s.131 for the meaning of 'proprietor in possession'.
3. Land Registration Act 2002, s.62(6).
4. Land Registration Rules 2003, r.124(1).

3.8. Dispositions of registered land

3.8.1. *Powers of disposition*

A registered proprietor is to be taken to have all the powers of an absolute owner unless any limitation of these powers is reflected by an entry on the register,[1] for example, a restriction. The purpose of the statutory provisions is to prevent the title of the buyer being challenged. They do not affect the lawfulness of the sale.[2] The Law Commission report preceding the Act illustrated the intended effect of these provisions with the example of trustees who have limited powers of sale, but who failed to enter a restriction on the register to reflect this limitation. If they then sell the land in breach of the terms of the trust they will remain personally liable for this breach. The buyer's title could not be challenged although he might be personally accountable in equity if he knew of the trustee's breach of trust at the time of the sale.[3]

3.8.2. *Registrable dispositions*

The Act sets out the dispositions that must be completed by registration if they are to operate at law.[4] These are:

(a) a transfer;

(b) the grant of a term of years absolute of an estate in land:

    (i) for a term of more than seven years from the date of the grant;

    (ii) taking effect in possession after the end of the period of three months beginning with the date of the grant;

    (iii) under which the right to possession is discontinuous;

    (iv) in pursuance of Part 5 of the Housing Act 1985 (the right to buy); or

    (v) in circumstances where section 171A of that Act applies (disposal by landlord which leads to a person no longer being a secure tenant);

(c) the grant of a lease of a franchise or manor;

(d) the express grant or reservation of an easement or other right falling within Law of Property Act 1925, s.1(2)(a), other than one which is capable of being registered under the Commons Registration Act 1965;

(e) the express grant or a reservation of a rentcharge or right of re-entry falling within Law of Property Act 1925, s.1(2)(b) or (e);

(f) the grant of a legal charge; and

(g) the transfer or sub-charge of a registered charge.[5]

3.8.3.
The requirement for registration applies also to transfers by operation of law except for:

(a) a transfer on the death or bankruptcy of an individual proprietor;

(b) a transfer on the dissolution of a corporate proprietor; and

(c) the creation of a legal charge which is a local land charge.[6]

.8.4. *Effect of dispositions on priority*

The general principle under the Act is that the priority of an interest in registered land is determined by its date of creation and not the date on which it is entered in the register.[7] There is a major exception, however, in the case of registrable dispositions (such as a transfer or charge) made for valuable consideration. In such cases, on completion of the disposition by registration, the disposition takes priority to an interest whose priority is not protected at the time of registration. The effect of these provisions is that registration of a disposition for valuable consideration takes effect subject only to:

(a) a registered charge;

(b) an interest the subject of a notice on the register;

(c) an overriding interest under Schedule 3 of the Act;

(d) an interest appearing from the register to be excepted from the effect of registration (for example, where the title is less than absolute); and

(e) where the land is leasehold, any interest incident to the leasehold estate (for example, the covenants contained in the registered lease).[8]

.8.5. *Relative priority of registered charges*

Registered charges rank as between themselves in the order shown in the register.[9] Any application to alter this priority must be made by, or with the consent of, the proprietor of any postponed registered charge and any other registered charge whose priority is affected by the alteration. But no consent is required from a person who has executed the instrument altering the priority of the charge.[10]

1. Land Registration Act 2002, ss.23 and 25.
2. Land Registration Act 2002, s.26.
3. *Land Registration for the Twenty-First Century* (Law Com 271), p.67.
4. Land Registration Act 2002, s.27(1).
5. Land Registration Act 2002, s.27(3).
6. Land Registration Act 2002, s.27(5).
7. Land Registration Act 2002, s.28(1).
8. Land Registration Act 2002, s.29.
9. Land Registration Act 2002, s.48.
10. Land Registration Rules 2003, r.102(1).

3.9. **Registered land: applications**

3.9.1. *The application*

Applications for registration of transfers, charges and other dispositions of registered land must be made on form AP1.[1] This is the 'default' form to be used when no other application form is prescribed.

3.9.2. Transfer of whole

The application for registration of a transfer of the whole of the seller's title (whether freehold or leasehold) should be lodged at the proper office within the 30 business day priority period conferred by the applicant's pre-completion official search certificate (see para. G3.10.2). The period of protection under the search cannot be extended (although a second search conferring a separate priority period can be made). The application should be accompanied by:

(a) the transfer in Form TR1 (or TR2 if the transfer is under a chargee's power of sale);

(b) the appropriate fee under the current Land Registration Fee Order; and

(c) in appropriate circumstances:

    (i) a completed Form DS1 (or reference in the Form AP1 to the use of the END system) in respect of the seller's mortgage;

    (ii) where the seller was the personal representative of a sole deceased proprietor an office copy or certified copy of the grant of representation;[2]

    (iii) where the transfer has been executed under a power of attorney, the original or a duly certified copy of the power, or a certificate by a conveyancer in Form 1;[3] and where the transfer is not made within one year of the power, appropriate evidence of non-revocation by statutory declaration or in Form 2;[4]

    (iv) a completed PD form where no stamp duty is payable (and the purchase deed is not a lease) (see para. G3.10.3).

3.9.3. Transfer of part

The transfer must be in Form TP1 (or TP2 if the transfer is under a chargee's power of sale). The transfer should include a plan signed by the seller identifying the land transferred.[5] The application should be lodged within the priority period referred to in para. G3.9.2 accompanied by the transfer and such documents listed in that paragraph as are relevant to the transaction.

3.9.4. Charges

A registered proprietor has power to mortgage the land in any way permitted by the general law but not by a mortgage by demise or sub-demise. He may also charge the land at law with the payment of money.[6] An application to register the charge should be made within the priority period conferred by the pre-completion official search certificate (see para. G3.9.2) and be accompanied by the charge and any requisite fee. The priority of lenders in registered land is governed by the order shown in the register.[7]

3.9.5. By far the best way of protecting a lender of registered land is by substantive registration of the charge when the chargee will be entered in the register as the proprietor of the charge.[8] On registration, a registered charge takes effect as a charge by way of legal mortgage and the proprietor of the charge can exercise all the powers of a legal mortgagee.[9]

3.9.6.   Alternatively, a charge can be protected by the entry of notice in the register (see para. G3.9.8) and any future buyer of the land would take subject to a charge in this way. However, where a charge is not a registered charge, in order to exercise a lender's power of sale, the chargee would need either to register the charge substantively (if it is capable of being registered in its own right), or to obtain an order of the court under the Law of Property Act 1925, s.90 and obtain substantive registration pursuant to that order.

3.9.7.   Where a lender wishes the Land Registry to note on the register an obligation to make further advances, an application to enter the obligation should be made in Form CH2 unless the form of the charge incorporating the obligation clause has been approved by the registrar or the application is contained in panel 7 of Form CH1.[10]

3.9.8.   *Notices*

A notice is used to protect interests that will not be overreached on a disposition (for example, restrictive covenants and equitable easements) and will therefore continue to affect the land. Certain interests are excluded from protection by way of notice.[11] The main excluded interests are:

    (a) an interest under a trust of land;

    (b) a lease for a term of three years or less which is not required to be registered; and

    (c) a restrictive covenant between lessor and lessee so far as it relates to the property leased.

A notice may be either an agreed or a unilateral notice.

3.9.9.   *Agreed notices*

An application for an agreed notice is to be made in Form AN1.[12] The proprietor's consent is normally required for an application for an agreed notice. An agreed notice may also be used without the proprietor's consent if the registrar is satisfied as to the validity of the claim.[13] In practice, this might be the case where there is an application relating to a document signed by the registered proprietor such as a contract for sale or an equitable charge.

3.9.10.   *Unilateral notices*

An application for a unilateral notice must be made on Form UN1.[14] A unilateral notice is entered without the consent of the registered proprietor. A unilateral notice must indicate that it is such a notice and identify who is the beneficiary of the notice. Where the registrar enters a unilateral notice in the register notice of the entry will be given to the registered proprietor who may at any time apply for its cancellation.[15] This is similar to the 'warning off' of a caution against dealings under the 1925 Act.

3.9.11. Restrictions

An application for a restriction is to be made in Form RX1 save where the application is for a standard form of restriction and the application is made in:

(a) the additional provisions panel of Forms TP1, TP2, TP3, TR1, TR2, TR3, TR4, TR5, AS1, AS2 or AS3;

(b) panel 7 of form CH1; or

(c) a charge, the form of which (including the application for the restriction) has first been approved by the registrar.

The standard forms of restriction are those listed in Schedule 4 to the Land Registration Rules 2003.

An application for a restriction must be accompanied by full details of the required restriction. If the restriction requires notice to be given to a person, requires a person's consent or certificate or is a standard form of restriction that refers to a named person, that person's address for service must be provided.

The application may be made by the registered proprietor or with his consent. A third party who can show a sufficient interest can also make an application.[16]

3.9.12. Duty to act reasonably

A person must not apply for entry of a notice or restriction without reasonable cause.[17] This duty of care is owed to any person who suffers damage in consequence of its breach.[18]

1. Land Registration Rules 2003, r.13.
2. Land Registration Rules 2003, rr.163(2) and 214.
3. Land Registration Rules 2003, r.61(1) and Sched. 3.
4. Land Registration Rules 2003, r.62 and Sched. 3.
5. Land Registration Rules 2003, r.213.
6. Land Registration Act 2002, s.23.
7. Land Registration Act 2002, s.48.
8. Land Registration Act 2002, Sched.2, para.8.
9. Land Registration Act 2002, s.51.
10. Land Registration Rules 2003, r.108.
11. Land Registration Act 2002, s.33.
12. Land Registration Rules 2003, r.81.
13. Land Registration Act 2002, s.34(3).
14. Land Registration Rules 2003, r.83.
15. Land Registration Act 2002, s.36.
16. Land Registration Rules 2003, rr.91 and 92.
17. Land Registration Act 2002, s.77(1).
18. Land Registration Act 2002, s.77(2).

3.10. **Applications generally**

3.10.1. Applications for first registration are dealt with in para. G3.4. Applications for registration of transfers, charges and other dispositions of registered land are dealt with in para. G3.9. This section deals with the more general matters which relate to all applications to the Land Registry.

3.10.2. *Delivery of applications*

An application for registration must be delivered to the proper Land Registry office.[1] A list of the Land Registry offices, and their respective geographical areas is given in Appendix XI.1. Care must be taken to send the application to the proper office. Lodging documents at the wrong office may result in loss of priority for the application or at worst no registration at all.

3.10.3. *Stamping of documents*

The Land Registry will not accept documents for registration unless they are correctly stamped with stamp duty and/or a Particulars Delivered stamp as appropriate.[2] However, where a document other than a lease is required to be produced to the Inland Revenue under Finance Act 1931 (for a PD stamp) but does not otherwise attract stamp duty, the document, with its completed Form LA451, may be sent direct to the Land Registry as part of an application for registration of the title and the Land Registry will deal with the production of the document as agents for the Inland Revenue. Separate submission of the document to the Inland Revenue in such cases is unnecessary.

3.10.4. *Time of delivery*

An application for registration is to be taken as made at the earlier of:

   (a) the time of the business day that notice of it is entered on the daylist;[3] or

   (b) (i) midnight on the day of receipt (if received before 12 noon on that day); or

        (ii) midnight on the day after receipt (if received at or on the day of receipt after 12 noon).[4]

3.10.5. *Address for service*

A registered proprietor must give the registrar at least one postal address for service, whether or not in the United Kingdom, to which the registrar may send notices and communications to him. Two further addresses for service may be given. They must be either a postal address, inside or outside the United Kingdom, a Document Exchange address in the United Kingdom (provided that delivery can be made on behalf of the Land Registry under existing arrangements between the Land Registry and the service provider), or an electronic address.[5] It is important that addresses for service are kept up to date.

3.10.6. Duty to disclose overriding interests

A person applying for either first registration or registration of a registrable disposition must provide the registrar with information as to certain overriding interests which affect the estate.[6] The information is to be provided in Form DI.

3.10.7. The provision of this information will enable the interests to be noted on the register and they will, as a result, lose their overriding status.

3.10.8. This disclosure obligation relates only to interests within the actual knowledge of the applicant; and does not extend to, for example:

(a) an interest arising under a trust;

(b) a lease for a term of three years or less which is not required to be registered;

(c) a local land charge;

(d) a public right; and

(e) on first registration, an interest that is apparent from the deeds and documents of title accompanying the application.

3.10.9. Capacity

Joint buyers are required to state on their application for registration whether they will hold the land as beneficial joint tenants or beneficial tenants in common. In the latter case a restriction in Form A will be entered in the proprietorship register of the title. Where the parties are to hold as tenants in common, a separate document may have been drawn up prior to completion indicating the proportionate shares which each tenant in common holds in the property because the register will not record the beneficial interests. This document is not submitted to the registry with the application for registration of the title but should be retained safely to avoid later disputes over the shares in the beneficial interests in the property.[7]

3.10.10. If a company is registered under the Companies Acts, the application must state the company's registered number.[8] In other cases, unless agreed with the registry's headquarters, a certified copy of the company's constitution should be lodged. Where the application includes a charge by such a company the applicant must produce to the registrar a certificate that the charge has been registered under section 395 of the Companies Act 1985.[9] In default, the registrar must enter a note in the register that the charge is subject to the provisions of that section.[10]

3.10.11. In other situations the solicitor may have to satisfy the registrar as to the capacity of the applicant to enter the transaction, for example, housing associations, charities, building societies.

3.10.12. If the applicant dies while an application for registration is pending, the application may be continued by any person who would be entitled to apply for registration, such as the deceased's personal representatives.[11] The application may be continued either in the name of the deceased or of his successor in title.

3.10.13. If the transferee of a registered title dies before registration of his interest has been completed, the deceased's equitable interest in the property passes to his personal representatives who may continue the application in their names on production of the grant of representation to the registrar.

3.10.14. *Applications not in order*

If an application is not in order the registrar may raise such requisitions as he considers necessary.[12] Any requisitions raised will:

(a) explain what is needed;

(b) state when the application will be cancelled if a full reply is not received (the period for complying with the requisitions will be not less than 20 business days from the date of the requisition); and

(c) explain what to do if a reply cannot be made by the cancellation date.

Extensions to the cancellation date can be made, particularly when the cause is outside the applicant's control. The Land Registry will need to know:

(a) the reason for the delay;

(b) what is being done to resolve the problem; and

(c) when it is expected that a full reply to the requisition can be supplied.

3.10.15. If an application appears to the registrar to be substantially defective, he may reject it on delivery or he may cancel it at any time thereafter.[13] Some examples of where this might occur are:

(a) Applications where the original transfer, lease, charge or other primary document is not lodged and no reasonable explanation for its absence is supplied.

(b) Dispositions for which a compulsory form is prescribed (for example, TR1 for a transfer of whole) where that form has not been used.

(c) Applications to note a deed which purports to be a deed of variation of a lease but which in fact extends the term of the lease or includes additional land in the extent demised. As a matter of law, such a deed takes effect as the surrender and re-grant of the lease and should therefore be the subject of an application for substantive registration.

(d) Applications that have been previously rejected or cancelled if the outstanding points remain unresolved.

3.10.16. *Objections*

Any person may object to an application to the registrar.[14] The objection must be in writing, signed by the objector or his conveyancer, state the ground for the objection and give the full name of the objector and the address to which communications may be sent.[15] The objection must be delivered to the appropriate office.

A person who objects to an application must not do so without reasonable cause; and owes a duty to any person who suffers damage in consequence of its breach.[16] If the objection is not groundless and cannot be disposed of by agreement it must be referred to the adjudicator.[17]

3.10.17. Completion of applications

Any entry in, removal of an entry from, or alteration of the register made as a result of an application has effect from the time of the making of the application.[18]

3.10.18. On completion of any application the registrar may retain all or any of the documents that accompanied the application and must return all other such documents to the applicant or as otherwise specified in the application.[19] If when making the application the applicant or his conveyancer requests the return of any of the documents sent with the application and provides certified copies of those particular documents with the application, the registrar must return the original documents so requested on completion of the application. On first registration, however, an applicant need only provide certified copies of any statutory declaration, subsisting lease, subsisting charge or the latest document of title.[20]

3.10.19. The registrar has power to destroy any documents, which accompanied an application and which have been retained by him, if he is satisfied that either he has made and retained a sufficient copy of the document or that its further retention is unnecessary.[21]

3.10.20. Where, on 13 October 2003, the registrar holds a document on which an entry on the register is or was founded, either the person who originally delivered that document to the registrar or, in certain circumstances, the registered proprietor, may within the period to 13 October 2008, ask for the return of the document.[22]

3.10.21. After 13 October 2008, the registrar may destroy any document held by him on 13 October 2003 if he is satisfied either that he has made and retained a sufficient copy of the document or that its further retention is unnecessary.[23]

1. Land Registration Act 2002, s.100(3) provides that the Lord Chancellor may by order designate a particular office of the Land Registry as the proper office for the receipt of applications or a specified description of application.
2. See above: para. G1.4.2 which deals with avoiding delays in stamping documents.
3. The daylist shows the date and time at which every pending application was made: see Land Registration Rules 2003, r.12.
4. Land Registration Rules 2003, r.15(1): and see Land Registration Rules 2003, r.15(2) and (3) as to receipt of applications on non-business days and as to the deemed delivery of applications.
5. Land Registration Rules 2003, r.198.
6. Land Registration Act 2002, s.71 and Land Registration Rules 2003, r.28 and r.57 and see para. A22.5 which deals with overriding interests.
7. See para. E1, The purchase deed.
8. Land Registration Rules 2003, r.181(1).
9. Land Registration Rules 2003, r.111(1).
10. Land Registration Rules 2003, r.111(2).
11. Land Registration Rules 2003, r.18.
12. Land Registration Rules 2003, r.16(1).
13. Land Registration Rules 2003, r.16(3).
14. Land Registration Act 2002, s.73(1).

5. Land Registration Rules 2003, r.19.
6. Land Registration Act 2002, s.77.
7. Land Registration Act 2002, s.73(7).
8. Land Registration Rules 2003, r.20.
9. Land Registration Rules 2003, r.203(1).
0. Land Registration Rules 2003, r.203(2)–(5).
1. Land Registration Rules 2003, r.203(6).
2. Land Registration Rules 2003, r.204(1)–(3).
3. Land Registration Rules 2003, r.204(6).

H1. Acting for the lender

See also: Mortgages: acting for lender and borrower, para. A11

1.1. Introduction

1.1.1. Matters relating to the solicitor who is acting for a lender client are dealt with in context in other sections of this book. The following paragraphs draw together some of those points in the form of checklists for ready reference.

1.1.2. In many cases the solicitor acting for the lender will also be acting for the borrower in a related sale or purchase transaction. In such a case the principles of conduct relating to conflict of interests and confidentiality must at all times be observed.[1]

1. See Mortgages: acting for lender and borrower, para. A11.

1.2. Instructions to act

1.2.1. Even where instructions are received from a lender for whom the solicitor acts frequently, it should not be assumed that the instructions in the current transaction are identical to those issued on previous occasions.

1.2.2. Instructions to act must be carefully checked in each particular case and any queries clarified with the lender. If at any time during the course of the transaction it appears that compliance with the lender's instructions will not be possible, further instructions must immediately be sought.

1.2.3. In many cases where the loan is connected to residential property the solicitor will be instructed to act in accordance with the terms of the Lenders' Handbook.[1] Part 1 of the Handbook contains provisions which are applicable to all transactions. These provisions may be varied by the specific requirements of an individual lender contained either in Part 2 of the Handbook and/or in special instructions supplied to the solicitor with the lender's letter of instruction. Where applicable, the Lenders' Handbook sets out the terms of the contract between the solicitor and the lender and the conditions must be closely observed.

1.2.4. A solicitor may only act for a lender where the lender's instructions do not extend beyond the requirements contained in Rule 6(3) of the Solicitors' Practice Rules 1990 (see Appendix I.1).

1. Part 1 of the CML Lenders' Handbook is reproduced in Appendix VIII.3. Part 2 of the Handbook is only available online at www.cml.org.uk.

1.3. Creation of new mortgage – checklist

1.3.1. (a) Check instructions to ensure that all conditions attached to the advance can be complied with by both the solicitor and the borrower.

(b) If the lender is not a building society, confirm with him the rate of charging for acting for him and who is to be responsible for payment of the solicitor's bill.

(c) Check that the terms of the contract to purchase are acceptable – does the purchase price in the contract accord with that shown on the lender's instructions?

(d) If the mortgage is being granted to a sole borrower, what are the lender's instructions relating to non-owning occupiers? Has any relevant consent form been signed?[1]

(e) Have adequate enquiries been made to ensure that there are no overriding interests over the property which will adversely affect the lender's security?

(f) Inform lender of exchange of contracts and of contractual completion date if necessary.

(g) Check that the property will be properly insured from the moment of exchange or completion (as appropriate).

(h) Has investigation of title been completed satisfactorily (including the results of pre-contract searches and enquiries) – have all the lender's specific requirements been met?

(i) Engross mortgage deed and obtain borrower's signature(s) to it. Where there are joint borrowers one or more of whom is not known personally to the solicitor, precautions should be taken to verify the signature of the unknown borrower(s) in order to guard against forgery, e.g. by requiring the document to be signed in the presence of the solicitor.[2]

(j) Engross and obtain borrower's signature to assignment of life policy (where appropriate).

(k) Ensure that life policy in terms which comply with lender's instructions is in existence.

(l) Are results of pre-completion searches satisfactory, including a clear result of a bankruptcy search against the names of the borrower(s) and a company search against a company seller?

(m) Send a report on title/certificate of title to the lender and request the advance cheque.[3]

(n) On receipt of advance cheque pay it into clients' account – ensure funds have been cleared before completion.

(o) Make arrangements for completion.

(p) If required, arrange for inspection of property immediately before completion to ensure vacant possession will be given.

(q) Arrange for transmission of funds on day of completion.

(r) Inform lender of completion.

(s) Obtain purchase deed and title deeds from borrower's solicitor on completion with cheque for stamp duty and Land Registry fees.

(t) Date and fill in blanks in mortgage deed and related documents.

(u) Send notice of assignment of life policy (in duplicate) to insurance company.

(v) Give notice to prior lender(s) (if second or subsequent mortgage).

(w) Attend to stamping of purchase deed (*ad valorem* and PD stamp as appropriate).

(x) Submit application for registration of title within relevant priority period.

(y) Keep lender informed of the reason for any delays at the Land Registry.

(z) Prepare schedule of deeds for lender.

(aa) Send deeds to lender (or as instructed) and request return of receipted schedule of deeds.

1. A signed deed or form of consent must be obtained from all occupants aged 17 or over (CML Lenders' Handbook, para. 7.3). Also note that the CML Lenders' Handbook states at para. 8.3 that the solicitor must not advise anyone who is intending to occupy the property regarding the signing of the consent. Arrangements must be made for them to see an independent adviser.

2. See the requirements relating to identification in CML Lenders' Handbook, para. 3. The signature must be checked against one of the documents specified in the Handbook.

3. For special procedure on the completion of a mortgage over a new property see para. I.1.7.

1.4. **Redemption of mortgage – checklist**

1.4.1. (a) Request redemption figure from lender and title deeds if unregistered.

(b) Make a search to check if there is a subsequent chargee to whom the title deeds should be handed on completion.

(c) Check instructions from lender on their receipt.

(d) In the case of a related sale prepare epitome of title and send to borrower's solicitor (if unregistered land and lender's solicitor is not also acting for borrower).

(e) In the case of a related sale keep in touch with borrower's solicitor about arrangements for completion.

(f) Prepare Form DS1 (or receipt in unregistered land) for signature by lender.

(g) Prepare reassignment of life policy (where relevant).

(h) Prepare undertaking for discharge of mortgage to be given to buyer's solicitor on completion.

(i) Prepare forms for discharge of land charges entries (second and subsequent mortgages of unregistered land).

(j) Obtain final redemption figure from lender and inform borrower's solicitor of the figure.

(k) Arrange with borrower's solicitor for actual payment on completion.

(l) On receipt of repayment money, clear draft through clients' account and account to lender in accordance with redemption statement.

(m) Hand over undertaking for discharge of mortgage to buyer's solicitor.

(n) Send Form DS1 or END1 (or receipt in unregistered land) and deed of reassignment of life policy to mortgagee for execution and return. In the case of non-building society lenders, request that documents are dated with the date that completion of the mortgagor's sale took place to avoid problems over inadvertent transfer of the mortgage.[1]

(o) On receipt of executed Form DS1 (or receipt), check it before sending to buyer's solicitor and request to be released from the undertaking given on completion.

(p) Return life policy to borrower.

1. See para. D2.9.2.

1.5.   Mortgage not simultaneous with purchase – checklist

1.5.1.   (a) Obtain official copy entries of the title/title deeds.

(b) Make relevant pre-contract searches and enquiries including a search to find out whether prior mortgages exist.[1]

(c) Make enquiries about non-owning occupiers and obtain signature of consent form/release of rights in accordance with lender's instructions.[2]

(d) Investigate title to the property.

(e) Check the state of the prior mortgage account (if relevant).

(f) Ensure compliance with Consumer Credit Act 1974, s.58 where applicable.[3]

(g) Draft, then engross mortgage deed.

(h) Send report on title/certificate of title to lender with request for advance cheque.

(i) Explain the effect of and obtain borrower's signature to mortgage deed.

(j) Make pre-completion searches, including bankruptcy search against name of borrower, and obtain clear results to searches.

(k) Ensure any conditions attached to offer of advance have been complied with.

(l) Arrange to complete.

(m) On completion hand advance money to mortgagor, date and fill in any blanks in mortgage deed.

(n) Protect lender's security by registration.

(o) Give notice to a prior lender (where relevant).

(p) Advise lender of completion of the mortgage.

1. See para. B10.
2. See para. H1.3.1.
3. See Second and subsequent mortgages, para. H3.

1.6. Buy to let mortgages

Occasionally a condition is attached to a buy to let mortgage to the effect that the new tenancy must be agreed and the start date set prior to the completion of the mortgage. This is not always possible to achieve and both the lender and the client must be kept informed of the position and the lender must be requested to withdraw the condition if it becomes clear that it cannot be complied with.

1.7. Incorrect redemption statements

Guidance has been issued jointly by the Law Society and Council of Mortgage Lenders in connection with problems arising out of incorrect redemption statements supplied by lenders. This guidance is set out in Appendix V.9.

H2. Sales by lenders

See also: Capacity, para. B7

2.1. Power of sale

2.1.1. A lender may sell property over which he enjoys a power of sale and convey in his own name provided his power has both arisen and become exercisable. The existence and exercise of the power are discussed above in para. B7.7.

2.1.2. A first lender sells free of all charges registered subsequent to his own; thus a buyer is not concerned with the discharge of second and subsequent mortgages when a power of sale is exercised by a first lender.[1]

2.1.3. If a second or subsequent lender wishes to sell he must either sell the property subject to any prior charges, or redeem them (thus becoming a first lender) but will overreach all charges which are subsequent to his own.

2.1.4. The lender must exercise his power in good faith for the purpose of obtaining repayment; subject to this, he can exercise his powers even if the exercise is disadvantageous to the borrower.[2] There is no wider duty in negligence.[3]

2.1.5. A lender must not sell to himself or to his nominee.[4] There is no rule that he cannot sell to a person connected with him[5] but the correctness of the price must plainly be beyond doubt, and the lender must have taken and acted on expert advice as to the best method of selling, what steps should reasonably be taken to make the sale a success, and what reserve price should be fixed.

2.1.6. It is usually inadvisable for the sale contract to be conditional or for an option to be granted, since there is a risk that the loan might be repaid and the borrower would then be entitled to a discharge of the mortgage. The borrower's equity of redemption, and his ability to redeem, is only destroyed when there is a binding unconditional contract for sale.[6]

2.1.7. If the mortgage is only over the beneficial interest of a joint owner, the lender will have to make application to the court under section 14 of Trusts of Land and Appointment of Trustees Act 1996 for an order for sale. This order will not necessarily be granted by the court.

. Law of Property Act 1925, s.104 and Land Registration Act 2002, s.52.
. *Kennedy* v. *De Trafford* [1897] AC 180.
. *Downsview Nominees* v. *First City Corp.* [1993] 3 All ER 626.
. *Farrar* v. *Farrars Ltd* (1888) 40 Ch 395.
. *Tse Kwong Lam* v. *Wong Chit Sen* [1983] 3 All ER 54, PC.
. *Property & Bloodstock Ltd* v. *Emerton* [1968] Ch 94.

2.2. Possession

2.2.1. Before selling the lender will normally take possession in order to be able to sell with vacant possession (or subject to any tenancies which bind him).

2.2.2. In the case of residential property it will be necessary to obtain a court order for possession unless the occupier leaves the premises voluntarily.[1]

2.2.3. A buyer from the lender is not concerned to see the court order authorising possession.

. Protection from Eviction Act 1977, s.2.

2.3. Price

2.3.1. Building societies are under a statutory duty to obtain the best price for the property.[1]

2.3.2. Other lenders must take reasonable precautions to obtain a proper price for the property.[2] Although there is a theoretical distinction between building societies and other lenders in relation to the price which they must obtain for the property, in practice the courts appear to apply similar criteria when applying each test.

2.3.3. Sales by lenders commonly take place by auction but there is no legal requirement to this effect. A sale by auction does not necessarily constitute evidence that the lender has obtained the best possible price for the property,[3] and the lender's duty in this respect is not discharged by placing the property for sale in the hands of reputable agents.[4]

2.3.4. A sale at a sum which is sufficient only to pay off the mortgage would be looked at carefully by the court.[5]

2.3.5. The fact that the property is resold to a third party shortly after the sale by the lender and at a substantially higher price than that obtained by the lender would also be viewed with suspicion by the court.[6]

2.3.6. The borrower can challenge the amount of costs claimed by the mortgagee by making an application to the court for the taxation of the lender's costs.[7]

1. Building Societies Act 1986, s.13(7).
2. *Cuckmere Brick Co. Ltd* v. *Mutual Finance Ltd* [1971] Ch 949.
3. *Tse Kwong Lam* v. *Wong Chit Sen* [1983] 3 All ER 54.

4. *Cuckmere Brick Co. Ltd* v. *Mutual Finance Ltd* [1971] Ch 949.
5. *Midland Bank Ltd* v. *Joliman Finance Ltd* (1967) 203 EG 612; *Predeth* v. *Castle Phillips Finance Co. Ltd* [1986] 2 EGLR 144, CA.
6. *Bank of Cyprus (London) Ltd* v. *Gill* [1980] 2 Lloyd's Rep. 51.
7. *Gomba Holdings (UK) Ltd* v. *Minories Finance (No.2)* [1992] 4 All ER 588.

2.4.   The sale transaction

2.4.1.   The sale follows the normal procedures for the sale of land, subject to any specific requirements or instructions given by the mortgagee client.

2.4.2.   Since the lender will have taken possession of the property (if at all) only shortly before exercising his power of sale, he will have little or no knowledge of the condition of the property and may not therefore be able to answer pre-contract enquiries as fully as the buyer would wish. The buyer should be advised of this fact and of any other special conditions attaching to the sale, e.g. requirement for payment of a full 10% deposit. A selling lender will commonly require the buyer to exchange contracts within a stated period, reserving the right to withdraw from the sale if this condition is not met. This type of condition is imposed because of the lender's duty to obtain the best price for the property. If exchange of contracts became delayed, property values might in the interim period have altered and the lender might find himself liable in an action for breach of trust if he continued with a prospective sale in circumstances where the market price of the property had risen and a better price would be obtainable elsewhere.

2.4.3.   The lender's duty to both the borrower and to subsequent lenders to obtain the best or proper price means that the lender is under an implicit duty to preserve the value of the property by ensuring that it remains in good physical order. For this reason, the buyer should not be allowed access or entry into possession before completion. Standard Condition 5.2 (occupation by the buyer) or any similar provision, should therefore normally be excluded from the contract. If not so excluded a buyer does not have a *right* to occupy; he may only do so with the seller's consent.

2.4.4.   The buyer can demand to see the mortgage deed under which the power of sale is being exercised in order to check the existence of the power and that it has arisen, but is not concerned to enquire whether circumstances exist which entitle the lender to exercise the power.

2.4.5.   In the case of registered land, the transfer must be in Form TR2.[1]

2.4.6.   The lender will need to consider which covenants for title (if any) he is prepared to give to the buyer in the purchase deed.

2.4.7.   On completion of a sale by a lender, the mortgage under which the power is exercised is not 'discharged' although the buyer takes free from it. Where the land is unregistered, the buyer will receive the mortgage deed and other title deeds but not a mortgage receipt. Where the land is registered, the buyer will not receive a Form DS1 or END1 in respect of the mortgage. Forms DS1 (mortgage deeds and/or receipts in unregistered land) relating to subsequent mortgages (if any) do not need to be handed over on completion since the sale by the lender overreaches these subsequent charges.

1. Land Registration Rules 2003, r.58 and Sched. 1.

2.5. Proceeds of sale

2.5.1. The selling lender will discharge the debt owing to him, including interest and the costs of the sale, from the proceeds of sale.

2.5.2. If any surplus then remains, the selling lender holds the surplus on behalf of and must account to a subsequent lender. It is essential that the selling lender makes a search at the Land Registry (registered land) or the Land Charges Department (unregistered land) to discover whether or not subsequent mortgages exist before accounting to the borrower for the surplus proceeds of sale. In registered land, the selling lender is taken to have notice of anything in the register immediately before the transfer.[1] The buyer from the lender is not concerned to see that the lender deals properly with the surplus.

2.5.3. When considering the application of the proceeds of sale, a lender must have regard to any other security he holds for the mortgage debt (e.g. an endowment policy). The lender who sells in possession may not recover his entire debt (or an unfair proportion of it) from one security rather than another, even if he regards the property as his primary security, where this is to the detriment of a second lender who only has one type of security. So, for example, the lender may not take his entire debt from the property and hand the endowment policy back to the borrower, where this would result in the second lender on the property receiving nothing. The selling lender must recover his debt pro rata against all available security in his hands to achieve fairness between himself and any subsequent lender(s) and between subsequent lenders *inter se*.[2]

2.5.4. In the event that there is a shortfall, the lender has a 12-year limitation period in which to bring an action against the borrower to recover the shortfall.

1. Land Registration Act 2002, s.54.
2. For a more detailed discussion of this rather esoteric doctrine of 'marshalling the assets' see *Fisher and Lightwood's Law of Mortgages*.

2.6. Administrative receivers

2.6.1. A properly appointed administrative receiver of a company (this person must be a licensed insolvency practitioner) has power to sell a company's property but is personally liable on all contracts he enters into, unless the contract otherwise provides. He owes a duty to both borrower and lender to take reasonable care to obtain the best price which circumstances permit when selling the assets.[1]

1. *Gosling v. Gaskell* [1897] AC 575.

2.7. Receiver appointed by lender

2.7.1. The receiver need not be a licensed insolvency practitioner unless his position is classified as that of an administrative receiver (i.e. his responsibilities extend to substantially the whole of the company's assets and he is appointed under floating as well as fixed charges). The receiver is agent for the borrower company and is personally liable on his contracts unless the contract otherwise provides. The receiver will not automatically take possession of the company's property but is entitled to collect income accruing from it. He must apply that income as directed by section 109 of Law of Property Act 1925. Rent collected by and in the hands of the borrower's managing agent may strictly not be classified as 'income' to which the receiver is entitled. To overcome this difficulty the receiver should as soon as practicable after his appointment give notice to all tenants and to the managing agent advising that all rent should be paid to the receiver as from that time. The receiver owes a duty to the borrower to carry out all rent reviews, lease renewals and other acts that a prudent landlord would do.[1] Where a receiver contracts to sell property owned by the borrower, the contract should provide for the purchase deed to be signed by the lender under his power of sale; this procedure will ensure that other interests in the property are overreached on completion.

1. See *Knight* v. *Lawrence* [1991] 1 EGLR 143.

H3. Second and subsequent mortgages

See also: Mortgages: acting for lender and borrower, para. A11
Capacity, para. B7
Sales by lenders, para. H2

3.1. Introduction

3.1.1. The creation of a second or subsequent mortgage will not necessarily occur simultaneously with the purchase of the property over which the mortgage is taken.

3.1.2. The solicitor acting for the borrower may also be instructed to act for the lender but not infrequently separate solicitors are instructed to act in this situation.

3.1.3. The procedures to be followed by the lender's solicitor broadly follow the steps to be taken in a normal purchase transaction (except that there is no contract) since full enquiries about the property and its title must be made on the lender's behalf to ensure that he will obtain a viable security for his loan.

3.1.4. A checklist of the steps to be taken when acting on a mortgage which is not simultaneous with a purchase is set out in para. H1.5.

3.1.5. Mortgages sometimes contain a condition prohibiting the borrower from creating further charges over the property without that lender's consent. In such a case the requisite consent should be sought and obtained at an early stage in the transaction. A mortgage created in breach of such a condition is not itself invalid but will render the borrower vulnerable to repayment of the first charge.

3.2. Registration of charges

3.2.1. On completion of a mortgage of registered land the charge must be protected by registration at the Land Registry within the priority period afforded by the lender's search.

3.2.2. The priority of registered charges in registered land depends on the order in which the charges are registered on the title; therefore registration within the priority period given by a pre-completion search certificate is essential.[1]

3.2.3. An equitable mortgage must be in writing and signed by both parties in order to satisfy Law of Property (Miscellaneous Provisions) Act 1989, s.2.[2]

3.2.4. An equitable mortgage of registered land should be protected by registration of a notice at the Land Registry. If not so protected the lender is at risk of losing his priority to the holder of a subsequently created legal charge.[3]

3.2.5. A charge created by a company, whether fixed or floating and whether over registered or unregistered land, must be registered at the Companies Registry under Companies Act requirements within 21 days of its creation.

3.2.6. In unregistered land a mortgage which is not accompanied by the deposit of title deeds must be protected by registration at the Land Charges Department by entry of a Class C(i) (for a legal mortgage) or Class C(iii) (for an equitable mortgage) land charge. By Law of Property Act 1925, s.198 registration constitutes actual notice to a third party for all purposes connected with the land; further, the date of registration governs the priority of mortgages. In order to effect registration at the earliest possible opportunity, a priority notice should be lodged at the Land Charges Department at least 15 working days before completion and the application for registration made within 30 working days of lodging the priority notice. This will ensure that registration is effective from the date of completion itself.

3.2.7. Notice of the mortgage should be given to prior lenders in order to ensure that they are actually aware of the existence of the new charge. The proprietor of a registered charge may make a further advance on the security of that charge ranking in priority to a subsequent charge if he has not received notice of the creation of the subsequent charge (from the subsequent chargee).[4]

1. Land Registration Act 2002, s.48 and see *Mortgage Corporation Ltd* v. *Nationwide Credit Corporation Ltd* [1994] Ch 49, CA.
2. *United Bank of Kuwait plc* v. *Sahib* [1996] NPC 12.
3. Land Registration Act 2002, s.29(1) and (2).
4. Land Registration Act 2002, s.49(1).

3.3. Power of sale

3.3.1. Provided that he has a power of sale and that it has both arisen and become exercisable[1] there is no legal reason why a second or subsequent lender should not sell the property in order to realise his security.

3.3.2. In practical terms he may experience difficulty in selling the property. Although he will sell free of incumbrances ranking in priority subsequent to his own, he cannot sell free of prior incumbrances (although he may be able to redeem these on completion if the proceeds of sale are sufficient). He should therefore make a search at the Land Registry (registered land) or the Land Charges Department (unregistered land) to establish which incumbrances, if any, have priority over his own.

3.3.3. The sale of a property which is subject to a subsisting mortgage is not an attractive marketable proposition and the price attainable on such a sale may be low as a reflection of the existence of the mortgage over the property. The selling lender may therefore either have to persuade his prior lender to join with him in exercising the power of sale (assuming that the price obtainable would then be sufficient to discharge both debts) or discharge the prior mortgage out of his own funds before selling thus placing himself in the position of first lender. A contract for sale by a subsequent lender cannot prevent the prior lender selling the property in the meantime. This would put the second lender in breach of his sale contract. He needs to come to an arrangement with the first lender before exchanging contracts. That could either involve him redeeming the first mortgage beforehand out of his own money, or agreeing to discharge it on completion out of the proceeds of sale.

1. See para. B7.7.

3.4. Consumer Credit Act 1974

3.4.1. Section 58 of Consumer Credit Act 1974 is primarily of concern when dealing with the creation of second or subsequent mortgages in favour of finance houses.

3.4.2. The section applies where:

(a) a mortgage is created over land;

(b) the mortgage is not taken out to finance the purchase of the land which is being mortgaged, i.e. a bridging loan or mortgage which is simultaneous with the purchase of land is not within this section;

(c) the lender is not exempt under Consumer Credit Act 1974, s.16 (most building societies, banks and insurance companies are exempt lenders);[1]

(d) the sum secured by the mortgage does not exceed £15,000.

3.4.3. Where this section applies the creditor (lender) must supply the debtor (borrower) with a copy of the prospective mortgage agreement and related documents, e.g. assignment of life policy. Having done this, he must allow seven days to elapse before sending a further copy of the agreement and related documents to the debtor for signature by him. A further period of seven days must then elapse before the creditor is permitted to contact the debtor for any reason. Thus the debtor is given a 14-day 'consideration period' which runs from the date when the first copies of the agreement and related documents are sent to him in which to consider the prospective transaction free of influence from the creditor and if desired to take legal advice. During the whole of this time the creditor must not contact the debtor except to send him the signature copies of the agreement and related documents, although he may speak to or otherwise communicate with the debtor if the debtor contacts him first. Any communication between the creditor and debtor during this period must only be at the instigation of the debtor.

3.4.4. The consideration period can come to an end before the expiry of the 14 days if within that time the debtor signs and returns the agreement to the creditor.

3.4.5. For the purposes of this section, communications sent to or made with the debtor by the creditor's solicitor would be treated as being communications made by the creditor himself.

3.4.6. Failure to comply with the section or breach of its provisions renders the agreement improperly executed. This means that it cannot be enforced without a court order under Consumer Credit Act 1974, s.127. Such a court order would not necessarily be granted.

3.4.7. Because of the seriousness of the consequences of non-compliance with section 58, it is imperative that creditors and their solicitors comply with its requirements and do not contact the debtor while the consideration period is running.

3.4.8. Where it appears that the loan will be subject to the provisions of section 58, it is best for the parties to be represented by separate solicitors in order to avoid the problems outlined in this paragraph. The section causes particular difficulty where the same solicitor is acting for both parties to the transaction since it means that during the consideration period the solicitor is unable to contact his debtor client, even to advise him about the terms of the loan agreement. It is uncertain whether in such circumstances contact made by the solicitor with the debtor about a matter unrelated to the loan would infringe the terms of the section, but it would seem advisable not to contact the debtor client at all during this period.

3.4.9. Where the loan is subject to Consumer Credit Act 1974 a proper default notice under section 87 of the Act must be served before enforcement of the security. The court may then make a time order under sections 129–130 of the Act (these sections are similar in their effect to Administration of Justice Act 1970, s.36).[2]

1. See Consumer Credit (Exempt Agreements) (No. 2) Order 1985 (S.I. 1985/757), as amended.
2. See *Southern & District Finance* v. *Barnes* [1995] NPC 52.

3.5. Tacking

3.5.1. Tacking is the name given to the process by which a lender makes a further advance to the borrower and claims priority for repayment of both the original loan and the further advance over intervening lenders whose mortgages were created after the first loan but before the further advance.

3.5.2. *Registered land*

Registered charges are to be taken to rank as between themselves in the order shown in the register.[1] However, this general rule is affected by the provisions contained in Land Registration Act 2002, s.49. Under this section a chargee can make a further advance ranking in priority to a subsequent charge:

(a) if he has not received notice from another chargee that a subsequent charge has been created;[2]

(b) if the advance is made pursuant to an obligation and this obligation is recorded in the register;[3] and

(c) where the parties to the original charge have agreed a maximum amount for which the charge is security and the agreement is entered on the register.[4]

In other cases, tacking is only possible with the agreement of the subsequent chargee.[5]

3.5.3. Unregistered land

Section 94 of Law of Property Act 1925 allows a mortgagee to tack a further advance in three cases:

(a) where the intervening lender agrees;

(b) where his mortgage imposes on him an *obligation* to make a further advance;

(c) where he had no notice of the intervening mortgage at the time of making the further advance. The registration of the intervening mortgage (whether legal or equitable) under Land Charges Act is notice for this purpose, except that if the first mortgage was made to secure a current account or other further advances, the mere registration of the intervening mortgage as a land charge is not of itself notice to the first lender to prevent tacking.

3.5.4. It follows from (c) above that a second or subsequent lender of unregistered land should (as well as registering his mortgage as a land charge) give express notice of his mortgage to any prior lender in order to prevent the tacking of further advances by the prior lender.

3.5.5. A further reason for giving such notice is to compel a first (or prior) lender to hand the title deeds to the later lender when the earlier mortgage is discharged. The earlier lender is bound to do this where he has notice of the later mortgage, but the mere registration of the mortgage as a land charge is not notice for this purpose.

1. Land Registration Act 2002, s.48.
2. Land Registration Act 2002, ss.49(1) and (2), and see Land Registration Rules 2003, r.107 as to when notice shall be treated as received.
3. Land Registration Act 2002, s.49(3).
4. Land Registration Act 2002, s.49(4).
5. Land Registration Act 2002, s.49(6).

3.6. **Consolidation**

3.6.1. Consolidation is the right of a lender to refuse to allow a mortgage on one property to be redeemed unless a mortgage on another property (or properties) is also redeemed. It is an equitable doctrine, based on the principle that it would be unfair to allow a borrower to redeem a mortgage over a valuable property and leave the lender with security on another property which was not worth the amount of the loan.

3.6.2.   As it is an equitable doctrine, the borrower must be seeking to exercise his equitable right to redeem, i.e. the legal date for redemption on all the mortgages sought to be consolidated must have passed, and all the mortgages must originally have been created by the same borrower. At least one of the mortgages must expressly reserve the right to consolidate, i.e. it must expressly exclude the effect of Law of Property Act 1925, s.93 which restricts consolidation.

3.6.3.   Provided the conditions set out in the preceding subparagraph are satisfied, a lender may consolidate provided that all the equities of redemption are in one hand (i.e. owned by the same person) and all the mortgages in another, or, that state of affairs having existed in the past, the equities (only) have become separated.

3.6.4.   Because a second mortgage of land is in principle a mortgage of the equity of redemption of the first mortgage, the right, where it exists, can be exercised not only against the transferees of the land, but also against subsequent lenders.

3.6.5.   A buyer who is taking land subject to an existing mortgage, or a subsequent lender of the land, should make enquiry as to the existence of mortgages on other land created by the same borrower, since the doctrine operates independently of notice and even the subsequent uniting of mortgages in one hand could cause prejudice to such a person.

3.6.6.   A chargee who has a right of consolidation in relation to a registered charge on registered land may apply to the registrar for entry of a notice in the individual register of the registered titles affected to show that the specified registered charges are consolidated. The application must be made in Form CC.[1]

1. Land Registration Act 2002, s.57 and Land Registration Rules 2003, r.110.

H4. Certificates of title

See also: Certificate of title (Appendix to SPR 6(3)), Appendix VII.2.
Report on proposed purchase (domestic), Appendix VII.10.
CLLS Certificate of title and short report on title, Appendix VII.2.

4.1. Definition

4.1.1. A certificate of title is written confirmation given by a solicitor or other person qualified in the law of the country in which the property is situated as to the ownership of land or any interest in land.

4.2. When will a certificate of title be required?

4.2.1. A certificate of title may be used in any case where confirmation as to the title to property is required and are increasingly requested by mortgage lenders (but see guidance on Rule 6(3) at Appendix V.13 and letters in Appendix VII.6 and VII.7). It may be appropriate to require that a certificate of title be given by or on behalf of the person who owns the land. As an alternative to a certificate it may be possible to deal with the title to the property by means of warranties given by the person owning the property or an investigation and report on the title by lawyers acting on behalf of the person who is seeking to ascertain the quality of the title.

4.2.2. Examples of situations where a certificate may be appropriate:

    (a) the purchase of shares in a company;

    (b) the purchase of assets from a company;

    (c) flotation, mortgage, debenture or other security arrangements made by companies;

    (d) occasionally on a straightforward house purchase, if required by the mortgage lender.

4.3. Contents of certificate

4.3.1. The person to whom the certificate is addressed is entitled to rely on its contents; thus the person giving the certificate can be held liable for inaccuracies in its contents. It is therefore important for the person giving the certificate to identify the recipient of the certificate and to know for what purpose the certificate is required. The giver may seek to limit his liability on the certificate to named recipients and/or to limit the validity of the certificate for a specified period, e.g. three months from its date.

4.3.2. The object of certification is not to give evidence of a perfect title but to provide an accurate description of the legal character of the property in question. Any material information or irregularities affecting the property should be stated in a schedule to the certificate.

4.3.3. To be of practical use to the recipient the certificate should deal with the following matters:

(a) ownership of the property;

(b) an adequate description of the property;

(c) its tenure with relevant details;

(d) the name of the current owner of the estate in land;

(e) whether the title to the land is good, marketable and unencumbered;

(f) whether there are any statutory orders, schemes or provisions detrimental to the property or its use;

(g) where appropriate, provisions relating to planning, highways, public health, etc., should be referred to;

(h) appropriate searches which have been made at the Land Registry, the Land Charges Department and the district council, and other relevant searches;

(i) which searches have not been carried out in order to give the recipient a complete picture of the title which he is accepting.

4.3.4. Although the certificate should be positive, a solicitor should qualify it to suit the circumstances where it has not been possible to obtain or to verify all the relevant information.

4.3.5. Where a certificate of title has been requested by a mortgage lender and the form has been provided by the lender, care must be taken to ensure that the certificate does not breach Rule 6(3). This Rule applies whenever the solicitor is acting for the lender (see the Law Society's Gazette, 22 August 2002 and Appendix V.13).

4.3.6. Where land is being purchased under right to buy legislation, the Land Registry is bound to accept a certificate of title supplied by the seller, the seller being obliged to indemnify the Registry if the certificate turns out to be inaccurate.

I. NEW PROPERTIES

I1. New property

See also: Value added tax, para. A16
Pre-contract searches and enquiries, para. B10
Plans, para. B21
Planning, para. B24
Sales of part, para. J1
Insurance, Appendix X

1.1.   Introduction

1.1.1.   A sale of a new property is a more complex transaction than the sale of an existing house or building, and some matters additional to those relevant to a sale of an existing house or building must be considered. The following paragraphs only deal with those matters which are exclusive to new properties.

1.2.   The contract

1.2.1.   Where the property comprises a plot on a new building estate the contract will often be in standard form and the seller will be reluctant to allow substantial amendments to that form.[1] The buyer's solicitor should ensure that the contract does not impose unnecessarily burdensome terms on the buyer, sufficiently protects his client's interests and complies with any conditions required by the buyer's lender. The seller may require the deposit to be paid to him as 'agent' and not as 'stakeholder'. The consequences of this requirement should be explained to the buyer and the lender's consent to such a contractual condition obtained.

1.2.2.   A contract for the sale of a new property will frequently be a sale of part of the seller's existing property and may comprise a plot on a new building estate. In either case adequate provision must be made in the contract for the grant and reservation of easements to the parties and the property being sold will usually be described by reference to a plan which should be coloured in accordance with the Land Registry requirements.[2]

1.2.3.   The contract should require the seller to complete the building works in accordance with the agreed specifications, planning permissions and plans submitted to the buyer. It may also contain a 'long stop' completion date requiring the builder to use his reasonable endeavours to complete the building works within a specified period so that, e.g. in the event of a prolonged strike by the workmen on site the buyer has the opportunity to rescind the contract. The buyer and his lender may wish to have a right to inspect the property during and at the completion of the building works.

1.2.4. Where the property being sold is in the course of construction it may not be possible for the seller to agree a definite completion date at the time of exchange since he will not be able to guarantee that the building works will be completed by a specified time. In such a case he may prefer to include a condition in the contract providing for completion of the transaction to take place within a specified number of days after completion of the building works.[3] This type of condition may give rise to difficulties from the buyer's point of view since if he is involved in a chain of transactions such a condition will make it difficult to synchronise the chain, unless similar conditions relating to completion are imposed in every transaction in the chain. The buyer should therefore be advised of this difficulty and warned of the possibility that in the event of the transactions not being synchronised the buyer may either have to complete his dependent sale first and move into tempo-rary accommodation pending completion of the new property, or be prepared to use bridging finance for the completion of the new property pending sale of the old one. Where completion is to take place within a specified number of days of completion of the building works, the buyer's solicitor should also ensure that the number of days provided by the contract gives the buyer's solicitor sufficient time in which to carry out his pre-completion searches and to arrange for the purchase price to be obtained and for a final inspection of the building by the buyer's lender's surveyor. In addition, the contract should provide that notice of the completion date cannot be given unless (as applicable) the home warranty cover note has been issued (see para. 1.7.2) and/or a completion certificate has been issued under the Building Regulations (see para. 1.3.2).

1.2.5. Provision may be made for the seller to rectify minor defects in the building within a specified time after completion, although where the property is to be covered by a structural defects policy (see para. I1.5) this matter will usually be covered by such a policy. A contract to build a building is a contract for services within Supply of Goods and Services Act 1982 which implies a condition that the builder will provide his services to a reasonable standard and within a reasonable time if no time is specified in the contract (see para. I1.7).

1.2.6. The buyer should consider whether the contract should provide for the builder to remove all builder's rubbish from the site before completion, to leave the prop-erty in a clean and tidy condition, for the erection of boundary fences, and if appropriate for the landscaping of the gardens and surrounding areas.

1.2.7. New restrictive covenants will frequently be imposed on the buyer by the contract. From the seller's point of view, the imposition of the covenants will be done to allow the seller to maximise his ability to sell the remainder of the houses in the development. From the buyer's point of view, the imposition of such covenants provides the buyer with the certainty that the estate will be developed and will remain in a saleable condition without having to worry about unsightly or undesirable alterations carried out by neighbours to their properties. The wording of the covenants should be checked to ensure that they do not impose an unnecessary or burdensome restriction on the buyer's use and enjoyment of the property and their significance explained to the buyer.[4]

1.2.8.   The plan attached to the purchase deed should be signed by the seller and by or on behalf of the buyer.

1.2.9.   Where there is to be a long delay between exchange of contracts and completion, the buyer's contract should be protected by registration.[5]

1. The terms of the contract may be subject to Unfair Terms in Consumer Contracts Regulations 1994, S.I. 1994/3159, see para. B11.11.
2. See Sales of part, para. J1 and Plans, para. B21.
3. The building works will be 'complete' on the issue of a certificate of practical completion or on certification by the seller's architect. Habitation certificates are not generally now issued on completion of a building.
4. See The purchase deed, para. E1.
5. See After exchange, para. C5.

1.3.   Planning permission

1.3.1.   The erection of a new building will normally require both express planning permission and building regulation consent. Copies of the relevant documents should be supplied to the buyer's solicitor prior to exchange of contracts and should be checked by the client or his surveyor to ensure (as far as possible) that the erection of the building complies with the permissions and with any restrictions or conditions attached to them. If on the face of the planning permission there are reserved matters requiring the further consent of the planning authority, compliance with such matters should be checked by the buyer's solicitor. Where there is a short-term condition attached to the permission which affects the right to occupy the property (e.g. the property shall not be occupied until all estate roads have been completed) the contract must be checked to ensure that the completion date specified in the contract can, if necessary, be adjusted to take account of this restriction on occupation. The contract may contain a warranty given by the seller to the effect that he has complied with all restrictions and conditions attached to the planning permission.

1.3.2.   In relation to work completed after 1 June 1992 it may be possible to obtain a certificate of completion of the building works from the local authority. The buyer should enquire whether such a certificate is available (see para. I1.7).

1.4.   Roads and drains

1.4.1.   *Roads*

The buyer's solicitor will need to check whether the roads and street lighting adjoining the property are publicly maintained or are intended to be so. Where the property forms part of a new building estate the seller (or developer) will frequently have entered into an agreement with the local highway authority under Highways Act 1980, s.38 whereby the highway authority will, after a certain period of time, adopt the highway and thereafter maintain it at public expense. Such an agreement should be supported by a bond which will guarantee sufficient money to allow the making up of the road to the proper standards required by the highway authority in case of default by the developer. Where appropriate a copy of the section 38 agreement and bond should be supplied to the buyer's solicitor with the draft contract and the buyer's solicitor should ask his client whether he wants his surveyor to check the bond to ensure that the amount guaranteed by it is adequate to cover the cost of the outstanding roadworks. In practice it is difficult to estimate the cost of the outstanding works and the buyer's solicitor may have to accept the bond which is offered without further investigation. The contract should contain provisions allowing the buyer and his employees, and others authorised by him, a right of access over the road pending its adoption. If no agreement and bond has been entered into, the road will remain in private ownership, maintainable at the expense of the owner. In such a case the buyer's solicitor must ensure that his client is given adequate rights of way to provide access to the property, and should ascertain that proper provisions are being made for the maintenance of the road and the likely cost of maintenance. The buyer and his lender must be advised accordingly. Where the property forms part of a small new estate it is common for the roads to remain in the ownership of the seller (or developer). From the buyer's point of view, the contract should then contain a covenant for maintenance by the road owner (at the shared cost of the buyer and owners of other houses on the estate), with provision for the house owners to carry out the work and recover any charges from other liable contributors in the event of default by the road owner. Such a provision may be dealt with by the imposition of an estate rentcharge under Rentcharges Act 1977.[1] In appropriate cases the client should be advised of any potential liability to road charges arising out of section 219 of Highways Act 1980 (where advance payments procedure has not been correctly followed by builder and local authority) or arising from the situation where (as is not uncommon) the local authority has released the builder from his bond in relation to part of the development but without formally adopting the roads in the part released.

1.4.2.   Drains

Except where the property is being built in a rural area, the seller will normally have entered into an agreement and bond with the water authority under Water Industry Act 1991, s.104 for the ownership and maintenance of the drains to be transferred to the water authority within a certain time after completion of the building works. Similar considerations apply here as in relation to the maintenance of highways (see para. I1.4.1). If the drainage system is to remain in private ownership a drainage survey may be desirable to ensure that the system under construction will be adequate to service the property.

1. See para. K15.

1.5.   Insurance against structural defects

1.5.1.   Most new residential properties will be offered with the benefit of structural defects insurance, e.g. the NHBC 'Buildmark' or similar scheme, which provides the buyer and his successors in title with insurance against structural defects in the property for a number of years after completion of the building. The contract will normally provide for such cover to be obtained by the seller without cost to the buyer and the appropriate insurance policy and other documentation should be supplied to the buyer on or before completion. Municipal Mutual Insurance Co. Ltd (MMI), underwriters to the Foundation 15 scheme, ceased to write new business under that scheme on 1 October 1992 but existing initial or final certificates issued before that date continue in force and are accepted by lenders. A summary of schemes appears in Appendix X.

1.5.2. The absence of such insurance cover may present the buyer with problems since it will frequently be a condition of the mortgage offer that cover is obtained. Even where the present buyer is not financing his purchase with the assistance of a mortgage, a subsequent buyer who buys the property within the first 10 years after its construction will expect to take the benefit of the policy, and thus the absence of such cover will restrict the potential both to mortgage and to resell the property.

1.5.3. The terms of the policies and their limitations should be examined in each case and their effect explained to the client. The explanatory notes furnished with the scheme documentation should be handed to the client.

1.5.4. It should be noted that subsidence is not generally covered by these schemes and so must be covered by the buyer's buildings insurance policy. The builder's liability under the schemes is often limited to the first two years after completion. After that time, the policy only covers structural defects. A structural survey of the property may be desirable immediately prior to the end of the two-year period.

1.5.5. Where a property is to be covered by a structural defects scheme a full survey may not be necessary, particularly if the property is still in the course of construction so that there is very little for the surveyor actually to survey. However, the usual mining and environmental searches (if applicable) should be undertaken. In some cases a surveyor may be asked to look at the plans for the prospective building to ensure that as far as can be ascertained the building is to be erected in accordance with the client's wishes and expectations.

1.5.6. *Assignment of policy*

The benefit of the policy can be assigned to a subsequent buyer of the property. NHBC will honour the policy in favour of a subsequent buyer irrespective of whether a formal assignment has taken place between the original and subsequent buyers. A formal assignment of the benefit of the policy may be desirable in other cases.

1.5.7. Where the property is being constructed under the supervision of an architect (e.g. under a JCT contract), a lender may accept an architect's certificate of completion of the building in place of a structural defects policy, although in such a case it may be desirable from the buyer's point of view for the contract to contain warranties given by the seller as to the proper design and construction of the building. The insurance cover carried by architects will only provide indemnity if the architect has a valid current policy at the time when liability is notified to the insurers. If therefore the architect has died or ceased to practise since completion of the building and before liability is discovered there may be no insurance policy in force to meet the claim and the architect's own assets or estate may be insufficient to cover the liability.

1.5.8. Defective Premises Act 1972 implies a term into a contract to purchase a building in the course of construction that the building when built will be habitable.

1.6. Payment of purchase price

1.6.1. The contract should state clearly whether the buyer is required to pay an additional price for extras (e.g. a coloured bathroom suite) and, if so, how much.

1.6.2. Some builders require the purchase price to be paid in stages as the building works progress. In such a case the buyer's lender must be informed of this fact and his agreement sought to release the mortgage advance in accordance with the builder's requirements. For the buyer's protection, he may seek an equitable charge over the property to the extent of the instalments paid by him. Such a charge must be registered and the contract to purchase should also be protected by registration as an estate contract since completion is unlikely to follow quickly after exchange of contracts in this situation. The lender's consent should be obtained to the form of the contract prior to exchange.

1.6.3. Any retention made by the buyer's mortgagee, e.g. in respect of outstanding roadworks must be discussed with the buyer and arrangements made to cover the resulting shortfall in time for completion.

1.6.4. Where the new property is a single building, i.e. not part of an estate development, it may be advantageous for the buyer initially to enter a contract to buy the site alone, and then to have a second contract for the builder to build the house or other building. In such a case the builder would expect to take a charge over the site to secure payment for the building works. There are possible stamp duty savings for the buyer if the two stages of the development are separated in this way.[1]

1. See below, Inland Revenue Practice Statement, App. IX.1.

1.7. Mortgages

1.7.1. It is usually a condition of the mortgage on a new property that the structural defects insurance must be in place before completion of the transaction and release of the mortgage funds. The following procedure has been agreed between the Council of Mortgage Lenders, the Law Society, the House Builders Federation, NHBC, Zurich Insurance and Premier Guarantee.

1.7.2. 'The lender will not release the mortgage funds until the conveyancer has received confirmation (a copy of the cover note or insurance certificate in the prescribed form) that the full New Home Warranty will be in place on or before completion. This revised approach will apply to transactions involving new properties being built or converted in accordance with the New Home Warranty scheme, and which exchange contracts on or after 1 April 2003. It will not apply to self-build schemes.'

1.7.3. The Certificate of Title cannot be sent to the lender until the solicitor has received the appropriate confirmation from the builder. See also para. 6.6.2 Lenders' Handbook.

1.7.4. Problems may be encountered when clients want to obtain occupation of the property as early as possible as this new procedure may lead to short delays. Clients should be advised at the outset that completion will not take place until this procedure has been carried out.

1.7.5. Problems may also be encountered in view of the fact that the confirmation will be issued provided there are no 'red' defects in the property. This means that the confirmation will be issued whilst there are still defects in the building, 'green' defects. Solicitors should request a list of the 'green' defects and the date by which the outstanding defects will be rectified. The client must be informed of their existence and of the time scale for correction.

1.8. Building estates

1.8.1. This paragraph does not deal in detail with site acquisition and development for which the reader should refer to a specialist work on the subject.

1.8.2. *Checklist for seller's solicitor*

(a) Has the site been inspected to ascertain the boundaries of each plot and the extent of easements and reservations?

(b) Has planning permission been obtained?

(c) Has a section 38 agreement and bond been obtained in respect of the roads?

(d) Has a section 104 agreement and bond been obtained in respect of sewers?

(e) Who is responsible for building regulation control and who will issue the certificate of completion of the building?

(f) Is the seller to make (and regularly update) pre-contract searches or will this be each buyer's responsibility?

(g) In residential cases will the Protocol be used; if so what variations to it are necessary to meet the present transactions? Remember to notify the buyer's solicitor of such variations.

(h) Will the property be covered by structural defects insurance? Has the builder registered and handed to his solicitor the appropriate documentation? (See para. I1.5.4.) Ensure that an unqualified (i.e. unconditional) certificate will be issued.

(i) Has an estate plan been prepared and approved by the Land Registry?

(j) Has the form of transfer been approved by the Land Registry? This is not essential but may save time and requisitions from the Land Registry at a later stage.

(k) Has all the necessary pre-contract documentation been prepared and duplicated for each plot? (See para. I1.8.3.)

(l) Have arrangements been made with the seller's lender to release the plots from the charge?

(m) Has the builder complied with Construction (Design and Management) Regulations 1994, S.I. 1994/3140 (e.g. the appointment of a planning supervisor)?

1.8.3. Documents to be prepared and sent to the prospective buyer's solicitor for each plot on receipt of instructions:

(a) Pre-contract enquiries with answers.

(b) Pre-contract searches with replies (where the seller is to undertake this task).

(c) Draft contract in duplicate (with buyer's name left blank).

(d) Draft transfer in duplicate with plan attached (annexed to contract, buyer's name left blank).

(e) Evidence of title.

(f) Requisitions on title with answers.

(g) Copies of relevant planning permissions and building regulation approval.

(h) Copies of relevant section 104 and section 38 agreements and bonds.

(i) Structural defects insurance documentation where appropriate.

(j) A copy of the plan of the property properly marked and coloured in accordance with Land Registry requirements, with a spare copy for search purposes.

(k) If desired, a general information sheet for the buyer containing *inter alia* address of local authorities and other bodies with whom searches may need to be conducted, explanation of the contract terms (including arrangements for deposit and completion), notification of whether the Protocol will be used (residential transactions) and of any variations to it.

(l) Covering letter.

2. Defects in new commercial buildings

2.1. Introduction

2.1.1. The owner or tenant of a new commercial building,[1] not being the party for whom the building was constructed or refurbished, will only be in a position to recover the cost of remedying defects to the building from the contractor or professional team (architect, engineer, etc.) if he has a contractual relationship with them.[2] He would, however, be able to sue the contractor or other professional in negligence for damages arising out of personal injury or damage to other property. To enable the subsequent owner to be able to sue the contractor or other professional for the cost of remedial works to the building, he needs to establish an enforceable contractual relationship with the contractor or professional who is to be sued.[3] This can be achieved either by creating new contracts between the subsequent owner/tenant and the contractor/professionals (these are usually called 'collateral warranties') or, where practical, by taking an assignment from the original owner of the building of his original contract(s) with the contractor/professionals. The subsequent owner/tenant might additionally seek a warranty from the original owner as to the condition of the building even in the current market, which may be difficult to obtain; sellers and landlords of new buildings understandably prefer the liability for defects to rest with the contractor/professionals.

2.1.2. Collateral warranties

A buyer or tenant of a new commercial building should, as a term of the contract, require the seller or landlord to procure that on completion collateral warranties in favour of the buyer/tenant are provided by the contractor and all professionals in the form approved by the buyer/tenant. In these the contractor/professionals warrant that they have to date exercised reasonable skill and care and (where work is unfinished at the time of the contract) agree to continue to do so. Other terms are generally included dealing with professional indemnity insurance, the limitation period, assignment and limitations on the warrantor's liability, for example where the defect was partly his fault and partly the fault of other parties.[4]

2.1.3. Assignment of original contracts

Where the whole development is being sold or let the buyer/tenant should consider requiring an assignment of the original contracts with the contractor/

professionals with a view to putting the buyer/tenant in a position to recover under these contracts for any breaches by the contractor/professionals.

2.1.4. In the following paragraphs references to 'A' are to the contractor, architect or other professional, 'B' is the original owner of the building who entered the construction (or as the case may be) contract with A (the 'A–B' contract), and C is the subsequent owner of the building who, having purchased from B, seeks to enforce a term of the A–B contract.

1. i.e. not covered by a structural insurance policy.
2. *Murphy* v. *Brentwood District Council* [1991] 1 AC 398; *Department of the Environment* v. *Thomas Bates & Son Ltd* [1991] 1 AC 499.
3. *Ibid.*
4. See, e.g. the precedents produced by the British Property Federation.

2.2. Method of assignment

2.2.1. The object of the assignment is a chose in action which, by section 136(1) of Law of Property Act 1925 must be in writing (between B and C) and notice of the assignment must be given to A. Notice of the assignment could be given by either B or C, but it is clearly in C's interests to ensure that it is done. A should be asked to sign and return one copy of the notice of assignment served on him in duplicate by C so that tangible evidence exists of the fact that notice was correctly given.

2.3. Types of assignment

2.3.1. The object of the exercise is to enable the benefit of the contract between A and B to be transferred to and enforced by C against A.

2.3.2. *Novation*

Where it is intended that obligations under the A–B contract should be assigned, a novation must take place. The assignment of one party's burdens or obligations can only be done with the consent of the other original contracting party. Therefore, for this to occur, a new contract, made between A, B, and C, will have to be entered into.

2.3.3. *Sub-contract*

A might enter a sub-contract with D (the sub-contractor) under which D agreed with A to perform some or all of A's obligations to B under the A–B contract. This is effectively an assignment of A's obligations without B's consent, but in this situation A always remains liable to B since the original contract between A and B has been neither novated nor discharged. Any defect in D's performance can therefore be remedied by an action by B against A. The main issue in this situation is whether B is bound to accept D's performance of the contract in A's place. Where the obligations to be performed by A are construed as 'personal services', B cannot be forced to accept performance from anyone other than the original contracting party, i.e. he is entitled to reject D's performance and treat A as being in breach of contract. An obligation to carry out building works has been held to be within the concept of personal services.[1]

2.3.4. *Assignment of benefits or rights*

Where there is a prohibition against the assignment of the benefit of the contract, that prohibition is effective to prevent the assignment unless the party with the burden of performance consents to it. Thus an assignment by A to C of the benefit of the A–B contract would require B's consent. This applies irrespective of whether the assignment is of accrued rights (e.g. existing breaches committed by B) or of future rights (e.g. the right to sue for breaches as and when they occur in the future).[2]

2.3.5.

If assignment is not possible (because B will not consent) C's remedy lies in persuading A to take direct action against B. The contract between A and C should contain warranties to this effect given by A. The damages recoverable by A on C's behalf are not restricted to A's losses (which may be nominal since he will no longer have an interest in the property) but can include reimbursement of losses suffered by C.[3] The contract between A and C should also contain a warranty given by A to hold any damages recovered on behalf of C.

1. See *Southway Group Ltd* v. *Wolff* [1991] EGCS 82 (CA).
2. *Linden Gardens Trust Ltd* v. *Lenesta Sludge Disposals Ltd*; *St Martins Property Corporation Ltd* v. *Sir Robert McAlpine Ltd* [1993] 3 WLR 408. See also *Darlington Borough Council* v. *Wiltshire Northern Ltd, The Times*, 4 July 1994 (CA). See also *Alfred McAlpine Construction Ltd* v. *Panatown Ltd, The Times*, 11 February 1998.
3. *Ibid.*

2.4. **Protection of subsequent owners**

2.4.1.
In view of the uncertainty demonstrated by the general law a subsequent owner of a building needs to ensure that he will have the right to recover his losses in the event of a later defect being discovered.

2.4.2.
In residential property transactions, the property will normally be covered by a structural defects insurance policy which should provide adequate protection for the buyer.

2.4.3.
In commercial situations a buyer from the original owner should ensure that his contract to purchase contains warranties given by the original owner, and that a valid novation or assignment with the contractor's consent takes place. Protection of the subsequent owner is a matter to which attention should be paid when the original owner is entering the original A–B contracts. If at that stage he can ensure that there is no prohibition against assignment in the A–B contract, the benefit of the A–B contract may more easily be assigned to C at a later stage.

2.4.4.
The distinction between the assignment of obligations and fruits of performance should not, however, be overlooked since the court seems to apply different rules to these two types of benefit.

2.5. Contracts (Rights of Third Parties) Act 1999

2.5.1.   The Contracts (Rights of Third Parties) Act 1999 permits a person or company who is not a contracting party to enforce a term of contract, as if he or it was a contracting party, unless the contract indicates that the actual parties did not intend such right of enforcement to arise. The term must be made for the third party's benefit and the third party must be identified in the contract by name, description or implication. The third party does not, however, have to be in existence at the time when the contract is made (e.g. a company not yet incorporated). The provisions of this Act may therefore provide a simpler method of enforcing warranties than that outlined above. Defences and exclusion clauses which would be available to a contracting party can be used against the third party who is seeking to enforce the contract. The Act can be expressly excluded from a contract. It should, however, be noted that where a third party is to benefit under the Act, the contract between the original contracting parties cannot be varied so as to affect the third party without the third party's consent. This provision, too, may be excluded from the contract.

J. SALES OF PART

J1. Sales of part

See also: Plans, para. B21
The purchase deed, para. E1

1.1. Introduction

1.1.1. A sale of part is a more complex transaction than the sale of the whole of the seller's interest in a particular piece of land, and some matters additional to those relevant to a sale of whole must be considered. The following paragraphs only deal with those matters which are exclusive to sales of part.

1.2. Description of the land

1.2.1. The description of the land in the seller's existing register and/or title deeds may not suffice to describe the part of the land being sold and a new, accurate description of the property must then be devised to describe the land in the particulars of sale of the contract. It will usually be necessary to identify the land by reference to a plan.[1] There may be circumstances in which it is useful for the seller's solicitor to inspect the property prior to drafting the contract.

1.2.2. *Retained land*

Reference will usually have to be made to the land which is to remain in the ownership of the seller after the sale off, e.g. in relation to easements and reservations; such land must therefore also be defined verbally in the contract and marked clearly on the plan attached to the contract.

1.2.3. Where the sale is of part of a registered title and comprises a plot on a building estate, the seller will frequently have deposited an estate plan at the Land Registry and the official copies which are issued will give a certificate of inspection in Form C1 in lieu of a title plan.[2] Where the estate plan procedure is used it is important that it is strictly adhered to in order to avoid difficulties. In addition the solicitor should emphasise to his builder client that if revisions are made on the ground to the layout shown on the approved estate plan, the builder should notify the solicitor immediately so that the solicitor can inform the Land Registry and submit a revised estate plan.

1. See para. J1.6.1 as to the Land Registry's requirements.
2. Land Registration Rules 2003, rr. 134 and 143.

1.3.   Grants and reservations

1.3.1.   On a sale of part of land Law of Property Act 1925, s.62 and the rule in *Wheeldon* v. *Burrows*[1] may give the buyer as easements certain rights over the land which are continuous and apparent, are necessary for the reasonable enjoyment of the land sold, and which had been and are at the time of the sale used by the seller for the benefit of the part sold. Although Law of Property Act 1925, s.62 and the rule in *Wheeldon* v. *Burrows*[2] will give the buyer such easements and quasi-easements as were previously enjoyed by the land before its division, the existence and extent of these implied rights may not be entirely clear and, for certainty, such matters should be dealt with expressly in the contract. Easements which pass by the operation of these provisions cannot give the buyer any right which the seller had no power to grant, and do not create any better title to any right than the seller is able to transfer. It will therefore usually be necessary to grant new express easements to the buyer, e.g. for a right of way or drainage. Express easements which are to arise in the future must comply with the perpetuity rule.

1.3.2.   Section 62 of Law of Property Act 1925 and the rule in *Wheeldon* v. *Burrows*[3] only operate in the buyer's favour. There is no reciprocal section or case which entitles the seller to easements over the land being sold off (other than easements of necessity). For this reason it is important to consider what rights the seller will need to exercise over the land being sold, e.g. passage of cables, drainage, etc., and to reserve these expressly in the contract.

1.3.3.   Rights of light and air may pass to the buyer under either Law of Property Act 1925, s.62 or the rule in *Wheeldon* v. *Burrows*.[4] The acquisition of such rights by the buyer may have adverse consequences for the seller since the buyer might be able by exercising such rights to prevent the seller from building on his retained land. It is therefore usually considered necessary to exclude the buyer's right to easements of light and air by an express condition in the contract which provides for the insertion of a provision to this effect in the purchase deed.[5] Standard Condition 3.3.2 and Standard Commercial Property Condition 3.4.2 both contain a provision to this effect.

1.3.4.   Standard Condition 3.3 and Standard Commercial Property Condition 3.3 both provide for the mutual grant of easements and reservations on a sale of part, but the rights given by this condition are limited and will in most cases be inadequate to deal effectively with the parties' requirements on a sale of part of land.

1.3.5   In registered land, a proprietor who claims the benefit of a legal easement or profit à prendre which has been acquired by implication (or prescription) may apply for it to be registered as appurtenant to the registered estate.[6]

1. (1879) 12 Ch. 31.
2. *Ibid.*
3. *Ibid.*
4. *Ibid.*

5. See Emmet and Farrand on Title, Chapter 15 (and Appendix X1.7).
6. Land Registration Rules 2003, r.74.

1.4. Imposition of new covenants[1]

1.4.1. In many cases the seller will wish to impose new covenants on the buyer, e.g. restricting the future use of the land. Provision for the imposition of new restrictions must be made expressly in the contract.

1.4.2. Covenants which are imposed on the sale of a new house on a building estate will usually comply with the terms of a building scheme.[2] In other cases, the enforceability of such restrictions against a subsequent purchaser of the land depends on their being negative in substance, expressly taken for the benefit of the seller's retained land, and registered on the charges register of the title (or as class D(ii) land charges in unregistered land).[3] Positive covenants may be indirectly enforced through a chain of indemnity covenants but their burden does not run with the land. Where the contract expressly provides for a covenant to benefit a subsequent owner the subsequent owner may be able to enforce the covenant (whether positive or negative) through the Contracts (Rights of Third Parties) Act 1999. This Act is not retrospective in operation.

1. See The purchase deed, para. E1.
2. See *Re Dolphin's Conveyance* [1970] 1 Ch 654.
3. *Tulk* v. *Moxhay* (1848) 2 Ph 774.

1.5. Consent of seller's lender

1.5.1. Where the land to be sold comprises part of the land which is mortgaged to the seller's lender, the seller must, at the earliest possible opportunity, obtain his lender's consent to the transaction. It should be ascertained from the lender whether the lender requires repayment of the whole or any part of the principal sums owing out of the proceeds of the sale of part and, if part, how much. Arrangements must be made for the lender to discharge the land being sold from the mortgage. In registered land the discharge is in Form DS3 (accompanied by a plan to show the extent of the land being released if not sufficiently defined on the title plan). In unregistered land the lender may either give a deed of release, or he may prefer to be joined as a party to the conveyance in order both to release the land being sold and to give a receipt for the money being paid to him. If the lender has taken a mortgage by way of deposit of the title deeds, he will give a consent to dealing on completion; no formal release is necessary in these circumstances.

1.6. The purchase deed

1.6.1. Registered land

A transfer of part will be drawn up to reflect the contract terms. The seller's title number is used in panel 2 of the transfer form, a new title number being allocated to the land sold off on registration of the sale of part. A transfer of part must have attached to it a plan identifying clearly the land dealt with. If the land dealt with is identified clearly on the title plan of the registered title, it may instead be described by reference to that title plan.[1] The transfer should be executed by the transferor; and by the transferee if it contains transferee's covenants or declarations or contains an application by the transferee (e.g. for a restriction). In the case of joint transferees, the transfer must be executed by each of them.[2] The transfer plan need only be signed by the transferor.[3] The buyer's pre-completion search at the Land Registry should be made on Form OS2 accompanied by a plan in duplicate or should refer to a Land Registry approved plan or plot number supplied by the seller.

1.6.2.   Unregistered land

The conveyance will reflect the terms of the contract. Although a plan is not essential in unregistered land, it is highly desirable in cases where only part of the seller's estate is being sold and should be signed by both parties. Since the seller will be retaining the documents of title an acknowledgement for production and undertaking for safe custody (where appropriate) of the deeds should be included in the conveyance.[4] Where the seller is selling other than as beneficial owner, only an acknowledgement will be given. The undertaking is not given by owners who are selling in a fiduciary capacity. Where the land is subject to a mortgage the seller may be required to give a covenant that he will give the statutory undertaking for safe custody of the deeds as and when they come into his possession. Where the buyer is entering into a covenant in the deed (whether for indemnity or to observe fresh restrictive covenants) he must execute the purchase deed.

1.6.3.   Commonly the draft purchase deed will be prepared by the seller and annexed to the draft contract so that the buyer in fact has no discretion over its contents.

1. Land Registration Rules 2003, rr.213(1) and (4).
2. See the prescribed forms of transfer in Land Registration Rules 2003, Sched. 1; and see Appendix XIII.1.
3. Land Registration Rules 2003, r.213(2).
4. See Law of Property Act 1925, s.64 and Standard Condition 4.5.5 and Standard Commercial Property Condition 4.5.5.

1.7.   Completion and post-completion

1.7.1.   Where the land is unregistered, the seller will not be handing over his title deeds to the buyer on completion; the buyer should therefore verify his abstract or epitome against the original deeds and mark his abstract or epitome as examined against the original.[1] Where the Protocol is used the seller is required to mark the abstract as examined against the original title deeds before sending it to the buyer. Even where the title to the land bought is to be registered immediately after completion this procedure is necessary so that the buyer can produce proper evidence of the title to the Land Registry with his application for first registration. Additionally, a memorandum of the sale off should be noted on the most recent of the seller's retained title deeds to prevent a second sale of the same land by the seller.[2] A note of any restrictive covenants imposed by the conveyance to the buyer (or a copy of that conveyance) should also be retained by the seller. New restrictive covenants will automatically be entered on the register of the new title on first registration.

1.7.2. Where the seller's title is already registered it is not necessary to provide for an acknowledgement for production of the deeds nor for a memorandum to be endorsed on the seller's deeds since the buyer will obtain his own title number on registration of the sale of part. An acknowledgement is needed where the sale is of part only of a lease or where the purchase deed is to be executed in duplicate. New restrictive covenants imposed or rights reserved by the transfer of part will automatically be entered on the charges register of the new title on registration.[3]

1.7.3. A lender who has custody of the title deeds will give an acknowledgement for their production. Such an acknowledgement may be contained in the deed of release supplied by the lender but is not necessary when dealing with registered land.

1.7.4. In some cases where new covenants are being imposed the contract will require the buyer to prepare the purchase deed in duplicate, the duplicate copy to be stamped and denoted at the buyer's expense and then handed to the seller as a record of the transaction. An acknowledgement for production is required in this situation.[4]

1. See Completion, section F.
2. See Law of Property Act 1925, s.200.
3. Land Registration Rules 2003, r.72(2).
4. See Standard Condition 4.5.5 and Standard Commercial Property Condition 4.5.5.

1.8. Checklist of matters to be considered on sale of part

1.8.1. Easements in the buyer's favour

    (a) To what extent will Law of Property Act 1925, s.62 and/or the rule in *Wheeldon* v. *Burrows* imply easements in the buyer's favour?[1]

    (b) Is it necessary to extend the implied easements by granting express rights to the buyer?[2]

    (c) What does the buyer need, for example:

        (i) rights of way;

        (ii) right to lay new cables/pipelines/drains;

        (iii) right to use/maintain existing or new pipelines/cables/drains?

1.8.2. *Rights of way*

(a) Will the right be to pass over the land in both directions or should it be restricted to one way only?

(b) Should the right be restricted, e.g. to a particular class of user, e.g. pedestrian only?

(c) Is the exercise of the right to be restricted, e.g. use only for a particular purpose or only at a specified time of day?

1.8.3. *All easements*

(a) Is the route of the right of way/drain, etc., specified on the plan?

(b) Who is liable for maintenance/repairs?

(c) Will it be necessary for the buyer to enter the seller's land to inspect the state of repair and/or to maintain?

(d) Should the buyer's access to inspect be restricted, e.g. a right to inspect on 24 hours' notice except in case of emergency?

(e) Should the buyer be under an obligation to cause no unnecessary damage and to make good any damage done while inspecting/maintaining?

(f) Where the buyer is to construct a new pipeline/cable, etc., should he be required to finish the construction works within a specified period after completion?

1.8.4. *Reservations*

(a) Remember the seller generally gets nothing under the implied grant rules.

(b) After completion will the seller need to continue to use a right of way/drain/pipeline/cable passing through the land being sold?

(c) If so, express reservations must be included in the contract by way of special condition. The same considerations in drafting apply as in paras. J1.8.2 and J1.8.3.

(d) Additionally, to protect the seller, it may be considered necessary to include a general reservations clause in his favour dealing with all easements, quasi-easements, etc., presently enjoyed by the land as a whole.

(e) Should rights of light and air be expressly reserved in order to preserve the seller's freedom to use the retained land in the future?[3]

1.8.5. *Existing covenants*

Is an indemnity clause required?[4]

1.8.6. *New covenants*[5]

(a) Should new restrictive covenants be imposed?

(b) If so, what type of restrictions will serve to protect the seller's land without imposing unnecessary constraints on the buyer?

(c) Consider:

   (i)   erection of new buildings on the land;

   (ii) use of the land;

   (iii) repair/maintenance of buildings or land;

   (iv) general covenant against nuisance.[6]

(d) Will the covenants be negative in nature?

(e) Do the words used ensure that the covenants will create an enforceable obligation?

1.8.7. *Description of the property in the contract*

(a) Does the wording of the particulars accurately describe the land being sold?

(b) Has the seller's retained land been precisely defined?[7]

(c) Is there reference in the particulars to a plan?

(d) Is the plan of sufficient size and scale to be able to delineate accurately both the area of land being sold and the routes of easements, etc.?

(e) Is a scale plan needed; if so is it accurate?

(f) If the plan is not to scale, do the particulars refer to the plan as being for identification purposes only? This phrase is not acceptable for transfers of part of registered land.

1.8.8. *Seller's lender*

(a) Will it be necessary to obtain the lender's consent to the sale – if so has this been obtained?

(b) How will the lender deal with the release of the land being sold from the mortgage?

1. Section 62 of Law of Property Act 1925 may operate to create easements over retained land where at the time of sale the two tenements are in separate occupation. Further, the rule in *Wheeldon* v. *Burrows* (1879) 12 Ch 31 will impliedly grant to the buyer as easements all rights which are continuous and apparent and reasonably necessary to the reasonable enjoyment of the property sold. These provisions will normally have the effect of giving the buyer fewer easements than he requires, but in some cases may give him more than the seller intends. It is therefore considered safer to negate the effect of these rules in the contract and to deal with easements by way of express grant.
2. Since the extent of the implied easements created by the implied grant rules is not always clear, these matters are better dealt with by way of express condition. Standard Condition 3.4 and Standard Commercial Property

Condition 3.4 deal briefly with easements but do not normally give adequate rights to the buyer; hence the need for express special conditions.

3. Standard Condition 3.4.2 and Standard Commercial Property Condition 3.4.2 reserve rights of light and air to the seller.

4. Standard Condition 4.5.4 and Standard Commercial Property Condition 4.5.4 requires indemnity covenants but it is common to include an indemnity clause by way of special condition in order specifically to draw the requirement to the buyer's attention. See The purchase deed, para. E1.

5. See The purchase deed, para. E1.

6. Nuisance is a tort actionable at common law; therefore the imposition of such a covenant may strictly be unnecessary.

7. Inspection of the property may assist with these matters. It may also be desirable to peg out the boundaries to the property or to ask a surveyor to confirm that it is possible to plot the site.

K. LEASEHOLDS

This section deals only with those matters where the considerations applicable to lease-hold property differ from the requirements outlined in other sections of this handbook relating to freehold land.

Some problem areas, e.g. licences to assign, are confined exclusively to the context of leaseholds and these are discussed within this section of the handbook.

A summary of the law relating to security of tenure is included, but the handbook does not contain a comprehensive guide to this topic.

The first group of paragraphs within this section deal with matters which are applicable to most leases, whether short or long and whether of business or residential premises. Then follow paragraphs dealing with specific types of lease or tenancy and, finally, paragraphs on specific points which affect leasehold land such as the right to buy, options, and liability on covenants. The topic of rentcharges is also included in this section.

K1. Acting on grant of lease

See also: Taking instructions, para. A1
Acting for the landlord, para. K2
Acting for the tenant, para. K3
Long-term residential tenancies, para. K6
Business premises, para. K7
Right to buy, para. K9
Code of Practice for Commercial Leases in England and Wales, Appendix VIII.4

1.1. Taking instructions

1.1.1. There are a number of key issues upon which thought, advice and instructions will be needed when acting on the grant or acceptance of a lease. There can be no standard approach; instead the details of the property and letting in question must be carefully considered.

1.1.2. Subject to the above, much of the information required by the landlord's solicitor from his client will be similar to that required from the seller in the case of a freehold transaction.

1.1.3. When acting for a landlord or tenant, a solicitor should draw his client's attention to, and explain, lease provisions which may be of importance to the client and influence the client's decision whether or not to accept the proposed terms.

1.1.4. *Code of Practice for Commercial Leases*

In appropriate cases, the client's attention should be drawn to the Code of Practice for Commercial Leases. The latest version of this voluntary code was introduced in April 2002 and contains 10 recommendations for landlords and tenants on the negotiation of business leases and a further 13 recommendations governing conduct during a lease.[1]

1. A copy of the Code can be obtained from www.commercialleasecodeew.co.uk and is reproduced at Appendix VIII.4.

1.2. Demised premises

1.2.1. The lease must clearly define the extent of the demised premises. A detached building standing in its own ground should cause no problems of description but care is needed when letting parts of a building, e.g. flats or suites of offices.

1.2.2. As far as possible express provision should be made relating to the ownership of walls, floors, ceilings, etc.[1] In the absence of express provision the following presumptions apply:

(a) external walls – these are included in the demise even if the landlord is responsible for their repairs;[2]

(b) internal walls – there is no presumption in respect of the internal boundary walls dividing one flat from another or the flat from common parts;

(c) floors and ceilings – the flat includes the ceiling at least to the underside of the floor joists to which the ceiling is attached;

(d) the ownership of the roof area should also be specifically dealt with since if this is not done it may be possible for the tenant of a top floor flat to claim occupation of the roof space and to carry out alterations to the roof space against the landlord's wishes.[3]

1. It is possible to create an 'eggshell' tenancy in which the demise only includes the airspace defined by reference to the area contained within the surfaces of the walls, floors and ceilings. See *Pumperninks of Piccadilly Ltd* v. *Land Securities Ltd* [2002] 21 EG 142.
2. *Sturge* v. *Hackett* [1962] 3 All ER 166.
3. See *Davies* v. *Yadegar* [1990] 09 EG 67 and *Haines* v. *Florensa* [1990] 09 EG 70.

1.3. Easements – Grant

1.3.1. Consideration must then be given to whether the tenant will require easements over the landlord's adjoining property in order to use the demised premises. The tenant might, e.g. need the right to use a private road in order to gain access to the premises or to use conducting media on the landlord's adjoining land to bring services from the mains supply to the demised premises. The tenant of a flat or suite of offices will certainly need such rights over the remainder of the building.[1]

1. Where such rights are not granted this will depress the rent at renewal under the Landlord and Tenant Act 1954 – see *J. Murphy & Sons Ltd* v. *Railtrack Plc* [2002] 19 EG 148.

1.4. Easements – Reservation

1.4.1. The landlord will need to consider if he or others claiming title under him will wish to exercise rights over the demised premises because, if so, an express reservation should be included. An example would be a driveway (part of) which is included within the demised premises but which is required to be used by the landlord and his other tenants.

1.5. Length of the term to be granted

1.5.1. Apart from the parties' wishes, consideration must be given to the stamp duty[1] consequences of the length of the term and also to the possible effect of security of tenure legislation on the lease which may affect the seller's ability to recover possession at the end of the term.[2] Where a short lease of a dwelling is to be granted the effect of the landlord's implied repairing obligations under Landlord and Tenant Act 1985, ss.11–14 must also be borne in mind (see para. K1.7.2). The term created must be of certain duration but, subject to security of tenure legislation, it may be made determinable on a certain event.[3]

1.5.2. Where a premium is paid on the grant of a lease not exceeding 50 years, for the purposes of taxation under Schedule A, the landlord is treated as receiving rent calculated by reference to a formula involving a multiplication of the premium and the length of the term.[4]

1. Although this is subject to new legislation, see para. K1.11.
2. See paras. K5, K7 and K8.
3. *Prudential Assurance Co. Ltd* v. *London Residuary Body* [1992] 3 All ER 504.
4. Income and Corporation Taxes Act 1988, s.34; and see *Hurlingham Estates Ltd* v. *Wilde* [1997] STC 627.

1.6. Amount of rent and frequency of reviews

1.6.1. Some statutory limitations on the amount of rent recoverable may be applicable where the lease is an assured shorthold tenancy or a protected or statutory tenancy (see para. K5).

1.6.2. Rent review provisions should be carefully checked by both landlord and tenant. In commercial leases reviews every five years or so are common. In long residential leases fixed increment reviews every 25–30 years are more usual. Without an enforceable rent review provision the landlord will not be able to increase the rent during the term of the lease. Rent review provisions are complex, but they must specify the period at which each review is to take place, and a formula for determining the amount of rent to be paid after each review date with a fall-back procedure (e.g. arbitration with a named office holder as the arbitrator) in case of dispute. A landlord prefers a clause which provides for 'upwards review' only so that the rent payable after the review date can never be less than that which was payable before the review date. It is also common to provide that the new rent, whenever determined, shall be payable from the review date in question so that where a rent review goes to arbitration and the new rent is not determined until some time after the actual review date, the tenant should be advised to place some money in a deposit account on each rent day so that he will be able to meet the cost of the reviewed rent when it is finally determined. Some leases will have break clauses which are operative in the tenant's favour at review dates, thus enabling the tenant to bring the lease to an end before the contractual term date if the rent payable after the review is more than he can afford to pay.

1.7. Common express covenants

1.7.1. To pay rent

The covenant should be clear as to the amount of rent, the intervals of payment, whether payable in advance or in arrear, whether the rent includes outgoings on the property, provisions for increase of the rent and payment of VAT.[1]

1.7.2. To repair

In certain cases the landlord will be obliged by statute to keep the structure and exterior of the premises in repair.[2] An express covenant to repair should precisely identify the obligations required of the party responsible for undertaking the repairs including, in the case of redecoration obligations, the intervals at which the work is to be undertaken. Where the demised premises form part of a larger building the landlord (or in the case of a flat perhaps a management company) will usually covenant to keep the structure and common parts of the building in repair. See the Law Society Standard Business Leases, of whole clause 5, of part clause 6 (see Appendix VII.11).

1.7.2.1. Gas appliances

Gas Safety (Installation and Use) Regulations 1994 (as amended by Gas Safety (Installation and Use) (Amendment) Regulations 1996) require gas appliances to be installed and maintained by competent personnel and regularly inspected. Landlords of residential premises only are under an obligation to carry out an annual inspection of such appliances (even where the lease places full repairing obligations on the tenant). Where an existing lease does not deal specifically with the responsibility for maintenance of such appliances, the landlord should ask the tenant to confirm in writing that the tenant will be responsible for ensuring that the installations are inspected each year. Where a new lease is being drafted, it should include a specific provision in the lease dealing with this responsibility. A full tenant's repairing covenant in the lease will not implicitly remove this obligation from the landlord. These provisions apply to leases for a term of less than seven years (including periodic tenancies). A lease which contains a land-lord's break clause, exercisable within the first seven years of the term, falls within these provisions but a lease which contains a tenant's option to renew which, if exercised, would extend the term beyond seven years does not.

1.7.2.2. Asbestos

The Control of Asbestos at Work Regulations 2002, regulation 4 come into force on 21 May 2004. They introduce a duty for the management of asbestos in non-domestic premises. Broadly the duty is imposed on those responsible for maintenance in the premises. The duties basically require an assessment as to whether there is asbestos in the premises, a decision as to whether it should be removed or properly maintained, and monitoring. Information has to be provided to those likely to come into contact with the asbestos, for example, contractors and the emergency services.

1.7.2.3. Disability Discrimination Act 1995

In outline, the Act imposes duties not to discriminate on the basis of disability on a number of categories of persons including employers. Much of the Act has come into force. One aspect of the Act which has caused concern to owners of property is in relation to obligations imposed on 'service providers'. These include anyone who provides goods, facilities or services to the public or a section of it. It may therefore include landlords who provide services in the form of common parts to tenants. One element of this is a duty to take reasonable steps to remove or alter a physical barrier which makes it unreasonably difficult for disabled persons to make use of facilities, a service, or obtain goods offered to others. Alternatively, in appropriate cases, the service provider may provide a reasonable alternative method of making the service etc. available to the disabled person. This aspect of the Act comes into force on 1 October 2004.

1.7.3. The extent of the repairing obligations imposed by the lease will vary from lease to lease but the following general principles are relevant:

(a) the wording of the clause must cover every part of the building and of the estate which it is intended to be covered. Usually this will mean that the clause(s) must cover five main areas (which may overlap): the demised premises, the structure (including roof, main walls and foundations), the common parts, the common conduits, and the exterior;

(b) the operative words of the clause(s) must be sufficient to cover all foreseeable repair activities. In this respect the wording of the clause should provide for the main areas of maintenance: repairing, cleaning, and decorating. Improvements to the property or major rebuilding effected by the landlord will not necessarily be covered by the wording of a covenant 'to repair' and thus, unless expressly included in the wording of the covenant, a landlord may be unable to recover their cost from the tenants;[3]

(c) the wording of the covenant(s) must leave no grey areas where liability for repair is uncertain, and should not have areas of overlap. Care should be taken with the liability for repair, etc., of walls, ceilings, floors and joists. Clarity in these areas is largely dependent on the clarity of the definition of the ownership of the various parts of the walls, floors, ceilings, etc., in the description of the property demised. The obligation to repair can then be defined in relation to ownership of the various parts. The lease should make it expressly clear whether the windows are part of the structure or of the demise;[4]

(d) the wording of the clause must clearly specify the apportionment of liability for repairs, etc., between landlord and tenant;

(e) where the lease requires the premises to be kept in 'good condition' this will require work to be done where the property is in a bad condition even though the property is not in disrepair.[5]

1.7.4. *Not to make improvements or alterations*

Such a covenant is commonly included in short leases of residential premises and leases of business premises in order to allow the landlord to retain control over his property and to ensure that no alterations are effected in breach of restrictive covenants on the landlord's title, or in breach of planning law or building regulation consent. Some improvements made by a tenant of business premises or agricultural land may commit the landlord to the payment of compensation when the tenant leaves the premises.[6] The covenant may be absolute, in which case the tenant is totally prohibited from making improvements or alterations unless the landlord grants a deed of variation of the lease. A qualified covenant means that the tenant must seek the landlord's prior consent to the alterations or improvements, such consent, in the case of improvements, not being unreasonably withheld by the landlord.[7] The landlord must not unreasonably withhold his consent where alterations to the premises are required by the tenant to adapt the premises for the needs of a disabled person.[8] Even in the case of an absolute covenant a tenant may seek the court's consent to the proposed improvements or alterations; in this respect the court's discretion will override an absolute covenant.[6] An absolute covenant is usually considered inappropriate in the context of the grant of a long lease (i.e. exceeding 21 years) of a house. See the Law Society Standard Business Leases, of whole clause 5, of part clause 6 (Appendix VII.11).

1.7.5. *Covenant restricting user*

Some restriction on the tenant's user of the premises is usually considered desirable for the same reasons as are cited in para. K1.7.4. The covenant may be absolute, in which case the tenant is totally prohibited from changing the use of the property unless the landlord grants a deed of variation of the lease. A qualified covenant means that the tenant must seek the landlord's prior consent to change of use, no premium being payable for giving consent.[9] There is no implied statutory proviso that the landlord's consent will not be unreasonably withheld. In the context of the lease of a dwelling house it may be appropriate to include an absolute covenant against any use except that as a private residence. In the case of business premises a very restrictive user clause (e.g. a clause which permits one specific type of business only) may have an adverse effect on the saleability of the premises and the amount of rent chargeable for them.[10]

1.7.6. *Covenant against alienation*

A covenant restricting the tenant's right to dispose of the property must be carefully drafted since such covenants are construed narrowly by the courts, e.g. a covenant preventing assignment alone will not prevent the tenant from granting a sub-lease of the property. The covenant may be absolute in form, in which case no alienation of the property will be possible unless the landlord specifically grants consent usually by granting a deed of variation of the lease. A qualified covenant is subject to the statutory restrictions and modifications which are explained in para. K11.[11] Except where the lease provides for payment of a premium as a condition of the granting of consent, no premium is payable for such consent.[12] In the context of the long lease of a dwelling house it is unusual to include a general restriction against alienation except during the last few years of the term.[13] In other cases such a restriction is common and desirable to ensure that the landlord retains some control over the occupiers of his property. See the Law Society Standard Business Leases, of whole clause 6, of part clause 7 (Appendix VII.11).

1.7.7. *Covenant to give notice of dealings to landlord*

Such a covenant is normally included in order to give the landlord notice of all dealings by the tenant with the property. The obligation for the tenant to give notice of dealings should specify the occasions on which the covenant is to operate, e.g. notice of assignment, sub-lettings, mortgage, change of ownership on death or bankruptcy of the tenant. The tenant is usually required to pay a small registration fee to the landlord with each notice served. See the Law Society Standard Business Leases, of whole clause 6, of part clause 7 (Appendix VII.11).

1.7.8. *Landlord's covenant for quiet enjoyment*

Such a covenant will be implied into the lease by the common law, but it is usual to find an express covenant to this effect. See the Law Society Standard Business Leases, of whole clause 10, of part clause 11. Damages for mental distress are not recoverable for breach of this covenant.[14]

1. See para. A16.7.
2. See Landlord and Tenant Act 1985, ss.11–14. Exceptionally a landlord may be under a common law implied duty to repair: see *Liverpool City Council* v. *Irwin* [1977] AC 239; *King* v. *South Northamptonshire District Council* [1992] 1 EGLR 53, CA.
3. See *Mullaney* v. *Maybourne Grange (Croydon) Management Ltd* [1986] 1 EGLR 70; *cf. Sutton (Hastoe) Housing Association* v. *Williams* [1988] 16 EG 75.
4. See *Holiday Fellowship Ltd* v. *Hereford* [1959] 1 All ER 433.
5. *Welsh* v. *Greenwich London Borough Council* [2002] 49 EG 118.
6. Part 1 Landlord and Tenant Act 1954.
7. Landlord and Tenant Act 1927, s.19(2).
8. Disability Discrimination Act 1995, s.22
9. Landlord and Tenant Act 1927, s.19(2).
10. A common device to attempt to alleviate the depressive effect on the value of the property for rent review purposes is to provide in the lease for this effect to be disregarded on such a review.
11. See Landlord and Tenant Act 1927, s.19(1), as amended by Landlord and Tenant Act 1987, and Landlord and Tenant (Covenants) Act 1995.
12. Law of Property Act 1925, s.144.
13. The CML Lenders' Handbook contains detailed requirements for the content of long term residential leases. See para. K6.6 and Appendix VIII.3.
14. *Branchett* v. *Beaney* [1992] 3 All ER 910.

1.8. Service charge

1.8.1. Leases of flats and of commercial premises will frequently require the tenant to pay a service charge for services, e.g. heating or cleaning and repair of the building of which the demised premises form part and the decoration of the common parts, provided by either the landlord or a management company. The service charge is usually expressed to be payable as 'additional rent', thus allowing the landlord to distrain for its non-payment. This device also enables the landlord to recover the sum due without the necessity of serving a section 146 notice. The tenant should ensure that the proportion of the charge which he is required to pay is fair in relation to the amount of the building which he occupies or enjoys rights over, and should ensure that the clause specifies precisely what services are to be supplied in return for the charge. A landlord may wish to provide for an estimate of the service charge to be payable in advance and for there to be a reconciliation at the end of the year. The landlord may also contemplate setting up a sinking fund to cater for major expenditure on the property. The tenant of a flat may be required to become a member of a residents' association or management company which will have responsibility for effecting the landlord's repairing covenants under the lease, but which also allows the tenants to control the expenditure to which they are committing themselves. Membership of a management company is normally restricted to the tenants of the block or estate and the covenant will require the tenant on assignment of his lease to require his assignee to take a transfer of the tenant's share in the management company. The landlord should be required to assume responsibilities for the management company's responsibilities under the lease until the company is set up and shares have been allotted to all the tenants. Statutory controls over service charges on dwellings are discussed in para. K6. The CML Lenders' Handbook requirements are considered in para. K6.6 and Part 1 of the Lenders' Handbook is reproduced in Appendix VIII.3. See also the Law Society Standard Business Lease of part clause 3 (reproduced in Appendix VII.11.).

1.8.2. Tenants are only obliged to pay for items agreed in the lease. The landlord should therefore be careful to include in the service charge provisions all the necessary expenditure which he may incur on the building. The clause must therefore encompass all the obligations which are covered by the landlord's covenants in the lease, e.g. repairs and decoration, insurance, services such as lifts, cleaning common parts, garden maintenance, etc. If the landlord may need in the future to make improvements to the property, this too should be covered by the clause. Provision for the tenants to contribute to a reserve fund or sinking fund will assist in the financing of major works and eliminate the burden of imposing a very large service charge in one particular year when major items such as a central heating system need to be renewed. The landlord's expenditure on bank interest and bank charges can only be recovered if the lease so permits.[1] Management charges need only be included where either the landlord will be carrying out his obligations himself or employing independent managing agents to do so. Professional fees are only recoverable under a service charge clause where they are properly incurred in respect of items which are chargeable under the service charge provisions.[2] It is advisable to include a sweeping-up clause to cover any omissions of specific items and to take account of any higher expectations in standards which were not anticipated at the commencement of the term.

1.8.3. In appropriate cases, the client's attention should be drawn to *The Guide to Good Practice relating to Service Charges in Commercial Properties*.[3]

1. *Frobisher (Second Investments) Ltd* v. *Kiloran Trust Co. Ltd* [1980] 1 All ER 488.
2. *Holding & Management Ltd* v. *Property Holding & Investment Trust plc* [1988] 2 All ER 702.
3. This can be downloaded from the web site of the Royal Institution of Chartered Surveyors at www.rics.org.uk.

1.9.　Proviso for forfeiture or re-entry

1.9.1.　The landlord's right to forfeit the lease for the tenant's breach of covenant is a valuable remedy which must be expressly included in the lease since such a right is not implied by the common law unless, exceptionally, the lease is made conditional on the due observance of the covenants. Without such a clause the landlord will be unable to remove the tenant from the premises during the currency of the lease term. It is usual to include a clause which gives the landlord the right to forfeit the lease on non-payment of rent by the tenant after a stated period (e.g. 21 days) and for breach of any other covenant in the lease. Forfeiture for the tenant's insolvency is common in non-residential leases but should not be included in the long lease of a dwelling house since such a provision is unacceptable to most mortgagees.[1] Forfeiture for breach of a covenant other than to pay rent must generally be preceded by service of a notice under Law of Property Act 1925, s.146 and may in certain cases be affected by Leasehold Property (Repairs) Act 1938. Repossession of an occupied dwelling house requires a court order.[2] In other cases a court order will be required if re-entry cannot be made peaceably.

1.9.2.　Forfeiture may also occur (even in the absence of an express proviso) where the tenant denies the landlord's title to the property. If a tenant makes a specific allegation that the landlord does not own the property or that a third party has better rights to the property than the landlord, this may be construed as a denial of the landlord's title and result in forfeiture.[3] A general denial of the landlord's title contained in a defence to proceedings brought by the landlord will not have this effect.[4]

1.9.3.　A tenant may not apply for relief against forfeiture for breach of covenant other than for non-payment of rent after a landlord has forfeited a lease by court proceedings and entry into possession of the property pursuant to the judgment obtained in those proceedings. Where, however, entry is regained peaceably, the tenant retains his right to apply for equitable relief against forfeiture even after the landlord has taken possession of the property.[5] An equitable tenant may claim relief against forfeiture.[6]

1.9.4.　If possession is resisted by the tenant when the landlord seeks to re-enter, there is a danger that a criminal offence under Criminal Law Act 1977, s.6 may be committed.

1.9.5.　Where the landlord seeks to forfeit following breach of a covenant against alienation by the tenant, any section 146 notice should be served on both the assignor (tenant) of the lease and on the purported assignee (person currently in possession).[7] This rule is complied with if the lease makes provision for the notice to be served on 'the tenant at the property' where the word 'tenant' is defined to include successors in title.

1.9.6. A notice under Law of Property Act 1925, s.146 is not required before forfeiting for non-payment of rent, and no formal demand is needed if the re-entry clause states that the landlord can re-enter if rent is in arrears 'whether or not formally demanded' or similar wording. Where the tenant is in breach of a repairing covenant and the landlord (acting under a power expressly given to him by the lease) effects the repairs himself and then seeks to recover the cost of the repairs from the tenant, it is not necessary to serve a section 146 notice and Leasehold Property (Repairs) Act 1938 does not apply. The action is for recovery of a liquidated sum only.[8]

1.9.7. If the landlord forfeits by legal proceedings, he can include a claim for arrears of rent, mesne profits, and interest. The county court will have jurisdiction if the amount claimed does not exceed £50,000.

1.9.8. Where the landlord is forfeiting by action (i.e. legal proceedings) in the county court,[9] the tenant can apply to the court for relief against forfeiture under County Courts Act 1984, s.138:

    (i) automatic relief if the tenant pays all arrears and costs of the action into court not less than five clear days before the return day of the landlord's proceedings;

    (ii) if relief is not obtained as above the court makes an order for possession on a future date (minimum four weeks) unless the tenant pays into court all arrears and costs by that date;

    (iii) even if a possession order is made and the landlord re-enters, the tenant or any person with an interest under the lease derived from the tenant's interest can apply to the court for relief within six months from the landlord's recovery of possession and the court may grant relief on terms it thinks fit.

1.9.9. These rules only apply to forfeiture for non-payment of rent and the court has a wider discretion in cases of other breaches of covenant.

1. The requirements of the CML Lenders' Handbook are considered at para. K6.6 and Part 1 is reproduced in Appendix VIII.3.
2. Protection from Eviction Act 1977, s.2.
3. *W.G. Clarke (Properties) Ltd* v. *Dupre Properties Ltd* [1992] Ch 297.
4. *Warner* v. *Sampson* [1959] 1 QB 297. Note also *Abidogun* v. *Frolan Health Care Ltd* [2001] 45 EG 138.
5. *Billson* v. *Residential Apartments* [1992] 1 AC 494, HL.
6. *High Street Investments* v. *Bellshore* [1996] NPC 20.
7. *Fuller* v. *Judy Properties* [1992] 1 EGLR 75 but see *Old Grovebury Manor Farm Ltd* v. *Seymour Plant Sales & Hire Ltd (No.2)* [1979] 3 All ER 504; and note *Brown & Root Technology* v. *Sun Alliance & London Assurance Co Limited* [1997] 18 EG 123.
8. *Jervis* v. *Harris* [1995] NPC 171.
9. Law of Property Act 1925, s.146(2), see e.g. *Crown Estate Commissioners* v. *Signet Group Plc* [1999] 2 EGLR 200.

1.10. Insurance

1.10.1. If the landlord is to insure the property (as would generally be the case in a lease of commercial premises) he should ensure that he is able to recover the amount of the premiums from the tenant and the tenant should be permitted to inspect the landlord's policy and the receipt for the last premium due. If the tenant is to insure the covenant should specify the risks against which the landlord wishes the policy to be effected and should give the landlord the right to inspect the policy, to see the receipt for the last premium due, and to insure in the case of the tenant's default. Where the premises comprise part of a building, the whole of which is owned by the landlord, the landlord will normally covenant to insure the structure and common parts of the building.

1.10.2. The lease must provide for both the unit and the common parts of the building to be properly insured. The lease may make provision for each tenant to insure his individual unit and for the landlord to insure the common parts of the building, but such an arrangement is not popular since it can lead to situations where not all tenants are insured for the same amounts or against the same risks with consequent difficulties in enforcing claims where it has become necessary for one tenant to claim against another. A more modern solution is for the landlord to covenant to insure all the units and the common parts together under a block policy, with a right to recover a proportionate part of the premium from each tenant. Incidental costs are sometimes also recoverable from tenants including the costs of regular valuations for insurance cover.

1.10.3. The insurance covenant in the lease should provide for an adequate level of cover and of risk to be maintained over the units and common parts, including the full costs of rebuilding or reinstatement and related professional fees, with reputable insurers. Consideration should be given to limiting liability where cover is unavailable in the open market at reasonable rates. Damage caused by terrorist activities is often excluded from cover in which case liability will fall on the party responsible for repair in the event of damage being caused by uninsured losses. Absolute covenants to insure are strictly construed so that, for example, where a landlord is under an absolute duty to insure against fire risks, he would have to reinstate the property even if the property burns down as a result of an excluded cause such as terrorist action.[1] The Law Society Standard Business Lease deals with this point (see Appendix VII.11). The tenants should have the right to a copy of the insurance policy or reasonable evidence of its existence and validity, and to inspect the original policy and the receipt (or reasonable evidence of payment) for the last premium due.

1.10.4. A tenant will wish the lease to provide for the landlord to use the proceeds of the policy to reinstate the premises in the event of their damage or destruction by an insured risk. Provision should also be made for the application of the policy money in the event of reinstatement not being possible.

1.10.5. It is also desirable that the landlord should maintain an occupiers' liability insurance policy in a situation where the landlord retains the ownership of common parts of the building.

1.10.6. It is preferable for the landlord to obtain a policy which cannot be vitiated by act or default of the tenants.

1.10.7. Landlords are sometimes able to secure the payment of commission for the placing of insurance cover with a particular insurance company. Except to the extent that the landlord provides services in respect of the insurance, this commission, in principle, belongs to the tenants.[2] Landlords may provide in the lease that they are to be permitted to retain this commission.

1. See *Enlayde Ltd* v. *Roberts* [1917] 1 Ch 109; *Moorgate Estates Ltd* v. *Trower* [1940] 1 All ER 195.
2. *Williams* v. *Southwark London Borough Council* [2000] EGCS 44.

1.11. Certificate of value

The Government propose to modernise the law relating to stamp duty. The enabling legislation is included in the Finance Bill 2003, with the detail to be contained in secondary legislation, which appears likely to be brought into force towards the end of 2003. The information given in this section relates to the stamp duty regime as it exists at the date of publication (see AAA Stamp Duty Land Tax).

1.11.1. The appropriate certificate of value should be included in the lease where the premium does not exceed the current stamp duty thresholds. However, the £60,000 threshold cannot be used if the annual rent exceeds £600.

1.11.2. Form of certificate of value:

'It is hereby certified that the transaction hereby effected does not form part of a larger transaction or of a series of transactions in respect of which the amount or value or the aggregate amount or value of the consideration other than rent exceeds [£60,000] [or as appropriate].'

1.12. Underleases

1.12.1. Most of the matters which are relevant when acting for the seller or buyer on grant of a lease will also be applicable to the grant of a sub-lease.

1.12.2. The head-tenant will be liable to his own landlord (the freeholder) on the covenants contained in his lease irrespective of whether the breach is committed by the head- or sub-tenant. To protect himself against liability for a breach committed by the sub-tenant, the head-tenant should impose on the sub-tenant obligations which are at least as onerous as those contained in the head-lease.

1.12.3. A sub-tenant will be directly liable to the freeholder in respect of breach of restrictive covenants which are contained in the head-lease since he will be deemed to know of those covenants through his entitlement to call for the head-lease as part of the evidence of title. Apart from this, the freeholder may choose as a term of the head-lease or by a condition attached to the grant of any necessary consent to the sub-lease to require the sub-tenant to enter into a direct covenant with the freeholder. This will put the freeholder in a strong position in relation to the enforcement of covenants contained in the head-lease because it has the effect of establishing the relationship of privity of contract between the freeholder and the sub-tenant.

1.12.4. The existence and validity of a sub-lease is dependent on the existence and validity of the head-lease out of which it is derived. If, therefore, the head-lease is forfeited, the sub-lease is also automatically forfeited although the sub-tenant may have the right to apply directly to the freeholder for relief against forfeiture even in circumstances where the head-tenant is unable to apply for relief. A lender (of the tenant or sub-tenant) has the same right to apply for relief against forfeiture as a sub-tenant.

1.12.5. Where the head-lease requires the prior consent of the freeholder to the grant of a sub-lease, the head-tenant should seek such consent at an early stage in the transaction and should not enter a binding contract for the grant of the sub-lease until it is certain that such consent will be forthcoming. The head-tenant's lender's consent may also be required to the grant of the sub-lease and this too should be obtained at an early stage in the transaction. Obtaining a landlord's consent to a sub-lease or assignment is discussed in para. K11.

1.12.6. Standard Condition 8.3 and Standard Commercial Property Condition 8.3 require the seller to apply for and pay for any necessary licence, the buyer (sub-tenant) supplying references and other information. In certain circumstances either party may rescind the contract if the consent is not forthcoming.[1]

1.12.7. In relation to leases granted or entered into on or after 11 May 2000 the Contracts (Rights of Third Parties) Act 1999 will in many cases allow direct enforcement of covenants between tenants and between a head landlord and a sub-tenant. The Act can be excluded if required.

1. See for example *Aubergine* v. *Lakewood* [2002] PLSCS 50.

1.13. Title

1.13.1. Under an open contract the tenant is not entitled to call for deduction of the free-hold reversionary title on the grant of a lease.[1] This rule is unsatisfactory, particularly where the lease is to be granted for a term in excess of 7 years, where a premium is to be paid for the grant of the lease or where a tenant is paying a significant rent for commercial premises. A lender who has taken a mortgage of a dwelling house will frequently not accept a lease as security for a loan unless the freehold title has been satisfactorily deduced,[2] and the absence of the freehold title will preclude the tenant and his successors from obtaining an absolute lease-hold title on the subsequent registration of the lease unless the freehold is already registered or the 'title shown' procedure has been used. The landlord should therefore be prepared to deduce his freehold title to the tenant in exactly the same way as if he were selling the freehold[3] and should include a condition in the contract to this effect. Standard Condition 8.2.4 and Standard Commercial Property Condition 8.2.4 require the landlord to deduce such title to the tenant as would enable the tenant to obtain an absolute title at the Land Registry where the grant in question is to be for a term which will exceed 21 years (but this will be amended to seven years in the next edition of the Conditions). This condition effectively means that the landlord is under an obligation in all circumstances to deduce his freehold reversionary title to the tenant.

1.13.2. In the case of sub-letting the sub-tenant is entitled to call for the head-lease out of which his sub-lease is to be derived and all subsequent assignments under which the lease has been held for the last 15 years. In the absence of a contractual condition to the contrary he is not entitled to call for production of the freehold title.[5] The sub-tenant's inability at common law to call for the deduction of the freehold title may cause problems if, e.g. a premium is being demanded for the grant of the sub-lease, or the sub-lease is to be mortgaged or requires registration with its own title. It should be noted that the sub-lease will not contain an implied covenant that any user clause in the sub-lease is either lawful or complies with a restriction on user in a superior title.[6] A solicitor who accepts a lease or sub-lease without checking the validity of the user clause would be liable to his client in negligence if, as a result, the client suffered loss. Standard Condition 8.2.4 and Standard Commercial Property Condition 8.2.4 require the head-tenant to deduce a title to the sub-tenant which will enable the sub-tenant to acquire registration of his sub-lease with an absolute title at the Land Registry where the sub-lease will exceed 21 years (but this will be amended to seven years in the next edition of the conditions)[4]. This condition therefore requires the head-tenant to produce the title to the freehold reversion to the sub-tenant on grant of the sub-lease. A head-tenant who did not call for deduction of the freehold title when he took his own lease may not be able to comply with this condition and will have to exclude it by special condition in the contract.

1.13.3. If the head-lease out of which the sub-lease is to be derived is registered with a separate title the sub-tenant is entitled to call for production of the head-lease. The sub-tenant will normally require the head-tenant to supply official copies of his registered title and the contract should contain a special condition to this effect.[7] Production of the title to the freehold is unnecessary if the head-lease is registered with an absolute title. In other cases, unless excluded by special condition, Standard Condition 8.2.4 and Standard Commercial Property Condition 8.2.4 will apply to the contract and the head-tenant may be obliged to deduce the reversionary title to the sub-tenant.

1. See Standard Condition 8.2.4, Standard Commercial Property Condition 8.2.4 and Law of Property Act 1925, s.44.
2. For details of the Lenders' Handbook requirements see para. K6.6 and Part 1, reproduced in Appendix VIII.3.
3. See Standard Condition 4.5.3 and Standard Commercial Property Condition 4.5.4.
4. The Land Registration Act 2002 reduces the period for registration of leases to those which are granted for a term of more than seven years. Appropriate amendments will be made to the Standard Conditions.
5. Law of Property Act 1925, s.44.
6. *Hill* v. *Harris* [1965] 2 QB 601.
7. In the absence of such a provision the sub-tenant will be able to inspect the registered title of the head tenant since the Land Register is open to the public.

1.14. Registration

1.14.1. A lease for 7 years or less is generally not capable of being registered with its own title at the Land Registry,[1] but the lease will normally take effect as an overriding interest under Land Registration Act 2002.[2] If there is concern about protecting the tenant's interest in the property an application for registration of a notice may be lodged against the landlord's title where the lease is for a term of more than three years from the date of the grant. A lease for a term of three years or less cannot be protected by notice.[3] In unregistered land a purchaser of the reversion is deemed to purchase with knowledge of the rights of occupiers, but an agreement for a lease may be registered as an estate contract (Class C(iv) land charge) and an application for the registration of a caution against first registration may be lodged at the Land Registry.[4]

1.14.2. On completion of the grant the tenant will make application for registration of the lease with a separate title. A notice in respect of the lease will be entered automatically in the register of the landlord's title.[5]

1. Except leases granted under Housing Act 1985, Part V, see K9.1.5, and see other exceptions in para. G3.
2. Land Registration Act 2002, Sched. 1 para. 1 and Sched. 3 para. 1.
3. Land Registration Act 2002, s.33.
4. Land Registration Act 2002, s.15.
5. Land Registration Act 2002, Sched. 2 para. 3(2)(b).

1.15. Surety

1.15.1. The landlord may require a surety to the lease as a condition of its grant. Where the proposed tenant is a small private company it is common to find that the directors of the company are asked to guarantee the company's obligations under the lease. In other circumstances a parent company may be asked to guarantee the obligations of a subsidiary company tenant. This gives the landlord additional protection under the lease since the sureties' obligations will be co-extensive with those of the principal debtor. If it is intended to enter a contract prior to the grant of the lease, the sureties should be made parties to that contract.

1.15.2. A buyer's solicitor who is also acting for the sureties to the lease must consider whether any conflict of interests exists or is likely to arise between the interests of his buyer client and the interests of the sureties. It may be in the best interests of the buyer to obtain a lease of the premises, which he can only do if he provides sureties to the lease (a pre-condition imposed by the landlord), but it may not be in the best interests of the sureties to enter into covenants with the landlord to guarantee performance of the buyer's obligations under the lease, e.g. as to payment of rent, repairs, etc., where the enforcement of the sureties' covenants would put the sureties' personal assets, such as a matrimonial home, at risk. Where such a conflict exists or is likely to arise, the sureties should receive independent advice about their potential liability.

.16. **Mortgages**

.16.1. If the freehold reversion is subject to a mortgage, the mortgage deed should be checked to see whether it requires the lender's consent to be obtained prior to the grant of a lease. If so, steps should be taken to obtain the lender's consent before a binding contract to grant the lease is created.[1] Failure to obtain such consent, where necessary, will put the seller into breach of his mortgage covenants, with the consequence that the principal sum under the mortgage will become due immediately. If consent is not required it should be checked that the lease is within the borrower's powers under Law of Property Act 1925, s.99.

. The borrower's powers of leasing can be extended by or excluded from the mortgage by agreement (Law of Property Act 1925, s.99) except in the case of a mortgage of an agricultural holding where they cannot be excluded and the mortgage cannot exclude the court's power to order a new tenancy of business premises under Pt. II Landlord and Tenant Act 1954.

.17. **Sub-sales**

.17.1. By Standard Condition 8.2.5 and Standard Commercial Property Condition 8.2.5 sub-sales are not permitted where the contract is for the grant of a lease.

.18. **Searches and enquiries before contract**

.18.1. When acting for a tenant on a long lease for a premium or on a commercial lease the same searches and enquiries as are relevant to a freehold purchase should be made. Searches are discussed above in para. B10. In the case of a commercial lease it may be convenient to use the Commercial Property Standard Enquiries.[1]

.18.2. Where a commercial lease is for a very short term at a low rent, or on short-term lettings of residential property, it is not usual for searches and enquiries to be made since the low risk attached to these lettings does not justify the expense of making the searches. In the latter case, however, the prospective tenant may feel it is prudent to make enquiries about the prospective landlord's solvency, particularly where the property is mortgaged, to avoid the risk of the landlord's lender seeking a possession order against the tenant if the landlord does not pay the mortgage.

. These enquiries have been drafted by the London Property Support Lawyers Group and are freely available at www.bpf.org.uk. An introduction and explanation appears at Appendix VIII.5.

.19. **The contract**

.19.1. A contract for the grant of the lease is normally entered into in the case of a purchase for a premium of a long-term residential lease but is not generally entered into on short-term lettings of residential premises nor on commercial leases where in both cases the parties directly enter negotiations on the draft lease. In the case of commercial lettings contracts are used to give early possession on terms, to deal with building work that may be required prior to completion or where in order to achieve quickly a binding commitment a contract is entered into which is expressed to be subject to some contingency, e.g. landlord's consent or grant of planning permission.

1.20. Drafting the lease

1.20.1. A lease for a term of over three years must be granted by deed to vest the legal estate in the tenant. A lease for three years or less, taking effect in possession at the best rent without a fine, may be granted orally or in writing.[1] To ensure certainty of terms between the parties it is recommended that all leases, no matter how short the term, should be in writing.

1.20.2. The lease is drafted by the seller's (landlord's) solicitor and annexed to the draft contract submitted to the buyer's (tenant's) solicitor. Except where the lease is to be for a term not exceeding three years, taking effect in possession and with no premium payable for its grant, the contract for the lease must satisfy Law of Property (Miscellaneous Provisions) Act 1989, s.2. Standard Condition 8.2 and Standard Commercial Property Condition 8.2 provide for the lease to be in the form annexed to the draft contract and for the seller to engross the lease and supply the buyer with the engrossment at least five working days before completion date. The length of the term and its commencement date must be expressly stated in the draft lease in order to satisfy Law of Property (Miscellaneous Provisions) Act 1989, s.2, or either or both could be stated in the contract.

1.20.3. Leases which are granted by the same landlord to different tenants of separate units all of which are in the common ownership of the landlord (e.g. flats within a block owned by the landlord) should be uniform in content. If this is not so, difficulty may subsequently be experienced in the management of the property and, where the letting scheme provides for mutual enforceability between tenants, enforcement of covenants against individual tenants. Subject to this, given the diversity of circumstances in which leases are granted, no two leases will ever be identical, and it is recommended that the seller's solicitor refers to a suitable precedent before embarking on the drafting of the lease.[2]

1.20.4. Where the lease is of business premises the Law Society Standard Business Leases for the whole or part of premises may be used. The texts of these are set out in Appendix VII.11.

1.20.5. Consideration should be given to whether the landlord should give covenants for title on the grant of the lease.[3]

1. Law of Property Act 1925, ss.52–54 and Law of Property (Miscellaneous Provisions) Act 1989, s.2.
2. See, e.g. *Encyclopaedia of Forms and Precedents (Vol. 22), Drafting and Negotiating Commercial Leases* by Murray Ross, *Practical Lease Precedents* by Trevor Aldridge.
3. Covenants can now be given on the grant of a lease: Law of Property (Miscellaneous Provisions) Act 1994 and see Covenants for title, para. M9.

K1.21. The Protocol

K1.21.1. The Protocol does not specifically refer to procedures on the grant of a lease. Since the procedure on grant of a lease is very similar to that applicable to a freehold transaction it is recommended that in appropriate cases when dealing with residential property the Protocol procedures are adhered to as closely as circumstances permit.

K1.22. Side letters

K1.22.1. A side letter (or letter of comfort) may take effect as a collateral contract. Such a letter may bind an assignee of the reversion, even if the assignee did not know of the letter or its contents.[1] It may, in certain circumstances, effect a variation of covenants.[2] Where a side letter has been used to vary the terms of a proposed subletting this should be disclosed to the landlord on an application for consent to the sub-letting.[3]

1. *System Floors* v. *Ruralpride* [1994] EGCS 162.
2. This topic is dealt with further in para K14.1.1.
3. *Allied Dunbar* v. *Homebase* [2002] PLSCS 123.

K2. Acting for the landlord

2.1.	**Taking instructions**	2.5.	**Completion and post-**
2.2.	**Drafting the lease**		**completion**
2.3.	**Preparing the package**	2.6.	**Apportionment of rent**
2.4.	**Engrossment and execution of lease**		

See also: Taking instructions, para. A1
Acting on grant of lease, para. K1
Acting for the tenant, para. K3
Long-term residential tenancies, para. K6
Business premises, para. K7
Right to buy, para. K9

2.1. Taking instructions

2.1.1. Much of the information required by the landlord's solicitor from his client will be similar to that required from the seller in the case of a freehold transaction. These matters are considered in paras. A1 and K1.

2.2. Drafting the lease

2.2.1. The lease is drafted by the seller's (landlord's) solicitor and annexed to the draft contract submitted to the buyer's (tenant's) solicitor. Except where the lease is to be for a term not exceeding three years, taking effect in possession and with no premium payable for its grant, the contract for the lease must satisfy Law of Property (Miscellaneous Provisions) Act 1989, s.2. Standard Condition 8.2 and Standard Commercial Property Condition 8.2 provide for the lease to be in the form annexed to the draft contract and for the seller to engross the lease and supply the buyer with the engrossment at least five working days before completion date. The length of the term and its commencement date must be expressly stated in the lease in order to satisfy Law of Property (Miscellaneous Provisions) Act 1989, s.2.

2.2.2. Where the lease is of business premises the Law Society Standard Business Leases for the whole or part of premises may be used. The texts of these are set out in Appendix VII.11.

.3. Preparing the package

Where the lease being granted is of a long-term residential property a sale package is commonly prepared in much the same way as in the sale of a freehold residential property.

.3.1. The contract

The particulars of sale must state that the property is leasehold and give details of the term to be vested in the tenant. The draft lease should be drafted and annexed to the contract. It is usual to include a condition requiring the tenant to accept the lease in the form annexed to the contract.[1] Incumbrances affecting the freehold title must be disclosed and indemnity taken from the tenant in respect of future breaches.[2] The landlord's solicitor should consider whether or not it is appropriate for his client to offer covenants for title to the tenant.[3]

.3.2. Checklist

The landlord's solicitor should send to the tenant's solicitor the following documents:

(a) draft contract with draft lease annexed;

(b) evidence of the freehold title;

(c) any relevant planning and building regulation consents;

(d) answers to pre-contract searches and enquiries (including in Protocol cases the Seller's Property Information Form and Seller's Leasehold Information Form), or in the case of a commercial property it may be convenient to send replies to the Commercial Property Standard Enquiries[4];

(e) where appropriate, evidence of the lender's consent to the grant of the lease;

(f) the memorandum and articles of any management company.

. See Standard Condition 8.2.3 and Standard Commercial Property Condition 8.2.3.
. See Standard Condition 4.5.4 and Standard Commercial Property Condition 4.5.4.
. See para. M9.
. The LPSLG Commercial Property Standard Enquiries are explained further in Appendix VIII.5, and may be downloaded from www.bpf.org.uk.

2.4. Engrossment and execution of lease

2.4.1. The lease is normally prepared in two parts (lease and counterpart) both engrossed by the landlord's solicitor.[1] If the landlord requires the tenant to pay a fee for the preparation of the engrossment this must be dealt with by special condition in the contract.

2.4.2. The landlord will sign the lease itself in readiness for completion; the counterpart should be sent to the tenant's solicitor at least five days before contractual completion date[2] for execution by the tenant. The requirements for execution of a deed are dealt with in section E above. The landlord's execution of the lease should expressly be made subject to a condition that the landlord can withdraw from the transaction if the tenant fails to complete. Once a deed is executed by the client and handed to his solicitor it may be impossible to unilaterally withdraw from the transaction. Although in most cases delivery will be conditional (or in escrow), the condition being payment of purchase price or the handing over of a counterpart. The signor will still, however, be bound on delivery unless the condition (escrow) fails. In some cases it may, however, be possible to show that the executed lease has been handed by the client to the solicitor for delivery at some later date, e.g. on the day of completion. In this case withdrawal is possible.[3]

1. Standard Condition 8.2.6 and Standard Commercial Property Condition 8.2.6.
2. Standard Condition 8.2.6 and Standard Commercial Property Condition 8.2.6.
3. See *Beesly* v. *Hallwood Estates Ltd* [1961] Ch 105; and *Johnsey Estates (1990) Ltd* v. *Newport Marketworld Ltd* [1996] EGCS 87.

2.5. Completion and post-completion

2.5.1.   On completion in addition to or in substitution for the matters relevant to a freehold transaction the landlord will receive:

(a) the counterpart lease executed by the tenant;

(b) any premium payable for the grant (less any deposit paid on exchange of contracts);

(c) an apportioned sum representing rent payable in advance under the lease and interim service charge. If the date from which the length of the term is calculated precedes the date of the lease itself, no rent can be recovered for this reason alone in respect of the period between the two dates.

2.5.2.   The landlord should give to the tenant:

(a) the lease executed by him;

(b) if not already done, properly marked or certified copies of the freehold title deeds (unregistered land);

(c) where relevant and if not already done, a certified copy of the consent of the landlord's lender to the transaction;

(d) share certificate relating to the management company.

2.5.3.   After completion the counterpart lease should be stamped with the appropriate duty. The landlord may receive notice in duplicate from the tenant, in accordance with the tenant's covenant to so do in the lease, of the tenant's mortgage of the property. One copy of the notice should be placed with the landlord's title deeds, the other receipted on behalf of the landlord and returned to the tenant's solicitor.

2.6.   Apportionment of rent

2.6.1. Neither the Standard Conditions of Sale nor the Standard Commercial Property Conditions provide for the apportionment of rent on completion of the grant of a lease; therefore an express special condition is required to deal with this matter.

2.6.2. Where the rent reserved by the lease is an annual rent payable quarterly in advance on the usual quarter days and the rent commencement date does not coincide with either the term commencement date or the usual quarter days, it is suggested that the apportionment of rent on completion of the grant of the lease should be made in accordance with the recommended method of calculation set out below. The quarter days are 25 March, 24 June, 29 September, and 25 December.

2.6.3. Where completion takes place at a date within a rent quarter (and where the lease remains in place), any apportionment of the quarter's rent should be treated as falling outside the scope of VAT, notwithstanding that an election to tax the rent has been, or will be, made. For further information, see the Law Society's *VAT Guide* at www.lawsoc.org/dcs/pdf/vatguide.pdf.

2.6.4. *Recommended method of calculation*

The following formula applies where the term year runs from a date which is a rent payment date.

2.6.5. The method of calculation is based on the view that, where a lease or tenancy agreement reserves an annual rent, the usual direction to pay the rent by equal quarterly payments will have been inserted for estate management convenience only and will not have been intended to convert the annual rent into a quarterly rent. This is important because the traditional quarters are of unequal duration and hence the daily amount of rent would differ between one quarter and another if it were calculated quarter by quarter.

2.6.6. The example used below to illustrate the methods is for a lease dated 8 March [20--] expressed to grant a term of 'ten years commencing on 29 September [20--] (the previous year)' and expressed to reserve 'a rent of £36,500 per annum payable by equal quarterly payments in advance on the usual quarter days (the first payment being a due proportion thereof for the period from the date hereof to the following quarter day to be paid on the execution hereof)'.

Initial payment

Step 1

Ascertain the 'term year'. In the example, the term year will begin on 29 September in one year and end on 28 September in the following year. If, instead, the term had been expressed as 'a term commencing on the date hereof and expiring on 28 September in ten years time', the 'term year' would probably (although it is a matter of intention evidenced by the wording used in the lease) commence on 8 March in one year and end on 7 March in the following year. If the term was expressed to run 'from' a particular date, it would be necessary to consider whether under the particular lease the term began on that date or on the next day, a question discussed in most of the reference books on leases.

Step 2

Count the number of days for which the tenant is liable to pay rent during the first term year. In the example, this would be from 8 March to 28 September inclusive, namely 205 days.

Step 3

Calculate the rent payable for that number of days on an annual basis. In our example, this would be 205/365 × £36,500 = £20,500.

Step 4

Calculate the rent that the tenant will have to pay on those rent payment days which will fall between the grant of the lease and the end of the first term year. In our example, there would be two such rent payment days, 25 March and 24 June, on each of which the tenant will have to pay one quarter's rent (£9,125) and therefore the total rent payable on those days will be 2 × £9,125 = £18,250.

Step 5

Deduct the sum calculated at step 4 from the sum calculated at step 3. The difference is the amount that the tenant must pay on the grant of the lease. In our example, this is £20,500 – £18,250 = £2,250. (Contrast this with the figure of £1,700 that would have been calculated by simply taking the number of days from 8 March to 24 March inclusive at a daily rate of £100 (calculated on an annual basis) or the figure of £1,723.61 that would have been calculated by taking those days as a fraction of the current quarter.)

Assignment of lease

Assume that the lease is assigned on 31 March in the second year of the term. The apportionment as between the assignor and the assignee is to be calculated as follows:

Step 1

Ascertain the term year.

Step 2

Count the number of days for which the present tenant is liable to pay the rent during the current term year down to the date of the assignment. In our example, this is from 29 September in year 1 to 31 March in year 2, namely 184 days.

Step 3

Calculate the rent payable for that number of days on an annual basis. In our example, this would be 184/365 × £36,500 = £18,400.

Step 4

Ascertain the amount of rent that will have been paid by the present tenant in respect of the current term year. In our example, the present tenant will have paid rent for the current year on 29 September in year 1, 25 December in year 1 and 25 March in year 2, namely 3 × £9,125 = £27,375.

Step 5

Compare the figures calculated at steps 3 and 4. If the former exceeds the latter, the present tenant must make an allowance of the difference to the assignee. If the latter exceeds the former, the assignee must make an allowance in favour of the present tenant. In our example, the present tenant has paid more rent than relates to his period of occupation during the current term year by the figure £27,375 – £18,400 = £8,975. This is the amount for which he is to be reimbursed by his assignee. (Contrast this with the sum of £8,400 that would have been calculated by simply applying the daily rate of £100 to the number of days between 31 March and the end of that quarter.)

On sale of reversion

Using our example, suppose that the landlord's interest was transferred to a new landlord on 30 April in the second year of the term. The apportionment of rental income between the old landlord and the new landlord is to be calculated as follows:

Step 1

Ascertain the term year.

Step 2

Count the number of days for which the old landlord is entitled to retain the rent received from the tenant in respect of the current term year. In our example, the old landlord is entitled to the rent for the period from 29 September in year 1 to 30 April in year 2, namely 214 days.

Step 3

Calculate the rent receivable for that number of days on an annual basis. In our example, this would be 214/365 × £36,500 = £21,400.

Step 4

Calculate the amount of rent actually received by the old landlord from the tenant in respect of the current term year. In our example, this rent should have been received on 29 September in year 1, 25 December in year 1 and 25 March in year 2, namely 3 × £9,125 = £27,375.

Step 5

Compare the figures calculated at steps 3 and 4. If the former exceeds the latter, the new landlord must make an allowance of the difference to the old landlord. If the latter exceeds the former, the old landlord must make an allowance of the difference to the new landlord. In our example, the old landlord has received more rent than relates to his period of ownership by the sum of £27,375 – £21,400 = £5,975. This is the amount which the old landlord must allow to the new landlord on transferring the reversion. (Contrast that with the sum of £5,400 that would have been calculated simply by taking the number of days between 30 April and the end of the current quarter and applying the daily rate of £100.)

2.6.7. For consistency, where the term expires by effluxion of time on a date other than the last day of a term year, the amount of the tenants' final payment of rent should be calculated on a basis similar to the apportionment of his initial payment on the grant of the lease.

2.6.8. Apportionment of rent where the term date does not commence on a rent payment date cannot be made according to the formula explained in para. K2.6.6. In most cases the most appropriate method of calculation in this situation will be what is sometimes called the 'surveyor's method'. This involves simply counting the days to immediately before the next payment date, and applying a daily rate computed on a yearly basis.

2.6.9. The illogicality of this approach is obvious. A daily rate for rent payable by, e.g. equal quarterly instalments is being calculated on a yearly basis and then applied to the residue of a particular quarter, which does not comprise exactly one-fourth of a year. A variation would be to calculate the daily rate for the particular quarter by reference to the total number of days in that quarter.

2.6.10. On either basis, it will be apparent that, should it be necessary to calculate an apportionment at a later date (e.g. when the lease is assigned or surrendered, or the reversion is transferred), to achieve a fair result it would be necessary to ascertain how much rent was actually paid under the apportionment at the grant of the lease and carry the calculation forward on that basis. This will usually be impractical, and the parties will have to be prepared to adopt each time a more rough and ready approach, such as the 'surveyor's method'.

2.6.11. However, since that method is entirely arbitrary and bears no logical relationship to the term/rent structure of the lease, it is recommended that leases should be drafted so that the term year commences on one of the recurring rent payment dates. Thus if rent is to be payable on the usual quarter days, the term year should commence on a quarter day. This will enable apportionments to be computed on a logical basis as set out in the standard formula above.

K3. Acting for the tenant

3.1. Before exchange

3.1.1. Taking instructions

The information required by the buyer's (tenant's) solicitor from his client will be similar to that required in a freehold transaction.[1] The client should be advised about the effect of any security of tenure provisions which may be applicable in the circumstances.[2]

3.1.2. The draft lease

The draft lease, prepared by the seller's (landlord's) solicitor, will be supplied to the tenant's solicitor with the draft contract. The contract will normally require the tenant to accept the draft in the form annexed to the contract;[3] therefore any queries or observations which are to be raised in connection with the lease must be finalised before contracts are exchanged. Even where the lease appears to contain 'usual' clauses appropriate to the particular transaction in hand, the document must be carefully examined by the tenant's solicitor to ensure that it does contain provisions which are adequate to protect his client's interests and contains no onerous clauses (e.g. in relation to repairing obligations or rent review) which may adversely affect the client. The length of the term will affect the amount of stamp duty payable on the lease by the tenant and this also should be considered.

3.1.3. Checklist

When checking the lease particular attention should be paid to the provisions relating to the following matters:

(a) the property to be demised;

(b) easements and reservations (particularly in the case of flats or other non-detached property: see para. K1);

(c) repairing obligations;

(d) rent and rent review provisions;

(e) provisions relating to service charges (see para. K1);

(f) insurance (who is to insure: landlord or tenant? do the insurance provisions accord with the tenant's mortgagee's instructions? what is covered by the policy both in terms of premises, amount of cover and risks insured against?);

(g) forfeiture clauses;

(h) covenants restricting alienation of the property;

(i) covenants restricting the use of the property;

(j) provisions relating to a management company or residents' association (is the tenant required to become a member of a management company which is limited by guarantee? will his liability to the management company terminate on assignment of the lease?);

(k) requirements for a surety or rent deposit scheme;

(l) are any of the covenants onerous?

(m) do the covenants adequately protect the tenant and his lender?

(n) are covenants for title being offered?

(o) requirements of the CML Lenders' Handbook (see K6.6).

NB: A brief summary of the most common express covenants found in leases is contained in para. K1.

3.1.4. *Searches*

The tenant's solicitor should usually undertake the same searches and enquiries as if he were buying the freehold.[4] Exceptionally, where a short tenancy agreement is being granted, it may be considered unnecessary to do such searches.

3.1.5. *Lender's requirements*

Where the lease provides security for a loan, the tenant's lender's requirements, contained in the instructions given to the solicitors acting for the lender, must be observed. The tenant's lender will frequently be concerned to see that the following conditions have been satisfied:

(a) the consent of the landlord's lender to the transaction has been obtained (where relevant);

(b) the length of the term to be granted provides adequate security for the loan The requirements in the CML Lenders' Handbook are considered at para. K6.6.1;

(c) the lease contains adequate insurance provisions relating both to the premises themselves and (where relevant) to common parts of the building and that the insurance provisions coincide with the lender's own requirements for insurance;

(d) normally title to the freehold reversion should be deduced. This will enable the lease to be registered with an absolute title at the Land Registry (where appropriate);

(e) the lease contains proper repairing covenants in respect both of the property itself and (where relevant) the common parts of the building;

(f) in the case of residential leases, that there is no provision for forfeiture on the insolvency of the tenant;

(g) where the lease is of part of a building or is, e.g. of one house on an estate comprising leasehold houses all owned by the same landlord, that the lease provides for mutual enforceability of covenants as between the tenants;

(h) where appropriate the landlord is giving the relevant covenants for title.

3.1.6. Where the lender's solicitor's instructions are governed by the Lenders' Handbook the requirements of the Handbook must be complied with. This is dealt with at para. K6.6 and Part 1 of the Lenders' Handbook is reproduced at Appendix VIII.3.

3.1.7. *Advising the client*

The tenant's obligations under the lease, which are often complex and extensive, should be clearly explained to him. In particular, the tenant (where relevant) should be warned of his continuing liability on the covenants in the lease notwithstanding the subsequent sale of the residue of the term to a third party[5] and of the danger of losing the lease through forfeiture for breach of covenant. A precontract report may be prepared and given to the client (as in freehold transactions).[6] The report should explain the main provisions of the terms of the lease and their effect on the tenant.

3.1.8. *Protocol*

The Protocol does not specifically refer to procedures on the grant of a lease. Since the procedure on grant of a lease is very similar to that applicable to a freehold transaction it is recommended that in appropriate cases when dealing with residential property the Protocol procedures are adhered to as closely as circumstances permit.

1. See Taking instructions, para. A1.
2. See paras. K6, K8 and K10.
3. See Standard Condition 8.2.3.
4. See para. B10 and para. E2.
5. See Liability on covenants in leases, para. K10.
6. See Preparing to exchange, para. C1.

3.2. Pre-completion and completion

3.2.1. The engrossment of the lease and counterpart will usually be prepared by the landlord's solicitor. The tenant, if the contract so provides, may be required on completion to pay a fee to the landlord for the preparation of the engrossment. By Standard Condition 8.2.6 and Standard Commercial Property Condition 8.2.6 the landlord is to deliver the engrossment of the counterpart lease to the tenant at least five working days before completion and by Standard Condition 8.2.7 and Standard Commercial Property Condition 8.2.7 the tenant is to execute the counterpart lease and deliver it to the landlord on completion. Execution should be made in escrow. Similar points apply in relation to execution of the counterpart as those relating to execution of the lease. This is discussed in para K2.4.2 and section E.

3.2.2. The tenant's solicitor should make pre-completion searches in the same way as if he were buying the freehold.[1]

3.2.3. Apportionments on completion may include amounts in respect of rent and service charge payable in advance under the provisions of the lease.

3.2.4. On completion the tenant should give to the landlord:

(a) the duly executed counterpart lease;

(b) any money due on completion, e.g. balance of premium (less deposit paid on exchange), apportioned sums payable in respect of rent and service charge, landlord's fee for engrossment of the lease.

3.2.5. The tenant should on completion receive from the landlord:

(a) the duly executed lease;

(b) where the landlord's title is unregistered, a marked abstract of the freehold title;

(c) where appropriate, consent to the dealing given by the landlord's mortgagee;

(d) share certificate and management company documents.

1. See Pre-completion, section E.

3.3. Post-completion

3.3.1. Stamp duty

The Government propose to modernise the law relating to stamp duty. The enabling legislation is included in the Finance Act 2003, with the detail to be contained in secondary legislation, which appears likely to be brought into force towards the end of 2003 (see AAA. Stamp Duty Land Tax).

At present the requirements are, briefly, that the lease must be lodged for stamping with duty at the appropriate rate within 30 days of completion but should in practice be presented for stamping at the earliest opportunity because other time-limits (e.g. in relation to registration of the lease itself) may also have to be complied with. Stamp duty on leases is assessed by reference to the amount of the premium, and the average rent with rates linked to the length of the term. A service charge reserved as rent for a fixed sum attracts duty in relation to its amount, but a service charge of an unascertained amount, perhaps to be ascertained by reference to the application of a formula contained within the lease attracts a fixed duty only. No duty is payable on a service charge which is payable to a third party, e.g. a management company. No stamp duty is payable where the premium on the lease does not exceed the current lowest stamp duty threshold and the average annual rent does not exceed £600 provided that an appropriate certificate of value is included in the lease.[1]

3.3.2.   If the lease is granted for a term of seven years or more, it falls within Finance Act 1931, s.28 and must be produced to the Inland Revenue in accordance with the requirements of that section.[2]

3.3.3.   *Registration of the lease*

Where applicable the lease must be registered at the Land Registry within the relevant priority period, or on first registration within two months of completion. The requirements for registration of a lease are outlined in para. K1.

3.3.4.   *Notice to landlord*

The lease will usually contain a covenant requiring the tenant to notify the landlord within a stated period of all dealings with the lease and to pay a fee to the landlord for registration of the notice. The creation of a mortgage by the tenant, depending on the wording of the covenant, may fall within this obligation. Where the tenant is obliged to give notice of dealings, this should be done by sending two copies of the notice, together with a cheque for the appropriate fee, to the landlord's solicitor or other person named in the covenant. The landlord should be asked to sign one copy of the notice and to return it to the tenant so that the receipted notice may be placed with the tenant's title deeds as evidence of compliance with this requirement.

3.3.5.   A tenant's lender may require a signed but otherwise blank stock transfer form and the tenant's share certificate to be lodged with him to ensure that the lender will be able to transfer the tenant's share in the management company in the event of the lender exercising his power of sale.

1. For form of certificate of value see para. K1.11. Also see Stamp duty and stamp duty savings, para. A14.
2. See Post-completion, section G.

K4. Acting for both parties

See also: Acting for both parties, para. A10
 Mortgages: acting for lender and borrower, para. A11
 Acting on grant of lease, para. K1
 Part 1 CML Lenders' Handbook, Appendix VIII.3.

4.1. Conflict of interests

4.1.1. A solicitor must not act where there is a conflict of interest between himself and his clients or between two of his clients (see paras. A10 and A11).

4.2. Rule 6 Solicitors' Practice Rules 1990

4.2.1. Specifically in relation to conveyancing Rule 6 Solicitors' Practice Rules 1990 prohibits a solicitor from acting for both landlord and tenant in the grant or assignment of a lease at arm's length. This rule and its exceptions are further discussed in para. A10 and Rule 6 is reproduced at Appendix I.1.

4.3. Acting for the client's lender

4.3.1. Generally, a solicitor may act for his landlord or tenant client and that client's lender provided that no conflict of interests exists or is likely to arise. See Mortgages: acting for lender and borrower, para. A11.

4.4. Sureties

4.4.1. A buyer's solicitor who is also acting for the sureties to the lease must consider whether any conflict of interest exists or is likely to arise between the interests of his buyer client and the interests of the sureties. It may be in the best interests of the buyer to obtain a lease of the premises, which he can only do if he provides sureties to the lease (a pre-condition imposed by the landlord), but it may not be in the best interests of the sureties to enter into covenants with the landlord to guarantee performance of the buyer's obligations under the lease, e.g. as to payment of rent, repairs, etc., where the enforcement of the sureties' covenants would put the sureties' personal assets, such as a matrimonial home, at risk. Where such a conflict exists, or is likely to arise, the sureties should receive independent advice about their potential liability.

4.4.2. Where a solicitor does act for a surety or guarantor he owes a duty of care to the surety or guarantor which is limited to exercising reasonable skill and care in carrying out the terms of the retainer.[1]

4.4.3. Under the terms of the Lenders' Handbook the solicitor who is acting for the borrower cannot also act for a guarantor, any borrower who does not personally benefit from the loan or anyone intending to occupy the property who is to consent to the mortgage. They must be independently advised.

4.4.4. The CML Lenders' Handbook also precludes the same fee earner in the same firm acting for the lender and borrower where the borrower is either the fee earner or a member of his or her immediate family. Consent may be given but in this case a separate fee earner of no less standing in the firm must act for the lender.

1. *Woodward* v. *Wolferstans* [1997] NPC 51.

K5. Short-term residential tenancies

See also: Taking instructions, para. A1
Acting on grant of lease, para. K1
Acting for the landlord, para. K2
Acting for the tenant, para. K3
Long-term residential tenancies, para. K6
Business premises, para. K7
Licence or tenancy, para. K12

5.1. Grant of lease

5.1.1. A lease for a term of over three years must be granted by deed to vest the legal estate in the tenant. A lease for three years or less, taking effect in possession at the best rent without a fine, may be granted orally or in writing.[1] To ensure certainty of terms between the parties it is recommended that all leases, no matter how short the term, should be in writing.

5.1.2. A contract for the grant of the lease is not generally entered into on short-term lettings of residential premises.

5.1.3. On short-term lettings of residential property it is not usual for searches and enquiries to be made since the low risk attached to these lettings does not justify the expense of making the searches. However, the prospective tenant may feel it is prudent to make enquiries about the prospective landlord's solvency, particularly where the property is mortgaged, to avoid the risk of the landlord's lender seeking a possession order against the tenant if the landlord does not pay the mortgage.

5.1.4. Where the lease is to be granted for a short term some of the considerations outlined in paras. K1, K2 and K3 will not be relevant. Frequently a formal contract for the grant of the lease is dispensed with and the landlord's solicitor simply submits a draft lease (sometimes referred to as a tenancy agreement) for approval by the tenant's solicitor. When the form of the lease or agreement is finalised and signed, the tenant will take possession of the premises. No premium is normally taken (and in some cases is not permitted by law) but a deposit which must not exceed one-sixth of the annual rent may be taken as security against damage to fixtures and fittings.

5.1.5. Where the premises are furnished, an inventory of the contents should be prepared by the landlord and agreed by the tenant.

5.1.6. If the rent is to be payable weekly, a rent book must be provided to the tenant.

5.1.7. The tenant's solicitor will not normally investigate title on his client's behalf, but the risks of omitting this step must be considered in each individual case. The terms of the tenancy agreement must be carefully scrutinised and their effect explained to the client. Particular attention should be paid to the effects of any security of tenure legislation on the tenancy.

5.1.8. A lease of seven years or less is generally not capable of being registered with its own title at the Land Registry,[2] but takes effect as an overriding interest.[3] If there is concern about protecting the tenant's interest in the property a notice may be entered against the landlord's title where the lease is for a term of more than three years from the date of the grant. A lease for a term of three years or less cannot be protected by notice.[4]

5.1.9. Where the title to the reversionary estate is unregistered a purchaser of the reversion will take subject to a lease. An agreement for a lease must be registered as an estate contract (C(iv) land charge) and a caution against first registration may be registered at the Land Registry.

1. Section 54(2) Law of Property Act 1925.
2. Except leases granted under Housing Act 1985, Part V, see K9.1.5. See exceptions in para. G3.
3. Land Registration Act 2002, Sched. 1, para. 1 and Sched. 3, para. 1.
4. Land Registration Act 2002, s.33.

5.2. Public sector tenants

5.2.1. Security for public sector tenants is provided by Part IV Housing Act 1985 (as amended by Housing Act 1988) under what are called 'secure tenancies'.

5.2.2. Subject to:

(a) a number of exceptions set out in Schedule 1 (e.g. tenancies granted for over 21 years and business tenancies within Part II Landlord and Tenant Act 1954);

(b) tenancies ceasing to be secure tenancies after the death of the tenant subject to certain limited succession rights;[1] and

(c) tenancies ceasing to be secure tenancies in consequence of an assignment or sub-letting other than one permitted by the Act,[2]

a tenancy under which a dwelling house is let as a separate dwelling is a secure tenancy at any time when the 'landlord condition' and the 'tenant condition' are both satisfied.

5.2.3.   The provisions apply to most licences as well as to tenancies.[3]

5.2.4.   The 'landlord condition'

The 'landlord condition' is that the interest of the landlord belongs to one of a number of bodies specified in Housing Act 1985, s.80, as modified by Housing Act 1988, s.35. These include local authorities and housing associations.

5.2.5.   The 'tenant condition'

The 'tenant condition' is that the tenant is an individual and occupies the house as his only or principal home or, where the tenancy is a joint tenancy, that each of the joint tenants is an individual and at least one of them occupies the house as his only or principal home.

5.2.6.   Where a secure tenancy for a term certain ends by effluxion of time or by an order terminating the tenancy in pursuance of a right of forfeiture, a periodic tenancy arises. A secure tenancy which is either a periodic tenancy or for a term certain but subject to termination by the landlord cannot usually be brought to an end by the landlord except by obtaining a court order for possession. The grounds for possession are set out in Schedule 2 Housing Act 1985.

5.2.7.   A secure tenancy ends on the death of the tenant, although provisions for succession to the tenancy after the death of the tenant are contained in Housing Act 1985, ss.87–90.

5.2.8.   A secure tenancy cannot generally be assigned, but there are limited exceptions to this rule, e.g. an assignment with the landlord's consent by way of exchange. A secure tenant cannot, without the landlord's consent, sub-let or part with the possession of part only of the house. In this case, the landlord must not unreasonably withhold his consent to the alienation and, if consent is unreasonably withheld, it is treated as having been given. If, however, the tenant parts with the possession of the whole house, or sub-lets the whole, the tenancy ceases to be a secure tenancy and cannot later revert to being one.

5.2.9.   Introductory tenancies

A local housing authority or housing action trust is empowered by Housing Act 1996, s.124 to operate an introductory tenancy regime.

5.2.10.   Where the scheme has been adopted by the local authority, the majority of all new periodic tenancies or licences, which would otherwise be secure, granted by such authorities will, instead, be 'introductory tenancies'. A new tenancy is one granted to a person (or persons) who immediately before its grant was not a secure tenant of the same or different premises and was not an assured tenant of a registered social landlord of the same or another dwelling house.

5.2.11.   An introductory tenancy remains such for a trial period of one year subject to certain earlier termination provisions contained in Housing Act 1996, s.125.

5.2.12. The landlord can bring an introductory tenancy to an end, after serving notice on the tenant, by obtaining a court order under Housing Act 1996, s.127. The tenant has the right to ask for a review of the landlord's decision to end the tenancy within 14 days of notice of possession proceedings being served on him. Subject to this, the possession ground is mandatory.

5.2.13. Provisions for succession to an introductory tenancy are contained in Housing Act 1996, ss.131–133. An introductory tenancy is not capable of assignment except under certain provisions of the Act which are similar to those for secure tenancies (e.g. assignments under the Matrimonial Causes Act 1973, s.24).

1. Housing Act 1985, ss.87–90.
2. Housing Act 1985, s.91.
3. Housing Act 1985, s.79.

5.3. Rent Act tenancies

5.3.1. A tenancy under which a dwelling house (including part of a house) was let as a separate dwelling before 15 January 1989 was (and will until termination of the tenancy continue to be) a protected tenancy under Rent Act 1977, unless that tenancy was excluded from the Act (see para. K5.3.3). Since 14 January 1989 no new Rent Act tenancies have come into being because on that date Rent Act 1977 was superseded by Housing Act 1988 (see para K5.4).

5.3.2. On the termination of a protected tenancy (e.g. by forfeiture or notice to quit), the person who at that time was the protected tenant will become a statutory tenant if and so long as he occupies the house as his residence. Although the terms of the protected tenancy apply to the statutory tenancy so far as they are consistent with the nature of the statutory tenancy, there are a number of differences between the two types of tenancy, such differences deriving from the fact that a protected tenancy is a proprietary right, while a statutory tenancy is merely a personal right of residence. A protected tenancy will vest in a tenant's trustee in bankruptcy and can be disclaimed by him (so ending the tenant's right of residence as against his landlord) but a statutory tenancy does not vest in a trustee in bankruptcy.

5.3.3. Exclusions from protection

These include:[1]

(a) tenancies of high rateable value dwellings;

(b) tenancies at low rents;

(c) holiday lettings;

(d) lettings by resident landlords;

(e) lettings by local authorities and housing associations;

(f) business tenancies within Part II Landlord and Tenant Act 1954; and

(g) licences.

5.3.4. Rent control[2]

Unless a rent is registered with the rent officer, a landlord who granted a protected tenancy can initially lawfully recover whatever amount of rent has been agreed between the parties. Such rent can be increased provided that the conditions in the Act relating to the making of a rent agreement are followed. It is open to the tenant to apply to the rent officer for the determination and registration of a 'fair rent', in which case the fair rent will be the maximum legally recoverable amount. An application for revision of the fair rent cannot normally be made within two years of the previous registration.

5.3.5. Recovery of possession

A court order is necessary in order to recover possession from a tenant who has security of tenure under Rent Act 1977.[3] Such an order can only be made where the court[4] is satisfied either that suitable alternative accommodation is available to the tenant or that one or more of the grounds for possession set out in Schedule 15 Rent Act 1977 has been established. Some of the grounds under Schedule 15 are mandatory and others are discretionary, i.e. the landlord must not only prove the existence of the ground, he must also satisfy the court that it is reasonable in all the circumstances to make an order for possession.

5.3.6. Protected shorthold tenancies

These were introduced by Housing Act 1980, enabling landlords to grant fixed-term tenancies for a minimum period of one year and a maximum period of five years giving the landlord the guaranteed right to possession at the end of the term provided certain conditions were satisfied. The fair rent provisions of Rent Act 1977 apply to such tenancies. No new protected shorthold tenancies have come into existence since 14 January 1989 when these provisions were superseded by Housing Act 1988.

5.3.7. Death of tenant

A protected tenancy is capable of devolution on the death of the tenant, subject to the rights to transmission of the tenancy to a member of the tenant's family. A statutory tenancy cannot pass by will or on intestacy since it is neither an estate in land nor a proprietary right. The transmission provisions contained in the Act apply equally to statutory tenancies.[5] On transmission the tenancy is converted into an assured tenancy (see para. K5.4).

5.3.8. Assignment and sub-letting

Whether or not a protected tenant can assign or sub-let the house or part of it depends on the terms of the tenancy. A statutory tenant cannot assign or sub-let the whole house without the consent of the landlord, although he may sub-let part unless he has agreed not to do so or the remainder is already sub-let.

5.3.9. *Premiums*

There is a general prohibition on the taking of a premium as a condition of or in connection with the grant, renewal, continuance or assignment of a protected tenancy. In relation to long tenancies, these rules are substantially modified by Rent Act 1977, s.127, as amended by Housing Act 1980, s.78 and Housing Act 1988, s.115.

1. See Rent Act 1977, ss.4–16.
2. Parts III and IV Rent Act 1977, as amended by Housing Act 1980.
3. Rent Act 1977, s.98.
4. The county court has jurisdiction over all matters under Rent Act 1977.
5. Rent Act 1977, Sched. 1, Pt. 1, as amended by Housing Act 1980, s.76 and Housing Act 1988, s.39.

5.4. Assured tenancies

5.4.1. *Introduction*

The definition of an assured tenancy is set out in Housing Act 1988, s.1. A tenancy under which a dwelling house is let as a separate dwelling will be an assured tenancy, if and so long as all of the following requirements are met:

(a) the tenant or each of joint tenants is an individual; and

(b) the tenant or at least one of joint tenants occupies the dwelling house as his only or principal home; and

(c) the tenancy is not specifically excluded by other provisions of the Act.

5.4.2. From the commencement date of Housing Act 1996, most new lettings will be assured shorthold tenancies (see para. K5.5) and not assured tenancies. However, a shorthold is merely a type of assured tenancy and so must comply with the definition of an assured tenancy as well as the extra requirements which make it a shorthold.

5.4.3. Tenancies which do not satisfy the definition of an assured tenancy (and so cannot be shortholds either) will not be subject to the provisions of Housing Act 1988. Instead, ordinary common law rules as to termination, etc., will apply. They will, however, be subject to Protection From Eviction Act 1977 (see para. K12.5.1).

5.4.4. *Constituent elements of an assured tenancy*

5.4.4.1. Tenancy

There must be a 'tenancy'; licences to occupy dwelling houses are excluded from protection. This distinction is dealt with in section K12.

5.4.4.2. Dwelling house

There is no statutory definition of 'dwelling house', and it will be a question of fact whether premises are a house or not, but any building designed or adapted for living in is capable of forming a dwelling house for these purposes.

5.4.4.3. Let as a separate dwelling

The premises, as well as being a dwelling house, must be let as a dwelling. So the purpose of the letting is relevant; thus if a building that would otherwise qualify as a dwelling house is let for business purposes, the tenant cannot claim that it is let on an assured tenancy merely because he decides to move in and live there.

5.4.4.4. There must be a letting as a dwelling. It has been established that this only permits of a singular construction (notwithstanding Interpretation Act 1978).[1] So if the let property comprises two or more residential units, each intended for separate occupation (e.g. the letting of the whole of a house converted into several flats), that tenancy cannot be an assured tenancy. The sub-letting of each of the individual flats could, however, be within the definition.

5.4.4.5. There must be a separate dwelling. This is intended to exclude lettings of accommodation which lacks some essential feature of a dwelling. The House of Lords have held that the presence of cooking facilities is not an essential feature of a dwelling.[2] However, Housing Act 1988, s.3 makes special provision for the situation where the tenant shares some of the essential features of a dwelling with others. Such a letting is deemed to be an assured tenancy (assuming that all the other conditions are met) even though the absence of essential facilities in the demised property would normally prevent the tenancy from fulfilling the statutory requirements. The tenant must, however, have the exclusive occupation of at least one room (otherwise it cannot be a tenancy), and if the other accommodation is shared with the landlord, the tenancy will be excluded from the definition of an assured tenancy for different reasons. Arrangements where each tenant is given exclusive occupation of his own bed-sitting room, but shares bathroom and kitchen with other tenants, will be deemed to be capable of being assured tenancies.

5.4.4.6. 'If and so long as'

The status of the tenancy is not to be determined once and for all at the commencement of the letting. Whether a tenancy is an assured tenancy can fluctuate according to changed circumstances. For example, one requirement of the definition is that the tenant must be occupying the house as his only or principal home. This may have been the case at the start of the tenancy, and so the tenancy would be assured, but if subsequently the tenant ceases to reside, the tenancy will no longer be assured. The tenant will thus lose his security of tenure.

5.4.4.7. The tenant must be an individual

Lettings to companies are excluded from the definition, even though an individual (e.g. a director or employee of the company) may be in occupation of the house. Any sub-letting by a company tenant could, however, qualify as an assured tenancy.

5.4.4.8. The tenant must occupy as his 'only or principal home'

It is possible for a person to have more than one 'home'. If that is the case, then it is a question of fact as to which is the tenant's principal home. Only a tenancy of the principal home can be an assured tenancy. Although the provision requires 'occupation', this does not mean continuous occupation. A mere temporary absence will not deprive a tenancy of its status as an assured tenancy.

5.4.5. *Tenancies excluded from the definition*

5.4.5.1. Tenancies entered into before the commencement of Housing Act 1988

Only lettings entered into on or after 15 January 1989 can be assured tenancies. Any pre-existing tenancy will, if it has any protection at all, still remain subject to the provisions of Rent Act 1977. There are, however, exceptions to this rule in some cases where a succession has taken place in relation to a pre-existing tenancy.

5.4.5.2. High value properties

For tenancies granted before 1 April 1990, a tenancy of a dwelling house with a rateable value in excess of £750 (£1,500 in Greater London) cannot be an assured tenancy. If the tenancy was granted on or after 1 April 1990, it cannot be an assured tenancy if the rent payable is £25,000 or more per annum.

5.4.5.3. Tenancies at a low rent

Lettings made before 1 April 1990 cannot be assured if the annual rent is less than two-thirds of the rateable value of the property. For tenancies granted on or after 1 April 1990, the exclusion applies to tenancies in which the rent does not exceed £250 per annum (£1,000 per annum in Greater London).

5.4.5.4. Business tenancies

A tenancy to which Part II of Landlord and Tenant Act 1954 applies cannot be an assured tenancy.[3]

5.4.5.5. Licensed premises

Premises licensed for the sale of alcohol for consumption on the premises, e.g. a public house, are excluded from the definition of an assured tenancy even if the tenant is residing on the premises.

5.4.5.6. Tenancies of agricultural land

A tenancy under which agricultural land exceeding two acres is let together with the house cannot be an assured tenancy (Housing Act 1988, Sched. 1, para. 6).

5.4.5.7. Tenancies of agricultural holdings

A tenancy under which a dwelling house is comprised in an agricultural holding (within the meaning of Agricultural Holdings Act 1986) or in a farm business tenancy under the Agricultural Tenancies Act 1995, and is occupied by the person responsible for the control of the farming of the holding cannot be an assured tenancy (Housing Act 1988, Sched. 1, para. 7).

5.4.5.8. Lettings to students

Lettings to students by specified educational bodies are outside the definition of an assured tenancy. This exception does not apply to lettings to students by landlords other than the specified universities and colleges.

5.4.5.9. Holiday lettings

A letting for the purpose of a holiday cannot be an assured tenancy.

5.4.5.10. Lettings by resident landlords

A letting by a resident landlord is excluded from the definition of an assured tenancy provided that certain conditions are satisfied (see para. K5.4.14).

5.4.5.11. Crown, local authority and housing association lettings

Crown, local authority and housing association lettings are excluded from the definition of an assured tenancy.

5.4.6. *Rents under assured tenancies*

5.4.6.1. The initial rent

There is no restriction on the amount of rent which can initially be charged on the grant of an assured tenancy. However, if the landlord subsequently wishes to increase the rent, he may not be able to do so unless he follows the correct procedure.

5.4.6.2. Statutory increases for assured periodic tenancies

Statutory increases for assured periodic tenancies are governed by Housing Act 1988, ss.13 and 14 which lay down a complicated procedure requiring the landlord to serve a notice (in the prescribed form) on the tenant. This can then be referred to the Rent Assessment Committee for arbitration if agreement as to the new rent cannot be reached between the parties. The Rent Assessment Committee must determine the rent at which the premises might reasonably be let in the open market. If there is an express term in the tenancy agreement permitting rent increases, this avoids the need to rely on the statutory procedure.

5.4.6.3. Rent increases for fixed-term assured tenancies (including shortholds)

There are no statutory provisions allowing an increase for fixed-term assured tenancies. In the absence of any express provision in the tenancy agreement, the landlord will be unable to increase the rent during the fixed term without the agreement of the tenant. Once the fixed term has ended and the tenant continues in possession as a statutory periodic tenant, then the above provisions of Housing Act 1988, ss. 13 and 14 will apply to enable the landlord to increase the rent, even if there is no express provision on the lease.

5.4.7. *Prohibition of assignment without consent*

If there is no such express provision against assignment in the lease, Housing Act 1988, s.15 may assist the landlord. The section only applies to periodic assured tenancies (including statutory periodic tenancies). It does not apply to fixed-term assured tenancies (including shortholds).

5.4.8. The term implied into a periodic assured tenancy is that the tenant must not without the consent of the landlord:

(a) assign the tenancy (in whole or in part); or

(b) sub-let or part with possession of all or part of the property.

Landlord and Tenant Act 1927, s.19 does not apply to this implied term and therefore the covenant is not subject to an implied proviso that consent will not be unreasonably withheld.

5.4.9. In the case of a periodic tenancy which is not a statutory periodic tenancy, these prohibitions do not apply if a premium was paid on the grant or renewal of the tenancy. 'Premium' is defined to include any pecuniary consideration in addition to rent and also includes returnable deposits exceeding one-sixth of the annual rent.

5.4.10. *Succession on death*

On the death of one of joint tenants, the tenancy will vest in the survivor(s). On the death of a sole tenant the tenancy will pass under his will or intestacy. Housing Act 1988, however, contains specific provisions in section 17 dealing with the succession to an assured periodic tenancy on the death of a sole tenant which will override these normal rules.

5.4.11. On the death of a sole periodic tenant the tenancy will vest in the tenant's spouse, notwithstanding the terms of the deceased's will, provided that immediately before the deceased tenant's death the spouse was occupying the dwelling house as his or her only or principal home. 'Spouse' is defined to include a person who was living with the tenant as his or her wife or husband as well as persons who were lawfully married. On the face of it, there can be no succession in favour of a person of the same sex who may have been co-habiting with the deceased tenant. However, in interpreting a similar provision in the Rent Act, the courts have held that this may extend to some types of same sex relationships.[4] This provision will not apply if the deceased tenant was himself a 'successor', as defined, i.e. the tenancy became vested in him:

(a) by virtue of this section; or

(b) under the will or intestacy of a former tenant; or

(c) he is the sole survivor of joint tenants; or

(d) he succeeded to the tenancy under the provisions of Rent Act 1977.

5.4.12. Only one statutory succession is possible. If there is no statutory succession, e.g. because there is no qualifying 'spouse', or there has already been a succession, or the tenancy is for a fixed term, the tenancy will then pass under the will or intestacy of the deceased in the normal way. However, on the death of a periodic assured tenant in such a situation, the landlord would be able to make use of one of the mandatory grounds in order to obtain possession.

5.4.13. Sub-lettings

Housing Act 1988, s.18 provides that in the case of a house lawfully sub-let on an assured tenancy, on the ending of the head lease, the sub-tenancy will still continue. The assured sub-tenant will then become the direct tenant of the head landlord with full security of tenure. However, this only applies to lawful sub-lettings. In the case of an unlawful sub-letting, the sub-tenant will have no security once the head lease has been determined and the head landlord will thus have an absolute right to possession.

5.4.14. Lettings by resident landlords

5.4.14.1. Qualifying conditions

The following qualifying conditions apply:

(a) the dwelling house which is let forms only part of a building; and

(b) the building is not a purpose-built block of flats; and

(c) the tenancy was granted by an individual (i.e. not a limited company) who at the time of the grant occupied another part of the same building as his only or principal home; and

(d) at all times since the tenancy was granted, the interest of the landlord has continued to belong to an individual who continued so to reside.

5.4.14.2. Continuity of residence

It is not sufficient for the landlord merely to have been in residence at the commencement of the tenancy; he must be in occupation throughout the tenancy. If he ceases to reside then the exception will cease to apply and the letting will once again be capable of being an assured tenancy with full security of tenure.

But if the tenancy was entered into on or after the commencement date of Housing Act 1996, the letting will become an assured shorthold tenancy. However, if the interest of the landlord is vested in two or more individuals, only one of those persons need be in residence at any one time.

5.4.14.3. Periods of absence disregarded

Certain periods of absence will be disregarded when deciding whether the landlord's occupation has been continuous:

    (a) a period of 28 days beginning with the date on which the interest of the landlord becomes vested at law and in equity in a new owner. If, during this 28 days, the new owner notifies the tenant in writing of his intention to occupy another part of the building as his only or principal home, the disregard will be extended up to six months from the change of ownership; and

    (b) any period not exceeding two years during which the interest of the landlord becomes and remains vested in:

        (i)   trustees as such; or

        (ii)   the Probate Judge under Administration of Estates Act 1925, s.9; or

        (iii) personal representatives of a deceased person acting in that capacity.

Throughout any period during which absence is disregarded (except in a situation where the house is vested in personal representatives), no order for possession can be made except one which might have been made if the tenancy were an assured tenancy. In other words, during these periods of deemed residence the letting becomes a quasi-assured tenancy and possession can only be obtained against the tenant if assured tenancy grounds can be established. However, as an exception to that rule, personal representatives of a deceased resident landlord will be able to recover possession without proving assured tenancy grounds, provided that the contractual term can be terminated.

5.4.14.4. Purpose-built blocks of flats

The resident landlord exception does not apply if the building is a purpose-built block of flats and the landlord occupies one flat in the block and lets one (or more) of the others. Such lettings are therefore capable of being assured tenancies.

A building is a purpose-built block of flats if *as constructed* it contained, and still contains, two or more flats.

'Flat' means a dwelling house which forms only part of a building and is separated horizontally from another dwelling house which forms part of the same building.

Housing Act 1988 makes it clear, however, that if the landlord occupies one flat in a purpose-built block and lets part of that flat, then the resident landlord exception can still apply.

5.4.14.5. Exceptions

A tenancy will be excluded from the resident landlord provisions if two conditions are both fulfilled:

(a) it was granted to a person who immediately before the grant was an assured tenant of the same house or of another house in the same building; and

(b) the landlord under the new tenancy and under the former tenancy is the same person. If either of the tenancies was granted by two or more persons, it is sufficient for this condition that the same person is the landlord or one of the landlords under each tenancy.

This is an anti-avoidance provision designed to ensure that a landlord does not deprive existing tenants of their protection as assured tenants by taking up possession himself and then granting a new tenancy to those existing tenants.

5.4.15. *Security of tenure*

5.4.15.1. Restriction on termination by landlord

An assured tenancy cannot be brought to an end by the landlord otherwise than by obtaining a court order for possession. Thus, in the case of a periodic assured tenancy, a notice to quit is of no effect. On the ending of a fixed-term assured tenancy (including a shorthold) otherwise than by an order of the court or by surrender, the tenant is entitled to remain in possession as a statutory periodic tenant. This statutory periodic tenancy will be on the same terms as the previous fixed-term tenancy.

5.4.15.2. Obtaining a court order

The landlord will only obtain a court order for possession if he follows the correct procedure and can establish one or more of the grounds for possession set out in Schedule 2 Housing Act 1988. Although some of these grounds are mandatory grounds, i.e. the court must order possession if the ground is established, many of them are discretionary grounds. With these, the court, on proof of the ground, may order possession only if it considers it reasonable to do so. The landlord must serve a notice on the tenant (a 'section 8 notice') in the prescribed form specifying the ground(s) upon which the landlord intends to rely and must give two weeks' notice of the landlord's intention to commence possession proceedings. (Sometimes two months' notice has to be given.) However, from the commencement of Housing Act 1996, if ground 14^5 is specified (whether or not with any other ground), then the proceedings can be commenced as soon as the section 8 notice has been served. The proceedings must then be commenced not earlier than the date specified and not later than 12 months from the date of service of the notice. It is possible for the court to dispense with the requirement for a section 8 notice (unless ground 8 is being relied upon), but only if it considers it just and equitable to do so.

5.4.15.3. In the case of a fixed-term assured tenancy, the landlord cannot normally obtain possession until after the end of the contractual fixed term (assuming that a ground for possession can then be established). However, as an exception to this, certain of the grounds for possession will be available to the landlord during the fixed term provided that the tenancy agreement contains a provision for it to be brought to an end on the ground in question. This provision can take any form at all, including a proviso for re-entry or a forfeiture clause. The grounds on which the landlord can obtain possession in this way during the fixed term are grounds 2, 8 and 10 to 15.

1. *Horford Investments Ltd* v. *Lambert* [1976] Ch 39.
2. *Ultratemp Venture Ltd* v. *Collins* [2001] 3 WLR 806.
3. See *Brewer* v. *Andrews* [1997] EGCS 19.
4. See *Fitzpatrick* v. *Sterling HL* [2000] 1 AC 27; and *Mendoza* v. *Ghadian* [2002] EWCA Civ 1533 (2002) *The Times*, November 14.
5. Ground 14 relates to the tenant being a nuisance or annoyance or there being illegal or immoral use.

5.5. Shorthold tenancies

5.5.1. Introduction

It is important to distinguish between the two types of shortholds. 'Old' short-holds were entered into before the commencement of s.96 of the Housing Act 1996 (28 February 1997). 'New' shortholds are those entered into on or after this date unless made pursuant to a contract made before that date.

5.5.2. In the case of an old shorthold, before the grant of the tenancy the landlord was required to serve a warning notice on the tenant in a prescribed form. An old shorthold was required to be for a fixed term for a minimum duration of at least six months. Providing these criteria were satisfied the landlord has an absolute right to recover possession, provided that he complies with the correct procedure.

5.5.3. From the commencement of s.96 of the Housing Act 1996, however, all new lettings (with certain exceptions) are deemed to be shortholds. The old conditions need no longer be complied with; the letting need not be for a fixed term, there is no need for a warning notice, etc. However, the landlord still has the same absolute right to possession as in an old shorthold.

5.5.4. Note, that 'old' shortholds continue as before and if one fails due to the conditions not having been complied with, e.g. no warning notice was served, the tenancy will still become a fully protected assured tenancy. This means that the conditions for the grant of an old shorthold are still of considerable practical importance even after the introduction of new shortholds.

5.5.5. The only disadvantage of a shorthold (whether new or old) from a landlord's point of view is the right given to the tenant to refer the rent initially payable to the Rent Assessment Committee. However, such Committee can only reduce the rent if it is 'significantly higher' than the rents under other comparable assured tenancies.

5.5.6   *An assured tenancy*

An assured shorthold tenancy must comply with all the requirements of an assured tenancy as it is merely a type of assured tenancy (see para. K5.4). It is therefore necessary for there to be a letting of a dwelling house to an individual who occupies the house as his only or principal home. In the same way none of the specific exclusions from the definition of an assured tenancy must apply. For example, high rental tenancies and lettings by resident landlords cannot be assured shortholds as they fall outside the definition of an assured tenancy.

5.5.7.   A shorthold cannot be granted to an existing tenant under an ordinary assured tenancy (or to one of joint tenants) if it is granted by the landlord under that existing tenancy. This is so even if the lettings are not of the same premises.

5.5.8.   *Old shortholds*

The qualifying conditions for shortholds entered into before the commencement date of Housing Act 1996 were set out in Section 20 Housing Act 1988. It provides that an assured shorthold tenancy is an assured tenancy which:

(a) is a fixed-term tenancy granted for a term of not less than six months; and

(b) contains no power for the landlord to terminate it during the first six months; and

(c) was preceded by the giving to the tenant of the prescribed shorthold notice.[1]

5.5.8.1.   Minimum six-month fixed term

The initial grant of an old shorthold could not be for a periodic term. It was required to be for a fixed term and for a minimum duration of six months. A letting for 'six months and then from month to month' is not a letting for a term certain and so cannot be an old shorthold, even though it is for longer than the minimum six months. There is, however, no maximum length. Many shortholds were granted for the minimum six-month period and, in such a case, care must be taken to ensure that the tenant is given a right to occupy for the minimum period. The six-month period will run from the date on which the tenancy is entered into; it cannot be backdated. So a tenancy granted 'from and including 1 January 1994 until 30 June 1994' but not actually executed until 15 January 1994 would not give the tenant the requisite six months' occupation from the date of grant and so could not be a shorthold.

5.5.8.2.   Problems are likely to arise where a tenancy agreement was drawn up containing a fixed termination date and there was then a delay in the agreement being executed so that by the time that it was executed there then remained less than six months until the prescribed termination date. Such a letting would amount to an ordinary assured tenancy giving the tenant full security of tenure.

5.8.3. No power for landlord to terminate during first six months

Even if a minimum period of six months was granted, any power, however expressed, which would or might allow the landlord to terminate the tenancy within the first six months of the tenancy will prevent the tenancy from amounting to a shorthold. Break clauses exercisable outside that period are not prohibited, but care must be taken with such clauses to ensure that they were only exercisable outside the initial six months; otherwise an ordinary assured tenancy will have been created giving the tenant full security of tenure. Note, however, that a forfeiture clause or a clause allowing termination on assured tenancy grounds 2, 8 and 10 to 15 will not breach this requirement even though it is exercisable during the first six months of the term. A term allowing the tenant to terminate during the first six months could have been validly included. Such a provision, however, will not be implied. A tenant entering into an old shorthold will, therefore, normally be contractually bound to pay the rent and perform the other obligations under the tenancy agreement for the full term entered into.

.5.8.4. Preceded by the giving of the prescribed shorthold notice

As the tenant under an assured shorthold has no security of tenure, he had to be served with a notice prior to the grant of the tenancy warning him of this fact. This notice must have been in the prescribed form.

.5.8.5. The notice must have been served before the tenancy agreement was entered into and not at the same time. Thus, it could not be included in the tenancy agreement itself. It was best to ensure that there was an adequate interval between the service of the notice and the signing of the tenancy agreement to give the tenant the opportunity of digesting the contents of the notice. However, it appears from *Bedding* v. *McCarthy* [1994] 41 EG 151 that an interval of a few hours between the service of the section 20 notice and the tenancy agreement being entered into would be sufficient. In the case of joint tenants, all of the prospective tenants should have been served. Common law rules as to service will apply (and not section 196 of Law of Property Act 1925) and so it is necessary to show that the notice actually came into the tenant's hands. It was advisable for a landlord to serve the notice in duplicate and to require all the prospective tenants to endorse one copy with an acknowledgement of receipt, and the date and time of receipt, and return this to the landlord before the tenancy agreement was entered into. Correct service of the current version of the shorthold notice was vital. The court has no power to dispense with these notice requirements even though it might be just and equitable to do so.

.5.9. *New shortholds*

.5.9.1. Definition

Shortholds entered into on or after the commencement date of Housing Act 1996 (otherwise than pursuant to a contract made before that date) are governed by Housing Act 1988, s.19A (as inserted by Housing Act 1996). This provides that any assured tenancy entered into on or after the commencement date will be a shorthold unless it falls within one of the specified exceptions.

5.5.9.2. There is no need for a shorthold to be for a fixed term and therefore it can be periodic. There is no longer any need for a shorthold to be preceded by a prescribed form of notice. There is also no prohibition on the landlord being able to terminate during the first six months. However, no order for possession using the shorthold ground can be made earlier than six months from the start of the tenancy, whether the tenancy is for a fixed term or is a periodic tenancy. This does not stop possession being obtained during the first six months using an assured tenancy ground because a new shorthold, like an old shorthold, is merely a type of assured tenancy.

5.5.9.3. Exceptions

All new assured tenancies granted on or after the commencement date of Housing Act 1996 (other than those granted pursuant to a contract made before that date) will be shortholds subject to certain exceptions,[2] which will take effect as ordinary assured tenancies. These are:

(1) Tenancies excluded by notice.

The landlord may serve a notice on the tenant either before or after the grant of the tenancy stating that the letting is not to be a shorthold.

(2) Tenancies containing a provision stating that the tenancy is not to be a shorthold.

(3) Lettings to existing assured tenants.

Where the landlord (or one of the landlords) under the existing assured tenancy grants a letting to an existing assured (i.e. not shorthold) tenant (whether alone or with others) the new letting will not be a shorthold. However, it is possible for the tenant to serve notice on the landlord before the new tenancy is entered into that he wants it to be a shorthold. This notice must be in a prescribed form.

5.5.10. *Duty of landlord to provide a statement of the terms of a shorthold tenancy*

Under Housing Act 1988, s.20A (as inserted by Housing Act 1996), the landlord is placed under a duty in certain circumstances to provide a tenant with written details of the following terms provided that they are not already evidenced in writing:

(a) the commencement date of the tenancy;

(b) the rent payable and the dates on which it is payable;

(c) any terms providing for rent review;

(d) the length of a fixed term tenancy.

The tenant must make a request to the landlord in writing for this information.

5.5.11. It is a criminal offence to fail to provide the information within 28 days, unless the landlord has reasonable excuse. On summary conviction, the penalty is to be a fine not exceeding level 4.

5.5.12. The right only exists where the terms are not already evidenced in writing. The provision will only apply to tenancies granted orally, or those granted in writing which makes no reference to one or more of the specified matters.

5.5.13. A statement provided by the landlord is not to be regarded as conclusive evidence as to what was agreed between the parties. The statement is the landlord's version of what was agreed; it is still open to the tenant to allege that any particular term was not agreed to by him.

5.5.14. These provisions only apply to new shortholds, i.e. those to which Housing Act 1988, s.19A applies. They do not apply to old shortholds. However, on the ending of an old shorthold any new letting between the same parties will be a new shorthold, and these provisions will then apply.

5.5.15. *Rent control*

The general principles are the same for both new or old shorthold, but the details differ.

5.5.16. Any existing registration of a 'fair rent' under the provisions of Rent Act 1977 can be ignored, as can any rental figure previously determined by the Rent Assessment Committee under these provisions. Therefore on the granting of the tenancy, the landlord can charge such rent for the premises as the market will bear. There is no statutory restriction on the amount of rent chargeable. However, an assured shorthold tenant can apply to the local Rent Assessment Committee for the determination of the rent which, in the Committee's opinion, the landlord might reasonably be expected to obtain under the shorthold tenancy.

5.5.17. If the tenant has an old shorthold, he can apply at any time during the tenancy.

5.5.18. If the tenant has a new shorthold, whether for a fixed term or a periodic letting, he cannot apply if more than six months have elapsed since the beginning of the tenancy. If the tenancy is a 'replacement tenancy', i.e. a second or subsequent shorthold between the same parties and of the same property, the application cannot be made if more than six months have elapsed from the commencement of the first shorthold between the parties.

5.5.19. *The effect of a determination by the Rent Assessment Committee*

If a rent is determined by the Committee, the effect again differs between old and new shortholds.

5.5.20. The rent assessed will become the maximum rent chargeable for the property throughout the remainder of the fixed term in the case of old shortholds and fixed-term new shortholds, despite anything to the contrary in the tenancy agreement.

No matter how long the unexpired term of the tenancy there is no provision for this figure to be increased during the fixed term.

5.5.21. Where a new shorthold is a periodic tenancy, the rent remains fixed throughout the tenancy. Once 12 months have expired, the landlord will be able to make an application under Housing Act 1988, ss.13 and 14 to increase the rent.[3]

5.5.22. With both old and new shortholds, once the rent has been determined by the Committee no further application for the fixing of a different figure can be made by either landlord or tenant. However, the rent determined by the Committee only has relevance to the particular tenancy in question. It will not limit the amount of rent chargeable under any subsequent letting, even if this is between the same parties. Further, in the absence of a further grant, on the ending of a fixed-term shorthold (whether old or new), a statutory periodic tenancy will arise and the provisions of Housing Act 1988 ss.13 and 14 will again apply to allow the landlord to increase the rent.

5.5.23. *When is an application to the Rent Assessment Committee not possible?*

The restrictions on tenants with new shortholds applying have been dealt with in para. K5.5.18.

5.5.24. As far as old shorthold tenants are concerned, it is not possible for the tenant to refer the rent to the Rent Assessment Committee once the original term of the shorthold has expired. This is so even if a new letting is entered into between the same parties and irrespective of whether an application was made during the original shorthold.

5.5.25. With both old and new shortholds, only one application to the Committee can be made. Once the rent has been determined by the Committee, it cannot be resubmitted for a further determination, even if the original determination was many years before and open market rents have fallen in the meantime.

5.5.26. *What happens when a shorthold expires?*

The tenant is allowed to remain in possession as a statutory periodic tenant when a fixed-term tenancy expires. However, the tenant will have no security of tenure. Under Housing Act 1988, s.21(1) the court must still make an order for possession if the landlord follows the correct procedure. This involves the service on the tenant of not less than two months' notice stating that the landlord requires possession.

5.5.27. *What happens if a new tenancy is granted?*

Although there are differences between new and old shortholds, the basic principle remains the same; if the parties are the same, any new tenancy of the same (or substantially the same) premises will be deemed to be a shorthold unless the landlord serves notice on the tenant that the new letting is not to be a shorthold.

.5.28. In the case of an old shorthold, the effect of this deeming provision is that the new tenancy will be a shorthold even though it does not comply with the normal requirements for an old shorthold. So no shorthold notice need have been served, the letting need not be for a fixed term, i.e. a periodic shorthold is permissible, and any fixed term need not be for a minimum period of six months. However, the new tenancy must still comply with the normal requirements for an assured tenancy, e.g. the tenant must still be occupying the house as his only or principal home.

.5.29. A further feature of a deemed shorthold following an old shorthold is that there is no right to refer the rent to the Rent Assessment Committee. This is the case whether or not an application was made to the Committee during the initial short-hold term. In the case of a tenancy following a new shorthold, the second tenancy will be a 'replacement tenancy' and an application to the Rent Assessment Committee cannot be made more than six months from the commencement of the original tenancy. So in the unlikely event of a new shorthold granted for three months, followed by a replacement tenancy granted for (say) six months, an application to the Rent Assessment Committee could be made during the first three months of that replacement tenancy.

5.5.30. In any event, if a rent was determined by the Rent Assessment Committee during the initial term this will not limit the amount of rent chargeable by the landlord under the new tenancy agreement.

5.5.31. How does the landlord obtain possession?

The landlord must apply to the court and obtain an order for possession unless the tenant leaves voluntarily. The court must order possession provided that the landlord follows the correct procedure. This involves the landlord serving a notice on the tenant (the 'section 21 notice') giving the tenant at least two months' notice that he requires possession.

5.5.32. Possession cannot be obtained using this shorthold procedure during the continuance of a fixed term; possession is only available after its expiry (although the procedure can be set in motion during the fixed term so that possession can be obtained as soon as it has ended). Note also that in the case of a new shorthold possession cannot be obtained within six months of the commencement of the term using the shorthold procedure. This is so whether the tenancy is a fixed term or is periodic.

5.5.33. Grounds for possession

A shorthold is a type of assured tenancy and so, during the term, the mandatory and discretionary grounds which apply to ordinary assured tenancies can also apply. Mandatory ground 8 and discretionary grounds 10 and 11 (all of which relate to rent arrears) can be used during the subsistence of the shorthold should the landlord be faced with a defaulting tenant. However, in the case of a fixed-term letting, as with other assured tenancies, these grounds can be used during the fixed term only if the tenancy agreement so provides.

5.5.34. In the case of a shorthold which is a periodic tenancy, the ordinary assured tenancy grounds will be available to a landlord without the need for any such provision in the tenancy agreement.

5.5.35. In the case of a fixed-term shorthold, however, it is always sensible to insert a provision allowing the landlord to terminate the tenancy on the specified grounds. In the case of an old shorthold, this is permissible despite the usual rule that there must be no power for the landlord to terminate within the first six months of the tenancy. This rule does not apply to termination because of a breach of the terms of the tenancy, e.g. non-payment of rent. Similarly, in the case of new shortholds, although possession cannot be obtained using the shorthold procedure within six months of the commencement, possession can be obtained during that period using the ordinary assured grounds provided that they are satisfied.

5.5.36. When the landlord is seeking to obtain possession on one of the ordinary assured grounds, then the procedure relevant to an ordinary assured tenancy should be followed, and not the shorthold procedure. In particular, this will mean that a section 8 notice will have to be served on the tenant before proceedings can be commenced, and not a section 21 notice.

1. In some circumstances the notice may be given to the tenant's agent, see *Yenula Properties Ltd* v. *Naida* [2002] EWCA Civ 719. The absence of details of the landlord may not be fatal if the details of the agent are given *Osborn and Co Ltd* v. *Dior* [2003] All ER (D) 185.
2. See Schedule 2A to the Housing Act 1988 as inserted by the Housing Act 1996.
3. New rules enable landlords to specify a date for annual increases; see Regulatory Reform (Assured Periodic Tenancies) (Rent Increases) Order 2003 and Assured Tenancies and Agricultural Occupancies (Forms) (Amendment) (England) Regulations 2003.

5.6. Long tenancies at low rents

5.6.1. Rent Act 1977 (as with previous Rent Acts) gave no protection to the tenant where the rent payable under the tenancy was less than two-thirds of the rateable value of the dwelling on the appropriate day (as defined in the Act), with the result that most tenants of dwellings under long tenancies at ground rents had no security of tenure when their contractual tenancies expired. Part I Landlord and Tenant Act 1954 extended to many such tenants the protection of Rent Act 1977 (and its predecessors) when their tenancies expired. Part I applied to a tenancy granted for over 21 years at a rent of less than two-thirds of the rateable value of the property where 'the circumstances (as respects the property comprised in the tenancy, the use of the property, and all other relevant matters) are such that on the coming to an end of the tenancy … the tenant would, if the tenancy had not been one at a low rent, be entitled by virtue of the Rent Acts to retain possession of the whole or part of the property comprised in the tenancy'.

5.6.2. *Security of tenure*

A long tenancy within Part I Landlord and Tenant Act 1954 is continued by Rent Act 1977 until determined in accordance with the statute. The landlord may terminate by notice expiring on or after the term date of the tenancy, but his notice must either propose a Rent Act statutory tenancy or state that he is seeking a court order for possession. The grounds on which an order for possession can be made are contained in section 12 and Schedule 3 Landlord and Tenant Act 1954, as amended by Leasehold Reform Act 1967, s.38.

5.6.3.   The Rent Act regime applicable on the termination of these long tenancies (unless the landlord obtains possession) is eventually to be replaced by the assured tenancy regime under section 186 and Schedule 10 Local Government and Housing Act 1989. However, in many cases such tenants may be able to extend their original leases or purchase a freehold interest. This is considered below in para. K9.

5.7.   Agricultural employees

5.7.1.   Security of tenure for farm workers living in accommodation provided by their employers is governed by either Rent (Agriculture) Act 1976 or Housing Act 1988, depending on the date of the grant of the tenancy.

5.7.2.   To gain the protection of the 1976 Act, the employee must generally have spent two years whole time in agriculture; he then becomes a protected occupier of the house. If as a result of a notice to quit or otherwise he ceases to be a protected occupier, he becomes a statutory tenant of the house under terms laid down by the Act.

5.7.3.   The court cannot make an order for possession of a house subject to a protected occupancy or statutory tenancy under the 1976 Act except on the grounds set out in the Act. Special provisions apply to the rehousing of agricultural employees. The provisions for rent control in the Act apply only to statutory tenancies.

5.7.4.   Farm workers who enjoyed the protection of Rent Act 1977 (e.g. because they were tenants paying an economic rent) were equated to those protected by the 1976 Act by Rent Act 1977, s.99.

5.7.5.   Farm workers with tenancies or licences granted before 15 January 1989 retain their protection under the 1976 Act. Tenancies or licences granted on or after that date are governed by Housing Act 1988. However, those tenants who were previously protected under the 1976 Act will, broadly, continue to enjoy the same regime of protection.[1] This Act introduced the assured agricultural occupancy, which qualifies for protection if it is an assured tenancy or would be such except for the fact that the rent (outside London) is less than £250 per annum or the fact that the house forms part of an agricultural holding and is occupied by the person responsible for the control of the farming. A licence to occupy which confers exclusive occupation and which fulfils the requisite conditions will also qualify. An assured shorthold is excluded from the definition, thus enabling the owner to create a tenancy giving a mandatory right to possession.

5.7.6.   In the case of tenancies or licences governed by Housing Act 1988, the main change is in regard to rent. The provisions of the Act in regard to the increase of rents under assured tenancies apply to assured agricultural occupancies, so that on a reference of a notice of increase of rent to a Rent Assessment Committee an open market rent can be fixed.

5.7.7. An occupier of agricultural land may apply to the housing authority concerned (i.e. the local housing authority as defined by Housing Act 1985) to rehouse a tenant on the ground that the land occupier requires the dwelling house to provide accommodation for an agricultural employee, the land occupier being unable to provide the present tenant with suitable alternative accommodation. The housing authority in reaching its decision on whether to rehouse the tenant must have regard to the advice tendered to them by the Agricultural Dwelling-House Advisory Committee.[2]

1. Housing Act 1988, s.34(4).
2. See Rent (Agriculture) Act 1976, ss.27–29.

K6. Long-term residential tenancies

6.1. Grant of lease

6.1.1. The grant or assignment of a long lease of a house or flat is similar to the grant or assignment of a lease of other premises. The matters to which particular attention needs to be paid when dealing with this type of lease are merely highlighted here.

6.1.2. The lease of a flat is frequently a complex document which should be specifically drafted to suit the individual requirements of the site. Except in the most straight-forward cases, copying a precedent directly from a book or the reuse of a lease drafted for another development will not suffice. The client's attention should be directed to the need for a site inspection before drafting of the lease is commenced so that the following points can be correctly dealt with in the lease:

(a) What is the structure of the building composed of? Repairing covenants must be drafted appropriately so that a covenant, e.g. 'to repair main walls and timbers' will be inappropriate where the building is of concrete construction.

(b) Access: the lease must deal with easements of access, e.g. is there a right of way over the drive from the public highway to the entrance of the flats, how does each tenant get from the door of the building to the door of his own flat, is there to be a lift, does each tenant require access to the dustbin area, etc.?

(c) Where do the mains services run? Which tenants need easements for pipes, cables, etc., to pass through another flat or common parts on the way to or from their own flat?

(d) Amenities: who is to have a garage or parking space, are these to be a part of the demise (i.e. a specific allocated space) or is there to be just a licence to use a garage/parking space (with no guarantee that a space will actually be available), use of gardens, is there communal central heating, is there an entry-phone system, is there a communal television or satellite aerial, are individual aerials to be permitted, is there a caretaker's flat?

(e) Service charges: what services are to be included in the charge, will all tenants have the benefit of all the services supplied, should the service charge be split equally between all the tenants or should some pay a greater proportion than others or should different proportions apply to different services?

(f) Check site and floor plans against the physical extent of the building both in relation to the whole building and individual flats, are they accurate, which tenants need which plans, are they coloured in accordance with Land Registry recommendations?

6.1.3. *Checklist of items to be sent to buyer's solicitor*

NB: Not all of the following will be relevant in every transaction:

(a) draft contract in duplicate;

(b) draft lease in duplicate;

(c) copy head lease;

(d) other evidence of superior and reversionary titles;

(e) draft agreement between landlord and management company for transfer of reversion to management company;

(f) copy memorandum and articles of management company;

(g) copy local authority search and enquiries with replies;

(h) copy planning permissions and building regulation consents;

(i) copy indemnity insurance policy covering defects in title, restrictive covenants, etc;

(j) copy of approved estate layout plan as deposited at the Land Registry;

(k) copy replies to enquiries before contract (Seller's Property Information Form and Additional Property Information Form in Protocol cases);

(l) copy insurance policy and schedules;

(m) copy guarantees, e.g. for repairs to structure;

(n) documentation relating to insurance against structural defects;

(o) estimated service charge calculation;

(p) audited accounts of the management company.

6.2. **Enforcement of covenants in flats**

6.2.1. The landlord for the time being can almost always enforce covenants in the lease against the tenant for the time being of each flat, because he enjoys privity of estate and in many cases also privity of contract with each tenant. Prima facie there is neither privity of contract nor of estate between the tenants and, although they will each be bound by identical covenants in their leases, without some device in the leases they cannot sue each other directly for breach of the tenants' covenants in their respective leases. It is advisable that the lease contains some method of allowing mutual enforceability of covenants between the tenants, particularly in relation to covenants concerning use, structural repair and noise.

6.2.2. This can be achieved either by taking a covenant in each lease that the landlord will if so requested by a tenant take action to enforce a breach of covenant committed by another tenant in the same block. Such a covenant usually requires the requesting tenant to provide a complete indemnity to the landlord against the costs of the action and provides an effective although cumbersome method of mutual enforceability of covenants. There are other schemes of varying complexity which attempt to ensure that one tenant can sue another. However, in practice none are now considered wholly satisfactory. Where the tenants are responsible for maintenance, insurance and repair of common parts, the CML Lenders' Handbook requires the key clauses in a lease to be enforceable by the landlord (or the management company) at the request of the tenant.[1]

1. See para. K6.6.

6.3. **Management schemes**

6.3.1. Any management scheme must ensure that the rights and obligations of both the landlord and the tenants under the lease are always enforceable. The landlord's objectives in setting up such a scheme are to provide for the maintenance and repair of the block. The type of scheme employed will depend on the landlord's particular requirements in relation to the flats concerned as recourse may have to be made to their rights under the Commonhold and Leasehold Reform Act 2002, which are considered in para. K6.9.

6.3.2. If the landlord is to retain the reversion of the block he may choose to carry out the landlord's functions personally or through a managing agent. From the landlord's point of view this arrangement has the disadvantage of the work involved and from the tenants' point of view it has the disadvantage that the tenants have only limited control over the way in which their block is managed as recourse may have to be made to their rights under the Commonhold and Leasehold Reform Act 2002, which are considered in para. K6.9.

6.3.3. Another type of arrangement is for the tenants to covenant with each other by separate deed of covenant to perform the obligations of repairing, etc., the common parts. Such a scheme is not binding on future assignees unless the lease obliges them to enter into similar deeds of covenant as a condition of their assignment.

6.3.4. Alternatively, the landlord may vest the reversion (with its obligations) in trustees (who would be representatives of the tenants) on trust for the tenants as a whole. This type of scheme is only suitable for the management of small blocks and saves the expense in that situation of setting up and running a management company.

6.3.5. Most larger blocks have schemes which entail the use of a management company. The landlord will transfer his reversion to the management company which will then assume the responsibility for performance of the landlord's covenants in the lease. Until transfer the landlord will be responsible for the management company's duties and should ideally expressly covenant to this effect in the lease. A management company can either be limited by shares or guarantee and is commonly purchased as a ready-made company. The management company should be a party to the lease and enter into direct covenants with the tenant for the performance of the maintenance obligations. Each tenant must be required to become a member of the company and to transfer his share in the company to an assignee on sale of the lease. Such a scheme allows the tenants to have absolute control over the management of their block, but carries with it the responsibility of performance of the maintenance obligations and duties in relation to the company itself under the Companies Acts. The landlord may reserve the right to take over the management company's responsibilities in the event of default by the company.

6.3.6. If maintenance is to be carried out by a maintenance trustee company, the tenant's solicitor should be satisfied as to the integrity of the trustee company. If this has been set up by a third party, the tenant will have no control over the company, and thus needs to be assured that the trustees (and any potential successors to the original trustees) are sound and responsible.

6.3.7. In relation to leases granted on or after May 11 2000, direct enforcement of the benefit of covenants between tenants may be possible without the device of a management scheme through the operation of the Contracts (Rights of Third Parties) Act 1999. However, the Act does not enable the burden of covenants to be passed to successors and is therefore unable to provide a satisfactory solution.

6.4. Other matters to be considered

6.4.1. The landlord may wish to reserve the right to prepare the engrossment of the lease himself. Such right must be expressly reserved in the contract and any fee payable by the tenant for the engrossment must be reasonable.

6.4.2. Where the landlord is to retain the reversion (and the liability for performance of the landlord's covenants in the lease) consideration may be given by the landlord to the appointment of reliable managing agents to carry out the landlord's duties under the lease.

6.4.3. On completion apportionments of the rent and service charge will have to be made. Apportionments of service charge will at this stage have to be made on an estimated basis and settled at the end of the first accounting period. The Standard Conditions of Sale do not provide for apportionments to be made on completion of the grant of a new lease and a special condition to such effect is necessary.

6.4.4. Where a management company is to perform the landlord's covenants under the lease, the company must be set up and share certificates (except where limited by guarantee) and the company books prepared in readiness for completion.

6.4.5. The term dates of all the leases should commence on the same date (irrespective of the dates of completion of the various leases) otherwise it becomes very difficult to know precisely when performance of some covenants is due, e.g. to decorate.

6.4.6. Apportionment of rent

This should be done by the method recommended by the Law Society explained in paras. K2.6.4–K2.6.7.

6.5. Maisonettes

6.5.1. Where a maisonette is being purchased, particular care needs to be exercised to ensure that the lease is quite specific as to the ownership and rights over the various parts of the property (especially common parts). Each tenant may be the freeholder of the other tenant's property; they will thus be jointly responsible for the maintenance and upkeep of the structure and common parts. A maintenance trustee company may be set up to deal with maintenance and repair. The CML Lenders' Handbook sets out specific requirements where there is a freehold flat or where one of the flat owners in the block owns the freehold in whole or in part. In many situations these arrangements may be acceptable to the lender where a building has been converted into not more than four flats.[1]

1. See CML Lenders' Handbook para. 5.5.3.

6.6. Lenders' requirements

6.6.1. The lenders' requirements may be found in a combination of documents depending on the nature of the transaction and whether the lender is a member of the Council of Mortgage Lenders. These documents are: the CML Lenders' Handbook England & Wales, 2nd edition, the mortgage offer, and instructions to the solicitor.

Part 1 of the Lenders' Handbook is a set of universal instructions to which all CML Lenders adhere. Individual lenders issue their own supplemental general instructions to their solicitors by use of Part 2 instructions. The current edition of Part 1 can be found at Appendix VIII.3. As the provisions of Part 2 change more regularly than Part 1, these are only available online at www.cml.org.uk. Solicitors are also recommended to check the web site for the latest version of both Parts. A lender is usually concerned with the following matters:

(a) to ensure that the lease contains proper provision for the mutual enforceability of covenants between tenants (Lenders' Handbook para. 5.10.6);

(b) to ensure that the property is leasehold and that the lease contains adequate repairing covenants relating to the flat itself, the exterior structure and the common parts of the building (Lenders' Handbook para. 5.10.4);

(c) that the lease contains adequate provision for the insurance of the whole building (Lenders' Handbook paras. 5.10.4. and 5.10.5);

(d) that the length of the term of the lease (or unexpired residue in the case of an assignment) is sufficient to permit a resale of the premises on the open market. A common period required by lenders is 55 years unexpired from completion and 30 years unexpired at the end of the mortgage term. Notification may be required if the minimum period is less than 70 years. A term which will have less than 20 years unexpired after the end of the mortgage term may be considered inadequate in the context of normal residential conveyancing;

(e) that the lease contains no provision for forfeiture on the insolvency of the tenant (Lenders' Handbook para. 5.10.2);

(f) that the lease contains no restrictions on alienation which may hinder a sale on the open market (Lenders' Handbook para. 5.10.3);

(g) that the lease is or will be registered at the Land Registry with an absolute leasehold title;

(h) where the tenant is to become a member of a management company, the mortgagee sometimes requires that a blank form of share transfer (signed by the mortgagor) and the tenant's share certificate is deposited with the lender to enable the lender to transfer that share to a buyer should he need to exercise his power of sale. A copy of the management company's memorandum and articles may also have to be deposited with the lender (Lenders' Handbook para. 5.12.1);

(i) that notices have been given to the landlord of the mortgage (Lenders' Handbook 5.10.11);

(j) that the lease reserves an appropriate ground rent and that receipts are provided for rent and service charge payments (Lenders' Handbook paras. 5.10.7 and 5.10.10);

(k) if the property being purchased is held under a sub-lease (so that the landlord's own interest is leasehold), it is desirable that the aggregate ground rents payable by the flats in the block should exceed the amount of rent payable by the landlord to the freeholder. If this is not the case the landlord will have little incentive to pay his own rent, and thus the sub-tenants of the flats would be put at risk from forfeiture of the head-lease. For this reason it is desirable that in any situation where sub-letting is permitted the tenant should be required to enter a covenant with his landlord not to sublet the whole at a rent lower than that payable under his own lease.

6.7. The Protocol

6.7.1. The Protocol makes no direct reference to the grant of a lease.

6.7.2. On the sale of an existing lease paragraph 2.14 requires the seller's solicitor to ask his client to produce, if possible:

    (a) a receipt or evidence from the landlord of the last payment of rent;

    (b) the maintenance charge accounts for the last three years, where appropriate, and evidence of payment;

    (c) details of the buildings insurance policy.

6.7.3. If any of these are lacking and are necessary to the transaction the solicitor should obtain them from the landlord. Investigation should also be made as to the necessity for a licence to assign, and whether any charge is payable to the management company on the change of ownership. The documents and information obtained in relation to the above matters should be given or communicated to the buyer's solicitor when the pre-contract documentation is sent to him (paragraph 4.4).

6.8. Service charges

6.8.1. Service charge accounts must be examined carefully and the buyer advised as to his potential liability under the lease.

6.8.2. Statutory provisions relating to service charges are now contained in Landlord and Tenant Act 1985, ss.18–30, as amended. The amendments made to these provisions by the Commonhold and Leasehold Reform Act 2002 have significantly enhanced tenants' rights in this respect. For the purposes of these provisions, a service charge is an amount payable by a tenant as part of or in addition to rent:

    (a) which is payable, directly or indirectly, for services, repairs, maintenance, improvements or insurance or the landlord's costs of management; and

    (b) the whole or part of which varies or may vary according to the relevant costs.

Provisions in relation to payments to a reserve fund (which allow 'savings' against future expenditure) are contained in the Landlord and Tenant Act 1987, ss.42–42B (as amended). These require such payments to be paid into a designated bank account and for the money to be held on trust for the tenants.[1]

6.8.3. The statutory provisions now apply to a lease of any dwelling (including houses as well as flats) except that they do not apply to lettings by certain bodies such as local authorities unless the tenancy is a long tenancy as defined in Landlord and Tenant Act 1985, s.26(2).

6.8.4. The statutes impose certain limitations and obligations on landlords which are not set out in detail here but which relate to the following:

(a) limitations on the amount recoverable;

(b) estimates for work to be done and the giving of notices;

(c) time-limits on making demands for service charges;

(d) the tenant's right to apply for a statement of account for costs incurred, an accountants certificate and to inspect the landlord's accounts;

(e) the landlord's duty to pass on requests for a summary of the relevant costs to a superior landlord;

(f) the right, in certain circumstances, to withhold a service charge;

(g) service charge contributions to be held in trust.

6.8.5. A buyer of the reversion on a lease reserving a service charge and a buyer of a lease subject to such a charge should be aware of the following matters:

(a) the statutory provisions outlined above;

(b) that the obligation to pay a service charge can arise only from an express provision in the lease and the extent of the obligation depends on the wording of such provision. Whether or not the landlord can recover from non-defaulting tenants his legal costs incurred in recovering rent and service charge contributions depends on the wording of the tenant's covenant, and the same is true in respect of a landlord's interest payments on money borrowed to finance the provision of works and services;

(c) ideally the landlord's obligation should match with the service charge provisions. If the obligations are not matched the landlord may find that he is obliged to provide more services than he can charge for or conversely that the tenants cannot force the landlord to, e.g. carry out repairs because the landlord's covenant does not extend to this matter;

(d) the manner in which the total service charge is to be apportioned between the various tenants;

(e) whether or not the landlord can require payment of a charge in advance of expenditure;

(f) the statutory provisions now apply to contribution covenants concerned with improvements as well as repairs;[2]

(g) where premises are let wholly or mainly as a dwelling for less than seven years, a service charge provision cannot cast on the tenant the cost of matters falling within the landlord's repairing obligation under Landlord and Tenant Act 1985, ss.11–16;

(h) a provision in the lease enabling the landlord to make an interim service charge is desirable. In the absence of such a provision a landlord may be disinclined to carry out expensive repairs or to provide services since he would have to bear the cost of these matters himself seeking recovery of the sums from the tenants at a later date.

6.8.6. The amount of service charge payable will be of particular concern to the buyer of a lease. The Protocol requires production of the maintenance accounts for the last three years which should give some indication of the amounts involved, although sums expended will frequently vary from year to year. A substantial sum recently spent on repairs and redecoration of the exterior of a building may indicate that a similar item should not recur for some time. In each case enquiry should be made of the particular circumstances relating to the building.

6.8.7. The apportionment of a service charge on a sale may create a problem as the amounts payable may not be determined at the time of completion. Standard Condition 6.3.5 provides that when any sums to be apportioned are not known or easily ascertainable a provisional apportionment is to be made on completion according to the best estimate available. As soon after completion as the amount is known, a final apportionment is to be made and notified to the other party and any resulting balance paid no more than 10 working days later, interest calculated at the contract rate being chargeable for late payment.

6.8.8. Sections 45–51 of the Housing Act 1985 (as amended by Landlord and Tenant Act 1987, s.41) contain restrictions on service charges where a house has been disposed of by a public sector authority other than under a long lease.

6.8.9. A landlord may not forfeit the lease of a dwelling house for failure to pay a service charge unless the amount of the service charge is agreed or admitted by the tenant or has been determined by a court or tribunal.[3]

1. *St. Mary's Mansions Ltd* v. *Limegate Investment Co Ltd, The Times*, 13 November 2002 (CA).
2. Commonhold and Leasehold Reform Act 2002, s.150 and Sched. 9.
3. Housing Act 1996, s.81.

6.9. Appointment of manager

6.9.1. Where a landlord has not complied with his obligations under the terms of the lease, a tenant of a flat may, after serving a preliminary notice on his landlord (and the landlord's lender where relevant), apply to the court under Part II Landlord and Tenant Act 1987 (as amended by Housing Act 1996) for the appointment of a manager to carry out the landlord's management functions. These provisions apply to premises where the building or part of a building consists of two or more flats except *inter alia* where the landlord is an exempt or resident landlord.

6.10. The Right to Manage

The Commonhold and Leasehold Reform Act 2002 creates a right to manage in favour of the tenants of flats. This right enables tenants to take over the management of their building without having to prove fault on the part of the landlord and without having to pay compensation. The right is exercised through a specific company which must be created in order to manage property, known as an RTM company.

6.10.1. *RTM Companies*[1]

These are defined by the Act in some detail but are essentially private companies limited by guarantee and all qualifying tenants are entitled to be members. Regulations will prescribe the content and form of the memorandum and articles of association of these companies.

6.10.2. *Qualifying conditions*

There are a number of qualifying conditions for exercising the right.

(a) The premises

The premises must consist of a self contained building or part, contain two or more flats and the total number of flats held by such tenants must be not less than two-thirds of the total number of flats in the premises.[2]

(b) Excluded premises.[3]

In outline this right to manage does not apply to premises if the internal floor area of non-residential parts exceeds 25% of the whole internal floor area. It also does not apply if there is a resident landlord and the premises do not contain more than four units. It does not apply if the local authority is the immediate landlord of any of the qualifying tenants.

6.10.3. *Qualifying tenants*[4]

A qualifying tenant must be a tenant of a flat under a long lease. However there are some exceptions so that, for example, the right does not apply to tenants of business premises. A long lease is again defined by the Act[5] but is essentially one granted for a term of more than 21 years.

6.10.4. *Claiming the right to manage*[6]

The right to manage is claimed by the RTM company giving notice inviting participation to those qualifying tenants who are not members of the RTM company. A 'claim notice' is then served on a specified number of interested parties including the landlord. A counter notice may then be served and if the claim is contested an application may be made to a leasehold valuation tribunal for a determination.

1. Commonhold and Leasehold Reform Act 2002, ss.73 and 74.
2. Commonhold and Leasehold Reform Act 2002, s.72(1).
3. Commonhold and Leasehold Reform Act 2002, Sched. 6.
4. Commonhold and Leasehold Reform Act 2002, s.75.
5. Commonhold and Leasehold Reform Act 2002, s.76.
6. Commonhold and Leasehold Reform Act 2002, ss.78 to 87.

K7. Business premises

See also: Value Added Tax, para. A16
Acting on grant of lease, para. K1
Assignment of leases, para. K11

7.1. Business tenancies

7.1.1. Part II Landlord and Tenant Act 1954 (as amended) established a comprehensive code of security of tenure for business tenants. The following paragraphs provide only an introduction to this very complex subject. It is proposed to make some minor changes to the legislation by means of delegated legislation and, at the time of writing a draft Regulatory Reform Order entitled *Statutory Instrument: The Regulatory Reform (Business Tenancies) (England and Wales) Order 2003* has been laid before Parliament. The Order is stated to come into force six months after the day on which it is made. However, difficulties have been encountered in the passage of the draft Order through the House of Lords Select Committee which will have serious implications for the timetable for implementation.[1] As it is now unclear if and when these changes will be made, the paragraphs below set out the current law without reference to the proposed amendments.

7.1.2. The Act applies to a tenancy where the property comprised in the tenancy is or includes premises which are occupied by the tenant and are so occupied for the purposes of a business carried on by him or for those and other purposes. It therefore will not apply to a licence (the distinction is dealt with in para. K12).

7.1.3. The word 'business' is widely defined to include a trade, profession or employment and includes any activity carried on by a body of persons, whether corporate or unincorporate.[2]

1. A copy can be obtained from www.cabinet-office.gov.uk/regulation/act/proposals.htm.
2. Landlord and Tenant Act 1954, s.23(2).

7.2.   Exclusions from the Act

7.2.1.   These include:

(a) agricultural holdings;

(b) mining leases;

(c) written service tenancies;

(d) tenancies at will;

(e) fixed term tenancies not exceeding six months unless the tenancy contains provision for renewing the term or for extending it beyond six months from its beginning. This exception also does not apply if the tenant has been in occupation for a period which, together with any period during which any predecessor in the carrying on of the business carried on by the tenant was in occupation exceeds twelve months;[1]

(f) tenancies for a term certain where the court's approval to the exclusion from protection has been obtained prior to the commencement of the tenancy.

7.2.2.   Subject to para. K7.2.1(f), where a tenancy is within the provisions of the Act it is not possible to exclude the operation of the Act by agreement between the parties.

1. Landlord and Tenant Act 1954, s.43. Considered in *Cricket Ltd* v. *Shaftsbury* [1999] 28 EG 127.

7.3.   Termination of tenancy

7.3.1.   A tenancy within the Act can only be determined by one of the methods prescribed by the Act. These include:

(a) forfeiture;

(b) notice to quit given by the tenant;

(c) immediate surrender;[1]

(d) service by the landlord of a notice under Landlord and Tenant Act 1954, s.25;

(e) a tenant's request for a new tenancy under Landlord and Tenant Act 1954, s.26;

(f) notice served under section 27 of the Act.

7.3.2.   Where the tenant has a periodic tenancy, his notice to quit will be of the length appropriate to the period of his tenancy (e.g. one month's notice for a monthly tenancy). In the case of a fixed-term tenancy, the tenant may serve a three-month notice under section 27 of the Act to expire on the term date or on any quarter day after the term date. Alternatively, the tenant may vacate before the end of the tenancy. It has been held[2] that where the tenant is not in occupation at the term date the Act does not apply to the tenancy.

7.3.3. A tenancy which is not determined by one of the above methods continues to run (despite expiry of a fixed term) on the same terms until terminated by one of these methods.

1. An agreement for the tenant to surrender his tenancy at some future time is void under Landlord and Tenant Act 1954, s.38 except if authorised by the court.
2. *Esselte AB* v. *Pearl Assurance* [1977] 02 EG 124; also note *Single Horse Properties Ltd* v. *Surrey County Council* [2002] 14 EG 126.

7.4. Landlord's notice

7.4.1. A notice to terminate a tenancy served by a landlord under Landlord and Tenant Act 1954, s.25 must be in a prescribed form and must specify a date (not earlier than the term date and not less than six nor more than 12 months ahead) on which the tenancy is to end. The notice must require the tenant to notify the landlord whether or not the tenant is willing to give up possession and must state whether the landlord would oppose the application to the court for a new tenancy and, if so, on what ground(s) – see para. K7.4.3.

7.4.2. If the tenant wants a new tenancy, he must notify the landlord to this effect within two months of the landlord's notice and should apply to the court for a new tenancy not less than two nor more than four months after service of the landlord's notice. A tenant's application to the court is a pending land action and should be protected by an entry in the register of pending land actions in the case of unregistered land. Where the land is registered a pending action should be protected by a notice.[1] If the tenant is in occupation of registered land, his application may be protected as an overriding interest under Land Registration Act 2002, Sched. 3, para. 2.

7.4.3. The landlord's grounds for opposing the grant of a new tenancy are contained in Landlord and Tenant Act 1954, s.30 and are briefly as follows:

   (a) breach of repairing obligations by the tenant;

   (b) persistent delay in paying rent;

   (c) substantial breaches of other obligations under the tenancy;

   (d) alternative accommodation;

   (e) possession of whole property required where tenant has a sub-tenancy of part;

   (f) landlord's intention to demolish or reconstruct the property;

   (g) landlord requires possession for his own purposes.[2]

7.4.4. The time-limits specified in the Act for service of notices and application to the court are construed strictly and in general no extension of those limits is permitted. Thus if a tenant fails to serve a counter-notice on the landlord within the prescribed period he will lose his right to a new tenancy. Similarly, the right to a new tenancy will be lost if the tenant does not make his application to the court *between* two and four months after service of the original notice terminating the tenancy.

1. Land Registration Act 2002, s.87(1)(a).
2. This ground is not available to a landlord whose interest was purchased or created within the five years preceding the termination date of the tenancy as specified in the notice terminating the tenancy (provided that the tenancy or series of tenancies was existing at the time of creation and has continued uninterrupted since that time).

7.5.   Tenant's request for a new tenancy

7.5.1.   A tenant's request for a new tenancy can be made only if the tenant originally had a tenancy for a term of years certain exceeding one year. It must be in prescribed form and must specify a date (not earlier than the term date and not less than six nor more than 12 months ahead) for the start of the new tenancy. If the landlord wishes to oppose the grant of a new tenancy, he must notify the tenant within two months, stating on which ground(s) he will rely (see para. K7.4.3). The tenant must then apply to the court for a new tenancy not less than two months and not more than four months from the service of his request (see para. K.7.4.4). A tenant's application to the court is a pending land action and should be protected by an entry in the register of pending land actions in the case of unregistered land. Where the land is registered a pending action should be protected by a notice. If the tenant is in occupation of registered land, his application may be protected as an overriding interest under Land Registration Act 2002, Sched. 3, para. 2.

7.6.   Application to the court

7.6.1.   Unless the landlord can establish one or more of the grounds for possession within section 30(1) of the Act,[1] a new tenancy must be ordered by the court comprising such holding (i.e. the part of the property occupied by the tenant), at such rent and on such other terms as the court orders (in the absence of agreement between the parties), although the new tenancy cannot, in the absence of agreement, exceed 14 years in length.[2]

1. See para. 7.4.3.
2. See ss.32–35 of the Act.

7.7.   Compensation

7.7.1.   If the landlord succeeds in obtaining possession, based on ground (e), (f), or (g) in para. K7.4.3, the tenant is entitled to compensation for giving up his tenancy.

7.7.2.   In certain circumstances a tenant of business premises may also be entitled to compensation for improvements effected by him under Landlord and Tenant Act 1927.

7.8.   Rent control

7.8.1.   There are no statutory limitations on the rent recoverable on the original grant of a tenancy of business premises, but on a renewal the court can fix a new rent failing agreement by the parties. The court also has power, on application, to fix an interim rent pending the outcome of proceedings.

7.9. Buying a business lease

7.9.1. A prospective assignee (purchaser) of a lease of business premises should (in addition to the usual matters to be considered on the assignment of a lease) pay careful attention to the following matters:

    (a) the rent review provisions contained in the lease;

    (b) the repairing obligations imposed by the lease;

    (c) any service charge provisions in the lease;

    (d) the VAT implications of the transaction;

    (e) whether the existing tenant has committed any breach of covenant which would give the landlord the right to determine the lease or to refuse a renewal of it;

    (f) the likelihood of a lease renewal being opposed by a landlord on other grounds, e.g. redevelopment;

    (g) the provisions relating to alienation of the lease.

7.10. Covenants restricting assignment

7.10.1. It is common for a business lease to prohibit an assignment without the landlord's consent.

7.10.2. Where a lease contains a covenant prohibiting assignment without the landlord's consent, that consent is not to be unreasonably withheld (section 19(1) Landlord and Tenant Act 1927). Guidelines for testing reasonableness are set out in the Court of Appeal decision in *International Drilling Fluids Ltd* v. *Louisville Investments (Uxbridge) Ltd*:[1]

    (a) the purpose of the covenant is to protect the landlord from an undesirable tenant or from an undesirable use being made of the premises;

    (b) a landlord cannot, therefore, refuse consent on grounds which have nothing to do with the relationship of landlord and tenant;

    (c) as long as the landlord's conclusions were those which a reasonable man might reach he does not have to prove they were justified;

    (d) it may be reasonable for a landlord to withhold consent on the grounds of the proposed use of the premises even though the proposed use of the premises is not prohibited by the lease;[2]

    (e) normally a landlord need have regard only to his own interests but it may be that the detriment caused to the tenant by withholding consent so outweighs the advantage to the landlord that it is unreasonable for consent to be withheld.

Subject to these considerations, whether a landlord is acting reasonably is a question of fact in each case. A lease which is 'old tenancy', i.e. one to which the Landlord and Tenant (Covenants) Act 1995 does not apply, cannot set out what is to be considered reasonable, although a condition precedent can be imposed.[3] Under the Landlord and Tenant Act 1988, a landlord must give consent within a reasonable time unless there is a reason for withholding it. Written reasons for refusal must be given within a reasonable time. The burden of proving that the withholding of consent is reasonable is on the landlord.

7.10.3 The above provisions have been amended[4] in relation to assignments of 'new tenancies' i.e. ones to which the Landlord and Tenant (Covenants) Act 1995 applies; broadly those granted on or after 1 January 1996 of commercial premises[5] and provides as follows:

7.10.4. A landlord may agree in advance with his tenant:

   (a) any circumstance in which he may withhold consent to a proposed assignment; or

   (b) any conditions subject to which his consent will be granted,

and if he withholds consent for these reasons he is not acting unreasonably. The agreement has to be made before the application for consent but does not have to be contained in the lease nor made at the same time as the lease.

The 1995 Act distinguishes between factual matters, for example:

   (a) the assignee must be a plc;

   (b) the assignee must have net assets equal to a specified multiplier of the rent;

   (c) the assignee must provide a rent deposit; or

   (d) the assignor must enter an AGA,

and discretionary matters, for example the assignee is, in the opinion of the landlord, of equal financial standing to the assignor.

In the latter case, the landlord's decision has to be arrived at reasonably, or the tenant must have the right to have the decision reviewed by an independent third party who is identifiable from the agreement and whose decision is conclusive.

7.10.5. The imposition of stringent conditions may have an adverse effect on the assessment of a revised rent or a subsequent review and/or may make it difficult for the tenant to assign the lease. In considering what conditions to impose, landlords are encouraged to have regard to the Code of Practice for Commercial Leases. This is set out in Appendix VIII.4. See also K1.1.4.

1. [1986] 1 All ER 321.
2. This principle was considered by the House of Lords in *Ashworth Frazer Limited* v. *Gloucester City Council* [2001] 46 EG 180.
3. See *Bocardo S.A.* v. *S & M Hotels* [1980] 1 WLR 17; *Vaux Group plc* v. *Lilley* [1991] 04 EG 136.
4. Landlord and Tenant (Covenants) Act 1995 inserting a new section 19(1A) into the Landlord and Tenant Act 1927.

. This provision applies to leases apart from leases of residential premises or those of agricultural property, see Landlord and Tenant Act 1927, s.19.

7.11. Professional arbitration on court terms (PACT)

7.11.1. The Royal Institution of Chartered Surveyors (RICS) and the Law Society have jointly agreed to offer a service providing private determination of lease renewals under the provisions of Landlord and Tenant Act 1954. This is claimed to provide a faster, cheaper and more efficient method of settling lease renewal disputes than in the courts by professionals who have the expertise to make decisions on technical matters.[1] A new edition of the Guidance Notes to the PACT scheme has been published in 2003 (see AA. New Developments in Conveyancing Practice).

7.11.2. The scheme is voluntary with referral by mutual agreement of the landlord and the tenant. Appointments of arbitrators and experts, experienced in landlord and tenant matters, is made by the President of the RICS or the President of the Law Society. The parties will need to protect their position under the Act and an application to the court will be made in the usual way to be followed by a consent order. Model consent orders are provided to be adapted to cover the needs of the particular case.

7.11.3. The nature of the dispute will dictate the expertise required. Sufficient information on the issue in dispute will be requested from the parties to enable the appropriate President to determine whether the services of a surveyor or solicitor or indeed both are required.

7.11.4. The primary aim is to settle rents where other terms have already been agreed. Other disputes can be referred to the scheme on matters of principle or drafting of a lease.

7.11.5. The tenant will retain the right to reject the tenancy which at present exists under the Act.

7.11.6. Parties will have the option of excluding or retaining a right of appeal to the court from the arbitrator's decision.

7.11.7. The system is designed to be flexible, giving the parties the right to settle their own procedure for determination of a dispute in a way not open to them in litigation.

7.11.8. *Using PACT – a summary of key issues*

1. Decide with the other party whether it would be advantageous to refer aspects of the lease renewal to a third party solicitor or arbitrator rather than a judge.

2. Identify which aspects of the renewal (if any) are agreed.

3. Decide which aspects to refer to the third party:

    (a) the interim rent;

    (b) the new rent;

    (c) other terms of the lease;

    (d) the detailed drafting of terms;

    (e) a combination of these.

4.   Choose which aspects are to be resolved by a third party solicitor and which by a third party surveyor.

5.   Choose the third party's capacity – arbitrator or expert?

6.   Draft court application making use of or adapting PACT model orders.

7.   Apply to court for consent.

8.   Apply for appointment of person adjudicating (if not agreed).

9.   Proceed with adjudication.

10. Receive award subject only to 'cooling off' rights and, in arbitration, any right of appeal.

1. As yet, there have been relatively few referrals to PACT so information as to the effectiveness of the scheme is unavailable.

K8. Agricultural tenancies

See also: Agricultural land, para. B8

8.1. Definitions

8.1.1. Many tenants of agricultural holdings which were created before 1 September 1995 enjoy security of tenure under Agricultural Holdings Act 1986. As from 1 September 1995, it is no longer possible to create a new agricultural tenancy which has the protection of the 1986 Act, unless it is a succession tenancy (see para. K8.5). Paragraphs K8.2–8.4 only apply to tenancies which were created before 1 September 1995.

8.1.2. The expression 'agricultural holding' is defined as the aggregate of land (whether agricultural land or not) comprised in a contract of tenancy which is a contract for an agricultural tenancy (not being a service tenancy).

8.1.3. In general, 'agricultural land' means land used for agriculture and so used for the purpose of a trade or business.

8.1.4. 'Contract of tenancy' means a letting of land or an agreement for letting land, for a term of years or from year to year.

8.2. Protection of short-term tenants and licensees

8.2.1. Under the Agricultural Holdings Act 1986, s.2 an agreement under which any land was let to a person for use as agricultural land for an interest less than a tenancy from year to year or under which a person was granted a licence to occupy land for use as agricultural land (in circumstances such that if his interest were a tenancy from year to year he would be the tenant of an agricultural holding) took effect (with the necessary modifications) as an agreement for the letting of land for a tenancy from year to year. The licence must not have been gratuitous and must have conferred occupation on the licensee.

8.3. Security of tenure

8.3.1. Subject to a provision dealing with the death of the tenant before the term date[1] a tenancy of an agricultural holding for two years or more continues as a tenancy from year to year unless written notice to quit is given by either party at least one year and not more than two years before the end of the tenancy.[2]

8.3.2. In consequence of Agricultural Holdings Act 1986, ss.2 and 3, a notice to quit is normally necessary to determine an agricultural letting for an interest less than a tenancy from year to year, a licence to occupy agricultural land, and a tenancy for two years or more. The importance of this is that the security of tenure provisions of Agricultural Holdings Act 1986 come into operation where notice to quit (the method of determination of periodic tenancies) is given to the tenant.

8.3.3. In general, if a notice to quit an agricultural holding or part of a holding is given to the tenant he has the right to serve a counter-notice on the landlord, requiring the landlord to obtain the consent of the Agricultural Land Tribunal to the operation of the notice to quit, which consent can only be given on certain grounds. The tenant's right to serve a counter-notice is excluded if the notice to quit is given and is expressed to be given on one of a number of grounds specified in Schedule 3 Agricultural Holdings Act 1986.

1. Agricultural Holdings Act 1986, s.4.
2. Agricultural Holdings Act 1986, s.3.

8.4. Other matters dealt with by Agricultural Holdings Act 1986

8.4.1. Agricultural Holdings Act 1986 deals with a large number of matters regulating the relationship between landlord and tenant, including the right of succession on the death or retirement of the tenant, the tenant's right to compensation for improvements, and arbitration as to rent.

8.5. Agricultural Tenancies Act 1995

8.5.1. Agricultural Tenancies Act 1995 applies to all agricultural tenancies granted after the commencement of the Act on 1 September 1995. It is not retrospective in effect and does not affect existing tenancies (or successions to those tenancies) granted under Agricultural Holdings Act 1986.

8.5.2. The words 'agriculture' and 'agricultural' have the same meaning as under the 1986 Act.

8.5.3. Tenancies created under the 1995 Act are called 'farm business tenancies'. Certain conditions must be satisfied for a tenancy to fall within this definition:

(a) **Business**

All or part of the land is farmed for the purposes of a trade or business and has been so farmed since the start of the tenancy.

(b) **Agriculture**

Having regard to a number of matters specified in the Act, the character of the tenancy is primarily or wholly agricultural.

(c) **Notice**

As an alternative to the agriculture condition, the parties can, before the grant of the tenancy, exchange written notices identifying the land and stating that the person giving the notice intends that the proposed tenancy is to be and remain a farm business tenancy. Even where such notices are exchanged, the character of the tenancy must be primarily or wholly agricultural at the start of the tenancy.

8.5.4. To be a farm business tenancy, condition (a) above must be satisfied, together with either (b) or (c). If (c) is used, the tenancy will remain a farm business tenancy so long as some part of the land is farmed, but other parts of the land may later be used for other business and non-agricultural purposes.

8.5.5. *Exclusions*

The following tenancies are excluded:

(a) tenancies granted before the commencement of the Act;

(b) tenancies granted under the succession on death or retirement provisions;

(c) tenancies granted to an existing tenant who is protected under the 1986 Act where a variation of the previous tenancy has the effect of an implied surrender and regrant.

8.5.6. *Security of tenure*

There is no security of tenure or right of renewal given to the tenant under the 1995 Act (other than as provided for in the agreement itself).

8.5.7. *Preparation of the agreement*

If the tenancy agreement is to be for a fixed term of three years or more, it must be made by deed (under the Law of Property Act 1925, s.52) and can only be prepared by 'accredited persons' – a barrister, solicitor, notary public, licensed conveyancer, a full member of the Central Association of Agricultural Valuers, or an Associate or Fellow of ISVA or RICS (Agricultural Tenancies Act 1995, s.35).

8.5.8. *Rent and rent review*

There are no statutory controls on rent. In relation to rent review, section 10 of the 1995 Act provides for a rent review to take place in accordance with the provisions of that section except where the provisions of section 9 are complied with. Section 9 applies to a tenancy which:

(a) expressly states that the rent is not to be reviewed during the term of the tenancy; or

(b) provides for a rent review at specified times, either:

  (i) by or to a specified amount; or

  (ii) in accordance with a specified formula (not upwards only) assessed by objective criteria.

8.5.8.1. Statutory review under section 10:

(a) either party can call for a review by notice to the other;

(b) the review date must not be less than 12 nor more than 24 months from service of a 'statutory review notice';

(c) if the parties have agreed a specified review date, the review date must be a date as from which rent could be varied under the agreement;

(d) if the parties have agreed in writing that the review date is to be a specified date, the review must be on that date;

(e) if there is no agreement as to the date of the review, the date is the anniversary of the beginning of the tenancy;

(f) subject to any agreement to the contrary, rent reviews may not take place at less than three-yearly intervals.

An independent expert or arbitrator is to be appointed to fix the reviewed rent. In default of agreement, the President of RICS is to appoint the arbitrator.

The reviewed rent on a statutory review is assessed on an open market formula (section 13). Tenant's improvements are broadly disregarded.

8.5.9. *Assignment*

The 1995 Act does not restrict assignment but section 19 of Landlord and Tenant Act 1927 does not apply to these tenancies.

8.5.10. *Agricultural covenants*

No agricultural covenants are implied by the 1995 Act. Such covenants must be expressly included in the agreement if required.

8.5.11. *Repairs and insurance*

The 1995 Act does not deal with these matters, thus appropriate clauses to deal with them must be included in the agreement.

8.5.12. *Termination*

(a) A fixed-term agreement for two years or less will expire automatically.

(b) Common law rules apply to periodic tenancies except that a yearly tenant needs to be given not less than one year's, and not more than two years' notice, expiring at the end of a year.

(c) For a fixed-term tenancy of more than two years, not less than 12 months' and not more than 24 months' notice to terminate on the term day must be given (otherwise the tenancy continues as a tenancy from year to year).

(d) Notices must be in writing.

8.5.13. *Compensation*

Compensation is payable for the tenant's improvements. These provisions cannot be excluded by the agreement. Improvements are categorised as follows:

(a) intangible advantages

Something which attaches to the holding and which the tenant has brought to the holding at his own expense, e.g. unimplemented planning permission or a water abstraction licence;

(b) physical improvements

(i) non-routine, e.g. building a shed,

(ii) routine (section 19(10) of the 1995 Act), e.g. 'tenant's right' (growing crops, etc.).

8.5.13.1. Conditions for claiming compensation

The landlord's consent must have been obtained (generally before or after the improvement was made). Appeal against the landlord's refusal of consent lies to an arbitrator (but in respect of non-routine physical improvements an appeal can only be lodged before the improvement has been made). There is no appeal against the landlord's refusal of consent to an application by the tenant for planning permission. The arbitrator cannot vary any conditions imposed by the landlord.

8.5.13.2. Amount of compensation (sections 20–27 of the 1995 Act)

The amount of compensation is the amount attributable to the improvement in the value of the holding at the termination of the tenancy. Appeal lies to an arbitrator under section 22 of the 1995 Act.

8.5.14. *Fixtures*

Tenant's fixtures can be removed by the tenant at the end of the tenancy. The tenant is under an obligation not to cause damage and to rectify any damage caused. The tenant need not give notice to the landlord of his intention to remove fixtures. If consent to an improvement was obtained, the tenant could alternatively claim compensation for the fixture as an improvement. The agreement should specify which fixtures are/are not tenant's fixtures.

8.5.15. *Dispute resolution*

The 1995 Act contains specific provisions for arbitration on rent review, improvements and compensation (see above). Other disputes are to be referred to arbitration unless the parties agree to a different procedure. The arbitrator is appointed with the consent of the parties (either on a joint reference or four weeks' notice by one party unchallenged by the other). In default of agreement, the President of RICS is to appoint the arbitrator. The court's jurisdiction is not excluded. The Arbitration Act 1996 applies to arbitrations under the 1995 Act.

K9. Right to buy

1. Public sector

1.1. Subject to certain conditions, a secure tenant normally has a right to buy.[1]

1.2. 'Right to buy' means:

   (a) if the dwelling is a house, and the landlord or a public sector head-landlord owns the freehold, the right to acquire the freehold;

   (b) if the landlord does not own the freehold or the dwelling is a flat, to be granted a lease of the premises.

1.3. To qualify, the tenant must usually have occupied the house or flat as a secure tenant for two years, although there are special provisions in Schedule 4 Housing Act 1985 relating to spouses and children. Schedule 5 Housing Act 1985 (as amended) contains a number of exceptions to the right to buy.

1.4. The price payable on exercise of the right is the price which the house would realise if sold on the open market by a willing seller, less any discount to which the buyer is entitled. The amount of the discount depends on the length of occupation of the secure tenant, but cannot usually be less than 32% nor more than 60% in the case of a house, or less than 44% or more than 70% in the case of a flat. This is subject to a maximum amount of the discount imposed by Housing Act 1985, s.131 and related to costs incurred in respect of the house.

1.5. If a tenant who has received a discount sells the property within three years, he will (except in certain specified cases) be required to repay to the landlord a proportionate part of the discount. This liability takes effect as a legal charge on the property. There are provisions in the legislation governing the form and effect of the conveyance/transfer or lease. There are service charge limits which the buyer can expect to see set out in the conveyance or lease. Where the title to the landlord's property is unregistered, the tenant does not need to examine a landlord's title because the landlord is required to supply the tenant with a certificate of title in the prescribed form, which certificate the Land Registry is bound to accept for the purposes of registration of the tenant's title. A lease taken by a tenant under the right to buy provisions needs to be registered even if for a term of 7 years or less since Land Registration Act 2002, s.4(1)(a) applies to it. If application for first registration is not made within two months, the lease will be void as regards the grant of the legal estate.[2] It takes effect as a contract made for valuable consideration to grant the lease concerned.[3] The contract may be protected as an overriding interest if the intended tenant is in occupation.[4]

1. Housing Act 1985, as amended by Housing and Planning Act 1988.
2. Land Registration Act 2002, s.7(1).
3. Land Registration Act 2002, s.7(2)(b).
4. Land Registration Act 2002, Sched. 1, para. 2.

9.2.   Leasehold Reform Act 1967

9.2.1.   Part I Leasehold Reform Act 1967 gives certain tenants the right compulsorily to buy out the landlord's freehold interest (enfranchisement) or to take an extended lease for an additional 50 years. The right to enfranchise can still be exercised after the grant of an extended lease. These provisions have been modified by Leasehold Reform Housing and Urban Development Act 1993, Housing Act 1996 and Commonhold and Leasehold Reform Act 2002 (see para. K9.3).

9.2.2.   *Qualifying conditions*

For the tenant to qualify, broadly the following conditions must be satisfied:

(a) his tenancy must be a long tenancy;

(b) the property had a rateable value other than nil at the date of commencement of the tenancy or otherwise at any time before 1 April 1990;

(c) the house must fall within the definition of that word in the 1967 Act;

(d) the tenant must have held the lease for the last two years.

9.2.3.   *Long tenancy*

A long tenancy is one granted for a term certain exceeding 21 years; but there are certain exceptions where shorter leases which have been extended beyond 21 years through renewal will qualify.

9.2.4.   *House*

A 'house' within the Act includes any building designed or adapted for living in and reasonably so called. The fact that part of the building is used for business purposes may not exclude the application of the Act. Where a building has been converted into flats or maisonettes, it depends on the structure of the conversion as to whether the converted units fall within the scope of the Act. If the result of the conversion is to produce a building which is divided horizontally, so that each tenant occupies the whole or part of one floor of the building, the units will be classed as flats which do not enjoy the benefit of the Act. If, however, the conversion has been made vertically, so that each tenant occupies a part of each floor of the building from the ground upwards, the individual units will be classed as houses, each of which may utilise the provisions of the Act. This will apply where parts of one overhang the other so that the division is not entirely vertical.

providing this is not to a material extent.[1] Flats, whether purpose built or otherwise, are not within the Act.

.2.5. *Residence qualification*

The former residence qualification has essentially been abolished. However, it may be relevant in other circumstances. So, for example, a person may be treated as having been the tenant of a house for two years if it was vested in trustees and he was beneficially entitled and permitted to occupy under the trust.[2] It is also relevant where the property has had a mixed use with business user.[3]

9.2.6. A notice served by a qualifying tenant on his landlord of his desire to purchase the freehold or to take an extended lease creates a contract between the parties capable of registration as a notice in registered land or a Class C(iv) land charge in unregistered land. The tenant's rights under the contract, even though he is in occupation, do not constitute an overriding interest in registered land.[4]

9.2.7. The benefit of a notice served by a tenant under a lease within the Act can be assigned, but only with the lease itself. A buyer who is buying a lease to which the Act applies should enquire whether the seller satisfies the qualifications under the Act. If he does so and the buyer wishes to enfranchise, the buyer should ask the seller to serve a notice on the landlord, and then to assign the benefit of such notice with the lease itself. In this way the buyer will be able to exercise his rights under the Act without having to establish his own period of residential qualification. Such a provision must be dealt with by special condition in the contract to purchase the lease.[5]

9.2.8. Details of the rights and obligations of the parties under the notice and of the procedures to be followed (e.g. form of transfer, etc.) are set out in the Act,[6] which also contains provisions dealing with the acquisition of intermediate reversions where the immediate landlord is not the freeholder. In many cases, however, the strict procedures under the Act are not followed and the procedure following service of the desire notice follows the ordinary steps in a normal purchase transaction. The payment of a deposit is often dispensed with although by written notice the landlord can demand a deposit not exceeding three times the annual rent or £25 whichever is greater. Since the service of notice by the tenant creates a contract between the parties[7] it is not open to the landlord subsequently to draw up a contract on, e.g. the Standard Conditions of Sale Form and to require the tenant to agree to the terms included in the landlord's contract. Where not agreed by the parties the terms of the contract are governed by Leasehold Reform (Enfranchisement and Extension) Regulations 1967.[8] Section 10 of the Act regulates the terms of the conveyance to the tenant. The tenant will take the property subject to legal easements and restrictive covenants of which he has notice, e.g. by registration. The general words implied by Law of Property Act 1925, s.62 cannot be excluded without the tenant's consent and certain more extensive rights as to support and access are implied. The purchase deed must also make reasonable provision for rights of way over and for the benefit of other property belonging to the landlord (where relevant). The landlord is only obliged to give one covenant for title; namely that he has not himself incumbered the property and must give the statutory acknowledgement relating to retained title deeds (in unregistered land) but need not give an undertaking for safe custody.[9]

9.2.9. The price payable on enfranchisement is the subject of two formulae, depending on the rateable/rental value of the property. Failing agreement between the parties the price is settled by the Lands Tribunal. Where premises have been brought into the Act by virtue of Leasehold Reform Housing and Urban Development Act 1993, the tenant must pay compensation to the landlord for loss of development value. Further amendments have been made to the calculation of the value of the property by CLRA 2002. These amendments require the tenant to pay one half of the marriage value except that if the unexpired term of the tenancy is more than 80 years there will be no marriage value.

9.2.10. Where an extended lease is taken, the rent under the extended term represents a ground rent for the property and may be subject to upwards revision after 25 years of the extension.

9.2.11. The tenant is responsible for payment of the landlord's costs, e.g. of valuation, deduction of title and the purchase deed.

9.2.12. Where the landlord's interest is subject to a mortgage, the lender must, on payment of the purchase price to him, release the property from the mortgage.

9.2.13. Where the Act applies it is non-excludable, although in certain limited circumstances a landlord may be able to defeat a tenant's claim to an extended lease because he intends to redevelop the premises, or to defeat a claim to enfranchise or to take an extended lease on the ground that he reasonably requires the property for occupation as the only or main residence of himself or an adult member of his family. In each case compensation is payable to the tenant by the landlord.

1. See *Malekshad* v. *Howard de Walden* [2002] All ER (D) 68; [2002] UKHL 49.
2. Leasehold Reform Act 1967, s.7(3) and (4) as amended by the Commonhold and Leasehold Reform Act 2002, s.138(6).
3. See Commonhold and Leasehold Reform Act 2002, s.140.
4. Leasehold Reform Act 1967, s.5(5) as amended by the Land Registration Act 2002, Schedule 11, para. 8(2).
5. Leasehold Reform Act 1967, s.5(2).
6. A new form has been introduced for landlords to reply to claims. See Leasehold Reform (Notices) (Amendment) (No.2) (England) Regulations 2002.
7. The tenant has a right to withdraw on ascertaining the purchase price. Leasehold Reform Act 1967, s.9(3)(b), as amended.
8. S.I. 1967/1879.
9. See Covenants for title, section M9.

9.3. Leasehold Reform Housing and Urban Development Act 1993

9.3.1. *Introduction*

This Act, as amended by Commonhold and Leasehold Reform Act 2002 (see section L. Commonhold), extends the rights to enfranchise/acquire an extended lease to the owners of flats and removes the rateable value limits which previously applied to houses under Leasehold Reform Act 1967. The Act also deals with some matters relating to public sector housing which are not dealt with in this book.

The majority of the amendments to the 1993 Act came into force on 26 July 2002, except for the new provisions in relation to RTE companies. This was by virtue of the Commonhold and Leasehold Reform Act 2002 (Commencement No.1, Savings and Transitional Provisions) (England) Order 2002. These amendments do not affect applications for collective enfranchisement or lease renewal that were made before 26 July 2002. This text sets out the new law and includes the provisions relating to RTE companies so that these can be dealt with. It therefore assumes that the RTE company provisions are in force. Until that happens the procedure is followed by a group of qualifying tenants known as a 'nominee purchaser'. In most cases this will, in fact, be a company formed by the tenants.

.3.2. *Collective enfranchisement*

(a) The right

The right is given to the tenants of a block of flats collectively to acquire the freehold of the block. The freehold is to be conveyed into the name of a company created by the tenants to buy the freehold known as an RTE company. The RTE company (a company limited by guarantee under section 122 of the Commonhold and Leasehold Reform Act 2002) must be formed before any further steps towards enfranchisement are taken. The RTE company must give notice to all the qualifying tenants under section 12A of the 1993 Act and invite their participation in the proposed enfranchisement. The conveyance can take place without the landlord's consent (subject to certain defences – see below). Certain qualifying conditions must be fulfilled (see para. K9.3.3). Not all the flats in the block need to be let on long leases, nor need all the premises be let exclusively for residential purposes for the Act to apply.

(b) Nature of the collective right

The nature of the collective right is for the tenants to have the freehold of the premises acquired on behalf of the participating qualifying tenants by the nominated RTE company at a price to be determined in accordance with the Act.

(c) Exercise of the collective right

Notice must be served on the reversioner by the RTE company as provided by s.13 of the 1993 Act.

To be entitled to give this notice the RTE company must have members who include a number of qualifying tenants which is not less than one-half of the total number of flats in the premises. Prior to the RTE company provisions being brought into force, in essence, the notice must be given by a number of qualifying tenants which is not less than one-half of the total number of flats.

(d) Landlord's grounds of opposition

The landlord can oppose the tenants' bid to enfranchise if the qualifying conditions are not met by the tenants. He may also oppose on the grounds that he wants to redevelop the whole or a substantial part of the premises but this ground is only available where not less than two-thirds of the long leases in the block are due to terminate within five years and the landlord cannot reasonably carry out the redevelopment without gaining possession.

(e) Qualifications

(i) Qualifying tenant
To qualify the tenant must be a 'tenant' of a 'flat' under a 'long lease'.

(ii) Tenant
Tenant includes a person holding a lease or tenancy, or an agreement for a lease or tenancy, and includes sub-leases/tenancies. Joint lease-holders are treated as one tenant.

(iii) Flat
A flat is defined as a separate set of premises but need not necessarily be all on the same floor level. The premises must form part of a building and be constructed or adapted for use as a dwelling. Additionally, either the whole or some material part of the premises must lie above or below some other part of the building. This defini-tion includes flats above shops, but may not apply to extensions, e.g. granny flats.[1]

(iv) Long lease
A long lease is one which is granted for a term of years certain exceeding 21 years. Provisions for determination within that period by either party do not affect this. The definition also includes most perpetually renewable leases, leases terminable by death or marriage, and leases granted under right to buy provisions and shared owner-ship leases where the tenant's total share is 100%, and new leases (of whatever length) granted on the expiry of an old long (i.e. 21 years plus) lease, and continuations under Landlord and Tenant Act 1954, Pt. I. Leases for less than 21 years which have been renewed without payment of a premium, taking the total term over 21 years, are also included within this definition.

(v) Rateable value
The property must have had a rateable value other than nil at the commencement of the tenancy or otherwise at any time before 1 April 1990.

(f) Excluded tenants

The following tenancies are excluded from the Act:[2]

(i) business tenancies;

(ii) where the immediate landlord is a charitable housing trust;

(iii) unlawful sub-lease out of non-qualifying superior lease;

(iv) tenants who do not satisfy the residence qualification.

(g) Interests included in the collective right

Tenants who enfranchise will obtain the freehold of the premises in which the flats are situated and:

(i) certain other property owned by the same freeholder ('appurtenant property'), e.g. garage, garden;

(ii) intermediate leasehold interests.

(h) Interests excluded from the collective right

Mineral rights owned by the freeholder are excluded from the collective right.

(i) Interests to be leased back

The Act contains provisions relating to certain interests which may (or in certain cases must) be leased back to the reversioner. They include the following:

(i) flats let by the freeholder on secure tenancies;

(ii) flats let by housing associations on tenancies other than secure tenancies;

(iii) units which are not flats let to qualifying tenants;

(iv) flat occupied by a resident landlord.

The items in (i) and (ii) above are subject to mandatory leaseback; (iii) and (iv) need only be leased back if the freeholder requires them. Schedule 9, Part IV of the Act contains detailed provisions dealing with the terms of the leaseback. Broadly this is to be a 999-year term at a peppercorn rent and will include the usual covenants but there will be no restrictions on alienation where the premises are residential.

(j) Price

The price which the tenants are to pay for the freehold comprises three elements:

(i) market value;

(ii) where the unexpired length of the leases held by participating members of the RTE company is 80 years or less, one-half of marriage value;

(iii) compensation;

plus landlord's reasonable costs. Where intermediate leases are also to be acquired, the price of each interest has to be separately calculated. A valuer's advice must be sought in relation to this matter.

(k) Market value

Market value is the price which might reasonably be expected to be paid if the property was sold on the open market by a willing seller to an arm's length buyer. The following assumptions also apply:

(i) the seller is selling the freehold subject to any leases subject to which the freeholder's interest is to be acquired by the buyer, but subject to any intermediate or other leases which are to be acquired by the buyer;

(ii) that the Act does not apply;

(iii) any increase in value caused by the participating tenant's improvements to the premises are to be disregarded.

(l) Marriage value

Marriage value is the increase in the value of the unencumbered freehold over the aggregate values of the freehold and any intermediate leasehold interest when held by the persons from whom they are to be acquired.

(m) Compensation

Compensation is payable to the freeholder for any loss or damage he may suffer as a result of the enfranchisement. It includes any diminution in the value of any other property owned by the landlord, including loss of development value. Schedule 11 Housing Act 1996 also provides for the tenant to pay compensation to the landlord if an unsuccessful claim is made within two years of the original term date of the lease. This provision came into effect on 15 January 1999.

(n) Premises

The flat must be in premises which either consist of a self-contained building or a self-contained part of a building whether or not the freehold of the whole building or of that part is owned by the same person. Self-contained means structurally detached. Buildings which are divided vertically may qualify under the Act. Premises where more than 25% is occupied or intended to be occupied for non-residential purposes are excluded. This last exclusion means that many flats above shops will not qualify under the Act. Resident landlords are excluded only if there are less than four flats in the block and they have owned the premises since their conversion or the block is not a purpose-built block.

9.3.3. *Advising in relation to collective enfranchisement*

(a) The first step is for the solicitor to find out whether the tenants and the building qualify under the Act. Information relating to these matters can be obtained by the service of various notices under section 11 of the Act:

(i)   on the immediate landlord (or person receiving rent on his behalf) to obtain the name and address of the freeholder and any superior leasehold interest;

(ii) on the freeholder to obtain the name and address of every person who is a tenant of the whole or any part of the building;

(iii) on the freeholder and/or other tenants to acquire information reasonably required in relation to the enfranchisement claim (e.g. as to how many other tenants qualify).

Service of these notices does not commit the tenant(s) to proceed and apart from payment for copies of documents the tenants are not required to pay for the provision of this information by the landlord. The landlord must respond to this request for information within 28 days. The tenants have a right to inspect and take copies of documents which might reasonably be required in connection with the enfranchisement claim (e.g. the landlord's title deeds). The landlord is obliged to disclose to the tenant(s) whether he has received initial notices under the Act from any other person.

(b) Having established that the tenants do qualify under the Act an RTE company must be formed and notice served by that company to all the tenants inviting their participation in the enfranchisement.

(c) **Costs of enfranchisement**

Taking any further steps towards enfranchisement is inevitably going to commit the tenants to the payments of their own solicitor's costs and also the reasonable costs of the landlord. Other expenses, e.g. in connection with the preparation of plans, valuation of the premises, the setting up of a company to purchase the freehold and possibly the expense of a court action to enforce the tenants' rights, will also be incurred. The tenants should be fully advised of the potential liability to costs and an arrangement for the payments of these costs by the qualifying tenants should be made before the matter proceeds further.

(d) **Plans**

If the tenants decide to proceed with their claim, a plan of the premises will be needed to accompany their initial notice (see (c)). It may be necessary to have this plan prepared by a surveyor.

(e) **Valuation**

The provisions for assessment of the price which the tenants have to pay for the freehold are complex and advice will be needed from a surveyor. An estimate of the price which the tenants may have to pay to acquire the freehold should be obtained from a suitably qualified surveyor at an early stage in the transaction to ensure that the tenants collectively will be able to afford to proceed with the transaction.

(f) **The initial notice**

To exercise rights under the Act the RTE company must serve an initial notice on the reversioner under section 13 of the Act (as revealed in answer to the enquiries noted in (a) above). The notice must be in writing and may be served by post. The Act prescribes the contents of the notice but not its form. Printed forms are available from law stationers. It must:

(i)   specify the premises with a plan;

(ii)   contain a statement of the grounds on which eligibility rests;

(iii)   specify other freehold or leasehold interests (if any) to be acquired;

(iv)   state which flats (if any) are subject to mandatory leaseback provisions;

(v)   specify the proposed purchase price of the freehold and any other interest specified in the notice;

(vi)   give the full names of all the qualifying tenants together with details of their leases;

(vii)   specify which tenants satisfy the residence qualification and how this is achieved;

(viii) give the name and address of the RTE company;

(ix)   specify a date by which the landlord must respond with his counter-notice (not less than two months).

The initial notice must be registered as an estate contract against the reversioner's title. A second notice cannot be served while a previously served notice is in force. If the notice is withdrawn (or is deemed to be withdrawn) no further notice can be served for 12 months. Once given, the notice remains in force until a binding contract is entered into or the notice is withdrawn or deemed to be withdrawn. Schedule 3, para. 15 of the Act contains provisions to overcome technical defects in the notice.

(g) **RTE company**

The initial notice must specify the name and address of an RTE company through whom negotiations for the acquisition of the freehold interest will be conducted and in whose name the freehold interest will ultimately be vested.

(h) **Landlord's rights and obligations when an initial notice is served**

Once notice has been served on the reversioner he has the immediate right of access to the premises for the purposes of valuation and to require evidence from the RTE company of title to the lease. The RTE company must respond to this request from the landlord within 21 days in default of which the notice is deemed to be withdrawn. The landlord is required to serve a counter-notice on the RTE company within the time-limit specified in the initial notice (not less than two months).[3] The counter-notice must either admit or deny the tenants' claim and, if the claim is denied, give the grounds of opposition.[4]

(i) Subsequent procedure

After service of the landlord's counter-notice, and assuming that the matter is to proceed, negotiations will then ensue between the RTE company and the reversioner for the completion of the acquisition. The form of the conveyance is prescribed by section 34 and Schedule 7. Provided the purchase price is paid to the landlord's lender, the property is discharged from the landlord's mortgage.[5] If the landlord fails to respond to the initial notice, after two months the tenants can apply to the court to determine the validity of the claim and the terms on which the freehold is to be acquired. If negotiations do not proceed, the initial notice is deemed to be withdrawn by the RTE company after a period of six months (or eight months after service by the landlord of his counter-notice).

(j) The Act contains no provisions enabling the time-limits prescribed within it to be extended.

9.3.4. *Individual acquisition of a long lease*

(a) Nature of the right

The tenant has the right to be granted a new lease to expire 90 years after expiry of the existing lease. The rent under the new lease is to be a peppercorn. A premium is payable for the grant. The new lease takes effect immediately in substitution for the tenant's existing lease. This right is available irrespective of the rights to collective enfranchisement.

(b) Entitlement to extension

The right to an extension applies to a qualifying tenant (as defined above) who has occupied the flat for the past two years. Companies cannot satisfy the residence requirement. Only one joint tenant need satisfy the residence requirement. A notice served by the personal representative of a deceased tenant cannot be served later than six months after the date of the grant.

(c) Landlord's defences

The landlord can oppose the tenant's request on the following grounds:

(i) that the tenant's existing lease is due to expire within five years; and

(ii) that the landlord intends to demolish/reconstruct the property and would be unable to do so without being given possession of the premises.

(d) Terms of new lease

The terms of the new lease will be the same as the existing lease except that the new rent is a peppercorn. The new lease takes effect immediately and is for a period which comprises the residue remaining on the old lease plus a further 90 years. Service charge provisions are to be included. The new lease will also contain a statement that the lease has been granted under the Act. Options which were included in the original lease will not be included in the new lease. The new lease will also contain a modification of the landlord's liability under his covenants and modifications to reflect defects in the existing lease. The new lease will include the landlord's right to apply to the court for possession for redevelopment purposes during the last 12 months of the original term or the last five years of the extension, subject to compensation being payable to the tenant.

(e) Premium

The amount of the premium payable by the tenant is the aggregate of:

(i) the diminution in the value of the landlord's interest;

(ii) where the unexpired term of the tenant's existing lease does not exceed 80 years, 50% of the marriage value;

(iii) compensation to landlord.

(f) Effect of grant of new lease

The grant of a new lease does not preclude a later application for collective enfranchisement. A further claim for another new lease can be brought in relation to any lease granted; subject to this, no security of tenure provisions apply once the original term date has passed.

9.3.5. Acting for a buyer of an individual flat

When acting for a buyer who is buying an existing lease which potentially qualifies under the Act, consideration should be given to raising enquiries of the seller to establish:

(a) whether the flat and the lease qualify under the Act;

(b) how many qualifying flats and qualifying tenants there are in the block;

(c) whether and when any initial notice has been served by an RTE company and if so how far negotiations have reached (a copy of the notice should be requested if not already supplied by the seller's solicitor);

(d) whether any steps have been taken by the seller to acquire an extension of his lease under the Act.

1. Considered in *Cadogan* v. *McGirk* [1996] 3 EG 175 in which a room on the 6th floor was not held to be part of a flat on the 2nd floor.
2. Leasehold Reform Housing and Urban Development Act 1993, s.5.
3. Failure to specify one of these options will render the counter notice invalid, see *Barman* v. *Mount Cook Land* [2001] 48 EG 128, CA.
4. Failure to give a counter notice will entitle the RTE company to apply to the court and acquire the freehold, s.25(1) and see *Willingale* v. *Gobalgrange* [2000] 18 EG 152 CA. Also, a new form of notice has recently been introduced. See Leasehold Reform (Collective Enfranchisement) (Counter-notices) (England) Regulations 2002.
5. The Leasehold Reform and Housing and Urban Development Act 1993, Sched. 8, para. 2.

9.4. Landlord and Tenant Act 1987

9.4.1. Landlord and Tenant Act 1987 (as amended) gives the tenants of certain premises the right of first refusal where the landlord intends to dispose of his interest in the premises. The Act applies where the landlord of premises which contain two or more flats held by qualifying tenants proposes to make a relevant disposal of the premises and provides that the landlord must first offer to make a disposal to a nominee of the qualifying tenants.

9.4.2. Premises

The provisions of the Act apply to premises consisting of the whole or part of a building which contains two or more flats held by qualifying tenants provided that the number of such flats exceeds 50% of the total number of flats in the building. The definition of a flat includes maisonettes and houses which have been converted into flats as well as purpose-built blocks. Premises which are used partly for non-residential purposes may be within the Act subject to a measurement limit. Thus premises which consist of a shop on the ground floor with two or more flats on the upper floors may qualify under the Act provided that the internal floor area of the shop represents less than 50% of the internal area of the whole building[1] and a nominee of the qualifying tenants who purchased the reversion of the flats would also therefore become the landlord of the shop. Where a landlord owns several blocks of flats with communal grounds on an estate development, each block is probably regarded as a separate building, the reversion of which may therefore be sold independently of the remainder of the estate.

9.4.3. Landlord

For the purposes of the Act a landlord is the immediate landlord of the qualifying tenants, or the superior landlord if the immediate landlord is himself a tenant under a tenancy for less than seven years or one terminable by his landlord within the first seven years.[2] Certain landlords are exempt and the provisions of the Act do not apply to, e.g. local authorities, urban development corporations or registered housing associations.[3] Resident landlords are also exempted from the provisions of the Act where the three following conditions are satisfied:

(a) the premises are not a purpose-built block of flats;

(b) the landlord occupies a flat in the premises as his only or principal residence;

(c) the landlord has been in occupation for the last 12 months.

9.4.4. Qualifying tenants

A tenant of a flat (including a company tenant) is a qualifying tenant unless his tenancy is:

(a) a protected shorthold tenancy;

(b) a business tenancy within Part II Landlord and Tenant Act 1954;

(c) an assured tenancy or an assured agricultural occupancy;

(d) a tenancy terminable on the cessation of the tenant's employment;

(e) of the flat and by virtue of one or more non-excluded tenancies he is also the tenant of at least two other flats contained in the same building;

(f) a sub-tenancy and his landlord is a qualifying tenant of the flat in question.

9.4.5. Relevant disposal

The word 'disposal' is defined in Landlord and Tenant Act 1987, s.4(3) as meaning a disposal whether by the creation or the transfer of an estate or interest. It includes the surrender of a tenancy and the grant of an option or right of pre-emption but excludes a disposal by will or under the intestacy rules.

9.4.6. A 'relevant disposal' is defined by Landlord and Tenant Act 1987, s.4(1) as a disposal by the landlord of any estate or interest (legal or equitable) in premises to which the Act applies, including a disposal of an interest in any common parts of the premises, other than the grant of a tenancy of a single flat with or without any appurtenant premises and subject to certain exceptions which are listed in para. K9.4.8.

9.4.7. A contract to sell is itself a relevant disposal. Further a disposal includes a disposal by the landlord's lender in selling or leasing the property, but not the creation of a mortgage. A conditional contract which is subject to the notice provisions being complied with at a later date is not valid.

9.4.8. Exceptions to 'relevant disposal'

By Landlord and Tenant Act 1987, s.4, the following are excluded from the definition of a relevant disposal:

(a) a disposal:

    (i) of an interest of a beneficiary in settled land;

    (ii) by way of the creation of a mortgage;

    (iii) of any incorporeal hereditament;

(b) a disposal to a trustee in bankruptcy or liquidator;

(c) a disposal in pursuance of an order under Matrimonial Causes Act 1973, s.24 or 24A, or Inheritance (Provision for Family and Dependants) Act 1975, s.2;

(d) a disposal in pursuance of a compulsory purchase order or agreement in lieu;

(e) a gift to a member of the landlord's family as defined in section 4(5) or to a charity;

(f) a disposal of functional land by one charity to another as defined in section 60;

(g) a disposal of trust property in connection with the appointment or discharge of a trustee;

(h) a disposal between members of the same family provided that at least one of the original owners still retains an interest;

(i) a disposal in pursuance of an option or right of pre-emption irrespective of the date of grant or of any other obligation created before 1 February 1988;

(j) a surrender of a tenancy in pursuance of any obligation contained in it;

(k) a disposal to the Crown;

(l) where the landlord is a body corporate, a disposal to an associated company.

9.4.9. *The landlord's offer*

Where a landlord proposes to make a relevant disposal of premises to which the Act applies, he must follow the procedure set out in section 5 of the Act which requires him to serve notice on the qualifying tenants of the flats in the premises. Different types of proposed disposal require different prescribed information to be inserted into the notice as set out in s.5A (normal sale by contract), s.5B (sale at auction), s.5C (grant of options and pre-emption rights), s.5D (sale of proceeding to completion without contract), and s.5E (wholly or partly for non-monetary consideration). The notice must:

(a) set out the principal terms proposed including the property and the estate or interest to be disposed of (the 'protected interest') and the consideration required;

(b) state that it constitutes an offer to dispose of the property on those terms which may be accepted by the requisite number of qualifying tenants (the offer is deemed by the Act to be 'subject to contract');

(c) specify a period for acceptance being at least two months beginning with the date of service; and

(d) specify a further period of at least two months beginning with the end of the period of acceptance within which a person or persons may be nominated to take the landlord's interest.

9.4.10. *The tenant's acceptance*

(a) The landlord's offer can be accepted by a simple majority of the qualifying tenants on the basis of one vote per flat let to qualifying tenants in the building. The tenants must nominate a person to deal with the landlord within the periods for acceptance and nomination specified in the landlord's notice.

(b) If a management company structure run by the tenants is already in place in the building, the management company may be nominated to purchase the landlord's interest. In other cases the tenants may consider forming a new company for this purpose.

(c) Acceptance by the qualifying tenants must be by written notice served on the landlord within the period specified in the offer. A single notice is served on behalf of all the accepting tenants which specifies the names and addresses of all the persons serving the notice.

(d) When the title is registered the acceptance notice is not protected as an overriding interest and should be protected by applying for entry of a notice.

9.4.11. Effects of acceptance

Once the acceptance notice has been served the landlord cannot dispose of the interest described in his offer to anyone other than the tenants' nominees during the 'protected period'. The procedure by which the tenants acquire their landlord's interest is not specified by the Act and will follow a normal conveyancing procedure. The 'protected period' is, in outline, the period beginning with the date of service of the acceptance notice and expiring at the end of the period for nominating a transferee specified in the offer notice plus three months if a transferee is nominated. If no nomination is made the landlord may dispose of his interest during the 12 months following expiry of the nomination period provided that the price is not less than that stated in the offer notice and the other terms of the disposal correspond with the terms of the offer to the tenants. Such a disposal may be by auction provided the reserve price is set to equate with the offer price. If no disposal occurs within this 12-month period, the landlord must serve a new offer notice on the tenants before attempting to dispose of the property. Acceptance of the offer does not create a binding contract since the offer itself is only subject to contract.

9.4.12. Rejection or counter-offer

If the tenants do not serve an acceptance notice or counter-offer within the period specified for acceptance in the landlord's offer notice, the landlord may dispose of his interest during the 12 months following the expiry of that period subject to the same conditions outlined in para. K9.4.11.

9.4.13. Disposals in breach of the Act

A new landlord who acquires a reversionary interest in flats from a seller who is in breach of the provisions of the Act can be required (on request made by a majority of the qualifying tenants) to supply details of the transaction to a nominee of the qualifying tenants. The qualifying tenants, by serving a purchase notice on the new landlord, can require him to dispose of his interest to a nominee of the qualifying tenants on the same terms as he acquired his interest. If the new landlord's interest is mortgaged, the property is discharged from the mortgage provided that the nominee pays the purchase price to the lender (even if the purchase price is less than the amount of the mortgage). A landlord who disposes of provisions in breach of the Act is also guilty of a criminal offence under Housing Act 1996.

9.4.14. *Advice to proposed buyers of reversionary interests*

A person who intends to purchase a reversionary interest direct from a landlord must before exchange of contracts check:

(a) whether or not the premises fall within the scope of the Act; and if they do

(b) whether the landlord has served notice on the qualifying tenants as required by the Act; and if so

(c) that either the tenants have rejected the landlord's offer or that the time-limits for acceptance have expired and the purchase transaction to the buyer can be completed within 12 months of the expiry of the acceptance period; and

(d) the terms on which the buyer is buying are similar to the terms of the offer which was made to the tenants.

9.4.15. Section 18 of Landlord and Tenant Act 1987 enables a prospective buyer to serve notice on tenants to ensure that rights of first refusal do not arise where it appears to the buyer that the disposal might be a relevant disposal of premises to which the Act applies. The notice must:

(a) set out the principal terms of the proposed disposal;

(b) invite the recipient to serve a notice stating:

   (i) whether an offer notice has been served;

   (ii) if not, whether he is aware of any reason why he is not entitled to such a notice, and

   (iii) whether he would wish to exercise any right of first refusal; and

(c) set out the effect of section 18(3) which says that, provided notices have been served on at least 80% of the tenants, and not more than 50% have replied within 28 days, or more than 50% have indicated that they do not regard themselves as entitled to an offer notice or would not wish to exercise a right of first refusal, the premises shall be treated as premises to which the Act does not apply.

9.4.16. *Auctions*

The notice procedures set out in para. K9.4.9 are modified where the landlord intends to dispose of the property at auction. Such notice must be served on the tenants between four to six months before the auction, giving the tenants at least two months to respond to the notice.[4]

1. This percentage is subject to alteration by Landlord and Tenant Act 1987, s.1.
2. Landlord and Tenant Act 1987, s.2.
3. Landlord and Tenant Act 1987, s.58.
4. Landlord and Tenant Act 1987, s.5B.

9.5. Compulsory acquisition by tenants of landlord's interest

9.5.1. Where a receiver or manager has been appointed under Part II Landlord and Tenant Act 1987 but this remedy proves to be inadequate, the majority of the qualifying tenants may in certain circumstances apply to the court under Part III Landlord and Tenant Act 1987 for an acquisition order which allows them to acquire their landlord's interest without his consent.

9.6. Registered social landlords

9.6.1. A tenant of a registered social landlord has the right to acquire the dwelling of which he is tenant under Housing Act 1996, s.16. The purchase price may be discounted by the landlord and similar provisions relating to the repayment of discount apply as to public sector tenants (para. K9.1).

K10. Liability on covenants in leases

10.1. Introduction

10.1.1. The general rule that an original tenant remains liable under his covenants throughout the term of the lease has been abolished by Landlord and Tenant (Covenants) Act 1995 but only in respect of new tenancies (as defined by the 1995 Act, see para. K10.1.2). The principle that only a party to a contract can sue or be sued on it has also been abrogated by the Contracts (Rights of Third Parties) Act 1999 which affects leases and assignments made on or after 11 May 2000.

10.1.2. *New tenancies*

A new tenancy is one which is granted on or after 1 January 1996, except those tenancies granted pursuant to:

(a) an agreement made before 1 January 1996; or

(b) a court order made before 1 January 1996; or

(c) an option granted before 1 January 1996.

An overriding lease granted under s.19 of the Landlord and Tenant (Covenants) Act 1995 (e.g. granted to a former tenant who has discharged the liability of a subsequent assignee) takes its status from that of the original lease.

Some leases granted on or after 1 January 1996 will not be new tenancies. Such a lease should make this clear by including a statement that the lease is not a new lease within the provisions of the 1995 Act.

A variation of a lease sometimes results in a deemed surrender and re-grant, e.g. where:

- extra land is included in the tenancy in return for additional rent;[1] or
- there is an extension of the term;[2]

but probably only in these situations.[3] The date of the surrender and re-grant will determine whether the lease deemed to be re-granted is a new one.

10.1.3. Paras. K10.2–K10.5 inclusive deal with old leases (i.e. those to which the 1995 Act does not apply). Para. K10.6 applies to all leases whenever granted. Paras. K10.7 onwards deal with new leases to which the provisions of the 1995 Act apply.

1. *Jenkin R. Lewis* v. *Kerman* [1971] Ch 477.
2. *Baker* v. *Merckel* [1960] 1 QB 657.
3. *Friends Provident Life Office* v. *British Railways Board* [1996] 1 All ER 336.

10.2.   Liability of original landlord and tenant

10.2.1. Unless released by the landlord the original tenant is liable on all the express and implied covenants in the lease for breaches committed at any time during the term of the lease. His liability is to the landlord for the time being since on a transfer of the reversion all rights of action attached to the reversion pass to the transferee including the right to sue for an existing breach of covenant.[1] The liability of the original tenant to the transferee of the reversion exists even though the tenant assigned the lease before the transfer of the reversion.[2]

10.2.2. The continuing liability of the original tenant may have serious consequences for him if an assignee of the lease cannot meet his obligations to the landlord. The original tenant remains liable for rent due after disclaimer of the lease on an assignee's insolvency,[3] and the release by the landlord of an assignee's surety does not release the original tenant since the latter has primary liability.[4] Although the landlord will normally only pursue the original tenant when the current assignee is unable to fulfil his commitments under the lease, the landlord's right of action against the original tenant is not confined to this situation.[5] The original tenant's liability does not, however, extend to arrears of rent accrued by an assignee during a statutory continuation of the term under Landlord and Tenant Act 1954, Pt. II unless the original tenant's covenant is expressed widely enough to cover this liability.[6]

10.2.3. The original landlord remains contractually bound to the original tenant throughout the term of the lease.[7] If an original landlord is unable through his own act or default (e.g. by transferring the reversion to a third party) to carry out an obligation imposed on him by the lease the landlord may be liable in damages to the tenant.[8]

10.2.4. Insurance against an original tenant's contingent liability under the covenants in the lease may be available from a few major insurance companies but is neither easy nor cheap to obtain because of the difficulty in quantifying the insurable risk.

1. Law of Property Act 1925, s.141 and see *Re King* [1963] Ch 459; *London and County (A. and D.) Ltd* v. *Wilfred Sportsman Ltd* [1971] Ch 764.
2. *Alresford Trading Co. Ltd* v. *Servansingh* [1971] 3 All ER 113.
3. *Warnford Investments* v. *Duckworth* [1979] Ch 127; *Hindcastle Limited* v. *Barbara Attenborough Associates Limited* [1996] 2 WLR 262; and *Active Estates Limited* v. *Parness* [2002] 36 EG 147.
4. *Allied London Investments Ltd* v. *Hambro Life Assurance Ltd* (1985) 50 P & CR 207.
5. *Norwich Union Life Assurance Society* v. *Low Profile Fashions Ltd* [1992] 21 EG 104.
6. *London City Corporation* v. *Fell; Herbert Duncan* v. *Cluttons (A Firm)* [1992] NPC 150, CA.
7. *Stuart* v. *Joy* [1904] 1 KB 362.
8. See, e.g. *Eagon* v. *Dent* [1965] 3 All ER 334 where a landlord sold the reversion to a third party and the original tenant who failed in his attempt to exercise an unregistered option against the buyer of the reversion recovered damages from the original landlord for breach of covenant.

10.3. Landlord and tenant for the time being

10.3.1. The relationship between a transferee of the reversion and the tenant for the time being and between an assignee of the lease and the landlord for the time being rests on the doctrine of privity of estate. Liability under this doctrine extends to breaches of covenants which touch and concern the land committed by a transferee of the reversion while he holds the reversion and by an assignee of the lease while the lease is vested in him. This means that an assignee may be liable to the landlord for a breach of covenant giving rise to continuing liability, committed by the assignor.

10.3.2. The doctrine embraces those covenants in the lease which affect the land demised and which also govern the landlord and tenant relationship as such, e.g. payment of rent, repairing covenants. While most covenants in leases will fall within the doctrine, including an option to renew the lease, it does not extend to purely personal obligations or to collateral obligations such as an option to purchase the reversion.[1]

10.3.3. An assignee of the lease will not be liable to the landlord for breaches of covenant committed after the date of an assignment of the lease by him to a third party unless, as is commonly required, he has entered into direct covenants with the landlord, in which case his liability will continue throughout the remainder of the term. In this respect the liability of an assignee is no different from that of an original tenant.

10.3.4. *Indemnity*

Irrespective of para. K10.3.3, an assignee of the lease may be called upon to indemnify his assignor in respect of any breach of covenant committed after the date of the assignment to him regardless of whether he has parted with the lease. On the transfer of a registered lease such an indemnity covenant is implied whether or not value was given for the assignment.[2] A similar indemnity provision is implied on the assignment of an unregistered lease, but only where value has been given for the assignment.[3] If the assignment of an unregistered lease is to be made for no valuable consideration an express indemnity covenant will be required by the assignor. At common law an original tenant who is sued by the landlord for a breach of covenant committed by an assignee can pursue a direct claim against that assignee.[4] Standard Condition 4.5.4 requires the purchase deed to contain an express indemnity covenant except where one is implied by law. The contractual exclusion of Law of Property Act 1925, s.77 does not negate the underlying common law obligation to reimburse.[5]

1. The benefit of an option to purchase the reversion may, however, pass to an assignee of the lease by assignment: see para. K13.
2. Land Registration Act 2002, Sched. 12, para. 20.
3. Law of Property Act 1925, s.77.
4. *Moule* v. *Garrett* (1872) LR 7 Exch. 101.
5. *Re Healing Research Trustee Co. Ltd* [1992] 2 All ER 481.

10.4. Liability between head-landlord and sub-tenant

10.4.1. No privity of estate exists between a head-landlord and a sub-tenant although a contractual relationship will exist between them if the sub-tenant has entered into direct covenants with the head-landlord (e.g. in a licence to sub-let). The sub-tenant will in any event be directly liable to the head-landlord on restrictive covenants in the head-lease of which the former had notice when he took his sub-lease. The sub-tenant is entitled to call for production of the head-lease on grant of the sub-lease to him (Law of Property Act 1925, s.44) and will be deemed to have notice of the contents of the head-lease even if he does not exercise his right under Law of Property Act 1925, s.44 to inspect it. Although it is very likely that an assignee of the sub-lease will have actual notice of restrictive covenants contained in the head-lease (and so assume liability on them), he is not fixed with constructive notice of the contents of the head-lease because, on the assignment to him, he is not entitled under the general law to call for production of the head-lease as part of his title. Also see the Contracts (Rights of Third Parties) Act 1999 and para K10.13.1.

10.5. Guarantors and sureties

10.5.1. The liability of a person who guarantees the performance of the tenant's obligations under the lease only arises if the original debtor defaults, but that liability may be extended by the terms of the guarantee to primary liability. The guarantor will have a continuing liability even though the lease has been disclaimed and the tenant's obligations terminated.[1]

10.5.2. The benefit of a tenant's surety's covenant passes automatically to a buyer of the reversion,[2] as does the benefit of a surety's covenant to accept a lease to replace one disclaimed on the tenant's insolvency.[3]

10.5.3. Where an assignee of the lease goes into liquidation and the landlord sues the original tenant for arrears of rent, the latter can pursue an action against the assignee's surety for reimbursement. Although both are liable to the landlord the surety's obligation is prior to that of the original tenant.[4] However, there is no obligation on the landlord to take action against the other parties before proceeding against the original tenant.[5]

1. *Hindcastle Limited* v. *Barbara Attenborough Associates Ltd* [1996] 2 WLR 262; and *Active Estates Limited* v. *Parness* [2002] 36 EG 147.
2. *P. & A. Swift Investments (A firm)* v. *Combined English Stores Group plc* [1989] AC 643.
3. *Coronation Street Industrial Properties* v. *Ingall Industries plc* [1989] 1 All ER 979.
4. *Becton Dickinson UK Ltd* v. *Zwebner* [1989] QB 208.
5. *Norwich Union Life Insurance Society* v. *Low Profile Fashions Limited* [1992] 1 EGLR 86.

10.6. Restriction on liability of former tenant or guarantor for rent or service charge

10.6.1. Where a landlord seeks to recover a 'fixed charge' from a former tenant or guarantor he must serve a written notice on the tenant within six months of the charge becoming due and in it inform the tenant that the charge is now due, and that the landlord intends to recover the sum specified in the notice plus, where payable, interest. The notice must comply with the Notices Regulations made pursuant to Landlord and Tenant (Covenants) Act 1995.[1]

10.6.2. Fixed charge

A fixed charge is rent, or a service charge as defined by section 18 of Landlord and Tenant Act 1985 (but without the statutory restrictions applicable to residential property) or any other liquidated sum payable in the event of a breach of covenant.

10.6.3. Effect of failure to comply

A landlord who fails to comply will not be able to recover the amounts from either the former tenant or a guarantor.

10.6.4. Amount of fixed charge unknown

The landlord can only recover the amount stated in the notice. If the rent is in the process of being reviewed, the notice must state that the liability may be greater than that specified, and once the amount is known a further notice must be served claiming the increased amount within three months.

10.6.5. Restriction of liability of former tenant or his guarantor where tenancy subsequently varied

(a) The effect of variations at common law

A variation may not bind the original tenant following the decision in *Friends Provident Life Office* v. *British Railways Board.*[2] If an assignee agrees a variation with the landlord, the variation does not alter the terms of the contract between the original parties to the lease. The original tenant is not released from liability, but the liability remains governed by the terms of the contract which he entered when he was granted the lease.

(b) **Section 18 of Landlord and Tenant (Covenants) Act 1995**

Section 18 relieves a former tenant of liability for any amount which is referable to a relevant variation made on or after 1 January, 1996. A relevant variation need not be contained in a deed. It is a variation which occurs where either a landlord has an absolute right to refuse it, or the lease has been altered after the assignment so as to deprive the landlord of a right of absolute refusal (e.g. a lease which prohibits a change of use without consent). To the extent that a guarantor remains liable despite the variation he will nevertheless not be liable to pay any amount referable to a relevant variation.

10.6.6. *Right of former tenant to overriding lease*

A person discharging a fixed charge has a right to require the landlord to grant him an overriding lease under the Landlord and Tenant (Covenants) Act 1995, s.19. An overriding lease is a reversionary lease granted for the remainder of the term usually plus a short term (e.g. a few days). Its terms are broadly identical to those of the relevant tenancy. It does not contain personal covenants or covenants which are spent, and covenants framed by reference to the beginning of the tenancy, e.g. repairing covenants, should be adjusted. To obtain an overriding lease the tenant must serve on the landlord a written request specifying the payment and claiming the right to the lease. The request must be made at the time of making the payment or within 12 months. The landlord must grant the lease within a reasonable time. The tenant has to deliver a counterpart and is liable for the landlord's reasonable costs. There is no obligation to grant an overriding lease if the original tenancy has been determined, or if an overriding lease has been granted or a request for one is still outstanding. Two or more requests for over-riding leases made on the same day are dealt with in the sequence in which the liability was incurred with a tenant having prior right to a guarantor. A tenant may withdraw his request or may fail to respond to a request from the landlord to take a lease within a reasonable time. In either case, the tenant will be liable for the landlord's costs. A request may be protected by the entry of a notice in registered land (or as an estate contract in unregistered land). It is possible to have tiers of overriding leases. Whether an overriding lease is a new lease or an old one depends upon the status of the original lease. It should state that it is an overriding lease granted under section 19 of Landlord and Tenant (Covenants) Act 1995 and whether or not it is a new tenancy for the purpose of section 1. Any right arising from such a request cannot be an overriding interest.[3] A landlord who fails to grant a reversionary lease may face a claim in tort for breach of statutory duty. A tenant who fails to deliver a counterpart lease cannot exercise rights under the overriding lease. These provisions are binding on mortgagees.

1. S.I. 1995/2964.
2. [1996] 1 All ER 336; and *Beegas Nominees* v. *BHP Petroleum Ltd* [1998] 31 EG 96.
3. Landlord and Tenant (Covenants) Act 1995, s.20(6) as amended by Land Registration Act 2002, Sched. 11, para. 33(4).

10.7. Covenants to which Landlord and Tenant (Covenants) Act 1995 applies

10.7.1. The 1995 Act applies to all covenants whether they are express, implied or imposed by law and whether or not they 'touch and concern the land', but not to those imposed pursuant to section 35, 155 or paragraph 1 of Schedule 6A Housing Act 1985, or paragraph 1 or 3 of Schedule 2 Housing Associations Act 1985. Most covenants in a lease do touch and concern the land, but see, for example, *Hua Chiao Commercial Bank Ltd* v. *Chiaphua Industries Ltd*.[1]

10.7.2. *Transmission of the benefit and burden*

An assignee now acquires the benefit and takes the burden of all the covenants. The assignor remains liable, and can sue, for breaches occurring before the assignment is made.[2] An assignor may, however, assign the benefit of a right.[3] The covenants are enforceable by and against any person entitled to the rents and profits and also by and against a mortgagee in possession.

10.7.3. *Exceptions*

(a) Personal covenants.

(b) A covenant which does not bind the assignor immediately before the assignment, for example, one that is of limited duration or which has been released.

(c) A covenant which relates to a part of the demised premises which is not included in the assignment.

(d) A covenant which needs to be protected by registration and has not been so protected (e.g. an option).

10.7.4. *The Landlord's right of re-entry*

A landlord's right of entry attaches to the reversion and passes on an assignment of it.[4]

1. [1987] AC 99 (PC).
2. *cf.* Law of Property Act 1925, s.141; and *Re King: Robinson* v. *Gray* [1963] Ch 459.
3. Landlord and Tenant (Covenants) Act 1995, s.23(2).
4. Landlord and Tenant (Covenants) Act 1995, s.4.

10.8. Tenant's release from covenants

10.8.1. A tenant who assigns the lease will be released from the burden and deprived of the benefit of the covenants from the moment the assignment is made. His guarantor is also released to the same extent.[1] The release is only from future observance of the covenants.

10.8.2. Exceptions

(a) An assignment in breach of covenant or by operation of law (e.g. devolution to PRs) is an 'excluded assignment'. The assignor is not released until the next assignment as long as it is not another excluded one.[2]

(b) A tenant who has entered an authorised guarantee agreement is similarly not released until the next non-excluded assignment.[3]

1. See the Landlord and Tenant (Covenants) Act 1995, s.24(2). It may be possible for the guarantor to guarantee the outgoing tenant's liability under any Authorised Guarantee Agreement he may give. The legal effectiveness of such a provision is unclear and is as yet unresolved by judicial authority.
2. Landlord and Tenant (Covenants) Act 1995, s.11(2).
3. See para. K10.9.

10.9. Authorised guarantee agreements

10.9.1. Where a lease contains a restriction on assignment, the landlord can, as a condition of his granting consent to the assignment, require the tenant to enter into an agreement which guarantees the performance of the lease covenants by the immediate assignee (called an 'authorised guarantee agreement'). The terms of the proposed agreement should be set out in the lease.

10.9.2. The agreement:

(a) can only guarantee the liability of the assignee;

(b) must cease when that assignee assigns the lease;

(c) may impose a primary liability;

(d) is void to the extent that it imposes obligations beyond those permitted[1];

(e) may require the tenant to accept a new lease where the old one is disclaimed as long as the tenancy is for no longer a period than the original term and its covenants are no more onerous.

10.9.3. Effect of disclaimers, vesting orders and reversionary leases

Where a tenant is granted a lease following disclaimer, or has a vesting order made in his favour under Insolvency Act 1986, or is granted an overriding lease, he may be required to enter a further AGA on its assignment.

1. Landlord and Tenant (Covenants) Act 1995, s.16(4)(a) and (b), and s.25.

10.10. Landlord's release from covenants

10.10.1. Need to serve notice

The landlord who assigns the reversion may apply for a release by serving a notice on the tenant either before or within four weeks beginning with the date of the assignment.[1]

0.10.2. *Contents of notice*

The tenant must be told about the proposed assignment or the fact that it has occurred and that the landlord is seeking a release from his covenants.

0.10.3. *Tenant's response*

A tenant may object to the landlord's release by serving a notice on the landlord within four weeks beginning with the date of service of the landlord's notice.

0.10.4. *Role of the court*

Unless the objection is withdrawn, the county court will decide whether it is reasonable for the landlord to be released.

0.10.5. *Date of release*

A landlord's release takes effect from the date of the assignment. Section 3(3A) Landlord and Tenant Act 1985 still applies: the liability of an assigning landlord is preserved until the tenant is notified of the change of landlord.

0.10.6. *Subsequent release*

A landlord who has not been released may make a fresh application on the next assignment of the reversion. He should, therefore, take an indemnity covenant from his buyer together with a covenant that the buyer will notify the landlord of his intention to re-sell the reversion.

0.10.7. Notices must comply with the Notices Regulations made pursuant to Landlord and Tenant (Covenants) Act 1995.[2]

1. Landlord and Tenant (Covenants) Act 1995, ss.6–8. Careful consideration needs to be given before taking this step in the case of multi-let properties as only obtaining the release by only some of the tenants will leave the landlord in an exposed position.
2. S.I. 1995/2964.

10.11. **Assignment of part**

10.11.1. The release of the assignor is only in respect of covenants which relate to the part sold except where the assignment is an excluded assignment.

10.11.2. *Apportionment of liability*

The assignor and the assignee remain bound by 'non-attributable' covenants, e.g. a covenant to pay rent or a service charge which is charged on the whole property, but they can agree between them how the liability is to be borne. The apportionment may bind the other party to the lease if a notice[1] is served either before or within four weeks beginning with the date of the assignment in question on the other party to the lease. The notice must inform him of the proposed assignment or the fact that it has occurred, the prescribed particulars of the agreement, and the request that the apportionment becomes binding on him. The apportionment will be binding if the recipient fails to serve a written notice[1] of objection within four weeks. If he does object, the parties to the agreement may apply to the county court for a declaration that it is reasonable for the apportionment to bind the other party to the lease. The recipient may also indicate consent to the apportionment or may withdraw a notice of objection. An apportionment which becomes binding does so from the date of the assignment.

10.11.3. Forfeiture or disclaimer limited to part only of demised premises

Where the landlord has a right to forfeit or there is a right for a liquidator or trustee in bankruptcy to disclaim a lease and where part only of the demised premises is affected, the forfeiture or disclaimer relates only to that part vested in the defaulting or insolvent tenant and not to the whole lease.[2]

1. The notices must comply with Landlord and Tenant (Covenants) Act 1995 (Notices) Regulations 1995, S.I. 1995/2964.
2. Landlord and Tenant (Covenants) Act 1995, s.21.

10.12. Exclusion of the 1995 Act

10.12.1. An agreement to exclude, modify or otherwise frustrate the operation of provisions in the 1995 Act is void.[1]

1. Landlord and Tenant (Covenants) Act 1995, s.25.

10.13. Contracts (Rights of Third Parties) Act 1999

10.13.1. The Contracts (Rights of Third Parties) Act 1999 affects leases and assignments made on or after May 11, 2000 and provides that where a contract made between A and B is intended to benefit C (e.g. a sub-tenant or assignee) C may sue on that contract as if he was an original contracting party. C, the third party, must be identified in the contract made between A and B by name, class or description. This will mean that covenants in a head lease may be directly enforceable as between tenants and as between a head landlord and sub-tenant or head landlord and an assignee where previously direct enforcement was not possible because of the doctrines of privity of contract and of estate. The right of enforcement is not for the whole contract but just those terms which are made for the benefit of a third party.

K11. Assignment of leases

See also: Taking instructions, para. A1
Estimate of costs, para. A8
Capacity, para. B7
Undertakings for bridging finance, para. B16
Pre-completion, section E
Completion, section F
Post-completion, section G
Right to buy, para. K9

NB: In this section the word 'lease' should be read to include the word 'sub-lease' where appropriate to the context.

11.1. Taking instructions

11.1.1. The information required by the seller's solicitor and buyer's solicitor will be similar to that needed in a freehold transaction (see para. A1) with the addition of details of the lease to be sold or bought. Of particular importance is the question of whether the landlord's consent to the transaction will be required (see para K.11.2.6). The seller's solicitor should check his own title, in particular to ensure that no outstanding breaches of covenant exist, before drafting the contract for sale.

11.1.2. The length of the residue of the term should be checked. Where the buyer is to obtain a mortgage on the property his lender will usually require that a minimum stated length of the term remains unexpired at the date of acquisition of the buyer's interest in order to provide the lender with adequate security for his loan. A lease with only a few years left unexpired is a wasting asset in the hands of the tenant and particularly in the case of residential property may prove difficult to sell unless the lease can be extended or enfranchised (see Right to buy, para. K9).

11.1.3. *Seller's solicitor*

The seller's solicitor should obtain from his client or, if not available from the client, from the landlord:

   (a) the receipt for the last rent due under the lease;

   (b) where relevant, evidence of payment of service charge over the past three years including the receipt for the last payment due;

(c) details of the insurance of the property including the receipt for the last premium due;

(d) details of any fee payable to a management company on the transfer of the lease (mainly applicable to retirement schemes);

(e) a copy of the memorandum and articles of association of any management company together with a copy of the seller's share certificate;

(f) copies of any side letters made between landlord and tenant which affect the terms of the lease.

11.1.3.1. Seller's checklist

Does the seller's solicitor have in his possession:

(a) evidence of the freehold title?

(b) licence permitting the current assignment and/or use of the property?

(c) insurance policy?

(d) latest rent review memo?

11.1.3.2. What consents are needed:

(a) from landlord?

(b) from lender?

11.1.3.3. Consider what statutes affect the current letting and the proposed sale. What impact does this legislation make on the proposed transaction?

11.1.3.4. Consider the terms of the existing lease, e.g. as to repairs, user, alterations, alienation, forfeiture, because the buyer's solicitor may raise points on these clauses.

11.1.3.5. Will it be necessary to obtain a release of the current sureties' liability from the landlord, or to obtain a deed of variation of the lease to reflect the current situation as between landlord and tenant?

11.1.3.6. If the lease to be assigned commenced before 1 January 1996, the assignor should be reminded of his continuing liability under the covenants in the lease.

11.1.3.7. If the lease to be assigned commenced after 1 January 1996, its terms should be checked to see whether the landlord requires the outgoing tenant to enter into an authorised guarantee agreement on assignment.

11.1.4. *Buyer's solicitor*

11.1.4.1. Checking the lease

On receipt of a copy of the lease from the seller's solicitor, the buyer's solicitor should check the lease carefully and advise his client about his responsibility under the various covenants in the lease. The lease may require an assignee to enter into direct covenants with the landlord which will create a contractual relationship between the landlord and the assignee and will make the assignee liable on all of the lease covenants for the remainder of the term, notwithstanding subsequent assignment of the lease to a third party (see para. K10).

1.1.4.2. Landlord's consent

If the landlord's consent to the transfer will be needed the buyer should be asked to supply his solicitor with the names and addresses of potential referees so that this information may be passed on to the seller's solicitor as quickly as possible in order to avoid any delay in obtaining the licence. References are commonly required from all or some of the following sources:

   (a) a current landlord;

   (b) the buyer's bankers;

   (c) the buyer's employer;

   (d) a professional person, e.g. accountant or solicitor;

   (e) a person or company with whom the buyer regularly trades;

   (f) three years' audited accounts in the case of a company or self-employed person.

1.1.4.3. A solicitor should only give a reference on behalf of his client if he knows the client well and trusts him. The landlord will rely on the information given in the reference in assessing the suitability of the buyer as a potential tenant and a misstatement made by a solicitor in the course of giving a reference may lead to liability to the landlord under the principles in *Hedley Byrne & Co. Ltd* v. *Heller and Partners Ltd* [1964] AC 465. It is thus common practice for a reference given by a solicitor to exclude liability or responsibility for its contents.

1.1.4.4. Surety

The landlord may also require a surety to the lease as a condition of the grant of a licence to assign. Consideration should be given as to who should stand surety under the lease. Where the proposed assignee is a company it is common to find that the directors of the company are asked to guarantee the company's obligations under the lease. Although the directors may be happy to do this since, unless they agree, they are unlikely to secure the landlord's consent to the assignment, they should be advised of the considerable personal liability which they are assuming by accepting such a role. This is particularly so if the assignee, by entering direct covenants with the landlord, will be assuming a contingent liability under the lease since the sureties' obligations will be co-extensive with those of the principal debtor. In this situation there may be a conflict between the interests of the company client (the prospective assignee) and those of the sureties (the company directors) and it may be advisable for the sureties to receive independent advice about their responsibilities in relation to the guarantee of the lease obligations.

11.1.4.5. Buyer's lender

The terms of the lease should be checked to ensure that it will be acceptable to the buyer's lender (see para K1) and where appropriate the provisions of the Lenders' Handbook must be observed.

11.2. Covenants against alienation

11.2.1. Covenants against alienation take many forms; they may restrict all or any of the following acts: assignment of the lease, sub-letting, sharing, parting with possession of the whole or any part of the property and creating a mortgage over the property. Such covenants are construed strictly by the courts so that when drafting a covenant it is essential that the covenant is worded to cover precisely the acts which it is intended to restrict, e.g. a covenant which prevents assignment will not restrict sub-letting and vice versa.

11.2.2. *Long residential leases*

A covenant which restricts assignment of a long lease of a house or flat, except during the final years of its term (e.g. during the last seven years of a 99-year lease), is not generally favoured by either buyers or their lenders since it unnecessarily restricts the saleability of the property and thus has an adverse effect on its market value. For this reason such a covenant is uncommon in such a lease and a buyer's solicitor should seek to remove such a restriction from the lease on grant.

11.2.3. Except in long residential leases the inclusion of some type of covenant against alienation is usual and acceptable and provides the landlord with some measure of control over the occupiers of his property. The precise effect of any covenant depends on its wording. The effect of Landlord and Tenant Act 1927, s.19(1)(*b*) on building leases should be noted.[1]

11.2.4. *Absolute covenants*

If the covenant is absolute, e.g. 'the tenant shall not assign or part with possession of the property', any assignment (or other dealing depending on the wording of the restriction), although effective, will be a breach of covenant by the tenant and may lead to forfeiture of the lease. An absolute covenant is not subject to any statutory restrictions on its operation except those imposed by Sex Discrimination Act 1975, Race Relations Act 1976 and Disability Discrimination Act 1995, and thus gives the landlord total control over the tenant's dealings with the lease, but is not popular with tenants since there is no guarantee that the tenant will be able to sell the lease should the need or desire to do so arise. The presence of an absolute covenant may therefore have a deflationary effect on the rent obtainable for the property. Where an absolute covenant exists, there is no objection to the tenant asking the landlord's permission to grant him a variation of the lease to permit assignment (or as the case may be), but there is no obligation on the landlord to accede to the tenant's request or to give reasons for his refusal.

11.2.5. *Qualified covenants*

A qualified covenant permits the tenant to assign provided that the tenant obtains the prior consent of the landlord to the dealing. This type of covenant is more acceptable to prospective tenants than an absolute covenant but does not give the landlord total control over the occupiers of his property since his discretion to refuse consent to a proposed assignee may be tempered by the application of statutory provisions which, where they apply, are non-excludable.

11.2.6. *Consent not to be unreasonably withheld*

In the case of a qualified covenant contained in a lease dated before 1 January 1996, the Landlord and Tenant Act 1927, s.19 adds to the covenant the non-excludable proviso that consent shall not be unreasonably withheld by the landlord.[2] The question of whether a landlord in refusing consent is acting 'unreasonably' presents problems for the tenant. If the tenant does apply for consent and the landlord unreasonably withholds his consent, the tenant may go ahead and assign (or as the case may be) without consent and the dealing will not constitute a breach of covenant by the tenant. The difficulty lies in knowing what is 'unreasonable' since a refusal which may appear to be unreasonable from the tenant's point of view may look very different when considered from the landlord's side. If the landlord does refuse consent the prospective assignee (or as the case may be) is unlikely to wish to proceed with the transaction without consent because he runs the risk of the lease being forfeited against him. One solution is for the tenant to seek a declaration from the court to the effect that the landlord is being unreasonable in withholding his consent but such a course of action is costly and time-consuming. Landlord and Tenant Act 1988 attempts to resolve some of the problems associated with the application of section 19 by providing that the landlord must, after having received a written request for consent, give his consent within a reasonable time unless it is reasonable for him to withhold his consent. He must serve written notice of his decision on the tenant within a reasonable time stating what conditions (if any) are attached to the consent or, if consent is refused, stating his reasons for withholding his consent. Breach of the landlord's duty under the Act is actionable in tort as a breach of statutory duty, giving a remedy to the tenant in damages.

11.2.7. *Offer to surrender*

Attached to some covenants against assignment is a proviso that should the tenant wish to assign he should first offer to surrender his lease to the landlord. Such a proviso (commonly known as an 'Adler clause' after the case of that name[3]) was held to be valid in *Bocardo S.A.* v. *S. & M. Hotels*,[4] but the effect of such a clause and the terms of any surrender need to be considered carefully by the tenant, especially since, in the case of business tenancies within Landlord and Tenant Act 1954, Pt. II, section 38 makes void an agreement which has the effect of precluding the tenant from making an application for a new tenancy under the Act. It may therefore be necessary in a commercial lease for landlord and tenant to obtain the consent of the court to an agreement to surrender.[5] Since Law of Property (Miscellaneous Provisions) Act 1989, s.2 requires a contract for the disposal of an interest in land to be in writing, it is arguable that to create an effective contract for surrender landlord and tenant must both sign a single document incorporating all the terms of the surrender or otherwise comply with the terms of the Act.[6]

11.2.8. Landlord and Tenant (Covenants) Act 1995

In relation to new tenancies (i.e. generally those granted on or after 1 January 1996) of commercial property[7] the provisions of section 19 of Landlord and Tenant Act 1927 are modified so that a landlord may agree in advance with his tenant:

(a) any circumstances in which the landlord may withhold his licence or consent to a proposed assignment; or

(b) any conditions subject to which such licence or consent may be granted.

A landlord who withholds consent because of the existence of any such circumstance or who imposes any such condition is not acting unreasonably.

The 1995 Act distinguishes between factual matters, for example:

(a) the assignee must be a plc;

(b) the assignee must have net assets equal to a specified multiplier of the rent;

(c) the assignee must provide a rent deposit; or

(d) the assignor must enter an AGA,

and discretionary matters, for example, the assignee is, in the opinion of the landlord, of equal financial standing to the assignor.

In discretionary matters, the landlord's decision has to be arrived at reasonably, or the tenant must have the right to have the decision reviewed by an independent third party, who is identifiable from the agreement, and whose decision is conclusive.

11.2.9. Demanding a premium for consent

Unless the lease specifically allows the landlord to charge a premium for giving his consent (an uncommon provision in modern leases) the landlord may not attach a condition to his consent requiring a premium to be paid by the tenant.[8]

11.2.10. Undertaking for landlord's costs

The landlord is entitled to ask the tenant to pay the landlord's solicitor's reasonable charges in connection with the preparation of the deed of consent (licence but may not demand a premium. Overcharging by the landlord's solicitor i unprofessional conduct. When the tenant's solicitor approaches the landlord' solicitor asking for consent to be given he should require the landlord's solicitor to provide a firm estimate of the costs of the application which should indicate whether or not VAT and disbursements are included in the estimate and should give a maximum fee which will be charged by the landlord in any event.[9] It may be difficult for the landlord's solicitor to quote a fixed figure at the outset of the transaction, but he should try to give the tenant's solicitor an accurate estimate of the likely costs and there is no objection to his qualifying the estimate by saying that it is given on the understanding that the matter proceeds to completion without any unforeseen difficulties or delays. The estimate should make it clear whether the tenant is to be responsible for the landlord's costs in any event, i.e. whether or not consent is forthcoming and whether or not the proposed assignment (or as the case may be) proceeds to completion. To assist the landlord in giving an accurate estimate the tenant's solicitor should be prepared to supply the landlord with such information as he requires, e.g. references about the proposed assignee (or as the case may be) as quickly as possible and preferably at the time when the application for consent is first made. A tenant's solicitor must advise his client of his potential liability to meet the landlord's costs and should not give an unqualified undertaking to meet the landlord's solicitors' costs of preparing the consent since he may be committing his client to an unquantified sum. An undertaking may be given, provided that the landlord has provided an estimate of costs, and subject to the prior approval of the tenant client.[10] It may be unreasonable for the landlord to insist on an undertaking as a pre-condition for dealing with the application for consent unless this is limited to a reasonable sum.[11] Where an undertaking has been given, the tenant's solicitor should obtain money on account from his client to ensure that he will be able to fulfil the undertaking. However, since Landlord and Tenant Act 1988 renders the landlord liable to the tenant in damages if an application for consent is not dealt with within a reasonable time, the landlord's solicitor should be wary of refusing to deal with the matter until such time as he receives an undertaking in respect of his costs.

11.2.11. *Standard Conditions of Sale*

Standard Condition 8.3 and Standard Commercial Property Condition 8.3 require the seller to apply for the landlord's consent at his own expense and to use his best endeavours to obtain such consent, the buyer providing all information and references reasonably required. Unless in breach of these obligations, either party may rescind the contract by notice if the consent has not been obtained four months after the original completion or if, by that time, consent has been given subject to a condition to which the buyer reasonably objects. The conditions do not require the assignee to enter into a direct covenant with the landlord. If the lease provides for the assignee to enter into a direct covenant, the contract should contain a special condition to this effect.

11.2.12. In view of the difficulties attached to covenants against alienation, contracts for a disposition which is dependent on consent being obtained should not be exchanged until it is certain that the landlord's consent will be forthcoming.

1. The effect of this is, broadly, that if the lease is for more than 40 years and made partly in consideration for construction work no consent to a dealing is required if this is done more than seven years before the end of the term. See *Vaux Group plc* v. *Lilley* [1991] 04 EG 136.
2. Section 19 does not apply to lettings of certain types of property e.g. agricultural holdings, see s.19(4).
3. *Adler* v. *Upper Grosvenor Street Investments* [1957] 1 All ER 229.
4. [1980] 1 WLR 17.
5. Landlord and Tenant Act 1954, s.38(4)(*b*) (added by Law of Property Act 1969, s.11).
6. *Proudread Ltd* v. *Microgen* (1995) NPC 120, CA.
7. Section 19(1A) of the 1927 Act does not apply to residential or agricultural tenancies.
8. Law of Property Act 1925, s.144.
9 See Estimate of costs, para. A8.
10. See section B16 Undertakings for bridging finance.
11. *Dong Bang Minerva* v. *Davina* [1996] 31 EG 87.

11.3. Preparing the package

11.3.1. The seller's solicitor should supply the buyer's solicitor with the following documents or information:

(a) the draft contract;

(b) a copy of the lease/sub-lease being purchased;

(c) a plan of the property (where appropriate);

(d) evidence of the seller's title;

(e) replies to pre-contract searches;

(f) details of the insurance of the property (including the receipt for the last premium due);

(g) details of any management company, including copies of the memorandum and articles of association;

(h) service charge accounts for the last three years including the receipt for the last sum payable (where appropriate);

(i) information about what steps have been taken to obtain the landlord's consent to the transaction (where appropriate);

(j) a request for references or such other information about the buyer as the landlord has indicated that he requires (where appropriate);

(k) answers to pre-contract enquiries. In Protocol cases the Seller's Property Information Form and Seller's Leasehold Information Form. In the case of commercial property replies to the Commercial Property Standard Enquiries should be supplied.[1]

1. The enquiries may be downloaded from www.bpf.org.uk. Also see para K1.18.1 and Appendix VIII.5.

11.4. The Protocol

11.4.1. The Protocol applies as in the case of a freehold transaction, but the seller should be asked to produce, if possible, a receipt or evidence from the landlord of the last payment of rent, the maintenance charge accounts for the last three years (where appropriate) and evidence of payment, and details of the buildings insurance policy. If a licence to assign is required, enquiry should be made of the landlord as to what references from the assignee are necessary. A copy of the lease, together with such of the above information as has been obtained and is relevant to the transaction, should be sent to the buyer's solicitor as soon as possible.

1.5. Title

1.5.1. *Lease registered with absolute title*

By Standard Condition 4.2.1 and Standard Commercial Property Condition 4.2.1, copies supplied must be official copy entries of the title. Since the title to the lease is guaranteed by the Land Registry there is no need for the buyer to investigate the title to the freehold or superior leases.

1.5.2. *Lease registered with good leasehold title*

By Standard Condition 4.2.1 and Standard Commercial Property Condition 4.2.1 copies supplied must be official copy entries of the title. Registration with a good leasehold title provides no guarantee of the soundness of the title to the freehold reversion and thus, although not entitled under the general law to do so, the buyer should insist on deduction of the superior title to him. Without deduction of the reversionary title the lease may be unacceptable to the buyer and/or his lender.[1] The reversionary title will be deduced by the appropriate method applicable to unregistered land.[2] As the register of title is open to public inspection a prospective tenant will in practice be able to find out a great deal about his proposed landlord's title (assuming it is registered).

1.5.3. *Unregistered lease*

A special condition should in appropriate cases be added to the contract requiring the seller to deduce the reversionary title to the buyer by the method appropriate to unregistered land.[3] The Standard Conditions of Sale do not require the seller to deduce a reversionary title in these circumstances.

1. See para. K1 for the reasons why a good leasehold title is considered to be inadequate. Note the special requirements in relation to good leasehold title contained in the Lenders' Handbook (Appendix VIII.3).
2. See Title, section D.
3. See Title, section D.

11.6. Preparing for completion

11.6.1. *The purchase deed*

The purchase deed (an assignment in unregistered land or a transfer in registered land) will be prepared by the buyer's solicitor. Even where the lease was granted informally the assignment must be by deed in order to transfer the legal estate in the land to the buyer.[1] An assignment of an unregistered lease will normally recite the brief history of the lease and the granting of any necessary consent to the present transaction, but is otherwise similar to a conveyance of freehold land. The form of transfer is the same as that used in freehold transactions. Execution of the purchase deed is discussed in para. E1.

11.6.2. Indemnity

If the assignor is to remain liable on the covenants in the lease after completion of the assignment, the purchase deed should include an express indemnity covenant from the buyer. Where Landlord and Tenant (Covenants) Act 1995 applies so as to release the assignor from future liability, no indemnity covenant is necessary; however, liability is commonly continued by an authorised guarantee agreement. If on an assignment of the reversion the assignor is not to be released from his covenants by the tenant (or there is a possibility that the tenant may refuse to give consent to the landlord's release), the assignor may wish to consider taking an express indemnity covenant from the buyer together with a covenant by the buyer to notify the assignor of the buyer's sale of the reversion to a third party within a specified time of completion of that further sale. This is to enable the first assignor to serve notice on the tenant renewing his request to be released from liability under the landlord's covenants in the lease. The assignor must serve notice on the tenant before or within four weeks after completion of an assignment if he wishes to be released from the landlord's covenants in the lease. The buyer should therefore be required to notify the assignor within seven days of completion of a further sale in order to give the assignor sufficient time to serve his notice on the tenants within the four-week period. It may be possible for a restriction to be entered on the register to prevent registration of a purchase until this has been done. In practice this solution is likely to be impractical.

11.6.3. Modification of covenants for title

If a seller is in breach of a repairing covenant in the lease, the lack of repair could involve him in liability to the buyer after completion under the covenants for title which will be implied in the purchase deed.[2] Since liability under the covenants is strict, and it is usual for the contract to contain a provision requiring the buyer to accept the property in its existing state of repair,[3] the contract should also provide for modification of the covenants for title in this respect. Such a contractual condition must be reflected by an express modification of the covenants in the purchase deed itself, if the Standard Conditions of Sale have not been used in the transaction.[4] A buyer who accepts a condition which restricts the seller's liability under the covenants for title must ensure that he is fully aware of the actual state of repair of the property (e.g. by inspection or survey) before contracts are exchanged since the effect of such a contractual condition is to take away the buyer's right to sue the seller in respect of a breach of repairing covenant.

11.6.4. *Pre-completion searches*

Where the lease is registered with an absolute title the buyer will make a pre-completion search at the Land Registry in the same way as if he were buying the freehold. Any other searches which would be appropriate to the purchase of a registered freehold should also be undertaken (see para. E2). Where the title to the lease is unregistered a Land Charges Department search against the names of the estate owners of the leasehold title should be made together with any other searches appropriate to the circumstances of the transaction (see para. E2). Where the freehold or other reversionary title has been deduced the names revealed through investigation of that title should also be included in the land charges search application. If the lease is registered with a good leasehold title, a search at the Land Registry must be made in respect of the registered title and a Land Charges Department search against the estate owners of an unregistered reversion. A company search should be carried out against the management company.

11.6.5. *Landlord's consent*

The landlord's solicitor will supply the engrossment of the licence which must be by deed if it is to contain covenants. If the licence requires the buyer to enter into a direct covenant with the landlord (and/or a management company) to observe and perform the covenants in the lease, the licence is usually drawn up in two parts, the landlord executing the original licence which will be given to the seller on completion for onwards transmission to the buyer, the buyer executing the counterpart which will be given to the landlord on completion.

11.6.6. *Apportionments*

Since it is unlikely that completion will take place on a day when rent and/or service charge become due under the lease it will be necessary for these sums to be apportioned on completion and the seller should supply the buyer with a completion statement which shows the amounts due and explains how they have been calculated. Copies of the rent and service charge receipts or demands should be supplied to the buyer with the completion statement so that the buyer can check the apportioned sums. In many cases it will not be possible to make an exact apportionment of service charge since the figures required in order to make this calculation will not be available. In such a case a provisional apportionment of the sum should be made on a 'best estimate' basis in accordance with Standard Condition 6.3.5 or Standard Commercial Property Condition 6.3.5 (see section F). These conditions, although of most relevance to the apportionment of service charges, are not confined in their application to service charges alone and can be used to make a provisional apportionment of any sums where the amount to be apportioned is not known or easily ascertainable. Where the seller's liability for unascertained service charges may be substantial and there is concern about enforcing his obligation to pay (e.g. where the seller is emigrating), it may be appropriate to negotiate a retention to be held by his solicitors pending the ascertainment of the service charge.

11.6.7. *Shares in management company*

Where appropriate the solicitor for the buyer should prepare a stock transfer form to be signed by the seller before completion in order to transfer the seller's management company share(s) to the buyer. If the management company is limited by guarantee (not shares) there will be no share certificate to transfer to the buyer but the buyer will need to write to the company and apply for membership after completion. If the amount of the guarantee is more than nominal the seller's liability under the guarantee continues for a year after he ceases to be a member and he should in such a case take an appropriate indemnity from the buyer.

1. Short leases do not have to be made by deed (Law of Property Act 1925, s.54), but the transfer of a legal estate in land must be by deed by Law of Property Act 1925, s.52. This includes the assignment of a short lease. See *Crago* v. *Julian* [1992] 1 All ER 744.
2. Land Registration Act 2002, Sched. 12, para 20; Law of Property Act 1925, s.76: see Capacity, para. B7.
3. See Standard Condition 3.2.1 and Standard Commercial Property Condition 3.2.1.
4. See Standard Condition 4.5.4 and Standard Commercial Property Condition 4.5.4.

11.7. Completion

11.7.1. The procedure on completion follows closely that in a freehold transaction (see section F).

11.7.2. The seller will hand to the buyer such of the following documents as are relevant to the transaction in hand:

    (a) the lease/sub-lease;

    (b) the purchase deed;

    (c) the landlord's licence;

    (d) marked abstract or other evidence of superior titles in accordance with the contract (lease not registered or not registered with absolute title);

    (e) Form DS1 or undertaking in respect of the seller's mortgage (unless the END system is being used);

    (f) copies of duplicate notices served by the seller and his predecessors on the landlord in accordance with a covenant in the lease requiring the landlord to be notified of any dispositions;

    (g) insurance policy (or copy if insurance is effected by the landlord) and receipt (or copy) relating to the last premium due;

    (h) rent and service charge receipts;

    (i) management company memorandum and articles;

    (j) seller's share certificate and completed stock transfer form.

11.7.3. The buyer should hand to the seller such of the following items as are appropriate to the transaction:

(a) money due in accordance with the completion statement;

(b) duly executed counterpart licence to assign;

(c) a release of deposit.

11.7.4. *Rent receipts*

Law of Property Act 1925, s.45(2) provides that on production of the receipt for the last rent due under the lease or sub-lease which he is buying a buyer must assume, unless the contrary appears, that the rent has been paid and the covenants performed under that and all superior leases. The buyer's solicitor should inspect the receipts on completion and also, where appropriate, receipts for payment of service charge. Standard Condition 6.6 and Standard Commercial Property Condition 6.6 entitle a buyer to assume that the correct person gave the receipt.

11.8. **Post-completion**

11.8.1. *Stamp duty*

The Government propose to modernise the law relating to stamp duty. The enabling legislation is included in the Finance Bill 2003, with the detail to be contained in secondary legislation, which appears likely to be brought into force on 1 December 2003. The information given in this section relates to the stamp duty scheme as it exists at the date of publication (See AAA. Stamp Duty Land Tax).

If the consideration for the sale does not exceed the current stamp duty threshold and a certificate of value is included in the purchase deed, no *ad valorem* duty will be payable on the deed. In other cases the purchase deed will bear duty at the same rates applicable to a conveyance of the freehold (see Stamping documents, para. G2). The licence to assign and its counterpart (whether or not made by deed) do not attract stamp duty. The stock transfer form must be stamped with the appropriate duty.

11.8.2. *Particulars delivered*

Irrespective of whether the purchase deed attracts stamp duty, the transfer of a lease or sub-lease which was granted for seven years or more must be produced to the Inland Revenue in accordance with Finance Act 1931, s.28 (see para. G2).

11.8.3. *Registered lease*

Where the lease is already registered at the Land Registry with separate title an application for registration of the transfer to the buyer should be made within the priority period afforded by the buyer's pre-completion search.

11.8.4. *Unregistered lease*

An unregistered lease or sub-lease which, at the date of the transfer to the buyer, still has over 7 years unexpired will need to be registered at the Land Registry within two months of the assignment. An application for first registration of title should therefore be made within this time-limit. An absolute title can be granted where:

(a) the registrar is of the opinion that the applicant's title to the lease is such that a willing buyer could properly be advised by a competent professional adviser to accept; and

(b) the registrar approves the lessor's title to grant the lease.[1]

If the title to the reversion is already registered, the lease will be noted against the superior title. In other cases the buyer may consider lodging a caution against first registration against the unregistered superior title in order to protect his interests against a subsequent buyer of the reversion. If the lease has 7 years or less unexpired it is generally incapable of registration with separate title but will take effect as an overriding interest.[2] It may be prudent to protect a term for more than three years by the entry of notice in the register of a superior title which is itself registered. A lease for three years or less cannot be so protected.[3]

11.8.5. *Notice to landlord*

The buyer's solicitor should give notice of the transfer (and of the buyer's mortgage if required) in accordance with any covenant to that effect in the lease. Two copies of the notice together with the appropriate fee should be sent to the landlord's solicitor (or other person specified in the covenant) and the landlord's solicitor should be asked to sign one copy of the notice as an acknowledgement of its receipt and to return the signed copy to the buyer's solicitor. The receipted notice should be kept with the buyer's title deeds as evidence of compliance with this covenant. The fee payable for service of the notice should have been included in the statement of account sent by the buyer's solicitor to his client before completion.

11.8.6. *Share transfer*

The duly stamped stock transfer form and seller's share certificate should be sent by the buyer's solicitor to the management company who will register the transfer of the share and issue a new share certificate in the buyer's name. The new share certificate should be kept with the buyer's title deeds. It will be necessary to check the requirements of the lender, where appropriate by means of the CML Lenders' Handbook, to see if the share certificate and other relevant documents should be sent to the lender. Where the management company is limited by guarantee the buyer should write to the company and apply for membership.

11.8.7. *Outstanding apportioned sums*

As soon as the figures are available the parties' solicitors should make an adjustment of the provisional apportionments which were made on completion. By Standard Condition 6.3.5 and Standard Commercial Property Condition 6.3.5 such outstanding sums must be settled within 10 working days of notification by one party to the other of the adjusted figures. The liability to account for the apportioned sums remains outstanding despite completion having taken place under Standard Condition 7.4 and Standard Commercial Property Condition 7.4. (see also para. K11.6.6).

1. Land Registration Act 2002, s.10(2).
2. Land Registration Act 2002, Sched. 1, para. 1 and Sched. 3, para. 1.
3. Land Registration Act 2002, s.33.

K12. Licence or tenancy

12.1. Importance of the distinction

12.1.1. The principal reason for distinguishing between a licence and a tenancy is that in general a licensee will not enjoy the benefit of security of tenure, whereas a tenant may be protected from eviction at the end of his contractual term by the operation of some statutory provision. A licensee is not protected under:

(a) Rent Act 1977;

(b) Housing Act 1988 (assured tenancies);

(c) Landlord and Tenant Act 1954, Pt. I (long tenancies);

(d) Local Government and Housing Act 1989, Sched. 10;

(e) Landlord and Tenant Act 1954, Pt. II (business tenancies).

12.1.2. Conversely, licensees do enjoy protection from eviction in the following situations:

(a) where the licensee would otherwise be a secure tenant under Housing Act 1985, s.79;

(b) under Rent (Agriculture) Act 1976; and

(c) generally where a person is granted a licence to occupy land for use as agricultural land under Agricultural Holdings Act 1986, s.2.

12.2. Licences

12.2.1. It is not always easy to determine whether an arrangement between two parties constitutes a licence or a tenancy. The modern starting point is usually accepted to be *Street* v. *Mountford*[1] where it was held as a general rule that if exclusive possession is given for a term at a rent (although the reservation of a rent is not essential to a tenancy), a tenancy will come into being, whatever the parties chose to call the arrangement and whatever they intended to be the result of that arrangement.

12.2.2. The giving of exclusive possession is essential to the creation of a tenancy, so that if the agreement genuinely denies this to the grantee, no tenancy will come into being. If, therefore, a clause is inserted into an agreement for the occupation of business premises, enabling the grantor to move the location of the grantee's occupied space or stall, such a right, being inconsistent with the creation of a tenancy, would generally ensure that the grantee became a licensee and not a tenant.[2]

12.2.3. The ability of the grantor to move the location of the grantee has more realism in the case of a business arrangement than in the context of residential premises, but in residential cases grantors have sometimes succeeded in denying the existence of a tenancy by using the device of requiring the grantee to share the accommodation either with other tenants or with the grantor himself (i.e. denying exclusive possession to the grantee). The courts will, however, not accept these devices at their face value, and will look into the reality of the situation; thus if a sharing arrangement is patently a sham in order to deprive the grantee of security of tenure, it is unlikely to succeed.[3]

1. [1985] AC 809.
2. *Dresden Estates Ltd* v. *Collinson* (1988) 55 P & CR 47.
3. See *Antoniades* v. *Villiers* [1988] 3 All E.R. 1058; *Aslan* v. *Murphy* (Nos. 1 & 2) [1989] 3 All ER 130; *Duke* v. *Wynne* [1989] 3 All ER 130; *A.G. Securities* v. *Vaughan* [1988] 3 All ER 1058; *Mikeover Ltd* v. *Brady* [1989] 3 All ER 618; *Westminster City Council* v. *Clarke* [1992] 2 AC 288, HL.

12.3. Lodgers

12.3.1. A genuine lodger is a recognised licensee and (apart from the denial of exclusive possession) special circumstances such as a family arrangement may negate a tenancy.

12.4. Possession before completion

12.4.1. In most circumstances a buyer who is let into occupation of the property before completion would be treated as a licensee.[1] Standard Condition 5.2 and Standard Commercial Property Condition 5.2 both provide that the buyer takes occupation as a licensee and not as a tenant.

1. But see *Bretherton* v. *Paton* [1986] 1 EGLR 172.

12.5. Notice to terminate

12.5.1. The length of notice necessary to determine a licence which is not protected by statute will normally be settled by agreement between the parties. In the absence of such agreement, reasonable notice must be given. Notice should always be given in writing so that it will be possible, if a dispute arises, to prove the existence and contents of the notice. Some record of posting or delivery should for the same reason be kept. Even where the licensee does not have the benefit of security of tenure, it may still be necessary to obtain a court order if the grantor seeks to regain possession.[1]

1. See, e.g. Protection from Eviction Act 1977, s.2 in the case of residential premises and Housing Act 1988, s.32.

K13. Options

See also: Form of contract, para. B11
Right to buy, para. K9

13.1. Introduction

13.1.1. An option for the tenant to renew the lease or to purchase the reversion may be included in some leases or may be granted to the tenant independently of the grant of the lease.

13.1.2. It is important that the price or rent to be paid on the exercise of the option is either fixed by the lease itself or is otherwise ascertainable by the operation of some effective formula (e.g. by reference to 'open market value at the time of the exercise of the option') in the absence of which the option may fail for uncertainty.

13.1.3 An option contained in a registrable lease should be protected by the entry of notice in the register. However, if the option is an overriding interest by virtue of the tenant's occupation,[1] the option will need to be disclosed on the application to register the lease.[2] Notice of the option would then be entered in the register automatically.[3] On an application for first registration of the lease, the option would also be noted on the register under the registrar's obligation to enter notice of burdens affecting the registered estate.[4]

13.1.4. If a lease out of a registered title is an overriding interest and is not registrable,[5] the option should be protected on the landlord's title by notice. If the tenant is in occupation, the option may be protected as an overriding interest.[6] It would be unwise to rely on protection as an overriding interest in case the tenant went out of occupation for any reason.

13.1.5. If the option is included in a separate document (i.e. not in the body of the lease out of a registered title) specific application would need to be made for its protection.

13.1.6. In unregistered land an option will not bind the buyer of the landlord's reversionary interest unless registered as an estate contract under Land Charges Act 1972. Where an option cannot be enforced against a buyer of the reversion through lack of registration, the tenant may be able to sue the original landlord for damages for breach of contract, who in turn may seek indemnity from the buyer under a contractual provision, e.g. Standard Condition 3.3.2. To protect his own interests the tenant should ensure that his option is registered as soon as possible after completion of its grant (the priority notice procedure may be used to ensure the date of registration is backdated to the date of grant). A landlord may choose to draft the option so that its validity is dependent on its registration within a stated period. Where a lease is granted out of an unregistered reversion, the option must be protected by registration under Land Charges Act 1972 even if the lease granted will itself be registered under the Land Registration Act 2002.

13.1.7. The grant of an option is a disposition of an interest in land within Law of Property (Miscellaneous Provisions) Act 1989, s.2 and so must satisfy the requirements for writing specified by that section.[7]

13.1.8. It is unusual to find options contained in long leases of dwellings which are granted at a low rent because, provided the qualifying conditions are satisfied, Leasehold Reform Act 1967 (as amended) or Leasehold Reform Housing and Urban Development Act 1993 will frequently give the tenant the right to an extended lease and/or to purchase the freehold reversion.[8]

1. Land Registration Act 2002, Sched. 1, para. 2 and Sched. 3, para. 2.
2. Land Registration Rules 2003, rr. 28 and 57.
3. Land Registration Act 2002, s. 37.
4. Land Registration Rules 2003, r. 35.
5. Land Registration Act 2002, Sched. 1, para. 1 and Sched. 3, para. 1.
6. Land Registration Act 2002, Sched. 1, para. 2 and Sched. 3, para. 2.
7. See Form of contract, para. B11; and note *Spiro* v. *Glencrown Properties Ltd.* [1991] 02 EG 167.
8. See Right to buy, para. K9.

13.2. Options to purchase the reversion

13.2.1. The perpetuity rule does not apply to an option to purchase the reversion provided that the option is contained in the lease itself and its exercise is restricted to the tenant and his successors in title either during the term of the lease or no later than one year after the end of the term. Any option which does not satisfy these requirements will fail for perpetuity unless confined within or exercised within 21 years from the date of the grant.[1]

13.2.2. An option to purchase the reversion is not within the doctrine of privity of estate, so that the mere fact that such a relationship exists between the landlord and an assignee of the lease does not automatically mean that the assignee can enforce the option. However, unless the lease restricts the assignability of the option, its benefit may be assigned to a third party,[2] so that an unrestricted option to purchase the reversion at any time during a term in excess of 21 years would fail for perpetuity after 21 years. In such a case the exercise of the option should be restricted to the tenant and his successors in title.

13.2.3. Although the benefit of such an option can be expressly assigned to an assignee of the lease (even after the assignment of the lease itself) and may pass to him by operation of law without express words of assignment,[3] it is recommended that in order to avoid doubt express words assigning the benefit of the option should be included in the document under which the benefit of the lease is transferred to the assignee.

. Perpetuities and Accumulations Act 1964. Different rules apply to leases granted before this Act came into force.
. *Re Button's Lease* [1964] Ch 263.
. *Griffith* v. *Pelton* [1958] Ch 205.

3.3. Options to renew

3.3.1. An option to renew a lease is not subject to the rule against perpetuities but a contract (which by definition includes an option) to renew a lease for a term exceeding 60 years is invalidated by Law of Property Act 1922.

3.3.2. Care must be taken in drafting such an option to ensure that it does not create a perpetually renewable lease, such leases being converted by Law of Property Act 1922 into terms for 2,000 years which are not terminable by a landlord's notice. To avoid creation of a perpetually renewable lease, the option to renew should be drafted to permit the tenant to renew 'on terms identical to those contained in the present lease *with the exception of the covenant to renew*'. Unless the words which are italicised in the previous sentence are included in the option clause, the new lease will also have to contain a further option to renew, thus creating a perpetually renewable lease.

3.3.3. An option to renew is within the doctrine of privity of estate so that provided the terms of exercise are complied with it can be enforced by the assignee who is in possession of the lease at the date when the option becomes exercisable.

3.3.4. If the exercise of the option is conditional on the tenant's performance of his covenants under the lease, the landlord can insist on strict compliance with the covenants and can refuse to grant the renewal even where the tenant's breach of covenant is merely technical and causes no loss to the landlord.[1] It is common for tenants to limit the strict application of this principle by providing that the breach must be 'material' before it would prevent an option being exercised, although it would appear that this qualification will not permit much departure from the need for strict compliance.[2]

1. See *West Country Cleaners (Falmouth) Ltd* v. *Saly* [1966] 3 All ER 210. See also *Little* v. *Courage Ltd, The Times*, 6 January 1995 (CA).
2. *Commercial Union Life Assurance Co Limited* v. *Label Ink Limited* [2001] L&TR 29.

3.4. Exercise of option

13.4.1. Unless there is provision to the contrary, time is automatically of the essence of the exercise of an option.[1]

13.4.2. Following initial uncertainty Law of Property (Miscellaneous Provisions) Act 1989 has been interpreted as permitting the exercise of an option by a single document signed by the grantee only.[2]

13.4.3. The exercised option is itself an estate contract capable of protection by registration as a notice in registered land or as a Class C(iv) land charge in unregistered land.

1. *United Scientific Holdings Ltd* v. *Burnley Borough Council* [1977] 2 All ER 62.
2. *Spiro* v. *Glencrown Properties Ltd* [1991] 1 All ER 600; followed in *Active Estates Ltd* v. *Parness* [2002] 36 EG 147.

K14. Variation of leases

14.1. Variation of lease

14.1.1. In some cases an informal variation of the terms of the lease (e.g. as to user) to be effective as between the landlord and tenant for the time being will be agreed between the parties. Such a variation is commonly effected by a side letter or informal agreement, leaving the terms of the lease itself unaltered.

14.1.2. Where a variation is made to a contract for the lease the variation may fall within the definition of the disposition of an interest in land within Law of Property (Miscellaneous Provisions) Act 1989, s.2. In essence, in this case the variation agreement must be in writing and signed by both parties and must contain all the terms of the contract between the parties or incorporate the document containing the terms by reference. It is possible for the agreement to be in two identical parts each of which is signed by one of the parties. The precise status of informal variations is uncertain in law.[1]

14.1.3. Where a side letter varies the terms of a lease after it has been granted it may not have to comply with the Law of Property (Miscellaneous Provisions) Act 1989, s.2.[2] In practice it is common for a variation to be personal to the tenant. In any event, the side letter should state whether the variation is for the benefit only of the signatories to the letter or is intended to bind and benefit their successors in title. Where the covenant is not personal the benefit may burden will run with the respective landlord and tenant interests.[3]

14.1.4. An application to register the variation of a registered lease must be accompanied by the instrument effecting the variation and evidence to satisfy the registrar that the variation has effect in law.[4]

1. See *Record* v. *Bell* [1991] 1 WLR 853; *McCausland* v. *Duncan Lawrie* [1996] NPC 94; *Jones* v. *Forest Fencing* [2001] PLSCS 249 and *Grossman* v. *Hooper* [2001] 2 EGLR 82. See also para. B11.1.3.
2. *Tootal Clothing Limited* v. *Guinea Properties Management Ltd* (1992). But cf. *Wright* v. *Robert Leonard (Developments) Ltd*. [1994] NPC 49 and *Paul Godden* v. *Merthyr Tydfil Housing Association* [1997] EWCA Civ 780.
3. See *Lotteryking Ltd* v. *AMEC Properties Ltd* [1995] 2 EGLR 13; *System Floors Ltd* v. *Ruralpride Ltd* [1995] 1 EGLR 48. Personal covenants do not appear to run with the respective landlord and tenant interests. As to this and the effect of the Landlord and Tenant (Covenants) Act 1995, see *BHP Petroleum (Great Britain) Ltd* v. *Chesterfield Properties Ltd* [2002] 1 All ER 821.
4. The Land Registration Rules 2003, r. 78.

14.2. Flats

14.2.1. Any party to a long lease of a flat may apply to the Leasehold Valuation Tribunal under Part IV Landlord and Tenant Act 1987 as amended by the Commonhold and Leasehold Reform Act 2002 for an order for the variation of the lease where the lease fails to make satisfactory provision for:

(a) repair or maintenance of the flat or building;

(b) insurance of the premises;

(c) repair or maintenance of installations;

(d) provision for maintenance of services;

(e) recovery by one party to the lease from another party of expenditure incurred for the benefit of the other party;

(f) computation of service charges under the lease.

14.2.2. The list of provisions which can be varied seemingly only applies to applications under section 35 of the 1987 Act, i.e. individual applications. It appears that applications under section 37, made by a majority of tenants, are not restricted to the items listed above.

14.2.3. Similar but more limited provisions apply to leases of dwellings other than flats in relation to insurance provisions only.

14.3. Surrender and re-grant

Where the variation of the lease extends or exchanges the premises contained in the original demise or extends the length of the original term (but probably only in these situations), it may be deemed to be a surrender of the original lease and a re-grant of a new lease on the varied terms.[1] The new lease created by the variation will be a 'new' lease and will therefore be subject to the provisions of Landlord and Tenant (Covenants) Act 1995. It is preferable in these circumstances to execute a new lease rather than a deed of variation. In the new lease the landlord may need to consider whether he should include provisions (in a lease of commercial premises) dealing with the terms on which he will be prepared to consent to an assignment of the lease (including provision for an authorised guarantee agreement) by the tenant.[2] He may also wish to consider whether an order should be sought excluding the new lease from the renewal provisions of the Landlord and Tenant Act 1954, Part 2.

1. See *Friends Provident Life Office* v. *British Railways Board* [1995] 38 EG 106.
2. See Landlord and Tenant (Covenants) Act 1995 and K10.

14.4. Effect of variation on former tenant

Where there has been a variation of a lease which variation the landlord has an absolute right to refuse or where the lease has been altered after an assignment so as to deprive the landlord of an absolute right of refusal (called a 'relevant variation' under section 18 of Landlord and Tenant (Covenants) Act 1995), a former tenant is not liable to pay any amounts under the covenants in the lease which are referable to the relevant variation. If, for example, a lease is varied after an assignment and the rent payable under the lease is increased, a former tenant who is sued by the landlord for rent unpaid by the assignee will only be liable for the amount of rent which was payable by the tenant before the variation and the former tenant cannot be held liable for the whole of the increased rent. A guarantor's liability under a variation is co-extensive with that of the tenant whose liability is being guaranteed.

K15. Rentcharges

15.1. Definition

15.1.1. A rentcharge is generally defined as being a periodic sum issuing out of land which arises other than out of a landlord/tenant relationship.

15.1.2. Since 22 August 1977 rentcharges have not, with limited exceptions, been able to be created (see the Rent Charges Act 1977, s.2).

15.1.3. If a rentcharge is created in fee simple or for a fixed term of years it is a legal interest which is binding on a subsequent buyer of the land charged irrespective of notice.

15.1.4. A rentcharge for life (e.g. created under a settlement) is equitable only.

15.2. Title

15.2.1. On a sale of unregistered land subject to a rentcharge, in the absence of a provision to the contrary in the contract, the document creating the rentcharge must be abstracted in addition to a 15-year-old good root of title and subsequent documentation.

15.2.2. On registration of land which is subject to a rentcharge, the rentcharge is noted in the charges register of the title to the land.

15.3. Transfer

15.3.1. The benefit of an existing rentcharge must be transferred by deed.[1] The benefit of a covenant for payment of the rentcharge must be expressly assigned.[2] In the absence of express assignment, the obligation to pay remains, but would be unenforceable by action for its recovery other than by distress or re-entry.

Where the rentcharge is registered, Form TR1 should be used and the necessary express assignment of the benefit of the covenant for payment should be inserted in the Additional Provisions Panel of Form TR1.
Grant v. *Edmondson* [1931] 1 Ch 1.

5.4. Extinction

5.4.1. The three main ways in which a rentcharge can come to an end are:

    (a) by release by the owner of the rentcharge to the owner of the land charged;

    (b) by merger when the owner of the rentcharge and the owner of the land charged become the same person;

    (c) by redemption under Law of Property Act 1925, s.191 or under the Rentcharges Act 1977.

5.4.2. Except for rentcharges which are created under Rentcharges Act 1977 (see para. K15.5), the 1977 Act provides that every rentcharge will be extinguished at the expiry of the period of 60 years from 22 August 1977 or on the date when it first becomes payable, whichever is later.

5.4.3. On compulsory redemption of a rentcharge and on proof that an applicant has paid the rentcharge price either to the person entitled to payment or into court, the Secretary of State will issue a redemption certificate. Where a rentcharge is redeemed by agreement or surrender, a deed of release should be drawn up and signed by the parties. Where the land subject to the rentcharge is registered, it is necessary to lodge the deed which ends the liability under the rentcharge at the Land Registry.

5.5. Creation of new rentcharges

5.5.1. Rentcharges Act 1977 prevents the creation of new rentcharges after 22 August 1977, except in the following circumstances:

    (a) where the creation of the charge has the effect of making the land on which it is charged settled land or land held on trust for sale, or where the creation of the charge would have that effect if the land were not already settled land or held on trust for sale;

    (b) creation of an estate rentcharge;

    (c) a rentcharge created under any Act in connection with works on land;

    (d) a rentcharge created under an order of the court.

15.6. Estate rentcharges

15.6.1. An estate rentcharge is a rentcharge created for the purposes either:

(a) of making covenants to be performed by the owner of the land affected enforceable by the rent owner against the owner for the time being of the land; or

(b) of meeting the costs of performance by the rent owner of covenants for the provision of services, the carrying out of maintenance or repairs, or effecting insurance or the making of a payment for the benefit of the land affected by the charge.

15.6.2. Rentcharges created under (a) above represent one method of providing for the effective enforcement of positive covenants.[1] Rentcharges under (b) above are a useful method of reserving service charges out of freehold sales, e.g. where a management company covenants to maintain amenity areas or to provide services, although some lenders may be reluctant to lend money on the security of a property which is subject to such a charge.

15.6.3. The rentcharge must represent a payment for the performance by the rent owner of a covenant (e.g. for insurance, etc., under (b) above) which is reasonable in relation to that covenant. If this provision is not complied with, the rentcharge will not be a valid estate rentcharge unless the amount reserved is only nominal.

It appears, however, that the wording of the rentcharge does not have to be expressed to require a reasonable sum, it is sufficient that the actual sum should be reasonable. Where the amount is no more than 100% of the expenditure incurred on behalf of owners of properties on an industrial estate this has been held to be reasonable.[2]

1. See The purchase deed, para. E1.
2. *Orchard Trading Estate Management Ltd* v. *Johnson Security Ltd* [2002] 2 EGLR 1.

15.7. Apportionment

15.7.1. By Rentcharges Act 1977, s.4, the owner of land affected by a rentcharge which also affects other land not owned by him may in certain circumstances apply to the Secretary of State for a certificate apportioning the rent between the two parcels of land. A similar procedure exists for the apportionment of a rentcharge on a sale of part of land.

15.7.2. By Standard Condition 4.4 and Standard Commercial Property Condition 4.4 the buyer is not entitled to object to an informal apportionment of a rentcharge as being a defect in title.

15.8. Registration of rentcharges

15.8.1. If a rentcharge capable of subsisting as a legal interest is granted out of a registered title, then, in accordance with the fundamental principles of registration of title, the disposition must be completed by registration to be legally effective. In other cases the compulsory registration provisions do not apply to rentcharges. They may, however, be registered voluntarily.[1]

15.8.2. If it appears to the registrar that a right to determine a registered rentcharge is exercisable he may enter notice of the fact in the register.[2] An application for such an entry must be supported by evidence to satisfy the registrar that the applicant has the right to determine the rentcharge and that the right is exercisable.[3]

---

1. Land Registration Act 2002, s.3.
2. Land Registration Act 2002, s.64.
3. Land Registration Rules 2003, r.125.

K16. Sale of tenanted property

See also: Long-term residential tenancies, para. K6
Business premises, para. K7
Right to buy, para. K9

16.1. Introduction

16.1.1. Where a sale is subject to a tenancy, the procedure and steps to be taken equate with those of a vacant possession transaction, but a number of additional matters need to be considered.

16.2. Disclosure of tenancies

16.2.1. It is an implied (and frequently expressed) term of a contract for the sale of land that vacant possession will be given to the buyer on completion. As this will not be the case where the sale is of tenanted property, the contract must include an express term saying that the sale is subject to a tenancy or tenancies, and a copy of the relevant lease or leases (sometimes called tenancy agreements) should be supplied to the buyer with the draft contract. An express condition will also provide that the buyer, having been supplied with copies of the relevant agreements, shall be deemed to purchase with full knowledge of their contents. Standard Condition 3.3.2(a) and Standard Commercial Property Condition 3.3.2 contain provisions to this effect.

16.3. Tenancy terminates before completion

16.3.1. If the tenancy to which the sale is subject comes to an end between contract and completion, the seller should not re-let the property without first consulting the buyer and obtaining his instructions. To re-let the property without the buyer's permission would frequently put the seller in breach of his fiduciary duty to the buyer. Standard Condition 3.3.2(b) provides that the seller is to inform the buyer without delay if any tenancy ends; the seller is then to act as the buyer directs, provided the latter agrees to indemnify the seller against all loss and expense. Standard Condition 3.3.2(c) provides that after the contract is made, the seller is to inform the buyer without delay of any change in the tenancy terms. Standard Commercial Property Conditions 3.3.4 contains similar provisions relating to commercial property.

6.4. Buyer's solicitor

6.4.1. The matters the buyer's solicitor should check include:

(a) the terms of the lease(s) or agreement(s) supplied by the seller's solicitor;

(b) the effect of any security of tenure legislation on the tenant(s);

(c) details of the landlord's obligations under the lease(s) or agreement(s), and in particular whether or not the seller has complied with such obligations;

(d) whether the tenant has complied with all his obligations under the lease or agreement (e.g. as to payment of rent and service charge) and, if not, what steps the seller has taken to enforce the agreement against the tenant;

(e) what variations have been made to the agreements and/or licences granted;

(f) details of any renewal applications or the exercise of an option made by the tenant;

(g) whether the tenants have a right of first refusal (see para. K9.4). This is also an important consideration for the seller's solicitor, since it is the seller who will be guilty of an offence if he fails to comply with the 1987 Act.

6.4.2. The buyer should be informed of the matters listed above and advised accordingly. If it is discovered that the landlord is in breach of any of his obligations (e.g. breach of a repairing covenant) the buyer's solicitor should require the seller to remedy the breach before completion. Alternatively the buyer may insist that the contract contains an express term providing that the seller will indemnify the buyer against liability for such breach since, on completion, the buyer will assume the seller's role as landlord and will thus be liable to the tenant for breaches of the landlord's covenants, even though such breach was committed before the buyer became the owner of the property. In the absence of an express provision for indemnity given by the seller, Standard Condition 3.3.2 and Standard Commercial Property Condition 3.3.7 will prevent the buyer from seeking indemnity from the seller in respect of a breach of covenant committed by the latter.

6.4.3. If the tenant has the benefit of security of tenure legislation, consideration should be given to the question of whether the buyer, on termination of the contractual tenancy, would be able to recover vacant possession of the property if he so wished. In certain circumstances the buyer may be precluded from relying on some of the statutory grounds for possession, e.g. a landlord who purchases premises which are subject to a business tenancy within Landlord and Tenant Act 1954, Pt. II will be unable to regain possession under section 30(1)(g) of that Act until he has owned his interest in the property for a period of five years. On termination of some tenancies the landlord may also be liable to pay compensation to the outgoing tenant, and this contingency should also be discussed with the buyer.

6.4.4. Full enquiries must be made in relation to the amount of rent payable by the tenant, any statutory restrictions on the amount of rent recoverable, and the provisions for review or increase of that rent. Enquiries should also be made to ensure that the rent payable under the lease or agreement has been paid to the date of completion and that no arrears exist. Standard Condition 3.3.2(e) provides that it is for the buyer to satisfy himself whether and how any legislation affects any tenancy and what rent is legally recoverable.

16.4.5. In certain circumstances a landlord who wishes to dispose of his reversionary interest in a block of flats must, before contracting to sell to a third party, first offer the reversion to the 'qualifying tenants'. Where these provisions apply, the buyer must ensure that the seller has correctly fulfilled his obligation to notify the qualifying tenants of their right to purchase the reversion, and that the time-limit for the tenants' right to exercise this option has elapsed. See also Right to buy, para. K9.

16.4.6. Where a tenancy is of a dwelling, and the lease is for a term not exceeding seven years, the landlord may be responsible for repairing the structure and exterior of the premises under Landlord and Tenant Act 1985, ss.11–14. Where these sections apply, they are generally non-excludable and in appropriate cases the buyer should be advised of his potential liability under these provisions.

16.5. Completion

16.5.1. In addition to the usual requirements on completion of the purchase of a freehold property, the buyer should receive:

 (a) the original lease(s) or tenancy agreement(s);

 (b) an authority signed by the seller and addressed to the tenant(s), authorising the tenant(s) to pay future rent to the buyer.

16.6. After completion

16.6.1. Where the premises which have been purchased consist of a dwelling, Landlord and Tenant Act 1985, s.3 requires the new landlord (the buyer) to give written notice of the assignment and of his name and address to the tenant not later than the next day on which rent is payable, or if that is within two months of the date of the assignment, the end of the period of two months. The seller remains liable for breaches of covenant occurring until written notice of the assignment is given to the tenant by either the seller or the buyer.

16.6.2. Landlord and Tenant Act 1987, s.48 also requires the landlord to provide the tenant with an address in England and Wales for service of notices. This section applies where the premises consist of or include a dwelling (including an agricultural holding[1]) but not to premises to which Landlord and Tenant Act 1954, Pt. II applies. Further, until such notice is given, any rent or service charge under the lease is treated as not being due, and is thus not recoverable by action by the buyer. It is therefore in the interests of both seller and buyer to ensure that such notice is given promptly after completion. Notice should be given to the tenant in duplicate, the tenant being requested to sign one copy and return it to the landlord who will, on receipt of the tenant's signed copy notice, have evidence of compliance with this provision.

6.6.3. Section 47 of Landlord and Tenant Act 1987 requires the landlord's name and address to be given on all demands for rent or any other sums payable under the tenancy. This will not satisfy the requirements of section 48.

6.6.4. Section 48 notices should be drafted in terms along the following lines:

Notification by landlord of address for service of notices.

To: (tenant's name)

(tenant's address)

Landlord and Tenant Act 1987, s.48

We (landlord's solicitors' or agents' name and address), on behalf of your landlord (landlord's name and address) hereby give you notice pursuant to section 48(1) of the Landlord and Tenant Act 1987 that your landlord's address for service of notices (including notices in proceedings) is as follows:

(landlord's address for service)

Signed
Dated this   day of   200

6.6.5. However, the Act does not make it clear to whom and at what point the notice should be given. The safest course is to give a section 48 notice to the original tenant on the grant of a new lease and to the assignee following every assignment of the lease.

6.6.6. Since most leases contain a covenant by the tenant to give the landlord a notice of assignment within a specified time after the disposition, the section 48 notice should be given to the new assignee as soon as the change of tenant becomes known. Alternatively managing agents or landlords should print the notice on every rent or service charge demand.

6.6.7. Section 48 notices do not have to be served personally on the tenant; delivery by post should be sufficient to meet the requirement that the landlord 'furnishes' the tenant with the information by notice.[2]

. *Dallhold Estates (UK) Pty Ltd* v. *Lindsey Trading Properties Inc., The Times*, 15 December 1993 (CA).
. Draft notice supplied by Tom Lumsden.

L1. Commonhold

See also:

1.1. Introduction

1.1.1. Parliament legislated for commonhold by Part 1 of the Commonhold and Leasehold Reform Act 2002 (the Act). The Act does not create any new tenures or estates. It does provide for a new way of organising ownership of freehold land. It is designed to deal with the problems that arise in freehold land when there are shared facilities and obligations, and thus is capable of being used when leases have, in the past, usually been the solution. It is intended to avoid the widely appreciated disadvantages of the long leasehold system, and, in the very long term, to replace it. It is expected to be used instead of leases in developments of residential property, and will often be the appropriate legal structure for mixed-use and purely commercial developments.

1.1.2. The foundations for commonhold are laid down in Part 1 of the Act which uses existing concepts of property, company, and trust law, but sets them out in a new way. The Act does introduce some new concepts, but its elements should be familiar to practitioners. Commonhold will be enhanced by further legislation to be made by statutory instruments, including many prescribed standard documents, and the structure will be completed by the work of practitioners making particular arrangements to meet the needs of particular schemes.

1.1.3. The Government hopes that commonhold will replace long leases as a method of owning residential property. It has concluded that long leases are a fundamentally unsatisfactory form of tenure for owner occupation. The added burdens for landlords and the increased rights for tenants in Part 2 of the Act will contribute to making commonhold a more attractive alternative than long leases. Foreign experience suggests that it will be widely used for mixed-use and commercial developments; and that its advantages will be reflected in the value of Units, and an enhanced aggregate value for Units and Common Parts by comparison with long leases and a reversion.

1.2. Types of scheme

1.2.1. While commonhold was primarily introduced to replace long leases of houses and flats it is not limited to residential use. It can be used for commercial and mixed use schemes, and should be examined in detail with clients and planners when considering developments of any size in which there will be any shared use of common facilities.

1.3. Standardisation

1.3.1. The Government intends that many of the documents and procedures for commonhold will be standardised.

1.3.2. Standardisation will be achieved by the use of prescribed documents for many of the elements of commonhold. These will be prescribed in statutory instruments to be laid before Parliament. The Lord Chancellor's Department has conducted an extensive consultation about the form and content of commonhold regulations.

1.3.3. There will be a variety of sanctions and devices to ensure compliance with regulations, including a requirement for a certificate for the directors on incorporation and on the making of certain changes to the Memorandum & Articles, and to the Community Statement. The most important matter to note is that attempted departures from central prescribed elements will be of no effect.

1.4. Structure

1.4.1. A commonhold will be divided into Common Parts and Units. Common Parts will belong to the Commonhold Association, and Units will belong to Unit Holders.

1.4.2. A Commonhold Association must be a company limited by guarantee and incorporated under the Companies Acts. It is expected that the liability of members will be limited to a contribution of £1 in the event of the Commonhold Association's insolvency. Most of the constitution, the Memorandum and Articles of Association, will be prescribed and any purported departure from the prescribed terms will be of no effect at law.

1.4.3. Membership of the Commonhold Association will be restricted to Unit Holders, after an initial phase for development. Unless joint Unit Holders decide otherwise, the first named Unit Holder in the Proprietorship Register of the title to the Unit will have the right to become a member of the Commonhold Association. Practitioners will need to advise clients who intend to hold Units jointly, and will need to take instructions about who should have the entitlement. This will reinforce the need to advise joint purchasers about the trusts on which they hold their property and to set them out clearly. Apart from the initial subscribers, members will not be able to resign but will cease to be members once they cease to be Unit Holders.

.4.4. The Commonhold Association will be managed by a Board of Directors chosen by the members in general meeting. The normal principles of company law and directors' duties will apply. Directors may, but need not, be members of the Commonhold Association. There may be circumstances in which non-member professionals, e.g. management surveyors or accountants, should be members of the Board of Directors.

.4.5. There are some special rules requiring a lack of dissent in general meeting for the Commonhold Association to do certain things, such as creating a charge by way of legal mortgage over the common parts. The Act refers to this requirement that some decisions must be made *nemine contradicente* as being unanimous. There are no restrictions on the identity, nationality, residence, or domicile of Unit Holders; and they may be natural or artificial persons. The legal estate in a Unit may be vested in up to four persons, or in any number of persons in trust for charitable purposes.

.5. Creating a commonhold

.5.1. Registered land

.5.1.1. The land from which a commonhold is to be created must be registered freehold land. A commonhold cannot be created from a leasehold estate. Any unregistered land to be included must first be registered.

.5.1.2. Following consultation, the Land Registry will introduce new forms and procedures to deal with commonhold transactions.

.5.1.3. (i) **Form CM1**

This will deal with the application to register the land as commonhold. If everything is in order, Land Registry will register titles for the Commonhold Common Parts and for each of the Units. The commonhold title will refer to the title numbers of each of the Units. Appropriate restrictions will be entered to reflect the statutory limitations on the powers of disposition of the registered proprietor and of the proprietor of any legal charge of the Common Parts. The title of each Unit will refer to the title of the Commonhold Common Parts so that official copies of it and of the current version of the Commonhold Association Memorandum and Articles of Association and Community Statement can be obtained. The title of each Unit will also contain appropriate restrictions to reflect the statutory limitations on the powers of disposition of the registered proprietor and of the proprietor of any legal charge of the Unit, i.e. that it can normally be transferred only as a whole, and that there may be restrictions on residential leasing.

1.5.1.4. (ii) **Form CM2**

This will be an application made during the transitional period to de-register the land as commonhold. The transitional period is the period during which a developer has registered the land as commonhold but there are no other Unit Holders.

1.5.1.5. (iii) **Form CM3**

This will be an application to register any variations to the Memorandum & Articles of Association of the Commonhold Association or of the Community Statement. Schedule 3 para. 3(1) to the Act provides that no amendment of the Memorandum & Articles of Association will have effect until registered. Any such application must be accompanied by a certificate by the directors that the variations comply with the Act and Regulations under it. Section 33 applies similar provisions to the Community Statement.

1.5.1.6. (iv) **Form CM4**

This will be an application to add land to the commonhold. Unless it is simply an addition to the Common Parts with no restrictions on use then an application with Form CM3 will also need to be made.

1.5.1.7. (v) **Form CM5**

This will be an application to terminate registration of the land as commonhold on termination of the commonhold under sections 43–55 of the Act.

1.5.2.   Non-agricultural land

1.5.2.1. Land that is agricultural, for which there is no test in the Act, cannot be converted into commonhold. It is not thought that agricultural use of land that is already commonhold would lead to its loss of that status or would otherwise be a breach of the Act.

1.5.3.   In touch with the ground

1.5.3.1. Land that is above ground level cannot be included in an application for conversion to commonhold unless all the land down to ground level is the subject of the same application (para. 1 of Schedule 2 to the Act). Any application should ensure that the land to be in the commonhold has adequate rights for foundations and services if it does not include land below ground level.

1.5.3.2. Commonhold land that is below ground level need not include any land above ground level.

1.5.3.3. The Act does not prohibit applications to remove land below a commonhold that would leave the commonhold out of touch with the ground. This is left to the good sense of practitioners and clients, which may not be an adequate protection in all cases. Regulations may deal with this anomaly.

1.5.4. *No land with contingent title*

1.5.4.1. Land that is subject to certain statutory rights of reverter cannot be included in an application for registration as commonhold. The relevant statutes are listed in para. 4 of Schedule 4 to the Act, but may be changed by Regulations.

1.5.5. *Consents*

1.5.5.1. Consent to conversion to commonhold must be obtained in prescribed form from:

- the freehold owners;
- any registered mortgagees of the freehold;
- any leasehold owners of leases of more than 21 years;
- any mortgagees of such leases;
- other persons to be prescribed, such as owners of options and rights of pre-emption protected by registration at the Land Registry.

1.5.5.2. Regulations may prescribe the duration of any consent.

1.5.5.3. In certain circumstances, such as where the person whose consent is necessary cannot be found, the Court may deem that consent has been given or may dispense with the need for consent.

1.5.5.4. When applying for consent, detailed proposals for dealing with any leases and mortgagees should be made, including substituted security and any appropriate compensation. It is to be expected that a long lease will be converted into a Unit, and a mortgage over a long lease should be made to apply to the Unit. It will not be necessary to redeem an existing mortgage over a lease and create a new one over a Unit, and unless the existing mortgage is unsatisfactory it will be futile or counterproductive to do so. A mortgage over the freehold should be redeemed and replaced with mortgages over Units. Mortgagees will, however, be able to impose such conditions as they wish. Any guidance in the CML Lenders' Handbook should be considered.

1.5.5.5. On conversion into commonhold all leases affecting the land will be extinguished. Former leaseholders from whom consent was not required and whose leases have been extinguished will have a right to compensation under the Act. Since the Act is silent, it is possible that any security of tenure (business or residential) that former leaseholders had may survive conversion to commonhold, which may be no less advantageous for landlord or tenant, and which could obviate any need for compensation. New leases and compensation should be dealt with expressly in any proposal for conversion.

1.5.5.6. Conversion is not compulsory and there are no sanctions for any refusal to consent. One hundred per cent agreement is required.

1.6. Forming the Commonhold Association

1.6.1. Company formation is a specialised area of law, and specialist advice should be obtained, although it is expected that 'off the shelf' companies that comply with the requirements of the Act will be available from company formation agents.

1.6.2. The form of the company and the form and contents of its constitution (Memorandum and Articles of Association) will be prescribed.

1.6.3. The directors will be required to certify to the Land Registry that the company meets the prescribed requirements, and will rely on advice from their solicitors (or other professional advisers) when doing so.

1.6.4. Prospective directors should be advised about:

- the extent of their duties under company law,

- the general principles of fiduciary duty, and

- the specific statutory duties and rights under the Act.

Directors' duties under section 35 are particularly important. The directors are to exercise their powers so far as possible so as to permit or facilitate the exercise by each Unit Holder of his rights, and the enjoyment by each Unit Holder of his freehold estate. Directors are also to try to prevent, remedy, or curtail any failure to discharge a Unit Holder's responsibilities.

1.6.5. Directors will have an unusual right to take no action if they reasonably believe that so doing would maintain harmonious relationships between Unit Holders, and would not cause any Unit Holder significant loss or disadvantage.

1.6.6. Parts of the Memorandum and Articles will not be prescribed, or options will be given. Practitioners will need to draft provisions reflecting the particular needs of each proposed commonhold.

1.7. The transitional period

1.7.1. In the case of new developments (unlike in a conversion of blocks of flats) there will not already be long leaseholders to become members of the Commonhold Association and Unit Holders on registration of the land as commonhold.

1.7.2. The freehold landowner will himself apply, with mortgagee's consent if appropriate. The commonhold will be registered without Unit Holders and will be in a transitional period during which the land can easily be deregistered if circumstances so demand, though with mortgagee's and any other required consents.

1.7.3. During the transitional period the rights and duties in the Community Statement do not apply (s.7(2)(b)) and it is expected that Regulations will provide that the functions of the Commonhold Association will not have effect or that the effect will be modified (s.8).

1.8. Developer's rights

1.8.1. If there are not already long leaseholders or other landowners who are seeking to convert their properties into a commonhold then it is likely that there will be a developer who is seeking to provide properties for the market to be sold as Units with shared facilities funded through the Assessment, and the affairs of the community managed through a Commonhold Association. Section 58 allows the transfer of developer's rights to a different person who is to carry on the development business.

1.8.2. Once a Unit has been registered with a different registered proprietor the transitional phase will come to an end, but it would be unfair fully to implement the commonhold while the development process is continuing, and a developer needs flexibility to respond to changing market circumstances. Sections 58 and 59 and Schedule 4 allow a Community Statement to make provision to facilitate the carrying on of 'development business'. That includes:

- building works on the commonhold, and on land removed from or added to the commonhold; marketing and sale of Units;

- addition of land to and removal of land from the commonhold;

- amendment of the Community Statement, including redefinition of the extent of a Unit;

- appointment and removal of directors.

1.8.3. When acting for a purchaser it will be important to check these rights carefully to ensure that facilities that are vital to the purchaser, such as secure parking, cannot be removed, and to advise if the development may turn out materially different from that envisaged. Anything that might add to the expense of a Unit should also be checked.

1.8.4. When drafting development rights practitioners should be careful to ensure that the developer's desire for flexibility does not impinge too much on the marketability of Units.

1.8.5. The developer will have rights during the development phase to appoint and maintain in office directors of his choosing. It will be important in the Articles (or in a members' agreement) to reserve matters that cannot be done without their approval as appropriate.

1.9. The Commonhold Community Statement

1.9.1. A commonhold must have a Commonhold Community Statement which sets out the rights and duties of Unit Holders in relation to the Commonhold Association. The rights belong to each Unit Holder; the duties should be enforceable by the Commonhold Association against each Unit Holder no matter when they arose.

1.9.2. The Commonhold Community Statement must also set out the rights and duties of the Commonhold Association.

1.9.3. Section 16 of the Act provides that a right or duty imposed by a Community Statement affect a new Unit Holder in the same way as they affected a former Unit Holder, and that a former Unit Holder is not to incur any liability or acquire any right under the Community Statement or because of anything done in accordance with section 20. It should be presumed that a new Unit Holder will acquire all the liabilities of the former Unit Holder to the Commonhold Association. Enquiries must be made of the Seller and of the Commonhold Association as to their extent, and they must be dealt with contractually as between Seller and buyer.

1.9.4. Much of the Community Statement will be prescribed, and so the contents will be found in all commonholds. Some parts will be prescribed as options, and the commonhold will have to choose which of the prescribed provisions to include. Other aspects will be left to individual drafting for each commonhold.

1.9.5. A Community Statement may not provide for anything resembling forfeiture, whether of a Unit or other land. It is not known whether regulations will prevent the imposition of forfeiture or pre-emption in any other arrangements such as a members' agreement or a rentcharge.

1.9.6. A Community Statement must define the extent of each Unit by reference to a plan that complies with prescribed standards.

1.9.7. A Community Statement must deal with:

- use of common parts,

- use of Units, and

- insurance repair and maintenance of Units – though such duties may be imposed on Unit Holders or the Commonhold Association.

1.9.8. A Community Statement may not restrict the transfer or legal mortgaging of Units, but may restrict leasing.

1.9.9. A Community Statement must include provisions about its amendment, and should contain provisions (by weighted voting or veto, if regulations permit) to protect changes to vital property interests, such as use of Units and proportions for contributions to the Commonhold Assessment.

1.10. Dealings with Units

1.10.1. A Commonhold Unit is a freehold parcel of land, and so all searches, enquiries and procedures applicable to other freehold land will apply. Additional matters will need to be checked and provided for. Nothing in the Memorandum & Articles of Association of a Commonhold Association or in the Commonhold

Statement is to restrict the right to transfer Units, but practitioners should check for other agreements (e.g. a members' agreement) that may do so, as well as for any restrictions on the register.

1.10.2. Search at Companies House

1.10.2.1. If the Commonhold Association does not exist the client must be advised not to proceed. The land will not qualify as commonhold, and so the peculiar incidents of commonhold land that make it workable, and mean that positive obligations bind Unit Holders without any further formality, will not apply. The Commonhold Association must be reinstated, or a successor Commonhold Association formed, before the client should proceed.

1.10.2.2. Check the Land Registry official copy Memorandum, Articles, and Community Statement. No amendments will take effect until registered and unless they comply with prescribed particulars. Ensure that all changes that required registration at Companies House have been registered.

1.10.3. Accounts, and other claims and liabilities

1.10.3.1. Obtain an account from the Commonhold Association of the Community Assessment for the Unit, and of any other claims against the Unit. Such an account should bind the Community Association and protect the buyer. Require payment, or make reductions to the price, apportionments, or contractual retentions as appropriate.

1.10.3.2. Check the annual budget and estimates. Check the accounts of the Association, and whether other Unit Holders are in arrears. Non-cooperation and arrears may render the property less attractive to a buyer, but are not fatal.

1.10.3.3. Check the company records at Companies House to see whether there is active participation in the Commonhold Association by Unit Holders. Non-participation could put its corporate existence at risk and make management difficult.

1.10.3.4. Check any reserve funds.

1.10.3.5. Check any restricted use areas to see that what the buyer requires from the Common Parts is available to him.

1.10.4. Dealings with part of a Unit

1.10.4.1. Dealings other than with the whole of a Unit require the consent of a Commonhold Association under ss. 21–24 of the Act. Any such consent is likely to be expensive because extensive changes will need to be made to the Community Statement redefining the Unit, adding another Unit, adjusting voting rights, and changing proportions for the Commonhold Assessment. The Commonhold Association should require an indemnity for costs from the applicant, ideally in the Community Statement, but otherwise on each application.

1.10.5. *Joint purchasers*

1.10.5.1. Advise joint purchasers about a choice of member, having checked any penalties for non-membership of the Commonhold Association. Regulations may prescribe or imply provisions governing the exercise of membership rights. If they do not then consider the inclusion of any express provisions in any trust deed governing joint ownership or whether the implied terms of any trust of land will suffice.

1.10.5.2. Notify the Commonhold Association of the transfer of the Unit as well as of the identity of member if the Unit Holders decide to take part in the Commonhold Association as members. There may be financial penalties for non-notification, as well as other agreements.

1.10.6. *Other agreements*

1.10.6.1. Consider any other agreements or restrictions binding on the members.

1.10.7. *Becoming a member*

1.10.7.1. The liability of members is to be limited, probably to £1 in the event of the Commonhold Association's insolvency. Regulations, or any particular Commonhold Community Statement, may require the eligible Unit Holder to become a member. The risks of participation will be minimal, and the costs of non-participation may be considerable because non-members will not have the right to take part in decisions about important matters such as mortgages, expenditure, changes to the Community Statement, and termination. Non-members will not have the 'unfair prejudice' protection of s.459 Companies Act 1985. If the choice remains then Unit Holders should be advised to exercise their right (under para. 7 of Schedule 3 to the Act) to membership of the Commonhold Association.

1.11. **Acting for the mortgagee of a unit**

1.11.1. Comply with the requirements of the CML Lenders' Handbook if applicable.

1.11.2. Regulations may make provision as to what constitutes notice to the Commonhold Association and the exercise of membership rights by mortgagees and receivers whom they appoint. In the absence of such provision, practitioners will need to ensure that these aspects are adequately covered, both in the constitutional documents of the Commonhold Association and in any mortgage of the Unit.

1.12. **Leasing**

1.12.1. *Common parts*

1.12.1.1. There will be no restrictions imposed under the Act on the power of the Commonhold Association to grant leases or let any of the Common Parts. It will be necessary to ensure that lettings do not interfere with any rights of any Unit Holders to use the parts to be let.

1.12.2. *Non-residential units*

1.12.2.1. There will be no restrictions imposed under the Act on the power of Unit Holders to grant leases or let non-residential units. Regulations, or the Commonhold Community Statement of a particular commonhold, may make provision for the enforcement of rights directly against a tenant of a Unit, and for tenants to exercise some of the rights of members of the Commonhold Association.

1.12.3. *Residential units*

1.12.3.1. Section 17 of the Act provides that regulations may impose restrictions on the powers of Unit Holders to grant leases or let residential Units. One possibility being considered is prohibiting the grant of a term of longer than seven (or 21) years. This is not likely to mean that a periodic tenancy will not be able to continue for more than seven years. There may be restrictions on the taking of premiums. Regulations, or the arrangements of a particular commonhold, may make provision for the enforcement of rights directly against a tenant of a Unit, and for tenants to exercise some of the rights of members of the Commonhold Association.

1.13. **Dealing with the Commonhold Association**

1.13.1. A Commonhold Association is not likely to have many assets of value. The Common Parts may be valuable in some cases, but will not often be so, and a person extending credit will not often be well advised to rely on a mortgage of them. Depending on what Regulations (ideally) or particular documentation (less than ideally) say, the Common Parts may be subject to easements in favour of the Units, and, if that is the case, would be of little real commercial use to a purchaser from a mortgagee of them.

1.13.2. The most important right is the right to recover the Commonhold Assessment from Unit Holders from time to time. If security is an important question then the potential creditor should check that the expenditure has been properly authorised, and should take an assignment of the right to collect the Commonhold Assessment. Any such security must be registered at Companies House under Companies Act 1985, s. 395.

1.13.3. If expenditure relates to the subject matter of a reserve fund the potential creditor should check its adequacy and take an assignment of it. Any such security must be registered at Companies House under Companies Act 1985, s. 395.

1.14. Termination

1.14.1. *Striking off*

1.14.1.1. Failure to file the matters prescribed by the Companies Acts as applicable to a company the size of the Commonhold Association will lead to it being struck off and losing its corporate existence as well as incurring civil and criminal liability by the officers of the company.

1.14.1.2. The most important consequence will be that the land will no longer be commonhold, and thus rights and duties between the Units and the Common Parts will be unenforceable. Participants must be warned about the importance of correct filing.

1.14.2. *Voluntary liquidation*

1.14.2.1. The members can put the Commonhold Association into voluntary liquidation if it is solvent. This requires the consent of 100 per cent of the membership. Alternatively, a vote of 80 per cent of the membership to put the association into voluntary liquidation may be passed but this needs to be ratified subsequently by court order.

1.14.2.2. An insolvency practitioner will be required to act as liquidator, and the scheme must deal with the rights and property interests involved.

1.14.3. *Insolvency*

1.14.3.1. The usual remedies of administration and receivership are available.

1.14.3.2. In an insolvent liquidation any reserve funds become available to the creditors. Except in insolvency, reserve funds can only be used for their specified purposes.

1.14.3.3. The Court may make provision for a successor association to take over the assets of the Commonhold Association. It is thought that the Court would not make such an order unless the successor association took over the liabilities of the insolvent association.

1.14.3.4. If Unit Holders or members were not willing to take over the liabilities, the land would lose the peculiar incidents of commonhold land, and rights and duties as between Units and Common Parts would become unenforceable. It is expected that the operation of easements and ordinary restrictive covenants within a commonhold will be excluded, and that enforcement of rights and duties will be exclusively through commonhold rights as set out in the Community Statement.

1.14.3.5. Specialist insolvency advice should be obtained, but Unit Holders are advised to ensure payment of the creditors of a Commonhold Association whenever possible.

1.15. **Alteration of the Register**

1.15.1. Section 6 of the Act imposes limits on the powers of the Land Registry to alter the Register where land has been wrongly registered as commonhold. The Court may grant a declaration that the land should not have been registered as commonhold, but can only do so on the application of a person who claims to have been adversely affected by the registration. On granting such a declaration the Court may make such order as appears to the Court to be appropriate; and, in particular, has power to order that the registration should continue or be altered, or that the land should cease to be commonhold. It can also require the directors or officers of the Commonhold Association to take specified steps, and may require compensation to be paid. In other cases the provisions as to alteration of the register, including rectification, set out in Schedule 4 to the Land Registration Act 2002 will apply.

1.16. **Disputes**

1.16.1. The Landlord and Tenant Act 1985 does not apply to the Commonhold Assessment and there can be no applications to the Leasehold Valuation Tribunal relating to the affairs of a Commonhold Association.

1.16.2. It is expected that all rights will be enforceable only through the Commonhold Association rather than by Unit Holders *inter se.*

1.16.3. Section 35 allows the directors to do nothing if they reasonably believe that so doing would be in the interests of harmonious relationships and would not cause significant loss or disadvantage. It requires them to have regard to the desirability of using arbitration, conciliation, or mediation instead of Court proceedings wherever possible.

1.16.4. Regulations may require participation in one or more ombudsman schemes.

M. DELAY AND REMEDIES

This section contains a brief summary of the matters which are relevant when there is either a delay in completion or a breach of contract. If court proceedings are contemplated reference should be made to a more detailed text which deals with such matters and the advice of a litigation specialist sought without delay.

M1. Delayed completion

1.1.	**Breach of contract**	1.4.	**Compensation for delay**
1.2.	**Time of the essence**	1.5.	**Service of a notice to**
1.3.	**Anticipating delay**		**complete**

See also: Breach of contract, para. M3
Specific performance, para. M4

1.1. Breach of contract

1.1.1. Any delay in completion beyond the contractual date will be a breach of contract entitling the innocent party to damages for his loss, but will not entitle him immediately to terminate the contract unless time was of the essence of the completion date.[1]

1. *Raineri* v. *Miles* [1981] AC 1050.

1.2. Time of the essence

1.2.1. At common law time is impliedly of the essence of the completion date where the subject matter of the contract makes it so, e.g. on the sale of a business as a going concern, or the sale of a wasting asset.[1] In such cases time will therefore be of the essence unless this implication is expressly negatived by a condition to the contrary in the contract.

1.2.2. By Standard Condition 6.1 and Standard Commercial Property Condition 6.1 time is not of the essence of the contract (but can be made so by express contractual condition) unless a notice to complete has been served.

1. See *Pips (Leisure Productions) Ltd* v. *Walton* (1982) 43 P & CR 415 (sale of a 21-year lease). It was also stated *obiter* in *Raineri* v. *Miles* [1981] AC 1050 that time might be considered to be of the essence in chain transactions.

1.3. Anticipating delay

1.3.1. Delay may occur owing to events outside the immediate control of the parties and their solicitors, e.g. postal delays or late receipt of funds from a lender. In such cases there is usually little doubt that completion will take place but it may be postponed for a few days beyond the contractual completion date.

1.3.2. Where delay is anticipated the client, his mortgagee and the other party's solicitor should be informed of the anticipated delay as soon as possible, and of its likely duration and, subject to the solicitor's duty of confidentiality, of the reason for the delay. This is particularly important in chain transactions where the delay in completion of one link in the chain may have serious consequences on the remainder of the transactions in the chain.

1.3.3. Any delay in completion may result in an adjustment being made to the repayment figure due on a seller's existing mortgage. This matter must, therefore, be resolved with the solicitors acting for the lender or the lender himself. Similarly, an advance cheque issued by the buyer's lender is usually delivered subject to the condition that it is used to complete the transaction within a stated number of days of its issue, failing which it must be returned to the lender and a fresh advance cheque issued in time for the rearranged completion date. Such an instruction must be observed by the solicitor acting for the buyer's lender.

1.3.4. Delay in completing one transaction may affect the client's ability to complete a related sale or purchase. If, e.g. completion of the client's sale becomes delayed, he will not have the necessary funds available with which to complete his synchronised purchase transaction, and failure to complete that purchase on the contractual date for completion will be a breach of contract involving the client at the very least in the payment of compensation for the delay. The client should be advised of the delay and of its consequences. Although the solicitor should do his best to ensure that any breach of contract is avoided, e.g. by arranging bridging finance so that the purchase transaction can be completed on time, he is also under a duty to act in his own client's best interests, and in these circumstances completion of the purchase with the assistance of bridging finance may not always represent the best course of action for the client to take. In the example under discussion, the client would probably not be able to utilise the advance cheque from his new mortgage to complete the purchase since there will commonly be a condition attached to it that the advance is conditional on the client's existing mortgage first being discharged. Not being able to utilise the new mortgage advance may result in a large sum being needed by way of bridging finance with a possible consequent heavy commitment to interest on the loan. Alternatively the client may choose to use bridging finance to pay off his first mortgage, thus releasing the mortgage funds for his purchase. Secondly, the client will be in the position of owning two houses until the sale of the first is completed, and if the sale transaction is not completed within a short space of time, this too will represent an onerous commitment for the client. The reason for the delay on the sale transaction and the likely period of delay in its completion must be taken into account when advising the client whether to complete the purchase on time, or to delay completion of the purchase thereby putting himself into breach of that contract. In the converse situation, where the sale can proceed but the purchase is delayed, completion of the sale transaction on the due date will result in the client becoming homeless for an uncertain length of time with consequent problems relating to alternative accommodation for the period of the delay, storage of furniture and other similar problems.

1.3.5. Any delay in completion will be a breach of contract for which the innocent party could recover damages but, where the delay is short, the amount of loss sustained by the breach is unlikely to justify the time and expense of an action for breach of contract. Compensation provisions under the contract may provide adequate redress for the innocent party in these circumstances. If not, an action for breach may be brought, but the amount of compensation received under the contract has to be credited against the amount claimed as damages.

1.4.   Compensation for delay

1.4.1.   The application of the common law provisions relating to payment of compensation for delay might not provide the innocent party with sufficient financial compensation for his loss and are usually replaced by specific contractual provisions providing for compensation. In default of a specific contractual clause dealing with the matter, the common law provisions as set out below would apply.

1.4.2.   *Common law provisions*

In addition to any action for damages, where the delay is the buyer's fault:

(a) the buyer pays the outgoings on the property from the contractual date for completion;

(b) the buyer is entitled to keep the income from the property (if any) from the date of completion;

(c) from the contractual date of completion, the buyer pays interest to the seller on the balance of the purchase price at the general equitable rate.[1]

1.4.3.   Where the delay is the seller's fault:

(a) the seller remains responsible for the outgoings on the property;

(b) he is entitled to keep whichever sum is the lesser of:

(i) the net income of the property; or

(ii) the amount of interest payable by the buyer, calculated as under (c) above.

1.4.4.   Since there will be no income generated by a property which is being sold with vacant possession, the application of these rules effectively means that the buyer has to pay interest when the delay is his fault, but not when the delay is caused by the seller.

1.4.5.   Standard Condition 7.3 provides for the payment of compensation at the 'contract rate' which is defined by Condition 1.1.1(g) as being 'the Law Society's interest rate from time to time in force' (see Appendix V.19), although the parties are free to substitute a different rate by special condition if they so wish.

1.4.6.   Under this condition, compensation is assessed using the 'concept of relative fault', so that whoever is most at fault for the delay pays the compensation; it is not simply a matter of the party who delayed in actual completion being liable to pay compensation. To calculate the liability for compensation, it is necessary to refer back to the timetable of events contained in Conditions 4.1.1 and 4.1.2 in order to establish whether the delay in completion has been caused by a delay in carrying out a procedural step earlier in the transaction. Delay occurring before completion is assessed by reference to the definition of a 'working day' contained in Condition 1.1.1(n) but this definition ceases to apply once completion date has passed, after which every day's delay counts towards the liability for compensation. Having apportioned the delay between the parties, the party who is most at fault for the delay pays compensation to the other for the period by which his delay exceeds the delay of the other party. Compensation under this provision is neither additional to nor in substitution for common law damages, but merely on account.

1.4.7. By Standard Conditions 6.1.2 and 6.1.3, where the sale is with vacant possession and the money due on completion is not paid by 2 p.m. on the day of actual completion (or such other time as may have been agreed by the parties), for the purposes of the compensation provisions only, completion is deemed to have taken place on the next following working day unless the seller had not vacated the property by 2 p.m. (or other agreed time). If this time-limit is not complied with the buyer may find himself liable to pay compensation to the seller under Standard Condition 7.3.

1.4.8. Condition 7.3.4 provides for cases in which the property is tenanted. It allows the seller to recover the income from the property in addition to any compensation to which it may be entitled under condition 7.3.1. While a provision to this effect is commonly encountered in contracts for the sale of commercial property, there is thought to be a risk that, if challenged, it would be struck down as a penalty. A particular source of difficulty is that the object of the compensation is to place the seller in the position it would have been in if the contract had been completed on time: if, however, the contract had been completed on time, the seller would not have received any income from the property following the completion date. The seller may, therefore, need to satisfy the court that the inclusion of the provision is justified by the particular circumstances of the sale.

1.4.9. Standard Commercial Property Condition 7.3 contains the compensation provisions under this form of contract. Condition 7.3 does not operate on the concept of relative fault and effectively only the buyer can be called upon to pay compensation for delayed completion. Where the seller is at fault the buyer is left to his remedy at common law, i.e. an action for damages.

1. According to *Esdaile* v. *Stephenson* (1822) 1 Sim & St 122, the general equitable rate is a mere 4% per annum, but more recently in *Bartlett* v. *Barclays Bank Trust Co. Ltd* [1980] Ch 515 interest was awarded based on the rate allowed on the court's short-term investment account under the Administration of Justice Act 1965.

1.5. Service of a notice to complete

1.5.1. Where it appears that the delay in completion is not likely to be resolved quickly (or at all), consideration may be given to the service of a notice to complete which will have the effect of making time of the essence of the contract so that if completion does not take place on the new completion date specified in the notice the aggrieved party may then terminate the contract forthwith, forfeit or recover his deposit (as the case may be) with accrued interest and commence an action for damages to recover his loss. This then gives the aggrieved party the certainty of knowing that on a stated date he can make a definite decision either to look for a new property to purchase (if a buyer), or resell the property elsewhere (as a seller). It must, however, be remembered that making time of the essence imposes a condition which binds both parties. If, therefore, between the date of service and new date for completion as specified by the notice, unforeseen events occur which result in the previously aggrieved party being unable to complete on the new date, the previously defaulting party could turn round and terminate the contract, leaving the aggrieved party in breach of contract himself. For this reason a notice to complete should never be served as an idle threat. The server must be sure that he will be able to comply with the new completion date himself before serving the notice.

1.5.2.   At common law, the service of a valid notice to complete can only be achieved where the notice specifies a 'reasonable time' for the new completion date, and the party serving the notice is himself ready, able and willing to complete. Both of these conditions present considerable difficulties for the server since it is difficult to assess the 'reasonable time' for the new completion date – a few days ahead may seem quite reasonable to a seller who is anxious to complete the sale, but a few weeks may seem more reasonable to a buyer whose mortgage arrangements have just fallen through. A seller may not be 'ready, able and willing' to complete if he has not discharged his subsisting mortgage over the property.[1] Since it is common practice for a seller to discharge his mortgage after completion, using part of the proceeds of sale with which to make repayment, this condition presents particular difficulties for a seller who wishes to serve a notice on a defaulting buyer. However, a seller will be 'ready, able and willing' to complete even though some of the administrative arrangements have yet to be made, e.g. obtaining charge certificates to hand over at completion. Charge certificates are not a matter of title and do not have to be in the seller's possession for him to complete.[2] Since the decision in *Behzadi* v. *Shaftesbury Hotels Ltd*[3] it seems that a notice to complete (making time of the essence) can be served immediately contractual completion date passes – there is no need for there to have been 'unreasonable delay'.

1.5.3.   The contract normally provides specifically for the service of a notice to complete, such clause being drafted to circumvent the common law problems outlined in the preceding paragraph. Standard Condition 6.8 and Standard Commercial Property Condition 6.8 are such conditions, and provided that the notice expressly refers to the fact that it is served under the provisions of the relevant condition, its service will be valid, the common law requirements being ousted by the specific contractual provisions.

1.5.4.   Standard Condition 6.8 and Standard Commercial Property Condition 6.8 provide that on service of a notice to complete, completion must take place within 10 working days (exclusive of the date of service) and makes time of the essence of the contract.

1.5.5.   Standard Condition 6.8.4 and Standard Commercial Property Condition 6.8.4 requires a buyer who has paid less than a 10% deposit to pay the balance of the full 10% immediately on receipt of a notice to complete.

.5.6. The parties' rights and obligations where a valid notice has been served but not complied with are governed by Standard Conditions 7.5 and 7.6 and Standard Commercial Property Conditions 7.5 and 7.6.

.5.7. Once served, a notice to complete cannot be withdrawn.

.5.8. If compliance with a first notice to complete is waived there is no reason why a second notice to complete, specifying an extended period for compliance should not be served on expiry of the initial notice, or why the period for compliance, with a first notice should not be extended by mutual agreement, but there is some doubt whether time would remain of the essence in such circumstances.

.5.9. Non-compliance with a notice to complete gives the aggrieved party the right to terminate the contract, but is not in itself an automatic termination of the contract.

.5.10. If it is necessary to serve a notice in a situation where the delay is caused by the death of one of the contracting parties, the notice should be addressed to the deceased and his personal representatives at the deceased's last known address. A further copy of the notice should be served on the Public Trustee.

. *Cole* v. *Rose* [1978] 3 All ER 1121.
. *Aero Properties* v. *Citycrest* [2002] All ER(D) 77.
. [1992] Ch 1.

M

M2. Rescission

See also: Conditional contracts, para. B13
Misrepresentation, para. M5

2.1. Introduction

2.1.1. The word rescission is used here in the context of contracts which involve a vitiating element, e.g. misrepresentation, fraud, mistake, and refers to the remedy which is available in these circumstances.

2.1.2. Rescission denotes the restoration of the parties to their pre-contract position by 'undoing' the contract and balancing the position of the parties with the payment of compensation by one party to the other. Damages in the conventional sense of that word are not payable since there will have been no breach of contract.

2.1.3. Since rescission is an equitable remedy, its operation is subject to the general equitable bars which are set out in more detail in para. M4.2.

2.2. Contractual right to rescind

2.2.1. No right to rescind exists except where there is a vitiating element in the contract or a specific contractual right to rescind. Therefore, unless there is a breach of contract entitling one party to terminate his obligations under it, the contract must be performed.

2.2.2. A right to rescind may be given by a specific contractual condition which will specify the circumstances in which the right is to operate and the parties' rights and obligations in the event of rescission taking place. Such a right may be granted, e.g. where the contract is conditional on the fulfilment of a condition.

2.2.3. Under the Standard Conditions of Sale, the right to rescind is available in three situations:

(a) where risk in the property remains with the seller and the property is rendered unusable between contract and completion (Condition 5.1);

(b) for misrepresentation (Condition 7.1);

(c) where a licence to assign is not forthcoming (Condition 8.3).

2.2.4. The Standard Commercial Property Conditions contain similar provisions with the exception of (a) above.

2.2.5. Where the right to rescind is exercised under one of the Conditions referred to in para. M2.2.3 or M2.2.4, the parties' rights on rescission are governed by Condition 7.2 of the Standard Conditions which provides for the repayment of the deposit to the buyer with accrued interest, the return of documents to the seller and the cancellation of any registration of the contract at the buyer's expense. Standard Commercial Property Condition 7.2 is similar in effect.

2.3. Restrictions on the use of contractual rescission clauses

2.3.1. The most commonly encountered type of contractual rescission clause is one which gives the seller the right to rescind if he is unable or unwilling to answer a requisition raised by the buyer. This type of clause is narrowly construed by the courts who will only permit the seller to rescind where the requisition reveals an incumbrance of which the seller was previously unaware and which he is unable to discharge. They thus provide an emergency escape route for a seller in the event that an unforeseen difficulty with the title arises, and cannot be relied on by a seller who had not taken proper care to investigate his own title before drafting the contract, nor where the seller changes his mind after exchange and decides not to go ahead with the contract.[1] The Standard Conditions of Sale (3rd edition) do not, however, contain this type of clause.

2.3.2. This type of clause was examined by the court in *Selkirk* v. *Romar Investments*[2] from which case it appears that the conditions set out below must be satisfied before the court will allow the seller to rely on the clause:

(a) the seller can show some title; if he can show no title at all his withdrawal from the contract will be a breach entitling the buyer to damages;

(b) at the date of the contract the seller was unaware of the defect of which the buyer complains;

(c) the defect is either irremovable or only removable at disproportionate expense;

(d) the seller relies on the condition definitely and within a reasonable time;

(e) the seller is reasonable in exercising his right to withdraw.

2.3.3. The right to rescind under this type of clause can only be exercised in response to requisitions which are raised on the title itself and not in relation to, e.g. the form of the purchase deed or administrative matters relating to completion. Law of Property Act 1925, ss. 42, 45 and 125 gives the buyer non-excludable rights to raise requisitions about certain matters affecting the title and a contractual rescission clause would not be effective in circumstances affected by one of these sections.[3]

1. See *Day* v. *Singleton* [1899] 2 Ch 320.
2. [1963] 3 All ER 994.
3. See Investigation of title, para. D2.

2.4.   Misrepresentation

2.4.1.   In certain circumstances rescission may be available for misrepresentation. This remedy is further discussed in para. M5.

2.5.   Misdescription

2.5.1.   Misdescription results from an error in the particulars of sale, e.g. misdescribing the tenure of the property or the physical extent of the land to be sold.

2.5.2.   If the misdescription is substantial the buyer may ask for rescission of the contract and compensation. A misdescription is substantial if its effect is substantially to deprive the buyer of his bargain.[1]

2.5.3.   If the misdescription is not substantial the buyer can be forced to complete but may seek compensation by way of an abatement from the purchase price.

2.5.4.   A misdescription of the property will usually also amount to a misrepresentation and it is more common nowadays to pursue a remedy under Misrepresentation Act 1967 than for misdescription.

1. See generally *Watson* v. *Burton* [1957] 1 WLR 19.

2.6.   Non-disclosure

2.6.1.   Non-disclosure arises out of the seller's failure to comply with his duty of disclosure. The seller's duty of disclosure is discussed in para. B5.

2.6.2.   Where the effect of the non-disclosure is substantial, i.e. its effect is substantially to deprive the buyer of his bargain, the buyer may seek rescission of the contract.

2.6.3.   If the non-disclosure is not substantial the buyer can be forced to complete but may seek compensation by way of an abatement to the purchase price.

2.7.   Mistake

2.7.1.   Where the parties have entered a contract under a fundamental mistake of fact, the contract is void at common law. The transaction will be set aside by the court and the buyer is entitled to recover any money paid. Examples of this principle are mainly confined to situations where the subject matter of the contract had been destroyed before the contract was made[1] or where the buyer unknowingly contracts to buy property which he already owns.[2]

2.7.2.   A mistake as to the quality of the subject matter of the contract will not normally have the effect of making the contract void at common law, although equity may in such circumstances refuse specific performance. If the effect of the mistake is to make the subject matter of the contract something entirely different from that which the parties thought it to be, the contract may be avoided.[3]

.7.3. A mistake as to the identity of the contracting parties seems not to affect a written contract for the sale of land. The court treats the parties named in the contract as being the correct parties to it and will enforce the contract on that basis.[4]

. i.e. *res extincta*: see, e.g. *Hitchcock* v. *Giddings* (1817) 4 Price 135.
. i.e. *res sua*: see, e.g. *Cooper* v. *Phibbs* (1865) 17 I Ch R 73.
. See generally *Bell* v. *Lever Bros Ltd* [1932] AC 161.
. *Hector* v. *Lyons* (1989) 58 P & CR 156. The principles relating to mistaken identity outlined in *Lewis* v. *Averay* (*No.2*) [1973] 2 All ER 229 are inapplicable in this situation.

.8. Limitation periods

.8.1. Where the right to rescind arises out of a contractual provision, it must be exercised within the time-limits given within the condition, or if no time is specified within a reasonable time. An action based on a contractual rescission clause is subject to the normal six-year limitation period under Limitation Act 1980 unless the contract was by deed when a 12-year limitation period would be available.

.8.2. Actions for rescission arising out of the general law principles, e.g. for misdescription are subject to the equitable doctrine of laches.

M3. Breach of contract

See also: Delayed completion, para. M1
Specific performance, para. M4
Misrepresentation, para. M5
Covenants for title, para. M9

3.1. Introduction

3.1.1. This section is intended as a brief overview of the subject under discussion. It is not intended to be used as a substitute for the advice of an experienced litigation solicitor. Prompt action by someone knowledgeable in the area of litigation is often required where problems arise in relation to a breach of contract.

3.1.2. Remedies for breach of contract depend on whether the breach is of a condition in the contract, entitling the aggrieved party to terminate the contract and/or claim damages, or of a warranty, entitling the aggrieved party to claim damages only.

3.1.3. A term of the contract will be a 'condition' if it is a major or fundamental term. Minor terms are classified as 'warranties'. In some cases it is not possible to classify a term as specifically falling into one or other of these categories until the consequences of the breach can be seen. Where the consequences are serious or far reaching, the unclassified term will be treated as a condition. In the converse situation it will be a warranty only. The terminology or labelling which the parties themselves have attached to the various terms of the contract is not conclusive as to their classification. In conveyancing contracts all terms are usually called 'conditions', but in law some of those terms would only have the status of warranties.[1]

3.1.4. An action on a simple contract, i.e. one not made by deed, has a limitation period under Limitation Act 1980 of six years running from the date of the breach. A limitation period of 12 years applies where the contract was made by deed. A three-year limitation period applies where the amount claimed includes damages for personal injury or death. In some cases, Latent Damage Act 1986 may extend the limitation period.

.1.5. On completion the terms of the contract merge with the purchase deed in so far as the two documents cover the same ground, and an action on the contract is no longer sustainable after completion except where it is based on a contract term which remains extant despite completion taking place. For this to happen the contract would generally have to contain a non-merger clause which expressly allowed a particular clause or clauses to remain alive after completion,[2] although sometimes the court may imply such an intention from the subject matter of the clause. If an action on the contract cannot be maintained, the buyer may have to attempt to pursue a remedy under the covenants for title or title guarantee (see para. M9).

.1.6. In any situation where the buyer suspects that the seller will or may default, consideration should be given to protecting the buyer's contract by entry of a notice (in registered land) or as a Class C(iv) land charge (if the seller's title is unregistered).

. See *Cehave* v. *Bremer* [1976] QB 44.
. See Standard Condition 7.4 and Standard Commercial Property Condition 7.4.

.2. Specific performance

.2.1. In sale of land cases an action for specific performance may provide an alternative remedy to an action for damages. This remedy is discussed in para. M4.

.3. Exclusion clauses

.3.1. An exclusion clause which purports to exclude liability under the contract must be incorporated in the contract if it is to be valid. In the case of a written contract, an exclusion clause contained within the writing is deemed to be incorporated whether or not the parties have read the document or were capable of reading it. In such circumstances illiteracy or inability to read English is no defence.[1]

.3.2. Exclusion clauses must be specifically drafted to fit the breach which has occurred; thus a clause which excludes liability for breach of condition will not protect against a breach of warranty and vice versa.[2]

.3.3. Any ambiguity in the wording of the clause will be construed against the party who is seeking to rely on the clause.

.3.4. The clause normally only affords protection to the parties to the contract. Therefore an action in tort may be brought against a third party who caused the loss of which the plaintiff complains. He will be unable to shelter behind the protection of the clause since he does not enjoy privity of contract with the plaintiff.[3]

.3.5. Exclusion clauses contained in contracts for the sale of land (except those relating to the exclusion of liability for misrepresentation) are not subject to the reasonableness test in Unfair Contract Terms Act 1977.

1. See *L'Estrange* v. *Graucob* [1934] 2 KB 394; *Thompson* v. *LMS Railway* [1930] 1 KB 41.
2. See *Curtis* v. *Chemical Cleaning Co.* [1951] 1 KB 805.
3. See *Adler* v. *Dickson* [1955] 1 QB 158.

3.4. Delayed completion

3.4.1. Unless time was of the essence of the completion date, or had been made so by service of a notice to complete, a completion which takes place later than the date specified in the contract does not of itself entitle the aggrieved party to terminate the contract.

3.4.2. Late completion will, however, be a breach of warranty entitling the aggrieved party to recover damages for any loss suffered as a result of the delay.[1]

1. *Raineri* v. *Miles; Wiejski (Third Party)* [1981] AC 1050 and see para. M1.4.

3.5. Damages for breach

3.5.1. Damages for breach of a contract for the sale of land are assessed under the normal contractual principles established in *Hadley* v. *Baxendale*.[1] Thus, subject to establishing causation, damages for losses naturally flowing from the breach may be claimed and in addition reasonably foreseeable consequential loss.

3.5.2. The quantum of damages under the consequential loss head are limited to loss which was reasonably foreseeable by the defaulting party in the light of the facts known by him (or by his agent) at the date when the contract was made (not at the date of the breach of contract).

3.5.3. The starting point for damages for breach of a contract for the sale of land is the difference between the contract and market prices of the property at the date of the breach. To this may be added actual financial loss suffered as a result of the breach, e.g. wasted conveyancing costs, legal costs involved in the purchase of another property, interest payable on a mortgage or bridging loan, costs of removal or storage of furniture, costs of alternative accommodation pending purchase of another property.[2]

3.5.4. Loss of development profit, or loss of profit on a sub-sale, can only be claimed if the defendant was aware of the plaintiff's proposals for the property at the time the contract was made.[3]

3.5.5. Where the buyer defaults and the seller makes a loss on the resale, that loss can be claimed as damages but, if the seller makes a profit on the resale, he would have to give credit for the amount of the profit in his action since he is only entitled to recover his financial loss and is not entitled to benefit from the buyer's breach. The purpose of contractual damages is to place the parties in the position in which they would have been had the contract been duly performed. There is no punitive element in the assessment of damages.

3.5.6. As a general principle of contractual damages, it is only possible to recover for financial loss, and no claim can be made in respect of mental distress suffered as a result of the defendant's breach. The practice of awarding a nominal sum in respect of damages for mental distress established by *Jarvis* v. *Swans Tours*[4] seems to be confined to leisure and pleasure contracts, e.g. holiday contracts and contracts for leisure activities.

3.5.7. Damages can normally only be claimed in respect of losses which have occurred since the contract was made; thus there is generally no possibility of recovering expenses incurred at the pre-contract stage of the transaction, e.g. for a wasted surveyor's report or search fees.[5]

3.5.8. The plaintiff must have attempted to mitigate his loss, e.g. by trying to purchase another similar property (as disappointed buyer) or by attempting to resell the property (as disappointed seller). The attempt to mitigate should be made; otherwise the award of damages may be reduced because of the failure to mitigate. If the plaintiff attempts to mitigate and in so doing increases his loss, the defendant will be liable for the increased loss.

3.5.9. Credit must be given in the claim for damages for any compensation received under Standard Condition 7.3 or similar provision or for any deposit forfeited by the seller (see para. M1).

3.5.10. Actions claiming a sum under £50,000 will be brought in the county court; above that limit, the High Court has jurisdiction. Actions brought in the county court for sums not exceeding £1,000 may be referred to arbitration (but not if there is a dispute over a point of law) in which case no costs are normally awarded in the action. In other county court cases, a successful litigant may be penalised as to costs if he does not recover more than £1,000 in his judgment, or does not recover more than the amount paid into court by the defendant prior to the hearing. The question of costs must be fully discussed with the client before the decision to start proceedings is taken, since in some cases the action for breach of contract may not be cost effective for the client.

. (1854) 9 Exch 341.
. See, e.g. *Beard* v. *Porter* [1948] 1 KB 321.
. *Diamond* v. *Campbell-Jones* [1961] Ch 22; *cf. Cottrill* v. *Steyning and Littlehampton Building Society* [1966] 2 All ER 295.
. [1973] QB 233; and see *Bliss* v. *South-East Thames Regional Health Authority* [1987] ICR 700.
. But see *Lloyd* v. *Stanbury* [1971] 2 All ER 267 where pre-contract expenditure including money spent on repairs to the property was recovered.

3.6. **Action in tort**

3.6.1. If an action in contract is not possible, e.g. a valid exclusion clause prevents the claim, an action in tort may be considered. The limitation period for such an action will usually be six years from the time the tort was committed, but a three-year limitation period applies where the claim includes damages for personal injury or death. Actions in tort may also be considered where it is desired to sue a third party who was not privy to the contract. Most actions of this type will lie in negligence which imposes a fairly onerous burden of proof on the plaintiff. The quantum of damages is assessed using different principles and in general damages for pure economic loss cannot be claimed.[1]

1. Damages are awarded following the principles laid down in *The Wagon Mound* [1961] AC 388. See *Junior Books* v. *Veitchi* [1983] 1 AC 520 and *Murphy* v. *Brentwood District Council* [1991] 1 AC 398 relating to economic loss.

3.7.   Misrepresentation

3.7.1.   Where an action on the contract cannot be sustained an action in misrepresentation may still be viable. This remedy is further discussed in para. M5.

3.8.   Freezing order

3.8.1.   Although not a conventional sale of land remedy, a freezing order could be obtained if it was suspected that the defendant was intending to remove his assets from the jurisdiction in order to avoid liability. Such an order would not provide a direct remedy but would protect the plaintiff's position as an interim measure. Prompt action is required. Where the land is registered, a freezing order should be reflected in the register by the entry of a restriction in Form AA.[1] A person who has applied to the court for a freezing order can apply for a restriction in Form CC.[2]

1. Land Registration Rules 2003, r.93 and Sched. 4.
2. Land Registration Rules 2003, r.93 and Sched. 4.

3.9.   Frustration

3.9.1.   Where the contract has become impossible of performance due to an unforeseen act which is beyond the control of both parties, the contract is frustrated and the parties' rights and obligations are terminated without there being liability for breach on either side. The parties' rights in this situation are, in the absence of specific contractual provision, governed by Law Reform (Frustrated Contracts) Act 1943 which aims to restore the parties to their pre-contract position without imposing penalties. Frustration is usually raised as a defence to an action for breach of contract and, if successfully pleaded, provides an absolute defence to the defendant.

3.9.2.   Although the general view is that the doctrine of frustration does not apply to contracts for the sale of land, dicta from the House of Lords in *National Carriers Ltd* v. *Panalpina (Northern) Ltd*[1] suggest otherwise. It is therefore possible that the defence of frustration might be allowed in a situation where, e.g. the land which was the subject of the sale was totally destroyed by landslip into the sea between the dates of contract and completion. If the land was destroyed before the date of the contract, the contract would be void for common mistake. Frustration would not apply where the property burned down between contract and completion. Neither does it apply where the property is subject to a compulsory acquisition order.[2]

1. [1981] AC 675.
2. *E. Johnson & Co (Barbados) Ltd* v. *NSR Ltd* [1996] EGCS 133.

.10. Return of deposit

.10.1. Where the buyer defaults on completion, the seller will wish to forfeit the deposit, but Law of Property Act 1925, s.49(2) gives the court an absolute discretion to order the return of the deposit to the buyer. A contractual clause attempting to negate the provisions of section 49 is of no effect.[1] If the deposit is more than 10% the buyer may be able to argue that it is not a reasonable amount and is a penalty, in which case the court may order its return to the buyer.

.10.2. Where the seller defaults on completion the buyer will have to bring an action under Law of Property Act 1925, s.49(2) to recover his deposit.

.10.3. Under section 49, the court appears to have power to return all of the deposit or none of it to the buyer. There is no discretion to order the return of part of the deposit even where this course of action would represent the most equitable way of dealing with the position between the parties. It seems, however, that the court may be prepared to order the return of the whole deposit to the buyer on condition that the buyer reimburse certain expenses to the seller, which would seem to be a fair way round the restrictions imposed by section 49.[2]

. *Country & Metropolitan Homes Surrey Ltd* v. *Topclaim Ltd* [1996] 3 WLR 525.
. See *Universal Corporation* v. *Five Ways Properties* [1979] 1 All ER 552; *James Macara Ltd* v. *Barclay* [1945] KB 148; cf. *Dimsdale Developments (South East) Ltd* v. *De Haan* (1984) 47 P & CR 1.

.11. Trade Descriptions Act 1968

.11.1. Under Trade Descriptions Act 1968, it is an offence to make a false statement in a contract for the supply of services (including land). The Act applies where the seller is acting in the course of a business and so would be applicable where, e.g. a buyer was purchasing land from a builder, but not in an ordinary residential purchase between private individuals. If an action in contract or misrepresentation cannot for some reason be sustained, it may be worth considering reporting a 'false statement', e.g. a misrepresentation about the quality of the property, to the local trading standards office and asking them to pursue a prosecution under the Act. Such a prosecution does not afford a direct remedy for the client. On conviction for the offence it would, however, be possible for the client to ask the court for a compensation order under Powers of Criminal Courts Act 1973, s.35. Where the conviction is obtained in the magistrates' court, the compensation order cannot exceed £2,000 in respect of each offence.[1]

. See *Breed* v. *Cluett* [1970] 2 QB 459 where such an order was obtained following a builder's conviction under this Act for making false statements about the availability of NHBC protection on a new house.

.12. Property Misdescriptions Act 1991

.12.1. This Act which came into force on 4 April 1993 creates a criminal offence which is committed where a false or misleading description is applied to certain aspects of the property as listed in regulations made under the Act in the course of an estate agency or property development business. The offence is of strict liability and can be committed by publishing a misleading photograph of property as well as by misdescribing property orally or in writing.[1] An action must generally be brought within three years of the alleged offence. Enforcement of the Act is through criminal proceedings brought by the Trading Standards Department for the area. Some estate agents are now seeking an indemnity from the seller in respect of liability under this Act. The seller should be advised not to accept such a clause.

1. In *Lewin* v. *Barratt Homes Ltd* [1999] EGCS 139 the defendants were held liable under this Act in relation to 'statements' made in photographs and through the display of a show house.

3.13. MIG policies

3.13.1. A lender who benefits from the proceeds of a MIG policy does not need to give credit for this sum when quantifying damages.[1]

1. *Europe Mortgage* v. *Halifax Estate Agencies* [1996] NPC 68.

3.14. Checklist

3.14.1. A client who is encountering problems with a property transaction will probably first seek the advice of the person who is advising him in the sale or purchase. A checklist of the main points to be considered when discussing the client's problems is set out below. These matters should be taken into consideration when deciding whether and how to pursue a remedy for breach of contract and cover the main points of information which will be needed by the litigation department if the matter is handed to them for further action. In addition to the matters listed below, the person taking instructions should obtain a complete history of the conveyancing transaction from the client, including a detailed timetable of the events leading to the present dispute, and should obtain from the client either the original documents relevant to the matter, or copies of them.

3.14.2. The following is a checklist of the main points to be considered:

    (a) Has there been a breach of contract?

    (b) If so, what type of breach, i.e. of condition or warranty?

    (c) What remedy does the client want, e.g. damages or specific performance?

    (d) Is there a valid exclusion clause which might prevent the claim?

    (e) When did the limitation period start to run?

    (f) What (approximately) is the total of the client's financial loss?

    (g) How much of that loss would be recoverable, bearing in mind the rules or remoteness of damage?

    (h) Would the costs of an action be justified?

    (i) Who should be sued, e.g. other party to the contract, solicitor, surveyor?

    (j) If a claim cannot be made in contract, is there a viable alternative action e.g. in tort or for misrepresentation?

M4. Specific performance

See also: Breach of contract, para. M3

4.1. Introduction

4.1.1. Although this is an equitable remedy which is granted at the discretion of the court, an order for specific performance is not uncommon in sale of land cases where, since no two pieces of land are identical, an award of damages would be inadequate compensation for the injured party's loss.[1]

4.1.2. The claim can be made either on its own, or in conjunction with a claim for damages or rescission, depending on the circumstances.

4.1.3. Specific performance cannot generally be awarded for breach of a contract to grant a loan (whether secured or unsecured).[2] It would not therefore be available where a lender, in breach of contract, withdrew his offer of mortgage.

. *Hall* v. *Warren* (1804) 9 Ves 605.
. *Rogers* v. *Challis* (1859) 27 Beav 175.

4.2. General bars to the award

4.2.1. As an equitable remedy, the award of a decree of specific performance is subject to the usual principles of equity. It will not therefore be awarded where:

(a) an award of damages would adequately compensate for the loss sustained by the breach;

(b) one of the contracting parties lacks full contractual capacity;

(c) the contract contains a vitiating element, e.g. mistake, fraud, illegality;

(d) the enforcement of the order would require the constant supervision of the court;

(e) a third party has acquired an interest for value in the property;

(f) the award would cause exceptional hardship to the guilty party;

(g) the seller cannot make good title.

4.3. Delay

4.3.1.   The Limitation Acts do not usually apply to equitable remedies, but the doctrine of laches (lapse of time) does. The remedy may therefore be barred if the innocent party is dilatory in seeking an award.[1]

4.3.2.   Unlike a common law action for breach of contract, the injured party can apply for a decree before a breach of contract has actually occurred (i.e. before contractual completion date) provided that he can show that a serious breach is likely to take place if the court does not intervene.[2]

4.3.3.   Laches will not bar the application where the buyer is already in possession of the property.[3]

1. *Lazard Brothers & Co. Ltd* v. *Fairfield Properties Co. (Mayfair) Ltd* (1977) 121 SJ 793.
2. *Marks* v. *Lilley* [1959] 2 All ER 647; *Hasham* v. *Zenab* [1960] AC 316, PC.
3. *Williams* v. *Greatrex* [1957] 1 WLR 31.

4.4. Damages in lieu

4.4.1.   Subject to the above principles the injured party always has the right to apply for a decree of specific performance, but there is no guarantee that an award will be forthcoming in any given circumstances. If, in a situation where specific performance would otherwise be available to the injured party, the court decides not to make such an order, it may award damages in lieu of specific performance under Supreme Court Act 1981, s.50. Such damages are assessed using normal contractual principles as outlined in para. M3.

4.4.2.   Where an award of specific performance has been made but has not been complied with, the injured party may return to the court asking the court to withdraw the order and to substitute the decree of specific performance with an award of damages.[1]

1. *Johnson* v. *Agnew* [1980] AC 367.

4.5. Standard Conditions of Sale and Standard Commercial Property Conditions

4.5.1.   Where a notice to complete has been served by the seller under Standard Condition 6.8 and is not complied with, by Standard Condition 7.5, the innocent party's right to apply for a decree of specific performance is not excluded. The Standard Commercial Property Conditions contain identical provisions.

M5. Misrepresentation

1. Definition

1.1. A misrepresentation is an untrue statement of fact which is relied on by the aggrieved party, which induces him to enter the contract, and as a result of which he suffers loss.

1.2. The statement must be of fact, not law.[1] A statement of opinion is not actionable unless it can be proved that the opinion was never genuinely held.[2]

1.3. A misrepresentation may be fraudulent, i.e. deliberately dishonest within the definition of fraud laid down in *Derry* v. *Peek*,[3] negligent, i.e. made carelessly without having checked the facts, but not necessarily negligent within the tortious meaning of that word, or innocent, i.e. a genuine and innocently made mistake.

1.4. The representation can be made by the seller's conduct. In *Taylor* v. *Hamer*[4] the seller was guilty of misrepresentation because her conduct had led the buyer to believe that certain items would be included in the sale. The items were present when the buyer inspected the property but were removed before exchange of contracts.

[1] The distinction between fact and law is not always clear; see *Solle* v. *Butcher* [1950] 1 KB 671; and *Pankhania* v. *Hackney London Borough* [2002] All ER(D) 22.
[2] *Edgington* v. *Fitzmaurice* (1885) 29 Ch 459.
[3] (1889) 14 App Cas 337.
[4] *Taylor* v. *Hamer* [2002] EWCA Civ 1130.

2. Fraudulent misrepresentation

2.1. Where the misrepresentation has been made fraudulently, the aggrieved party may bring an action in tort for deceit which may result in rescission of the contract and damages.

2.2. The party who alleges fraud must prove fraud. This places a very onerous burden of proof on the plaintiff in the action and, except where the evidence of fraud is indefeasible, it is more usual to treat the misrepresentation as having been made negligently and to pursue a remedy under Misrepresentation Act 1967.

5.3.   Actions under Misrepresentation Act 1967

5.3.1.   The claimant must show that he has an action in misrepresentation as defined in para. M5.1, after which the burden of proof shifts to the defendant who, in broad terms, has to disprove negligence.

5.3.2.   A misrepresentation is negligent if the defendant cannot prove that he had grounds for belief and did believe the statement he made was true up to the time the contract was made. There is therefore a duty to correct a statement which, although being true at the time when it was made, subsequently becomes untrue.

5.3.3.   The remedies for a negligent misrepresentation are rescission of the contract and damages.

5.3.4.   If the defendant successfully establishes the defence of grounds and belief outlined in para. M5.3.2, thus showing that the misrepresentation was truly innocent, rescission is available, but not damages.

5.3.5.   Although Misrepresentation Act 1967 allows a party to ask for rescission of the contract, the award of the remedy remains within the equitable jurisdiction of the court and is thus discretionary and subject to the equitable bars.[1]

5.3.6.   If none of the equitable bars applies, but nevertheless the court decides not to grant rescission, it may instead award damages in lieu of rescission to the plaintiff.[2]

5.3.7.   Damages under Misrepresentation Act 1967 are awarded on a tortious basis[3] under Misrepresentation Act 1967, s.2(2).

5.3.8.   An award of damages can be made under both the subsections of section 2, i.e. an award in lieu of rescission and an award to compensate the claimant for his loss, subject to the overriding principle that the claimant cannot recover more than his actual loss; thus the awards under the two subsections are not cumulative.

5.3.9.   Rescission is only likely to be awarded where the result of the misrepresentation is substantially to deprive the claimant of his bargain.[4]

5.3.10.   An action in misrepresentation does not arise out of the contract, since the misrepresentation is a non-contractual statement which has the effect of inducing the contract. Neither does it arise out of tort. The limitation periods prescribed by Limitation Act 1980 do not therefore apply in this situation and it seems that the limitation period for an action based on misrepresentation relies on the equitable doctrine of laches.

5.3.11.   Where a misrepresentation has become incorporated as a minor term of the contract it is possible by Misrepresentation Act 1967, s.1 to treat the statement as a mere representation and to pursue a remedy under Misrepresentation Act 1967. This option would benefit the claimant by giving him the right to ask for rescission of the contract as well as damages. If his action were confined to breach of a minor contractual term his only available remedy would be damages.

. The equitable bars are listed in para. M4.2.
. Misrepresentation Act 1967, s.2(1).
. *Chesneau* v. *Interhome, The Times,* 9 June 1983, CA; and see *Royscott Trust* v. *Rogerson* [1991] 2 QB 297.
. See *Gosling* v. *Anderson, The Times,* 8 February 1972; *cf. Museprime Properties Ltd* v. *Adhill Properties Ltd* (1990) 61 P & CR 111.

5.4. Imputed knowledge

5.4.1. Knowledge gained by a solicitor in the course of a transaction is deemed to be known by the solicitor's client whether or not this is in fact the case. Thus where a solicitor makes an incorrect reply to pre-contract enquiries, basing his reply on an erroneous assessment of the title deeds, the solicitor's knowledge and also his misstatement is attributable to the client who will be liable to the buyer in misrepresentation.[1] In such a situation the solicitor would be liable to his own client in negligence.

5.4.2. The converse situation is also true. If, for example, the seller makes a misrepresentation to the buyer personally, but the misrepresentation is later corrected in correspondence between the seller's solicitors and the buyer's solicitors, the buyer is deemed to know of the correction (even if not actually told by his solicitor) and would not in these circumstances be able to sustain an action for misrepresentation against the seller.[2]

. *Cemp Properties* v. *Dentsply* [1989] 35 EG 99.
2. *Strover* v. *Harrington* [1988] Ch 390.

5.5. Exclusion clauses

5.5.1. By Misrepresentation Act 1967, s.3, as amended by Unfair Contract Terms Act 1977, s.8, any clause which purports to limit or exclude liability for misrepresentation is only valid in so far as it satisfies the reasonableness test laid down in section 11 and Schedule 2 Unfair Contract Terms Act 1977.

5.5.2. The reasonableness test is applied subjectively, in the light of the circumstances which were known to the parties at the time when the contract was made. It therefore depends on the circumstances of each particular case as to whether the exclusion clause is valid in that situation. There is no guarantee that any given form of wording will satisfy the test unless and until the clause is subjected to the scrutiny of the court. Such clauses therefore require great care in drafting. Fraudulent misrepresentation should (if required) be excluded by express wording to this effect.

5.5.3. Standard Condition 7.1 purports to limit the seller's liability for, *inter alia,* misrepresentation. The validity of this clause is subject to its satisfying the reasonableness test on the facts of each particular case. Standard Commercial Property Condition 7.1 contains an identical provision which will not be subject to the reasonableness test unless one of the parties to the contract is dealing as a consumer (i.e. is a private individual buying or leasing for a non-business purpose).

5.5.4. The majority of misrepresentation actions arising out of property transactions appear to result from erroneous replies to pre-contract enquiries. Some standard forms of pre-contract enquiries (but not the Seller's Property Information Form used in Protocol transactions) have an exclusion clause printed on them. This exclusion clause is also subject to the reasonableness test.[1]

1. See *Walker* v. *Boyle* [1982] 1 All ER 634 where an exclusion clause contained in a then current edition of a standard form of pre-contract enquiries failed the reasonableness test. In the same case, the exclusion clause contained in the 19th edition of the National Conditions of Sale was held to be invalid for the same reason.

M6. Other causes of action

See also: Rectification and indemnity, para. M7
Solicitor's negligence, para. M10

6.1. Introduction

6.1.1. In certain circumstances it may be possible or necessary to seek a remedy from someone other than a party to the contract. Such action will normally have to be brought in tort since no privity of contract will exist between the potential parties to the action.

6.1.2. A non-exhaustive list of suggestions of alternative sources of action which might be relevant if an action on the contract was unavailable is included here.

6.2. Solicitor's liability

6.2.1. A solicitor who is guilty of bad professional work may be reprimanded by the Office for the Supervision of Solicitors who additionally may order the solicitor to rectify a mistake at his own expense or to waive his costs or repay costs to the client. The Office can also order the solicitor to pay compensation of up to £5,000 to the client.

6.2.2. A solicitor who has been negligent in the conduct of a client's affairs can be sued in negligence.

6.2.3. If a client has suffered loss as a result of default by a solicitor which loss cannot be recovered from any other source, the Solicitors' Compensation Fund may be able to assist.

6.2.4. A solicitor's duty of care is owed not only to his own client, but in certain circumstances to third parties as well.[1] It may therefore be possible in some circumstances for an aggrieved buyer to sue his seller's solicitor in negligence[2] although the court has held that in a normal conveyancing transaction the seller's solicitor does not owe a duty of care to the buyer.[3]

6.2.5. Where the solicitor's own client had been held liable for, e.g. breach of contract in circumstances where the breach was caused by the party's solicitor, the solicitor can be required to indemnify the client against his liability for damages.[4]

1. See *Ross* v. *Caunters* [1980] 1 Ch 297 but see *Murphy* v. *Brentwood District Council* [1991] 1 AC 398.
2. See, e.g. *Wilson* v. *Bloomfield* (1979) 123 SJ 860 (CA).
3. *Gran Gelato Ltd* v. *Richcliff Ltd* [1992] Ch 560.
4. e.g. *Cemp Properties* v. *Dentsply* [1989] 35 EG 99.

6.3. Breach of warranty of authority

6.3.1. Where an agent acts outside the scope of his authority he will be liable to the third party for breach of warranty of authority.[1]

6.3.2. A solicitor or estate agent who exceeds his client's authority may thus be sued by a third party.[2]

1. *Yonge* v. *Toynbee* [1910] 1 KB 215.
2. *Suleman* v. *Shahsavari* [1989] 2 All ER 460; *Penn* v. *Bristol and West Building Society* [1997] 3 All ER 470.

6.4. Estate agents

6.4.1. An estate agent may be liable for misrepresentation occurring in the particulars of sale of the property.

6.4.2. Liability may also exist if the agent exceeds his authority as under para. M6.3.

6.4.3. An estate agent who is authorised to *sell* the property (but not one who is merely empowered to procure a buyer) may have authority to receive the contract deposit.[1]

6.4.4. As far as pre-contract deposits are concerned, unless there is express authority from the seller to take and hold a pre-contract deposit, such sum must be held on behalf of the buyer. If the pre-contract deposit is lost, e.g. where an estate agent absconds with the money, the loss falls on the buyer except where the agent was expressly authorised to take the pre-contract deposit.[2]

6.4.5. The estate agent's duty to the seller is similar to the common law duties which exist between an agent and his principal.[3]

6.4.6. The estate agent's duty is owed to his principal, i.e. the seller client, and generally he owes no duty to the buyer.[4] There may also in some circumstances be a liability in relation to the pre-contract deposit, or in negligence under *Hedley Byrne* v. *Heller* principles.[5]

6.4.7. Similar remedies to those afforded under Trade Descriptions Act 1968 lie under the Property Misdescriptions Act 1991 against an estate agent (including a solicitor who is acting as an estate agent) who misdescribes a property which he is selling. This Act creates a criminal offence which is committed where a false or misleading description is applied to property in the course of an estate agency or property development business. The offence is of strict liability and can be committed by publishing a misleading photograph of property as well as by misdescribing property orally or in writing. An action must generally be brought within three years of the alleged offence. Enforcement of the Act is through criminal proceedings brought by the Trading Standard Department for the area.

1. *Boote* v. *R.T. Shiels & Co.* [1978] 1 NZLR 445.
2. *Sorrell* v. *Finch* [1977] AC 728.
3. But see *Luxor* v. *Cooper* [1941] AC 108; *cf. Prebble (P.G.) & Co.* v. *West* (1969) 211 EG 831.
4. *McCulloch* v. *Lane Fox, The Times,* 22 December 1995 (CA).
5. [1964] AC 465.

6.5.   Surveyors

6.5.1.   A surveyor owes his client a duty to perform his contract with reasonable skill and care. This common law duty has been replaced by the implied term to the same effect under Supply of Goods and Services Act 1982, s.13 but the surveyor's duty, and thus his liability, are necessarily limited by the extent of the instructions given to him.

6.5.2.   If the problem with the survey stems from the results of a valuation report, the surveyor will generally have been instructed by the client's lender, and so there will probably be no contractual relationship between the client and the surveyor; thus any liability which does exist will necessarily be in tort. If however the contract between the lender and the valuer contemplates that the buyer will have the benefit of the valuation report, it may be possible for the buyer to sustain an action against the valuer in contract under the Contracts (Rights of Third Parties) Act 1999.

6.5.3.   In other cases a contractual relationship between the client and the surveyor will or may exist, giving the choice of action under either contract or tort.

6.5.4.   An exclusion clause purporting to exclude liability for the survey will be construed narrowly against the party seeking to rely on it and will only be valid in so far as it is fair and reasonable in the context of the particular contract in which it is included.[1]

6.5.5.   A surveyor who prepares a valuation report for a lender in the knowledge (express or implied) that the buyer will see the report and may rely on it in deciding whether or not to proceed with his purchase owes a duty of care to the buyer.[2] This duty will not, however, apply in every case. Where, for example, it is reasonable for the surveyor to assume that the buyer would be obtaining his own independent survey – which may be a fair assumption for him to make where the property is at the top end of the property market – or where the buyer is experienced in property matters, the surveyor may be entitled to shelter behind the protection of his exclusion clause and thus avoid liability.[3]

6.5.6.   Where a surveyor is sued, the quantum of damages is usually limited to the difference between what the property was actually worth at the date of the contract and what it would have been worth if the survey report had been accurate (not what the client paid for the property, or the cost of repairs). Thus, in some circumstances, the amount of damages recoverable will not equate with the client's loss. For example, the difference in value may be only a few thousand pounds, but the cost of repairs to put the property right at the date of the action may be huge, and the client can only recover the smaller sum representing the difference in value.[4] Loss in value to the property which is attributable to the fall in value of the property market is not generally recoverable as a head of loss.[5] The lender's contributory negligence (e.g. in relying on the valuation without checking it) may reduce the award made against the surveyor.[6]

6.5.7.   There is no doubt that a valuer owes a duty to the seller to provide a valuation which is as accurate as circumstances allow – a duty of skill and care is owed to the seller. If the valuer's error results in there being an undervalue of the property, the measure of damages will usually be the difference between the sale price and the market value of the property. If on the other hand an over-valuation is given, full contractual damages within *Hadley* v. *Baxendale*[7] principles will be payable to the seller, including loss caused by his inability to sell the property within a reasonable time, if this has been a consequence of the over-valuation.

6.5.8.   The cause of action by a lender in respect of a negligent valuation arises when the loss crystallises, i.e. at the date when the security is sold.[8]

6.5.9.   The RICS appraisal and valuation manual ('The Red Book') contains mandatory guidelines for surveyors to follow when undertaking surveys and valuations of all types of property. Non-observance of these guidelines may be evidence of negligence.

1. The reasonableness test in Unfair Contract Terms Act 1977, s.11 must be satisfied.
2. *Smith* v. *Eric Bush* [1990] 1 AC 831; and see *Qureshi* v. *Liassides* (unreported) (1995) EG 123 (case comment).
3. *Stevenson* v. *Nationwide Building Society* (1984) 272 EG 663.
4. *Philips* v. *Ward* [1956] 1 All ER 874; and see *Watts* v. *Morrow, The Independent*, 20 August 1991.
5. *Banque Bruxelles Lambert S.A.* v. *Eagle Star Insurance* [1995] 12 EG 144, CA reversed on appeal to the House of Lords *sub nomine South Australia Asset Management (Pty) Ltd* v. *York Montague* [1996] NPC 100 and see *Platform Home Loans* v. *Oyston* [1999] EGCS 26, HL.
6. *Ibid.*
7. (1854) 9 Exch 341.
8. *First National Commercial Bank* v. *Humberts, The Times*, 27 January 1995, CA.

6.6.   Dangerous substances

6.6.1.   There may be heavy liability (in financial terms) to third parties in tort, in negligence[1] or under Environmental Protection Act 1990 if, e.g. untreated sewage escapes into a waterway and pollutes the water.

1. Subject to foreseeability: *Cambridge Water Company* v. *Eastern Counties Leather plc* [1994] 1 All ER 53.

6.7.   Local searches

6.7.1.   In certain circumstances compensation may be claimed under Local Land Charges Act 1975, s.10, where there has been an error in an official search (see para. B10).

6.8.   The Land Registry

6.8.1.   In certain circumstances compensation may be claimed from the Land Registry where a person suffers loss by reason of rectification of the register or a mistake in an official search (see para. M7).

6.9.   Covenants in freehold land

6.9.1.   Where restrictive covenants have been validly annexed to land, the person with the benefit of those covenants (who may be a successor in title of the original covenantee) will be able to enforce the covenants by injunction and/or damages against either the present estate owner of the land which bears the burden of the covenants or the original covenantor. The original covenantor may, in turn, be able to recover his loss from his immediate successor in title through an indemnity covenant.

6.9.2.   In certain circumstances it may be possible to make an *ex parte* application to the Lands Tribunal under Law of Property Act 1925, s.84 for the modification or release of an obsolete restrictive covenant and so remove the potential liability under it.

6.9.3.   The burden of positive covenants does not run with freehold land and can only be enforced directly between the original contracting parties.[1] An original covenantor who is held liable in this way may seek to recoup his own loss if an indemnity covenant was taken from his immediate successor in title.[2]

6.9.4.   Covenants entered into on or after 11 May 2000 and which are clearly expressed to be taken for the benefit of successors in title to the land may be enforceable by successors under the Contracts (Rights of Third Parties) Act 1999. This Act applies to both positive and negative covenants.

1. *Rhone* v. *Stephens, The Times*, 18 March 1994, HL.
2. See Rentcharges, para. K15.

6.10.   Covenants in leasehold land

6.10.1.   Although both positive and restrictive covenants are enforceable, liability is limited by the doctrines of privity of contract and of estate. It may not therefore always be possible for a head-landlord to take direct action against a sub-tenant since neither privity of contract nor of estate exist in this situation. However, covenants entered into on or after 11 May 2000 may benefit from the Contracts

(Rights of Third Parties) Act 1999 which amends the law relating to privity of contract and will allow direct enforcement between e.g. a head landlord and a sub-tenant.

6.10.2. Similarly, in the absence of special provisions in the lease, it is not generally possible for one tenant directly to sue a fellow tenant for breach of one of the covenants contained in their leases, and the enforcement of the covenant against the offending tenant frequently has to be brought by the landlord at the request of the injured tenant. However, covenants entered into on or after 11 May 2000 may benefit from the Contracts (Rights of Third Parties) Act 1999 which amends the law relating to privity of contract and will allow direct enforcement between tenants.

6.10.3. Liability on leasehold covenants is further discussed in paras. K6 (Long-term residential tenancies) and K10 (Liability on covenants in leases).

6.11. Estate agent's commission

6.11.1. The following points are relevant to the estate agent's entitlement to his commission and when it becomes payable.

6.11.2. The contract between the agent and the seller must be absolutely clear as to what is included in the price. For example does the fee quoted include, e.g. advertising, valuation, agent's expenses, VAT, or are these to be added to the bill?

6.11.3. In the absence of express provision in the contract no charge can be made for abortive work.[1]

6.11.4. As a general principle, an agent's entitlement to his fee depends on his introduction of a ready, able and willing buyer. This means someone who is prepared and able to go ahead to completion not merely a 'subject to contract' offer.[2]

6.11.5. It is in the estate agent's interests to ensure that the contract is quite specific as to the time when his fee for the estate agency work becomes due, and that the fee becomes payable as soon as a binding contract is entered into with the buyer – not on condition that completion takes place. This type of provision (commonly found in estate agent's contracts) ensures that the commission is still payable even if the contract is terminated between exchange and completion or completion fails to take place.[3]

6.11.6. The courts interpret the expressions 'the agent is to find a buyer' or 'the agent is to introduce a buyer' as meaning that the buyer must actually sign the contract before the commission becomes due.[4]

6.11.7. Three conditions must all be satisfied before the agent can claim his commission:

(a) the agent must introduce a person who enters a valid binding contract. This means a contract which satisfies the requirements of Law of Property (Miscellaneous Provisions) Act 1989, s.2 and the contract is not otherwise voidable for mistake, fraud, etc.;

(b) the buyer must be willing and able (financially) to complete. The buyer's ability in this respect is judged at contractual date for completion, so if there is a dispute about the agent's entitlement to his fee the contractual completion date must be allowed to pass before proceedings for the commission are commenced. This is so even if, under the contract with the seller, commission became payable on exchange of contracts;

(c) the agent must be the effective cause of the sale. This means that he must be able to show that his introduction of the buyer led to the formation of the contract of sale between the seller and buyer.

6.11.8. If the buyer fails to complete the contract and is in breach of his contract with the seller, unless commission was expressly due on exchange, no completion means no commission. If, however, the seller successfully claims damages from the buyer for breach, the agent may be entitled to recover a *quantum meruit* out of the seller's damages.[5]

6.11.9. Where two agents are instructed by the seller, there is frequently an argument about which of the agents is entitled to the commission for the sale. The principle here is that commission is payable to the first agent to secure a buyer who enters a binding contract.[6]

6.11.10. If it is the seller who withdraws from the sale, no contract means no commission, unless the contract contains express provision to the contrary. It makes no difference in this situation if the seller rescinds after the contract is made (even if the seller is in breach).

6.11.11. If a sole agency is agreed with the client, it is important that the terms of that agreement are fully and clearly explained to the client so he cannot complain of being misled if things go wrong. The danger as far as the client is concerned is that he does not understand what a sole agency means, instructs a second agent who sells the property and then feels aggrieved because both agents claim to be entitled to commission. If a sole agency agreement is expressed in terms using the phrase 'sole agent', the seller is not entitled to instruct another agent to sell the property, but there is nothing to prevent him from contracting a private sale and in that way depriving the agent of his commission. On the other hand, if the expression 'sole right to sell' is used this prohibits the seller from contracting a private sale on his own initiative. This latter phrase is therefore much more restrictive of the seller's rights than the former and would merit explicit explanation of its implications to the client. The term 'sole selling agent' is construed as meaning 'sole agent', so the seller is not prevented from contracting a private sale if this phrase is used.

6.11.12. If the seller withdraws his instructions from the agent before a sale contract is entered into, this is not a breach of the sole agency contract (the seller is entitled to change his mind and this is a normal and acceptable risk attached to estate agency) but a *sale* contracted elsewhere will be and the sole agent can then claim damages for the breach.

6.11.13. An agent who is himself in breach of his duty to his client may forfeit his right to commission.

6.11.14. Estate Agents (Provision of Information) Regulations 1991 require estate agents to inform their clients in writing of the terms of the agreement between themselves and their clients including, where appropriate, the meaning of 'sole agency' and 'sole selling rights'. The Regulations have adopted definitions of these two phrases which are similar to the explanations contained in para. M6.11.11.

1. *Lott* v. *Outhwaite* (1893) 10 TLR 76.
2. *Luxor* v. *Cooper* [1941] AC 108.
3. *Poole* v. *Clarke & Co.* [1945] 2 All ER 445; *cf. Midgely Estates Ltd* v. *Hand* [1952] 2 QB 432.
4. *Jones* v. *Lowe* [1945] KB 73.
5. *Boots* v. *E. Christopher & Co.* [1952] 1 KB 89.
6. *A.A. Dickson & Co.* v. *O'Leary* (1979) 254 EG 731 suggests that the seller cannot be made liable to pay commission twice over.

6.12. Timeshare properties

6.12.1. The Timeshare Act 1992 gives the prospective buyer of a timeshare property a 14-day 'cooling off' period during which he has the right to cancel the contract.[1] The Act only applies where the buyer is buying from the developer and not to 'secondhand' timeshares.

6.12.2. Notice of the buyer's right to cancel must be given by the seller in prescribed form. Failure to give the correct notice renders the contract unenforceable and the seller is guilty of a criminal offence punishable by a fine. Enforcement of the Act is the responsibility of the local weights and measures office.

6.12.3. The Timeshare Regulations[2] extend the Timeshare Act to rights acquired as the result of share ownership and rights under collective investment schemes. The Act is also extended to cover properties within the EU, Iceland, Norway, Liechtenstein and Switzerland, where the buyer is a private individual (not acting in the course of a business) who is normally resident in the UK.

6.12.4. A seller is required to provide any person on request with a document containing information on the property. This information will form part of the contract if a contract is subsequently entered into by an individual buyer acting in a private (i.e. non-business) capacity.

6.12.5. The contract must contain certain minimum information relating to the nature of the property, the price and recurring cover and charges. A buyer who is resident in the UK is entitled to have a copy of the contract in English.

1. This period may be extended to three months and 10 days if certain information is not provided to the buyer.
2. S.I. 1997/1081.

6.13. Squatters

6.13.1. A summary procedure for the eviction of squatters exists under Order 24 of County Court Rules or under Criminal Justice and Public Order Act 1994, ss.72–75. The 1994 Act applies to both residential and commercial property.

M7. Rectification and indemnity

7.1. Rectification of the contract

7.1.1.   Where the parties have reached agreement over a particular matter, but in error that matter is either omitted from the written contract, or is wrongly recorded in the written agreement, an application for rectification of the contract in order to correct the error can be made.[1] Under Law of Property (Miscellaneous Provisions) Act 1989, s.2(4) where rectification is ordered the court has a discretion to determine the date on which the contract comes into operation. If a term is missing from the contract, there is no contract.

1. See *Wright* v. *Robert Leonard Developments Ltd* [1994] EGCS 69.

7.2. Rectification of the purchase deed

7.2.1.   Where a term of the contract is either omitted from, or inaccurately represented in, the purchase deed an application for rectification of the deed may be made to the court. Rectification relates back to the date when the original document was executed and there is no need to draw up an amended deed. The order granting rectification is often endorsed on the affected deed.[1] Rectification is an equitable remedy and is thus subject to the equitable bars.

1. For examples of the court's discretion to rectify see, e.g. *Craddock Bros* v. *Hunt* [1923] 2 Ch 136; *Wilson* v. *Wilson* [1969] 3 All ER 945; *Riverlate Properties Ltd* v. *Paul* [1975] Ch 133.

7.3. Rectification of documents by the Adjudicator

7.3.1.   The Adjudicator[1] has power, on application, to make any order which the High Court could make for the rectification or setting aside of a document which:

(a) effects a qualifying disposition of a registered estate or charge;

(b) is a contract to make such a disposition; or

(c) effects a transfer of an interest which is the subject of a notice in the register.[2]

A qualifying disposition is a registrable disposition or one which creates an interest which may be the subject of a notice in the register.[3]

1. See para. A22.9.4 as to the Office of the Adjudicator to the Land Registry.
2. Land Registration Act 2002, s.108(2).
3. Land Registration Act 2002, s.108(3).

7.4. Rectification of the register

7.4.1.   Rectification in the Land Registration Act 2002 has a narrower definition than in the previous law. It is limited to an alteration in the register which involves the correction of a mistake and prejudicially affects the title of a registered proprietor.[1] When such rectification occurs, the proprietor may be entitled to indemnity.

7.4.2.   The court has power to make an order for rectification of the register:

(a) to correct a mistake;

(b) to bring the register up to date; or

(c) to give effect to any estate, right or interest excepted from the effect of registration.[2]

7.4.3.   Rectification cannot be ordered against a proprietor without his consent in relation to land in his possession unless:

(a) the proprietor has by fraud or lack of proper care caused or substantially contributed to the mistake; or

(b) it would for any other reason be unjust for the alteration not to be made.[3]

Land is in the possession of a proprietor if it is physically in his possession. A proprietor is treated as being in possession of land which is physically in the possession of certain other people, for example, the proprietor's tenant or licensee.[4]

7.4.4.   Where the court has power to make an order for rectification it must do so unless there are exceptional circumstances which justify its not doing so.[5]

7.4.5.   The registrar has power to rectify the register without the need for the matter to be considered by the court. He can rectify the register for the same purposes, and subject to the same limitations, as the court has power to order it.[6]

1. Land Registration Act 2002, Sched. 4, para. 1.
2. Land Registration Act 2002, Sched. 4, para. 2.
3. Land Registration Act 2002, Sched. 4, para. 3(2).
4. Land Registration Act 2002, s.131.
5. Land Registration Act 2002, Sched. 4, paras.3(3).
6. Land Registration Act 2002, Sched. 4, paras. 5 and 6.

7.5. Indemnity

7.5.1.   Subject to the exceptions contained in the Land Registration Act 2002 a person is entitled to be indemnified by the registrar if he suffers loss by reason of:

(a) a rectification of the register;

(b) a mistake whose correction would involve rectification of the register;

(c) a mistake in an official search;

(d) a mistake in an official copy;

(e) a mistake in a document kept by the registrar which is not an original and is referred to in the register;

(f) the loss or destruction of a document lodged at the registry for inspection or safe custody;

(g) a mistake in the cautions register; or

(h) failure by the registrar to perform his duty under section 50 of the Land Registration Act 2002 (duty of notification of overriding statutory charges).[1]

7.5.2. Indemnity is not payable for any loss suffered by a claimant wholly or partly as a result of his own fraud or lack of proper care.[2]

7.5.3. No indemnity is payable on account of any mines or minerals, or the existence of any right to work or get mines or minerals, unless it is noted in the register that the title to the registered estate concerned includes the mines or minerals.[3]

7.5.4. Indemnity may be claimed for costs or expenses reasonably incurred by the claimant with the consent of the registrar.[4]

7.5.5. For limitation purposes, the claim must be made within six years of the time when the claimant knows, or but for his own default might have known, of the existence of his claim.[5]

7.5.6. A claim for indemnity should initially be made to the registrar. However, a person may apply to the court for the determination of any question as to whether he is entitled to an indemnity and its amount.[6]

7.5.7. Where the register is not rectified, the amount of indemnity payable cannot exceed the value of the estate or interest at the time when the mistake which caused the loss was made. Where the register is rectified, the amount of indemnity is limited to the value of the estate or interest immediately before rectification of the register (but as if there were to be no rectification).[7]

7.5.8. There are provisions for the payment of interest on the amount of any indemnity so paid.[8]

7.5.9. Where an indemnity is paid there are provisions which entitle the registrar to either recover the amount paid from any person who caused or substantially contributed to the loss by his fraud or to enforce any rights of action for the purpose of recovering the amount paid.[9]

1. Land Registration Act 2002, Sched. 8, para. 1.
2. Land Registration Act 2002, Sched. 8, para. 5.
3. Land Registration Act 2002, Sched. 8, para. 2.
4. Land Registration Act 2002, Sched. 8, para. 3 and as to costs in non-rectification cases see Land Registration Act 2002, Sched. 4, para. 9.
5. Land Registration Act 2002, Sched. 8, para. 8.
6. Land Registration Act 2002, Sched. 8, para. 7.
7. Land Registration Act 2002, Sched. 8, para. 6.
8. Land Registration Rules 2003, r.195.
9. Land Registration Act 2002, Sched. 8, para. 10.

M8. Liens

8.1.	Seller's lien	8.3.	Solicitor's lien
8.2.	Buyer's lien	8.4.	Abortive transactions

8.1. Seller's lien

8.1.1. The seller has an equitable lien over the property being sold to the extent of the unpaid purchase price.[1]

8.1.2. The lien arises immediately there is a binding contract for sale and is discharged on completion to the extent that the purchase price is paid at that time.[2]

8.1.3. By Law of Property Act 1925, s.68 the presence of a receipt clause in the purchase deed is evidence (but not conclusive evidence) of the discharge of the seller's lien. In registered land, in the absence of an adverse entry on the register of the title (or protection of the lien as an overriding interest) a subsequent purchaser of the land will take free from the lien.[3]

8.1.4. To protect the lien against a subsequent buyer, it should be registered as a notice on the register of the title in registered land, or as a Class C(iii) land charge in unregistered land pursuant to a priority notice. The lien may take effect as an overriding interest in registered land if (unusually) the person with its benefit is in occupation of the land.[4] An unpaid seller who is in actual occupation may be estopped from claiming that the lien is an overriding interest if he has warranted, in answer to pre-contract enquiries, that vacant possession will be given on completion.[5]

8.1.5. The lien is enforceable by foreclosure[6] or by a court order for sale of the property.[7]

8.1.6. If the seller has agreed to permit the buyer to leave part of the purchase price outstanding on mortgage, the purchase deed should not contain a receipt clause. The buyer should enter a covenant to pay the money to the seller and to enter a formal mortgage if required. If the seller has taken a mortgage to secure the outstanding moneys, this will displace the lien. Where it appears from the transfer that further moneys are payable by the buyer to the seller but it is intended that the seller should not have a lien on the property, it is desirable for an express waiver to be included in the transfer. Where the buyer is entering another mortgage to assist with his purchase of the property, care needs to be exercised to ensure that the priorities of the lender's and seller's charges are correctly maintained; a lender will not normally cede priority to the seller's lien. It may be preferable to include a receipt clause in the document and to execute a formal mortgage in the seller's favour.

8.1.7. If the transfer cites the non-payment and contains a provision for a charge over the land this charge will take priority over a formal mortgage created by the buyer in favour of a third party immediately after completion.

8.1.8. By Standard Condition 6.5.1 and Standard Commercial Property Condition 6.5.1 the seller is not entitled to a lien over the title deeds after completion. If the seller wishes to reserve such a lien this provision must be expressly excluded by contractual condition.

1. *Mackreth* v. *Symmons* (1808) 15 Ves 329.
2. *London & Cheshire Insurance Co. Ltd* v. *Laplagrene Property Co. Ltd* [1971] Ch 499.
3. *Ibid.*
4. Land Registration Act 2002, Sched. 1, para. 2 and Sched. 3, para. 2.
5. *UCB Finance* v. *France* [1995] NPC 144.
6. *Hughes* v. *Griffin* [1969] 1 All ER 460.
7. *Williams* v. *Aylesbury & Buckingham Rail Co.* (1874) 9 Ch App 684.

8.2. Buyer's lien

8.2.1. The buyer has a similar lien over the property to the extent of any deposit paid by him. This lien can be registered as a notice in registered land or as a Class C(iii) land charge in unregistered land (see para. B17.12).

8.3. Solicitor's lien

8.3.1. At common law a solicitor has a lien over his client's property until his costs are paid. He may also ask the court to direct that property recovered by the solicitor in an action brought on the client's behalf should be retained by the solicitor as security against the solicitor's costs.

8.3.2. The common law lien attaches to all deeds, papers and other personal property of the client which comes into the solicitor's possession with the client's consent. Such property must have been received by the solicitor in his capacity as solicitor. No lien attaches to a client's will. A buyer's solicitor must have received documents over which he exercises his lien in his capacity as buyer's solicitor and not, e.g. as lender's solicitor.

8.3.3. The lien is restricted to costs due to the solicitor in respect of work done on the client's instructions. The solicitor is entitled to retain the client's property until his costs are paid in full.

8.3.4. The existence of the lien does not entitle the solicitor to sell or otherwise dispose of the client's property.

8.3.5. Despite the existence of a lien the Law Society has power to order a solicitor to hand over papers to one of its officers where there is an intervention in a solicitor's practice under Solicitors Act 1974, Sched. 1 and the court also has power to order papers to be delivered.[1]

8.3.6.   On termination of the retainer where the client has instructed another solicitor to act for him, the first solicitor should hand over papers and documents to the second solicitor, subject to obtaining a satisfactory undertaking from the second solicitor in respect of payment of the first solicitor's costs.

8.3.7.   A solicitor has no lien against the official receiver or a trustee in bankruptcy.[2]

8.3.8.   A further type of lien exists by virtue of Solicitors Act 1974, s.73 which empowers the court to make a charging order over real or personal property belonging to the client as security for the solicitor's taxed costs (see para. N1).

8.3.9.   No lien can be exercised over property which is held by the solicitor in the capacity of stakeholder.[3]

8.3.10   Under the terms of the Lenders' Handbook the lender's solicitor is not entitled to exercise a lien over the title deeds.

1. Solicitors Act 1974, s.68.
2. See *Re Toleman and England, ex p. Bramble* (1880) 13 Ch 885.
3. *Rockeagle Ltd* v. *Alsop Wilkinson* [1992] Ch 47.

8.4.   Abortive transactions

8.4.1.   A draft contract and other papers supplied by the seller's solicitor to the buyer's solicitor belong to the seller until contracts for the transaction are exchanged. If therefore the transaction is aborted before exchange takes place the buyer's solicitor should comply with a request for return of those papers made by the seller's solicitor. This is notwithstanding any contrary instructions issued by the buyer to his own solicitor. For the avoidance of doubt the seller's solicitor may choose to indicate in his covering letter to the buyer's solicitor that he expects such papers to be returned to him on request if the transaction does not proceed to exchange.

M9. Covenants for title

See also: Capacity, para. B7
The purchase deed, para. E1

9.1. Introduction

9.1.1. On completion of the transaction the contract merges with the purchase deed in so far as the two documents cover the same ground, and in general an action arising out of the contract is not possible after completion has taken place. The principal post-completion remedy available to the buyer will be an action for breach of the title guarantee which was introduced by the Law of Property (Miscellaneous Provisions) Act 1994. This applies to all transactions completed on or after the 1 July 1995.

9.1.2. As an exception to the general rule outlined in the preceding paragraph, an action arising out of the contract is sustainable after completion in circumstances where a clause or clauses of the contract have been expressed in such a way that they do not merge with the purchase deed on completion.[1] In appropriate circumstances an action in misrepresentation would also be available since this action does not derive from the contract itself.

9.1.3. For transactions completed before 1 July 1995 the principal post-completion remedy is an action for breach of the covenants for title. The exact nature of the covenants implied into the purchase deed depends upon the capacity in which the seller transferred the land. The appropriate law is contained in Law of Property Act 1925, s.76 (as modified by Land Registration Act 1925, s.24). If a seller purported to convey in a capacity other than that which he in fact possessed, e.g. a trustee purported to sell as a beneficial owner, it is likely that no covenants of title will have passed in the purchase deed. The benefit of a covenant for title is annexed to and passes with the land. So if A sells to B, B's successor in title can enforce the covenant for title given by A provided the action is brought within the appropriate limitation period of 12 years.

1. See Standard Condition 7.4 and Standard Commercial Property Condition 7.4.

9.2. Title guarantee

9.2.1. The seller can sell with either full or limited title guarantee irrespective of the capacity in which he could have sold the property under the pre 1 July 1995 law,

Law of Property (Miscellaneous Provisions) Act 1994. The guarantees apply to the sale of both freehold and leasehold property and on the grant of a lease. They can also be used on the transfer of personal property including intellectual property and rights in shares.

9.2.2.   On the front of the Standard Contract form the seller should specify whether he sells with full or limited title guarantee. Should the seller fail to specify the nature of the title guarantee Standard Condition 4.5.2 and Standard Commercial Property Condition 4.5.2, provide that the seller will sell with full title guarantee.

9.2.3.   The warranties given under the full and limited guarantees can be amended in the agreement. If the seller is concerned about encumbrances he should disclose them in the contract and ensure that the buyer agrees to take the property subject to them. See also Standard Condition 4.5.3. Under s.6 of the 1994 Act (as amended by the Land Registration Act 2002) the sale of a registered title will also be subject to any matters entered on the register of title at the time of the disposition. As a result any such matters will not be covered by the title guarantee.

9.2.4.   If the seller is a beneficial owner, he will usually provide full title guarantee. If the seller is a trustee, personal representative or mortgagee, he will usually provide a limited title guarantee.

9.2.5.   Full title guarantee

Where the full guarantee is given the seller warrants that:

(a) he has the right to dispose of the property in the manner purported;

(b) he will at his own cost do all he reasonably can to give his transferee the title he purports to give;

(c) he disposes of his whole interest where that interest is registered;

(d) he disposes of the whole lease where the interest is leasehold;

(e) he disposes of a freehold where it is unclear from the face of the documents whether the interest is freehold or leasehold;

(f) in the case of a subsisting lease he covenants that the lease is still subsisting and that there is no subsisting breach which might result in forfeiture;

(g) in the case of a mortgage of a property which is subject to a rentcharge or lease, that the mortgagor will observe and perform the obligations under the rentcharge or lease;

(h) that the person giving the disposition is disposing of it free from all charges and encumbrances (whether monetary or not) and from all other rights exercisable by third parties, not being rights which the transferor does not and could not reasonably be expected to know about.

9.2.6.   Under (b) the seller is promising to put right any defects in title, for example, he will execute any further documents needed to ensure that the buyer receives the title he contracted to buy.

9.2.7. As a result of the warranty in (e) a seller who is selling a leasehold estate must expressly state in the contract that the estate is leasehold. The seller can do this on the front page of the Standard Conditions of Sale form. The warranty in (f) applies on the sale of an existing lease. The seller should modify this covenant to ensure that he will not be liable to the buyer for any breach of any of the tenant's covenants relating to the physical state and condition of the property. Standard Condition 3.2.2 and Standard Commercial Property Condition 3.2.2 modify this implied warranty by providing that the property is sold subject to any subsisting breach of a condition or tenant's obligation relating to the physical state of the property which renders the lease liable to forfeiture. Standard Condition 3.2.3 and Standard Commercial Property Condition 3.2.3 contain a similar provision on the grant of a sub-lease.

9.2.8. The warranty in (h) applies to any encumbrances created by the seller or by his predecessors unless the encumbrances are disclosed in the contract or on the title of a registered property.

9.2.9. *Limited title guarantee*

Where limited title guarantee is given, all the above warranties apply except for (h), which is replaced with the following:

  (h) that the transferor has not charged or encumbered the property by a charge or encumbrance which still exists, that he has not granted any third party rights which still subsist and that he is not aware that anyone else has done so since the last disposition for value.

The seller therefore warrants that he has not encumbered the property but he does not warrant that his predecessor has not done so.

9.2.10. *Assignment of the guarantee*

The title guarantee runs with the land and is enforceable by the buyer's successors in title.

9.2.11. *Remedies*

A breach of title guarantee is actionable as a breach of contract. However, the remedies available may be restricted. Once completion has taken place, or a third party has acquired an interest in the property, e.g. a lender, it is unlikely that rescission will be granted. Damages will therefore be the usual remedy although the seller may be ordered to execute documents to perfect a defective title.

M10. Solicitor's negligence

10.1. Introduction

10.1.1. Where a solicitor has been negligent the client must seek redress through a civil action against the solicitor.

10.1.2. Where a client or third party makes a claim against a solicitor (or gives notice of intention to make such a claim) and the claim is one in respect of which indemnity is provided by the solicitor's insurance the solicitor must as soon as practicable notify his insurers and co-operate with them in order to enable the claim to be dealt with in the appropriate manner. Where top-up indemnity cover is maintained the terms of that policy should also be considered.

10.2. Action to be taken by solicitor

10.2.1. If a solicitor discovers an act or omission which would justify a claim by a client (or third party) against him he should:

    (a) contact his insurers;

    (b) inform the client (or third party) in order to enable him to take independent legal advice;

    (c) seek the advice of his insurers as to any further communication with the client (or third party); and

    (d) confirm any oral communication in writing.

10.2.2. If a client makes a claim against his solicitor or notifies his intention of doing so, or if the solicitor discovers an act or omission which would justify such a claim, the solicitor is under a duty to inform his client that he should seek independent advice.

10.2.3. If the client refuses to seek independent advice the solicitor should decline to act further for the client unless he is satisfied that no conflict of interest exists.

10.2.4. The solicitor should not admit liability or settle a claim without the consent of his insurers.

10.2.5. Where the solicitor is asked to hand papers over to another solicitor who is giving independent advice to the client about the claim, the solicitor should keep copies of the original documents for his own reference. If the first solicitor has a lien over the client's papers he may, as an alternative to taking copies, ask the second solicitor to give an undertaking for the production of the papers should they be required.

N. COSTS

N1. Costs

See also: Estimate of costs, para. A8

1.1. The basis of charging

1.1.1. Costs in non-contentious matters including conveyancing are governed by Solicitors' (Non-Contentious Business) Remuneration Order 1994 (see Appendix XII.3).

1.1.2. Rule 3 Solicitors' (Non-Contentious Business) Remuneration Order 1994 provides that the remuneration shall be 'such sum as may be fair and reasonable having regard to all the circumstances of the case'. The following matters must be taken into account:

(a) the complexity of the matter or the difficulty or novelty of the questions raised;

(b) the skill, labour, specialised knowledge and responsibility involved;

(c) the time spent on the business;

(d) the number and importance of the documents prepared or perused, without regard to length;

(e) the place where and the circumstances in which the business or any part thereof is transacted;

(f) the amount or value of any money or property involved;

(g) whether any land involved is registered land;

(h) the importance of the matter to the client; and

(i) the approval (express or implied) of the entitled person or the express approval of the testator to:

(i) the solicitor undertaking all or any part of the work giving rise to the costs; or

(ii) the amount of the costs.

1.1.3. On taking instructions the solicitor should give his client the best information he can about the likely cost of the matter including when costs will be charged and whether or not such costs will be deducted from money held by the solicitor on the client's behalf. Where possible an estimate should be given to the client; in other cases the solicitor should give the client a general forecast of the approximate costs to be incurred. Where no estimate has been given and the solicitor has not arranged an agreed fee for the work, the client must be told how the solicitor's charges are to be calculated, e.g. on an hourly rate basis or as a percentage of the value of the transaction. Information should also be given to the client about the nature and cost of disbursements.

1.1.4.   Practice Rule 15 (solicitors' costs information and client care code), Solicitors' Practice Rules 1990 as amended (see Appendix I.1) and the Law Society's Practice Management Standards should also be followed. Failure to observe these standards is regarded as inadequate professional services by the Office for the Supervision of Solicitors.

1.1.5.   By Supply of Goods and Services Act 1982, s.15 the contract between solicitor and client contains an implied term that the client will pay the solicitor a reasonable sum for his services; however, the matter of costs should be dealt with expressly. It is the solicitor's duty to raise the issue of costs if the client does not enquire.

1.1.6.   When confirming the client's instructions the solicitor should record whether a fee has been agreed, and if so what it covers and whether it includes VAT and disbursements.

1.1.7.   Where the client has imposed an upper limit on costs, a solicitor who exceeds that limit without the client's authority will not be able to recover his costs in so far as they exceed the agreed maximum sum. The client must be informed as soon as possible if it appears that the limit imposed on the costs will be insufficient and instructions obtained as to whether the client wishes the solicitor to continue with the matter. If the solicitor continues to act and exceeds the limit imposed by the client on the costs to be incurred the amount of the bill in excess of the agreed amount will be disallowed if the client applies for a remuneration certificate or taxation. The solicitor may also be guilty of professional misconduct in these circumstances.

1.1.8.   The amount of costs being incurred on a client's behalf should be reviewed regularly. It is recommended that the client should be informed at least every six months of the amount of costs incurred to date and where appropriate an interim bill should be delivered.

1.1.9.   A solicitor may, at the outset of the retainer, require the client to make a payment on account of costs and disbursements to be incurred. The solicitor must make his acceptance of the instructions conditional on the client's advance payment. Unless he does this the solicitor will not be able to justify the termination of the retainer if the client does not make the interim payment.

1.1.10.   A solicitor may charge interest on the whole or outstanding part of an unpaid bill with effect from one month after delivery of the bill, provided that notice has been given to the client informing him of his right to apply for a remuneration certificate and taxation of the bill. The rate of interest chargeable is that which is payable on judgment debts.

1.1.11. A solicitor must not take advantage of the client by overcharging for work done or to be done. Overcharging the client may be professional misconduct. If a taxing officer allows less than one-half of the sum charged he is under a duty to report the matter to the Law Society. The solicitor is responsible for ensuring that the amount of the bill is fair and reasonable and cannot escape liability by delegating the preparation of the bill to a costs draftsman.

1.1.12. Unless there is an agreement to the contrary, a solicitor is personally responsible for paying the proper costs of any professional agent or other person whom he instructs on behalf of his client, whether or not he receives payment from his client.

1.1.13. Costs which are taken by way of deduction from money which the solicitor is holding on the client's behalf cannot be transferred from clients' account to office account without the consent of the client.

1.1.14. In the absence of agreement to the contrary a solicitor will charge on a *quantum meruit* basis (or for a reasonable sum under Supply of Goods and Services Act 1982, s.15) for abortive work.

1.2. Agreements for charges

1.2.1. Solicitors Act 1974, s.57 allows a solicitor to make an agreement with a client for costs in a non-contentious matter.

1.2.2. In order to be enforceable under the Act, the agreement must fully comply with the provisions of section 57. Thus the agreement must:

    (a) be in writing;

    (b) embody all the terms of the agreement;

    (c) be signed by the party to be charged or his agent, i.e. the client;

    (d) be reasonable in amount and be in lieu of ordinary profit costs.

1.2.3. Remuneration may be by a gross sum, commission, percentage, salary or otherwise, and should state whether the agreed remuneration is to be inclusive of disbursements and VAT. The agreement should specifically set out the method by which the remuneration is to be calculated.

1.2.4. An agreement which complies with section 57 is enforceable under the ordinary principles of contract law.

1.2.5. If the costs are ultimately taxed and the client raises an objection to the agreement on the grounds that it is unfair or unreasonable, the taxing officer may enquire into the facts and the court may set the agreement aside or reduce the amount payable and give such consequential directions as it thinks fit.

1.3. VAT

1.3.1. When giving an estimate or quotation for costs the solicitor should make it clear to the client whether or not VAT is included in the quoted sum.

1.3.2. If VAT is not mentioned it is presumed that the quotation or estimate is VAT inclusive.

1.3.3. Where an individual or firm is registered for VAT the firm's VAT registration number must appear on the bills issued by the firm or, if a separate tax invoice is issued, on the tax invoice.

1.3.4. The VAT registration number is also required to appear on any bill or fee note produced on a taxation of costs *inter partes*.

1.3.5. Stamp duties are exempt from VAT (see paras. A14 and A16).

1.3.6. Where the client's bill is reduced by the amount of commission which a solicitor has earned, e.g. on an endowment policy taken out by the client, VAT should be charged on the gross amount of the bill but in practice is sometimes only charged on the net sum.

1.3.7. Fees for telegraphic transfers, when passed on by a solicitor to his or her client, must bear VAT at the standard rate.

1.4. Delivery of bill

1.4.1. A solicitor is under a duty to render a bill of costs to his client within a reasonable time of concluding the matter to which the bill relates.

1.4.2. It is recommended practice to submit a bill to the client as soon as possible after the conclusion of the transaction and it is particularly important to do so where the solicitor is already holding sums of money on his client's behalf and is waiting for the client's approval of the bill before deducting his costs and accounting to the client for the balance, or where the client has asked for the papers and the solicitor is claiming a lien over them until his costs are met.

1.4.3. In residential conveyancing purchase transactions the bill is usually submitted to the client before completion on the understanding that the solicitor's charges are paid in full before completion. In sale transactions, the solicitor's costs are usually deducted from money held by the solicitor on the client's behalf before the balance is remitted to the client. If the client refuses to allow payment of costs by deduction the solicitor must nevertheless complete the transaction since he is obliged to fulfil his retainer.

1.4.4. A solicitor's bill of costs should contain sufficient information to identify the matter to which it relates and the period covered.

1.4.5. The form of the bill should comply with Solicitors Act 1974, s.69 and must be signed by the solicitor personally or by one of the partners in the firm. The signature may be either that of the solicitor signing the bill or made in the name of the firm. Alternatively the letter which accompanies and refers to the bill should be so signed. Unless this provision is complied with the solicitor will be unable to sue on the bill. A form of signature such as, e.g. 'signed A. Smith, a partner in A. Smith & Co.' is recommended to ensure that it can be proved in evidence (should it be necessary to sue) that the bill was signed by a solicitor and not merely by an unqualified assistant. Disbursements should be separately itemised in the bill.

1.4.6. A solicitor must not sue or threaten to sue unless he has first informed the client in writing of his right to require a remuneration certificate and of his right to seek taxation of the bill. The form of notice to be given to the client should be in the following wording:

> 'This constitutes notice of your right under paragraph 1 of Article 3 of the Solicitors' (Non-Contentious Business) Remuneration Order 1994 to require me within one month of the receipt hereof to obtain a certificate from the Law Society stating that in their opinion the costs charged are fair and reasonable or, as the case may be, what lesser sum would be fair and reasonable. Also there are provisions in sections 70, 71, and 72 of the Solicitors Act 1974 relating to taxation of costs which give you the right to have the bill checked by an officer of the High Court.'

1.4.7. This notice must be given even where costs are payable by deduction from money already held by the solicitor on behalf of the client.

1.5. Remuneration certificate

1.5.1. A client or residuary beneficiary of an estate where all the personal representatives are solicitors who is dissatisfied with his solicitor's bill may require the solicitor to apply to the Law Society for a remuneration certificate which will either state that in the opinion of the Law Society the sum charged by the solicitor is fair and reasonable, or what lesser sum would be fair and reasonable. If the sum stated in the remuneration certificate is less than the amount of the bill, the client need only pay the amount stated in the certificate. An application for a remuneration certificate is free of charge to the client. A client applying for a remuneration certificate must pay half the costs plus paid disbursements and VAT unless the solicitor agrees to waive this requirement.

1.5.2. The client is not entitled to require a remuneration certificate where:

(a) a period of more than one month has expired after the date on which he was notified of his right to such a certificate; or

(b) a bill has been delivered and paid (otherwise than by deduction without authority); or

(c) the High Court has ordered the bill to be taxed; or

(d) the bill exceeds £50,000, exclusive of VAT and disbursements.

1.5.3.   In addition to or as an alternative to a remuneration certificate the client may apply to have his bill taxed by the High Court.

1.5.4.   Except as below, the right to a remuneration certificate applies to the client in relation to his own solicitor's costs; it is not therefore available to a third party who has agreed to be responsible for another person's solicitor's costs. Where a third party is to pay the solicitor's bill, e.g. where a tenant is to pay his landlord's solicitor's costs, the tenant's solicitor should agree the fee to be paid at the outset of the transaction. Alternatively the third party can apply for a third party taxation within three months of delivery of the bill (see para. N1.6). A residuary beneficiary of an estate where the personal representatives are all solicitors may apply for a remuneration certificate.

1.6.   Taxation of costs

1.6.1.   The right to taxation of the bill by the High Court is in addition to or may be used by the client as an alternative to an application for a remuneration certificate. The costs of an application for taxation must be borne by the client.

1.6.2.   If in a non-contentious matter a taxing officer allows less than one-half of the sum charged to the client by the bill, he is under a duty to bring the facts of the case to the attention of the Law Society.

1.6.3.   A third party who is responsible for paying the costs of another can apply for a third party taxation within three months of delivery of the bill.

1.7.   Lender's costs

1.7.1.   The solicitor should consider making a separate charge for legal work carried out on behalf of the lender client.

1.7.2.   The solicitor should agree his charges with the lender client at the outset of the transaction.

1.7.3.   Under the terms of the Lenders' Handbook the borrower client is responsible for the lender's solicitor's costs (see Appendix VIII.3).

1.8.   Commissions

1.8.1.   Under Rule 10 Solicitors' Practice Rules 1990, a solicitor must normally account to his client for any commission received by him which exceeds £20. Thus where the solicitor introduces a client to an insurance company for the purposes of the client obtaining an insurance policy, and as a result of that introduction the solicitor receives commission from the insurance company, that commission will be subject to Rule 10. The solicitor is only entitled to keep a commission which exceeds £20 if, having disclosed its receipt and the amount to the client, the client agrees that the solicitor may keep the money. If the amount is not known, the solicitor must have disclosed the basis of the calculation of the commission to the client.

.8.2.   The rule does not apply where the solicitor acts as agent for a building society or other financial institution and a member of the public, whom the solicitor has not advised as a client about the investment of the money, deposits money with the solicitor.

.8.3.   Stock Exchange commissions fall within the scope of the rule.

.8.4.   The amount of any commission earned by the solicitor should be shown on the client's bill.

.9.   Recovery of charges

.9.1.   A solicitor may sue a client who does not pay his solicitor's bill provided that the conditions in the following paragraphs have been complied with.

.9.2.   A bill of costs in the proper form must have been delivered to the client.

.9.3.   In a non-contentious matter, a solicitor may not sue the client until the expiration of one month from the delivery of the bill, unless the solicitor had been given leave to do so on the grounds set out in Solicitors Act 1974, s.69. A solicitor must not sue or threaten to sue unless he has first informed the client in writing of his right to require a remuneration certificate and of his right to seek taxation of the bill. A statutory demand in bankruptcy can, however, be made within one month of an unpaid bill being presented.[1]

.9.4.   A lien exists by virtue of Solicitors Act 1974, s.73 which empowers the court to make a charging order over real or personal property belonging to the client as security for the solicitor's taxed costs.

. *Re A Debtor (No. 88 of 1991)* [1992] 4 All ER 301.

1.10.   Court of Protection work

1.10.1.   Fixed costs are payable for all conveyancing matters in the Court of Protection.

1.10.2.   Two elements will be allowable, as follows:

   (a) a sum of £146 in every case to cover correspondence with the Court of Protection, the preparation of the certificate or affidavit of value, and all other work solely attributable to the Court of Protection; together with

(b) a value element of 0.5% of the consideration up to £400,000 and 0.25% thereafter, with a minimum sum for this element of £282.

1.10.3. As well as a fee for both the above elements, VAT and disbursements will be allowed.

1.10.4. Fixed costs will apply to conveyancing of all types of property.

1.10.5. If solicitors wish, they may choose to have their costs taxed, rather than to accept fixed costs. It should, however, be emphasised that agreed costs will not be an option, save in exceptional circumstances.

APPENDICES

1. LAW SOCIETY RULES

1.1. Solicitors' Practice Rules 1990[1]

Rules dated 18th July 1990

made by the Council of the Law Society,

with the concurrence of the Master of the Rolls under section 31 of the Solicitors Act 1974 and section 9 of the Administration of Justice Act 1985

and the approval of the Lord Chancellor under Part II of Schedule 4 to the Courts and Legal Services Act 1990,

- *regulating the English and Welsh practices of solicitors, registered European lawyers, registered foreign lawyers and recognised bodies;*

- *and, in respect of Rule 12 only, regulating:*

  the practices of solicitors and recognised bodies in any part of the world;

  the practices of registered European lawyers in any part of the United Kingdom; and

  the practices of registered foreign lawyers in England and Wales;

  in the conduct of investment business in, into or from the United Kingdom.

Rule A (Scope of the rules)

(1)   These rules apply to all forms of practice of a solicitor of the Supreme Court.

(2)   The rules also extend to all regulated individuals and all regulated practices – see Rule 18(2) (interpretation).

(3)   The rules do not apply to practice from an office outside England and Wales – except for Rule 12 (investment business), the geographical scope of which is set out in the rule.

Rule 1 (Basic principles)

A solicitor shall not do anything in the course of practising as a solicitor, or permit another person to do anything on his or her behalf, which compromises or impairs or is likely to compromise or impair any of the following:

(a)   the solicitor's independence or integrity;

(b)   a person's freedom to instruct a solicitor of his or her choice;

(c)   the solicitor's duty to act in the best interests of the client;

(d)   the good repute of the solicitor or of the solicitor's profession;

(e)   the solicitor's proper standard of work;

(f)   the solicitor's duty to the Court.

1. With consolidated amendments to 1 March 2003.

Rule 2 (Publicity)

Solicitors may at their discretion publicise their practices, or permit other persons to do so, or publicise the businesses or activities of other persons, provided there is no breach of these rules and provided there is compliance with a Solicitors' Publicity Code promulgated from time to time by the Council of the Law Society with the concurrence of the Master of the Rolls.

Rule 3 (Introductions and referrals)

Solicitors may accept introductions and referrals of business from other persons and may make introductions and refer business to other persons, provided there is no breach of these rules and provided there is compliance with a Solicitors' Introduction and Referral Code promulgated from time to time by the Council of the Law Society with the concurrence of the Master of the Rolls.

Rule 4 (Employed solicitors)

(1) (a) Solicitors who are employees of non-solicitors shall not as part of their employment do for any person other than their employer work which is or could be done by a solicitor acting as such, save as permitted by an Employed Solicitors Code promulgated from time to time by the Council of the Law Society with the concurrence of the Master of the Rolls.

(b) In sub-paragraph (a) above, 'employee' includes a solicitor of the Supreme Court or registered European lawyer practising in house as the director of a company which is not a recognised body, and 'employer' and 'employment' shall be construed accordingly.

(c) Solicitors who are employees of:

(i) a registered European lawyer practising as sole principal;

(ii) a lawyers' partnership which includes a solicitor of the Supreme Court, registered European lawyer or recognised body; or

(iii) a recognised body;

are not 'employees of non-solicitors' for the purpose of this rule, and are therefore not subject to paragraph (1) of the rule.

(2) (a) Solicitors of the Supreme Court or registered European lawyers who are employees of a registered European lawyer practising as sole principal shall not draw or prepare any instrument or papers, or make any application or lodge any document, relating to the conveyancing of land or the administration of estates, which is reserved to qualified persons by the Solicitors Act 1974, or supervise or assume responsibility for any such work, unless the principal is a registered European lawyer qualified to do the work under regulation 12 or 13 of the European Communities (Lawyer's Practice) Regulations 2000.

(b) Solicitors of the Supreme Court or registered European lawyers who are employees of a regulated practice which is a partnership all of whose members are foreign lawyers and/or European lawyers' recognised bodies shall not do or supervise or assume responsibility for any of the work referred to in paragraph (2)(a) of this rule unless the partnership has at least one member who or which is

(i) a registered European lawyer qualified to do the work under regulation 12 or 13 of the European Communities (Lawyer's Practice) Regulations 2000; or

(ii) a company (a recognised body) with a director who is such a person; or

(iii) a limited liability partnership (a recognised body) with a member who is such a person.

(c) Registered European lawyers who are directors of a European lawyers' recognised body which is a company, or solicitors of the Supreme Court or registered European lawyers who

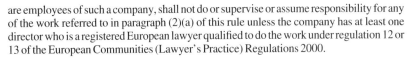

are employees of such a company, shall not do or supervise or assume responsibility for any of the work referred to in paragraph (2)(a) of this rule unless the company has at least one director who is a registered European lawyer qualified to do the work under regulation 12 or 13 of the European Communities (Lawyer's Practice) Regulations 2000.

(d) Registered European lawyers who are members of a European lawyers' recognised body which is a limited liability partnership, or solicitors of the Supreme Court or registered European lawyers who are employees of such a limited liability partnership, shall not do or supervise or assume responsibility for any of the work referred to in paragraph (2)(a) of this rule unless the limited liability partnership has at least one member who or which is:

(i) a registered European lawyer qualified to do the work under regulation 12 or 13 of the European Communities (Lawyer's Practice) Regulations 2000; or

(ii) a company (a recognised body) with a director who is such a person; or

(iii) another limited liability partnership (a recognised body) with a member who is such a person.

(e) In sub-paragraphs (b) to (d) above, 'European lawyers' recognised body' means:

(i) a recognised body which is a company and which has no director who is a solicitor of the Supreme Court; or

(ii) a recognised body which is a limited liability partnership and has no member who or which is:

(A) a solicitor of the Supreme Court; or

(B) a company (a recognised body) with a director who is a solicitor of the Supreme Court; or

(C) another limited liability partnership (a recognised body) with a member who is a solicitor of the Supreme Court.

Rule 5 (Providing services other than as a solicitor)

Solicitors must comply with the Solicitors' Separate Business Code in controlling, actively participating in or operating (in each case alone, or by or with others) a business which:

(a) provides any service which may properly be provided by a solicitor's practice, and

(b) is not itself:

(i) a regulated practice as defined in Rule 18(2) of these rules; or

(ii) a practice permitted to solicitors of the Supreme Court under the Solicitors' Overseas Practice Rules; or

(iii) a practice in Scotland or Northern Ireland permitted to registered European lawyers under the Solicitors' Overseas Practice Rules.

Rule 6 (avoiding conflicts of interest in conveyancing, property selling and mortgage related services)

(1) *(General)*

This rule sets out circumstances in which a solicitor may act for more than one party in conveyancing, property selling or mortgage related services, in connection with:

(i) the transfer of land for value at arm's length;

(ii) the grant or assignment of a lease, or some other interest in land, for value at arm's length; or

(iii) the grant of a mortgage of land.

The rule must be read in the light of the notes.

Notes

(i) *'Solicitor' (except where the notes specify otherwise)* **means a regulated individual or regulated practice, and any associated practice, and includes a SEAL;** *and*

- *'associated practices' are practices with at least one principal in common;*

- *a 'principal' is an individual or body corporate who or which is:*

  (a) *a sole practitioner,*

  (b) *in the case of a practice which is a partnership*

    (A) *a partner in the practice (including a partner who is not qualified to do conveyancing, such as a registered foreign lawyer),*

    (B) *a director of or shareowner in a company which has a share capital and which is a partner in the practice,*

    (C) *a director or member of a company which does not have a share capital and which is a partner in the practice, and*

    (D) *a member of a limited liability partnership which is a partner in the practice,*

  (c) *in the case of a practice which is a company with a share capital, a director of or shareowner in the company, and the company itself,*

  (d) *in the case of a practice which is a company without a share capital, a director or member of the company, and the company itself,*

  (e) *in the case of a practice which is a limited liability partnership:*

    (A) *a member of the practice,*

    (B) *the limited liability partnership itself,*

    (C) *a director of or shareowner in a company which has a share capital and which is a member of the practice,*

    (D) *a director or member of a company which does not have a share capital and which is a member of the practice, and*

    (E) *a member of another limited liability partnership which is a member of the practice;*

- *a 'SEAL' (Solicitors' Estate Agency Limited) means a recognised body which:*

  (a) *does not undertake conveyancing;*

  (b) *is owned jointly by at least four participating practices which do not have any principals in common and none of which has majority control; and*

  (c) *is conducted from accommodation physically divided from, and clearly differentiated from that of any participating practice; and*

- *a 'participating practice' means a solicitor's private practice one or more of whose principals is a shareowner in the SEAL (if the SEAL is a company with a share capital) or a member of the SEAL (if the SEAL is a company without a share capital or a limited liability partnership).*

(*ii*) *'Property selling' means negotiating the sale for the seller.*

(*iii*) *'Mortgage related services' means advising on or arranging a mortgage, or providing mortgage-related financial services, for a buyer; and*

- *'seller' and 'buyer' include lessor and lessee.*

(*iv*) *Whether a transaction is 'at arm's length' will depend on the relationship between the parties and the context of the transaction, and will not necessarily follow from the fact that a transaction is at market value, or is stated to be on arm's length terms.*

A transaction would not usually be at arm's length, for example, if the parties are:

- *related by blood, adoption or marriage;*

- *the settlor of a trust and the trustees;*

- *the trustees of a trust and its beneficiary or the beneficiary's relative;*

- *personal representatives and a beneficiary;*

- *the trustees of separate trusts for the same family;*

- *a sole trader or partners and a limited company set up to enable the business to be incorporated;*

- *associated companies (i.e. where one is a holding company and the other is its subsidiary within the meaning of the Companies Act 1985, or both are subsidiaries of the same holding company); or*

- *a local authority and a related body within the meaning of paragraph 6(b) of the Employed Solicitors' Code 1990.*

(*v*) *'Mortgage' includes a remortgage.*

(*vi*) *Nothing in the rule allows a solicitor to act in breach of Rule 6A(5) (acting for seller and one of two prospective buyers), or any other rule or principle of professional conduct.*

(*vii*) *Nothing in the rule allows a registered foreign lawyer or a registered European lawyer to undertake conveyancing unless, in the case of a registered European lawyer, he or she is authorised to do so under regulation 12 of the European Communities (Lawyer's Practice) Regulations 2000 – see Rule 4(2), note (ja) to Rule 13, Rule 18(1)(b)(iv) and note (ii) to Rule 18(1) of these rules, and Rules 4(3) and 5(6) of the Solicitors' Incorporated Practice Rules.*

(2) ***(Solicitor acting for seller and buyer)***

(a) A solicitor must not act for seller and buyer:

(i) without the written consent of both parties;

(ii) if a conflict of interest exists or arises; or

(iii) if the seller is selling or leasing as a builder or developer.

(b) Otherwise, a solicitor may act for seller and buyer, but only if:

(i) both parties are established clients; or

(ii) the consideration is £10,000 or less and the transaction is not the grant of a lease; or

(iii) there is no other qualified conveyancer in the area whom either the seller or the buyer could reasonably be expected to consult; or

(iv) seller and buyer are represented by two separate offices in different localities, and:

(A) different solicitors, who normally work at each office, conduct or supervise the transaction for seller and buyer; and

    (B)   no office of the practice (or an associated practice) referred either client to the office conducting his or her transaction; or

  (v)   the only way in which the solicitor is acting for the buyer is in providing mortgage related services; or

  (vi) the only way in which the solicitor is acting for the seller is in providing property selling services through a SEAL.

(c)   When a solicitor's practice (including a SEAL) acts in the property selling for the seller and acts for the buyer, the following additional conditions must be met:

    (i)   different individuals must conduct the work for the seller and the work for the buyer; and if the individuals conducting the work need supervision, they must be supervised by different solicitors; and

    (ii)   the solicitor must inform the seller in writing, before accepting instructions to deal with the property selling, of any services which might be offered to a buyer, whether through the same practice or any practice associated with it; and

    (iii) the solicitor must explain to the buyer, before the buyer gives consent to the arrangement:

        (A)   the implications of a conflict of interest arising; and

        (B)   the solicitor's financial interest in the sale going through; and

        (C)   if the solicitor proposes to provide mortgage related services to the buyer through a SEAL which is also acting for the seller, that the solicitor cannot advise the buyer on the merits of the purchase.

Notes

(i)   If a builder or developer acquires a property in part exchange, and sells it on without development, he or she is not, for the purpose of this rule, selling 'as a builder or developer'.

(ii)   The test of whether a person is an 'established client' is an objective one; that is, whether a reasonable solicitor would regard the person as an established client.

- *A seller or buyer who is instructing the solicitor for the first time is not an established client.*

- *An individual related by blood, adoption or marriage to an established client counts as an established client.*

- *A person counts as an established client if selling or buying jointly with an established client.*

(iii) The consideration will only count as £10,000 or less if the value of any property given in exchange or part exchange is taken into account.

(iv) Even where none of the other exceptions apply, a SEAL may act for the seller, and provide mortgage related services to the buyer; one of the participating practices may do the buyer's conveyancing, and another participating practice may do the seller's conveyancing.

(v)   'Solicitor'

- *in paragraph (2)(b)(iv)(A), means any solicitor of the Supreme Court or registered European lawyer who is conducting or supervising the transaction; and*

- *in paragraph (2)(c)(i), means the solicitor of the Supreme Court or registered European lawyer who is supervising the transaction;*

and if the work is conveyancing, the registered European lawyer must in each case be qualified to do conveyancing under regulation 12 of the European Communities (Lawyer's Practice) Regulations 2000 – see Rule 18(1)(b)(iv) and note (ii) to Rule 18(1).

(3) *(Solicitor acting for lender and borrower)*

(a) A solicitor must not act for both lender and borrower on the grant of a mortgage of land:

   (i) if a conflict of interest exists or arises;

   (ii) on the grant of an individual mortgage of land at arm's length;

   (iii) if, in the case of a standard mortgage of property to be used as the borrower's private residence only, the lender's mortgage instructions extend beyond the limitations contained in paragraphs (3)(c) and (3)(e), or do not permit the use of the certificate of title required by paragraph (3)(d); or

   (iv) if, in the case of any other standard mortgage, the lender's mortgage instructions extend beyond the limitations contained in paragraphs (3)(c) and (3)(e).

(b) A solicitor who proposes to act for both lender and borrower on the grant of a standard mortgage of land, must first inform the lender in writing of the circumstances if:

   (i) the solicitor or a member of his or her immediate family is a borrower; or

   (ii) the solicitor proposes to act for seller, buyer, and lender in the same transaction.

(c) A solicitor acting for both lender and borrower in a standard mortgage may only accept or act upon instructions from the lender which are limited to the following matters:

   (i) taking reasonable steps to check the identity of the borrower (and anyone else required to sign the mortgage deed or other document connected with the mortgage) by reference to a document or documents, such as a passport, precisely specified in writing by the lender;

   following the guidance in the Law Society's 'green card' warning on property fraud and 'blue card' warning on money laundering;

   checking that the seller's solicitors or licensed conveyancers (if unknown to the solicitor) appear in a current legal directory or hold practising certificates issued by their professional body;

   and, in the case of a lender with no branch office within reasonable proximity of the borrower, carrying out the money laundering checks precisely specified in writing by the lender;

   (ii) making appropriate searches relating to the property in public registers (for example, local searches, commons registration searches, mining searches), and reporting any results specified by the lender or which the solicitor considers may adversely affect the lender; or effecting search insurance;

   (iii) making enquiries on legal matters relating to the property reasonably specified by the lender, and reporting the replies;

   (iv) reporting the purchase price stated in the transfer and on how the borrower says that the purchase money (other than the mortgage advance) is to be provided; and reporting if the solicitor will not have control over the payment of all the purchase money (other than a deposit paid to an estate agent or a reservation fee paid to a builder or developer);

   (v) reporting if the seller or the borrower (if the property is already owned by the borrower) has not owned or been the registered owner of the property for at least six months;

   (vi) if the lender does not arrange insurance, confirming receipt of satisfactory evidence that the buildings insurance is in place for at least the sum required by the lender and covers the risks specified by the lender; giving notice to the insurer of the lender's interest and requesting confirmation that the insurer will notify the lender if the policy is not renewed or is cancelled; and supplying particulars of the insurance and the last premium receipt to the lender;

(vii)   investigating title to the property and appurtenant rights; reporting any defects revealed, advising on the need for any consequential statutory declarations or indemnity insurance, and approving and effecting indemnity cover if required by the lender; and reporting if the solicitor is aware of any rights needed for the use or enjoyment of the property over other land;

(viii)   reporting on any financial charges (for example, improvement or repair grants or Housing Act discounts) secured on the property revealed by the solicitor's searches and enquiries which will affect the property after completion of the mortgage;

(ix)   in the case of a leasehold property, confirming that the lease contains the terms stipulated by the lender and does not include any terms specified by the lender as unacceptable; obtaining a suitable deed of variation or indemnity insurance if the terms of the lease are unsatisfactory; enquiring of the seller or the borrower (if the property is already owned by the borrower) as to any known breaches of covenant by the landlord or any superior landlord and reporting any such breaches to the lender; reporting if the solicitor becomes aware of the landlord's absence or insolvency; making a company search and checking the last three years' published accounts of any management company with responsibilities under the lease; if the borrower is required to be a shareholder in the management company, obtaining the share certificate, a blank stock transfer form signed by the borrower and a copy of the memorandum and articles of association; obtaining any necessary consent to or prior approval of the assignment and mortgage; obtaining a clear receipt for the last payment of rent and service charge; and serving notice of the assignment and mortgage on the landlord;

(x)   if the property is subject to a letting, checking that the type of letting and its terms comply with the lender's requirements;

(xi)   making appropriate pre-completion searches, including a bankruptcy search against the borrower, any other person in whom the legal estate is vested and any guarantor;

(xii)   receiving, releasing and transmitting the mortgage advance, including asking for any final inspection needed and dealing with any retentions and cashbacks;

(xiii)   procuring execution of the mortgage deed and form of guarantee as appropriate by the persons whose identities have been checked in accordance with any requirements of the lender under paragraph (3)(c)(i) as those of the borrower, any other person in whom the legal estate is vested and any guarantor; obtaining their signatures to the forms of undertaking required by the lender in relation to the use, occupation or physical state of the property; and complying with the lender's requirements if any document is to be executed under a power of attorney;

(xiv)   asking the borrower for confirmation that the information about occupants given in the mortgage instructions or offer is correct; obtaining consents in the form required by the lender from existing or prospective occupiers of the property aged 17 or over specified by the lender, or of whom the solicitor is aware;

(xv)   advising the borrower on the terms of any document required by the lender to be signed by the borrower;

(xvi)   advising any other person required to sign any document on the terms of that document or, if there is a conflict of interest between that person and the borrower or the lender, advising that person on the need for separate legal advice and arranging for him or her to see an independent conveyancer;

(xvii) obtaining the legal transfer of the property to the mortgagor;

(xviii) procuring the redemption of (A) existing mortgages on property the subject of any associated sale of which the solicitor is aware, and (B) any other mortgages secured against a property located in England or Wales made by an identified lender where an identified account number or numbers or a property address has been given by the lender;

(xix) ensuring the redemption or postponement of existing mortgages on the property, and registering the mortgage with the priority required by the lender;

(xx) making administrative arrangements in relation to any collateral security, such as an endowment policy, or in relation to any collateral warranty or guarantee relating to the physical condition of the property, such as NHBC documentation;

(xxi) registering the transfer and mortgage;

(xxii) giving legal advice on any matters reported on under this paragraph (3)(c), suggesting courses of action open to the lender, and complying with the lender's instructions on the action to be taken;

(xxiii) disclosing any relationship specified by the lender between the solicitor and borrower;

(xxiv) storing safely the title deeds and documents pending registration and delivery to or as directed by the lender;

(xxv) retaining the information contained in the solicitor's conveyancing file for at least six years from the date of the mortgage.

(d) In addition, a solicitor acting for both lender and borrower in a standard mortgage of property to be used as the borrower's private residence only:

(i) must use the certificate of title set out in the Appendix, or as substituted from time to time by the Council with the concurrence of the Master of the Rolls ('the approved certificate'); and

(ii) unless the lender has certified that its mortgage instructions are subject to the limitations contained in paragraphs (3)(c) and (3)(e), must notify the lender on receipt of instructions that the approved certificate will be used, and that the solicitor's duties to the lender are limited to the matters contained in the approved certificate.

(See also note (iii) below.)

(e) The terms of this rule will prevail in the event of any ambiguity in the lender's instructions, or discrepancy between the instructions and paragraph (3)(c) or the approved certificate.

Anti-avoidance

(f) (i) Subject to paragraph (3)(f)(ii), a solicitor who is acting only for the borrower in a standard mortgage of property must not accept or act upon any requirements by way of undertaking, warranty, guarantee or otherwise of the lender, the lender's solicitor or other agent which extend beyond the limitations contained in paragraph (3)(c).

(ii) Provided the property is not to be used solely as the borrower's private residence, paragraph (3)(f)(i) does not prevent the borrower's solicitor from giving any form of certificate of title recognised from time to time by the Council of the Law Society (a 'recognised certificate'). Additions or amendments which arise from the individual transaction may be made to the text of a recognised certificate but, to the extent to which they create an increased or additional obligation, must not extend beyond the limitations contained in paragraph (3)(c).

Notes

(i) *A mortgage is a 'standard mortgage' where (1) it is provided in the normal course of the lender's activities; (2) a significant part of the lender's activities consists of lending; and (3) the mortgage is on standard terms. An 'individual mortgage' is any other mortgage.*

- *A mortgage will not be on standard terms if material terms in any of the documents relating to the mortgage transaction are negotiated between the lender's solicitor and the borrower's solicitor contemporaneously with effecting the mortgage. In commercial transactions, the element of negotiation will often relate to the facility letter or facility agreement rather than the mortgage deed itself.*

- *Provided there has been no contemporaneous negotiation of material terms between the parties' solicitors, a mortgage will be on standard terms where the lender uses a prescribed form of mortgage deed. Minor variations, such as the usual clause limiting the liability of trustee mortgagors, are not regarded as material and do not alter the nature of these terms as standard.*

- *In addition to its normal standard terms, a lender may have a different set or sets of standard terms applicable to specialised types of borrower, such as registered social landlords. Provided these terms are applied by the lender to all equivalent specialist borrowers or have been agreed between the lender and a specialist borrower as applicable to all transactions between them, they will constitute standard terms for the purposes of the rule.*

- *The lender and the borrower must be separately represented on the grant of an individual mortgage at arm's length (see paragraph (3)(a)(ii)). The rest of the rule is not then applicable.*

- *A solicitor may act for both lender and borrower in a standard mortgage, provided (1) there is no conflict of interests; (2) the mortgage instructions do not go beyond the limits set out in paragraph (3)(c); and (3) in the case of a property to be used solely as the borrower's private residence, the approved certificate of title set out in the Appendix is used (see paragraphs (3)(a)(iii)–(iv) and note (iv)).*

- *The limitations of paragraph (3)(c) also apply to a standard mortgage where the lender and the borrower are separately represented (see paragraph (3)(f)(i) which includes certificates of title). However, paragraph (3)(f)(ii) allows the borrower's solicitor, in a transaction where the property is not to be used solely as the borrower's private residence, to give a certificate of title in any form recognised by the Law Society. A solicitor also remains free to give any other form of certificate which complies with the rule.*

- *There may be cases where the lapse of time between the mortgage offer and completion (for example, when new properties are added) results in use of an earlier edition of a recognised certificate. That is acceptable.*

(ii) *A solicitor will not be in breach of paragraphs (3)(a)(iii)–(iv) or (c) if the lender has certified that its mortgage instructions and documents sent pursuant to those instructions are subject to the limitations set out in paragraphs (3)(c) and (e), and certifies any subsequent instructions and documents in the same way. If there is no certification, a solicitor acting in a transaction involving the charge of property to be used solely as the borrower's private residence must notify the lender that the approved certificate of title will be used and that the solicitor's duties to the lender will be limited accordingly (see paragraph (3)(d)(ii)). In other types of transaction, the solicitor should draw the lender's attention to the provisions of paragraphs (3)(c) and (e) and state that he or she cannot act on any instructions which extend beyond the matters contained in paragraph (3)(c).*

(iii) *As an alternative to printing the approved certificate for each transaction, it is acceptable for a lender to use a short form certificate of title which incorporates the approved certificate by reference. The form must include in the following order:*

- *the title 'Certificate of Title';*

- *the contents of the details box in the order set out in the approved certificate (use of two columns is acceptable) but with details not required shaded out or stated not to be required; and*

- *the wording 'We, the conveyancers named above, give the Certificate of Title set out in the Appendix to Rule 6(3) of the Solicitors' Practice Rules 1990 as if the same were set out in full, subject to the limitations contained in it.'*

Administrative details, such as a request for cheque, may follow the Certificate of Title.

(iv) *The approved certificate is only required for a transaction where the property is to be used solely as the borrower's private residence. The approved certificate need not, therefore, be used for investment properties such as blocks of flats, business premises such as shops (even if living accommodation is attached), or 'buy to let mortgages' on properties which are not intended for owner-occupation.*

(v) *'Solicitor' in paragraph (3)(b)(i) means any principal in the practice (or an associated practice), and any solicitor of the Supreme Court or registered European lawyer who is conducting or supervising the transaction, whether or not he or she is a principal; and*

- *'immediate family' means spouse, children, parents, brothers and sisters.*

'Solicitor' in sub-paragraphs (i)–(xxv) of paragraph (3)(c) means the practice instructed and any solicitor of the Supreme Court or registered European lawyer conducting or supervising the transaction.

(vi) *The lender must be informed of the circumstances, in accordance with paragraph (3)(b) so that the lender can decide whether or not to instruct the solicitor.*

(vii) *A lender's instructions (see paragraph (3)(c)(xxiii)) may require a wider disclosure of a solicitor's circumstances than paragraph (3)(b) requires; and a solicitor must assess whether the circumstances give rise to a conflict. For example, there will be a conflict between lender and borrower if the solicitor becomes involved in negotiations relating to the terms of the loan. A conflict might arise from the relationship a solicitor has with the borrower – for example, if the solicitor is the borrower's creditor or debtor or the borrower's business associate or co-habitant.*

(viii) *In relation to paragraph (3)(f)(ii), the limitations contained in paragraph (3)(c) will not apply to the insertion into a recognised certificate of any information required by that certificate. For example, where the recognised certificate requires details of the parties' repairing obligations under a lease of the property, the borrower's solicitor may provide a summary of the relevant terms of the lease despite the general limitation contained in paragraph (3)(c)(ix). However, any additions or amendments to the text of a recognised certificate to suit a particular transaction must not, to the extent to which they create an increased or additional obligation, extend beyond the limitations contained in paragraph (3)(c).*

(ix) *Many lenders require their solicitor to check the vires of corporate borrowers and that the correct procedures have been followed to ensure the validity of the mortgage. Paragraph (3)(c)(xiii) enables lenders to impose duties on solicitors in relation to the execution of the mortgage and guarantee. Within this context it is perfectly proper for a lender to require a solicitor to obtain such information as the circumstances may require in relation to the capacity of, or execution of documents by, the borrower, third party mortgagor or guarantor; for instance, by way of certified copy minutes or an opinion from a foreign lawyer as to the validity and enforceability of the security or guarantee given by a foreign registered company. There is no reason why solicitors should not assist corporate clients by drafting minutes or board resolutions. Solicitors should not, however, themselves certify the validity or passing of resolutions unless they were present at the meeting and have verified that it was convened and held strictly in accordance with all relevant requirements.*

(x)   *Paragraph (3)(c)(xx) allows a solicitor to accept instructions from a lender to carry out administrative arrangements in relation to any collateral security. This expression includes associated debentures, collateral warranties, second charges, rent assignments, charges over rent income and deeds of priority. The administrative arrangements necessarily include the preparation and execution of the relevant documents and subsequent registration.*

[Please note: The Certificate of Title has been extracted to form Appendix VII.2.]

Rule 6A (Seller's solicitor dealing with more than one prospective buyer)

(1)   This rule applies to the conveyancing of freehold and leasehold property. The rule is to be interpreted in the light of the notes.

Notes

(i)   *Rule 6A applies to all conveyancing of land, whether the transaction is of a 'commercial' or 'domestic' nature.*

(ii)   *Rule 6A does not set terms for a contract race. It lays down requirements which must be met when a solicitor is instructed to deal with more than one prospective buyer. The rule imposes no obligation on the seller's solicitor to exchange contracts with the first buyer to deliver a signed contract and deposit. It will be a matter of law whether or not the seller has entered into a contractual obligation to exchange with the buyer 'first past the post', or whether the whole matter remains 'subject to contract'.*

(2)   Where a seller instructs a solicitor to deal with more than one prospective buyer, the solicitor (with the client's consent) shall immediately disclose the seller's decision, if possible by telephone or fax, to the solicitor or other conveyancer acting for each prospective buyer or direct to the prospective buyer if acting in person. Such disclosure, if made by telephone, shall at once be confirmed by letter or fax. If the seller refuses to authorise disclosure, the solicitor shall immediately cease to act. Each prospective buyer must be notified each time a decision is taken to deal with any further prospective buyer.

Notes

(i)   *It is the seller's decision to deal with more than one prospective buyer which must be notified. The seller's solicitor must not wait until contracts are actually submitted but must notify the appropriate parties immediately upon receiving instructions to deal with a prospective buyer (other than the first).*

(ii)   *A solicitor will have been instructed to deal with a prospective buyer where the solicitor is asked to submit a draft contract or to provide any other documentation or information (e.g. a plan or a note of the Land Registry title number) in order to facilitate the conveyancing of the premises to the prospective buyer. The rule does not, however, cover activities normally performed by an estate agent, such as issuing particulars of sale, showing prospective buyers round the property, and negotiating the price.*

(iii) *The rule will apply where the contracts are to contain non-identical terms (e.g. where one contract is to include additional land). It will also apply where the contracts are to relate to different interests in the same property where the sale of one such interest would affect the sale of the other. For example, a party negotiating to take a lease of premises will be affected by another party negotiating to buy the freehold with vacant possession, since the sale of one precludes the sale of the other. On the other hand, the rule would not apply where the seller is proposing to grant a lease and to effect a simultaneous sale of the freehold reversion subject to that lease, since neither transaction precludes the other.*

(iv)   *Where a prospective buyer has retained an unqualified conveyancer, solicitors are reminded to consult the Council guidance on dealing with unqualified conveyancers (Annex 25A in the 1999 edition of 'The Guide to the Professional Conduct of Solicitors'). However, so far as Rule 6A is concerned, the obligations in paragraph (2) will be met by disclosure either to the prospective buyer direct or to the unqualified conveyancer.*

(3)   The obligations in paragraph (2) of this rule apply where a seller client, to the solicitor's knowledge, deals (whether directly or through another solicitor or other conveyancer) with another prospective buyer (or with that buyer's solicitor or other conveyancer).

Note

> *'Deals with another prospective buyer' should be interpreted in the light of note (ii) to paragraph (2).*

(4)   A solicitor shall not act for more than one of the prospective buyers.

Notes

(i)   *'Prospective buyers' should be interpreted in the light of note (ii) to paragraph (2).*

(ii)   *This part of the rule recognises the inevitable conflict of interest which makes it impossible for a solicitor to act for more than one of the prospective buyers.*

(5)   A solicitor shall not act for both the seller and one of the prospective buyers, even in a case which would fall within Rule 6(2)(b) of these rules.

Notes

(i)   *'Prospective buyers' should be interpreted in the light of note (ii) to paragraph (2).*

(ii)   *Clearly a solicitor must not act for both where it is known at the time of taking instructions on behalf of the buyer that there is more than one prospective buyer. In addition, this part of the rule does not permit a solicitor to continue to act for both in a case falling within Rule 6(2), where another prospective buyer is introduced during the course of the transaction because of the significant inherent conflict; the solicitor would find it impossible to reconcile the interests of both clients if, for example, it was in the seller's best interests to exchange with the other prospective buyer.*

(6)   For the purposes of this rule a prospective buyer shall continue to be treated as such until either the prospective buyer or the seller gives written notice (either by letter or by fax) of withdrawal from the transaction, such notice to be between solicitors or other conveyancers save where such notice is given by or to a prospective buyer acting in person.

Notes

(i)   *Solicitors should take particular care where a contract has been submitted but nothing has been heard from the prospective buyer's solicitor for some time. If the seller decides to deal with another buyer, the rule must still be complied with unless the seller's solicitor has already given notice of withdrawal.*

(ii)   *Where a prospective buyer has retained an unqualified conveyancer, the provisions of paragraph (6) should be interpreted in the light of note (iv) to paragraph (2).*

(7) This rule does not apply to a proposed sale by auction or tender. The rule does, however, apply to require disclosure to a prospective buyer by private treaty of instructions to offer the property by auction or tender.

Rule 7 (Fee sharing, partnership and corporate practice)

(1) A solicitor shall not share or agree to share his or her professional fees with any person except:

    (a) a practising solicitor;

    (b) a practising lawyer of another jurisdiction (other than a lawyer who has been struck off the register of foreign lawyers or the register of European lawyers, or whose registration has been suspended);

    (ba) a non-registered European lawyer partner in a partnership permitted by paragraph (6)(c) of this rule;

    (bb) a body corporate wholly owned and controlled, for the purpose of practising law, by lawyers within sub-paragraph (b) above, but without the involvement of registered European lawyers or registered foreign lawyers practising as such as directors, members or owners of shares;

    (bc) a body corporate permitted under Rule 9(1)(a) of the Solicitors' Overseas Practice Rules;

    (c) the solicitor's *bona fide* employee, which provision shall not permit under the cloak of employment a partnership prohibited by paragraph (6) of this rule; or

    (d) a retired partner or predecessor of the solicitor or the dependants or personal representatives of a deceased partner or predecessor.

(2) Notwithstanding paragraph (1) of this rule a solicitor who instructs an estate agent as sub-agent for the sale of properties may remunerate the estate agent on the basis of a proportion of the solicitor's professional fee.

(3) The exceptions set out in paragraphs 2 to 9 of the Employed Solicitors Code shall where necessary also operate as exceptions to this rule but only to permit fee sharing with the solicitor's employer (as defined in Rule 4(1) of these rules).

(4) A solicitor who works as a volunteer in a law centre or advice service operated by a charitable or similar non-commercial organisation may pay to the organisation any fees or costs that he or she receives under the legal aid scheme.

(5) For the purposes of sub-paragraph (1)(d) above, the references to a retired or deceased partner shall be construed,

    (a) in relation to a recognised body which is a company with a share capital, as meaning a retired or deceased director of or shareowner in that body,

    (b) in relation to a recognised body which is a company without a share capital, as meaning a retired or deceased director or member of the body, and

    (c) in relation to a recognised body which is a limited liability partnership, as meaning

        (i) a retired or deceased member of the body, or

        (ii) a retired or deceased director of or shareowner in a company which is or was a member of the body, or

        (iii) a retired or deceased member of a limited liability partnership which is or was a member of the body.

(6) Solicitors of the Supreme Court, registered European lawyers and recognised bodies are permitted to practise in the following types of partnership only:

(a) a partnership consisting of solicitors of the Supreme Court and/or registered European lawyers and/or recognised bodies;

(b) a partnership consisting of solicitors of the Supreme Court and/or registered European lawyers, together with registered foreign lawyers; and

(c) a partnership consisting of registered European lawyers with or without registered foreign lawyers, together with non-registered European lawyers who are based at offices in member states but outside England and Wales.

(d) In paragraph (6)(c) above:

(i) 'non-registered European lawyer' means a member of a legal profession which is covered by the Establishment of Lawyers Directive 98/5/EC, but who is not:

(A) a solicitor of the Supreme Court, registered European lawyer or registered foreign lawyer,

(B) a barrister of England and Wales, Northern Ireland or the Irish Republic, or

(C) a Scottish advocate; and

(ii) 'member state' means a state to which the Establishment of Lawyers Directive 98/5/EC applies.

(7) A solicitor of the Supreme Court or registered European lawyer shall not practise through any body corporate except a recognised body, or save as permitted under Rule 4 of these rules.

Rule 8 (Contingency fees)

(1) A solicitor who is retained or employed to prosecute or defend any action, suit or other contentious proceeding shall not enter into any arrangement to receive a contingency fee in respect of that proceeding, save one permitted under statute or by the common law.

(2) Paragraph (1) of this rule shall not apply to an arrangement in respect of an action, suit or other contentious proceeding in any country other than England and Wales to the extent that the local lawyer would be permitted to receive a contingency fee in respect of that proceeding.

Rule 9 (Claims assessors)

(1) A solicitor shall not, in respect of any claim or claims arising as a result of death or personal injury, either enter into an arrangement for the introduction of clients with or act in association with any person (not being a solicitor) whose business or any part of whose business is to make, support or prosecute (whether by action or otherwise, and whether by a solicitor or agent or otherwise) claims arising as a result of death or personal injury and who in the course of such business solicits or receives contingency fees in respect of such claims.

(2) The prohibition in paragraph (1) of this rule shall not apply to an arrangement or association with a person who solicits or receives contingency fees only in respect of proceedings in a country outside England and Wales, to the extent that a local lawyer would be permitted to receive a contingency fee in respect of such proceedings.

Rule 10 (Receipt of commissions from third parties)

(1) Solicitors shall account to their clients for any commission received of more than £20 unless, having disclosed to the client in writing the amount or basis of calculation of the commission or (if the

precise amount or basis cannot be ascertained) an approximation thereof, they have the client's agreement to retain it.

(2) Where the commission actually received is materially in excess of the amount or basis or approximation disclosed to the client the solicitor shall account to the client for the excess.

(3) This rule does not apply where a member of the public deposits money with a solicitor who is acting as agent for a building society or other financial institution and the solicitor has not advised that person as a client as to the disposition of the money.

Rule 11

[repealed]

Rule 12 (Investment business)

(1) Without prejudice to the generality of the principles embodied in Rule 1 of these rules, solicitors shall not in connection with investment business:

    (a) be appointed representatives; or

    (b) have any arrangement with other persons under which the solicitors could be constrained to recommend to clients or effect for them (or refrain from doing so) transactions in some investments but not others, with some persons but not others, or through the agency of some persons but not others; or to introduce or refer clients or other persons with whom the solicitors deal to some persons but not others.

(2) Solicitors shall not alone, or by or with others, control, actively participate in or operate any separate business which is an appointed representative, unless it is the appointed representative of an independent financial adviser.

(3) [deleted]

(4) This rule shall have effect in relation to the conduct of investment business in, into or from the United Kingdom by:

    (a) a solicitor of the Supreme Court or recognised body practising from an office anywhere in the world;

    (b) a registered European lawyer practising from an office anywhere in the United Kingdom; or

    (c) a registered foreign lawyer practising from an office in England and Wales.

(5) In this rule 'investment business' means any 'regulated activity' as defined in the Financial Services and Markets Act 2000; and 'appointed representative' and 'investment' have the meanings given in that Act.

Rule 13 (Supervision and management of a practice)

[See also Annex A at page 74.]

In this rule, words in italics are defined in the notes.

(1) The *principals* in a practice must ensure that their practice is supervised and managed so as to provide for:

    (a) compliance with *principal* solicitors' duties at law and in conduct to exercise proper *supervision* over their admitted and unadmitted staff;

(b) adequate *supervision* and direction of clients' matters;

(c) compliance with the requirements of sections 22(2A) and 23(3) of the Solicitors Act 1974, section 9(4) of the Administration of Justice Act 1985 and section 84(2)(c) of the Immigration and Asylum Act 1999 as to the direction and *supervision* of unqualified persons;

(d) effective *management* of the practice generally.

2) Every practice must have at least one *principal* who is a solicitor *qualified to supervise.*

3) (a) Except as provided in (b) below, every office of the practice must have at least one solicitor *qualified to supervise,* for whom that office is his or her *normal place of work.*

(b) Without prejudice to the requirements of paragraph (1) of this rule, an office which undertakes only property selling and ancillary mortgage related services as defined in rule 6 of these rules, survey and valuation services, must be managed and supervised to the following minimum standards:

(i) the day-to-day control and administration must be undertaken by a suitably qualified and experienced office manager who is a fit and proper person to undertake such work; and for whom that office is his or her normal place of work; and

(ii) the office must be supervised and managed by a solicitor *qualified to supervise,* who must visit the office with sufficient frequency and spend sufficient time there to allow for adequate control of and consultation with staff, and if necessary consultation with clients.

4) This rule is to be interpreted in the light of the notes, and is subject to the transitional provisions set out in note (k).

5) (a) This rule applies to private practice, and to solicitors employed by a law centre.

(b) The rule also applies to other employed solicitors, but only:

(i) if they advise or act for members of the public under the legal aid scheme; or

(ii) if, in acting for members of the public, they exercise any *right of audience* or *right to conduct litigation,* or supervise anyone exercising those rights.

Notes

(a) *Principals' responsibility for the practice*

Principals are responsible at law and in conduct for their practices, and compliance with the rule does not derogate from this responsibility. Under rule 6 of these rules, property selling or mortgage related services to one party to a conveyance, and conveyancing services for the other party, may not be supervised by the same solicitor.

(b) *'Supervision' and 'management'*

(i) *'Supervision' refers to the professional overseeing of staff and the professional overseeing of clients' matters.*

(ii) *'Management' is a wider concept, which encompasses the overall direction and development of the practice and its day-to-day control and administration. Management functions include business efficiency as well as professional competence.*

(iii) *Operationally, supervision and management may be delegated within an established framework for reporting and accountability. However, the responsibility under paragraph (1)(a) of the rule, and the responsibility referred to in note (a) above, remain with the principals.*

(iv) 'With sufficient frequency' in paragraph (3)(b)(ii) would normally mean daily; but if the office is open at weekends it may be possible to defer consultations with clients until a weekday and be available only at need to staff.

(c) *Evidence of effective supervision and management*

Where a question arises as to compliance with paragraph (1) of the rule, principals will be expected to be able to produce evidence of a systematic and effective approach to the supervision and management of the practice. Such evidence may include the implementation by the practice of one or more of the following:

(i) guidance on the supervision and execution of particular types of work issued from time to time by the Law Society including guidance on solicitors' responsibilities for the supervision of clerks exercising rights of audience under section 27(2)(e) of the Courts and Legal Services Act 1990;

(ii) the practice's own properly documented management standards and procedures;

(iii) practice management standards promoted from time to time by the Law Society;

(iv) accounting standards and procedures promoted from time to time by the Law Society;

(v) external quality standards such as BS EN ISO 9000 or Investors in People; and

(vi) in the case of solicitors employed by a law centre, any management standards or procedures laid down by its management committee.

(d) *'Qualified to supervise'*

A solicitor is qualified to supervise if he or she:

(i) has held practising certificates for at least 36 months within the last ten years; and

(ii) has completed the training specified from time to time by the Law Society for the purpose of the rule.

(e) *'Normal place of work'*

(i) A solicitor's 'normal place of work' is the office from which he or she normally works, even though the day-to-day demands of practice may often take the solicitor out of the office.

(ii) If a solicitor normally works from a particular office for a part of the working week, that office is his or her 'normal place of work' for that part of the week. The solicitor may have a different 'normal place of work' for another part of the week.

(iii) A solicitor who has a different 'normal place of work' for different parts of the week could be the sole solicitor qualified to supervise at different offices at different times in the week. However, no solicitor can be the sole solicitor qualified to supervise at two different offices for the same part of the week.

(iv) For compliance with paragraph (3) of the rule, an office must, for every part of the working week, have a solicitor qualified to supervise for whom that office is his or her 'normal place of work' for that part of the week. This could be a different solicitor for different parts of the week.

(v) The working week of an office includes early mornings, late evenings and weekends if work is carried on, and if so the office must have a solicitor qualified to supervise for those times. However, it is not required that the solicitor qualified to supervise normally works at those times, provided that he or she:

(A) is available for emergency consultation, and

(B) pays occasional visits to the office during such times.

(f) *Working away from the office*

It is particularly important that systems of supervision and management encompass the work of:

   (i) *those persons from time to time working away from the office – e.g. at home, visiting clients, at court, at a police station, at a consulting room open only for a few hours per week, or staffing a stand at an exhibition;*

   (ii) *any person who normally works away from the office, such as a teleworker or homeworker.*

(g) *Absence of solicitor qualified to supervise, or office manager*

   (i) *When the solicitor qualified to supervise at an office is away on holiday, on sick leave, etc., suitable arrangements must be in place to ensure that any duties to clients and others are fully met. A similar standard applies to the absence of an office manager with responsibility for the day-to-day control and administration of a property selling office.*

   (ii) *If the solicitor qualified to supervise will be away for a month or more, the arrangements will normally need to include the provision of another solicitor qualified to supervise at that office. A similar standard applies to the absence of an office manager with responsibility for the day-to-day control and administration of a property selling office.*

(h) *'Right of audience' and 'right to conduct litigation'*

'Right of audience' and 'right to conduct litigation' are to be interpreted in accordance with Part II and section 119 of the Courts and Legal Services Act 1990 – see Rule 18(2)(fe).

(i) *'Principals'*

   (i) *'Principal', in Rule 13(1) and notes (a)–(c), means:*

      (A) *a sole practitioner;*

      (B) *if the practice is a partnership, an individual or recognised body who or which is a partner in the practice;*

      (C) *if the practice is a recognised body which is a company, the company and its directors;*

      (D) *if the practice is a recognised body which is a limited liability partnership, the limited liability partnership and its members.*

   (ii) *'Principal', in Rule 13(2) and note (j), means an individual who is:*

      (A) *a sole practitioner;*

      (B) *if the practice is a partnership, a partner in the practice;*

      (C) *if the practice is a recognised body which is a company, a director of the company;*

      (D) *if the practice is a recognised body which is a limited liability partnership:*

         (I) *a member of the body; or*

         (II) *a director of a company (a recognised body) which is a member of the body; or*

         (III) *a member of a limited liability partnership (a recognised body) which is a member of the body.*

(ia) *Registered European lawyers*

   (i) *A registered European lawyer may fulfil the role of a 'solicitor qualified to supervise' for the purpose of paragraph (2) or (3) of the rule or note (k)(ii)(C) below, provided that he or she has:*

(A) *practised as a lawyer for at least 36 months within the last ten years; and*

(B) *completed any training specified from time to time by the Law Society under note (d)(ii) above.*

(ii) *A solicitor of the Supreme Court who was formerly a registered European lawyer will be a 'solicitor qualified to supervise' if he or she has:*

(A) *practised as a lawyer for at least 36 months within the last ten years; and*

(B) *completed the training specified from time to time by the Law Society under note (d)(ii) above.*

(j) *Registered foreign lawyers*

(i) *A registered foreign lawyer who is a principal in the practice may fulfil the role of a 'solicitor qualified to supervise' for the purpose of paragraph (2) of the rule, provided that:*

(A) *the practice has at least one principal who is a solicitor of the Supreme Court or registered European lawyer; and*

(B) *the practice does not exercise or assume responsibility for any right of audience or any right to conduct litigation; and*

(C) *the registered foreign lawyer has practised as a lawyer for at least 36 months within the last ten years; and*

(D) *he or she has completed the training specified under note (d)(ii) above.*

(ii) *A registered foreign lawyer who is a principal in the practice may fulfil the role of a 'solicitor qualified to supervise' for the purpose of paragraph (3) of the rule or note (k)(ii)(C) below, provided that:*

(A) *no right of audience or right to conduct litigation is exercised or supervised from that office; and*

(B) *the practice has at least one principal who is a solicitor of the Supreme Court or registered European lawyer; and*

(C) *the registered foreign lawyer has practised as a lawyer for at least 36 months within the last ten years; and*

(D) *he or she has completed the training specified under note (d)(ii) above.*

(ja) *Conveyancing and probate*

A registered foreign lawyer, or a registered European lawyer (unless qualified to do conveyancing or probate work under regulation 12 or 13 of the European Communities (Lawyer's Practice) Regulations 2000), may not supervise conveyancing or probate work for the purposes of section 22(2A) or 23(3) of the Solicitors Act 1974 or section 9(4) of the Administration of Justice Act 1985, but may, subject to the requirements of the rule, fulfil the role of a 'solicitor qualified to supervise' in a practice or at an office where such work is done.

(k) *Transitional provisions*

For a period of 10 years from 23rd December 1999:

(i) *a solicitor of the Supreme Court, registered European lawyer or registered foreign lawyer who would not satisfy the requirements for a solicitor qualified to supervise can nevertheless fulfil that role for the purpose of paragraph (2) of the rule or note (k)(ii)(C) below, provided that:*

(A) *immediately before 12th December 1996 he or she was qualified to supervise an office under Practice Rule 13(1)(a) as it then stood, or any waiver of that rule; and*

(B) *any requirements of that rule or of any waiver continue to be met;*

(ii) *a person who would not satisfy the requirements for a solicitor qualified to supervise can nevertheless fulfil that role for the purpose of paragraph (3) of the rule, provided that:*

(A) *immediately before 12th December 1996 he or she was managing or employed to manage an office in compliance with Practice Rule 13(1)(b) as it then stood, or any waiver of that rule; and*

(B) *any requirements of that rule or of any waiver continue to be met; and*

(C) *the office is attended on a daily basis by a solicitor qualified to supervise.*

Rule 14 (Structural surveys and formal valuations)

Solicitors may not provide structural surveys or formal valuations of property unless the work is carried out by a principal, director, member (in the case of a limited liability partnership) or employee who is a chartered surveyor or who holds another professional qualification approved by the Council

Rule 15 (Costs information and client care)

Solicitors shall:

(a) give information about costs and other matters, and

(b) operate a complaints handling procedure,

in accordance with a Solicitors' Costs Information and Client Care Code made from time to time by the Council of the Law Society with the concurrence of the Master of the Rolls, but subject to the notes.

Notes

(i) *A serious breach of the code, or persistent breaches of a material nature, will be a breach of the rule, and may also be evidence of inadequate professional services under section 37A of the Solicitors Act 1974.*

(ii) *Material breaches of the code which are not serious or persistent will not be a breach of the rule, but may be evidence of inadequate professional services under section 37A.*

(iii) *The powers of the Office for the Supervision of Solicitors on a finding of inadequate professional services include:*

(a) *disallowing all or part of the solicitor's costs; and*

(b) *directing the solicitor to pay compensation to the client up to a limit of £5,000.*

(iv) *Non-material breaches of the code will not be a breach of the rule, and will not be evidence of inadequate professional services under section 37A.*

(v) *Registered foreign lawyers practising in partnership with solicitors of the Supreme Court or registered European lawyers, or as members of recognised bodies which are limited liability partnerships, or as directors of recognised bodies which are companies, although subject to Rule 15 as a matter of professional conduct, are not subject to section 37A. However, such solicitors, registered European lawyers and recognised bodies are subject to section 37A for professional services provided by the firm.*

Rule 16 (Cross-border activities within the European Community)

[See also Annex B at page 77.]

(1) In relation to cross-border activities within the European Community solicitors shall, without prejudice to their other obligations under these rules or any other rules, principles or requirements of conduct, observe the rules codified in articles 2 to 5 of the CCBE Code of Conduct for Lawyers in the European Community adopted on 28th October 1988, as interpreted by article 1 (the preamble) thereof and the Explanatory Memorandum and Commentary thereon prepared by the CCBE's Deontology Working Party and dated May 1989, and the notes to this rule.

(2) In this rule:

    (a) 'cross-border activities within the European Community' means:

        (i) all professional contacts with lawyers of member states other than the United Kingdom; and

        (ii) the professional activities of the solicitor in a member state other than the United Kingdom, whether or not the solicitor is physically present in that member state;

    (b) 'lawyers' means members of legal professions covered by the Lawyers' Services Directive 77/249/EEC as amended and applied from time to time; and

    (c) 'member state' means a state to which the Lawyers' Services Directive 77/249/EEC applies.

Notes

(i) The Council's view is that a solicitor will fulfil his or her obligations under articles 2 to 5 of the code by observing the corresponding rules, principles and requirements of conduct otherwise applicable to solicitors (including these rules), and in addition articles 2.5 (incompatible occupations), 5.2 (co-operation among lawyers of different member states), 5.3 (correspondence between lawyers), 5.6 (change of lawyer) and 5.9 (disputes among lawyers in different member states), being articles having no such corresponding provision. This view is subject to any authoritative ruling to the contrary at Community level.

(ii) The Lawyers' Services Directive 77/249/EEC applies to the countries of the European Union, and to Iceland, Liechtenstein, Norway and Switzerland.

(iii) For the purpose of Rule 16:

    (a) professional contacts with a registered European lawyer, or a lawyer registered with one of the other Law Societies or Bars of the United Kingdom under the Establishment of Lawyers Directive 98/5/EC, are to be regarded as professional contacts with a lawyer of the United Kingdom, and not as professional contacts with a lawyer of another member state; and

    (b) professional contacts with a solicitor of the Supreme Court, or other United Kingdom lawyer, established in a host member state under the Establishment of Lawyers Directive 98/5/EC, are to be regarded as professional contacts with a lawyer of that member state, and not as professional contacts with a lawyer of the United Kingdom; but

    (c) professional contacts and professional activities taking place within a practice are not to be regarded as 'European cross-border activities'.

Rule 16A (Solicitors acting as advocates)

Any solicitor of the Supreme Court or registered European lawyer acting as advocate shall at all times comply with the Law Society's Code for Advocacy.

Rule 16B (Choice of advocate)

(1)   A solicitor shall not make it a condition of providing litigation services that advocacy services shall also be provided by that solicitor or by the solicitor's firm or the solicitor's agent.

(2)   A solicitor who provides both litigation and advocacy services shall as soon as practicable after receiving instructions and from time to time consider and advise the client whether having regard to the circumstances including:

(i)   the gravity, complexity and likely cost of the case;

(ii)   the nature of the solicitor's practice;

(iii)   the solicitor's ability and experience;

(iv)   the solicitor's relationship with the client;

the best interests of the client would be served by the solicitor, another advocate from the solicitor's firm, or some other advocate providing the advocacy services.

Rule 16C (Powers of the Law Society)

(1)   Any solicitor must at the time and place fixed by the Law Society produce any documents held by the solicitor or held under the solicitor's control:

(a)   in connection with the solicitor's practice; or

(b)   in connection with any trust of which the solicitor is or formerly was a trustee,

for inspection by a person appointed by the Society for the purpose of ascertaining whether the solicitor is complying with rules, codes or guidance made or issued by the Council of the Law Society.

(2)   A requirement for production under paragraph (1) above must be in writing, and left at or sent by registered post or recorded delivery to the most recent address held by the Society's Regulation and Information Services Department, or delivered by the Society's appointee. If sent through the post, receipt will be deemed 48 hours (excluding Saturdays, Sundays and Bank Holidays) after posting.

(3)   Documents held electronically must be produced in the form required by the Society's appointee.

(4)   The Society's appointee is entitled to seek verification from clients, staff and the banks, building societies or other financial institutions used by the solicitor. The solicitor must, if necessary, provide written permission for the information to be given.

(5)   The Society's appointee is not entitled to take original documents away but must be provided with photocopies on request.

(6)   The Society may use any information obtained under this rule in proceedings before the Solicitors' Disciplinary Tribunal and, if the information indicates that the solicitor or an employee of the solicitor may have committed a serious criminal offence, may disclose the information for use in investigating the possible commission of a criminal offence and in any subsequent prosecution. In the case of a registered European lawyer or registered foreign lawyer, the information may also be sent to the competent authority in that lawyer's home state or states. In the case of a solicitor of the Supreme Court who is established in another state under the Establishment of Lawyers Directive 98/5/EC, the report may also be sent to the competent authority in the host state.

(7)   In paragraph (6) of this Rule, 'an employee of the solicitor' includes a director of a recognised body which is a company, or a member of a recognised body which is a limited liability partnership.

Rule 17 (Waivers)

In any particular case or cases the Council of the Law Society shall have power to waive in writing any of the provisions of these rules for a particular purpose or purposes expressed in such waiver, and to revoke such waiver.

Rule 18 (Application and interpretation)

(1) *(Application to foreign lawyers)*

(a) For the avoidance of doubt, neither registration in the register of foreign lawyers, nor anything in these rules or in any other rules made under Part II of the Solicitors Act 1974 or section 9 of the Administration of Justice Act 1985, shall entitle any registered foreign lawyer:

    (i) to exercise any right of audience or right to conduct litigation, or supervise or assume responsibility for the exercise of any such right, unless:

        (A) the right is not reserved by law to any category of persons but is open to any individual; or

        (B) the right is an immigration service which could have been provided by an individual who is neither a lawyer nor a legal executive but is registered with the Office of the Immigration Services Commissioner, and the registered foreign lawyer is practising as a regulated individual; or

    (ii) to draw or prepare any instrument or papers, or make any application or lodge any document, whether relating to contentious proceedings, the conveyancing of land, the transfer of other property or the administration of estates, which is reserved to qualified persons by the Solicitors Act 1974, or to supervise or assume responsibility for any such work; unless he or she does the work

        (A) as a director of a recognised body which is a company, at the direction and under the supervision of a director or employee of the body or

        (B) as a member of a recognised body which is a limited liability partnership, at the direction and under the supervision of a member or employee of the body

        in accordance with section 9(4) of the Administration of Justice Act 1985 and without breach of Rule 4(2) of these rules; or

    (iii) to hold him- or herself out as a registered foreign lawyer, or as regulated by or registered with the Law Society, in connection with a sole practice as a foreign lawyer, or any other practice or business where he or she is not practising as a regulated individual.

(b) For the avoidance of doubt, neither registration in the register of European lawyers, nor anything in these rules or in any other rules made under Part II of the Solicitors Act 1974 or section 9 of the Administration of Justice Act 1985, shall entitle any registered European lawyer:

    (i) to exercise any right of audience, unless:

        (A) the right of audience is one which a solicitor of the Supreme Court could exercise without a higher courts qualification, and the registered European lawyer is instructed with, and appears in conjunction with, a solicitor of the Supreme Court or a barrister in accordance with regulation 11 of the European Communities (Lawyer's Practice) Regulations 2000; or

        (B) the right of audience is one which a solicitor of the Supreme Court could not exercise without a higher courts qualification, and the registered European lawyer has a relevant higher courts qualification, and he or she is instructed with, and appears in conjunction with, a solicitor of the Supreme Court who has a relevant higher courts qualification or a barrister in accordance with regulation 11 of the European Communities (Lawyer's Practice) Regulations 2000; or

(C) the registered European lawyer is exercising the right of audience as an employee, and the same right of audience could be exercised by an unqualified employee; or

(D) the right of audience is not reserved by law to any category of persons but is open to any individual; or

(ii) to exercise any right to conduct litigation, or to supervise or assume responsibility for the exercise of any such right, unless:

(A) he or she is instructed with, and acts in conjunction with, a solicitor of the Supreme Court, or a barrister entitled to exercise the right to conduct that litigation, in accordance with regulation 11 of the European Communities (Lawyer's Practice) Regulations 2000; or

(B) the right to conduct the litigation is not reserved by law to any category of persons but is open to any individual; or

(C) the right to conduct litigation is an immigration service which could have been provided by an individual who is neither a lawyer nor a legal executive but is registered with the Office of the Immigration Services Commissioner; or

(iii) to draw or prepare any instrument relating to contentious proceedings which is reserved to qualified persons by the Solicitors Act 1974, or to supervise or assume responsibility for any such work, unless:

(A) he or she is instructed with, and acts in conjunction with, a solicitor of the Supreme Court or barrister in accordance with regulation 11 of the European Communities (Lawyer's Practice) Regulations 2000; or

(B) he or she draws or prepares the instrument

(I) as an employee, at the direction and under the supervision of an employer or fellow employee in accordance with section 22(2A) of the Solicitors Act 1974 or

(II) as a director or employee of a recognised body which is a company, at the direction and under the supervision of a director or employee of the body in accordance with section 9(4) of the Administration of Justice Act 1985 or

(III) as a member or employee of a recognised body which is a limited liability partnership, at the direction and under the supervision of a member or employee of the body in accordance with section 9(4) of the Administration of Justice Act 1985; or

(iv) to draw or prepare any instrument or papers, or make any application or lodge any document, relating to the conveyancing of land or the administration of estates, which is reserved to qualified persons by the Solicitors Act 1974, or to supervise or assume responsibility for any such work; unless:

(A) he or she is qualified to do so under regulation 12 or 13 of the European Communities (Lawyer's Practice) Regulations 2000; or

(B) he or she draws or prepares the instrument or papers, makes the application or lodges the document:

(I) as an employee, at the direction and under the supervision of an employer or fellow employee in accordance with section 22(2A) or 23(3) of the Solicitors Act 1974 or

(II) as a director or employee of a recognised body which is a company, at the direction and under the supervision of a director or employee of the body in accordance with section 9(4) of the Administration of Justice Act 1985, and without breach of Rule 4(2) of these rules, or

(III) as a member or employee of a recognised body which is a limited liability partnership, at the direction and under the supervision of a member or employee of the body in accordance with section 9(4) of the Administration of Justice Act 1985, and without breach of Rule 4(2) of these rules.

(c) All the principles and requirements of conduct affecting solicitors shall apply in all respects, *mutatis mutandis*:

    (i) to a registered European lawyer established in the United Kingdom; and

    (ii) to a registered foreign lawyer practising as a partner in a partnership permitted by Rule 7(6)(b) or (c) or as a director of a recognised body which is a company or as a member of a recognised body which is a limited liability partnership;

as they apply to a solicitor of the Supreme Court.

(d) When a registered European lawyer becomes a solicitor of the Supreme Court, any separate practice which he or she may conduct in England and Wales as a lawyer of a state, other than the United Kingdom, to which the Establishment of Lawyers Directive 98/5/EC applies shall be deemed to be that of a solicitor of the Supreme Court practising as such, and these rules and all other rules, principles and requirements of conduct affecting solicitors shall apply in all respects, *mutatis mutandis*, to that practice.

Notes

(i) *When a registered European lawyer exercises a right to conduct litigation in conjunction with a solicitor of the Supreme Court who is not in the same firm, it is essential that all concerned should be clear which of the two firms has overall responsibility for the conduct of the matter. Accordingly, it must be made clear to the court, the client and all other parties which is the correct address for correspondence. Only this address, and not the address of the other firm, should be used for all normal purposes. A similar situation may arise when a European lawyer conducts litigation in England and Wales under the Lawyers' Services Directive 77/249/EEC.*

(ii) *Registered European lawyers qualified in Denmark, Finland, Iceland, the Irish Republic, Liechtenstein, Norway and Sweden are entitled to do reserved conveyancing work in England and Wales.*

(iii) *Registered European lawyers qualified in Austria, Denmark, Finland, Germany, Iceland, the Irish Republic, Liechtenstein, Norway and Sweden are entitled to do reserved probate work in England and Wales.*

(2) (*Interpretation*)

In these rules, except where the context otherwise requires:

    (a) 'arrangement' (in the singular) means any express or tacit agreement between a solicitor and another person whether contractually binding or not;

    (b) 'contentious proceeding' is to be construed in accordance with the definition of 'contentious business' in section 87 of the Solicitors Act 1974;

    (c) 'contingency fee' means any sum (whether fixed, or calculated either as a percentage of the proceeds or otherwise howsoever) payable only in the event of success in the prosecution or defence of any action, suit or other contentious proceeding;

    (ca) 'director' means the director of a company;

    (d) 'firm' includes a sole practitioner or a recognised body;

    (da) 'foreign lawyer' means an individual who is not a solicitor of the Supreme Court but is a member, and entitled to practise as such, of a legal profession regulated within a jurisdiction outside England and Wales;

(db) 'limited liability partnership' means a limited liability partnership formed by being incorporated under the Limited Liability Partnerships Act 2000;

(dc) 'partnership' means an unincorporated partnership, and does not include a limited liability partnership;

(e) 'person' includes a body corporate or unincorporated association or group of persons;

(f) 'recognised body' means a body corporate for the time being recognised by the Council under the Solicitors' Incorporated Practice Rules from time to time in force;

(fa) 'registered European lawyer' means an individual registered with the Law Society under regulation 17 of the European Communities (Lawyer's Practice) Regulations 2000; and 'register of European lawyers' means the register maintained by the Society for that purpose;

(fb) 'registered foreign lawyer' means an individual registered with the Law Society under section 89 of the Courts and Legal Services Act 1990; and 'register of foreign lawyers' means the register maintained by the Society for that purpose;

(fc) 'regulated individual' means:

    (i) a solicitor of the Supreme Court;

    (ii) a registered European lawyer who is established in the United Kingdom; or

    (iii) a registered foreign lawyer practising as a partner in a partnership permitted by Rule 7(6)(b) or (c) or as a director of a recognised body which is a company or as a member of a recognised body which is a limited liability partnership;

(fd) 'regulated practice' means:

    (i) the sole practice of a solicitor of the Supreme Court, or of a registered European lawyer who is established in the United Kingdom;

    (ii) a partnership permitted by Rule 7(6);

    (iii) a recognised body, whether practising alone or as a member of a partnership or as a member of a limited liability partnership; or

    (iv) an in-house practice of solicitors of the Supreme Court, and/or of registered European lawyers who are established in the United Kingdom;

(fe) 'right of audience' and 'right to conduct litigation' are to be construed in accordance with Part II and section 119 of the Courts and Legal Services Act 1990;

(ff) 'shareowner' means a member of a body corporate which is a company with a share capital, a beneficial owner of a share in the body held by a member as nominee, or a member of or beneficial owner of a share in a company holding or owning shares in the body;

(g) **'solicitor'** includes any regulated individual and any regulated practice – except in the phrase 'solicitor of the Supreme Court', and except in Rule 6 (avoiding conflicts in conveyancing, etc.), which has its own definitions;

(ga) **'solicitor of the Supreme Court'** means an individual who is a solicitor of the Supreme Court of England and Wales; and

(h) words in the singular include the plural, words in the plural include the singular, and words importing the masculine or feminine gender include the neuter.

Rule 19 (Repeal and commencement)

1) The Solicitors' Practice Rules 1988 are hereby repealed.

2) These rules shall come into force on 1st September 1990.

I.2. Solicitors' Accounts Rules 1998: Part C – Interest

Rule 24 – When interest must be paid

(1) When a solicitor holds money in a separate designated client account for a client, or for a person funding all or part of the solicitor's fees, the solicitor must account to the client or that person for all interest earned on the account.

(2) When a solicitor holds money in a general client account for a client, or for a person funding all or part of the solicitor's fees (or if money should have been held for a client or such other person in a client account but was not), the solicitor must account to the client or that person for a sum in lieu of interest calculated in accordance with rule 25.

(3) A solicitor is not required to pay a sum in lieu of interest under paragraph (2) above:

    (a) if the amount calculated is £20 or less;

    (b) (i) if the solicitor holds a sum of money not exceeding the amount shown in the left hand column below for a time not exceeding the period indicated in the right hand column:

Amount	Time
£1,000	8 weeks
£2,000	4 weeks
£10,000	2 weeks
£20,000	1 week

       (ii) if the solicitor holds a sum of money exceeding £20,000 for one week or less, unless it is fair and reasonable to account for a sum in lieu of interest having regard to all the circumstances;

    (c) on money held for the payment of counsel's fees, once counsel has requested a delay in settlement;

    (d) on money held for the Legal Aid Board;

    (e) on an advance from the solicitor under rule 15(2)(b) to fund a payment on behalf of the client in excess of funds held for that client; or

    (f) if there is an agreement to contract out of the provisions of this rule under rule 27.

(4) If sums of money are held intermittently during the course of acting, and the sum in lieu of interest calculated under rule 25 for any period is £20 or less, a sum in lieu of interest should still be paid if it is fair and reasonable in the circumstances to aggregate the sums in respect of the individual periods.

(5) If money is held for a continuous period, and for part of that period it is held in a separate designated client account, the sum in lieu of interest for the rest of the period when the money was held in a general

lient account may as a result be £20 or less. A sum in lieu of interest should, however, be paid if it is fair nd reasonable in the circumstances to do so.

5) (a) If a solicitor holds money for a client (or person funding all or part of the solicitor's fees) in an account opened on the instructions of the client (or that person) under rule 16(1)(a), the solicitor must account to the client (or that person) for all interest earned on the account.

(b) If a solicitor has failed to comply with instructions to open an account under rule 16(1)(a), the solicitor must account to the client (or the person funding all or part of the solicitor's fees) for a sum in lieu of any net loss of interest suffered by the client (or that person) as a result.

7) This rule does not apply to controlled trust money.

Notes

Requirement to pay interest

(i) *The whole of the interest earned on a separate designated client account must be credited to the account. However, the obligation to pay a sum in lieu of interest for amounts held in a general client account is subject to the de minimis provisions in rule 24(3)(a) and (b). Section 33(3) of the Solicitors Act 1974 permits solicitors to retain any interest earned on client money held in a general client account over and above that which they have to pay under these rules. (See also note (viii) to rule 15 on aggregation of accounts.)*

(ii) *There is no requirement to pay a sum in lieu of interest on money held on instructions under rule 16(1)(a) in a manner which attracts no interest.*

(iii) *Accounts opened in the client's name under rule 16(1)(b) (whether operated by the solicitor or not) are not subject to rule 24, as the money is not held by the solicitor. All interest earned belongs to the client. The same applies to any account in the client's own name operated by the solicitor as signatory under rule 11.*

(iv) *Money subject to a trust which is not a controlled trust is client money (see rule 13, note (vii)), and rule 24 therefore applies to it.*

De minimis provisions (rule 24(3)(a) and (b))

(v) *The sum in lieu of interest is calculated over the whole period for which money is held (see rule 25(2)); if this sum is £20 or less, the solicitor need not account to the client. If sums of money are held in relation to separate matters for the same client, it is normally appropriate to treat the money relating to the different matters separately, so that, if any of the sums calculated is £20 or less, no sum in lieu of interest is payable. There will, however, be cases when the matters are so closely related that they ought to be considered together – for example, when a solicitor is acting for a client in connection with numerous debt collection matters.*

Administrative charges

(vi) *It is not improper to charge a reasonable fee for the handling of client money when the service provided is out of the ordinary.*

Unpresented cheques

(vii) *A client may fail to present a cheque to his or her bank for payment. Whether or not it is reasonable to recalculate the amount due will depend on all the circumstances of the case. A reasonable charge may be made for any extra work carried out if the solicitor is legally entitled to make such a charge.*

Liquidators, trustees in bankruptcy, Court of Protection receivers and trustees of occupational pension schemes

(viii) *Under rule 9, Part C of the rules does not normally apply to solicitors who are liquidators, etc. Solicitors must comply with the appropriate statutory rules and regulations, and rules 9(3) and (4) as appropriate.*

Joint accounts

(ix) *Under rule 10, Part C of the rules does not apply to joint accounts. If a solicitor holds money jointly with a client, interest earned on the account will be for the benefit of the client unless otherwise agreed. If money is held jointly with another solicitors' practice, the allocation of interest earned will depend on the agreement reached.*

Requirements for controlled trust money (rule 24(7))

(x) *Part C does not apply to controlled trust money. Under the general law, trustees of a controlled trust must account for all interest earned. For the treatment of interest on controlled trust money in a general client account, see rule 13, note (xi)(b), rule 15(2)(d) and note (vi) to rule 15. (See also note (viii) to rule 15 on aggregation of accounts.)*

Rule 25 – Amount of interest

(1) Solicitors must aim to obtain a reasonable rate of interest on money held in a separate designated client account, and must account for a fair sum in lieu of interest on money held in a general client account (or on money which should have been held in a client account but was not). The sum in lieu of interest need not necessarily reflect the highest rate of interest obtainable but it is not acceptable to look only at the lowest rate of interest obtainable.

(2) **The sum in lieu of interest** for money held in a general client account (or on money which should have been held in a client account but was not) **must be calculated**:

- **on the balance or balances held over the whole period for which cleared funds are held**

- **at a rate not less than (whichever is the higher of) the following**:

  (i) the rate of interest payable on a separate designated client account for the amount or amounts held, or

  (ii) the rate of interest payable on the relevant amount or amounts if placed on deposit on similar terms by a member of the business community

  at the bank or building society where the money is held.

(3) If the money, or part of it, is held successively or concurrently in accounts at different banks or building societies, the relevant bank or building society for the purpose of paragraph (2) will be whichever of those banks or building societies offered the best rate on the date when the money was first held.

(4) If, contrary to the rules, the money is not held in a client account, the relevant bank or building society for the purpose of paragraph (2) will be a clearing bank or building society nominated by the client (or other person on whose behalf client money is held).

Notes

(i) *The sum in lieu of interest has to be calculated over the whole period for which money is held – see rule 25(2). The solicitor will usually account to the client at the conclusion of the client's matter, but might in some cases consider it appropriate to account to the client at intervals throughout.*

(ii) *When looking at the period over which the sum in lieu of interest must be calculated, it will usually be unnecessary to check on actual clearance dates. When money is received by cheque and paid out by cheque, the normal clearance periods will usually cancel each other out, so that it will be satisfactory to look at the period between the dates when the incoming cheque is banked and the outgoing cheque is drawn.*

(iii) *Different considerations apply when payments in and out are not both made by cheque. So, for example, the relevant periods would normally be:*

- *from the date when a solicitor receives incoming money in cash until the date when the outgoing cheque is sent;*

- *from the date when an incoming telegraphic transfer begins to earn interest until the date when the outgoing cheque is sent;*

- *from the date when an incoming cheque or banker's draft is or would normally be cleared until the date when the outgoing telegraphic transfer is made or banker's draft is obtained.*

(iv) *The sum in lieu of interest is calculated by reference to the rates paid by the appropriate bank or building society (see rule 25(2) to (4)). Solicitors will therefore follow the practice of that bank or building society in determining how often interest is compounded over the period for which the cleared funds are held.*

(v) *Money held in a client account must be immediately available, even at the sacrifice of interest, unless the client otherwise instructs, or the circumstances clearly indicate otherwise. The need for access can be taken into account in assessing the appropriate rate for calculating the sum to be paid in lieu of interest, or in assessing whether a reasonable rate of interest has been obtained for a separate designated client account.*

Rule 26 – Interest on stakeholder money

When a solicitor holds money as stakeholder, the solicitor must pay interest, or a sum in lieu of interest, on the basis set out in rule 24 to the person to whom the stake is paid.

Note

For contracting out of this provision, see rule 27(2) and the notes to rule 27.

Rule 27 – Contracting out

(1) In appropriate circumstances a client and his or her solicitor may by a written agreement come to a different arrangement as to the matters dealt with in rule 24 (payment of interest).

(2) A solicitor acting as stakeholder may, by a written agreement with his or her own client and the other party to the transaction, come to a different arrangement as to the matters dealt with in rule 24.

Notes

(i) *Solicitors should act fairly towards their clients and provide sufficient information to enable them to give informed consent if it is felt appropriate to depart from the interest provisions. Whether it is appropriate to contract out depends on all the circumstances, for example, the size of the sum involved or the nature or status or bargaining position of the client. It might, for instance, be appropriate to contract out by standard terms of business if the client is a substantial commercial entity and the interest involved is modest in relation to the size of the transaction. The larger the sum of interest involved, the more there would be an onus on the solicitor to show that a client who had accepted a contracting out provision was properly informed and had been treated fairly. Contracting out is never appropriate if it is against the client's interests.*

(ii) In principle, a solicitor-stakeholder is entitled to make a reasonable charge to the client for acting as stakeholder in the client's matter.

(iii) Alternatively, it may be appropriate to include a special provision in the contract that the solicitor-stakeholder retains the interest on the deposit to cover his or her charges for acting as stakeholder. This is only acceptable if it will provide a fair and reasonable payment for the work and risk involved in holding a stake. The contract could stipulate a maximum charge, with any interest earned above that figure being paid to the recipient of the stake.

(iv) Any right to charge the client, or to stipulate for a charge which may fall on the client, would be excluded by, for instance, a prior agreement with the client for a fixed fee for the client's matter, or for an estimated fee which cannot be varied upwards in the absence of special circumstances. It is therefore not normal practice for a stakeholder in conveyancing transactions to receive a separate payment for holding the stake.

(v) A solicitor-stakeholder who seeks an agreement to exclude the operation of rule 26 should be particularly careful not to take unfair advantage either of the client, or of the other party if unrepresented.

Rule 28 – Interest certificates

Without prejudice to any other remedy:

(a) any client, including one of joint clients, or a person funding all or part of a solicitor's fees, may apply to the Society for a certificate as to whether or not interest, or a sum in lieu of interest, should have been paid and, if so, the amount; and

(b) if the Society certifies that interest, or a sum in lieu of interest, should have been paid, the solicitor must pay the certified sum.

Notes

(i) Applications for an interest certificate should be made to the Office for the Supervision of Solicitors (OSS). It is advisable for the client (or other person) to try to resolve the matter with the solicitor before approaching the OSS.

(ii) If appropriate, the OSS will require the solicitor to obtain an interest calculation from the relevant bank or building society.

1.3.   Solicitors' Anti-Discrimination Rule 1995[1]

Rule dated 18th January 1995 made by the Council of the Law Society with the concurrence of the Master of the Rolls under section 31 of the Solicitors Act 1974 and section 9 of the Administration of Justice Act 1985, regulating the professional conduct of solicitors, registered European lawyers, registered foreign lawyers and recognised bodies in England and Wales.

(1)   Solicitors must not discriminate on grounds of race, sex or sexual orientation, and must not discriminate unfairly or unreasonably on grounds of disability, in their professional dealings with clients, staff, other solicitors, barristers or other persons.

(2)   Principal solicitors in private practice must operate a policy dealing with the avoidance of such discrimination, and solicitors with management responsibilities in employed practice must use reasonable endeavours to secure the operation of such a policy.

(3)   Principal solicitors in private practice who have not developed and adopted their own policy dealing with the avoidance of such discrimination will be deemed to have adopted the model anti-discrimination policy for the time being promoted for such purposes by the Law Society.

(4)   (a)   Paragraph (1) applies to a registered European lawyer, or to a registered foreign lawyer practising in partnership with a solicitor or registered European lawyer or as director of a recognised body which is a company or as a member of a recognised body which is a limited liability partnership, or to a recognised body, as it applies to a solicitor, and

  (b)   paragraphs (2) and (3) apply to a registered European lawyer who is a principal in private practice, or to a registered foreign lawyer practising in partnership with a solicitor or registered European lawyer, or to a recognised body, as they apply to a principal solicitor in private practice.

(5)   This rule comes into force on 18th July 1995.

---

1. With consolidated amendments to 6 April 2001.

II.   LAW SOCIETY CODES
II.1.   Solicitors' Introduction and Referral Code 1990[1]

Code dated 18th July 1990 promulgated by the Council of the Law Society with the concurrence of the Master of the Rolls under Rule 3 of the Solicitors' Practice Rules 1990, regulating the introduction of clients to and by solicitors, registered European lawyers, registered foreign lawyers and recognised bodies practising in England and Wales.

Introduction

(1)   This code states the principles to be observed in relation to the introduction of clients by third parties to solicitors or by solicitors to third parties.

(2)   The code does not apply to introductions and referrals between lawyers.

(3)   Non-compliance, evasion or disregard of the code could represent not only a breach of Practice Rule 3 (introductions and referrals) but also a breach of Practice Rule 1 (basic principles) or one of the other practice rules, and conduct unbefitting a solicitor of the Supreme Court or other lawyer.

(4)   Those wishing to advertise the services of solicitors to whom they refer work should be encouraged to publicise their adherence to the code by means of a notice on the following lines:

> 'We comply with the Solicitors' Introduction and Referral Code published by the Law Society, and any solicitor [or registered European lawyer] to whom we may refer you is an independent professional from whom you will receive impartial and confidential advice. You are free to choose another solicitor [or registered European lawyer].'

(5)   In this code all references to individual practice rules are references to the Solicitors' Practice Rules 1990 and all words have the meanings assigned to them in Rule 18 of those rules.

(6)   The code will come into force on 1st September 1990.

Section 1: The basic principles

(1)   Solicitors must always retain their professional independence and their ability to advise their clients fearlessly and objectively. Solicitors should never permit the requirements of an introducer to undermine this independence.

(2)   In making or accepting introductions or referrals, solicitors must do nothing which would be likely to compromise or impair any of the principles set out in Practice Rule 1:

(a)   the solicitor's independence or integrity;

(b)   a person's freedom to instruct a solicitor of his or her choice;

(c)   the solicitor's duty to act in the best interests of the client;

(d)   the good repute of the solicitor or the solicitors' profession;

(e)   the solicitor's proper standard of work;

(f)   the solicitor's duty to the Court.

1. With consolidated amendments to 1 December 2001.

(3) Practice Rule 9 prevents a solicitor from entering into any arrangement with a claims assessor for the introduction of personal injury clients to the solicitor.

(4) Practice Rule 12 makes provision in respect of introductions and referrals in the field of investment business. In particular the rule prevents a solicitor from acting as an appointed representative as defined in the Financial Services and Markets Act 2000 other than by having a separate business which is the appointed representative of an independent financial adviser.

Note

> *An independent financial adviser is a financial adviser authorised under the Financial Services and Markets Act 2000, or subsequent relevant legislation, who is not constrained to recommend to clients or effect for them transactions in some investments but not others, with some persons but not others; or to refrain from doing so.*

Section 2: Introduction or referral of business to solicitors

(1) Solicitors may discuss and make known to potential introducers the basis on which they would be prepared to accept instructions and the fees they would charge to clients referred.

(2) Solicitors should draw the attention of potential introducers to the provisions of this code and the relevant provisions of the Solicitors' Publicity Code.

(3) Solicitors must not reward introducers by the payment of commission or otherwise. However, this does not prevent normal hospitality. A solicitor may refer clients to an introducer provided the solicitor complies with Section 4 below.

(4) Solicitors should not allow themselves to become so reliant on a limited number of sources of referrals that the interests of an introducer affect the advice given by the solicitor to clients.

(5) Solicitors should be particularly conscious of the need to advise impartially and independently clients referred by introducers. They should ensure that the wish to avoid offending the introducer does not colour the advice given to such clients.

(6) Where a tied agent refers to a solicitor a client who is proposing to take out a company life policy, the solicitor should, where necessary, have regard to the suitability of that policy in each particular case.

(7) Solicitors must ensure that they alone are responsible for any decisions taken in relation to the nature, style or extent of their practices.

(8) This code does not affect the need for the solicitor to communicate directly with the client to obtain or confirm instructions, in the process of providing advice and at all appropriate stages of the transaction.

(9) Each firm should keep a record of agreements for the introduction of work.

(10) Each firm should conduct a review at six-monthly intervals, which should check:

    (a) that the provisions of this code have been complied with;

    (b) that referred clients have received impartial advice which has not been tainted by the relationship between the firm and the introducer; and

    (c) the income arising from each agreement for the introduction of business.

(11) Where, so far as can be reasonably ascertained, more than 20 per cent of a firm's income during the period under review arises from a single source of introduction of business, the firm should consider whether steps should be taken to reduce that proportion.

(12) Factors to be taken into account in considering whether to reduce the proportion include:

(a)   the percentage of income deriving from that source;

(b)   the number of clients introduced by that source;

(c)   the nature of the clients and the nature of the work; and

(d)   whether the introducer could be affected by the advice given by the solicitor to the client.

Section 3: Solicitor agreeing to be paid by a third party to do work for the third party's customers other than conveyancing work

(1)   In addition to the other provisions of this code the following requirements should be observed in relation to agreements for the introduction of clients/business to solicitors under which the solicitor agrees with the introducer to be paid by the introducer to do work other than conveyancing work for the introducer's customers.

(2)   The terms of the agreement should be set out in writing and a copy available for inspection by the Law Society or the Office for the Supervision of Solicitors.

(3)   The solicitor may agree to be remunerated by the introducer either on a case by case basis or on a hourly, monthly or any other appropriate basis.

(4)   The solicitor should ensure that any agreement between the introducer and customer for the provision of services under this section includes:

(a)   express mention of the independence of the solicitor's professional advice;

(b)   a provision that control of the professional work should remain in the hands of the solicitor subject to the instructions of the client; and

(c)   a provision that information disclosed by the client to the solicitor should not be disclosed to the introducer unless the client consents.

Section 3A: Contractual referrals for conveyancing

(1)   In addition to the other provisions of this code the following requirements must be observed in relation to agreements for the introduction of clients/business to solicitors under which the solicitor agrees with the introducer to be paid by the introducer to provide conveyancing services for the introducer's customers.

Agreements for referrals

(2)   Solicitors may enter into agreements under this section for referrals for conveyancing services only with introducers who undertake in such agreements to comply with the terms of this code.

(3)   Referrals under this section must not be made where the introducer is a seller or seller's agent and the conveyancing services are to be provided to the buyer.

(4)   The agreement between the solicitor and the introducer must be set out in writing. A copy of the agreement and of records of the six-monthly reviews carried out under paragraph 10 of Section 2 of this code in relation to transactions under the agreement must be retained by the solicitor for production on request to the Law Society or the Office for the Supervision of Solicitors.

(5)   If the solicitor has reason to believe that the introducer is breaching terms of the agreement required by this section the solicitor must take all reasonable steps to procure that the breach is remedied. If the introducer persists in breaches the solicitor must terminate the agreement in respect of future referrals.

(6)   The agreement between the introducer and the solicitor must not include any provisions which would:

(a) compromise, infringe or impair any of the principles set out in Rule 1 of the Solicitors' Practice Rules or any duties owed by the solicitor to the introducer's customer by virtue of the solicitor/client relationship and/or the requirements of professional conduct; or

(b) restrict the scope of the duties which the solicitor owes to the customer in relation to the services agreed to be provided by virtue of the professional relationship between solicitor and client; or

(c) interfere with or inhibit the solicitor's responsibility for the control of the professional work.

Publicity as to conveyancing services

(7) In publicity material of the introducer which includes reference to any service that may be provided by the solicitor, any reference to the charge for the conveyancing services must be clearly expressed and must not be misleading. It must be clear whether disbursements and VAT are included.

Notice to customer

(8) Before making a referral the introducer must give the customer in writing:

(a) details of the conveyancing service to be provided under the terms of the referral;

(b) notification of:

    (i) the charge payable by the customer to the introducer for the conveyancing services;

    (ii) the liability for VAT and disbursements and how these are to be discharged; and

    (iii) what charge if any is to be made if the transaction does not proceed to completion or if the solicitor is unable to continue to act;

(c) notification of the amount the introducer will be paying to the solicitor for the provision of conveyancing services relating to the customer's transaction;

(d) a statement to the effect that the charge for conveyancing services will not be affected whether or not the customer takes other products or services offered by the introducer, and that the availability and price of other services will not be affected whether the customer chooses to instruct a solicitor (or registered European lawyer) under the referral or decides to instruct another solicitor or conveyancer; and

(e) a statement to the effect that the advice and service of the solicitor (or registered European lawyer) to whom the customer is to be referred will remain independent and subject to the instructions of the customer.

Solicitor's terms of business

(9) Where a solicitor accepts instructions on referral under this section the solicitor (or registered European lawyer) must provide the client with written terms of business which must include:

(a) details of the conveyancing service to be provided under the referral and if appropriate any other services the solicitor is to provide and on what terms;

(b) a statement that any advice given by the solicitor (or registered European lawyer) will be independent and that the client is free to raise questions on all aspects of the transaction;

(c) confirmation that information disclosed by the client to the solicitor (or registered European lawyer) will not be disclosed to the introducer unless the client consents; but that where the solicitor (or registered European lawyer) is also acting for the introducer in the same matter and a conflict of interest arises, the solicitor (or registered European lawyer) might be obliged to cease acting.

Definition

(10) In this section references to a conveyancing service or services include services to be provided to the introducer if the solicitor is also to be instructed to act for the introducer.

Section 4: Referral of clients by solicitors

(1) If a solicitor recommends that a client use a particular firm, agency or business, the solicitor must do so in good faith, judging what is in the client's best interest. A solicitor should not enter into any agreement or association which would restrict the solicitor's freedom to recommend any particular firm, agency or business.

(2) The referral to a tied agent of a client requiring life insurance would not discharge the solicitor's duty to give his client independent advice. In such circumstances, any referral should be to an independent intermediary.

(3) If the best interests of the client require it, a solicitor may refer a client requiring a mortgage to a tied agent, provided that the client is informed that the agent offers products from only one company.

(4) In relation to commission received for the introduction of clients' business to third parties, Practice Rule 10 applies.

II.2. Solicitors' Separate Business Code 1994 (extracts)[1]

Code dated 4th February 1994 made by the Council of the Law Society with the concurrence of the Master of the Rolls under rule 5 of the Solicitors' Practice Rules 1990, regulating the circumstances in which practising solicitors, registered European lawyers, registered foreign lawyers and recognised bodies, practising in England and Wales, may provide certain services other than through their practices.

Section 4: Safeguards and exceptions – separate businesses generally

Requirements:

(2) A solicitor who has a separate business must ensure:

(a) that the name of any practice of the solicitor has no substantial element in common with the name of that separate business;

(b) that the words 'solicitor(s)', 'attorney(s)' or 'lawyer(s)', or any equivalent expressions in another language, are not used in connection with the solicitor's involvement with that separate business;

(c) that paperwork and records relating to customers of the separate business are kept separately from paperwork and records relating to clients of the solicitor (whether or not those customers are also clients of the solicitor);

(d) that all clients referred by any English or Welsh practice of the solicitor to the separate business are informed in writing of the solicitor's interest in the business and that, as customers of the separate business, they do not enjoy the statutory protections attaching to clients of a solicitor (or a registered European lawyer, a recognised body, or a lawyer's partnership regulated by the Law Society, as the case may be);

(e) that where the separate business shares premises, office accommodation or reception staff with any English or Welsh practice of the solicitor, all customers of the separate business are informed in writing that, as customers of the separate business, they do not enjoy the statutory protections attaching to the clients of a solicitor (or a registered European lawyer, a recognised body, or a lawyer's partnership regulated by the Law Society, as the case may be); and

(f) that the solicitor does not hold on the client account of the solicitor's practice money held for customers of the separate business as such; or money held for the separate business.

Section 5: Safeguards and exceptions – particular businesses

(2) Estate agency

Requirements:

A solicitor who has a separate business providing estate agency:

(a) must comply with Section 4(1) and 2(a), (b), (c) and (f); and

(b) must ensure that the separate business is conducted from accommodation physically divided and clearly differentiated from that of any practice of the solicitor in England and Wales; and

1. With consolidated amendments to 13 January 2003.

(c)   must ensure that all clients referred by any English or Welsh practice of the solicitor to the separate business are informed of the solicitor's interest in the business and that, as customers of the separate business, they do not enjoy the statutory protections attaching to clients of a solicitor (or a registered European lawyer, a recognised body, or a lawyer's partnership regulated by the Law Society, as the case may be) by the following steps:

   (i)   in a personal interview or telephone call and

   (ii)   in writing confirming the contents of that interview or call; and

(d)   must ensure that (without prejudice to (b) above) where the separate business shares premises or reception staff with any English or Welsh practice of the solicitor, all customers of the separate business are informed that, as customers of the separate business, they do not enjoy the statutory protections attaching to clients of a solicitor (or a registered European lawyer, a recognised body, or a lawyer's partnership regulated by the Law Society, as the case may be) by the following steps:

   (i)   in a personal interview or telephone call and

   (ii)   in writing confirming the contents of that interview or call; and

(e)   without prejudice to Practice Rule 6, must not act in the conveyance for the buyer of any property sold through the separate business, unless:

   (i)   the solicitor's practice shares ownership of the separate business with at least one other firm, or other business, in which the solicitor or the solicitor's practice have no financial interest; and

   (ii)   neither the solicitor nor anyone else working in the practice is dealing with or has dealt with the sale of the seller's property for the separate business; and

   (iii)   the buyer has given written consent to the solicitor acting, after the solicitor has explained his or her financial interest in the sale going through.

II.3. Solicitors' Publicity Code 2001[1]

Code dated 16 November 2001 promulgated by the Council of the Law Society with the concurrence of the Master of the Rolls under rule 2 of the Solicitors' Practice Rules 1990, regulating the publicity of:

- solicitors, registered European lawyers and recognised bodies practising in England and Wales; and

- registered foreign lawyers practising in England and Wales in partnership with solicitors or registered European lawyers.

Section 1 – General principles

(a) Misleading or inaccurate publicity

Publicity must not be misleading or inaccurate.

(b) Clarity as to charges

Any publicity as to charges or a basis of charging must be clearly expressed. It must be clear whether disbursements and VAT are included.

(c) Name of firm

A private practice must not use a name or description which is misleading. It would be misleading for a name or description to include the word 'solicitor(s)', if none of the principals or directors (or members in the case of a limited liability partnership) is a solicitor.

(d) Unsolicited visits or telephone calls

    (i)   Practitioners must not publicise their practices by making unsolicited visits or telephone calls to a member of the public.

    (ii)   'Member of the public' does not include:

        (A)   a current or former client;

        (B)   another lawyer;

        (C)   an existing or potential professional or business connection; or

        (D)   a commercial organisation or public body.

(e) Addresses to the court

It is not proper for practitioners to distribute to the press, radio or television copies of a speech or address to any court, tribunal or inquiry, except at the time and place of the hearing to persons attending the hearing to report the proceedings.

---

1. With consolidated amendments to 13 January 2003.

f) *International aspects of publicity*

Publicity intended for a jurisdiction outside England and Wales must comply with:

   (i)   the provisions of this code; and

   (ii)   the rules in force in that jurisdiction concerning lawyers' publicity.

Publicity intended for a jurisdiction where it is permitted will not breach this paragraph through being incidentally received in a jurisdiction where it is not permitted.

g) *Practitioners' responsibility for publicity*

A practitioner must not authorise any other person to conduct publicity for the practitioner's practice in a way which would be contrary to this code.

h) *Application*

This section of the code applies to all forms of publicity including stationery, advertisements, brochures, directory entries, media appearances, press releases promoting a practice, and direct approaches to potential clients and other persons, and whether conducted in person, in writing, or in electronic form.

Section 2 – Professional stationery

  a)   The letterhead of a private practice must bear the words 'regulated by the Law Society'.

  b) (i)   The letterhead of:

      (A) a sole principal must include the name of the sole principal;

      (B) a partnership of 20 or fewer persons must include a list of the partners;

      (C) a recognised body which is a company with a sole director must include the name of the director, identified as director.

    (ii)   The letterhead of:

      (A) a partnership of more than 20 persons must include either a list of the partners,

      (B) a recognised body which is a limited liability partnership must include either a list of the members, identified as members,

      (C) a recognised body which is a company with more than one director must include either a list of the directors, identified as directors,

      or a statement that the list is open to inspection at the office.

    (iii) (A) On the letterhead of a recognised body which is an unlimited company; or

      (B) in the list of partners referred to in sub-paragraph (i) or (ii) above, if a partnership has an unlimited company as a member; or

      (C) in the list of members referred to in sub-paragraph (ii) above, if a limited liability partnership has an unlimited company as a member;

      it shall be stated, either as part of the unlimited company's name or otherwise, that the unlimited company is a body corporate.

  c)   In a private practice, if the partners (or directors in the case of a company, or members in the case of a limited liability partnership) comprise both solicitors and foreign lawyers, the list referred to in (b)(i) or (ii) above must:

(i)   in the case of any solicitor, identify him or her as a solicitor;

(ii)   in the case of any lawyer or notary of a state (other than the UK) covered by the Establishment of Lawyers Directive 98/5/EC:

   (A)   identify the European jurisdiction(s) – local or national as appropriate – under whose professional title he or she is practising;

   (B)   give the professional title, expressed in an official language of the European state(s) concerned; and

   (C)   if the lawyer is a registered European lawyer, refer to his or her registration with the Law Society; and

(iii) in the case of any registered foreign lawyer not included in (c)(ii) above, indicate his or her professional qualification(s) as a lawyer and the country or jurisdiction of qualification.

(d)   Whenever a registered European lawyer is named on the letterhead used by any private or in-house practice, there must be compliance with paragraph (c)(ii) above.

Section 3 – Interpretation and repeal

(a)   In this code, words have the meanings assigned to them in rule 18 of the Solicitors' Practice Rules 1990, except that:

(i)   'letterhead' includes a fax heading; and

(ii)   'solicitor' means a solicitor of the Supreme Court.

(b)   This code replaces the Solicitors' Publicity Code 1990.

II.4.   Solicitors' Costs Information and Client Care Code[1]

1.   Introduction

(a)   This code replaces the written professional standards on costs information for clients (see paragraphs 3–6) and the detail previously contained in Practice Rule 15 (client care) (see paragraph 7).

(b)   The main object of the code is to make sure that clients are given the information they need to understand what is happening generally and in particular on:

    (i)   the cost of legal services both at the outset and as a matter progresses; and

    (ii)   responsibility for clients' matters.

(c)   The code also requires firms to operate a complaints handling procedure.

(d)   It is good practice to record in writing:

    (i)   all information required to be given by the code including all decisions relating to costs and the arrangements for updating costs information; and

    (ii)   the reasons why the information required by the code has not been given in a particular case.

(e)   References to costs, where appropriate, include fees, VAT and disbursements.

2.   Application

(a)   The code is of general application, and it applies to registered foreign lawyers as well as to solicitors of the Supreme Court and registered European lawyers (subject to note (v) to Practice Rule 15). However, as set out in paragraph 2(b), parts of the code may not be appropriate in every case, and solicitors should consider the interests of each client in deciding which parts not to apply in the particular circumstances.

(b)   The full information required by the code may be inappropriate, for example:

    (i)   in every case, for a regular client for whom repetitive work is done, where the client has already been provided with the relevant information, although such a client should be informed of changes; and

    (ii)   if compliance with the code may at the time be insensitive or impractical. In such a case relevant information should be given as soon as reasonably practicable.

(c)   Employed solicitors should have regard to paragraphs 3–6 of the code where appropriate, e.g. when acting for clients other than their employer. Paragraph 7 does not apply to employed solicitors.

---

1. The Solicitors' Costs Information and Client Care Code appears as principle 13.02 in *The Guide to the Professional Conduct of Solicitors 1999*, published by the Law Society, and include consolidated amendments to 6 April 2001.

(d) Solicitors should comply with paragraphs 3–6 of the code even where a client is legally aided if the client may have a financial interest in the costs because contributions are payable or the statutory charge may apply or they may become liable for the costs of another party.

(e) The code also applies to contingency fee and conditional fee arrangements and to arrangements with a client for the solicitor to retain commissions received from third parties.

3. Informing the client about costs

(a) Costs information must not be inaccurate or misleading.

(b) Any costs information required to be given by the code must be given clearly, in a way and at a level which is appropriate to the particular client. Any terms with which the client may be unfamiliar, for example 'disbursement', should be explained.

(c) The information required by paragraphs 4 and 5 of the code should be given to a client at the outset of, and at appropriate stages throughout, the matter. All information given orally should be confirmed in writing to the client as soon as possible.

4. Advance costs information – general

The overall costs

(a) The solicitor should give the client the best information possible about the likely overall costs, including a breakdown between fees, VAT and disbursements.

(b) The solicitor should explain clearly to the client the time likely to be spent in dealing with a matter, if time spent is a factor in the calculation of the fees.

(c) Giving 'the best information possible' includes:

    (i) agreeing a fixed fee; or

    (ii) giving a realistic estimate; or

    (iii) giving a forecast within a possible range of costs; or

    (iv) explaining to the client the reasons why it is not possible to fix, or give a realistic estimate or forecast of, the overall costs, and giving instead the best information possible about the cost of the next stage of the matter.

(d) The solicitor should, in an appropriate case, explain to a privately paying client that the client may set an upper limit on the firm's costs for which the client may be liable without further authority. Solicitors should not exceed an agreed limit without first obtaining the client's consent.

(e) The solicitor should make it clear at the outset if an estimate, quotation or other indication of cost is not intended to be fixed.

Basis of firm's charges

(f) The solicitor should also explain to the client how the firm's fees are calculated except where the overall costs are fixed or clear. If the basis of charging is an hourly charging rate, that must be made clear.

(g) The client should be told if charging rates may be increased.

Further information

(h) The solicitor should explain what reasonably foreseeable payments a client may have to make either to the solicitor or to a third party and when those payments are likely to be needed.

(i) The solicitor should explain to the client the arrangements for updating the costs information as set out in paragraph 6.

Client's ability to pay

(j) The solicitor should discuss with the client how *and when* any costs are to be met, and consider:

    (i)   whether the client may be eligible and should apply for legal aid (including advice and assistance);

    (ii) whether the client's liability for their own costs may be covered by insurance;

    (iii) whether the client's liability for another party's costs may be covered by pre-purchased insurance and, if not, whether it would be advisable for the client's liability for another party's costs to be covered by after the event insurance (including in every case where a conditional fee or contingency fee arrangement is proposed); and

    (iv) whether the client's liability for costs (including the costs of another party) may be paid by another person e.g. an employer or trade union.

Cost-benefit and risk

(k) The solicitor should discuss with the client whether the likely outcome in a matter will justify the expense or risk involved including, if relevant, the risk of having to bear an opponent's costs.

5. **Additional information for particular clients**

Legally aided clients

(a) The solicitor should explain to a legally aided client the client's potential liability for the client's own costs and those of any other party, including:

    (i)   the effect of the statutory charge and its likely amount;

    (ii) the client's obligation to pay any contribution assessed and the consequences of failing to do so;

    (iii) the fact that the client may still be ordered by the court to contribute to the opponent's costs if the case is lost even though the client's own costs are covered by legal aid; and

    (iv) the fact that even if the client wins, the opponent may not be ordered to pay or be capable of paying the full amount of the client's costs.

Privately paying clients in contentious matters (and potentially contentious matters)

(b) The solicitor should explain to the client the client's potential liability for the client's own costs and for those of any other party, including:

    (i)   the fact that the client will be responsible for paying the firm's bill in full regardless of any order for costs made against an opponent;

    (ii) the probability that the client will have to pay the opponent's costs as well as the client's own costs if the case is lost;

    (iii) the fact that even if the client wins, the opponent may not be ordered to pay or be capable of paying the full amount of the client's costs; and

    (iv) the fact that if the opponent is legally aided the client may not recover costs, even if successful.

Liability for third party costs in non-contentious matters

(c) The solicitor should explain to the client any liability the client may have for the payment of the costs of a third party. When appropriate, solicitors are advised to obtain a firm figure for or agree a cap to a third party's costs.

6. **Updating costs information**

The solicitor should keep the client properly informed about costs as a matter progresses. In particular, the solicitor should:

(a) tell the client, unless otherwise agreed, how much the costs are at regular intervals (at least every six months) and in appropriate cases deliver interim bills at agreed intervals;

(b) explain to the client (and confirm in writing) any changed circumstances which will, or which are likely to, affect the amount of costs, the degree of risk involved, or the cost-benefit to the client of continuing with the matter;

(c) inform the client in writing as soon as it appears that a costs estimate or agreed upper limit may or will be exceeded; and

(d) consider the client's eligibility for legal aid if a material change in the client's means comes to the solicitor's attention.

7. **Client care and complaints handling**

Information for clients

(a) Every solicitor in private practice must ensure that the client:

(i) is given a clear explanation of the issues raised in a matter and is kept properly informed about its progress (including the likely timescale);

(ii) is given the name and status of the person dealing with the matter and the name of the principal, or director (in the case of a recognised body which is a company), or member (in the case of a registered body which is a limited liability partnership) responsible for its overall supervision;

(iii) is told whom to contact about any problem with the service provided; and

(iv) is given details of any changes in the information required to be given by this paragraph.

Complaints handling

(b) Every principal in private practice (or, in the case of a recognised body, the body itself) must:

(i) ensure the client is told the name of the person in the firm to contact about any problem with the service provided;

(ii) have a written complaints procedure and ensure that complaints are handled in accordance with it; and

(iii) ensure that the client is given a copy of the complaints procedure on request.

III. LAW SOCIETY PROTOCOL AND FORMULAE

III.1 National Conveyancing Protocol (4th edition) for domestic freehold and leasehold property

Acting for the seller

1. **The first step**

   The seller should inform the solicitor as soon as it is intended to place the property on the market so that delay may be reduced after a prospective purchaser is found.

2. **Preparing the package: assembling the information**

   On receipt of instructions, the solicitor should then immediately take the following steps, at the seller's expense:

2.1 Whenever possible instructions should be obtained from the client in person.

2.2 Check the client's identity if the client is not known to you.

2.3 Give the client information as to costs, information relating to the name and status of the person who will be carrying out the work and, if that person is not a partner, the name of the partner who has overall responsibility for the matter. Give any other information necessary to comply with Rule 15 of the Solicitors' Practice Rules 1990 and Solicitors' Costs Information and Client Care Code 1999. If given orally this information should be confirmed in writing.

2.4 Give the seller details of whom to contact in the event of a complaint about the firm's services (Rule 15).

2.5 Consider with client whether to make local authority and other searches so that these can be supplied to the buyer's solicitor as soon as an offer is made. If thought appropriate request a payment on account in relation to disbursements.

2.6 Ascertain the whereabouts of the deeds and, if not in the solicitor's custody, obtain them.

2.7 Ask the seller to complete the Seller's Property Information Form.

2.8 Obtain such original guarantees with the accompanying specification, planning decisions, building regulation approvals and certificates of completion as are in the seller's possession and copies of any other planning consents that are with the title deeds or details of any highway and sewerage agreements and bonds or any other relevant certificates relating to the property (e.g. structural engineer's certificate or an indemnity policy).

2.9 Give the seller the Fixtures, Fittings and Contents Form, with a copy to retain, to complete and return prior to the submission of the draft contract.

2.10 If the title is unregistered make an index map search.

2.11 If so instructed requisition a local authority search and enquiries and any other searches (e.g. mining or commons registration searches).

2.12 Obtain details of all mortgages and other financial charges of which the seller's solicitor has notice including, where applicable, improvement grants and discounts repayable to a local authority. Redemption figures should be obtained at this stage in respect of all mortgages on the property so that cases of negative equity or penalty redemption interest can be identified at an early stage.

2.13 Ascertain the identity of all people aged 17 or over living in the dwelling and ask about any financial contribution they or anyone else may have made towards its purchase or subsequent improvement. All persons identified in this way should be asked to confirm their consent to the sale proceeding.

2.14 In leasehold cases, ask the seller to complete the Seller's Leasehold Information Form and to produce, if possible:

(1) A receipt or evidence from the landlord of the last payment of rent.

(2) The maintenance charge accounts for the last three years, where appropriate, and evidence of payment.

(3) Details of the buildings insurance policy.

If any of these are lacking, and are necessary for the transaction, the solicitor should obtain them from the landlord. At the same time investigate whether a licence to assign is required and, if so, enquire of the landlord what references or deeds of covenant are necessary and, in the case of some retirement schemes, if a charge is payable to the management company on change of ownership.

3. **Preparing the package: the draft documents**

As soon as the title deeds are available, and the seller has completed the Seller's Property Information Form and, if appropriate, the Seller's Leasehold Information Form, the solicitor shall:

3.1 If the title is unregistered:

(1) Make a land charges search against the seller and any other appropriate names.

(2) Make an index map search in the Land Registry (if not already obtained – see 2.10) in order to verify that the seller's title is unregistered and ensure that there are no interests registered at the Land Registry adverse to the seller's title.

(3) Prepare an epitome of title. Mark copies or abstracts of all deeds which will not be passed to the buyer's solicitor as examined against the original.

(4) Prepare and mark as examined against the originals copies of all deeds, or their abstracts, prior to the root of title containing covenants, easements, etc., affecting the property.

(5) Check that all plans on copied documents are correctly coloured.

3.2 If the title is registered, obtain office copy entries of the register and copy documents incorporated or referred to in the certificate.

3.3 Prepare the draft contract and complete the second section of the Seller's Property Information Form and, if appropriate, the Seller's Leasehold Information Form.

3.4 Check contract package is complete and ready to be sent out to the buyer's solicitor.

3.5 Deal promptly with any queries raised by the estate agent.

4. **Buyer's offer accepted**

When made aware that a buyer has been found the solicitor shall:

4.1 Check with the seller agreement on the price and, if appropriate, that there has been no change in the information already supplied (Seller's Property Information Form, Seller's Leasehold Information Form and Fixtures, Fittings and Contents Form). Also check the seller's position on any related purchase.

.2   Inform the buyer's solicitor that the Protocol will be used.

.3   Ascertain the buyer's position on any related sale and in the light of that reply, ask the seller for a proposed completion date.

.4   Send to the buyer's solicitor as soon as possible the contract package to include:

(1)   Draft contract.

(2)   Office copy entries of the registered title (including office copies of all documents mentioned), or the epitome of title (including details of any prior matters referred to but not disclosed by the documents themselves) and the index map search.

(3)   The Seller's Property Information Form with copies of all relevant planning decisions, guarantees, etc.

(4)   The completed Fixtures, Fittings and Contents Form. Where this is provided it will form part of the contract and should be attached to it.

(5)   In leasehold cases

(i)   the Seller's Leasehold Information Form, with all information about maintenance charges and insurance and, if appropriate the procedure (including references required) for obtaining the landlord's consent to the sale;

(ii) a copy of the lease.

(6)   If available, the local authority search and enquiries and any other searches made by the seller's solicitor.

If any of these documents are not available the remaining items should be forwarded to the buyer's solicitor as soon as they are available.

4.5   Inform the estate agent when the draft contract has been submitted to the buyer's solicitor.

4.6   Ask the buyer's solicitor if a 10 per cent deposit will be paid and, if not, what arrangements are proposed.

4.7   If and to the extent that the seller consents to the disclosure, supply information about the position on the seller's own purchase and of any other transactions in the chain above, and thereafter, of any change in circumstances.

4.8   Notify the seller of all information received in response to the above.

4.9   Inform the estate agent of any unexpected delays or difficulties likely to delay exchange of contracts.

Acting for the buyer

5.   The first step

On notification of the buyer's purchase the solicitor should then immediately take the following steps, at the buyer's expense:

5.1   Wherever possible instructions should be obtained from the client in person.

5.2   Check the client's identity if the client is not known to you.

5.3   Give the client information as to costs, information relating to the name and status of the person who will be carrying out the work and, if that person is not a partner, the name of the partner who has overall responsibility for the matter. Give any other information necessary to comply with

Rule 15 of the Solicitors' Practice Rules 1990 and Solicitors' Costs Information and Client Care Code 1999. If given orally this information should be confirmed in writing.

5.4 Give the client details of whom to contact in the event of a complaint about the firm's services (Rule 15).

5.5 Request a payment on account in relation to disbursements.

5.6 Confirm to the seller's solicitor that the Protocol will be used.

5.7 Ascertain the buyer's position on any related sale, mortgage arrangements and whether a 10 per cent deposit will be provided.

5.8 If and to the extent that the buyer consents to the disclosure, inform the seller's solicitor about the position on the buyer's own sale, if any, and of any connected transactions, the general nature of the mortgage application, the amount of deposit available and if the seller's target date for completion can be met, and thereafter, of any change in circumstances.

On receipt of the draft contract and other documents:

5.9 Notify the buyer that these documents have been received, check the price and send the client a copy of the Fixtures, Fittings and Contents Form and, if appropriate, a copy of the filed plan for checking.

5.10 Make a local authority search with the usual part one enquiries and any additional enquiries relevant to the property.

5.11 Make a commons registration search, if appropriate.

5.12 Make mining enquiries and drainage enquiries if appropriate and consider any other relevant searches, e.g. environmental searches.

5.13 Check the buyer's position on any related sale and check that the buyer has a satisfactory mortgage offer and all conditions of the mortgage are or can be satisfied.

5.14 Check the buyer understands the nature and effect of the mortgage offer and duty to disclose any relevant matters to the lender.

5.15 Advise the buyer of the need for a survey on the property.

5.16 Confirm approval of the draft contract and return it approved as soon as possible, having inserted the buyer's full names and address, subject to any outstanding matters.

5.17 At the same time ask only those specific additional enquiries which are required to clarify some point arising out of the documents submitted or which are relevant to the particular nature or location of the property or which the buyer has expressly requested. Any enquiry, including those about the state and condition of the building, which is capable of being ascertained by the buyer's own enquiries or survey or personal inspection should not be raised. Additional duplicated standard forms should not be submitted; if they are, the seller's solicitor is under no obligation to deal with them nor need answer any enquiry seeking opinions rather than facts.

5.18 If a local authority search has been supplied by the seller's solicitors with the draft contract, consider the need to make a local authority search with the usual part one enquiries and any additional enquiries relevant to the property. (The local authority search should not be more than three months' old at exchange of contracts nor six months' old at completion.)

5.19 Ensure that buildings insurance arrangements are in place.

5.20 Check the position over any life policies referred to in the lender's offer of mortgage.

5.21 Check with the buyer if property is being purchased in sole name or jointly with another person. If a joint purchase check whether as joint tenants or tenants in common and advise on the difference in writing.

Both parties' solicitor

6.   **Prior to exchange of contracts**

If acting for the buyer

When all satisfactory replies received to enquiries and searches:

6.1   Prepare and send to the buyer a contract report and invite the buyer to make an appointment to call to raise any queries on the contract report and to sign the contract ideally in the presence of a solicitor.

6.2   When the buyer signs the contract check:

(1)   Completion date.

(2)   That the buyer understands and can comply with all the conditions on the mortgage offer if appropriate.

(3)   That all the necessary funds will be available to complete the purchase.

If acting for the seller

6.3   Advise the seller on the effect of the contract and ask the seller to sign it, ideally in the presence of the solicitor.

6.4   Check the position on any related purchase so that there can be a simultaneous exchange of contracts on both the sale and purchase.

6.5   Check completion date.

7.   **Relationship with the buyer's lender**

On receipt of instructions from the buyer's lender:

7.1   Check the mortgage offer complies with Practice Rule 6(3)(c) and (e) and is certified to that effect.

7.2   Check any special conditions in the mortgage offer to see if there are additional instructions or conditions not normally required by Practice Rule 6(3)(c).

7.3   Go through any special conditions in the mortgage offer with the buyer.

7.4   Notify the lender if Practice Rule 6(3)(b) or 1.13 or 1.14 of the CML Lenders' Handbook ('Lenders' Handbook') are applicable.

7.5   Consider whether there are any conflicts of interest which prevent you accepting instructions to act for the lender.

7.6   If you do not know the borrower and anyone else required to sign the mortgage, charge or other document, check evidence of identity (Practice Rule 6(3)(c)(*i*)).

7.7   Consider whether there are any circumstances covered by the Law Society's:

(1)   Green Card on property fraud

(2)   Blue Card on money laundering

(3)   Pink Card on undertakings

7.8   If you do not know the seller's solicitor/licensed conveyancer check that they appear in a legal directory or are on the record of their professional body (see Practice Rule 6(3)(c)(*i*) and the Lenders' Handbook).

7.9   Carry out any other checks required by the lender provided they comply with Practice Rule 6(3)(c).

7.10   At all times comply with the requirements of Practice Rule 6(3) and the Lenders' Handbook and ensure if a conflict of interest arises you cease to act for the lender.

8.   Exchange of contracts

On exchange, the buyer's solicitor shall send or deliver to the seller's solicitor:

8.1   The signed contract with all names, dates and financial information completed.

8.2   The deposit provided in the manner prescribed in the contract. Under the Law Society's Formula C the deposit may have to be sent to another solicitor nominated by the seller's solicitor.

8.3   If contracts are exchanged by telephone the procedures laid down by the Law Society's Formulae A, B or C must be used and both solicitors must ensure (unless otherwise agreed) that the undertakings to send documents and to pay the deposit on that day are strictly observed.

8.4   The seller's solicitor shall, once the buyer's signed contract and deposit are held unconditionally, having ensured that the details of each contract are fully completed and identical, send the seller's signed contract on the day of exchange to the buyer's solicitor in compliance with the undertaking given on exchange.

8.5   Notify the client that contracts have been exchanged.

8.6   Notify the seller's estate agent or property seller of exchange of contracts and the completion date.

9.   Between exchange and the day of completion

As soon as possible after exchange and in any case within the time limits contained in the Standard Conditions of Sale:

9.1   The buyer's solicitor shall send to the seller's solicitor, in duplicate:

     (1)   Completion Information and Requisitions on Title Form.

     (2)   Draft conveyance/transfer or assignment incorporating appropriate provisions for joint purchase.

     (3)   Other documents, e.g. draft receipt for purchase price of fixtures, fittings and contents.

9.2   As soon as possible after receipt of these documents the seller's solicitor shall send to the buyer's solicitor:

     (1)   Replies to Completion Information and Requisitions on Title Form.

     (2)   Draft conveyance/transfer or assignment approved.

     (3)   If appropriate, completion statement supported by photocopy receipts or evidence of payment of apportionments claimed.

     (4)   Copy of licence to assign from the landlord if appropriate.

9.3   The buyer's solicitor shall then:

     (1)   Engross the approved draft conveyance/transfer or assignment.

     (2)   Explain the effect of that document to the buyer and obtain the buyer's signature to it (if necessary).

     (3)   Send it to the seller's solicitor in time to enable the seller to sign it before completion without suffering inconvenience.

     (4)   If appropriate prepare any separate declaration of trust, advise the buyer on its effect and obtain the buyer's signature to it.

     (5)   Advise the buyer on the contents and effect of the mortgage deed and obtain the buyer's

signature to that deed. If possible, and in all cases where the lender so requires, a solicitor should witness the buyer's signature to the mortgage deed.

(6)   Send the certificate of title (complying with Rule 6(3)(d)) to the lender.

(7)   Take any steps necessary to ensure that the amount payable on completion will be available in time for completion including sending to the buyer a completion statement to include legal costs, Land Registry fees and other disbursements and, if appropriate, stamp duty.

(8)   Make the Land Registry and land charges searches and, if appropriate, a company search.

9.4   The seller's solicitor shall:

(1)   Request redemption figures for all financial charges on the property revealed by the deeds/office copy entries/land charges search against the seller.

(2)   On receipt of the engrossment of the conveyance/transfer or assignment, after checking the engrossment to ensure accuracy, obtain the seller's signature to it after ascertaining that the seller understands the nature and contents of the document. If the document is not to be signed in the solicitor's presence the letter sending the document for signature should contain an explanation of the nature and effect of the document and clear instructions relating to the execution of it.

(3)   On receipt of the estate agent's or property seller's commission account obtain the seller's instructions to pay the account on the seller's behalf out of the sale proceeds.

10.   Relationship with the seller's estate agent or property seller

Where the seller has instructed estate agents or property seller, the seller's solicitor shall take the following steps:

10.1   Inform them when the draft contracts are submitted (see 4.5).

10.2   Deal promptly with any queries raised by them.

10.3   Inform them of any unexpected delays or difficulties likely to delay exchange of contracts (see 4.9).

10.4   Inform them when exchange has taken place and the date of completion (see 8.6).

10.5   On receipt of their commission account send a copy to the seller and obtain instructions as to arrangements for payment (see 9.4(3)).

10.6   Inform them of completion and, if appropriate, authorise release of any keys held by them (see 11.3(1)).

10.7   If so instructed pay the commission (see 9.4(3) and 11.6(2)).

11.   Completion: the day of payment and removals

11.1   If completion is to be by post, the Law Society's Code for Completion shall be used, unless otherwise agreed.

11.2   As soon as practicable and not later than the morning of completion, the buyer's solicitor shall advise the seller's solicitor of the manner and transmission of the purchase money and of steps taken to despatch it.

11.3   On being satisfied as to the receipt of the balance of the purchase money, the seller's solicitor shall:

(1)   Notify the estate agent or property seller that completion has taken place and authorise release of the keys.

(2) Notify the buyer's solicitor that completion has taken place and the keys have been released.

(3) Date and complete the transfer.

(4) Despatch the deeds including the transfer to the buyer's solicitor with any appropriate undertakings.

11.4 The seller's solicitor shall check that the seller is aware of the need to notify the local and water authorities of the change in ownership.

11.5 After completion, where appropriate, the buyer's solicitor shall give notice of assignment to the lessor.

11.6 Immediately after completion, the seller's solicitor shall:

(1) Send to the lender the amount required to release the property sold.

(2) Pay the estate agent's or property seller's commission if so authorised.

(3) Account to the seller for the balance of the sale proceeds.

11.7 Immediately after completion, the buyer's solicitor shall:

(1) Date and complete the mortgage document.

(2) Confirm completion of the purchase and the mortgage to the buyer.

(3) Pay stamp duty on the purchase deed, if appropriate.

(4) Deal with the registration of the transfer document and mortgage with the Land Registry within the priority period of the search.

(5) If appropriate, send a notice of assignment of a life policy to the insurance company.

(6) On receipt of the land or charge certificate from the Land Registry check its contents carefully and supply a copy of the certificate to the buyer.

(7) Send the charge certificate to the lender or deal with the land certificate in accordance with the buyer's instructions.

III.2. The Law Society's formulae for exchanging contracts by telephone, fax or telex[1]

Introduction

It is essential that an agreed memorandum of the details and of any variations of the formula used should be made at the time and retained in the file. This would be very important if any question on the exchange were raised subsequently. Agreed variations should also be confirmed in writing. The serious risks of exchanging contracts without a deposit, unless the full implications are explained to and accepted by the seller client, are demonstrated in *Morris* v. *Duke-Cohan & Co.* (1975) 119 SJ 826.

As those persons involved in the exchange will bind their firms to the undertakings in the formula used, solicitors should carefully consider who is to be authorised to exchange contracts by telephone or telex and should ensure that the use of the procedure is restricted to them. Since professional undertakings form the basis of the formulae, they are only recommended for use between firms of solicitors and licensed conveyancers.

Law Society telephone/telex exchange – Formula A (1986)

(for use where one solicitor holds both signed parts of the contract):

A completion date of ……………..… is agreed. The solicitor holding both parts of the contract confirms that he or she holds the part signed by his or her client(s), which is identical to the part he or she is also holding signed by the other solicitor's client(s) and will forthwith insert the agreed completion date in each part.

Solicitors mutually agree that exchange shall take place from that moment and the solicitor holding both parts confirms that, as of that moment, he or she holds the part signed by his or her client(s) to the order of the other. He or she undertakes that day by first class post, or where the other solicitor is a member of a document exchange (as to which the inclusion of a reference thereto in the solicitor's letterhead shall be conclusive evidence) by delivery to that or any other affiliated exchange, or by hand delivery direct to that solicitor's office, to send his or her signed part of the contract to the other solicitor, together, where he or she is the purchaser's solicitor, with a banker's draft or a solicitor's client account cheque for the deposit amounting to £……

Note:

1. A memorandum should be prepared, after use of the formula, recording:

   (a) date and time of exchange;

   (b) the formula used and exact wording of agreed variations;

   (c) the completion date;

---

1. Formulae A and B: 9 July 1986, revised January 1996. Formula C: 15 March 1989, revised January 1996. This text appears in *The Guide to the Professional Conduct of Solicitors 1999* as Annex 25D.

(d)   the (balance) deposit to be paid;

(e)   the identities of those involved in any conversation.

Law Society telephone/telex exchange – Formula B (1986)

(for use where each solicitor holds his or her own client's signed part of the contract):

A completion date of ……………. is agreed. Each solicitor confirms to the other that he or she holds a part contract in the agreed form signed by the client(s) and will forthwith insert the agreed completion date.

Each solicitor undertakes to the other thenceforth to hold the signed part of the contract to the other's order, so that contracts are exchanged at that moment. Each solicitor further undertakes that day by first class post, or, where the other solicitor is a member of a document exchange (as to which the inclusion of a reference thereto in the solicitor's letterhead shall be conclusive evidence) by delivery to that or any other affiliated exchange, or by hand delivery direct to that solicitor's office, to send his or her signed part of the contract to the other together, in the case of a purchaser's solicitor, with a banker's draft or a solicitor's client account cheque for the deposit amounting to £…… .

Notes:

1.   A memorandum should be prepared, after use of the formula, recording:

(a)   date and time of exchange;

(b)   the formula used and exact wording of agreed variations;

(c)   the completion date;

(d)   the (balance) deposit to be paid;

(e)   the identities of those involved in any conversation.

2.   Those who are going to effect the exchange must first confirm the details in order to ensure that both parts are identical. This means in particular, that if either part of the contract has been amended since it was originally prepared, the solicitor who holds a part contract with the amendments must disclose them, so that it can be confirmed that the other part is similarly amended.

9th July 1986, revised January 1996

Law Society telephone/fax/telex exchange – Formula C (1989)

Part I

The following is agreed:

Final time for exchange: pm

Completion date:

Deposit to be paid to:

Each solicitor confirms that he or she holds a part of the contract in the agreed form signed by his or her client, or, if there is more than one client, by all of them. Each solicitor undertakes to the other that:

(a) he or she will continue to hold that part of the contract until the final time for exchange on the date the formula is used, and

(b) if the vendor's solicitor so notifies the purchaser's solicitor by fax, telephone or telex (whichever was previously agreed) by that time, they will both comply with part II of the formula.

he purchaser's solicitor further undertakes that either he or she or some other named person in his or er office will be available up to the final time for exchange to activate part II of the formula on receipt f the telephone call, fax or telex from the vendor's solicitors.

art II

ach solicitor undertakes to the other henceforth to hold the part of the contract in his or her possession o the other's order, so that contracts are exchanged at that moment, and to despatch it to the other on at day. The purchaser's solicitor further undertakes to the vendor's solicitor to despatch on that day, r to arrange for the despatch on that day of, a banker's draft or a solicitor's client account cheque for e full deposit specified in the agreed form of contract (divided as the vendor's solicitor may have pecified) to the vendor's solicitor and/or to some other solicitor whom the vendor's solicitor nominates, o be held on formula C terms.

To despatch' means to send by first class post, or, where the other solicitor is a member of a document xchange (as to which the inclusion of a reference thereto in the solicitor's letterhead is to be conclusive vidence) by delivery to that or any other affiliated exchange, or by hand delivery direct to the recipient olicitor's office. 'Formula C terms' means that the deposit is held as stakeholder, or as agent for the endor with authority to part with it only for the purpose of passing it to another solicitor as deposit in a elated property purchase transaction on these terms.

Notes:

.   Two memoranda will be required when using formula C. One needs to record the use of part I, and a second needs to record the request of the vendor's solicitor to the purchaser's solicitor to activate part II.

.   The first memorandum should record:

(a) the date and time when it was agreed to use formula C;

(b) the exact wording of any agreed variations;

(c) the final time, later that day, for exchange;

(d) the completion date;

(e) the name of the solicitor to whom the deposit was to be paid, or details of amounts and names if it was to be split; and

(f) the identities of those involved in any conversation.

.   Formula C assumes the payment of a full contractual deposit (normally 10%).

.   The contract term relating to the deposit must allow it to be passed on, with payment direct from payer to ultimate recipient, in the way in which the formula contemplates. The deposit must ultimately be held by a solicitor as stakeholder. Whilst some variation in the formula can be agreed this is a term of the formula which must *not* be varied, unless all the solicitors involved in the chain have agreed.

.   If a buyer proposes to use a deposit guarantee policy, formula C will need substantial adaptation.

.   It is essential prior to agreeing part I of formula C that those effecting the exchange ensure that both parts of the contract are identical.

7. Using formula C involves a solicitor in giving a number of professional undertakings. These must be performed precisely. Any failure will be a serious breach of professional discipline. One of the undertakings may be to arrange that someone over whom the solicitor has no control will do something (i.e. to arrange for someone else to despatch the cheque or banker's draft in payment of the deposit). An undertaking is still binding even if it is to do something outside the solicitor's control [see **18.04**, p.353 of *The Guide to the Professional Conduct of Solicitors 1999*].

8. Solicitors do not as a matter of law have an automatic authority to exchange contracts on a formula C basis, and should always ensure that they have the client's express authority to use formula C. A suggested form of authority is set out below. It should be adapted to cover any special circumstances:

I/We.. understand that my/our sale and purchase of........................… are both part of a chain of linked property transactions, in which all parties want the security of contracts which become binding on the same day.

I/We agree that you should make arrangements with the other solicitors or licensed conveyancers involved to achieve this.

I/We understand that this involves each property-buyer offering, early on one day, to exchange contracts whenever, later that day, the seller so requests, and that the buyer's offer is on the basis that it cannot be withdrawn or varied during that day.

I/We agree that when I/we authorise you to exchange contracts, you may agree to exchange contracts on the above basis and give any necessary undertakings to the other parties involved in the chain and that my/our authority to you cannot be revoked throughout the day on which the offer to exchange contracts is made.

15th March 1989, revised January 1996

III.3. The Law Society's code for completion by post[1]

Preamble

The code provides a procedure for postal completion which practising solicitors may adopt by reference. It may also be used by licensed conveyancers.

Before agreeing to adopt this code, a solicitor must be satisfied that doing so will not be contrary to the interests of the client (including any mortgagee client).

When adopted, the code applies without variation, unless agreed in writing in advance.

PROCEDURE

General

1. To adopt this code, all the solicitors must expressly agree, preferably in writing, to use it to complete a specific transaction.

2. On completion, the seller's solicitor acts as the buyer's solicitor's agent without any fee or disbursements.

Before completion

3. The seller's solicitor will specify in writing to the buyer's solicitor before completion the mortgages or charges secured on the property which, on or before completion, will be redeemed or discharged to the extent that they relate to the property.

4. The seller's solicitor *undertakes*:

    (i)   to have the seller's authority to receive the purchase money on completion;

          and

    (ii) on completion to have the authority of the proprietor of each mortgage or charge specified under paragraph 3 to receive the sum intended to repay it,

          BUT

          if the seller's solicitor does not have all the necessary authorities then:

    (iii) to advise the buyer's solicitor no later than 4pm on the working day before the completion date that they do not have all the authorities or immediately if any is withdrawn later; and

    (iv) not to complete until he or she has the buyer's solicitor's instructions.

5. Before the completion date, the buyer's solicitor will send the seller's solicitor instructions as to any of the following which apply:

    (i)   documents to be examined and marked;

    (ii) memoranda to be endorsed;

---

1. 1984, revised 1998. This text appears in *The Guide to the Professional Conduct of Solicitors 1999* as Annex 25E.

(iii) undertakings to be given;

(iv) deeds, documents (including any relevant undertakings) and authorities relating to rents, deposits, keys, etc. to be sent to the buyer's solicitor following completion; and

(v) other relevant matters.

In default of instructions, the seller's solicitor is under no duty to examine, mark or endorse any document.

6. The buyer's solicitor will remit to the seller's solicitor the sum required to complete, as notified in writing on the seller's solicitor's completion statement or otherwise, or in default of notification as shown by the contract. If the funds are remitted by transfer between banks, the seller's solicitor will instruct the receiving bank to telephone to report immediately the funds have been received. Pending completion, the seller's solicitor will hold the funds to the buyer's solicitor's order.

7. If by the agreed date and time for completion the seller's solicitor has not received the authorities specified in paragraph 4, instructions under paragraph 5 and the sum specified in paragraph 6, the seller's solicitor will forthwith notify the buyer's solicitor and request further instructions.

Completion

8. The seller's solicitor will complete forthwith on receiving the sum specified in paragraph 6, or at a later time agreed with the buyer's solicitor.

9. When completing, the seller's solicitor *undertakes*:

(i) to comply with the instructions given under paragraph 5; and

(ii) to redeem or obtain discharges for every mortgage or charge so far as it relates to the property specified under paragraph 3 which has not already been redeemed or discharged.

After completion

10. The seller's solicitor *undertakes*:

(i) immediately completion has taken place to hold to the buyer's solicitor's order every item referred to in (iv) of paragraph 5 and not to exercise a lien over any such item;

(ii) as soon as possible after completion, and in any event on the same day,

(a) to confirm to the buyer's solicitor by telephone or fax that completion has taken place; and

(b) to send written confirmation and, at the risk of the buyer's solicitor, the items listed in (iv) of paragraph 5 to the buyer's solicitor by first class post or document exchange.

Supplementary

11. The rights and obligations of the parties, under the contract or otherwise, are not affected by this code.

12. (i) References to the seller's solicitor and the buyer's solicitor apply as appropriate to solicitors acting for other parties who adopt the code.

(ii) When a licensed conveyancer adopts this code, references to a solicitor include a licensed conveyancer.

13. A dispute or difference arising between solicitors who adopt this code (whether or not subject to any variation) relating directly to its application is to be referred to a single arbitrator agreed between the solicitors. If they do not agree on the appointment within one month, the President of the Law Society may appoint the arbitrator at the request of one of the solicitors.

NOTES TO THE CODE

This code will apply to transactions where the code is adopted after 1st July 1998.

The object of this code is to provide solicitors with a convenient means for completion on an agency basis when a representative of the buyer's solicitor is not attending at the office of the seller's solicitor.

As with the Law Society's formulae for exchange of contracts by telephone and fax, the code embodies professional undertakings and is only recommended for adoption between solicitors and licensed conveyancers.

Paragraph 2 of the code provides that the seller's solicitors will act as agents for the buyer's solicitors without fee or disbursements. The convenience of not having to make a specific appointment on the date of completion for the buyer's solicitors to attend to complete personally will offset the agency work that the seller's solicitor has to do and any postage payable in completing under the code. Most solicitors will from time to time act for both sellers and buyers. If a seller's solicitor does consider that charges and/or disbursements are necessary in a particular case this would represent a variation in the code and should be agreed in writing before the completion date.

In view of the decision in *Edward Wong Finance Company Limited* v. *Johnson, Stokes and Master* [1984] A.C. 1296, clause 4(ii) of the code requires the seller's solicitors to undertake on completion to have authority of the proprietor of every mortgage or charge to be redeemed to receive the sum needed to repay such charge.

Paragraph 11 of the code provides that nothing in the code shall override any rights and obligations of the parties under the contract or otherwise.

The buyer's solicitor is to inform the seller's solicitor of the mortgages or charges which will be redeemed or discharged (see paragraph 3 above) and is to specify those for which an undertaking will be required on completion (paragraph 5(iii)). The information may be given in reply to requisitions on title. Such a reply may also amount to an undertaking.

Care must be taken if there is a sale and sub-sale. The sub-seller's solicitor may not hold the title deeds nor be in a position to receive the funds required to discharge the seller's mortgage on the property. Enquiries should be made to ascertain if the monies or some part of the monies payable on completion should, with either the authority of the sub-seller or the sub-seller's solicitor, be sent direct to the seller's solicitor and not to the sub-seller's solicitor.

Care must also be taken if there is a simultaneous resale and completion and enquiries should be made by the ultimate buyer's solicitor of the intermediate seller's solicitor as to the price being paid on that purchase. Having appointed the intermediate seller's solicitor as agent the buyer's solicitor is fixed with the knowledge of an agent even without having personal knowledge (see the Society's 'green card' warning on property fraud at Annex 25G, p.501).

10. If the seller's solicitor has to withdraw from using the code, the buyer's solicitor should be notified of this not later than 4pm on the working day prior to the completion date. If the seller's solicitor's authority to receive the monies is withdrawn later the buyer's solicitor must be notified immediately.

These notes refer only to some of the points in the code that practitioners may wish to consider before agreeing to adopt it. Any variation in the code must be agreed in writing before the completion date.

IV. LAW SOCIETY WARNING CARDS

IV.1. Contaminated Land Warning Card

Warning – To All Solicitors – Contaminated Land Liabilities

The advice contained on this Card is not intended to be a professional requirement for solicitors. Solicitors should be aware of the requirements of Part IIA of the Environmental Protection Act 1990 but they themselves cannot provide their clients with conclusive answers. They must exercise their professional judgement to determine the applicability of this advice to each matter in which they are involved and, where necessary, they should suggest to the client obtaining specialist advice. In the view of the Law Society the advice contained in this Card conforms to current best practice.

Solicitors should be aware that environmental liabilities may arise and consider what further enquiries and specialist assistance the client should be advised to obtain.

Contaminated land

1. The contaminated land regime was brought into effect in England on 1 April 2000. It applies to all land, whether residential, commercial, industrial or agricultural. It can affect owners, occupiers, developers, and lenders. The legislation, which is contained in Part IIA, Environmental Protection Act 1990 and in regulations and statutory guidance issued under it (see Contaminated Land (England) Regulations 2000 SI 2000/227 and DETR Guidance on Contaminated Land April 2000) is retrospective. It covers existing and future contamination.

   The National Assembly is expected shortly to introduce similar regulations regarding contaminated land in Wales.

2. Local authorities must inspect and identify seriously contaminated sites. They can issue remediation notices requiring action to remediate contamination, in the absence of a voluntary agreement to do so. In certain cases ('Special Sites') responsibility for enforcement lies with the Environment Agency.

   A negative reply to the standard local authority enquiries from the local authority may merely mean the site has not been inspected. It does not necessarily mean there is no problem.

   Compliance can be costly, and may result in expenditure which could exceed the value of the property.

   Liability falls primarily on those who 'cause or knowingly permit' contamination (a Class A person). If the authority cannot identify a Class A person, liability falls on a Class B person, the current owner, or occupier of the land. Class B persons include lenders in possession. There are complex exclusion provisions for transferring liability from one party to another. Some exclusions apply only on the transfer of land, or the grant of a lease. The applicability of any relevant exclusion needs to be considered before entering such transactions.

   In every transaction you must consider whether contamination is an issue.

Conveyancing transactions

In purchases, mortgages and leases, solicitors should:

1.   Advise the client of potential liabilities associated with contaminated land.

Generally clients should be advised of the possibility and consequences of acquiring interests in contaminated land and the steps that can be taken to assess the risks.

2.   Make specific enquiries of the seller.

In all commercial cases, and if contamination is considered likely to be a risk in residential cases (e.g. redevelopment of brown field land):

3.   Make enquiries of statutory and regulatory bodies.

4.   Undertake independent site history investigation, e.g. obtaining site report from a commercial company.

In commercial cases, if there is a likelihood that the site is contaminated:

5.   Advise independent full site investigation.

6.   Consider use of contractual protections and the use of exclusion tests.

This may involve specific disclosure of known defects, possibly coupled with price reduction, requirements on seller to remedy before completion, and in complex cases the use of warranties and indemnities.

Unresolved problems, consider

7.   Advising withdrawal, and noting advice;

8.   Advising insurance (increasingly obtainable for costs of remediation of undetected contamination and any shortfall in value because of undisclosed problems).

Specific transactions

1.   Leases

     Consider if usual repair and statutory compliance clauses transfer remediation liability to tenant, and advise.

2.   Mortgages

     Advise lender, if enquiries reveal potential for or existence of contamination, and seek instructions.

     In enforcement cases, consider appointment of receivers, rather than steps resulting in lender becoming mortgagee in possession, and so treated as a Class B person.

3.   Share sales and asset purchases

     Consider recommending the obtaining of specialist technical advice on potential liabilities, use of detailed enquiries, warranties and indemnities.

Other relevant legislation

Other legislation and common law liabilities (e.g. nuisance) may also be relevant when advising on environmental matters including:

Water Resources Act 1991
Groundwater Regulations 1998
Pollution Prevention and Control (England and Wales) Regulations 2000

Further information

Law Society's *Environmental Law Handbook* (4th Edition 2001)

DETR's Website www.detr.gov.uk

IV.2. Money Laundering Warning Card ('Blue Card')[1]

Be on your guard

Your firm, whatever its size or nature of practice, could be a target for criminals wishing to launder the proceeds of their crime through legal transactions. You might commit a criminal offence if you help them by missing the warning signs.

The Proceeds of Crime Act 2002 means that if you fail to report to the National Criminal Intelligence Service you will be judged by the standard of whether a reasonable solicitor should have been suspicious in all the surrounding circumstances. Learning to spot warning signals is more important than ever before.

The criminal law and regulatory requirements are undergoing rapid change. Keep up to date by reading Law Society guidance and interim updates which can be found at *www.lawsociety.org.uk*.

What does this mean in practice?

You will need to ask your clients more questions. By June 2003 most solicitors will be legally required to establish the identity of most clients. Honest clients should be happy to assist. Make sure you and your colleagues receive some training about money laundering.

Know your client

- Check the identity of new clients and be wary of clients who are reluctant to provide such details.
- Where possible meet new clients in person. Be cautious about third parties introducing clients who you do not meet.

If anything about the circumstances, particularly these warning signals, give cause for concern **then ask more questions**. The answers may deal with your initial cause for concern. If they do not, then the answers may give foundation to a suspicion and you may have to consider whether or not to make a report under the legislation.

Causes for concern can include the following:

Unusual settlement requests

Anything that is unusual or unpredictable or otherwise gives cause for concern should lead you to **ask more questions** about the source of the funds. Remember, proceeds of crime can arrive through the banking system as well.

Think carefully if any of the following are proposed or occur:

- Settlements by cash
- Surprise payments by way of third party cheque
- Money transfers where there is a variation between the account holder or the signatory

1. The Money Laundering Warning Card was issued in 2002.

- Requests to make regular payments out of client account
- Settlements which are reached too easily

Unusual instructions

- Why has the client chosen your firm? Could the client find the same service nearer their home?
- Are you being asked to do something that does not fit in with the normal pattern of your business?
- Be cautious if instructions change without a reasonable explanation
- Be cautious about transactions which take an unusual turn

Use of your client account

- Using solicitors' client accounts to transmit money is useful to money launderers
- Do not provide a banking facility if you do not undertake any related legal work
- Be cautious if you are instructed to do legal work, receive funds into your client account, but then the instructions are cancelled and you are asked to return the money either to your client or a third party

Remember you may still be assisting a money launderer even though the money does not pass through your firm's bank accounts

Suspect territory

- If you are instructed in transactions with an international element you can refer to the Financial Action Task Force (www.oecd.org/fatf) who produce up to date information about different countries
- Be cautious if a client is introduced through an overseas bank or third party based in countries where the production of drugs, drug trafficking, or terrorism may be prevalent.
- Take care if funds are being routed into and out of the UK without a logical explanation

Loss making transactions

- Be alert to instructions which could lead to some financial loss to your client or a third party without a logical explanation, particularly where your client seems unconcerned
- Be cautious about confusing movements of funds between different accounts, institutions or jurisdictions without apparent reason

The better you know your client and the full details of and reasons for the transaction before accepting the retainer, and particularly before accepting funds, the less likely you are to become involved in money laundering.

What if you are suspicious?

In many situations, the law will require you to make an official disclosure to:

The National Criminal Intelligence Service
Spring Gardens
Vauxhall
London SE11 5EF
Tel: 020 7238 8282
Fax: 020 7238 8286.

Helpful guidance notes about money laundering are issued by:

The Joint Money Laundering Steering Group
Pinners Hall
105–108 Old Broad Street
London, EC2N 1EX
Tel: 020 7216 8800
Fax: 020 7216 8811.

Confidential advice can be obtained from:

The Professional Adviser
Professional Ethics
The Law Society
Ipsley Court
Berrington Close
Redditch, B98 0TD
DX 19114 Redditch
Tel: 0870 6062577
Fax: 0207 320 5897

IV.3. Property Fraud Warning Card II ('Green Card')[1]

This card has been updated to take account of knowledge gained from criminal prosecutions and suggestions from the profession.

Could you be involved or implicated?

Could you be unwittingly assisting in a fraud? The general assumption is that if there has been a property fraud a solicitor must have been involved. Solicitors should therefore be vigilant to protect both their clients and themselves. Steps can be taken to minimise the risk of being involved or implicated in a fraud (see below).

Could you spot a property fraud?

The signs to watch for include the following (but this list is not exhaustive):

- **Fraudulent buyer or fictitious solicitors** – especially if the buyer is introduced to your practice by a third party [for example a broker or estate agent] who is not well known to you. Beware of clients whom you never meet and solicitors not known to you.

- **Unusual instructions** – for example a solicitor being instructed by the seller to remit the net proceeds of sale to anyone other than the seller.

- **Misrepresentation of the purchase price** – ensure that the true cash price actually to be paid is stated as the consideration in the contract and transfer and is identical to the price shown in the mortgage instructions and in the report on title to the tender.

- **A deposit or any part of purchase price paid direct** – a deposit, or the difference between the mortgage advance and the price, paid direct, or said to be paid direct, to the seller.

- **Incomplete contract documentation** – contract documents not fully completed by the seller's representative, i.e. dates missing or the identity of the parties not fully described or financial details not fully stated.

- **Changes in the purchase price** – adjustments to the purchase price, particularly in high percentage mortgage cases, or allowances off the purchase price, for example, for works to be carried out.

- **Unusual transactions** – transactions which do not follow their normal course or the usual pattern of events:

  (a) client with current mortgage on two or more properties

  (b) client using alias

  (c) client buying several properties from same person or two or more persons using same solicitor

  (d) client reselling property at a substantial profit, for which no explanation has been provided.

1. © The Law Society 2002.

What steps can I take to minimise the risk of fraud?

Be vigilant. If you have any doubts about a transaction, consider whether any of the following steps could be taken to minimise the risk of fraud:

- **Verify the identify and bona fides of your client and solicitor's firm you do not know** – meet the clients where possible and get to know them a little. Check that the solicitor's firm and office address appear in the *Directory of Solicitors and Barristers* or contact the Law Society's Records Office [Tel: 0870 606 2555].

- **Question unusual instructions** – if you receive unusual instructions from your client discuss them with your client fully.

- **Discuss with your client any aspects of the transaction which worry you** – if, for example, you have any suspicion that your client may have submitted a false mortgage application or references, or if the lender's valuation exceeds the actual price paid, discuss with your client. If you believe that the client intends to proceed with a fraudulent application, you must refuse to continue to act for the buyer and the lender.

- **Check that the true price is shown in all documentation** – check that the actual price paid is stated in the contract, transfer and mortgage instructions. Where you are also acting for a lender, tell your client that you will have to cease acting unless the client permits you to report to the lender all allowances and incentives.

- **Do not witness pre-signed documentation** – no document should be witnessed by a solicitor or his or her staff unless the person signing does so in the presence of the witness. If the document is pre-signed ensure that it is pre-signed in the presence of a witness.

- **Verify signatures** – consider whether signatures on all documents connected with a transaction should be examined and compared with signatures on any other available documentation.

- **Make a company search** – where a private company is the seller, or the seller has purchased from a private company in the recent past, and you suspect that the sale may not be on proper arm's length terms, you should make a search in the Companies Register to ascertain the names and addresses of the officers and shareholders, which can then be compared with the names of those connected with the transactions and the seller and buyer.

Remember that, even where investigations result in a solicitor ceasing to act for a client, the solicitors will still owe a duty of confidentiality which would prevent the solicitors from passing on information to the lender. It is only where the solicitor is satisfied that there is a strong *prima facie* case that the client was using the solicitor to further a fraud or other criminal purpose that the duty of confidentiality would not apply.

Any failure to observe these signs and to take the appropriate steps may be used in court as evidence against you if you and your client are prosecuted, or if you are sued for negligence.

Further guidance can be obtained from the Law Society's Practice Advice Service [Tel: 0870 606 2522]

IV.4. Undertakings Warning Card ('Pink Card')[1]

Cost to the profession

The giving of sloppy or negligent undertakings is a considerable drain on the Solicitors' Indemnity Fund and the Compensation Fund. SIF estimate that such undertakings cost in excess of £5 million per annum. However, many undertakings may result in a liability within the deductible (i.e. excess) – exposing solicitors to considerable personal liability. Your work is made easier because people know they can rely on a solicitor's undertaking. However, it can be a two-edged sword. The wide and routine use of undertakings can result in a lack of care. The profession can no longer afford to underwrite the bill!

Remember – there is **no** obligation on a solicitor to give an undertaking, even to assist the progress of a client's matter.

Financial guarantees

Think twice before standing guarantor for a client – you could be personally liable for a substantial sum. There can be cases where SIF provides no cover if an undertaking is given which amounts to a bare guarantee of the financial obligations of a client or third party. Moreover, you would have no cover from SIF if you give an undertaking to a lender to repay money which you have borrowed and which you then re-lend to a client who subsequently defaults.

Be **SMART** when giving undertakings – make sure they are:

S Specific

Undertakings should refer to a particular task or action which has been clearly identified and defined. Do not give general or open-ended undertakings, such as an undertaking to discharge 'all outstanding mortgages on a property' or the 'usual undertaking'. Make sure that any undertaking to pay monies out of a fund is qualified by the proviso that the fund comes into your hands, **and** that it is sufficient.

M Measurable

Undertakings should include agreed measures or steps which are understood by both parties and can easily be monitored or checked, so that there can be no dispute as to whether an undertaking has been fully discharged. If an undertaking involves the payment of a sum of money, make sure the amount is clear or that it is easy to calculate. Ambiguous undertakings will be construed in favour of the recipient.

A Agreed

Undertakings should be expressly agreed by both the person giving and the person receiving them and should be confirmed in writing. They may be given orally or in writing and need not necessarily include the word 'undertake' – beware of inadvertent undertakings.

---

1. © The Law Society May 1993.

R Realistic

Undertakings should be achievable. Before giving an undertaking consider carefully whether you will be able to implement it. If any events must happen before you will be able to implement your undertaking, it is good practice to spell out those events on the face of the undertaking. An undertaking is still binding even if it is to do something outside your control. As **you** give the undertaking – you **can** stay in control.

T Timed

Undertakings should indicate when, or on the happening of which event, they will be implemented. In the absence of an express term, there is an implied term that an undertaking will be performed within a reasonable time, having regard to its nature.

General points

Costs

- Don't ask other solicitors to provide an undertaking in terms you wouldn't give yourself. This applies particularly to undertakings as to costs: it's unfair to expect another solicitor to give an open-ended undertaking to pay your costs. Be prepared to give an upper limit or agree a basis of charging.

- An undertaking to pay another party's costs is generally discharged if the matter does not proceed to completion. If you intend some other arrangement, make this clear.

Conveyancing

- The Law Society's formulae for exchange of contracts and its Code for Completion by Post contain certain undertakings. Are you sure that you and your staff really know what undertakings they are giving in a normal conveyancing transaction?

- Make sure that each of your replies to requisitions on title concerning mortgages specifies exactly which mortgages or charges you intend to discharge. Vague replies will probably result in you being liable to discharge all charges – whether you know of them or not.

- Do not give unconditional undertakings without sufficient enquiry into the amount owed on prior charges – don't always rely on what your client tells you.

- If your ability to comply with an undertaking depends upon action to be taken by another solicitor, make sure that he or she will be able to comply, e.g. by obtaining an undertaking to a similar effect.

- Beware of bank 'standard form' undertakings – they sometimes go beyond what is in your control – it may be necessary to amend them.

Good management

- Principals are responsible for undertakings given by staff. Clear guidance should be given to staff, specifying those permitted to give undertakings and prescribing the manner in which they can be given. Find out how safe you are by doing an 'undertaking audit' - ask staff to check files for undischarged undertakings. Note how many have been given in a sloppy or negligent manner and calculate the size of the potential claims if things go wrong. Then introduce a system to put things right. This might be to:

  - draw up standard undertakings for use, where possible, by all fee-earners, with any deviation from the norm to be authorised by a partner;

  - have all undertakings checked by another fee-earner prior to being given (or at least those which amount to a financial obligation);

- confirm all telephone undertakings (given or received) in writing;
- make sure that undertakings are not overlooked by:
  - copying undertakings and attaching them to the file;
  - indicating on the file cover, using coloured labels, that an undertaking has been given and its date.

The Guide to the Professional Conduct of Solicitors has a chapter about undertakings which contains useful guidance – please read it!

BE SMART!

V. LAW SOCIETY GUIDANCE

V.1. Accepting undertakings on completion following the Court of Appeal decision in *Patel v. Daybells*[1]

Accepting Undertakings On Completion

The first instance decision in *Patel* v. *Daybells* [2000] All ER(D) 1004 caused consternation among conveyancers. It held that it was negligent for a buyer's solicitor to accept an undertaking for Form 53 (now DS1), save in exceptional circumstances. The Court of Appeal ([2001] EWCA Civ 1229) has now upheld the decision that the solicitor in the case was not negligent, but reversed the reasoning – the acceptance of a solicitor's undertaking for a DS1 will not normally be negligent. But does this mean a return to business as usual?

The Court of Appeal held that 'conformity to a common (or even universal) professional practice is not an automatic defence against liability; the practice must be demonstrably reasonable and responsible'. This involves considering the risks involved and how to avoid them. The Court of Appeal was satisfied that the legal profession had considered the risks of accepting an undertaking and that in the standard case it was reasonable to rely on the existence of compulsory insurance, the Compensation Fund and the summary procedure for enforcing undertakings when assessing the extent of that risk. Other relevant factors were: the Council of Mortgage Lenders' advice to its members to discharge a mortgage even where insufficient funds were sent, if this was due to the lender's error; and the problems which would ensue if the buyer's solicitor had to communicate directly with the seller's lender.

Exceptional cases

The 'exceptional circumstances' in which it might be negligent for a buyer's solicitor to accept an undertaking were not specified by the Court of Appeal, although the court made it clear that the fact that the seller's solicitor was a sole practitioner did not make the transaction exceptional.

The court referred in detail to the expert evidence on behalf of the buyer's solicitor that it would not be normal or advisable to rely on an undertaking in two situations, but did not expressly endorse these as the relevant 'exceptional circumstances'. The two situations mentioned are:

● Where the amount required to redeem the seller's mortgage exceeds the minimum level of solicitors' indemnity insurance (currently £1m per claim); or

● Where the mortgagee is not a member of the Council of Mortgage Lenders.

Minimising the risks in exceptional cases

The risk of accepting an undertaking for a DS1 is that it might not be forthcoming (e.g. because of the fraud or negligence of the seller's solicitor or because of problems in identifying the amount required to redeem the mortgage). Default by the seller's solicitor is dealt with by the requirement for compulsory

1. This guidance was issued by the Law Society's Conveyancing and Land Law Committee in May 2002.

insurance and, ultimately, the Compensation Fund. Only where the figures exceed the compulsory level of insurance might the buyer's solicitor need to take additional steps to deal with that risk. The risk of a dispute with the lender should not normally be a problem where the lender is a member of the CML. Even disputes not covered by the CML's advice may not put the buyer's solicitor at risk: the Law Society's recommended form of undertaking puts an absolute obligation on the seller's solicitor to discharge the relevant mortgage. It is therefore the seller's solicitor who is at risk if the DS1 is not forthcoming: his obligations can be summarily enforced and are backed by compulsory insurance and in certain cases, the Compensation Fund.

In each of the exceptional cases mentioned in *Patel* v. *Daybells* the matter comes back to the safeguards put in place by the profession. The only variable is the level of insurance cover and that is only relevant in the case of large mortgages. Normally the buyer's solicitor does not know the amount of the debt (and the Court of Appeal disapproved of the idea that the buyer's solicitor should have to make such enquiries). It is common to ask in preliminary enquiries for confirmation that the sale price exceeds the amount secured on the mortgage. Provided the sale price is not more than £1m, such confirmation should give the buyer's solicitor the necessary comfort to accept an undertaking from the seller's solicitor. In larger transactions the buyer's solicitor may wish to take additional steps before or instead of accepting an undertaking.

- The buyer's solicitor could ask the seller's solicitor to get express written confirmation from the lender that he has been appointed the lender's agent for the receipt of the redemption money. This places the risk of default or dispute with the lender and avoids the buyer having to investigate either the details of the mortgage or the seller's solicitor's insurance.

- The buyer's solicitor could insist on sending the redemption money direct to the lender. The buyer's solicitor should ask to see the redemption statement as independent evidence of the figure. The Court of Appeal disapproved of the buyer making such enquiries in the standard case but in an exceptional case, where large sums are involved, this may be inevitable. As this information is confidential to the seller, the seller's solicitor should get instructions before revealing it. However, this solution does not deal with the problem of a dispute over the amount required to redeem. It may also be difficult to arrange in the case of an 'all moneys' mortgage. If this course is followed, Standard Condition 6.7 should be amended (or, if using the Standard Commercial Property Conditions, expand condition 6.7). In either case, the issue must be addressed before exchange.

- Where the amount of the mortgage debt exceeds the minimum indemnity insurance (as will often be the case in commercial transactions), a buyer's solicitor might only accept an undertaking for DS1 if coupled with a warranty from the seller's solicitor that his insurance cover exceeds the amount required to redeem the mortgage.

- Finally, there is no obligation to accept an undertaking in place of performance of the obligation. Indeed, solicitors have often been unwilling to accept an undertaking for the DS1 in the case of a mortgage to a non-institutional or overseas lender or in the case of a private loan. However, if that is the buyer's solicitor's position, a contract condition that the DS1 must be available on completion will be necessary. In many cases this will not be a realistic option as institutional lenders' procedures do not include issuing the DS1 in escrow.

Before the buyer's solicitor accepts an undertaking where the expert evidence in *Patel* v. *Daybells* stated it would not be normal practice to do so, it is essential to explain the risks to the buyer and get clear instructions that the buyer is willing to take them.

Even where the lender is separately represented, the buyer's solicitor should consider whether there are any exceptional circumstances making it unwise (or potentially negligent) to accept an undertaking (or at least without evidence of the lender's solicitor's authority to accept the redemption money).

ENDs

The use of Electronic Notifications of Discharge (END) presents a particular problem as there is never a paper DS1 to be handed over: the buyer's solicitor is always reliant on an undertaking by the seller's solicitor to forward the redemption money and the END form to the lender, who then sends the discharge notification directly to the Land Registry. Even where the transaction might fall into the category of exceptional cases the buyer's solicitor will ultimately have no choice but to accept the undertaking and will have to take such steps as are available (e.g. split payments, evidence of the seller's solicitor's authority, evidence of sufficient insurance cover).

V.2. CON 29 Enquiries of Local Authority: Guidance Notes (2002)

These notes were prepared by the Law Society in consultation with the various bodies listed below. Both parts of the new form are reproduced here.

Introduction

These notes are for the guidance of both the legal profession and local authorities.

These notes generally apply both to enquiries submitted on paper and those submitted electronically through a service provider using an NLIS channel.

Two new forms, CON 29 Part I (2002) and CON 29 Part II (2002), comprising Standard Enquiries and Optional Enquiries, will come into force on 1 July 2002 and will replace CON 29 (2000 revision).

The joint working party of the Law Society and the Local Government Association, which has been established for many years to keep the forms under review, was enlarged by the addition of representatives of bodies including government departments, NLIS, RICS, CML, CLC and Water UK, and has worked in conjunction with the DTLR's Advisory Group on the House Buying and Selling Review. These notes have been prepared in consultation with those bodies.

The last main revision of the Enquiries occurred in 1994, with an interim revision in 2000 concerning contaminated land. The latest review takes into account recent and proposed changes in legislation and practice, including the use of electronic searching and sellers' packs. Where practicable and appropriate, questions which were formerly optional have been moved into the standard list.

Among the principles adopted during the revision were that that the enquiries should:

(a) be relevant and beneficial to potential buyers, mortgagees and tenants;

(b) be capable of answer by authorities using reasonably modern systems;

(c) be capable of an objective answer;

(d) exclude matters on the local land charges register and those no longer within the jurisdiction of local authorities;

(e) exclude references to specific Acts of Parliament where the subject matter can be adequately described generically.

Drainage is now controlled by local sewerage undertakers in almost every local authority area and a separate standard form of drainage and water search (CON 29DW) has been agreed with Water UK for submission to those undertakers. Thus, for the reason given at (d) above, the drainage questions numbered 2.1–2.5 and 37 and 38 on the old version of CON 29 have been omitted. However, the questions on agreements for combined drainage and on agreements and consents for building over sewers have been retained since those old agreements and consents may still be recorded in local authority records. The Law Society recommends that enquirers submit the separate drainage and water searches to the local sewerage undertaker, in addition to submitting the Standard Enquiries to the local authority.

Since all smoke control orders are registerable as local land charges, the old separate question 15 on CON 29 has been omitted.

Time is important in land transactions. Enquirers should ensure that forms are completed properly and are accompanied by clear plans and the appropriate fee. Local authorities should process them as speedily as possible. Except when using electronic transmissions through an NLIS channel, first class mail or the document exchange (DX) should be used by both enquirers and local authorities.

Format

The questions have been divided between two forms, largely (but not exactly) following the division of CON 29 into Part I and Part II. The form of Standard Enquiries contains questions considered to be relevant in every case, and should be the minimum used for inclusion in sellers' packs. Questions which are likely to be appropriate only to certain types of property or location are set out separately in the Optional Enquiries.

The form of Standard Enquiries is to be submitted by enquirers in every case, together with the search of local land charges registers on form LLC1. Enquirers who wish to raise one or more of the optional questions should also submit, at the same time, the form of Optional Enquiries, indicating those questions to be answered and paying the appropriate increased fee.

The questions on the Standard Enquiries form have been grouped so that questions asking for positive information (about planning matters, road adoption, etc) are at the beginning and those seeking a negative response (about the absence of potentially adverse matters) are grouped together after them.

Style of replies

Local authorities are requested to reply to the enquiries on a separate sheet of paper or electronically, in each case to be issued in the name of the appropriate officer of the local authority.

In order to be as user-friendly as possible, the replies should preferably be fully textual so that they can be understood by lay people. Alternatively the replies should set out the heading of each question (taken from the enquiry form) before giving a short form of reply.

The replies should include the informative statements mentioned below. These cover matters mentioned in footnotes to the old form together with some new information. Setting them out in the replies should make them more conspicuous than relying on footnotes to the enquiry form.

Front pages

As before, the address boxes A and F on the front of the forms are positioned for use in window envelopes.

The property description box (Box B) now has fields for the address conforming to NLIS, including the unique property reference number (UPRN) allocated by the National Land and Property Gazeteer (NLPG).

As before, any roadway, footway or footpath which abuts or directly gives access to (or means of escape from) the property but which is not included in the address in Box B should be inserted by the enquirer in Box C. Where a road mentioned in Box B is believed by the enquirer to be an adopted public highway, the enquirer is requested not to insert into Box B or Box C details of other public roads into which that road runs unless there is a specific reason for doing so in the particular case, since this can delay the processing of the search.

As stated in Box D, a plan must be attached to the form(s) and both the form and the plan are to be submitted in duplicate.

Fees

The fees charged by the particular local authority can be discovered from that authority, the Law Society, the selected NLIS channel or from certain published directories.

Local authorities' fees for Optional Enquiries are fixed on the basis that they will be submitted at the same time as Standard Enquiries. Higher fees may be charged and delays may occur if they are submitted separately.

Footnotes, words and phrases

The footnotes on the Standard Enquiries form should be read. They also apply to the Optional Enquiries where relevant to them.

The footnotes draw attention to the following:

(a) The replies will relate to the property as described in Box B (and any additional roads, etc. in Box C) but generally not to adjoining or nearby property.

(b) Where the word 'area' is used in any question, it means whatever size of area is used for the particular designation or application to which the question relates and which happens to include the property; it could be the whole of the local authority's area, or just part of it, or even a larger area.

(c) The records to be referred to by the local authority when processing the enquiries are to be those of that authority and (where there has been a change of authority) its predecessor, and in appropriate cases the records of the county council.

(d) Questions about decisions or approvals include those made by committees or officers acting under delegated powers, and in relation to the council's own acts 'approval' includes a decision to proceed with the relevant matter.

(e) Any references in the questions to particular Acts of Parliament or regulations are to be read as including former Acts or regulations which they have replaced and also present and future amendments of the stated Acts or regulations.

Liability

The footnotes specify that the local authority will give replies based on information available to its officers, but neither the authority nor any officer will accept liability for errors except in the case of negligence.

As at present, liability in negligence will extend for the benefit of the persons submitting the enquiries (or the persons on whose behalf they are submitted) and also any other person who buys, rents or takes a mortgage over the property, knowing of the replies (directly or through another, such as solicitor or licensed conveyancer) when entering into that transaction. This means that, in addition to buyers/tenants/mortgagees, those sellers who submit the enquiries will be entitled to rely on the replies, as will persons who make the enquiries before they acquire an interest in the property indirectly (e.g. by buying the share capital of a company which owns the property).

Part I: Standard Enquiries

Question 1.1

An extended version of old question 7 and asks the local authority to provide a list of approvals, refusals, certificates and pending applications relating to the property in respect of the matters set out in the question, covering both planning matters and building regulations.

As previously, references to specific types of planning documents include the equivalent documents under previous planning legislation (e.g. references to certificates of lawfulness of use should include established use certificates).

The reply, except where there are no such matters, should comprise a list which includes the nature of the document, its date and reference, and the description of development or use (as set out in the document itself).

The reply should also state how copy documents can be obtained, including contact details and fees.

Those authorities who currently provide a detailed 'planning history' which includes the above information should continue to do so in relation to the planning aspects of the question.

Item (g) on the list in this question takes account of Building Regulation 16A, which applies from 1 April 2002 where building work in an existing building consists only of the installation of replacement windows, rooflights, or roof windows, or of a replacement door which, together with its frame, has more than 50 per cent of its internal face area glazed. That work may be carried out, without building regulation approval, by a person who is registered under the Fenestration Self-Assessment Scheme (FENSA) by the Glass and Glazing Federation, but that person must lodge with the local authority, within ten days of completing the work, a certificate that the work complies with the applicable requirements of Schedule 1 of the Building Regulations; the certificate can be sent electronically or on paper.

In *all* cases, the reply should also contain the statement:

> '*Informative*: (1) This reply does not cover other properties in the vicinity of the property. (2) As from 1 April 2002 the installation of a replacement window, rooflight or roof window or specified type of glazed door must either have building regulation approval or be carried out and certified by a person who is registered under the Fenestration Self-Assessment Scheme by the Glass and Glazing Federation.'

Local authorities who store FENSA certificates should supply details of any which relate to the property. Those who do not store should add after the last sentence the words 'The owner or occupier of the property should be asked to produce any such certificate.'

Where the local authority's records of a particular type of document do not extend back before a certain date, the reply to the relevant part of the question should include the statement:

> '*Informative*: The Council's records of [*specify the type of document*] do not extend back before [*insert date*] and this reply covers only the period since that date.'

Where a computer system is used to reply to the enquiries but the computerisation does not include records before a certain date, the reply to the relevant part of the question should include the statement:

> '*Informative*: The Council's computerised records of [*specify the type of document*] do not extend back before [*insert date*] and this reply covers only the period since that date. Prior records would have to be searched manually at additional cost.'

V.2. LAW SOCIETY GUIDANCE

Where the practice of issuing the particular type of document does not extend back before a certain date, the reply to the relevant part of the question should include the statement:

'*Informative*: The Council did not issue [*specify the type of document*] before [*insert date*].'

If building control for the property is currently being administered by an outside body (e.g. the NHBC for a new residential development in the course of construction) this should be stated in the reply, and in that case (but *not* where the council is administering building control or already holds copies of all consents and certificates) adding the statement:

'*Informative*: The seller or developer should be asked to provide evidence of compliance with building regulations.'

Question 1.2

This is based on old questions 1.1–1.6 and asks about two matters that may be in any type of development plan. The first is designation of land use (e.g. town centre/shopping) affecting either just the property or the area it is in. The second is any specific proposal for the property itself.

The question covers all types of development plan created by all levels of local authority under the town and country planning legislation, and whether currently adopted or proposed. In this context 'proposed' means formally published for consultation or submitted for statutory approval.

The reply should state the development plan in which the policy or proposal is contained and include a short summary of the policy or proposal and how to obtain more details.

The reply should include the statement:

'*Informative*: This reply reflects policies or proposals in any existing development plan and in any formally proposed alteration or replacement plan, but does not include policies contained in planning guidance notes.'

Question 2

This is based on old questions 3.1–3.3 and relates to the roads, footways and footpaths mentioned by the enquirer in Box B and, if used, Box C.

Where none of them is currently a 'highway maintainable at the public expense' within (a), the replies to (b) and (c) should be as detailed as possible and should if possible specify the nearest road which is a highway maintainable at public expense.

The reply should include the statement :

'*Informative*: If a road, footpath or footway is not a highway, there may be no right to use it. The Council cannot express an opinion, without seeing the title plan of the property and carrying out an inspection, whether or not any existing or proposed highway directly abuts the boundary of the property.'

Question 3

This covers those questions to which generally the satisfactory answer, from the buyer's viewpoint, is that there are none affecting the property. It asks whether the property is affected by any of the matters listed in 13 individual sub-paragraphs numbered 3.1–3.13.

The reply can either be given globally in respect of all the matters covered by question 3 or an individual reply can be given to each sub-paragraph.

Question 3.1

This is based on old question 1.7 concerning land in a category specified in Town and Country Planning Act 1990 Sched. 13 paras. 5 and 6, as being required for public purposes.

Question 3.2

This is based on old question 4.3, concerning land to be acquired for highway construction or improvement.

Question 3.3

This sub-question (a) is based on old question 2.3.1 concerning combined drainage agreements. Sub-question (b) is taken from old question 2.3.2 relating to consents or agreements for building over or close to sewers.

Although drainage matters are now mainly handled by water companies, local authorities will often have records on the above matters dating from before privatisation of the water industry.

The reply should include the statement:

> '*Informative*: Enquiries about drainage should also be made of the local sewerage undertaker.'

Question 3.4

This is based on old questions 4.1.1, 4.1.2, 4.2 and 4.4, concerning road schemes. Because of the different stages of planning at which road schemes are notified, it has been necessary to continue references to centre lines as well as limits of construction.

Question 3.5

This is based on old question 16, concerning light railways, etc. This question is now extended to include tramways.

Question 3.6

This based on old (Part II) questions 19 and 20, concerning road closure and traffic schemes. This question is now extended to include traffic calming (e.g. road humps), residents' parking, minor widening/improvement, pedestrian crossings, cycle tracks and bridge construction.

The reply should include the statement:

> '*Informative*: In some circumstances, road closure orders can be obtained by third parties from magistrates courts or can be made by the Secretary of State for Transport, without involving the Council.'

Question 3.7

This is based on old question 5, concerning outstanding notices under certain legislation. Notices under the Health and Safety at Work legislation are now included. The old reference to 'informal' notices has been dropped in view of uncertainty as to what comprised an informal notice. The question is now limited to formal statutory notices.

Question 3.8

This is based on old question 6, concerning proceedings for breach of building regulations.

Question 3.9

This is an update of old questions 8, 9 and 10, concerning notices, orders, directions and proceedings under the Town and Country Planning Act. The question is limited to 'subsisting' matters, so anything which is defunct or no longer capable of implementation can be omitted.

For London Boroughs, the reply should include the statement:

> '*Informative*: The Historic Buildings and Monuments Commission (also called English Heritage) also have power to issue building preservation notices for listed buildings in London Boroughs and enquiry should also be made of them if appropriate.'

Question 3.10

This is based on old question 12. It covers both those conservation areas which were designated before 31 August 1974 (since which time they have been registrable as a local land charge) and cases where there is a subsisting resolution to create a conservation area but registration as a local land charge has not yet taken place.

Question 3.11

This is based on old question 13, concerning compulsory purchase.

Question 3.12

This is based on old question 16A, concerning contaminated land. The reply should include the statement:

> '*Informative*: A negative reply does not imply that the property or any adjoining or adjacent land is free from contamination or from the risk of it, and the reply may not disclose steps taken by another council in whose area adjacent or adjoining land is situated.'

Question 3.13

This is based on old (Part II) question 36, concerning the presence of radon gas. The question has been updated to reflect the current regime under which the National Radiological Protection Board designates Radon Affected Areas, being areas where 1% or more of properties are estimated to be at or above the radon Action Level of 200 becquerels per cubic metre of air. The NRPB publishes maps of these areas, on behalf of the Government. Local authorities should be aware of any Radon Affected Areas within their area.

Prior to 1999, protective measures required under building regulations were initially a sump or sub-floor ventilation; radon barriers were only required in areas of highest risk. Under current guidance (BR211 *Radon: Guidance on Protective Measures for New Dwellings*) there are two levels of protection, basic and full. Basic protection should be provided where there is a 3% or greater probability of exceeding Action Level and comprises a barrier across the ground floor of a building. Where radon levels may be much higher than Action Level, full protection should be provided incorporating sub-floor depressurisation or ventilation in addition to the barrier. Local authority building control departments will be familiar with the building regulation requirements.

If the property is in Devon, Cornwall, Somerset, Northamptonshire or Derbyshire and was built between 1992 and 1999, the present owner may know if it has radon protection. For new homes in England and Wales built in affected areas as shown on the maps in the 1999 edition of BR211, the builder or building control body should know what type of radon protection has been provided.

If the reply is positive (but *not* if the reply is negative), the reply should include the statement :

'*Informative*: Radon Affected Areas are designated by the National Radiological Protection Board. It is recommended that the level of radon gas should be measured in all properties within Radon Affected Areas. The present owner or (for a new property) the builder should be asked whether protective measures were incorporated in the construction of the property; whether radon levels have been measured in the property; whether the results were at or above the Action Level (prescribed by the NRPB) and if so whether remedial measures were installed and whether the radon levels were re-tested and confirmed the effectiveness of the measures.'

A guide containing further information about Radon Affected Areas is available free from DEFRA Warehouse Publications, Admail 6000, London SW1A 2XX (tel. 08459 556000, fax 020 8957 5012) or from DEFRA Radioactive Substances Division, Zone 4/E7, Ashdown House, 123 Victoria Street, London SW1E.

Part II: Optional Enquiries

The following new questions (italicised) are based on questions from the previous CON 29 Enquiries of Local Authority (2000):

- *Question 4* on question 17, concerning proposals to construct nearby roads, as approved by planning permission granted to private developers.

- *Question 6* on question 21, concerning consent for advertisements.

- *Question 7* on question 22, concerning completion notices affecting uncompleted development.

- *Question 8* on question 23, concerning parks and countryside.

- *Question 9* on question 24, concerning pipelines.

- *Question 10* on question 25, concerning the control of houses in multiple occupation.

- *Question 11* on question 26, concerning noise abatement zones.

- *Question 12* on question 27, concerning urban development areas.

- *Question 13* on question 28, concerning enterprise zones.

- *Question 14* on question 29, concerning inner urban improvement areas.

- *Question 15* on question 30, concerning simplified planning zones.

- *Question 16* on question 31, concerning land maintenance notices.

- *Question 17* on question 32, concerning mineral consultation areas.

- *Question 18* on question 33, concerning hazardous substance consents.

The following questions have received more substantial amendment since the 2000 edition.

Question 5

This is based on old question 18, concerning public paths or byways. Inclusion of this in the Standard Enquiries was considered but was ultimately rejected as being inappropriate at this time. The reply should include the statement:

'*Informative*: The definitive map does not show every public footpath or byway.'

Question 19

This is based on old question 34, concerning environmental and pollution notices (other than those covered by the contaminated land question). As before, the question concerns both formal and informal notices. The reply should include informal notices such as letters sent by the council concerning complaints and letters giving notice of inspections or investigations, where this could lead to the service of a formal statutory notice.

Question 20

This is based on old question 35, concerning food safety notices. As before, the question concerns both formal and informal notices. The reply should include informal notices such as letters sent by the council concerning complaints and letters giving notice of inspections or investigations, where this could lead to the service of a formal statutory notice.

Question 21

This is a new question reflecting the power to serve notices under the Hedgerows Regulations 1997 and the record that local authorities are required to maintain under them.

V.3.   CON 29DW Standard Drainage and Water Enquiries: Guidance Notes (2002)

GUIDANCE NOTES

The guidance set out below has been prepared by the water service companies and the Law Society in 2002.

These notes are for the guidance of both the legal profession and water service companies.

These notes generally apply both to enquiries submitted on paper and those submitted electronically through a service provider using a channel of NLIS.

The new form CON 29DW (2002) will be accepted by all water service companies in England and Wales from 1 April 2002.

The Law Society recommends that enquirers submit the separate drainage and water search, CON 29DW, to the local sewerage undertaker, on all occasions in addition to submitting CON 29, Standard Enquiries, to the local authority.

The joint working party of the Law Society and the Local Government Association, which has been established for many years to keep the forms under review, was enlarged by the addition of representatives of bodies including government departments, NLIS, RICS, CML, CLC and Water UK, and has worked in conjunction with the DTLR's Advisory Group on the House Buying and Selling Review. These notes have been prepared in consultation with those bodies.

Among the principles adopted during the revision were that the enquiries should:

(a)   be relevant and beneficial to potential buyers, mortgagees and tenants;

(b)   be capable of answer by companies using modern systems;

(c)   be capable of an objective answer;

(d)   exclude references to specific Acts of Parliament where the subject matter can be adequately described generically.

Drainage is now controlled by regional sewerage undertakers in almost every local authority area and the new form of drainage and water search has been agreed with Water UK for submission to those undertakers. The old drainage questions numbered 2.1–2.5 and 37 and 38 on CON 29 are omitted from the 2002 edition, with the exception of the questions on combined drainage and building over sewer agreements and consents, since old agreements may still be recorded in local authority records.

Time is important in land transactions. Enquirers should ensure that forms are completed properly and are accompanied by clear plans and the appropriate fee. Water service companies should process them as speedily as possible. First class mail or the document exchange (DX) or Internet services should be used by both enquirers and companies.

Format

The form of standard enquiries contains questions considered to be relevant in every case, and should be the minimum used for inclusion in sellers' packs.

Style of replies

Water service companies are to reply to the enquiries in a fully textual form so that they can be understood by lay people. The reply is to be signed by the appropriate company officer.

The replies should include as a minimum the standard answers and informative statements mentioned below.

Front pages

The property description box now has fields for the address conforming to NLIS, including the unique property reference number.

· Where a property is less than 5 years old, or it is believed that sewers serving it may still be subject to a statutory agreement to adopt them, the requested developer details should be completed.

A location plan must be provided with all enquiries.

Fees

The fees charged by the particular water service company can be obtained either from that company or from the Law Society or from *www.drainageandwater.co.uk*.

Liability

Drainage and water enquiries are subject to standard terms and conditions for all water service companies. Water service companies accept liability for negligence, subject to certain limitations, for incorrect replies.

Standard Enquiries

The following pages detail the range of possible standard answers and informative statements that will be contained in water service company replies:

Question 1.1

● A copy of the statutory sewer map is provided; or

● No plan is provided, as there are no public sewers in the vicinity of the property.

Notes: The company is not generally responsible for rivers, watercourses, ponds, culverts or highway drains. If any of these are shown on the copy extract they are shown for information only. Sewers indicated on the extract of the public sewer map as being subject to an agreement under section 104 of the Water Industry Act 1991 are not an 'as constructed' record. It is recommended that these details are checked with the developer, if any. Assets other than public sewers may be shown on the copy extract, for information only.

Question 1.2

● The company's records indicate that foul water from the property does drain to the public sewerage system; or

● The company's records indicate that foul water from the property does *not* drain to the public sewerage system; or

● This enquiry appears to relate to a plot of land or a recently built property. It is recommended that drainage proposals are checked with the developer.

Notes: The company is not responsible for those private drains and sewers which connect the property to the public sewerage system, and does not hold details of these. The property owner will normally have sole responsibility for private drains serving the property and may have shared responsibility, with other users, if the property is served by a private sewer which also serves other properties. These may pass through land outside of the control of the seller; the buyer may wish to investigate whether separate rights or easements are needed for their inspection, repair or renewal.

An extract from the public sewer map is enclosed. This will show known public sewers in the vicinity of the property and it should possible to estimate the likely length and route of any private drains and/or sewers connecting the property to the public sewerage system.

If foul water does not drain to the public sewerage system the property may have private facilities in the form of a cesspit, septic tank or other type of treatment plant.

Question 1.3

● The company's records indicate that surface water from the property does drain to the public sewerage system; or

● The company's records indicate that surface water from the property does *not* drain to the public sewerage system; or

● This enquiry appears to relate to a plot of land or a recently built property. It is recommended that drainage proposals are checked with the developer.

Notes: The company is not responsible for private drains and sewers that connect the property to the public sewerage system and does not hold details of these. The property owner will normally have sole responsibility for private drains serving the property and may have shared responsibility, with other users, if the property is served by a private sewer which also serves other properties. These may pass through land outside of the control of the seller; the buyer may wish to investigate whether separate rights or easements are needed for their inspection, repair or renewal.

An extract from the public sewer map is enclosed. This will show known public sewers in the vicinity of the property and it should be possible to estimate the likely length and route of any private drains and/or sewers connecting the property to the public sewerage system.

In some cases company records do not distinguish between foul and surface water connections to the public sewerage system. If on inspection the buyer finds that the property is not connected for surface water drainage, the property may be eligible for a rebate of the surface water drainage charge. Details can be obtained from the company.

If surface water does not drain to the public sewerage system the property may have private facilities in the form of a soakaway or private connection to a watercourse.

Question 1.4

● The company's records indicate that the sewers serving the development, of which this property forms part, are not the subject of an application for adoption under section 104 of the Water Industry Act 1991. Where the property is part of an established development it would not normally be subject to an adoption agreement under section 104 of the Water Industry Act 1991; or

● The company's records indicate that certain sewers serving the development, of which this property forms part, are the subject of an application for adoption by the company under section 104 of the Water Industry Act 1991 [*and one of the following*]:

(a) An application for a statutory adoption agreement has been received.

(b) A statutory adoption agreement is currently in preparation.

(c) A statutory adoption agreement is in place. The maintenance period has not commenced.

(d) A statutory adoption agreement is in place. The maintenance period has commenced. The agreement is [supported by a bond/subject of a bond waiver / not supported by a bond or bond waiver].

Notes: Where the property is part of a very recent or ongoing development and the sewers are not the subject of an adoption application, buyers should consult with the developer to ascertain the extent of private drains and sewers for which they will hold maintenance and renewal liabilities. Final adoption is subject to the developer complying with the terms of the adoption agreement under section 104 of the Water Industry Act 1991.

Question 2.1

●   The public sewer map indicates that there is a public sewer running within the boundary of the property; or

●   The public sewer map indicates that there is a sewer subject to an agreement under section 104 of the Water Industry Act 1991 running within the boundary of the property; or

●   The public sewer map does not show any public sewers within the boundary of the property. However, historically, it has not been a requirement for all public sewers to be recorded on the public sewer map. It is therefore possible for unidentified public sewers to exist.

Notes: The boundary of the property has been determined by reference to the Ordnance Survey record. The presence of a public sewer running within the boundary of the property may restrict further development. The company has a statutory right of access to carry out work on its assets, subject to notice. This may result in employees of the company or its contractors needing to enter the property to carry out work.

Sewers indicated on the extract of the public sewer map as being subject to an agreement under section 104 of the Water Industry Act 1991 are not an 'as constructed' record. It is recommended that these details be checked with the developer, if any.

Question 2.2

●   The public sewer map indicates a public sewer within 30.48 metres (100 feet) of the building(s) within the property. (See supplied extract from the public sewer map.)

●   The public sewer map indicates that there is a sewer, subject to an agreement under section 104 of the Water Industry Act 1991, within 30.48 metres (100 feet) of the building(s) within the property. (See supplied extract from the public sewer map.)

●   The public sewer map does not indicate any public sewers within 30.48 metres (100 feet) of the building(s) within the property. However, historically it has not been a requirement for all public sewers to be recorded on the public sewer map. It is therefore possible for unidentified public sewers to exist.

Notes: The presence of a public sewer within 30.48 metres (100 feet) of the building(s) within the property can result in the local authority requiring a property to be connected to the public sewer. Sewers indicated on the extract of the public sewer map as being subject to an agreement under section 104 of the Water Industry Act 1991 are not an 'as constructed' record. It is recommended that these details are checked with the developer. The measure is estimated from the Ordnance Survey record, between the building(s) within the boundary of the property and the nearest public sewer.

Question 2.3

●   The company's records confirm that there is a statutory agreement in respect of building over a public sewer at this property; or

●   The company's records confirm that there is a consent in respect of building over a public sewer at this property; or

●   The company's records indicate that there is not a statutory agreement or consent in respect of building over a public sewer at this property. For historical reasons the company may not be aware of some agreements or consents which have been entered into by the local authority.

Question 3.1

●   The water supply for this area is provided by [*company name and address*] and a copy of the map of waterworks is provided; or

●   The water supply for this area is provided by the company and a copy of the map of waterworks is provided; or

●   A plan has not been attached, as there are no vested water mains in the vicinity of the property.

Notes: Assets other than vested water mains may be shown on the plan, for information only. The company is not responsible for private supply pipes connecting the property to the public water main and does not hold details of hese. These may pass through land outside of the control of the seller, or may be shared with adjacent properties. The buyer may wish to investigate whether separate rights or easements are needed for their inspection, repair or renewal. If an extract of the public water main record is enclosed. This will show known public water mains in the vicinity of the property. It should be possible to estimate the likely length and route of any private water supply pipe connecting the property to the public water network.

Question 3.2

- The company supplies water to this area; or

  The water supply for this area is provided by [*company name and address*].

Question 3.3

- The water supply for this area is provided by [*company name and address*] whose records indicate that the property is connected to mains water supply; or

  The company records indicate that the property is connected to the mains water supply; or

  The water supply for this area is provided by [*company name and address*] whose records indicate that the property is not connected to mains water supply; or

- The company records indicate that the property is not connected to the mains water supply; or

  This enquiry relates to a plot of land or a recently built property. It is recommended that the water supply proposals are checked with the developer.

Question 3.4

- The water supply for this area is provided by [*company name and address*] whose records indicate that there is a vested water main within the boundary of the property; or

- The map of waterworks indicates that there is a vested water main within the boundary of the property; or

- The water supply for this area is provided by [*company name and address*] whose records do not show any vested water mains within the boundary of the property; or

- The map of waterworks does not show any vested water mains within the boundary of the property.

Notes: The boundary of the property has been determined by reference to the Ordnance Survey record. The presence of a vested water main within the boundary of the property may restrict further development within it. The company has a statutory right of access to carry out work on its assets, subject to notice. This may result in employees of the company or its contractors needing to enter the property to carry out work.

Question 4.1

The answer to this question will be company specific, however any reply should include details of:

- Which services are charged for;

- Whether charges are measured or unmeasured;

- Which companies charge and what services they charge for.

Following a change of occupation, in what circumstances will charges be measured or unmeasured?

Notes: Measured (metered) charges will apply where the buyer makes a change of use of the property or where the buyer's use of water falls within certain categories specified by the water company.

V.4. CON 29M Coal Mining Search: Guidance Notes 2003[1]

1 INTRODUCTION

1.1 A coal mining search should be made by solicitors when acting on the occasion of any dealing with land in coal mining areas ('affected areas'), including purchase, mortgage, further advance or before any development takes place. For those solicitors not using the National Land Information Service (NLIS) or other electronic means, the search should be made using form CON 29M (2003) which is approved by the Law Society and the Coal Authority. The search should be made before the exchange of contracts or any binding obligation is entered into.

1.2 Solicitors are recommended to submit a plan of the property with every coal mining search. Plans should be marked with the full boundary of the property and not just the property building footprint or other lesser area. Solicitors should retain a copy of the search form and the plan.

1.3 These Guidance Notes should be read in conjunction with the Coal Authority's Terms and Conditions 2003 and User Guide 2003.

2 PRELIMINARY ENQUIRIES

2.1 If the property is in an affected area (see User Guide 2003, para. 2), a solicitor should make a search on form CON 29M (2003) and raise an additional preliminary enquiry of the seller. The enquiry should ask whether during the ownership of the seller, or to the seller's knowledge his predecessors in title, the property has sustained coal mining subsidence damage and if so how any claim was resolved (by making good or payment in respect of the cost of remedial, merged or redevelopment works, or otherwise).

2.2 If the mining report discloses a current stop notice or the withholding of consent to a request for preventive works affecting the property a solicitor should ask preliminary enquiries of the seller as to the present position.

3 REPRODUCTION OF FORMS

3.1 The form CON 29M (2003) and enquiries are the copyright of the Law Society which has granted to solicitors a non-exclusive licence to reproduce them. Any such form must follow precisely and in all respects the printed version.

3.2 Any reproduction of the form CON 29M (2003) which does not comply with these requirements will be rejected by the Coal Authority.

4 MINING SURVEYS AND SITE INVESTIGATION

4.1 Disclosure of a disused mine shaft or adit in a mining report, the existence of recorded or possible unrecorded shallow coal workings and/or any other coal mining related hazard identified within the mining report, should be brought to the attention of the client.

If further information or advice is required in addition to that available from the Coal Authority, then solicitors should in these circumstances explain to clients that there are experienced mining surveyors and structural engineers able to advise as to what further enquiries, surveys or investigation should be made.

1. © The Law Society 2003. Conveyancers should also read The User Guide and Terms and Conditions which also appear in *Coal Mining Searches: Directory & Guidance* (The Law Society, 2003).

4.2   If a lender is involved in the transaction, solicitors should establish that the surveyor or engineer selected is acceptable to the lender.

4.3   In most cases, but not all, any shaft or adit will be owned by the Coal Authority and not the adjacent surface landowner. Clients should be advised accordingly and reminded that in these cases the permission of the Coal Authority must be sought before carrying out any works to locate, treat or in any other way interfere with former coal workings including disused coal mine shafts or adits.

5   DEALING WITH LENDERS

5.1   If domestic property which is the subject of a coal mining search is to be charged as security for a loan, a copy of the mining report should be sent to the lender as soon as received depending on the result and the lender's instructions. The solicitor should not comment substantively on the replies within the mining report but should recommend that they are referred to the lender's valuer to review.

5.2   Provided that a copy of the mining report has been so provided solicitors are not obliged to make any other reference to the replies in any mining report on title to a lender save to refer to the existence of the search and the mining report.

5.3   The Royal Institution of Chartered Surveyors, the Council of Mortgage Lenders and the Association of British Insurers have been consulted with regard to these Guidance Notes in respect of, surveys of, loans granted on security of, and insurance of, domestic properties in areas affected by coal mining, and each such organisation has prepared separate guidance to its own members.

5.4   With regard to non-domestic property a similar procedure should be adopted. Solicitors should, however, refer to the replies to the additional enquiries included in the mining reports for non-residential, commercial or development sites as these deal with legal matters (namely the withdrawal of support and the existence of working facilities orders).

5.5   When also acting for the lender solicitors should, in all cases, check whether the instructions from that lender require the solicitor to deal with the mining report in any other manner. If so, the solicitor should explain to the lender the basis upon which the solicitor is recommended by these paragraphs to proceed. It is important that solicitors should not attempt to perform the function of the client's valuer or surveyor with regard to the mining report.

6   IMPLEMENTATION OF FORM CON 29M (2003)

6.1   The new form CON 29M (2003) will be available from 26 May 2003. The Coal Authority will continue to accept the 1998 form until 1 July 2003.

6.2   From 30 April 2003, all mining reports requested from the Coal Authority will be prepared in accordance with the Law Society's Guidance 2003, the User Guide 2003 and the Terms and Conditions 2003.

V.5. Council Statement: Landlords' Solicitors' Costs[1]

Reproduced from the Law Society's Gazette, December 19, 1984, at pp.3556–7

Both the Professional Purposes and Non-Contentious Business Departments of The Law Society regularly receive complaints and requests for guidance from solicitors as to the practice where landlords seek to pass liability for their solicitors' costs to a lessee or assignor. The Council hope that this statement will help to resolve the problems that can arise.

Grants of leases

It is, of course, common for a prospective lessee to agree to pay the landlord's solicitor's costs relating to the grant of the lease. The most frequent problem is that the amount of the landlord's solicitor's costs comes as a surprise to the lessee and/or his solicitor. This problem can be mitigated and often avoided if the lessee's solicitor seeks an estimate of the landlord's solicitor's costs at the outset and informs his client forthwith. If it is thought that the estimate is unreasonably high, negotiations can take place immediately, before either party has been involved in any substantial amount of work relating to the grant of the lease.

If a landlord's solicitor is asked for an estimate, then he should do his best to give a firm estimate, although it would usually be reasonable to add that the estimate could be exceeded if matters did not proceed quickly and without unforeseen complications. If the landlord is not prepared to depart substantially from the draft form of lease submitted to the lessee's solicitor, the landlord's solicitor should make this plain and should also state, if it be the case, that his estimate is based on the assumption that attempts will not be made to make substantial changes.

Licences to assign

The second situation where problems arise is where a proposed assignor needs a licence to assign from a superior landlord or a succession of superior landlords. It is sometimes appropriate that the proposed assignor should pay the costs and disbursements of such landlord(s) in relation to such licence(s), especially where the lease itself obliges him to pay (as to which s.144, Law of Property Act 1925 and s.19, Landlord and Tenant Act 1927 are relevant).

The Council express no view on whether in any given case there is a legal obligation on a proposed assignor to bear his landlord's costs. However, where the solicitor for the assignor asks the landlord's solicitor for such a licence, the Council do not regard it as professionally improper for the landlord's solicitor to ask for a professional undertaking that, whether or not the matter proceeds, the assignor's solicitor will pay his costs and disbursements in relation to the required licence. Whether the assignor's solicitor is willing to give the undertaking is a matter for his professional judgment in all the circumstances.

It is often vital to assignors that there should be no delay in obtaining any necessary licences. This will no doubt be a factor in their solicitor's decision whether to give the undertaking. The Council do

---

1. © The Law Society 1984. This statement first appeared in The Law Society's Gazette on 19 December 1984.

mphasise, however, that where solicitors give an undertaking, it will stand to be construed strictly and at compliance with it will be a charge on their resources unless they are put in funds by their client.

will be prudent for an assignor's solicitor to seek an estimate of the amount of costs and disbursements at are to be covered by his proposed undertaking. It follows that time can be saved if landlords' licitors include an estimate of the amount when asking for the undertaking. They should certainly do eir best to give a firm estimate on request, although again it would usually be reasonable to add that e estimate could be exceeded if matters did not proceed quickly and without unforeseen mplications.

ther licences

he principles in the last section of this statement should usually apply also where landlords are asked r licences to underlet, change use, carry out alterations, etc.

emuneration certificates or taxations of costs

Vhether a lease is being granted or a licence has been applied for, the client on whose behalf the relevant osts have been incurred is the landlord. The fact that a third party is liable to pay such costs does not of self create an entitlement to seek a Remuneration Certificate under the Solicitors' Remuneration Order 972. As a matter of practice, the Law Society will accept an application for a remuneration certificate such circumstances, but *only* if the landlord gives his consent. In appropriate cases, the Council would ope that landlords' solicitors will encourage their clients to give such consent.

here is judicial authority for saying that an undertaking to pay reasonable costs means costs to be taxed not agreed – *Zaniewski* v. *Scales* (1969) 113 SJ 525. If the landlord is unwilling to give his consent, e paying party is entitled to apply to the High Court for a taxation of the bill under s.71, Solicitors Act 974. The client should be warned of the estimated expense of such an application and as to whether uch expense might be disproportionate to the amount of the bill in dispute. Further, the client's attention hould be drawn to the provisions of s.70(9) relating to payment of the costs of the taxation proceedings.

V.6. Dealing with licensed conveyancers[1]

A solicitor may normally deal with a licensed conveyancer as if the conveyancer were a solicitor, subject to the best interests of the solicitor's client.

1. Licensed conveyancers are permitted to practise in partnership with other licensed conveyancers, or with other persons (although not with solicitors). Licensed conveyancers may also practise through the medium of a 'recognised body', i.e. a body corporate recognised by the Council for Licensed Conveyancers.

2. The identity of firms of licensed conveyancers can be checked in the *Directory of Solicitors and Barristers*. In cases of doubt contact the Council for Licensed Conveyancers [16 Glebe Road, Chelmsford, Essex CM1 1QG. DX 121925 Chelmsford 6. Tel: 01245 349599. Fax: 01245 341300].

3. Licensed conveyancers are subject to conduct and accounts rules similar to those which apply to solicitors. They are covered by compulsory indemnity insurance and contribute to a compensation fund. In dealings with licensed conveyancers, it should normally be possible to proceed as if the licensed conveyancer were a solicitor and bound by the same professional obligations. For example, if it is agreed to use the Law Society's code for exchange of contracts by telephone, it is understood that any failure to respect the code would expose the licensed conveyancer to disciplinary proceedings; this also applies to the Society's code for completion by post, and reliance on undertakings. Since licensed conveyancers may practise in partnership or association with others, it is important to ensure that the other party's representative is a licensed conveyancer, or a person working immediately under the supervision of a licensed conveyancer.

---

1. The following text appears as principle 25.06 in *The Guide to the Professional Conduct of Solicitors 1999* published by the Law Society.

V.7.   Dealing with unqualified conveyancers[1]

Effect of section 22 of the Solicitors Act 1974

1.   Section 22 of the Solicitors Act 1974 (see Annex 2A at p.45 in the Guide) makes it an offence for an unqualified person to draw or prepare, *inter alia*, a contract for sale or a transfer, conveyance, lease or mortgage relating to land in expectation of fee, gain or reward. Qualified persons under this section are solicitors, barristers, notaries public, licensed conveyancers, some public officers and, for unregistered conveyancing, Scottish solicitors.

2.   It is inevitable that an unqualified person who undertakes a conveyancing transaction in the course of a conveyancing business will commit an offence under section 22, unless the drawing or preparation of the relevant documents is undertaken by a qualified person. In such circumstances, the unqualified conveyancer's client is likely, albeit unwittingly, to be guilty of aiding and abetting the offence. The solicitor acting for the other party could also be guilty of procuring the commission of an offence by inviting or urging the unqualified person to provide a draft contract or transfer or to progress the transaction.

3.   Solicitors should therefore refuse to have any dealings with any unqualified person carrying on a conveyancing business unless there is clear evidence that offences under section 22 will not be committed.

4.   It is recommended that, at the outset of any transaction, the solicitor should write to the unqualified conveyancer drawing attention to this guidance and saying that the solicitor cannot enter into any dealings with him or her unless there is clear evidence that no offences will be committed. An example of satisfactory evidence would be a letter from a qualified person confirming that he or she will prepare the relevant documents. The solicitor should also immediately report to his or her own client and explain why he or she cannot deal with the unqualified conveyancer unless clear evidence is forthcoming.

Draft letter to unqualified conveyancer

'We are instructed to act for the seller/buyer in connection with the above transaction and understand that you have been instructed by the buyer/seller. Please confirm that you are a solicitor or licensed conveyancer. If not, please state who will prepare the contract/conveyance/transfer for you; we need to receive written confirmation from a qualified person that he or she will personally settle the contract/conveyance/transfer.

As you know, it is an offence for an unqualified person to prepare a contract for sale or a transfer, conveyance or mortgage relating to land in expectation of fee, gain or reward. We have been advised by the Law Society that we should not deal with an unqualified person carrying on a conveyancing business unless clear evidence is provided that offences under section 22 of the Solicitors Act 1974 will not be committed. The written confirmation referred to above, if explicit and unequivocal, could provide such evidence.

---

1. The following text appears as Annex 25A in *The Guide to the Professional Conduct of Solicitors 1999*, published by the Law Society. Cross references to paragraphs in the *Guide* include page references from the *Guide*.

We regret that unless you are a solicitor or licensed conveyancer, we cannot deal with you until the evidence required above is provided.'

Draft letter to client of solicitor

'Thank you for your instructions relating to the above transactions. There is unfortunately a problem. The buyer/seller appears to have instructed an unqualified conveyancer to act for him/her and this could lead to the conveyancer, his/her client and myself being involved in the commission of criminal offences under the Solicitors Act 1974. The Law Society, my professional body, has advised solicitors not to deal with unqualified conveyancers because of the possibility of committing criminal offences.

I have therefore written to the firm acting for the buyer/seller asking for confirmation whether or not they are unqualified conveyancers and, if they are, whether they will be making arrangements to prevent the commission of such offences. If they cannot satisfy me about this, the buyer/seller will have to instruct a solicitor or licensed conveyancer, or deal with me direct.'

Further help

1.   Solicitors should first check with the Council for Licensed Conveyancers whether a person is a licensed conveyancer, since a licensed conveyancer can normally be dealt with as if a solicitor (see **25.06**, p.472 in the Guide).

2.   The Society can help practitioners dealing with unqualified conveyancers if the above guidance and the practice notes below do not cover the situation. Telephone calls and written requests for guidance should be made to the Practice Advice Service – for contact details see p.xv.

3.   The Professional Adviser (for contact details, see p.xv) has responsibility for investigating and prosecuting non-solicitors who appear to be in breach of the Solicitors Act 1974. Solicitors are asked to report (without submitting their files) any case where there is *prima facie* evidence of breaches of the Solicitors Act.

4.   For assistance in those cases where the solicitor has clear evidence that no offences under section 22 will be committed, there is set out below a series of practice notes relating to the problems which might arise in a transaction in which the other party is represented by an unqualified conveyancer. These practice notes give advice only and it is for solicitors to decide for themselves what steps should properly be taken in any particular situation.

PRACTICE NOTES

(applicable only where evidence is provided of compliance with section 22)

General

1.   Any undertaking which unqualified agents may offer in the course of a transaction is not enforceable in the same way as an undertaking given by a solicitor or licensed conveyancer. Solicitors should therefore never accept such undertakings.

2.   Solicitors are under no duty to undertake agency work by way of completions by post on behalf of unqualified persons, or to attend to other formalities on behalf of third parties who are not clients, even where such third parties offer to pay the agent's charges.

3.   The Council also suggests that in cases where a solicitor is dealing with an unqualified conveyancer, the solicitor should bear in mind the line of decisions starting with *Hedley Byrne* v. *Heller*

1964] AC 465, which extends the duty of care owed by a solicitor to persons who are not clients, but who rely and act on the solicitor's advice to his or her knowledge.

4. Solicitors must decide in each case whether special provisions should be incorporated in the draft contract to take account of the problems which arise by reason of the other party having no solicitor or licensed conveyancer, e.g. that the seller should attend personally at completion if represented by an unqualified agent. All such matters must be considered prior to exchange of contracts since contractual conditions cannot, of course, be imposed subsequently.

5. The protection provided by section 69 of the Law of Property Act 1925 only applies when a document containing a receipt for purchase money is handed over by a solicitor or licensed conveyancer or the seller himself or herself. Thus it should be considered whether the contract should provide either for the seller to attend personally at completion, or for an authority signed by the seller, for the purchase money to be paid to his or her agent, to be handed over on completion.

Acting for the seller: buyer not represented by a solicitor or licensed conveyancer

Completion

6. It is important to ensure that the deeds and keys are passed to the person entitled to receive them, i.e. the buyer. If an authority on behalf of the buyer is offered to the seller's solicitor, it is for the solicitor to decide whether or not to accept it, bearing in mind that no authority, however expressed, can be irrevocable. Again it is worth considering at the outset whether the point should be covered by express condition in the contract (see practice note 4 above).

Acting for the buyer: seller not represented by a solicitor or licensed conveyancer

Preliminary enquiries and requisitions on title

7. It may be prudent to require and ensure that replies to all preliminary enquiries and requisitions are signed by the seller.

Payment of deposit

8. Difficulties may arise in connection with payment of the deposit where there is no estate agent involved to whom the deposit may be paid as stakeholder in the ordinary way. The deposit may be paid direct to the seller, but this cannot be recommended since it is equivalent to parting with a portion of the purchase money in advance of investigation of the title and other matters.

9. Some unqualified agents insist that the deposit be paid to them. The Council does not recommend this. If a solicitor is obliged to pay the deposit to unqualified agents, he or she should inform the client of the risks involved, and obtain specific instructions before proceeding.

10. An alternative is for the deposit to be paid to the buyer's solicitor as stakeholder. The buyer's solicitor should insist on this where possible. If the seller will not agree to this, it may be possible to agree to place the deposit in a deposit account in the joint names of the buyer's solicitor and the seller, or in a deposit account in the seller's name, with the deposit receipt to be retained by the buyer's solicitor.

Payment of purchase money

11. As referred to in practice note 5 above, the buyer's solicitor should ensure that all the purchase money, including any deposit, is paid either to the seller or to the seller's properly authorised agent.

Matters unresolved at completion

12.   Whilst it is unusual to leave any issues revealed by searches and other enquiries outstanding at completion, undertakings relating to their discharge or resolution may on occasions be given between solicitors or licensed conveyancers. Such undertakings should not be accepted from unqualified agents for the reason mentioned in practice note 1 above.

Power of attorney

13.   Unqualified agents sometimes obtain a power of attorney to enable themselves or their employees to conduct certain aspects of the transaction. It is clearly important to ensure that such powers are valid, properly granted, and effective for all relevant purposes.

Acting for the lender: borrower not represented by a solicitor or licensed conveyancer

14.   The lender's solicitor often finds himself or herself undertaking much of the work which a borrower's solicitor would do. Whilst the client's interests are paramount, the solicitor must ensure that he or she does not render the unqualified agent additional assistance in a way which might establish a solicitor/client relationship either with the unqualified conveyancer or with the borrower, or leave the solicitor open to a negligence claim either from the solicitor's lender client or from the borrower.

Advances

15.   As regards the drafting and preparation of the instrument of transfer by the borrower's representative, the lender's solicitor is not obliged to undertake work which would normally be done by the borrower's solicitor. Solicitors are reminded, however, that it is of paramount importance to their lender client that good title is conveyed to the borrower.

16.   The importance of paying mortgage advances only to those properly entitled to receive them is a reason for insisting either that the borrower attends personally on completion, or that a signed authority from the borrower in favour of his or her agent is received on completion. Section 69 of the Law of Property Act 1925 is a relevant consideration in this context (see practice note 5 above).

Redemptions

17.   On completion, cheques or drafts should be drawn in favour of solicitors or licensed conveyancers or their clients, and not endorsed over to some intermediate party. The deeds should normally be handed over to the borrower personally, unless he or she provides a valid authority for them to be handed to a third party.

18.   Any issues of doubt or difficulty must be referred to the lender/client for detailed instructions. Where the lender is a building society and its solicitor considers that the totality of the work involved justifies a charge in excess of the building society's guideline fee, he or she should seek the approval of the lender/client, supported if necessary by a bill of costs containing sufficient detail of the work and the time spent on it.

16th March 1988, revised December 1995

V.8. Gifts of property guidelines[1]

Introduction

Elderly people or those nearing retirement may seek advice from solicitors as to the advantages and disadvantages of transferring their home or other property to relatives, even though in some cases they still intend to live in the home. The solicitor's advice will of course vary, according to the individual circumstances of the client, their motivation for making such a gift, and what they are hoping to achieve by it.

The following guidelines are designed to assist solicitors, both to ensure that their clients fully understand the nature, effects, benefits, risks and foreseeable consequences of making such a gift, and also to clarify the solicitor's role and duty in relation to such transactions. In particular, consideration is given to the implications of making gifts of property on possible future liability for the payment of fees for residential or nursing home care. This area of law is still under review by the Government, so solicitors should be aware that the law may change.

Whilst these guidelines generally refer to the making of 'gifts' they apply with equal force to situations where the disposal of property at a significant undervalue is contemplated.

The need for legal advice

The Law Society is aware of a number of non-solicitor legal advice services which are marketing schemes for elderly people to effect a gift of property with the intention of avoiding the value of that property being taken into account to pay for residential care. Some make unjustified claims as to the effectiveness of the schemes, or fail to take into account the individual circumstances of clients. Seldom do these schemes highlight the other risks involved in making a gift of the home to members of the family.

These guidelines are also intended to assist solicitors to stress the need for clients to obtain proper legal advice, and to highlight the risks of using unqualified advisers.

Who is the client?

The solicitor must first be clear as to who s/he is acting for, especially where relatives purport to be giving instructions on behalf of an elderly person. In most cases, it will be the elderly person who owns the home or property so if the solicitor is to act in a transfer the elderly person will be the client. This will be the assumption for the purpose of these guidelines. It is important to recognise that there is an inevitable conflict of interest between the elderly person and anyone who stands to gain from the transaction, so the elderly person should receive independent advice.

The solicitor acting for the elderly person should see the client alone, to satisfy him/herself that the client is acting freely, to confirm the client's wishes and intentions, and to gauge the extent, if any, of family or other influence (see Principle 12.05 of *The Guide to the Professional Conduct of Solicitors 1999*). It

1. © The Law Society 2000. This Appendix was originally published as guidance from the Law Society's Mental Health and Disability Committee, and was called 'Gifts of Property: Implications for future liability to pay for long term care'.

may be necessary to spend some time with the client, talking about wider issues, in order to evaluate these aspects, clarify the family circumstances, and assess whether the client has the mental capacity to make the gift (see Appendix A on p. 111 below for details of the relevant test of capacity).

If the client is not already known to the solicitor, it may also be advisable to check whether another solicitor has previously acted for the client, and if so, to seek the client's consent to contact that solicitor, in case there are factors to be taken into account which are not immediately apparent.

The client's understanding

It is important to ensure that the client understands the nature of a gift, that this is what is intended and the long-term implications. Before making any such gift clients should in particular understand:

(a)   that the money or property they intend to give away is theirs in the first place;

(b)   why the gift is being made;

(c)   whether it is a one-off, or part of a series of gifts;

(d)   the extent of the gift in relation to the rest of their money and property;

(e)   that they are making an outright gift rather than, say, a loan or acquiring a share in a business or property owned by the recipient;

(f)   whether they expect to receive anything in return and, if so, how much, or on what terms (e.g. someone who is giving away their house might expect to be able to carry on living there rent-free for the rest of their life: but who pays for the insurance and upkeep?);

(g)   whether they intend the gift to take effect immediately, or at a later date – perhaps when they die, or go into residential care;

(h)   that, if the gift is outright, they cannot assume that the money or property would be returned to them on request;

(i)   the effect that making the gift could have on their future standard of living;

(j)   the effect that the gift could have on other members of the family who might have expected eventually to inherit a share of the money or property;

(k)   the possibility that the recipient could die first, or become involved in divorce or bankruptcy proceedings, in which case the money or property given away could end up belonging to somebody else;

(l)   that the donor and recipient could fall out and even become quite hostile to one another;

(m)   whether they have already made gifts to the recipient or other people; and

(n)   any other foreseeable consequences of making or not making the gift (some of which are considered below).

The client's objectives

The solicitor should establish why the gift of property is being contemplated, and whether the client's objectives will in fact be achieved by the making of the gift or could be achieved in some other way. In establishing the client's objectives, the following matters may be relevant:

(a)   If the objective is to ensure that a particular relative (e.g. a child) inherits the client's home rather than someone else, this can equally well be achieved by making a will.

(b)   If the objective is to avoid inheritance tax on the death of the client, a rough calculation should be made of the client's likely estate to assess the amount of tax which may be payable, and whether other tax saving measures could be considered. The client might not appreciate that the value of the property, together with the remainder of the estate, may not exceed the level at which inheritance tax becomes payable.

The client might also not be aware that if s/he intends to continue living in the home after giving it away, there may be no inheritance tax saving because of the 'reservation of benefit' rules. The consequence might also be to increase the liability to inheritance tax on the death of the relative to whom the gift has been made if s/he dies before the client. Again, other schemes to mitigate these vulnerabilities should be considered.

(c)   If the objective is to relieve the elderly client of the worry and responsibility of home ownership, other ways of achieving this should be discussed, such as making an Enduring Power of Attorney.

(d)   If the client volunteers that a significant part of his/her objective is to try to avoid the value of the home being taken into account in various forms of means-testing, the implications and possible consequences should be explained to the client. These matters are considered in the following paragraphs in relation to liability to pay for long-term care. Alternative measures should also be discussed. The solicitor may also need to consider her/his own position.

Other reasons for transferring the home

There may, of course, be good reasons for transferring the home, or a share in the home, to a relative or another person quite apart from the desire to avoid means-testing. If such reasons exist the transfer should be effected sooner rather than later and it would be worthwhile reciting the reason in the transfer deed. For example:

(a)   the home has not been vested in the appropriate names in the first place (e.g. it was funded in whole or in part by a son or daughter but vested in the name of the parent);

(b)   a daughter has given up a well paid job to live in the home and care for an infirm parent in the expectation of inheriting the home on the death of the parent;

(c)   the parent has for some years been unable to meet the outgoings or pay for alterations or improvements to the home and these have been funded by a son in the expectation of inheriting the home on the death of the parent;

(d)   the home comprises part of a family business (e.g. a farm) which would no longer be viable if the home was 'lost'.

If the home is already vested in the joint names of the infirm elderly person and another occupier, or can for justifiable reasons be transferred by the elderly person into joint names, the beneficial interest of the elderly person may, on a means assessment, have little value when subject to the continued rights of occupation of the co-owner.

Severance of a joint tenancy

If the home is vested in the joint names of an elderly couple it may be worth considering a severance of the joint tenancy with a view to preserving at least a one-half share for the family. Each spouse can then make a will leaving his or her one-half share to the children. This provides some protection in the event that a caring spouse dies before an infirm spouse but there may be vulnerability to a claim under Inheritance (Provision for Family and Dependants) Act 1975. It is possible to sever the joint tenancy even after the infirm spouse has become mentally incapable.

Implications of making the gift

A proper assessment of the implications of making a gift of the home, both for the client and for her/his relative(s) can best be achieved by listing the possible benefits and risks. These may include the following:

Possible benefits

(a) a saving of inheritance tax, probate fees and costs on the death of the client. Although in most cases the existence of a potential liability for inheritance tax will mean that a gift of the home by itself will not avoid vulnerability to means-testing, the high value of homes particularly in London may create this situation;

(b) avoiding the need to sell the home to pay for charges such as residential care or nursing home fees, thus securing the family's inheritance;

(c) avoiding the value of the home being taken into account in means-testing for other benefits or services.

Possible risks

(a) the value of the home may still be taken into account under the anti-avoidance measures in relation to means-testing;

(b) the capital gains tax owner-occupier exemption will apply to the gift, but may be lost thereafter and there will be no automatic uplift to the market value of the home on the client's death;

(c) the client may never need residential or nursing home care (it has been estimated that less than 6% of people aged 75–85 need residential care), so the risks of giving away the home may outweigh any potential benefits to be achieved;

(d) if the client does eventually need residential or nursing home care but no longer has the resources to pay the fees him/herself because of the gift, the local authority may only pay for a basic level of care (e.g. a shared room in a home of its choice), so the client may be dependent on relatives to top up the fees if a better standard of care is desired;

(e) the relatives to whom the gift has been made may fail to keep their side of the understanding, whether deliberately or through no fault of their own. For example, they may:

    (i) fail to support the client (e.g. by not topping up residential care fees);

    (ii) seek to move the client prematurely into residential care in order to occupy the home themselves or to sell it;

    (iii) die suddenly without making suitable provision for the client;

    (iv) run into financial difficulties because of unemployment or divorce or become bankrupt and in consequence be unable to support the client;

(f) the home may be lost on the bankruptcy, divorce or death of the relative to whom it has been given, resulting in the client being made homeless if s/he is still living there;

(g) there may be no inheritance tax saving whilst the client continues to live in the home, yet there could be a liability for inheritance tax if the relative dies before the client;

(h) the relative to whom the home has been gifted may lose entitlement to benefits and/or services (e.g. social security benefits, legal aid) due to personal means-testing if not living in the home;

(i) the local authority may decide, having regard to the client's ownership of the notional capital value of the home, rather than the property itself, that s/he is not entitled to certain community care services, or even to be funded at all for residential care should this be needed.

Anti-avoidance measures

The client can be given no guarantees that there is a fool-proof way of avoiding the value of the home being taken into account in means-testing, since the anti-avoidance measures in the law enable some gifts to be ignored by the authorities and even set aside by the court. Not only are these measures subject to change from time to time, but it is also unclear how far the authorities will go in order to pursue contributions they believe to be owing to them.

In most cases, the intention behind making the gift is the most important factor. Where the intention is clearly to create or increase entitlement to financial support from the local authority, measures can be taken to impose a charge on the asset given away in the hands of the recipients or even to recover the asset itself. However, it is necessary that the authority concerned believe that this was a 'significant' part of the client's intention in making the gift. Using one of the marketed schemes which have been advertised specifically to help people to avoid local authority means-testing may make clear the client's intention.

Charges for residential and nursing home care

At present, a major cause for concern among many older clients is the fear of having to sell their homes in order to pay for residential or nursing home care in the future, and they may wish to take steps to protect their families' inheritance. In giving advice on this matter, it is important that solicitors are familiar with the key points summarised in para. 21.7 below, including:

(a) the eligibility criteria for NHS-funded nursing home care;

(b) the charging and funding arrangements by local authorities for residential and nursing home care (when applicable);

(c) when care must be provided free of charge; and

(d) if charges may be made, the means-testing rules which apply.

Implications of the 'notional capital' rule

Where the local authority believe that property has been given away by the client with the intention of creating or increasing entitlement to help with residential care fees, or nursing home fees where these are payable, then it may decide that the client has 'notional capital' equivalent in value to that of the property given away. If that notional capital value exceeds the capital cut-off (currently £16,000, see para. 21.7 below) the authority may decide that the client is not entitled to any assistance (or any continuing assistance) with the home care fees.

In such cases it would be the client who then had to take action if s/he wished to challenge the decision. This may involve the use of the local authority's complaints procedures, as well as the Ombudsman or a judicial review. These may all entail significant legal expense and anxiety for the client as the outcome could not be guaranteed. If a judicial review is necessary it would be the client who had to establish that the authority's decision was *Wednesbury* unreasonable (i.e. the burden of proof would be on the client).[2]

Enforcing payment of fees for residential and nursing home care

Having assessed someone as being in need of residential or nursing home care and then provided that care, the local authority cannot withdraw that provision simply because the resident does not pay assessed contributions. However, where charges may legally be made, the authority can take steps to recover contributions, and in assessing ability to pay, may take into account property that has been given away for the purpose of avoiding means-testing.

The enforcement provisions available to local authorities are as follows:

(a) taking proceedings in the Magistrates' Court to recover sums due as a civil debt (National Assistance Act 1948, s.56);

---

2. See *Robertson* v. *Fife* (Court of Session) 12/1/2000 [http://www.scotscourt.gov.uk/index1.htm].

(b) imposing a charge on any property belonging to the resident, with interest chargeable from the day after death (HASSASSA Act 1983, s.22 and s.24);

(c) imposing a charge on property transferred by the resident within 6 months of going to residential care, or whilst in care, with the intention of avoiding contributions (HASSASSA Act 1983, s.21).

Once the debt for unpaid contributions reaches £750, insolvency proceedings could be taken to declare the resident bankrupt, whereupon transactions at an undervalue may be set aside within two years, or within five years if the person made bankrupt was insolvent at the time of the transaction, which is unlikely (Insolvency Act 1986, ss.339–341).

Under other provisions, a gift may be set aside without time limit and without bankruptcy, if the court is satisfied that the transfer was made for the purpose of putting assets beyond the reach of a potential creditor or otherwise prejudicing the creditor's interests (Insolvency Act 1986, ss.423–425). This provision is exceptionally wide, and the court has extensive powers to restore the position to that which it would have been had the gift not been made.

Although some local authorities have threatened to use insolvency proceedings, few have actually done so, perhaps because of lack of expertise or the prospect of bad publicity. However, with increasing pressures on local authority resources to provide community care services, there is no guarantee they will not do so in the future.

The burden of proof remains on the local authority to establish that the purpose behind the gift of the property was to avoid means-testing. But it may be difficult for the donor or his/her relatives to give evidence as to the donor's intentions, and if another purpose of the gift cannot be established or indicated the judge may conclude that it must have been to avoid means-testing.

The purpose of the gift will have been discussed in advance with the solicitor, and it would be prudent for the solicitor to retain evidence of the advice given in order to protect him/herself in the event of a subsequent family dispute or professional negligence claim. The file notes and correspondence will normally be covered by legal professional privilege or at least by the duty of confidentiality. The court will not usually order discovery of a solicitor's file unless there is *prima facie* evidence of fraud, but has done so in similar circumstances on the basis of public policy considerations.[3] It is possible that a trustee in bankruptcy, or a local authority bringing proceedings under the Insolvency Act 1986, ss.423–425, may persuade the court to override privilege.

In *Yule v South Lanarkshire Council* [1999] 1 CCLR 546 Lord Philip held that a local authority was entitled to take account of the value of an elderly woman's home transferred to her daughter over 18 months before the woman entered residential care. The Court held that there was no time limit on local authorities when deciding whether a person had deprived themselves of assets for the purposes of avoiding residential care fees.

The solicitor's duty

The solicitor's role is more than just drawing up and registering the necessary deeds and documents to effect the making of the gift. S/he has a duty to ensure that the client fully understands the nature, effect, benefits, risks and foreseeable consequences of making the gift. The solicitor has no obligation to advise the client on the wisdom or morality of the transaction, unless the client specifically requests this.

The Professional Ethics Division of the Law Society has advised that the solicitor should follow his/her client's instructions, provided that by doing so, the solicitor will not be involved in a breach of the law or a breach of the principles of professional conduct. Reference is made to Principle 12.02 of

3. *Barclays Bank plc v. Eustice* [1995] 1 WLR 1238.

The Guide to the Professional Conduct of Solicitors 1999, which indicates when instructions must be refused. Solicitors will want to satisfy themselves in each individual case that no breach of the law is involved in the proposed transaction. Having advised the client as to the implications and possible consequences of making the gift, the decision whether or not to proceed remains with the client.

Solicitors must also be aware of the possible conflict of interest, or significant risk of such a conflict, between the donor and recipient of a gift. While there is no general rule of law that a solicitor should never act for both parties in a transaction where their interests might conflict, Principle 15.01 of *The Guide to the Professional Conduct of Solicitors 1999* states: 'A solicitor or firm of solicitors should not accept instructions to act for two or more clients where there is a conflict or a significant risk of a conflict between the interests of the clients.' Given the potentially vulnerable position of an elderly client, the solicitor will have to consider carefully whether he can act for the donor and the recipient or whether there is an actual or significant risk of conflict. If the solicitor has initially advised the donor alone as to all the implications of the gift and is satisfied that there is no undue influence and that the donor has capacity, the solicitor may be able to act for both clients in the conveyancing.

If the solicitor is asked to act for both parties, the solicitor should make them both aware of the possibility of a conflict of interest and advise one of them to consider taking independent advice. S/he should also explain that as a result of any conflict of interest, a solicitor acting by agreement for both parties may be unable to disclose all that s/he knows to each of them or to give advice to one of them which conflicts with the interests of the other and may have to cease acting for both. Both parties must be content to proceed on this basis, be competent to do so and give their consent in writing. However, if any doubt remains, the solicitor would be advised not to act for both parties.

FURTHER READING

The Elderly Client Handbook: The Law Society's Guide to Acting for Older People, Gordon R. Ashton (Second Edition, 2000), Law Society.

Elderly People and the Law, Gordon R. Ashton (1995), Butterworths.

Butterworths Older Client Law Service, Gordon R. Ashton (ed.) (1998 loose-leaf), Butterworths.

Community Care and the Law, L. Clements (Third Edition, 2000), Legal Action Group.

The Guide to the Professional Conduct of Solicitors, The Law Society (Eighth edition, 1999), The Law Society.

Age Concern Fact Sheets available from Age Concern England, FREEPOST, (SWB 30375), Ashburton, Devon TQ13 7ZZ. Tel: 0800 00 99 66:

No. 10: *Local authority charging procedures for residential and nursing home care.*
No. 11: *Financial support for people in residential and nursing home accommodation prior to 1 April 1993.*
No. 38: *Treatment of the former home as capital for people in residential and nursing home care.*
No. 39: *Paying for care in a residential or nursing home if you have a partner.*
No. 40: *Transfer of assets and paying for care in a residential or nursing home.*

Appendix A – Capacity to make a gift[4]

The relevant test of capacity to make a gift is set out in the judgment in *Re Beaney (Deceased)* [1978] 1 WLR 770. In that case a 64-year-old widow with three grown up children owned and lived in a three-bedroom semi-detached house. Her elder daughter lived with her. In May 1973, a few days after being admitted to hospital suffering from advanced dementia, the widow signed a deed of gift transferring the

---

4. Adapted from British Medical Association/Law Society, *Assessment of Mental Capacity: Guidance for Doctors and Lawyers* (1995), BMA.

house to her elder daughter. The widow died intestate the following year, and her son and younger daughter applied successfully to the court for a declaration that the transfer of the house was void and of no effect because their mother was mentally incapable of making such a gift. The judge in the case set out the following criteria for capacity to make a lifetime gift:

'The degree or extent of understanding required in respect of any instrument is relative to the particular transaction which it is to effect. ... Thus, at one extreme, if the subject matter and value of a gift are trivial in relation to the donor's other assets, a low degree of understanding will suffice. But, at the other, if its effect is to dispose of the donor's only asset of value and thus, for practical purposes, to pre-empt the devolution of his estate under [the donor's] will or ... intestacy, then the degree of understanding required is as high as that required for a will, and the donor must understand the claims of all potential donees and the extent of the property to be disposed of.'

It is arguable that, when someone makes a substantial gift, a further point should be considered, namely, the effect that disposing of the asset could have on the donor for the rest of his or her life.

Appendix B – Paying for residential and nursing home care[5]

Charges

Individuals who can afford to pay for a place in a residential care or nursing home may arrange this independently, though it is advisable to seek a 'needs' assessment prior to entering residential or nursing care in order to achieve continuity if local authority funding may be needed in future:

(a)   if met with a refusal to assess in advance, point out that the assessment of need for care provision does not depend upon the need for funding;

(b)   it may also be wise to ensure that the particular home is willing to accommodate residents on local authority funding.

Those who enter such a home through an arrangement made by the local authority must pay or contribute to the cost, whether the authority provides or buys in the accommodation:

(a)   each authority must fix a standard weekly charge for its own homes which should represent the true economic cost of providing the accommodation – many have a standard scale of fees geared to their eligibility criteria;

(b)   where the authority purchases a place from an independent home the weekly charge to the resident should represent the cost of the place to the authority;

(c)   residents must generally contribute in accordance with their resources up to the appropriate charge, but no one will be required to pay more;

(d)   the authority either:

(i)   pays the full fee to the home and collects the resident's contribution; or

(ii)   pays its share whilst the resident and any third party pay the balance;

(e)   a contract with the authority or the home should state what is included in the charge and what are extras.

Where a health authority arranges a place in a nursing home under a contractual arrangement the individual remains an NHS patient and no charge is made but social security benefits may be withdrawn or reduced. It is important to ascertain whether a move from hospital to a private nursing home also involves a transfer of responsibility from the health authority to social services.

5. Adapted from Gordon R. Ashton, *The Elderly Client Handbook: The Law Society's Guide to Acting for Older People* (Second Edition 2000), Law Society.

Means-testing

When the resident cannot afford the full charge an assessment is made of ability to pay and this is reviewed annually but a resident should ask for re-assessment at any time if this would be beneficial:

(a)   the assessment relates to both income and capital:

   (i)   since April 1993 assessment has been brought largely into line with that for income support, though local authorities retain some discretion;

   (ii)   the capital cut-off point is £16,000 but capital above £10,000 will result in a tariff income (an attempt to apply a lower financial threshold before acknowledging need failed in *R. v. Sefton Metropolitan Borough Council, ex p. Help the Aged* ([1997] 1 CCLR 57, CA);

   (iii)   notional capital and notional income rules apply as for income support;

(b)   assessment relates only to the means of the resident (unlike for income support where spouses and partners are generally assessed together):

   (i)   there is no power to oblige a spouse/partner to take part but spouses are liable to maintain each other (National Assistance Act 1948, s.42) and court action may be taken against a liable relative (s.43);

   (ii)   jointly owned property may be deemed to be owned in equal shares (but query whether it has a value if a home is occupied by the joint owner);

   (iii)   since 1996 one-half of occupational and private pensions of the resident are re-routed back to the non-resident spouse;

(c)   the value of the resident's home is disregarded during a temporary stay or:

   (i)   if occupied by a spouse/partner, or a relative who is aged 60 or over or incapacitated;

   (ii)   if occupied by someone else and the local authority exercises its discretion;

(d)   there is a minimum charge payable by all residents and the assessment determines what should be paid above this, but all residents retain a personal expenses allowance (revised annually):

   (i)   to be used by the resident for expenditure of personal choice such as stationery, personal toiletries, treats (e.g. sweets, drinks, cigarettes) and presents;

   (ii)   the authority has a discretion to increase the amount, but it should not be used for top-up to provide more expensive accommodation;

(e)   authorities should carry out a benefits check because they have an incentive to ensure that people in homes are receiving maximum state benefits:

   (i)   this should only be with the informed consent of the resident;

   (ii)   income support will include a residential allowance (not for local authority homes).

Power to charge?

In two main situations (see *R. v. North and East Devon Health Authority ex p. Coughlan* [1999] 2 CCLR 285; *R. v. Borough of Richmond ex p. Watson* [1999] 2 CCLR 402) no charges may be made for the care of an individual:

(a)   where, following discharge from detention under one of the longer treatment sections of the Mental Health Act 1983 (usually s.3 or s.37), he or she requires residential or nursing home care as a result of mental disorder:

   (i)   no charge may be made for care as this is deemed 'aftercare' service provision under Mental Health Act 1983, s.117;

(ii) that section places a joint duty on the health and local authorities to provide the services required free of charge, unless it is decided by both that the person is no longer in need of these by virtue of their mental disorder;

(b) (only applicable to placements in nursing homes) where his or her need is primarily a health care need:

(i) the health authority must fund the entire cost of the placement and the local authority has no power to purchase such care and pass the costs to the client;

(ii) the only exception is where the nursing care is 'merely ancillary or incidental to the provision of the accommodation' in a nursing home. This will depend on the level and type of care. Most nursing homes placements will be the responsibility of the NHS because a client will not be placed there unless their primary need is for nursing care, i.e. health care.

Regulations and guidance

National Assistance (Assessment of Resources) Regulations 1992, as amended.

Circular LAC (99)9: *Charging for Residential Accommodation Guide* (CRAG).

Copies are available from the Department of Health, PO Box 777, London SE1 6XH; fax: 01623 724 524; e-mail: doh@prologistics.

V.9.   Incorrect redemption statements[1]

The guidance set out below has been issued jointly by the Law Society and Council of Mortgage Lenders in connection with problems arising out of incorrect redemption statements supplied by lenders.

Guidance notes

Problems relating to mortgage redemption statements have caused difficulties for lenders and solicitors (this expression to include licensed conveyancers) for a number of years. In 1985 the Building Societies Association and the Law Society issued detailed advice to their respective members on this subject because of the difficulties which were apparent at that time.

The advice comprised paras. 9 to 13 of BSA circular No. 3155. Those paragraphs are now replaced by the new guidance set out below.

In recent months, the Council of Mortgage Lenders (CML) has received a number of enquiries in respect of redemption statements provided by lenders to solicitors acting for the lender (who will often also act for the seller). This guidance refers to some of the circumstances which can produce errors and problems, and the consequences which this can have for the solicitor in the conveyancing transaction. It also suggests certain practical measures designed to reduce problems in this area. Accordingly, it is of importance to all lenders and covers:

(a)   the function and importance of solicitors' undertakings;

(b)   the general principle that lenders should seal a discharge where a redemption statement was incorrect;

(c)   ways in which lenders might overcome the difficulty caused when the borrower prematurely stops payments;

(d)   similar proposals as to the problem of dishonoured cheques;

(e)   suggestions for overcoming difficulties sometimes presented by multiple mortgage accounts;

(f)   information to be provided to banks for inclusion in telegraphic transfers; and

(g)   the importance of returning the sealed discharge promptly.

Terms of reference

This guidance applies to England and Wales; separate guidance for Scotland and Northern Ireland will follow, if necessary.

Redemption on sale

The guidance applies primarily to redemption of a mortgage on sale of the security and, consequently, the lender's/seller's solicitor is required to give an undertaking to the buyer's solicitor that the charge will be discharged.

---

1. This guidance was first published in 1993. It may be updated in 2003/4 to take account of flexible mortgages.

Remortgages

It is appreciated that an undertaking will also be given on a remortgage and that, accordingly, the guidance should be interpreted as including this situation.

Simple redemption

Much of the guidance is inapplicable to a straightforward redemption (without sale or remortgage) as no undertaking is given. However, even in redemption *per se*, solicitors and lenders will no doubt wish to provide accurate information and deal promptly with their respective responsibilities.

Solicitors' undertakings

The solicitor acting for the seller will need, on completion, to satisfy the buyer's solicitor that the mortgage on the property being sold has been or will be discharged. In theory the buyer's solicitor will wish to see the mortgage discharged before the purchase money is paid. However, where the monies to repay the mortgage are being provided wholly or partly by the proceeds of sale, then the mortgage cannot be paid off until after completion.

Most lenders will not seal the discharge (this expression to include sealing the vacating receipt on a mortgage deed or sealing of Form DS1) until they receive the redemption money. This leaves the buyer's solicitor with a problem in that he or she has to be satisfied that the mortgage will be discharged and that he or she will obtain the receipted mortgage or Land Registry Form DS1 or END1. This problem is solved by the use of the solicitor's undertaking.

On completion, the seller's/lender's solicitor will provide the buyer's solicitor with a written undertaking to redeem the mortgage(s) in a form recommended by the Law Society similar to that set out below:

'In consideration of your today completing the purchase of . . . . we hereby undertake forthwith to pay over to . . . . [the lender] the money required to redeem the mortgage/legal charge dated . . . . and to forward the receipted mortgage/legal charge to you as soon as it is received by us from . . . . [the lender].'

Incorrect redemption statements

Before completion of a sale, the lender's seller's solicitor will obtain a redemption statement calculated to the date of redemption. He or she will sometimes request the daily figure for interest which will be added if completion is delayed. If the lender supplies an incorrect redemption statement, the solicitor is likely to forward insufficient money to redeem the mortgage. The lender might be unwilling to discharge the mortgage and, if the solicitor is not holding more funds on behalf of the borrower, the solicitor would be in breach of his or her undertaking.

Problem areas

Problems with redemption statements can arise for a number of reasons:

(a)   a lender might simply make a mistake in calculating the redemption figure;

(b)   difficulties could be caused by the cancellation of standing orders or direct debit payments or by borrowers' cheques being dishonoured; and

(c)   there might be misunderstanding between a lender and the solicitor.

Some of the more common practical problems are outlined below.

Cancellation

A difficulty arises if the mortgage payments are made by standing order and, shortly before completion, the borrower stops the payments without notice to the lender. There will be a shortfall if the lender assumed, without making this assumption clear, that the next payment would be paid and made the redemption figure calculation accordingly.

If this is the case, and the solicitor has acted in good faith and with no knowledge that a payment has been or is likely to be cancelled, the view of the CML is that the lender should seal the discharge. This is to avoid the solicitor being in breach of his or her undertaking to the buyer's solicitor. (The lender would then have to recoup the money from the borrower.)

This difficulty is less likely to arise where payments are made by direct debit because the lender is the originator of the debit and therefore has control over the raising of any future direct debits from the borrower's bank account.

However, there is no guarantee that direct debits will be honoured and they may be returned on the grounds of insufficient funds or that the customer has closed his or her account or instructed his or her bank to cancel the direct debit.

Some lenders overcome this problem by excluding any future payments due when calculating the redemption figure. In other words, they 'freeze' the account balance at the day of the redemption calculation. The disadvantages of this are that (if the payment has not been cancelled) the borrower has to pay a higher redemption figure and the lender has to make a refund to the borrower after redemption.

An alternative is for the lender on the redemption statement to make it clear to the solicitor that it is assumed that the next payment will be made and that, if it is not paid, the mortgage will not be discharged until the balance is received. This gives the solicitor an early chance to address his or her and his or her borrower client's mind to this situation and to ensure that sufficient monies will be available to redeem the mortgage. Indeed, this would also serve as a reminder to the solicitor to warn the borrower client of the importance of continuing the payments in the normal way up to completion.

Uncleared cheques

This is a very similar situation to that of standing orders and direct debits. The CML's view is that if the lender does not notify the solicitor that it is assumed that the borrower's cheque will clear then, provided that the solicitor acts in good faith and without knowledge that the cheque would be or is likely to be dishonoured, the lender should seal the discharge. Exceptions to this are if the lender:

(a) prepares the redemption statement on the assumption that the cheque will not clear and informs the solicitor of this, probably, in a note on the statement. This has the disadvantages described above, or

(b) notifies the solicitor that a cheque has been received and that, if it does not clear by the date of redemption, the mortgage will not be discharged until the balance is received.

Separate loan account

The lender may have more than one loan secured on the property. For example, in addition to the principal mortgage, there could be a secured personal loan which is a regulated agreement under Consumer Credit Act 1974 and/or a further advance conducted on a separate account basis. In such cases, there will be more than one account number.

On a sale, as all mortgage accounts will be repaid, multiplicity of accounts should not present a problem unless the solicitor does not know and is unable to specify every account and has no notice or cause to query the matter and the lender fails to cross-check the matter internally.

However, it is possible, for example, on certain remortgages, that it is the intention of the borrower and the lender that not all mortgages will be discharged and replaced. If so, when requesting the redemption statement, the solicitor should make it clear to the lender which mortgages the borrower wishes to redeem. The solicitor should inform the lender of any mortgages of which he or she is aware which are outstanding with the lender but which are not being redeemed. The solicitor should also quote all relevant account numbers if known as far as possible and ensure that the redemption statement received from the lender includes all the mortgages which are intended to be redeemed.

The lender should have its own internal cross-checking system but it is vital that the solicitor (who will, after all, be acting for the lender in most cases) is as clear as possible about the mortgage account(s) being redeemed. It is suggested that the solicitor should if possible, and time permits, send a copy of the redemption statement to the borrower to check agreement on the amount shown as due to the lender. Solicitors should be encouraged to ask for a statement at the earliest possible date.

Telegraphic transfers

Lenders could request that solicitors adopt procedures to assist in the identification of telegraphic transfers. When mortgages are being redeemed the telegraphic transfer which a lender receives is often difficult to identify and to match to a particular account.

The administrative difficulties which are caused by the inability to identify the money would be overcome if solicitors provided to the bank the information to be included in the telegraphic transfer, i.e. the borrower's mortgage account number and the firm's name and address.

Delay

Lenders are sometimes criticised for delay in providing a form of discharge after redemption of the mortgage. It is recognised that most lenders can and do return the receipted mortgage or Form DS1 promptly and that solicitors can apply for registration to protect priority. However, unless there is good reason for the delay, e.g. a solicitor sending the form to the wrong office of the lender, lenders will no doubt deal promptly with this important procedure.

It is suggested that lenders should aim to return the receipted mortgage or Form DS1 within seven days, and if there is likely to be a delay beyond that period they should notify the seller's solicitor. This would enable the buyer's solicitor to lodge an application with the Land Registry pending receipt of receipted mortgage or sealed Form DS1, although it is hoped that this would only be necessary in exceptional circumstances.

The CML view

Many of the difficulties described above would be reduced if as a matter of course solicitors gave lenders correct information about the borrower, the property, the account number(s), etc., and lenders, in turn, operated internal cross-checking systems and provided accurate and complete redemption statements showing clearly the last payment to be taken into account and, systems permitting, details of all the borrower's accounts relating to the property which represent mortgages to be discharged.

If the solicitor, relying on an incorrect redemption statement provided by the lender, sends insufficient money to redeem a mortgage, the lender should discharge the mortgage. (However, the lender might wish to make it clear that the release was not intended to discharge the borrower from his or her outstanding personal liability. This might prevent the borrower from successfully claiming estoppel against the lender.)

Such cases do not occur frequently; when they do, it is generally because of a clerical or administrative error on the part of the lender, such as by omitting one month's interest or an insurance premium, and the amount is usually small. Nevertheless, where it appears that there has been an error, the solicitor should immediately draw this to the lender's notice and should pursue his or her borrower client actively for any shortfall.

Very rare cases could arise where general guidance of this kind is inapplicable, for example, if there is such a major discrepancy in the redemption figure that the borrower, and, perhaps, his or her solicitor, could not reasonably have believed in the accuracy of the statement.

Conclusion

Where there is an incorrect redemption statement, which is clearly due to an error by the lender or lack of clarification, it is unreasonable that a solicitor should be put in breach of his or her undertaking. The undertaking given to the buyer's solicitor is a vital part of the conveyancing process. It is the CML's view, in such cases, that the lender should seal the discharge.

The Law Society and the Council for Licensed Conveyancers agree with the views expressed in these paragraphs. It is hoped that some of the practical measures referred to above will be implemented to avoid difficulties on redemption.

V.10. Insolvency (No. 2) Act 1994: counsel's opinion[1]

Section 339 of the 1986 Act gives the court power, on the application of the trustee in bankruptcy, to set aside an undervalue transaction, i.e. a gift or transfer for significantly low consideration, should the maker of the gift or transfer become bankrupt within five years after the date of the undervalue transaction. Section 342 provides protection, in certain conditions, against the use of section 339 powers. However, in its 1986 form, it was too restrictive. It left exposed to the risk of section 339 proceedings not only those who had benefited from undervalue transactions, but also those who had subsequently acquired, in good faith and for value, by way of genuine open market purchases, any property which had previously been the subject of an undervalue transaction. The 1994 Act overcame this problem by removing the 1986 Act's requirement that a buyer of – or, strictly, the acquirer of an interest in – property had to acquire not only in good faith and for value, but also without notice of the previous undervalue transaction, in order to get a title unchallengeable under section 339. With most types of property, a subsequent good faith buyer is unlikely to have notice of a previous undervalue transaction affecting it, and this generally applies to land as long as its title is registered. However, where title is unregistered, a buyer will inevitably have notice of a previous undervalue transaction. There is still a substantial amount of unregistered land in the UK and difficulties caused by section 339 are common. To the extent that the 1994 Act brought about protection for the good faith and for value acquirer, its effect was wholly beneficial. Unfortunately, as the price paid for removing the 'without notice' requirement, section 2(2) of the Act (which inserted new subsection (2A) into section 342 of the 1986 Act) made two exceptions to the improved protection. One of these is of little significance since it applies to an acquirer who is an 'associate of', or is 'connected with' (both terms are defined by the 1986 Act) either the undervalue transferor or transferee. However, the other exception, the 'dual notice' exception, gives rise to the main question which has been raised about the 1994 Act. These are counsel's views on this and other questions about the Act's effect.

Question 1

What is the effect of the 'dual notice' exception on the person who will for convenience be called the 'subsequent acquirer' (i.e. a person acquiring on the open market from the undervalue transferee, and also any further person who later acquires on the open market from that person)? The dual notice exception (section 342(2A) of the 1986 Act as amended by the 1994 Act) says that, where a subsequent acquirer of an interest in property has notice both of a previous undervalue transaction and of bankruptcy proceedings (i.e. a petition which leads to a bankruptcy order; or an actual bankruptcy order) against the undervalue transferor, the acquirer will be presumed to acquire other than in good faith, until he or she shows otherwise. The problem which this exception causes arises thus: A transfers a property at an undervalue to B; B sells on the open market to C who buys in good faith; C, some time later, wants to sell to D, another open market and good faith buyer. C knew of the undervalue transaction between A and B (though, with current land registration rules, this is perhaps unlikely to happen very often) but, at the time when he or she bought, there were no bankruptcy proceedings against A, so C acquired an unquestionably good title. However, by the time C sells to D, bankruptcy proceedings have begun against A, and D knows of the previous undervalue transaction (though this is even more unlikely under the current land registration regime). What is D's position as to possible section 339 proceedings? Counsel's view is that D is, in practice, at no risk if he acquires in these circumstances (provided that, in reality, he acts in good faith). Counsel says that this is an issue which must be looked at in context.

---

1. In 1995 the Law Society obtained the opinion of leading counsel, Gabriel Moss Q.C. These paragraphs set out his views.

The underlying purpose of the legislation is to protect the *bona fide* buyer in good faith and for value, i.e. the buyer in the ordinary course of buying and selling property, while preventing creditors being cheated. Counsel is also confident that no court would deprive D of an interest bought in good faith and for value, for the benefit of the creditors of A, since it would be outrageously unfair to do so. Counsel is also confident that the courts would be concerned to interpret the legislation so as to achieve a fair result. He refers to the observation of Sir Donald Nicholls V-C in *Paramount Airways Ltd (No.2)* [1992] 3 All ER 1 (CA) in support of the view that 'the court will ensure that it does not seek to exercise oppressively or unfairly the very wide jurisdiction conferred by the sections' (in that case, sections 238 to 241). In fact, counsel thinks it highly unlikely that, in practice, any trustee in bankruptcy would even consider trying to challenge D since it would be a waste of the assets of the bankrupt's estate to do so. However, should this unlikely situation occur, counsel's view is that there are three bases on which an application should be resisted.

(i) Under the 'shelter' rule: this rule, which is not widely known, is illustrated in *Wilkes* v. *Spooner* [1911] 2 KB 473 (CA). It says, broadly, that a person who acquires property in good faith and for value can pass on as good a title as he or she has to another person who also acquires in good faith. In *Wilkes* v. *Spooner*, a person acquired land which was subject to various covenants. However, as he had acquired without notice of them, but in good faith and for value, he was not bound by them. By the time he came to sell, the covenants had come to light, but he claimed that, because of the 'shelter' principle, he could sell free of them to another good faith buyer. The Court of Appeal agreed. In counsel's view, this principle applies equally to property in the undervalue transaction context – and, indeed, some of the drafting of section 342 may, he thinks, be a somewhat clumsy attempt to reflect the 'shelter' rule.

(ii) On the grounds that D's title is 'derived' from that of C section 342(2)(*a*) of the 1986 Act (as amended) says that no order made under section 339 shall prejudice an interest acquired in good faith and for value, nor any interest 'derived' from that interest. What 'derived' means in this context is unclear, but counsel thinks that its use may have been intended to replicate the 'shelter' rule. If this is the effect of the term, D's interest would be protected by reason of being 'derived' from that of C. It is possible, however, that interests such as those of subsequent buyers were not intended to be treated as 'derived' interests and that the term was meant to cover only interests such as those acquired by inheritance.

(iii) On the grounds, simply, that he or she had acquired in good faith and for value. In a normal open market transaction, there would be no question that the buyer had acquired his or her interest in this way. However, new subsection (2A) of section 342 (inserted by the 1994 Act) creates an artificial presumption against good faith where the dual notice exception applies, even in relation to such a transaction. Counsel's view, however, is that a court would ask no more of D, in order to displace this presumption, than to show that his purchase was at arm's length and for value, i.e. that it was a normal, open market purchase. Thus, in the highly unlikely event of a challenge, the presumption against good faith would be easily rebutted. Only where there was actual evidence calling D's good faith into question could there be any prospect of a serious challenge by a trustee. If D had bought on the open market, this would be a highly unusual situation – indeed, it is difficult to imagine its arising.

Question 2

What does 'notice' mean in this context (i.e. as to notice of a previous undervalue transaction but, in particular, notice of bankruptcy proceedings)? Counsel's view is that actual notice is notice in this context, both as to bankruptcy proceedings and previous undervalue transactions. As to statutory notice of bankruptcy proceedings, an acquirer of an interest in unregistered land will have notice of any information recorded either in the register of pending actions or in the register of writs and orders – sections 5 and 6 Land Charges Act 1972. Although there is some question (because of the wording of sections 5 and 6, and also of section 198 Law of Property Act 1925) as to whether this notice would be effective against an acquirer, because it would not be recorded against the name of a bankrupt with any present connection with the property concerned, the prudent view is to assume that it would do so. As to registered land, the acquirer will have notice only of what appears on the land register. Section 59 Land Registration Act 1955 says that a writ, order, etc. has effect against registered land only if lodged as provided by that Act, so that it is shown on the registered title; and section 14 Land Charges Act 1972 excludes that Act's effect as to any matter relating to registered land. Nevertheless, counsel suggests that, where a prospective buyer of registered land has notice of an undervalue transaction – but only then – it would be prudent to carry out a bankruptcy search against the undervalue transferor, if known, as failure to do so might cause difficulties in rebutting the presumption against good faith (section 342(2A)) should the issue arise.

Question 3

What is the effect of the 1994 Act on mortgagees? In counsel's view, exactly the same as on the acquirer of any other kind of interest. A mortgagee acquires an interest in property. In a normal mortgage of domestic property to a bank or building society, the mortgagee clearly acquires its interest in good faith and gives value. The mortgagee's interest is thus protected by section 342(2)(*a*) as amended. This applies regardless of whether the mortgagor is B, the undervalue transferee; or C, the first subsequent good faith and for value buyer; or D, the next subsequent good faith and for value buyer. Similarly, a mortgagee exercising its power of sale would be able to pass good title to a subsequent acquirer, for the same reasons that a subsequent freehold buyer (C or D) can do so. The Law Society has received queries about the effect of section 339 and the 1994 Act where property which is the subject of an undervalue transaction is transferred subject to an existing mortgage. In this situation, no section 339 issue arises at all, as far as the mortgaged interest is concerned, because the mortgage agreement was entered into before the undervalue transaction took place. Though the trustee in bankruptcy could apply under section 339 for the return of the property itself – in practice, the equity which would have been the subject of an undervalue transaction – the mortgagee's interest would remain intact (as it would have had the mortgage been created after the undervalue transaction, in the event of section 339 proceedings).

Question 4

Where A transfers property at an undervalue to A (self) and B jointly or in common; or A and B transfer jointly either to A or B alone, does the section 342(2)(*a*) protection operate in relation to C, the subsequent acquirer, or is it disapplied by the exclusion contained in section 342(2)(*a*) of an interest acquired from 'that individual', i.e. the undervalue transferor. Counsel's view is that C is not excluded from the protection given by section 342(2)(*a*) because of having acquired from 'that individual'. Where A, as sole owner, transfers to himself and B jointly, what happens is that A transfers the whole of the legal estate in the property, but only that part of his beneficial interest which passes to B. In this context, what Insolvency Act 1986 is concerned with is the beneficial, not the legal, interest in the property which is the subject of an undervalue transaction. Thus, when A and B then sell to C (a good faith and for value buyer), what C acquires is A's beneficial interest which has not been the subject of an undervalue transaction, and B's beneficial interest which has been but which C obviously does not acquire from 'that individual'). Thus, the interest acquired by C comes within the section 342(2)(*a*) protection to the extent that it is acquired from B, and is outside section 339 altogether to the extent that it is acquired from A. Similarly, when A and B transfer jointly owned property to B, and B then sells to C, the same principle applies. That is, since the only transfer to which section 339 and section 342(2)(*a*) are material is that of A's beneficial interest to B and, as C is acquiring from B and not A, he or she is not affected by the 'other than that individual' exclusion.

V.11. Mortgage fraud – variation in purchase price[1]

This guidance deals with the solicitor's duty in conduct when acting for lender and borrower when there is some variation in the purchase price.

Professional Ethics is frequently asked to advise on a solicitor's duty to the lender in conduct when there is some variation in the purchase price of a property of which the lender may be unaware. The Society has therefore prepared the following guidance (which is supported by the Council of Mortgage Lenders) on the professional conduct issues involved.

Solicitors acting contemporaneously for a buyer and a lender should consider their position very carefully if there is any change in the purchase price, or if the solicitors become aware of any other information which they would reasonably expect the lender to consider important in deciding whether, or on what terms, it would make the mortgage advance available. In such circumstances the solicitor's duty to act in the best interests of the lender would require him or her to pass on such information to the lender.

Solicitors have a duty of confidentiality to clients, but this does not affect their duty to act in the best interests of each client. Therefore any such information concerning variations to the purchase price should be forwarded to the lender with the consent of the buyer. If the buyer will not agree to the information being given to the lender, then there will be a conflict between the solicitor's duty of confidentiality to the buyer and the duty to act in the best interests of the lender. Solicitors must therefore cease acting for the lender and must consider carefully whether they are able to continue acting for the buyer, bearing in mind **15.02** note 1, p.314 in the Guide and also **12.02** note 1 referred to below.

Solicitors must not withhold information relevant to a transaction from any client. Where the client is a lender, this includes not only straightforward price reductions but may also include other allowances (e.g. for repairs, payment of costs, the inclusion of chattels in the price and incentives of the kind offered by builders such as free holidays and part-subsidisation of mortgage payments) which amount to a price reduction and which would affect the lender's decision to make the advance. Solicitors should not attempt to arbitrate on whether the price change is material but should notify the lender. It is recommended that solicitors advise their clients as soon as practicable that it would be regarded as fraud to misrepresent the purchase price and that a solicitor is under a duty to inform the lender of the true price being paid for a property.

Solicitors who are party to an attempt to deceive a lender may be exposing both the buyer and themselves to criminal prosecution and/or civil action and will be liable to be disciplined for having breached the principles of professional conduct (see **12.02** note 1, p.245 in the Guide). If a solicitor is aware that his or her client is attempting to perpetrate fraud in any form he or she must immediately cease acting for that client.

---

1. 12th December 1990, updated February 1999. This text appears in *The Guide to the Professional Conduct of Solicitors 1999* as Annex 25F.

V.12. Mortgages and life policies[1]

Solicitors should refer a client who is likely to need an endowment policy, or similar life insurance with an investment element, to an independent intermediary authorised to give investment advice.

1. Where clients may need life insurance, solicitors should either act as independent intermediaries themselves, or introduce the client to another independent intermediary. The duty to give independent advice is not normally discharged by referring a client to an appointed representative, i.e. a tied agent. See also section 4 of the Solicitors' Introduction and Referral Code 1990 (Annex 11B at p.243).

2. Although a mortgage of land is not an investment under the Financial Services Act 1986, solicitors who advise on or make arrangements in respect of mortgages where an endowment policy or pension policy is to be used as additional security may be caught by the Act. A mere referral to an independent intermediary is not caught by the Act, but solicitors should assess the client's needs and consider factors such as speed and reliability of administration, availability, interest rates and general terms. Referral to a mortgage provider who is a tied agent may result in the client not receiving independent investment advice. If the client's interests dictate a referral to a tied agent, the client should be informed that the agent can offer investment products from a single company only.

3. Solicitors should be aware of the Financial Services Act status of persons to whom clients are referred, as many banks, building societies, estate agents and insurance agents are appointed representatives of particular insurance companies and are unable to offer independent advice.

4. A client who is proposing to take out a company life policy or other financial product without independent advice may be referred to a solicitor by the life office, bank, building society or other tied agent. It is not a solicitor's duty to force clients to take independent advice, if they do not wish to do so. However, solicitors should be prepared to make enquiries of a client if the proposed policy seems unsuitable and, if appropriate, provide independent advice, or refer the client to an independent intermediary. The solicitor will need to consider and discuss with the client whether obtaining independent advice will involve additional cost or delay or prejudice the proposed purchase. See also section 2(6) of the Solicitors' Introduction and Referral Code 1990 (Annex 11B at p.239).

5. Similar considerations arise where the referral is by an independent financial adviser who has persuaded the client to enter into an obviously inappropriate scheme. Whilst a solicitor is not under a duty to re-advise, or to offer investment business advice as part of a conveyancing retainer, there may be a general duty in relation to the conveyancing retainer to give advice on the legal implications. See also **25.10** note 5, p.477.

6. All home income or equity release schemes, whereby homes are mortgaged to raise a capital sum for investment, carry an element of risk. Two home income plans sold to the elderly a few years ago have given rise to a number of claims against advisers, including solicitors. Reference may be made to *Using Your Home as Capital* by Cecil Hinton, published by Age Concern, for an account of these schemes – the 'investment bond income scheme' and the 'roll-up loan scheme'. So far as

---

1. The following text is taken from Chapter 25, 25.09 of *The Guide to the Professional Conduct of Solicitors 1996*, published by the Law Society. Cross-references to paragraphs in the Guide include page references from the Guide.

they can, solicitors should dissuade clients from entering into any scheme of this kind without expert and independent advice.

7. Rule 12 of the Solicitors' Practice Rules 1990 (see **27.21**, p.533) provides that solicitors shall not, in connection with investment business, be appointed representatives or operate any separate business which is an appointed representative, unless it is an appointed representative of an independent financial adviser. Solicitors' agency arrangements with building societies or other financial institutions which are tied agents, and the business transacted at the solicitor's agency office, must be confined to non-investment business. A solicitor operating a building society agency, etc., if asked about mortgages, should consider whether the customer needs independent advice.

8. The Society has a group licence covering credit brokerage by solicitors, limited to activities arising in the course of practice. Solicitors who arrange mortgages will be carrying on credit brokerage within the meaning of the Consumer Credit Act 1974.

9. Solicitors who advertise that they are able to arrange mortgages must comply with the Consumer Credit (Advertisements) Regulations 1989 (S.I. 1989 no. 1125). Such an advertisement, provided it contains no details of amounts due in repayment of the mortgage, will be an intermediate credit advertisement for the purpose of the regulations which provide that the following information must be contained in the advertisement:

   (a) the name of the solicitors and a postal address or telephone number;

   (b) a statement in the following form:

   > 'Your home is at risk if you do not keep up repayments on a mortgage or other loan secured on it.'

   This statement must be in capital letters and afforded no less prominence than the statement relating to the ability to arrange mortgages.

   (c) the amount of any arrangement fee payable or a statement of its methods of calculation;

   (d) a statement that individuals may obtain on request a quotation in writing about the terms on which the solicitors are prepared to do business, e.g. 'written details on request'.

10. Solicitors who act as mortgage intermediaries, i.e. who advise clients on which mortgage to apply for after reviewing a range of mortgage products, need to register with the Mortgage Code Register of Intermediaries, and to comply with the Mortgage Code. Note that although paragraph 11(2) of the code merely requires intermediaries to give details of mortgage arrangement fees over £250, rule 10 of the Solicitors' Practice Rules 1990 (see **14.13**, p.283) requires solicitors to account to clients for commission received of more than £20 unless the client has agreed otherwise. For the purpose of completing the registration form, firms may obtain their FSA number from Regulation and Information Services (see p.xv for contact details). The Law Society's group consumer credit licence number is G900001 and covers categories A, C, D and E. Firms wishing to register should contact the Mortgage Code Register of Intermediaries (see p.xv for contact details).

V.13. Practice Rule 6(3) and lenders' certificates of title[1]

It has come to the Law Society's attention that a number of lenders are asking solicitors to sign certificates of title that would put solicitors in breach of practice rule 6(3). This rule applies both where a solicitor is acting for the lender – whether or not a member of the Council of Mortgage Lenders (CML) – and borrower, and also where the solicitor is acting solely for the borrower but carries out work (such as providing a certificate of title) for the lender.

The Society is approaching individual lenders directly and will be referring the matter to the CML where appropriate. Solicitors are reminded that where they are able to act for the lender and the borrower in a standard mortgage, the lender's instructions must not extend beyond the limitations contained in paragraphs 3(c) and 3(e) of the rules and that these apply to all types of transaction.

In any transactions which are exclusively residential, solicitors must use the approved certificate of title set out in the appendix to rule 6(3). The solicitor is reminded that the lender should certify that its mortgage instructions comply with the rule (see note (ii) to the rule).

If the lender's mortgage instructions are not certified the solicitor in a residential transaction should notify the lender on receipt of the instructions that the approved certificate of title will be used and that the solicitor's duties to the lender are limited to matters in the certificate.

In other types of transaction the solicitor should notify the lender that the solicitor cannot act on any instructions which extend beyond the limitations contained in the rule. Solicitors are reminded that a suggested form of letter has been published along with other guidance (see [1999] *Gazette*, 29 September, 36). It is preferable that the lender positively confirms that it accepts the position.

Solicitors are also reminded that in circumstances where the lender's mortgage instructions are certified as complying with the rule, but a solicitor maintains that one or more of the instructions extend beyond the limitations of that rule, an offending instruction should never be accepted. The position should be clarified with the lender. Again, a suggested form of letter has been published in the *Gazette*.

The guidance and suggested forms of letters can be found on the Society Web site (*www.lawsociety.org.uk*) under the conveyancing section.

For additional information about the operation of the rule, contact the Society's professional ethics department on 0870 606 2577. Those who are aware of lenders that are requesting solicitors to sign certificates that would put them in breach of rule 6(3) should write to: Policy Advisers, Conveyancing & Land Law Committee, 113 Chancery Lane, London WC2A 1PL or DX 56 Lon/Chancery Lane giving details and enclosing copies of the offending title certificate.

---

1. © The Law Society 2002. This article appeared in the Law Society's *Gazette* on 22 August 2002.

V.14. Practice Rule 6(3) solicitor acting for lender and borrower[1]

Practice rule 6(3) deals with a solicitor acting for both lender and borrower. In addition to its existing requirements it will, with effect from 1 October 1999, define the scope of a solicitor's retainer with a lender whenever the solicitor acts for the borrower as well.

Rule 6(3) was first amended on 29 September 1998 and again on 29 April 1999. The earlier version will never become effective. The final version was printed in the *Gazette* on 6 May 1999

Questions and answers

Q.1 Why is it necessary to change the rule by defining the scope of a solicitor's retainer with a lender when the solicitor is also acting for the borrower?

A.1 Solicitors have traditionally acted for both lender and borrower in matters of title where the lender's and borrower's interests coincide. Undertaking more tasks for the lender client has led to an increased risk of conflict between the interests of lender and borrower. In addition, the ambit of the solicitor's duties to lender clients has been widening to include matters beyond the normal role of the conveyancing solicitor.

The Law Society has addressed this problem by producing a new version of practice rule 6(3) which sets out the type of mortgage instructions which may be given when the solicitor is also acting for the borrower. A number of major lenders, under the auspices of the Council of Mortgage Lenders, have also produced standard mortgage instructions ('the CML lenders' handbook') to comply with the new rule 6(3).

Q.2 What is the commencement date?

A.2 The new version of the rule applies to transactions where mortgage instructions are first issued on or after 1 October 1999.

Q.3 When does the rule apply?

A.3 The rule applies when the same solicitor or firm of solicitors (including an associated practice) acts for both borrower and lender. Although the rule does not apply if the parties are separately represented, note paragraph (3)(f). This is an anti-avoidance provision which prohibits a borrower's solicitor from giving assurances or undertakings which go beyond the matters set out in the rule.

Q.4 What about the current restrictions?

A.4 These remain unchanged:

- acting for both lender and borrower is never allowed if there is a conflict of interest – paragraph (3)(a)(i);

1. © The Law Society 1999. This article appeared in the Law Society's *Gazette* on 29 September 1999. The article was produced by Ken Byass and Ed Nally (council members) in conjunction with Law Society staff.

- acting for both lender and borrower is never allowed on the grant of a private mortgage of land at arm's length – paragraph (3)(a)(ii) and note (i);

- a solicitor must disclose to an institutional lender certain relationships (i.e., solicitor is a borrower or related to a borrower) – paragraph (3)(b)(i) and notes (v)–(vii); and

- a solicitor must notify an institutional lender if the solicitor will be acting for seller, buyer and lender – paragraph (3)(b)(ii).

Q.5 Assuming there is no conflict of interest, is it still possible to act for both the lender and the borrower in an institutional mortgage?

A.5 Yes, but the new rule 6(3) imposes certain safeguards to reduce the risk of a conflict of interest arising:

- the lender's instructions must not extend beyond the limitations contained in paragraphs (3)(c) and (3)(e) – this applies to all types of transaction (residential, commercial or mixed); and

- in addition, the approved certificate of title set out in the appendix to rule 6(3) must be used for exclusively residential transactions – paragraph (3)(d) and note (iii).

Q.6 How should a solicitor act if a conflict of interest nevertheless arises?

A.6 A solicitor always has a duty to act with honesty and integrity and with regard to the best interests of the client (both lender and borrower). If a conflict of interests arises between the lender and the borrower (e.g., the solicitor becomes aware that the borrower intends to let the property without the lender's knowledge or consent), the solicitor will have to stop acting for the lender (and possibly also for the borrower) unless the borrower is prepared to allow disclosure. If the borrower does not consent to disclosure, the solicitor cannot breach his or her duty of confidentiality but will have to tell the lender that he or she can no longer act for professional reasons (if the CML lenders' handbook is being used, the solicitor must tell the lender that the retainer has been terminated for conflict reasons).

Q.7 How should a solicitor ensure that the mortgage instructions comply with the rule?

A.7 The lender should certify that its mortgage instructions comply with the rule and, if this certification has been given, the solicitor need take no further action – note (ii). If the lender gives such a certificate, you may rely upon it whether or not the instructions do in fact comply with the rule. If a lender has given a certificate relating to its standard instructions, you may assume that the certificate applies also to the specific instructions relating to the individual transaction with which you are dealing. You do not need to ask the lender to confirm this. It is not the Law Society's intention to give confirmations in respect of instructions. The rule provides that it is for the lender concerned to satisfy itself that its instructions comply and give a certificate accordingly. The many and varied permutations of lending instructions, and the frequency of change of those instructions, make individual confirmations by the Law Society impracticable.

Q.8 What is the CML lenders' handbook?

A.8 The CML lenders' handbook, which contains standard mortgage instructions, was discussed by the Law Society and the Council of Mortgage Lenders representing the interests of major institutional lenders. The Law Society believes that the CML lenders' handbook should be adopted as a standard by the residential lending industry. The CML lenders' handbook is certified as complying with the rule.

Q.9 What if the lender's mortgage instructions are not certified?

A.9 The following steps should be taken:

- in a residential transaction, the solicitor must notify the lender on receipt of instructions that the approved certificate of title will be used, and that the solicitor's duties to the lender are limited to the matters contained in the approved certificate – paragraph (3)(d) and note (ii); and

- for other types of transaction, the solicitor should notify the lender that the solicitor cannot act on any instructions which extend beyond the matters contained in the rule – note (ii).

So, if you are instructed by the lender and the borrower, and if the lender has not given the certificate that its instructions comply with the rule, you must write to the lender on receipt of instructions. [A suggested form of draft letter was included with this guidance when published in the Law Society's Gazette. It has been extracted for reproduction in this Handbook to form *Appendix VII.6.*]

If the lender positively confirms that it accepts the position (or if, in the absence of a response, the lender can be taken to have tacitly accepted the position), then your instructions are limited to the matters described in the rule and, in the case of a residential property, you must give a certificate of title in the form prescribed by the rule in full. You must not use the lender's own report on title in these circumstances.

A positive confirmation by the lender as to what it does or does not accept is far preferable and safer for the solicitor than a tacit acceptance. For this reason, you may well judge it best not to proceed to a binding exchange of contracts unless you have the confirmation from the lender that you require.

If the lender at any time refuses to accept the limitation of its instructions, you must cease to act.

Q.10 What if the lender's mortgage instructions are certified as complying with the rule but the solicitor believes some instructions extend beyond the limitations of the rule?

A.10 You should acknowledge receipt of instructions and confirm that you are happy to act for the lender. However, you may feel it prudent as a matter of clarity only to:

- point out that the lender has certified that the instructions are subject to the limitations of practice rule 6(3)(c) and (e);

- point out that some instructions conflict with paragraph (3)(c) and accordingly are not comprised in the instructions given and will not be referred to in the certificate of title; and

- list the offending instructions.

[A suggested form of draft letter was included with this guidance when published in the Law Society's Gazette. It has been extracted for reproduction in this Handbook to form *Appendix VII.7.*]

You must never accept an offending instruction and never attempt to carry it out. If the lender insists on you doing so, you will be unable to act for the lender.

Q.11 What if a solicitor is acting for the borrower only but the lender's solicitor requires the borrower's solicitor to give undertakings which relate to matters outside those listed in paragraph (3)(c)?

A.11 You must decline to accept or act upon any such requirements – paragraph (3)(f).

Q.12 What can a solicitor be asked to do under rule 6?

A.12 You should note that the rule states what a lender can ask a solicitor to do. Accordingly, it should be viewed as a series of possible (but not compulsory) areas of work. If you are in doubt, read through the list of requirements which lenders are permitted to make as set out in the rule – paragraph (3)(c). If what you are being asked to do does not obviously fall within one of those permitted requirements, then the lender is asking you to go beyond the rule. It is in these circumstances that you need to send a letter along the lines of the draft form marked 'B' referred to in question and answer 10 above.

Q.13 What is the lender banned from asking?

A.13 It is important to note that the rule states what a lender is permitted to require of a solicitor. It is not possible to give a comprehensive list of what a lender may not require. However, the following examples indicate that the lender has gone beyond what is permitted by the rule:

(i)   A requirement for a certificate of title in any form other than that permitted by the rule (but remember that the rule permits the use of an abbreviated certificate – note (iii)).

(ii)   A requirement that the solicitor inspect the property at any stage (for instance, to confirm that works have been carried out or that the seller has vacated), or a requirement which cannot be satisfied without an inspection by or on behalf of the solicitor.

(iii) A requirement that the solicitor express an opinion outside the solicitor's expertise (for instance, that a property has been built in accordance with applicable building regulations or defined plans and specifications).

(iv)   A requirement under which the solicitor guarantees that something will be done in the future (for instance, that the property will be occupied within one month of completion).

(v)   A condition requiring the discharge of unspecified mortgages (for instance, to the effect that all other mortgages owed by the borrower must be discharged on completion or that all credit cards of the borrower must be paid in full on completion). A condition requiring the discharge of specified mortgages is, however, in order.

(vi)   A requirement that the solicitor carry out any function more appropriate to a surveyor or valuer (for instance, to confirm that the property is free from contamination).

Q.14 What happens if a solicitor breaches the rule?

A.14 As with other practice rules, a breach of rule 6(3) will be a disciplinary offence. You should never, therefore, accept instructions from a lender which go beyond the limitations set out in the rule. In addition, if the property mortgaged is to be used by the borrower as his or her residence, you may only give a certificate of title in the form set out in the appendix to the rule. It is in order (if the lender so requires) to use an abbreviated certificate which incorporates by reference the full certificate set out in the appendix to the rule – note (iii).

Q.15 The rule is drafted in the form of a rule with notes. What is the status of the notes?

A.15 The notes have equal force with the rules – see rule 6(1) (General) which states that: 'The rule must be read in the light of the notes'.

Q.16 The approved certificate of title is required for any transaction where the property is to be used as a private residence only. Does this include 'buy to let mortgages' on properties which are not intended for owner-occupation?

A.16 No. Note (iv) to the rule states that the approved certificate is only required if the property is to be occupied by the owner. 'Buy to let mortgages' are regarded as 'commercial'. There is nothing, however, to prevent a lender from using the approved certificate of title for commercial and mixed transactions if it so wishes.

Q.17 What about borrowers who work from home or run small businesses from home?

A.17 These remain residential transactions and both the rule and the approved certificate of title apply. This contrasts with the purchase of a shop with living accommodation attached or indeed any other form of mixed commercial/residential user, which is subject to the rule but not the approved certificate of title.

Q.18 Can the lender incorporate the approved certificate of title by reference in their own style of certificate on title?

A.18 Yes, provided the certificate follows the requirements set out in note (iii) to the rule.

Q.19 What if the lender does not require the solicitor to carry out everything contained in the approved certificate of title (e.g. the lender has its own arrangements for stamping and registration)?

A.19 The rule sets the parameters of the instructions a lender may give to a solicitor who is acting for both the lender and borrower. The lender is, therefore, free to select from the type of instructions listed in the rule and could shade out parts of the certificate not required.

Alternatively, a lender might simply instruct you not to carry out something you would normally be expected to do, in which case you will need to amend the certificate of title:

- if the full form certificate of title is being used, delete the paragraphs which do not apply and point this out to the lender in a covering letter;

- if an abbreviated form of certificate of title is being used (see note (iii) of the rule), add to the main wording after 'as if the same were set out in full' words along the lines of 'except for paragraph(s) …', and point this out to the lender in a covering letter.

The certificate of title should not be altered other than to delete provisions not required by the lender.

Q.20 In the case of a borrower who is not an individual (for example, a company, partnership, club, society, pension trust, charity, friendly society), may the lender's instructions include advice on whether the borrower has the power to borrow and purchase property?

A.20 Yes. Confirming that the borrower has the necessary powers, ascertaining which individuals can exercise those powers on behalf of the borrower, and advising on procedures which must be followed (for example, resolutions approving the transaction, shareholder approval and procedures required under the Companies Acts) are matters of title. They relate to the borrower's powers and satisfy conditions precedent to vesting a legal estate in the lender. They are perfectly proper requirements because, if they are not satisfied, the mortgage will be invalid and the lender's instructions to procure execution of a valid mortgage will not have been complied with. They are covered partly by paragraph (3)(c)(vii) and partly by paragraph (3)(c)(xiii).

Q.21 In the case of a shared ownership property, may the lender issue instructions relating to a mortgage protection clause/mortgage indemnity clause?

A.21 Yes. The rule allows for confirmation of the lease terms required by the lender and for obtaining prior approval of the mortgage – paragraph (3)(c)(ix).

Q.22 What type of search should be carried out under paragraph (3)(c)(ii)?

A.22 It is a matter of judgement as to which searches a solicitor thinks it appropriate to undertake to protect the interests of both the lender and the borrower. A lender is, however, free to stipulate the searches it requires, or to say that it is prepared to rely on search insurance (although that might not be acceptable to the borrower client).

Q.23 Can the solicitor enquire who is living at the property and who will be living there after completion?

A.23 Under paragraph (3)(c)(xiv) the lender may instruct the solicitor to ask the borrower for confirmation that the information about occupants given in the mortgage instructions or offer is correct. Instructions may also cover obtaining the consent of any existing or prospective occupier of whom the solicitor is aware, in addition to those listed in the instructions.

Q.24 Does paragraph (3)(c)(xiii) cover completion of relevant information in the mortgage deed/form of guarantee?

A.24 Yes. In order to procure execution of the mortgage deed/form of guarantee, it must be completed fully and accurately.

Q.25 Can the lender ask the solicitor under paragraph (3)(c)(xvi) to ensure that the non-borrower required to sign the mortgage deed or other document receives independent legal advice?

A.25 No. A solicitor can advise a person to take independent legal advice but cannot force him or her to do so, or oversee the advice given by another solicitor. The instructions may, however, require the solicitor to arrange for the signatory to see an independent conveyancer.

Q.26 What is meant by 'administrative arrangements' in paragraph (3)(c)(xx)?

A.26 This covers anything necessary in relation to the collateral security; e.g., asking the life company to issue the policy; arranging the legal assignment of the policy (including any prior reassignment); registering notice of the lender's interest; notifying the NHBC of the need for the solicitor to receive the NHBC documentation.

Q.27 Does paragraph (3)(c)(xxii) envisage the solicitor making a recommendation as to the course of action to be taken?

A.27 Yes. It also covers complying with the lender's instructions on the action to be taken following the advice.

Q.28 Some lenders may be prepared to accept a possessory title but paragraph (2)(i) of the approved certificate of title seems to require absolute title. Is that correct?

A.28 Paragraph (2) of the approved certificate of title must always be read in the light of the opening words: 'Except as otherwise disclosed to you in writing'. It is always open to the lender to accept a lesser title on disclosure.

Q.29 I am not clear about the disclosure requirements in the rule as opposed to the provisions in the approved certificate of title and CML lenders' handbook. Is there an inconsistency?

A.29 There is, unfortunately, an inconsistency between the existing disclosure requirements of paragraph (3)(b)(i) of the rule and paragraph (2)(ix) of the approved certificate of title. The combined effect means that you should at the outset of a transaction ascertain the following:

- is any principal in the practice or an associated practice a borrower?

- is any solicitor conducting or supervising the transaction a borrower?

- is any solicitor working in the practice which undertakes the transaction a borrower?
- is a member of the immediate family (spouse, child, parent, brother or sister) of any of the above categories a borrower?

If the answer is 'yes' to any of these questions, the lender should be informed in writing. This is so that the lender is aware of potential conflicts of interest and can decide whether it wants to instruct another firm to act on its behalf.

In practice, for those lenders who use it, the CML lenders' handbook will decide whether or not the firm may act and, if so, who within the firm will be permitted to do the work. The rule recognises at paragraph (3)(c)(xxiii) that a lender's instructions may require a wider disclosure, and indeed the CML lenders' handbook contains a much wider definition of immediate family.

Paragraph 1.13 of the handbook will not allow a sole practitioner to act if he or she or a member of his or her immediate family is a borrower. Immediate family is defined as a spouse, co-habitee, parent, sibling, child, step-parent, step-child, grandparent, grandchild, parent-in-law or child-in-law.

Paragraph 1.14 of the handbook will not allow a firm to act if the partner or fee-earner dealing with the transaction or a member of his or her immediate family (as defined) is a borrower, unless the lender concerned allows such firms to act (consult part 2 of the handbook) and a different partner or fee-earner of no less standing within the firm acts for the lender.

Conclusion

The introduction of the new version of rule 6(3) is designed to introduce certainty and reasonableness into the relationship between lenders and solicitors. The Law Society hopes and expects that solicitors and lenders will co-operate with one another in an effective and common sense way in the best interests of their clients.

For queries on Practice Rule 6(3) contact the Professional Ethics division; Tel: 0870 606 2577 or Practice Advice; Tel: 0870 606 2522.

V.15   Practice Rule 6(3) solicitor acting for lender and borrower in commercial transactions[1]

The new version of rule 6(3) of the Solicitors' Practice Rules 1990 came into effect on 1 October 1999. The rule has always applied to both residential and commercial conveyancing transactions. It has always required separate representation in a private mortgage at arm's length (where the terms have been individually negotiated) and, subject to the overriding principle that a solicitor can never act for two parties when there is a conflict of interest, allowed joint representation in an institutional mortgage (a mortgage on standard terms).

Additionally, since 1 October 1999, the rule allows joint representation only if the lender's mortgage instructions do not extend beyond the matters set out in paragraph 6(3)(c). An anti-avoidance provision (paragraph (f)) applies the same restrictions to any requirements imposed on the borrower's solicitor when the parties are separately represented in an institutional mortgage.

Effect of anti-avoidance provision

As indicated in previously published notes ([2000] Gazette, 30 March 47 and 15 December 47), the anti-avoidance provision created an anomaly in that:

- Commercial conveyancers acting just for the borrower in a private mortgage continued to be free to give whatever form of certificate of title was considered appropriate, including the 'industry standard' City of London Law Society's land law sub-committee certificate (CLLS certificate) – so long as no retainer was thereby created between solicitor and lender, as the rule requires separate representation;

- Commercial conveyancers acting just for the borrower in an institutional mortgage had to ensure that any certificate they gave did not extend beyond the limitations set out in the rule.

This anomaly caused problems for commercial conveyancers, because it was not clear whether or not the CLLS certificate went beyond the rule. The CLLS certificate is designed for use in commercial transactions where the parties are separately represented but the borrower's solicitor provides a certificate of title to the lender. The certificate is of general application and is used across the country.

'Private' and 'institutional' mortgages

A further problem was that the expressions 'private mortgage' and 'institutional mortgage' as used in the rule caused confusion. The expression 'private mortgage', when used colloquially, has a narrower meaning than that used in the rule.

Therefore, the Law Society Council has made an amendment rule – new paragraph (f)(ii) and notes (i) and (viii) – which came into effect on 27 April 2001. The expression 'private mortgage' has been replaced by 'individual mortgage'. The expression 'institutional mortgage' has been replaced by

1. © The Law Society 2001. This guidance appeared in the Law Society's *Gazette* on 7 June 2001.

'standard mortgage'. A standard mortgage is specifically defined in a revised note (i). Any mortgage not falling within this definition is an individual mortgage.

In addition, where a solicitor is acting only for the borrower but gives a certificate of title to the lender, the rule amends paragraph (f) and inserts a new note (viii) to allow, in cases where the property is not to be used solely as the borrower's private residence, the use of any form of certificate of title recognised from time to time by the Law Society Council. Paragraphs (a)(iii) and (d) and note (iv) have also been amended for consistency of expression. Note (iv) has been expanded to clarify the distinction between 'residential' and 'commercial'.

On 2 May 2001, the council recognised the CLLS certificate and the short form report on title also issued by the City of London Law Society's land law sub-committee for voluntary use in this type of transaction. The 4th edition of the CLLS certificate is printed in the revised volume 38 of Butterworth's Encyclopedia of Forms and Precedents. Both the CLLS certificate and CLLS report are available on the City of London Law Society's Web site at: www.citysolicitors.org.uk. There is a link to this site from the Law Society's Web site at: www.lawsociety.org.uk – see 'commercial' under 'specialisms'.

Additions or amendments which arise from the individual transaction may be made to the text of any recognised certificate but, to the extent to which they create an increased or additional obligation, they must not extend beyond the limitations contained in paragraph (c).

The result of the change to paragraph (f) is that solicitors acting only for the borrower in a standard mortgage where the property is not to be used solely as the borrower's private residence can use either a recognised form of certificate or any other form of certificate which complies with paragraph (c). In cases of separate representation where the property is to be used solely as the borrower's private residence, a recognised certificate may not be used and any certificate given must comply with paragraph (c).

Solicitors acting for both lender and borrower in a standard mortgage are unaffected by this change. In cases where the property is to be used solely as the borrower's private residence, the approved certificate set out in the appendix to the rule must continue to be used. In cases where the property is not to be used solely as the borrower's private residence, any certificate given must comply with paragraph (c).

As before, solicitors acting for the borrower in an individual mortgage at arm's length may continue to give certificates of title in whatever form they wish, provided no retainer is created between borrower's solicitor and lender. This is because the rule requires separate representation for this type of mortgage and the rest of the rule does not then apply.

Other issues

Guidance is now given in new notes (ix)–(x) on checking corporate capacity and obtaining collateral security as these are tasks routinely carried out as part of commercial lending transactions.

The amended version of the rule is printed at the end of this note. *Significant changes are highlighted in italic.*

For additional information contact the Law Society's Professional Ethics Department, tel: 0870 606 2577.

Rule 6(3) of the Solicitors' Practice Rules 1990

(3) *(Solicitor acting for lender and borrower)*

    (a) A solicitor must not act for both lender and borrower on the grant of a mortgage of land:

        (i) if a conflict of interest exists or arises;

        (ii) on the grant of an *individual mortgage* of land at arm's length;

(iii) if, in the case of a *standard* mortgage of property to be used as the borrower's private residence only, the lender's mortgage instructions extend beyond the limitations contained in paragraphs (3)(c) and (3)(e), or do not permit the use of the certificate of title required by paragraph (3)(d); or

(iv) if, in the case of any other *standard* mortgage, the lender's mortgage instructions extend beyond the limitations contained in paragraphs (3)(c) and (3)(e).

(b) A solicitor who proposes to act for both lender and borrower on the grant of a *standard* mortgage of land, must first inform the lender in writing of the circumstances if:

(i) the solicitor or a member of his or her immediate family is a borrower; or

(ii) the solicitor proposes to act for seller, buyer, and lender in the same transaction.

(c) A solicitor acting for both lender and borrower in a *standard* mortgage may only accept or act upon instructions from the lender which are limited to the following matters:

(i) taking reasonable steps to check the identity of the borrower (and anyone else required to sign the mortgage deed or other document connected with the mortgage) by reference to a document or documents, such as a passport, precisely specified in writing by the lender; following the guidance in the Law Society's 'green card' warning on property fraud and 'blue card' warning on money laundering; checking that the seller's solicitors or licensed conveyancers (if unknown to the solicitor) appear in a current legal directory or hold practising certificates issued by their professional body; and, in the case of a lender with no branch office within reasonable proximity of the borrower, carrying out the money-laundering checks precisely specified in writing by the lender;

(ii) making appropriate searches relating to the property in public registers (for example, local searches, commons registration searches, mining searches), and reporting any results specified by the lender or which the solicitor considers may adversely affect the lender; or effecting search insurance;

(iii) making enquiries on legal matters relating to the property reasonably specified by the lender, and reporting the replies;

(iv) reporting the purchase price stated in the transfer and on how the borrower says that the purchase money (other than the mortgage advance) is to be provided; and reporting if the solicitor will not have control over the payment of all the purchase money (other than a deposit paid to an estate agent or a reservation fee paid to a builder or developer);

(v) reporting if the seller or the borrower (if the property is already owned by the borrower) has not owned or been the registered owner of the property for at least six months;

(vi) if the lender does not arrange insurance, confirming receipt of satisfactory evidence that the buildings insurance is in place for at least the sum required by the lender and covers the risks specified by the lender; giving notice to the insurer of the lender's interest and requesting confirmation that the insurer will notify the lender if the policy is not renewed or is cancelled; and supplying particulars of the insurance and the last premium receipt to the lender;

(vii) investigating title to the property and appurtenant rights; reporting any defects revealed, advising on the need for any consequential statutory declarations or indemnity insurance, and approving and effecting indemnity cover if required by the lender; and reporting if the solicitor is aware of any rights needed for the use or enjoyment of the property over other land;

(viii) reporting on any financial charges (for example, improvement or repair grants or Housing Act discounts) secured on the property revealed by the solicitor's searches and enquiries which will affect the property after completion of the mortgage;

(ix) in the case of a leasehold property, confirming that the lease contains the terms stipulated by the lender and does not include any terms specified by the lender as unacceptable; obtaining a suitable deed of variation or indemnity insurance if the terms of the lease are unsatisfactory; enquiring of the seller or the borrower (if the property is already owned by the borrower) as to any known breaches of covenant by the landlord or any superior landlord and reporting any such breaches to the lender; reporting if the solicitor becomes aware of the landlord's absence or insolvency; making a company search and checking the last three years' published accounts of any management company with responsibilities under the lease; if the borrower is required to be a shareholder in the management company, obtaining the share certificate, a blank stock transfer form signed by the borrower and a copy of the memorandum and articles of association; obtaining any necessary consent to or prior approval of the assignment and mortgage; obtaining a clear receipt for the last payment of rent and service charge; and serving notice of the assignment and mortgage on the landlord;

(x) if the property is subject to a letting, checking that the type of letting and its terms comply with the lender's requirements;

(xi) making appropriate pre-completion searches, including a bankruptcy search against the borrower, any other person in whom the legal estate is vested and any guarantor;

(xii) receiving, releasing and transmitting the mortgage advance, including asking for any final inspection needed and dealing with any retentions and cashbacks;

(xiii) procuring execution of the mortgage deed and form of guarantee as appropriate by the persons whose identities have been checked in accordance with any requirements of the lender under paragraph (3)(c)(i) as those of the borrower, any other person in whom the legal estate is vested and any guarantor; obtaining their signatures to the forms of undertaking required by the lender in relation to the use, occupation or physical state of the property; and complying with the lender's requirements if any document is to be executed under a power of attorney;

(xiv) asking the borrower for confirmation that the information about occupants given in the mortgage instructions or offer is correct; obtaining consents in the form required by the lender from existing or prospective occupiers of the property aged 17 or over specified by the lender, or of whom the solicitor is aware;

(xv) advising the borrower on the terms of any document required by the lender to be signed by the borrower;

(xvi) advising any other person required to sign any document on the terms of that document or, if there is a conflict of interest between that person and the borrower or the lender, advising that person on the need for separate legal advice and arranging for him or her to see an independent conveyancer;

(xvii) obtaining the legal transfer of the property to the mortgagor;

(xviii) procuring the redemption of (a) existing mortgages on property the subject of any associated sale of which the solicitor is aware, and (b) any other mortgages secured against a property located in England or Wales made by an identified lender where an identified account number or numbers or a property address has been given by the lender;

(xix) ensuring the redemption or postponement of existing mortgages on the property, and registering the mortgage with the priority required by the lender;

(xx) making administrative arrangements in relation to any collateral security, such as an endowment policy, or in relation to any collateral warranty or guarantee relating to the physical condition of the property, such as National Housebuilding Council (NHBC) documentation;

(xxi)   registering the transfer and mortgage;

(xxii) giving legal advice on any matters reported on under this paragraph (3)(c), suggesting courses of action open to the lender, and complying with the lender's instructions on the action to be taken;

(xxiii) disclosing any relationship specified by the lender between the solicitor and borrower;

(xxiv) storing safely the title deeds and documents pending registration and delivery to or as directed by the lender;

(xxv)   retaining the information contained in the solicitor's conveyancing file for at least six years from the date of the mortgage.

(d)   In addition, a solicitor acting for both lender and borrower in a *standard* mortgage of property to be used as the borrower's private residence only:

   (i)   must use the certificate of title set out in the appendix, or as substituted from time to time by the Council with the concurrence of the Master of the Rolls, ('the approved certificate'); and

   (ii) unless the lender has certified that its mortgage instructions are subject to the limitations contained in paragraphs (3)(c) and (3)(e), must notify the lender on receipt of instructions that the approved certificate will be used, and that the solicitor's duties to the lender are limited to the matters contained in the approved certificate. (See also note (iii) below.)

(e)   The terms of this rule will prevail in the event of any ambiguity in the lender's instructions, or discrepancy between the instructions and paragraph (3)(c) or the approved certificate.

Anti-avoidance

(f)(i) *Subject to paragraph (3)(f)(ii),* a solicitor who is acting only for the borrower in a *standard* mortgage of property must not accept or act upon any requirements by way of undertaking, warranty, guarantee or otherwise of the lender, the lender's solicitor or other agent which extend beyond the limitations contained in paragraph (3)(c).

(f)(ii) *Provided the property is not to be used solely as the borrower's private residence, paragraph (3)(f)(i) does not prevent the borrower's solicitor from giving any form of certificate of title recognised from time to time by the Council of the Law Society (a 'recognised certificate'). Additions or amendments which arise from the individual transaction may be made to the text of a recognised certificate but, to the extent to which they create an increased or additional obligation, must not extend beyond the limitations contained in paragraph (3)(c).*

Notes

(i)   *A mortgage is a 'standard mortgage' where (1) it is provided in the normal course of the lender's activities; (2) a significant part of the lender's activities consists of lending; and (3) the mortgage is on standard terms. An 'individual mortgage' is any other mortgage.*

   •   *A mortgage will not be on standard terms if material terms in any of the documents relating to the mortgage transaction are negotiated between the lender's solicitor and the borrower's solicitor contemporaneously with effecting the mortgage. In commercial transactions, the element of negotiation will often relate to the facility letter or facility agreement rather than the mortgage deed itself.*

   •   *Provided there has been no contemporaneous negotiation of material terms between the parties' solicitors, a mortgage will be on standard terms where the lender uses a prescribed form of mortgage deed. Minor variations, such as the usual clause limiting the liability of trustee mortgagors, are not regarded as material and do not alter the nature of these terms as standard.*

- *In addition to its normal standard terms, a lender may have a different set or sets of standard terms applicable to specialised types of borrower, such as registered social landlords. Provided these terms are applied by the lender to all equivalent specialist borrowers or have been agreed between the lender and a specialist borrower as applicable to all transactions between them, they will constitute standard terms for the purposes of the rule.*

- *The lender and the borrower must be separately represented on the grant of an individual mortgage at arm's length (see paragraph (3)(a)(ii)). The rest of the rule is not then applicable.*

- *A solicitor may act for both lender and borrower in a standard mortgage, provided (1) there is no conflict of interests; (2) the mortgage instructions do not go beyond the limits set out in paragraph (3)(c); and (3) in the case of a property to be used solely as the borrower's private residence, the approved certificate of title set out in the appendix is used (see paragraphs (3)(a)(iii)–(iv) and note (iv)).*

- *The limitations of paragraph (3)(c) also apply to a standard mortgage where the lender and the borrower are separately represented (see paragraph (3)(f)(i) which includes certificates of title). However, paragraph (3)(f)(ii) allows the borrower's solicitor, in a transaction where the property is not to be used solely as the borrower's private residence, to give a certificate of title in any form recognised by the Law Society. A solicitor also remains free to give any other form of certificate which complies with the rule.*

- *There may be cases where the lapse of time between the mortgage offer and completion (for example, when new properties are added) results in use of an earlier edition of a recognised certificate. That is acceptable.*

(ii) A solicitor will not be in breach of paragraphs (3)(a)(iii)–(iv) or (c) if the lender has certified that its mortgage instructions and documents sent pursuant to those instructions are subject to the limitations set out in paragraphs (3)(c) and (e), and certifies any subsequent instructions and documents in the same way. If there is no certification, a solicitor acting in a transaction involving the charge of property to be used solely as the borrower's private residence must notify the lender that the approved certificate of title will be used and that the solicitor's duties to the lender will be limited accordingly (see paragraph (3)(d)(ii)). In other types of transaction, the solicitor should draw the lender's attention to the provisions of paragraphs (3)(c) and (e) and state that he or she cannot act on any instructions which extend beyond the matters contained in paragraph (3)(c).

(iii) As an alternative to printing the approved certificate for each transaction, it is acceptable for a lender to use a short form certificate of title which incorporates the approved certificate by reference. The form must include in the following order:

- the title 'Certificate of Title';

- the contents of the details box in the order set out in the approved certificate (use of two columns is acceptable) but with details not required shaded out or stated not to be required; and

- the wording 'We, the conveyancers named above, give the Certificate of Title set out in the appendix to rule 6(3) of the Solicitors' Practice Rules 1990 as if the same were set out in full, subject to the limitations contained in it.'

Administrative details, such as a request for cheque, may follow the Certificate of Title.

(iv) The approved certificate is only required for a transaction where the property is to be used solely as the borrower's private residence. The approved certificate need not, therefore, be used for investment properties such as blocks of flats, business premises such as shops (even if living accommodation is attached), or 'buy to let mortgages' on properties which are not intended for owner-occupation.

(v)   'Solicitor' in paragraph (3)(b)(i) means any principal in the practice (or an associated practice), and any solicitor of the Supreme Court or registered European lawyer who is conducting or supervising the transaction, whether or not he or she is a principal; and 'immediate family' means spouse, children, parents, brothers and sisters. 'Solicitor' in sub-paragraphs (i)–(xxv) of paragraph (3)(c) means the practice instructed and any solicitor of the Supreme Court or registered European lawyer conducting or supervising the transaction.

(vi) The lender must be informed of the circumstances, in accordance with paragraph (3)(b) so that the lender can decide whether or not to instruct the solicitor.

(vii) A lender's instructions (see paragraph (3)(c)(xxiii)) may require a wider disclosure of a solicitor's circumstances than paragraph (3)(b) requires; and a solicitor must assess whether the circumstances give rise to a conflict. For example, there will be a conflict between lender and borrower if the solicitor becomes involved in negotiations relating to the terms of the loan. A conflict might arise from the relationship a solicitor has with the borrower – for example, if the solicitor is the borrower's creditor or debtor or the borrower's business associate or co-habitant.

(viii) *In relation to paragraph (3)(f)(ii), the limitations contained in paragraph (3)(c) will not apply to the insertion into a recognised certificate of any information required by that certificate. For example, where the recognised certificate requires details of the parties' repairing obligations under a lease of the property, the borrower's solicitor may provide a summary of the relevant terms of the lease despite the general limitation contained in paragraph (3)(c)(ix). However, any additions or amendments to the text of a recognised certificate to suit a particular transaction must not, to the extent to which they create an increased or additional obligation, extend beyond the limitations contained in paragraph (3)(c).*

(ix) *Many lenders require their solicitor to check the vires of corporate borrowers and that the correct procedures have been followed to ensure the validity of the mortgage. Paragraph (3)(c)(xiii) enables lenders to impose duties on solicitors in relation to the execution of the mortgage and guarantee. Within this context it is perfectly proper for a lender to require a solicitor to obtain such information as the circumstances may require in relation to the capacity of, or execution of documents by, the borrower, third party mortgagor or guarantor; for instance, by way of certified copy minutes or an opinion from a foreign lawyer as to the validity and enforceability of the security or guarantee given by a foreign registered company.*

There is no reason why solicitors should not assist corporate clients by drafting minutes or board resolutions. Solicitors should not, however, themselves certify the validity or passing of resolutions unless they were present at the meeting and have verified that it was convened and held strictly in accordance with all relevant requirements.

(x)   *Paragraph (3)(c)(xx) allows a solicitor to accept instructions from a lender to carry out administrative arrangements in relation to any collateral security. This expression includes associated debentures, collateral warranties, second charges, rent assignments, charges over rent income and deeds of priority.*

The administrative arrangements necessarily include the preparation and execution of the relevant documents and subsequent registration.

Appendix

Approved certificate for standard residential mortgage where solicitor acting for lender and borrower not reproduced here (see appendix VIII.2).

Flowchart – Law Society practice rule 6(3) (acting for lender and borrower)

Note: covers both residential and commercial transactions (residential – where property is to be used as the borrower's private residence only; commercial – all other property).

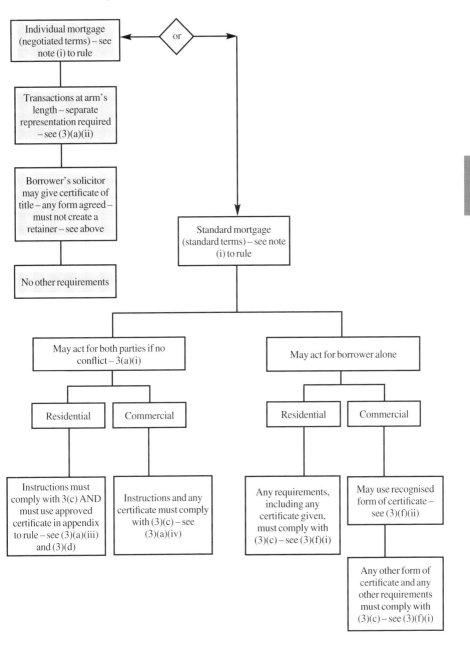

V.16. Property selling[1]

26.01 Solicitors selling property

Property selling as part of practice

1. Property selling is work which a solicitor may properly carry on in the course of his or her professional practice. Section 1(2)(a) of the Estate Agents Act 1979 exempts from that Act 'things done in the course of his profession by a practising solicitor or a person employed by him'. However, solicitors must comply with the Property Misdescriptions Act 1991 and regulations made under it. A solicitor's property selling work is covered by the Solicitors' Indemnity Rules, and the solicitor's earnings from property selling must be included in his or her gross fee returns.

2. If a solicitor sells property as part of his or her practice, the seller will be his or her client. The solicitor's relationship with and the work carried out for the client will be subject to the same law and professional rules binding on solicitors in relation to their other work. (This contrasts with the situation where a solicitor sells property through a separate business – see **26.17**, p.520.)

3. A solicitor may sell property either as an activity of his or her general practice or through a practice formed especially for that purpose, and either alone or with other firms of solicitors. If solicitors from two or more different practices form a partnership for the purpose of property selling, it will be a distinct practice for all purposes, including the indemnity rules, the accounts rules, the practice rules and conflict of interests.

Competence

4. If a solicitor's firm does not have the resources, competence or experience to handle property of a particular value or character, the solicitor must, as in the case of any work which the solicitor does not feel competent to handle, decline instructions and advise the client to consult another property seller, possibly a specialist agent.

Incorporated practices

5. A solicitor's property selling practice may be a company (recognised body). The guidance in this chapter applies equally to a recognised body and its directors, employees and shareholders. The rules vary slightly in relation to a 'SEAL' (see 26.02 below).

Fee sharing with estate agents

6. Solicitors are prohibited from sharing fees, or practising in partnership, with estate agents. However, a solicitor may instruct an estate agent as sub-agent and pay the sub-agent on the basis of a proportion of the solicitor's fee, or accept instructions to act as the sub-agent of an estate agent. (See rule 7 of the practice rules at **3.03**, p.68.)

---

1. The following text is taken from Chapter 26 of *The Guide to the Professional Conduct of Solicitors 1999*, published by the Law Society. Cross-references to paragraphs in the *Guide*, other than Chapter 26, include page references from the *Guide*.

26.02 'SEALs'

1. A 'SEAL' (Solicitors' Estate Agency Limited) is a special type of jointly owned solicitors' incorporated practice. Rule 6 of the practice rules (see **25.01**, p.455) defines a SEAL as a recognised body which:

   (a) does not undertake conveyancing;

   (b) is owned jointly by at least four participating practices which do not have any principals in common and none of which own a controlling majority of the shares; and

   (c) is conducted from accommodation physically divided from, and clearly differentiated from that of any participating practice.

   A participating practice is defined as a practice one or more of whose principals is a member of, or a beneficial owner of a share in, the SEAL.

2. There can be advantages for conveyancing solicitors who undertake property selling through a SEAL rather than as an adjunct to their conveyancing practice (see **26.06** notes 8 and 14, pp.512 and 513).

26.03 Description of property selling work

1. The name of a solicitor's estate agency practice must comply with practice rule 11 at **3.04**, p.69.

2. Practice rule 11 also requires that the word 'solicitor(s)' or the words 'regulated by the Law Society' appear on the firm's letterhead.

3. A property selling practice or a property selling department may be described as 'solicitors and estate agents', 'estate agents', a 'property centre' or by any other suitable description. For appearance under 'Estate Agents' in a directory, see **26.07** note 6, p.514.

26.04 Staff

1. In property selling, a solicitor may employ staff experienced in estate agency. Rule 7(1) of the practice rules (see **3.03**, p.68) allows a solicitor to share fees with his or her *bona fide* employee, whether or not a solicitor. Thus, property selling negotiations may be paid on a commission basis.

2. Paragraph 7 of the publicity code (see Annex 11A at p.233) allows any member of staff to be named in publicity (including stationery), but the status of a staff member who is not a solicitor with a current practising certificate must be unambiguously stated.

26.05 Supervision

A solicitor may open a branch office with, for example, a street-level window purely for the purpose of property selling. A branch office must be staffed and supervised in accordance with practice rule 13 (supervision and management – see **3.08**, p.73). An application for a waiver will also be considered in the case of an office at which the only work carried out is property selling, surveying and mortgage related services. See also **26.14** notes 4–5, p.519 as regards a property display centre.

26.06 Conflict of interests

Connected persons

1. The requirements in notes 4 and 9–12 below are similar to those imposed on estate agents by the Estate Agents (Provision of Information) Regulations 1991 (S.I. 1991 no. 859) and the Estate Agents (Undesirable Practices) (No. 2) Order 1991 (S.I. 1991 no. 1032).

2. Reference throughout **26.06** to a connected person includes:

(a)   any of the solicitor's family, meaning a spouse, former spouse, reputed spouse, brother, sister, uncle, aunt, nephew, niece, direct descendant, parent or other direct ancestor;

(b)   any employee of the solicitor and any family of an employee;

(c)   any partner in an associated practice as defined in rule 6 of the practice rules (i.e. where two or more practices have at least one common principal), any employee of that practice and any family of an employee;

(d)   any company of which the solicitor is a director or employee or in which the solicitor, either alone or with any other connected person or persons is entitled to exercise, or control the exercise of, one-third or more of the voting power at any general meeting;

(e)   any company of which any of the persons mentioned in (a), (b) and (c) above is a director or employee or in which any of them, either alone or with any other connected person or persons, is entitled to exercise, or control the exercise of, one-third or more of the voting power at any general meeting;

(f)   any other 'associate' of the solicitor as defined in section 32 of the Estate Agents Act 1979.

3.   Reference throughout **26.06** to a solicitor's partners includes those with whom he or she carries on a joint property selling practice, and partners in an associated practice – see note 2(c) above and practice rule 6 at **25.01**, p.455 for the meaning of 'associated practice'.

Notification to client when connected person has interest in property

4.   A solicitor must always place the client's interests first. In addition to the requirements of **15.04**, p.316, the solicitor should promptly inform the client in writing whenever the solicitor or, to his or her knowledge, any connected person has, or is seeking to acquire, a beneficial interest in the property or in the proceeds of sale of any interest in the property.

Avoiding conflicts of interest

5.   A solicitor and his or her partners who act in the sale of a property may be faced with insuperable problems of conflict of interests. In accordance with the general principles of professional conduct, a solicitor must not act (nor continue to act) if a conflict of interests exists, arises or is likely to arise (see **15.01**, p.314).

6.   The solicitor who or whose partners act in the sale of a property, even if not in the conveyancing, must not act also for the buyer in the negotiations.

Acting for the buyer

7.   The solicitor who acts in the sale is always free to act for the seller in the conveyancing as well, or the seller may choose to instruct different solicitors. However, rule 6 of the practice rules generally prevents a solicitor from acting for both seller and buyer in conveyancing, property selling or mortgage related services, subject to certain important exceptions (see **25.01**, p.455 and note 14 below). Where these exceptions apply and the solicitor acts for both the buyer and the seller in the same transaction, rule 6 imposes specific conditions, including a full explanation of the position to both clients.

8.   An effect of rule 6(2)(b)(v) and (vi) is to allow a SEAL to act for the seller, and provide mortgage related services to the buyer, whilst one of the participating practices in the SEAL does the buyer's conveyancing, and another participating practice does the seller's conveyancing.

Notification to client of sale instructions from prospective buyer

9.   Apart from cases governed by rule 6, questions of conflict may arise where the solicitor and his or her partners act also for parties in related transactions. Where a prospective buyer has made an offer for a client's property, the solicitor must promptly inform the client in writing if, to the

solicitor's knowledge, he or she or any connected person has also been instructed by the buyer to sell an interest in land, and that sale is necessary to enable the buyer to buy from the client or results from that prospective purchase.

Notification of offers to client

10. A solicitor must promptly send to the client written accurate details (other than those of a description which the client has indicated in writing he or she does not wish to receive) of any offer the solicitor has received from a prospective buyer in respect of an interest in the property.

Duties to buyers

11. In addition to the general requirements of **17.01**, p.346 (a solicitor must not use his or her position as a solicitor to take unfair advantage either for the solicitor or another person), a solicitor must promptly and in writing inform any person negotiating to acquire or dispose of any interest in the property whenever the solicitor or, to his or her knowledge, any connected person has a beneficial interest in the property or in the proceeds of sale of any interest in it. The solicitor should not enter into negotiations with a prospective buyer until that disclosure has been made.

12. A solicitor must not discriminate against a prospective buyer because he or she has not or is unlikely to instruct the solicitor to sell an interest in land, which sale is necessary to enable the buyer to buy from the solicitor's client or results from that prospective purchase.

13. A solicitor acting for a seller of property may need to contact the buyer direct but the communication should be restricted to the solicitor's estate agency function. Communications about legal matters should so far as possible be through the buyer's solicitor, and the buyer should not be led to believe that he or she is receiving legal advice from the seller's solicitor.

Mortgages for buyers

14. In order to facilitate the sale of properties, solicitors sometimes wish to assist buyers to obtain mortgages. Under the rule 6 exceptions, a solicitor or two associated practices may, in certain circumstances and subject to certain conditions, act for the seller in the sale of a property and for the buyer in respect of a mortgage. In particular:

   • a solicitor may do the seller's conveyancing and property selling, whilst providing only mortgage related services to the buyer; or

   • a SEAL may do the property selling for the seller and provide mortgage related services to the buyer, whilst two participating firms do the conveyancing for seller and buyer.

15. Even in cases to which the rule 6 exceptions do not apply, a solicitor may, acting as solicitor for the seller, arrange (in a particular case or as part of a scheme) with a building society or other financial institution that a mortgage will be available on a property (subject to the buyer's status). The solicitor may inform a prospective buyer of the availability of the mortgage but (unless one of the rule 6 exceptions applies) must make it clear in writing that the solicitor cannot advise or act for the prospective buyer in respect of the mortgage, that the mortgage may not be the only one available and that he or she should consult his or her own solicitor.

16. Where a solicitor wishes to advise on mortgages linked with a life policy, the solicitor must comply with the Financial Services Act 1986. It is likely that in order to give such advice the solicitor will require authorisation under that Act (see Chapter 27, p.522).

26.07 Publicity

1. A solicitor may publicise his or her property selling service or properties for sale, subject to the provisions of the Solicitors' Publicity Code 1990 (see Annex 11A, p.229). For the effect of the publicity code on the naming of staff in publicity, see **26.04** note 2, p.510.

2.   Paragraph 3 of the publicity code at p.230, which contains the prohibition on unsolicited visits or unsolicited telephone calls, nevertheless permits an unsolicited visit or telephone call to publicise a specific commercial property or properties the solicitor has for sale or to let.

3.   Paragraph 4 of the publicity code (at p.231) permits the naming or identification of a client in advertisements, with the client's written consent, where the naming or identification is not likely to prejudice the client's interests. Subject to these provisions therefore, a solicitor may name a client in advertising property for sale or to let on that client's behalf.

4.   In publicising properties for sale, solicitors must comply with the Property Misdescriptions Act 1991 and regulations made under it.

Composite fees

5.   Where a solicitor publicises a composite fee for a package of property selling and conveyancing, paragraph 5(d) of the publicity code (at p.231) provides that he or she must be willing if required:

(a)   to quote separate fees for the individual services (which may total more than the composite fee); and

(b)   to carry out one service only on the basis of the separate fee.

A solicitor is 'required' for this purpose if he or she has a clear indication that a prospective client may wish to give instructions in respect of only one service in the package.

Directories

6.   An entry or advertisement of a solicitor who provides a property selling service may appear in a directory, such as the Yellow Pages, under the classification 'Estate Agents', provided that 'solicitor(s)' appears in a description of the practice appearing in the entry or advertisement itself. See paragraph 8 of the publicity code (at p.234).

Flag advertising

7.   A reference may be made in publicity to the solicitor's membership of an organisation or association of solicitors, but if an advertisement does not name the solicitor's firm it must comply with paragraph 10 of the publicity code (at p.234).

Arranging mortgages

8.   A solicitor may advertise the ability to arrange mortgages but will need to comply with relevant consumer credit regulations. See **25.09** notes 9 and 10 (pp.475 and 476) and also **26.06** note 16 (p.513).

26.08 Introductions and referrals

1.   Rule 3 of the practice rules (see **11.04**, p.224) allows solicitors to enter into arrangements for the introduction and referral of clients to and from the solicitor's practice, subject to compliance with the Solicitors' Introduction and Referral Code 1990 (see Annex 11B, p.238). The code provides *inter alia* that a solicitor may not reward an introducer by the payment of commission or otherwise (see section 2(3) of the code).

Investment business and mortgages

2.   Rule 12 of the practice rules (see **27.21**, p.533) places conditions on the ability of a solicitor to enter into arrangements for introductions and referrals in the field of investment business. In particular, a solicitor cannot act as an appointed representative, as defined in the Financial Services Act 1986, unless he or she is an appointed representative of an independent financial adviser.

3.   In accepting or making referrals in the field of mortgages or investment business, solicitors must comply with **25.09**, p.474.

26.09 Remuneration

Statement as to remuneration

1.   When accepting instructions to act in the sale of a property, a solicitor must give the client a written statement setting out their agreement as to the amount of the solicitor's fee or the method of its calculation, the circumstances in which it is to become payable, the amount of any disbursements to be charged separately (or the basis on which they will be calculated) and the circumstances in which they may be incurred, and as to the incidence of VAT. It should state the identity of the property, the interest to be sold and the price to be sought. This requirement is similar to that imposed on estate agents by the Estate Agents Act 1979 and enables the client to be clear as to the proposed basis of charging.

2.   The statement should also deal with whether or not the solicitor is to have 'sole agency' or 'sole selling rights' and, if so, explain the intention and effect of those terms (or any similar terms used) in the following manner:

(a)   **Sole selling rights**

'You will be liable to pay a fee to us, in addition to any other costs or charges agreed, in each of the following circumstances:

●   if unconditional contracts for the sale of the property are exchanged in the period during which we have sole selling rights, even if the buyer was not found by us but by another agent or by any other person, including yourself; or

●   if unconditional contracts for the sale of the property are exchanged after the expiry of the period during which we have sole selling rights but to a buyer who was introduced to you during that period or with whom we had negotiations about the property during that period.'

(b)   **Sole agency**

'You will be liable to pay a fee to us, in addition to any other costs or charges agreed, if unconditional contracts for the sale of the property are exchanged at any time:

●   with a buyer introduced by us with whom we had negotiations about the property in the period during which we have sole agency; or

●   with a buyer introduced by another agent during the period of our sole agency.'

These requirements and those in notes 3–5 below are similar to the obligations imposed on estate agents by the Estate Agents (Provision of Information) Regulations 1991 (S.I. 1991 no. 859).

3.   If reference is made to a 'ready, willing and able' buyer (or similar term), the statement should contain the following explanation:

'A buyer is a "ready, willing and able" buyer if he or she is prepared and is able to exchange unconditional contracts for the purchase of your property. You will be liable to pay a fee to us, in addition to any other costs or charges agreed, if such a buyer is introduced by us in accordance with your instructions and this must be paid even if you subsequently withdraw and unconditional contracts for sale are not exchanged, irrespective of your reasons.'

4.   If, by reason of the provisions of the statement in which any of the terms referred to above appear, any of the prescribed explanations is in any way misleading, the content of the explanation should be altered so as accurately to describe the liability of the client to pay a fee in accordance with those provisions. Subject to this requirement, the prescribed explanations should be reproduced

prominently, clearly and legibly without any material alterations or additions and should be given no less prominence than that given to any other information in the statement apart from the heading, practice names, names of the parties, numbers or lettering subsequently inserted.

5. The statement must be given at the time when communication commences between the solicitor and the client or as soon as is reasonably practicable thereafter, provided that this is before the client is committed to any liability towards the solicitor.

Commission – remuneration certificates and taxation

6. The Society does not make any recommendation about property selling commissions. Commission charged on property sales is, however, subject to the Society's remuneration certificate procedure, unless the client signs a non-contentious business agreement in accordance with section 57 of the Solicitors Act 1974 (see Annex 14A, p.284), and to taxation by the Court.

Commission from third party

7. Commission paid by a third party, e.g. by an insurance company where the client takes out an endowment policy, is distinct from the remuneration paid by the client to the solicitor in relation to the property transaction. The solicitor must deal with commission from a third party in accordance with rule 10 of the practice rules (see **14.13**, p.283). An exception is where commission has been received for the referral of a prospective buyer who is merely browsing; rule 10 only comes into operation when a buyer expresses interest in a specific property.

Composite fees

8. A solicitor may quote or publicise a composite fee for property selling and conveyancing but should be prepared to quote separate fees if asked. The separate fees may total more than the composite fee. See **26.07** note 5, p.514.

26.10 Interest earned on preliminary deposits

A preliminary deposit is usually held on behalf of and is fully refundable to the buyer. The Solicitors' Accounts Rules apply only to interest arising on client and stakeholder money. However, as a matter of good practice, solicitors should consider, when refunding a preliminary deposit, whether it is appropriate to pay interest to the buyer. Regulation 7 of the Estate Agents (Accounts) Regulations 1981 (S.I. 1981 no. 1520) provides that estate agents must account to the buyer where the preliminary deposit exceeds £500, and the interest actually earned on it, or which could have been earned if it had been kept in a separate deposit account, is at least £10. In that case, the agent must account for all interest earned, or for the interest which could have been earned in a separate deposit account. Solicitors could follow these regulations themselves. Alternatively, they could refer to the Solicitors' Accounts Rules (see Annex 28B, p.684).

26.11 Practice rule 14 (structural surveys and formal valuations)

'Solicitors may not provide structural surveys or formal valuations of property unless:

(a) the work is carried out by a principal or employee who is a chartered surveyor or who holds another professional qualification approved by the Council; and

(b) the appropriate contribution has been paid to the Solicitors' Indemnity Fund.'

Solicitors' Practice Rules 1990, rule 14

26.12 Structural surveys and formal valuations – additional guidance

A solicitor may carry out structural surveys and formal valuations of property as part of his or her practice. Rule 44 of the Solicitors' Indemnity Rules 1998 (see Annex 29A at p.837) details the additional contribution payable and provides that any practice intending to undertake this work must immediately notify Solicitors Indemnity Fund Limited.

26.13 Joint property selling practice

1. For a joint property selling practice, see **26.01** note 3 (p.509).

2. Firms wishing to set up such a joint practice may wish to set it up as a SEAL because the participating firms in a SEAL will be less constrained under practice rule 6 (see **26.02**, p.509, and **26.06** notes 7 and 8, p.512).

26.14 Property display centre

1. As an alternative to setting up a SEAL or other form of joint property selling practice, a number of independent firms of solicitors (the participating firms) may join together to carry on a joint property display centre (PDC) to publicise properties in the sale of which an individual participating firm is instructed. In this way, the participating firms may avoid some of the constraints which arise under practice rule 6 in the case of a joint property selling practice.

2. A PDC which observes the requirements set out in note 3 below is regarded as an administrative extension of the practices of the participating firms. It is not regarded either as a department or branch office of all or any of the participating firms, or as a joint property selling practice. The address of a PDC should be notified to Regulation and Information Services (see p.xv for contact details) under section 84(1) of the Solicitors Act 1974 (see **2.09**, p.40) as a business address of all the participating firms. Although it may involve a partnership for administrative purposes between participating firms, a PDC is not a partnership for the purposes of carrying on a solicitors' practice.

Characteristics and functions of a PDC

3. (a) A PDC can have no clients; it may merely carry out certain activities on behalf of the participating firms. Only individual participating firms may be instructed in the sale of a property.

   (b) A PDC is a place where the principal activity carried on is the display and dissemination of information about properties which the individual participating firms have for sale.

   (c) No part of a solicitor's professional practice may be carried on at a PDC. In particular no negotiations may be conducted there; prospective buyers must be referred to the individual participating firm instructed in the sale of the property in question. Instructions to sell a property may only be accepted at offices of participating firms. To avoid problems with practice rule 6 (see **26.06**, p.510) the participating firms must operate totally independently so far as their professional business, including property selling, is concerned.

   (d) A PDC is inherently an administrative extension of the practices of the participating firms, not a separate entity.

   (e) The participating firms may wish to establish a joint service company to carry out support functions connected with the running of the PDC, e.g. hiring premises and equipment. The service company (as with a service company established by an individual firm of solicitors) cannot carry on any legal practice or have any dealings with the property selling or property buying public (see **3.19**, p.88).

   (f) Having regard to rule 1(b) and (c) of the practice rules (see **1.01**, p.1), a participating firm may not make it a condition that a prospective buyer instructs another participating firm in his or her conveyancing or any other matter.

Supervision and management

4.   As no part of a solicitor's practice is carried on at a PDC, rule 13 of the practice rules (supervision and management) does not apply. Note that the participating firms are nevertheless responsible for the activities of the PDC staff and have a duty to supervise them.

A single firm PDC

5.   A single firm of solicitors could establish its own PDC where no negotiations or any other part of the firm's practice was conducted. Rule 13 would not apply to such a PDC. The firm would nevertheless be responsible for the activities of its PDC staff and would have a duty to supervise them.

26.15 Joint property display centre – publicity

1.   Paragraph 10 of the Solicitors' Publicity Code 1990 governs 'flag advertising' (see Annex 11A at p.234). This term includes any advertising by a joint PDC which does not name the firm or firms whose services are being advertised.

2.   Any advertising under the logo of or in the name of a joint PDC, if it does not name the firm or firms whose services are being advertised, must include the word 'solicitor(s)' (see paragraph 10 of the publicity code at p.234) and the PDC's address (or some other address at which the names of all the participating firms are available). A name such as 'Solicitors' Property Centre' or 'Solicitors' Property Centre, Craxenford' (provided it is not misleading or inaccurate) may appear on the PDC premises, advertisements or stationery.

3.   On the PDC premises the PDC name must be accompanied by the names of the participating firms (either outside or visible from outside the premises) and the word 'solicitor(s)'. The PDC stationery must be used only in connection with activities which a PDC may properly undertake in accordance with **26.14** note 3, p.518. In particular it must not be used in connection with negotiations.

4.   For the reasons stated in **26.14** note 3, p.518, the name of a service company (e.g. 'Solicitors' Property Centre Ltd') should not appear on the PDC itself or in its advertisements or any stationery used for writing to the property buying and selling public.

5.   An individual participating firm advertising in its own name may refer to its membership of the PDC or include the PDC logo in its advertisements. The firm's stationery may include the PDC logo or refer to the firm's membership of the PDC. Notepaper used for a solicitor's professional business, including notepaper used in negotiating a sale of property, must include the name of the firm and not merely the name of the PDC.

6.   'For Sale' boards and particulars of properties for sale may, at the discretion of the participating firms, either be the boards and particulars of an individual participating firm or the boards and particulars of the PDC. Boards and particulars of the PDC must comply with notes 2–4 above. An individual participating firm may use the PDC name and/or logo on its boards or particulars in addition to the firm's own name.

26.16 Joint property display centre – referrals

In practice a prospective client may either first approach an individual participating firm or the PDC itself. A joint PDC must not accept instructions on behalf of participating firms. However, rule 3 of the practice rules (see **11.04**, p.224) allows a PDC to refer prospective clients to the participating firms. In the light of rule 1(b) of the practice rules (see **1.01**, p.1) a prospective client should be asked to make his or her own choice from amongst the participating firms. If he or she decides not to make a choice, the method whereby a participating firm is selected for a referral is a matter for the participating firms. Note, however, that if a member of the PDC staff is asked for a recommendation (rather than for a referral), the recommendation must only be given on the basis of a genuine belief that the firm concerned should be recommended.

16.17 Selling property through a separate business

1. Rule 5 of the practice rules and the Solicitors' Separate Business Code 1994 (see **3.20**, p.89 and Annex 3E, p.129) permit a solicitor to conduct property selling through a separate business, subject to the provisions of section 5(2) of the code at p.132.

2. A solicitor with a separate estate agency business may do conveyancing for its buyers, but only if:

   • the estate agency is owned jointly with another practice or business; and

   • the solicitor does not do the seller's conveyancing, or does the seller's conveyancing under one of the rule 6 exceptions; and

   • the buyer and the seller give their written informed consent; and

   • different individuals deal with the work for them.

3. A solicitor with a separate estate agency business which provides mortgage related services to a buyer may, nevertheless, do conveyancing for the seller.

V.17. Tax on bank and building society interest – practice information[1]

Since April 1996, savings income received by an individual, the estate of a deceased person or an interest in possession trust has been taxable at the lower rate (20%), unless in the case of an individual his or her total income makes him or her liable to higher rate tax, rather than the basic rate of tax (section 73 of the Finance Act 1996 inserting a new section 1A into the Income and Corporation Taxes Act 1988). This is relevant to the tax treatment of bank and building society interest received by solicitors.

The Solicitors' Accounts Rules 1998, Part C

Under this part of the rules ('the interest provisions'), a solicitor who is required to account for interest to a client may do so by either of two methods. He or she may:

(a) account to the client for the interest earned on the client's money in a separate designated client account; or

(b) pay to the client a sum in lieu of interest when the money is held in a general client account.

These two procedures are referred to as Method A and Method B respectively.

Deduction of tax at source

The tax deduction at source rules apply, broadly, to separate designated client accounts, e.g. accounts held for individuals who are ordinarily resident in the U.K.

Interest on general client accounts, whether with a bank or a building society, is paid gross.

When opening any separate designated client account the solicitor must provide the necessary information for the bank or building society to decide whether or not deduction of tax at source is appropriate.

Tax treatment of interest – Method A

Method A applies to separate designated client accounts. Where tax is deducted at source by the bank or building society interest will be received by the solicitor net, and he or she will simply pass it on to the client net – no tax deduction certificate is required. Interest from separate designated client accounts is taxable as savings income. The client, when making his or her tax return, will declare the interest as having been received under deduction of tax, and will only be liable to be assessed in relation to higher rate tax in respect of it (since he or she will have a tax credit for the lower rate of tax). If the client is for any reason not liable to income tax, he or she can recover any tax deducted from the interest. In those circumstances the solicitor must, on being required by the client, obtain a certificate of deduction of tax from the bank or building society and deliver this to the client. The client's position is, therefore, for practical purposes, the same as that which arises where he or she receives interest from a building society or bank on a deposit of his or her own.

1. The following text appears as Annex 28D in *The Guide to the Professional Conduct of Solicitors 1999*, published by the Law Society.

Where the client is not liable to tax or is not ordinarily resident (NOR) in the U.K. the bank or building society will pay the interest gross provided that it holds the relevant declaration. Declarations of non-ordinary residence can be completed by either the solicitor or the client but declarations of non-liability by U.K. residents will normally be completed by the client. However, in view of the difficulty of obtaining complete information about an overseas client, solicitors may feel that it is more appropriate for the client concerned to make the declaration, especially since it contains an undertaking to notify the bank or building society should circumstances change.

Where the tax deduction at source rules do not apply, the solicitor will receive interest from the bank or building society gross and may account to the client for it gross, even if the client is non-resident. The client will be assessed on the gross receipt (but a non-resident client may, by concession, not be assessed) and (unless the solicitor has been acting as the client's agent for tax purposes – see below under 'Solicitors as agents') the solicitor himself or herself will not be assessed in respect of the interest.

Tax treatment of interest – Method B

Where Method B is used, deduction of tax at source does not apply to the solicitor's general client account at either a bank or building society, and interest is therefore paid to the solicitor gross. When making a payment to the client of a sum in lieu of interest under the interest provisions, the solicitor should make the payment gross even if the client is not ordinarily resident. The Revenue's view is that such payments may be treated as within Case III of Schedule D, so that the lower rate of tax on savings income may apply where appropriate. The client will be assessed to income tax on his or her receipt, but a non-resident may, by concession, not be assessed.

Wherever payments are made by solicitors to clients under Method B they can, in practice, be set off against the solicitor's Case III assessment on gross interest received on general client account deposits; if the payments exceed the interest received, a Case II deduction can be claimed for the excess.

Stake money

Since 1st June 1992, stake money has been included in the definition of 'client money'. Interest will be payable to the person to whom the stake is paid using either Method A or B above. But there will still be circumstances in which payment is not possible until a later tax year. Where this situation looks likely to arise, e.g. if the stake is held pending the outcome of litigation, the deposit would normally be placed in a general client account until it is established to whom the stake is to be paid. Because, in the meantime, interest will be included in the solicitor's Case III assessment, it is again important to make provision for the tax liability to be met out of the interest as it arises.

Tax treatment of interest – money paid into court

The position of money paid into court is covered by the Supreme Court Funds Rules as amended. Where any order for payment out of money paid into court is made, the order should provide for the disposal of any interest accrued to the date of the judgment or order, and for interest accruing thereafter up to the date the money is paid out in accordance with the order. In the absence of such provision, interest accruing between the date of the payment into court, and its acceptance or the judgment or order for payment out, goes to the party who made the payment in, and interest from the date of the judgment or order follows the capital payment.

Where interest is paid to a party to proceedings in respect of money held in court, it should be paid to the client gross, even if he or she is non-resident. The client will normally be assessable under Case III, but the solicitor will not, unless exceptionally he or she is assessable as the client's agent.

Solicitors as agents

Where a solicitor acts for tax purposes as agent for a non-resident client, the solicitor will remain liable to be assessed on behalf of the client in relation to interest earned in a separate designated client account, where Method A is used, unless he or she is an agent without management or control of the interest, in which case, under Extra Statutory Concession B13, no assessment will be made on him or her. Where the solicitor is assessable, the charge may, if appropriate, be to higher rate tax, so the solicitor will need to retain tax at the client's marginal rate of income tax from interest received gross from a bank or building society before remitting it to the client. This is the case even though the account would not be subject to deduction of tax at source since the client would have completed a declaration of non-liability due to his or her non-residence. No question of the solicitor being taxed as an agent will arise where the interest in question has been earned in a general client account, or on stake money, but it could very exceptionally do so in relation to money held in court.

Determination of whether a solicitor has management or control for the purposes of the extra statutory concession will depend on the nature of the solicitor's relationship with the client. Under the Finance Act 1995, a person not resident in the U.K. is assessable and chargeable to income tax in the name of an agent if the agent has management or control of the interest. Acting as a solicitor in giving advice or in conducting a transaction on the client's instructions will not of itself give management or control nor usually would the holding of a power of attorney on behalf of the client for a specific purpose, e.g. concluding a specified purchase or sale. If a client had no fixed place of business in the U.K., and his or her solicitor had, and habitually exercised, an authority to conclude contracts on behalf of the client, this would give rise to the client having a permanent establishment in the U.K., and accordingly the client would be taxable. In essence, the solicitor would be deemed to have management and control if he or she were effectively carrying on the client's business in the U.K., rather than merely acting as a solicitor, even regularly. Therefore, in order for the agency principle to apply, the solicitor/client relationship would normally have to go beyond a solicitor's usual representative capacity. It should be noted that where interest arises in connection with the receipt of rents on behalf of the non-resident, the solicitor would be chargeable as agent in relation to the rent.

For a more detailed analysis of when solicitors can be taxed as agents, see [1991] *Gazette*, 1 May, 15 (article by John Avery Jones).

If a solicitor is assessable on behalf of the client, he or she has a general right to reimbursement, out of the client's money coming into his or her hands, for any tax for which the client is liable and in respect of which the solicitor has been charged. For the exercise of this right see the Finance Act 1995.

Trusts

Deduction of tax at source may apply depending upon the type of trust and where the investment is held. But it can only apply where money is held in a separate designated client account. The income of trusts where none of the beneficiaries is ordinarily resident in the U.K. will not be subject to deduction of tax at source, even if a separate designated client account is used, provided that the appropriate declaration has been made.

Administration of estates

Interest on money held for U.K. resident personal representatives will, if placed in a separate designated client account, be subject to deduction of tax at source unless a declaration is made by the solicitor or the personal representatives that the deceased was not resident in the U.K. immediately before his death.

AIDE-MEMOIRE OF NORMAL SITUATIONS

Type of account	Payment of interest by bank or building society	Consequences
A Designated – where subject to tax deduction	Net	Pay net to client, who gets basic rate tax credit. No further tax deductions for residents (unless solicitor is assessable as an agent).
B Designated – where paid gross (client money generally)	Gross	Pay gross to client who is assessable on payment as gross income. No deduction of tax for non-residents (unless the solicitor is assessable as agent).
C Bank and building society general client account – always paid gross (client money generally and stake money)	Gross	Pay gross to client who in turn is assessable on payment as gross income; in practice solicitor assessed on interest after setting-off this payment. No deduction of tax for non-residents.

4th March 1992, revised February 1999

V.18. Undue Influence – solicitors' duties post Etridge[1]

Introduction

Many negligence claims have arisen as a result of solicitors viewing their role in the execution of third party charge documentation as little more than a formality. The important House of Lords decision in *Royal Bank of Scotland* v. *Etridge* was delivered on 11th October 2001 and as a result all conveyancing lawyers should consider carefully their procedures when faced with a transaction where a third party provides security for another person's borrowing. The risk to solicitors' professional indemnity cover remains acute. Etridge involved a wife claiming that she had charged her interest in the matrimonial home as a result of the undue influence of her husband. Whilst the decision has to some extent clarified the scope of the solicitors' duties and set out what is required of the lender this arrangement does still present all parties with exposure to risk and this has not in any way been reduced following the House of Lords decision.

Can you advise?

Whilst Etridge does contemplate that the same solicitor can act for both parties and the lender in an administrative capacity, the first decision for the solicitor is whether he or she should be acting at all. The risk of conflict is extreme when attempting to reconcile Lord Nicholls' comments concerning the provision of full information with a client who in many cases may not wish for the documentation to be fully explained. When the third party realises that the home will be at risk to secure the other person's borrowing, there may be some reluctance to sign.

If advising the third party the solicitor will be acting for the third party alone and so must consider carefully whether there is a conflict of duty or interest and whether it would be in the best interests of that client to accept the instructions. If the third party is a wife she may well have an interest in supporting the husband's business as it is the source of the family's income. In such cases the wife may, despite the risks, have a good reason to sign the charge.

Many solicitors will, however, be reluctant to advise in such circumstances. The Law Lords stressed the importance of bank finance in the business world and stated that 'finance raised by second mortgages on the principal's home is a significant source of capital for the start up of small businesses'. So in order to facilitate the development of embryonic businesses, solicitors will no doubt still be asked to witness charge documentation. What steps should the solicitor take to ensure that the obligation of independent advice is properly discharged?

Who is your client?

The solicitor must ensure that the client wishes and intends to instruct the solicitor. It must be established that there is no conflict of interest and that it is the third party (and not the borrower) who is the client.

---

1. © The Law Society. This guidance was issued by the Law Society's Conveyancing and Land Law Committee in May 2002.

Full financial information

The solicitor must obtain full financial information concerning the borrower's account. This will normally include (para 79 of Lord Nicholls' judgment) information on the purpose for the new facility, the current indebtedness, the amount of the current overdraft facility, and the amount and terms of any new borrowing together with a copy of any application form. Lord Nicholls stated that:

'…it should become routine practice for banks if relying on confirmation from a solicitor for their protection to send to the solicitor the necessary financial information'.

Expertise

The solicitor must be satisfied that he or she has the necessary expertise to interpret or advise on the detailed financial information.

Advice

The solicitor must explain to the client the purpose for which the solicitor has become involved and that the bank, should it ever become necessary, will rely upon the solicitor's involvement to counter any suggestion that the client did not properly understand the implications of the transaction (para 64). After explaining the documents, it is the client's rather than the solicitor's decision as to whether or not to proceed.

Core Minimum Requirements

Lord Nicholls summarised at paragraph 65 of the judgment the core minimum requirements for advice which typically will include:

- the nature of the documents and the risk that the client will lose the home if the borrower's business does not prosper, and even the possibility that the client could be made bankrupt;

- the seriousness of the risks involved by reference to the purpose, amount and terms of the new facility and whether the client understands the value of the property being charged and if there are any other assets out of which repayment could be made if the business fails;

- the fact that the lender may alter the terms of the loan including increasing the amount borrowed without reference to the client;

- asking whether the client is content for the solicitor to write to the bank confirming that the solicitor has explained the nature of the documents to the client and the practical implications they may have;

- discussing whether the client wishes the solicitor to negotiate with the bank on the terms of the transaction (e.g. limitation on the amount borrowed);

- providing the advice at a face to face meeting in the absence of the borrower and giving the advice using non-technical language;

- explaining that the client does have a choice on whether to sign the charge/guarantee or to consent to mortgage with the decision being up to the client alone.

However, it must be appreciated that additional requirements may become appropriate depending on the specific facts of the case. It should be appreciated by the solicitor that 'the solicitor's task is an important one. It is not a formality' (Lord Nicholls, para 65). To comply properly with the House of Lord's judgment guidance is likely to take several chargeable hours.

Confirmation

The advice given should be recorded in a full attendance note and confirmed in detail in writing in a letter sent promptly after the meeting. A draft letter is available on the Law Society website and is reproduced in Appendix VII.8.

Summary

All conveyancing solicitors should be certain that before advising on third party charges:

(1) they have the necessary expertise.

(2) there is no conflict.

(3) there is no suspicion of undue influence or impropriety.

(4) the bank provides full financial information.

(5) the advice covers, at the very least, the core minimum requirements.

(6) the advice is confirmed in writing.

In addition the solicitor should check if the firm's indemnity insurers have any additional requirements or have issued any guidance.

Finally it is up to the solicitor to exercise his or her skill and judgement in each individual case to decide whether to act. A solicitor who is acting for the borrower should not agree to advise the third party if there is a real possibility that the advice would be that the third party should not execute the charge/guarantee or consent to mortgage.

V.19. The Law Society interest rate

The Law Society interest rate is the 'contract rate' in the Standard Conditions of Sale first published in 1990. The Law Society interest rate is 4% above Barclays Bank base rate. Rates are as at close of business on the day indicated.

This information is provided for your use and it is your responsibility to check its accuracy and application. No liability is accepted to third parties.

Please note: For the current rate ring the Library Enquiry Line on 0870 606 2511. A message giving the current rate is accessible even when the Library is closed.

Date	Rate	Date	Rate
10 July 2003	7.50%	30 October 1996	10.00%
06 February 2003	7.75%	06 June 1996	9.75%
08 November 2001	8.00%	08 March 1996	10.00%
04 October 2001	8.50%	18 January 1996	10.25%
18 September 2001	8.75%	13 December 1995	10.50%
02 August 2001	9.00%	02 February 1995	10.75%
10 May 2001	9.25%	07 December 1994	10.25%
05 April 2001	9.50%	12 September 1994	9.75%
08 February 2001	9.75%	08 February 1994	9.25%
10 February 2000	10.00%	23 November 1993	9.50%
13 January 2000	9.75%	26 January 1993	10.00%
04 November 1999	9.50%	13 November 1992	11.00%
08 September 1999	9.25%	16 October 1992	12.00%
10 June 1999	9.00%	22 September 1992	13.00%
08 April 1999	9.25%	17 September 1992	14.00%
04 February 1999	9.50%	16 September 1992	16.00%
07 January 1999	10.00%	05 May 1992	14.00%
11 December 1998	10.25%	04 September 1991	14.50%
05 November 1998	10.75%	12 July 1991	15.00%
09 October 1998	11.25%	24 May 1991	15.50%
04 June 1998	11.50%	12 April 1991	16.00%
06 November 1997	11.25%	22 March 1991	16.50%
07 August 1997	11.00%	27 February 1991	17.00%
10 July 1997	10.75%	13 February 1991	17.50%
06 June 1997	10.50%	08 October 1990	18.00%
06 May 1997	10.25%	30 April 1990	19.00%

VI. LAW SOCIETY CLIENT LEAFLETS

VI.1. About the Client's Charter and Client's Guides

Introduction

As part of its campaign to raise standards in the profession, the Law Society has developed a Client's Charter, to raise public awareness about what they can expect from their solicitor and a series of Client's Guides.

The Client's Charter, Your Guide to Buying a Home, and Your Guide to Using a Solicitor are reproduced in Appendices VI.2–VI.4 to this edition of the *Conveyancing Handbook*.

The Client's Charter

The Client's Charter explains in simple terms what to expect from a solicitor and how to complain if things go wrong. Endorsed by the Plain English Campaign, the Charter is based on the Guide to the Professional Conduct of Solicitors.

Marketing

The Client's Charter and Client's Guides, which were approved by the Council in 2002, were launched on 17 March 2003 at the Law Society. The Law Society has also issued releases to the national and regional press.

A3 size posters will also be available to help promote the Charter.

Distribution of the Client's Charter and Client's Guides

Solicitors firms will receive an initial pack consisting of 100 Charters and a pack of the 11 guides with an order form. Copies of the Client's Charter will also be sent to all Citizens' Advice Bureaux, MP's surgeries, Libraries and Law Centres.

The Client's Guides

To complement the Client's Charter the Law Society have produced a range of guides containing information about common legal problems. The 11 guides in the series are:

- Your guide to buying a home
- Your guide to renting out your property
- Your guide to renting a home
- Your guide to making a will
- Your guide to getting a divorce
- Your guide to problems at work
- Your guide to setting up in business

- Your guide to making a personal injury claim
- Your guide to financial matters for the elderly
- Your guide to setting up home with your partner
- Your guide to using a solicitor

Translations

The Charter and the Guides will be available in English, Welsh, Arabic, Chinese, Greek, Hindi, Turkish, Vietnamese, Bengali, Punjabi, Gujarati, Urdu and Somali. The guides will eventually be available via the web site in all available languages. These languages were recommended to the Society by the Commission for Racial Equality.

How do solicitors order the guides?

Solicitors will be able to order the guides, which are initially **free of charge** (although CABx, Law Centres and MPs will always receive them free of charge), from a distribution company. To order:

By email law.society@alphamail.co.uk
By fax: 01444 871355
By post: Data Department, Alpha Mail Ltd. 18 Victoria Way, Burgess Hill, West Sussex RH15 9NF.

How do members of the public order the guides?

Members of the public can obtain copies by sending an email to customerguides@lawsociety.org.uk or by phoning the customer guide line on 020 7316 5605.

VI.2. Your Guide to Buying a Home[1]

Getting advice

Buying a home is always an exciting prospect, but without the help of a solicitor it can also be a legal minefield. Your solicitor is qualified in all areas of property law and is there to help you avoid potential problems and to protect your interests at every step, from making an offer to getting the keys to the door.

This is a guide to the services you can expect from your solicitor when buying a home.

Finding a solicitor

Ideally you should contact your solicitor as soon as you think about buying a home. If you do not already have a solicitor, call the Law Society on 0870 606 6575. Or you can visit our website at www.solicitors-online.com and search under 'Conveyancing residential' to get details of solicitors in your area.

Costs

Charges can vary between solicitors and will depend on the type and difficulty of the sale. Before you decide who to use, check with a few firms of solicitors to compare their fees. You should bear in mind that you may have to pay more for a more experienced solicitor, so the cheapest quote is not always your best option. Remember that you will also need to pay a variety of other expenses such as stamp duty, VAT, Land Registry fees and other search fees.

What your solicitor will need from you

Once you have chosen a solicitor, they will ask you for a variety of details and documents. These could include:

- some personal identification;
- the price of the property;

  any factors that may influence the exact time you want to buy the property (for example: to coincide with school holidays); and
- how you are planning to pay for the property.

They will also need to know whether:

- you have applied for a mortgage;
- you plan to carry out work on the property;
- you are buying with someone else;
- the seller is buying another property; and
- you have a property to sell.

1. © The Law Society 2003. Your Guide to Buying a Home and other client leaflets were launched by the Law Society on 17 March 2003. See Appendix VI.1 for details.

Contacting the seller's solicitor

Your solicitor will then contact the seller's solicitor, who will in turn supply your solicitor with a draft contract and a copy of the title deeds to the property. With these will be a form listing the fittings and contents which will be included when you buy the property. You will need to check this list carefully.

Searches

Your solicitor will make various searches, including enquiries with the local authority. These can help to reveal any planning issues affecting the property, such as road improvements and details of any planning permission granted on the property. Your solicitor may also carry out flooding, mining and contaminated land searches if necessary. If any of these searches show matters of concern, your solicitor will let you know.

Leasehold properties

If the property is leasehold (particularly common when buying a flat), there will be detailed lease terms and conditions. Your solicitor will need to check these carefully and will also make enquiries with the seller's solicitor or the managing agents of the property about what service charges and management costs you will have to pay.

Survey advice

If you are applying for a mortgage, your mortgage lender will need an independent valuation of the property. Usually they will appoint their own surveyor to do this, but you will have to pay for it. Remember that this is a valuation and not a survey.

You should consider appointing your own surveyor (possibly the same person as the valuer) to carry out a survey on the property as it is up to you to satisfy yourself that the property is structurally sound before you buy it. If the survey reveals that building work is needed, you should tell your solicitor as this may allow you to renegotiate the price.

Mortgage deed and terms

Your mortgage lender will also need a mortgage deed. You should read the mortgage deed, offer letter and mortgage conditions very carefully. Your solicitor will explain them to you.

Signing the contract

Your solicitor will then report back to you on all the investigations he or she has made for you so far. If you are still happy to go ahead, your solicitor will finalise the terms of the contract and explain it to you. You then need to sign the contract and provide the deposit money – usually between 5% and 10% of the purchase price.

Exchanging contracts

This is the crucial moment of the agreement between you and the seller. Your solicitor and the seller's solicitor exchange contracts so that you have the contract the seller has signed and the seller has the contract you have signed. If you want to withdraw from buying the property after this stage, you may have to pay financial penalties. The solicitors will also set the date for completing the sale at this stage.

Final balance

Between exchanging contracts and completion, your solicitor will take the mortgage money from your lender and the rest of the money from you. This will include costs, VAT, Land Registry fees and stamp duty (if any). At this stage your solicitor will carry out final searches and make arrangements with the seller's solicitor for paying off any existing mortgages on the property. Your solicitor will also prepare the transfer deed and send it to the seller's solicitor for signing.

Completion

This is the final stage in the conveyancing process when your solicitor hands over the money to the seller and the keys are released to you. Your solicitor will pay the stamp duty and Land Registry fees for you and register your ownership at the Land Registry. This registers the interest of your mortgage lender and records you as the new legal owner of the property.

Related legal matters

Buying a property may introduce other related legal matters. For example:

- if you are buying a home with someone you are not married to, you may need to enter into a 'deed of trust' to set out what share of the property each person owns;

- if you do not have a will, you should consider making one; and

- if you do have a will, you may need to update it.

In all cases your solicitor can offer you legal advice as part of a complete professional service.

VI.3. The Client's Charter – Your solicitor's customer care standards[1]

Whatever legal service you need, you have the right to be treated with care and professionalism by your solicitor. The Client's Charter is your guide to what to expect from your solicitor in terms of customer care.

Working together

Whilst your solicitor has various duties to you as their client, they can only give their best advice and service if the information you give them is accurate and complete.

A solicitor will:

- put your interests first when representing you;

- be polite and considerate in their dealings with you;

- find out from the start what you are hoping to achieve, and aim to make sure that your expectations are realistic;

- make every effort to explain things clearly, and in terms you can understand, keeping jargon to a minimum;

- agree with you the type of service you can expect to receive;

- tell you who will be handling your work;

- explain what the costs are likely to be;

- keep you informed of costs throughout so that you can work out if a particular course of action is worth following financially;

- respond to your letters and phone calls;

- tell you about any developments and update you on progress as work proceeds;

- give you a clear bill which shows the work done and the amount charged;

- treat all clients fairly, and not discriminate against anyone; because of his or her race, sex, sexual orientation (sexuality) or disability; and

- keep what you tell them confidential, and refuse to act for anyone else if doing so could compromise that confidentiality.

This is a summary of the main rules and principles that apply to all solicitors.

PLEASE NOTE: Other legal and professional duties may occasionally affect the ability of your solicitor to meet all these standards. For example, the legal duty to release information about money laundering or the solicitor's duty to the court can override the duty of confidentiality or the duty to put your interest first.

1. © The Law Society 2003. The Client's Charter and other client leaflets were launched by the Law Society on 17 March 2003. See Appendix VI.1 for details.

What to do if you have a complaint

Most people have a good experience with their solicitor, but things do sometimes go wrong. That is why there is a clear and effective complaints procedure in place.

Every solicitor's firm has to have their own complaints procedure, and you should use this procedure first before going elsewhere.

If this does not provide a satisfactory resolution, you should complain to the Office for the Supervision of Solicitors, Victoria Court, No 8 Dormer Place, Leamington Spa, CV32 5AE. Phone: 0845 608 6565.

After this, if you are still not satisfied, you can take your complaint to the Office of the Legal Services Ombudsman, 3rd Floor Sunlight House, Quay Street, Manchester M3 3JZ. Phone: 0161 839 7262. Email: lso@olso.gsi.gov.uk

For a list of solicitors in your area and lots of other information on legal issues, visit the Law Society's website at: www.lawsociety.org.uk

You can find details of the rules which apply to solicitors, including the circumstances when your solicitor may not be able to meet all the terms of the Charter, at www.guide-online.lawsociety.org.uk

VI.4. Your Guide to Using a Solicitor[1]

Most of us will seek legal advice at some stage in our lives. The Law Society aims to make this process as easy and straightforward as possible. To do this, we offer access, through our website or helpline, to a database of solicitors in England and Wales and a wealth of information on legal issues. We have also published a Client's Charter, which sets out standards of service and administrative procedures for legal professionals to follow. This is with one aim: to help you get the most from your solicitor.

Janet Paraskeva
Chief Executive, The Law Society

Choosing a solicitor

Finding a list of solicitors in your area is easy using the Law Society's helpline or website. Call 0870 606 6575 or visit www.solicitors-online.com to start your search, but think carefully about what type of service you need. Here are just some of the issues you should consider:

What sort of legal help do I need?

A firm of solicitors may offer services in a wide range of legal subjects, although more and more individual solicitors are specialising in only one or two subjects. If your usual firm of solicitors cannot help you with all your needs, they will be happy to refer you to another solicitor. Or, if you prefer, they can get the advice of a specialist on your behalf.

How can I be sure they are qualified to help me?

All solicitors in private practice must hold a practising certificate issued by the Law Society. This guarantees that the solicitor is qualified to practise and has insurance to protect you if anything goes wrong. If you want to be sure, ask to see the certificate (which should be on display in your solicitor's office) or contact the Law Society to check.

You can also ask your solicitor whether the firm has received any quality awards to prove that they have good standards of practice in place. If the firm has received the Law Society's 'Lexcel' quality award, the Law Society will be able to confirm this.

Individual solicitors might also be members of 'Quality assured panels' set up by the Law Society to cover a number of legal subjects. To be asked to join these panels, solicitors must show that they have considerable specialist knowledge. You can find a list of panel members on the Law Society's website.

Where is the firm based?

Where a firm is based is obviously an issue of convenience, particularly for elderly, sick or disabled people. Do you need to use a firm that is close to where you live? If so, this will narrow your search. Some solicitors are happy to visit you at home, so if you find travelling difficult, it's well worth asking about this.

---

1. © The Law Society 2003. Your guide to using a solicitor, the Client's Charter and other Client's Guides were launched by the Law Society on 17 March 2003. See Appendix VI.1 for details.

Do they do legal aid work?

If you are on a low income or receiving benefits, you may be eligible for legal aid. You can find this out by contacting your nearest Citizens' Advice Bureau or Law Centre. As some firms do legal aid work and some do not, if you are eligible for this kind of funding, you will need to narrow your search to firms that do. There is a list of these available on the Community Legal Service website at www.justask.org.uk

Legal aid is managed by The Legal Services Commission, which makes sure that all solicitors' firms that offer legal aid meet high quality standards.

Do they work on a conditional fee basis?

For certain types of case, including personal injury, your solicitor may be prepared to work on a conditional fee basis. This is more commonly known as a 'no win, no fee' arrangement. If you win the case, your solicitor's fees will mostly be paid by the other side. If you lose, you do not have to pay your solicitor's fees. You may be asked to take out an insurance policy to pay for the other side's costs if you lose. There are various types of conditional fee arrangement, but not all solicitors firms are prepared to work on this basis.

Will they be sympathetic?

If you need to see a solicitor about a personal matter, such as a relationship breakdown, you will want to choose someone who makes you feel comfortable. Most solicitors will be sympathetic and understanding if you are distressed, but you may prefer to deal with someone who is the same sex as you. Don't be afraid to say that this is what you want.

Will they speak my language?

If English is not your first language, you should mention this when you are trying to find a solicitor. If enough warning is given, a firm can arrange for an interpreter to be present at your meetings.

Making an appointment

Once you have found a suitable firm, you need to make an appointment. Let them know if there's anyone you need to bring to the meeting with you and ask if you should bring any documents with you, such as proof of identity or income.

Be prepared

The more preparation you do before the meeting, the more you'll get out of it. Make a list of the main points you want to make or the questions you want to ask. Get together any paperwork that is relevant and put it in some kind of order so you can refer to it quickly. This will make it quicker and easier for your solicitor to understand your circumstances and give you proper advice.

At the meeting

Check how long the meeting will last so that you don't suddenly find that 'time is up' before you've made all your points. Have your notes in front of you, tick off each point as it is covered, and don't be afraid to ask if anything is said that you do not understand.

Finally, ask your solicitor to send you a letter after the meeting to summarise the advice you've been given, and confirm the following details:

- That he or she has taken on the work.
- The name of the person in the firm who will be dealing with your case day to day.

- The amount of time the firm will need to see your case through.
- An estimate of costs and any agreed spending limit.
- Any more information you need to supply.

Solicitors' charges

Legal advice, like anything else you buy, costs money, but its value can be enormous. Charges vary between solicitors, and will depend on the expertise and experience of the individual solicitor as well as how complicated the work is.

Before making a decision about which firm to use, you may want to 'shop around'. Decide on what sort of solicitor you need to speak to and get quotes from several. Many solicitors charge little or nothing for a short first interview. It is worth asking.

However, price is not the only thing you have to consider. Above all, try to find a solicitor who you are comfortable with and whose advice you feel you understand.

Fixed or hourly rate?

Solicitors don't always charge a fixed fee for a particular job. The bill will often be worked out on an hourly basis, so the longer it takes, the more it costs. A solicitor must give you a cost estimate at the outset, usually at the first interview.

If an hourly rate is quoted, you may want to agree a fixed spending limit. If the costs look likely to go over this limit your solicitor will contact you to warn you and get your agreement to continue.

Keeping in touch

Once you have appointed a solicitor, they must consult you at every important stage, to check how you want to proceed. Similarly, you need to tell your solicitor about any changes to your personal circumstances which could affect the case. This includes any changes in your financial position which could alter your eligibility for legal aid.

Customer service

Everyone is entitled to expect a certain standard of service from their solicitor. This is why the Law Society has produced 'the Client's Charter' – a set of principles of customer care for solicitors. You can get a copy of this by visiting the Law Society's website at www.lawsociety.org.uk

VII. LAW SOCIETY FORMS AND PRECEDENTS

VII.1. Agreed form of wording with banks for undertaking for bridging finance[1]

FORM No. 4 (BRIDGING FINANCE)

Undertaking by solicitor (with form of authority from client) to account to bank for net proceeds of sale of the existing property, the bank having provided funds in connection with the purchase of the new property.

Authority from client(s)

[Date] ....

To .... [name and address of solicitors]

I/We hereby irrevocably authorise and request you to give an undertaking in the form set out below and accordingly to pay the net proceeds of sale after deduction of your costs to

.... Bank plc .... Branch.

Signature of client(s). ....

Undertaking

[Date] ....

To .... Bank plc

If you provide facilities to my/our client ....

for the purchase of the freehold/leasehold property (the new property)

.... [description of property]

pending the sale by my/our client of the freehold/leasehold property (the existing property)

.... [description of property]

---

1. The following text appears in *The Guide to the Professional Conduct of Solicitors 1999* as part of Annex 25C.

I/we undertake:

1. That any sums received from you or your customer will be applied solely for the following purposes:

   (a) in discharging the present mortgage(s) on the existing property *[delete if not applicable]*;

   (b) in acquiring a good marketable title to the new property, subject to the mortgage mentioned below *[delete if not applicable]*;

   (c) in paying any necessary deposit, legal fees, costs and disbursements in connection with the purchase.

The purchase price contemplated is £. .... gross.

I/We are informed that a sum of £ .... is being advanced on mortgage by .... *[delete if not applicable]*. The amount required from my/our client for the transaction including the deposit and together with costs, disbursements and apportionments is not expected to exceed £..............

2. To hold to your order when received by me/us the documents of title of the existing property pending completion of the sale (unless subject to any prior mortgage(s)) and of the new property (unless subject to any prior mortgage(s)).

3. To pay to you the net proceeds of sale of the existing property when received by me/us. The sale price contemplated is £........... and the only deductions which will have to be made at present known to me/us are:

   (i) the deposit (if not held by me/us),

   (ii) the estate agents' commission,

   (iii) the amount required to redeem any mortgages and charges, which so far as known to me/us at present do not exceed £.............,

   (iv) the legal fees, costs and disbursements relating to the transaction.

4. To advise you immediately of any subsequent claim by a third party upon the net proceeds of sale of which I/we have knowledge.

NOTES:

(1) If any deductions will have to be made from the net proceeds of sale other than those shown above, these must be specifically mentioned.

(2) It would be convenient if this form of undertaking were presented in duplicate so that a copy could be retained by the solicitor.

VII.2. Certificate of Title (Appendix to SPR 6(3))[1]

Details Box

TO: (Lender)	
Lender's Reference or Account No:	
The Borrower:	
Property:	
Title Number:	
Mortgage Advance:	
Price stated in transfer:	
Completion Date:	
Conveyancer's Name & Address:	
Conveyancer's Reference:	
Conveyancer's bank, sort code and account number:	
Date of instructions:	

WE THE CONVEYANCERS NAMED ABOVE CERTIFY as follows:

(1) If so instructed, we have checked the identity of the Borrower (and anyone else required to sign the mortgage deed or other document connected with the mortgage) by reference to the document or documents precisely specified in writing by you.

(2) Except as otherwise disclosed to you in writing:

    (i) we have investigated the title to the Property, we are not aware of any other financial charges secured on the Property which will affect the Property after completion of the mortgage and, upon completion of the mortgage, both you and the mortgagor (whose identity has been checked in accordance with paragraph (1) above) will have a good and marketable title to the Property and to appurtenant rights free from prior mortgages or charges and from onerous encumbrances which title will be registered with absolute title;

    (ii) we have compared the extent of the Property shown on any plan provided by you against relevant plans in the title deeds and/or the description of the Property in any valuation which you have supplied to us, and in our opinion there are no material discrepancies;

    (iii) the assumptions stated by the valuer about the title (its tenure, easements, boundaries and restrictions on use) in any valuation which you have supplied to us are correct;

    (iv) if the Property is leasehold the terms of the lease accord with your instructions, including any requirements you have for covenants by the Landlord and/or a management company and/or by a deed of mutual covenant for the insurance, repair and maintenance of the structure, exterior and common parts of any building of which the Property forms part, and we have or will obtain on or before completion a clear receipt for the last payment of rent and service charge;

    (v) we have received satisfactory evidence that the buildings insurance is in place, or will be on completion, for the sum and in the terms required by you;

    (vi) if the Property is to be purchased by the Borrower:

1. © The Law Society 1999. This Certificate is an appendix to Solicitors' Practice Rule 6(3), see Appendix I.1.

VII

(a) the contract for sale provides for vacant possession on completion;

(b) the seller has owned or been the registered owner of the Property for not less than six months;

(c) we are not acting on behalf of the seller;

(vii) we are in possession of: (A) either a local search or local search insurance and (B) such other searches or search insurance as are appropriate to the Property, the mortgagor and any guarantor, in each case in accordance with your instructions;

(viii) nothing has been revealed by our searches and enquiries which would prevent the Property being used by any occupant for residential purposes;

(ix) neither any principal nor any other solicitor or registered European lawyer in the practice giving this certificate nor any spouse, child, parent, brother or sister of such a person is interested in the Property (whether alone or jointly with any other) as mortgagor.

WE :

(a) undertake, prior to use of the mortgage advance, to obtain in the form required by you the execution of a mortgage and a guarantee as appropriate by the persons whose identities have been checked in accordance with paragraph (1) above as those of the Borrower, any other person in whom the legal estate is vested and any guarantor; and, if required by you:

to obtain their signatures to the forms of undertaking required by you in relation to the use, occupation or physical state of the Property;

to ask the Borrower for confirmation that the information about occupants given in your mortgage instructions or offer is correct; and

to obtain consents in the form required by you from any existing or prospective occupier(s) aged 17 or over of the Property specified by you or of whom we are aware;

(b) have made or will make such Bankruptcy, Land Registry or Land Charges Searches as may be necessary to justify certificate no. (2)(i) above;

(c) will within the period of protection afforded by the searches referred to in paragraph (b) above:

(i) complete the mortgage;

(ii) arrange for stamping of the transfer if appropriate;

(iii) deliver to the Land Registry the documents necessary to register the mortgage in your favour and any relevant prior dealings;

(iv) effect any other registrations necessary to protect your interests as mortgagee;

(d) will despatch to you such deeds and documents relating to the Property as you require with a list of them in the form prescribed by you within ten working days of receipt by us of the Charge Certificate from the Land Registry;

(e) will not part with the mortgage advance (and will return it to you if required) if it shall come to our notice prior to completion that the Property will at completion be occupied in whole or in part otherwise than in accordance with your instructions;

(f) will not accept instructions, except with your consent in writing, to prepare any lease or tenancy agreement relating to the Property or any part of it prior to despatch of the Charge Certificate to you;

(g) will not use the mortgage advance until satisfied that, prior to or contemporaneously with the transfer of the Property to the mortgagor, there will be discharged (A) any existing mortgage on property the subject of an associated sale of which we are aware and (B) any other mortgages made by a lender identified by you secured against a property located in England or Wales where you have given either an account number or numbers or a property address;

(h) will notify you in writing if any matter comes to our attention before completion which would render the certificate given above untrue or inaccurate and, in those circumstances, will defer completion pending your authority to proceed and will return the mortgage advance to you if required;

(i) we confirm that we have complied, or will comply, with your instructions in all other respects to the extent that they do not extend beyond the limitations contained in paragraph (3)(c) of rule 6 of the Solicitors' Practice Rules 1990.

OUR duties to you are limited to the matters set out in this certificate and we accept no further liability or responsibility whatsoever. The payment by you to us (by whatever means) of the mortgage advance or any part of it constitutes acceptance of this limitation and any assignment to you by the Borrower of any rights of action against us to which the Borrower may be entitled shall take effect subject to this limitation.

Signature Box

SIGNED on behalf of **THE CONVEYANCERS**	....
NAME of Authorised Signatory	....
QUALIFICATION of Authorised Signatory	....
DATE of Signature	....

VII

VII.3. Client Care Letters (Appendix to the Costs Information and Client Care Code)[1]

General notes for guidance

These letters and terms and conditions of business are *examples* of how solicitors can provide client care and costs information to their clients.

They are designed to assist solicitors in compliance with the Solicitors' Costs Information and Client Care Code 1999 which is incorporated into the Solicitors' Practice (Costs Information and Client Care) Amendment Rule 1999 made on 3 March 1999 which comes into force on 3 September 1999.

The letters were prepared as part of a lengthy process of consultation and with the benefit of Plain English advice. Whilst the Society hopes that they will help solicitors in the design and content of their client care and costs information, there may be situations where the letters require amendments (to reflect, for example, The Consumer Protection (Distance Selling Regulations 2000).

FORMAT OF LETTERS

• It is for the solicitor to decide whether to send a client a letter or a covering letter containing important information relevant to that client together with the firm's standard terms of business. Any of these example documents could be adapted for use in another format and practitioners are encouraged to adopt their own style. However, do always have regard to the provisions of the Code.

• Some of the individual letters may appear lengthy to clients in which case, consider sending shorter client care letters enclosing leaflets containing more general information, for example, about storage of papers and deeds/documents, or additional information, such as, an explanation of the client's rights to challenge a bill.

• Alternatively, it may be helpful to produce terms of business set out over the two sides of one sheet of paper only.

• The matters covered in these documents are mainly presented in general form. Always check whether there is a need to adapt the wording in an individual case.

• These examples are not intended to be exhaustive. Do consider what other provisions may be appropriate for your firm. For example, if you wish to give clients an option to make payments on account by standing order and/or by credit card.

CONTENTS OF LETTERS

Introduction

The introductory paragraph of the letters introduces the people responsible for the client's work. It is vital to put the status of the fee earner not only to comply with the solicitors practice rule obligations, but also following *Pilbrow* v. *Pearless De Rougemont & Company* (Court of Appeal, 16 March 1999) where failure to tell the client the status of the non-solicitor fee earner rendered the whole bill unenforceable. Remember the term legal executive only applies to a fellow of the institute.

1. © The Law Society 1999. The full Code is reproduced here in Appendix II.4.

Charges and Expenses

1.   The Code Requirements

The Code requires solicitors to discuss with clients how any costs are to be met at the outset of, and at appropriate stages throughout the matter, and to confirm any such advice in writing as soon as possible.

This is very much a matter for the practitioners in each individual case. Whilst terms of business can inform the client, matters should be discussed with them as well. Details such as whether the client's liability for costs (their own or another party's) may be covered by insurance or by an employer or trade union may be better covered in correspondence. Likewise advice on whether the likely outcome in a matter will justify the expense or risk involved including, if relevant, the risk of having to bear an opponent's cost.

2.   Rule 48.8 of the Civil Procedure Costs Rules

In litigation matters, to ensure compliance with Rule 48.8 of the Civil Procedure Costs Rules the written document providing for solicitor and client costs to be greater than those recoverable from another party must be signed by the client. Failure to do so will result in costs being limited to the amount allowed from an opponent under S.74(3) of the Solicitors Act 1974.

3.   Hourly Rates

In respect of hourly rates, the client should be told in advance if those rates are to be reviewed for any reason.

It is generally assumed both in the letters for use in contentious and non-contentious cases that an hourly rate (whether a blended/composite rate or a rate for each type of fee earner) will be presented as a single charging rate which adequately reflects the relevant factors and the weight to be attached to them. It can often be confusing to refer to 'mark-up' or 'care and attention'.

Where the solicitor's charges are based on hourly rates, consider whether you prefer to charge routine letters sent out and consideration of letters received at six and three minutes per page or letter respectively.

4.   Telephone Calls

Clients frequently complain that they did not expect to have to pay for telephone calls which they make to their solicitor. It may be desirable to ensure that the client understands clearly their liability for costs in this respect.

5.   Money held on account

Whilst not included in the Code, it is often necessary to discuss with clients the terms of investment of any money held on account. Do make clear how a deposit will be invested and what interest it will earn. A charge by a solicitor for calculating and crediting interest to a client cannot be provided for in a retainer letter or terms of business.

Billing Arrangements

1.   Indemnity Cover

If you propose to show the cost of indemnity cover as a separate item in a bill do make it clear in the opening client care letter, terms of business or any estimate. Any wording is adequate provided it is clear. For example:

'Our basic charges for acting for you in your purchase/sale/mortgage are (however you normally charge, a fixed fee, an hourly rate, whatever). In addition we are members of the Solicitors Indemnity Fund which means we are covered for claims arising out of your transaction and you are protected by comprehensive professional indemnity arrangements. We make a separate charge of £X + VAT per purchase as a contribution towards the cost of that cover.'

2.   *Costs of a third party*

In non-contentious cases it may also be necessary to explain to the client any liability the client may have for the payment of the costs of a third party.

3.   *Disclosure of Charging Rates*

Solicitors doing contentious work should always bear in mind the question of the disclosure of their charging arrangements with the client to the court, including in relation to interim bills. In addition, the Lord Chancellor will be consulting shortly on a range of measures which will include:

● compulsory notification by solicitors to their clients of their actual charging rate;

● at an early stage in all civil proceedings, solicitors will be expected to provide their clients, and the court, with an estimate of their costs to date and the full costs likely to be incurred to trial; and

in addition to the above, at a later stage in civil cases, solicitors will be expected to provide an estimate of their costs to date and the full costs likely to be incurred to trial. Solicitors may be expected to adhere to this final estimate – or face not recovering costs incurred above it.

NON-CONTENTIOUS

NOTES FOR GUIDANCE

Client Care and Costs Information Letter – Conveyancing

Fixed Fee

● This is intended for use where a fixed fee is being paid which is clearly intended to be fixed and there will be no need to update the costs information. If possible a fixed indication of the disbursements should be given as well.

● Practitioners may also wish to include a request for a payment of costs on account.

● Remember to keep clients properly informed about their matter at the outset and as the transaction progresses, including the likely timescale, as well as giving costs information.

● Unless, at the outset of a retainer, the client has been required to make a payment or payments on account of costs before completion of the retainer, you should not refuse to complete a transaction for the client if the sole reason for that refusal is that the client has not paid the costs. This example letter therefore says that payment of the bill is due after completion. Guidance can be found at **25.17** page 408 of *The Guide to the Professional Conduct of Solicitors* 7th edition.

LETTER THREE: CLIENT CARE AND COSTS INFORMATION LETTER – CONVEYANCING

Fixed Fee

Date

Dear [   ]

This letter explains the basis on which we will carry out all the work necessary in the [sale/purchase] of [   ]. [The charges set out below do not cover any work for your mortgage lenders.]

People responsible for your work

[   ] will carry out most of the work in this matter. [She/He] is a [grade of fee earner] specialising in property law and residential conveyancing. [She/He] is supervised by [   ], [status] who is ultimately responsible for the work.

[[   ] [grade of fee earner] will also work on the matter on your behalf.] If you need to telephone, please ask to speak to [   ] [or   ]. If they are unavailable, please leave a message with their secretary.

We will try to avoid changing the people who handle your work but if this cannot be avoided, we will inform you promptly who will be handling the matter [and why the change was necessary].

Charges and expenses

We will charge you £ [   ]

We will add VAT to our charge at the rate that applies when the work is done. At present, VAT is 17.5%.

We set out below the other things you are likely to have to pay for, an estimate of their cost, and when payment for them is likely to be needed:

Expense	When payment is likely to be needed	Cost £

VAT is payable on certain expenses.

Your overall charges are therefore likely to be £[   ]. We will discuss with you how you are to pay these charges.

If this firm does not complete the work, we will charge you £[   ] per hour for each hour of work. We will charge for writing letters, and for making and taking telephone calls in units of 1/10th of an hour. Our charges for considering letters received will be in units of 1/20th of an hour. Our total charge will not exceed £[fixed fee/firm's abortive fee]. Our bill will also include VAT and expenses.

We will inform you if any unforeseen extra work becomes necessary – for example, due to unexpected difficulties or if your requirements or the circumstances change significantly during the matter. We will also inform you in writing of the estimated cost of the extra work before incurring extra costs. We will attempt to agree an amended charge with you. If we cannot reach agreement, we will do no further work and charge you on an hourly basis for work to date, as set out earlier.

It is normal practice to ask clients to make payments on account from time to time. These payments help to meet our expected charges and expenses, and help to avoid delaying progress in the matter.

We will need £[   ] to enable us to pay expenses before we start work on your matter. We will then pay expenses as they become due. We may request further payments on account of expenses as the matter progresses. These amounts will be shown as paid on your final bill.

Bills

We will send you a bill for our charges and expenses [normally after the exchange of contracts]. Payment of the bill is due after completion. If you are a purchaser and you have agreed with the lenders to pay their costs, we will send you a copy of their bill if we are instructed to act for your lenders.

If sufficient funds are available on completion and we have sent you a bill, we will usually deduct our charges from the funds.

If you do not pay our bill on completion of the [sale/purchase], payment is due within 28 days of our sending you the bill. If you do not pay the bill within 28 days, we will charge interest on it at [   ]% per year or a daily basis, from [the date of the bill] [the date on which payment of our bill is due].

If you have any query about the bill, you should contact [   ] straight away.

Storage of papers and deeds

After completing the [sale/purchase], we are entitled to keep all your papers and documents while money is owing to us. We will keep our file of papers (except for any of your papers which you ask to be returned to you) for no more than [   ] years and on the understanding that we have your authority to destroy the file [   ] years after sending you our final bill. We will not destroy documents you ask us to deposit in safe custody.

We do not normally make a charge for retrieving stored papers or deeds in response to continuing or new instructions to act for you. However, we reserve the right to make a charge based on the time we spend on reading papers, writing letters or other work necessary to comply with the instructions.

Termination

You may terminate your instructions to us in writing at any time. For example, you may decide you cannot give us clear or proper instructions on how to proceed, or you may lose confidence in our work.

We are entitled to keep all your papers and documents while money is owing to us.

We expect to receive instructions from your lenders to act on their behalf. If so, we will have to pass them information you give us that might be relevant to their decision whether to finance the purchase. If you tell us things that you do not want the lenders to know and they are relevant to the lenders, we may have to stop acting for the lenders and possibly also for you.

We will decide to stop acting for you only with good reason and on giving you reasonable notice.

If you or we decide that we will stop acting for you, you will pay our charges on an hourly basis and expenses as set out earlier.

Raising queries or concerns with us

We are confident that we will give you a high quality service in all respects. However, if you have any queries or concerns about our work for you, please take them up first with [   ]. If that does not resolve the problem to your satisfaction or you would prefer not to speak to [   ], then please take it up with [   ] or this firm's client care partner who is [   ].

All firms of solicitors are obliged to attempt to resolve problems that clients may have with the service provided. It is therefore important that you immediately raise your concerns with us. We value you and would not wish to think you have any reason to be unhappy with us.

Conclusion

Your continuing instructions will amount to your acceptance of these terms of business, but please sign and date the enclosed copy of this letter and return it to us immediately. Then we can be confident that you understand the basis on which we will act for you.

We hope that by sending this letter to you we have addressed your immediate queries about the day-to-day handling of your work and our terms of business. However, if you have any queries, please do not hesitate to contact [   ].

This is an important document which we would urge you to keep in a safe place for future reference.

Yours faithfully

NOTES FOR GUIDANCE

Client Care and Costs Information Letter – Conveyancing

Hourly Rates

- The last three paragraphs of the notes for guidance for the Client Care and Costs Information Letter – Conveyancing – Fixed Fee are also relevant to this letter.

- The letter assumes that you will not wish to review the hourly rates or deliver interim bills in view of the likely timescale involved.

- The letter provides an explanation of the arrangements for updating cost information as necessary.

LETTER FOUR: CLIENT CARE AND COSTS INFORMATION LETTER – CONVEYANCING

Hourly Rates

Date

Dear [   ]

This letter explains the basis on which we will carry out all the work necessary in the [sale/purchase] of [   ]. [The charges set out below do not cover any work for your mortgage lenders.]

People responsible for your work

[   ] will carry out most of the work in this matter. [She/He] is a [grade of fee earner] specialising in property law and residential conveyancing. [She/He] is supervised by [   ], [status] who is ultimately responsible for the work.

[[   ] [grade of fee earner] will also work on the matter on your behalf.] If you need to telephone, please ask to speak to [   ] [or   ]. If they are unavailable, please leave a message with their secretary.

We will try to avoid changing the people who handle your work but if this cannot be avoided, we will inform you promptly who will be handling the matter [and why the change was necessary].

Charges and expenses

Our charges are based on the time spent dealing with a case. Time spent on your affairs will include meetings with you; considering, preparing and working on papers; correspondence; and making and receiving telephone calls.

We will charge you [£   ] per hour for each hour of work by [   ] [and [£   ] per hour for work by[   ]]. Routine letters and routine telephone calls made and received will be charged for in units of 1/10th of an hour. Our charges for considering routine letters received will be in units of 1/20th of an hour. Other letters and calls will be charged for on a time basis.

[plus explanation of value element where relevant]

We will add VAT to our charge at the rate that applies when the work is done. At present, VAT is 17.5%.

We set out below the other things that you are likely to have to pay for, an estimate of their cost and when payment for them is likely to be needed:

Expense	When payment is likely to be needed	Cost £

VAT is payable on certain expenses.

We believe that the time we are likely to spend on your matter will be [   ]. We estimate that your total charges and expenses will be about £ [   ]. [This estimate is not intended to be fixed.] We will update you on the position as to your charges and expenses every [   ] months and inform you if it appears that any estimate may be exceeded.

We will discuss with you how you are to pay these charges.

If this firm does not complete the work, we will charge you for the work done and expenses incurred.

We will inform you if any unforeseen extra work becomes necessary – for example, due to unexpected difficulties or if your requirements or the circumstances significantly change during the matter. We will also inform you in writing of the estimated cost of the extra work before incurring extra costs.

We will need £[   ] to enable us to pay expenses before we start work on the matter. We will then pay expenses as they become due. We may request further payments on account of expenses as the matter progresses. These amounts will be shown as paid on your final bill.

Bills

We will send you a bill for our charges and expenses [normally after the exchange of contracts]. Payment of the bill is due after completion. If you are a purchaser and you have agreed with the lenders to pay their costs, we will send you a copy of their bill if we are instructed to act for your lenders.

If sufficient funds are available on completion and we have sent you a bill, we will usually deduct our charges from the funds.

If you do not pay our bill on completion, payment is due within 28 days of our sending you the bill. If you do not pay the bill within 28 days, we will charge interest on it at [   ]% per year or a daily basis, from [the date of the bill] [the date on which payment of our bill is due].

If you have any query about the bill, you should contact [   ] straight away.

Storage of papers and deeds

After completing the [sale/purchase], we are entitled to keep all your papers and documents while money is owing to us. We will keep our file of papers (except for any of your papers which you ask to be returned to you) for no more than [   ] years and on the understanding that we have your authority to destroy the file [   ] years after sending you our final bill. We will not destroy documents you ask us to deposit in safe custody.

We do not normally make a charge for retrieving stored papers or deeds in response to continuing or new instructions to act for you. However, we reserve the right to make a charge based on the time we spend on reading papers, writing letters or other work necessary to comply with the instructions.

Termination

You may terminate your instructions to us in writing at any time. For example, you may decide you cannot give us clear or proper instructions on how to proceed, or you may lose confidence in our work.

We are entitled to keep all your papers and documents while money is owing to us.

We expect to receive instructions from your lenders to act on their behalf. If so, we will have to pass them information you give us that might be relevant to their decision whether to finance the purchase. If you tell us things that you do not want the lenders to know and they are relevant to the lenders, we may have to stop acting for the lenders and possibly also for you.

We will decide to stop acting for you only with good reason and on giving you reasonable notice.

If you or we decide that we will stop acting for you, you will pay our charges on an hourly basis and expenses as set out earlier.

Raising queries or concerns with us

We are confident that we will give you a high quality service in all respects. However, if you have any queries or concerns about our work for you, please take them up first with [   ]. If that does not resolve the problem to your satisfaction or you would prefer not to speak to [   ], then please take it up with [   ] or this firm's client care partner who is [   ].

All firms of solicitors are obliged to attempt to resolve problems that clients may have with the service provided. It is therefore important that you immediately raise your concerns with us. We value you and would not wish to think you have any reason to be unhappy with us.

Conclusion

Your continuing instructions will amount to your acceptance of these terms of business, but please sign and date the enclosed copy of this letter and return it to us immediately. Then we can be confident that you understand the basis on which we will act for you.

We hope that by sending this letter to you we have addressed your immediate queries about the day-to-day handling of your work and our terms of business. However, if you have any queries, please do not hesitate to contact [   ].

This is an important document which we would urge you to keep in a safe place for future reference.

Yours faithfully

**TERMS OF BUSINESS THREE: NON-CONTENTIOUS BUSINESS
AGREEMENT – CONVEYANCING**

Fixed Fee

Date of agreement:

1. **This agreement is a legally binding contract between you and us. Before you sign and return it to us, please read it carefully.**

2. The agreement is between us, [   ] of [   ], and you, [   ] of [   ].

3. The agreement relates to work we are to carry out in connection with your [sale/purchase] of [   ] [excluding   ]. It does not relate to any other work you might ask us to do.

4. We will charge you £[   ].

5. We will add VAT to our charge at the rate that applies when the work is done. At the date of the agreement, VAT is 17.5%.

6. We set out below the other things that you will have to pay for, and an estimate of their cost:

Expense	*Cost £*
Search fees	
Stamp duty	
Land Registry fee	

   VAT is payable on certain expenses.

   Note: This is a non-exhaustive list. Solicitors are advised to provide as much detail as possible and to list all reasonably anticipated disbursements. If other expenses might be payable this should be made clear.

7. Your total charges and expenses for the [sale/purchase] will therefore be [about] £[   ]. This figure does not cover any work we do for your mortgage lenders.

8. If this firm does not complete the work, we will charge you £[   ] per hour for each hour of work. We will charge for writing letters, and for making and taking telephone calls in units of 1/10th of an hour. Our charges for considering letters received will be in units of 1/20th of an hour. Our total charge will not exceed £[fixed fee]. Our bill will also include VAT and expenses.

9. Payment is due to us within 28 days of our sending you the bill. If sufficient funds are available on completion of the [sale/purchase], we will usually deduct our charges from the funds.

10. The agreement is a non-contentious business agreement under Section 57 of the Solicitors Act 1974. If you sign it, you will not be able to ask the Law Society to check the bill. You will have the right to get our bill reviewed by a court if you claim that the agreement as a whole is unfair or unreasonable.

11. If the [sale/purchase] is not completed and you disagree with the bill but do not object to the agreement as a whole, you may ask a court to assess the reasonableness of the time spent, but not the hourly rates.

12. We will begin work when you tell us that you accept our terms by signing and returning to us the attached duplicate of the agreement [and by letting us have £[   ] on account of expenses. We will then pay expenses as they become due.]

....
[Name of Firm]

I accept the above terms

....
[Name of Client/s]

NOTES FOR GUIDANCE

Costs Agreement – Conveyancing

Fixed Fee

- This is intended to be an example of how to provide costs information to clients in a very simple form.

- It is not intended to be a non-contentious business agreement but allows the solicitor to review and vary the fixed fee as necessary.

- The other information required to be given by the Code will need to be set out for the client elsewhere.

TERMS OF BUSINESS FOUR: COSTS AGREEMENT – CONVEYANCING

Fixed Fee

Date of agreement:

1. **The agreement is a legally binding contract between you and us. Before you sign and return it to us, please read it carefully.**

2. The agreement is between us, [   ] of [   ], and you, [   ] of [   ].

3. The agreement relates to all the work we are to carry out in connection with your [sale/purchase] of [   ] but not to any other work you might ask us to do.

4. We will charge you £[   ].

5. We will add VAT to our charge at the rate that applies when the work is done. At the date of the agreement, VAT is 17.5%.

6. We set out below the other things that you will have to pay for, and an estimate of their cost:

Expense	*Cost £*
Search fees	
Stamp duty	
Land Registry fee	

    VAT is payable on certain expenses.

    Note: This is a non-exhaustive list. Solicitors are advised to provide as much detail as possible and to list all reasonably anticipated disbursements. If other expenses might be payable this should be made clear.

7. Your total charges and expenses for the [sale/purchase] will therefore be about £[   ]. This figure does not cover any work we do for your mortgage lenders.

8. If this firm does not complete the work, we will charge you £[   ] per hour for each hour of work. We will charge for writing letters, and for making and taking telephone calls in units of 1/10th of an hour. Our charges for considering letters received will be in units of 1/20th of an hour. Our total charge will not exceed £[fixed fee]. Our bill will also include VAT and expenses.

9. We will inform you of any unforeseen extra work – for example, due to unexpected difficulties or if your requirements or the circumstances change significantly during the matter. We will also inform you in writing of the estimated cost of the extra work when it arises and before incurring extra costs. We will attempt to agree an amended charge with you and will ask you to sign a note of this to be annexed to the agreement. If you do not agree our charge for the extra work, we may terminate the agreement and charge you on an hourly basis for work to date, as set out earlier.

10. We will begin work when you tell us that you accept our terms by signing and returning to us the attached duplicate of the agreement [and by letting us have £[   ] on account of expenses. We will then pay expenses as they become due.]

....
[Name of Firm]

I accept the above terms

....
[Name of Client/s]

VII.4. CON 29 Enquiries of Local Authority (parts I & II)[1]

Part I: Standard Enquiries of a Local Authority

The following text comprises the complete standard enquiries taken from form CON 29 introduced on 1 July 2002.

1. PLANNING AND BUILDING REGULATIONS

1.1. Planning and building regulation decisions and pending applications

What applications for any of the following (if applicable) have been granted, refused or are now pending:

(a) planning permissions;

(b) listed building consents;

(c) conservation area consents;

(d) certificates of lawfulness of use or development;

(e) building regulation approvals;

(f) building regulation completion certificates;

(g) certificate of compliance of a replacement window, rooflight, roof window or glazed door?

How can copies of any of the above be obtained?

1.2. Planning designations and proposals

What designations of land use for the property or the area, and what specific proposals for the property, are contained in any current adopted or proposed development plan?

2. ROADS

Which of the roads, footways and footpaths mentioned in Boxes B and C are:

(a) highways maintainable at public expense;

(b) subject to a current legal agreement for adoption and, if so, is the agreement supported by a bond or other financial security;

(c) to be made up at the cost of the frontagers under a current Council resolution;

(d) to be adopted without cost to the frontagers under a current Council resolution?

3. OTHER MATTERS

Apart from matters entered on the registers of local land charges, do any of the following matters apply to the property? How can copies of relevant documents be obtained?

1. © The Law Society 2002. Also see Appendix V.2.

CON 29 Part I   (This form must be submitted in duplicate)

STANDARD ENQUIRIES OF LOCAL AUTHORITY
(2002 Edition)

The Law Society

Please type or use BLOCK LETTERS

A.

To (Local Authority address):	For Local Authority Completion only
	Search No:
	The replies are attached
	Signed:
	Proper Officer
	Dated:

B.

Address of the land/property.

NLPG UPRN:

Address 1:

Address 2:

Street:

Locality:

Town/Village:

County:

Post Code:

C.

Other roadways, footways and footpaths:

D.

Note: A plan in duplicate (see note D) must be attached. This form may be returned if the land/property cannot easily be identified.

Optional enquires to be answered: YES / NO
(If so, please attach Optional Enquiries form)

Are any Additional enquiries attached?   YES / NO

E.

Fees of £
are enclosed / NLIS transfer (delete as applicable)

Signed:

Dated:

Reference:

Tel No:

Fax No:

E-mail Contact:

F.

Please reply to:

DX Address:

Notes

A. Enter name and address of Council for the area to whom this form has been officially submitted. If the property is near a local authority boundary, consider raising certain enquiries (e.g. road schemes) with the adjoining Council.

B. Enter address and description of the property. Please quote the NLPG UPRN (Unique Property Reference Number) where known.

C. Enter name and/or mark on plan any other roadways, footpaths and footways abutting the property (in addition to those entered in Box B) to which a reply to enquiry 2 and 3.6 is required.

D. A duplicate plan is required for all searches. If required, the Optional Enquiries form, ticked where necessary, should be attached along with the relevant fee. Additional enquiries must be attached on a separate sheet in duplicate and an additional fee will be charged for any that the Council is willing to answer.

E. Details of fees can be obtained from the Council, your chosen NLIS Channel or The Law Society

F. Enter the name and address / DX address of the person or company lodging this form.

© Law Society 2002

3.1. Land required for public purposes

Inclusion of the property in a category of land required for public purposes within Schedule 13, paras. 5 and 6 of the Town and Country Planning Act 1990.

3.2. Land to be acquired for road works

Inclusion of the property in land to be acquired for an approved scheme of Highway construction or improvement.

3.3. Drainage agreements and consents

(a) An agreement under the Building Act 1984, s.22 for drainage of any part of the property in combination with another building through a private sewer.

(b) Statutory agreement or consent for a building or extension to a building on the property to be constructed over or in the vicinity of a drain, sewer or disposal main.

Note: The sewerage undertaker for the area should also be asked about 3(b) and drainage generally.

3.4. Nearby road schemes

Location of any part of the property within 200 metres of:

(a) the centre line of a new trunk road or special road specified in an order, draft order or scheme notified to the Council by the appropriate Secretary of State; or

(b) the centre line of a proposed alteration or improvement to an existing road, notified to the Council by the appropriate Secretary of State, involving the construction of a subway, underpass, flyover, footbridge, elevated road or dual carriageway (whether or not within existing highway limits); or

(c) the limits of construction of a proposed alteration or improvement to an existing road, notified to the Council by the appropriate Secretary of State, involving the construction of a roundabout (other than a mini roundabout) or widening by the construction of one or more additional traffic lanes; or

(d) the limits of construction of an approved new road to be constructed by the Council or an approved alteration or improvement by the Council to an existing road involving the construction of a subway, underpass, flyover, footbridge, elevated road or dual carriageway (whether or not within existing highway limits) or the construction a roundabout (other than a mini roundabout) or widening by the construction of one or more additional traffic lanes; or

(e) the centre line of the possible route of a new road under proposals published for public consultation by the Council or by the appropriate Secretary of State; or

(f) the limits of construction of a possible alteration or improvement to an existing road involving the construction of a subway, underpass, flyover, footbridge, elevated road or dual carriageway (whether or not within existing highway limits) or the construction a roundabout (other than a mini roundabout) or widening by the construction of one or more additional traffic lanes, under proposals published for public consultation by the Council or by the appropriate Secretary of State.

Note: A mini-roundabout is a roundabout having a one-way circulatory carriageway around a flush or slightly raised circular marking less than 4 metres in diameter and with or without flared approaches.

3.5. Nearby railway schemes

Location of any part of the property within 200 metres of the centre line of a proposed railway, tramway, light railway or monorail.

3.6. Traffic schemes

Approval by the Council of any of the following, not yet implemented, in respect of such of the roads, footways and footpaths mentioned in Box B (and, if applicable, Box C) which abut the boundaries of the property:

(a) permanent stopping up or diversion;

(b) waiting or loading restrictions;

(c) one way driving;

(d) prohibition of driving;

(e) pedestrianisation;

(f) vehicle width or weight restriction;

(g) traffic calming works e.g. road humps;

(h) residents parking controls;

(i) minor road widening or improvement;

(j) pedestrian crossings;

(k) cycle tracks;

(l) bridge construction.

3.7. Outstanding notices

Current statutory notices relating to the property under legislation relating to building works, environment, health and safety at work, housing, highways or public health, other than those falling elsewhere within 3.1. to 3.13.

3.8. Infringement of building regulations

Proceedings authorised by the Council for infringement of the Building Regulations in respect of the property.

3.9. Notices, orders, directions and proceedings under Planning Acts

Subsisting notices, orders, directions, or proceedings, or those which the Council has decided to issue, serve, make or commence in the following categories (other than those which are shown in the Official Certificate of Search or which have been withdrawn or quashed) relating to the property:

(a) enforcement notice;

(b) stop notice;

(c) listed building enforcement notice;

(d) breach of condition notice;

(e) planning contravention notice;

(f) other notice relating to breach of planning control;

(g) listed building repairs notice;

(h) order for compulsory acquisition of a listed building with a minimum compensation provision;

(i) building preservation notice;

(j) direction restricting permitted development;

(k)　order revoking or modifying a planning permission or discontinuing an existing planning use;

(l)　tree preservation order;

(m)　proceedings for breach of a statutory planning agreement.

3.10.　Conservation area

Creation of the area before 31 August 1974 as a conservation area or a subsisting resolution to designate the area as a conservation area.

3.11.　Compulsory purchase

Inclusion of the property in land which is subject to an enforceable order or resolution for compulsory purchase.

3.12.　Contaminated land

(a)　Entry relating to the property in the register maintained under section 78R(1) of the Environmental Protection Act 1990.

(b)　Notice relating to the property served or resolved to be served under section 78B(3).

(c)　Consultation with the owner or occupier of the property having taken place, or being resolved to take place under s.78G(3) in relation to anything to be done on the property as a result of adjoining or adjacent land being contaminated land.

(d)　Entry in the register, or notice served or resolved to be served under section 78B(3) in relation to any adjoining or adjacent land, which has been identified as contaminated land because it is in such a condition that harm or pollution of controlled waters might be caused on the property.

3.13.　Radon gas

Location of the property in a Radon Affected Area.

Notes

The following notes further explain the Standard Enquiries of the new CON 29.

1.　Unless otherwise indicated, matters will be disclosed only if they apply directly to the property described in Box B.

2.　'Area' means any area in which the property is located.

3.　References to 'the Council' include any predecessor Council and also any council committee, sub-committee or other body or person exercising powers delegated by the Council and their 'approval' includes their decision to proceed. The replies given to certain enquiries cover knowledge and actions of both the District Council and County Council.

4.　References to the provisions of particular Acts of Parliament or Regulations include any provisions which they have replaced and also include existing or future amendments or re-enactments.

5.　The replies will be given in the belief that they are in accordance with information presently available to the officers of the replying Council, but none of the Councils or their officers accept legal responsibility for an incorrect reply, except for negligence. Any liability for negligence will extend to the person who raised the enquiries and the person on whose behalf they were raised. It will also extend to any other person who has knowledge (personally or through an agent) of the replies before the time when he purchases, takes a tenancy of, or lends money on the security of the property or (if earlier) the time when he becomes contractually bound to do so.

6.　This form should be read in conjunction with the guidance notes available separately.

Part II: Optional Enquiries of a Local Authority (2002)

The following text comprises the enquiries from the new CON 29 to be introduced on 1 July 2002.

4. ROAD PROPOSALS BY PRIVATE BODIES

What proposals by others,[1] still capable of being implemented, have the Council approved for any of the following, the limits of construction of which are within 200 metres of the property:

(a)   The construction of a new road; or

(b)   The alteration or improvement of an existing road, involving the construction, whether or not within existing highway limits, of a subway, underpass, flyover, footbridge, elevated road, dual carriageway, the construction of a roundabout (other than a mini roundabout)[2] or the widening of an existing road by the construction of one or more additional traffic lanes?

Notes

1.   This enquiry refers to proposals by bodies or companies (such as private developers) other than the Council (and where appropriate the County Council) or the Secretary of State.
2.   A mini roundabout is a roundabout having a one-way circulatory carriageway around a flush or slightly raised circular marking less than 4 metres in diameter and with or without flared approaches.

5. PUBLIC PATHS OR BYWAYS

5.1.   Is any public path, bridleway or road used as a public path or byway which abuts on, or crosses the property shown in a definitive map or revised definitive map prepared under Part IV of the National Parks and Access to the Countryside Act 1949 or Part III of the Wildlife and Countryside Act 1981?

5.2.   If so, please mark its approximate route on the attached plan.

6. ADVERTISEMENTS

Entries in the register

6.1.   Please list any entries in the register of applications, directions and decisions relating to consent for the display of advertisements.

6.2.   If there are any entries, where can that register be inspected?

Notices, proceedings and orders

6.3.   Except as shown in the Official Certificate of Search:

(a)   Has any notice been given by the Secretary of State or served in respect of a direction or proposed direction restricting deemed consent for any class of advertisement?

(b)   Have the Council resolved to serve a notice requiring the display of any advertisement to be discontinued?

(c)   If a discontinuance notice has been served, has it been complied with to the satisfaction of the Council?

(d)   Have the Council resolved to serve any other notice or proceedings relating to a contravention of the control of advertisements?

(e)   Have the Council resolved to make an order for the special control of advertisements for the area?

7. COMPLETION NOTICES

Which of the planning permissions in force have the Council resolved to terminate by means of a completion notice under section 94 of the Town and Country Planning Act 1990?

CON 29 Part II (This form must be submitted in duplicate)

OPTIONAL ENQUIRIES OF LOCAL AUTHORITY
(2002 Edition)
Please type or use BLOCK LETTERS

The Law Society

A.

To (Local authority address):

For Local Authority Completion only

Search No:

The replies are attached

Signed:

Proper Officer
Dated:

B.

Address of the land/property:

NLPG UPRN:

Address 1:

Address 2:

Street:

Locality:

Town/Village:

County:

Post Code:

C.

OPTIONAL ENQUIRIES, please tick as required:
(Note: questions 1-3 can be found on the CON 29 Part I Standard Enquiries of Local Authority)

☐ 4. Road proposals by private bodies

☐ 5. Public paths or byways

☐ 6. Advertisements

☐ 7. Completion Notices

☐ 8. Parks and countryside

☐ 9. Pipelines

☐ 10. Houses in multiple occupation

☐ 11. Noise Abatement

☐ 12. Urban development Areas

☐ 13. Enterprise Zones

☐ 14. Inner urban improvement areas

☐ 15. Simplified planning zones

☐ 16. Land maintenance notices

☐ 17. Mineral consultation areas

☐ 18. Hazardous substance consents

☐ 19. Environmental and pollution notices

☐ 20. Food safety notices

☐ 21. Hedgerow notices

D.

Fees of £
Are enclosed / NLIS transfer (delete as applicable)

Signed:

Dated:

Reference:

Tel no:

Fax No:

E-Mail contact:

Notes

A.   Enter name and address of Council for the area to whom this form has been officially submitted. If the property is near a local authority boundary, consider raising certain enquiries (e.g. road schemes) with the adjoining Council.

B.   Enter address and description of property. Please quote the NLPG UPRN (Unique Property Reference Number) where known.

C.   Tick where required.

D.   A fee will be charged for any enquiries that the Council is willing to answer. Details of fees can be obtained from the Council, your chosen NLIS Channel or the Law Society.

E.   Enter the name and address / DX address of the person or company lodging this form.

IMPORTANT NOTICE: A plan in duplicate must also be attached. This form may be returned if the land/property cannot be easily identified.

E.

Please reply to:

DX Address:

© Law Society 2002

VII

8. PARKS AND COUNTRYSIDE

Areas of outstanding natural beauty

8.1 Has any order under section 87 of the National Parks and Access to the Countryside Act 1949 been made?

National Parks

8.2. Is the property within a National Park designated under section 7 of the National Parks and Access to the Countryside Act 1949?

9. PIPELINES

Has a map been deposited under section 35 of the Pipelines Act 1962, or Schedule 7 of the Gas Act 1986, showing a pipeline laid through, or within 100 feet (30.48 metres) of the property?

10. HOUSES IN MULTIPLE OCCUPATION

Is the property included in a registration of houses scheme (houses in multiple occupation) under section 346 of the Housing Act 1985, containing control provisions as authorised by section 347 of that Act?

11. NOISE ABATEMENT

Noise abatement zone

11.1. Have the Council made, or resolved to make, any noise abatement zone order under section 63 of the Control of Pollution Act 1974 for the area?

Entries in register

11.2. Has any entry been recorded in the Noise Level Register kept pursuant to section 64 of the Control of Pollution Act 1974?

11.3. If there is any entry, how can copies be obtained and where can that Register be inspected?

12. URBAN DEVELOPMENT AREAS

12.1. Is the area an urban development area designated under Part XVI of the Local Government, Planning and Land Act 1980?

12.2. If so, please state the name of the urban development corporation and the address of its principal office.

13. ENTERPRISE ZONES

Is the area an enterprise zone designated under Part XVIII of the Local Government, Planning and Land Act 1980?

14. INNER URBAN IMPROVEMENT AREAS

Have the Council resolved to define the area as an improvement area under section 4 of the Inner Urban Areas Act 1978?

15. SIMPLIFIED PLANNING ZONES

15.1. Is the area a simplified planning zone adopted or approved pursuant to section 83 of the Town and Country Planning Act 1990?

15.2. Have the Council approved any proposal for designating the area as a simplified planning zone?

16. LAND MAINTENANCE NOTICES

Have the Council authorised the service of a maintenance notice under section 215 of the Town and Country Planning Act 1990?

17. MINERAL CONSULTATION AREAS

Is the area a mineral consultation area notified by the county planning authority under Schedule 1, para. 7 to the Town and Country Planning Act 1990?

18. HAZARDOUS SUBSTANCE CONSENTS

18.1. Please list any entries in the register kept pursuant to section 28 of the Planning (Hazardous Substances) Act 1990.

18.2. If there are any entries:

   (a)   How can copies of the entries be obtained?

   (b)   Where can the register be inspected?

19. ENVIRONMENTAL AND POLLUTION NOTICES

What outstanding statutory or informal notices have been issued by the Council under the Environmental Protection Act 1990 or the Control of Pollution Act 1974?

Note: This enquiry does not cover notices under Part IIA or Part III of the EPA, to which enquiries 3.12 or 3.7 apply.

20. FOOD SAFETY NOTICES

What outstanding statutory notices or informal notices have been issued by the Council under the Food Safety Act 1990?

21. HEDGEROW NOTICES

21.1. Please list any entries in the record maintained under regulation 10 of the Hedgerows Regulations 1997.

21.2. If there are any entries:

   (a)   How can copies of the matters entered be obtained?

   (b)   Where can the record be inspected?

Note

This form should be read in conjunction with the guidance notes available separately.

VII.5.   CON 29DW Standard Drainage and Water Enquiries[1]

Terms and Conditions

Customer and Clients are asked to note these terms, which govern the basis on which this drainage and water report is supplied

Definitions

'Company' means the water service company or their data service provider producing the Report.

'Order' means any request completed by the Customer requesting the Report.

'Report' means the drainage and/or water report prepared by The Company in respect of the Property.

'Property' means the address or location supplied by the Customer in the Order.

'Customer' means the person, company, firm or other legal body placing the Order, either on their own behalf as Client, or, as an agent for a Client.

'Client' means the person, company or body who is the intended recipient of the Report with an actual or potential interest in the Property.

Agreement

1.   The Company agrees to supply the Report to the Customer and the Client subject to these terms. The scope and limitations of the Report are described in paragraph 2 of these terms. Where the Customer is acting as an agent for the Client then the Customer shall be responsible for bringing these terms to the attention of the Client. The Customer and Client agree that the placing of an Order for a Report indicates their acceptance of these terms.

The Report

2.   Whilst The Company will use reasonable care and skill in producing the Report, it is provided to the Customer and the Client on the basis that they acknowledge and agree to the following:

2.1   The information contained in the Report can change on a regular basis so The Company cannot be responsible to the Customer and the Client for any change in the information contained in the Report after the date on which the Report was produced and sent to the Client.

2.2   The Report does not give details about the actual state or condition of the Property nor should it be used or taken to indicate or exclude actual suitability or unsuitability of the Property for any particular purpose, or relied upon for determining saleability or value, or used as a substitute for any physical investigation or inspection. Further advice and information from appropriate experts and professionals should always be obtained.

2.3   The information contained in the Report is based upon the accuracy of the address supplied by the Customer or Client.

2.4   The Report provides information as to the location and connection of existing services and should not be relied on for any other purpose. The Report may contain opinions or general advice to the

1. © Law Society 2002. Also see the Guidance Notes in Appendix V.3.

CON 29DW

STANDARD DRAINAGE & WATER ENQUIRIES
(England & Wales, 2002 Edition)

To :

Your Details.

Date of request:_____

Reference: _____

Company name:_____

Contact name : _____

Full postal address:_____

_____

_____

D.X. No:_____

Tel. No:_____

Fax. No_____

E-mail _____

Enter address and description of the land/property.

UPRN:_____Address 1:_____Address 2:_____

Street:_____Locality:_____

Town/Village:_____County:_____Post Town:_____

Post Code:_____Current Occupant or Business name: _____

The details below should be completed if the property is less than 5 years old.

Name of developer:_____Site Name & Phase:_____

_____Off Site Road Name:_____

A location plan must be enclosed.

Fee enclosed of £

Signed:

Official use	**STANDARD ENQUIRIES INCLUDE:**
	1.1 Please provide a copy extract from the public sewer map
	1.2 Does Foul drainage from the property drain to a public sewer?
	1.3 Does surface water from the property drain to a public sewer?
	1.4 Is any sewer serving or which is proposed to serve the property the subject of a current statutory agreement or an application for such an agreement? If so, what stage of the adoption process has been reached, and is the agreement supported by a bond?
	2.1 Does the public sewer map show any public sewer within the boundary of the property?
	2.2 Does the public sewer map show a public sewer within 30.48 metres (100 feet) of the buildings within the property?
	2.3 Is there a current statutory agreement or consent to erect a building or extension on the property over or in the vicinity of a public sewer or disposal main?
	3.1 Please provide a copy extract from the public water main map
	3.2 Which company supplies water to this area?
	3.3 Is the property connected to mains water supply?
	3.4 Does the map of waterworks show any vested water mains or assets within the boundary of the property?
	4.1 What is the basis for charging for sewerage and water supply at this property?

Completed by: Date:

© Law Society 2002

The Law Society

Customer and the Client and The Company cannot ensure that any such opinion or general advice is accurate, complete or valid and accepts no liability therefor.

2.5 The position and depth of apparatus shown on any maps attached to the Report are approximate, and are furnished as a general guide only, and no warranty as to its correctness is given or implied. The exact positions and depths should be obtained by excavation trial holes and the maps must not be relied on in the event of excavation or other works made in the vicinity of The Company's apparatus.

Liability

3.1 The Company shall not be liable to the Client for any failure, defect or non-performance of its obligations arising from any failure of or defect in any machine, processing system or transmission link or anything beyond The Company's reasonable control or the acts or omissions of any party for whom The Company are not responsible.

3.2 Where the Customer sells this report to a Client (other than in the case of a bona fide legal adviser recharging the cost of the Report as a disbursement) The Company shall not in any circumstances (whether for breach of contract, negligence or any other tort, under statute or statutory duty or otherwise at all) be liable for any loss or damage whatsoever and the Customer shall indemnify the Company in respect of any claim by the Client.

3.3 Where a report is requested for an address falling within a geographical area where two different Companies separately provide Water and Sewerage Services, then it shall be deemed that liability for the information given by either Company will remain with that Company in respect of the accuracy of the information supplied. A Company supplying information which has been provided to it by another Company for the purposes outlined in this agreement will therefore not be liable in any way for the accuracy of that information and will supply that information as agent for the Company from which the information was obtained.

3.4 The Report is produced for use in relation to individual domestic property transactions and if used other than in relation to individual domestic property transactions for example in relation to commercial developments of domestic properties or commercial properties for intended occupation by third parties the Company's entire liability (except to the extent provided by clause 3.5) in respect of all causes of action arising by reason of or in connection with the Report (whether for breach of contract, negligence or any other tort, under statute or statutory duty or otherwise at all) shall be limited to £5,000.

3.5 The Company shall accept liability for death or personal injury arising from its negligence.

Copyright and Confidentiality

4.1 The Customer and the Client acknowledge that the Report is confidential and is intended for the personal use of the Client. The copyright and any other intellectual property rights in the Report shall remain the property of The Company. No intellectual or other property rights are transferred or licensed to the Customer or the Client except to the extent expressly provided.

4.2 The Customer or Client is entitled to make copies of the Report (other than any maps contained in, or attached to the Report, where no copying is permitted).

4.3 The Customer and Client agree (in respect of both the original and any copies made) to respect and not to alter any trademark, copyright notice or other property marking which appears on the Report.

4.4 The maps contained in the Report are protected by Crown Copyright and must not be used for any purpose outside the context of the Report.

4.5 The Customer and the Client agree to indemnify The Company against any losses, costs, claims and damage suffered by The Company as a result of any breach by either of them of the terms of paragraphs 4.1 to 4.4 inclusive.

Payment

5.1　Unless otherwise stated all prices are inclusive of VAT. The Customer shall pay for the price of the Report specified by The Company, without any set off, deduction or counterclaim. Unless the Customer or Client has an account with The Company for payment for Reports, The Company must receive payments for Reports in full before the Report is produced. Where a customer orders an expedited search for 24 hour return, payment must be made in full to The Company within 48 hours of placing the Order. For Customers or Clients with accounts, payment terms will be as agreed with The Company.

General

6.1　If any provision of these terms is or becomes invalid or unenforceable, it will be taken to be removed from the rest of these terms to the extent that it is invalid or unenforceable. No other provision of these terms shall be affected.

6.2　These terms shall be governed by English law and all parties submit to the exclusive jurisdiction of the English courts.

6.3　Nothing in this notice shall in any way restrict the Customer or Client's statutory or any other rights of access to the information contained in the Report.

VII.6. Letter to lender if lender's instructions do not contain a certificate that it complies with Rule 6(3)[1]

To [Lender]

Re: Application Number:
Property:
Borrower:

Dear Sir,

Thank you for your instructions of .... relating to this matter. Since it is intended that we should act on behalf of the borrower as well as yourselves, the provisions of Solicitors' Practice Rule 6(3) will apply. Under the terms of this rule, unless a lender's mortgage instructions contain a certificate given by the lender that such instructions are subject to the limitations contained in paragraph (3)(c) and (3)(e) of the Practice Rule, we are under an obligation to give you a notification which limits our responsibilities to you.

We have read your instructions and cannot see the certificate referred to above. Accordingly, we notify you that our duties to you under your instructions will be limited to the matters contained in the certificate of title set out in the appendix to rule 6(3) and no more. We must draw to your attention the final paragraph of the certificate which states as follows:

'Our duties to you are limited to the matters set out in this certificate and we accept no further liability or responsibility whatsoever. The payment by you to us (by whatever means) of the mortgage advance or any part of it constitutes acceptance of this limitation and any assignment to you by the borrower of any rights of action against us to which the borrower may be entitled shall take effect subject to this limitation.'

You will understand that we are professionally bound by the requirements of this rule and are unable to depart from the requirement. Accordingly, if you are unable to accept this limitation we regret that you will have to instruct somebody else to act on your behalf. Will you please confirm your acceptance of the position.

Yours faithfully,

---

1. © The Law Society 1999. This letter originally appeared as 'Appendix A' to the guidance published in the Law Society's Gazette 'Practice rule 6(3) solicitor acting for lender and borrower' on 29 September 1999. The full article appears here in Appendix V.14. The companion to this letter, 'Appendix B' to the original article, is also reproduced here in Appendix VII.7.

VII.7. Letter to lender if lender's instructions (either general or specific to the transaction) appear to go beyond the limitations of Rule 6(3)[1]

To [Lender]

Application Number:
Property:
Borrower:

Dear Sir,

Thank you for your instructions of .... related to this matter, in accordance with which we shall be pleased to act.

As you will be aware, as solicitors we are bound by the requirements of Solicitors' Practice Rule 6(3) which limits the duties which we can undertake to a lender in cases (such as this one) where we are also acting for the borrower.

Although you have certified that your mortgage instructions are subject to the limitations contained in paragraphs (3)(c) and (3)(e) of Practice Rule 6, we are concerned that your instructions may fall outside the terms of the rule in certain respects which we mention in this letter.

We draw to your attention that since this is a residential property, the certificate of title will be in the form set out in the appendix to rule 6(3), the concluding paragraph of which reads as follows:

'*Our duties to you are limited to the matters set out in this certificate and we accept no further liability or responsibility whatsoever. The payment by you to us (by whatever means) of the mortgage advance or any part of it constitutes acceptance of this limitation and any assignment to you by the borrower of any rights of action against us to which the borrower may be entitled shall take effect subject to this limitation.*'

You will understand that we are professionally bound by the requirements of this rule and are unable to depart from the same. Accordingly, we respectfully point out that the instructions referred to below

---

1. © The Law Society 1999. This letter originally appeared as 'Appendix B' to the guidance published in the Law Society's Gazette 'Practice rule 6(3) solicitor acting for lender and borrower' on 29 September 1999. The full article appears here in Appendix V.14.

appear to us to conflict with paragraph (3)(c). The contractual effect of your certificate is to exclude any obligation (even if it is specifically stated in your instructions) which goes beyond the limitations of Practice Rule 6(3). The certificate of title will be accordingly given subject to such exclusion.

List of offending conditions:

[insert list here]

Yours faithfully,

VII.8. Model letter to wife where charging home to secure loan to husband or his business[1]

To be amended as necessary

Dear [   ]

This letter confirms the advice that [I] [we] gave you at our meeting [today] in respect of the proposal that your [freehold][leasehold] property known as [   ] (the Property) is to be mortgaged to [   ] (the Lender) to secure a loan from the Lender to [   ] (the Borrower).

The Lender requires that you are given this advice so that, if you sign [the mortgage] [and related documents] [a consent to mortgage] you will not be able to claim afterwards that you are not legally bound by [it] [them].

(1)   The Property is owned [in your sole name] [in the Borrower's sole name] [in the joint names of yourself and [   ]] and you [both] will be required to sign [the mortgage] [and related documents] [the consent to mortgage] in favour of the Lender.

(2)   Enclosed is a copy of the form of mortgage [and the mortgage conditions that are incorporated into it] [and related documents], which please read carefully and ask [me] [us] if you have any questions. The following is a summary of the main provisions and implications, but does not cover everything.

(3)   The mortgage is [initially] required to give the Lender security for a loan [of £   ] [a loan facility of up to £   ] to be provided to the Borrower.

[However, the mortgage will be on 'all monies' terms and will also give the Lender security over the Property for:

   (1)   any further loan or increased facility that the Borrower (individually or jointly with you or anyone else) may in future obtain from the Lender while the mortgage remains in existence, even if this is done without your knowledge or consent;

   (2)   any existing loans from the Lender to the Borrower (individually or jointly with you or anyone else), even if you do not know about them;

   (3)   any existing or future loans that you yourself may obtain (individually or jointly with anyone else) from the Lender while the mortgage remains in existence;

   (4)   any sums owing to the Lender, at any time while the mortgage remains in existence, by any other person or company if you or the Borrower has already given, or shall in future give, a guarantee for those sums to the Lender, and even if the Borrower has given or shall give such a guarantee without your knowledge and consent;

---

1. © The Law Society 2002. This model letter was issued by the Law Society's Conveyancing and Land Law Committee. It originally appeared as an appendix to the guidance – 'Undue influence – solicitors' duties post Etridge', which is reproduced here as Appendix V.18.

    (5)   interest on all such sums as charged by the Lender;

    (6)   *[anything else]*.

According to the terms of the loan the Lender can demand repayment at [any time,] [on fixed dates,] [by instalments,] *[set out repayment requirements]* .

(4)   During the subsistence of the mortgage, [you] [the Borrower] must:

    (1)   keep the Property insured in accordance with the Lender's requirements;

    (2)   keep the Property in good repair;

    (3)   not make any structural alterations or changes of use without the Lender's consent;

    (4)   not let the Property or take in lodgers without the Lender's consent;

    (5)   comply with all covenants and restrictions affecting the Property ;

    (6)   *[anything else]*.

(5)   The mortgage will give the Lender a [first] charge over the Property as security for all the sums mentioned in paragraph (3) above. You could lose the Property if the Borrower's business does not prosper, or if the borrowing is increased unwisely. This is because, if any loan repayment or interest charge is not paid on time, the Lender would be entitled to enforce the mortgage by taking court proceedings to evict you and any other occupiers from the Property and sell the Property in order to obtain repayment. Alternatively the Lender could appoint a receiver to take possession of the Property from you and any other occupiers.

(6)   [The Lender reserves the right to transfer the benefit of the mortgage to another lender.]

(7)   [In addition, the mortgage will contain a covenant by you to pay all sums falling within paragraph (3) above if the Borrower fails to pay them [up to a maximum of £   plus interest charged by the Lender]. This means that [up to that level] you will be a guarantor for the liabilities of the Borrower to the Lender, you will be personally liable for those sums, you could be sued by the Lender for them and, if the value of the Property and your other assets is insufficient to meet those sums, you could be made bankrupt as well as losing the Property.]

(8)   *[Any other features of the mortgage needing comment?]*

The above legal advice relates to the effect of the proposed mortgage documents and the types of risks that arise. [However, [I am] [we are] not qualified to assess the likelihood of those risks actually materialising. That depends largely on the financial standing and prospects of the Borrower [and his business], although you should also consider whether the sums secured could be repaid from the sale value of the Property and your other assets. Therefore, before you decide whether to agree to sign [the mortgage] [the consent to mortgage], you should get help on assessing the risks by taking advice on those important financial aspects from a chartered accountant or other qualified professional financial adviser who should be independent of the Borrower].

You do not have to agree to these arrangements at all if you consider that the risks are too great or if you think that these arrangements are of no advantage to you. If you are generally willing but find particular terms unacceptable, it may be possible to negotiate variations of those terms with the Lender in order to make them acceptable to you. These decisions are yours and yours alone.

[As you know, [I am] [my firm is] also acting for the Borrower in this matter [and also for the Lender in an administrative capacity] but I have given you this advice independently. Nevertheless you should consider whether you want further legal advice from a completely separate solicitor before you make a final decision in connection with the mortgage].

Please sign paragraph (A) at the end of the enclosed copy of this letter to acknowledge that you have been given, and have understood, this advice.

If and when you decide that you will enter into the mortgage and will not require the Lender to vary any of the terms, please also sign paragraph (B) to confirm that decision and to allow the Lender to be told that you have received this advice.

Yours [   ]

ACKNOWLEDGEMENTS

(A) I confirm that I have read this letter and have received and understood the advice given in it.

Signed: .... Date: ....

(B) I confirm that that I have decided, of my own free will, to enter into the mortgage, I do not require the Lender to vary any of the terms, [I do not require any further legal advice,] and I agree that the Lender may be told that I have received the advice in this letter.

Signed: .... Date: ....

VII.9. Recommended form of undertaking for discharge of building society mortgages[1]

'In consideration of your today completing the purchase of .... WE HEREBY UNDERTAKE forthwith to pay over to the .... Building Society the money required to redeem the mortgage/legal charge dated .... and to forward the receipted mortgage/legal charge to you as soon as it is received by us from the .... Building Society.'

---

1. The following text appears in *The Guide to the Professional Conduct of Solicitors 1999* as Annex 25B.

VII.10. Report on proposed purchase (domestic)[1]

**Of the property known as
15 High Hill, Harkley, Herts**

prepared for Mr and Mrs Harvey Hart

1. The Property

The Property is known as 15 High Hill, Harkley, Herts HH1 2ZZ. A copy of the Land Registry title plan is attached [*not produced in this book*] showing the extent of the property edged in red.

Land Registry title plans are to a small scale and are not intended to show the precise location of each boundary; these should be checked on site and any significant discrepancies referred to us so that we can seek clarification from the sellers.

2. Title

The Property is freehold. The title number is HH123456. It is registered at the Land Registry with 'absolute' title, which means that ownership is guaranteed by the Registry. You should inspect the property to ensure that it is only occupied by the seller and his immediate family and let us know if this is not the case. The property is being sold to you with full vacant possession on completion.

3. Rights passing with the Property

The Property has the benefit of a right of way over the alleyway at the rear of the Property, marked in brown on the Land Registry plan, leading to the road known as Hall Hollow. This right is on foot only, so there is no right to drive vehicles (or ride bicycles or horses) along it. The deeds do not make provision for any person to be responsible for maintaining or clearing the alleyway but do provide for the owner of the Property to pay a fair contribution towards any expenditure on such matters. The sellers state that they are not aware of anyone carrying out such works and have not been asked to pay anything in this regard. If the alleyway needs maintaining so that you can walk along it, as a matter of general law the right of way would give you the right to do necessary maintenance, but wholly at your own cost.

4. Rights over the Property

The owner of the property known as 13 High Hill has a right of way on foot across the south-west corner of the rear garden of the Property, to enable him to pass between the end of his garden and the alleyway. The route is marked in blue on the Land Registry plan. This right was apparently granted because the alleyway stops level with the west boundary of the Property and does not run behind the garden of number 13. The sellers state that the neighbour has never exercised this right during their 8 years of ownership of the Property; however, this does not mean that the right has legally lapsed.

---

1. This Report has been written by Frances Silverman and the Editorial Board of the Conveyancing Handbook.

5. Covenants

A number of restrictive covenants were imposed on the owner of the Property when the plot was sold to the original house builder in 1898. It appears that similar covenants were imposed on all the plots in the street, and these covenants may still be enforceable by one house owner against another; if you purchase the Property, you may be obliged to observe them, and you may be entitled to require the neighbouring owners to observe them. The following is a summary of those that may still be relevant:

(1) not to park any caravan or similar vehicle on the Property;

(2) not to erect more than one single house on the Property, apart from a greenhouse or other usual outbuilding;

(3) not to use any house for business use but only as a private dwelling;

(4) not to cause nuisance or annoyance to neighbours.

Even if these covenants are not strictly enforceable in law, planning restrictions imposed by the local authority may in practice have a similar effect.

A positive covenant was also imposed in 1898, requiring the owner of the Property to maintain the fence on the east boundary of the Property. We have marked this fence with the letter 'T' on the attached copy of the Land Registry plan. Whilst it is unlikely that anyone could legally enforce compliance with this covenant, in practice you should be prepared to maintain this fence, and the other fences bounding the Property, at your own cost.

6. Information from the Sellers

The solicitors acting for the sellers, Henry and Hetty Hodgson, have supplied us with a package of information under the Law Society TransAction scheme. We attach copies of the following items supplied to us in that package:

(a) **Seller's Property Information Form**
This gives information about boundaries, disputes, notices, guarantees, services, rights and other matters. Our comments are:

(1) the information on boundaries must be read subject to our comment about the eastern fence, in paragraph 5 of this Report;

(2) the building work mentioned in reply to question 10.3 of the Form did not need planning permission, but future enlargement of the building might.

(b) **List of Fixtures Fittings and Contents**
This indicates which items at the Property are included in the sale and which are not. Please let us know if anything stated to be excluded was in fact supposed to be included, or if you reach agreement with the sellers to buy any of the excluded items.

We understand that this sale is dependent upon the sellers buying another property, but their solicitors tell us that this is progressing well and they hope to be in a position to exchange contracts on both transactions at the end of next month.

7. Information from the Local Authority, etc.

We have made a search in the Register of Local Land Charges and have raised enquiries with the local council, and have obtained the following information which relates to the property which you are intending to buy. A separate search would be needed to obtain information relating to neighbouring properties:

(1) High Hill and Hall Hollow are publicly maintained roads, but the rear alleyway is not;

(2) there are no current plans for road improvements or new roads within 200 metres of the Property;

(3) foul drainage is believed to be connected to the public sewer but the means of connection is not known (a drain running between a house and the public sewer is not maintained at public expense and you should consult your surveyor as to the likelihood of your having to repair or maintain any drain connected to the property).

None of the other replies by the council to our enquiries need to be drawn to your attention.

Because of the location of the Property, we have also made a search with British Coal in order that you or your surveyor can assess the risk of future subsidence due to coal extraction beneath the Property. A statutory compensation scheme is available if you suffer damage as a result of mining works. British Coal has given the following response:

(1) Two seams of coal have been mined at an approximate depth of 200 metres under or near the Property, the last working being in 1990.

(2) There are presently no workings taking place within influencing distance of the Property.

(3) Although coal exists unworked, British Coal states that the possibility of future working is considered unlikely.

8. Outgoings

The Property is in band F for council tax purposes. The annual water charge (currently £XXX) is payable to Hartford Water Company. The water supply at the Property is not metered.

9. The Purchase Contract

This is in a form incorporating the Standard Conditions of Sale, which are widely used for this type of transaction. The main provisions of the contract are:

(1) The purchase price is £XXX,XXX. (No VAT will be payable on this.) The price includes the items shown on the list attached to the contract, which corresponds with the list of Fixtures, Fittings and Chattels mentioned above.

(2) On exchange of contracts, you must pay a deposit of £XX,XXX. If we cannot complete your purchase of the Property due to the Hodgsons' default, you will become entitled to the return of the deposit (and may be able to claim damages for your loss). However, under the Standard Conditions of Sale, all or part of the deposit money can be used by Mr and Mrs Hodgson to pay the deposit on their new property, and only the remainder, if any, will be retained by their solicitors as 'stakeholder' until we satisfactorily complete the purchase. Whilst this arrangement has become common practice, we must warn you that in the event of the matter not completing, it may be more difficult to obtain repayment of deposit money which has been used by the Hodgsons in that way, than if the whole deposit was retained by their solicitors until completion; on the other hand, very few house purchases totally fail to complete (though completion is occasionally delayed), and you may be prepared to take this risk rather than insisting that the Hodgsons incur the expense of obtaining separate bridging finance for the deposit on their new property. Please discuss this with us if you are concerned about it.

(3) The completion date will be inserted just before contracts are exchanged. We will discuss it with you at that time so that a date acceptable to both you and the Hodgsons can be fixed. This date will then be the date on which the transaction is to be completed: the Hodgsons must vacate the Property on that date, if they do not vacate earlier, and we must send the completion

money to their solicitors to reach their bank account by 2 p.m. that afternoon. You will be liable to pay daily interest at X% per year above bank base rate if cleared funds are not made available to us in time to remit the completion money early enough, so we will need to receive the funds (other than the loan from your Building Society, mentioned below) from you either by cheque in favour of this firm reaching us at least five working days before the completion date, or by bank transfer into this firm's bank account preferably on the day before the completion date. Nearer the time, we will let you know how much we require; this will include a sum to cover our fees, disbursements paid or payable by us (including stamp duty of £X,XXX and registration fees of £XXX) and VAT.

(4) You are buying the Property in its actual state and condition. You must be satisfied about this from your own inspection of the Property and from your surveyor's report. If you expect the sellers to remedy (or pay for the remedy of) any defects, this will have to be agreed with them before contracts are exchanged and special provisions added to the contract. Your lender has asked us to point out to you that the valuation undertaken by their surveyor may not reveal all the defects in the Property.

(5) The Property remains at the sellers' risk until completion, and the sellers must hand it over in its present condition, except for fair wear and tear. You would be entitled to withdraw from the transaction, with the return of your deposit, if the Property was so badly damaged before the completion date as to make it unusable, and the sellers would have a similar right if the damage was caused by a risk against which they could not have been expected to insure.

10. Mortgage

We have received instructions from the Highland Building Society to act for them on a mortgage loan to assist you in buying the Property. We have to report to them on the result of our investigations about the Property and also on any discrepancies between the details of the transaction known to us and the details you gave the Society with your mortgage application (e.g. as to the purchase price). So far, the documents supplied to us do not show any such discrepancies.

The main terms of the proposed mortgage are:

(1) The loan will be £XX,XXX.

(2) Interest is variable at the discretion of the Society, but will initially be at the rate of X% per year.

(3) The loan is repayable, with interest, over XX years, by monthly instalments comprising a mixture of capital and interest. Initially the instalments will be £XXX per month, but this is variable and the Society will recalculate the amount as a result of changes in the rate of interest. You will be required to pay the instalments by bank standing order. Failure to pay any instalments will entitle the Society to call for immediate repayment of the entire loan.

(4) The loan will be to both of you, and you will both be individually legally responsible for ensuring that the instalment payments are duly made and that the other provisions of the mortgage, mentioned below, are observed.

(5) The loan and interest will be secured on a first legal mortgage over the Property. This will give the Society various rights if you fail to pay the instalments, including the right to apply to the court to evict you and your family so that the Society can sell the Property in order to recoup the outstanding loan and any unpaid interest. If the sale proceeds exceed the amount due to the Society, the surplus will be paid to you (or to any second lender), but if there is a shortfall the Society can sue you for it.

(6) The mortgage will impose a number of standard obligations and restrictions, the most important being:

(a) you must keep the Property in good repair;

(b) you must insure the Property with insurers agreed between you and the Society;

(c) you must not alter the Property, or change its use, without the Society's prior consent;

(d) you must not let any part of the Property without the Society's prior consent;

(e) no second or subsequent mortgage must be taken out without the Society's prior consent.

(7) The mortgage will be security for any future loans you may borrow from the Society, as well as for the loan mentioned above.

The full text of the mortgage terms are set out in the enclosed book from the Society, and we recommend that you read them.

11. Environmental matters

We have/have not made enquiries relating to environmental matters affecting the property. [Our enquiries revealed the following information (*set out details*).]

Please ask us if you have any queries about this report or on any other aspect of this transaction.

12. Joint purchase

[*Where there are two or more buyers explain the difference between joint tenancy and tenancy in common and request the buyers to confirm their choice to you.*]

(Name of solicitors)

VII

VII.11. Standard Business Lease (of whole and of part)

Licences

The Law Society holds the copyright in the leases and grants licences to print the documents. The printed forms are available from law stationers and from the Law Society's shop. However, it is intended that solicitors who wish to do so will be licensed to produce the leases on their word processors but it is on the understanding that:

1.   The format of the standard leases is adopted as closely as practicable in the form of the printed lease.

2.   No alterations or additions whatsoever are to be made to the text of the standard clauses. This means that cll 1 to 14.6 of the lease of the whole building and cll 1 to 17.6 of the lease of part of the building are to be reproduced without any amendment whatsoever.

3.   The lease must contain a statement that it is in the form of the Law Society Business Lease.

4.   All variations, whether being amendments or additional clauses, must be set out at the end of the document in an additional page to be attached to the lease which will deal with all alterations and variations to the standard clauses and any additional provisions required. It is essential that neither alterations nor deletions are made to the text itself.

5.   The licence to reproduce the lease does not extend to printing the lease. Local law societies will be granted a licence to print both forms of the leases on favourable terms should they wish to do so.

6.   Photocopies of the leases must not be used other than as file copies.

The Law Society business leases (whole and part of building) are set out on the following pages.

THE LAW SOCIETY

DATE _____

LANDLORD _____

OF _____

_____

LETS TO

TENANT _____

OF _____

THE PROPERTY KNOWN AS

PROPERTY _____

_____

RESIDENTIAL [WHICH INCLUDES
ACCOMMODATION

_____]

FOR THE PERIOD STARTING ON

LEASE PERIOD _____

AND ENDING ON

_____

FOR USE (EXCEPT ANY RESIDENTIAL ACCOMODATION) AS

USE ALLOWED _____

OR ANY OTHER USE TO WHICH THE LANDLORD CONSENTS (AND THE LANDLORD IS

NOT ENTITLED TO WITHHOLD THAT CONSENT UNREASONABLY)

THE TENANT PAYING THE LANDLORD RENT AT THE RATE OF

_____ POUNDS

RENT

(£ _____)

A YEAR BY THESE INSTALMENTS:

(A) ON THE DATE OF THIS LEASE, A PROPORTIONATE SUM FOR THE PERIOD

STARTING ON

_____ TO

_____ AND THEN

(B) EQUAL MONTHLY INSTALMENTS IN ADVANCE ON THE

_____ DAY OF EACH MONTH

RENT DAYS

THE RENT MAY BE INCREASED (UNDER CLAUSE 8) WITH EFFECT FROM EVERY

RENT REVIEW DATES   ANNIVERSARY OF THE START OF THE LEASE PERIOD

This lease is granted on the terms printed on pages 2 to 4, as added to or varied by any terms appearing on any attached continuation page

© The Law Society   **L.S.2 (Whole) 5/96**

1

TENANT'S OBLIGATIONS

1 PAYMENTS

1. The Tenant is to pay the Landlord:

1.1 the rent

1.2 the amount of every premium which the Landlord pays to insure the property under this lease, to be paid within 14 days after the Landlord gives written notice of payment (and this amount is to be paid as rent)

and the following sums on demand:

1.3 a fair proportion (decided by a surveyor the Landlord nominates) of the cost of repairing maintaining and cleaning:

party walls, party structures, yards, gardens, roads, paths, gutters, drains, sewers, pipes, conduits, wires, cables and things used or shared with other property

1.4 the cost (including professional fees) of any works to the property which the Landlord does after the Tenant defaults

1.5 the costs and expenses (including professional fees) which the Landlord incurs in:

(a) dealing with any application by the Tenant for consent or approval, whether or not it is given

(b) preparing and serving a notice of a breach of the Tenant's obligations, under section 146 of the Law of Property Act 1925, even if forfeiture of this lease is avoided without a court order

(c) preparing and serving schedules of dilapidations either during the lease period or recording failure to give up the property in the appropriate state or repair when this lease ends

1.6 interest at the Law Society's interest rate on any of the above payments when more than fourteen days overdue, to be calculated from its due date

and in making payment under this clause:

(a) nothing is to be deducted or set off

(b) any value added tax payable is to be added.

2

2. The Tenant is also to make the following payments, with value added tax where payable:

2.1 all periodic rates, taxes and outgoings relating to the property, including any imposed after the date of this lease (even if of a novel nature), to be paid promptly to the authorities to whom they are due

2.2 the cost of the grant, renewal or continuation of any licence or registration for using the property for the use allowed, to be paid promptly to the appropriate authority when due

2.3 a registration fee of £20 for each document which this lease required the Tenant to register, to be paid to the Landlord's solicitors when presenting the document for registration

3 USE

3. The Tenant is to comply with the following requirements as to the use of the property and any part of it and is not to authorise or allow anyone else to contravene them:

3.1 to use the property, except any residential accommodation, only for the use allowed

3.2 to use any residential accommodation only as a home for one family

3.3 not to do anything which might invalidate any insurance policy covering the property or which might increase the premium

3.4 not to hold an auction sale in the property

3.5 not to use the property for any activities which are dangerous, offensive, noxious, illegal or immoral, or which are or may become a nuisance or annoyance to the Landlord or to the owner or occupier of any neighbouring property

3.6 not to display any advertisements on the outside of the property or which are visible from the outside unless the Landlord consents (and the Landlord is not entitled to withhold that consent unreasonably)

3.7 not to overload the floors or walls of the property

3.8 to comply with the terms of every Act of Parliament, order, regulation, bye-law, rule, licence and registration authorising or

regulating how the property is used, and to obtain, renew and continue any licence or registration which is required

4 ACCESS

4. The Tenant is to give the Landlord, or anyone authorised by him in writing, access to the property:

4.1 for these purposes:

(a) inspecting the condition of the property, or how it is being used

(b) doing works which the Landlord is permitted to do under clause 5.8(c)

(c) complying with any statutory obligation

(d) viewing the property as a prospective buyer or mortgagee or, during the last six months if the lease period, as a prospective tenant

(e) valuing the property

(f) inspecting, cleaning or repairing neighbouring property, or any sewers, drains, pipes, wires, cables serving neighbouring property

4.2 and only on seven days' written notice except in an emergency

4.3 and during normal business hours except in an emergency

4.4 and the Landlord is promptly to make good all damage caused to the property and any goods there in exercising these rights

5 CONDITION AND WORK

5. The Tenant is to comply with the following duties in relation to the property:

5.1 to maintain the state and condition of the property but the Tenant need not alter or improve it except if required under clause 5.7

5.2 to decorate the inside and outside of the property:

(a) in every fifth year of the lease period

(b) in the last three months of the lease period (however it ends) except to the extent that it has been decorated in the previous year

and on each occasion the Tenant is to use the colours and the types of finish used previously

5.3 but the Tenant need only make good damage caused by an insured risk to the extent that the insurance money has not been paid because of any act or default of the Tenant

5.4 not to make any structural alterations, external alterations or additions to the property

5.5 not to make any other alterations unless with the Landlord's consent in writing (and the Landlord is not entitled to withhold that consent unreasonably)

5.6 to keep any plate glass in the property insured for its full replacement cost with reputable insurers, to give the Landlord details of that insurance on request, and to replace any plate glass which becomes damaged

5.7 to do the work to the property which any authority acting under an Act of Parliament requires, even if it alters or improves the property. Before the Tenant does so, the Landlord is to:

(a) give his consent in writing to the work

(b) contribute a fair proportion of the cost of the work taking into account any value to him of the work

5.8 if the Tenant fails to do any work which this lease requires him to do and the Landlord gives him written notice to do it, the Tenant is to:

(a) start the work within two months, or immediately in case of emergency, and

(b) proceed diligently with the work

(c) in default, permit the Landlord to do the work

5.9 any dispute arising under clause 5.7(b) is to be decided by arbitration under clause 14.5

6 TRANSFER ETC.

6. The Tenant is to comply with the following:

6.1 the Tenant is not to share occupation of the property and no part of it is to be transferred, sublet or occupied separately from the remainder

L.S.2(Whole)/2

2

6.2 the Tenant is not to transfer or sublet the whole of the property unless the Landlord gives his written consent in advance, and the Landlord is not entitled to withhold that consent unreasonably

6.3 any sublease is to be in terms which are consistent with this lease, but is not to permit the sub-tenant to underlet

6.4 within four weeks after the property is transferred mortgaged or sublet, the Landlord's solicitors are to be notified and a copy of the transfer mortgage or sublease sent to them for registration with the fee payable under clause 2.3

6.5 if the Landlord requires, a tenant who transfers the whole of the property is to give the Landlord a written guarantee, in the terms set out in the Guarantee Box, that the Transferee will perform his obligations as Tenant

7   OTHER MATTERS

7. The Tenant:

7.1 is to give the Landlord a copy of any notice concerning the property or any neighbouring property as soon as he receives it

7.2 is to allow the Landlord, during the last six months of the lease period, to fix a notice in a reasonable position on the outside of the property announcing that it is for sale or to let

7.3 is not to apply for planning permission relating to the use or alteration of the property unless the Landlord gives written consent in advance

8   RENT REVIEW

8.1 On each rent review date, the rent is to increase to the market rent if that is higher than the rent applying before that date

8.2 The market rent is the rent which a willing tenant would pay for the property on the open market, if let to him on the rent review date by a willing landlord on a lease on the same terms as this lease without any premium and for a period equal to the remainder of the lease period, assuming that at that date:

(a) the willing tenant takes account of any likelihood that he would be entitled to a new lease of the property when the lease ends, but does not take account of any goodwill belonging to anyone who had occupied the property

(b) the property is vacant and had not been occupied by the Tenant or any sub-tenant

(c) the property can immediately be used

(d) the property is in the condition required by this lease and any damage caused by any of the risks insured under clause 11 has been made good

(e) during the lease period no tenant nor sub-tenant has done anything to the property to increase or decrease its rental value and "anything" includes work done by the Tenant to comply with clause 5.7, but nothing else which the Tenant was obliged to do under this lease

8.3 If the Landlord and the Tenant agree the amount of the new rent, a statement of that new rent, signed by them, is to be attached to this lease

8.4 If the Landlord and the Tenant have not agreed the amount of the new rent two months before the rent review date, either of them may require the new rent to be decided by arbitration under clause 14.5

8.5

(a) The Tenant is to continue to pay rent at the rate applying before the rent review date until the next rent day after the new rent is agreed or decided

(b) Starting on that rent day, the Tenant is to pay the new rent

(c) On that rent day, the Tenant is also to pay any amount by which the new rent since the rent review date exceeds the rent paid, with interest on that amount at 2% below the Law Society's interest rate.

9   DAMAGE

9. If the property is damaged by any of the risks to be insured under clause 11 and as a result of that damage the property, or any part of it, cannot be used for the use allowed:

9.1 the rent, or a fair proportion of it, is to be suspended for three years or until the property is fully restored, if sooner

9.2 if at any time it is unlikely that the property will be fully restored within three years from the date of the damage, the Landlord (so long as he has not delayed the restoration) or the Tenant can end this lease by giving one month's notice to the other during the three

year period, in which case

(a) the insurance money belongs to the Landlord and

(b) the Landlord's obligation to make good damage under clause 11 ceases

9.3 a notice given outside the time limits in clause 9.2 is not effective

9.4 the Tenant cannot claim the benefit of this clause to the extent that the insurers refuse to pay the insurance money because of his act or default

9.5 any dispute arising under any part of this clause is to be decided by arbitration under clause 14.5

LANDLORD'S OBLIGATIONS AND FORFEITURE RIGHTS

10   QUIET ENJOYMENT

10. While the Tenant complies with the terms of this lease, the Landlord is to allow the Tenant to possess and use the property without lawful interference from the Landlord or any trustee for the Landlord

11   INSURANCE

11. The Landlord agrees with the Tenant:

11.1 the Landlord is to keep the property (except the plate glass) insured with reputable insurers to cover:

(a) full rebuilding, site clearance, professional fees, value added tax and three years' loss of rent

(b) against fire, lightning, explosion, earthquake, landslip, subsidence, heave, riot, civil commotion, aircraft, aerial devices, storm, flood, water, theft, impact by vehicles, damage by malicious persons and vandals and third party liability and any other risks reasonably required by the Landlord

so far as cover is available at the normal insurance rates for the locality and subject to reasonable excesses and exclusions

11.2 and to take all necessary steps to make good as soon as possible damage to the property caused by insured risks except to the extent that the insurance money is not paid because of the act or default of the Tenant

11.3 and to give the Tenant at his request once a year particulars of the policy and evidence from the insurer that it is in force

11.4 and that the Tenant is not responsible for any damage for which the Landlord is compensated under the insurance policy

12   FORFEITURE

12. This lease comes to an end if the Landlord forfeits it by entering any part of the property, which the Landlord is entitled to do whenever:

(a) payment of any rent is fourteen days overdue, even if it was not formally demanded

(b) the Tenant has not complied with any of the terms in this lease

(c) the Tenant if any individual (and if more than one, any of them) is adjudicated bankrupt or an interim receiver of his property is appointed

(d) the Tenant if a company (and if more than one, any of them) goes into liquidation (unless solely for the purpose of amalgamation or reconstruction when solvent), or has an administrative receiver appointed or has an administration order made in respect of it

The forfeiture of this lease does not cancel any outstanding obligation of the Tenant or a Guarantor

13   END OF LEASE

13. When this lease ends the Tenant is to:

13.1 return the property to the Landlord leaving it in the state and condition in which this lease required the Tenant to keep it

13.2 (if the Landlord so requires) remove anything the Tenant fixed to the property and make good any damage which that causes

L.S.2(Whole)/3

3

VII

GENERAL

14 PARTIES' RESPONSIBILITY

14.1 Whenever more than one person or company is the Landlord, the Tenant or the Guarantor, their obligations can be enforced against all or both of them jointly and against each individually

LANDLORD

14.2

(a) The obligations in this lease continue to apply to the Landlord until he is released by the Tenant or by a declaration of the court

(b) The current owner of the Landlord's interest in the property must comply with the Landlord's obligations in this lease

TENANT

14.3

(a) A transfer of this lease releases the Tenant from any future obligations under it. This does not apply in the case of a transfer made without the Landlord's consent or as a result of the Tenant's death or bankruptcy

(b) After a transfer, the Tenant's successor must comply with the Tenant's obligations in this lease

SERVICE OF NOTICES

14.4 The rules about serving notices in Section 196 of the Law of Property Act 1925 (as since amended) apply to any notice given under this lease

ARBITRATION

14.5 Any matter which this lease requires to be decided by arbitration is to be referred to a single arbitrator under the Arbitration Acts. The Landlord and the Tenant may agree the appointment of the arbitrator, or either of them may apply to the President of the Royal Institution of Chartered Surveyors to make the appointment.

HEADINGS

14.6 The headings do not form part of this lease

STAMP DUTY

15. This lease has not been granted to implement an agreement for a lease

GUARANTEE BOX

The terms in this box only take effect if a guarantor is named and then only until the Tenant transfers this lease with the Landlord's written consent. The Guarantor must sign this lease.

'Guarantor':

of

agrees to compensate the Landlord for any loss incurred as a result of the Tenant failing to comply with an obligation in this lease during the lease period or any statutory extension of it. If the Tenant is insolvent and this lease ends because it is disclaimed, the Guarantor agrees to accept a new lease, if the Landlord so requires, in the same form but at the rent then payable. Even if the Landlord gives the Tenant extra time to comply with an obligation, or does not insist on strict compliance with terms of this lease, the Guarantor's obligation remains fully effective.

THIS DOCUMENT CREATES LEGAL RIGHTS AND LEGAL OBLIGATIONS. DO NOT SIGN IT UNTIL YOU HAVE CONSULTED A SOLICITOR. THERE IS A CODE OF PRACTICE CONCERNING COMMERCIAL LEASES IN ENGLAND AND WALES PUBLISHED UNDER THE AUSPICES OF THE DEPARTMENT OF THE ENVIRONMENT.

Signed as a deed by/on behalf of the
Landlord and delivered in the presence of:

....

Witness

....

Witness's occupation and address

.... Landlord

Signed as a deed by/on behalf of the
Tenant and delivered in the presence of:

....

Witness

....

Witness's occupation and address

.... Tenant

Signed as a deed by/on behalf of the
Guarantor and delivered in the presence of:

....

Witness

....

Witness's occupation and address

.... Guarantor

THE LAW SOCIETY

L.S.2(Whole)/4

4

THE LAW SOCIETY

DATE

LANDLORD

OF

LETS TO

TENANT

OF

THE PROPERTY KNOWN AS

PROPERTY

WHICH IS PART OF

BUILDING

(WHICH, WHEN REFERRED TO IN THIS LEASE, INCLUDES ITS GROUNDS) FOR THE PERIOD STARTING ON

AND ENDING ON

LEASE PERIOD

FOR USE AS

USE ALLOWED

OR ANY OTHER USE TO WHICH THE LANDLORD CONSENTS (AND THE LANDLORD IS

NOT ENTITLED TO WITHHOLD THAT CONSENT UNREASONABLY)

THE TENANT PAYING THE LANDLORD RENT AT THE RATE OF

POUNDS

RENT

(£   )

A YEAR BY THESE INSTALMENTS:

(A) ON THE DATE OF THIS LEASE, A PROPORTIONATE SUM FOR THE PERIOD

STARTING ON

TO

AND THEN

(B) EQUAL MONTHLY INSTALMENTS IN ADVANCE ON THE

DAY OF EACH MONTH

RENT DAYS

THE RENT MAY BE INCREASED (UNDER CLAUSE 9) WITH EFFECT FROM EVERY

RENT REVIEW DATES   ANNIVERSARY OF THE START OF THE LEASE PERIOD

This lease is granted on the terms printed on pages 2 to 5, as added to or varied by any terms appearing on page 6 or any attached continuation page

© The Law Society   **L.S.1 (Part) 5/96**

1

THE LAW SOCIETY BUSINESS LEASE (PART OF BUILDING)

VII

TENANT'S OBLIGATIONS

1 PAYMENTS

1. The Tenant is to pay the Landlord:

1.1 the rent

1.2 the service charge in accordance with clause 3 (and this is to be paid as rent)

and the following sums on demand:

1.3 a fair proportion (decided by a surveyor the Landlord nominates) of the cost of repairing maintaining and cleaning:

party walls, party structures, yards, gardens, roads, paths, gutters, drains, sewers, pipes, conduits, wires, cables and things used or shared with other property

1.4 the cost (including professional fees) of any works to the property which the Landlord does after the Tenant defaults

1.5 the costs and expenses (including professional fees) which the Landlord incurs in:

(a) dealing with any application by the Tenant for consent or approval, whether or not it is given

(b) preparing and serving a notice of a breach of the Tenant's obligations, under section 146 of the Law of Property Act 1925, even if forfeiture of this lease is avoided without a court order

(c) preparing and serving schedules of dilapidations either during the lease period or recording failure to give up the property in the appropriate state of repair when this lease ends

1.6 interest at the Law Society's interest rate on any of the above payments when more than fourteen days overdue, to be calculated from its due date

and in making payments under this clause:

(a) nothing is to be deducted or set off

(b) any value added tax payable is to be added

2

2. The Tenant is also to make the following payments, with value added tax where applicable:

2.1 all periodic rates, taxes and outgoings relating to the property, including any imposed after the date of this lease (even if of a novel nature), to be paid promptly to the authorities to whom they are due

2.2 the cost of the grant, renewal or continuation of any licence or registration for using the property for the use allowed, to be paid promptly to the appropriate authority when due

2.3 a registration fee of £20 for each document which this lease requires the Tenant to register to be paid to the Landlord's solicitors when presenting the document for registration

3 SERVICE CHARGE

3. The Landlord and the Tenant agree that:

3.1 the service charge is the Tenant's fair proportion of each item of the service costs

3.2 the service costs:

(a) are the costs which the Landlord fairly and reasonably incurs in complying with his obligations under clauses 12 and 13

(b) include the reasonable charges of any agent contractor consultant or employee whom the Landlord engages to provide the services under clauses 12 and 13

(c) include interest at no more than the Law Society's interest rate on sums the Landlord borrows to discharge his obligations under clauses 12 and 13

3.3 the Tenant is to pay the Landlord interim payments on account of the service charge within 21 days of receiving a written demand setting out how it is calculated

3.4 an interim payment is to be the Tenant's fair proportion of what the service costs are reasonably likely to be in the three months following the demand

3.5 the Landlord is not entitled to demand interim payments more than once in every three months

3.6 the Landlord is to keep full records of the service costs and at least once a year is to send the Tenant an account setting out, for the period since the beginning of the lease period or the last account as the case may be:

(a) the amount of the service costs

(b) the service charge the Tenant is to pay

(c) the total of any interim payments the Tenant has paid

(d) the difference between the total interim payments and the service charge

3.7 within 21 days after the Tenant receives the account, the amount mentioned in clause 3.6(d) is to be settled by payment between the parties except that the Landlord is entitled to retain any overpayment towards any interim payments he has demanded for a later accounting period

3.8 the Landlord is either:

(a) to have the account certified by an independent chartered accountant, or

(b) to allow the Tenant to inspect the books records invoices and receipts relating to the service costs

3.9 disagreements about the amounts of the service charge or the service costs are to be decided by arbitration under clause 17.5

4 USE

4. The Tenant is to comply with the following requirements as to the use of the building and any part of it, and is not to authorise or allow anyone else to contravene them:

4.1 to use the property only for the use allowed

4.2 not to obstruct any part of the building used for access to the property or any other part of the building

4.3 not to do anything which might invalidate any insurance policy covering any part of the building or which might increase the premium

4.4 not to hold an auction sale in the property

4.5 not to use any part of the building for any activities which are dangerous, offensive, noxious, illegal or immoral, or which are or may become a nuisance or annoyance to the Landlord or to the owner or occupier of any other part of the building or of any neighbouring property

4.6 not to display any advertisements on the outside of the property or which are visible from outside the property unless the Landlord consents (and the Landlord is not entitled to withhold that consent unreasonably)

4.7 not to overload the floors or walls of the property

4.8 to comply with the terms of every Act of Parliament, order, regulation, bye-law, rule, licence and registration authorising or regulating how the property is used, and to obtain, renew and continue any licence or registration which is required

5 ACCESS

5. The Tenant is to give the Landlord, or anyone authorised by him in writing, access to the property:

5.1 for these purposes:

(a) inspecting the condition of the property, or how it is being used

(b) doing works which the Landlord is permitted to do under clauses 6.11(c) or 13

(c) complying with any statutory obligation

(d) viewing the property as a prospective buyer, tenant or mortgagee

(e) valuing the property

(f) inspecting, cleaning or repairing neighbouring property, any sewers, drains, pipes, wires, cables serving the building or any neighbouring property

5.2 and only on seven days' written notice except in an emergency

5.3 and during normal business hours except in an emergency

5.4 and the Landlord is promptly to make good all damage caused to the property and any goods there in exercising these rights

L.S.1/2

2

6 CONDITION AND WORK

6. The Tenant is to comply with the following duties in relation to the property:

6.1 to maintain the state and condition of the inside of the property but the Tenant need not alter or improve it except if required in clause 6.10

6.2 to decorate the inside of the property:

(a) in every fifth year of the lease period

(b) in the last three months of the lease period (however it ends) except to the extent that it has been decorated in the previous year

6.3 where the property has a shop front to maintain and decorate it

6.4 when decorating, the Tenant is to use the colours and the types of finish used previously

6.5 but the Tenant need only make good damage caused by an insured risk to the extent that the insurance money had not been paid because of any act or default of the Tenant

6.6 the inside of the property is to include all ceilings, floors, doors, door frames, windows, window frames and plate glass and the internal surfaces of all walls but is to exclude joists immediately above the ceilings and supporting floors

6.7 not to make any structural alterations or additions to the property

6.8 not to make any other alterations unless with the Landlord's consent in writing (and the Landlord is not entitled to withhold that consent unreasonably)

6.9 to keep any plate glass in the property insured for its full replacement cost with reputable insurers, to give the Landlord details of that insurance on request, and to replace any plate glass which becomes damaged

6.10 to do the work to the property which any authority acting under an Act of Parliament requires even if it alters or improves the property. Before the Tenant does so, the Landlord is to:

(a) give his consent in writing to the work

(b) contribute a fair proportion of the cost of the work taking into account any value to him of that work

6.11 if the Tenant fails to do any work which this lease requires him to do and the Landlord gives him written notice to do it, the Tenant is to:

(a) start the work within two months, or immediately in case of emergency, and

(b) proceed diligently with the work

(c) in default, permit the Landlord to do the work

6.12 any dispute arising under clause 6.10(b) is to be decided by arbitration under clause 17.5

7 TRANSFER ETC.

7. The Tenant is to comply with the following:

7.1 the Tenant is not to share occupation of the property and no part of it is to be transferred, sublet or occupied separately from the remainder

7.2 the Tenant is not to transfer or sublet the whole of the property unless the Landlord gives his written consent in advance, and the Landlord is not entitled to withhold that consent unreasonably

7.3 any sublease is to be on terms which are consistent with this lease, but is not to permit the sub-tenant to underlet

7.4 within four weeks after the property is transferred mortgaged or sublet, the Landlord's solicitors are to be notified and a copy of the transfer mortgage or sublease sent to them for registration with the fee payable under clause 2.3

7.5 if the Landlord requires, a Tenant who transfers the whole of the property is to give the Landlord a written guarantee, in the terms set out in the Guarantee Box, that the Transferee will perform his obligations as Tenant

8 OTHER MATTERS

8. The Tenant:

8.1 is to give the Landlord a copy of any notice concerning the property or any neighbouring property as soon as he receives it

8.2 is to allow the Landlord, during the last six months of the lease period, to fix a notice in a reasonable position on the outside of the property announcing that it is for sale or to let

8.3 is not to apply for planning permission relating to the use or alteration of the property unless the Landlord gives written consent in advance

9 RENT REVIEW

9.1 On each rent review date, the rent is to increase to the market rent if that is higher than the rent applying before that date

9.2 The market rent is the rent which a willing tenant would pay for the property on the open market, if let to him on the rent review date by a willing landlord on a lease on the same terms as this lease without any premium and for a period equal to the remainder of the lease period, assuming that at that date:

(a) the willing tenant takes account of any likelihood that he would be entitled to a new lease of the property when the lease ends, but does not take account of any goodwill belonging to anyone who had occupied the property;

(b) the property is vacant and had not been occupied by the Tenant or any sub-tenant;

(c) the property can immediately be used;

(d) the property is in the condition required by this lease and any damage caused by any of the risks insured under clause 12 has been made good;

(e) during the lease period no Tenant or Sub-Tenant has done anything to the property to increase or decrease its rental value and "anything" includes work done by the Tenant to comply with clause 6.10, but nothing else which the Tenant was obliged to do under this lease

9.3 If the Landlord and the Tenant agree the amount of the new rent, a statement of that new rent, signed by them, is to be attached to this lease

9.4 If the Landlord and the Tenant have not agreed the amount of the new rent two months before the rent review date, either of them may require the new rent to be decided by arbitration under clause 17.5

9.5

(a) The Tenant is to continue to pay rent at the rate applying before the rent review date until the next rent day after the new rent is agreed or decided

(b) Starting on that rent day, the Tenant is to pay the new rent

(c) On that rent day, the Tenant is also to pay any amount by which the new rent since the rent review date exceeds the rent paid, with interest on that amount at 2% below the Law Society's interest rate

10 DAMAGE

10. If the property is or the common parts are damaged by any of the risks to be insured under clause 12 and as a result of that damage the property, or any part of it, cannot be used for the use allowed:

10.1 the rent, or a fair proportion of it, is to be suspended for three years or until the property or the common parts are fully restored, if sooner

10.2 if at any time it is unlikely that the property or the common parts will be fully restored within three years from the date of the damage, the Landlord (so long as he has not wilfully delayed the restoration) or the Tenant may end this lease by giving one month's notice to the other during the three year period, in which case

(a) the insurance money belongs to the Landlord and

(b) the Landlord's obligation to make good damage under clause 12 ceases

10.3 a notice given outside the time limits in clause 10.2 is not effective

10.4 The Tenant cannot claim the benefit of this clause to the extent that the insurers refuse to pay the insurance money because of his act or default

10.5 any dispute arising under any part of this clause is to be decided by arbitration under clause 17.5

LANDLORD'S OBLIGATIONS AND FORFEITURE RIGHTS

11 QUIET ENJOYMENT

11. While the Tenant complies with the terms of this lease, the Landlord is to allow the Tenant to possess and use the property without lawful interference from the Landlord, anyone who derives title from the Landlord or any trustee for the Landlord

VII

L.S.1/3

3

12 INSURANCE

12. The Landlord agrees with the Tenant:

12.1 the Landlord is to keep the building (except the plate glass) insured with the reputable insurers to cover

(a) full rebuilding, site clearance, professional fees, value added tax and three years' loss of rent

(b) against fire, lightning, explosion, earthquake, landslip, subsidence, heave, riot, civil commotion, aircraft, aerial devices, storm, flood, water, theft, impact by vehicles, damage by malicious persons and vandals and third party liability and any other risks reasonably required by the Landlord

so far as cover is available at the normal insurance rates for the locality and subject to reasonable excesses and exclusions

12.2 and to take all necessary steps to make good as soon as possible damage to the building caused by insured risks except to the extent that the insurance money is not paid because of the act or default of the Tenant

12.3 and to give the Tenant at his request once a year particulars of the policy and evidence from the insurer that it is in force

12.4 and that the Tenant is not responsible for any damage for which the Landlord is compensated under the insurance policy

13 SERVICES

13. The Landlord is to comply with the following duties in relation to the building:

13.1 to maintain the state and condition (including the decorations) of:

(a) the structure, outside, roof, foundations, joists, floor slabs, load bearing walls, beams and columns of the building

(b) those parts of the building which tenants of more than one part can use ("the common parts")

13.2 to decorate the common parts and the outside of the building every five years, using colours and types of finish reasonably decided by the Landlord

13.3 to pay promptly all periodic rates, taxes and outgoings relating to the common parts, including any imposed after the date of this lease (even if of a novel nature)

13.4 to pay or to contribute to the cost of repairing, maintaining and cleaning party walls, party structures, yards, gardens, roads, paths, gutters, drains, sewers, pipes, conduits, wires, cables and other things used or shared with the other property

13.5 to provide the services listed on page 5, but the Landlord is not to be liable for failure or delay caused by industrial disputes, shortage of supplies, adverse weather conditions or other causes beyond the control of the Landlord

14 FORFEITURE

14. This lease comes to an end if the Landlord forfeits it by entering any part of the property, which the Landlord is entitled to do whenever:

(a) payment of any rent is fourteen days overdue, even if it was not formally demanded

(b) the Tenant has not complied with any of the terms in this lease

(c) the Tenant if an individual (and if more than one, any of them) is adjudicated bankrupt or an interim receiver of his property is appointed

(d) the Tenant if a company (and if more than one, any of them) goes into liquidation (unless solely for the purpose of amalgamation or reconstruction when solvent), or had an administrative receiver appointed or had an administration order made in respect of it

The forfeiture of this lease does not cancel any outstanding obligation of the Tenant or a Guarantor

15 END OF LEASE

15. When this lease ends the Tenant is to:

15.1 return the property of the Landlord leaving it in the state and condition in which this lease requires the Tenant to keep it

15.2 (if the Landlord so requires) remove anything the Tenant fixed to the property and make good any damage which that causes

PROPERTY RIGHTS

16 BOUNDARIES

16.1 This lease does not let to the Tenant the external surfaces of the outside walls of the property and anything above the ceilings and below the floors

FACILITIES

16.2 The Tenant is to have the use, whether or not exclusive, of any of the following facilities:

the right for the Tenant and visitors to come and go to and from the property over the parts of the building designed or designated to afford access to the property, the rights previously enjoyed by the property for shelter and support and for service wires, pipes and drains to pass through them, and the right to park vehicles in any designated parking area subject to any reasonable rules made by the Landlord

16.3 The Landlord is to have the rights previously enjoyed over the property by other parts of the building for shelter and support and for service wires, pipes and drains to pass through it, and the right for the Landlord and his tenants and their visitors to come and go to and from the other parts of the building over the parts of the property designated for that purpose

GENERAL

17 PARTIES' RESPONSIBILITY

17.1 Whenever more than one person or company is the Landlord, the Tenant or the Guarantor, their obligations can be enforced against all or both of them jointly and against each individually

LANDLORD

17.2

(a) The obligations in this lease continue to apply to the Landlord until he is released by the Tenant or by a declaration of the court

(b) The current owner of the Landlord's interest in the property must comply with the Landlord's obligations in this lease

TENANT

17.3

(a) A transfer of this lease releases the Tenant from any future obligations under it. This does not apply in the case of a transfer made without the Landlord's consent or as a result of the Tenant's death or bankruptcy

(b) After a transfer, the Tenant's successor must comply with the Tenant's obligations in this lease

SERVICE OF NOTICE

17.4 The rules about serving notices in Section 196 of the Law of Property Act 1925 (as since amended) apply to any notice given under this lease

ARBITRATION

17.5 Any matter which this lease requires to be decided by arbitration is to be referred to a single arbitrator under the Arbitration Acts. The Landlord and the Tenant may agree the appointment of the arbitrator, or either of them may apply to the President of the Royal Institution of Chartered Surveyors to make the appointment

HEADINGS

17.6 The headings do not form part of this lease

18 STAMP DUTY

This lease has not been granted to implement an agreement for a lease

L.S.1/4

4

SERVICES

These are the services mentioned in clause 13.5
(delete or add as required)

Cleaning of the common parts

Lighting of the common parts

Heating of the common parts

Lift maintenance

Hot and cold water to wash hand basins in the common parts

Porterage

Fire extinguishers in the common parts

Heating in the property

Window cleaning for the building

Furnishing the common parts

GUARANTEE BOX

The terms in this box only take effect if a guarantor is named and then only until the Tenant transfers this lease with the Landlord's written consent. The Guarantor must sign this lease.

'Guarantor':

of

agrees to compensate the Landlord for any loss incurred as a result of the Tenant failing to comply with an obligation in this lease during the lease period or any statutory extension of it. If the Tenant is insolvent and this lease ends because it is disclaimed, the Guarantor agrees to accept a new lease, if the Landlord so requires, in the same form but at the rent then payable. Even if the Landlord gives the Tenant extra time to comply with an obligation, or does not insist on strict compliance with terms of this lease, the Guarantor's obligation remains fully effective.

THIS DOCUMENT CREATES LEGAL RIGHTS AND LEGAL OBLIGATIONS. DO NOT SIGN IT UNTIL YOU HAVE CONSULTED A SOLICITOR. THERE IS A CODE OF PRACTICE CONCERNING COMMERCIAL LEASES IN ENGLAND AND WALES PUBLISHED UNDER THE AUSPICES OF THE DEPARTMENT OF THE ENVIRONMENT.

VII

Signed as a deed by/on behalf of the
Landlord and delivered in the presence of:

....
Landlord

....

Witness

....

Witness's occupation and address

Signed as a deed by/on behalf of the
Tenant and delivered in the presence of:

....
Tenant

....

Witness

....

Witness's occupation and address

Signed as a deed by/on behalf of the
Guarantor and delivered in the presence of:

....
Guarantor

....

Witness

....

Witness's occupation and address

VII.12.　Standard Commercial Property Conditions of Sale (1st edition)[1]

CONTRACT

(Incorporating the Standard Commercial Property Conditions (First Edition))

Contract date	:
Seller	:
Buyer	:
Property **(freehold/leasehold)**	:
Root of title/Title Number	:
Incumbrances on the Property	:
Completion date	:
Contract rate	:
Purchase price	:
Deposit	:
Amount payable for chattels	:

The Seller will sell and the Buyer will buy the Property for the Purchase price.

The Contract continues on the back page.

WARNING	**Signed**
This is a formal document, designed to create legal rights and legal obligations. Take advice before using it.	Authorised to sign on behalf of Seller/Buyer

---

1. See section AA. New Developments in Conveyancing Practice for information regarding the updating of the conditions.

STANDARD COMMERCIAL PROPERTY CONDITIONS
(FIRST EDITION)

1. GENERAL

1.1 **Definitions:**

1.1.1 In these conditions:

(a) 'accrued interest' means:

   (i) if money has been placed on deposit or in a building society share account, the interest actually earned

   (ii) otherwise, the interest which might reasonably have been earned by depositing the money at interest on seven days' notice of withdrawal with a clearing bank

less, in either case, any proper charges for handling the money

(b) 'clearing bank' means a member of CHAPS Clearing Limited

(c) 'completion date', unless otherwise defined, has the meaning given in condition 6.1.1

(d) 'contract rate', unless otherwise defined is the Law Society's interest rate from time to time in force

(e) 'direct credit' means a direct transfer of cleared funds to an account nominated by the seller's solicitor and held at a clearing bank

(f) 'lease' includes sub-lease, tenancy and agreement for a lease or sub-lease

(g) 'notice to complete' means a notice requiring completion of the contract in accordance with condition 6

(h) 'public requirement' means any notice, order or proposal given or made (whether before or after the date of the contract) by a body acting on statutory authority

(i) 'requisition' includes objection

(j) 'service charge' has the meaning given to it by section 18 of the Landlord and Tenant Act 1985 (disregarding the words 'of a dwelling')

(k) 'solicitor' includes barrister, certificated notary public, licensed conveyancer and recognised body under sections 9 or 32 of the Administration of Justice Act 1985

(l) 'transfer' includes conveyance and assignment

(m) 'working day' means any day from Monday to Friday (inclusive) which is not Christmas Day, Good Friday or a statutory Bank Holiday.

1.1.2 When used in these conditions the terms 'absolute title' and 'office copies' have the special meanings given to them by the Land Registration Act 1925.

1.2 **Joint parties**

If there is more than one seller or more than one buyer, the obligations which they undertake can be enforced against them all jointly or against each individually.

1.3 **Notices and documents**

1.3.1 A notice required or authorised by the contract must be in writing.

1.3.2 Giving a notice or delivering a document to a party's solicitor has the same effect as giving or delivering it to that party.

1.3.3 Transmission by fax is a valid means of giving a notice or delivering a document where delivery of the original document is not essential.

1.3.4 Subject to conditions 1.3.5 to 1.3.7, a notice is given and a document delivered when it is received.

1.3.5 If a notice or document is received after 4.00 p.m. on a working day, or on a day which is not a working day, it is to be treated as having been received on the next working day.

1.3.6 Unless the actual time of receipt is proved, a notice or document sent by the following means is to be treated as having been received before 4.00 p.m. on the day shown below:

    (a) by first class post: two working days after posting

    (b) by second class post: three working days after posting

    (c) through a document exchange: on the first working day after the day on which it would normally be available for collection by the addressee.

1.3.7 Where a notice or document is sent through a document exchange, then for the purposes of condition 1.3.6 the actual time of receipt is:

    (a) the time when the addressee collects it from the document exchange or, if earlier

    (b) 8.00 a.m. on the first working day on which it is available for collection at that time.

1.4 VAT

1.4.1 An obligation to pay money includes an obligation to pay any value added tax chargeable in respect of that payment.

1.4.2 All sums made payable by the contract are exclusive of value added tax.

1.5 Assignment and Sub-sales

1.5.1 The buyer is not entitled to transfer the benefit of the contract.

1.5.2 The seller may not be required to transfer the property in parts or to any person other than the buyer.

2. FORMATION

2.1 Date

2.1.1 If the parties intend to make a contract by exchanging duplicate copies by post or through a document exchange, the contract is made when the last copy is posted or deposited at the document exchange.

2.1.2 If the parties' solicitors agree to treat exchange as taking place before duplicate copies are actually exchanged, the contract is made as so agreed.

2.2 Deposit

2.2.1 The buyer is to pay a deposit of 10 per cent of the purchase price no later than the date of the contract.

2.2.2 Except on a sale by auction the deposit is to be paid by direct credit and is to be held by the seller's solicitor as stakeholder on terms that on completion it is paid to the seller with accrued interest.

2.3 **Auctions**

2.3.1 On a sale by auction the following conditions apply to the property and, if it is sold in lots, to each lot.

2.3.2 The sale is subject to a reserve price.

2.3.3 The seller, or a person on its behalf, may bid up to the reserve price.

2.3.4 The auctioneer may refuse any bid.

2.3.5 If there is a dispute about a bid, the auctioneer may resolve the dispute or restart the auction at the last undisputed bid.

2.3.6 The auctioneer is to hold the deposit as agent for the seller. If any cheque tendered in payment of all or part of the deposit is dishonoured when first presented, the seller may, within seven working days of being notified that the cheque has been dishonoured, give notice to the buyer that the contract is discharged by the buyer's breach.

3 **MATTERS AFFECTING THE PROPERTY**

3.1 **Freedom from incumbrances**

3.1.1 The seller is selling the property free from incumbrances, other than those mentioned in condition 3.1.2.

3.1.2 The incumbrances subject to which the property is sold are:

(a) those mentioned in the contract

(b) those discoverable by inspection of the property before the contract

(c) those the seller does not and could not reasonably know about

(d) matters, other than monetary charges or incumbrances, disclosed or which would have been disclosed by the searches and enquiries which a prudent buyer would have made before entering into the contract

(e) public requirements.

3.1.3 After the contract is made, the seller is to give the buyer written details without delay of any new public requirement and of anything in writing which it learns about concerning any incumbrances subject to which the property is sold.

3.1.4 The buyer is to bear the cost of complying with any outstanding public requirement and is to indemnify the seller against any liability resulting from a public requirement.

3.2 **Physical state**

3.2.1 The buyer accepts the property in the physical state it is in at the date of the contract unless the seller is building or converting it.

3.2.2 A leasehold property is sold subject to any subsisting breach of a condition or tenant's obligation relating to the physical state of the property which renders the lease liable to forfeiture.

3.2.3 A sub-lease is granted subject to any subsisting breach of a condition or tenant's obligation relating to the physical state of the property which renders the seller's own lease liable to forfeiture.

3.3 **Leases affecting the property**

3.3.1 The following provisions apply if any part of the property is sold subject to a lease.

3.3.2 The seller having provided the buyer with full details of each lease or copies of the documents embodying the lease terms, the buyer is treated as entering into the contract knowing and fully accepting those terms.

3.3.3 (a) The seller is to inform the buyer without delay if the seller learns of any application by the tenant in connection with the lease.

(b) The seller is not to agree to any application by the tenant nor to grant or withhold licences, consents or approvals required under the lease without the consent of the buyer.

(c) The buyer is not to withhold its consent or attach conditions to the consent where to do so might place the seller in breach of an obligation to the tenant or a statutory duty.

(d) In all other circumstances the seller is to act as the buyer reasonably directs, and the buyer is to indemnify it against all consequent loss and expense.

3.3.4 The seller is not to agree to any proposal to change the lease terms without the consent of the buyer and is to inform the buyer without delay of any change which may be proposed or agreed.

3.3.5 The seller is to manage the property in accordance with the principles of good estate management until completion.

3.3.6 The seller is to inform the buyer without delay if the lease ends and is not to serve any notice to end the lease.

3.3.7 The buyer is to indemnify the seller against all claims arising from the lease after actual completion; this includes claims which are unenforceable against a buyer for want of registration.

3.3.8 If the property does not include all the land let, the seller may apportion the rent and, if the lease is a new tenancy, the buyer may require the seller to apply under section 10 of the Landlord and Tenant (Covenants) Act 1995 for the apportionment to bind the tenant.

3.4 Retained land

3.4.1 The following provisions apply where after the transfer the seller will be retaining land near the property.

3.4.2 The buyer will have no right of light or air over the retained land, but otherwise the seller and the buyer will each have the rights over the land of the other which they would have had if they were two separate buyers to whom the seller had made simultaneous transfers of the property and the retained land.

3.4.3 Either party may require that the transfer is to contain appropriate express terms.

4 TITLE AND TRANSFER

4.1 Timetable

4.1.1 The following are the steps for deducing and investigating the title to the property to be taken within the following time limits:

Step	Time Limit
1. The seller is to send the buyer evidence of title in accordance with condition 4.2	Immediately after making the contract
2. The buyer may raise written requisitions	Six working days after either the date of the contract or the date of delivery of the seller's evidence of title on which the requisitions are raised whichever is the later
3. The seller is to reply in writing to any requisitions raised	Four working days after receiving the requisitions

Step	Time Limit
4. The buyer may make written observations on the seller's replies	Three working days after receiving the replies

The time limit on the buyer's right to raise requisitions applies even where the seller supplies incomplete evidence of its title, but the buyer may, within six working days from delivery of any further evidence, raise further requisitions resulting from that evidence. On the expiry of the relevant time limit the buyer loses its right to raise requisitions or make observations.

4.1.2 The parties are to take the following steps to prepare and agree the transfer of the property within the following time limits:

Step	Time Limit
A. The buyer is to send the seller a draft transfer	At least twelve working days before completion date
B. The seller is to approve or revise that draft and either return it or retain it for use as the actual transfer	Four working days after delivery of the draft transfer
C. If the draft is returned the buyer is to send an engrossment to the seller	At least five working days before completion date

4.1.3 Periods of time under conditions 4.1.1 and 4.1.2 may run concurrently.

4.1.4 If the period between the date of the contract and completion date is less than 15 working days, the time limits in conditions 4.1.1 and 4.1.2 are to be reduced by the same proportion as that period bears to the period of 15 working days. Fractions of a working day are to be rounded down except that the time limit to perform any step is not to be less than one working day.

4.2 Proof of title

4.2.1 The evidence of registered title is office copies of the items required to be furnished by section 110(1) of the Land Registration Act 1925 and the copies, abstracts and evidence referred to in section 110(2).

4.2.2 The evidence of unregistered title is an abstract of the title, or an epitome of title with photocopies of the relevant documents.

4.2.3 Where the title to the property is unregistered, the seller is to produce to the buyer (without cost to the buyer):

(a) the original of every relevant document, or

(b) an abstract, epitome or copy with an original marking by a solicitor of examination against the original or against an examined abstract or against an examined copy.

4.3 Defining the property

4.3.1 The seller need not:

(a) prove the exact boundaries of the property

(b) prove who owns fences, ditches, hedges or walls

(c) separately identify parts of the property with different titles

further than it may be able to do from information in its possession.

4.3.2 The buyer may, if to do so is reasonable, require the seller to make or obtain, pay for and hand over a statutory declaration about facts relevant to the matters mentioned in condition 4.3.1. The form of the declaration is to be agreed by the buyer, who must not unreasonably withhold its agreement.

4.4 Rents and rentcharges

The fact that a rent or rentcharge, whether payable or receivable by the owner of the property, has been or will on completion be, informally apportioned is not to be regarded as a defect in title.

4.5 Transfer

4.5.1 The buyer does not prejudice its right to raise requisitions, or to require replies to any raised, by taking any steps in relation to the preparation or agreement of the transfer.

4.5.2 If the contract makes no provision as to title guarantee, then subject to condition 4.5.4 the seller is to transfer the property with full title guarantee.

4.5.3 The transfer is to have effect as if the disposition is expressly made subject to all matters to which the property is sold subject under the terms of the contract.

4.5.4 If after completion the seller will remain bound by any obligation affecting the property and disclosed to the buyer before the contract is made, but the law does not imply any covenant by the buyer to indemnify the seller against liability for future breaches of it:

(a) the buyer is to covenant in the transfer to indemnify the seller against liability for any future breach of the obligation and to perform it from then on, and

(b) if required by the seller, the buyer is to execute and deliver to the seller on completion a duplicate transfer prepared by the buyer.

4.5.5 The seller is to arrange at its expense that, in relation to every document of title which the buyer does not receive on completion, the buyer is to have the benefit of:

(a) a written acknowledgement of the buyer's right to its production, and

(b) a written undertaking for its safe custody (except while it is held by a mortgagee or by someone in a fiduciary capacity).

5 PENDING COMPLETION

5.1 Responsibility for property

5.1.1 Unless condition 5.1.2 or condition 8.1.3 applies:

(a) the seller is under no obligation to the buyer to insure the property

(b) if payment under a policy effected by or for the buyer is reduced, because the property is covered against loss or damage by an insurance policy effected by or for the seller, the purchase price is to be abated by the amount of that reduction.

5.1.2 If the contract provides that the policy insuring the property against loss or damage effected by or for the seller should continue in force after exchange of contracts, the seller is to:

(a) do everything required to continue to maintain the policy, including to pay promptly any premium which falls due

(b) increase the amount or extent of the cover as requested by the buyer, if the insurers agree and the buyer pays the additional premium

(c) permit the buyer to inspect the policy, or evidence of its terms, at any time

(d) obtain or consent to an endorsement on the policy of the buyer's interest, at the buyer's expense

(e) pay to the buyer immediately on receipt, any part of an additional premium which the buyer paid and which is returned by the insurers

(f) if before completion the property suffers loss or damage:

   (i) pay to the buyer on completion the amount of policy moneys which the seller has received; and

   (ii) if no final payment has then been received, assign to the buyer, at the buyer's expense, all rights to claim under the policy in such form as the buyer reasonably requires; and pending execution of the assignment, hold any policy moneys received in trust for the buyer

and the buyer is to pay the seller a proportionate part of the premium which the seller paid in respect of the period from the date when the contract is made to the date of actual completion.

5.1.3 (a) The following provisions apply if any part of the property transferred is subject to a lease.

   (b) On completion the seller is to cancel the insurance policy relating to the property.

   (c) The seller is to pay the buyer immediately on receipt the amount of the refund of premium received which relates to any part of the premium which was paid or reimbursed by a tenant or third party.

   (d) The buyer is to hold the money paid subject to the rights of that tenant or third party.

5.1.4 Section 47 of the Law of Property Act 1925 does not apply.

5.2 Occupation by buyer

5.2.1 If the buyer is not already lawfully in the property, and the seller agrees to let the buyer into occupation, the following terms apply.

5.2.2 The buyer is a licensee and not a tenant. The terms of the licence are that the buyer:

   (a) cannot transfer it

   (b) is to pay or indemnify the seller against all outgoings and other expenses in respect of the property

   (c) is to pay the seller a fee calculated at the contract rate on the purchase price (less any deposit paid) for the period of the licence

   (d) is entitled to any rents and profits from any part of the property which the buyer does not occupy

   (e) is to keep the property in as good a state of repair as it was in when the buyer went into occupation (except for fair wear and tear) and is not to alter it

   (f) is not to infringe a statutory requirement relating to it

   (g) is to quit the property when the licence ends.

5.2.3 The licence ends on the earliest of: completion date, rescission of the contract or when five working days' notice given by one party to the other takes effect.

5.2.4 If the buyer is in occupation of the property after the licence has come to an end and the contract is subsequently completed the buyer is to pay the seller compensation for its continued occupation calculated at the same rate as the fee mentioned in condition 5.2.2(c).

5.2.5 The buyer's right to raise requisitions is unaffected.

6.   COMPLETION

6.1   Date

6.1.1   Completion date is twenty working days after the date of the contract but time is not of the essence of the contract unless a notice to complete has been served.

6.1.2   If the money due on completion is received after 2.00 p.m., completion is to be treated, for the purposes only of conditions 6.3 and 7.3, as taking place on the next working day.

6.2   Place

Completion is to take place in England and Wales, either at the seller's solicitor's office or at some other place which the seller reasonably specifies.

6.3   Apportionments

6.3.1   Subject to condition 6.3.7 income and outgoings of the property are to be apportioned between the parties so far as the change of ownership on completion will affect entitlement to receive or liability to pay them.

6.3.2   If the whole property is sold with vacant possession or the seller exercises its option in condition 7.3.4, apportionment is to be made with effect from the date of actual completion; otherwise, it is to be made from completion date.

6.3.3   In apportioning any sum, it is to be assumed that the buyer owns the property from the beginning of the day on which the apportionment is to be made.

6.3.4   A sum to be apportioned is to be treated as accruing:

(a)   from day to day throughout the period for which it is payable or receivable, even if it is payable by instalments, and

(b)   at the rate from time to time applicable during the period for which the apportionment is made.

6.3.5   When a sum to be apportioned is not known or easily ascertainable at completion, a provisional apportionment is to be made according to the best estimate available. As soon as the amount is known, a final apportionment is to be made and notified to the other party. Any resulting balance is to be paid no more than ten working days later, and if not then paid the balance is to bear interest at the contract rate from then until payment.

6.3.6   Compensation payable under condition 5.2.4 is not to be apportioned.

6.3.7   This provision applies where any lease subject to which the property is sold obliges the tenant to pay a service charge.

(a)   On completion the buyer is to pay the seller the amount of any service charge expenditure already incurred by the seller but not yet due from the tenant.

(b)   On completion the seller is to credit the buyer with service charge payments already recovered from the tenant but not yet incurred by the seller.

6.3.8   Condition 6.3.9 applies if:

(a)   any part of the property is sold subject to a lease

(b)   on completion any rent or service charge payable under the lease is due but not paid

(c)   the contract does not provide that the buyer is to assign to the seller the right to collect any arrears due to the seller under the terms of the contract, and

(d)   the seller is not entitled to recover any arrears from the tenant.

6.3.9   (a)   The buyer is to seek to collect all the arrears in the ordinary course of management, but need not take legal proceedings or distrain

      (b)   A payment made on account of arrears is to be apportioned between the parties in the ratio of the sums owed to each, unless the tenant exercises its right to appropriate the payment in some other manner

      (c)   Any part of a payment on account of arrears received by one party but due to the other is to be paid no more than ten working days after the receipt of cash or cleared funds and, if not then paid, the sum is to bear interest at the contract rate until payment.

6.4   Amount payable

The amount payable by the buyer on completion is the purchase price (less any deposit already paid to the seller or its agent) adjusted to take account of:

  (a)   apportionments made under condition 6.3

  (b)   any compensation to be paid under condition 7.3

  (c)   any sum payable under condition 5.1.2.

6.5   Title deeds

6.5.1   As soon as the buyer has complied with all its obligations on completion the seller must part with the documents of title.

6.5.2   Condition 6.5.1 does not apply to any documents of title relating to land being retained by the seller after completion.

6.6   Rent receipts

The buyer is to assume that whoever gave any receipt for a payment of rent or service charge which the seller produces was the person or the agent of the person then entitled to that rent or service charge.

6.7   Means of payment

The buyer is to pay the money due on completion by direct credit and by an unconditional release of any deposit held by a stakeholder.

6.8   Notice to complete

6.8.1   At any time on or after the completion date, a party who is ready, able and willing to complete may give the other a notice to complete.

6.8.2   A party is ready, able and willing:

  (a)   if it could be, but for the default of the other party, and

  (b)   in the case of the seller, even though a mortgage remains secured on the property, if the amount to be paid on completion enables the property to be transferred freed of all mortgages (except those to which the sale is expressly subject).

6.8.3   The parties are to complete the contract within ten working days of giving a notice to complete, excluding the day on which the notice is given. For this purpose, time is of the essence of the contract.

6.8.4   On receipt of a notice to complete:

(a) if the buyer paid no deposit, it is forthwith to pay a deposit of 10 per cent

(b) if the buyer paid a deposit of less than 10 per cent, it is forthwith to pay a further deposit equal to the balance of that 10 per cent.

7   REMEDIES

7.1   Errors and omissions

7.1.1   If any plan or statement in the contract, or in the negotiations leading to it, is or was misleading or inaccurate due to an error or omission, the remedies available are as follows.

7.1.2   When there is a material difference between the description or value of the property as represented and as it is, the injured party is entitled to damages.

7.1.3   An error or omission only entitles the injured party to rescind the contract:

(a) where that error or omission results from fraud or recklessness, or

(b) where that party would be obliged, to its prejudice, to transfer or accept property differing substantially (in quantity, quality or tenure) from that which the error or omission had led it to expect.

7.2   Rescission

If either party rescinds the contract:

(a) unless the rescission is a result of the buyer's breach of contract the deposit is to be repaid to the buyer with accrued interest

(b) the buyer is to return any documents received from the seller and is to cancel any registration of the contract

(c) the seller's duty to pay any returned premium under condition 5.1.2(e) (whenever received) is not affected.

7.3   Late completion

7.3.1   If the buyer defaults in performing its obligations under the contract and completion is delayed, the buyer is to pay compensation to the seller.

7.3.2   Compensation is calculated at the contract rate on the purchase price (less any deposit paid) for the period between completion date and actual completion, but ignoring any period during which the seller was in default.

7.3.3   Any claim by the seller for loss resulting from delayed completion is to be reduced by any compensation paid under this contract.

7.3.4   Where the sale is not with vacant possession of the whole property and completion is delayed, the seller may give notice to the buyer, before the date of actual completion, that it will take the net income from the property until completion as well as compensation under condition 7.3.1.

7.4   After completion

Completion does not cancel liability to perform any outstanding obligation under the contract.

7.5   Buyer's failure to comply with notice to complete

7.5.1   If the buyer fails to complete in accordance with a notice to complete, the following terms apply.

7.5.2   The seller may rescind the contract, and if it does so:

(a) it may

(i)　forfeit and keep any deposit and accrued interest

(ii)　resell the property

(iii)　claim damages

(b)　the buyer is to return any documents received from the seller and is to cancel any registration of the contract.

7.5.3　The seller retains its other rights and remedies.

7.6　Seller's failure to comply with notice to complete

7.6.1　If the seller fails to complete in accordance with a notice to complete, the following terms apply.

7.6.2　The buyer may rescind the contract, and if it does so:

(a)　the deposit is to be repaid to the buyer with accrued interest

(b)　the buyer is to return any documents it received from the seller and is, at the seller's expense, to cancel any registration of the contract.

7.6.3　The buyer retains its other rights and remedies.

8.　LEASEHOLD PROPERTY

8.1　Existing leases

8.1.1　The following provisions apply to a sale of leasehold land.

8.1.2　The seller having provided the buyer with copies of the documents embodying the lease terms, the buyer is treated as entering into the contract knowing and fully accepting those terms.

8.1.3　The seller is to comply with any lease obligations requiring the tenant to insure the property.

8.2　New leases

8.2.1　The following provisions apply to a grant of a new lease.

8.2.2　The conditions apply so that:

'seller' means the proposed landlord

'buyer' means the proposed tenant

'purchase price' means the premium to be paid on the grant of a lease.

8.2.3　The lease is to be in the form of the draft attached to the contract.

8.2.4　If the term of the new lease will exceed 21 years, the seller is to deduce a title which will enable the buyer to register the lease at HM Land Registry with an absolute title.

8.2.5　The seller may not be required to grant a lease to any person other than the buyer.

8.2.6　The seller is to engross the lease and a counterpart of it and is to send the counterpart to the buyer at least five working days before completion date.

8.2.7　The buyer is to execute the counterpart and deliver it to the seller on completion.

8.3   Landlord's consent

8.3.1   The following provisions apply if the property is leasehold and the terms of the lease require a reversioner whether or not immediate (a 'landlord') to consent to an assignment or sub-letting.

8.3.2   The seller is to:

(a)   apply for the consent at its expense, and to use all reasonable efforts to obtain it

(b)   give the buyer notice forthwith on obtaining the consent

(c)   enter into an authorised guarantee agreement if the lease so requires.

8.3.3   Where the landlord lawfully requires, the buyer is to:

(a)   use reasonable endeavours to provide promptly all information and references

(b)   covenant directly with the landlord to observe the tenant's covenants and the conditions in the seller's lease

(c)   use reasonable endeavours to provide guarantees of the performance and observance of the tenant's covenants and the conditions in the seller's lease

(d)   execute or procure the execution of the licence.

8.3.4   If the landlord's consent has not been obtained by the original completion date:

(a)   the time for completion is to be postponed until five working days after the seller gives written notice to the buyer that the consent has been obtained or four months from the original completion date whichever is the earlier

(b)   the postponed date is to be treated as the completion date.

8.3.5   At any time after four months from the original completion date, either party may rescind the contract by notice to the other if:

(a)   consent has still not been given, and

(b)   no declaration has been obtained from the court that consent has been unreasonably withheld.

8.3.6   Neither party may object to a consent subject to a condition:

(a)   which under section 19(1A) of the Landlord and Tenant Act 1927 is not regarded as unreasonable,

(b)   which is lawfully imposed under an express term of the lease.

8.3.7   If the contract is rescinded under condition 8.3.5 the seller is to remain liable for any breach of condition 8.3.2 and the buyer is to remain liable for any breach of condition 8.3.3 but in all other respects neither party is to be treated as in breach of contract and condition 7.2 applies.

8.3.8   A party in breach of its obligations under condition 8.3.2 or 8.3.3 cannot rescind under condition 8.3.5 for so long as its breach is a cause of the consent's being withheld.

9.   CHATTELS

9.1   The following provisions apply to any chattels which are to be sold.

9.2   Whether or not a separate price is to be paid for the chattels, the contract takes effect as a contract for sale of goods.

9.3   Ownership of the chattels passes to the buyer on actual completion but they are at the buyer's risk from the contract date.

SPECIAL CONDITIONS

1. This Contract incorporates the Standard Commercial Property Conditions (First Edition). Where there is a conflict between those Conditions and any other provision of this Contract, that other provision prevails.

2. The Property is sold subject to the Incumbrances on the Property and the Buyer will raise no requisition on them.

3. The Property is sold with vacant possession on completion.

(or) 3. The Property is sold subject to the following leases or tenancies:

4. The chattels at the Property and set out on the attached list are included in the sale.

Seller's Solicitors   :

Buyer's Solicitors   :

VII.13.   Standard Conditions of Sale (3rd edition)[1]

AGREEMENT

(Incorporating the Standard Conditions of Sale (Third Edition))

Agreement date :

Seller :

Buyer :

Property :
(freehold/leasehold)

Root of title/Title Number :

Incumbrances on the Property :

Title Guarantee :
(full/limited)

Completion date :

Contract rate :

Purchase price :

Deposit :

Amount payable for chattels :

Balance :

The Seller will sell and the Buyer will buy the Property for the Purchase price.

The Agreement continues on the back page.

WARNING	**Signed**
This is a formal document, designed to create legal rights and legal obligations. Take advice before using it.	Seller/Buyer

---

1. See section AA. New Developments in Conveyancing Practice for information regarding the updating of the conditions.

STANDARD CONDITIONS OF SALE (THIRD EDITION)
(NATIONAL CONDITIONS OF SALE 23RD EDITION, LAW SOCIETY'S
CONDITIONS OF SALE 1995)

1.   GENERAL

1.1   **Definitions**

1.1.1   In these conditions:

(a)   'accrued interest' means:

    (i)   if money has been placed on deposit or in a building society share account, the interest actually earned

    (ii)   otherwise, the interest which might reasonably have been earned by depositing the money at interest on seven days' notice of withdrawal with a clearing bank

    less, in either case, any proper charges for handling the money

(b)   'agreement' means the contractual document which incorporates these conditions, with or without amendment

(c)   'banker's draft' means a draft drawn by and on a clearing bank

(d)   'clearing bank' means a bank which is a member of CHAPS Limited

(e)   'completion date', unless defined in the agreement, has the meaning given in condition 6.1.1

(f)   'contract' means the bargain between the seller and the buyer of which these conditions, with or without amendment, form part

(g)   'contract rate', unless defined in the agreement, is the Law Society's interest rate from time to time in force

(h)   'lease' includes sub-lease, tenancy and agreement for a lease or sub-lease

(i)   'notice to complete' means a notice requiring completion of the contract in accordance with condition 6

(j)   'public requirement' means any notice, order or proposal given or made (whether before or after the date of the contract) by a body acting on statutory authority

(k)   'requisition' includes objection

(l)   'solicitor' includes barrister, duly certificated notary public, recognised licensed conveyancer and recognised body under sections 9 or 32 of the Administration of Justice Act 1985

(m)   'transfer' includes conveyance and assignment

(n)   'working day' means any day from Monday to Friday (inclusive) which is not Christmas Day, Good Friday or a statutory Bank Holiday.

1.1.2   When used in these conditions the terms 'absolute title' and 'office copies' have the special meanings given to them by the Land Registration Act 1925.

1.2   **Joint parties**

If there is more than one seller or more than one buyer, the obligations which they undertake can be enforced against them all jointly or against each individually.

1.3   **Notices and documents**

1.3.1   A notice required or authorised by the contract must be in writing.

1.3.2   Giving a notice or delivering a document to a party's solicitor has the same effect as giving or delivering it to that party.

1.3.3   Transmission by fax is a valid means of giving a notice or delivering a document where delivery of the original document is not essential.

1.3.4   Subject to conditions 1.3.5 to 1.3.7, a notice is given and a document delivered when it is received.

1.3.5   If a notice or document is received after 4.00pm on a working day, or on a day which is not a working day, it is to be treated as having been received on the next working day.

1.3.6   Unless the actual time of receipt is proved, a notice or document sent by the following means is to be treated as having been received before 4.00pm on the day shown below:

(a)   by first-class post: two working days after posting

(b)   by second-class post: three working days after posting

(c)   through a document exchange: on the first working day after the day on which it would normally be available for collection by the addressee.

1.3.7   Where a notice or document is sent through a document exchange, then for the purposes of condition 1.3.6 the actual time of receipt is:

(a)   the time when the addressee collects it from the document exchange or, if earlier

(b)   8.00am on the first working day on which it is available for collection at that time.

1.4   **VAT**

1.4.1   An obligation to pay money includes an obligation to pay any value added tax chargeable in respect of that payment.

1.4.2   All sums made payable by the contract are exclusive of value added tax.

2.   **FORMATION**

2.1   **Date**

2.1.1   If the parties intend to make a contract by exchanging duplicate copies by post or through a document exchange, the contract is made when the last copy is posted or deposited at the document exchange.

2.1.2   If the parties' solicitors agree to treat exchange as taking place before duplicate copies are actually exchanged, the contract is made as so agreed.

2.2   **Deposit**

2.2.1   The buyer is to pay or send a deposit of 10 per cent of the purchase price no later than the date of the contract. Except on a sale by auction, payment is to be made by banker's draft or by a cheque drawn on a solicitors' clearing bank account.

2.2.2   If before completion date the seller agrees to buy another property in England and Wales for his residence, he may use all or any part of the deposit as a deposit in that transaction to be held on terms to the same effect as this condition and condition 2.2.3.

2.2.3   Any deposit or part of a deposit not being used in accordance with condition 2.2.2 is to be held by the seller's solicitor as stakeholder on terms that on completion it is paid to the seller with accrued interest.

2.2.4   If a cheque tendered in payment of all or part of the deposit is dishonoured when first presented, the seller may, within seven working days of being notified that the cheque has been dishonoured, give notice to the buyer that the contract is discharged by the buyer's breach.

2.3   Auctions

2.3.1   On a sale by auction the following conditions apply to the property and, if it is sold in lots, to each lot.

2.3.2   The sale is subject to a reserve price.

2.3.3   The seller, or a person on his behalf, may bid up to the reserve price.

2.3.4   The auctioneer may refuse any bid.

2.3.5   If there is a dispute about a bid, the auctioneer may resolve the dispute or restart the auction at the last undisputed bid.

3.   MATTERS AFFECTING THE PROPERTY

3.1   Freedom from incumbrances

3.1.1   The seller is selling the property free from incumbrances, other than those mentioned in condition 3.1.2.

3.1.2   The incumbrances subject to which the property is sold are:

(a)   those mentioned in the agreement

(b)   those discoverable by inspection of the property before the contract

(c)   those the seller does not and could not know about

(d)   entries made before the date of the contract in any public register except those maintained by HM Land Registry or its Land Charges Department or by Companies House

(e)   public requirements.

3.1.3   After the contract is made, the seller is to give the buyer written details without delay of any new public requirement and of anything in writing which he learns about concerning any incumbrance subject to which the property is sold.

3.1.4   The buyer is to bear the cost of complying with any outstanding public requirement and is to indemnify the seller against any liability resulting from a public requirement.

3.2   Physical state

3.2.1   The buyer accepts the property in the physical state it is in at the date of the contract, unless the seller is building or converting it.

3.2.2   A leasehold property is sold subject to any subsisting breach of a condition or tenant's obligation relating to the physical state of the property which renders the lease liable to forfeiture.

3.2.3   A sub-lease is granted subject to any subsisting breach of a condition or tenant's obligation relating to the physical state of the property which renders the seller's own lease liable to forfeiture.

3.3 Leases affecting the property

3.3.1 The following provisions apply if the agreement states that any part of the property is sold subject to a lease.

3.3.2 (a) The seller having provided the buyer with full details of each lease or copies of the documents embodying the lease terms, the buyer is treated as entering into the contract knowing and fully accepting those terms.

(b) The seller is to inform the buyer without delay if the lease ends or if the seller learns of any application by the tenant in connection with the lease; the seller is then to act as the buyer reasonably directs, and the buyer is to indemnify him against all consequent loss and expense.

(c) The seller is not to agree to any proposal to change the lease terms without the consent of the buyer and is to inform the buyer without delay of any change which may be proposed or agreed.

(d) The buyer is to indemnify the seller against all claims arising from the lease after actual completion; this includes claims which are unenforceable against a buyer for want of registration.

(e) The seller takes no responsibility for what rent is lawfully recoverable, nor for whether or how any legislation affects the lease.

(f) If the let land is not wholly within the property, the seller may apportion the rent.

3.4 Retained land

3.4.1 The following provisions apply where after the transfer the seller will be retaining land near the property.

3.4.2 The buyer will have no right of light or air over the retained land, but otherwise the seller and the buyer will each have the rights over the land of the other which they would have had if they were two separate buyers to whom the seller had made simultaneous transfers of the property and the retained land.

3.4.3 Either party may require that the transfer contain appropriate express terms.

4. TITLE AND TRANSFER

4.1 Timetable

4.1.1 The following are the steps for deducing and investigating the title to the property to be taken within the following time limits:

Step	Time Limit
1. The seller is to send the buyer evidence of title in accordance with condition 4.2	Immediately after making the contract
2. The buyer may raise written requisitions	Six working days after either the date of the contract or the date of delivery of the seller's evidence of title on which the requisitions are raised whichever is the later
3. The seller is to reply in writing to any requisitions raised	Four working days after receiving the requisitions
4. The buyer may make written observations on the seller's replies	Three working days after receiving the replies

The time limit on the buyer's right to raise requisitions applies even where the seller supplies incomplete evidence of his title, but the buyer may, within six working days from delivery of any further evidence, raise further requisitions resulting from that evidence. On the expiry of the relevant time limit the buyer loses his right to raise requisitions or make observations.

4.1.2 The parties are to take the following steps to prepare and agree the transfer of the property within the following time limits:

Step	Time Limit
A. The buyer is to send the seller a draft transfer	At least twelve working days before completion date
B. The seller is to approve or revise that draft and either return it or retain it for use as the actual transfer	Four working days after delivery of the draft transfer
C. If the draft is returned the buyer is to send an engrossment to the seller	At least five working days before completion date

4.1.3 Periods of time under conditions 4.1.1 and 4.1.2 may run concurrently.

4.1.4 If the period between the date of the contract and completion date is less than 15 working days, the time limits in conditions 4.1.1 and 4.1.2 are to be reduced by the same proportion as that period bears to the period of 15 working days. Fractions of a working day are to be rounded down except that the time limit to perform any step is not to be less than one working day.

4.2 Proof of title

4.2.1 The evidence of registered title is office copies of the items required to be furnished by section 110(1) of the Land Registration Act 1925 and the copies, abstracts and evidence referred to in section 110(2).

4.2.2 The evidence of unregistered title is an abstract of the title, or an epitome of title with photocopies of the relevant documents.

4.2.3 Where the title to the property is unregistered, the seller is to produce to the buyer (without cost to the buyer):

(a) the original of every relevant document, or

(b) an abstract, epitome or copy with an original marking by a solicitor of examination either against the original or against an examined abstract or against an examined copy.

4.3 Defining the property

4.3.1 The seller need not:

(a) prove the exact boundaries of the property

(b) prove who owns fences, ditches, hedges or walls

(c) separately identify parts of the property with different titles

further than he may be able to do from information in his possession.

4.3.2 The buyer may, if it is reasonable, require the seller to make or obtain, pay for and hand over a statutory declaration about facts relevant to the matters mentioned in condition 4.3.1. The form of the declaration is to be agreed by the buyer, who must not unreasonably withhold his agreement.

4.4 Rents and rentcharges

The fact that a rent or rentcharge, whether payable or receivable by the owner of the property, has been or will on completion be, informally apportioned is not to be regarded as a defect in title.

4.5   Transfer

4.5.1   The buyer does not prejudice his right to raise requisitions, or to require replies to any raised, by taking any steps in relation to the preparation or agreement of the transfer.

4.5.2   If the agreement makes no provision as to title guarantee, then subject to condition 4.5.3 the seller is to transfer the property with full title guarantee.

4.5.3   The transfer is to have effect as if the disposition is expressly made subject to all matters to which the property is sold subject under the terms of the contract.

4.5.4   If after completion the seller will remain bound by any obligation affecting the property, but the law does not imply any covenant by the buyer to indemnify the seller against liability for future breaches of it:

(a)   the buyer is to covenant in the transfer to indemnify the seller against liability for any future breach of the obligation and to perform it from then on, and

(b)   if required by the seller, the buyer is to execute and deliver to the seller on completion a duplicate transfer prepared by the buyer.

4.5.5   The seller is to arrange at his expense that, in relation to every document of title which the buyer does not receive on completion, the buyer is to have the benefit of:

(a)   a written acknowledgement of his right to its production, and

(b)   a written undertaking for its safe custody (except while it is held by a mortgagee or by someone in a fiduciary capacity).

5.   PENDING COMPLETION

5.1   Responsibility for property

5.1.1   The seller will transfer the property in the same physical state as it was at the date of the contract (except for fair wear and tear), which means that the seller retains the risk until completion.

5.1.2   If at any time before completion the physical state of the property makes it unusable for its purpose at the date of the contract:

(a)   the buyer may rescind the contract

(b)   the seller may rescind the contract where the property has become unusable for that purpose as a result of damage against which the seller could not reasonably have insured, or which it is not legally possible for the seller to make good.

5.1.3   The seller is under no obligation to the buyer to insure the property.

5.1.4   Section 47 of the Law of Property Act 1925 does not apply.

5.2   Occupation by buyer

5.2.1   If the buyer is not already lawfully in the property, and the seller agrees to let him into occupation, the buyer occupies on the following terms.

5.2.2   The buyer is a licensee and not a tenant. The terms of the licence are that the buyer:

(a)   cannot transfer it

(b)   may permit members of his household to occupy the property

(c)   is to pay or indemnify the seller against all outgoings and other expenses in respect of the property

(d)   is to pay the seller a fee calculated at the contract rate on the purchase price (less any deposit paid) for the period of the licence

(e) is entitled to any rents and profits from any part of the property which he does not occupy

(f) is to keep the property in as good a state of repair as it was in when he went into occupation (except for fair wear and tear) and is not to alter it

(g) is to insure the property in a sum which is not less than the purchase price against all risks in respect of which comparable premises are normally insured

(h) is to quit the property when the licence ends.

5.2.3 On the creation of the buyer's licence, condition 5.1 ceases to apply, which means that the buyer then assumes the risk until completion.

5.2.4 The buyer is not in occupation for the purposes of this condition if he merely exercises rights of access given solely to do work agreed by the seller.

5.2.5 The buyer's licence ends on the earliest of: completion date, rescission of the contract or when five working days' notice given by one party to the other takes effect.

5.2.6 If the buyer is in occupation of the property after his licence has come to an end and the contract is subsequently completed he is to pay the seller compensation for his continued occupation calculated at the same rate as the fee mentioned in condition 5.2.2(d).

5.2.7 The buyer's right to raise requisitions is unaffected.

6. COMPLETION

6.1 Date

6.1.1 Completion date is twenty working days after the date of the contract but time is not of the essence of the contract unless a notice to complete has been served.

6.1.2 If the money due on completion is received after 2.00pm, completion is to be treated, for the purposes only of conditions 6.3 and 7.3, as taking place on the next working day.

6.1.3 Condition 6.1.2 does not apply where the sale is with vacant possession of the property or any part and the seller has not vacated the property or that part by 2.00pm on the date of actual completion.

6.2 Place

Completion is to take place in England and Wales, either at the seller's solicitor's office or at some other place which the seller reasonably specifies.

6.3 Apportionments

6.3.1 Income and outgoings of the property are to be apportioned between the parties so far as the change of ownership on completion will affect entitlement to receive or liability to pay them.

6.3.2 If the whole property is sold with vacant possession or the seller exercises his option in condition 7.3.4, apportionment is to be made with effect from the date of actual completion; otherwise, it is to be made from completion date.

6.3.3 In apportioning any sum, it is to be assumed that the seller owns the property until the end of the day from which apportionment is made and that the sum accrues from day to day at the rate at which it is payable on that day.

6.3.4 For the purpose of apportioning income and outgoings, it is to be assumed that they accrue at an equal daily rate throughout the year.

6.3.5 When a sum to be apportioned is not known or easily ascertainable at completion, a provisional apportionment is to be made according to the best estimate available. As soon as the amount is known, a final apportionment is to be made and notified to the other party. Any resulting balance is to be paid no more than ten working days later, and if not then paid the balance is to bear interest at the contract rate from then until payment.

6.3.6 Compensation payable under condition 5.2.6 is not to be apportioned.

6.4   Amount payable

The amount payable by the buyer on completion is the purchase price (less any deposit already paid to the seller or his agent) adjusted to take account of:

(a)   apportionments made under condition 6.3

(b)   any compensation to be paid or allowed under condition 7.3.

6.5   Title deeds

6.5.1 The seller is not to retain the documents of title after the buyer has tendered the amount payable under condition 6.4.

6.5.2 Condition 6.5.1 does not apply to any documents of title relating to land being retained by the seller after completion.

6.6   Rent receipts

The buyer is to assume that whoever gave any receipt for a payment of rent or service charge which the seller produces was the person or the agent of the person then entitled to that rent or service charge.

6.7   Means of payment

The buyer is to pay the money due on completion in one or more of the following ways:

(a)   legal tender

(b)   a banker's draft

(c)   a direct credit to a bank account nominated by the seller's solicitor

(d)   an unconditional release of a deposit held by a stakeholder.

6.8   Notice to complete

6.8.1 At any time on or after completion date, a party who is ready able and willing to complete may give the other a notice to complete.

6.8.2 A party is ready able and willing:

(a)   if he could be, but for the default of the other party, and

(b)   in the case of the seller, even though a mortgage remains secured on the property, if the amount to be paid on completion enables the property to be transferred freed of all mortgages (except those to which the sale is expressly subject).

6.8.3 The parties are to complete the contract within ten working days of giving a notice to complete, excluding the day on which the notice is given. For this purpose, time is of the essence of the contract.

6.8.4 On receipt of a notice to complete:

(a)   if the buyer paid no deposit, he is forthwith to pay a deposit of 10 per cent

(b)   if the buyer paid a deposit of less than 10 per cent, he is forthwith to pay a further deposit equal to the balance of that 10 per cent.

7. REMEDIES

7.1 Errors and omission

7.1.1 If any plan or statement in the contract, or in the negotiations leading to it, is or was misleading or inaccurate due to an error or omission, the remedies available are as follows.

7.1.2 When there is a material difference between the description or value of the property as represented and as it is, the injured party is entitled to damages.

7.1.3 An error or omission only entitles the injured party to rescind the contract:

(a) where it results from fraud or recklessness, or

(b) where he would be obliged, to his prejudice, to transfer or accept property differing substantially (in quantity, quality or tenure) from what the error or omission had led him to expect.

7.2 Rescission

If either party rescinds the contract:

(a) unless the rescission is a result of the buyer's breach of contract the deposit is to be repaid to the buyer with accrued interest

(b) the buyer is to return any documents he received from the seller and is to cancel any registration of the contract.

7.3 Late completion

7.3.1 If there is default by either or both of the parties in performing their obligations under the contract and completion is delayed, the party whose total period of default is the greater is to pay compensation to the other party.

7.3.2 Compensation is calculated at the contract rate on the purchase price, or (where the buyer is the paying party) the purchase price less any deposit paid, for the period by which the paying party's default exceeds that of the receiving party, or, if shorter, the period between completion date and actual completion.

7.3.3 Any claim for loss resulting from delayed completion is to be reduced by any compensation paid under this contract.

7.3.4 Where the buyer holds the property as tenant of the seller and completion is delayed, the seller may give notice to the buyer, before the date of actual completion, that he intends to take the net income from the property until completion. If he does so, he cannot claim compensation under condition 7.3.1 as well.

7.4 After completion

Completion does not cancel liability to perform any outstanding obligation under this contract.

7.5 Buyer's failure to comply with notice to complete

7.5.1 If the buyer fails to complete in accordance with a notice to complete, the following terms apply.

7.5.2 The seller may rescind the contract, and if he does so:

(a) he may

(i) forfeit and keep any deposit and accrued interest

(ii) resell the property

(iii) claim damages

(b)   the buyer is to return any documents he received from the seller and is to cancel any registration of the contract.

7.5.3   The seller retains his other rights and remedies.

7.6   Seller's failure to comply with notice to complete

7.6.1   If the seller fails to complete in accordance with a notice to complete, the following terms apply.

7.6.2   The buyer may rescind the contract, and if he does so:

(a)   the deposit is to be repaid to the buyer with accrued interest

(b)   the buyer is to return any documents he received from the seller and is, at the seller's expense, to cancel any registration of the contract.

7.6.3   The buyer retains his other rights and remedies.

8.   LEASEHOLD PROPERTY

8.1   **Existing leases**

8.1.1   The following provisions apply to a sale of leasehold land.

8.1.2   The seller having provided the buyer with copies of the documents embodying the lease terms, the buyer is treated as entering into the contract knowing and fully accepting those terms.

8.1.3   The seller is to comply with any lease obligations requiring the tenant to insure the property.

8.2   **New leases**

8.2.1   The following provisions apply to a grant of a new lease.

8.2.2   The conditions apply so that:

'seller' means the proposed landlord

'buyer' means the proposed tenant

'purchase price' means the premium to be paid on the grant of a lease.

8.2.3   The lease is to be in the form of the draft attached to the agreement.

8.2.4   If the term of the new lease will exceed 21 years, the seller is to deduce a title which will enable the buyer to register the lease at HM Land Registry with an absolute title.

8.2.5   The buyer is not entitled to transfer the benefit of the contract.

8.2.6   The seller is to engross the lease and a counterpart of it and is to send the counterpart to the buyer at least five working days before completion date.

8.2.7   The buyer is to execute the counterpart and deliver it to the seller on completion.

8.3   **Landlord's consent**

8.3.1   The following provisions apply if a consent to assign or sub-let is required to complete the contract.

8.3.2   (a)   The seller is to apply for the consent at his expense, and to use all reasonable efforts to obtain it.

(b)   The buyer is to provide all information and references reasonably required.

8.3.3   The buyer is not entitled to transfer the benefit of the contract.

8.3.4 Unless he is in breach of his obligation under condition 8.3.2, either party may rescind the contract by notice to the other party if three working days before completion date:

(a) the consent has not been given or

(b) the consent has been given subject to a condition to which the buyer reasonably objects.

In that case, neither party is to be treated as in breach of contract and condition 7.2 applies.

9. CHATTELS

9.1 The following provisions apply to any chattels which are to be sold.

9.2 Whether or not a separate price is to be paid for the chattels, the contract takes effect as a contract for sale of goods.

9.3 Ownership of the chattels passes to the buyer on actual completion.

SPECIAL CONDITIONS

1. (a) This Agreement incorporates the Standard Conditions of Sales (Third Edition). Where there is a conflict between those Conditions and this Agreement, this Agreement prevails.

   (b) Terms used or defined in this Agreement have the same meaning when used in the Conditions.

2. The Property is sold subject to the Incumbrances on the Property and the Buyer will raise no requisitions on them.

3. Subject to the terms of this Agreement and to the Standard Conditions of Sale, the Seller is to transfer the Property with the title guarantee specified on the front page.

4. The chattels on the Property and set out on any attached list are included in the sale.

5. The Property is sold with vacant possession on completion.

(or) 5. The Property is sold subject to the following leases or tenancies:

Seller's Solicitors   :

Buyer's Solicitors   :

VIII. FORMS AND GUIDANCE FROM OTHER ORGANISATIONS

VIII.1. Association for Payment Clearing Services – an overview[1]

The Association for Payment Clearing Services was set up in 1985 as a non-statutory association of major banks and building societies and has become the umbrella body at the heart of the UK payments industry. APACS provides the forum for banks and building societies to discuss non-competitive issues relating to money transmission.

Within the APACS umbrella are three clearing companies which manage the major UK payment clearing systems and to maintain their operational efficiency and financial integrity:

- Cheque and Credit Clearing Company which oversees the paper clearing.

- CHAPS Clearing Company which provides electronic same-day clearings in sterling and euro.

- BACS which operates the bulk electronic clearing.

A range of other senior industry groups also operate under the umbrella of APACS: Card Payments Group, Cash Services Group, Liquidity Managers Group, Electronic Commerce Group and the Currency Clearings Committee.

In addition, APACS forecasts payment trends, conducts market research and maintains a large body of statistics. The Association also formulates payments industry standards.

Planning has also been undertaken to ensure that, when and if HM Government decides the UK will join EMU, there will be a smooth transition from sterling to euro.

APACS provides the single industry voice to the public and to the media on all non-competitive payment matters.

Although APACS is often described as the governing body for the whole payment system this is not strictly correct as there are a number of different constituent parts.

These entities are:

- Association for Payment Clearing Services

- BACS Ltd

- Cheque and Credit Clearing Company Ltd

- CHAPS Clearing Company Ltd

- APACS (Administration) Ltd

1. The material in this appendix is reproduced with the permission of the Association for Payment Clearing Services.

In broad terms, the three Clearing Companies, BACS Ltd, Cheque and Credit Clearing Company Ltd, and CHAPS Clearing Company Ltd are responsible for the operation of, and future developments within, the clearings that they run. Each has its own Board of Directors. The Association for Payment Clearing Services is responsible for overseeing these key areas, and covering other relevant payment issues. The governing body is the APACS Council. Staff, facilities and premises for all these bodies (except BACS Ltd) are provided by APACS (Administration) Ltd. It has a Board of Directors drawn by custom from Council Members.

Membership of APACS, the Clearing Companies, Card Payments Group, Cash Services Group and Liquidity Managers Group

Members	APACS	BACS	Cheque and credit	CHAPS Sterling	CHAPS Euro	Card payments group	Cash Services Group	Liquidity Managers Group
Abbey National	X	X	X	–	X	X	X	X
ABN AMRO Bank N.V.	X	–	–	X	X	–	–	X
Bank of America NA	X	–	–	–	X	–	–	X
Bank of England	X	X	X	X	X	–	X	X
Bank of Scotland (HBOS)	X	X	X	X	X	X	X	X
The Bank of Tokyo – Mitsubishi Ltd	X	–	–	–	X	–	–	X
Barclays Bank	X	X	X	X	X	X	X	X
Capital One Bank (Europe) Plc	X	–	–	–	–	X	–	–
Citibank	X	–	–	X	X	–	–	X
Clydesdale Bank Plc	X	X	X	X	–	X	–	X
Co-operative Bank Plc (The)	X	X	X	X	X	X	X	X
Coutts & Co	X	X	–	–	–	–	–	–
Den norske Bank AS	X	–	–	–	X	–	–	X
Deutsche Bank	X	–	–	X	X	–	–	X
Dresdner Bank AG	X	–	–	–	X	–	–	X
Egg Banking Plc	X	–	–	–	–	X	–	–
Girobank Plc	X	X	X	–	–	X	X	–
HFC Bank Plc	X	–	–	–	–	X	–	–
HSBC Bank Plc	X	X	X	X	X	X	X	X
JP Morgan AG	X	–	–	–	X	–	–	X
Lloyds TSB Bank Plc	X	X	X	X	X	X	X	X
MBNA Europe Bank	X	–	–	–	–	X	–	–
Morgan Stanley Dean Witter Bank Limited	X	–	–	–	–	X	–	–
National Australia Bank Ltd	X	–	–	–	X	–	–	X
National Westminster Bank Public Limited Company	X	X	X	X	X	X	X	X
Nationwide Building Society	X	X	X	–	–	X	X	–
Northern Rock Plc	X	X	–	–	–	–	–	–
The Royal Bank of Scotland Public Limited Company	X	X	X	X	X	X	X	X
Royal Mail Group Plc	X	–	–	–	–	–	X	–
Standard Chartered Bank	X	–	–	X	X	–	–	X
Wachovia Bank, National Association	X	–	–	–	X	–	–	X
Woolwich	X	–	–	–	–	X	–	–
Members	**32**	**14**	**12**	**13**	**20**	**17**	**12**	**21**

VIII.2. CLLS Certificate of Title and Short Report on Title[1]

Introduction

Certificates of title are used in many different transactions. These include secured loans, mortgage debenture stock issues, acquisitions of companies and businesses, flotations and privatisations.

As users will know, the sub-committee produced a first draft of the certificate of title, with a view to reducing as much as possible the negotiation that used to take place over the form of such certificates.

This objective seems to have been achieved, in that now the certificate is accepted as the standard by many firms in the UK.

Some lenders insist on the certificate being used. In their 1995 report on streamlining commercial property transactions, the Investment Property Forum working party drew attention to it.

Dissemination of each new edition of the certificate has been a problem in the past. However, this has been overcome by:

(a)   publishing in the *Encyclopaedia of Forms and Precedents* (Butterworths);

(b)   publishing on the City of London Law Society web site (www.citysolicitors.org).

The fourth edition incorporates a number of changes suggested by users. Comments on the certificate can be made either to Butterworths, or to the administrator at the City of London Law Society. The sub-committee plans to issue the next edition in 2003.

General points

A considerable amount of the information contained in the certificate will be based on information provided by the owner of the property. To this extent, the certificate replaces the normal enquiries before contract. This means that the solicitors giving the certificate will have to liaise closely with the owner of the property to obtain this information. Those advising the recipient of the certificate may also wish to suggest to their client that the owner of the property warrants the accuracy of the information. Obviously, this warranty cannot appear in the certificate itself but could be included in the document dealing with the transaction in connection with which the certificate is being given.

Inevitably different circumstances will require different forms of certificate, so it is not suggested that the draft can be used unchanged in every case. Indeed, there will be transactions where use of a certificate, even generally in the form of the draft, will not be appropriate but which will require a certificate in a quite different, and probably shorter, form. Having said that, when it is appropriate to use the draft, it is intended to be a comprehensive form of certificate which strikes a reasonable balance between the interests of those to whom it is addressed and the solicitors by whom it is given.

Often the certificate will be given to a lender providing finance for the company to purchase the property. In this case, the company's knowledge of the property will be slight and it will be relying on the information provided by the seller's solicitors.

---

1. © City of London Law Society. This Appendix comprises extracts from the notes to the City of London Law Society 4th edition.

The certificate deals with this by including an optional reference to the seller, as well as, or instead of, the company, in the appropriate places.

The certificate has been prepared on the basis that the recipient will take his own professional advice on its contents if he considers it necessary to do so. From discussions which some members of the sub-committee have had with other solicitors in the past, it is clear that some solicitors used to take the view that a certificate of title should be in a form in which the recipient could rely on it without needing to take his own professional advice. Putting the same point in another way, this school of thought used to take the view that not only should the certificate highlight problems, it should also provide some assessment of the risks arising from these problems.

The sub-committee has always disagreed with this view. The members of the sub-committee have always considered that the function of the certificate is to provide specific information about the property. The recipient of the certificate, with the help of his own professional advisers, can then decide whether the property is one which can be accepted for the transaction in question.

However, if the recipient of the certificate, or those advising him, reasonably consider that more information needs to be provided by the firm giving the certificate to enable a proper assessment to be made of any risks disclosed by the certificate, the recipient or those advising him should be entitled to ask for this information.

Another point which sometimes arises in relation to a certificate is whether the certificate should annex copies of documents, or extracts from documents, or whether it should summarise the effect of those documents without attaching copies of them. The sub-committee's view is that normally the certificate should summarise any relevant documents and that it should not be necessary to annex copies of them to it. The certificate is intended to replace an investigation of title by the recipient's solicitors. If they have to read, not only the certificate, but also a bundle of documents attached to it, the point of the certificate is to some extent lost.

Having said that, the sub-committee appreciates that there are circumstances when a document, or a part of a document, is so important and so complex that it cannot be summarised accurately. The sub-committee believes that such circumstances are rare, but where they do exist, it would be appropriate for the document, or an extract from it, to be annexed to the certificate.

The sub-committee appreciates that this certificate of title may not be appropriate where the property is held under a rack rent lease and has no capital value. In these circumstances, a shorter version of the certificate may be appropriate or even a certificate or report in a quite different form.

The sub-committee has established a working party which is actively considering what form of certificate or report is appropriate in relation to properties of this type, with a view to producing a draft.

With the increase in stamp duty to 3.5% on purchases above £500,000, property is now more frequently bought in the name of a company specially formed for that purpose, a special purpose vehicle or SPV. Those giving a certificate of title may wish to consider whether, in these circumstances, it is appropriate for the certificate to be given to the SPV. If subsequently the shares in the SPV are sold, rather than the property itself being sold, the liability of the firm giving the certificate will continue for the benefit of a second purchaser. Had the property itself been sold, as has normally happened in the past, liability would effectively have ceased on sale.

Since the introduction on 1st October, 1999 of the new Rule 6(3) of the Solicitors' Practice Rules, concerns have been expressed as to whether the certificate can be given in its present form when it is being used for secured lending transactions.

Rule 6(3)(a) prohibits a solicitor from acting for both borrower and lender in the following circumstances, among others:

(a)   on the grant of a private mortgage of land at arm's length.

(b)   in the case of an institutional mortgage of property to be used other than as a private residence only, if the lender's mortgage instructions extend beyond the limitations in paragraphs (3)(c) and (3)(e).

Rule 6(3)(f) prohibits a solicitor who is acting only for the borrower in an institutional mortgage from accepting or acting on any requirement of the lender which extends beyond these limitations.

The notes to the rule state that an institutional mortgage is a mortgage on standard terms, provided by an institutional lender in the normal course of its activities and a private mortgage is any other mortgage.

In discussions with the Law Society, they have confirmed informally that, clearly, there is no problem in the lender's solicitor giving a certificate in the form of the CLLS certificate to his own client, the lender, if the borrower and the lender are separately represented and the mortgage is a private mortgage. In practice, the lender's solicitor would be more likely to give the lender a report on the title rather than the certificate.

They have also given a preliminary view that, so long as there is no retainer between the borrower's solicitor and the lender, the rule would not prevent the borrower's solicitor giving the lender a certificate of title in the form of the CLLS certificate if the lender is separately represented and the mortgage is a private mortgage.

If and to the extent that rule 6(3) prohibits the borrower's solicitors giving the certificate to the lender on an institutional mortgage, whether or not the parties are separately represented, the Law Society is considering whether this can be permitted and, if so, on what basis. This note will be updated as and when further information is available.

VIII

VIII.3. The CML Lenders' Handbook for England and Wales (2nd Edition) Part 1

Part 1 of the CML Lenders' Handbook for England and Wales is reproduced in this appendix with the kind permission of the Council of Mortgage Lenders. Part 2 of the Handbook for England and Wales and the editions of the Handbook for Scotland and the Isle of Man are only available online (at www.cml.org.uk). Solicitors are advised to always check the CML website for the latest version of the Handbook.

INTRODUCTION

The CML Lenders' Handbook provides comprehensive instructions for solicitors and licensed conveyancers acting on behalf of lenders in conveyancing transactions. The Lenders' Handbook was developed by seven major lenders (Halifax, Abbey National, Cheltenham & Gloucester, Woolwich, Nationwide, Alliance & Leicester and Natwest Mortgage Services) together with the CML in close consultation with the Law Society. The Lenders' Handbook complies with the requirements of the Solicitors' Practice Rules 1990.

The Lenders' Handbook is divided into two parts:

Part 1 sets out the main instructions and guidance which must be followed by conveyancers.

Part 2 details each lender's specific requirements which arise from those instructions.

Use of the Lenders' Handbook is not mandatory for lenders. A list of lenders who have adopted the Lenders' Handbook is available in Part 2. The instructions from individual lenders will indicate if the conveyancer is being instructed in accordance with the Lenders' Handbook. Where this is the case, conveyancers should follow the instructions in the Lenders' Handbook and not any checklist or aide memoire produced by a third party.

Only members of the CML and their subsidiaries are permitted to instruct in accordance with the Lenders' Handbook.

The second edition of the Lenders' Handbook

The second edition of the Lenders' Handbook came into effect on 1 October 2002. Conveyancers instructed by lenders on or after 1 October 2002 must use the second edition. Conveyancers instructed prior to 1 October 2002 must continue to use the first edition of the Lenders' Handbook (dated July 1999 and last amended June 2000) until the transaction is complete. The first edition is available online at www.cml.org.uk and was reproduced in Appendix XI of the Conveyancing Handbook 2001 (8th edition).

Queries on the Lenders' Handbook and Solicitors' Practice Rules

If a conveyancer has a query on the Lenders' Handbook, this must be raised with the instructing lender and not the Council of Mortgage Lenders. For queries on the Solicitors' Practice Rules, please contact the Law Society's Professional Ethics (0870 606 2577) or the Law Society's Practice Advice Service (0870 606 2522).

AMENDMENTS TO THE FIRST EDITION OF THE CML LENDER'S HANDBOOK FOR ENGLAND AND WALES

This section outlines the changes which have been made to the first edition of the CML Lenders' Handbook for England & Wales published in July 1999. These amendments have been made in consultation with the Law Society of England & Wales, the Council of Licensed Conveyancers and mortgage lenders. The second edition incorporates the amendments made in October 1999 and June 2000.

General (paragraph 1.16)

This is a new instruction at the request of the Law Society which reiterates the conveyancer's duty to the borrower client.

Communication (paragraph 2.3)

This paragraph now makes it clear that if a conveyancer does need to refer a matter to the lender, certain information must be provided. This includes identifying the issue and the extent to which it is not covered in the Handbook, a concise summary of the legal risks and a recommendation on how the lender should protect its interests. This should help streamline the process and make it transparent as to what information is required. Lenders have seen many cases where an issue is covered in the Handbook but this has not been identified by the conveyancer.

Safeguards (paragraph 3.1)

This section reminds licensed conveyancers that they should also refer to any guidance issued by the Council. The original text simply reminded solicitors to follow guidance issued by the Law Society.

Identity checks (paragraph 3.3)

With regard to identity checks, the list of documentary evidence has been updated to include the new UK Photo-card driving licence.

Searches and Reports (paragraph 5.2.3)

This instruction now requires all searches (except where there is a priority period) to be not more than six months old at completion. The earlier instruction adopted a two-pronged approach requiring searches to be not more than three months old at exchange and not more than six months old at completion. This had led to cases where searches met one part of the criteria but not the other. This amendment should result in a more straightforward approach.

Envrionmental search reports (paragraph 5.2.5)

Many lenders do not want conveyancers to send them a copy of environmental or contaminated land reports which may have been commissioned for the buyer. Lenders can now set out in Part 2 whether they do want to see such reports. Where this is not the case, the Handbook also makes it clear that the conveyancer does not need to make these enquiries on the lender's behalf.

Personal searches of local authorities (paragraph 5.2.6)

In recent years, there has been an expansion in the number of companies providing local authority search information. The Handbook has been updated to reflect this position and now refers to personal searches, searches carried out by private search organisations and search insurance. Lenders will be able to indicate which they will accept in Part 2.

Indemnity insurance (paragraph 5.2.7)

Where lenders do accept searches under paragraph 5.2.6, then paragraph 5.2.7 sets out what indemnity insurance should be in position.

Planning and Building Regulations (paragraph 5.3)

This paragraph has been updated so that the conveyancer not only has to look at potential breaches of planning and building consents but also to check that the property has the benefit of any necessary planning consents to begin with.

Good and Marketable Title (paragraph 5.4.2)

The layout has been updated for ease of reference.

Flying Freeholds, Freehold Flats and other Freehold Arrangements (paragraph 5.5)

This paragraph has been updated to incorporate some of the many different freehold flat arrangements which arise in different parts of the country. Many of the examples refer to properties split into not more than four flats. In some parts of the country, there may be properties with more than four flats. In this scenario, the conveyancer should refer the matter to the lender in accordance with paragraph 2.3.

Restrictive Covenants (paragraph 5.7)

The text in paragraph 5.7.1 has been amended to cross-refer to paragraph 5.7.2 and the circumstances where indemnity insurance would not be required where there is an enforceability risk on the breach of a restrictive covenant.

Leasehold Property (paragraph 5.10.4)

The layout has been amended to split earlier paragraphs in the Handbook which had been very long.

Mutual enforceability covenants (paragraph 5.10.6.3)

This has been amended at the request of the Law Society to make it clear that lenders only require mutual enforceability covenants where one or more of the tenants in the building are responsible for the insurance, maintenance and repair of the common services.

Indemnity insurance to remedy a defect in a lease (paragraph 5.10.9)

Lenders can now stipulate in Part 2 whether they will accept indemnity insurance to remedy a defect in a lease. We do not expect many lenders to amend their existing lending policies on this issue, as indemnity insurance has provided an effective form of recourse in such circumstances and has assisted the mortgageability of these properties.

Notice of the mortgage (paragraph 5.10.11)

In some cases, conveyancers are unable to obtain receipt of the notice of the mortgage as served on the landlord. In such cases, then as a last resort, suitable evidence of service of the notice can now be provided.

Management Company (paragraph 5.11.1)

In recognition that many management companies may not have a formal interest in a property, the Handbook has been amended to refer to a 'legal right to enter' to maintain and repair the common parts. This should allow greater flexibility.

Management Company check (paragraph 5.11.2)

This paragraph has been updated to confirm that a conveyancer must check that the Management Company is registered at Companies House and obtain the last three years' published accounts or the accounts from inception if it has only been formed in the last three years.

Powers of Attorney (paragraph 5.13)

The paragraph confirms that in the case of joint borrowers, neither borrower can appoint the other as their attorney.

New Properties (paragraph 6.6)

The layout has been amended and divided into two sections. The first deals with new properties built or converted under a new home warranty scheme. The second deals with new properties built or converted under the supervision of a professional consultant. For new home warranty schemes, an additional scheme has been included, Premier Guarantee which has recently entered the market. It will be for each lender to decide whether they accept this warranty. If additional schemes are launched in the future, lenders can also set out in Part 2 which they accept (see paragraph 6.6.1.2). The Handbook has also been amended to allow lenders to set out in Part 2 (paragraph 6.6.2) what new home warranty scheme documentation should be sent to them. With more lenders pursuing the dematerialisation of documentation relating to a mortgage transaction, it is clear that lenders' requirements will differ.

The paragraphs on the supervision of work by a professional consultant have been changed to reflect amendments to the names of the professional building organisations. The Consultant's Certificate has also been updated in consultation with these professional bodies and in particular the RICS and RIBA.

Roads and Sewers (paragraph 6.7.3)

This paragraph has been added to provide that where there is an agreement between the developer and the lender whereby the lender will not require a retention in connection with roads and sewers, the conveyancer should seek confirmation from the developer that this is still in position. In practice, the developer's conveyancer will put together the developer's title package and so will have this information.

Insurance (paragraph 6.13.6)

Some lenders no longer require conveyancers to check the individual risks contained in a policy and it is expected that more lenders will pursue a similar approach in the future. This paragraph has been made a Part 2 issue, to reflect this change in lender requirements. The list of risks remains largely unaltered; however, accidental breakage of glass and sanitary ware has been removed and coverage of professional fees, demolition and site clearance costs has been added.

The Loan and Certificate of Title (paragraph 10.2)

This paragraph now provides additional information so that the conveyancer can identify how the mortgage will be paid, whether by cheque or electronically and the minimum number of days notice required. Lenders will also set out in Part 2 whether there are any standard deductions made from the mortgage, so the position is clear to the conveyancer.

Title Deeds (paragraph 14.2.1)

Reference to the schedule of title deeds being in 'triplicate' has been deleted reflecting changes in lender practice.

Discharge (paragraph 17.2)

This paragraph has been updated so that lenders will set out in Part 2 whether the discharge will be via a DS1 or direct with the Land Registry.

AMENDMENT TO THE SECOND EDITION OF THE CML LENDERS' HANDBOOK FOR ENGLAND AND WALES

On 1 April 2003, the CML amended 6.6.2 of the Lenders' Handbook to read:

'Before you send us the certificate of title, you must obtain a copy of a new home warranty provider's cover note from the developer. The cover note must confirm that the property has received a satisfactory final inspection and that the new home warranty will be in place on or before completion. This will only apply where exchange of contracts occurs on or after 1 April 2003. This does not apply to self-build schemes. Check part 2 to see what new home warranty documentation should be sent to us on completion.'

The new home warranty providers

The new home warranty providers are currently doing much work to ensure that the necessary procedures are in place in the run-up to implementation. This includes guidance to builders on inspection standards, so that builders will only apply for a final inspection once all the standards have been met.

The developers

The HBF is looking at what changes should be made to builders' contracts for sale to reflect the revised approach and address any concerns that conveyancers may have regarding time constraints and liability. Builders will need to:

- Ensure that the property is completed to the required standard before applying for the final inspection by the new home warranty provider;

- Supply the cover note immediately to the buyer's conveyancer;

- Bear in mind when formulating the legal completion date in the contracts for sale that the conveyancer will be unable to submit the certificate of title to the lender until the conveyancer has received the cover note; and the lender will have a minimum notice period of five working days (in some cases longer) for the release of mortgage funds after receipt of the certificate of title, and;

- Request their lawyers to make the necessary amendments to the legal documentation for the sale of new properties as a result of the changes in approach and timing referred to earlier.

It is clear that this is a significant change in approach to improve standards and all the parties are working together to achieve smooth implementation.

PART 1 – INSTRUCTIONS AND GUIDANCE

Those lenders who instruct using the CML Lenders' Handbook certify that these instructions have been prepared to comply with the requirements of Rule 6 (3) of the Solicitors' Practice Rules 1990.

1. GENERAL

1.1 The CML Lenders' Handbook is issued by the Council of Mortgage Lenders. Your instructions from an individual lender will indicate if you are being instructed in accordance with the Lenders' Handbook. If you are, the general provisions in part 1 and any specific requirements in part 2 must be followed.

1.2 References to 'we' and 'our' means the lender from whom you receive instructions.

1.3 The Lenders' Handbook does not affect any responsibilities you have to us under the general law or any practice rule or guidance issued by your professional body from time to time.

1.4 The standard of care which we expect of you is that of a reasonably competent solicitor or licensed conveyancer acting on behalf of a mortgagee.

1.5 The limitations contained in rule 6(3)(c) and (e) of the Solicitors' Practice Rules 1990 apply to the instructions contained in the Lenders' Handbook and any separate instructions.

1.6 You must also comply with any separate instructions you receive for an individual loan.

1.7 If the borrower and the mortgagor are not one and the same person, all references to 'borrower' shall include the mortgagor.

1.8 References to 'borrower' (and, if applicable, 'guarantor' or, expressly or impliedly, the mortgagor) are to each borrower (and guarantor or mortgagor) named in the mortgage instructions/offer (if sent to the conveyancer). This applies to references in the Lenders' Handbook and in the certificate of title.

1.9 References to 'mortgage offer' include any loan agreement, offer of mortgage or any other similar document.

1.10 If you are instructed in connection with any additional loan (including a further advance) then you should treat references to 'mortgage' and 'mortgage offer' as applying to such 'additional loan' and 'additional loan offer' respectively.

1.11 In any transaction during the lifetime of the mortgage when we instruct you, you must use our current standard documents in all cases and must not amend them without our written consent. We will send you all the standard documents necessary to enable you to comply with our instructions, but please let us know if you need any other documents and we will send these to you. Check part 2 to see who you should contact. If you consider that any of the documentation is inappropriate to the particular facts of a transaction, you should write to us (see part 2) with full details and any suggested amendments.

1.12 In order to act on our behalf your firm must be a member of our conveyancing panel. You must also comply with any terms and conditions of your panel appointment.

1.13 If you or a member of your immediate family (that is to say, a spouse, co-habitee, parent, sibling, child, step-parent, step-child, grandparent, grandchild, parent-in- law, or child-in-law) is the borrower and you are a sole practitioner, you must not act for us.

1.14 Your firm or company must not act for us if the partner or fee earner dealing with the transaction or a member of his immediate family is the borrower, unless we say your firm may act (see part 2) and a separate fee earner of no less standing or a partner within the firm acts for us.

1.15 If there is any conflict of interest, you must not act for us and must return our instructions.

1.16 Nothing in these instructions lessens your duties to the borrower.

2.   COMMUNICATIONS

2.1   All communications between you and us should be in writing quoting the mortgage account or roll number, the surname and initials of the borrower and the property address. You should keep copies of all written communication on your file as evidence of notification and authorisation. If you use PC fax or e-mail, you should keep a paper copy.

2.2   If you require deeds or information from us in respect of a borrower or a property then you must first of all have the borrower's authority for such a request. If there is more than one borrower, you must have the authority of all the borrowers.

2.3   If you need to report a matter to us, you must do so as soon as you become aware of it so as to avoid any delay. If you do not believe that a matter is adequately provided for in the Handbook, you should identify the relevant Handbook provision and the extent to which the issue is not covered by it. You should provide a concise summary of the legal risks and your recommendation on how we should protect our interest. After reporting a matter you should not complete the mortgage until you have received our further written instructions. We recommend that you report such matters before exchange of contracts because we may have to withdraw or change the mortgage offer.

3.   SAFEGUARDS

3.1   You must follow the guidance in the Law Society's Green Card (mortgage fraud) and Pink Card (undertakings) and, to the extent that they apply, comply with the Money Laundering Regulations 1993 (see the Law Society's Blue Card). Licensed conveyancers must follow any guidance issued by the Council for Licensed Conveyancers.

3.2   If you are not familiar with the seller's solicitors or licensed conveyancers, you must verify that they appear in a legal directory or they are currently on record with the Law Society or Council for Licensed Conveyancers as practising at the address shown on their note paper.

3.3   Unless you personally know the signatory of a document, you must ask the signatory to provide evidence of identity, which you must carefully check. You should check the signatory's identity against one of the documents from list A or two of the documents in list B:

List A

–   a valid full passport; or

–   a valid H M Forces identity card with the signatory's photograph; or

–   a valid UK Photo-card driving licence; or

–   any other document listed in the additional list A in part 2.

List B

–   a cheque guarantee card, credit card (bearing the Mastercard or Visa logo), American Express or Diners Club card, debit or multi-function card (bearing the Switch or Delta logo) issued in the United Kingdom with an original account statement less than three months old; or

–   a firearm and shot gun certificate; or

–   a receipted utility bill less than three months old; or

–   a council tax bill less than three months old; or

–   a council rent book showing the rent paid for the last three months; or

–   a mortgage statement from another lender for the mortgage accounting year just ended; or

–   any other document listed in the additional list B in part 2.

You should check that any document you use to verify a signatory's identity appears to be authentic and current, signed in the relevant place. You should take a copy of it and keep the copy on your file. You should also check that the signatory's signature on any document being used to verify identity matches the signatory's signature on the document we require the signatory to sign and that the address shown on any document used to verify identity is that of the signatory.

3.4 All your duties to us under the Lenders' Handbook in relation to identifying signatories of documents will be satisfied by you complying with paragraphs 3.1, 3.2 and 3.3.

4. VALUATION OF THE PROPERTY

4.1 Valuation

4.1.1 Check part 2 to see whether we send you a copy of the valuation report or if you must get it from the borrower. If you are sent, or are required to obtain, a copy of the valuation report:

4.1.1.1 you must take reasonable steps to verify that there are no discrepancies between the description of the property as valued and the title and other documents which a reasonably competent conveyancer should obtain, and, if there are, you must tell us immediately; and

4.1.1.2 you should take reasonable steps to verify that the assumptions stated by the valuer about the title (for example, its tenure, easements, boundaries and restrictions on its use) in the valuation are correct. If they are not, please let us know as soon as possible (see part 2) as it will be necessary for us to check with the valuer whether the valuation needs to be revised. We are not expecting you to assume the role of valuer. We are simply trying to ensure that the valuer has valued the property based on correct information.

4.1.2 We recommend that you should advise the borrower that there may be defects in the property which are not revealed by the inspection carried out by our valuer and there may be omissions or inaccuracies in the report which do not matter to us but which would matter to the borrower. We recommend that, if we send a copy of a valuation report that we have obtained, you should also advise the borrower that the borrower should not rely on the report in deciding whether to proceed with the purchase and that he obtains his own more detailed report on the condition and value of the property, based on a fuller inspection, to enable him to decide whether the property is suitable for his purposes.

4.2 Re-inspection

Where the mortgage offer states that a final inspection is needed, you must ask for the final inspection at least 10 working days before the advance is required. Failure to do so may cause delay in the issue of the advance. Your certificate of title must be sent to us in the usual way (see part 2).

5. TITLE

5.1 Surrounding Circumstances

5.1.1 Please report to us (see part 2) if the owner or registered proprietor has been registered for less than six months or the person selling to the borrower is not the owner or registered proprietor unless the seller is:

5.1.1.1 a personal representative of the registered proprietor; or

5.1.1.2 an institutional mortgagee exercising its power of sale; or

5.1.1.3 a receiver, trustee-in-bankruptcy or liquidator; or

5.1.1.4 developer or builder selling a property acquired under a part-exchange scheme.

5.1.2 If any matter comes to the attention of the fee earner dealing with the transaction which you should reasonably expect us to consider important in deciding whether or not to lend to the borrower (such as whether the borrower has given misleading information to us or the information which you might reasonably expect to have been given to us is no longer true) and you are unable to disclose that information to us because of a conflict of interest, you must cease to act for us and return our instructions stating that you consider a conflict of interest has arisen.

5.2 Searches and Reports

5.2.1 In carrying out your investigation, you must make all usual and necessary searches and enquiries. We must be named as the applicant in the Land Registry search.

5.2.2 In addition, you must carry out any other searches which may be appropriate to the particular property, taking into account its locality and other features (see also paragraph 5.2.5).

5.2.3 All searches except where there is a priority period must not be more than six months old at completion.

5.2.4 You must make a mining search (such as a coal, tin, china clay or brine search) where it is reasonable to believe that the property could be affected by underground workings. The search must not be more than six months old at completion. In the case of a coal mining search, if the results of the search from the Coal Authority are such that the property is not affected by any of the matters mentioned in the report then we do not need to be notified of its contents. Subject to that, you should advise us if any entries are revealed in the same way as you would advise the borrower. You should not simply send us a copy of the mining search.

5.2.5 You must advise us of any contaminated land entries revealed in the local authority search. Check part 2 to see if we want to receive environmental or contaminated land reports (as opposed to contaminated land entries revealed in the local authority search). If we do not, you do not need to make these enquiries on our behalf.

5.2.6 For local authority searches under paragraph 5.2.1, check part 2 to see if we accept:

5.2.6.1 personal searches; or

5.2.6.2 searches carried out by private search organisations; or

5.2.6.3 search insurance.

5.2.7 If we do accept personal searches, searches carried out by private search organisations or search insurance, you must ensure:

5.2.7.1 a suitably qualified search agent carries out the personal search and has indemnity insurance that adequately protects us; or

5.2.7.2 the private search organisation's indemnity insurance adequately protects us; or

5.2.7.3 the search insurance policy adequately protects us.

You must be satisfied that you will be able to certify that the title is good and marketable.

5.3 Planning and Building Regulations

5.3.1 You must by making appropriate searches and enquiries take all reasonable steps (including any further enquiries to clarify any issues which may arise) to ensure:

5.3.1.1 the property has the benefit of any necessary planning consents; and

5.3.1.2 there is no evidence of any breach of the conditions of that or any other consent or certificate affecting the property; and

5.3.1.3 that no matter is revealed which would preclude the property from being used as a residential property or that the property may be the subject of enforcement action.

5.3.2 If there is such evidence and the seller (or the borrower in the case of a remortgage) is not providing a sufficient undertaking to satisfy those outstanding conditions by completion, then this must be reported to us (see part 2). Check part 2 to see if copies of planning permissions, building regulations and other consents or certificates should be sent to us.

5.3.3 If the property will be subject to any enforceable restrictions, for example under an agreement (such as an agreement under section 106 of the Town and Country Planning Act 1990) or in a planning permission, which, at the time of completion, might reasonably be expected materially to affect its value or its future marketability, you should report this to us (see part 2).

5.4 Good and Marketable Title

5.4.1 The title to the property must be good and marketable free of any restrictions, covenants, easements, charges or encumbrances which, at the time of completion, might reasonably be expected to materially adversely affect the value of the property or its future marketability (but excluding any matters covered by indemnity insurance) and which may be accepted by us for mortgage purposes. Our requirements in respect of indemnity insurance are set out in paragraph 9. You must also take reasonable steps to ensure that, on completion, the property will be vested in the borrower.

5.4.2 Good leasehold title will be acceptable if:

5.4.2.1 a marked abstract of the freehold and any intermediate leasehold title for the statutory period of 15 years before the grant of the lease is provided; or

5.4.2.2 you are prepared to certify that the title is good and marketable when sending your certificate of title (because, for example, the landlord's title is generally accepted in the district where the property is situated); or

5.4.2.3 you arrange indemnity insurance. Our requirements in respect of indemnity insurance are set out in paragraph 9.

5.4.3 A title based on adverse possession or possessory title will be acceptable if:

5.4.3.1 there is satisfactory evidence by statutory declaration of adverse possession for a period of at least 12 years. In the case of lost title deeds, the statutory declaration must explain the loss satisfactorily;

5.4.3.2 we will also require indemnity insurance where there are buildings on the part in question or where the land is essential for access or services;

5.4.3.3 we may not need indemnity insurance in cases where such title affects land on which no buildings are erected or which is not essential for access or services. In such cases, you must send a plan of the whole of the land to be mortgaged to us identifying the area of land having possessory title. We will refer the matter to our valuer so that an assessment can be made of the proposed security. We will then notify you of any additional requirements or if a revised mortgage offer is to be made.

5.5 Flying Freeholds, Freehold Flats and other Freehold Arrangements

5.5.1 If any part of the property comprises or is affected by a flying freehold or the property is a freehold flat, check part 2 to see if we will accept it as security.

5.5.2 If we are prepared to accept a title falling within 5.5.1:

5.5.2.1 (unless we tell you not to in part 2) you must report to us that the property is a freehold flat or flying freehold; and

5.5.2.2   the property must have all necessary rights of support, protection, and entry for repair as well as a scheme of enforceable covenants that are also such that subsequent buyers are required to enter into covenants in identical form; and

5.5.2.3   you must be able to certify that the title is good and marketable; and

5.5.2.4   in the case of flying freeholds, you must send us a plan of the property clearly showing the part affected by the flying freehold.

If our requirements in 5.5.2.2 are not satisfied, indemnity must be in place at completion (see paragraph 9).

Other freehold arrangements

5.5.3   Unless we indicate to the contrary (see part 2), we have no objection to a security which comprises a building converted into not more than four flats where the borrower occupies one of those flats and the borrower or another flat owner also owns the freehold of the building and the other flats are subject to long leases.

5.5.3.1   If the borrower occupying one of the flats also owns the freehold, we will require our security to be:

5.5.3.1.1   the freehold of the whole building subject to the long leases of the other flats; and

5.5.3.1.2   any leasehold interest the borrower will have in the flat the borrower is to occupy.

5.5.3.2   If another flat owner owns the freehold of the building, the borrower must have a leasehold interest in the flat the borrower is to occupy and our security must be the borrower's leasehold interest in such flat.

5.5.3.3   The leases of all the flats should contain appropriate covenants by the tenant of each flat to contribute towards the repair, maintenance and insurance of the building. The leases should also grant and reserve all necessary rights and easements. They should not contain any unduly onerous obligations on the landlord.

5.5.4   Where the security will comprise:

5.5.4.1   one of a block of not more than four leasehold flats and the borrower will also own the freehold jointly with one or more of the other flat owners in the building; or

5.5.4.2   one of two leasehold flats in a building where the borrower also owns the freehold reversion of the other flat and the other leaseholder owns the freehold reversion in the borrower's flat;

check part 2 to see if we will accept it as security and if so, what our requirements will be.

5.6   **Restrictions on Use and Occupation**

You must check whether there are any material restrictions on the occupation of the property as a private residence or as specified by us (for example, because of the occupier's employment, age or income), or any material restrictions on its use. If there are any restrictions, you must report details to us (see part 2). In some cases, we may accept a restriction, particularly if this relates to sheltered housing or to first time buyers.

5.7   **Restrictive Covenants**

5.7.1   You must enquire whether the property has been built, altered or is currently used in breach of a restrictive covenant. We rely on you to check that the covenant is not enforceable. If you are unable to provide an unqualified certificate of title as a result of the risk of enforceability you must ensure (subject to paragraph 5.7.2) that indemnity insurance is in place at completion of our mortgage (see paragraph 9).

5.7.2   We will not insist on indemnity insurance:

5.7.2.1   if you are satisfied that there is no risk to our security; and

5.7.2.2   the breach has continued for more than 20 years; and

5.7.2.3   there is nothing to suggest that any action is being taken or is threatened in respect of the breach.

5.8   **First Legal Charge**

On completion, we require a fully enforceable first charge by way of legal mortgage over the property executed by all owners of the legal estate. All existing charges must be redeemed on or before completion, unless we agree that an existing charge may be postponed to rank after our mortgage. Our standard deed or form of postponement must be used.

5.9   **Other Loans**

You must ask the borrower how the balance of the purchase price is being provided. If you become aware that the borrower is not providing the balance of the purchase price from his own funds and/or is proposing to give a second charge over the property, you must report this to us if the borrower agrees (see part 2), failing which you must return our instructions and explain that you are unable to continue to act for us as there is a conflict of interest.

5.10   **Leasehold Property**

5.10.1   Our requirements on the unexpired term of a lease offered as security are set out in part 2.

5.10.2   There must be no provision for forfeiture on the insolvency of the tenant or any superior tenant.

5.10.3   The only situations where we will accept a restriction on the mortgage or assignment (whether by a tenant or a mortgagee) of the lease is where the person whose consent needs to be obtained cannot unreasonably withhold giving consent. The necessary consent for the particular transaction must be obtained before completion. If the lease requires consent to an assignment or mortgage to be obtained, you must obtain these on or before completion (this is particularly important if the lease is a shared ownership lease). You must not complete without them.

5.10.4   You must take reasonable steps to check that:

5.10.4.1   there are satisfactory legal rights, particularly for access, services, support, shelter and protection; and

5.10.4.2   there are also adequate covenants and arrangements in respect of the following matters, buildings insurance, maintenance and repair of the structure, foundations, main walls, roof, common parts, common services and grounds (the 'common services').

5.10.5   You should ensure that responsibility for the insurance, maintenance and repair of the common services is that of:

5.10.5.1   the landlord; or

5.10.5.2   one or more of the tenants in the building of which the property forms part; or

5.10.5.3   the management company – see paragraph 5.11.

5.10.6   Where the responsibility for the insurance, maintenance and repair of the common services is that of one or more of the tenants;

5.10.6.1   the lease must contain adequate provisions for the enforcement of these obligations by the landlord or management company at the request of the tenant.

5.10.6.2   In the absence of a provision in the lease that all leases of other flats in the block are in, or will be granted in, substantially similar form, you should take reasonable steps to check that the leases of the other flats are in similar form. If you are unable to do so, you should effect indemnity insurance (see paragraph 9). This is not essential if the landlord is responsible for the maintenance and repair of the main structure.

5.10.6.3   We do not require enforceability covenants mutual or otherwise for other tenant covenants.

5.10.7   We have no objection to a lease which contains provision for a periodic increase of the ground rent provided that the amount of the increased ground rent is fixed or can be readily established and is reasonable. If you consider any increase in the ground rent may materially affect the value of the property, you must report this to us (see part 2).

5.10.8   You should enquire whether the landlord or managing agent foresees any significant increase in the level of the service charge in the reasonably foreseeable future and, if there is, you must report to us (see part 2).

5.10.9   If the terms of the lease are unsatisfactory, you must obtain a suitable deed of variation to remedy the defect. We may accept indemnity insurance (see paragraph 9). See part 2 for our requirements.

5.10.10   You must obtain on completion a clear receipt or other appropriate written confirmation for the last payment of ground rent and service charge from the landlord or managing agents on behalf of the landlord. Check part 2 to see if it must be sent to us after completion. If confirmation of payment from the landlord cannot be obtained, we are prepared to proceed provided that you are satisfied that the absence of the landlord is common practice in the district where the property is situated, the seller confirms there are no breaches of the terms of the lease, you are satisfied that our security will not be prejudiced by the absence of such a receipt and you provide us with a clear certificate of title.

5.10.11   Notice of the mortgage must be served on the landlord and any management company immediately following completion, whether or not the lease requires it. If you cannot obtain receipt of the notice then, as a last resort, suitable evidence of the service of the notice on the landlord should be provided. Check part 2 to see if a receipted copy of the notice or evidence of service must be sent to us after completion.

5.10.12   We will accept leases which require the property to be sold on the open market if re-building or reinstatement is frustrated provided the insurance proceeds and the proceeds of sale are shared between the landlord and tenant in proportion to their respective interests.

5.10.13   You must report to us (see part 2) if it becomes apparent that the landlord is either absent or insolvent. If we are to lend, we may require indemnity insurance (see paragraph 9). See part 2 for our requirements.

5.10.14   If the leasehold title is registered but the lease has been lost, we are prepared to proceed provided you have checked an M Land Registry produced copy of the registered lease. Whilst this will not be an office copy of the lease you may accept it as sufficient evidence of the lease and its terms when approving the title for mortgage purposes provided it is, on its face, a complete copy.

5.11   **Management Company**

5.11.1   In paragraph 5.11 the meanings shall apply:

- 'management company' means the company formed to carry out the maintenance and repair of the common parts;

- 'common parts' means the structure, main walls, roof, foundations, services grounds and any other common areas serving the building or estate of which the property forms part.

If a management company is required to maintain or repair the common parts, the management company should have a legal right to enter the property;

if the management company's right to so enter does not arise from a leasehold interest, then the tenants of the building should also be the members of the management company.

If this is not the case, there should be a covenant by the landlord to carry out the obligations of the management company should it fail to do so.

5.11.1.1 For leases granted before 1 September 2000:

If the lease does not satisfy the requirements of paragraph 5.11.1 but: you are nevertheless satisfied that the existing arrangements affecting the management company and the maintenance and repair of the common parts are sufficient to ensure the adequate maintenance and repair of the common parts; and

you are able to provide a clear certificate of title,

then we will rely on your professional judgement.

5.11.2 You should make a company search and verify that the company is in existence and registered at Companies House. You should also obtain the management company's last three years' published accounts (or the accounts from inception if the company has only been formed in the past three years). Any apparent problems with the company should be reported to us (see part 2). If the borrower is required to be a shareholder in the management company, check part 2 to see if you must arrange for the share certificate, a blank stock transfer form executed by the borrower and a copy of the memorandum and articles of association to be sent to us after completion (unless we tell you not to). If the management company is limited by guarantee, the borrower (or at least one of them if two or more) must become a member on or before completion.

5.12 Insolvency Considerations

5.12.1 You must obtain a clear bankruptcy search against each borrower (and each mortgagor or guarantor, if any) providing us with protection at the date of completion of the mortgage. You must fully investigate any entries revealed by your bankruptcy search against the borrower (or mortgagor or guarantor) to ensure that they do not relate to them.

5.12.2 Where an entry is revealed against the name of the borrower (or the mortgagor or guarantor):

5.12.2.1 you must certify that the entry does not relate to the borrower (or the mortgagor or guarantor) if you are able to do so from your own knowledge or enquiries; or

5.12.2.2 if, after obtaining office copy entries or making other enquiries of the Official Receiver, you are unable to certify that the entry does not relate to the borrower (or the mortgagor or guarantor) you must report this to us (see part 2). We may as a consequence need to withdraw our mortgage offer.

5.12.3 If you are aware that the title to the property is subject to a deed of gift or a transaction at an apparent undervalue completed within five years of the proposed mortgage then you must be satisfied that we will acquire our interest in good faith and will be protected under the provisions of the Insolvency (No 2) Act 1994 against our security being set aside. If you are unable to give an unqualified certificate of title, you must arrange indemnity insurance (see paragraph 9).

5.12.4   You must also obtain clear bankruptcy searches against all parties to any deed of gift or transaction at an apparent undervalue.

5.13   **Powers of Attorney**

5.13.1   If any document is being executed under power of attorney, you must ensure that the power of attorney is, on its face, properly drawn up, that it appears to be properly executed by the donor and that the attorney knows of no reason why such power of attorney will not be subsisting at completion. Where there are joint borrowers the power should comply with section 25 of the Trustee Act 1925, as amended by section 7 of the Trustee Delegation Act 1999, or with section 1 of the Trustee Delegation Act 1999 with the attorney making an appropriate statement under section 2 of the 1999 Act. In the case of joint borrowers, neither borrower may appoint the other as attorney.

5.13.2   A power of attorney must not be used in connection with a regulated loan under the Consumer Credit Act 1974.

5.13.3   Check part 2 to see if:

5.13.3.1   the original or a certified copy of the power of attorney must be sent to us after completion;

5.13.3.2   where the power of attorney is a general power of attorney and was completed more than 12 months before the completion of our mortgage, you must send us a statutory declaration confirming that it has not been revoked.

5.14   **Title Guarantee**

Whilst we recommend that a borrower should try to obtain a full title guarantee from the seller, we do not insist on this. We, however, require the borrower to give us a full title guarantee in the mortgage deed. The mortgage deed must not be amended.

6.   THE PROPERTY

6.1   **Mortgage Offer and Title Documents**

6.1.1   The loan to the borrower will not be made until all relevant conditions of the mortgage offer which need to be satisfied before completion have been complied with and we have received your certificate of title.

6.1.2   You must check your instructions and ensure that there are no discrepancies between them and the title documents and other matters revealed by your investigations.

6.1.3   You should tell us (see part 2) as soon as possible if you have been told that the borrower has decided not to take up the mortgage offer.

6.2   **Boundaries**

These must be clearly defined by reference to a suitable plan or description. They must also accord with the information given in the valuation report, if this is provided to you. You should check with the borrower that the plan or the description accords with the borrower's understanding of the extent of the property to be mortgaged to us. You must report to us (see part 2), if there are any discrepancies.

6.3   **Purchase Price**

6.3.1   The purchase price for the property must be the same as set out in our instructions. If it is not, you must tell us (unless we say differently in part 2). You must tell us (unless we say differently in part 2) if the contract provides for:

6.3.1.1   a cashback to the buyer; or

6.3.1.2   part of the price is being satisfied by a non-cash incentive to the buyer.

       This may lead to the mortgage offer being withdrawn or amended.

6.3.2   You must report to us (see part 2) if you will not have control over the payment of all of the purchase money (for example, if it is proposed that the borrower pays money to the seller direct) other than a deposit held by an estate agent or a reservation fee of not more than £500 paid to a builder or developer.

6.4   Vacant Possession

       Unless otherwise stated in your instructions, it is a term of the loan that vacant possession is obtained. The contract must provide for this. If you doubt that vacant possession will be given, you must not part with the advance and should report the position to us (see part 2).

6.5   Properties Let At Completion

6.5.1   Where the property, or part of it, is already let, or is to be let at completion, then the letting must comply with the details set out in the mortgage offer or any consent to let we issue. If no such details are mentioned, you must report the position to us (see part 2).

6.5.2   Check part 2 for whether counterparts or certified copies of all tenancy agreements and leases in respect of existing tenancies must be sent to us after completion.

6.6   New Properties – Building Standards Indemnity Schemes

6.6.1   If the property is newly built, or newly converted, or to be occupied for the first time, you must ensure that it was built or converted under whichever of the following is acceptable to us (see part 2):

6.6.1.1   the National House-Building Council (NHBC) Buildmark scheme; or

6.6.1.2   the Zurich Municipal Newbuild scheme; or

6.6.1.3   Zurich Municipal Rebuild scheme; or

6.6.1.4   the Housing Association Property Mutual (HAPM) scheme; or

6.6.1.5   the Premier Guarantee for Private Housing and Completed Housing; or

6.6.1.6   any other new home warranty schemes.

6.6.2   Before you send us the certificate of title, you must obtain a copy of a new home warranty provider's cover note from the developer. The cover note must confirm that the property has received a satisfactory final inspection and that the new home warranty will be in place on or before completion. This will only apply where exchange of contracts occurs on or after 1 April 2003. This does not apply to self-build schemes. Check part 2 to see what new home warranty documentation should be sent to us on completion.

6.6.3   We do not insist that notice of assignment of the benefit of the new home warranty agreement be given to the builder in the case of a second and subsequent purchase(s) during the period of the insurance cover. Check part 2 to see if any assignments of building standards indemnity schemes which are available should be sent to us after completion.

6.6.4   Check part 2 to see if we will accept the monitoring of a newly built or newly converted property to be occupied for the first time by a professional consultant. You should ensure that the professional consultant properly completes the lender's Professional Consultant's Certificate which forms an appendix to this Handbook or such other form as the instructing lender may provide. The professional consultant should also confirm to you that he has appropriate experience in the design or monitoring of the construction or conversion of residential buildings and has one or more of the following qualifications:

6.6.4.1   fellow or member of the Royal Institution of Chartered Surveyors (FRICS or MRICS); or

6.6.4.2   fellow or member of the Institution of Structural Engineers (F.I.Struct.E or M.I.Struct.E); or

6.6.4.3   fellow or member of the Chartered Institute of Building (FCIOB or MCIOB); or

6.6.4.4   fellow or member of the Architecture and Surveying Institute (FASI or MASI); or

6.6.4.5   fellow or member of the Association of Building Engineers (FB.Eng or MB.Eng); or

6.6.4.6   member of the British Institute of Architectural Technologists (MBIAT); or

6.6.4.7   architect registered with the Architects Registration Board (ARB). An architect must be registered with the Architects Registration Board, even if also a member of another institution, for example the Royal Institute of British Architects (RIBA); or

6.6.4.8   fellow or member of the Institution of Civil Engineers (FICE or MICE).

6.6.5   At the time he issues his certificate of practical completion, the consultant must have professional indemnity insurance in force for each claim for the greater of either:

6.6.5.1   the value of the property once completed; or

6.6.5.2   £250,000 if employed directly by the borrower or, in any other case, £500,000.

If we require a collateral warranty from any professional adviser, this will be stated specifically in the mortgage instructions.

6.6.6   Check part 2 to see if the consultant's certificate must be sent to us after completion.

6.7   Roads and Sewers

6.7.1   If the roads or sewers immediately serving the property are not adopted or maintained at public expense, there must be a suitable agreement and bond in existence or you must report to us (see part 2 for who you should report to).

6.7.2   If there is any such agreement, it should be secured by bond or deposit as required by the appropriate authority to cover the cost of making up the roads and sewers to adoptable standards, maintaining them thereafter and procuring adoption.

6.7.3   If there is an arrangement between the developer and the lender whereby the lender will not require a retention, you must obtain confirmation from the developer that the arrangement is still in force.

6.8   Easements

6.8.1   You must take all reasonable steps to check that the property has the benefit of all easements necessary for its full use and enjoyment. This would include, for example, rights of way (both vehicular and pedestrian), the use of services and any necessary rights of entry for repair. All such rights must be enforceable by the borrower and the borrower's successors in title. If they are not, you must report to us (see part 2).

6.8.2   If the borrower owns adjoining land over which the borrower requires access to the property or in respect of which services are provided to the property, this land must also be mortgaged to us.

6.9   Release of Retentions

6.9.1   If we make a retention from an advance (for example, for repairs, improvements or road works) we are not obliged to release that retention, or any part of it, if the borrower is in breach of any of his obligations under the mortgage, or if a condition attached to the retention has not been met or if the loan has been repaid in full. You should, therefore, not give an unqualified undertaking to pay the retention to a third party.

6.9.2   Check part 2 to see who we will release the retention to.

6.10   Neighbourhood Changes

The local search or the enquiries of the seller or the seller's conveyancer should not reveal that the property is in an area scheduled for redevelopment or in any way affected by road proposals. If it is, please report this to us (see part 2).

6.11   Rights of Pre-emption and Restrictions on Resale

You must ensure that there are no rights of pre-emption, restrictions on resale, options or similar arrangements in existence at completion which will affect our security. If there are, please report this to us (see part 2).

6.12   Improvement and Repair Grants

Where the property is subject to an improvement or repair grant which will not be discharged or waived on completion, check part 2 to see whether you must report the matter to us.

6.13   Insurance

Where we do not arrange the insurance, you must:

6.13.1   report to us (see part 2) if the property is not insured in accordance with our requirements (one of our requirements, see part 2, will relate to whether the property is insured in the joint names of us and the borrower or whether our interest may be noted);

6.13.2   arrange that the insurance cover starts from no later than completion;

6.13.3   check that the amount of buildings insurance cover is at least the amount referred to in the mortgage offer (if the property is part of a larger building and there is a common insurance policy, the total sum insured for the building must be not less than the total number of flats multiplied by the amount set out in the mortgage offer for the property);

6.13.4   ensure that the buildings insurance cover is index linked;

6.13.5   ensure that the excess does not exceed the amount set out in part 2;

6.13.6   Check part 2 to see if we require you to confirm that all the following risks are covered in the insurance policy:

6.13.6.1   fire;

6.13.6.2   lightning;

6.13.6.3   aircraft;

6.13.6.4   explosion;

6.13.6.5   earthquake;

6.13.6.6   storm;

6.13.6.7   flood;

6.13.6.8   escape of water or oil;

6.13.6.9   riot;

6.13.6.10   malicious damage;

6.13.6.11   theft or attempted theft;

6.13.6.12 falling trees and branches and aerials;

6.13.6.13 subsidence;

6.13.6.14 heave;

6.13.6.15 landslip;

6.13.6.16 collision;

6.13.6.17 accidental damage to underground services;

6.13.6.18 professional fees, demolition and site clearance costs; and

6.13.6.19 public liability to anyone else.

6.13.7   Check part 2 to see if we require you to obtain before completion the insurer's confirmation that the insurer will notify us if the policy is not renewed or is cancelled or if you do not obtain this, report to us (see part 2).

6.13.8   Check part 2 to see if we require you to send us a copy of the buildings insurance policy and the last premium receipt to us.

7.   OTHER OCCUPIERS

7.1   Rights or interests of persons who are not a party to the mortgage and who are or will be in occupation of the property may affect our rights under the mortgage, for example as overriding interests.

7.2   If your instructions state the name of a person who is to live at the property, you should ask the borrower before completing the mortgage that the information given by us in our mortgage instructions or mortgage offer about occupants is correct and nobody else is to live at the property.

7.3   Unless we state otherwise (see part 2), you must obtain a signed deed or form of consent from all occupants aged 17 or over of whom you are aware who are not a party to the mortgage before completion of the mortgage.

7.4   We recognise that in some cases the information given to us or you by a borrower may be incorrect or misleading. If you have any reason to doubt the accuracy of any information disclosed, you should report it to us (see part 2) provided the borrower agrees; if the borrower does not agree, you should return our instructions.

8.   SEPARATE REPRESENTATION

Unless we otherwise state (see part 2), you must not advise:

8.1   any borrower who does not personally benefit from the loan; or

8.2   any guarantor; or

8.3   anyone intending to occupy the property who is to execute a consent to the mortgage,

and you must arrange for them to see an independent conveyancer. If we do allow you to advise any of these people, you must only do so after recommending in the absence of any other person interested in the transaction that such person obtains independent legal advice. Any advice that you give any of these people must also be given in the absence of any other person interested in the transaction. You should be particularly careful if the matrimonial home is being charged to secure a business debt.

9.   INDEMNITY INSURANCE

You must effect an indemnity insurance policy whenever the Lenders' Handbook identifies that this is an acceptable or required course to us to ensure that the property has a good and marketable title at completion. This paragraph does not relate to mortgage indemnity insurance. The draft policy should not be sent to us unless we ask for it. Check part 2 to see if the policy must be sent to us after completion. Where indemnity insurance is effected:

9.1 you must approve the terms of the policy on our behalf; and

9.2 the limit of indemnity must meet our requirements (see part 2); and

9.3 the policy must be effected without cost to us; and

9.4 you must disclose to the insurer all relevant information which you have obtained; and

9.5 the policy must not contain conditions which you know would make it void or prejudice our interests; and

9.6 you must provide a copy of the policy to the borrower and explain to the borrower why the policy was effected and that a further policy may be required if there is further lending against the security of the property; and

9.7 you must explain to the borrower that the borrower will need to comply with any conditions of the policy and that the borrower should notify us of any notice or potential claim in respect of the policy; and

9.8 the policy should always be for our benefit and, if possible, for the benefit of the borrower and any subsequent owner or mortgagee. If the borrower will not be covered by the policy, you must advise the borrower of this.

10. THE LOAN AND CERTIFICATE OF TITLE

10.1 You should not submit your certificate of title unless it is unqualified or we have authorised you in writing to proceed notwithstanding any issues you have raised with us.

10.2 We shall treat the submission by you of the certificate of title as a request for us to release the mortgage advance to you. Check part 2 to see if the mortgage advance will be paid electronically or by cheque and the minimum number of days notice we require. See part 2 for any standard deductions which may be made from the mortgage advance.

10.3 You are only authorised to release the loan when you hold sufficient funds to complete the purchase of the property and pay all stamp duties and registration fees to perfect the security as a first legal mortgage or, if you do not have them, you accept responsibility to pay them yourself. You must hold the loan on trust for us until completion. If completion is delayed, you must return it to us when and how we tell you (see part 2).

10.4 You should note that although your certificate of title will be addressed to us, we may at some time transfer our interest in the mortgage. In those circumstances, our successors in title to the mortgage and persons deriving title under or through the mortgage will also rely on your certificate.

10.5 If, after you have requested the mortgage advance, completion is delayed you must telephone or fax us immediately after you are aware of the delay and you must inform us of the new date for completion (see part 2).

10.6 See part 2 for details of how long you can hold the mortgage advance before returning it to us. If completion is delayed for longer than that period, you must return the mortgage advance to us. If you do not, we reserve the right to require you to pay interest on the amount of the mortgage advance (see part 2).

10.7 If the mortgage advance is not returned within the period set out in part 2, we will assume that the mortgage has been completed, and we will charge the borrower interest under the mortgage. We may make further payments and advances without reference to you.

11.   THE DOCUMENTATION

11.1   The Mortgage

The mortgage incorporates our current mortgage conditions and, where applicable, loan conditions. If the mortgage conditions booklet is supplied to you with your instructions you must give it to the borrower before completion of the mortgage.

11.2   Explanation

You should explain to each borrower (and any other person signing or executing a document) his responsibilities and liabilities under the documents referred to in 11.1 and any documents he is required to sign.

11.3   Signing and Witnessing of Documents

It is considered good practice that the signature of a document that needs to be witnessed is witnessed by a solicitor, legal executive or licensed conveyancer. All documents required at completion must be dated with the date of completion of the loan.

12.   INSTALMENT MORTGAGES AND MORTGAGE ADVANCES RELEASED IN INSTALMENTS

12.1   Introduction

12.1.1   If the cost of the building is to be paid by instalments as work progresses (for example, under a building contract) the amount of each instalment which we will be able to release will be based on a valuation made by our valuer at the time. Whilst we will not be bound by the terms of any building contract we will meet the reasonable requirements of the borrower and the builder as far as possible.

12.1.2   The borrower is expected to pay for as much work as possible from his own resources before applying to us for the first instalment. However, we may, if required, consider advancing a nominal sum on receipt of the certificate of title to enable the mortgage to be completed so long as the legal estate in the property is vested in the borrower.

12.1.3   The borrower is responsible for our valuer's fees for interim valuations as well as the first and final valuations.

12.2   Applications for Part of the Advance

As in the case of a normal mortgage account, cheques for instalment mortgages will be made payable and sent to you. However, instalment cheques (apart from the first which will be sent to you to enable you to complete the mortgage) can be made payable to and sent direct to the borrower on request.

12.3   Requests for Intermediate Cheques

To allow time for a valuation to be carried out, your request should be sent to us (see part 2) at least 10 days before the cheque is required.

12.4   Building Contract as Security

We will not lend on the security of a building contract unless our instructions to you specifically state to the contrary. As a result, the mortgage must not be completed and no part of the advance released until the title to the legal estate in the property has been vested in the borrower.

13.   MORTGAGE INDEMNITY INSURANCE OR HIGH LOAN TO VALUE FEE

You are reminded to tell the borrower that we (and not the borrower) are the insured under any mortgage indemnity or similar form of insurance policy and that the insurer will have a subrogated right to claim against the borrower if it pays us under the policy. Different lenders call the various schemes of this type by different names. They may not involve an insurance policy.

14.   AFTER COMPLETION

14.1   **Application to HM Land Registry**

14.1.1   You must register our mortgage at HM Land Registry. Before making your Land Registry application for registration, you must place a copy of the Land or Charge Certificate relating to the property on your file together with certified copies of the transfer, mortgage deed and any receipt or DS1 from a previous mortgagee.

14.1.2   Our mortgage conditions and mortgage deed have been deposited at HM Land Registry and it is therefore unnecessary to submit a copy of the mortgage conditions on an application for registration.

14.1.3   Where the loan is to be made in instalments or there is any deferred interest retention or stage release, check part 2 to see whether you must apply to the Land Registry on form 113 for entry of a notice on the register that we are under an obligation to make further advances. If the Land Registry code 'CHOBL' appears on the mortgage deed (it is usually in the top right hand corner) there is no need to submit a form 113.

14.1.4   The application for registration must be received by the Land Registry during the priority period afforded by your original Land Registry search made before Completion and, in any event, in the case of an application for first registration, within two months of completion.

14.2   **Title Deeds**

14.2.1   All title deeds, searches, enquiries, consents, requisitions and documents relating to the property in your possession must be held to our order and you must not create or exercise any lien over them. Unless otherwise instructed, they must be sent to us (see part 2) with the schedule supplied by us as soon as possible after completion. We expect them to be lodged, in any event, within three months of completion. If it is not possible to return the deeds to us within this period you should advise us in writing with a copy of any correspondence from HM Land Registry explaining the delay.

14.2.2   You must only send us documents we tell you to (see part 2). You should obtain the borrower's instructions concerning the retention of documents we tell you not to send us.

14.3   **Your Mortgage File**

14.3.1   For evidential purposes you must keep your file for at least six years from the date of the mortgage before destroying it. Microfiching or data imaging is suitable compliance with this requirement. It is the practice of some fraudsters to demand the conveyancing file on completion in order to destroy evidence that may later be used against them. It is important to retain these documents to protect our interests. Where you are processing personal data (as defined in the Data Protection Act 1998) on our behalf, you must:

14.3.1.1   take such security measures as are required to enable you to comply with obligations equivalent to those imposed on us by the seventh data protection principle in the 1998 Act; and

14.3.1.2 process such personal data only in accordance with our instructions. In addition, you must allow us to conduct such reasonable audit of your information security measures as we require to ensure your compliance with your obligations in this paragraph.

14.3.2 Subject to any right of lien or any overriding duty of confidentiality, you should treat documents comprising your file as if they are jointly owned by the borrower and the lender and you should not part with them without the consent of both parties. You should on request supply certified copies of documents on the file or a certified copy of the microfiche to either the borrower or the lender, and may make a reasonable charge for copying and certification.

15.   LEGAL COSTS

Your charges and disbursements are payable by the borrower and should be collected from the borrower on or before completion. You must not allow non-payment of fees or disbursements to delay the stamping and registration of documents. The Law Society recommends that your costs for acting on our behalf in connection with the mortgage should, in the interest of transparency, be separately identified to the borrower.

16.   TRANSACTIONS DURING THE LIFE OF THE MORTGAGE

16.1   **Requests for Deeds**

All requests for deeds should be made in writing and sent to us (see part 2). In making such a request you must have the consent of all of the borrowers to apply for the deeds.

16.2   **Further Advances**

16.2.1 Our mortgage secures further advances. Consequently, when a further advance is required for alterations or improvements to the property we will not normally instruct a member of our conveyancing panel.

16.2.2 If additional land is to be mortgaged or the further advance is required for some other purpose (for example, to purchase a spouse's equitable or other interest in the property), you may receive instructions to act for us in connection with that transaction.

16.3   **Transfers of Equity**

16.3.1 You must approve the transfer (which should be in the Land Registry's standard form) and, if we require, the deed of covenant on our behalf. Check part 2 to see if we have standard forms of transfer and deed of covenant. When drafting or approving a transfer, you should bear in mind:

16.3.1.1 although the transfer should state that it is subject to the mortgage (identified by date and parties), it need give no details of the terms of the mortgage;

16.3.1.2 the transfer need not state the amount of the mortgage debt. If it does, the figure should include both principal and interest at the date of completion, which you must check (see part 2 for where to obtain this);

16.3.1.3 there should be no statement that all interest has been paid to date.

16.3.2 You must ensure that every person who will be a borrower after the transfer covenants with us to pay the money secured by the mortgage, except in the case of:

16.3.2.1 an original party to the mortgage (unless the mortgage conditions are being varied); or

16.3.2.2 a person who has previously covenanted to that effect.

16.3.3 Any such covenant will either be in the transfer or in a separate deed of covenant. In a transfer, the wording of the covenant should be as follows, or as close as circumstances permit: 'The new borrower agrees to pay the lender all the money due under the mortgage and will keep to all the terms of the mortgage.' If it is in the transfer, you must place a certified copy of the transfer with the deeds (unless we tell you not to in part 2).

16.3.4 If we have agreed to release a borrower or a guarantor and our standard transfer form (if any) includes no appropriate clause, you must add a simple form of release. The release clause should be as follows, or as close as circumstances permit: 'The lender releases ... from [his/her/their] obligations under the mortgage.' You should check whether a guarantor who is to be released was a party to the mortgage or to a separate guarantee.

16.3.5 You must obtain the consent of every guarantor of which you are aware to the release of a borrower or, as the case may be, any other guarantor.

16.3.6 You must only submit the transfer to us for execution if it releases a party. All other parties must execute the transfer before it is sent to us. See part 2 for where the transfer should be sent for sealing. Part 2 also gives our approved form of attestation clause.

16.4 Properties To Be Let After Completion

16.4.1 You should advise the borrower that any letting of the property is prohibited without our prior consent. If the borrower wishes to let the property after completion then an application for consent should be made to us (see part 2). Check part 2 to see whether it is necessary to send to us a copy of the proposed tenancy when making the application.

16.4.2 If the application for our consent is approved and we instruct you to act for us, you must approve the form of tenancy agreement on our behalf.

16.4.3 Please also note that:

16.4.3.1 an administration fee will be payable for our consideration of the application whether or not consent is granted; and

16.4.3.2 the proposed rent should cover the borrower's gross mortgage payments at the time; and

16.4.3.3 we reserve the right to charge a higher rate of interest to the borrower in certain circumstances or change the terms of the mortgage.

16.5 Deeds of Variation, Rectification, Easement or Option Agreements

16.5.1 If we consent to any proposal for a deed of variation, rectification, easement or option agreement, we will rely on you to approve the documents on our behalf.

16.5.2 Our consent will usually be forthcoming provided that you first of all confirm in writing to us (see part 2) that our security will not be adversely affected in any way by entering into the deed. If you are able to provide this confirmation then we will not normally need to see a draft of the deed. If you cannot provide confirmation and we need to consider the matter in detail then an additional administration fee is likely to be charged.

16.5.3 Whether we are a party to the deed or give a separate deed or form of consent is a matter for your discretion. It should be sent to us (see part 2) for sealing or signing with a brief explanation of the reason for the document and its effect together with your confirmation that it will not adversely affect our security.

16.6 Deeds of Postponement or Substitution

If we agree to enter into an arrangement with other lenders concerning the order of priority of their mortgages, you will be supplied with our standard form of deed or form of postponement or substitution. We will normally not agree to any amendments to the form. In no cases will we postpone our first charge over the property.

17.   REDEMPTION

17.1   **Redemption Statement**

17.1.1   When requesting a redemption statement you should quote the expected repayment date and whether you are acting for the borrower or have the borrower's authority to request the redemption statement in addition to the information mentioned in paragraph 2.1. You should request this at least five working days before the expected redemption date. You must quote all the borrower's mortgage account or roll numbers of which you are aware when requesting the repayment figure. You must only request a redemption statement if you are acting for the borrower or have the borrower's written authority to request a redemption statement.

17.1.2   To guard against fraud please ensure that if payment is made by cheque then the redemption cheque is made payable to us and you quote the mortgage account or roll number and name of borrower.

17.2   **Discharge**

On the day of completion you should send the discharge and your remittance for the repayment to us (see part 2). Check part 2 to see if we discharge via a DS1 form or direct with the Land Registry.

VIII.4. Code of Practice for Commercial Leases in England and Wales (2nd edition)[1]

This updated Code and Explanatory Guide has been produced, at the request of the Department for Transport, Local Government and the Regions, by the Commercial Leases Working Group comprising the Association of British Insurers, Association of Property Bankers, British Retail Consortium, British Property Federation, Confederation of British Industry, Forum of Private Business, Law Society, National Association of Corporate Real Estate Executives (UK chapter), Property Market Reform Group, Royal Institution of Chartered Surveyors and Small Business Bureau. In addition, this code has received support from the British Council for Offices, the British Chambers of Commerce, Council for Licensed Conveyancers and the Federation of Small Businesses.

This Code replaces the First Edition produced by the Commercial Leases Group in December 1995.

Introduction

This updated Code contains recommendations for landlords and tenants when they negotiate new leases of business premises and where they deal with each other during the term of a lease.

The Code consists of twenty-three recommendations which an industry-wide working party, including landlord and tenant representatives, consider reflect current 'best practice' for landlords and tenants negotiating a business tenancy.

Explanatory guidance notes provide the background to each of the recommendations.

Landlords and tenants should have regard to the recommendations of this Code when they negotiate lease renewals. Under current legislation if a court has to fix terms for a new lease it may decide not to change the terms from those in the existing lease.

Negotiating a business tenancy (lease)

- **Recommendation 1; Renting premises:**
  Both landlords and tenants should negotiate the terms of a lease openly, constructively and considering each other's views.

- **Recommendation 2; Obtaining professional advice:**
  Parties intending to enter into leases should seek early advice from property professionals or lawyers.

- **Recommendation 3; Financial matters:**
  Landlords should provide estimates of any service charges and other outgoings in addition to the rent. Parties should be open about their financial standing to each other, on the understanding that information provided will be kept confidential unless already publicly available or there is proper need for disclosure. The terms on which any cash deposit is to be held should be agreed and documented.

1. © Commercial Leases Working Group 2002.

- **Recommendation 4; Duration of lease:**
  Landlords should consider offering tenants a choice of length of term, including break clauses where appropriate and with or without the protection of the Landlord and Tenant Act 1954. Those funding property should make every effort to avoid imposing restrictions on the length of lease that landlords, developers and/or investors may offer.

- **Recommendation 5; Rent and value added tax:**
  Where alternative lease terms are offered, different rents should be appropriately priced for each set of terms. The landlord should disclose the VAT status of the property and the tenant should take professional advice as to whether any VAT charged on rent and other charges is recoverable.

- **Recommendation 6; Rent Review:**
  The basis of rent review should generally be to open market rent. Wherever possible, landlords should offer alternatives which are priced on a risk-adjusted basis, including alternatives to upwards only rent reviews; these might include up/down reviews to open market rent with a minimum of the initial rent, or another basis such as annual indexation. Those funding property should make every effort to avoid imposing restrictions on the type of rent review that landlords, developers and/or investors may offer.

- **Recommendation 7; Repairs and services:**
  The tenant's repairing obligations, and any repair costs included in service charges, should be appropriate to the length of the term and the condition and age of the property at the start of the lease. Where appropriate the landlord should consider appropriately priced alternatives to full repairing terms.

- **Recommendation 8; Insurance:**
  Where the landlord is responsible for insuring the property, the policy terms should be competitive. The tenant of an entire building should, in appropriate cases, be given the opportunity to influence the choice of insurer. If the premises are so damaged by an uninsured risk as to prevent occupation, the tenant should be allowed to terminate the lease unless the landlord agrees to rebuild at his own cost.

- **Recommendation 9; Assigning and subletting:**
  Unless the particular circumstances of the letting justify greater control, the only restriction on assignment of the whole premises should be obtaining the landlord's consent which is not to be unreasonably withheld. Landlords are urged to consider requiring Authorised Guarantee Agreements only where the assignee is of lower financial standing than the assignor at the date of the assignment.

- **Recommendation 10; Alterations and changes of use:**
  Landlord's control over alterations and changes of use should not be more restrictive than is necessary to protect the value of the premises and any adjoining or neighbouring premises of the landlord. At the end of the lease the tenant should not be required to remove and make good permitted alterations unless this is reasonably required.

Conduct during a lease

- **Recommendation 11; Ongoing relationship:**
  Landlords and tenants should deal with each other constructively, courteously, openly and honestly throughout the term of the lease and carry out their respective obligations fully and on time. If either party faces a difficulty in carrying out any obligations under the lease, the other should be told without undue delay so that the possibility of agreement on how to deal with the problem may be explored. When either party proposes to take any action which is likely to have significant consequences for the other, the party proposing the action, when it becomes appropriate to do so, should notify the other without undue delay.

- **Recommendation 12; Request for consents:**
  When seeking a consent from the landlord, the tenant should supply full information about his/her proposal. The landlord should respond without undue delay and should where practicable give the tenant an estimate of the costs that the tenant will have to pay. The landlord should ensure that the request is passed promptly to any superior landlord or mortgagee whose agreement is needed and should give details to the tenant so that any problems can be speedily resolved.

- **Recommendation 13; Rent review negotiation:**
  Landlords and tenants should ensure that they understand the basis upon which rent may be reviewed and the procedure to be followed, including the existence of any strict time limits which could create pitfalls. They should obtain professional advice on these matters well before the review date and also immediately upon receiving (and before responding to) any notice or correspondence on the matter from the other party or his/her agent.

- **Recommendation 14; Insurance:**
  Where the landlord has arranged insurance, the terms should be made known to the tenant and any interest of the tenant covered by the policy. Any material change in the insurance should be notified to the tenant. Tenants should consider taking out their own insurance against loss or damage to contents and their business (loss of profits etc.) and any other risks not covered by the landlord's policy.

- **Recommendation 15; Varying the lease – effect on guarantors:**
  Landlords and tenants should seek the agreement of any guarantors to proposed material changes to the terms of the lease, or even minor changes which could increase the guarantor's liability.

- **Recommendation 16; Holding former tenants and their guarantors liable:**
  When previous tenants or their guarantors are liable to a landlord for defaults by the current tenant, landlords should notify them before the current tenant accumulates excessive liabilities. All defaults should be handled with speed and landlords should seek to assist the tenant and guarantor in minimising losses. An assignor who wishes to remain informed of the outcome of rent reviews should keep in touch with the landlord and the landlord should provide the information. Assignors should take professional advice on what methods are open to them to minimise their losses caused by defaults by the current occupier.

- **Recommendation 17; Release of landlord on sale of property:**
  Landlords who sell their interest in premises should take legal advice about ending their ongoing liability under the relevant leases.

- **Recommendation 18; Repairs:**
  Tenants should take the advice of a property professional about their repairing obligations near the end of the term of the lease and also immediately upon receiving a notice to repair or a schedule of dilapidations.

- **Recommendation 19; Business Rates:**
  Tenants or other ratepayers should consider if their business rates assessment is correct or whether they need to make an appeal. They should refer to the DTLR Business Rates – a Guide or obtain advice from a rating specialist. The RICS provides a free rating help line service (see below) and advice is available also from the Institute of Revenues Rating and Valuation (IRRV).

- **Recommendation 20; Service charges:**
  Landlords should observe the Guide to Good Practice on Service Charges in Commercial Properties. Tenants should familiarise themselves with that Guide and should take professional advice if they think they are being asked to pay excessive service charges.

- **Recommendation 21; Dispute resolution:**
  When disputes arise, the parties should make prompt and reasonable efforts to settle them by agreement. Where disputes cannot be settled by agreement, both sides should always consider speed and economy when selecting a method of dispute resolution. Mediation may be appropriate before embarking on more formal procedures.

- **Recommendation 22; Repossession by the landlord:**
  Tenants threatened with repossession or whose property has been repossessed will need professional advice if they wish to try to keep or regain possession. Similarly, landlords should be clear about their rights before attempting to operate a forfeiture clause and may need professional advice.

- **Recommendation 23; Renewals under the Landlord and Tenant Act 1954:**
  The parties should take professional advice on the Landlord and Tenant Act 1954 and the PACT (Professional Arbitration on Court Terms) scheme at least six months before the end of the term of the lease and also immediately upon receiving any notice under the Act from the other party or their agent. Guidance on the Act can be found in the Department for Transport, Local Government and the Region's 'Guide to the Landlord and Tenant Act 1954'.

A CODE OF PRACTICE FOR COMMERCIAL LEASES IN ENGLAND AND WALES – EXPLANATORY GUIDE

The Code of Practice for Commercial Leases consists of the Recommendations set out in this Guide. This Guide gives a brief explanation of the background to the recommendations. Further sources of advice and explanation are listed at the end.

Negotiating a business tenancy (lease)

- **Renting premises**
  Roughly a third of business premises in the UK are occupied by rent-paying tenants holding a lease (also called a 'tenancy') of the premises. Tenants should choose premises suitable for their short to medium term business plans, in respect of size, location, property and the terms of the lease. Premises might be rented, depending on the individual circumstances, either by the owner granting a new lease, by an existing tenant assigning the lease or by an existing tenant granting a sublease. The terms of a lease should reflect the type, location and condition of the property, the needs and status of the parties, and the state of the property market. All the terms in a commercial lease are normally negotiable.

  For business reasons, the landlord or the tenant may wish to keep the details of their transaction confidential, but parties should avoid unnecessary secrecy. This will help the availability of market data.

Recommendation 1: Both landlords and tenants should negotiate the terms of a lease openly, constructively and considering each other's views.

- **Obtaining professional advice**
  Unless landlords and tenants are fully experienced in these matters they will benefit from the advice of professional property advisers. Each party should be separately advised by independent advisers as the same person should not advise both parties. Tenants should not place reliance on advice offered by a letting agent acting for the landlord.

  The main recognised property professionals are chartered surveyors regulated by the Royal Institution of Chartered Surveyors (RICS) and solicitors regulated by the Law Society and Licensed Conveyancers regulated by the Council for Licensed Conveyancers.

  A surveyor can conduct, or assist in, the negotiations and can advise on the terms, including the appropriate level of rent taking into account the other terms of the letting, the location, size and quality of the property, the state of the property market, the level of business rates and other outgoings, and other relevant matters. A building surveyor can advise about the present condition of the property and about any necessary repairs. For lettings of part of a building, this can include advice about the need for major repairs and renewals of the structure or common parts which might increase service charges. A solicitor can negotiate the detailed text of the lease once the main terms have been agreed. Lease documents often run to many pages and there are no standard forms of lease. A solicitor can also check important matters such as town planning and the landlord's ownership of the property.

Recommendation 2: Parties intending to enter into leases should seek early advice from property professionals or lawyers.

- **Financial matters**
  The tenant should find out about the total cost of occupying the premises – rent, service charges, insurance, business rates, utility costs etc. – and ensure that they can be afforded within the budget of the business.

  As the landlord will wish to assess the tenant's ability to pay those costs, particularly the rent and any service charge, the tenant should provide written references from accountants, trade suppliers and any previous landlord. If the tenant is a limited company, the landlord may also wish to see audited accounts for the last few years' trading. If this information does not exist or fails to show that the tenant has an adequate financial standing, the landlord may refuse to accept that tenant or may require guarantees from financially viable guarantors, covering not only the rent but also all other liabilities under the lease.

  The landlord may also require a cash deposit, frequently of three or six months' rent. This 'rent deposit' will generally be required as security for service charges and the cost of remedying disrepair or other defaults as well as rent. There should be a proper written agreement covering the amount deposited, whether it can vary, who can hold it, how and when it can be paid over to the landlord or returned to the tenant and which party will receive any interest accruing.

  The drawing up of commercial leases involves legal costs. The question of payment is a matter for negotiation between the parties. The Costs of Leases Act 1958 provides that, in the absence of agreement, each side pays its own costs.

Recommendation 3: Landlords should provide estimates of any service charges and other outgoings in addition to the rent. Parties should be open about their financial standing to each other, on the understanding that information provided will be kept confidential unless already publicly available or there is proper need for disclosure. The terms on which any cash deposit is to be held should be agreed and documented.

- **Duration of lease**
  The length of the letting is called the 'term'. Leases are commonly granted for three, five, ten or fifteen year terms, but can be for terms of twenty or twenty-five years or more. A lease carries the protection of the Landlord and Tenant Act 1954, unless the parties agree to its exclusion. If the tenant occupies all or part of the premises when the lease ends, the Act enables a tenant to ask the county court to order the landlord to grant a new lease at a market rent.

  The landlord can refuse to grant a new lease in certain circumstances set out in the Act, for example if the tenant has seriously defaulted under the lease, or if the property is to be redeveloped or used for the landlord's own business. The tenant can ask the county court to examine the landlord's refusal to grant a new lease. In some cases, the tenant may be entitled to be paid compensation if a new lease is refused. If the lease excludes the Act, the tenant will not have the right to seek a new lease through the courts when the term expires.

  Leases can contain a provision (break clause) allowing either the landlord or the tenant (or both) to terminate the lease at a specified date without waiting for the term to expire. This may be advantageous to the party who wishes to end the lease early – such as a tenant who wants to vacate without finding an assignee or subtenant, or a landlord who wants to redevelop – but early termination may cause problems and/or loss to the other party.

Recommendation 4: Landlords should consider offering tenants a choice of length of term, including break clauses where appropriate and with or without the protection of the Landlord and Tenant Act 1954. Those funding property should make every effort to avoid imposing restrictions on the length of lease that landlords, developers and/or investors may offer.

- **Rent and value added tax**

    The appropriate level of rent will depend upon the state of the property market, the location, type, age, size, character and condition of the premises and the terms on which the lease is to be granted, especially the duration of the lease and the burden of repairing obligations. Rent is usually payable by quarterly instalments in advance; the usual quarter days being 25 March, 24 June, 29 September and 25 December.

    One quarter of the yearly rent will usually be payable on these dates. This is not invariable. In some cases, particularly for short term lettings, monthly payments might be appropriate. Value Added Tax (VAT) will be payable on the rent (and on service charges) if the landlord has elected to waive the building's exemption from VAT. If the landlord has not already done this, it could be done at any time during the lease unless the lease forbids it. If this waiver is made, VAT will be payable by the tenant in addition to the rent and service charge. Many tenants will be entitled to recover the VAT through their business VAT returns.

Recommendation 5: Where alternative lease terms are offered, different rents should be appropriately priced for each set of terms. The landlord should disclose the VAT status of the property and the tenant should take professional advice as to whether any VAT charged on rent and other charges is recoverable.

- **Rent Review**

    For leases over five years, it is usual for the rent to be reviewed at stated intervals. Usually rent is reviewed to open market rent level – the rent that a new tenant would pay if the property was being let in the open market at the time of the review (the most appropriate basis for review). Alternatives include fixed increases or linking the rent to a published index (such as the Index of Retail Prices) or to the annual turnover of the tenant's business at the premises. Reviews to open market rent normally occur every five years whilst rents linked to indices or turnover are commonly recalculated annually.

    Not all these methods of review are suitable for every tenant or appropriate to every type of property or business. If the review is on 'upwards only' terms, the rent will not reduce at review but will remain at its existing level even if the market rent or index has fallen. Tenants may find that they would have to pay a higher initial rent where the rent review is to be up or down compared with upwards only, as this transfers the risk of downward movements to the landlord. Financers of property require landlords to ensure that rental income will not fall below a particular level and this may restrict a landlord's ability to agree an upwards/downwards basis.

Recommendation 6: The basis of rent review should generally be to open market rent. Wherever possible, landlords should offer alternatives which are priced on a risk-adjusted basis, including alternatives to upwards only rent reviews; these might include up/down reviews to open market rent with a minimum of the initial rent, or another basis such as annual indexation. Those funding property should make every effort to avoid imposing restrictions on the type of rent review that landlords, developers and/or investors may offer.

- **Repairs and services**

    Leases generally state which party will be responsible for carrying out, or for meeting the cost of, repairing and maintaining the fabric and services of the property. The degree to which these burdens are placed on the tenant should take into account the initial condition of the premises and the duration of the lease.

A 'full repairing' lease makes the tenant of an entire building responsible for all internal and external repairs and redecoration that become necessary during the term. This includes the roof, foundations, main walls and other structural parts, irrespective of whether or not they are in good condition at the start of the lease. A 'full repairing' lease for part of a building requires the tenant to maintain and decorate the inside of the premises and to pay, through a service charge, towards the landlord's costs of maintaining and repairing the common parts and structure and providing services such as porterage, lifts, central heating, etc. Such obligations might require the tenant to carry out, or pay towards the cost of, work to remedy an inherent construction defect which becomes apparent during the term.

Alternatives to 'full repairing' terms might include limiting the tenant's repairs to the maintenance of the property in its existing condition, excluding certain categories of repair, and the remediation of inherent defects. The scope or amount of any service charge can be limited or there can be a fixed rent which is inclusive of service costs.

If the lease refers to the existing condition of the property, it will be in both parties' interests for a schedule of condition (which can be photographic) to be professionally prepared and kept with the lease documents. Professional advice should be sought when the tenant is required to carry out initial improvements and repairs, as there may be implications for tax and rent review.

Recommendation 7: The tenant's repairing obligations, and any repairs costs included in service charges, should be appropriate to the length of the term and the condition and age of the property at the start of the lease. Where appropriate the landlord should consider appropriately priced alternatives to full repairing terms.

- **Insurance**
  It is usual for the landlord to insure the building and require the tenants to pay the premiums. In the case of multi-occupied buildings, each tenant would be expected to contribute towards the total insurance premium; this may be included in the service charge or may be charged separately. Leases may give the landlord discretion to choose the insurer. Alternatives include allowing the tenant to influence the selection of the insurer (if their lease covers the entire building), or providing that the landlord must arrange the insurance on competitive rates.

  The lease should contain provisions covering the situation where there is damage by an uninsured risk or where there is a large excess. These risks vary from time to time and might include terrorist damage. If suitable provisions are not included in the lease the tenant might have to meet the cost of rebuilding in that situation.

  Alternatives include allowing the tenant to terminate the lease following uninsured damage, although it may be appropriate to allow the landlord to choose to rebuild at his own cost in order to keep the lease in force.

Recommendation 8: Where the landlord is responsible for insuring the property, the policy terms should be competitive. The tenant of an entire building should, in appropriate cases, be given the opportunity to influence the choice of insurer. If the premises are so damaged by an uninsured risk as to prevent occupation, the tenant should be allowed to terminate the lease unless the landlord agrees to rebuild at his own cost.

- **Assigning and subletting**
  There are two ways in which the tenant may pass on the lease obligations to a third party; one is by assignment (selling, giving away or paying someone to take over, the lease) and the other is by subletting (remaining as tenant of the lease with the lease obligations but granting a sublease to another tenant who undertakes the same or similar obligations). Leases generally control assignment and subletting. Most require the tenant to obtain the landlord's

consent (which cannot be unreasonably withheld) but some leases completely prohibit certain acts such as subletting part of the premises.

A new lease, and an existing lease granted since 1995, may expand the landlord's right to control assignments by imposing credit ratings or other financial criteria for assignees. It may also require the assigning tenant to stand as guarantor for any assignee by giving the landlord an 'Authorised Guarantee Agreement'; alternatives include giving this guarantee only if it is reasonably required by the landlord, such as where the assignee is of lower financial standing than the assigning tenant.

Recommendation 9: Unless the particular circumstances of the letting justify greater control, the only restriction on assignment of the whole premises should be obtaining the landlord's consent which is not to be unreasonably withheld. Landlords are urged to consider requiring Authorised Guarantee Agreements only where the assignee is of lower financial standing than the assignor at the date of the assignment.

- **Alterations and changes of use**
  Leases generally restrict the tenant's freedom to make alterations and often impose tighter control over external and structural alterations than over internal non-structural alterations or partitioning. The lease may absolutely prohibit the work.

  Alternatives may require the landlord's consent which must not be unreasonably withheld, or may permit the particular type of alteration without consent. The lease may entitle the landlord to require the tenant to reinstate the premises (remove alterations) at the end of the lease; or alternatively reinstatement need only take place if it is reasonable for the landlord to require it.

  The permitted use of the premises may be very narrowly defined or there may be a wide class of use. Consent for changes of use can be at the landlord's discretion or, alternatively, the lease may provide that consent is not to be unreasonably withheld.

  If the provisions of the lease are very restrictive this can hinder the assignment of the lease or the subletting of the property to a different business.

Recommendation 10: Landlord's control over alterations and changes of use should not be more restrictive than is necessary to protect the value of the premises and any adjoining or neighbouring premises of the landlord. At the end of the lease the tenant should not be required to remove and make good permitted alterations unless this is reasonably required.

Conduct during a lease

- **Ongoing relationship**
  The relationship between landlord and tenant will continue after the lease has been signed; for example, there may be rent review negotiations or discussions about varying the terms. The landlord may be contemplating planning applications, redevelopment, improvements or making changes in the provision of services.

Recommendation 11: Landlords and tenants should deal with each other constructively, courteously, openly and honestly throughout the term of the lease and carry out their respective obligations fully and on time. If either party faces a difficulty in carrying out any obligations under the lease, the other should be told without undue delay so that the possibility of agreement on how to deal with the problem may be explored. When either party proposes to take any action which is likely to have significant consequences for the other, the party proposing the action, when it becomes appropriate to do so, should notify the other without undue delay.

- **Request for consents**
  There may be occasions when the tenant seeks a consent (licence) from the landlord, when for example, the tenant proposes to assign the lease, grant a sublease, change the use of the

property, make alterations or display signs. The effect on the landlord will vary with the exact details. In some cases, the landlord will have to pass the request to a superior landlord or to a mortgagee. Most leases require the tenant to pay any costs incurred by the landlord in dealing with such an application.

Recommendation 12: When seeking a consent from the landlord, the tenant should supply full information about his/her proposal. The landlord should respond without undue delay and should where practicable give the tenant an estimate of the costs that the tenant will have to pay. The landlord should ensure that the request is passed promptly to any superior landlord or mortgagee whose agreement is needed and should give details to the tenant so that any problems can be speedily resolved.

- **Rent review negotiation**
  Many leases contain provisions for the periodic review of rent; these may be highly technical and may lay down procedures and time limits.

Recommendation 13: Landlords and tenants should ensure that they understand the basis upon which rent may be reviewed and the procedure to be followed, including the existence of any strict time limits which could create pitfalls. They should obtain professional advice on these matters well before the review date and also immediately upon receiving (and before responding to) any notice or correspondence on the matter from the other party or his/her agent.

- **Insurance**
  Directly or indirectly, the tenant will usually pay the cost of insuring the premises and the lease will state whether the tenant or the landlord has to arrange this. Where the landlord has arranged insurance, the terms should be made known to the tenant and any interest of the tenant covered by the policy.

  Sometimes the lease allows the landlord or the tenant to end the lease if the premises are very badly damaged. If damage occurs but is covered by the insurance, there may be important questions about how, why and by whom the insurance money is spent and the parties should take professional advice as soon as the damage occurs.

Recommendation 14: Where the landlord has arranged insurance, the terms should be made known to the tenant and any interest of the tenant covered by the policy. Any material change in the insurance should be notified to the tenant. Tenants should consider taking out their own insurance against loss or damage to contents and their business (loss of profits etc.) and any other risks not covered by the landlord's policy.

- **Varying the lease – effect on guarantors**
  A guarantor may not be liable if the terms of the lease are changed without the guarantor's consent. In some cases the variation may release a guarantor from all liability.

Recommendation 15: Landlords and tenants should seek the agreement of any guarantors to any proposed material changes to the terms of the lease, or even minor changes which could increase the guarantor's liability.

- **Holding former tenants and their guarantors liable**
  A tenant who assigns a lease may remain liable for a period for any subsequent breach of the lease terms including failure to pay rent. This liability may also apply to a guarantor for the former tenant. Where payment is made to the landlord under this liability, the former tenant may be entitled to take an overriding lease of the property in order to have some control over the current tenants; legal advice can be obtained about these matters. In certain circumstances, insurance against losses following an assignment may be possible. Landlords must notify previous tenants about arrears of rent and service charges within six months of the amount becoming due, in order to make them liable.

Recommendation 16: When previous tenants or their guarantors are liable to a landlord for defaults by the current tenant, landlords should notify them before the current tenant accumulates excessive liabilities. All defaults should be handled with speed and landlords should seek to assist the tenant and guarantor in minimising losses. An assignor who wishes to remain informed of the outcome of rent reviews should keep in touch with the landlord and the landlord should provide the information. Assignors should take professional advice on what methods are open to them to minimise their losses caused by defaults by the current occupier.

- **Release of landlord on sale of property**
  A landlord who sells his interest in the building may remain liable to the tenants to perform any obligations in the lease (for example, in repairing or insuring the building) in the event of failure on the part of the new landlord.

  It is possible, in certain circumstances, for landlords to terminate their obligations on selling the property through provisions in the lease or, in some cases by seeking the agreement of their tenants and, in the event of objection, decision by a county court.

Recommendation 17: Landlords who sell their interest in premises should take legal advice about ending their ongoing liability under the lease.

- **Repairs**
  The landlord may be entitled to serve a notice requiring the tenant to undertake repairing obligations which the tenant has failed to carry out. This notice may be served near or at the end of the term or earlier. The list of repairs is called a 'schedule of dilapidations'. Disagreements about these are not uncommon and the law on repairing obligations is complex.

Recommendation 18: Tenants should take the advice of a property professional about their repairing obligations near the end of the term of the lease and also immediately upon receiving a notice to repair or a schedule of dilapidations.

- **Business Rates**
  Uniform Business Rates (UBR) are payable to local authorities and are the responsibility of the occupier (the ratepayer) of the property. In certain circumstances the amount payable can be reduced by appealing against the business rates assessment.

  Ratepayers should be aware time limits apply to certain appeal procedures and advice on these may be obtained from a rating specialist, who is usually a chartered surveyor.

Recommendation 19: Tenants or other ratepayers should consider if their business rates assessment is correct or whether they need to make an appeal. They should refer to the DTLR Business Rates – a Guide or obtain advice from a rating specialist. RICS provides a free rating help line service and advice is available also from the Institute of Revenues Rating and Valuation (IRRV)

- **Service charges**
  Where the lease entitles the landlord to levy a service charge, details of the services covered are usually set out in the lease and it may contain provisions requiring the landlord to act reasonably or economically. Some leases lay down strict time limits for the tenant to query service charges. Several leading property industry and professional bodies have agreed a Guide to Good Practice in relation to service charges which is available free.

Recommendation 20: Landlords should observe the Guide to Good Practice on Service Charges in Commercial Properties. Tenants should familiarise themselves with that Guide and should take professional advice if they think they are being asked to pay excessive service charges.

- **Dispute resolution**
  Disputes between landlords and tenants can be expensive, time-consuming and divisive. If the lease does not state how a particular dispute is to be settled, the parties may have to go to court. Leases often provide for certain types of dispute to be resolved by particular procedures; for example, it is common to provide that a dispute about rent review is to be referred to an independent surveyor acting either as an arbitrator or as an expert.

Professional advice should be obtained about any procedures laid down in the lease.

The parties can agree to appoint a mediator to try to resolve a particular dispute even though the lease does not provide for it. The mediator will consult both parties separately and advise them on the strengths or weaknesses of their case and work towards a settlement. Mediators should be able to keep costs down and achieve an outcome within a short timescale; but if mediation fails, delay and cost will have been incurred and the parties still have to resort to the formal procedures of arbitration, expert determination or court proceedings.

Recommendation 21: When disputes arise, the parties should make prompt and reasonable efforts to settle them by agreement. Where disputes cannot be settled by agreement, both sides should always consider speed and economy when selecting a method of dispute resolution. Mediation may be appropriate before embarking on more formal procedures.

- **Repossession by the landlord**

  The lease will contain a clause giving the landlord the right ('forfeiture' or 're-entry') to repossess the property if the tenant breaks any obligations under the lease or becomes insolvent. When a landlord seeks repossession under a forfeiture clause, the tenant (or sub-tenant) may be entitled to claim 'relief from forfeiture' from a court, i.e. the right to retain the property despite the breach.

Recommendation 22: Tenants threatened with repossession or whose property has been repossessed will need professional advice if they wish to try to keep or regain possession. Similarly, landlords should be clear about their rights before attempting to operate a forfeiture clause and may need professional advice.

- **Renewals under the Landlord and Tenant Act 1954**

  Unless it is excluded, this Act may give the tenant a right to renew the lease when it ends (see under Duration of lease). It contains procedures and time limits that must be strictly followed by both landlords and tenants. Disputes under the Act about whether the tenant should be granted a new lease and about its terms are adjudicated by the county court, but the parties may agree to ask the court to refer all or some aspects to be decided by an independent surveyor or solicitor under the Professional Arbitration on Court Terms scheme operated by the RICS and the Law Society.

Recommendation 23: The parties should take professional advice on the Landlord and Tenant Act 1954 and the PACT scheme at least six months before the end of the term of the lease and also immediately upon receiving any notice under the Act from the other party or their agent. Guidance on the Act can be found in the Department for Transport, Local Government and the Regions, 'Guide to the Landlord and Tenant Act 1954'.

Property advice

For a selection of local professional property advisers who could represent you call: The Royal Institution of Chartered Surveyors' (RICS) Contact Centre on 020 7222 7000.

For a free rent review and lease renewal helpline service for businesses not already professionally represented call the RICS on 020 7334 3806. For the rating helpline call 020 7222 7000. Rating advice also available from the Institute of Revenues Rating and Valuation on 020 7831 3505.

Also free from the RICS: 'Rent review – a guide for small businesses'. Send a large stamped, self addressed envelope to Corporate Communications, The Royal Institution of Chartered Surveyors, 12 Great George Street, London SW1P 3AD, or contact the RICS Rent Review and Lease Renewal helpline on 020 7334 3806.

For a 'Guide to Good Practice on Service Charges in Commercial Properties', contact the RICS Commercial Property Faculty at the address above (with a large stamped SAE) or the website found at www.servicechargeguide.co.uk.

Legal advice

For a free Guide to the Landlord and Tenant Act 1954 write to the

Department for Transport, Local Government and the Regions,
Eland House,
Bressenden Place,
London SW1E 5DU.

For information on local solicitors who could represent you, call The Law Society on 020 7242 1222.

For information on local licensed conveyancers who could represent you, call The Council for Licensed Conveyancers on 01245 349599.

Property owners

The trade association which looks after the interests of property owners is:

The British Property Federation,
1 Warwick Row,
7th Floor,
London SW1E 5ER,
Tel: 020 7828 0111
Fax: 020 7834 3442.

Occupiers

Several trade associations look after the interests of occupiers, including the British Retail Consortium and the Property Market Reform Group.

The BRC can be contacted on 020 7854 8900.

Contact details for the PMRG and other organisations supporting the code may be obtained from the Commercial Leases Working Group Secretariat.

The Secretariat for the Commercial Leases Working Group can be contacted at:

Policy Unit
The Royal Institution of Chartered Surveyors
12 Great George Street
Parliament Square
London
SW1P 3AD
United Kingdom

T. +44 (0)20 7695 1535
F. +44 (0)20 7334 3795

www.rics.org

VIII.5. Commercial Property Standard Enquiries (an overview)[1]

The newly launched Commercial Property Standard Enquiries (CPSEs) aim to speed up commercial property transactions for lawyers and, more importantly, clients. They are available free of charge through the British Property Federation (BPF) Web site and the Practical Law Company (PLC) Property Law Web site (www.bpf.org.uk and www.practicallaw.com).

The CPSEs have been prepared by the London Property Support Lawyers Group, whose members are drawn from about 20 major law firms, both London and national. Helpful input was also received from a number of other firms and interested parties. The project was sponsored by the BPF, whose endorsement is a valuable demonstration that the CPSEs will benefit owners and managers of property and not just lawyers.

The documents

The CPSEs so far comprise:

- CPSE 1 – general enquiries for all commercial transactions, whether freehold or leasehold, vacant or tenanted;

- CPSE 2 – supplemental enquiries for property subject to commercial tenancies;

- CPSE 3 – supplemental enquiries on the grant of a lease;

- CPSE 4 – supplemental enquiries on the assignment of a lease;

- STER – solicitor's title and exchange requirements;

- SCR – solicitor's completion requirements;

- RQ – buyer's request for replies to CPSEs.

Each document is accompanied by guidance notes to help both lawyers and clients understand the purpose of the enquiry, why it is raised and how it should be answered. Further supplemental enquiries are planned, covering residential tenancies (for example, for the common situation of a flat over a shop), newly constructed buildings, agricultural property and mixed-use premises where the residential tenants have a right of first refusal under the Landlord and Tenant Act 1987.

The benefits of standardisation

Although standardised documentation has many benefits, commercial conveyancing has traditionally employed few standard documents, unlike residential conveyancing where the TransAction scheme is well established. Some of the benefits are listed below:

- Sellers will be asked the same enquiries in all transactions, and will not have to wrestle with obscure questions to deal with different firms' concerns. This is particularly useful when

---

1. This was originally published as an article in the Law Society's *Gazette* on 14 October 2002. The article was written by Emma Slessenger of Dechert and Peter JG Williams of Eversheds.

selling or letting units on a development. Buyers can, of course, ask additional questions specific to the transaction or the property;

● Where sellers wish to prepare a package of information in advance (as recommended by the Investment Property Forum and likely to become commonplace following the introduction of the CPSEs), they can be confident that they are covering what the buyer will want to know with a minimum of additional enquiries;

● Buyers will benefit from faster turnaround times and should receive information in one bite, rather than having to ask obvious follow-up questions;

● Making the information-gathering exercise easier will help to speed up the whole trans- action and is in tune with developments like National Land Information Service and e-conveyancing;

● The CPSEs also help prevent important issues from being overlooked and can act as a basic form of quality control.

Drafting principles

Dealing with preliminary enquiries is probably the lawyer's and the client's least favourite part of any transaction. Even without disturbing the caveat emptor principle, the information-gathering exercise can be made more effective by limiting it to the legitimate concerns of the buyer which the seller can accept are appropriate and reasonable. With this aim in mind, the following drafting criteria were used:

● Questions must be universally relevant. For example, mining is irrelevant when buying an office block in central London. Such questions will, of course, be perfectly appropriate in mining areas;

● Generally enquiries should not duplicate information obtained by searches, inspection or survey. However, some questions checking the seller's personal knowledge of the absence of problems can be useful and some enquiries (for example, on planning) supplement official information;

● Questions about matters of title were removed. In response to consultation comments, the STER form was created as a skeleton checklist for lawyers;

● Contract amendments (for example, is the transaction a sub-sale, obligations on the seller not to make a VAT election) were removed from the enquiries;

● Generally, the seller should not be expected to answer questions about adjoining or neighbouring property. An obvious exception is in relation to rights over or in favour of neighbouring land, which are included in the CPSEs. More extensive questions are also relevant when the property concerned is a unit on a development or part of a building;

● As far as possible, duplication is avoided, although there is some inevitable overlap, such as between questions about various kinds of disputes and the general disputes enquiry;

● Two types of enquiry were rejected: those which ask for details which are rarely available (for example, floorloading) and those asking for the seller's opinion (for example, about the adequacy of plant or equipment serving the property).

The guidance notes also help to keep the enquiries short. Examples of what might be relevant and summaries of the law could be put in the notes rather than the question. The notes are also used to suggest follow-up action, including situations which should be referred to specialists.

How to use the CPSEs

The CPSEs can be used straight from the Web site or may be downloaded onto a firm's own network in PDF format, but they must be used as they appear on screen (including displaying the BPF logo) if they are to be described as the CPSEs. In particular, it is vital that questions are not altered or omitted. The CPSEs will only work if everyone is using the same form.

However, practitioners may send additional enquiries contained in a separate document with the relevant CPSEs. These might be particular concerns of the client or the lawyer, enquiries relevant in certain areas of the country or to certain properties, or enquiries arising out of the particular transaction. Any additional enquiries must be clearly identified as such and not just tacked on to the CPSEs.

Equally, a practitioner might choose not to ask the CPSE question on a particular topic (such as where it is known that a particular enquiry is irrelevant or insufficiently detailed for a known problem). In that case, simply tell the seller that you are asking CPSE 1 but omitting a particular question and, if appropriate, that you are also asking the additional enquiries attached. The CPSE form must not be amended.

With the e-conveyancing revolution approaching, paper can be saved by not sending hard copies at all, but merely referring the seller's solicitor to the Web site. A form of request (RQ) is available on the Web site. This simply asks the seller's solicitors to reply to the specified enquiries (CPSE 1 and whichever of CPSE 2, CPSE 3 and CPSE 4 are relevant to the transaction). Copies of the enquiries will probably continue to be printed for the report on title and to keep with the deeds.

A working group of property support lawyers will keep the enquiries up to date. A new edition is planned for autumn 2003 which will take account of the complete rewriting of land registration law, among other developments.

VIII

IX.   STAMP DUTY

IX.1.   Inland Revenue Statement of Practice on the sale of new houses[1]

STAMP DUTY: NEW BUILDINGS

This Statement sets out the practice the Board of Inland Revenue will apply in relation to the stamp duty chargeable in certain circumstances on the conveyance or lease of a new or partly constructed building. It affects transactions where, at the date of the contract for sale or lease of a building plot, building work has not commenced or has been only partially completed on that site but where that work has started or has been completed at the time the conveyance or lease is executed.

This Statement reflects the advice the Board have received on this subject in the light of the decision in the case of **Prudential Assurance Company Limited v IRC** (**[1993] 1 WLR 211**). The Statement does not apply to the common situation where the parties have entered into a contract for the sale of a new house and that contract is implemented by a conveyance of the whole property. This Statement replaces the Statements of Practice issued in 1957 and 1987 (SP 10/87) on this subject which are now withdrawn.

The Board are advised that, whilst each case will clearly depend on its own facts, the law is as follows:

1.   Two transactions/two contracts

Where the purchaser or lessee is entitled under the terms of a contract to a conveyance or lease of land alone in consideration of the purchase price or rent of the site and a second genuine contract for building works is entered into as a separate transaction, the ad valorem duty on the conveyance or lease will be determined by the amount of the purchase price or rent which the purchaser or lessee is obliged to pay under the terms of the first contract. In these circumstances it does not matter whether any building work has commenced at the date of the conveyance or lease. The consideration chargeable to ad valorem duty will still be only that passing for the land.

2.   One transaction/two contracts

Where there is one transaction between the parties but this is implemented by two contracts, one for the sale or lease of the building plot and one for the building works themselves, the amount of ad valorem duty charged on the instrument will depend on the amount of the consideration, which in turn will depend on whether those contracts can be shown to be genuinely independent of each other.

   (i)   If the two contracts are so interlocked that they cannot be said to be genuinely capable of independent completion (and in particular where if default occurs on either contract, the other is then not enforceable) ad valorem duty will be charged on the total consideration for the land and buildings, whether completed or not, as if the parties had entered into only one contract.

   (ii)   If the two contracts are shown to be genuinely independent of each other, ad valorem duty will be charged by reference to the consideration paid or payable for the land and any building

1. 12 July 1993.

works on that land at the date of execution of the instrument. It follows that, where the instrument is executed after the building works are completed, ad valorem duty will be charged on the consideration for the land and the completed building(s).

3. Sham or artificial transactions

This Statement does not apply to cases where the transaction concerned, or any part of it, involves a sham or artificial transaction.

4. Contracts already entered into

Where unconditional contracts have been entered into before or within 28 days of the date of this Statement and the duty payable on the resulting conveyance or lease would have been less under the earlier Statements of Practice, the Stamp Office will accept duty in the lesser amount. In such cases the instrument should be submitted together with all the evidence to support the claim that unconditional contracts were entered into within this transitional period.

5. Procedure for submitting documents

Where a person accepts that a conveyance or lease of a building plot is chargeable on the total price paid or payable for the land and the completed building, it should be submitted for stamping in the usual way together with a covering letter giving the aggregate price and a payment for the duty appropriate to that price.

Where the total price does not exceed the amount up to which the instrument is liable to nil duty (currently £60,000) and a certificate of value is included in the instrument, a conveyance may be sent direct to the Land Registry in England and Wales or, in Scotland, to the Keeper of the Registers of Scotland. A lease will need to be stamped in respect of the rent.

Where the total price exceeds the threshold at which duty becomes payable but the taxpayer takes the view that duty is payable on some smaller sum, the instrument should be submitted to the Stamp Office. This applies even where the taxpayer believes that the amount potentially chargeable to ad valorem duty is below the threshold and a certificate of value is included in the instrument. The instrument should be accompanied by a copy of the agreement(s) for sale etc. and a letter stating the amount which the taxpayer regards as chargeable consideration, identifying separately any amount attributable to building work. Details of any contractual arrangements not covered by the agreement(s) should also be given in the covering letter.

This Statement does not affect in any way a taxpayer's rights of appeal.

IX.2. Stamp Duty Form 22: Apportionment of consideration under agreement for sale

	A		B
Amount of consideration payable in Cash or Bills	£	**Legal Estates in Freehold Property**	£
Amount of consideration payable in Shares, Debentures etc	£	**Fixed Plant and Machinery in Freehold Property**	£
Liabilities assumed by the Purchaser:		**Legal Estates in Leasehold Property**	£
Amounts due on mortgages of Freeholds and/or Leaseholds, including interest to date of sale	£	**Fixed Plant and Machinery in Leasehold Property**	£
Hire Purchase Debts for Goods acquired	£	**Equitable interests in Freehold or Leasehold Property**	£
Other liabilities of the Vendor	£	**Loose Plant and Machinery, Stock-in-Trade and other Chattels**	£
		(Only Plant and Machinery in an actual state of severance, i.e. not fixed to the premises at the date of the Agreement for Sale, must be included in this figure)	
Any other consideration	£	**Goods, Wares and Merchandise subject to Hire Purchase Agreements (Written Down Value)**	£
		Goodwill and Benefit of Contracts	£
		Patents, Designs, Trade Marks, Licences, etc.	£
		Book Debts	£
		Cash in Hand and at Bank on Current Account	£
		Cash on Deposit	£
		Shares, Debentures and other investments	£
		Other property viz	£
	£		£

Please note that Column A should equal Column B.

I hereby certify that the particulars shown in this form are in every respect fully and truly stated according to the best of my judgment and belief, and that the Loose Plant and Machinery included in the above apportionment were in a state of severance at the date of the sale agreement.

This certificate should be signed by the Vendor or Purchaser (the Secretary in the case of a Company) or by an Accountant or Solicitor acting in the sale.

Signed . . . . Date . . . .

Address . . . .

IX

IX.3. Inland Revenue Statement of Practice on disadvantaged areas relief[1]

This Statement of Practice is intended as guidance for those claiming exemption from stamp duty in respect of transfers of property situated in designated areas ('Disadvantaged Areas Relief') and explains how Inland Revenue Stamp Taxes will interpret the extension to the relief introduced with effect from 10 April 2003.

The relief is one of a number of measures set out in the Government's Urban White Paper *'Our Towns and Cities: The Future: Delivering an Urban Renaissance'* published in November 2000. The measure is designed to stimulate the physical, economic and social regeneration of the UK's most disadvantaged areas by attracting development and by encouraging the purchase of residential and commercial property by individuals and businesses. The areas eligible for relief were designated 'Enterprise Areas' by the Chancellor in his 2002 Pre-Budget Report. In addition to the relief, a range of other Government policies designed to support enterprise and economic regeneration, including the Community Investment Tax Relief, will benefit these areas, helping to support the development of new and existing businesses.

Introduction

1. Disadvantaged Areas Relief (provided for by section 92 of, and Schedule 30 to, the Finance Act 2001) was introduced on 30 November 2001 and was initially only available for conveyances or transfers on sale (of both residential and commercial property) for which the consideration did not exceed £150,000. Stamp duty in respect of conveyances or transfers of commercial property in disadvantaged areas was abolished in consequence of the Stamp Duty (Disadvantaged Areas) (Application of Exemptions) Regulations 2003 ('the Regulations'), which have effect in relation to instruments executed on or after 10 April 2003. Thereafter the £150,000 limit applies only in relation to residential property.

2. Finance Act 2002 inserted the following provisions in Finance Act 2001 to distinguish residential from other property and to provide for differing stamp duty exemptions:

    ● Section 92A which enables stamp duty relief in designated disadvantaged areas in respect of all properties to be varied depending on whether or not the property is 'residential';

    ● Section 92B which defines 'residential property' for the purposes of the relief. Non-residential property, in respect of which unlimited relief is available, is therefore defined in the Act by exclusion. The section also sets out particular building uses that are specifically included within, or specifically excluded from, the definition.

3. In most cases there will be no difficulty in practice in establishing whether or not a property is 'residential'. This statement sets out in more detail the Stamp Office's approach to borderline cases and gives guidance on the practical application of the legislation. The annexed flowchart provides a quick guide for simpler cases as to whether property constitutes 'residential property'.

---

1. © Crown 2003. This Statement of Practice (SP1/2003) from the Inland Revenue can be found on their web site at www.inlandrevenue.gov.uk

Certification

4　Claims for unlimited relief must be accompanied by a certificate stating either that none of the land in question is residential property or, if part is residential, the proportion that is non-residential (together with the usual certificate of value for the remainder).

- *Residential property*: Section 92A(4) of Finance Act 2001, together with the Regulations, provides that the exemption will only apply if the document is certified to the effect that the amount or value of the consideration does not exceed £150,000.

- *Non-residential property*: Subsection (2) of section 92 of Finance Act 2001 provides that the exemption will only apply if the document is certified to the Commissioners as being an instrument on which stamp duty is not chargeable by virtue of subsection (1) of that section.

5.　The following are suggested forms of words for particular certificates:

- *Residential Property*: 'I/We hereby certify that the transaction effected by this instrument does not form part of a larger transaction or series of transactions in respect of which the amount or value of the consideration exceeds £150,000 and that stamp duty is not chargeable thereon by virtue of the provisions of sections 92 and 92A of the Finance Act 2001.'

- *Non-residential Property*: 'I/We hereby certify that this is an instrument in respect of non-residential property on which stamp duty is not chargeable by virtue of the provisions of section 92 of the Finance Act 2001.'

- *Mixed Use Property*: 'I/We hereby certify that the transaction effected by this instrument is in respect of property part of which is residential property, and which does not form part of a larger transaction or series of transactions in respect of which the amount or value of the consideration relating to the residential part exceeds £150,000 so that stamp duty is not chargeable by virtue of sections 92 and 92A of the Finance Act 2001, and part of which is non-residential property on which stamp duty is not chargeable by virtue of the provisions of section 92 of the Finance Act 2001. The basis upon which the allocation between residential and non-residential parts has been made is as follows: …'

6.　While the legislation does not specifically require the certificate to be included as part of the document, it is suggested that it should be so included. If the person submitting the document for stamping does not provide a certificate, either in the document or separately in writing, exemption will not be granted.

7.　Appropriate contemporaneous evidence should be retained to support any certificate provided. Estate agents' specifications, site plans, planning applications or permissions, marketing material and photographs may all provide relevant information.

8.　Anyone falsely certifying a document with a view to obtaining relief that is not due will be committing a stamp duty fraud.

The meaning of residential property

9.　Section 92B defines 'residential property' as a building which:

- is used as a dwelling, **or**

- is suitable for use as a dwelling, **or**

- is in the process of being constructed or adapted for such use.

If a property meets any one of these separate tests it will be treated as residential property and be subject to the £150,000 limit for relief, as will any garden or grounds belonging to it or any interests or rights attaching to it. Each element of the definition is considered in turn below.

The question of whether and to what extent a building and grounds are defined as residential property for stamp duty purposes may also have implications for its treatment for capital gains tax and local authority rates.

Use as a dwelling

10. Where a building is in use at the date of execution of the relevant instrument, it will be a question of fact whether and to what extent it is used as a dwelling. Use at the date the instrument is executed overrides any past or intended future uses for this purpose.

11. Where the property in question is in use as a dwelling at the date of execution, it is residential property for the purposes of the relief unless it is part of a multiple transaction qualifying for relief under the Regulations (see paragraphs 35 to 39 below).

12. For the treatment of buildings put to both residential and non-residential use, see paragraphs 17 and 18 below.

Suitable for use as a dwelling

13. The suitability test applies to the state of the building at the time the instrument is executed, having regard to the facilities available and any history of use. For example, the Inland Revenue will not regard an office block as 'suitable for use as a dwelling', but a house which has been used as an office without particular adaptation may well be so.

14. If a building is not in use at the date of execution but its last use was as a dwelling, it will be taken to be 'suitable for use as a dwelling' and treated as residential property for the purposes of the relief, unless evidence is produced to the contrary (see paragraph 15).

15. Whether a building is suitable for use as a dwelling will depend upon the precise facts and circumstances. The simple removal of, for example, a bathroom suite or kitchen facilities will not be regarded as rendering a building unsuitable for use as a dwelling. Where it is claimed that a previously residential property is no longer suitable for use as a dwelling, perhaps because it is derelict or has been substantially altered, the claimant will need to provide evidence that this is the case. See also paragraph 29.

16. Where a building has been used partly for residential purposes and partly for another purpose, its overall suitability for use as a dwelling will be judged from the facilities available at the date of execution of the relevant document. For example, if two rooms of a house were in use as a dentist's surgery and waiting room at the date of execution, the Inland Revenue would nevertheless normally consider this property suitable for use as a dwelling unless the claimant provided evidence to the contrary. In other words, the interaction of the Regulations with section 92B(1) enables a building that is used only partly as a dwelling to be nevertheless suitable for use wholly as a dwelling, with the effect that the £150,000 limit applies to the whole of the consideration. Where only a distinct part of the building is used and suitable for use as a dwelling, that part will be residential property for the purposes of the relief and the mixed use provisions will apply (paragraphs 17 and 18).

Mixed use

17. Where only part of a building (and land or interest relating to it) is 'residential property' within section 92B(1), the consideration 'shall be apportioned on such basis as is just and reasonable' between the residential and non-residential elements. The £150,000 limit is then applied only to the residential portion, in accordance with the appropriate certification (regulation 5 of the Regulations). For example:

A property situated wholly within a disadvantaged area is bought for

   (a) £200,000

   (b) £400,000

50 per cent of the property is 'residential property' on the basis of a just and reasonable apportionment.

Relief is conferred by section 92 FA 2001, applied in conjunction with regulation 5 of the Regulations. Paragraph (3) of regulation 5 calls for an apportionment of the total consideration between residential and non-residential elements. Paragraph (4) confirms that relief applies to the residential property element only where the consideration attributed to it does not exceed £150,000. In these examples:

(a) £100,000 is attributed to the residential property element, so relief is due. The part of the land that is not residential property is also exempt under the normal operation of section 92 FA 2001. So no duty is payable.

(b) the £200,000 attributed to the residential property element is not exempt, because of regulation 5(4), but attracts duty at the rate of 1 per cent (stamp duty payable £2,000). The non-residential property element is exempt as above.

18. The 'just and reasonable' test is necessarily subjective, and each case will be considered on its merits. Apportionment might be on the basis of the percentage areas quoted in planning applications, where appropriate, or alternatively of floor space relating to the respective uses. Other methods of apportionment will be considered as part of a claim.

Specific cases

19. Some types of communal or institutional building are used neither as dwellings nor for commercial purposes. The legislation therefore outlines how these are classified for the purposes of relief, specifically including some such buildings within the definition of 'dwelling' (section 92B(2)) and specifically excluding others (section 92B(3)). If they do not fall within any of the specific categories of section 92B(3), most residential institutions will come within section 92B(2)(d) and will be treated as dwellings by default.

20. Categories of building use specifically included within the definition of 'use as a dwelling' (so that transfers of such buildings only qualify for relief if the consideration does not exceed £150,000) (section 92B(2)) are:

(a) residential accommodation for school pupils, for example accommodation blocks in boarding schools;

(b) residential accommodation for students, other than that within section 92B(3)(b). Student accommodation provided by private landlords is 'a dwelling', as is accommodation leased to students by universities or colleges in flats or houses rather than in halls of residence (see section 92B(3)(b));

(c) residential accommodation for members of any of the armed forces, including accommodation for their families (section 92B(2)(c));

(d) an institution that is the sole or main residence of at least 90 per cent of its residents and does not fall within any of the categories referred to in section 92B(3) (see section 92B(2)(d) and also paragraph 21). This would include, for example,

● sheltered accommodation for the elderly where no nursing or personal care is provided

● accommodation for religious communities (subject to the rules regarding mixed use; see paragraphs 17 and 18).

21. Categories of building use specifically excluded from the definition of 'use as a dwelling' (so that transfers of such buildings in a disadvantaged area will qualify for unlimited relief) (section 92B(3)) are:

(a) a home or other institution providing residential accommodation for children;

(b) a hall of residence for students in further or higher education. This is not defined in the legislation but in practice property provided by a university or similar establishment will be judged on the facts (number of inhabitants, type of facilities, availability of communal areas);

(c) a home or other institution providing residential accommodation with personal care for persons in need of personal care by reason of old age, disablement, past or present dependence on alcohol or drugs or past or present mental disorder;

(d) a hospital or hospice;

(e) a prison or similar establishment, or

(f) a hotel or inn or similar establishment.

22. The specific inclusions and exclusions set out in paragraphs 20 and 21 apply not only to a building's actual use at the date of the transfer, but to the uses for which it is suitable at that date. Where, however, a building is being put to one of the non-residential uses specified in section 92B(3), this overrides any suitability for another use (section 92B(4)). For example, a building used as a children's home may also be suitable for use as a school boarding house, but this will not preclude a claim to unlimited relief.

23. Where a vacant building is suitable for at least one of the uses specified in section 92B(2) and at least one specified in section 92B(3), the tiebreaker in section 92B(5) determines, for the purposes of the relief, the use for which it is 'most suitable'. Whether or not a vacant building has one or more uses for which it is most suitable is a question of fact. Evidence supporting such uses should be provided with the claim for relief.

24. Where there is a single use for which a building is most suitable, the fact that it is also suitable for another use will be discounted.

25. If there are a number of uses for which a building is most suitable and they all come within either of the two subsections, any other use for which the building is suitable will be discounted.

26. Where no most suitable use can be shown, the default will be to classify the building as residential property and apply the £150,000 limit.

27. Land and buildings that are not suitable for any use at the date of execution will be treated as residential property if they are 'in the process of being constructed or adapted for such use' - see paragraphs 28 and 29.

Process of being constructed or adapted for use as a dwelling

28. Undeveloped land is in essence non-residential, but land may be 'residential property' for the purposes of disadvantaged areas relief if a residential building is being built on it at the date the instrument is executed. The process of construction is taken as commencing when the builders first start work. A development of six or more dwellings is deemed to be non-residential under regulation 6 of the Regulations, even if in the process of construction at the date of the instrument (see paragraph 35).

29. Where (at the date the relevant instrument is executed) an existing building is being adapted for, or restored to, domestic use, it is 'residential property' for the purposes of the relief. This may apply, for example, where a derelict building is being made fit for habitation, or where a previously non-residential building is being converted to a dwelling. Again, the process is taken as commencing when the builders start work.

The garden or grounds of a building used etc. as a dwelling

30. Section 92B(1)(b) includes within the definition of residential property 'land that is or forms part of the garden or grounds of a building within paragraph (a) (including any building or structure on such land)'. The test the Inland Revenue will apply is similar to that applied for the purposes of the

capital gains tax relief for main residences (section 222(3) of the Taxation of Chargeable Gains Act 1992). The land will include that which is needed for the reasonable enjoyment of the dwelling having regard to the size and nature of the dwelling.

31. A caravan or houseboat is not a 'building' for this purpose.

32. Commercial farmland is not within the definition of residential property. A farmhouse situated on agricultural land would be dealt with under the mixed use provisions (paragraphs 17 and 18).

33. Outhouses on land within the section 92B(1)(b) definition will also be 'residential property' unless it can be demonstrated that they have a specific non-residential purpose. Where a distinct non-residential use can be demonstrated, the mixed use provisions will apply.

Interest in or rights over residential property

34. The treatment of interests in, or rights over, land or buildings for the purposes of disadvantaged areas relief will follow that of the land or buildings to which they relate.

Six or more separate dwellings transferred by single contract

35. The Regulations provide that 'where there is a single contract for the conveyance, transfer or lease of land comprising or including six or more separate dwellings, none of that land counts as residential property…'Accordingly the transaction will qualify for unlimited relief. This recognises that commercial developers and institutional landlords, for example, frequently deal in numerous properties at one time. The fact that those properties may individually be 'residential property' does not detract from the inherently commercial nature of the transaction itself.

36. To qualify as 'separate', the dwellings must be self-contained. So for example, flats within a block, sharing some common areas but each with their own amenities, will qualify as separate dwellings. Rooms let within a house will not constitute separate dwellings if tenants share amenities such as a kitchen and bathroom.

37. A transaction in respect of six or more such dwellings must be carried out by means of a single contract in order to qualify for relief. Several instruments may however be presented for stamping if the properties are held under separate title.

38. Qualifying multiple transactions will be treated as non-residential property for the purposes of relief, even where the proportionate consideration for individual dwellings exceeds the £150,000 limit for residential property. It is not a condition of relief that multiple transactions comprise only dwellings.

39. The fact that some of the six or more dwellings within the single contract are outside a designated disadvantaged area will not prevent them from constituting a non-residential transaction. However relief will only be available for the portion of the land situated within the disadvantaged area.

Property only partly within a disadvantaged area

40. Schedule 30 to Finance Act 2001, together with the Regulations, determines how property situated partly within and partly outside a designated disadvantaged area is to be treated for the purposes of the relief. Such cases are relatively rare in practice. Queries may be referred to Inland Revenue (Stamp Taxes) for guidance.

Lease Duty

41. Relief is also available from duty on the rental element of new leases executed on or after 10 April 2003. Rental leases of residential property shall be eligible for relief where the average annual rent is no more than £15,000 and/ or where any premium does not exceed £150,000. For nonresidential property, full relief is available for the rental element of leases as well as for any premium.

Other issues

42. The extended relief applies to documents executed on or after 10 April 2003, irrespective of whether the contract was entered into before or after that date. There is no scope to reclaim stamp duty already paid in respect of transfers executed on or before 9 April 2003.

X.   INSURANCE

X.1.   Countrywide Legal Indemnities[1]

Over the past few years, and especially since the introduction of the Mortgage Lenders' Handbook, the use of legal indemnity insurance by solicitors to overcome a wide variety of property title related problems has grown significantly.

Countrywide Legal Indemnities assists solicitors with problems including:

- Restrictive Covenants
- Defective Titles
- Rights of Way
- Lack of legal easements
- Adverse Possession
- The Insolvency Act
- Defective Lease problems
- Lack of Building Regulation Consent

In 1997, discussions between Countrywide and the Law Society resulted in the establishment of a specifically endorsed service aimed at providing conveyancing solicitors with a complete solution to all their legal indemnity needs.

The Defective Title Insurance Scheme

In establishing the Defective Title Insurance Scheme, the Law Society sought to cater for the predicted rise in demand for legal indemnity insurance and provide its members with access to a fast, efficient and comprehensive source of legal indemnity policies.

The Benefits

Solicitors need to know that the precise cover they require is available and that it can be obtained at a reasonable cost in a quick and efficient manner. The Defective Title Insurance Scheme provides solicitors with the comfort that this is all possible and routinely available from Countrywide's large team of expert underwriters.

More specifically, solicitors can take advantage of the following benefits:

- A guaranteed 24-hour response to all written enquiries, with most being answered by fax in a matter of hours.
- Instant advice and premium quotations over the phone followed by faxed confirmation the same day.

---

1. This appendix has been prepared by Countrywide Legal Indemnities.

- Direct access to fully-trained legal indemnity underwriters with the expertise and experience to advise on even the largest and most complicated risks.

- Confirmation of cover over the telephone for a large number of commonly encountered risks.

- A comprehensive range of covers, some exclusive to Countrywide.

- A flexible underwriting approach. Countrywide will do everything possible to arrange the exact cover required, even for the most unusual of circumstances.

- Highly competitive premiums.

'On-Cover'

Alternatively, solicitors have the option of using 'On-Cover', Countrywide's unique legal indemnity Cover Note Pack. 'On-Cover' enables solicitors to issue their own legal indemnity Cover Notes in a wide variety of circumstances. Once in receipt of a copy of a Cover Note issued in this way, Countrywide prepare and despatch a full policy document within two working days.

A constantly improving service

In response to a steady flow of feedback from its own customers and regular research into the behaviour, attitudes and requirements of conveyancing solicitors in general, Countrywide constantly reviews its range of products and services. In addition to the launch of 'On-Cover', recent innovations have included the provision of a Lack of Building Regulation Consent indemnity. This policy alleviates the time and expense of having to discover whether or not Building Regulation Consent was granted for work on residential properties, where work was carried out more than 12 months ago. Full details are available on request. Countrywide also works closely with the Law Society, responding to the comments and suggestions of its members.

Home Environmental Liability Policy (H.E.L.P.)

Since 1 April 2000 all property owners have had a potential liability in respect of the costs of undertaking remediation works in respect of contaminated land identified by the local authority under part IIA of the Environmental Protection Act 1990.

Countrywide's Home Environmental Liability Policy (H.E.L.P.) provides cover for a range of potential costs and liabilities associated with such remediation work. Full details and a copy of the policy wording are available on request.

No risk is too large or too complicated

While the majority of policies issued by Countrywide relate to individual residential properties, an increasing amount of enquiries received relate to large housing and commercial developments. These types of risk not only involve much larger amounts of money but usually a considerably higher degree of complexity. Fortunately, Countrywide have the expertise and experience to deal quickly and efficiently with such cases, and can also offer very large limits of indemnity to cater for most circumstances.

Arranging cover couldn't be easier:

Countrywide can be contacted by telephone, fax, DX and post and are currently developing an on-line and e-mail service. For 'simple' or routinely encountered risks, solicitors can use the 'On-Cover' pack if they prefer.

For further information, advice or premium indications or to request an 'On-Cover' pack, please contact:

Countrywide Legal Indemnities
St Crispins
Duke Street
Norwich NR3 1PD
DX: 5261 Norwich
Tel: 01603 617617
Fax: 01603 622933

or visit: www.countrywidelegal.co.uk

Countrywide Legal Indemnities is a member of the General Insurance Standards Council. All Policies are underwritten by Liberty Legal Indemnities at Lloyd's.

X.2.   Foundation 15

Note

Municipal Mutual Insurance ceased writing new business, including Foundation 15, on 1 October 1992. Consequently Foundation 15 is no longer available for new properties. Existing properties with an **Initial** Certificate dated prior to 1 October 1992 continue in force and are accepted by mortgagees generally. It should be noted that **Final** Certificates for these properties may well be dated after 1 October 1992 as these properties are physically completed, and such policies are all valid.

Foundation 15 (F.15) is a New Home Structural Guarantee available from Municipal Mutual Insurance (MMI). It provides cover for a period of 15 years and is fully accepted by building societies, banks and other mortgage lenders. The guarantee is issued by builders and developers who are registered with F.15; the scheme as a whole consists of a set of Rules, Technical Standards and an Inspection Service, and the insurance policy entitled 'Scheme Details'.

The cover provided is in 3 stages:

(i)   *During Building:* the protection covers the deposit, or at the insurer's option, the cost of putting right defects when construction is not completed in accordance with the Requirements (e.g. if the developer becomes insolvent).

(ii) *First 2 Years:* the primary responsibility is on the developer to correct Damage and Defects. However, if he fails to comply with this responsibility, the buyer may claim directly on the insurer.

(iii) *Up to 15 Years:* MMI insures against Major Damage and Defects, generally relating to the structure of the new home.

The Scheme Details provide a glossary of all the terms used; the more important relate to the scope of cover and the insured. Included is damage caused by ground movement, and property covered includes common parts, separate or integral garage or other permanent building, footpath or drive, retaining or boundary wall and drainage system (including pipes, channels, gullies or inspection chambers for which the buyer is responsible). The insured is the original buyer (or successor in title), or any mortgagee in possession or lessor (other than the developer or builder).

When an F.15 registered builder commences work, the single premium is paid to MMI. The company immediately issues the policy (Scheme Details) together with an Initial Certificate which identifies the particular property covered; three Initial Certificates are produced – one each for the buyer, mortgagee and builder. All are sent to the builder to be distributed as required via a buyer's solicitor. Also produced at this time is a Buyer's Details form, to be completed on exchange of contracts. This information is used to produce the Final Certificate. The Initial Certificate is the evidence that a property is covered by the Scheme, and exchange of contracts can safely proceed in the knowledge that the protection 'during building' is in place.

When construction is completed to the satisfaction of the F.15 surveyor, a Final Certificate is issued. This date commences the 15 year guarantee period. Again, this is produced as a set of three. If contracts have been exchanged and the buyer details are known, then the buyer's name appears on the Final Certificate. If contracts are exchanged after physical completion, a revised Final Certificate can be issued, to include the buyer's details.

The Scheme is administered from the Head Office at Southwood, through a regional office network covering England, Wales and Scotland.

There is a telephone hot-line (01252 377474) dedicated to F.15 for urgent enquiries, otherwise enquiries should be addressed to the Administration Manager, Building Guarantee Department, Municipal Mutual Insurance Ltd, Southwood Crescent, Farnborough, Hants, GU14 0NJ.

X.3. National House-Building Council Scheme (NHBC)[1]

NHBC standards

The NHBC provides a scheme under which houses are designed and built to a set of standards by builders on its register. The NHBC scheme is split into two major parts:

1. the builder's obligations;

2. NHBC's undertakings – the insurance policy.

The builder's obligations are:

1. to build in accordance with NHBC requirements;

2. to remedy any defect which results from a breach of NHBC's technical requirements during the two year initial guarantee period.

NHBC's undertakings are:

1. to cover loss resulting from the builder's insolvency prior to completion of the home;

2. to make good loss resulting from the builder's failure during the first two year period to put right defects;

3. to cover loss resulting from a defined list of defects or major damage to the structure or damage to the below ground drainage system during the third to tenth years – structural guarantee period.

There are a number of different sets of documents in circulation depending on the date that the relevant home was registered for cover under the scheme. The generic name for the scheme is the Buildmark and it has been in operation since 1988.

The Buildmark Scheme

The Buildmark Scheme consists of four principal documents:

- the Offer and Acceptance Form;

- the Copy Offer Form;

- the Buildmark book;

- the Ten Year Notice, or combined Ten Year Notice and Final Certificate – or for houses registered after 1 April 1999 – the Insurance Certificate.

Under the Buildmark Scheme it is essential that the home owner receives the documents; they are not, with the exception of the lender's copy of the Ten Year Notice or Certificate, sent to the building society. When the home receives its final inspection NHBC will issue the Ten Year Notice or certificate (or Ten Year Notice and Final Certificate). This will be sent in duplicate direct to the home owner's solicitors provided the Acceptance Form has not been completed and returned to NHBC. One copy of the Ten

---

1. The material in this appendix is reproduced with the permission of the National House-Building Council.

Year Notice is sent to the purchaser for retention with the Buildmark book and Offer Form and the other copy is sent to the lender if applicable.

Cover under the Buildmark for pre-completion insolvency cover is now 10% of the contract sum or £10,000 whichever is the greater. Under the post-completion builders' liability period and the structural guarantee period cover is based upon the market value of the home as shown in the Acceptance Form or £500,000 for newly built homes or £250,000 for conversions whichever is the less. Under both schemes the builder must be a current member of the NHBC Register to be able to offer valid cover on exchange of contract. It is important to check if in any doubt before exchange of contract.

For homes registered after 1 April 1999 the start date for full cover has changed to the date of legal completion of the sale of the home, or (in Scotland) date of entry. However for homes registered on or after 1 January 2003 the start date has changed again and is now the date of legal completion (or date of entry) or the date on which NHBC issues its Insurance Certificate, whichever is the later.

The NHBC customer services department (telephone 01494 735363) will be able to say which version of Buildmark applies.

NHBC has now introduced a variation of the Buildmark Scheme for housing associations called Buildmark Choice.

Claims

Claims are dealt with in offices at Milton Keynes and York (north of England, Scotland, Northern Ireland and the Isle of Man only). The claims office will arrange a resolution meeting with the builder at the home where there are defects which are the responsibility of the builder having arisen during the first two year period. Where a claim is made during the structural guarantee period an inspection will be carried out to ascertain if the claim is valid, and, if so, what work must be done by the NHBC. Disputes about insurance claims may be referred to the Financial Ombudsman Service.

Where building control is carried out by NHBC a fourth element of insurance cover under Buildmark comes into operation. It covers the cost of work needed if there is a breach of the building regulations resulting in an imminent danger to the physical health and safety of an occupier. It is subject to a £200 index-linked excess.

From 1999 to 2002 NHBC provided cover against the costs of cleaning up contamination of the plot. The cover only operates if a remediation notice is served under the Environmental Protection Act 1990. From 2003 that cover is only available for homes where NHBC carried out building control.

Building control

A subsidiary company, NHBC Building Control Services Ltd has been appointed by the Secretary of State for Environment as an approved inspector under Part II of the Building Act 1984. Under the Act a builder may opt to have his work inspected by the building control company for the purposes of compliance with the building regulations in substitution for the Local Authority. Supervision by the building control company will not affect the completion by the Local Authority of local searches and enquiries although many authorities note that an initial notice is in force.

NHBC's Head Office is at Buildmark House, Chiltern Avenue, Amersham, Bucks HP6 5AP, DX 50712, Tel: 0870 241 4302, Fax: 01494 735201, web: www.nhbc.co.uk.

X.4. Premier Guarantee

Introduction

The Premier Guarantee consists of a comprehensive range of housing related warranties recognised by all major mortgage lenders. The Premier Guarantee range of warranties include:

- completed houses
- new homes – new builds and conversions
- social housing
- self build
- Ireland

The schemes are underwritten by Liberty Legal Indemnities (syndicate 190) one of two Lloyd's syndicates operated by Liberty Syndicates, who are a wholly owned subsidiary of Liberty Mutual.

Changes in conveyancing rules

Where a mortgage is required, it is vital that you check that the warranty policy insurance certificate is in place. As part of the changes required by the CML as of 1 April 2003, a 'cover note' from The Premier Guarantee may be provided as an alternative.

Completed house scheme

The owners on newly constructed houses do not always receive long-term security against the risks of latent defects.

The most common reasons being:

- the builder was not registered with one of the alternative providers of warranties
- the owner had been promised an architects certificate but did not receive it when the house was completed; and
- the original owner had elected not to take out a warranty.

This causes problems, should the original owner attempt to sell the house within a period of 10 years, as banks and building societies acting on behalf of potential purchasers understandably ask for an acceptable warranty to protect their interests. The Premier Guarantee have recognised this and responded by providing a warranty that can protect the interest of either the purchaser or the original owner.

The Premier Guarantee for completed housing protects all parties with a financial interest in the property and is assignable to future owners.

Cover summary

- The cost of complete or partial rebuilding or rectifying work to the housing unit, which has been affected by major damage.

- The cost of repairing, replacing or rectifying any part of the waterproof envelope, as a result of ingress of water caused by a defect in the design, workmanship, materials or the waterproofing elements of the housing unit.

- The cost of making good any defects in the new chimneys and flues, causing imminent danger to the health and safety of occupants.

Additional Extensions

- Additional costs to comply with local authorities or building regulations

- Alternative accommodation cost

- Debris removal costs

- Professional fees

Financial Limits

The financial limits for this section are index linked in accordance with Condition 5 of the Policy:

(i)   £750,000 for any one housing unit.

(ii) £350,000 for any housing unit that has been converted or refurbished.

(iii) A maximum of £1.25 million for all housing units in one continuous structure.

The standard excess is £1,000.

The Limit of Indemnity and excess are increased in line with the RICS building index or 5 per cent per annum compound, whichever is the lesser.

From the date of receipt by the Insurer of a satisfactory condition survey on the housing unit for the balance of a 10-year period from the date of completion of original construction.

The policy is assignable to all parties acquiring a future insurable interest in the housing unit.

Banks and building societies with an interest in a housing unit are automatically insured and an endorsement noting their interest will be issued if required.

Housing scheme – Speculatively built houses

The Premier Guarantee for housing is aimed specifically at house-builders and developers, providing a 10-year insurance warranty on new housing developments.

To demonstrate that the audit function carried out on behalf of the Insurer will improve the standard of new housing constructed in the country we have established a network of qualified and experienced surveyors across the UK and Ireland. The surveyors have had to provide a technical manual that can be issued to builders that contains information on all building standards and building regulations that should be met when constructing housing.

Summary of cover and financial limits

Section 3.1 – Cover during the Construction Period

- Deposit refunded to policyholder in the event the developer becomes insolvent prior to work starting.

- Deposit refunded or housing unit completed (Underwriters option) in the event the developer becomes insolvent after work has started.

- Cover for the deposit is limited to 10 per cent or £10,000 whichever is the greater.

Note: issuance of cover under this section is subject to the outcome of various financial checks.

Section 3.2 – Defects Insurance Period (Years 1–2)

Provides for the cost of repairing, replacing or rectifying any defect in the new housing unit, which is formally notified to Underwriters within six months of the expiry of the defects insurance period.

The policy will only pay a claim where the developer has refused to respond to the claim or use the conciliation service or where the developer has become insolvent. Under the conciliation service an independent expert or arbitrator will be appointed by the President of the Royal Institute of Chartered Surveyors and will be subject to fixed maximum costs.

The financial limits for this section index linked in accordance with Condition 5 of the policy

(i)   £750,000 for any one new housing unit.

(ii) £350,000 for any new housing unit that has been converted or refurbished.

(iii) A maximum of £1.25 million for all new housing units in one continuous structure.

Section 3.3 – Structural Insurance Period (Years 3–10)

- Cover the cost of complete or partial rebuilding or rectifying work to the new housing unit, which has been affected by major damage.

- The cost of making good any defect in the design materials or workmanship in the new drainage system.

- The cost of repairing, replacing or rectifying any part of the new waterproof envelope, as a result of ingress of water caused by a defect in the design, workmanship, materials or the waterproofing elements of the new housing unit.

- The cost of making good any defects in the new chimneys and flues, causing imminent danger to the health and safety of occupants.

The financial limits for this section index linked in accordance with Condition 5 of the policy:

(i)   £750,000 for any one new housing unit.

(ii) £350,000 for any new housing unit that has been converted or refurbished.

(iii) A maximum of £1.25 million for all new housing units in one continuous structure.

Note: it is possible to increase the financial limit on continuous structures for an additional premium.

Section 3.4 – Contaminated land (Years 3–10)

Covers claims notified to Underwriters during the construction period in respect of remediation expenses incurred in treating or isolating or removing any substance from the policyholders land in accordance with any statutory notice.

The financial limits for this section index linked in accordance with Condition 5 of the policy:

- £50,000 for any one new housing unit.

- £250,000 for all new housing units situated at any one new development.

Note: this section is not automatically provided for conversions and/or refurbishments.

In addition, in the event of a valid claim under Sections 3.2, 3.3 or 3.4 of the Policy, the Insurer will pay within the Limit of Indemnity:

- Additional costs
- Alternative accommodation costs
- Fees
- Removal of debris

The maximum the insurer will pay for any claim relating to common parts will be the amount the policyholder has a legal liability to contribute towards the cost of repairs, rectification or rebuilding works. Claims are subject to the financial limits for the individual sections detailed above and in respect of claims made under Section 3.3 of the policy the minimum claim value and/or excess.

For New Build there is a minimum claim value of £500 and for conversions/renovations there is an excess of £1,000.

The limit of indemnity and excess are increased in line with the RICS building index or 5 per cent per annum compound, whichever is the lesser.

Eight years from the expiry of the defects insurance period and as specified in the final certificate for each new housing unit.

In the event of a new housing unit not being sold by the developer at the date of issue of the certificate of approval the insurer agrees to issue the final certificate in the interest of the developer. The period of insurance will commence on the date specified in the final certificate.

The policy is assignable to all parties acquiring a future insurable interest in the housing unit.

Banks and building societies with an interest in a housing unit are automatically insured and an endorsement noting their interest will be issued if required.

For further information on The Premier Guarantee range of warranties, please contact The Premier Guarantee at Brook House, Brook Terrace, West Kirby, Wirral CH48 4DX Tel: 0151–625–3883 Fax: 0151–625–6167 or e-mail insurance@thepremierguarantee.co.uk.

X.5. Zurich '10' New Home Warranty: solicitor and conveyancer's guide[1]

The Zurich new home warranty policy is recognised by all major mortgage lenders. Our reputation is based on providing a high level of standard cover and an opportunity for your client, the new homeowner, to benefit from additional cover.

Where a mortgage is required, it is vital that you check that the warranty policy Insurance Certificate is in place. As part of the changes required by the CML as of April 1 2003, a Zurich Cover Note may be provided as an alternative. As a precaution we would recommend that you confirm cover with us before proceeding to completion on the basis of the Cover Note alone. Call or email us – we can advise immediately.

HAVE I RECEIVED ALL THE FOLLOWING KEY DOCUMENTATION?

The developer or their solicitor should pass all the following documentation to you.

Building Period Certificate

For exchange of contracts only. Please make sure that the developer named on the certificate is the same as the vendor and contact us if the names differ. Policy schedule details are given on the back.

'10' Warranty Policy Document

Details cover given on the new home and should be read alongside the policy schedule.

Insurance Certificate (or Cover Note if appropriate)

Essential at purchase contract completion. This is required for the draw down of mortgage funds. Completion of contracts should not occur without this or alternative authority from Zurich that cover is in place.

The Common Parts Certificate

Applicable for the purchase of apartments only. It is possible that this may not be available at the same time as the Insurance Certificate. The purchase can still be completed but warranty policy cover for areas of shared ownership will not be available until the Common Parts Certificate has been issued.

The Zurich offer

Giving your client the opportunity to extend their policy cover and take advantage of free buildings insurance cover.

---

1. This appendix has been contributed by Zurich Insurance.

Homeowner's guide

Offers valuable information regarding your client's new home, key information on what to do when problems arise, as well as details on how to make a claim should they need to.

Buyer's Details form

We need this document completed to make sure the contract exchange date is correctly entered, so that the full policy term is given to your client. In the interests of good customer care we also need the policyholder's name and correct postal address.

WHAT LEVEL OF COVER IS AVAILABLE?

Our warranty policy cannot meet every contingency but we have taken care in specifying the level of cover in the policy document and accompanying schedule. It is important that you check these documents carefully to ensure that the level of cover meets that offered by the developer under the terms of the purchase contract.

Some outline detail of standard cover is given here but this is a guide only. For full details it is important to consult the policy document.

The Zurich '10' warranty policy is an insurance against the developer's failure to honour some specific obligations to your client and afterwards insurance against latent defects in the construction of the new home. It provides cover for both newly built homes and conversions. If the date of exchange of contracts is later than the effective date of the Insurance Certificate, and providing we are informed (see 'The Buyer's Details Form'), the policy term will run from the later date (clause 4.1).

The Building Period

This provides protection against loss of deposit up to 10% of the contract purchase price where the developer has failed due to bankruptcy, insolvency or fraud (see Part One).

The Developer's Warranty Period

Begins at the effective date of the Insurance Certificate or exchange of contracts, whichever is the later. The period of cover will be specified in the schedule but will usually be 2 years for a newly built home and 1 year for a conversion. During this time the developer undertakes to put right damage or defects under the terms of cover stated in the policy (see Part Two).

Insurance Cover

Where the developer unjustifiably refuses to meet their obligations under the Developer's warranty or fails due to bankruptcy, liquidation or fraud, we will step in. From the end of the Developer's Warranty we provide cover for damage affecting the structural stability of the new home – as specifically defined in the policy – caused by a latent defect. It is essential that the policy and schedule be read together to be sure of the cover and the period which applies.

One area of insurance which only the developer can provide is Environmental Impairment cover. Not all properties may be at risk. Developers choosing to provide this cover may do so as a precautionary measure and as a benefit for their customers.

Environmental Impairment Insurance is for the life of the policy and to meet the clean up costs incurred by a homeowner in complying with a Statutory Enforcement Notice issued by the Environment Agency or other approved body.

If this cover has been provided, it will be listed on the policy schedule (see Part Five).

WHAT IS THE ZURICH OFFER?

It is possible that your client's developer may have already provided additional cover as part of the sale. If this is not the case, your client may wish to add to the level of cover themselves.

Three important advantages are available to Zurich warranty policyholders.

Homeowners have the option to extend warranty policy cover for a further five years at the end of the policy term. In the final year of the policy's life, your client should apply to Zurich for a premium quotation (clause 6.1).

The range of additional cover includes extended defects cover and buy back option. For full details consult the Zurich offer leaflet and Part Six of the '10' policy document.

Three months free buildings insurance may be available to your client. Check the policy schedule to see if they are entitled to this. In order to benefit from cover, your client must arrange and activate this by calling 0500 600509.

Special note

The information provided in this brochure is a guide only to the warranty policy. For full details, please consult the policy document, Zurich '10' new home Solicitor & Conveyancer's Guide

Free buildings insurance*

The Zurich '10' year warranty policy now comes with three months free buildings insurance for homebuyers on their new home.

This will help cover the cost of insuring their new home while they still have to insure their old home, between exchange and completion of contracts.

Our buildings insurance is accepted by all major mortgage lenders and really should take some of the stress out of moving for your client.

If you need to know more, please contact us on

6 Southwood Crescent
Farnborough
Hampshire
GU14 0NL
Tel: 01252 377474
Fax: 01252 372989
Email: building.guarantee@uk.zurich.com

*The free insurance is buildings insurance for a period of three months and homebuyers can arrange this by quoting their Zurich Building Period Certificate reference number. There is no requirement for homebuyers to purchase any other insurance policy from Zurich Insurance Company. The three months free buildings insurance normally applies to freehold properties only. Provision of cover for all financial services products bought from us and the three months free building insurance is subject to individual assessment. Full details of the cover are available on request. Terms and conditions apply. The free insurance must be activated before or at completion of contracts. Calls may be recorded or monitored for quality control or security purposes.

XI. DIRECTORY

XI.1. The Land Registry – head and district registries

Head Office (HQ)
32 Lincoln's Inn Fields
London WC2A 3PH

Tel: 020 7917 8888
Fax: 020 7955 0110
DX: 1098 Lond/Chancery Lane WC2

District Registries

Birkenhead (BR)

*For titles in **Cheshire**, **Halton**, and **Warrington**
and the London Boroughs of **Kensington and
Chelsea/Hammersmith and Fulham***
The Birkenhead (Rosebrae) District Land
   Registry
Rosebrae Court
Woodside Ferry Approach
Birkenhead
Merseyside CH41 6DU

Tel: 0151 472 6666
Fax: 0151 472 6789
DX: 24270 Birkenhead-4

*For titles in **Merseyside**, **Staffordshire** and
Stoke-on-Trent (BH)*
The Birkenhead (Old Market) District Land
   Registry
Old Market House
Hamilton Street
Birkenhead
Merseyside CH41 5FL

Tel: 0151 473 1110
Fax: 0151 473 0251
DX: 14300 Birkenhead-3

Coventry (CO)

The Coventry District Land Registry
Leigh Court
Torrington Avenue
Tile Hill
Coventry CV4 9XZ

Tel: 024 7686 0860
Fax: 024 7686 0021
DX: 18900 Coventry-3

Croydon (CR)

The Croydon District Land Registry
Sunley House
Bedford Park
Croydon CR9 3LE

Tel: 020 8781 9100
Fax: 020 8781 9110
DX: 2699 Croydon-3

Durham (DB)

*For titles in **Cumbria** and **Surrey***
The Durham (Boldon House) District Land
   Registry
Boldon House
Wheatlands Way
Pity Me
Durham DH1 5GJ

Tel: 0191 301 2345
Fax: 0191 301 2300
DX: 60860 Durham-6

*For titles in **Darlington**, **Durham**, **Hartlepool**,
Middlesbrough, **Redcar and Cleveland**,
Northumberland, **Stockton-on-Tees** and **Tyne
& Wear** (DS)*
The Durham (Southfield House) District Land
   Registry
Southfield House
Southfield Way
Durham DH1 5TR

Tel: 0191 301 3500
Fax: 0191 301 0020
DX: 60200 Durham-3

Gloucester (GL)

The Gloucester District Land Registry
Twyver House
Bruton Way
Gloucester GL1 1DQ

Tel: 01452 511111
Fax: 01452 510050
DX: 7599 Gloucester-3

Harrow **(HA)**

The Harrow District Land Registry
Lyon House
Lyon Road
Harrow
Middlesex HA1 2EU

Tel: 020 8235 1181
Fax: 020 8862 0176
DX: 4299 Harrow-4

Kingston-Upon-Hull **(HL)**

The Kingston-Upon-Hull District Land
  Registry
Earle House
Colonial Street
Hull HU2 8JN

Tel: 01482 223244
Fax: 01482 224278
DX: 26700 Hull-4

Lancashire **(LA)**

The District Land Registry of Lancashire
Wrea Brook Court
Lytham Road
Warton
Lancashire
PR4 1TE

Tel: 01772 836700
Fax: 01772 836970
DX: 721560 Lytham St Annes 6

Leicester **(LT)**

The Leicester District Land Registry
Westbridge Place
Leicester LE3 5DR

Tel: 0116 265 4000
Fax: 0116 265 4008
DX: 11900 Leicester-5

Lytham **(LY)**

The Lytham District Land Registry
Birkenhead House, East Beach
Lytham St. Annes
Lancs FY8 5AB

Tel: 01253 849849
Fax: 01253 840000
DX: 14500 Lytham St. Annes-3

Nottingham East **(NE)**

The Nottingham (East) District Land Registry
Robins Wood Road
Nottingham NG8 3RQ

Tel: 0115 906 5353
Fax: 0115 936 0036
DX: 716126 Nottingham-26

Nottingham (West) **(NW)**

The Nottingham (West) District Land Registry
Chalfont Drive
Nottingham NG8 3RN

Tel: 0115 935 1166
Fax: 0115 935 0038
DX: 10298 Nottingham-3

Peterborough **(PB)**

The Peterborough District Land Registry
Touthill Close
City Road
Peterborough PE1 1XN

Tel: 01733 288288
Fax: 01733 280022
DX: 12598 Peterborough-4

Plymouth **(PL)**

The Plymouth District Land Registry
Plumer House
Tailyour Road
Crownhill
Plymouth PL6 5HY

Tel: 01752 636000
Fax: 01752 636161
DX: 8299 Plymouth-4

Portsmouth **(PM)**

The Portsmouth District Land Registry
St Andrew's Court
St Michael's Road
Portsmouth
Hampshire PO1 2JH

Tel: 023 9276 8888
Fax: 023 9276 8768
DX: 83550 Portsmouth-2

Stevenage (SV)

The Stevenage District Land Registry
Brickdale House
Swingate
Stevenage
Herts SG1 1XG

Tel: 01438 788889
Fax: 01438 785460
DX: 6099 Stevenage-2

Swansea (SW)

The Swansea District Land Registry
Tŷ Bryn Glas
High Street
Swansea SA1 1PW

Tel: 01792 458877
Fax: 01792 473236
DX: 33700 Swansea-12

Telford (TF)

The Telford District Land Registry
Parkside Court
Hall Park Way
Telford TF3 4LR

Tel: 01952 290355
Fax: 01952 290356
DX: 28100 Telford-2

Tunbridge Wells (TW)

The Tunbridge Wells District Land Registry
Forest Court
Forest Road
Tunbridge Wells
Kent TN2 5AQ

Tel: 01892 510015
Fax: 01892 510032
DX: 3999 Tunbridge Wells-2

Weymouth (WY)

The Weymouth District Land Registry
Melcombe Court
1 Cumberland Drive
Weymouth
Dorset DT4 9TT

Tel: 01305 363636
Fax: 01305 363646
DX: 8799 Weymouth-2

York (YK)

The York District Land Registry
James House
James Street
York YO10 3YZ

Tel: 01904 450000
Fax: 01904 450086
DX: 61599 York-2

Wales/Cymru (WA)

Cofrestrfa Tir Ddosbarthol Cymru/
The District Land Registry for Wales
Tŷ Cwm Tawe
Phoenix Way
Llansamlet
Swansea SA7 9FQ

Tel: 01792 355000
Fax: 01792 355055
DX: 82800 Swansea-2

Telephone Service Centres
National number
0845 308 4545

XI.2. Local authorities of England and Wales

Adur District Council
Civic Centre
Ham Road
Shoreham-by-Sea BN43 6PR

Tel: 01273 263 000
Fax: 01273 454 847
DX: 59765 Shoreham-by-Sea

Allerdale Borough Council
Allerdale House
New Bridge Road
Workington
Cumbria CA14 3YJ

Tel: 01900 326 333
Fax: 01900 326 346
DX: 62861 Workington-1

Alnwick District Council
Allerburn House
Denwick Lane
Alnwick NE66 1YY

Tel: 01665 510 505
Fax: 01665 605 099
DX: 67809 Alnwick

Amber Valley Borough Council
PO Box 15
Town Hall
Market Place
Ripley
DE5 3XE

Tel: 01773 841 357
Fax: 01773 841 396
DX: 16888 Ripley

Anglesey County Council
Council Offices
Llangefni LL77 7TW

Tel: 01248 752 566
Fax: 01248 752 412
DX: 701771 Llangefni

Arun District Council
Civic Centre
Maltravers Road
Littlehampton BN17 5LF

Tel: 01903 737 500
Fax: 01903 716 019
DX: 57406 Littlehampton

Ashfield District Council
Council Offices
Urban Road
Kirkby-in-Ashfield
Nottingham NG17 8DA

Tel: 01623 450 000
Fax: 01623 457 585
(no DX)

Ashford Borough Council
Civic Centre
Tannery Lane
Ashford TN23 1PL

Tel: 01233 330 284
Fax: 01233 330 284
DX: 30204 Ashford (Kent)

Aylesbury Vale District Council
4 Great Western Street
Aylesbury HP20 2TW

Tel: 01296 585 039
Fax: 01296 585 585
DX: 4130 Aylesbury-1

Babergh District Council
Council Offices
Corks Lane
Hadleigh
Ipswich IP7 6SJ

Tel: 01473 822 801
Fax: 01473 825 742
DX: 85055 Babergh

Barnsley Metropolitan Borough Council
Town Hall
Church Street
Barnsley S70 2TA

Tel: 01226 773 054
Fax: 01226 773 097
DX: 12266 Barnsley-l

Barrow-in-Furness Borough Council
Town Hall
Duke Street
Barrow-in-Furness LA14 2LD

Tel: 01229 894 900
Fax: 01229 894 217
DX: 63917 Barrow-in-Furness

Basildon District Council
Basildon Centre
St Martin's Square
Basildon SS14 1DL

Tel: 01268 294 168
Fax: 01268 294 162
DX: 53008 Basildon

Basingstoke & Deane Borough Council
Civic Offices
London Road
Basingstoke RG21 4AH

Tel: 01256 844 844
Fax: 01256 841 945
DX: 3008 Basingstoke-1

Bassetlaw District Council
Queen's Buildings
Potter Street
Worksop S80 2AH

Tel: 01909 533 277
Fax: 01909 535 524
DX: 723180 Worksop-3

Bath and North East Somerset
District Council
Trimbridge House
Trim Street
Bath BA1 2DP

Tel: 01225 477 092
Fax: 01225 477 655
DX: 8047 Bath

Bedford Borough Council
Town Hall
St Paul's Square
Bedford MK40 1SJ

Tel: 01234 221 619
Fax: 01234 221 689
DX: 5600 Bedford

Berwick-upon-Tweed Borough Council
Council Offices
Wallace Green
Berwick-upon-Tweed TD15 1ED

Tel: 01289 330 044
Fax: 01289 330 540
DX: 67798 Berwick

Birmingham City Council
PO Box 28
Alpha Tower
Suffolk Street
Birmingham B1 1TU

Tel: 0121 303 3529
Fax: 0121 303 4708
DX: 715472 Birmingham-41

Blaby District Council
Council Offices
Desford Road
Narborough LE19 2EP

Tel: 0116 275 0555
Fax: 0116 272 7596
DX: 706890 Narborough

Blackburn with Darwen Borough Council
Town Hall
King William Street
Blackburn BB1 7DY

Tel: 01254 585 242
Fax: 01254 585 289
(no DX)

Blackpool Borough Council
PO Box 11
Town Hall
Blackpool FY1 1NB

Tel: 01253 477 400
Fax: 01253 477 403
(no DX)

Blaenau Gwent County Borough Council
Municipal Offices
Civic Centre
Ebbw Vale NP23 6XB

Tel: 01495 350 555
Fax: 01495 301 255
DX: 43956 Ebbw Vale

Blyth Valley Borough Council
Dinsdale House
75 Marine Terrace
Blyth NE24 2LN

Tel: 01670 542 212
Fax: 01670 542 205
(no DX)

Bolsover District Council
Sherwood Lodge
Bolsover
Chesterfield S44 6NF

Tel: 01246 240 000
Fax: 01246 242 424
(no DX)

Bolton Metropolitan Borough Council
Town Hall
Civic Centre
Bolton BL1 1RU

Tel: 01204 333 333
Fax: 01204 331 060
DX: 716633 Bolton-10

Boston Borough Council
Municipal Buildings
West Street
Boston PE21 8QR

Tel: 01205 314 200
Fax: 01205 364 604
DX: 26823 Boston

Bournemouth Borough Council
Town Hall
Bourne Avenue
Bournemouth BH2 6DY

Tel: 01202 451 451
Fax: 01202 451 005/6
DX: 7615 Bournemouth

Bracknell Forest Borough Council
Seymour House
38 Broadway
Town Square
Bracknell RG12 1AU

Tel: 01344 424 642
Fax: 01344 352 236
DX: 33611 Bracknell

Bradford Metropolitan District Council
City Hall
Bradford BD1 1HY

Tel: 01274 752 238
Fax: 01274 741 230
DX: 11758 Bradford-1

Braintree District Council
Causeway House
Bocking End
Braintree CM7 9HB

Tel: 01376 557 789
Fax: 01376 552 626
DX: 56210 Braintree

Breckland District Council
Elizabeth House
Walpole Loke
Dereham
Norfolk NR19 1EE

Tel: 01362 656 384
Fax: 01362 690 817
DX: 45058 Dereham

Brentwood Borough Council
Town Hall
Ingrave Road
Brentwood CM15 8AY

Tel: 01277 261 111
Fax: 01277 260 836
DX: 5001 Brentwood-1

Bridgend County Borough Council
Civic Offices
Angel Street
Bridgend CF31 4WB

Tel: 01656 643 124
Fax: 01656 657 899
(no DX)

Bridgnorth District Council
Westgate
Bridgnorth WV16 5AA

Tel: 01746 713 100
Fax: 01746 764 414
DX: 23207 Bridgnorth

Brighton & Hove City Council
2nd Floor
Brighton Town Hall
Bartholomew Square
Brighton BN1 1JA

Tel: 01273 292 007
Fax: 01273 291 948
DX: 2704 Brighton-1

Bristol City Council
Council House
College Green
Bristol BS1 5TR

Tel: 0117 922 3506
Fax: 0117 922 3440
DX: 7827 Bristol-1

Broadland District Council
Thorpe Lodge
1 Yarmouth Road
Thorpe St Andrew
Norwich NR7 0DU

Tel: 01603 431 133
Fax: 01603 300 087
DX: 134740 Norwich-4

Bromsgrove District Council
Council Offices
Burcot Lane
Bromsgrove B60 1AA

Tel: 01527 873 232
Fax: 01527 881 414
DX: 17279 Bromsgrove

Broxbourne Borough Council
Borough Offices
Bishop's College
Churchgate
Cheshunt EN8 9XQ

Tel: 01992 785 555
Fax: 01992 785 578
(no DX)

Broxtowe Borough Council
Council Offices
Foster Avenue
Beeston
Nottingham NG9 1AB

Tel: 0115 917 3285
Fax: 0115 917 3131
DX: 11663 Beeston

Burnley Borough Council
Town Hall
Manchester Road
Burnley BB11 1JA

Tel: 01282 425 011
Fax: 01282 452 536
DX: 23863 Burnley

Bury Borough Council
Town Hall
Knowsley Street
Bury BL9 0SW

Tel: 0161 253 5243
Fax: 0161 253 5248
(no DX)

Caerphilly County Borough Council
Council Offices
Ystrad Fawr
Ystrad Mynach CF82 7SF

Tel: 01443 863 143
Fax: 01443 863 204
DX: 145140 Caerphilly-5

Calderdale Metropolitan Borough Council
Crossley House
Crossley Street
Halifax HX1 1UG

Tel: 01422 393 053
Fax: 01422 393 090
(no DX)

Cambridge City Council
The Guildhall
Market Square
Cambridge CB2 3QJ

Tel: 01223 457 417
Fax: 01223 457 409
DX: 5854 Cambridge

Cannock Chase Council
Civic Centre
PO Box 28
Beecroft Road
Cannock WS11 1BG

Tel: 01543 462 621
Fax: 01543 462 317

Canterbury City Council
Development Services
Land Charges
Military Road
Canterbury CT1 1YW

Tel: 01227 862 181
Fax: 01227 862 020
DX: 99713 Canterbury-3

Caradon District Council
Luxstowe House
Liskeard PL14 3DZ

Tel: 01579 341 420
Fax: 01579 341 001

Cardiff County Council
County Hall
Atlantic Wharf
Cardiff CF10 4UW

Tel: 029 2087 2000
Fax: 029 2087 3519
DX: 200753 Cardiff Bay

Carlisle City Council
Civic Centre
Rickergate
Carlisle CA3 8QG

Tel: 01228 817 024
Fax: 01228 817 048
DX: 63037 Carlisle

Carmarthenshire County Council
3 Spilman Street
Carmarthen SA31 1LE

Tel: 01267 228 726
Fax: 01267 228 815
DX: 51403 Carmarthen

Carrick District Council
Carrick House
Pydar Street
Truro TR1 1EB

Tel: 01872 224 201
Fax: 01872 242 104
DX: 81232 Truro

Castle Morpeth Borough Council
Council Offices
The Kylins
Loansdean
Morpeth NE61 2EQ

Tel: 01670 535 000
Fax: 01670 535 005

Castle Point Borough Council
Council Offices
Kiln Road
Thundersley
Benfleet
Essex SS7 1TF

Tel: 01268 882 438
Fax: 01268 755 332
DX: 39603 Hadleigh

Ceredigion County Council
Town Hall
Aberystwyth SY23 2EB

Tel: 01970 633 057
Fax: 01970 633 059
DX: 92401 Aberaeron

Charnwood Borough Council
Macaulay House
5 Cattle Market
Loughborough LE11 3DH

Tel: 01509 634 993
Fax: 01509 211 703
DX: 19628 Loughborough

Chelmsford Borough Council
Civic Centre
Duke Street
Chelmsford CM1 1JE

Tel: 01245 606 859
Fax: 01245 606 559
DX: 123305 Chelmsford-7

Cheltenham Borough Council
Municipal Offices
The Promenade
Cheltenham GL50 1PP

Tel: 01242 262 626
Fax: 01242 264 236
DX: 7406 Cheltenham-1

Cherwell District Council
Bodicote House
White Post Road
Bodicote
Banbury OX15 4AA

Tel: 01295 252 535
Fax: 01295 263 143
DX: 24224 Banbury

Chester City Council
The Forum
Chester CH1 2HF

Tel: 01244 402 585
Fax: 01244 310 071
DX: 722411 Chester-17

Chester-le-Street District Council
Civic Centre
Newcastle Road
Chester-le-Street DH3 3UT

Tel: 0191 387 1919
Fax: 0191 387 1583
(no DX)

Chesterfield Borough Council
Town Hall
Rose Hill
Chesterfield S40 1LP

Tel: 01246 345 345
Fax: 01246 345 252
DX: 12356 Chesterfield-1

Chichester District Council
East Pallant House
East Pallant
Chichester PO19 1TY

Tel: 01243 534 664
Fax: 01243 534 673
DX: 30340 Chichester

Chiltern District Council
Council Offices
King George V Road
Amersham HP6 5AW

Tel: 01494 732 007
Fax: 01494 586 509
DX: 50711 Amersham

Chorley Borough Council
Town Hall
Market Street
Chorley PR7 1DP

Tel: 01257 515 151
Fax: 01257 515 150
DX: 18411 Chorley

Christchurch Borough Council
Civic Offices
Bridge Street
Christchurch BH23 1AZ

Tel: 01202 495 140
Fax: 01202 482 060
(no DX)

Colchester Borough Council
PO Box 884
Town Hall
High Street
Colchester CO1 1FR

Tel: 01206 282 248
Fax: 01206 282 287
DX: 3612 Colchester-1

Congleton Borough Council
Westfields
Middlewich Road
Sandbach CW11 1HZ

Tel: 01270 763 231
Fax: 01270 769 323
DX: 15658 Sandbach

Conwy County Borough Council
Bodlondeb
Bangor Road
Conwy LL32 8DU

Tel: 01492 574 000
Fax: 01492 592 114
DX: 24628 Conwy

Copeland Borough Council
PO Box 19
The Council Offices
Catherine Street
Whitehaven CA28 7NY

Tel: 01946 852 585
Fax: 01946 852 788
DX: CBC 62904 Whitehaven

Corby Borough Council
Grosvenor House
George Street
Corby NN17 1QB

Tel: 01536 402 551
Fax: 01536 464 109
DX: 12915 Corby

Cotswold District Council
Council Offices
Trinity Road
Cirencester GL7 1PX

Tel: 01285 623 000
Fax: 01285 623 900
DX: 144420 Cirencester-2

Coventry City Council
Records and Land Charges
Council House
Earl Street
Coventry CV1 5RR

Tel: 024 7683 3059
Fax: 024 7683 3204
DX: 18868 Coventry-2

Craven District Council
Council Offices
Granville Street
Skipton BD23 1PS

Tel: 01756 700 600
Fax: 01756 700 658
DX: 21767 Skipton

Crawley Borough Council
Town Hall
The Boulevard
Crawley RH10 1UZ

Tel: 01293 438 278
Fax: 01293 438 605
DX: 57139 Crawley-1

Crewe & Nantwich Borough Council
Municipal Buildings
Earle Street
Crewe CW1 2BJ

Tel: 01270 537 125
Fax: 01270 537 009
DX: 725221 Crewe-8

Dacorum Borough Council
Civic Centre
Marlowes
Hemel Hempstead HP1 1HH

Tel: 01442 228 000
Fax: 01442 228 264
DX: 8804 Hemel Hempstead

Darlington Borough Council
Town Hall
Darlington DL1 5QT

Tel: 01325 388 336
Fax: 01325 388 318
DX: 69280 Darlington-6

Dartford Borough Council
Civic Centre
Home Gardens
Dartford DA1 1DR

Tel: 01322 343 434
Fax: 01322 343 422
DX: 31908 Dartford

Daventry District Council
Civic Offices
Lodge Road
Daventry NN11 5AF

Tel: 01327 302 505
Fax: 01327 300 011
DX: 21965 Daventry

Denbighshire County Council
Russell House
Churton Road
Rhyl LL18 3DP

Tel: 01824 706 378/9
Fax: 01824 706 398
DX: 17367 Rhyl

Derby City Council
Council House
Corporation Street
Derby DE1 2FS

Tel: 01332 255 469
Fax: 01332 255 540
DX: 723460 Derby 20

Derbyshire Dales District Council
Town Hall
Bank Road
Matlock DE4 3NN

Tel: 01629 580 580
Fax. 01629 761 148
DX: 27259 Matlock

Derwentside District Council
Civic Centre
Medomsley Road
Consett DH8 5JA

Tel: 01207 218 210
Fax: 01207 218 200
(no DX)

Doncaster Metropolitan Borough Council
PO Box 71
Copley House
Waterdale
Doncaster DN1 3EQ

Tel: 01302 734 638
Fax: 01302 734 637
DX: 12569 Doncaster-1

Dover District Council
Council Offices
White Cliffs Business Park
Dover
Kent CT16 3PJ

Tel: 01304 872 354
Fax: 01304 872 300
DX: 6312 Dover

Dudley Metropolitan Borough Council
3 St James's Road
Dudley DY1 1HZ

Tel: 01384 815 336
Fax: 01384 814 084
DX: 12767 Dudley

Durham City Council
4 Saddler Street
Durham City
Durham DH1 3NZ

Tel: 0191 301 8861
Fax: 0191 386 0625
DX: 60239 Durham

District of Easington Council
Council Offices
Seaside Lane
Easington Village
Peterlee SR8 3TN

Tel: 0191 527 0501
Fax: 0191 527 0076
(no DX)

East Cambridgeshire District Council
The Grange
Nutholt Lane
Ely CB7 4PL

Tel: 01353 665 555
Fax: 01353 668 803
DX: 41001 Ely

East Devon District Council
Council Offices
Knowle
Sidmouth EX10 8HL

Tel: 01395 516 551
Fax: 01395 517 507
DX: 48705 Sidmouth

East Dorset District Council
Council Offices
Furzehill
Wimborne BH21 4HN

Tel: 01202 886 201
Fax: 01202 841 390
DX: 140871 Wimborne-2

East Hampshire District Council
Penns Place
Petersfield GU31 4EX

Tel: 01730 234 251
Fax: 01730 234 263
DX: 100403 Petersfield

East Hertfordshire District Council
Council Offices
1 The Causeway
Bishop's Stortford CM23 2EN

Tel: 01279 655 261
Fax: 01279 757 582
DX: 50431 Bishop's Stortford

IX

East Lindsey District Council
Tedder Hall
Manby Park
Louth LN11 8UP

Tel: 01507 329 408
Fax: 01507 600 206
(no DX)

East Northamptonshire District Council
East Northamptonshire House
Cedar Drive
Thrapston
Northants NN14 4LZ

Tel: 01832 742 141
Fax: 01832 734 839
DX: 701611 Thrapston

East Riding of Yorkshire Council
County Hall
Cross Street
Beverley HU17 9BA

Tel: 01482 887 700
Fax: 01482 393 175
DX: 28318 Beverley

East Staffordshire Borough Council
Grain Warehouse
Burton-on-Trent DE14 2JJ

Tel: 01283 508 318
Fax: 01283 508 388
DX: 700336 Burton-on-Trent-2

Eastbourne Borough Council
Town Hall
Grove Road
Eastbourne BN21 4UG

Tel: 01323 415 015
Fax: 01323 415 994
DX: 6921 Eastbourne

Eastleigh Borough Council
Civic Offices
Leigh Road
Eastleigh SO50 9YN

Tel: 023 8068 8000
Fax: 023 8062 9277
DX: 122381 Eastleigh-2

Eden District Council
Town Hall
Penrith CA11 7QF

Tel: 01768 864 671
Fax: 01768 890 470
(no DX)

Ellesmere Port & Neston Borough Council
Council Offices
4 Civic Way
Ellesmere Port
Cheshire CH65 0BE

Tel: 0151 356 6425
Fax: 0151 356 6437
(no DX)

Elmbridge Borough Council
Civic Centre
High Street
Esher KT10 9SD

Tel: 01372 474 195
Fax: 01372 474 973
DX: 36302 Esher

Epping Forest District Council
Civic Offices
323 High Street
Epping CM16 4BZ

Tel: 01992 564 000
Fax: 01992 578 018
DX: 40409 Epping

Epsom & Ewell Borough Council
Town Hall
The Parade
Epsom KT18 5BY

Tel: 01372 732 000
Fax: 01372 732 149
DX: 30713 Epsom-1

Erewash Borough Council
Town Hall
Ilkeston DE7 5RP

Tel: 0115 907 1144
Fax: 0115 907 1121
DX: 10318 Ilkeston

Exeter City Council
Civic Centre
Paris Street
Exeter EX1 1JJ

Tel: 01392 265 137
Fax: 01392 265 165
(no DX)

Fareham Borough Council
PO Box 13
Civic Offices
Civic Way
Fareham PO16 7PU

Tel: 01329 236 100
Fax: 01329 822 732
DX: 40814 Fareham

Fenland District Council
Fenland Hall
County Road
March PE15 8NQ

Tel: 01354 622 207
Fax: 01354 622 259
DX: 30955 March

Flintshire County Council
County Hall
Mold
Flintshire CH7 6NR

Tel: 01352 702 334
Fax: 01352 700 289
DX: 708590 Mold-4

Forest Heath District Council
District Offices
College Heath Road
Mildenhall
Suffolk IP28 7EY

Tel: 01638 719 319
Fax: 01638 716 493
(no DX)

Forest of Dean District Council
Council Offices
High Street
Coleford GL16 8HG

Tel: 01594 812 337
Fax: 01594 812 330
DX: 94102 Coleford

Fylde Borough Council
Town Hall
Lytham St Annes FY8 1LW

Tel: 01253 721 222
Fax: 01253 713 113
(no DX)

Gateshead Borough Council
Civic Centre
Regent Street
Gateshead NE8 1HH

Tel: 0191 433 3000
Fax: 0191 478 2755
DX: 60308 Gateshead-1

Gedling Borough Council
Civic Centre
Arnot Hill Park
Arnold
Nottingham NG5 6LU

Tel: 0115 901 3912
Fax: 0115 901 3920
(no DX)

Gloucester City Council
Council Offices
North Warehouse
The Docks
Gloucester GL1 2EP

Tel: 01452 522 232
Fax: 01452 396 140
DX: 7516 Gloucester-1

Gosport Borough Council
Town Hall
High Street
Gosport PO12 1EB

Tel: 023 9258 4242
Fax: 023 9254 5295
DX: 136567 Gosport-2

Gravesham Borough Council
Civic Centre
Windmill Street
Gravesend DA12 1AU

Tel: 01474 564 422
Fax: 01474 337 546
DX: 6804 Gravesham Borough Council

Great Yarmouth Borough Council
Town Hall
Hall Quay
Great Yarmouth NR30 2QF

Tel: 01493 856 100
Fax: 01493 846 332
DX: 41121 Great Yarmouth-1

Guildford Borough Council
Council Offices
Millmead House
Millmead
Guildford GU2 4BB

Tel: 01483 444 080
Fax: 01483 444 996
DX: 2472 Guildford-1

Gwynedd Council
Council Offices
Shirehall Street
Caernarfon LL55 1SH

Tel: 01286 672 255
Fax: 01286 673 993
DX: 713560 Caernarfon-5

Halton Borough Council
Municipal Buildings
Kingsway
Widnes WA8 7QF

Tel: 0151 424 2061
Fax: 0151 471 7527
DX: 24302 Widnes-1

Hambleton District Council
Civic Centre
Stone Cross
Northallerton DL6 2UU

Tel: 01609 779 977
Fax: 01609 767 228
DX: 61650 Northallerton-1

Harborough District Council
Council Offices
Adam & Eve Street
Market Harborough
Leicestershire LE16 7AG

Tel: 01858 821 333
Fax: 01858 821 336
DX: 27317 Market Harborough

Harlow District Council
Town Hall
Southgate
Harlow
Essex CM20 1HJ

Tel: 01279 446 611
Fax: 01279 446 767
DX: 40550 Harlow-1

Harrogate Borough Council
Council Offices
Crescent Gardens
Harrogate HG1 2SG

Tel: 01423 568 954
Fax: 01423 556 010
DX: 11962 Harrogate-1

Hart District Council
Civic Offices
Harlington Way
Fleet
Hampshire GU51 4AE

Tel: 01252 622 122
Fax: 01252 774 409
DX: 32632 Fleet

Hartlepool Borough Council
Civic Centre
Victoria Road
Hartlepool TS24 8AY

Tel: 01429 266 522
Fax: 01429 523 005
DX: 60669 Hartlepool-1

Hastings Borough Council
Town Hall
Queens Road
Hastings TN34 1QR

Tel: 01424 781 729
Fax: 01424 781 743
DX: 7055 Hastings

Havant Borough Council
Civic Offices
Civic Centre Road
Havant
Hampshire PO9 2AX

Tel: 023 9247 4174
Fax: 023 9248 0263
DX: 50005 Havant

Herefordshire Council
PO Box 237
Brockington
35 Haford Road
Hereford HR1 1ZY

Tel: 01432 260 477
Fax: 01432 383 409
DX: 135297 Hereford-3

Hertsmere Borough Council
Civic Offices
Elstree Way
Borehamwood
Herts WD6 1WA

Tel: 020 8207 2277
Fax: 020 8207 7555
DX: 45602 Borehamwood

High Peak Borough Council
Council Offices
Hayfield Road
Chapel-en-le-Frith
High Peak SK23 0QJ

Tel: 01663 751 751
Fax: 01663 751 042

Hinckley & Bosworth Borough Council
Council Offices
Argents Mead
Hinckley LE10 1BZ

Tel: 01455 238 141
Fax: 01455 635 692
DX: 716429 Hinckley

Horsham District Council
Council Offices
Park House
North Street
Horsham
West Sussex RH12 1RL

Tel: 01403 215 100
Fax: 01403 215 487
DX: 57609 Horsham-6

Huntingdon District Council
Pathfinder House
St Mary's Street
Huntingdon PE29 3TN

Tel: 01480 388 388
Fax: 01480 388 061
DX: 80929 Huntingdon-1

Hyndburn Borough Council
Council Offices
Scaitcliffe House
Ormerod Street
Accrington BB5 0PF

Tel: 01254 388 111
Fax: 01254 392 597

Ipswich Borough Council
Civic Centre
Civic Drive
Ipswich IP1 2EE

Tel: 01473 432 000
Fax: 01473 432 226
DX: 3225 Ipswich-1

Isle of Wight Council
County Hall
High Street
Newport
Isle of Wight PO30 1UD

Tel: 01983 823 220
Fax: 01983 823 224
DX: 56361 Newport IOW

Kennet District Council
Browfort
Bath Road
Devizes SN10 2PE

Tel: 01380 724 911
Fax: 01380 720 835
DX: 42909 Devizes

Kerrier District Council
Council Offices
Dolcoath Avenue
Camborne TR14 8SX

Tel: 01209 614 000
Fax: 01209 614 099

Kettering Borough Council
Municipal Offices
Bowling Green Road
Kettering NN15 7QX

Tel: 01536 534 220
Fax: 01536 410 795
DX: 12816 Kettering

King's Lynn & West Norfolk Borough
Council
King's Court
Chapel Street
King's Lynn PE30 1EX

Tel: 01553 692 722
Fax: 01553 616 728
DX: 57825 King's Lynn

Kingston upon Hull City Council
Guildhall
Alfred Gelder Street
Kingston upon Hull HU1 2AA

Tel: 01482 615 058
Fax: 01482 613 258
DX: 11934 Hull-1

Kirklees Metropolitan Council
Council Offices
49/51 Huddersfield Road
Holmfirth HD7 3ER

Tel: 01484 222 410
Fax: 01484 222 450
DX: 708620 Holmfirth

Knowsley Council
Municipal Buildings
Archway Road
Huyton
Knowsley L36 9YU

Tel: 0151 443 3558
Fax: 0151 443 3550
DX: 713891 Huyton-3

Lancaster City Council
Town Hall
Dalton Square
Lancaster LA1 1PJ

Tel: 01524 582 035
Fax: 01524 582 030
DX: 63531 Lancaster

Leeds City Council
Civic Hall
Leeds LS1 1UR

Tel: 0113 247 4015
Fax: 0113 224 3279
DX: 715295 Leeds-33

Leicester City Council
New Walk Centre
Welford Place
Leicester LE1 6ZG

Tel: 0116 252 6356
Fax: 0116 285 8993
DX: 10908 Leicester-1

Lewes District Council
Southover House
Southover Road
Lewes BN7 1DW

Tel: 01273 471 600
Fax: 01273 484 121
DX: 3118 Lewes-1

Lichfield District Council
District Council House
Frog Lane
Lichfield WS13 6YU

Tel: 01543 308 000
Fax: 01543 309 899
(no DX)

Lincoln City Council
City Hall
Beaumont Fee
Lincoln LN1 1DF

Tel: 01522 873 291
Fax: 01522 567 934
(no DX)

Liverpool City Council
Municipal Buildings
Dale Street
Liverpool L69 2DH

Tel: 0151 225 4776
Fax: 0151 225 4774
DX: 712364 Liverpool-10

Luton Borough Council
Town Hall
George Street
Luton LU1 2BQ

Tel: 01582 546 438
Fax: 01582 547 137
DX: 5926 Luton-1

Macclesfield Borough Council
PO Box 44
Town Hall
Macclesfield SK10 1DX

Tel: 01625 500 500
Fax: 01625 504 203
DX: 25010 Macclesfield-2

Maidstone Borough Council
London House
5–11 London Road
Maidstone ME16 8HR

Tel: 01622 602 251
Fax: 01622 602 372
DX: 4819 Maidstone-1

Maldon District Council
District Council Offices
Princes Road
Maldon CM9 5DL

Tel: 01621 875 734
Fax: 01621 852 575
DX: 41264 Maldon

Malvern Hills District Council
Council House
Avenue Road
Malvern
Worcs WR14 3AF

Tel: 01684 892 700
Fax: 01684 862 473
DX: 17608 Malvern

Manchester City Council
PO Box 532
Town Hall
Manchester M60 2LA

Tel: 0161 234 3143
Fax: 0161 234 4099
DX: 714441 Manchester-23

Mansfield District Council
Civic Centre
Chesterfield Road South
Mansfield NG19 7BH

Tel: 01623 463 463
Fax: 01623 463 900

Medway Council
Civic Centre
High Street
Strood
Rochester
Kent ME2 4AU

Tel: 01634 332 733
Fax: 01634 332 703
DX: 56006 Strood

Melton Borough Council
Council Offices
Nottingham Road
Melton Mowbray LE13 0UL

Tel: 01664 567 771
Fax: 01664 410 283
DX: 26764 Melton Mowbray-1

Mendip District Council
Council Offices
Cannards Grave Road
Shepton Mallet BA4 5BT

Tel: 01749 343 399
Fax: 01749 344 050
DX: 43001 Shepton Mallet

Merthyr Tydfil County Borough Council
Ty Keir Hardie
Riverside Court
Avenue de Clichy
Merthyr Tydfil CF47 8LW

Tel: 01685 725 108
Fax: 01685 725 060

Mid Bedfordshire District Council
The Limes
Dunstable Street
Ampthill
Bedford MK45 2JU

Tel: 01525 402 051
Fax: 01525 406 288
DX: 36903 Ampthill

Mid Devon District Council
7 St Peter Street
Tiverton
Devon EX16 6NU

Tel: 01884 234 309
Fax: 01884 234 318
DX: 49011 Tiverton

Mid Suffolk District Council
Council Offices
High Street
Needham Market IP6 8DL

Tel: 01449 720 711
Fax: 01449 721 946

Mid Sussex District Council
Oaklands
Oaklands Road
Haywards Heath
West Sussex RH16 1SS

Tel: 01444 458 166
Fax: 01444 477 461
DX: 300320 Haywards Heath-1

Middlesbrough Borough Council
PO Box 99A
Town Hall
Russell Street
Middlesbrough TS1 2QQ

Tel: 01642 263 551
Fax: 01642 263 656
DX: 60532 Middlesbrough

Milton Keynes Council
Civic Offices
PO Box 111
1 Saxon Gate East
Milton Keynes MK9 3HG

Tel: 01908 252 317
Fax: 01908 252 211
DX: 31406 Milton Keynes-1

Mole Valley District Council
Pippbrook
Dorking RH4 1SJ

Tel: 01306 885 001
Fax: 01306 876 821
DX: 57306 Dorking

Monmouthshire County Council
County Hall
Cwmbran NP44 2XH

Tel: 01633 644 073
Fax: 01633 644 205
DX: 131331 Cwmbran-2

Neath Port Talbot County Borough Council
Civic Centre
Port Talbot SA13 1PJ

Tel: 01639 763 333
Fax: 01639 763 370
DX: 135226 Port Talbot-2

New Forest District Council
Appletree Court
Lyndhurst SO43 7PA

Tel: 023 8028 5383
Fax: 023 8028 5223
DX: 123010 Lyndhurst-2

Newark & Sherwood District Council
Administration Dept
Kelham Hall
Newark
Notts NG23 5QX

Tel: 01636 650 000
Fax: 01636 655 229

Newcastle-under-Lyme Borough Council
Civic Offices
Merrial Street
Newcastle-under-Lyme ST5 2AG

Tel: 01782 717 717
Fax: 01782 711 032
DX: 20959 Newcastle-under-Lyme

Newcastle upon Tyne City Council
Civic Centre
Barras Bridge
Newcastle upon Tyne NE99 2BN

Tel: 0191 232 8520
Fax: 0191 211 4887
DX: 62552 Jesmond

Newport County Borough Council
Civic Centre
Newport NP20 4UR

Tel: 01633 244 491
Fax: 01633 244 721
DX: 33238 Newport-1

North Cornwall District Council
3/5 Barn Lane
Bodmin PL31 1LZ

Tel: 01208 893 333
Fax: 01208 265 683
(no DX)

North Devon District Council
Civic Centre
North Walk
Barnstaple EX31 1EA

Tel: 01271 388 406
Fax: 01271 343 968
(no DX)

North Dorset District Council
'Nordon'
Salisbury Road
Blandford Forum DT11 7LL

Tel: 01258 484 021
Fax: 01258 484 388
DX: 142920 Blandford Forum-2

North East Derbyshire District Council
Council House
Saltergate
Chesterfield S40 1LF

Tel: 01246 231 111
Fax: 01246 550 213

North East Lincolnshire Borough Council
Municipal Offices
Town Hall Square
Grimsby DN31 1HU

Tel: 01472 324 032
Fax: 01472 324 022
DX: 13536 Grimsby-1

North Hertfordshire District Council
Council Offices
Gernon Road
Letchworth SG6 3JF

Tel: 01462 474 220
Fax: 01462 474 227
DX: 31317 Letchworth

North Kesteven District Council
PO Box 3
District Council Offices
Kesteven Street
Sleaford
Lincolnshire NG34 7EF

Tel: 01529 414 155
Fax: 01529 305 808
DX: 26909 Sleaford-1

North Lincolnshire Council
Pitwood House
Ashby Road
Scunthorpe DN16 1AB

Tel: 01724 296 246
Fax: 01724 281 705
DX: 14717 Scunthorpe-1

North Norfolk District Council
PO Box 1
Council Offices
Holt Road
Cromer NR27 9PZ

Tel: 01263 513 811
Fax: 01263 515 042
DX: 31008 Cromer

North Shropshire District Council
Edinburgh House
New Street
Wem
Shrewsbury SY4 5DB

Tel: 01939 232 771
Fax: 01939 238 404
DX: 27386 Wem

North Somerset District Council
Town Hall
PO Box 147
Weston-super-Mare BS23 1LR

Tel: 01934 888 888
Fax: 01934 634 884
DX: 8411 Weston-super-Mare

North Tyneside Borough Council
14 Northumberland Square
North Shields
Tyne and Wear NE30 1PZ

Tel: 0191 200 5416
Fax: 0191 200 5858

North Warwickshire Borough Council
PO Box 5
The Council House
South Street
Atherstone CV9 1BD

Tel: 01827 719 235
Fax: 01827 719 225
DX: 23956 Atherstone

North West Leicestershire District Council
Council Offices
Coalville LE67 3FJ

Tel: 01530 454 545
Fax: 01530 454 647
DX: 23662 Coalville

North Wiltshire District Council
Monkton Park
Chippenham SN15 1ER

Tel: 01249 706 111
Fax: 01249 443 158
DX: 34208 Chippenham

Northampton Borough Council
Cliftonville House
Bedford Road
Northampton NN4 7NR

Tel: 01604 238 930
Fax: 01604 838 503
DX: 703139 Northampton-6

Norwich City Council
City Hall
St Peter's Street
Norwich NR2 1NH

Tel: 01603 622 233
Fax: 01603 213 000
DX: 5278 Norwich-1

Nottingham City Council
The Guildhall
Burton Street
Nottingham NG1 4BT

Tel: 0115 915 4571
Fax: 0115 915 4995
DX: 719182 Nottingham-34

Nuneaton & Bedworth Borough Council
Town Hall
Coton Road
Nuneaton CV11 5AA

Tel: 024 7637 6222
Fax: 024 7637 6435
DX: 16458 Nuneaton-1

Oadby & Wigston Borough Council
Council Offices
Station Road
Wigston LE18 2DR

Tel: 0116 257 2606
Fax: 0116 288 7828

Oldham Borough Council
PO Box 33
Civic Centre
West Street
Oldham OL1 1UL

Tel: 0161 911 4849
Fax: 0161 911 4820
DX: 710000 Oldham

Oswestry Borough Council
Council Offices
Castle View
Oswestry SY11 1JR

Tel: 01691 677 209
Fax: 01691 677 348
DX: 26610 Oswestry

Oxford City Council
The Town Hall
PO Box 1191
Blue Boar Street
Oxford OX1 4YS

Tel: 01865 252 213
Fax: 01865 252 694
DX: 4309 Oxford

Pembrokeshire County Council
PO Box 27
County Hall
Haverfordwest
Pembrokeshire SA61 1TP

Tel: 01437 775 788
Fax: 01437 776 493
DX: 98295 Haverfordwest

Pendle Borough Council
Town Hall
Market Street
Nelson BB9 7LG

Tel: 01282 661 661
Fax: 01282 661 630
DX: 14669 Nelson

Penwith District Council
Council Offices
St Clare
Penzance TR18 3QW

Tel: 01736 336 546
Fax: 01736 336 575
DX:144380 Penzance-3

Peterborough City Council
Town Hall
Bridge Street
Peterborough PE1 1HQ

Tel: 01733 563 141
Fax: 01733 452 537
DX: 12310 Peterborough-1

Plymouth City Council
Property Registration Section (Floor 1)
Civic Centre
Plymouth PL1 2EW

Tel: 01752 668 000
Fax: 01752 601 394
DX: 8278 Plymouth-2

Borough of Poole
Civic Centre
Poole
Dorset BH15 2RU

Tel: 01202 633 633
Fax: 01202 262 818
DX: 123820 Poole

Portsmouth City Council
Civic Offices
Guildhall Square
Portsmouth PO1 2AL

Tel: 023 9282 2251
Fax: 023 9283 4076
DX: 2244 Portsmouth-1

Powys County Council
County Hall
Llandrindod Wells
Powys LD1 5LG

Tel: 01597 826 000
Fax: 01597 826 230

Preston Borough Council
Town Hall
Lancaster Road
Preston PR1 2RL

Tel: 01772 906 119
Fax: 01772 906 323

Purbeck District Council
Westport House
Worgret Rd
Wareham BH20 4PP

Tel: 01929 556 561
Fax: 01929 557 360
(no DX)

Reading Borough Council
Civic Offices
Civic Centre
Reading RG1 7TD

Tel: 0118 939 0362
Fax: 0118 939 0320
DX: 40124 Reading (Castle St)

Redcar & Cleveland Borough Council
Town Hall
Fabian Road
South Bank
Middlesbrough TS6 9AR

Tel: 01642 444 408
Fax: 01642 444 594
DX: 60041 Normanby

Redditch Borough Council
Town Hall
Alcester Street
Redditch B98 8AH

Tel: 01527 534 008
Fax: 01527 65216
DX: 19106 Redditch

Reigate & Banstead Borough Council
Town Hall
Castlefield Road
Reigate RH2 0SH

Tel: 01737 276 065
Fax: 01737 276 070
DX: 54102 Reigate-2

Restormel Borough Council
Central Services
39 Penwinnick Road
St Austell PL25 5DR

Tel: 01726 223 300
Fax: 01726 223 301
DX: 144560 St Austell-3

Ribble Valley Borough Council
Council Offices
Church Walk
Clitheroe BB7 2RA

Tel: 01200 425 111
Fax: 01200 414 488
DX: 15157 Clitheroe

Richmondshire District Council
Springwell House
Frenchgate
Richmond DL10 4JG

Tel: 01748 829 100
Fax: 01748 822 535
DX: 65047 Richmond

Rochdale Borough Council
Telegraph House
Baillie Street
Rochdale OL16 1JH

Tel: 01706 647 474
Fax: 01706 864 185
DX: 22831 Rochdale

Rochford District Council
Council Offices
South Street
Rochford SS4 1BW

Tel: 01702 318 133
Fax: 01702 318 183
DX: 39751 Rochford

Rossendale Borough Council
Town Hall
Rawtenstall
Rossendale BB4 7LZ

Tel: 01706 217 777
Fax: 01706 244 504

Rother District Council
Town Hall
Town Hall Square
Bexhill-on-Sea TN39 3JX

Tel: 01424 787 878
Fax: 01424 787 879
DX: 8103 Bexhill-on-Sea

Rotherham Borough Council
Land Charges Department
Bailey House
Rawmarsh Road
Rotherham S60 1TD

Tel: 01709 823 890
Fax: 01709 823 865
(no DX)

Rugby Borough Council
PO Box 16
Town Hall
Evreux Way
Rugby CV21 2LA

Tel: 01788 533 560
Fax: 01788 533 567
DX: 713161 Rugby-2

Runnymede Borough Council
Civic Offices
Station Road
Addlestone
Surrey KT15 2AH

Tel: 01932 838 383
Fax: 01932 855 135
DX: 46350 Addlestone

Rushcliffe Borough Council
The Civic Centre
Pavilion Road
West Bridgford
Nottingham NG2 5FE

Tel: 0115 981 9911
Fax: 0115 945 5882
DX: 719907 West Bridgford

Rushmoor Borough Council
Council Offices
Farnborough Road
Farnborough GU14 7JU

Tel: 01252 398 398
Fax: 01252 524 017
DX: 122250 Farnborough-2

Rutland County Council
Catmose
Oakham
Rutland LE15 6HP

Tel: 01572 722 577
Fax: 01572 758 307
DX: 28340 Oakham

Ryedale District Council
Ryedale House
Old Malton Road
Malton YO17 7HH

Tel: 01653 600 666
Fax: 01653 696 801
DX: 723621 Malton-2

St Albans City and District Council
Civic Centre
St Peter's Street
St Albans AL1 3JE

Tel: 01727 866 100
Fax: 01727 845 658
DX: 6178 St Albans-1

St Edmundsbury Borough Council
Borough Offices
Angel Hill
Bury St Edmunds IP33 1XB

Tel: 01284 763 233
Fax: 01284 757 124
DX: 57223 Bury St Edmunds

St Helens Borough Council
Victoria Square
St Helens WA10 1HP

Tel: 01744 456 000
Fax: 01744 733 337
DX: 19484 St Helens-7

Salford City Council
Civic Centre
Chorley Road
Swinton M27 5DA

Tel: 0161 793 3124
Fax: 0161 794 6480
DX: 712100 Swinton-2

Salisbury District Council
Legal Property Services
Bourne Hill
Salisbury SP1 3UZ

Tel: 01722 434 232
Fax: 01722 434 539
DX: 58026 Salisbury

Sandwell Metropolitan Borough Council
PO Box 2374
The Sandwell Council House
Oldbury
Warley
West Midlands B69 3DE

Tel: 0121 569 3207
Fax: 0121 569 3241
DX: 710070 Sandwell

Scarborough Borough Council
Town Hall
St Nicholas Street
Scarborough YO11 2HG

Tel: 01723 232 323
Fax: 01723 500 636
DX: 719232 Scarborough-5

Sedgefield Borough Council
Council Offices
Spennymoor
County Durham DL16 6JQ

Tel: 01388 816 166
Fax: 01388 817 251
(no DX)

Sedgemoor District Council
Bridgwater House
King Square
Bridgwater TA6 3AR

Tel: 01278 435 435
Fax: 01278 446 412
DX: 80619 Bridgwater

Sefton Council
2nd Floor
Crown Buildings
9–11 Eastbank Street
Southport PR8 1DL

Tel: 0151 934 2018
Fax: 0151 934 2267
(no DX)

Selby District Council
Civic Centre
Portholme Road
Selby YO8 4SB

Tel: 01757 292 194
Fax: 01757 292 229
DX: 27408 Selby

Sevenoaks District Council
Council Offices
Argyle Road
Sevenoaks
Kent TN13 1HG

Tel: 01732 227 000
Fax: 01732 227 176
DX: 30006 Sevenoaks

Sheffield City Council
Town Hall
Pinstone Street
Sheffield S1 2HH

Tel: 01142 734 033
Fax: 01142 736 399
DX: 10580 Sheffield-1

Shepway District Council
Civic Centre
Castle Hill Avenue
Folkestone CT20 2QY

Tel: 01303 852 543
Fax: 01303 852 293
DX: 4912 Folkestone

Shrewsbury & Atcham Borough Council
Guildhall
Dogpole
Shrewsbury SY1 1ER

Tel: 01743 281 000
Fax: 01743 281 040
DX: 19723 Shrewsbury

Slough Borough Council
Town Hall
Bath Road
Slough SL1 3UQ

Tel: 01753 875 039
Fax: 01753 875 057
DX: 42270 Slough West

Solihull Metropolitan Borough Council
PO Box 8893
Solihull B91 3TX

Tel: 0121 704 6013
Fax: 0121 704 8260
DX: 144142 Solihull-23

South Bedfordshire District Council
District Offices
High Street North
Dunstable LU6 1LF

Tel: 01582 472 222
Fax: 01582 474 009
DX: 57012 Dunstable

South Buckinghamshire District Council
Council Offices
Windsor Road
Slough SL1 2HN

Tel: 01753 533 333
Fax: 01753 512 771
DX: 42266 Slough West

South Cambridgeshire District Council
South Cambridgeshire Hall
9–11 Hills Road
Cambridge CB2 1PB

Tel: 01223 443 063
Fax: 01223 443 149
DX: 5848 Cambridge

South Derbyshire District Council
Civic Offices
Civic Way
Swadlincote
Derbyshire DE11 0AH

Tel: 01283 221 000
Fax: 01283 595 854
DX: 23912 Swadlincote

South Gloucestershire District Council
Civic Centre
High Street
Kingswood BS15 9TR

Tel: 01454 863 064
Fax: 01454 863 005
DX: 43359 Kingswood

South Hams District Council
Follaton House
Plymouth Road
Totnes TQ9 5NE

Tel: 01803 861 127
Fax: 01803 866 151
DX: 300050 Totnes-2

South Holland District Council
PO Box 8
Priory Road
Spalding PE11 2XE

Tel: 01775 761 161
Fax: 01775 710 772
(no DX)

South Kesteven District Council
Council Offices
St Peter's Hill
Grantham NG31 6PZ

Tel: 01476 406 080
Fax: 01476 406 000
DX: 27024 Grantham

South Lakeland District Council
South Lakeland House
Lowther Street
Kendal
Cumbria LA9 4UQ

Tel: 01539 733 333
Fax: 01539 740 300
DX: 63428 Kendal-1

South Norfolk District Council
South Norfolk House
Swan Lane
Long Stratton
Norwich NR15 2XE

Tel: 01508 533 633
Fax: 01508 533 695
DX: 130080 Long Stratton-2

South Northamptonshire Council
Council Offices
Springfields
Towcester NN12 6AE

Tel: 01327 322 322
Fax: 01327 322 074
DX: 16938 Towcester

South Oxfordshire District Council
Council Offices
Benson Lane
Crowmarsh Gifford
Wallingford
Oxford OX10 8AY

Tel: 01491 823 621
Fax: 01491 823 625
DX: 144122 Wallingford-2

South Ribble Borough Council
Civic Centre
West Paddock
Leyland PR25 1DH

Tel: 01772 421 491
Fax: 01772 625 319

South Shropshire District Council
Stone House
Corve Street
Ludlow SY8 1DG

Tel: 01584 813 000
Fax: 01584 813 128
DX: 709050 Ludlow-3

South Somerset District Council
PO Box 25
Council Offices
Brympton Way
Yeovil BA20 2DS

Tel: 01935 462 191
Fax: 01935 462 666

South Staffordshire District Council
Council Offices
Wolverhampton Road
Codsall
Wolverhampton WV8 1PX

Tel: 01902 696 116
Fax: 01902 696 149
DX: 18036 Codsall

South Tyneside Metropolitan Borough
  Council
Town Hall & Civic Offices
Westoe Road
South Shields
Tyne and Wear NE33 2RL

Tel: 0191 427 1717
Fax: 0191 455 0208
DX: 60850 South Shields-4

Southampton City Council
Civic Centre
Southampton SO14 7LY

Tel: 023 8083 2247
Fax: 023 8083 4359
DX: 115710 Southampton-17

Southend-on-Sea Borough Council
Land Charges Department
PO Box 6
Civic Centre
Victoria Avenue
Southend-on-Sea SS2 6ER

Tel: 01702 215 114
Fax: 01702 534 982
DX: 2812 Southend

Spelthorne Borough Council
Council Offices
Knowle Green
Staines TW18 1XB

Tel: 01784 446 236
Fax: 01784 463 356
DX: 98044 Staines-2

Stafford Borough Council
Civic Centre
Riverside
Stafford ST16 3AQ

Tel: 01785 619 000
Fax: 01785 619 473
DX: 723320 Stafford-7

Staffordshire Moorlands District Council
Moorlands House
Stockwell Street
Leek ST13 6HQ

Tel: 01538 483 470
Fax: 01538 483 474
DX: 16361 Leek

Stevenage Borough Council
Daneshill House
Dane Street
Stevenage SG1 1HN

Tel: 01438 242 242
Fax: 01438 242 197
DX: 6022 Stevenage-1

Stockport Metropolitan Borough Council
Town Hall
Edward Street
Stockport SK1 3XE

Tel: 0161 480 4949
Fax: 0161 477 9530
DX: 22605 Stockport-2

Stockton-on-Tees Borough Council
PO Box 11
Municipal Buildings
Church Road
Stockton-on-Tees TS18 1LD

Tel: 01642 393 146
Fax: 01642 393 129
DX: 60611 Stockton

Stoke-on-Trent City Council
PO Box 631
Civic Centre
Glebe Street
Stoke-on-Trent ST4 1RN

Tel: 01782 232 775
Fax: 01782 232 171
DX: 21058 Stoke-on-Trent

Stratford-upon-Avon District Council
Elizabeth House
Church Street
Stratford-upon-Avon CV37 6HX

Tel: 01789 267 575
Fax: 01789 260 261
DX: 700737 Stratford-upon-Avon-2

Stroud District Council
Council Offices
Ebley Mill
Westward Road
Stroud GL5 4UB

Tel: 01453 766 321
Fax: 01453 754 957

Suffolk Coastal District Council
Council Offices
Melton Hill
Woodbridge IP12 1AU

Tel: 01394 383 789
Fax: 01394 444 692
DX: 41400 Woodbridge

Sunderland City Council
Civic Centre
Burdon Road
Sunderland SR2 7DN

Tel: 0191 553 1018
Fax: 0191 553 1020
DX: 60729 Sunderland

Surrey Heath Borough Council
Surrey Heath House
Knoll Road
Camberley GU15 3HD

Tel: 01276 707 305
Fax: 01276 707 337
DX: 32722 Camberley

Swale Borough Council
Swale House
East Street
Sittingbourne ME10 3HT

Tel: 01795 424 341
Fax: 01795 417 327
DX: 59900 Sittingbourne-2

Council of the City and County of Swansea
County Hall
Swansea SA1 3SM

Tel: 01792 636 150
Fax: 01792 636 763
DX: 82807 Swansea-2

Tameside Metropolitan Borough Council
Council Offices
Wellington Road
Ashton-under-Lyne OL6 6DL

Tel: 0161 342 3064
Fax: 0161 342 3111
(no DX)

Tamworth Borough Council
Marmion House
Lichfield Street
Tamworth B79 7BZ

Tel: 01827 709 709
Fax: 01827 709 259
(no DX)

Tandridge District Council
Council Offices
Station Road East
Oxted RH8 0BT

Tel: 01883 732 878
Fax: 01883 722 015
DX: 39359 Oxted

Taunton Deane Borough Council
Deane House
Belvedere Road
Taunton TA1 1HE

Tel: 01823 356 315
Fax: 01823 356 329
(no DX)

Teesdale District Council
Teesdale House
Galgate
Barnard Castle DL12 8EL

Tel: 01833 696 201
Fax: 01833 637 269
(no DX)

Teignbridge District Council
Forde House Council Offices
Brunel Road
Newton Abbot TQ12 4XX

Tel: 01626 361 101
Fax: 01626 215 169
DX: 121075 Newton Abbot-5

Telford & Wrekin Council
Civic Offices
Telford TF3 4LD

Tel: 01952 202 100
Fax: 01952 201 174
DX: 712120 Telford-5

Tendring District Council
88–90 Pier Avenue
Clacton-on-Sea CO15 1TN

Tel: 01255 254 100
Fax: 01255 254 147
DX: 34662 Clacton-on-Sea

Test Valley Borough Council
Council Offices
Duttons Road
Romsey
Hants SO51 8XG

Tel: 01794 527 700
Fax: 01794 527 724
DX: 45917 Romsey

Tewkesbury Borough Council
Council Offices
Gloucester Road
Tewkesbury GL20 5TT

Tel: 01684 295 010
Fax: 01684 272 039
DX: 11406 Tewkesbury

Thanet District Council
PO Box 9
Council Offices
Cecil Street
Margate CT9 1XZ

Tel: 01843 577 000
Fax: 01843 296 671
DX: 30555 Margate

Three Rivers District Council
Three Rivers House
Northway
Rickmansworth WD3 1RL

Tel: 01923 776 611
Fax: 01923 896 119
DX: 38271 Rickmansworth

Thurrock Council
Civic Offices
New Road
Grays RM17 6SL

Tel: 01375 652 652
Fax: 01375 652 782
DX: 141040 Grays-3

Tonbridge & Malling Borough Council
Central Services
Gibson Building
Gibson Drive
Kingshill
West Malling ME19 4LZ

Tel: 01732 876 124
Fax: 01732 873 530
DX: 92854 West Malling

Torbay Council
Town Hall
Castle Circus
Torquay TQ1 3DS

Tel: 01803 201 201
Fax: 01803 201 032
DX: 59006 Torquay-1

Torfaen County Borough Council
Civic Centre
Pontypool NP4 6YB

Tel: 01495 766 394
Fax: 01495 766 396
DX: 44257 Pontypool

Torridge District Council
Riverbank House
Bideford EX39 2QG

Tel: 01237 428 700
Fax: 01237 425 972
DX: 53606 Bideford

Trafford Borough Council
Trafford Town Hall
Talbot Road
Stretford
Trafford M32 0YU

Tel: 0161 912 1212
Fax: 0161 912 4294

Tunbridge Wells Borough Council
Town Hall
Tunbridge Wells TN1 1RS

Tel: 01892 526 121
Fax: 01892 554 027
DX: 3929 Tunbridge Wells-1

Tynedale Council
Hexham House
Hexham NE46 3NH

Tel: 01434 652 200
Fax: 01434 652 421
DX: 63216 Hexham

Uttlesford District Council
Council Offices
London Road
Saffron Walden CB11 4ER

Tel: 01799 510 418
Fax: 01799 510 392
DX: 200307 Saffron Walden

Vale of Glamorgan County Council
Civic Offices
Holton Road
Barry CF63 4RU

Tel: 01446 709 417
Fax: 01446 709 193
DX: 38553 Barry

Vale of White Horse District Council
The Abbey House
Abbey Close
Abingdon OX14 3JE

Tel: 01235 520 202
Fax: 01235 554 960
DX: 35863 Abingdon

Vale Royal Borough Council
The Drumber
Winsford
Cheshire CW7 1AH

Tel: 01606 867 619
Fax: 01606 867 665
DX: 722042 Winsford-2

Wakefield Metropolitan District Council
County Hall
Bond Street
Wakefield WF1 2QW

Tel: 01924 305 260
Fax: 01924 305 263
(no DX)

Walsall Metropolitan Borough Council
Civic Centre
Darwall Street
Walsall WS1 1DG

Tel: 01922 650 000
Fax: 01922 623 234
(no DX)

Wansbeck District Council
Wansbeck Square
Ashington NE63 9XL

Tel: 01670 814 444
Fax: 01670 817 170

Warrington Borough Council
Town Hall
Sanky Street
Warrington WA1 1UH

Tel: 01925 444 400
Fax: 01925 442 044
DX: 17760 Warrington-1

Warwick District Council
Riverside House
Milverton Hill
Leamington Spa CV32 5HZ

Tel: 01926 456 607/8
Fax: 01926 456 609
DX: 29123 Leamington Spa-1

Watford Borough Council
Town Hall
Watford WD17 3EX

Tel: 01923 226 400
Fax: 01923 278 100
DX: 4514 Watford-1

Waveney District Council
Town Hall
High Street
Lowestoft NR32 1HS

Tel: 01502 562 111
Fax: 01502 589 327
DX: 41220 Lowestoft

Waverley Borough Council
The Burys
Godalming
Surrey GU7 1HR

Tel: 01483 523 710
Fax: 01483 523 261
DX: 58303 Godalming-1

Wealden District Council
Council Offices
Pine Grove
Crowborough TN6 1DH

Tel: 01892 602 431
Fax: 01892 602 523
DX: 36860 Crowborough

Wear Valley District Council
Civic Centre
Crook
County Durham DL15 9ES

Tel: 01388 765 555
Fax: 01388 766 660

Wellingborough Borough Council
Swanspool House
Wellingborough NN8 1BP

Tel: 01933 229 777
Fax: 01933 231 540
DX: 12865 Wellingborough

Welwyn Hatfield District Council
The Council Offices
The Campus
Welwyn Garden City
Hertfordshire AL8 6AE

Tel: 01707 357 000
Fax: 01707 357 373
DX: 30075 Welwyn Garden City-1

West Berkshire District Council
Council Offices
Market Street
Newbury RG14 5LD

Tel: 01635 519 469
Fax: 01635 519 431
DX: 30825 Newbury

West Devon Borough Council
Kilworthy Park
Drake Road
Tavistock PL19 0BZ

Tel: 01822 813 600
Fax: 01822 813 634
DX: 82405 Tavistock

West Dorset District Council
Stratton House
58–60 High West Street
Dorchester DT1 1UZ

Tel: 01305 252 213
Fax: 01305 261 639
DX: 8724 Dorchester

West Lancashire District Council
Council Offices
52 Derby Street
Ormskirk L39 2DF

Tel: 01695 577 177
Fax: 01695 585 082
(no DX)

West Lindsey District Council
26 Spital Terrace
Gainsborough DN21 2HG

Tel: 01427 615 411
Fax: 01427 678 778
DX: 27214 Gainsborough

West Oxfordshire District Council
Council Offices
Woodgreen
Witney OX28 1NB

Tel: 01993 702 941
Fax: 01993 770 255

West Somerset District Council
20 Fore Street
Williton
Taunton TA4 4QA

Tel: 01984 632 291
Fax: 01984 635 325
DX: 117701 Williton

West Wiltshire District Council
Bradley Road
Trowbridge BA14 0RD

Tel: 01225 776 655
Fax: 01225 770 316
DX: 116891 Trowbridge-3

Weymouth & Portland Borough Council
Council Offices
North Quay
Weymouth DT4 8TA

Tel: 01305 838 202
Fax: 01305 760 971
(no DX)

Wigan Council
Legal Services Department
Town Hall
Library Street
Wigan WN1 1YN

Tel: 01942 244 991
Fax: 01942 827 154
DX: 702075 Wigan-2

Winchester City Council
City Offices
Colebrook Street
Winchester SO23 9LJ

Tel: 01962 848 281
Fax: 01962 843 069
DX: 120400 Winchester-5

Royal Borough of Windsor & Maidenhead
Town Hall
St Ives Road
Maidenhead SL6 1RF

Tel: 01628 798 888
Fax: 01628 776 031
DX: 6422 Maidenhead-1

Metropolitan Borough of Wirral
Town Hall
Brighton Street
Wallasey CH44 8ED

Tel: 0151 638 7070
Fax: 0151 691 8468
DX: 708630 Seacombe

Woking Borough Council
Civic Offices
Gloucester Square
Woking
Surrey GU21 6YL

Tel: 01483 743 035
Fax: 01483 750 537
DX: 2931 Woking

Wokingham District Council
PO Box 151
Shute End
Wokingham
Berkshire RG40 1WH

Tel: 0118 974 6000
Fax: 0118 978 9078
DX: 33506 Wokingham

Wolverhampton City Council
Civic Centre
St Peter's Square
Wolverhampton WV1 1RG

Tel: 01902 555 028
Fax: 01902 554 970
(no DX)

Worcester City Council
Guildhall
Worcester WR1 2EY

Tel: 01905 722 024
Fax: 01905 722 031
(no DX)

Worthing Borough Council
Town Hall
Chapel Road
Worthing BN1 1HA

Tel: 01903 239 999
Fax: 01903 221 039
DX: 142963 Worthing-10

Wrexham County Borough Council
PO Box 1284
Guildhall
Wrexham LL11 1WF

Tel: 01978 292 021
Fax: 01978 292 207
DX: 26672 Wrexham

Wychavon District Council
Civic Centre
Queen Elizabeth Drive
Pershore
Worcestershire WR10 1PT

Tel: 01386 565 000
Fax: 01386 561 092
DX: 25934 Pershore

Wycombe District Council
District Council Offices
Queen Victoria Road
High Wycombe HP11 1BB

Tel: 01494 421 225
Fax: 01494 461 292
DX: 4411 High Wycombe-1

Wyre Borough Council
Civic Centre
Breck Road
Poulton-le-Fylde FY6 7PU

Tel: 01253 891 000
Fax: 01253 899 000
(no DX)

Wyre Forest District Council
Civic Centre
Stourport-on-Severn DY13 8UJ

Tel: 01562 820 505
Fax: 01299 879 688
(no DX)

City of York Council
9 St Leonard's Place
York YO1 7ET

Tel: 01904 613 161
Fax: 01904 551 378
DX: 61585 York-1

London Boroughs
Barking & Dagenham
Town Hall
Barking IG11 7LU

Tel: 020 8227 3203
Fax: 020 8227 3698
DX: 8511 Barking

Barnet
Town Hall
The Burroughs
Hendon
London NW4 4BG

Tel: 020 8359 2489
Fax: 020 8359 2493
DX: 59318 Hendon

Bexley
Civic Offices
Broadway
Bexleyheath
Kent DA6 7LB

Tel: 020 8303 7777
Fax: 020 8319 9612
DX: 31807 Bexleyheath-1

Brent
Brent House
349 High Road
Wembley
Middlesex HA9 6BZ

Tel: 020 8937 1234
Fax: 020 8937 5348
DX: 148840 Wembley Central-3

Bromley
Civic Centre
Stockwell Close
Bromley
Kent BR1 3UH

Tel: 020 8464 3333
Fax: 020 8313 4345
DX: 5727 Bromley-1

Camden
Town Hall
Judd Street
London WC1H 9LU

Tel: 020 7974 5277
Fax: 020 7974 2546
DX: 2106 Euston

Corporation of London
PO Box 270
Guildhall
London EC2P 2EJ

Tel: 020 7332 1435
Fax: 020 7332 1806
DX: 121784 Guildhall

Croydon
Taberner House
Park Lane
Croydon
Surrey CR9 3JS

Tel: 020 8760 5639
Fax: 020 8760 5662
DX: 136018 Croydon-17

Ealing
Perceval House
14–16 Uxbridge Road
Ealing
London W5 2HL

Tel: 020 8579 2424
Fax: 020 8825 6040
DX: 5106 Ealing

Enfield
Civic Centre
Silver Street
Enfield
Middlesex EN1 3XA

Tel: 020 8379 4125
Fax: 020 8379 4172
DX: 90615 Enfield-1

Greenwich
Peggy Middleton House
1st Floor
50 Woolwich New Road
London SE18 6HQ

Tel: 020 8921 5088
Fax: 020 8921 5370
DX: 400852 Woolwich-5

Hackney
Dorothy Hodgkin House
12 Reading Lane
London E8 1HJ

Tel: 020 8356 8295
Fax: 020 8356 8298
DX: 124200 Hackney-3

Hammersmith & Fulham
Town Hall Extension
King Street
London W6 9JU

Tel: 020 8576 5392
Fax: 020 8753 1196
DX: 32759 Hammersmith-2

Haringey
Land Charges Department
Alexander House
10 Station Road
London N22 7TR

Tel: 020 8489 0000
Fax: 020 8489 3948
DX: 35651 Wood Green-l

Harrow
PO Box 2
Civic Centre
Station Road
Harrow
Middlesex HA1 2UH

Tel: 020 8863 5611
Fax: 020 8424 1557
DX: 30450 Harrow-3

Havering
Ballard Chambers
26 High Street
Romford
Essex RM1 1HR

Tel: 01708 434 343
Fax: 01708 432 482
DX: 138121 Romford-4

Hillingdon
Civic Centre
High Street
Uxbridge
Middlesex UB8 1UW

Tel: 01895 250 111
Fax: 01895 277 029
DX: 45125 Uxbridge

Hounslow
Civic Centre
Lampton Road
Hounslow
Middlesex TW3 4DN

Tel: 020 8583 2000
Fax: 020 8583 2092
DX: 3505 Hounslow

Islington
Town Hall
Upper Street
Islington
London N1 2UD

Tel: 020 7527 3297
Fax: 020 7527 3370
DX: 122230 Upper Islington

Kensington & Chelsea
Room 306
Town Hall
Hornton Street
London W8 7NX

Tel: 020 7361 3554
Fax: 020 7361 3464
DX: 84016 Kensington High Street-2

Kingston upon Thames
The Guildhall
High Street
Kingston upon Thames
Surrey KT1 1EU

Tel: 020 8547 4634
Fax: 020 8547 5127
DX: 31515 Kingston Upon Thames

Lambeth
Room 24
Town Hall
Brixton
London SW2 1RW

Tel: 020 7926 2178/9
Fax: 020 7926 2361
DX: 132672 Brixton-2

Lewisham
5th Floor
Laurence House
1 Catford Road
Catford
London SE6 4RU

Tel: 020 8695 6000
Fax: 020 8314 3127
DX: 139501 Lewisham-4

Merton
Merton Civic Centre
London Road
Morden
Surrey SM4 5DX

Tel: 020 8545 3350
Fax: 020 8545 3672
DX: 41650 Morden

Newham
Town Hall Annex
328 Barking Road
East Ham
London E6 2RP

Tel: 020 8472 1430
Fax: 020 8557 8981
DX: 4706 East Ham

Redbridge
852 Cranbrook Road
Barkingside
Ilford
Essex IG6 1HZ

Tel: 020 8478 3020
Fax: 020 8708 7022

Richmond upon Thames
Civic Centre
44 York St
Twickenham
Middlesex TW1 3BZ

Tel: 020 8891 7774
Fax: 020 8891 7702
DX: 200027 Twickenham

Southwark
Central House
Town Hall
Peckham Road
London SE5 8UB

Tel: 020 7525 7392
Fax: 020 7525 7396
DX: 136148 Peckham-2

Sutton
24 Denmark Road
Carshalton
Surrey SM5 2JG

Tel: 020 8770 5106
Fax: 020 8770 6201
DX: 134341 Sutton-11

Tower Hamlets
41–47 Bow Road
London E3 2BS

Tel: 020 7364 5000
Fax: 020 7364 5350
DX: 55653 Bow

Waltham Forest
Legal Services Department
Sycamore House
Town Hall
Forest Road
Walthamstow
London E17 4JA

Tel: 020 8925 5237
Fax: 020 8523 4967
DX: 124540 Waltham Forest

Wandsworth
Room 84
Town Hall
Wandsworth High Street
London SW18 2PU

Tel: 020 8871 6000
Fax: 020 8871 7664
DX: 59054 Wandsworth North

Westminster
Westminster City Hall
64 Victoria Street
London SW1E 6QP

Tel: 020 7641 2413
Fax: 020 7641 2761
DX: 2310 Victoria SW1

XI.3. Probate Registries – head and district registries

Principal Registry

First Avenue House
42–49 High Holborn
London WC1V 6NP

Tel: 020 7947 7000
Fax: 020 7947 6946
DX: 941 Lond/Chancery Ln

District Registries

Birmingham
The Priory Courts
33 Bull Street
Birmingham B4 6DU

Tel: 0121 681 3414
Fax: 0121 236 2465
DX: 701990 Birmingham-7

Brighton
William Street
Brighton
East Sussex BN2 2LG

Tel: 01273 684 071
Fax: 01273 625 845
DX: 98073 Brighton-3

Bristol
The Crescent Centre
Temple Back
Bristol BS1 6EP

Tel: 0117 927 3915/926 4619
Fax: 0117 925 3549
DX: 94400 Bristol-5

Ipswich
8 Arcade Street
Ipswich
Suffolk IP1 1EJ

Tel: 01473 284 260
Fax: 01473 231 951
DX: 3279 Ipswich

Leeds
3rd Floor
Coronet House
Queen Street
Leeds LS1 2BA

Tel: 0113 243 1505
Fax: 0113 247 1893
DX: 26451 Leeds Park Sq

Liverpool
The Queen Elizabeth II
Law Courts
Derby Square
Liverpool L2 1XA

Tel: 0151 236 8264
Fax: 0151 227 4634
DX: 14246 Liverpool-1

Manchester
9th Floor, Astley House
23 Quay Street
Manchester M3 4AT

Tel: 0161 834 4319
Fax: 0161 832 2690
DX: 14387 Manchester-1

Newcastle upon Tyne
2nd Floor
Plummer House
Croft Street
Newcastle upon Tyne NE1 6NP

Tel: 0191 261 8383
Fax: 0191 230 4868
DX: 61081 Newcastle 14

Oxford
St Aldates
Oxford OX1 1LY

Tel: 01865 793 050
Fax: 01865 793 090
DX: 96454 Oxford-4

XI

Winchester
4th Floor
Cromwell House
Andover Road
Winchester
Hants SO23 7EW

Tel: 01962 853 046
Fax: 01962 840 796
DX: 96900 Winchester-2

Probate Registry of Wales
PO Box 474
2 Park Street
Cardiff CF10 1TB

Tel: 029 2037 6479
Fax: 029 2037 6466
DX: 122782 Cardiff-13

Sub-Registries

Bangor
Council Offices
Ffordd Gwynedd
Bangor LL57 1DT

Tel: 01248 362 410
Fax: 01248 364 423
DX: 23186 Bangor-2

Bodmin
Market Street
Bodmin
Cornwall PL31 2JW

Tel: 01208 72279
DX: 81858 Bodmin

Carlisle
Courts of Justice
Earl Street
Carlisle CA1 1DJ

Tel: 01228 521 751
Fax: 01228 590 588
DX: 63034 Carlisle

Carmarthen
14 King Street
Carmarthen SA31 1BL

Tel: 01267 236 238
Fax: 01267 229 067
DX: 51420 Carmarthen

Chester
5th Floor
Hamilton House
Hamilton Place
Chester CH1 2DA

Tel: 01244 345 082
Fax: 01244 346 243
DX: 22162 Chester (Northgate)

Exeter
Finance House
Barnfield Road
Exeter
Devon EX1 1QR

Tel: 01392 274 515
DX: 8380 Exeter-1

Gloucester
2nd Floor
Combined Court Building
Kimbrose Way
Gloucester GL1 2DG

Tel: 01452 522 585
Fax: 01452 421 849
DX: 98663 Gloucester-5

Lancaster
Mitre House
Church Street
Lancaster LA1 1HE

Tel: 01524 36625
Fax: 01524 35561
DX: 63509 Lancaster

Leicester
90 Wellington Street
Leicester LE1 6HG

Tel: 0116 285 3380
Fax: 0116 285 3382
DX: 17403 Leicester-3

Lincoln
360 High Street
Lincoln LN5 7PS

Tel: 01522 523 648
Fax: 01522 539 903
DX: 703233 Lincoln-6

Maidstone
Law Courts
Barker Road
Maidstone
Kent ME16 8EQ

Tel: 01622 202 000
Crown Court Fax: 01622 202 001
County Court Fax: 01622 202 002
DX: 130065 Maidstone-7

Newcastle
2nd Floor
Plummer House
Croft Street
Newcastle upon Tyne
NE1 6NP

Tel: 0191 261 8383
Fax: 0191 230 4868
DX: 61081 Newcastle-14

Norwich
Norwich Combined Court Centre
The Law Courts
Bishopgate
Norwich NR3 1UR

Tel: 01603 728 200
Fax: 01603 760 863
DX: 97385 Norwich-5

Nottingham
Buttdyke House
33 Park Row
Nottingham NG1 6GR

Tel: 0115 941 4288
Fax: 0115 950 3383
DX: 10055 Nottingham

Peterborough
1st Floor, Crown Building
Rivergate
Peterborough PE1 1EJ

Tel: 01733 562 802
Fax: 01733 313 016
DX: 12327 Peterborough-1

Sheffield
PO Box 832
The Law Courts
50 West Bar
Sheffield S3 8YR

Tel: 0114 281 2596
Fax: 0114 281 2598
DX: 26054 Sheffield-2

Stoke on Trent
Combined Court Centre
Bethesda Street
Hanley
Stoke on Trent ST1 3BP

Tel: 01782 854 065
Fax: 01782 274 916
DX: 20736 Hanley-1

York
1st Floor
Castle Chambers
Clifford Street
York YO1 9RG

Tel: 01904 666 777
Fax: 01904 666 776
DX: 61543 York-21

XI.4. The Law Society of England and Wales

The Law Society of England and Wales
113 Chancery Lane
London WC2A 1PL

Tel: 020 7242 1222
Fax: 020 7831 0344
DX: 56 Lond/Chancery Ln
Web: lawsociety.org.uk

Business Centre and Shop

Sells legal books, forms and reports from the Law Society and other legal publishers. Also stocks a range of gifts and cards.

Business Centre and Shop
The Law Society
113 Chancery Lane
London WC2A 1PL

Tel: 020 7320 5640
DX: 56 Lond/Chancery Ln
Email: marilyn.redgrave@lawsociety.org.uk

Corporate Affairs

This unit have launched the Client's Charter and Customer Guides in March 2003.

Corporate Affairs
The Law Society
113 Chancery Lane
London WC2A 1PL

Tel: 020 7316 5605
DX: 56 Lond/Chancery Ln
Email: customerguides@lawsociety.org.uk
Email: law.society@alphamail.co.uk (for orders of 100+ guides)

Conveyancing & Land Law Policy

Conveyancing & Land Law Policy
113 Chancery Lane
London WC2A 1PL

DX: 56 Lond/Chancery Ln

Directories

Publishers of the Law Society's Directory of Solicitors & Barristers; the Charities and Appeals Directory; and Easter Legacy (nb. Sweet & Maxwell are publishers of the Law Society's Directory of Expert Witnesses).

Directories
The Law Society
113 Chancery Lane
London WC2A 1PL

Tel: 020 7320 5763 (advertising)
DX: 56 Lond/Chancery Ln

Law Society Publishing

Publishers of legal books and forms, including the Guide to the Professional Conduct of Solicitors (see Marston Book Services for ordering information).

Publishing
The Law Society
113 Chancery Lane
London WC2A 1PL

Tel: 020 7320 5876
Fax: 020 7404 1124
DX: 56 Lond/Chancery Ln
Web: publishing.lawsociety.org.uk

Marston Book Services

Distributors for Law Society Publishing. Books and forms may be ordered using the details below.

PO Box 312
Abingdon
Oxon OX14 4YH

Tel: 01235 465 656
Fax: 01235 465 660
Email: law.society@marston.co.uk
Web: marston.co.uk

Gazette

The Law Society's free magazine for members. Write to the editor, send press releases or call to advertise.

The Gazette
The Law Society
113 Chancery Lane
London WC2A 1PL

Tel: 020 7320 5854 (advertising)
Fax: 020 7316 5777 (advertising)
DX: 56 Lond/Chancery Ln
Web: lawgazette.co.uk

Library and Information Services

The Library Enquiries line can give information about its stock of books, journals, looseleafs and electronic products and answer general enquiries about locating legal information, whether a case has been overruled, or whether a statutory instrument is in force. The delivery service line may be used to order a particular document. The Library can also supply the Law Society's Interest Rate (past and present) – see Appendix V.19 – and publish helpful guides to finding legal information. The Library also produce a current awareness bulletin.

113 Chancery Lane
London WC2A 1PL

Tel: 0870 606 2511 (enquiries)
Tel: 020 7320 5920 (document delivery service)
DX: 56 Lond/Chancery Ln
Web: library.lawsociety.org.uk

Office for the Supervision of Solicitors

OSS
The Law Society
Victoria Court
8 Dormer Place
Leamington Spa
Warwickshire CV32 5AE

Tel: 0845 608 6565 (helpline)
Fax: 01926 431 435
E-mail: enquiries@lawsociety.org.uk
Web: oss.lawsociety.org.uk

Practice Advice

The Practice Advice Service is a support service for members and may help with: problems of legal practice and procedure, solicitors' costs, the policy and practice of the Law Society, and multi-party actions (it cannot give legal advice).

The Practice Advice Service also produces free information booklets: Payment by Results; Contentious Costs; Non-Contentious Costs; Police Station Advisers' Accreditation Scheme; Solicitors Specialist Associations and Networks; Enduring Powers of Attorney; Money Laundering; Setting up in Practice; Gifts of Property.

The Practice Advice Service
The Law Society
113 Chancery Lane
London WC2A 1PL

Tel: 0870 606 2522 (9 to 5)
Fax: 020 7316 5541
DX: 56 Lond/Chancery Ln
Email: lib-pas@lawsociety.org.uk

Professional Ethics

Among other services, Professional Ethics run an advice line for conduct issues and maintain a web site containing the entire and updated, Guide to the Professional Conduct of Solicitors. Free booklets containing updated Rules may be ordered by calling their helpline.

Professional Ethics
The Law Society
Ipsley Court
Berrington Close
Redditch
Worcs B98 0TD

Tel: 0870 606 2577 (11am–4pm)
Email: professional.ethics@lawsociety.org.uk
Web: guide-on-line.lawsociety.org.uk

Property Section

The Section aims to address the needs and concerns of both residential and commercial property solicitors. It offers a number of resources, including a quarterly issued magazine entitled 'Property in Practice' – a journal dedicated to the issues facing practitioners and which covers key issues that practitioners need to be aware of. The Section also offers an electronic email alert service. A subscription form may be downloaded from the Law Society's web site – lawsociety.org.uk

Property Section
The Law Society
113 Chancery Lane
London WC2A 1PL

Email: propertysection@lawsociety.org.uk.

Strategic Research Unit (SRU)

*SRU (previously called the Research and Policy Planning Unit) conducts, commissions and manages research. The focus of the Unit's work is determined by the Law Society's strategic priorities, the needs of the solicitors' profession, changes to the legal environment and the public interest. Reports are available to buy from the **Business Centre and Shop** or to download from the Law Society's website.*

XI.5. All other addresses

AIG Europe (UK) Ltd

The AIG Building
58 Fenchurch Street
London EC3M 4AB

Tel: 020 7954 7000
Fax: 020 7954 7001

Association of British Insurers

51 Gresham Street
London EC2V 7HQ

Tel: 020 7600 3333
Fax: 020 7696 8999

British Gas

Head Office

Centrica
Millstream
Maidenhead Road
Windsor
Berkshire FL4 5GD

Tel: 01753 494 000
Fax: 01753 494 001

British Geological Survey

Kingsley Dunham Centre
Keyworth
Nottingham NG12 5GG

Tel: 0115 936 3100
Fax: 0115 936 3593

British Property Federation

7th Floor
1 Warwick Row
London SW1E 5ER

Tel: 020 7828 0111
Fax: 020 7834 3442

BRB (Residuary) Ltd

Whittles House
14 Pentonville Road
London N1 9RP

Tel: 020 7904 5100
Fax: 020 7904 5092

British Sugar PLC

Oundle Road
Peterborough PE2 9QU

Tel: 01733 563 171
Fax: 01733 563 068

British Waterways Board (BWB)

Headquarters

Willow Grange
Church Road
Watford
Herts WD1 74QA

Tel: 01923 226 422
Fax: 01923 226 081

Regional Offices

Midlands & South West
Peels Wharf
Lichfield Street
Fazeley
Tamworth B78 3QZ

Tel: 01827 252 000
Fax: 01827 288 071

North East
Firms Wharf
Neptune Street
Leeds LS9 8PB

Tel: 0113 281 6800
Fax: 0113 281 6886

North West
Navigation Road
Northwich CW8 1BH

Tel: 01606 723 800
Fax: 01606 871 471

Certa

America House
2 America Square
London EC3N 2LU

Tel: 020 7903 6500
Fax: 020 7903 6588

**Charities Commissioners for England
and Wales**

Central Register of Charities
Harmsworth House
13–15 Bouverie Street
London EC4Y 8DP

Tel: 0870 333 0123
Fax: 020 7674 2300

Northern Office
2nd Floor
20 King's Parade
Queen's Dock
Liverpool L3 4DQ

Tel: 0870 333 0123
Fax: 0151 703 1555

**Cheshire Brine Subsidence
Compensation Board**

Cheshire Brine Board
Richard House
80 Lower Bridge Street
Chester CH1 1SW

Tel: 01244 602 576
DX: 717532 Chester-15

Church Commissioners for England

1 Millbank
Westminster
London SW1P 3JZ

Tel: 020 7898 1000
Fax: 020 7898 1001

Coal Authority

Mining Reports Dept
200 Lichfield Lane
Mansfield
Nottingham NG18 4RG

Tel: 01623 427 162
Fax: 01623 638 338
DX: 716176 Mansfield-5

Companies House

Companies House
Crown Way
Cardiff CF14 3UZ

Tel: 029 2038 8588
Fax: 029 2038 0900
DX: 33050 Cardiff-1

Cornwall Consultants Ltd

Parc Vean House
Coach Lane
Redruth
Cornwall TR15 2TT

Tel: 01209 313 511
Fax: 01209 313 512

Council for Licensed Conveyancers

16 Glebe Road
Chelmsford
Essex CM1 1QG

Tel: 01245 349 599
Fax: 01245 341 300
DX: 121925 Chelmsford-6

Council of Mortgage Lenders

3 Savile Row
London W1S 3PB

Tel: 020 7437 0655
Fax: 020 7734 6416
DX: 81550 Savile Row W1

Countrywide Legal Indemnities

St Crispins
Duke Street
Norwich NR3 1PD

Tel: 01603 617 617
Fax: 01603 617 117
DX: 5245 Norwich

Court of Protection

Public Guardianship Office
Protection Division
Archway Tower
2 Junction
London N19 5SZ

Tel: 020 7664 7000
Fax: 020 7664 7705
DX: 141150 Archway-2

Crown Estate

16 Carlton House Terrace
London SW1Y 5AH

Tel: 020 7210 4377
Fax: 020 7210 4236

Drinking Water Inspectorate

Floor 2/A2
Ashdown House
123 Victoria Street
London SW1E 6DE

Tel: 020 7944 5956
Fax: 020 7944 5969

Duchy of Cornwall

10 Buckingham Gate
London SW1E 6LA

Tel: 020 7834 7346
Fax: 020 7931 9541

Duchy of Lancaster

1 Lancaster Place
Strand
London WC2E 7ED

Tel: 020 7836 8277
Fax: 020 7836 3098

Electricity Companies

Aquila
Whittington Hall
Whittington Road
Worcester WR5 7RB

Tel: 0845 735 3637
Fax: 01905 761 464

AES Kilroot Power
Kilroot Power Station
Larne Road
Co Antrim BT38 7LX

Tel: 028 9335 1644
Fax: 028 9335 1086

BNFL Magnox Generation
Berkeley Centre
Berkeley GL13 9PB

Tel: 01453 810 451
Fax: 01453 812 529

British Energy
East Kilbride
G74 5PR

Tel: 01355 262 000
Fax: 01355 262 262

East Midlands Electricity
Herald Way
Pegasus Business Park
Castle Donington
DE74 2CU

Tel: 0800 096 3080
Fax: 02476 425 805

Edison Mission Energy
Lansdowne House
Berkeley Square
London W1J 6ER

Tel: 020 7312 4000
Fax: 020 7312 4040

Entergy
Equitable House
47 King William Street
London EC1R 4JD

Tel: 020 7337 8200
Fax: 020 7337 8201

International Power
Senator House
85 Queen Victoria Street
London EC4V 4DP

Tel: 020 7320 8600
Fax: 020 7320 8700

IVO Energy
101 Wigmore Street
London W1H 9AB

Tel: 020 7616 1500
Fax: 020 7616 1515

LE Group
Templer House
81–87 High Holborn
London WC1V 6NU

Tel: 020 7242 9050
Fax: 020 7242 2815

MANWEB Scottish Power
Wilderspool Causeway
Warrington
WA4 6QD

Tel: 0845 272 1212
Fax: 01925 422 233

Manx Electricity Authority
PO Box 177
Douglas
Isle of Man IM99 1PS

Tel: 01624 687 687
Fax: 01624 687 612

Northern Electric Plc
Carliol House
Market Street
Newcastle upon Tyne NE1 6NE

Tel: 0191 221 2000
Fax: 0191 210 2001

North Western Electricity (NORWEB)
Powergen
Wherstead Park
PO Box 40
Ipswich IP9 2AQ

Tel: 01473 688 688
(no Fax)

Powergen
PO Box 40
Wherstead Park
Ipswich IP9 2AQ

Tel: 01473 688 688
(no Fax)

Seeboard
Forest Gate
Brighton Road
Crawley RH11 9BH

Tel: 01293 565 888
Fax: 01293 657 327

South Wales Electricity (SWALEC)
Cardiff Gate Business Park
Malt House Lane
Pontprennau
Cardiff CF24 8AW

Tel: 0800 052 5252
Fax: 029 2024 9752

South Western Electricity Board
Osprey Road
Exeter EX2 7HZ

Tel: 0800 365 000
Fax: 01454 448 911

Scottish & Southern Energy PLC
200 Dunkeld Road
Perth PH1 3AQ

Tel: 01738 456 000
Fax: 01738 456 520

Yorkshire Electricity
Wetherby Road
Scarcroft
Leeds LS14 3HS

Tel: 0113 289 2123
Fax: 0113 289 5611

Energy and Environmental Programme

Royal Institute of International Affairs
Chatham House
10 St James's Square
London SW1Y 4LE

Tel: 020 7957 5700
Fax: 020 7957 5710

Energy Watch

Head Office

4th Floor
Artillery House
Artillery Row
London SW1P 1RT

Tel: 020 7799 8340
Fax: 020 7799 8341

Regional Offices

Birmingham
Civic House
156 Great Charles Street
Birmingham B3 3HN

Tel: 0845 906 0708

Bournemouth
3rd Floor
Rooddis House
6–12 Old Christ Church Road
Bournemouth BH1 1LG

Tel: 0845 906 0708

Cardiff
5th Floor (West Wing)
St David's House
Wood Street
Cardiff CF10 1ER

Tel: 0845 906 0708

London & South East
3rd Floor
Artillery House
Artillery Row
London SW1P 1RT

Tel: 0845 906 0708

North East
7th Floor
Pearl Assurance House
7 New Bridge Street
Newcastle upon Tyne NE1 8AQ

Tel: 0845 906 0708

North West
Boulton House
Chorlton Street
Manchester M1 3HY

Tel: 0845 906 0708

Scotland
Delta House
50 West Nile Street
Glasgow G1 2NP

Tel: 0845 906 0708

Environment Agency

Head Office

Rio House
Waterside Drive
Aztec West
Almondsbury
Bristol BS32 4UD

Tel: 01454 624 400
Fax: 01454 624 409
DX: 121225 Almondsbury-2

Regional Offices

Anglian Region
Kingfisher House
Goldhay Way
Orton Goldhay
Peterborough PE2 5ZR

Tel: 01733 371 811
Fax: 01733 231 840

Midlands Region
Sapphire East
550 Streetsbrook Road
Solihull B91 1QT

Tel: 0121 711 2324
Fax: 0121 711 5824

North East Region
Phoenix House
Global Avenue
Leeds LS11 8TG

Tel: 0113 213 4600
Fax: 0113 213 4609

North West Region
Richard Fairclough House
PO Box 12
Knutsford Road
Lexford
Warrington WA4 1HG

Tel: 01925 653 999
Fax: 01925 415 961

South West Region
Manley House
Kestrel Way
Exeter EX2 7LQ

Tel: 01392 444 000
Fax: 01392 444 238

Southern Region
Guildbourne House
Chatsworth Road
Worthing
West Sussex BN11 1LD

Tel: 01903 820 692
Fax: 01903 821 832

Thames Region
Kings Meadow House
Kings Meadow Road
Reading RG1 8DQ

Tel: 0118 953 5000
Fax: 0118 950 0388

Welsh Region
Rivers House/Plas-yr-Avon
St Mellons Business Park
St Mellons
Cardiff CF3 0EY

Tel: 029 2077 0088
Fax: 029 2036 2487

West Region
SEPA
5 Redwood Crescent
Peel Park
East Kilbride G74 5PP

Tel: 01355 574 200
Fax: 01355 574 688

GroundSure Ltd

Suite 14, Fourth Floor
New England House
New England Business Centre
Brighton BN1 4GH

Tel: 01273 819 500
Fax: 01273 377 902
DX: 30262 Brighton Preston Rd

Hays Document Exchange

DX House
Ridgeway
Iver SL0 9JQ

Tel: 01753 630 630
Fax: 01753 631 631
DX: 1 Iver

Imerys

John Keay House
St Austell
Cornwall PL25 4DJ

Tel: 01726 74482
Fax: 01726 623 019

**Inland Revenue Capital Taxes
Office**

Ferrers House
PO Box 38
Castle Meadow Road
Nottingham NG2 1BB

Tel: 0115 974 2400
Fax: 0115 974 2432
DX: 701201 Nottingham-4 (non-cash)
    701205 Nottingham-4 (cash)
    701202 Nottingham-4 (pre-grant)

Inland Revenue Stamp Offices

Belfast Stamp Office
Third Floor
Dorchester House
52–58 Great Victoria Street
Belfast BT2 7QE

Tel: 02890 505 312
Fax: 02890 505 130
DX: 2003 Belfast-2

Birmingham Stamp Office
5th Floor
Norfolk House
Smallbrook Queensway
Birmingham B5 4LA

Tel: 0121 633 3313
Fax: 0121 643 8381
DX: 15001 Birmingham-1

Bristol Stamp Office
First Floor
The Pithay
All Saints Street
Bristol BS1 2NY

Tel: 0117 927 2022
Fax: 0117 925 3599
DX: 7899 Bristol-1

Edinburgh Stamp Office
Grayfield House
Spur X
4 Bankhead Avenue
Edinburgh EH11 4BF

Tel: 0131 442 3161
Fax: 0131 442 3038
DX: 543303 Edinburgh-33
LP: 18 Edinburgh-2

London

Personal callers

Ground Floor
South West Wing
Bush House
Strand
London WC2B 4QN

Tel: 020 7438 7452
Fax: 020 7438 7302

Manchester Stamp Office
Upper 5th Floor
The Royal Exchange
Exchange Street
Manchester M2 7ED

Tel: 0161 834 8020
Fax: 0161 834 9503
DX: 14430 Manchester-2

Newcastle Stamp Office
4th Floor
Weardale House
Washington
Tyne & Wear NE37 1LW

Tel: 0191 261 1199
Fax: 0191 201 7392
DX: 61021 Newcastle-upon-Tyne

Worthing Stamp Office

Postal applications

Ground Floor
Room 35
East Block
Barrington Road
Worthing
West Sussex BN12 4XJ

Tel: 01903 508 962
Fax: 01903 508 953
DX: 3799 Worthing-1

Insolvency Practitioners Control Unit

Insolvency Service
1st–2nd Floor
Ladywood House
45–46 Stephenson Street
Birmingham B2 4UP

Tel: 0121 698 4000
Fax: 0121 698 4402
DX: 713895 Birmingham-37

Institute of Legal Executives

Kempston Manor
Kempston MK42 7AB

Tel: 01234 841 000
Fax: 01234 840 373
DX: 124780 Kempston-2

Intervention Board Executive Agency

Kings House
33 Kings Road
Reading RG1 3BU

Tel: 0118 958 3626
Fax: 0118 959 7736

Kaolin and Ball Clay Association Ltd

John Keay House
St Austell
Cornwall PL25 4DJ

Tel. 01726 74482
Fax. 01726 623 019

Land Charges Department (the Land Registry)

Plumer House
Tailyour Road
Crownhill
Plymouth PL6 5HY

Tel: 01752 636 666
Fax: 01752 636 699
DX: 8249 Plymouth-3

Landmark Information Group Ltd

7 Abbey Court
Eagle Way
Exeter EX2 7HY

Tel: 01392 441 700
Fax: 01392 441 709

Lands Tribunal

48/49 Chancery Lane
London WC2A 1JR

Tel: 020 7947 7200
Fax: 020 7947 7215
DX: 44452 Strand

Leasehold Valuation Tribunal

10 Alfred Place
London WC1E 7LR

Tel: 020 7446 7738
Fax: 020 7637 1250

Local Government Association

Local Government House
Smith Square
London SW1P 3HZ

Tel: 020 7664 3000

Milk Marque

Clarendon House
14 St. Andrew Street
Droitwich
Worcester
WR9 8DY

Tel: 01905 776 679
Fax: 01905 797 335

National Association of Estate Agents

Arbon House
21 Jury Street
Warwick
Warwickshire CV34 4EH

Tel: 01926 496 800
Fax: 01926 400 953
DX: 18120 Warwick

National Criminal Intelligence Service (NCIS)

Economic Crime Branch
PO Box 8000
London SE11 5EN

Tel: 020 7238 8271
Fax: 020 7238 8286

National House-Building Council (NHBC)

Head Office

Buildmark House
Chiltern Avenue
Amersham
Bucks HP6 5AP

Tel: 01494 434 477
Fax: 01494 728 521
DX: 50712 Amersham

Regional Offices

North of England
Buildmark House
George Cayley Drive
Clifton
York YO30 4GG

Tel: 01904 691 666
Fax: 01904 698 001

Scotland
42 Colinton Road
Edinburgh EH10 5BT

Tel: 0131 313 1001
Fax: 0131 313 1211

South of England
Ash House
Dencora Business Park
Breckland
Milton Keynes MK14 6ET

Tel: 0870 241 4302
Fax: 0870 241 4759

National Radiological Protection Board (NRPB)

Radon Survey
Chilton
Didcot
Oxon OX11 0RQ

Tel: 01235 831 600
Fax: 01235 833 891
NRPB Radon Freephone: 0800 614 529

Network Rail

Headquarters

40 Melton Street
London NW1 2EE

Tel: 020 7557 8020
Fax: 020 7557 9121

Regional Offices

Network Rail
Arena Point
1 Hunts Bank
Manchester M3 1RT

Tel: 0161 838 1234
Fax: 0161 838 1237

Network Rail
Buchanan House
58 Port Dundas Rd
Glasgow G4 0LQ

Tel: 0141 335 2424
Fax: 0141 335 2070
DX: 500953 Cowcaddens

Network Rail
Bristol & Exeter House
Lower Approach Road
Temple Meads
Bristol BS1 6QS

Tel: 0117 934 8170
Fax: 0117 934 8777
DX: 138083 Bristol Temple Meads-2

Network Rail Spacia

The Hop Exchange
26 Southwark Street
London SE1 1TU

Tel: 020 7645 3000
Fax: 020 7645 3023

NLIS Searchflow

Crown House
Home Gardens
Dartford DA1 1DZ

Tel: 0870 990 9945
Fax: 0870 990 9949

Ordnance Survey

Customer Service Centre
Romsey Road
Southampton SO16 4GU

Tel: 023 8030 5030
Fax: 023 8079 2615

Pollution Legal Liability

Environment Impairment Liability
 (EIL) Dept
AIG Europe (UK) Ltd
The AIG Building
58 Fenchurch Street
London EC3M 4AB

Tel: 020 7280 8998
Fax: 020 7623 3762

Premier Guarantee

Brook House
Brook Terrace
West Kirby
CH48 4DX

Tel: 0151 625 3883
Fax: 0151 625 6171
DX: 27186 Hoylake

Public Guardianship Office

Archway Tower
2 Junction Road
London N19 5SZ

Tel: 020 7664 7000
Fax: 020 7664 7705

Public Records Office

Ruskin Avenue
Kew
Richmond
Surrey TW9 4DU

Tel: 020 8876 3444
Fax: 020 8878 8905

Bourne Avenue
Hayes
Middlesex UB3 1RF

Tel: 020 8573 3831
Fax: 020 8569 2751

Rail Property Ltd

Headquarters

Whittles House
14 Pentonville Road
London N1 9RP

Tel: 020 7904 5100
Fax: 020 7904 5132

Regional Offices

North Eastern Rail Property Ltd
Hudson House
Toft Green
York YO1 6HP

Tel: 01904 524 848
Fax: 01904 524 862
DX: 65525 York-12

Registry of Friendly Societies

25 The North Colonnade
Canary Wharf
London E14 5HF

Tel: 020 7676 1000
Fax: 020 7676 1099

Rent Assessment Panels

Eastern Rent Assessment and
   Leasehold Valuation Panel
Great Eastern House
Second Floor
Tennison Road
Cambridge CB1 2TR

Tel: 01223 505 112/0845 100 2616
Fax: 01223 505 116

London
10 Alfred Place
London WC1E 7LR

Tel: 020 7446 7700
Fax: 020 7637 1250

Midlands
2nd Floor
East Wing
Ladywood House
45–46 Stephenson Street
Birmingham B2 4DH

Tel: 0121 643 8336
Fax: 0121 643 7605

Northern
20th Floor
Sunley Tower
Piccadilly Plaza
Manchester M1 4BE

Tel: 0161 237 9491
Fax: 0161 237 3656

Scotland (Glasgow)
3rd Floor
140 West Campbell Street
Glasgow G2 4TZ

Tel: 0141 572 1170
Fax: 0141 572 1171

Southern
1st Floor
1 Market Avenue
Chichester
West Sussex PO19 1JU

Tel: 01243 779 394
Fax: 01243 779 389

Wales
1st Floor West Wing
Southgate House
Wood Street
Cardiff CF10 1EW

Tel: 029 2023 1687
Fax: 029 2023 1646

Royal Courts of Justice

Strand
London WC2A 2LL

Tel: 020 7947 6000
DX: 44450 Strand

Royal Institute of British Architects

66 Portland Place
London W1B 1AD

Tel: 020 7580 5533
Fax: 020 7255 1541

**Royal Institution of Chartered
Surveyors**

12 Great George Street
Parliament Square
London SW1P 3AD

Tel: 020 7222 7000
Fax: 020 7222 9430
DX: 2348 Victoria SW1

Rural Payments Agency

Milk Quotas
PO Box 277
Exeter EX5 1WB

Tel: 01392 266466
Fax: 01392 266489

Sugar Bureau

Duncan House
Dolphin Square
London SW1V 3PW

Tel: 020 7828 9465
Fax: 020 7821 5393

Sitescope Limited

Imperial House
21–25 North Street
Bromley BR1 1SS

Tel: 0870 754 4410
Fax: 0870 606 1701

TM Property Service Ltd

Delta 200
Delta Business Park
Swindon
Wiltshire SN5 7XP

Tel: 0870 740 5007
Fax: 0870 741 0426

TransAction Online

Ground Floor
Clare House
Langley Business Centre
Station Road
Langley
Berkshire SL3 8DS

Tel: 0800 0854 951
Fax: 01753 214 599
DX: 47057 Langley

Treasury Solicitor

Dept. of HM Procurator General and
Treasury Solicitor
Queen Anne's Chambers
28 Broadway
London SW1H 9JS

Tel: 020 7210 3000
Fax: 020 7222 6006

Water Service Companies

AWG
Anglian House
Ambury Road
Huntington PE29 3NZ

Tel: 01480 323 000
Fax: 01480 323 115

Northumbrian Water
Abbey Road
Pity Me
Durham DH1 5FJ

Tel: 0191 383 2222
Fax: 0191 384 1920
DX: 717040 Durham-15

Severn Trent Water
2297 Coventry Road
Birmingham B26 3PU

Tel: 0121 722 4000
Fax: 0121 722 4800

South West Water
Peninsular House
Rydon Lane
Exeter EX2 7HR

Tel: 01392 446 688
Fax: 01392 434 966
DX: 119850 Exeter-10

Southern Water
Southern House
Yeoman Road
Worthing
West Sussex BN13 3NX

Tel: 01903 264 444
Fax: 01903 691 435
DX: 400500 Goring-by-Sea-3

Thames Water Utilities Ltd
Blake House
Manor Farm Road
Reading
Berks RG2 0JN

Tel: 0118 925 1515
Fax: 0118 923 6657
DX: 132045 Reading-11

United Utilities
Dawson House
Liverpool Road
Great Sankey
Warrington WA5 3LW

Tel: 01925 234 000
Fax: 01925 236 932

Welsh Water
Pentwyn Road
Nelson
Treharris
Mid Glamorgan CF46 6LY

Tel: 01443 452 300
Fax: 01443 452 323

Wessex Water PLC
Operation Centre
Claverton Down Road
Claverton Down
Bath BA2 7WW

Tel: 01225 526 000
Fax: 01225 528 000

Yorkshire Water
PO Box 52
Bradford BD3 7YD

Tel: 0845 124 2424
Fax: 01274 372 800

Water Supply Companies

Bournemouth & West Hampshire Water plc
George Jessel House
Francis Avenue
Bournemouth BH11 8NB

Tel: 01202 590 059
Fax: 01202 597 022

Bristol Water plc
PO Box 218
Bridgwater Road
Bristol BS99 7AU

Tel: 0117 966 5881
Fax: 0117 963 4576

Cambridge Water Company
41 Rustat Road
Cambridge CB1 3QS

Tel: 01223 247 351
Fax: 01223 214 052

Cholderton & District Water Company
Estate Office
Cholderton
Salisbury
Wiltshire SP4 0DR

Tel: 01980 629 203
Fax: 01980 629 307

Dee Valley Water
Packsaddle
Wrexham Road
Rhostyllen
Wrexham
Clwyd LL14 4EH

Tel: 01978 846 946
Fax: 01978 846 888

Essex & Suffolk Water Company
Hall Street
Chelmsford
Essex CM2 0HH

Tel: 01245 491 234
Fax: 01245 212 345

Folkestone & Dover Water Services Ltd
The Cherry Garden
Cherry Garden Lane
Folkestone
Kent CT19 4QB

Tel: 01303 298 800
Fax: 01303 276 712

Hartlepool Water plc
3 Lancaster Road
Hartlepool TS24 8LW

Tel: 01429 868 555
Fax: 01429 858 000

Mid Kent Water plc
Rockfort Road
Snodland
Kent ME6 5AH

Tel: 01634 240 313
Fax: 01634 242 764

Portsmouth Water Ltd
PO Box 8
West Street
Havant
Hants PO9 1LG

Tel: 023 9249 9888
Fax: 023 9245 3632

South East Water plc
1–3 Church Road
Haywards Heath
West Sussex RH16 3NY

Tel: 01444 448 200
Fax: 01444 413 200

South Staffordshire Group plc
Green Lane
Walsall
W Midlands WS2 7PD

Tel: 01922 638 282
Fax: 01922 631 779

Sutton & East Surrey Water plc
London Road
Redhill
Surrey RH1 1LJ

Tel: 01737 772 000
Fax: 01737 766 807

Tendring Hundred Water
Services Ltd
Mill Hill
Manningtree
Essex CO11 2AZ

Tel: 01206 399 200
Fax: 01206 399 210

Three Valleys Water plc
PO Box 48
Bishops Rise
Hatfield
Herts AL10 9HL

Tel: 01707 268 111
Fax: 01707 277 333

Yorkshire Water Services Ltd
Western House
Western Way
Halifax Road
Bradford BD6 2SZ

Tel: 01274 691 111
Fax: 01274 604 764

Zurich Insurance

Building Guarantee Dept
6 Southwood Crescent
Farnborough
Hants GU14 0NJ

Tel: 01252 522 000
Fax: 01252 372 989

XI.6.   Guide to conveyancing information online

The links in this Appendix are grouped into the following areas: featured sites; Government sites; A–Z of conveyancing-related sites; and Publishers. The links are not intended to be comprehensive or to confer any endorsement by the Law Society. Some links will inevitably become broken during the lifetime of this book so conveyancers are also directed to the portal sites: **venables.co.uk**, **infolaw.co.uk**, **lawinblackandwhite.com**, and **links4lawyers.co.uk**.

FEATURED SITES

British Property Federation   **bpf.org.uk**

The publications section contains pdf files of the following documents: BPF Short Term Commercial Lease; BPF & BCO Model Clauses for an FRI Office Lease of Whole; Code of Practice for Commercial Leases; Code of Practice for Commercial Leases: Compliance Checklist; Commercial Property Standard Enquiries; Service Charges in Commercial Property; Code of Practice.

Code for Commercial Leases   **commercialleasecodeew.co.uk**

This new Code is a voluntary document that has been prepared by a cross industry working group representing all sides of the property industry. The Code makes ten detailed recommendations when negotiating a lease and another thirteen on conduct over the duration of the lease.

Council of Mortgage Lenders   **cml.org.uk**

Part 1 of the CML Lenders' Handbook England & Wales 2nd edition is reproduced in Appendix VIII.3 of this Handbook. Part 2 is only available on the CML web site. The CML site also includes the Lender's Handbook for Scotland and for the Isle of Man

Epolitix   **epolitix.com**

A free site dedicated to improving communication between the electorate and their representatives. Of most use to conveyancers for its 'Legislation Watch' service.

Inland Revenue   **inlandrevenue.gov.uk**

- Disadvantaged Areas Relief   inlandrevenue.gov.uk/so/pcode_search.htm
- Modernising consultation 2002   inlandrevenue.gov.uk/so/modern.htm
- Stamp Taxes Manual   inlandrevenue.gov.uk/so/manual.htm
- Stamp Taxes Office   inlandrevenue.gov.uk/so/
- Stamp Taxes Office leaflets   inlandrevenue.gov.uk/leaflets/stof.htm
- Budget and Finance Bill   inlandrevenue.gov.uk/so/budget2003.htm
- Group relief clawback   inlandrevenue.gov.uk/budget2003/pn05.htm
- Disadvantaged Areas SP1/2003   inlandrevenue.gov.uk/pdfs/sp1_2003.htm

The Inland Revenue web site will contain all the necessary information to explain the transitional and final details of the new stamp duty land tax and the disadvantaged areas relief. Statements of Practice, leaflets, press releases, forms, and links to the legislation can all be found on the site.

Office of Deputy Prime Minister **odpm.gov.uk**

- Business lease reform   urban.odpm.gov.uk/property
- Commonhold & Leasehold Reform Act   housing.odpm.gov.uk/information/
                                               leasehold reform/
- Compulsory Purchase Orders circular   planning.odpm.gov.uk/circulars/02_03/
- Housing Bill (consultation)   housing.odpm.gov.uk/information/consult/
                                               housingbill/
- Planning and Compulsory Purchase   planning.odpm.gov.uk/consult/greenpap/
                                               greenind.htm
- Right to buy   housing.odpm.gov.uk/information/index01.htm
- Home Information Pack   housing.odpm.gov.uk/hbs/infopack/

The ODPM site will be of particular use to solicitors wishing to follow progress of Home Information Packs.

Land Registry **landreg.gov.uk**

- Commonhold   landreg.gov.uk/legislation/content/
                                           commonhold/
- E-Conveyancing   landreg.gov.uk/e-conveyancing/
- Land Registry Direct   landregistrydirect.gov.uk
- Land Registration Act 2002   landreg.gov.uk/lract2002/
- Land Registration Rules 2003   landreg.gov.uk/lract2002/content/rules/
- Legislation   landreg.gov.uk/legislation
- Publications (forms and leaflets, etc.) landreg.gov.uk/publications/
- Land Register Online   landregisteronline.gov.uk

The Land Registry has set up several sites of interest to solicitors, including Landregistrydirect; Legislation and Landregister Online. The new 'pilot' site, Land Register Online, allows members of the public to download copies of the register and perform a search of the Index Map.

Law Society of England & Wales **lawsociety.org.uk**

- Directory of Solicitors & Barristers   solicitors-online.com
- Gazette   lawgazette.co.uk
- Guide Online   guide-on-line.lawsociety.org.uk

Relevant guidance can be found in the 'conveyancing residential' section and in the guide-on-line site, where you may select 'Browse the Guide' and 'Chapter 32 Information Packs and Updated Rules' to view updated materials from the Guide to the Professional Conduct of Solicitors 1999. Also of relevance to conveyancers are: consultations; list of indemnity insurers; membership of the new Property Section; Law Society Publishing; and Practice Advice Service publications; and the Law Society's VAT Guide, available in pdf.

National Land Information Service (NLIS)   nlis.org.uk

- NLIS Searchflow (channel)   searchflow.co.uk
- TM Property Search (channel)   tmproperty.co.uk
- TransAction online (channel)   transaction-online.co.uk

A government initiative to provide electronic access to land and property information currently held by such diverse organisations as the Land Registry, the Coal Authority, local authorities and the Environment Agency.

Royal Institute of Chartered Surveyors   **rics.org.uk/**

- Commercial Property Newsletter   rics.org/com/
- Common Auction Conditions   rics.org/property_auctions/
- Property Solutions Guide   rics.org/about_us/property_solutions/
- Residential Property Newsletter   rics.org/res/
- RICS Books   ricsbooks.com/

The RICS books site holds information on The Red Book – RICS Appraisal and Valuation Standards.

GOVERNMENT SITES

Cabinet Office   **cabinet-office.gov.uk**

The site includes pages on the Regulatory Reform Act 2001, which the government is planning to use in order to reform the Landlord and Tenant Act 1954. Progress of the reform to this Act can be viewed at **cabinet-office.gov.uk/regulation/act/proposals.htm**.

Charities Commissioners (E&W)   **charity-commission.gov.uk**

Council for Licensed Conveyancers   **theclc.gov.uk**

This site includes: a directory of licensed conveyancers; the CLC guide to professional conduct; practice notes; and the CLC Chronicle.

Court of Protection   **publictrust.gov.uk/court.html**

Crown Estate   **crownestate.co.uk**

Customs and Excise   **hmce.gov.uk**

This site includes: VAT forms and leaflets and Budget notices.

Department for Transport   **dft.gov.uk**

DEFRA   **defra.gov.uk**

Drinking Water Inspectorate   **dwi.gov.uk**

Insolvency Service   **insolvency.gov.uk**

Environment Agency   **environment-agency.gov.uk**

Financial Services Authority   **fsa.gov.uk**

Highways Agency   **highways.gov.uk**

Housing Corporation   **housingcorp.gov.uk**

Law Commission   **lawcom.gov.uk**

Local Government Association   **lga.gov.uk**

Lord Chancellor's Department	**lcd.gov.uk**
● Commonhold	lcd.gov.uk/civil/commonhold.htm
● Land Registration	lcd.gov.uk/civil/landreg.htm

> This site includes: guidance on unfair terms in tenancy agreements; response to the LCD's 'In the Public Interest?' consultation; distance selling regulations information; unfair terms in consumer agreements information. Now the Department of Constitutional Affairs.

National Statistics	**statistics.gov.uk**
Office of Fair Trading	**oft.gov.uk**
Ordnance Survey	**ordsvy.gov.uk**
Public Records Office	**pro.gov.uk**
Rent Service	**therentservice.gov.uk**
Treasury	**hm-treasury.gov.uk**

> Includes: Money Laundering regulations (drafts and consultations).

A–Z OF CONVEYANCING-RELATED WEB SITES

AIG Europe (UK) Ltd	**aigeurope.co.uk**
Association of British Insurers	**abi.gov.uk**
Association of Geographical Information	**agi.org.uk**
A.W. & C. Barsby	**barsby.com**

> Company owned by barristers publishing in property law where the books are kept updated online.

British Gas	**house.co.uk**
British Geological Society	**bgs.ac.uk**
British Sugar PLC	**britishsugar.co.uk**
British Waterways Board (BWB)	**britishwaterways.co.uk**
Certa	**certa.com**
Chartered Institute of Building	**ciob.org.uk**

> Includes: Dispute Resolution Services (DRS) and the Construction Best Practice Programme.

Chartered Institute of Housing	**cih.org**
● HouseMark gateway	housemark.co.uk
● Housing Law Direct	housinglawdirect.com
Church Commissioners	**cofe.anglican.org/commissioners/**
City of London Law Society (CLLS)	**citysolicitors.org**

> The CLLS Long Form Certificate of Title and CLLS Short Form Report on Title are both available to view and download from this website.

Commercial Property Direct   **rimer.butterworths.co.uk/proponl/**
(don't add 'www')

Subscription service from Butterworths including access to: Hill & Redman; Ross; Tolley's Property Taxation; Tolley's Capital; Allowances; Tolley's Stamp Duties; Halsbury's commentary.

Countrywide Legal Indemnities   **countrywidelegal.co.uk**

Drainage and Water   **drainageandwater.co.uk**

Includes: Fees and contact information for Water Service Companies.

Elexica (Simmons and Simmons)   **elexica.com**

Register for free access to a wide range of materials including property checklists, property email circular, and property updates.

Energy Watch   **energywatch.org.uk**

English Heritage   **english-heritage.org.uk**

ESRI (UK)   **esri.co.uk**

Estates Gazette   **egi.co.uk**

Subscriber service. The legal section includes: Lands Tribunal decisions since 1996; Legal articles from 1986; Estates Gazette Law Reports; Estates Gazette Planning Law Reports; Practice points (free); E-conveyancing information (free).

Fenestration Self-Assessment Scheme   **fensa.org.uk**

GroundSure Ltd   **groundsure.com**

Hays Document Exchange   **haysdx.co.uk**

House Builders Federation   **hbf.org.uk**

Independent Housing Ombudsman   **ihos.org.uk**

Web site includes information on the tenancy deposit scheme.

Institute of Legal Executives   **ilex.org.uk**

Landmark Information Group Ltd   **landmark-information.co.uk**

Lands Tribunal   **courtservice.gov.uk/tribunals/
lands_frm.htm**

Includes: cases; decisions; fees; and rules.

LEASE   **lease-advice.org**

The site of the Leasehold Advisory Service includes: Leasehold Valuation Tribunal decisions; and commentary on the Commonhold and Leasehold Reform Act.

Legislation (general)	**hmso.gov.uk/legis.htm**
● Bills before Parliament	parliament.the-stationery-office.co.uk/ pa/pabills.htm
● Hansard	parliament.uk/hansard/hansard.cfm
● The Stationery Office	tso.co.uk
● House of Commons	parliament.uk/about_commons/ about_commons.cfm
● House of Lords	parliament.uk/about_lords/about_lords.cfm

Marplus **marplus.co.uk**

National Criminal Intelligence Service **ncis.co.uk**

National Radiological Protection Board **nrpb.co.uk**

National Association of Estate Agents **naea.co.uk**

National House Building Council (NHBC) **nhbc.co.uk**

See this site for details on new homes structural defects insurance.

Network Rail **networkrail.co.uk**

Practical Law Company Property Law **property.practicallaw.com/home/** (don't add 'www')

Subscription service including: practice notes; precedents; drafting notes; commercial property standard enquiries; know-how index; email circular.

Premier Guarantee Ltd **thepremierguarantee.co.uk**

See this site for details on new homes structural defects insurance.

Property Forum **thepropertyforum.net/forum/**

The web site includes news items; resources; discussion groups; and an email circular.

Property Litigation Association **pla.org.uk**

Royal Institute of British Architects **riba.org**

Royal Mail **royalmail.com**

The web site offers a free postcode and address finder.

Royal Town Planning Institute **rtpi.org.uk**

Service Charges in Commercial Property **servicechargeguide.co.uk/**

Sitescope **sitescope.co.uk**

Solicitors Property Group **solicitorspropertygroup.co.uk/**

The site includes the Solicitors Property Sellers' Code of Practice.

Sugar Bureau	**sugar-bureau.co.uk**
Westlaw UK Landlord and Tenant	**westlaw.co.uk/landt.htm**

Subscription service includes: landlord and tenant reports from 1998; unreported cases from 1999; selected cases from the law reports from 1865; Westlaw UK legislation from 1267; Woodfall: Landlord & Tenant; full text of Landlord & Tenant Review and Property Law Bulletin; and a news service.

Zurich	**zurich.co.uk**

See this site for details on new homes structural defects insurance.

PUBLISHERS

Conveyancing Forms Suppliers

• Everyform	**everyform.co.uk**
• Laserform	**laserform.co.uk**
• Law Society Bookshop	**lawsociety.org.uk**
• Oyez Straker Legal Forms	**oyezstraker.co.uk**
• Shaw & Sons Ltd	**shaws.co.uk/professional_forms.htm**
• Stat Plus	**statplus.co.uk**

Books and Journals Publishers

• Butterworths	**butterworths.com**
• Cavendish	**cavendish.co.uk**
• EMIS Professional Publishing	**emispp.com**
• Estates Gazette	**egi.co.uk**
• Hart	**hartpub.co.uk**
• Incorporated Council of Law Reporting	**lawreports.co.uk**
• Jordans	**jordanspublishing.co.uk**
• LAG	**lag.org.uk**
• Law Society Publishing	**lawsociety.org.uk**
• Northumbria Legal Press	**nlp.unn.ac.uk** (don't add 'www')
• Oxford University Press	**oup.co.uk**
• RICS Books	**ricsbooks.com**
• Sweet & Maxwell	**smlawpub.co.uk**
• The Stationery Office	**tso.co.uk**

XI.7. Conveyancing publications in print

This Appendix holds details of publications relevant to conveyancing which is available in print. It is not intended to be comprehensive or to confer any endorsement from the Law Society. It replaces the 'Further Reference' lists that appeared at the end of chapters in previous editions of the *Conveyancing Handbook*. Many important documents are now only available as pdf files on the Internet so another list has been compiled for online information at Appendix XI.6.

To order, call the Law Society's Business Centre on Tel. 020 7320 5640 or Hammicks Legal Bookshops on Tel. 0207 405 5711. If you can't find what you're looking for, call the Law Society's Library on Tel. 0870 606 2522.

FORMS

These forms may be ordered through the Law Society's Business Centre (Tel. 020 7320 5640) or through any of the Law Society's approved stationery suppliers: Everyform, Oyez Office Supplies, Laserform, Peapod Solutions, Shaw and Sons, and Stat Plus Ltd.

- *CON 29 (Part I) Standard Enquiries of Local Authority 2002*
- *CON 29 (Part II) Optional Enquiries of Local Authority 2002*
- *CON 29M (2003) Coal Mining Search*
- *CON 29DW (2002) Standard Drainage and Water Enquiries*
- *Fixtures, Fittings and Contents Form 2nd edition*
- *Completion Information and Requisitions on Title*
- *Seller's Property Information Form 3rd edition (SPIF)*
- *Seller's Leasehold Information Form 2nd edition (SLIF)*
- *Standard Business Lease (whole of building)*
- *Standard Business Lease (part of building)*
- *Standard Conditions of Sale 3rd edition**
- *Standard Commercial Conditions of Sale 1st edition**

*At the time of going to press, revisions are planned to the Standard Conditions of Sale and the Standard Commercial Conditions of Sale (see AA. New Developments in Conveyancing Practice).

GUIDANCE FROM THE LAW SOCIETY

The appendices of the *Conveyancing Handbook* collect most of the guidance relevant to conveyancers (see Appendix I, II, III, IV, V and VI) but there are several other publications listed below. See Appendix XI.4 for contact details of the Practice Advice Service and the Strategic Research Unit.

- *Coal Mining Searches: Directory and Guidance*, The Coal Authority and The Law Society, Law Society Publishing 2003

- *Guide to the National Conveyancing Protocol,* The Law Society, Law Society Publishing 2002

- *Guide to the Professional Conduct of Solicitor* 8ᵗʰ edition, The Law Society, Law Society Publishing 1999 (updated online at www.guide-on-line.lawsociety.org.uk)

- *Money Laundering Legislation: Guidance for solicitors,* Professional Ethics, The Law Society, Law Society Publishing 1999*

- *Money Laundering Legislation: Guidance for solicitors (update),* Professional Ethics, The Law Society, Law Society Publishing 2002*

- Practice Advice Service publications:

  — *Non-Contentious Costs*

  — *Enduring Powers of Attorney*

  — *Money Laundering*

  — *Gifts of Property*

- Strategic Research Unit Publications:

  — *Annual Statistical Report 2002,* The Law Society 2002

  — *The Conveyancing Market 1999,* Law Society 1999

  — *Client Views: Client's experiences of using a solicitor for personal matters,* Law Society 2000

- *Solicitors' Accounts Manual 8ᵗʰ edition.* The Law Society 2001

*The Law Society's guidance on Money Laundering will be updated following the publication of new regulations in 2003. Check the Law Society's web site for details.

COUNCIL OF MORTGAGE LENDERS

Part 1 of the *Lenders' Handbook for England and Wales* 2ⁿᵈ edition (is reproduced in Appendix VIII.3).

The first edition of the *Lenders' Handbook for England and Wales* was published in as a booklet (when it was distributed free with the Law Society's Gazette). The revisions to the first edition and subsequent editions are available online at www.cml.org.uk.

NATIONAL RADIOLOGICAL PROTECTION BOARD

See Appendix XI.5 for contact details.

- *NRPB Response Statement R3/02,* NRPB 2002 (re: CON 29 searches)

- *NRPB-W26 Radon Atlas of England and Wales,* NRPB

- *NRPB–R308 Radon in Dwellings in Northern Ireland: Atlas and 1999 Review,* NRPB

GENERAL TITLES ON CONVEYANCING

- *An Introduction to Residential Conveyancing,* H. Barraclough, EMIS 1999

- *A Practical Approach to Conveyancing* 5th edition, R. Abbey and M. Richards, OUP, 2003.

- *A Practical Approach to Commercial Conveyancing,* R. Abbey and M. Richards, OUP 2003.

- *Conveyancing Forms and Procedures 3rd edition,* S. Buckingham with A. Colby, Law Society Publishing 2001

- *The Conveyancers Yearbook 2003,* R. Hewitson, Shaw & Sons 2003

PRECEDENTS FOR CONVEYANCERS

- *Encyclopaedia of Forms and Precedents,* Butterworths.

- *Commercial Property Development Precedents,* Heller, Levine and Cuthbert, Sweet & Maxwell

- *Precedents for the Conveyancer,* J.E. Adams, Sweet & Maxwell

- *Practical Conveyancing Precedents,* T.M. Aldridge, Sweet & Maxwell

- *Parker's Modern Conveyancing Precedents,* Butterworths

- *Practical Lease Precedents,* T. Aldridge, Sweet & Maxwell (looseleaf)

LOOSELEAFS ON CONVEYANCING

- *Butterworths Property Law Service,* J. Hullah, H. Barraclough, T. Smithers, P. Stevens and D. Clarke

- *Emmet and Farrand on Title,* J. Farrand and A. Clarke, Sweet & Maxwell

- *Practical Conveyancing Precedents,* T. Aldridge, Sweet & Maxwell

- *Ruoff and Roper: Registered Conveyancing,* R.B. Roper, C. West, R. Fearnley, J. Donaldson and F. Twambley, Sweet & Maxwell

- *Sweet & Maxwell's Conveyancing Practice,* P.H. Kenny, Sweet & Maxwell

LOOSELEAFS ON LANDLORD AND TENANT

- *Handbook of Business Tenancies,* D. Williams, C.M. Brand and C. Hubbard, Sweet & Maxwell

- *Hill and Redman's Law of Landlord and Tenant,* Butterworths

- *Landlord and Tenant Factbook,* E. Slessenger and G. Baxter, Sweet & Maxwell

- *Landlord and Tenant Reports,* N. Dowding, J. Driscoll, P. Williams, C. Wilson and C. Padley, Sweet & Maxwell

- *Leasehold Law, T. Aldridge, Sweet & Maxwell*

- *Woodfall: Landlord and Tenant,* K. Lewison, J. Brock, N. Dowding, P. Morgan and M. Rodger, Sweet & Maxwell

JOURNALS

- *Conveyancer and Property Lawyer,* Sweet & Maxwell

- *Estates Gazette,* The Estates Gazette

- *Journal of Planning and Environment Law,* Sweet & Maxwell

- *Landlord and Tenant Review,* Sweet & Maxwell

- *Practical Lawyer,* Legalease

- *Property in Practice* (magazine of the Property Section), The Law Society

- *Property Law Bulletin,* Sweet & Maxwell

SPECIALIST CONVEYANCING TOPICS

Agricultural Land and Tenancies

- *Agricultural Precedents Handbook,* N. Davies, G. Smith, A. Sydenham, Jordans 2001

- *Council Regulation* (EEC) 3590/92 (O.J. L.405, 31.12.92, p.1), as amended

● . *Commission Regulation* (EEC) 536/93 (O.J. L.57, 10.3.93, p.12), as amended

● *Dairy Produce Quotas Regulations 1997* (S.I. 1997/733 and 1997/1093)

● *Farms and Estates: A Conveyancing Handbook,* C. Jessel, Jordans 1999

● The Guide to Milk Quotas, The Rural Payments Agency

● *Muir Watt and Moss: Agricultural Holdings,* J. Moss, Sweet & Maxwell 1998

● *Scammell and Densham's Law of Agricultural Holdings,* H.A.C. Densham, Butterworths 1996

Cohabitants

● *Cohabitants and the Law 3ʳᵈ edition,* A. Barlow, Butterworths 2001

● *Cohabitants,* S.Dewar and J. Parker, Sweet & Maxwell 1995

● *Cohabitation Law, Practice and Precedents,* D. Lush, H. Wood and D. Bishop, Family Law 2001

● *Cohabitation Law and Precedents,* J. Craig and P. Pearson, Sweet & Maxwell

● *The Property Rights of Cohabitees,* J. Mee, Hart Publishing 1999

Commonhold

● *Commonhold Law,* T. Aldridge, Sweet & Maxwell 2002

● *Commonhold: The New Law.* D. Clarke, Jordans 2002

● *Commonhold: Law and practice,* G. Fetherstonhaugh, M. Sefton and E. Peters

● *Furber: The Commonhold and Leasehold Reform Act 2002,* J. Furber, J. Karas, J. Evans and T. Scott, Butterworths 2002

Costs

● *Cook on Costs: A guide to legal remuneration in civil contentious and non-contentious business 2002/03,* M. Cook, Butterworths 2002

● *Non-Contentious Costs,* Practice Advice Service, The Law Society 1999

Covenants

● *Blackstone's Guide to Covenants for Title: Understanding the New Law,* P. Kenny, OUP 1995.

● *Preston and Newsom: Restrictive Covenants Affecting Freehold Land,* G.L. Newsom, Sweet & Maxwell, 1998

● *The Restrictive Covenant in the Control of Land Use,* D. Sabey and A. Everton, Dartmouth 1999.

● *Restrictive Covenants over Freehold Land: A practitioner's guide,* A. Francis, Sweet & Maxwell 1999.

● *Scammell: Land Covenants,* E. Scammell, Butterworths 1996

Easements and Boundaries

● *Boundaries and Easements 3ʳᵈ edition,* C. Sara, Sweet & Maxwell 2002

● *Boundaries, Walls and Fences 8ᵗʰ edition,* T. Aldridge, Sweet & Maxwell 1997

● *Gale on the Law of Easements 17ᵗʰ edition,* J. Gaunt & P. Morgan, Sweet & Maxwell 2002

Elderly Clients and Gifts of Property

- *Butterworths Older Client Law Service*, G.Ashton (ed.), Butterworths
- *Elderly Client Handbook 3rd edition*, G. Ashton, Law Society Publishing 2000
- *Elderly People and the Law*, G. Ashton, Butterworths 2002

Environmental

- *Conveying Contaminated Land: Developing issues*, M. Edwards, C. Deansley, D. Cuckson, EMIS Professional Publishing 1997
- *Environmental Law Handbook*, T. Hellawell, Law Society Publishing 2002
- *Waite and Jewell: Environmental Law in Property Transactions*, A. Waite and T. Jewell, Butterworths 1997.

Land Registration Act 2002

- *Blackstone's Guide to the Land Registration Act 2002*, R. Abbey and M. Richards, Oxford University Press 2002
- *The Land Registration Act 2002 'A Practical Guide*, I. Clarke, Sweet & Maxwell 2002
- *Registered Land: the new law: A guide to the Land Registration Act 2002*, C. Harpum and J. Bignell, Jordans 2002
- *The Land Registration Act 2002*, D. Ainger, F. Barlow, G. Hill, R. Wallington, R. Dew and T. Harry, Butterworths 2003

Mortgages

- *Fisher and Lightwood's Law of Mortgage*, E.L.G. Tyler, Butterworths, 1999
- *The Law of Mortgages*, Cousins and Clarke, Sweet & Maxwell 2001
- *Mortgage Fraud*, C. Osborn, EMIS 1995

Planning

- *An Outline of Planning Law*, D. Heap, Sweet & Maxwell 1996
- *Butterworths Planning Law Service*, Butterworths
- *Encyclopaedia of Planning Law and Practice*, Sweet & Maxwell
- *Planning Law for Conveyancers*, C.M. Brand and D.W. Williams, Sweet & Maxwell
- *Planning Law for Conveyancers*, D. Forbes, EMIS 1999
- *Practical Approach to Planning Law 8th edition*, V. Moore, OUP 2002
- *Telling and Duxbury: Planning Law and Procedure*, R.M.C. Duxbury, Butterworths 2002
- *The Building Regulations Explained and Illustrated*, V. Powell-Smith, Blackwell Science 1990

Property selling

- *Estate Agents and Property Misdescriptions Acts*, J.R. Murdoch, Estates Gazette, 1993
- *Regulating the Sale of Property*, R. Rowell and J. Hancock, EMIS 1993

Searches and enquiries

- Directory of Local Authorities 2003, *Sweet & Maxwell 2003*
- *Enquiries of Local Authorities and Water Companies: A Practical Guide*, K.M. Pugsley, Callow Publishing 2002
- *Garners Local Land Charges 12th edition*, J. Boothroyd, Shaw & Sons 1998

Tax

- *Capital Gains Tax 99–00*, D. Bertram, Accountancy Books
- *Monroe and Nock on the Law of Stamp Duties*, R. Nock, Sweet & Maxwell
- *Sergeant and Sims on Stamp Duty* B.J. Sims and M. Quinlan, Butterworths 1996
- *Tolley's Stamp Duties and Stamp Duty Reserve Tax 2002–3*, P. Cannon, Tolley 2002
- *Tolley's VAT on Construction Land and Property*, A. Buckett, Tolley
- *Understanding Stamp Duty on Property*, R. Nock, Law Society Publishing 2003
- *Understanding VAT on Property*, D. Jordan, Law Society Publishing 2002
- *Whitehouse and Stuart-Buttle: Revenue Law Principles and Practice*, C. Whitehouse, Butterworths
- *Whiteman on Capital Gains Tax*, Whiteman, Gammie and Herbert, Sweet & Maxwell 2002

LANDLORD AND TENANT (GENERAL)

- *Aldridge's Residential Lettings* 11th edition, T. Aldridge, Sweet & Maxwell 1998
- *Bamford: Amending a Commercial Lease*, K. Bamford, Butterworths 1998
- *Butterworths Business Landlord and Tenant Handbook*, K. Bradford, P. Matthews and P. Withers, Butterworths, 1998
- *Drafting Business Leases 6th Edition*, K. Lewison, Sweet & Maxwell 1996
- *Drafting Residential Leases*, C. Bennett, Sweet & Maxwell 1995
- *Handbook of Residential Tenancies*, J. Driscoll, D. Williams and C. Boston, Sweet & Maxwell

LANDLORD AND TENANT (SPECIALIST TOPICS)

- *Brooke and Curtis: Commercial Leasing*, N. Brooke and M. Curtis, Butterworths 1998
- *Cawthorn and Barraclough: The Sale and Management of Flats: Practice and Precedents*, Barraclough, Butterworths 1996
- *Commercial Leases*, M.J. Ross, Butterworths
- *Dilapidations: The Law and Practice 2nd edition*, N. Dowding and K. Reynolds, Sweet & Maxwell 2002
- *Drafting and Negotiating Rent Review Clauses*, M. Kemp, Sweet & Maxwell 1996
- *Hague on Leasehold Enfranchisement 4th edition*, A. Radevsky and D. Greenish, Sweet & Maxwell 2003
- *Handbook of Rent Review*, K. Reynolds, G. Fetherstonhaugh, R. Bernstein, Sweet & Maxwell
- *Handbook of Dilapidations*, D. Williams, E. Shapiro and J. Thom, Sweet & Maxwell
- *Law of Flats 3rd edition*, T.M. Aldridge, Sweet & Maxwell 1994

- *Leasehold Liability: Landlord and Tenant (Covenants) Act 1985*, P. Rogers, S. Fogel and A. Riley, E. Slessenger, Jordans 2000

- *Leasehold Valuation Tribunals: A Practical Guide*, S. Gallagher, Sweet & Maxwell 2003

- *Megarry's Assured Tenancies*, T.M. Fancourt, Sweet & Maxwell, 1999

- *Possession and Lease Renewal of Business Premises* 3rd edition, G. Webber, Sweet & Maxwell 2003

- *Renewal of Business Tenancies* 2nd edition, K. Reynolds and W. Clarke, Sweet & Maxwell 2002

- *Resident-owned Flats*, Tabbush, Sweet & Maxwell 1994

- *Service Charges: Law and Practice,* P. Freedman and E. Shapiro, Sweet & Maxwell 2003

XII. STATUTORY MATERIALS

XII.1. Land Charges Fees Rules 1990 (S.I. 1990/327)[1]

1990 No. 327

LAND CHARGES

The Land Charges Fees Rules 1990

Made	*21st February 1990*
Coming into force	*2nd April 1990*

The Lord Chancellor, with the concurrence of the Treasury, in exercise of the powers conferred on him by sections 9(1), 10(2), 16(1) and 17(1) of the Land Charges Act 1972(**a**) hereby makes in the following rules:

1. (1) These Rules may be cited as the Land Charges Fees Rules 1990 and shall come into force on 2nd April 1990.

   (2) In these Rules, unless the context otherwise requires –

   'the Act' means the Land Charges Act 1972;

   'credit account' means an account authorised by the Registrar for the purpose of providing credit facilities for the payment of fees;

   'fee' means a fee specified in Schedule 1;

   'Schedule' means a schedule to these Rules;

   'written application' in Schedule 1 does not include an application made by teleprinter or facsimile transmission.

2. The fees specified in Schedule 1 shall be payable under the Act.

3. Every fee which accompanies an application is to be paid in money in accordance with the Land Charges (Fees) Order 1990(**b**) and shall, except as mentioned in Rule 4 or as the Registrar may otherwise allow, be paid in cash or by means of a postal order crossed and made payable to H.M. Land Registry.

4. (1) Any person or firm having a credit account may request the Registrar, on any application, to debit the requisite fee to that account.

   (2) When a person or firm having a credit account makes an application which is not accompanied by any fee and does not contain a request for the fee to be debited to that account, the Registrar may, if he thinks fit, nevertheless accept the application and debit the fee to that person's or that firm's account.

   (3) If the Registrar debits a fee to a credit account, this shall be treated as due payment of that fee.

(**a**) 1972 c.61.
(**b**) S.I. 1990/323.
1. Incorporating amendments made by the Land Charges Fees (Amendment) Rules 1994 (S.I. 1994/286).

(4) Credit accounts shall be authorised and maintained in accordance with the provisions set out in Schedule 2.

5. The Land Charges Fees Order 1985(c) so far as made under powers conferred by the Act is hereby revoked.

Dated 16th February 1990   *Mackay of Clashfern*, C.

We concur

David Lightbown
Stephen Dorrell

Dated 21st February 1990   *Two of the Lord Commissioners of Her Majesty's Treasury*

SCHEDULE 1   Rule 2

Service		Amount of Fee
1. Registration, renewal, rectification or cancellation of an entry in any register	per name	£1
2. Certificate of cancellation	per name	£1
3. Entry of priority notice	per name	£1
4. Inspection of an entry in the register	per entry	£1
5. Office copy of an entry in the register (including any plan) whether the application is made in writing or by telephone or teleprinter or facsimile transmission or to the registrar's computer system by means of the applicant's remote terminal	per copy	£1
6. Official search in the index (including issue of printed certificate of result):–		
written application	per name	£1
telephone application	per name	£2
teleprinter application	per name	£2
facsimile transmission application	per name	£2
Application made to the registrar's computer system by means of the applicant's remote terminal	per name	£2
7. Official search in the index (including visual display of result of search and issue of printed certificate of such result)	per name	£2

SCHEDULE 2   Rule 4(4)

PROVISION OF CREDIT ACCOUNTS

1. The Registrar may, as he thinks fit, authorise any person or firm to use a credit account for the purpose of the payment of fees but may withdraw or suspend any such authorisation at any time without giving any reason therefor.

2. The Registrar may also at any time terminate or suspend all credit accounting facilities generally.

(c) S.I. 1985/358.

3. A statement of account shall be sent by the Registrar to each account holder at the end of each calendar month or at such other period as the Registrar shall direct either in any particular case or generally.

4. On receipt of the statement and if no question arises thereon the account holder shall pay by cheque any sum due on his account promptly, and in any event within ten days of its receipt.

5. Cheques shall be made payable to H.M. Land Registry and sent to the Accounts Section, Land Charges Department, Burrington Way, Plymouth, PL5 3LP or at such other address as the Registrar shall direct.

XII.2. Stamp Duty (Exempt Instruments) Regulations 1987 (S.I. 1987/516)¹

1987 No. 516

TAXES

The Stamp Duty (Exempt Instruments) Regulations 1987

Made	*24th March 1987*
Laid before the House of Commons	*26th March 1987*
Coming into force	*1st May 1987*

Note. – FA 1985, s. 87 (2) provides that instruments which would otherwise be chargeable with stamp duty of a fixed amount under any provision specified in regulations shall not be so charged if they are of a kind specified in regulations and certified to be instruments of that kind.

These regulations specify the provisions under which, subject to conditions, that duty shall not be charged; specify the instruments (executed on or after 1 May 1987) in relation to which the exemption is available; and provide for the certification requirements.

Regulation 1 provides the title and commencement date.

Regulation 2 provides the conditions for the exemption.

Regulation 3 provides for the requirements for the certificate and the conditions which have to be fulfilled.

Regulation 4 introduces the Schedule which specifies the instruments which may qualify for the exemption provided by regulation 2.

Regulation 5 dispenses with the requirement of adjudication in accordance with the Stamp Act 1891, s. 12 as required by FA 1985, ss. 82(5) and 84(9).

The Treasury, in exercise of the powers conferred on them by section 87(2) of the Finance Act 1985, hereby make the following regulations:

1. These regulations may be cited as the Stamp Duty (Exempt Instruments) Regulations 1987 and shall come into force on 1st May 1987.

In these Regulations 'life policy' means—

(a) **any policy of insurance on a human life, or on the happening of a contingency dependent upon a human life, except a policy of insurance for a payment only upon the death of a person otherwise than from a natural cause, or**

(b) **a grant or contract for the payment of an annuity upon a human life.**

Inserted by SI 1999/2539, reg 3. Date in force: 1 October 1999

---

1. Incorporating amendments made by The Stamp Duty (Exempt Instruments) (Amendments) Regulations 1999 (S.I. 1999/2539).

2. (1) An instrument which—

(a) is executed on or after 1st May 1987,

(b) is of a kind specified in the Schedule hereto for the purposes of this regulation, and

(c) is certified by a certificate which fulfils the conditions of regulation 3 to be an instrument of that kind,

shall be exempt from duty under the provisions specified in paragraph (2) of this regulation.

(2) The provisions specified are—

(a) **the following paragraphs of Part III of Schedule 13 to the Finance Act 1999—**

(i) **paragraph 16 (conveyance or transfer otherwise than on sale),**

(ii) **paragraph 17 (declaration of use or trust),**

(iii) **paragraph 18 (dispositions in Scotland);**

(b) **sections 83(2) and 84(8) of the Finance Act 1985.**

Para (2): sub-para (a) substituted by SI 1999/2539, reg 4. Date in force: 1 October 1999.

3. The certificate—

(a) shall be in writing and—

(i) be included as part of the instrument, or

(ii) be endorsed upon or, where separate, be physically attached to the instrument concerned;

(b) shall contain a sufficient description of—

(i) the instrument concerned where the certificate is separate but physically attached to the instrument, and

(ii) the category in the Schedule hereto into which the instrument falls;

(c) (i) shall be signed by the transferor or grantor or by his solicitor or duly authorised agent, and

(ii) where it is not signed by the transferor or grantor or by his solicitor, it shall contain a statement by the signatory of the capacity in which he signs, that he is authorised so to sign and that he gives the certificate from his own knowledge of the facts stated in it.

4. The Schedule to these regulations shall have effect for the specification of instruments for the purposes of regulation 2.

5. An instrument which is certified in accordance with these regulations shall not be required under section 82(5) or section 84(9) of the Finance Act 1985 to be stamped in accordance with section 12 of the Stamp Act 1891 with a particular stamp denoting that it is duly stamped or that it is not chargeable with any duty.

SCHEDULE

Regulation 4

An instrument which effects any one or more of the following transactions only is an instrument specified for the purposes of regulation 2—

A. The vesting of property subject to a trust in the trustees of the trust on the appointment of a new trustee, or in the continuing trustees on the retirement of a trustee.

B. The conveyance or transfer of property the subject of a specific devise or legacy to the beneficiary named in the will (or his nominee).

C. The conveyance or transfer of property which forms part of an intestate's estate to the person entitled on intestacy (or his nominee).

D. The appropriation of property within section 84(4) of the Finance Act 1985 (death: appropriation in satisfaction of a general legacy of money) or section 84(5) or (7) of that Act (death: appropriation in satisfaction of any interest of surviving spouse and in Scotland also of any interest of issue).

E. The conveyance or transfer of property which forms part of the residuary estate of a testator to a beneficiary (or his nominee) entitled solely by virtue of his entitlement under the will.

F. The conveyance or transfer of property out of a settlement in or towards satisfaction of a beneficiary's interest, not being an interest acquired for money or money's worth, being a conveyance or transfer constituting a distribution of property in accordance with the provisions of the settlement.

G. The conveyance or transfer of property on and in consideration only of marriage to a party to the marriage (or his nominee) or to trustees to be held on the terms of a settlement made in consideration only of the marriage.

H. The conveyance or transfer of property within section 83(1) of the Finance Act 1985 (transfers in connection with divorce etc.).

I. The conveyance or transfer by the liquidator of property which formed part of the assets of the company in liquidation to a shareholder of that company (or his nominee) in or towards satisfaction of the shareholder's rights on a winding-up.

J. The grant in fee simple of an easement in or over land for no consideration in money or money's worth.

K. The grant of a servitude for no consideration in money or money's worth.

L. The conveyance or transfer of property operating as a voluntary disposition inter vivos for no consideration in money or money's worth nor any consideration referred to in section 57 of the Stamp Act 1891 (conveyance in consideration of a debt etc.).

M. The conveyance or transfer of property by an instrument within section 84(1) of the Finance Act 1985 (death: varying disposition).

N.   The declaration of any use or trust of or concerning a life policy, or property representing, or benefits arising under, a life policy.

Category N: inserted by SI 1999/2539, reg 5. Date in force: 1 October 1999.

XII.3. Solicitors' (Non-Contentious Business) Remuneration Order 1994 (S.I. 1994/2616)

1994 No. 2616

SOLICITORS

The Solicitors' (Non-Contentious Business) Remuneration Order 1994

Made	*5th October 1994*
Laid before Parliament	*10th October 1994*
Coming into force	*1st November 1994*

The Lord Chancellor, the Lord Chief Justice, the Master of the Rolls, the President of the Law Society, the president of Holborn law society and the Chief Land Registrar (in respect of business done under the Land Registration Act 1925(**a**)), together constituting the committee authorised to make orders under section 56 of the Solicitors Act 1974(**b**), in exercise of the powers conferred on them by that section and having complied with the requirements of section 56 (3), hereby make the following Order:

Citation, commencement and revocation

1. (1) This Order may be cited as the Solicitors' (Non-Contentious Business) Remuneration Order 1994.

(2) This Order shall come into force on 1st November 1994 and shall apply to all non-contentious business for which bills are delivered on or after that date.

(3) The Solicitors' Remuneration Order 1972(**c**) is hereby revoked except in its application to business for which bills are delivered before this Order comes into force.

Interpretation

2. In this Order:

'client' means the client of a solicitor;

'costs' means the amount charged in a solicitor's bill, exclusive of disbursements and value added tax, in respect of non-contentious business or common form probate business;

'entitled person' means a client or an entitled third party;

'entitled third party' means a residuary beneficiary absolutely and immediately (and not contingently) entitled to an inheritance, where a solicitor has charged the estate for his professional costs for acting in the administration of the estate, and *either*

(**a**) 1925 c.21.
(**b**) 1974 c.47, as modified by the Administration of Justice Act 1985 (c.61), Schedule 2, paragraphs 22 and 23.
(**c**) S.I. 1972/1139.

(a) the only personal representatives are solicitors (whether or not acting in a professional capacity); or

(b) the only personal representatives are solicitors acting jointly with partners or employees in a professional capacity;

'paid disbursements' means disbursements already paid by the solicitor;

'recognised body' means a body corporate recognised by the Council under section 9 of the Administration of Justice Act 1985(**d**);

'remuneration certificate' means a certificate issued by the Council pursuant to this Order;

'residuary beneficiary' includes a person entitled to all or part of the residue of an intestate estate;

'solicitor' includes a recognised body and shall apply to registered European lawyers (S.I. 2000/1119);

'the Council' means the Council of the Law Society.

Solicitors' costs

3. A solicitor's costs shall be such sum as may be fair and reasonable to both solicitor and entitled person, having regard to all the circumstances of the case and in particular to:

(a) the complexity of the matter or the difficulty or novelty of the questions raised;

(b) the skill, labour, specialised knowledge and responsibility involved;

(c) the time spent on the business;

(d) the number and importance of the documents prepared or perused, without regard to length;

(e) the place where and the circumstances in which the business or any part thereof is transacted;

(f) the amount or value of any money or property involved;

(g) whether any land involved is registered land;

(h) the importance of the matter to the client; and

(i) the approval (express or implied) of the entitled person or the express approval of the testator to:

    (i) the solicitor undertaking all or any part of the work giving rise to the costs; or

    (ii) the amount of the costs.

Right to certification

4. (1) Without prejudice to the provisions of sections 70, 71, and 72 of the Solicitors Act 1974 (which relate to taxation of costs), an entitled person may, subject to the provisions of this Order, require a solicitor to obtain a remuneration certificate from the Council in respect of a bill which has been delivered where the costs are not more than £50,000.

(2) The remuneration certificate must state what sum, in the opinion of the Council, would be a fair and reasonable charge for the business covered by the bill (whether it be the sum charged or a lesser sum). In the absence of taxation the sum payable in respect of such costs is the sum stated in the remuneration certificate.

(**d**) 1985 c.61.

Disciplinary and other measures

5. (1) If on a taxation the taxing officer allows less than one half of the costs, he must bring the facts of the case to the attention of the Council.

(2) The provisions of this Order are without prejudice to the general powers of the Council under the Solicitors Act 1974.

Commencement of proceedings against a client

6. Before a solicitor brings proceedings to recover costs against a client on a bill for non-contentious business he must inform the client in writing of the matters specified in article 8, except where the bill has been taxed.

Costs paid by deduction

7. (1) If a solicitor deducts his costs from monies held for or on behalf of a client or of an estate in satisfaction of a bill and an entitled person objects in writing to the amount of the bill within the prescribed time, the solicitor must immediately inform the entitled person in writing of the matters specified in article 8, unless he has already done so.

(2) In this article and in article 10, 'the prescribed time' means:

(a) in respect of a client, three months after delivery of the relevant bill, or a lesser time (which may not be less than one month) specified in writing to the client at the time of delivery of the bill; or

(b) in respect of an entitled third party, three months after delivery of notification to the entitled third party of the amount of the costs, or a lesser time (which may not be less than one month) specified in writing to the entitled third party at the time of such notification.

Information to be given in writing to entitled person

8. When required by articles 6 or 7, a solicitor shall inform an entitled person in writing of the following matters:

(a) where article 4(1) applies:

(i) that the entitled person may, within one month of receiving from the solicitor the information specified in this article or (if later) of delivery of the bill or notification of the amount of the costs, require the solicitor to obtain a remuneration certificate; and

(ii) that (unless the solicitor has agreed to do so) the Council may waive the requirements of article 11(1), if satisfied from the client's written application that exceptional circumstances exist to justify granting a waiver;

(b) that sections 70, 71 and 72 of the Solicitors Act 1974 set out the entitled person's rights in relation to taxation;

(c) that (where the whole of the bill has not been paid, by deduction or otherwise) the solicitor may charge interest on the outstanding amount of the bill in accordance with article 14.

Loss by client of right to certification

9. A client may not require a solicitor to obtain a remuneration certificate:

(a) after a bill has been delivered and paid by the client, other than by deduction;

(b) where a bill has been delivered, after the expiry of one month from the date on which the client was informed in writing of the matters specified in article 8 or from delivery of the bill if later;

(c)   after the solicitor and client have entered into a non-contentious business agreement in accordance with the provisions of section 57 of the Solicitors Act 1974;

(d)   after a court has ordered the bill to be taxed.

Loss by entitled third party of right to certification

10.   An entitled third party may not require a solicitor to obtain a remuneration certificate:

(a)   after the prescribed time (within the meaning of article 7(2)(b)) has elapsed without any objection being received to the amount of the costs;

(b)   after the expiry of one month from the date on which the entitled third party was (in compliance with article 7) informed in writing of the matters specified in article 8 or from notification of the costs if later;

(c)   after a court has ordered the bill to be taxed.

Requirement to pay a sum towards the costs

11. (1)   On requiring a solicitor to obtain a remuneration certificate a client must pay to the solicitor the paid disbursements and value added tax comprised in the bill together with 50% of the costs unless:

(a)   the client has already paid the amount required under this article, by deduction from monies held or otherwise; or

(b)   the solicitor or (if the solicitor refuses) the Council has agreed in writing to waive all or part of this requirement.

(2)   The Council shall be under no obligation to provide a remuneration certificate, and the solicitor may take steps to obtain payment of his bill if the client, having been informed of his right to seek a waiver of the requirements of paragraph (1), has not:

(a)   within one month of receipt of the information specified in article 8, either paid in accordance with paragraph (1) or applied to the Council in writing for a waiver of the requirements of paragraph (1); or

(b)   made payment in accordance with the requirements of paragraph (1) within one month of written notification that he has been refused a waiver of those requirements by the Council.

Miscellaneous provisions

12. (1)   After an application has been made by a solicitor for a remuneration certificate the client may pay the bill in full without invalidating the application.

(2)   A solicitor and entitled person may agree in writing to waive the provisions of sub-paragraphs (a) or (b) of articles 9 or 10.

(3)   A solicitor may take from his client security for the payment of any costs, including the amount of any interest to which the solicitor may become entitled under article 14.

Refunds by solicitor

13. (1)   If a solicitor has received payment of all or part of his costs and a remuneration certificate is issued for less than the sum already paid, the solicitor must immediately pay to the entitled person any refund which may be due (after taking into account any other sums which may properly be payable to the solicitor whether for costs, paid disbursements, value added tax or otherwise) unless the solicitor has applied for an order for taxation within one month of receipt by him of the remuneration certificate.

(2) Where a solicitor applies for taxation, his liability to pay any refund under paragraph (1) shall be suspended for so long as the taxation is still pending.

(3) The obligation of the solicitor to repay costs under paragraph (1) is without prejudice to any liability of the solicitor to pay interest on the repayment by virtue of any enactment, rule of law or professional rule.

Interest

14. (1) After the information specified in article 8 has been given to an entitled person in compliance with articles 6 or 7, a solicitor may charge interest on the unpaid amount of his costs plus any paid disbursements and value added tax, subject to paragraphs (2) and (3) below.

(2) Where an entitlement to interest arises under paragraph (1), and subject to any agreement made between a solicitor and client, the period for which interest may be charged may run from one month after the date of delivery of a bill, unless the solicitor fails to lodge an application within one month of receipt of a request for a remuneration certificate under article 4, in which case no interest is payable in respect of the period between one month after receiving the request and the actual date on which the application is lodged.

(3) Subject to any agreement made between a solicitor and client, the rate of interest must not exceed the rate for the time being payable on judgment debts.

(4) Interest charged under this article must be calculated, where applicable, by reference to the following:

(a) if a solicitor is required to obtain a remuneration certificate, the total amount of the costs certified by the Council to be fair and reasonable plus paid disbursements and value added tax;

(b) if an application is made for the bill to be taxed, the amount ascertained on taxation;

(c) if an application is made for the bill to be taxed or a solicitor is required to obtain a remuneration certificate and for any reason the taxation or application for a remuneration certificate does not proceed, the unpaid amount of the costs shown in the bill or such lesser sum as may be agreed between the solicitor and the client, plus paid disbursements and value added tax.

Application by solicitor

15. A solicitor, when making an application for a remuneration certificate in accordance with the provisions of this Order, must deliver to the Council the complete relevant file and working papers, and any other information or documentation which the Council may require for the purpose of providing a remuneration certificate.

EXPLANATORY NOTE

(This note is not part of the Order)

Section 56 of the Solicitors Act 1974 establishes a Committee with power to make general orders regulating the remuneration of solicitors in respect of non-contentious business. Paragraph 22(2) of Schedule 2 to the Administration of Justice Act 1985 modifies the section so that references to solicitors include references to recognised bodies (solicitors' incorporated practices recognised under section 9 of the Administration of Justice Act 1985). This Order sets out the rights of solicitors' clients and residuary beneficiaries of certain estates to require the solicitor charging the client or estate to obtain a certificate from the Law Society as to the reasonableness of his costs. The Order prescribes requirements in relation to information to be given in writing to clients and beneficiaries who are entitled to require a solicitor to obtain a certificate, and lays certain obligations on clients, beneficiaries and solicitors.

XII.4. Land Registration Act 2002 (selected schedules)[1]

Schedule 1 Unregistered interests which override first registration

Leasehold estates in land

1 A leasehold estate in land granted for a term not exceeding seven years from the date of the grant, except for a lease the grant of which falls within section 4(1)(d), (e) or (f).

Interests of persons in actual occupation

2 An interest belonging to a person in actual occupation, so far as relating to land of which he is in actual occupation, except for an interest under a settlement under the Settled Land Act 1925 (c. 18).

Easements and profits a prendre

3 A legal easement or profit a prendre.

Customary and public rights

4 A customary right.

5 A public right.

Local land charges

6 A local land charge.

Mines and minerals

7 An interest in any coal or coal mine, the rights attached to any such interest and the rights of any person under section 38, 49 or 51 of the Coal Industry Act 1994 (c. 21).

8 In the case of land to which title was registered before 1898, rights to mines and minerals (and incidental rights) created before 1898.

9 In the case of land to which title was registered between 1898 and 1925 inclusive, rights to mines and minerals (and incidental rights) created before the date of registration of the title.

Miscellaneous

10 A franchise.

11 A manorial right.

12 A right to rent which was reserved to the Crown on the granting of any freehold estate (whether or not the right is still vested in the Crown).

13 A non-statutory right in respect of an embankment or sea or river wall.

14 A right to payment in lieu of tithe.

1. © Crown 2002. Schedules 1, 3–6, 8 and 12 are reproduced here.

Schedule 3 Unregistered interests which override registered dispositions

Leasehold estates in land

1   A leasehold estate in land granted for a term not exceeding seven years from the date of the grant, except for–

(a)   a lease the grant of which falls within section 4(1)(d), (e) or (f);

(b)   a lease the grant of which constitutes a registrable disposition.

Interests of persons in actual occupation

2   An interest belonging at the time of the disposition to a person in actual occupation, so far as relating to land of which he is in actual occupation, except for–

(a)   an interest under a settlement under the Settled Land Act 1925 (c. 18);

(b)   an interest of a person of whom inquiry was made before the disposition and who failed to disclose the right when he could reasonably have been expected to do so;

(c)   an interest–

(i)   which belongs to a person whose occupation would not have been obvious on a reasonably careful inspection of the land at the time of the disposition, and

(ii)   of which the person to whom the disposition is made does not have actual knowledge at that time;

(d)   a leasehold estate in land granted to take effect in possession after the end of the period of three months beginning with the date of the grant and which has not taken effect in possession at the time of the disposition.

Easements and profits a prendre

3   (1)   A legal easement or profit a prendre, except for an easement, or a profit a prendre which is not registered under the Commons Registration Act 1965 (c. 64), which at the time of the disposition–

(a)   is not within the actual knowledge of the person to whom the disposition is made, and

(b)   would not have been obvious on a reasonably careful inspection of the land over which the easement or profit is exercisable.

(2)   The exception in sub-paragraph (1) does not apply if the person entitled to the easement or profit proves that it has been exercised in the period of one year ending with the day of the disposition.

Customary and public rights

4   A customary right.

5   A public right.

Local land charges

6   A local land charge.

Mines and minerals

7   An interest in any coal or coal mine, the rights attached to any such interest and the rights of any person under section 38, 49 or 51 of the Coal Industry Act 1994 (c. 21).

8 In the case of land to which title was registered before 1898, rights to mines and minerals (and incidental rights) created before 1898.

9 In the case of land to which title was registered between 1898 and 1925 inclusive, rights to mines and minerals (and incidental rights) created before the date of registration of the title.

Miscellaneous

10 A franchise.

11 A manorial right.

12 A right to rent which was reserved to the Crown on the granting of any freehold estate (whether or not the right is still vested in the Crown).

13 A non-statutory right in respect of an embankment or sea or river wall.

14 A right to payment in lieu of tithe.

Schedule 4 Alteration of the Register

Introductory

1 In this Schedule, references to rectification, in relation to alteration of the register, are to alteration which–

    (a) involves the correction of a mistake, and

    (b) prejudicially affects the title of a registered proprietor.

Alteration pursuant to a court order

2 (1) The court may make an order for alteration of the register for the purpose of–

    (a) correcting a mistake,

    (b) bringing the register up to date, or

    (c) giving effect to any estate, right or interest excepted from the effect of registration.

    (2) An order under this paragraph has effect when served on the registrar to impose a duty on him to give effect to it.

3 (1) This paragraph applies to the power under paragraph 2, so far as relating to rectification.

    (2) If alteration affects the title of the proprietor of a registered estate in land, no order may be made under paragraph 2 without the proprietor's consent in relation to land in his possession unless–

    (a) he has by fraud or lack of proper care caused or substantially contributed to the mistake, or

    (b) it would for any other reason be unjust for the alteration not to be made.

    (3) If in any proceedings the court has power to make an order under paragraph 2, it must do so, unless there are exceptional circumstances which justify its not doing so.

    (4) In sub-paragraph (2), the reference to the title of the proprietor of a registered estate in land includes his title to any registered estate which subsists for the benefit of the estate in land.

4 Rules may–

    (a) make provision about the circumstances in which there is a duty to exercise the power under paragraph 2, so far as not relating to rectification;

(b)   make provision about the form of an order under paragraph 2;

(c)   make provision about service of such an order.

Alteration otherwise than pursuant to a court order

5   The registrar may alter the register for the purpose of–

     (a)   correcting a mistake,

     (b)   bringing the register up to date,

     (c)   giving effect to any estate, right or interest excepted from the effect of registration, or

     (d)   removing a superfluous entry.

6   (1)   This paragraph applies to the power under paragraph 5, so far as relating to rectification.

     (2)   No alteration affecting the title of the proprietor of a registered estate in land may be made under paragraph 5 without the proprietor's consent in relation to land in his possession unless–

         (a)   he has by fraud or lack of proper care caused or substantially contributed to the mistake, or

         (b)   it would for any other reason be unjust for the alteration not to be made.

     (3)   If on an application for alteration under paragraph 5 the registrar has power to make the alteration, the application must be approved, unless there are exceptional circumstances which justify not making the alteration.

     (4)   In sub-paragraph (2), the reference to the title of the proprietor of a registered estate in land includes his title to any registered estate which subsists for the benefit of the estate in land.

7   Rules may–

     (a)   make provision about the circumstances in which there is a duty to exercise the power under paragraph 5, so far as not relating to rectification;

     (b)   make provision about how the register is to be altered in exercise of that power;

     (c)   make provision about applications for alteration under that paragraph, including provision requiring the making of such applications;

     (d)   make provision about procedure in relation to the exercise of that power, whether on application or otherwise.

Rectification and derivative interests

8   The powers under this Schedule to alter the register, so far as relating to rectification, extend to changing for the future the priority of any interest affecting the registered estate or charge concerned.

Costs in non-rectification cases

9   (1)   If the register is altered under this Schedule in a case not involving rectification, the registrar may pay such amount as he thinks fit in respect of any costs or expenses reasonably incurred by a person in connection with the alteration which have been incurred with the consent of the registrar.

     (2)   The registrar may make a payment under sub-paragraph (1) notwithstanding the absence of consent if–

         (a)   it appears to him:

      (i)   that the costs or expenses had to be incurred urgently, and

      (ii)   that it was not reasonably practicable to apply for his consent, or

   (b)   he has subsequently approved the incurring of the costs or expenses.

Schedule 5 Land Registry network

Access to network

1 (1)   A person who is not a member of the land registry may only have access to a land registry network under authority conferred by means of an agreement with the registrar.

  (2)   An agreement for the purposes of sub-paragraph (1) ("network access agreement") may authorise access for–

    (a)   the communication, posting or retrieval of information,

    (b)   the making of changes to the register of title or cautions register,

    (c)   the issue of official search certificates,

    (d)   the issue of official copies, or

    (e)   such other conveyancing purposes as the registrar thinks fit.

  (3)   Rules may regulate the use of network access agreements to confer authority to carry out functions of the registrar.

  (4)   The registrar must, on application, enter into a network access agreement with the applicant if the applicant meets such criteria as rules may provide.

Terms of access

2 (1)   The terms on which access to a land registry network is authorised shall be such as the registrar thinks fit, subject to sub-paragraphs (3) and (4), and may, in particular, include charges for access.

  (2)   The power under sub-paragraph (1) may be used, not only for the purpose of regulating the use of the network, but also for–

    (a)   securing that the person granted access uses the network to carry on such qualifying transactions as may be specified in, or under, the agreement,

    (b)   such other purpose relating to the carrying on of qualifying transactions as rules may provide, or

    (c)   enabling network transactions to be monitored.

  (3)   It shall be a condition of a network access agreement which enables the person granted access to use the network to carry on qualifying transactions that he must comply with any rules for the time being in force under paragraph 5.

  (4)   Rules may regulate the terms on which access to a land registry network is authorised.

Termination of access

3 (1)   The person granted access by a network access agreement may terminate the agreement at any time by notice to the registrar.

  (2)   Rules may make provision about the termination of a network access agreement by the registrar and may, in particular, make provision about–

    (a)   the grounds of termination,

    (b)   the procedure to be followed in relation to termination, and

    (c)   the suspension of termination pending appeal.

  (3)   Without prejudice to the generality of sub-paragraph (2)(a), rules under that provision may authorise the registrar to terminate a network access agreement if the person granted access–

    (a)   fails to comply with the terms of the agreement,

    (b)   ceases to be a person with whom the registrar would be required to enter into a network access agreement conferring the authority which the agreement confers, or

    (c)   does not meet such conditions as the rules may provide.

Appeals

4   (1)   A person who is aggrieved by a decision of the registrar with respect to entry into, or termination of, a network access agreement may appeal against the decision to the adjudicator.

  (2)   On determining an appeal under this paragraph, the adjudicator may give such directions as he considers appropriate to give effect to his determination.

  (3)   Rules may make provision about appeals under this paragraph.

Network transaction rules

5   (1)   Rules may make provision about how to go about network transactions.

  (2)   Rules under sub-paragraph (1) may, in particular, make provision about dealings with the land registry, including provision about–

    (a)   the procedure to be followed, and

    (b)   the supply of information (including information about unregistered interests).

Overriding nature of network access obligations

6   To the extent that an obligation not owed under a network access agreement conflicts with an obligation owed under such an agreement by the person granted access, the obligation not owed under the agreement is discharged.

Do-it-yourself conveyancing

7   (1)   If there is a land registry network, the registrar has a duty to provide such assistance as he thinks appropriate for the purpose of enabling persons engaged in qualifying transactions who wish to do their own conveyancing to do so by means of the network.

  (2)   The duty under sub-paragraph (1) does not extend to the provision of legal advice.

Presumption of authority

8   Where–

    (a)   a person who is authorised under a network access agreement to do so uses the network for the making of a disposition or contract, and

    (b)   the document which purports to effect the disposition or to be the contract–

       (i)   purports to be authenticated by him as agent, and

       (ii)   contains a statement to the effect that he is acting under the authority of his principal,

he shall be deemed, in favour of any other party, to be so acting.

Management of network transactions

9 (1) The registrar may use monitoring information for the purpose of managing network transactions and may, in particular, disclose such information to persons authorised to use the network, and authorise the further disclosure of information so disclosed, if he considers it is necessary or desirable to do so.

(2) The registrar may delegate his functions under sub-paragraph (1), subject to such conditions as he thinks fit.

(3) In sub-paragraph (1), "monitoring information" means information provided in pursuance of provision in a network access agreement included under paragraph 2(2)(c).

Supplementary

10 The registrar may provide, or arrange for the provision of, education and training in relation to the use of a land registry network.

11 (1) Power to make rules under paragraph 1, 2 or 3 is exercisable by the Lord Chancellor.

(2) Before making such rules, the Lord Chancellor must consult such persons as he considers appropriate.

(3) In making rules under paragraph 1 or 3(2)(a), the Lord Chancellor must have regard, in particular, to the need to secure–

(a) the confidentiality of private information kept on the network,

(b) competence in relation to the use of the network (in particular for the purpose of making changes), and

(c) the adequate insurance of potential liabilities in connection with use of the network.

12 In this Schedule–

'land registry network' means a network provided under section 92(1);

'network access agreement' has the meaning given by paragraph 1(2);

'network transaction' means a transaction carried on by means of a land registry network;

'qualifying transaction' means a transaction which–

(a) involves registration, and

(b) is capable of being effected electronically.

Schedule 6 Registration of Adverse Possessor

Right to apply for registration

1 (1) A person may apply to the registrar to be registered as the proprietor of a registered estate in land if he has been in adverse possession of the estate for the period of ten years ending on the date of the application.

(2) A person may also apply to the registrar to be registered as the proprietor of a registered estate in land if–

(a) he has in the period of six months ending on the date of the application ceased to be in adverse possession of the estate because of eviction by the registered proprietor, or a person claiming under the registered proprietor,

(b) on the day before his eviction he was entitled to make an application under sub-paragraph (1), and

(c) the eviction was not pursuant to a judgment for possession.

(3) However, a person may not make an application under this paragraph if–

    (a) he is a defendant in proceedings which involve asserting a right to possession of the land, or

    (b) judgment for possession of the land has been given against him in the last two years.

(4) For the purposes of sub-paragraph (1), the estate need not have been registered throughout the period of adverse possession.

Notification of application

2 (1) The registrar must give notice of an application under paragraph 1 to–

    (a) the proprietor of the estate to which the application relates,

    (b) the proprietor of any registered charge on the estate,

    (c) where the estate is leasehold, the proprietor of any superior registered estate,

    (d) any person who is registered in accordance with rules as a person to be notified under this paragraph, and

    (e) such other persons as rules may provide.

(2) Notice under this paragraph shall include notice of the effect of paragraph 4.

Treatment of application

3 (1) A person given notice under paragraph 2 may require that the application to which the notice relates be dealt with under paragraph 5.

(2) The right under this paragraph is exercisable by notice to the registrar given before the end of such period as rules may provide.

4 If an application under paragraph 1 is not required to be dealt with under paragraph 5, the applicant is entitled to be entered in the register as the new proprietor of the estate.

5 (1) If an application under paragraph 1 is required to be dealt with under this paragraph, the applicant is only entitled to be registered as the new proprietor of the estate if any of the following conditions is met.

(2) The first condition is that–

    (a) it would be unconscionable because of an equity by estoppel for the registered proprietor to seek to dispossess the applicant, and

    (b) the circumstances are such that the applicant ought to be registered as the proprietor.

(3) The second condition is that the applicant is for some other reason entitled to be registered as the proprietor of the estate.

(4) The third condition is that–

    (a) the land to which the application relates is adjacent to land belonging to the applicant,

    (b) the exact line of the boundary between the two has not been determined under rules under section 60,

    (c) for at least ten years of the period of adverse possession ending on the date of the application, the applicant (or any predecessor in title) reasonably believed that the land to which the application relates belonged to him, and

    (d) the estate to which the application relates was registered more than one year prior to the date of the application.

(5)   In relation to an application under paragraph 1(2), this paragraph has effect as if the reference in sub-paragraph (4)(c) to the date of the application were to the day before the date of the applicant's eviction.

Right to make further application for registration

6   (1)   Where a person's application under paragraph 1 is rejected, he may make a further application to be registered as the proprietor of the estate if he is in adverse possession of the estate from the date of the application until the last day of the period of two years beginning with the date of its rejection.

(2)   However, a person may not make an application under this paragraph if–

(a)   he is a defendant in proceedings which involve asserting a right to possession of the land,

(b)   judgment for possession of the land has been given against him in the last two years, or

(c)   he has been evicted from the land pursuant to a judgment for possession.

7   If a person makes an application under paragraph 6, he is entitled to be entered in the register as the new proprietor of the estate.

Restriction on applications

8   (1)   No one may apply under this Schedule to be registered as the proprietor of an estate in land during, or before the end of twelve months after the end of, any period in which the existing registered proprietor is for the purposes of the Limitation (Enemies and War Prisoners) Act 1945 (8 & 9 Geo. 6 c. 16)–

(a)   an enemy, or

(b)   detained in enemy territory.

(2)   No-one may apply under this Schedule to be registered as the proprietor of an estate in land during any period in which the existing registered proprietor is–

(a)   unable because of mental disability to make decisions about issues of the kind to which such an application would give rise, or

(b)   unable to communicate such decisions because of mental disability or physical impairment.

(3)   For the purposes of sub-paragraph (2), 'mental disability' means a disability or disorder of the mind or brain, whether permanent or temporary, which results in an impairment or disturbance of mental functioning.

(4)   Where it appears to the registrar that sub-paragraph (1) or (2) applies in relation to an estate in land, he may include a note to that effect in the register.

Effect of registration

9   (1)   Where a person is registered as the proprietor of an estate in land in pursuance of an application under this Schedule, the title by virtue of adverse possession which he had at the time of the application is extinguished.

(2)   Subject to sub-paragraph (3), the registration of a person under this Schedule as the proprietor of an estate in land does not affect the priority of any interest affecting the estate.

(3)   Subject to sub-paragraph (4), where a person is registered under this Schedule as the proprietor of an estate, the estate is vested in him free of any registered charge affecting the estate immediately before his registration.

(4) Sub-paragraph (3) does not apply where registration as proprietor is in pursuance of an application determined by reference to whether any of the conditions in paragraph 5 applies.

Apportionment and discharge of charges

10 (1) Where–

    (a) a registered estate continues to be subject to a charge notwithstanding the registration of a person under this Schedule as the proprietor, and

    (b) the charge affects property other than the estate,

the proprietor of the estate may require the chargee to apportion the amount secured by the charge at that time between the estate and the other property on the basis of their respective values.

(2) The person requiring the apportionment is entitled to a discharge of his estate from the charge on payment of–

    (a) the amount apportioned to the estate, and

    (b) the costs incurred by the chargee as a result of the apportionment.

(3) On a discharge under this paragraph, the liability of the chargor to the chargee is reduced by the amount apportioned to the estate.

(4) Rules may make provision about apportionment under this paragraph, in particular, provision about–

    (a) procedure,

    (b) valuation,

    (c) calculation of costs payable under sub-paragraph (2)(b), and

    (d) payment of the costs of the chargor.

Meaning of 'adverse possession'

11 (1) A person is in adverse possession of an estate in land for the purposes of this Schedule if, but for section 96, a period of limitation under section 15 of the Limitation Act 1980 (c. 58) would run in his favour in relation to the estate.

(2) A person is also to be regarded for those purposes as having been in adverse possession of an estate in land–

    (a) where he is the successor in title to an estate in the land, during any period of adverse possession by a predecessor in title to that estate, or

    (b) during any period of adverse possession by another person which comes between, and is continuous with, periods of adverse possession of his own.

(3) In determining whether for the purposes of this paragraph a period of limitation would run under section 15 of the Limitation Act 1980, there are to be disregarded–

    (a) the commencement of any legal proceedings, and

    (b) paragraph 6 of Schedule 1 to that Act.

Trusts

12 A person is not to be regarded as being in adverse possession of an estate for the purposes of this Schedule at any time when the estate is subject to a trust, unless the interest of each of the beneficiaries in the estate is an interest in possession.

Crown foreshore

13   (1)   Where–

(a)   a person is in adverse possession of an estate in land,

(b)   the estate belongs to Her Majesty in right of the Crown or the Duchy of Lancaster or to the Duchy of Cornwall, and

(c)   the land consists of foreshore,

paragraph 1(1) is to have effect as if the reference to ten years were to sixty years.

(2)   For the purposes of sub-paragraph (1), land is to be treated as foreshore if it has been foreshore at any time in the previous ten years.

(3)   In this paragraph, 'foreshore' means the shore and bed of the sea and of any tidal water, below the line of the medium high tide between the spring and neap tides.

Rentcharges

14   Rules must make provision to apply the preceding provisions of this Schedule to registered rentcharges, subject to such modifications and exceptions as the rules may provide.

Procedure

15   Rules may make provision about the procedure to be followed pursuant to an application under this Schedule.

Schedule 8 Indemnities

Entitlement

1   (1)   A person is entitled to be indemnified by the registrar if he suffers loss by reason of–

(a)   rectification of the register,

(b)   a mistake whose correction would involve rectification of the register,

(c)   a mistake in an official search,

(d)   a mistake in an official copy,

(e)   a mistake in a document kept by the registrar which is not an original and is referred to in the register,

(f)   the loss or destruction of a document lodged at the registry for inspection or safe custody,

(g)   a mistake in the cautions register, or

(h)   failure by the registrar to perform his duty under section 50.

(2)   For the purposes of sub-paragraph (1)(a)–

(a)   any person who suffers loss by reason of the change of title under section 62 is to be regarded as having suffered loss by reason of rectification of the register, and

(b)   the proprietor of a registered estate or charge claiming in good faith under a forged disposition is, where the register is rectified, to be regarded as having suffered loss by reason of such rectification as if the disposition had not been forged.

(3)   No indemnity under sub-paragraph (1)(b) is payable until a decision has been made about whether to alter the register for the purpose of correcting the mistake; and the loss suffered by reason of the mistake is to be determined in the light of that decision.

Mines and minerals

2   No indemnity is payable under this Schedule on account of–

    (a)   any mines or minerals, or

    (b)   the existence of any right to work or get mines or minerals,

unless it is noted in the register that the title to the registered estate concerned includes the mines or minerals.

Costs

3   (1)   In respect of loss consisting of costs or expenses incurred by the claimant in relation to the matter, an indemnity under this Schedule is payable only on account of costs or expenses reasonably incurred by the claimant with the consent of the registrar.

    (2)   The requirement of consent does not apply where–

       (a)   the costs or expenses must be incurred by the claimant urgently, and

       (b)   it is not reasonably practicable to apply for the registrar's consent.

    (3)   If the registrar approves the incurring of costs or expenses after they have been incurred, they shall be treated for the purposes of this paragraph as having been incurred with his consent.

4   (1)   If no indemnity is payable to a claimant under this Schedule, the registrar may pay such amount as he thinks fit in respect of any costs or expenses reasonably incurred by the claimant in connection with the claim which have been incurred with the consent of the registrar.

    (2)   The registrar may make a payment under sub-paragraph (1) notwithstanding the absence of consent if–

       (a)   it appears to him–

          (i)   that the costs or expenses had to be incurred urgently, and

          (ii)   that it was not reasonably practicable to apply for his consent, or

       (b)   he has subsequently approved the incurring of the costs or expenses.

Claimant's fraud or lack of care

5   (1)   No indemnity is payable under this Schedule on account of any loss suffered by a claimant–

       (a)   wholly or partly as a result of his own fraud, or

       (b)   wholly as a result of his own lack of proper care.

    (2)   Where any loss is suffered by a claimant partly as a result of his own lack of proper care, any indemnity payable to him is to be reduced to such extent as is fair having regard to his share in the responsibility for the loss.

    (3)   For the purposes of this paragraph any fraud or lack of care on the part of a person from whom the claimant derives title (otherwise than under a disposition for valuable consideration which is registered or protected by an entry in the register) is to be treated as if it were fraud or lack of care on the part of the claimant.

Valuation of estates etc.

6   Where an indemnity is payable in respect of the loss of an estate, interest or charge, the value of the estate, interest or charge for the purposes of the indemnity is to be regarded as not exceeding–

    (a)   in the case of an indemnity under paragraph 1(1)(a), its value immediately before rectification of the register (but as if there were to be no rectification), and

(b)   in the case of an indemnity under paragraph 1(1)(b), its value at the time when the mistake which caused the loss was made.

Determination of indemnity by court

7   (1)   A person may apply to the court for the determination of any question as to–

(a)   whether he is entitled to an indemnity under this Schedule, or

(b)   the amount of such an indemnity.

(2)   Paragraph 3(1) does not apply to the costs of an application to the court under this paragraph or of any legal proceedings arising out of such an application.

Time limits

8   For the purposes of the Limitation Act 1980 (c. 58)–

(a)   a liability to pay an indemnity under this Schedule is a simple contract debt, and

(b)   the cause of action arises at the time when the claimant knows, or but for his own default might have known, of the existence of his claim.

Interest

9   Rules may make provision about the payment of interest on an indemnity under this Schedule, including–

(a)   the circumstances in which interest is payable, and

(b)   the periods for and rates at which it is payable.

Recovery of indemnity by registrar

10   (1)   Where an indemnity under this Schedule is paid to a claimant in respect of any loss, the registrar is entitled (without prejudice to any other rights he may have)–

(a)   to recover the amount paid from any person who caused or substantially contributed to the loss by his fraud, or

(b)   for the purpose of recovering the amount paid, to enforce the rights of action referred to in sub-paragraph (2).

(2)   Those rights of action are–

(a)   any right of action (of whatever nature and however arising) which the claimant would have been entitled to enforce had the indemnity not been paid, and

(b)   where the register has been rectified, any right of action (of whatever nature and however arising) which the person in whose favour the register has been rectified would have been entitled to enforce had it not been rectified.

(3)   References in this paragraph to an indemnity include interest paid on an indemnity under rules under paragraph 9.

Interpretation

11   (1)   For the purposes of this Schedule, references to a mistake in something include anything mistakenly omitted from it as well as anything mistakenly included in it.

(2)   In this Schedule, references to rectification of the register are to alteration of the register which–

    (a)   involves the correction of a mistake, and

    (b)   prejudicially affects the title of a registered proprietor.

Schedule 12 Transition

Existing entries in the register

1   Nothing in the repeals made by this Act affects the validity of any entry in the register.

2   (1)   This Act applies to notices entered under the Land Registration Act 1925 (c. 21) as it applies to notices entered in pursuance of an application under section 34(2)(a).

    (2)   This Act applies to restrictions and inhibitions entered under the Land Registration Act 1925 as it applies to restrictions entered under this Act.

    (3)   Notwithstanding their repeal by this Act, sections 55 and 56 of the Land Registration Act 1925 shall continue to have effect so far as relating to cautions against dealings lodged under that Act.

    (4)   Rules may make provision about cautions against dealings entered under the Land Registration Act 1925.

    (5)   In this paragraph, references to the Land Registration Act 1925 include a reference to any enactment replaced (directly or indirectly) by that Act.

3   An entry in the register which, immediately before the repeal of section 144(1)(xi) of the Land Registration Act 1925, operated by virtue of rule 239 of the Land Registration Rules (S.I. 1925/1093) as a caution under section 54 of that Act shall continue to operate as such a caution.

Existing cautions against first registration

4   Notwithstanding the repeal of section 56(3) of the Land Registration Act 1925, that provision shall continue to have effect in relation to cautions against first registration lodged under that Act, or any enactment replaced (directly or indirectly) by that Act.

Pending applications

5   Notwithstanding the repeal of the Land Registration Act 1925, that Act shall continue to have effect in relation to an application for the entry in the register of a notice, restriction, inhibition or caution against dealings which is pending immediately before the repeal of the provision under which the application is made.

6   Notwithstanding the repeal of section 53 of the Land Registration Act 1925, subsections (1) and (2) of that section shall continue to have effect in relation to an application to lodge a caution against first registration which is pending immediately before the repeal of those provisions.

Former overriding interests

7   For the period of three years beginning with the day on which Schedule 1 comes into force, it has effect with the insertion after paragraph 14 of–

    '15. A right acquired under the Limitation Act 1980 before the coming into force of this Schedule.'

8   Schedule 3 has effect with the insertion after paragraph 2 of–

    '2A (1) An interest which, immediately before the coming into force of this Schedule, was an overriding interest under section 70(1)(g) of the Land Registration Act 1925 by virtue of a person's receipt of rents and profits, except for an interest of a person of whom inquiry was made before the disposition and who failed to disclose the right when he could reasonably have been expected to do so.

(2) Sub-paragraph (1) does not apply to an interest if at any time since the coming into force of this Schedule it has been an interest which, had the Land Registration Act 1925 (c. 21) continued in force, would not have been an overriding interest under section 70(1)(g) of that Act by virtue of a person's receipt of rents and profits.'

9　(1)　This paragraph applies to an easement or profit a prendre which was an overriding interest in relation to a registered estate immediately before the coming into force of Schedule 3, but which would not fall within paragraph 3 of that Schedule if created after the coming into force of that Schedule.

(2)　In relation to an interest to which this paragraph applies, Schedule 3 has effect as if the interest were not excluded from paragraph 3.

10　For the period of three years beginning with the day on which Schedule 3 comes into force, paragraph 3 of the Schedule has effect with the omission of the exception.

11　For the period of three years beginning with the day on which Schedule 3 comes into force, it has effect with the insertion after paragraph 14 of–

'15. A right under paragraph 18(1) of Schedule 12.'

12　Paragraph 1 of each of Schedules 1 and 3 shall be taken to include an interest which immediately before the coming into force of the Schedule was an overriding interest under section 70(1)(k) of the Land Registration Act 1925.

13　Paragraph 6 of each of Schedules 1 and 3 shall be taken to include an interest which immediately before the coming into force of the Schedule was an overriding interest under section 70(1)(i) of the Land Registration Act 1925 and whose status as such was preserved by section 19(3) of the Local Land Charges Act 1975 (c. 76) (transitional provision in relation to change in definition of 'local land charge').

Cautions against first registration

14　(1)　For the period of two years beginning with the day on which section 15 comes into force, it has effect with the following omissions–

(a)　in subsection (1), the words 'Subject to subsection (3),', and

(b)　subsection (3).

(2)　Any caution lodged by virtue of sub-paragraph (1) which is in force immediately before the end of the period mentioned in that sub-paragraph shall cease to have effect at the end of that period, except in relation to applications for registration made before the end of that period.

(3)　This paragraph does not apply to section 15 as applied by section 81.

15　(1)　As applied by section 81, section 15 has effect for the period of ten years beginning with the day on which it comes into force, or such longer period as rules may provide, with the omission of subsection (3)(a)(i).

(2)　Any caution lodged by virtue of sub-paragraph (1) which is in force immediately before the end of the period mentioned in that sub-paragraph shall cease to have effect at the end of that period, except in relation to applications for registration made before the end of that period.

16　This Act shall apply as if the definition of 'caution against first registration' in section 132 included cautions lodged under section 53 of the Land Registration Act 1925 (c. 21).

Applications under section 34 or 43 by cautioners

17　Where a caution under section 54 of the Land Registration Act 1925 is lodged in respect of a person's estate, right, interest or claim, he may only make an application under section 34 or 43 above in respect of that estate, right, interest or claim if he also applies to the registrar for the withdrawal of the caution.

Adverse possession

18 (1) Where a registered estate in land is held in trust for a person by virtue of section 75(1) of the Land Registration Act 1925 immediately before the coming into force of section 97, he is entitled to be registered as the proprietor of the estate.

(2) A person has a defence to any action for the possession of land (in addition to any other defence he may have) if he is entitled under this paragraph to be registered as the proprietor of an estate in the land.

(3) Where in an action for possession of land a court determines that a person is entitled to a defence under this paragraph, the court must order the registrar to register him as the proprietor of the estate in relation to which he is entitled under this paragraph to be registered.

(4) Entitlement under this paragraph shall be disregarded for the purposes of section 131(1).

(5) Rules may make transitional provision for cases where a rentcharge is held in trust under section 75(1) of the Land Registration Act 1925 immediately before the coming into force of section 97.

Indemnities

19 (1) Schedule 8 applies in relation to claims made before the commencement of that Schedule which have not been settled by agreement or finally determined by that time (as well as to claims for indemnity made after the commencement of that Schedule).

(2) But paragraph 3(1) of that Schedule does not apply in relation to costs and expenses incurred in respect of proceedings, negotiations or other matters begun before 27 April 1997.

Implied indemnity covenants on transfers of pre-1996 leases

20 (1) On a disposition of a registered leasehold estate by way of transfer, the following covenants are implied in the instrument effecting the disposition, unless the contrary intention is expressed–

(a) in the case of a transfer of the whole of the land comprised in the registered lease, the covenant in sub-paragraph (2), and

(b) in the case of a transfer of part of the land comprised in the lease–

(i) the covenant in sub-paragraph (3), and

(ii) where the transferor continues to hold land under the lease, the covenant in sub-paragraph (4).

(2) The transferee covenants with the transferor that during the residue of the term granted by the registered lease the transferee and the persons deriving title under him will–

(a) pay the rent reserved by the lease,

(b) comply with the covenants and conditions contained in the lease, and

(c) keep the transferor and the persons deriving title under him indemnified against all actions, expenses and claims on account of any failure to comply with paragraphs (a) and (b).

(3) The transferee covenants with the transferor that during the residue of the term granted by the registered lease the transferee and the persons deriving title under him will–

(a) where the rent reserved by the lease is apportioned, pay the rent apportioned to the part transferred,

(b)   comply with the covenants and conditions contained in the lease so far as affecting the part transferred, and

(c)   keep the transferor and the persons deriving title under him indemnified against all actions, expenses and claims on account of any failure to comply with paragraphs (a) and (b).

(4)   The transferor covenants with the transferee that during the residue of the term granted by the registered lease the transferor and the persons deriving title under him will–

(a)   where the rent reserved by the lease is apportioned, pay the rent apportioned to the part retained,

(b)   comply with the covenants and conditions contained in the lease so far as affecting the part retained, and

(c)   keep the transferee and the persons deriving title under him indemnified against all actions, expenses and claims on account of any failure to comply with paragraphs (a) and (b).

(5)   This paragraph does not apply to a lease which is a new tenancy for the purposes of section 1 of the Landlord and Tenant (Covenants) Act 1995 (c. 30).

XII.5. Land Registration Rules 2003 (extracts)[1] S.I. 2003/1417

SCHEDULE 3

rule 61

SCHEDULE 3 FORMS REFERRED TO IN RULE 206

Form 1 – Certificate as to execution of power of attorney (rule 61)

Date of power of attorney: ....

Donor of power of attorney:...

Donee of power of attorney:...

I/We ....

of...

certify that

- the power of attorney ('the power') is in existence [and is made under (*state statutory provision under which the power is made if applicable*)],

- the power is dated (*insert date*),

- I am/we are satisfied that the power is validly executed as a deed and authorises the attorney to execute the document on behalf of the donor of that power, and

- I/we hold [the instrument creating the power] *or* [a copy of the power by means of which its contents may be proved under section 3 of the Powers of Attorney Act 1971] *or* [a document which under section 4 of the Evidence and Powers of Attorney Act 1940 or section 7(3) of the Enduring Powers of Attorney Act 1985 is sufficient evidence of the contents of the power].

Signature of

conveyancer .... Date...........................

Form 2 – Statutory declaration/certificate as to non-revocation for powers more than 12 months old at the date of the disposition for which they are used (rule 62)

Date of power of attorney: ....

Donor of power of attorney:...

I/We...

of...

---

1. © Crown 2003. Schedules 3, 4, 6, and 9 are reproduced here.

do solemnly and sincerely [declare] *or* [certify] that at the time of completion of the ....
to me/us/my client/I/we/my client had no knowledge:

- of a revocation of the power, or

- of the death or bankruptcy of the donor or, if the donor is a corporate body, its winding up or dissolution, or

- of any incapacity of the donor where the power is not a valid enduring power, or

Where the power is in the form prescribed for an enduring power:

- that the power was not in fact a valid enduring power, or

- of an order or direction of the Court of Protection which revoked the power, or

- of the bankruptcy of the attorney, or

Where the power was given under section 9 of the Trusts of Land and Appointment of Trustees Act 1996:

- of an appointment of another trustee of the land in question, or

- of any other event which would have the effect of revoking the power, or

- of any lack of good faith on the part of the person(s) who dealt with the attorney, or

- that the attorney was not a person to whom the functions of the trustees could be delegated under section 9 of the Trusts of Land and Appointment of Trustees Act 1996, or

Where the power is expressed to be given by way of security:

- that the power was not in fact given by way of security, or

- of any revocation of the power with the consent of the attorney, or

- of any other event which would have had the effect of revoking the power.

Where a certificate is given:

Signature of
conveyancer .... Date...............................; or

Where a Statutory Declaration is made:

And I/we make this solemn declaration conscientiously believing the same to be true and by virtue of the provisions of the Statutory Declarations Act 1835.

Signature of
Declarant(s) .... Date...............................

DECLARED at..before me, a person entitled to administer oaths.

Name ....

Address...

Qualification..

Signature ....

Form 3 – Statutory declaration/certificate in support of power delegating trustees' functions to a beneficiary (rule 63)

Date of power of attorney: ....

Donor of power of
attorney:...

I/We ....

of..

do solemnly and sincerely [declare] *or* [certify] that at the time of completion of the ....
to me/us/my client/I/we/my client had no knowledge —

• of any lack of good faith on the part of the person(s) who dealt with the attorney, or

• that the attorney was not a person to whom the functions of the trustees could be delegated under section 9 of the Trusts of Land and Appointment of Trustees Act 1996.

Where a certificate is given :

Signature of
conveyancer .... Date.............................., or

Where a Statutory Declaration is made:

And I/we make this solemn declaration conscientiously believing the same to be true and by virtue of the provisions of the Statutory Declarations Act 1835.

Signature of
Declarant(s)... Date....................................

DECLARED at .... before me, a person entitled to administer oaths.

Name ....

Address...

Qualification...

Signature ....

Form 4 – Certificate as to Vesting in an Incumbent or other Ecclesiastical Corporation (rule 174)

(*Date*). This is to certify that the registered estate (*or* registered charge *or* that part of the registered estate) comprised in a [*describe the transfer*] under the provisions of [*state the Act or Measure*] (if such transfer were a conveyance under such Act or Measure), vests in the incumbent of .... (*or* the bishop of .... *as the case may be*) and his successors immediately (*or as the case may be*) upon the happening of the event following, namely, the [*state event*]

(To be sealed be the Church Commissioners)

Form 5 – The Like Certificate under rule 175

(*Date*). This is to certify that the [*describe Scheme, instrument or transfer, &c.*] operates to vest immediately (*or*, on publication in the 'London Gazette', *or at some subsequent period, as the case may be*), the registered estate (*or* registered charge *or* that part of the registered estate [*include description by reference to a plan or to the register if possible*]) in the [*describe the corporation or person*].

(To be sealed by the Church Commissioners)

Form 6 – Transfer where the Tenant for Life is already registered as proprietor (rule 186 and paragraph 5 of Schedule 7)

(*Date*). Pursuant to a trust deed of even date herewith, [made between A.B. (*name of tenant for life*) and C.D. and E.F. (*names of trustees of the Settlement*)], I, the said A.B., hereby declare as follows:

(a) The land is vested in me upon the trusts from time to time affecting it by virtue of the said trust deed.

[(b) The said C.D. and E.F. are the trustees of the Settlement.

(c) The following powers relating to land are expressly conferred by the said trust deed in extension of those conferred by the Settled Land Act 1925 (*fill in the powers, if any*).]

(d) I have the power to appoint new trustees of the Settlement.

(To be executed as a deed)

SCHEDULE 4

rule 91

STANDARD FORMS OF RESTRICTION

Form A (Restriction on dispositions by sole proprietor)

No disposition by a sole proprietor of the registered estate (except a trust corporation) under which capital money arises is to be registered unless authorised by an order of the court.

Form B (Dispositions by trustees – certificate required)

No disposition *[or specify details]* by the proprietors of the registered estate is to be registered unless they make a statutory declaration, or their conveyancer gives a certificate, that the disposition *[or specify details]* is in accordance with *[specify the disposition creating the trust]* or some variation thereof referred to in the declaration or certificate.

Form C (Dispositions by personal representatives – certificate required)

No disposition by *[name]*, the *[executor or administrator]* of *[name]* deceased, other than a transfer as personal representative, is to be registered unless he makes a statutory declaration, or his conveyancer gives a certificate, that the disposition is in accordance with the terms *[of the will of the deceased or the law relating to intestacy as varied by a deed dated specify details of deed or specify appropriate details]* or *[some variation or further variation]* thereof referred to in the declaration or certificate, or is necessary for the purposes of administration.

Form D (Parsonage, church or churchyard land)

No disposition of the registered estate is to be registered unless made in accordance with *[the Parsonages Measure 1938 (in the case of parsonage land) or the New Parishes Measure 1943 (in the case of church or churchyard land)]* or some other Measure or authority.

Form E (Non-exempt charity – certificate required)

No disposition by the proprietor of the registered estate to which section 36 or section 38 of the Charities Act 1993 applies is to be registered unless the instrument contains a certificate complying with section 37(2) or section 39(2) of that Act as appropriate.

Form F (Land vested in official custodian on trust for non-exempt charity – authority required)

No disposition executed by the trustees of *[charity]* in the name and on behalf of the proprietor shall be registered unless the transaction is authorised by an order of the court or of the Charity Commissioners, as required by section 22(3) of the Charities Act 1993.

Form G (Tenant for life as registered proprietor of settled land, where there are trustees of the settlement)

No disposition is to be registered unless authorised by the Settled Land Act 1925, or by any extension of those statutory powers in the settlement, and no disposition under which capital money arises is to be registered unless the money is paid to *(name)* of *(address)* and *(name)* of *(address)*, (the trustees of the settlement, who may be a sole trust corporation or, if individuals, must number at least two but not more than four) or into court.

Note – If applicable under the terms of the settlement, a further provision may be added that no transfer of the mansion house (shown on an attached plan or otherwise adequately described to enable it to be fully identified on the Ordnance Survey map or title plan) is to be registered without the consent of the named trustees or an order of the court.

Form H (Statutory owners as trustees of the settlement and registered proprietors of settled land)

No disposition is to be registered unless authorised by the Settled Land Act 1925, or by any extension of those statutory powers in the settlement, and, except where the sole proprietor is a trust corporation, no disposition under which capital money arises is to be registered unless the money is paid to at least two proprietors.

Note – This restriction does not apply where the statutory owners are not the trustees of the settlement.

Form I (Tenant for life as registered proprietor of settled land – no trustees of the settlement)

No disposition under which capital money arises, or which is not authorised by the Settled Land Act 1925 or by any extension of those statutory powers in the settlement, is to be registered.

Form J (Trustee in bankruptcy and beneficial interest – certificate required)

No disposition of the *[*registered estate *or* registered charge dated *[date]]* is to be registered without a certificate signed by the applicant for registration or his conveyancer that written notice of the disposition was given to *[name of trustee in bankruptcy]* (the trustee in bankruptcy of *[name of bankrupt person]*) at *[address for service]*.

Form K (Charging order affecting beneficial interest – certificate required)

No disposition of the *[*registered estate *or* registered charge dated *[date]]* is to be registered without a certificate signed by the applicant for registration or his conveyancer that written notice of the disposition was given to *[name of person with the benefit of the charging order]* at *[address for service]*, being the person with the benefit of *[an interim]* *[a final]* charging order on the beneficial interest of *(name of judgment debtor)* made by the *(name of court)* on *(date)* *(Court reference....)*.

Form L (Disposition by registered proprietor of a registered estate or proprietor of charge – certificate required)

No disposition *[or specify details]* of the registered estate [(other than a charge)] by the proprietor of the registered estate *[, or by the proprietor of any registered charge,]* is to be registered without a certificate

[signed by [name] of [address] (or *[his conveyancer] or specify appropriate details*))]

or

[signed on behalf of [name] of [address] by *[its secretary or conveyancer or specify appropriate details]]*

that the provisions of *[specify clause, paragraph or other particulars]* of *[specify details]* have been complied with.

Form M (Disposition by registered proprietor of registered estate or proprietor of charge – certificate of registered proprietor of specified title number required)

No disposition *[or specify details]* of the registered estate *[(other than a charge)]* by the proprietor of the registered estate *[or by the proprietor of any registered charge]* is to be registered without a certificate signed by the proprietor for the time being of the estate registered under title number *[title number]* [(or his conveyancer *or specify appropriate details*)] or, if appropriate, signed on such proprietor's behalf by *[its secretary or conveyancer or specify appropriate details]*, that the provisions of *[specify clause, paragraph or other particulars]* of *[specify details]* have been complied with.

Form N (Disposition by registered proprietor of registered estate or proprietor of charge – consent required)

No disposition *[or specify details]* of the registered estate *[(other than a charge)]* by the proprietor of the registered estate *[or by the proprietor of any registered charge]* is to be registered without a written consent

[signed by [name] of [address] (or *[his conveyancer] or specify appropriate details*))]

or

[signed on behalf of [name] of [address] by *[its secretary or conveyancer or specify appropriate details]]*.

Form O (Disposition by registered proprietor of registered estate or proprietor of charge – consent of registered proprietor of specified title number required)

No disposition *[or specify details]* of the registered estate *[(other than a charge)]* by the proprietor of the registered estate *[or by the proprietor of any registered charge]* is to be registered without a written consent signed by the proprietor for the time being of the estate registered under title number *[title number]*, [(or his conveyancer, *or specify appropriate details*)] or, if appropriate, signed on such proprietor's behalf by *[its secretary or conveyancer or specify appropriate details]*.

Form P (Disposition by registered proprietor of registered estate or proprietor of charge – consent of proprietor of specified charge required)

No disposition *[or specify details]* of the registered estate *[(other than a charge)]* by the proprietor of the registered estate *[or by the proprietor of any registered charge]* is to be registered without a written consent signed by the proprietor for the time being of the charge dated *[date]* in favour of *[chargee]* referred to in the charges register *[*(or his conveyancer *or specify appropriate details*)*]* or, if appropriate, signed on such proprietor's behalf by *[*its secretary or conveyancer *or specify appropriate details]*.

Form Q (Disposition by registered proprietor of registered estate or proprietor of charge – consent of personal representative required)

No disposition *[or specify details]* of *[*the registered estate *or* the registered charge dated *[date]* (referred to above)*]* by the proprietor *[*of the registered estate *or* of that registered charge*]* is to be registered after the death of *[name of the current proprietor(s) whose personal representative's consent will be required]* without the written consent of the personal representatives of the deceased.

Form R (Disposition by registered proprietor of registered estate or proprietor of charge – evidence of compliance with club rules required)

No disposition *[or specify details]* of the registered estate *[*(other than a charge)*]* by the proprietor of the registered estate *[*or by the proprietor of any registered charge*]* is to be registered unless authorised by the rules of the *[name of club]* of *[address]* as evidenced *[*by a resolution of its members *or* by a certificate signed by its secretary or conveyancer *[or specify appropriate details]]*.

Form S (Disposition by proprietor of charge – certificate of compliance required)

No disposition *[or specify details]* by the proprietor of the registered charge dated *[date]* (referred to above) is to be registered without a certificate

*[*signed by *[name]* of *[address]* (or *[*his conveyancer*]* or specify appropriate details)*]*

or

*[*signed on behalf of *[name]* of *[address]* by *[*its secretary or conveyancer *or specify appropriate details]*,

that the provisions of *[specify clause, paragraph or other particulars]* of *[specify details]* have been complied with.

Form T (Disposition by proprietor of charge – consent required)

No disposition *[or specify details]* by the proprietor of the registered charge dated *[date]* (referred to above) is to be registered without a written consent

*[*signed by *[name]* of *[address]* (or *[*his conveyancer*]* or specify appropriate details)*]*

or

*[*signed on behalf of *[name]* of *[address]* by *[*its secretary or conveyancer *or specify appropriate details]*.

Form U (Section 37 of the Housing Act 1985)

No transfer or lease by the proprietor of the registered estate or by the proprietor of any registered charge is to be registered unless a certificate by *[specify relevant local authority]* is given that the transfer or lease is made in accordance with section 37 of the Housing Act 1985.

Form V (Section 157 of the Housing Act 1985)

No transfer or lease by the proprietor of the registered estate or by the proprietor of any registered charge is to be registered unless a certificate by *[specify relevant local authority or housing association etc]* is given that the transfer or lease is made in accordance with section 157 of the Housing Act 1985.

Form W (Paragraph 4 of Schedule 9A to the Housing Act 1985)

No disposition (except a transfer) of a qualifying dwellinghouse (except to a qualifying person or persons) is to be registered without the consent of the Secretary of State given under section 171D(2) of the Housing Act 1985 as it applies by virtue of the Housing (Preservation of Right to Buy) Regulations 1993.

Form X (Section 81 or 133 of the Housing Act 1988 or section 173 of the Local Government and Housing Act 1989)

No disposition by the proprietor of the registered estate or in exercise of the power of sale or leasing in any registered charge (except an exempt disposal as defined by section 81(8) of the Housing Act 1988) is to be registered without the consent of the Secretary of State to that disposition under the provisions of (*as appropriate* [section 81 of that Act] *or* [section 133 of that Act] *or* [section 173 of the Local Government and Housing Act 1989]).

Form Y (Section 13 of the Housing Act 1996)

No transfer or lease by the proprietor of the registered estate or by the proprietor of any registered charge is to be registered unless a certificate by *[specify relevant registered social landlord]* is given that the transfer or lease is made in accordance with section 13 of the Housing Act 1996.

Form AA (freezing order on the registered estate)

Under an order of the *(name of court)* made on *(date)* *(claim no)* no disposition by the proprietor of the registered estate is to be registered except under a further order of the Court.

Form BB (freezing order on charge)

Under an order of the *(name of court)* made on *(date)* *(claim no)* no disposition by the proprietor of the charge is to be registered except under a further order of the Court.

Form CC (application for freezing order on the registered estate)

Pursuant to an application made on *(date)* to the *(name of court)* for a freezing order to be made under *(statutory provision)* no disposition by the proprietor of the registered estate is to be registered except with the consent of *(name of the person applying)* or under a further order of the Court.

Form DD (application for freezing order on charge)

Pursuant to an application made on *(date)* to the *(name of the court)* for a freezing order to be made under *(statutory provision)* no disposition by the proprietor of the registered charge dated *(date)* (referred to above) is to be registered except with the consent of *(name of the person applying)* or under a further order of the Court.

Form EE (restraint order or interim receiving order on the registered estate)

Under (*as appropriate* [a restraint order] *or* [an interim receiving order]) made under (*statutory provision*) on (*date*) (*claim no*) no disposition by the proprietor of the registered estate is to be registered without the consent of (*name of the prosecutor or other person who applied for the order*) or under a further order of the Court.

Form FF (restraint order or interim receiving order on charge)

Under (*as appropriate* [a restraint order] *or* [an interim receiving order]) made under (*statutory provision*) on (*date*) (*claim no*) no disposition by the proprietor of the registered charge dated (*date*) (referred to above) is to be registered without the consent of (*name of the prosecutor or other person who applied for the order*) or under a further order of the Court.

Form GG (application for restraint order or interim receiving order on the registered estate)

Pursuant to an application for (*as appropriate* [a restraint order] *or* [an interim receiving order]) to be made under (*statutory provision*) and under any order made as a result of that application, no disposition by the proprietor of the registered estate is to be registered without the consent of (*name of the prosecutor or other person applying*) or under a further order of the Court.

Form HH (application for restraint order or interim receiving order on charge)

Pursuant to an application for (*as appropriate* [a restraint order] *or* [an interim receiving order]) to be made under (*statutory provision*) and under any order made as a result of that application no disposition by the proprietor of the registered charge dated (*date*) (referred to above) is to be registered without the consent of (*name of the prosecutor or other person applying*) or under a further order of the Court.

SCHEDULE 6

rule 145

INFORMATION TO BE INCLUDED IN CERTAIN RESULTS OF OFFICIAL SEARCHES

Part 1

INFORMATION TO BE INCLUDED IN THE RESULT OF AN OFFICIAL SEARCH OF THE INDEX MAP

A.   The date and time of the official search certificate.

B.   A description of the land searched.

C.   The reference (if any) of the applicant or the person to whom the search is being sent: limited to 25 characters including spaces.

D.   Whether there is :

   (i)   a pending application for first registration (other than of title to a relating franchise).

   (ii)   a pending application for a caution against first registration (other than where the subject of the caution is a relating franchise).

   (iii) a registered estate in land.

   (iv)   a registered rentcharge.

(v)   a registered profit a prendre in gross.

(vi) a registered affecting franchise, or

(vii) a caution against first registration (other than where the subject of the caution is a relating franchise).

and, if there is such a registered estate or caution, the title number.

Part 2
INFORMATION TO BE INCLUDED IN THE RESULT OF AN OFFICIAL SEARCH OF THE INDEX OF RELATING FRANCHISES AND MANORS

A.   The date and time of the official search certificate.

B.   The administrative area(s) searched.

C.   The reference (if any) of the applicant or the person to whom the search is being sent: limited to 25 characters including spaces.

D.   Whether there is a verbal description of:

(i)   a pending application for first registration of title to a relating franchise.

(ii) a pending application for a caution against first registration where the subject of the caution is a relating franchise.

(iii) a registered franchise which is a relating franchise.

(iv) a registered manor, or

(v)   a caution against first registration where the subject of the caution is a relating franchise.

and the title numbers of any such registered estates and cautions arranged by administrative area.

Part 3
INFORMATION TO BE INCLUDED IN THE RESULT OF AN OFFICIAL SEARCH OF AN INDIVIDUAL REGISTER OF A REGISTERED TITLE

A.   The title number.

B.   The date and time of the official search certificate.

C.   If the official search certificate is part of a registered title, a short description of the property or plot number on the approved estate plan.

D.   The applicant's name.

E.   The applicant's, or his agent's, reference (if any): limited to 25 characters including spaces.

F.   Details of any relevant adverse entries made in the individual register since the end of the day specified in the application as the search from date.

G.   Notice of the entry of any relevant pending application affecting the registered title entered on the day list (other than an application to designate a document as an exempt information document under rule 136).

H.   Notice of the entry of any relevant official search the priority period of which has not expired.

I.   If the official search is with priority, the date and time at which the priority expires.

J.   If the official search is without priority, a statement that the certificate will not confer on the applicant priority for any registrable disposition.

Part 4

INFORMATION TO BE INCLUDED IN THE RESULT OF AN OFFICIAL SEARCH
WITH PRIORITY IN RELATION TO A PENDING APPLICATION FOR FIRST
REGISTRATION

A.   The title number allotted to the pending application for first registration.

B.   The date and time of the official search certificate.

C.   If the official search is of part, a short description of the property.

D.   The applicant's name.

E.   The applicant's, or his agent's, reference (if any): limited to 25 characters including spaces.

F.   The full name of the person who has applied for first registration.

G.   The date and time at which the pending application for first registration was entered on the day list.

H.   Notice of the entry of any relevant pending application affecting the estate sought to be registered and entered on the day list subsequent to the date and time at which the pending application for first registration was entered on the day list (other than an application to designate a document as an exempt information document under rule 136).

I.   Notice of the entry of any relevant official search the priority period of which has not expired affecting the pending application for first registration.

J.   The date and time at which priority expires.

Part 5

INFORMATION TO BE INCLUDED IN THE RESULT OF AN OFFICIAL SEARCH
BY A MORTGAGEE FOR THE PURPOSE OF SECTION 56(3) OF THE FAMILY LAW
ACT 1996

A.   The title number.

B.   The date and time of the official search certificate.

C.   The mortgagee's name.

D.   The mortgagee's, or his agent's, reference (if any): limited to 25 characters including spaces.

E.   Whether, at the date of the official search certificate, a matrimonial home rights notice or matrimonial home rights caution has been registered against the registered title searched and if so the date of registration and the name of the person in whose favour the notice or caution was registered.

F.   Whether there is a pending application for the entry of a matrimonial home rights notice entered on the day list.

SCHEDULE 9

rule 206(3)

FORMS OF EXECUTION

Note: All dispositions other than assents must be executed as a deed. In the case of an assent the words 'as a deed' may be omitted.

A. Where the instrument is to be executed personally by an individual:

Signed as a deed by *(full name of individual)* in the presence of:

> *Signature*

Signature of witness...

Name (in BLOCK CAPITALS)

....

Address..

....

B. Where the instrument is to be executed by an individual directing another to sign on his behalf:

Signed as a deed by *(full name of person signing)* at the direction and on behalf of *(full name of individual)* in [his][her] presence and in the presence of:

> *Sign here the name of the individual and your own name,*
> *eg:* John Smith by Jane Brown

Signature of first witness...

Name (in BLOCK CAPITALS)

....

Address..

....

Signature of second witness..

Name (in BLOCK CAPITALS) ....

Address..

....

C. Where the instrument is to be executed by a company registered under the Companies Acts, or an unregistered company, using its common seal:

The common seal of *(name of company)* was affixed in the presence of:

> *Common seal of company*

....

Signature of director

....

Signature of secretary

D. Where the instrument is to be executed by a company registered under the Companies Acts, or an unregistered company, without using a common seal:

Signed as a deed by *(name of company)*
acting by [a director and its secretary]
[two directors]

Signature
Director
Signature
[Secretary] [Director]

E. Where the instrument is to be executed on behalf of an overseas company without using a common seal:

Signed as a deed on behalf of *(name of company)*, a company incorporated in *(territory)*, by *(full name(s) of person(s) signing)*, being [a] person[s] who, in accordance with the laws of that territory, [is][are] acting under the authority of the company.

Signature(s)
Authorised [signatory] [signatories]

Note: In the case of an overseas company having a common seal, the form of execution appropriate to a company registered under the Companies Acts may be used, with such adaptations as may be necessary, in place of execution by a person or persons acting under the authority of the company.

F. Where the instrument is to be executed by a limited liability partnership incorporated under the Limited Liability Partnerships Act 2000, without using a common seal:

Signed as a deed by *(name of limited liability partnership)* acting by two members

Signature
Member
Signature
Member

XII.6. Land Registration Fees Order 2003 (S.I. 2003/2092)

2003 No. 2092

LAND REGISTRATION, ENGLAND AND WALES

The Land Registration Fee Order 2003

Made 11th August 2003
Coming into force in accordance with article 1(1)

The Lord Chancellor, with the advice and assistance of the Rule Committee appointed in pursuance of section 127 of the Land Registration Act 2002[(a)], and the Treasury, in exercise of the powers conferred on them by section 102 of that Act and sections 2 and 3 of the Public Offices Fees Act 1879[(b)] hereby make and concur in the following Order:

PART 1

General

Citation, commencement and interpretation

1. (1) This Order may be cited as the Land Registration Fee Order 2003 and shall come into force on the day that section 1 of the Act comes into force.

(2) In this Order unless the context otherwise requires:

'account holder' means a person or firm holding a credit account,

'the Act' means the Land Registration Act 2002,

'charge' includes a sub-charge,

'credit account' means an account authorised by the registrar under article 15(1),

'large area application' is as defined in article 6(1),

'large scale application' is as defined in article 6(1),

'premium' means the amount or value of any monetary consideration given by the lessee as part of the same transaction in which a lease is granted by way of fine, premium or otherwise, but, where a registered leasehold estate of substantially the same land is surrendered on the grant of a new lease, the premium for the new lease shall not include the value of the surrendered lease,

'profit' means a profit à prendre in gross,

'monetary consideration' means a consideration in money or money's worth (other than a nominal consideration or a consideration consisting solely of a covenant to pay money owing under a mortgage),

(a) 2002 c.9.
(b) 1879 c.58.

'the rules' means the Land Registration Rules 2003[(c)] and a rule referred to by number means the rule so numbered in the rules,

'rent' means the largest amount of annual rent the lease reserves within the first five years of its term that can be quantified at the time an application to register the lease is made,

'Scale 1' means Scale 1 in Schedule 1,

'Scale 2' means Scale 2 in Schedule 2,

'scale fee' means a fee payable in accordance with a scale set out in Schedule 1 or 2 whether or not reduced in accordance with article 2(6),

'scale fee application' means an application which attracts a scale fee, or which would attract such a fee but for the operation of article 6,

'Schedule' means a Schedule to this Order,

'share', in relation to land, means an interest in that land under a trust of land,

'surrender' includes a surrender not made by deed,

'voluntary application' means an application for first registration (other than for the registration of title to a rentcharge, a franchise or a profit) which is not made wholly or in part pursuant to section 4 of the Act (when title must be registered).

(3) Expressions used in this Order have, unless the contrary intention appears, the meaning which they bear in the rules.

PART 2

Scale fees

Applications for first registration and applications for registration of a lease by an original lessee

2. (1) The fee for an application for first registration is payable under Scale 1 on the value of the estate in land comprised in the application assessed under article 7 unless the application is:

    (a) for the registration of title to a lease by the original lessee or his personal representative, where paragraph (2) applies,

    (b) for the first registration of a rentcharge, where paragraph (4) applies,

    (c) for the first registration of a franchise or a profit, where paragraph (5) applies,

    (d) a voluntary application, where paragraph (6) applies, or

    (e) a large scale application or a large area application, where article 6 applies.

(2) The fee for an application for the registration of title to a lease (whether or not it is a registrable disposition) by the original lessee or his personal representative is payable under Scale 1:

    (a) on an amount equal to the sum of the premium and the rent, or

    (b) where:

        (i) there is no premium and;

        (ii) either there is no rent or the rent cannot be quantified at the time the application is made,

(c) S.I. 2003/1447.

on the value of the lease assessed under article 7 subject to a minimum fee of £40, unless either of the circumstances in paragraph (3) applies.

(3) Paragraph (2) shall not apply if the application is:

   (a) a voluntary application, where paragraph (6) applies, or

   (b) a large scale application or a large area application, where article 6 applies.

(4) The fee for an application for the first registration of a rentcharge is £40.

(5) The fee for an application for the first registration of a franchise or a profit is payable under Scale 1 on the value of the franchise or the profit assessed under article 7.

(6) The fee for a voluntary application is the fee which would otherwise be payable under paragraphs (1) and (2) for applications to which those paragraphs apply reduced by 25 per cent and, where the reduced fee would be a figure which includes pence, the fee must be adjusted to the nearest £10.

Transfers of registered estates for monetary consideration, etc.

3. (1) Subject to paragraphs (2), (3) and (4), the fee for an application for the registration of:

   (a) a transfer of a registered estate for monetary consideration,

   (b) a transfer for the purpose of giving effect to a disposition for monetary consideration of a share in a registered estate,

   (c) a surrender of a registered leasehold estate for monetary consideration, other than a surrender to which paragraph (3) of Schedule 4 applies,

is payable under Scale 1 on the amount or value of the consideration.

(2) Paragraph (1) shall not apply if the application is:

   (a) a large scale application, where article 6 applies, or

   (b) for the registration of a transfer of a matrimonial home made pursuant to an order of the court, where article 4(1)(h) applies.

(3) Where a sale and sub-sale of a registered estate are made by separate deeds of transfer, a separate fee is payable for each deed of transfer.

(4) Where a single deed of transfer gives effect to a sale and a sub-sale of the same registered estate a single fee is assessed upon the greater of the monetary consideration given by the purchaser and the monetary consideration given by the sub-purchaser.

(5) The fee for an application to cancel an entry in the register of notice of an unregistered lease which has determined is payable under Scale 1 on the value of the lease immediately before its determination.

Transfers otherwise than for monetary consideration, etc.

4. (1) Unless the application is a large scale application (where article 6 applies), the fee for an application for the registration of:

   (a) a transfer of a registered estate otherwise than for monetary consideration (unless paragraph (2) applies),

   (b) a surrender of a registered leasehold estate otherwise than for monetary consideration,

   (c) a transmission of a registered estate on death or bankruptcy,

   (d) an assent of a registered estate (including a vesting assent),

   (e) an appropriation of a registered estate,

(f)   a vesting order or declaration to which section 27(5) of the Act applies,

(g)   an alteration of the register (unless paragraph (3) applies), or

(h)   a transfer of a matrimonial home (being a registered estate) made pursuant to an order of the Court, is payable under Scale 2 on the value of the registered estate which is the subject of the application, assessed under article 7, but after deducting from it the amount secured on the registered estate by any charge subject to which the registration takes effect.

(2)   Where a transfer of a registered estate otherwise than for monetary consideration is for the purpose of giving effect to the disposition of a share in a registered estate the fee for an application for its registration is payable under Scale 2 on the value of that share.

(3)   In any application for alteration of the register:

     (a)   if it appears to the registrar that the fee is excessive, he may reduce it, and

     (b)   if it appears to him unreasonable that the applicant should pay a fee, he may waive it.

Charges of registered estates

5.   (1)   The fee for an application for the registration of a charge is payable under Scale 2 on the amount of the charge assessed under article 8 unless it is an application to which paragraphs (2), (3) or (4) apply.

(2)   No fee is payable for an application to register a charge lodged with or before the completion of a scale fee application ('the primary application') that will result in the chargor being registered as proprietor of the registered land included in the charge unless:

     (a)   the charge includes a registered estate which is not included in the primary application, where paragraph (4) applies, or

     (b)   the primary application is a voluntary application, in which case this paragraph shall apply only if the application to register the charge accompanies the primary application.

(3)   No fee is to be paid for an application to register a charge made by a predecessor in title of the applicant that is lodged with or before completion of an application for first registration of the estate included in the charge.

(4)   Where a charge also includes a registered estate which is not included in the primary application any fee payable under Scale 2 is to be assessed on an amount calculated as follows:

$$\frac{\text{Value of the additional property}}{\text{Value of all the property included in the charge}} \times \text{Amount secured by the charge}$$

(5)   The fee for an application for the registration of:

     (a)   the transfer of a registered charge for monetary consideration, or

     (b)   a transfer for the purpose of giving effect to the disposition for monetary consideration of a share in a registered charge,

is payable under Scale 2 on the amount or value of the consideration.

(6)   The fee for an application for the registration of the transfer of a registered charge otherwise than for monetary consideration is payable under Scale 2 on:

     (a)   the amount secured by the registered charge at the time of the transfer or,

     (b)   where the transfer relates to more than one charge, the aggregate of the amounts secured by the registered charges at the time of the transfer.

(7) The fee for an application for the registration of a transfer for the purpose of giving effect to a disposition otherwise than for monetary consideration of a share in a registered charge is payable under Scale 2 on:

    (a) the proportionate part of the amount secured by the registered charge at the time of the transfer or,

    (b) where the transfer relates to more than one charge, the proportionate part of the aggregate of the amounts secured by the registered charges at the time of the transfer.

(8) This article takes effect subject to article 6 (large scale applications).

Large scale applications, etc.

6. (1) In this article:

    (a) 'large area application' means an application for first registration which relates to land having a total area exceeding 100 hectares,

    (b) 'large scale application' means a scale fee application which relates to 20 or more land units, other than:

        (i) a large area application, or

        (ii) a low value application,

    (c) 'low value application' means a scale fee application, other than an application for first registration, where the value of the land or the amount of the charge to which it relates (as the case may be) does not exceed £30,000,

    (d) 'land unit' means

        (i) the land registered under a single title number, or

        (ii) on a first registration application, a separate area of land not adjoining any other unregistered land affected by the same application.

(2) Unless the application is one in respect of a charge lodged with another application and falls within article 5(2), the fee for a large scale application is the greater of:

    (a) the scale fee, and

    (b) a fee calculated on the following basis:

        (i) where the application relates to not more than 500 land units, £10 for each land unit, or

        (ii) where the application relates to more than 500 land units, £5,000 plus £5 for each land unit in excess of 500, up to a maximum of £40,000.

(3) The fee for a large area application is the Scale 1 fee and if the registrar considers that the cost of the work involved in dealing with the application would substantially exceed the scale fee otherwise payable, he may direct that an additional fee be paid but the fee is not to exceed the cost of the work involved.

(4) If a large area application or a large scale application is a voluntary application, the fee payable under this article is reduced in accordance with article 2(6).

PART 3

Valuation

Valuation (first registration and registered estates)

7. (1) For the purposes of this Order, the value of the estate in land, franchise, profit or share is the maximum amount for which, in the registrar's opinion, it could be sold in the open market free from any charge:

   (a) in the case of a surrender, at the date immediately before the surrender,

   (b) in any other case, at the date of the application.

   (2) As evidence of the amount referred to in paragraph (1), the registrar may require a written statement signed by the applicant or his conveyancer or by any other person who, in the registrar's opinion, is competent to make the statement.

   (3) Where an application for first registration is made on:

   (a) the purchase of a leasehold estate by the reversioner,

   (b) the purchase of a reversion by the leaseholder, or

   (c) any other like occasion,

   and an unregistered interest is determined, the value of the land is the combined value of the reversionary and determined interests assessed in accordance with paragraphs (1) and (2).

Valuation (charges)

8. (1) On an application for registration of a charge, the amount of the charge is:

   (a) where the charge secures a fixed amount, that amount,

   (b) where the charge secures further advances and the maximum amount that can be advanced or owed at any one time is limited, that amount,

   (c) where the charge secures further advances and the total amount that can be advanced or owed at any one time is not limited, the value of the property charged,

   (d) where the charge is by way of additional or substituted security or by way of guarantee, an amount equal to the lesser of:

   (i)   the amount secured or guaranteed, and

   (ii) the value of the property charged,

   (e) where the charge secures an obligation or liability which is contingent upon the happening of a future event ('the obligation'), and is not a charge to which sub-paragraph (d) applies, an amount equal to:

   (i)   the maximum amount or value of the obligation, or

   (ii) if that maximum amount is greater than the value of the property charged, or is not limited by the charge, or cannot be calculated at the time of the application, the value of the property charged.

   (2) Where a charge of a kind referred to in paragraph (1)(a) or (1)(b) is secured on unregistered land or other property as well as on a registered estate or registered charge, the fee is payable on an amount calculated as follows:

$$\frac{\text{Value of the registered estate or registered charge}}{\text{Value of all the property charged}} \times \text{Amount of the charge}$$

(3) Where one deed contains two or more charges made by the same chargor to secure the same debt, the deed is to be treated as a single charge, and the fee for registration of the charge is to be paid on the lesser of:

    (a) the amount of the whole debt, and

    (b) an amount equal to the value of the property charged.

(4) Where one deed contains two or more charges to secure the same debt not made by the same chargor, the deed is to be treated as a separate single charge by each of the chargors and a separate fee is to be paid for registration of the charge by each chargor on the lesser of:

    (a) the amount of the whole debt, and

    (b) an amount equal to the value of the property charged by that chargor.

(5) In this article 'value of the property charged' means the value of the registered estate or the amount of the registered charge or charges affected by the application to register the charge, less the amount secured by any prior registered charges.

PART 4

Fixed Fees and Exemptions

Fixed fees

9. (1) Subject to paragraphs (2), (3) and (4), the fees for the applications and services specified in Schedule 3 shall be those set out in that Schedule.

    (2) The fee for an application under rule 140 shall be the aggregate of the fees payable for the services provided, save that the maximum fee for any one application shall be £200.

    (3) The registrar may, if he thinks fit, waive any fee or part of a fee or any category of fee payable under this article.

    (4) If:

        (a) having regard to the extent of the land to which an application for a search of the index map relates, or

        (b) in an application for the determination of the exact line of a boundary under rule 118,

    the registrar considers that the cost of the work involved in dealing with that application would substantially exceed any fee otherwise payable under this Order, such additional fee shall be payable as the registrar shall direct as appropriate to cover the excess cost of the work involved.

    (5) Notification of the additional fee under paragraph (4) shall be given to the applicant and, if he then elects to withdraw his application, no fee shall be payable.

Exemptions

10. No fee is payable in respect of any of the applications and services specified in Schedule 4.

PART 5

General and Administrative Provisions

Refund of fees

11. (1) Where an amount exceeding the fee payable under this Order has been paid, there shall be refunded any excess remaining after the deduction, if the registrar so directs, of an amount not exceeding £10 in respect of the cost of repayment.

(2) Where the person or firm lodging the application is an account holder, any amount to be refunded under paragraph (1) may at the discretion of the registrar be repaid to the account holder by crediting the amount to the account holder's credit account.

(3) If any application is cancelled or withdrawn no part of the fee shall be refunded unless:

(a) the registrar so directs, or

(b) article 9(5) applies.

Cost of surveys, advertisements and special enquiries

12. Unless the registrar directs otherwise, the applicant is to meet the costs of any survey, advertisement or other special enquiry that the registrar requires to be made or published in dealing with an application.

Applications not otherwise referred to

13. Upon an application for which no other fee is payable under this Order and which is not exempt from payment, there shall be paid such fee (if any) not exceeding a fee in accordance with Scale 1 on the value of the registered estate or on the amount of the charge as the registrar shall direct having regard to the work involved.

Method of payment

14. (1) Fees payable under this Order shall be collected in money.

(2) Except where the registrar otherwise permits, every fee shall be paid by means of a cheque or postal order crossed and made payable to the Land Registry.

(3) Where there is an agreement with the applicant, a fee may be paid by direct debit to such bank account of the Land Registry as the registrar may from time to time direct.

(4) Where the amount of the fee payable on an application is immediately quantifiable, the fee shall be payable on delivery of the application.

(5) Where the amount of the fee payable on an application is not immediately quantifiable, the applicant shall pay the sum of £40 towards the fee when the application is made and shall lodge at the same time an undertaking to pay on demand the balance of the fee due, if any.

(6) Where an outline application is made, the fee payable shall be the fee payable under paragraph (9) of Part 1 of Schedule 3 in addition to the fee otherwise payable under this Order.

Credit accounts

15. (1) Any person or firm may, if authorised by the registrar, use a credit account in accordance with this article for the payment of fees for applications and services of such kind as the registrar shall from time to time direct.

(2) To enable the registrar to consider whether or not a person or firm applying to use a credit account may be so authorised, that person or firm shall supply the registrar with such information and evidence as the registrar may require to satisfy him of the person or firm's fitness to hold a credit account and the ability of the person or firm to pay any amounts which may become due from time to time under a credit account.

(3) To enable the registrar to consider from time to time whether or not an account holder may continue to be authorised to use a credit account, the account holder shall supply the registrar, when requested to do so, with such information and evidence as the registrar may require to satisfy him of the account holder's continuing fitness to hold a credit account and the continuing ability of the account holder to pay any amounts which may become due from time to time under the account holder's credit account.

(4) Where an account holder makes an application where credit facilities are available to him, he may make a request, in such manner as the registrar directs, for the appropriate fee to be debited to the account holder's credit account, but the registrar shall not be required to accept such a request where the amount due on the account exceeds the credit limit applicable to the credit account, or would exceed it if the request were to be accepted.

(5) Where an account holder makes an application where credit facilities are available to him, and the application is accompanied neither by a fee nor a request for the fee to be debited to his account, the registrar may debit the fee to his account.

(6) A statement of account shall be sent by the registrar to each account holder at the end of each calendar month or such other interval as the registrar shall direct.

(7) The account holder must pay any sums due on his credit account before the date and in the manner specified by the registrar.

(8) The registrar may at any time and without giving reasons terminate or suspend any or all authorisations given under paragraph (1).

(9) In this article 'credit limit' in relation to a credit account authorised for use under paragraph (1) means the maximum amount (if any) which is to be due on the account at any time, as notified by the registrar to the account holder from time to time, by means of such communication as the registrar considers appropriate.

Signed by the authority of the Lord Chancellor

Dated   Parliamentary Secretary
                                          Department for Constitutional Affairs

                                          Two of the Lord Commissioners
Dated   of Her Majesty's Treasury

SCHEDULE 1

Articles 2, 3, 13 & 14

SCALE 1

NOTE 1: Where the amount or value is a figure which includes pence, it may be rounded down to the nearest £1.
NOTE 2: The third column, which sets out the reduced fee payable where article 2(6) (voluntary registration: reduced fees) applies, is not part of the scale.

Amount or value £	Fee £	Reduced fee where article 2(6) (voluntary registration: reduced fees) applies £
0–50,000	40	30
50,001–80,000	60	45
80,001–100,000	100	75
100,001–200,000	150	110
200,001–500,000	250	190
500,001–1,000,000	450	340
1,000,001 and over	750	560

SCHEDULE 2

Articles 4, 5 & 14

SCALE 2

NOTE: Where the amount or value is a figure which includes pence, it may be rounded down to the nearest £1.

Amount or value £	Fee £
0–100,000	40
100,001–200,000	50
200,001–500,000	70
500,001–1,000,000	100
1,000,001 and over	200

SCHEDULE 3

Articles 9 & 14

PART 1

FIXED FEE APPLICATIONS

Fee

(1) To register:
- (a) a standard form of restriction contained in Schedule 4 of the rules, or
- (b) a notice (other than a notice to which section 117(2)(b) of the Act applies), or
- (c) a new or additional beneficiary of a unilateral notice, or
- (d) an entry for which no other provision is made by this Order and for which the registrar considers a fee should be paid:
  - – total fee for up to three registered titles £40
  - – additional fee for each subsequent registered title £20

Provided that no such fee is payable if, in relation to each registered title affected, the application is accompanied by a scale fee application or another application which attracts a fee under this paragraph.

(2) To register a restriction in a form not contained in Schedule 4 of the rules – for each registered title £80

(3) To register a caution against first registration (other than a caution to which section 117(2)(a) of the Act applies) £40

(4) To alter a cautions register – for each individual cautions register £40

(5) To close or partly close a registered leasehold or a registered rentcharge title other than on surrender – for each registered title closed or partly closed £40

Provided that no such fee is payable if the application is accompanied by a scale fee application.

(6) To upgrade from one class of registered title to another £40

Provided that no such fee is payable if the application for upgrading is accompanied by a scale fee application.

(7) To cancel an entry in the register of notice of an unregistered rentcharge which has determined – for each registered title affected £40

Provided that no such fee is payable if the application is accompanied by a scale fee application.

(8) To enter or remove a record of a defect in title pursuant to section 64(1) of the Act . . .   £40

Provided that no such fee is payable if the application is accompanied by a scale fee application.

(9) An outline application to secure priority for a dealing with registered land which cannot be protected by an official search with priority of the register:
  (a) where delivered by direct access to the registrar's computer system by means of a remote terminal £2
  (b) where delivered by any other means £4

Such fee is payable in addition to any other fee which is payable in respect of the application.

(10) For an order in respect of a restriction under section 41(2) of the Act – for each registered title affected £40

(11) To register a person in adverse possession of a registered estate – for each registered title affected £100

(12) For registration as a person entitled to be notified of an application for adverse possession – for each registered title affected £40

(13) Subject to article 9(4), for the determination of the exact line of a boundary under rule 118 – for each registered title affected £80

PART 2

SERVICES – INSPECTION AND COPYING

(1) Inspection of the following, including in each case the making of a copy, on any one occasion when a person gains access to the registrar's computer system by means of a remote terminal under rule 132:
  (a) for each individual register £2
  (b) for each title plan £2
  (c) for any or all of the documents referred to in an individual register (other than the documents referred to in paragraph (7) below) £2
  (d) for each individual caution register £2
  (e) for each caution plan £2
  (f) for any other document kept by the registrar which relates to an application to him – per document £2

(2) Inspection (otherwise than under paragraph (1) above):
  (a) for each individual register £4
  (b) for each title plan £4
  (c) for any or all of the documents referred to in an individual register (other than the documents referred to in paragraph (7) below) £4
  (d) for each individual caution register £4
  (e) for each caution plan £4
  (f) for any other document kept by the registrar which relates to an application to him – per document £4

(3) Official copy in respect of a registered title:
  (a) for each individual register
    (i) where requested from a remote terminal £2
    (ii) where requested by any other permitted means £4

    (b) for each title plan:
        (i)   where requested from a remote terminal £2
        (ii) where requested by any other permitted means £4

(4) Official copy in respect of a cautions register:
    (a) for each individual caution register:
        (i)   where requested from a remote terminal £2
        (ii) where requested by any other permitted means £4
    (b) for each caution plan
        (i)   where requested from a remote terminal £2
        (ii) where requested by any other permitted means £4

(5) Official copy of any or all of the documents referred to in an individual register (other than documents referred to in paragraph (7) below) – for each registered title:
    (a) where requested from a remote terminal £2
    (b) where requested by any other permitted means £4

(6) Official copy of any other document kept by the registrar which relates to an application to him – for each document:
    (a) where requested from a remote terminal £2
    (b) where requested by any other permitted means £4

(7) Where permitted (being unavailable as of right) inspection or official copy (or both) of a transitional period document – for each document £8

(8) Copy of an historical edition of an individual register – for each title £8

(9) Application to the registrar to ascertain the title number or numbers (if any) under which the estate is registered where the applicant seeks to inspect or to be supplied with an official copy of an individual register or of a title plan and the applicant has not supplied a title number, or the title number supplied does not relate to any part of the land described by the applicant £4

PART 3

SERVICES – SEARCHES

(1) An official search of an individual register or of a pending first registration application made to the registrar by means of a remote terminal communicating with the registrar's computer system – for each title £2

(2) An official search of an individual register by a mortgagee for the purpose of section 56(3) of the Family Law Act 1996[a] made to the registrar by means of a remote terminal communicating with the registrar's computer system – for each title £2

(3) An official search of an individual register or of a pending first registration application other than as described in paragraphs (1) and (2) – for each title £4

(4) The issue of a certificate of inspection of a title plan – for each registered title affected . £4

(5) Subject to article 9(4), an official search of the index map:
    (a) where any part of the land to which the search relates is registered – for each registered title in respect of which a result is given £4
    (b) where no part of the land to which the search relates is registered – for each application £4

(a) 1996 c. 27

(6) Search of the index of proprietors' names – for each name £10

(7) Official search of the index of relating franchises and manors – for each administrative area:
    (a) where requested from a remote terminal £2
    (b) where requested by any other permitted means £4

PART 4

SERVICES – OTHER INFORMATION

(1) Application to be supplied with the name and address of the registered proprietor of a registered title identified by its postal address – for each application £4

(2) Application for return of a document under rule 204 . . . . £8

(3) Application for day list information on any one occasion when a person gains access to the registrar's computer system by means of a remote terminal – for each title £1

(4) Application that the registrar designate a document an exempt information document . £20

(5) Application for an official copy of an exempt information document under rule 137 . . £40

SCHEDULE 4

Article 10

EXEMPTIONS

No fee is payable in respect of:

(1) reflecting a change in the name, address or description of a registered proprietor or other person referred to in the register, or in the cautions register, or changing the description of a property,

(2) giving effect in the register to a change of proprietor where the registered estate or the registered charge, as the case may be, has become vested without further assurance (other than on the death or bankruptcy of a proprietor) in some person by the operation of any statute (other than the Act), statutory instrument or scheme taking effect under any statute or statutory instrument,

(3) registering the surrender of a registered leasehold estate where the surrender is consideration or part consideration for the grant of a new lease to the registered proprietor of substantially the same premises as were comprised in the surrendered lease and where a scale fee is paid for the registration of the new lease,

(4) registering a discharge of a registered charge,

(5) registering a matrimonial home rights notice, or renewal of such a notice, or renewal of a matrimonial home rights caution under the Family Law Act 1996,

(6) entering in the register the death of a joint proprietor,

(7) cancelling the registration of a notice (other than a notice in respect of an unregistered lease or unregistered rentcharge), caution against first registration, caution against dealings, including a withdrawal of a deposit or intended deposit, inhibition, restriction, or note,

(8) the removal of the designation of a document as an exempt information document,

(9) approving an estate layout plan or any draft document with or without a plan,

(10) an order by the registrar (other than an order under section 41(2) of the Act),

(11) deregistering a manor,

(12) an entry in the register of a note of the dissolution of a corporation,

(13) registering a restriction in form A in Schedule 4 to the rules.

EXPLANATORY NOTE

(This note is not part of the Order)

This Order is made under the Land Registration Act 2002 (2002 c.9) ('the Act'). The Act repeals the Land Registration Act 1925 (1925 c.21). The Order, which prescribes land registry fees, performs a similar function to the Land Registration Fees Order 2003 (SI 2003/165) made under the Land Registration Act 1925.

Article 2 and Schedule 1 set the application fees for first registration and for registration of leases by an original lessee. Article 3 and Schedule 1 set the fees for transfers for value of registered land, and article 4 and Schedule 2, such transfers not for value. Article 5 and Schedule 2 set the fees for the registration of charges. Article 6 makes provision about the fees for large scale and large area applications. Articles 7 and 8 make provisions about how to value the estate or charge being registered.

Article 9 and Schedule 3 prescribe the set fees for the listed applications. Article 10 and Schedule 4 set out a list of applications for which there is no fee. Article 12 makes provision about meeting the cost of additional enquiries in dealing with an application. Article 13 deals with the payment of fees for applications in any other case. Articles 11, 14 and 15 deal with refunds, payment methods, and the operation of credit accounts, respectively.

XIII. THE LAND REGISTRY

XIII.1. Land Registry forms and guidance

The Land Registration Rules 2003 includes prescribed forms for applying to the Land Registry in Schedule 1. Use of the new forms and the old forms will be governed by a Transitional Order. A CD-ROM has been prepared by the Land Registry and distributed to their credit account customers and those who have registered their interest by telephone or website.

All forms, Practice Bulletins, and Practice Guides may be downloaded in Word or PDF format from the Land Registry website www.landreg.gov.uk.

Commonly used LRR 2003 Forms

*Solicitors should use the new forms whenever possible, but may continue to use the old forms under transitional arrangements to be governed by a Transitional Order and explained in a Land Registry Bulletin. The anticipated arrangements are outlined in Land Registry Practice Guide 46 – Land Registry Forms (1 March 2003).

Code	Name	Date	Replaces
OC1	Application for official copies of register/plan or certificate in Form CI	6 July 2003	Form 109*
OC2	Application for official copies of documents only	6 July 2003	Form 110*
SIM	Application for an official search of the index map	6 July 2003	Form 96*
OS1	Application by purchaser for official search with priority of the whole of the land in a registered title or a pending first registration application	6 July 2003	Form 94A*
OS2	Application by purchaser for official search with priority of part of the land in a registered title or a pending first registration	6 July 2003	Form 94B*
OS3	Application for official search without priority of the land in a registered lease	6 July 2003	Form 94C*
TP1	Transfer of part of registered title(s)	6 July 2003	Form TP1*
TP2	Transfer of part of registered title(s) under power of sale	6 July 2003	Form TP2*
TP3	Transfer of whole of registered title(s)	6 July 2003	Form TP3*
TR1	Transfer of whole of registered title(s)	6 July 2003	Form TR1*
TR2	Transfer of whole of registered title(s) under power of sale	6 July 2003	Form TR2*
TR3	Transfer of sale	6 July 2003	Form TR3*
TR4	Transfer of portfolio of charges	6 July 2003	Form TR4*

Code	Name	Date	Replaces
TR5	Transfer of portfolio of whole titles	6 July 2003	Form TR5*
DS1	Cancellation of entries relating to a registered charge	6 July 2003	Form DS1*
DS2	Application to cancel entries relating to a registered charge	6 July 2003	Form DS2*
DS3	Release of part of the land from a registered charge	6 July 2003	Form DS3*
AP1	Application to change the register	6 July 2003	Form AP1*
FR1	First registration application	6 July 2003	Form FR1*

Other LRR 2003 Forms

* Solicitors should use the new forms whenever possible, but may continue to use the old forms under transitional arrangements to be governed by a Transitional Order and explained in a Land Registry Bulletin. The anticipated arrangements are outlined in Land Registry Practice Guide 46 – Land Registry Forms (1 March 2003).

Code	Name	Date	Replaces
ADV1	Application for registration of a person in adverse possession under Schedule 6 to the Land Registration Act 2002	6 July 2003	(New)
ADV2	Application to be registered as a person to be notified of an application for adverse possession	6 July 2003	(New)
AN1	Application to enter an agreed notice	6 July 2003	(New)
AS1	Assent of whole of registered title(s)	6 July 2003	Form AS1*
AS2	Assent of charge	6 July 2003	Form AS2*
AS3	Assent of part of registered title(s)	6 July 2003	Form AS3*
CC	Entry of a note of consolidation of charges	6 July 2003	(New)
CCD	Application to cancel a caution against dealings	6 July 2003	(New)
CCT	Application to cancel a caution against first registration	6 July 2003	(New)
CH1	Legal charge of a registered estate	6 July 2003	(New)
CH2	Application to enter an obligation to make further advances	6 July 2003	Form 113
CH3	Application to note agreed maximum amount of security	6 July 2003	(New)
CI	Certificate of inspection of title plan	6 July 2003	Form 102
CIT	Application in connection with court proceedings, insolvency and tax liability	6 July 2003	(New)
CN1	Application to cancel notice of an unregistered lease or rentcharge	6 July 2003	Form CN1*
CS	Continuation sheet for use with application and disposition forms	6 July 2003	Form CS

Code	Name	Date	Replaces
CT1	Caution against first registration	6 July 2003	Form CT1*
DB	Application to determine the exact line of a boundary	6 July 2003	**(New)**
DI	Disclosable overriding interests	6 July 2003	**(New)**
DL	List of documents	6 July 2003	Form DL*
EX1	Application for the registrar to designate a document as an exempt information document	6 July 2003	**(New)**
EX1A	Reasons for exemption in support of an application to designate a document as an exempt information document	6 July 2003	**(New)**
EX2	Application for official copy of an exempt information document	6 July 2003	**(New)**
EX3	Application to remove the designation of a document as an exempt information document	6 July 2003	**(New)**
HC1	Application for copies of historical edition(s) of the register/title plan held in electronic form	6 July 2003	**(New)**
MH1	Application for registration of a notice of matrimonial home rights	6 July 2003	Form MH1*
MH2	Application for renewal of registration of a notice or a caution in respect of matrimonial home rights	6 July 2003	Form MH2*
MH3	Application by mortgagee for official search in respect of matrimonial home rights	6 July 2003	Form MH3*
NAP	Notice to the registrar in respect of an adverse possession application	6 July 2003	**(New)**
PIC	Application for a personal inspection under section 66 of the Land Registration Act 2002	6 July 2003	Form 111*
PN1	Application for a search in the index of proprietor's names	6 July 2003	Form 104
PRD1	Request for the production of documents	6 July 2003	**(New)**
RX1	Application to enter a restriction	6 July 2003	Form 75/76
RX2	Application for an order that a restriction be disapplied or modified	6 July 2003	**(New)**
RX3	Application to cancel a restriction	6 July 2003	**(New)**
RX4	Application to withdraw a restriction	6 July 2003	Form 77
SC	Application for noting the overriding priority of a statutory charge	6 July 2003	**(New)**
SIF	Application for an official search of the index of relating franchises and manors	6 July 2003	**(New)**
UN1	Application to enter a unilateral notice	6 July 2003	**(New)**
UN2	Application to remove a unilateral notice	6 July 2003	**(New)**

XIII

Code	Name	Date	Replaces
UN3	Application to be registered as beneficiary of an existing unilateral notice	6 July 2003	**(New)**
UN4	Application for the cancellation of a unilateral notice	6 July 2003	**(New)**
UT1	Application for upgrading of title	6 July 2003	Form 6*
WCT	Application to withdraw a caution	6 July 2003	Form WCT*

Practice bulletins

Code	Name	Date
LRPB001	Lost or destroyed certificates – effect of LRA	1 March 2003
LRPB002	Land and charge certificates – effect of LRA 2002	1 March 2003

Practice guides

Code	Name	Date
LRPG001	First registrations	1 March 2003
LRPG002	First registration of title where deeds have been lost or destroyed	1 March 2003
LRPG003	Cautions against first registration	1 March 2003
LRPG004	Adverse possession of registered land under the new provisions of the Land Registration Act 2002	1 March 2003
LRPG005	Adverse possession of unregistered land and transitional provisions for registered land in the Land Registration Act 2002	1 March 2003
LRPG006	Devolution on the death of a registered proprietor	1 March 2003
LRPG007	Entry of price paid or value stated on the register	1 March 2003
LRPG008	Execution of deeds	
LRPG009	Powers of attorney and registered land	1 March 2003
LRPG010	Official searches of the Index Map	1 March 2003
LRPG011	Inspection and applications for official copies	1 March 2003
LRPG012	Official searches and outline applications	1 March 2003
LRPG013	Official searches of the index relating to franchises and manors	1 March 2003
LRPG014	Charities	1 March 2003
LRPG015	Overriding interests and their disclosure	1 March 2003
LRPG016	Profits à prendre in gross	
LRPG017	Souvenir land	1 March 2003
LRPG018	Franchises	
LRPG019	Notices, restrictions and the protection of third party interest in the register	1 March 2003
LRPG020	Applications under the Family Law Act 1996	1 March 2003

Code	Name	Date
LRPG021	Using transfer forms for less straightforward applications	1 March 2003
LRPG022	Manors	1 March 2003
LRPG023	[Topic not yet allocated]	
LRPG024	Private trusts of land	
LRPG025	Leases – when to register	1 March 2003
LRPG026	Leases – determination	1 March 2003
LRPG027	The Leasehold Reform Legislation	
LRPG028	Extension of leases	1 March 2003
LRPG029	Registration of legal charges and deeds of variation of charge	1 March 2003
LRPG030	Approval of mortgage documentation	
LRPG031	Discharges of charges	1 March 2003
LRPG032	Applications affecting one or more Land Registry office	
LRPG033	Large scale applications (calculation of fees)	
LRPG034	Personal insolvency	1 March 2003
LRPG035	Corporate insolvency	
LRPG036	Administration and receivership	1 March 2003
LRPG037	Objections and disputes	
LRPG038	Costs	
LRPG039	Rectification and indemnity	
LRPG040	Land Registry plans: A summary of Land Registry plans records, pre-registration requirements, other plans related services	1 March 2003
LRPG041	Developing estates – registration services	1 March 2003
LRPG041-S1	Developing estates – registration services. Supplement 1 Estate boundary approval	1 March 2003
LRPG041-S2	Developing estates – registration services. Supplement 2 Estate plan approval	1 March 2003
LRPG041-S3	Developing estates – registration services. Supplement 3 Approval of draft transfers and leases	1 March 2003
LRPG041-S4	Developing estates – registration services. Supplement 4 Plot sales, transfers and leases	1 March 2003
LRPG041-S5	Developing estates – registration services. Supplement 5 Detailed plan requirements and surveying specifications – guidance for surveyors	1 March 2003
LRPG041-S6	Developing estates – registration services. Supplement 6 Voluntary application to note overriding interests	1 March 2003
LRPG042	Upgrading the class of title	1 March 2003
LRPG043	Applications in connection with court proceedings, insolvency and tax liability	

Code	Name	Date
LRPG044	Fax facilities	
LRPG045	[Topic not yet allocated]	
LRPG046	Land Registry forms	1 March 2003
LRPG047	Transfers of public housing estates	
LRPG048	Implied covenants	
LRPG049	Rejection of applications for registrations	
LRPG050	Requisition and cancellation procedures	
LRPG051	Areas served by Land Registry offices	
LRPG052	Easements claimed by prescription and statutory rights of way for vehicles	1 March 2003
LRPG053	Schemes titles	1 March 2003
LRPG054	Acquisition of land by General Vesting Declaration	
LRPG055	Address for service	1 March 2003
LRPG056	[Topic not yet allocated]	
LRPG057	Exempting documents from the general right to inspect and copy	1 March 2003

Index

Environmental Law Handbook

5th edition

Trevor Hellawell

This essential manual for non-specialists explains the important ways in which environmental law affects everyday property, financial and business transactions.

Focusing on how environmental law applies within particular contexts, the book covers the major liabilities, ways of maximising protection for clients, insurance against the main risks and the use of environmental consultants.

New to this edition:
- updated throughout with particular attention to environmental liabilities and searches
- a revised chapter on property transactions which includes the Law Society's Warning Card on contaminated land
- a new section on Contaminated Land Insurance
- new developments in EU law, including the Environmental Liability Directive.

1 85328 891 8   November 2002   256 pages   £34.95

Available from Marston Book Services:
Tel. 01235 465 656.

The Law Society

Understanding Stamp Duty on Property

7th edition

Reg Nock

This book is an updated and much-expanded edition of the popular practitioner title, *Stamp Duty for Conveyancers* (FT Law & Tax). The seventh edition has been entirely restructured to concentrate on land and property transactions and the needs of advisers.

It is clearly structured to explain this complex tax in easy-to-follow terms, and includes:

- explanation of where modernisation is likely to have an impact
- a chapter outlining the anticipated new provisions
- illustrative examples from everyday practice
- advice on how to avoid common pitfalls
- drafting and structuring techniques
- reference materials from the Inland Revenue.

1 85328 880 2   April 2003   336 pages   £39.95

Available from Marston Book Services:
Tel. 01235 465 656.

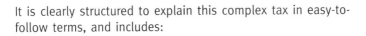

The Law Society

Coal Mining Searches

5th edition

The Coal Authority
and *The Law Society*

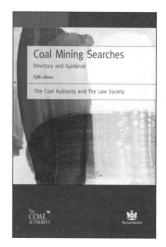

The Coal Authority has worked
with the Association of British
Insurers, the Council of Mortgage
Lenders, the Law Society of
England and Wales, and the Royal
Institution of Chartered Surveyors
to produce a search suitable for the
needs of conveyancers.

This fifth edition has been significantly updated and continues
to help conveyancers to determine whether a coal mining search
is required.

It also outlines the various methods now available to order and
receive mining reports, including through the National Land
Information Service and other online services. The book includes
supporting guidance, a directory showing "affected areas" and a
copy of form CON 29M (2003).

1 85328 910 8   March 2003   88 pages   £19.95

Available from Marston Book Services:
Tel. 01235 465 656.

The Law Society